HOLT McDOUGAL

Literature

Grade 7

SIR GAWAIN
AND THE
GREEN KNIGHT

COMMON CORE
EDITION

Typeset in *The Sans* from LucasFonts.

ACKNOWLEDGMENTS

STUDENT GUIDE TO ACADEMIC SUCCESS

D. Mark Singletary: "Pro Athletes' Salaries Aren't Overly Exorbitant" by Mark Singletary, from *New Orleans City Business,* March 25, 2002. Copyright © 2002 by D. Mark Singletary. Reprinted with permission of the author.

Justin Hjelm: "Do Professional Athletes Get Paid Too Much?" by Justin Hjelm. Copyright © 2004 by Justin Hjelm. Used by permission of the author.

Pantheon Books: "The War of the Wall," from *Deep Sightings and Rescue Missions* by Toni Cade Bambara. Copyright © 1996 by the Estate of Toni Cade Bambara. Used by permission of Pantheon Books, a division of Random House, Inc.

Piri Thomas: Excerpt from *Stories from El Barrio* by Piri Thomas. Copyright © 1978 by Piri Thomas. Reprinted by permission of the author.

Acknowledgments are continued at the back of the book, following the Index of Titles & Authors.

ART CREDITS

COVER, TITLE PAGE

top left © Kit Houghton/Corbis; *top right* © Randy Faris/Corbis; *bottom center* The Granger Collection, New York; *background, The Titanic,* Gordon Johnson. Oil on paper. © Margaret Johnson/SuperStock; *bottom left* Ken Kinzie/HMH Publishers.

Art Credits are continued at the back of the book, following the Acknowledgments.

Printed in the U.S.A.

ISBN 978-0-547-61837-1

8 9 10   0868   20 19 18 17 16 15

4500527384   B C D E F G

HOLT McDOUGAL

Literature

Grade 7

Janet Allen

Arthur N. Applebee

Jim Burke

Douglas Carnine

Yvette Jackson

Carol Jago

Robert T. Jiménez

Judith A. Langer

Robert J. Marzano

Mary Lou McCloskey

Donna M. Ogle

Carol Booth Olson

Lydia Stack

Carol Ann Tomlinson

Special Contributor: Kylene Beers

HOLT McDOUGAL

HOUGHTON MIFFLIN HARCOURT

SENIOR PROGRAM CONSULTANTS

JANET ALLEN Reading and Literacy Specialist; creator of the popular "It's Never Too Late"/"Reading for Life" Institutes. Dr. Allen is an internationally known consultant who specializes in literacy work with at-risk students. Her publications include *Tools for Content Literacy; It's Never Too Late: Leading Adolescents to Lifelong Learning; Yellow Brick Roads: Shared and Guided Paths to Independent Reading; Words, Words, Words: Teaching Vocabulary in Grades 4–12;* and *Testing 1, 2, 3 . . . Bridging Best Practice and High-Stakes Assessments.* Dr. Allen was a high school reading and English teacher for more than 20 years.

ARTHUR N. APPLEBEE Leading Professor, School of Education at the University at Albany, State University of New York; Director of the Center on English Learning and Achievement. During his varied career, Dr. Applebee has been both a researcher and a teacher, working in institutional settings with children with severe learning problems, in public schools, as a staff member of the National Council of Teachers of English, and in professional education. He was elected to the International Reading Hall of Fame and has received, among other honors, the David H. Russell Award for Distinguished Research in the Teaching of English.

JIM BURKE Lecturer and Author; Teacher of English at Burlingame High School, Burlingame, California. Mr. Burke is a popular presenter at educational conferences across the country and is the author of numerous books for teachers, including *School Smarts: The Four Cs of Academic Success; The English Teacher's Companion; Reading Reminders; Writing Reminders;* and *ACCESSing School: Teaching Struggling Readers to Achieve Academic and Personal Success.* He is the recipient of NCTE's Exemplary English Leadership Award and was inducted into the California Reading Association's Hall of Fame.

DOUGLAS CARNINE Professor of Education at the University of Oregon; Director of the Western Region Reading First Technical Assistance Center. Dr. Carnine is nationally known for his focus on research-based practices in education, especially curriculum designs that prepare instructors of K–12 students. He has received the Lifetime Achievement Award from the Council for Exceptional Children and the Ersted Award for outstanding teaching at the University of Oregon. Dr. Carnine frequently consults on educational policy with government groups, businesses, communities, and teacher unions.

YVETTE JACKSON Executive Director of the National Urban Alliance for Effective Education. Nationally recognized for her work in assessing the learning potential of underachieving urban students, Dr. Jackson is also a presenter for the Harvard Principal Center and is a member of the Differentiation Faculty of the Association for Supervision and Curriculum Development. Dr. Jackson's research focuses on literacy, gifted education, and cognitive mediation theory. She designed the Comprehensive Education Plan for the New York City Public Schools and has served as their Director of Gifted Programs.

CAROL JAGO Teacher of English with thirty-two years of experience at Santa Monica High School in California; Author and nationally known Lecturer; and Past President of the National Council of Teachers of English. With varied experience in standards assessment and secondary education, Ms. Jago is the author of numerous books on education and is active with the California Association of Teachers of English, editing its scholarly journal *California English* since 1996. Ms. Jago also served on the planning committee for the 2009 NAEP Framework and the 2011 NAEP Writing Framework.

ROBERT T. JIMÉNEZ Professor of Language, Literacy, and Culture at Vanderbilt University. Dr. Jiménez's research focuses on the language and literacy practices of Latino students. A former bilingual education teacher, he is now conducting research on how written language is thought about and used in contemporary Mexico. Dr. Jiménez has received several research and teaching honors, including two Fulbright awards from the Council for the International Exchange of Scholars and the Albert J. Harris Award from the International Reading Association.

JUDITH A. LANGER Distinguished Professor at the University at Albany, State University of New York; Director of the Center on English Learning and Achievement; Director of the Albany Institute for Research in Education. An internationally known scholar in English language arts education, Dr. Langer specializes in developing teaching approaches that can enrich and improve what gets done on a daily basis in classrooms. Her publications include *Getting to Excellent: How to Create Better Schools* and *Effective Literacy Instruction: Building Successful Reading and Writing Programs.*

ROBERT J. MARZANO Senior Scholar at Mid-Continent Research for Education and Learning (McREL); Associate Professor at Cardinal Stritch University in Milwaukee, Wisconsin; President of Marzano & Associates. An internationally known researcher, trainer, and speaker, Dr. Marzano has developed programs that translate research and theory into practical tools for K–12 teachers and administrators. He has written extensively on such topics as reading and writing instruction, thinking skills, school effectiveness, assessment, and standards implementation.

DONNA M. OGLE Professor of Reading and Language at National-Louis University in Chicago, Illinois; Past President of the International Reading Association. Creator of the well-known KWL strategy, Dr. Ogle has directed many staff development projects translating theory and research into school practice in middle and secondary schools throughout the United States and has served as a consultant on literacy projects worldwide. Her extensive international experience includes coordinating the Reading and Writing for Critical Thinking Project in Eastern Europe, developing integrated curriculum for a USAID Afghan Education Project, and speaking and consulting on projects in several Latin American countries and in Asia.

CAROL BOOTH OLSON Senior Lecturer in the Department of Education at the University of California, Irvine; Director of the UCI site of the National Writing Project. Dr. Olson writes and lectures extensively on the reading/writing connection, critical thinking through writing, interactive strategies for teaching writing, and the use of multicultural literature with students of culturally diverse backgrounds. She has received many awards, including the California Association of Teachers of English Award of Merit, the Outstanding California Education Research Award, and the UC Irvine Excellence in Teaching Award.

CAROL ANN TOMLINSON Professor of Educational Research, Foundations, and Policy at the University of Virginia; Co-Director of the University's Institutes on Academic Diversity. An internationally known expert on differentiated instruction, Dr. Tomlinson helps teachers and administrators develop effective methods of teaching academically diverse learners. She was a teacher of middle and high school English for 22 years prior to teaching at the University of Virginia. Her books on differentiated instruction have been translated into eight languages.

SPECIAL CONTRIBUTOR:
KYLENE BEERS Special Consultant; Former Middle School Teacher; nationally known Lecturer and Author on reading and literacy; and former President of the National Council of Teachers of English. Dr. Beers is the nationally known author of *When Kids Can't Read: What Teachers Can Do* and co-editor of *Adolescent Literacy: Turning Promise into Practice,* as well as articles in the *Journal of Adolescent and Adult Literacy.* Former editor of *Voices from the Middle,* she is the 2001 recipient of NCTE's Richard W. Halley Award, given for outstanding contributions to middle-school literacy.

ENGLISH LEARNER SPECIALISTS

MARY LOU McCLOSKEY Past President of Teachers of English to Speakers of Other Languages (TESOL); Director of Teacher Development and Curriculum Design for Educo in Atlanta, Georgia. Dr. McCloskey is a former teacher in multilingual and multicultural classrooms. She has worked with teachers, teacher educators, and departments of education around the world on teaching English as a second and foreign language. She is author of *On Our Way to English, Voices in Literature, Integrating English,* and *Visions: Language, Literature, Content.* Her awards include the Le Moyne College Ignatian Award for Professional Achievement and the TESOL D. Scott Enright Service Award.

LYDIA STACK International ESL consultant. Her areas of expertise are English language teaching strategies, ESL standards for students and teachers, and curriculum writing. Her teaching experience includes 25 years as an elementary and high school ESL teacher. She is a past president of TESOL. Her awards include the James E. Alatis Award for Service to TESOL (2003) and the San Francisco STAR Teacher Award (1989). Her publications include *On Our Way to English; Wordways: Games for Language Learning;* and *Visions: Language, Literature, Content.*

CURRICULUM SPECIALIST

WILLIAM L. McBRIDE Curriculum Specialist. Dr. McBride is a nationally known speaker, educator, and author who now trains teachers in instructional methodologies. A former reading specialist, English teacher, and social studies teacher, he holds a Masters in Reading and a Ph.D. in Curriculum and Instruction from the University of North Carolina at Chapel Hill. Dr. McBride has contributed to the development of textbook series in language arts, social studies, science, and vocabulary. He is also known for his novel *Entertaining an Elephant,* which tells the story of a burned-out teacher who becomes re-inspired with both his profession and his life.

MEDIA SPECIALISTS

DAVID M. CONSIDINE Professor of Instructional Technology and Media Studies at Appalachian State University in North Carolina. Dr. Considine has served as a media literacy consultant to the U.S. government and to the media industry, including Discovery Communications and Cable in the Classroom. He has also conducted media literacy workshops and training for county and state health departments across the United States. Among his many publications are *Visual Messages: Integrating Imagery into Instruction,* and *Imagine That: Developing Critical Viewing and Thinking Through Children's Literature.*

LARKIN PAULUZZI Teacher and Media Specialist; trainer for the New Jersey Writing Project. Ms. Pauluzzi puts her extensive classroom experience to use in developing teacher-friendly curriculum materials and workshops in many different areas, including media literacy. She has led media literacy training workshops in several districts throughout Texas, guiding teachers in the meaningful and practical uses of media in the classroom. Ms. Pauluzzi has taught students at all levels, from Title I Reading to AP English IV. She also spearheads a technology club at her school, working with students to produce media and technology to serve both the school and the community.

LISA K. SCHEFFLER Teacher and Media Specialist. Ms. Scheffler has designed and taught media literacy and video production curriculum, in addition to teaching language arts and speech. Using her knowledge of mass communication theory, coupled with real classroom experience, she has developed ready-to-use materials that help teachers incorporate media literacy into their curricula. She has taught film and television studies at the University of North Texas and has served as a contributing writer for the Texas Education Agency's statewide viewing and representing curriculum.

TEACHER ADVISORS

These are some of the many educators from across the country who played a crucial role in the development of the tables of contents, the lesson design, and other key components of this program:

Virginia L. Alford, MacArthur High School, San Antonio, Texas

Yvonne L. Allen, Shaker Heights High School, Shaker Heights, Ohio

Dave T. Anderson, Hinsdale South High School, Darien, Illinois

Kacy Colleen Anglim, Portland Public Schools District, Portland, Oregon

Jordana Benone, North High School, Torrance, California

Patricia Blood, Howell High School, Farmingdale, New Jersey

Marjorie Bloom, Eau Gallie High School, Melbourne, Florida

Edward J. Blotzer, Wilkinsburg Junior/Senior High School, Wilkinsburg, Pennsylvania

Stephen D. Bournes, Evanston Township High School, Evanston, Illinois

Barbara M. Bowling, Mt. Tabor High School, Winston-Salem, North Carolina

Kiala Boykin-Givehand, Duval County Public Schools, Jacksonville, Florida

Laura L. Brown, Adlai Stevenson High School, Lincolnshire, Illinois

Cynthia Burke, Yavneh Academy, Dallas, Texas

Hoppy Chandler, San Diego City Schools, San Diego, California

Gary Chmielewski, St. Benedict High School, Chicago, Illinois

Delorse Cole-Stewart, Milwaukee Public Schools, Milwaukee, Wisconsin

Kathy Dahlgren, Skokie, Illinois

Diana Dilger, Rosa Parks Middle School, Dixmoor, Illinois

L. Calvin Dillon, Gaither High School, Tampa, Florida

Dori Dolata, Rufus King High School, Milwaukee, Wisconsin

Jon Epstein, Marietta High School, Marietta, Georgia

Helen Ervin, Fort Bend Independent School District, Sugar Land, Texas

Sue Friedman, Buffalo Grove High School, Buffalo Grove, Illinois

Chris Gee, Bel Air High School, El Paso, Texas

Paula Grasel, The Horizon Center, Gainesville, Georgia

Rochelle L. Greene-Brady, Kenwood Academy, Chicago, Illinois

Christopher Guarraia, Centreville High School, Clifton, Virginia

Michele M. Hettinger, Niles West High School, Skokie, Illinois

Elizabeth Holcomb, Forest Hill High School, Jackson, Mississippi

Jim Horan, Hinsdale Central High School, Hinsdale, Illinois

James Paul Hunter, Oak Park-River Forest High School, Oak Park, Illinois

Susan P. Kelly, Director of Curriculum, Island Trees School District, Levittown, New York

Beverley A. Lanier, Varina High School, Richmond, Virginia

Pat Laws, Charlotte-Mecklenburg Schools, Charlotte, North Carolina

Diana R. Martinez, Treviño School of Communications & Fine Arts, Laredo, Texas

Natalie Martinez, Stephen F. Austin High School, Houston, Texas

Elizabeth Matarazzo, Ysleta High School, El Paso, Texas

Carol M. McDonald, J. Frank Dobie High School, Houston, Texas

Amy Millikan, Consultant, Chicago, Illinois

Eileen Murphy, Walter Payton Preparatory High School, Chicago, Illinois

Lisa Omark, New Haven Public Schools, New Haven, Connecticut

Kaine Osburn, Wheeling High School, Wheeling, Illinois

Andrea J. Phillips, Terry Sanford High School, Fayetteville, North Carolina

Cathy Reilly, Sayreville Public Schools, Sayreville, New Jersey

Mark D. Simon, Neuqua Valley High School, Naperville, Illinois

Scott Snow, Seguin High School, Arlington, Texas

Jane W. Speidel, Brevard County Schools, Viera, Florida

Cheryl E. Sullivan, Lisle Community School District, Lisle, Illinois

Anita Usmiani, Hamilton Township Public Schools, Hamilton Square, New Jersey

Linda Valdez, Oxnard Union High School District, Oxnard, California

Nancy Walker, Longview High School, Longview, Texas

Kurt Weiler, New Trier High School, Winnetka, Illinois

Elizabeth Whittaker, Larkin High School, Elgin, Illinois

Linda S. Williams, Woodlawn High School, Baltimore, Maryland

John R. Williamson, Fort Thomas Independent Schools, Fort Thomas, Kentucky

Anna N. Winters, Simeon High School, Chicago, Illinois

Tonora D. Wyckoff, North Shore Senior High School, Houston, Texas

Karen Zajac, Glenbard South High School, Glen Ellyn, Illinois

Cynthia Zimmerman, Mose Vines Preparatory High School, Chicago, Illinois

Lynda Zimmerman, El Camino High School, South San Francisco, California

Ruth E. Zurich, Brown Deer High School, Brown Deer, Wisconsin

COMMON
CORE

OVERVIEW
Student Edition

LESSONS WITH EMBEDDED COMMON CORE INSTRUCTION

COMMON CORE

Look for the COMMON CORE symbol throughout the book. It highlights targeted objectives to help you succeed in mastering the knowledge and skills you will need for college or for a career.

© Getty Images

COMMON CORE CONTENTS

COMMON CORE

CONTENTS IN BRIEF

STUDENT RESOURCE BANK

Online at

Log in to learn more at thinkcentral.com, where you can access most program resources in one convenient location.

LITERATURE AND READING CENTER
- Author Biographies
- *PowerNotes* Presentations with Video Trailers
- Professional Audio Recordings of Selections
- Graphic Organizers
- Analysis Frames
- NovelWise

WRITING AND GRAMMAR CENTER
- Interactive Student Models*
- Interactive Graphic Organizers*
- Interactive Revision Lessons*
- *GrammarNotes* Presentations and Practice

also available on WriteSmart CD-ROM

VOCABULARY CENTER
- *WordSharp* Interactive Vocabulary Tutor
- Vocabulary Practice Copy Masters

MEDIA AND TECHNOLOGY CENTER
- MediaScope: Media Literacy Instruction
- Digital Storytelling
- Speaking and Listening Support

RESEARCH CENTER
- Writing and Research in a Digital Age
- Citation Guide

Assessment Center
- Program Assessments
- Level Up Online Tutorials
- Online Essay Scoring

MORE TECHNOLOGY

Student One Stop

Access an electronic version of your textbook, complete with selection audio and worksheets.

Media Smart DVD-ROM

Sharpen your critical viewing and analysis skills with these in-depth interactive media studies.

Weaving a Story
PLOT, CONFLICT, AND SETTING

• FICTION • INFORMATIONAL TEXT • POETRY • DRAMA • MEDIA

Vocabulary Strategies

Latin roots: *uni, p. 44*
Antonyms as context clues, *p. 63*
Prefixes that mean "not," *p. 74*

Latin roots: *viv* and *vit, p. 94*
Analogies, *p. 120*
Suffixes that form adjectives, *p. 131*

Personality Tests
ANALYZING CHARACTER AND POINT OF VIEW

• FICTION • INFORMATIONAL TEXT • POETRY

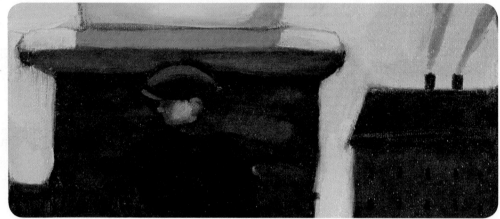

TEXT ANALYSIS WORKSHOP: CHARACTER AND POINT OF VIEW 184

Vocabulary Strategies

Similes, *p.214*
Context clues, *p. 233*
Multiple-meaning words, *p. 246*

Latin roots: *cred*, *p. 264*
Using reference aids, *p. 274*
Idioms, *p. 286*

Lessons to Learn
UNDERSTANDING THEME

• FICTION • POETRY • DRAMA • MEDIA

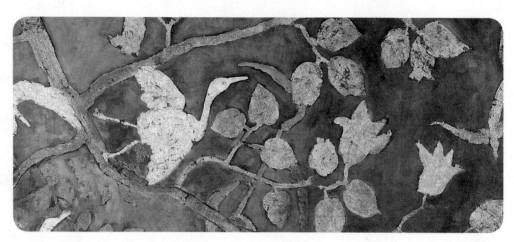

Vocabulary Strategies

Latin roots: *pel, p. 336*
Denotations and connotations, *p. 348*

General context clues, *p. 366*
Forms of the prefix *in-, p. 385*

Finding a Voice
MOOD, TONE, AND STYLE

• FICTION • INFORMATIONAL TEXT • POETRY • MEDIA

INFORMATIONAL TEXT: LITERARY NONFICTION

> ### Vocabulary Strategies
>
> Latin roots: *pend, p. 480*   Using a thesaurus, *p. 503*
> Greek roots: *therm, p. 490*

Picture the Moment
APPRECIATING POETRY

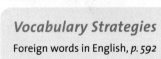

Vocabulary Strategies
Foreign words in English, *p. 592*

COMMON CORE
UNIT 6

Sharing Our Stories
MYTHS, LEGENDS, AND TALES

Vocabulary Strategies

Foreign words in English, *p. 659*
Using a dictionary, *p. 672*
Analogies, *p. 688*

Using a glossary, *p. 704*
General context clues, *p. 731*
Dictionary entries, *p. 741*

Writing a Life
BIOGRAPHY AND AUTOBIOGRAPHY

• INFORMATIONAL TEXT • MEDIA • DRAMA • POETRY

STANDARDS FOCUS

Characteristics of Biographies and Autobiographies, Distinguish Diaries from Fictional Adaptations

HISTORY Video link at thinkcentral.com
Biography, Identify Chronological Order

Synthesize, Draw Conclusions

Personal Essay, Connect

Author's Purpose and Theme, Make Inferences

Reading Fluency

Vocabulary Strategies

Words with Anglo-Saxon roots, *p. 799*   Anglo-Saxon affixes, *p. 825*
Connotations and meaning, *p. 812*   Latin roots: *spec, p. 845*

Face the Facts
INFORMATION, ARGUMENT, AND PERSUASION
• INFORMATIONAL TEXT • MEDIA

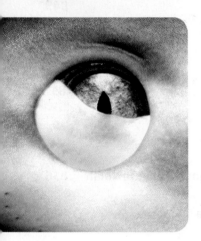

Vocabulary Strategies

Content-specific words, *p. 916*   Specialized vocabulary, *p. 940*   Greek roots: *aut, p. 975*
Prefixes and *vert, p. 927*   Idioms, *p. 966*   Analogies, *p. 982*

Investigation and Discovery
THE POWER OF RESEARCH

STANDARDS FOCUS
Use Reference Materials and Technology, Evaluate Sources

Research, Synthesize

Selections by Genre

DRAMA

NONFICTION

AUTOBIOGRAPHIES/MEMOIRS

BIOGRAPHIES

ESSAYS

EXPLANATORY/FUNCTIONAL TEXTS

NARRATIVE NONFICTION

Features

STUDENT GUIDE TO ACADEMIC SUCCESS

STUDENT GUIDE

© Jupiterimages/Getty Images

The Common Core for Uncommon Achievement

Carol Jago

"If you don't know where you are going, any road will get you there." – Lewis Carroll

The Common Core State Standards make clear where students are going. They describe what today's children need to know and be able to do to thrive in post-secondary education and the workplace. By focusing on results — the destination — rather than on the how — the means of transportation — the Common Core allows for a variety of teaching methods and many different classroom approaches. The challenge for teachers is to turn the daily journey towards this destination into an intellectual adventure.

One way to think about the Common Core is as a kind of GPS device to situate curriculum. While some students may choose the road less traveled, the objective is fixed. When students become lost through a wrong turn, teachers recalculate the route, providing a calm and confident voice that guides all students to academic achievement and deep literacy.

Shared Responsibility for Students' Literacy Development

The Common Core State Standards insist that the responsibility for helping students achieve literacy is not the sole responsibility of the English teacher. The introduction states clearly that, "instruction in reading, writing, speaking, listening, and language (should) be a shared responsibility within the school" (4). Citing NAEP Reading assessment test specification guidelines, the Common Core recommends that 55% of what students read in grade 8 and 70% in grade 12 should be informational text. These percentages are not meant to reflect the balance of reading materials in English class alone but rather the totality of what students should be reading across the curriculum in history/social studies, science, and technical subjects as well as in English. Given the type of reading that will be required of students in college and of graduates in the workplace, this distribution is both relevant and practical.

Understanding of Other Perspectives and Cultures

The Common Core also makes clear the importance of literature in the education of America's children. "Through reading great classic and contemporary works of literature representative of a variety of periods, cultures, and worldviews, students can vicariously inhabit worlds and have experiences much different from their own" (7). Reading literature demands that readers look inward, examine their beliefs in light of new information, consider the world through different eyes, take time for reflection. Such reading is a key to student learning.

The Purpose of Exemplar Texts

To describe the quality and complexity of the works students should read at each grade level, the Common Core offers lists of "exemplar texts." While some may choose to treat the texts on these lists as required reading, such usage would represent a misunderstanding of their purpose. "The choices should serve as useful guideposts in helping educators select texts of similar complexity, quality, and range for their own classrooms. They expressly do not represent a partial or complete reading list" (Appendix B, 2). The poems, stories, novels, and nonfiction that appear on the Common Core lists are intended as models for guiding — not dictating — text selection.

The Difference Between Persuasion and Argument

The Common Core writing standards describe the types and purposes for writing that students need to master. You will find extended definitions of argument, informative/explanatory writing, and narrative writing in Appendix A. Of particular note is the distinction the Common Core draws between persuasion and argument. "When writing to persuade, writers employ a variety of persuasive strategies. One common strategy is an appeal to the credibility, character, or authority of the writer (or speaker). A logical argument, on the other hand, convinces the audience because of the perceived merit and reasonableness of the claims and proofs offered rather than either the emotions the writing evokes in the audience or the character or credentials of the writer" (24). Because of its importance for college and workplace readiness, argument holds a special place in the Common Core writing standards.

> *One way to think about the Common Core is as a kind of GPS device …*

Complex Literary and Informational Texts

Throughout the Common Core document you will notice the anchor standard, "Read and comprehend complex literary and informational texts independently and proficiently." It isn't enough for students to read with a teacher by their side. They need to be able, often with a little help from their friends or from the habits of mind they learned from their teachers, to read for themselves. They need to be able, like Huck Finn, to head out for the territory on their own. Such a journey requires confidence in one's ability to navigate uncharted waters and to overcome challenges their teachers can't foresee or even imagine. As we guide students on the academic adventure that is middle and high school, let us never forget that the path we tread is the path to intellectual freedom.

WORKS CITED

Common Core State Standards for English Language Arts and History/Social Studies, Science, & Technical Subjects. 2010.

Appendix B. Common Core State Standards for English Language Arts and History/Social Studies, Science, & Technical Subjects. 2010.

Carol Jago has taught middle and high school for over 30 years and was a member of the Common Core Initiative feedback team. She is the Past President of the National Council of Teachers of English.

Understanding the Common Core State Standards

What are the English Language Arts Common Core State Standards?

The Common Core State Standards for English Language Arts indicate what you should know and be able to do by the end of your grade level. These understandings and skills will help you be better prepared for future classes, college courses, and a career. For this reason, the standards for each strand in English Language Arts (such as reading informational text or writing) directly relate to the College and Career Readiness Anchor Standards for each strand. The Anchor Standards broadly outline the understandings and skills you should learn by the end of middle school so that you are well-prepared for high school, for college, or for a career.

How do I learn the English Language Arts Common Core State Standards?

Your textbook is closely aligned to the English Language Arts Common Core State Standards. Every time you learn a concept or practice a skill, you are working on mastery of one of the standards. Each unit, each selection, and each workshop in your textbook connects to one or more of the standards for English Language Arts listed on the following pages.

The English Language Arts Common Core State Standards are divided into five strands: Reading Literature, Reading Informational Text, Writing, Speaking and Listening, and Language.

Reading Literature (RL)

This strand concerns the literary texts you will read at this grade level: stories, drama, and poetry. The Common Core State Standards stress that you should read a range of texts of increasing complexity as you progress through middle school.

Reading Informational Text (RI)

Informational text includes a broad range of literary nonfiction, including exposition, argument, and functional text, such as personal essays, speeches, opinion pieces, memoirs, and historical and technical accounts. The Common Core State Standards stress that you will also read a range of informational texts of increasing complexity as you progress from grade to grade.

Writing (W)

The Writing strand focuses on your generating three types of texts: arguments, informative or explanatory texts, and narratives, as well as using the writing process and technology to develop and share your writing. The Common Core State Standards also emphasize research and specify that you should write routinely for both short and extended time frames.

Speaking and Listening (SL)

The Common Core State Standards focus on comprehending information presented in a variety of media and formats, on participating in collaborative discussions, and on presenting knowledge and ideas clearly.

Language (L)

The standards in the Language strand address the conventions of Standard English grammar, usage, and mechanics; knowledge of language; and vocabulary acquisition and use.

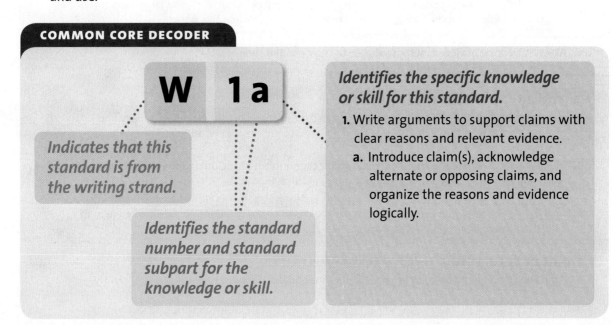

COMMON CORE DECODER

W 1a

Indicates that this standard is from the writing strand.

Identifies the standard number and standard subpart for the knowledge or skill.

Identifies the specific knowledge or skill for this standard.

1. Write arguments to support claims with clear reasons and relevant evidence.
   a. Introduce claim(s), acknowledge alternate or opposing claims, and organize the reasons and evidence logically.

COMMON CORE

English Language Arts
Common Core State Standards

Listed below are the English Language Arts Common Core State Standards that you are required to master by the end of grade 7. We have provided a summary of the concepts you will learn on your way to mastering each standard. The CCR anchor standards and grade-specific standards for each strand work together to define college and career readiness expectations—the former providing broad standards, the latter providing additional specificity.

College and Career Readiness Anchor Standards for Reading

COMMON CORE STATE STANDARDS

KEY IDEAS AND DETAILS

1. Read closely to determine what the text says explicitly and to make logical inferences from it; cite specific textual evidence when writing or speaking to support conclusions drawn from the text.

2. Determine central ideas or themes of a text and analyze their development; summarize the key supporting details and ideas.

3. Analyze how and why individuals, events, and ideas develop and interact over the course of a text.

CRAFT AND STRUCTURE

4. Interpret words and phrases as they are used in a text, including determining technical, connotative, and figurative meanings, and analyze how specific word choices shape meaning or tone.

5. Analyze the structure of texts, including how specific sentences, paragraphs, and larger portions of the text (e.g., a section, chapter, scene, or stanza) relate to each other and the whole.

6. Assess how point of view or purpose shapes the content and style of a text.

INTEGRATION OF KNOWLEDGE AND IDEAS

7. Integrate and evaluate content presented in diverse formats and media, including visually and quantitatively, as well as in words.

8. Delineate and evaluate the argument and specific claims in a text, including the validity of the reasoning as well as the relevance and sufficiency of the evidence.

9. Analyze how two or more texts address similar themes or topics in order to build knowledge or to compare the approaches the authors take.

RANGE OF READING AND LEVEL OF TEXT COMPLEXITY

10. Read and comprehend complex literary and informational texts independently and proficiently.

Reading Standards for Literature, Grade 7 Students

The College and Career Readiness Anchor Standards for Reading apply to both literature and informational text.

COMMON CORE STATE STANDARD	WHAT IT MEANS TO YOU
KEY IDEAS AND DETAILS	
1. Cite several pieces of textual evidence to support analysis of what the text says explicitly as well as inferences drawn from the text.	You will use information from the text to support its main ideas—both those that are stated directly and those that are suggested.
2. Determine a theme or central idea of a text and analyze its development over the course of the text; provide an objective summary of the text.	You will analyze a text's main ideas and themes by showing how they unfold throughout the text. You will also summarize the main idea of the text as a whole without adding your own ideas or opinions.
3. Analyze how particular elements of a story or drama interact (e.g., how setting shapes the characters or plot).	You will analyze how different parts of a story or drama affect each other.
CRAFT AND STRUCTURE	
4. Determine the meaning of words and phrases as they are used in a text, including figurative and connotative meanings; analyze the impact of rhymes and other repetitions of sounds (e.g., alliteration) on a specific verse or stanza of a poem or section of a story or drama.	You will analyze specific words, phrases, and patterns of sound in the text to determine what they mean and how they contribute to the text's larger meaning.
5. Analyze how a drama's or poem's form or structure (e.g., soliloquy, sonnet) contributes to its meaning.	You will analyze how the form of a drama or poem affects its meaning.
6. Analyze how an author develops and contrasts the points of view of different characters or narrators in a text.	You will analyze how an author contrasts the perspectives of different characters or the points of view of narrators in a text.
INTEGRATION OF KNOWLEDGE AND IDEAS	
7. Compare and contrast a written story, drama, or poem to its audio, filmed, staged, or multimedia version, analyzing the effects of techniques unique to each medium (e.g., lighting, sound, color, or camera focus and angles in a film).	You will compare and contrast how events and information are presented in visual and non-visual texts.
8. (Not applicable to literature)	
9. Compare and contrast a fictional portrayal of a time, place, or character and a historical account of the same period as a means of understanding how authors of fiction use or alter history.	You will recognize and analyze how an author draws from and uses historical source material.
RANGE OF READING AND LEVEL OF TEXT COMPLEXITY	
10. By the end of the year, read and comprehend literature, including stories, dramas, and poems, in the grades 6–8 text complexity band proficiently, with scaffolding as needed at the high end of the range.	You will read and understand grade-level appropriate literary texts by the end of grade 7.

Spotlight on Common Core

 COMMON CORE **RL 6** Analyze how an author develops and contrasts the points of view of different characters or narrators in a text.

Literature: Analyzing Point of View

The Common Core State Standards require you to analyze how writers develop the points of view of different characters or narrators in a story. In literature, the narrator is the one who tells the story. Sometimes the narrator is a character in the story and sometimes he or she is not. The writer's choice of a narrator is referred to as **point of view**. There are three types of point of view:

- In **first-person point of view**, the narrator is a character in the story and uses the pronouns *I, me, we,* and *us*. He or she describes his or her own thoughts and feelings and relates events as he or she experiences them. This type of narrator does not know what other characters are thinking or feeling.
- In **second-person point of view**, the narrator tells the story to another character and uses the pronoun *you*. The narrator is also a character in the story, stating his or her thoughts and explaining events to the other characters. This type of narration creates a sense of intimacy between the narrator and the reader but is rarely used.
- In **third-person point of view**, the narrator is not a character in the story. The characters are referred to as *he, she, they, him, her,* and *them*. Third-person point of view is referred to as **limited** if the narrator tells the thoughts and feelings of only one character. Third-person point of view is referred to as **omniscient**, or all-knowing, if the narrator reveals the thoughts and feelings of all the characters.

In this book, you will be asked to analyze the point of view used in a story. Study the following example.

> Read the following excerpt from "The War of the Wall" by Toni Cade Bambara. Then answer the questions that follow.
>
> > Me and Lou had no time for courtesies. We were late for school. So we just flat out told the painter lady to quit messing with the wall. It was our wall, and she had no right coming into our neighborhood painting on it.
>
> 1. From what point of view is this excerpt told? Explain how you can tell.
> 2. What can you tell about the personality of the character who is narrating? What do you know about the other characters?

LEARN HOW Analyzing Point of View In choosing a story's point of view, the writer controls the amount and type of information that is shared with the reader. With first-person point of view, the reader only sees events through one character's eyes. Sometimes the writer may experiment with point of view by having different characters narrate, in first person, different sections or chapters of the story. In third-person omniscient point of view, the writer allows the reader a view into the thinking of all the characters.

In the following excerpt from Piri Thomas' short story "Amigo Brothers," notice how Thomas develops point of view by contrasting the thoughts of the two characters.

1. What is the point of view of the excerpt?

The evening before the big fight, Tony made his way to the roof of his tenement. In the quiet early dark, he peered over the ledge. Six stories below, the lights of the city blinked, and the sounds of cars mingled with the curses and the laughter of children in the street. He tried not to think of Felix, feeling he had succeeded in psyching his mind. But only in the ring would he really know. To spare Felix hurt, he would have to knock him out, early and quick.

> The writer focuses on the character Tony using pronouns *his* and *he*.

Up in the South Bronx, Felix decided to take in a movie in an effort to keep Antonio's face away from his fists. The flick was *The Champion* with Kirk Douglas, the third time Felix was seeing it.

The champion was getting beat, his face being pounded into raw, wet hamburger. His eyes were cut, jagged, bleeding, one eye swollen, the other almost shut. He was saved only by the sound of the bell.

Felix became the champ and Tony the challenger.

> The writer focuses on the thoughts and actions of the character Felix.

As you read the literature throughout this book, identify the point of view by looking at who is telling the story. Ask yourself how much he or she knows about the characters in the story.

Reading Standards for Informational Text, Grade 7 Students

COMMON CORE STATE STANDARD	WHAT IT MEANS TO YOU
KEY IDEAS AND DETAILS	
1. Cite several pieces of textual evidence to support analysis of what the text says explicitly as well as inferences drawn from the text.	You will cite information from the text to support its main ideas—both those that are stated directly and those that are suggested.
2. Determine two or more central ideas in a text and analyze their development over the course of the text; provide an objective summary of the text.	You will analyze the development of at least two of a text's main ideas by showing how they progress throughout the text. You will also summarize the text as a whole without adding your own ideas or opinions.
3. Analyze the interactions between individuals, events, and ideas in a text (e.g., how ideas influence individuals or events, or how individuals influence ideas or events).	You will analyze the ways in which individuals, events, and ideas in the text interact with one another.
CRAFT AND STRUCTURE	
4. Determine the meaning of words and phrases as they are used in a text, including figurative, connotative, and technical meanings; analyze the impact of a specific word choice on meaning and tone.	You will analyze specific words and phrases in the text to determine both what they mean and how they affect the text's tone and meaning as a whole.
5. Analyze the structure an author uses to organize a text, including how the major sections contribute to the whole and to the development of the ideas.	You will examine the major sections of a text and analyze how each one contributes to the whole.

Reading Standards for Informational Text, Grade 7 Students, continued

COMMON CORE STATE STANDARD	WHAT IT MEANS TO YOU
6. Determine an author's point of view or purpose in a text and analyze how the author distinguishes his or her position from that of others.	You will understand the author's point of view and analyze how the author sets his or her position apart from others.
INTEGRATION OF KNOWLEDGE AND IDEAS	
7. Compare and contrast a text to an audio, video, or multimedia version of the text, analyzing each medium's portrayal of the subject (e.g., how the delivery of a speech affects the impact of the words).	You will compare and contrast text to an audio, video, or multimedia version of the text.
8. Trace and evaluate the argument and specific claims in a text, assessing whether the reasoning is sound and the evidence is relevant and sufficient to support the claims.	You will evaluate the strength of the author's claims and reasoning and identify any faults or weaknesses in them.
9. Analyze how two or more authors writing about the same topic shape their presentations of key information by emphasizing different evidence or advancing different interpretations of facts.	You will compare and contrast at least two different authors' treatments of the same subject.
RANGE OF READING AND LEVEL OF TEXT COMPLEXITY	
10. By the end of the year, read and comprehend literary nonfiction in the grades 6–8 text complexity band proficiently, with scaffolding as needed at the high end of the range.	You will demonstrate the ability to read and understand grade-level appropriate literary nonfiction texts by the end of grade 7.

Spotlight on Common Core

COMMON CORE

RI 9 Analyze how two or more authors writing about the same topic shape their presentations of key information by emphasizing different evidence or advancing different interpretations of facts.

Informational Text: Comparing Texts on the Same Topic

The Common Core State Standards require you to analyze texts with different viewpoints and conclusions based on the same information. Two writers may choose the same topic but come to very different conclusions, depending on how they shape the topic.

There are two major ways that writers shape their texts:

- by choosing which pieces of evidence to emphasize and
- by deciding what that evidence means.

The writer makes those decisions based on the **treatment**, or the way a topic is going to be handled, and the **scope**, the particular information that will be included. The writer will select a form, decide on a purpose, and choose a tone, or attitude, toward the subject.

Throughout this book, you will be asked to analyze informational texts that present different viewpoints and offer different conclusions. Study the following example:

Read the following editorial excerpts. Then answer the questions that follow.

from **"Pro Athletes' Salaries Aren't Overly Exorbitant"**
by Mark Singletary

The historical argument for paying exorbitant salaries to athletes is the brevity [shortness] of their careers. All of these athletes are a busted knee, concussion or torn rotator cuff away from the end of their career, and very few sports offer guaranteed contracts that go beyond the season when the injury occurs.

Our fans are important to the economic health of our ball club. My teammates and I are responsible for finding and keeping fans. If I am a star, it can rightly be assumed the fans come to see me play.

When the fans come to see the stars perform, the value of the franchise increases. I'm pretty smart and understand all this and how it relates to me. I also know what I make and how that relates to others that play my game.

So, it seems to me that even though I love the game, even though just playing the game is huge compensation [payment] and very, very satisfying, I want things to be fair.

Fair is fair. And fair is that the athletes deserve what the fans are willing to pay.

The owners probably don't care what the athletes make, as long as they can pass the cost on to sponsors and ticket buyers. The intelligence in sports ownership is the ability to predict exactly where the fans and sponsors lose interest.

Until that time, it seems fair to allocate as much as possible to the players that make the games entertaining.

from **"Do Professional Athletes Get Paid Too Much?"**
by Justin Hjelm

For nearly a century, superstar athletes have demanded and received salaries grossly out of proportion with the average income of their times. What makes modern times different and more disturbing is that even the role players in professional sports are pulling in an exorbitant amount of money.

Fifty years ago, only the 40-home-run outfielder would make a huge salary. Now, however, the utility infielder who comes in as a defensive replacement three times a week makes ten times more than the average working man.

Nolan Ryan broke ground in 1979, becoming the first athlete to receive a $1-million-a-year contract. It took over a century for baseball to reach this milestone income figure, and just 25 years later a $1 million contract offer is considered an insult.

continued

The contracts of professional athletes have gone unchecked for too long, and now athletes are among the wealthiest people in our nation.

Athletes are paid far too much for simply playing games. Essentially, as anyone can tell you, sports are entertainment. We pay to see these athletes perform at the highest level.

It is a sad commentary on our societal values that these entertainers are raking in seven-figure salaries while teachers, police officers, and fire fighters make less than one percent of the income of some athletes. Entertainment is a necessary thing, but it is not needed nearly as much as countless other occupations are.

What kind of message are we sending our children with these backward values?

1. What facts does each writer emphasize?

2. How do the writers' interpretations of the same fact or facts differ?

LEARN HOW Comparing Texts on the Same Topic   No writer can include all the facts about a topic in a single piece of writing. Instead, writers choose the facts that best relate to the point they are trying to make. Even the facts they include are not treated equally. The facts that best support the writer's point are emphasized, while others are played down. When comparing texts on the same topic, first note the facts that each writer chooses to emphasize. Look at one writer's answer to the first question.

1. What facts does each writer emphasize?

> 1. Singletary emphasizes the facts that athletes' careers are short and that the entertainment they provide brings in large amounts of money. Hjelm emphasizes the fact that athletes' salaries are out of proportion to those of average people.

Even when writers include the same facts, they may not agree on what those facts mean. Look at one writer's answer to the second question.

2. How do the writers' interpretations of the same fact or facts differ?

> 2. Singletary and Hjelm agree that sports are entertainment, and that the business of entertainment brings in large amounts of money. Singletary interprets this fact to mean that sports are worth the money they bring in. Hjelm interprets the same fact as meaning that our society's values are misguided.

As you compare texts on the same topic throughout the book, be sure to look at which pieces of evidence writers choose to include and how they interpret that evidence.

College and Career Readiness Anchor Standards for Writing

COMMON CORE STATE STANDARDS

TEXT TYPES AND PURPOSES

1. Write arguments to support claims in an analysis of substantive topics or texts, using valid reasoning and relevant and sufficient evidence.

2. Write informative/explanatory texts to examine and convey complex ideas and information clearly and accurately through the effective selection, organization, and analysis of content.

3. Write narratives to develop real or imagined experiences or events using effective technique, well-chosen details, and well-structured event sequences.

PRODUCTION AND DISTRIBUTION OF WRITING

4. Produce clear and coherent writing in which the development, organization, and style are appropriate to task, purpose, and audience.

5. Develop and strengthen writing as needed by planning, revising, editing, rewriting, or trying a new approach.

6. Use technology, including the Internet, to produce and publish writing and to interact and collaborate with others.

RESEARCH TO BUILD AND PRESENT KNOWLEDGE

7. Conduct short as well as more sustained research projects based on focused questions, demonstrating understanding of the subject under investigation.

8. Gather relevant information from multiple print and digital sources, assess the credibility and accuracy of each source, and integrate the information while avoiding plagiarism.

9. Draw evidence from literary or informational texts to support analysis, reflection, and research.

RANGE OF WRITING

10. Write routinely over extended time frames (time for research, reflection, and revision) and shorter time frames (a single sitting or a day or two) for a range of tasks, purposes, and audiences.

Writing Standards, Grade 7 Students

COMMON CORE STATE STANDARD	WHAT IT MEANS TO YOU
TEXT TYPES AND PURPOSES	
1. Write arguments to support claims with clear reasons and relevant evidence.	You will write and develop arguments with clear reasons and strong evidence that include
a. Introduce claim(s), acknowledge alternate or opposing claims, and organize the reasons and evidence logically.	**a.** a clear organization of claims and counterclaims
b. Support claim(s) with logical reasoning and relevant evidence, using accurate, credible sources and demonstrating an understanding of the topic or text.	**b.** strong, accurate support for claims
c. Use words, phrases, and clauses to create cohesion and clarify the relationships among claim(s), reasons, and evidence.	**c.** use of cohesive words, phrases, and clauses to link information
d. Establish and maintain a formal style.	**d.** a formal style
e. Provide a concluding statement or section that follows from and supports the argument presented.	**e.** a strong concluding statement that summarizes the argument
2. Write informative/explanatory texts to examine a topic and convey ideas, concepts, and information through the selection, organization, and analysis of relevant content.	You will write clear, well-organized, and thoughtful informative and explanatory texts with
a. Introduce a topic clearly, previewing what is to follow; organize ideas, concepts, and information, using strategies such as definition, classification, comparison/contrast, and cause/effect; include formatting (e.g., headings), graphics (e.g., charts, tables), and multimedia when useful to aiding comprehension.	**a.** a clear introduction and organization, including headings and graphic organizers (when appropriate)
b. Develop the topic with relevant facts, definitions, concrete details, quotations, or other information and examples.	**b.** sufficient supporting details and background information
c. Use appropriate transitions to create cohesion and clarify the relationships among ideas and concepts.	**c.** cohesive transitions to link ideas
d. Use precise language and domain-specific vocabulary to inform about or explain the topic.	**d.** precise language and relevant vocabulary
e. Establish and maintain a formal style.	**e.** a formal style
f. Provide a concluding statement or section that follows from and supports the information or explanation presented.	**f.** a strong conclusion that restates the importance or relevance of the topic

Writing Standards, Grade 7 Students, continued

COMMON CORE STATE STANDARD	WHAT IT MEANS TO YOU
3. Write narratives to develop real or imagined experiences or events using effective technique, relevant descriptive details, and well-structured event sequences.	You will write clear, well-structured, detailed narrative texts that
a. Engage and orient the reader by establishing a context and point of view and introducing a narrator and/or characters; organize an event sequence that unfolds naturally and logically.	**a.** draw your readers in with a clear topic that unfolds logically
b. Use narrative techniques, such as dialogue, pacing, and description, to develop experiences, events, and/or characters.	**b.** use narrative techniques to develop and expand on events and/or characters
c. Use a variety of transition words, phrases, and clauses to convey sequence and signal shifts from one time frame or setting to another.	**c.** use a variety of transition words to clearly signal shifts between time frames or settings
d. Use precise words and phrases, relevant descriptive details, and sensory language to capture the action and convey experiences and events.	**d.** use precise words and sensory details that keep readers interested
e. Provide a conclusion that follows from and reflects on the narrated experiences or events.	**e.** have a strong conclusion that reflects on the topic

PRODUCTION AND DISTRIBUTION OF WRITING

4. Produce clear and coherent writing in which the development, organization, and style are appropriate to task, purpose, and audience. (Grade-specific expectations for writing types are defined in standards 1–3 above.)	You will produce writing that is appropriate to the task, purpose, and audience for whom you are writing.
5. With some guidance and support from peers and adults, develop and strengthen writing as needed by planning, revising, editing, rewriting, or trying a new approach, focusing on how well purpose and audience have been addressed.	With help from peers and adults, you will revise and refine your writing to address what is most important for your purpose and audience.
6. Use technology, including the Internet, to produce and publish writing and link to and cite sources as well as to interact and collaborate with others, including linking to and citing sources.	You will use technology to share your writing and to provide links to other relevant information.

RESEARCH TO BUILD AND PRESENT KNOWLEDGE

7. Conduct short research projects to answer a question, drawing on several sources and generating additional related, focused questions for further research and investigation.	You will conduct short research projects to answer a question using multiple sources and generating topics for further research.
8. Gather relevant information from multiple print and digital sources, using search terms effectively; assess the credibility and accuracy of each source; and quote or paraphrase the data and conclusions of others while avoiding plagiarism and following a standard format for citation.	You will effectively conduct searches to gather information from different sources and assess the strength of each source, following a standard format for citation.

Writing Standards, Grade 7 Students, continued

COMMON CORE STATE STANDARD	WHAT IT MEANS TO YOU
9. Draw evidence from literary or informational texts to support analysis, reflection, and research. • Apply *grade 7 Reading standards* to literature (e.g., "Compare and contrast a fictional portrayal of a time, place, or character and a historical account of the same period as a means of understanding how authors of fiction use or alter history"). • Apply *grade 7 Reading standards* to literary nonfiction (e.g. "Trace and evaluate the argument and specific claims in a text, assessing whether the reasoning is sound and the evidence is relevant and sufficient to support the claims").	You will paraphrase, summarize, quote, and cite primary and secondary sources to support your analysis, reflection, and research.
RANGE OF WRITING 10. Write routinely over extended time frames (time for research, reflection, and revision) and shorter time frames (a single sitting or a day or two) for a range of discipline-specific tasks, purposes, and audiences.	You will write for many different purposes and audiences both over short and extended periods of time.

Spotlight on Common Core

COMMON CORE

W 10 Write routinely over extended time frames (time for research, reflection, and revision) and shorter time frames (a single sitting or a day or two) for a range of discipline-specific tasks, purposes, and audiences. **W 4** Produce clear and coherent writing in which the development, organization, and style are appropriate to task, purpose, and audience.

Writing: Maintaining Clarity and Coherence

The Common Core State Standards require you to write in a variety of forms and situations. You might be asked to spend a month writing a research paper or thirty minutes writing a diary entry. No matter how long you take or what your final product, your writing will be better if you start with a plan. Here are some questions you can use to make a plan for any writing task.

- **What is my final product?**
  What are you being asked to write? A wiki entry? A persuasive essay? A literary analysis? Think about how long it will be and what it should contain.

- **What is my purpose for writing?**
  Is your purpose to support an argument, to inform or explain, or to tell about real or imagined experiences or events?

- **What is my topic?**
  Has your teacher assigned a topic, given you a choice, or allowed you to choose your own? When you have selected a topic, begin to think about what you know and what you need to find out. Try filling in a chart like this one.

I already know ...	I need to find out ...	I can get this information from ...
Abraham Lincoln was the president who signed the Emancipation Proclamation.	how he made his decision to sign.	a biography of Abraham Lincoln.

- **Who is my audience?**
  Think about what your audience needs to know to understand your topic. You should also think about what you are comfortable sharing with your audience. If you are writing for a few close friends, you might say things you would not want to say if you were posting comments on the Internet. Finally, choose vocabulary and a style that are right for your audience.

- **How long do I have to write?**
  Make sure you don't take on more than you have time to do. Look at the "I need to find out" column of your chart. Can you find the information you need in the time allowed? Make sure you leave plenty of time to revise, edit, and proofread your writing.

Now that your plan is in place, it is time to produce a clear, coherent piece of writing with development, organization, language, and style that fit your purpose, task, and audience. A piece of writing is **coherent** when every part of it goes together in a logical way. After you have written your first draft, use the chart below to evaluate your writing.

DEVELOPMENT	WHAT DOES IT LOOK LIKE?
• Strong, memorable introduction and concluding section • **Controlling idea or thesis statement** • Support (logical reasoning and relevant evidence, including facts, definitions, concrete details, and quotations)	One of the greatest challenges of our times is providing for the energy needs of the earth's people. Our population is growing, and so is the amount of energy used by each person. Old sources of energy such as oil and coal simply can't keep up with the demand. Some new sources of energy such as solar panels and wind turbines aren't efficient enough to provide more than a fraction of what is needed. **Our only practical option to power the future is nuclear fission.**

ORGANIZATION	WHAT DOES IT LOOK LIKE?
• Logical organization (makes sense for the purpose and audience) • Formatting, graphics, and multimedia to help aid comprehension, if necessary • **Patterns, such as definition, classification, comparison/contrast, cause/effect, and sequence of events to help readers understand the relationship between ideas** • Words, phrases, and clauses, including appropriate transitions, to link sections of text and create cohesion, or flow	After Fidel Castro took over the government of Cuba, he confiscated people's private property. Some of this property belonged to U.S. companies. He tried to start revolutions in other countries and made agreements with socialist governments. **Because of these actions, the U.S. decided to stop most trade with Cuba.** The government stopped companies from buying sugar from Cuba or selling any goods except for food and medicine to Cuba.

LANGUAGE/STYLE	WHAT DOES IT LOOK LIKE?
• Appropriate style and tone (formal for academic tasks and some real-world writing) • **Precise words and phrases, relevant descriptive details, and sensory language** • Strong command of grammar, usage, capitalization, punctuation	On the second day, I woke up **with my thighs and calves aching.** My whole body felt **stiff.** Only the **savory smell of eggs and bacon** cooking over a campfire coaxed me from my sleeping bag. I crawled out of my tent to see the sun rising between two mountain peaks. **The sky was covered with broad strokes of pink, orange, and yellow.** In an instant, I forgot all about my tired muscles.

College and Career Readiness Anchor Standards for Speaking and Listening

COMPREHENSION AND COLLABORATION

1. Prepare for and participate effectively in a range of conversations and collaborations with diverse partners, building on others' ideas and expressing their own clearly and persuasively.

2. Integrate and evaluate information presented in diverse media and formats, including visually, quantitatively, and orally.

3. Evaluate a speaker's point of view, reasoning, and use of evidence and rhetoric.

PRESENTATION OF KNOWLEDGE AND IDEAS

4. Present information, findings, and supporting evidence such that listeners can follow the line of reasoning and the organization, development, and style are appropriate to task, purpose, and audience.

5. Make strategic use of digital media and visual displays of data to express information and enhance understanding of presentations.

6. Adapt speech to a variety of contexts and communicative tasks, demonstrating command of formal English when indicated or appropriate.

Speaking and Listening Standards, Grade 7 Students

COMMON CORE STATE STANDARD	WHAT IT MEANS TO YOU
COMPREHENSION AND COLLABORATION	
1. Engage effectively in a range of collaborative discussions (one-on-one, in groups, and teacher-led) with diverse partners on grade 7 topics, texts, and issues, building on others' ideas and expressing their own clearly.	You will actively participate in a variety of discussions in which you
a. Come to discussions prepared, having read or researched material under study; explicitly draw on that preparation by referring to evidence on the topic, text, or issue to probe and reflect on ideas under discussion.	a. have read any relevant material beforehand and have come to the discussion prepared
b. Follow rules for collegial discussions, track progress toward specific goals and deadlines, and define individual roles as needed.	b. work with others to establish goals and processes within the group
c. Pose questions that elicit elaboration and respond to others' questions and comments with relevant observations and ideas that bring the discussion back on topic as needed.	c. ask and respond to questions and make observations that bring the discussion back to topic as needed
d. Acknowledge new information expressed by others and, when warranted, modify their own views.	d. respond to different perspectives and adjust your own views if necessary
2. Analyze the main ideas and supporting details presented in diverse media and formats (e.g., visually, quantitatively, orally) and explain how the ideas clarify a topic, text, or issue under study.	You will analyze main ideas and details of various media and relate them to a topic under study.

Speaking and Listening Standards, Grade 7 Students, continued

COMMON CORE STATE STANDARD	WHAT IT MEANS TO YOU
3. Delineate a speaker's argument and specific claims, evaluating the soundness of the reasoning and the relevance and sufficiency of the evidence.	You will evaluate a speaker's argument and identify any false reasoning or evidence.
PRESENTATION OF KNOWLEDGE AND IDEAS	
4. Present claims and findings, emphasizing salient points in a focused, coherent manner with pertinent descriptions, facts, details, and examples; use appropriate eye contact, adequate volume, and clear pronunciation.	You will organize and present information to your listeners in a logical sequence and engaging style that is appropriate to your task and audience.
5. Include multimedia components and visual displays in presentations to clarify claims and findings and emphasize salient points.	You will use digital media to enhance and add interest to presentations.
6. Adapt speech to a variety of contexts and tasks, demonstrating command of formal English when indicated or appropriate.	You will adapt the formality of your speech appropriately.

Spotlight on Common Core

COMMON
CORE

SL 3 Delineate a speaker's argument and specific claims, evaluating the soundness of the reasoning and the relevance and sufficiency of the evidence.

Speaking and Listening: Evaluating an Argument

The Common Core State Standards require you to do the following:

- Identify the elements of a speaker's argument and its specific claim(s). A basic argument consists of a **claim**, which is the speaker's position on an issue or problem, and the reasons and evidence offered to support that claim.
- Evaluate the soundness of the speaker's reasoning. In other words, determine whether the speaker's reasoning is good or flawed by errors in logic.
- Determine whether the speaker has provided enough relevant evidence to prove his or her claim is true or valid. **Relevant evidence** consists of facts, examples, and other details that prove a specific claim is most likely true or valid. Irrelevant evidence has no bearing on the claim.

In this book, you will be asked to delineate and evaluate arguments in speeches you read, deliver, or hear. To prepare yourself to do this, study the following example.

Read the following text from a speech by John F. Kennedy. Then answer the questions that follow.

from **"We choose to go to the Moon . . ."**
by John F. Kennedy

President John F. Kennedy gave this speech in 1962 at Rice University in Houston, Texas.

Those who came before us made certain that this country rode the first waves of the industrial revolutions, the first waves of modern invention, and the

continued

first wave of nuclear power, and this generation does not intend to founder in the backwash of the coming age of space. We mean to be a part of it—we mean to lead it. For the eyes of the world now look into space, to the moon and to the planets beyond, and we have vowed that we shall not see it governed by a hostile flag of conquest, but by a banner of freedom and peace. We have vowed that we shall not see space filled with weapons of mass destruction, but with instruments of knowledge and understanding.

Yet the vows of this Nation can only be fulfilled if we in this Nation are first, and, therefore, we intend to be first. . . .

We set sail on this new sea because there is new knowledge to be gained, and new rights to be won, and they must be won and used for the progress of all people. . . .

The growth of our science and education will be enriched by new knowledge of our universe and environment, by new techniques of learning and mapping and observation, by new tools and computers for industry, medicine, the home as well as the school. Technical institutions, such as Rice, will reap the harvest of these gains.

. . . [T]he space effort itself, while still in its infancy, has already created a great number of new companies, and tens of thousands of new jobs. Space and related industries are generating new demands in investment and skilled personnel, and this city and this State, and this region, will share greatly in this growth. What was once the furthest outpost on the old frontier of the West will be the furthest outpost on the new frontier of science and space.

1. What is President Kennedy's basic argument? Identify his claim, reasons, and evidence in your answer.

2. Does he provide enough relevant evidence to support his claim?

LEARN HOW Evaluating an Argument The questions that follow the speech ask you to delineate and evaluate Kennedy's argument.

To delineate the argument, you would first identify Kennedy's claim, which is his position on the U.S. space program. Next, you would note the reasons and evidence he presents to support this claim. Finally, you would present these basic elements of claim, reasons, and evidence in an organized way. You could do this in a chart or in a paragraph. To evaluate his argument you would look at the evidence you found in the speech to see if there is enough relevant evidence to convince you to agree with his position, or claim.

Here are two examples of how one student responded to these questions.

1. What is President Kennedy's basic argument? Identify his claim, reasons, and evidence in your answer.

Claim	We should aggressively support the U.S. space program.		
Reasons	to ensure that freedom and peace are extended to the moon and planets	to gain new rights and knowledge for all people	to create new industries and jobs
Evidence		New techniques of mapping and observation will be developed. New tools and computers will be developed.	A great number of new companies have been created. Tens of thousands of new jobs have been created. This city, state, and region will benefit.

The writer correctly realizes that there is no evidence to support this reason.

The writer finds two likely predictions to back up this reason.

In support of this reason the writer finds two facts and one likely prediction.

2. Does he provide enough relevant evidence to support his claim?

Kennedy provides three good reasons to back up his claim that we should aggressively support the U.S. space program. These are (1) to ensure that we establish freedom and peace on the moon and planets beyond, (2) to gain new rights and knowledge, and (3) to create new industries and jobs. He gives no evidence to support his first reason, however. He does make a few likely predictions to support his second reason, though, and he backs up his third reason with facts and another likely prediction. In my opinion, Kennedy offers enough good reasons and relevant evidence to convince me that we should aggressively support the U.S. space program.

College and Career Readiness Anchor Standards for Language

COMMON CORE STATE STANDARDS

CONVENTIONS OF STANDARD ENGLISH

1. Demonstrate command of the conventions of standard English grammar and usage when writing or speaking.

2. Demonstrate command of the conventions of standard English capitalization, punctuation, and spelling when writing.

KNOWLEDGE OF LANGUAGE

3. Apply knowledge of language to understand how language functions in different contexts, to make effective choices for meaning or style, and to comprehend more fully when reading or listening.

College and Career Readiness Anchor Standards for Language, continued

VOCABULARY ACQUISITION AND USE

4. Determine or clarify the meaning of unknown and multiple-meaning words and phrases by using context clues, analyzing meaningful word parts, and consulting general and specialized reference materials, as appropriate.

5. Demonstrate understanding of word relationships and nuances in word meanings.

6. Acquire and use accurately a range of general academic and domain-specific words and phrases sufficient for reading, writing, speaking, and listening at the college and career readiness level; demonstrate independence in gathering vocabulary knowledge when considering a word or phrase important to comprehension or expression.

Language Standards, Grade 7 Students

COMMON CORE STATE STANDARD	WHAT IT MEANS TO YOU

CONVENTIONS OF STANDARD ENGLISH
1. Demonstrate command of the conventions of standard English grammar and usage when writing or speaking.
  a. Explain the function of phrases and clauses in general and their function in specific sentences.
  b. Choose among simple, compound, complex, and compound-complex sentences to signal differing relationships among ideas.
  c. Place phrases and clauses within a sentence, recognizing and correcting misplaced and dangling modifiers.
	You will correctly understand and use the conventions of English grammar and usage, including
	
	  a. explaining the function of phrases and clauses
	
	  b. using a variety of sentence structures
	
	  c. correctly placing phrases and clauses in sentences

2. Demonstrate command of the conventions of standard English capitalization, punctuation, and spelling when writing.
  a. Use a comma to separate coordinate adjectives (e.g., *It was a fascinating, enjoyable movie* but not *He wore an old[,] green shirt*).
  b. Spell correctly.
	You will correctly use the conventions of English capitalization, punctuation, and spelling, including
	
	  a. commas
	
	  b. spelling

KNOWLEDGE OF LANGUAGE
3. Use knowledge of language and its conventions when writing, speaking, reading, or listening.
  a. Choose language that expresses ideas precisely and concisely, recognizing and eliminating wordiness and redundancy.
	You will apply your knowledge of language in different contexts by
	  a. choosing precise and concise language to avoid wordiness or stating the same thing more than once

Language Standards, Grade 7 Students, continued

COMMON CORE STATE STANDARD	WHAT IT MEANS TO YOU
VOCABULARY ACQUISITION AND USE	
4. Determine or clarify the meaning of unknown and multiple-meaning words and phrases based on grade 7 reading and content, choosing flexibly from a range of strategies.	You will understand the meaning of grade-level appropriate words and phrases by
a. Use context (e.g., the overall meaning of a sentence or paragraph; a word's position or function in a sentence) as a clue to the meaning of a word or phrase.	**a.** using context clues
b. Use common, grade-appropriate Greek or Latin affixes and roots as clues to the meaning of a word (e.g., *belligerent, bellicose, rebel*).	**b.** using Greek or Latin roots
c. Consult general and specialized reference materials (e.g., dictionaries, glossaries, thesauruses), both print and digital, to find the pronunciation of a word or determine or clarify its precise meaning or its part of speech.	**c.** using reference materials
d. Verify the preliminary determination of the meaning of a word or phrase (e.g., by checking the inferred meaning in context or in a dictionary).	**d.** inferring and verifying the meanings of words in context
5. Demonstrate understanding of figurative language, word relationships, and nuances in word meanings.	You will understand figurative language, word relationships, and slight differences in word meanings by
a. Interpret figures of speech (e.g., literary, biblical, and mythological allusions) in context.	**a.** interpreting figures of speech in context
b. Use the relationship between particular words (e.g., synonym/antonym, analogy) to better understand each of the words.	**b.** analyzing relationships between words
c. Distinguish among the connotations (associations) of words with similar denotations (definitions) (e.g., *refined, respectful, polite, diplomatic, condescending*).	**c.** distinguishing among words with similar definitions
6. Acquire and use accurately grade-appropriate general academic and domain-specific words and phrases; gather vocabulary knowledge when considering a word or phrase important to comprehension or expression.	You will learn and use grade-appropriate vocabulary.

Spotlight on Common Core

 COMMON CORE L 5a Interpret figures of speech (e. g., literary, biblical, and mythological allusions) in context.

Vocabulary: Figures of Speech

The Common Core State Standards require you to figure out the meaning of figures of speech as you read. A **figure of speech** is an imaginative way of using words to express ideas that are not literally true. Here's an example:

At the track meet, Ming ran like the wind.

Ming did not really run at the same speed as the wind blows. The figure of speech means that Ming ran fast.

There are several kinds of figures of speech. Four of the most common are similes, metaphors, personification, and allusion. All of them are types of comparisons.

A **simile** compares two unlike things using the word *like* or *as*.

> That cheese smells like dirty socks.
> (The writer compares cheese to socks, using the word *like*.)

> Juan is as hungry as a bear.
> (The writer compares Juan to a bear, using the word *as*.)

A **metaphor** compares two unlike things without using *like* or *as*.

> His smile is a ray of sunshine.
> (The writer compares a smile to the sun.)

> The prairie's mane of long, yellow grass rippled in the breeze.
> (The writer compares the grass to an animal's mane.)

Personification describes an object, animal, or idea as though it were human. It compares non-human things with humans.

> The old house's floorboards groaned under his weight.
> (The writer compares floorboards to people, who can groan. Objects do not groan.)

> The mountain goat danced across the meadow.
> (The writer compares a mountain goat to people, who can dance. Animals do not dance.)

An **allusion** is a reference to knowledge from outside the work. An allusion can refer to another work of literature, the Bible, mythology, film, or popular culture. It invites a comparison of a person, place, thing, idea, or situation to something from the readers' previous experience.

> Olive loves to play Cupid; she is always trying to set her friends up on dates.
> (Cupid is a mythological figure who makes people fall in love. The writer compares Olive to Cupid.)

> Our football team will enter the lions' den when they play the Kilgore Cougars in their home stadium on Saturday.
> (In the Bible, Daniel was thrown into a den of lions for continuing to practice his faith. The writer compares the football team to Daniel.)

Throughout this book, you will read poems, stories, and novel excerpts that use figures of speech.

LEARN HOW Interpreting Figures of Speech in Context When you come across a figure of speech you don't understand, ask yourself these questions.

- What is the context for the figure of speech?
- What two things is the figure of speech comparing?

Read this paragraph and interpret each of the underlined figures of speech.

1 I was having a horrible time at the school dance. The ice cream smelled like the inside of the janitor's closet.
2 The cake was a dried-out kitchen sponge. Even worse, I felt too shy to talk with anyone.
3 Then Leticia turned into my own personal Tinker Bell. She came up to me and took my arm. She turned and waved at Maya.
4 Before I knew it, Maya and I were dancing. Suddenly all the gymnasium's fairy lights were winking just at me.

Here are one writer's interpretations of the figures of speech.

> *1. The context tells me the narrator is having a bad time. This simile compares the smell of the ice cream with the smell of a janitor's closet. The figure of speech means that the ice cream smells bad. It tells me one reason why the narrator is having a bad time.*
>
> *2. This metaphor compares a cake with a kitchen sponge. The figure of speech means that the cake is dry. It tells me another reason why the narrator is having a bad time.*
>
> *3. The context tells me that something happens to change the narrator's bad time. This allusion compares Leticia to Tinker Bell. Tinker Bell is a character from the book Peter Pan. She is a fairy who uses magic to help her friends. The figure of speech means that Leticia helps the narrator in a way that seems magical. It tells why the narrator is no longer having a bad time.*
>
> *4. The context tells me that the narrator is now having a good time. This figure of speech personifies the lights decorating the gym. It compares the lights with people winking. The figure of speech means that the gym seems like a friendly place. Because the narrator is having fun, everything around him seems friendly.*

As you read the literature in this book, interpret figures of speech by looking at their context and asking yourself what two things they compare.

Spotlight on Common Core

L 1b Choose among simple, compound, complex, and compound-complex sentences to signal differing relationships among ideas.

Grammar: Sentence Types

The Common Core State Standards require you to choose the sentence types that best express your ideas and how those ideas are related. Before you look at the four types of sentences, you need to know about their building blocks: clauses.

There are two kinds of clauses: main clauses and subordinate clauses. Both kinds of clauses have a subject and a verb.

A **main clause** can stand by itself as a complete sentence. It has a subject and a verb.

> <u>Mikhail</u> <u>likes</u> funny movies.
>   subj. verb

A **subordinate clause** cannot stand by itself as a sentence. It has a subject and a verb and a word that makes the clause dependent.

> unless <u>they</u> <u>make</u> fun of people
>   subj. verb

> <u>that</u> <u>make</u> him laugh
> subj. verb

Subordinate clauses start with a dependent word. This dependent word can be a conjunction, such as *unless*, or a pronoun, such as *that*. If you take away the conjunction or turn the pronoun into a noun, you can change a subordinate clause to a main clause.

> They make fun of people. (remove the conjunction *unless*)

Movies make him laugh. (change the pronoun *that* to the word *Movies*)

Throughout this book, you will be asked to write responses to a variety of prompts and tasks. Whenever you write, you must choose the sentence types that best express your ideas.

LEARN HOW Writing Simple, Compound, Complex, and Compound-Complex Sentences
Look at these definitions and examples of the four sentence types. They are made up of different combinations of main and subordinate clauses. You can use them as models to write your own sentences.

A **simple sentence** has one main clause and no subordinate clauses.
<u>Michaela will try out for the volleyball team</u>.
                main clause

A **compound sentence** has two or more main clauses and no subordinate clauses.
<u>Michaela will try out for the volleyball team</u> and <u>Lindsey will try out for the debate team</u>.
         main clause   main clause

A **complex sentence** has one main clause and one or more subordinate clauses.
<u>Michaela will try out for the volleyball team</u> <u>if she brings up her grade in English</u>.
        main clause   subordinate clause

Note that you can also add the subordinate clause to the beginning of the sentence. When the subordinate clause comes first, it is followed by a comma.
<u>If she brings up her grade in English</u>, <u>Michaela will try out for the volleyball team</u>.
      subordinate clause   main clause

A **compound-complex sentence** has two or more main clauses and one or more subordinate clauses.
<u>Michaela will try out for the volleyball team</u> <u>if she brings up her grade in English</u> and
      main clause   subordinate clause
<u>Lindsey will try out for the debate team</u> <u>if she brings up her grade in Geometry</u>.
     main clause   subordinate clause

Now try using the clauses below to write a simple sentence, a compound sentence, a complex sentence, and a compound-complex sentence.

- that have surprising endings
- after he does his homework
- Eli prefers to read mystery stories
- Thomas likes to skateboard

Here are one writer's sentences.

Simple: Thomas likes to skateboard.
Compound: Thomas likes to skateboard, but Eli prefers to read mystery stories.
Complex: Thomas likes to skateboard after he does his homework.
Compound-complex: Thomas likes to skateboard, but Eli prefers to read mystery stories that have surprising endings.

Whenever you are asked to write throughout this book, make sure you use a variety of sentence types to express your ideas.

The Power of Ideas

INTRODUCING
THE ESSENTIALS

- Genres Workshop
- Reading Strategies Workshop
- Academic Vocabulary Workshop
- Writing Process Workshop

What Are Life's Big Questions?

We all wrestle with the big questions in life, including the ones shown here. That's because such questions prompt us to think about certain experiences—for example, love, growing up, and loss—that affect all our lives, no matter who we are or where we come from. Through our experiences, we come closer to answering these questions, making sense of the world, and understanding ourselves. But powerful literature holds some answers too.

What is COURAGE?

Courage helps people face big challenges, such as protecting their families or fighting life-threatening illnesses. It can also take courage to do something small, like talk to someone who intimidates you. This book is filled with brave characters—among them a pet mongoose and a shy seventh grader—who can teach you what true courage is.

Is life always FAIR?

If you've ever single-handedly lost a team championship or gotten blamed for something that wasn't your fault, you've probably realized that life can feel completely unfair. Read Ernest Lawrence Thayer's poem "Casey at the Bat" or Chaim Potok's story "Zebra," and you'll discover that you're not alone in feeling this way.

Where is HOME?

"Home is where the heart is," as the old saying goes. The place you call home doesn't have to be the house where you live. Rather, home can be wherever you feel most comfortable and secure. Think about all the places that people might call home—for example, a certain country or a hiding place that nobody else knows about. Then ask yourself: Where is home?

Can we achieve the IMPOSSIBLE?

In many Hollywood action movies, the hero emerges victorious despite impossible odds. Some stories in this book star real-life heroes whose astonishing achievements can make us believe that anything is possible. However, tales as ancient as Greek myths warn us about what can happen if we set our sights too high. Is the impossible really within our reach?

Exploring Text Types

The big questions in life are not easy to answer, but people keep trying. For centuries, writers have searched for answers to such questions, exploring their ideas through stories, poems, and plays. As readers, we turn to literary and nonfiction texts to see how others see the world and to learn about ourselves.

The Genres

COMMON CORE

Included in this workshop:
RL 1, RL 2, RL 3, RL 4, RL 5, RL 6,
RI 1, RI 3

Literature and nonfiction include a variety of genres that have many purposes. Some are meant to be read; others are meant to be performed. Formats such as blockbuster movies and advertisements are not what you would expect to find in a book. They are important to analyze, though, since they communicate many ideas and messages in today's world.

In this book you will explore questions and ideas in many genres. By reading everything from dramas and newspaper articles to poetry and short stories, you will be able to discuss and write about such ideas as survival and happiness. First, review the characteristics of each genre.

GENRES AT A GLANCE

STORIES
Stories portray made-up characters and events.
- short stories
- novels
- novellas
- folk tales

POETRY
Poetry is a type of literature in which words are chosen and arranged in a compact, precise way to create specific effects.
- haiku
- free-verse poems
- narrative poems

DRAMA
Dramas are stories that are meant to be performed.
- comedies
- historical dramas
- teleplays

NONFICTION
Nonfiction tells about real people, places, and events.
- autobiographies
- essays
- news articles
- biographies
- speeches
- opinion pieces

TYPES OF MEDIA

The word *media* refers to communication that reaches many people.
- feature films
- advertising
- news blogs

STORIES

Whether it is a book by your favorite author or a story that your friend invented, a story starts as an idea in someone's imagination. Sometimes stories are also inspired by real people and events.

Good stories keep readers interested by weaving together many elements. These elements include **plot** (the action of the story), **characters** (the persons or animals involved in the action), **setting** (where and when the action takes place), and **theme** (the big idea behind the story—what the story is *really* about). Three types of fiction are short stories, novels, and novellas.

- A **short story** is a brief work of fiction that can usually be read in one sitting. It often focuses on a single event or a few main characters.

- A **novel** is a much longer work of fiction that can take several days or even weeks to read. Because they are longer than short stories, novels have room to develop more complex characters and plots.

- A **novella** is longer than a short story but shorter than a novel.

Read the Model In the novel *The Cay,* a young boy named Phillip and his mother flee their home in the Caribbean. After their ship is attacked, Phillip goes blind from an injury and gets lost at sea. Soon he finds himself stranded on a remote island. His only companions are an island man named Timothy and a cat. Notice the story elements that the author uses to explore the idea of survival.

---

from

The Cay

Novel by **Theodore Taylor**

The palm fronds above me rattled in the breeze, and there were other noises from the underbrush. I knew Stew Cat was around somewhere, but it didn't sound like him.

I wondered if Timothy had checked for snakes. There were also
5 scorpions on most Caribbean islands, and they were deadly. I wondered if there were any on our cay.

During those first few days on the island, the times I spent alone were terrible. It was, of course, being unable to see that made all the sounds so frightening. I guess if you are born blind, it is not so bad. You grow
10 up knowing each sound and what it means.

Suddenly, the tears came out. I knew it was not a manly thing to do, something my father would have frowned on, but I couldn't stop.

Close Read

1. Using terms from the Literary Terms list, describe what's happening in this scene.

2. **Exploring a Big Question** Phillip will probably have to overcome his fear if he wants to survive. What qualities might help him stay alive on this solitary island?

POETRY

Poetry is all around you—in the nursery rhymes you learned as a child, in the lyrics of the songs you listen to, in greeting-card messages, and in this book. Poetry is very different from stories, starting with the way words are arranged on the page. In poetry, ideas are expressed through a series of **lines,** which are often grouped into **stanzas.** Often, the **form** or structure of a poem contributes to its meaning.

Many poems are meant to be heard, not just read. For that reason, the way a poem sounds is as important as the way it looks on the page. Poets often experiment with sound devices, including **rhythm** and **rhyme,** to emphasize important words and create musical effects.

Read the Model A powerful poem can make readers look at something ordinary—a thumbprint, for example—in a new way. Read this poem aloud so that you can hear its rhythm and rhyme. What is the poet saying about the idea of individuality?

LITERARY TERMS FOR POETRY

- form
- line
- stanza
- rhythm
- rhyme
- speaker
- imagery

Thumbprint

Poem by **Eve Merriam**

On the pad of my thumb
are whorls, whirls, wheels
in a unique design:
mine alone.
5   What a treasure to own!
My own flesh, my own feelings.
No other, however grand or base,
can ever contain the same.
My signature,
10   thumbing the pages of my time.
My universe key,
my singularity.
Impress, implant,
I am myself,
15   of all my atom parts I am the sum.
And out of my blood and my brain
I make my own interior weather,
my own sun and rain.
Imprint my mark upon the world,
20   whatever I shall become.

Close Read

1. How can you tell that "Thumbprint" is a poem? Cite specific evidence to support your answer.

2. **Exploring a Big Question** A thumbprint is one of many things that distinguishes one person from another. What other qualities or characteristics make an individual unique?

DRAMA

Good stories can take different forms. For example, **drama** is meant to be performed before an audience. As a result, a drama does not include long descriptions of settings or characters' thoughts. Instead, the story is developed through **dialogue** and actions—what the characters say and do. The structure of a drama is also different from that of a short story or novel. A drama is made up of **scenes** and **acts,** rather than chapters and parts.

A drama also includes notes to help the actors and the director perform it as the writer intended. These instructions, or **stage directions,** describe the setting and how the characters should look, talk, and act. Stage directions are often printed in *italic* type.

Read the Model *A Young Lady of Property* is about Wilma, a teenager who dreams of leaving her home and becoming a movie star. Wilma also wants to leave so that she doesn't have to deal with Mrs. Leighton, her father's girlfriend. In this excerpt Wilma reveals her plan to her father. As you read, think about the idea of ambition.

> ### LITERARY TERMS FOR DRAMA
> - plot
> - character
> - act
> - scene
> - dialogue
> - stage directions

from

A Young *Lady* of Property

Drama by **Horton Foote**

Lester. Say hello to Mrs. Leighton.

Wilma (*most ungraciously*). Hello, Mrs. Leighton.

Mrs. Leighton (*most graciously*). Hello, Wilma.

Lester. What are you doing hanging around the streets, Wilma?

5 **Wilma.** Waiting to see if I have a letter.

Lester. What kind of letter, Wilma?

Wilma. About getting into the movies. Arabella and I saw an ad in the *Houston Chronicle* about a Mr. Delafonte who is a famous Hollywood director.

10 **Lester.** Who is Mr. Delafonte?

Wilma. The Hollywood director I'm trying to tell you about. He's giving screen tests in Houston to people of beauty and talent, and if they pass they'll go to Hollywood and be in the picture shows.

Lester. Well, that's all a lot of foolishness, Wilma. You're not going to

15 Houston to take anything.

Wilma. But, Daddy . . . I . . .

Lester. You're fifteen years old and you're gonna stay home. . . .

Close Read

1. How does Wilma treat Mrs. Leighton? How does Mrs. Leighton act toward Wilma? Explain how you can tell.

2. **Exploring a Big Question** Wilma's desire to become a movie star is an ambition that many other teens may share. What other ambitions do young people have? Explain why such ambitions are appealing.

NONFICTION

Through **literary nonfiction,** such as autobiographies and speeches, you can learn about historic events, inspiring people, and ground-breaking topics. **Informational text,** such as signs, textbooks, instruction manuals, magazine articles, and other writing that conveys factual information, is also a source for learning about the world. For these reasons, you need to become a critical reader of all types of nonfiction.

TERMS FOR NONFICTION
- purpose
- organization
- main idea
- argument

TYPE OF NONFICTION	CHARACTERISTICS	
AUTOBIOGRAPHY/ BIOGRAPHY The true story of a person's life, told by that person (autobiography) or by someone else (biography)	• Helps readers learn about events and experiences in a person's life • Is told from the first-person point of view (autobiography) or the third-person point of view (biography)	
ESSAY A short piece of writing about a single, focused subject	• Has one or more of the following purposes: to express feelings, to inform, to entertain, to persuade • Uses either formal or informal language	 Homeless Anna Quindlen
SPEECH An oral presentation of the speaker's ideas or beliefs	• Is intended to express feelings, to inform, to entertain, or to persuade • Achieves its power through well-chosen language as well as the speaker's voice and gestures	
NEWS/FEATURE ARTICLES Informational writing in newspapers and magazines. News articles report on recent events. Feature articles provide in-depth coverage of interesting people, topics, and trends.	• Are primarily intended to inform or entertain • Often use examples, statistics, quotations from sources, and graphic aids to present information	 **TheHoriz** DO PROFESSIONAL **ATHLETES GET PAID TOO MUCH?** JUSTIN HJELM *Staff Reporter*
CONSUMER DOCUMENTS Instructional manuals and other printed materials for products and services	• Are intended to inform consumers about how to use a product or service • Often include illustrations, diagrams, and step-by-step directions	**How to operate your digital camera**  on/off

MODEL 1: AUTOBIOGRAPHY

As you read this excerpt from an autobiography by author Walter Dean Myers, notice how he describes his feelings. Through his descriptions, what do you learn about the idea of overcoming obstacles?

from **BAD BOY**

Autobiography by
Walter Dean Myers

    I knew in my heart that I would have some difficulties in life because of my speech problems, and I also knew that I wouldn't always be able to solve them by punching somebody out. But I didn't want to make my speech the focus of my life. If I couldn't speak well, I could
5 still communicate by writing. If the words didn't come easily from my mouth, they would, I hoped, eventually come from my writing.

    I never understood my speech problem. The words I spoke sounded clear to me. When a teacher or classmate asked me to say something more clearly, I didn't know what to do. Reading aloud in front of an
10 audience was especially difficult for me. After a while I dreaded reading even a sports page to my friends. My stomach would tighten up, and I would become so nervous I could hardly read at all.

Close Read

1. What challenges did young Myers face because of his speech problem? Look for descriptions of his feelings.

2. **Exploring a Big Question** Myers realized early on that he had to deal with his problem. Do you think that all obstacles can be overcome with enough effort? Why or why not?

MODEL 2: FEATURE ARTICLE

Stress, the idea in this article, is something that many people experience. How does the article help you understand the reactions that Myers describes in his autobiography?

Stress

YOUR HEALTH

    Stress is a part of life, whether you are young or old or in-between. Even children experience stress. But what can you do to prevent stress from taking over? The first step is to understand what stress is.

    Stress is the body's way of reacting to certain challenging events. The
5 events that cause stress are referred to as *stressors.* They include physical dangers, like climbing a steep mountain, or emotional challenges, such as performing in front of an audience.

    Most of the time, we don't like feeling stress. But a certain amount of stress can be a good thing, leading to heightened focus and increased
10 stamina and alertness. . . .

Close Read

1. How are the boxed details in this article different from the kinds of details that Myers uses to describe the stress he felt as a child?

2. **Exploring a Big Question** Life is full of stressful situations. What other events or factors in life can cause stress?

9

TYPES OF MEDIA

Movies allow you to experience everything from time travel to heroic adventures. The news informs you about what's happening in the world. Ads promise that your life will improve if you buy certain products. Media messages like these influence your life in many ways. That's why you need to become **media literate**—that is, learn how to "read" the media as carefully as you would a work of literature.

TYPE OF MEDIA	CHARACTERISTICS	
FEATURE FILMS Motion pictures that tell stories	• Are meant to entertain and to make a profit • Use camera shots, sound effects, music, actors, and sets to tell stories • Are at least one hour long	
NEWS MEDIA Reports of recent events in newspapers and magazines and on TV, the radio, and the Web	• Are intended to inform and to create a loyal audience • Medium (TV, radio, or print) affects how information is presented • Need to be closely examined for accuracy and bias	
TV SHOWS Dramas, sitcoms, and other programs broadcast on television	• Are meant to inform and entertain • Use visuals, sound effects, and music to create entertaining stories • Are usually 30 to 60 minutes long	
ADVERTISING The promotion of products, services, and ideas using print and broadcast media	• Is designed to persuade a target audience to buy a product or agree with an idea • Uses persuasive techniques, visuals, and sounds to convey a message	
WEB SITES Collections of pages on the World Wide Web	• Use text, graphics, audio, and video to present information • Include hyperlinks and menus that allow users to navigate to the information they are looking for	 Dickens and Too Many S DICKENS BIOGRAPHY → BOOKS BY DICKENS → THE STORY BEHIND A C Dickens' cherished little Christmas story, the bes of all of his books, began life as the result of the of money. In the fall of 1843 Dickens and his wife, K fifth child. Requests for money from his family, a Devonshire Terrace home, and lagging sales from of *Martin Chuzzlewit* had left Dickens seriously s As the idea for the story took shape and the Dickens became engrossed in the book. He wr

Literature and Nonfiction Strategies

 Jot your reactions and observations in your **Reader/Writer Notebook.**

❶ Ask Yourself the Right Questions

One skill that can help you analyze any text is the ability to ask good questions. This book will show you what good questions are, so that you can begin to craft them yourself.

Where to Look	What You'll Find
Text Analysis Workshops (at the beginning of every unit) ▶	Interactive practice models and Close Read questions
Side notes and discussion questions ▶	Questions that focus on the analysis of literary and nonfiction elements
Analysis Frames **THINK**central Go to **thinkcentral.com.** KEYWORD: HML7-11 ▶	Guided questions for analyzing different genres

❷ Make Connections

For any text to have real meaning for you, you have to make connections. Here are some ways to do just that:

- **Connect to Your Life** What does it take to survive? What makes an individual unique? Consider how experiences in your own life can help you explore big questions like these and the key ideas at the heart of them.

- **Connect to Other Subjects** Surviving on an island, managing stress, living in ancient times—the subjects you read about can help you learn about the world. If a subject interests you, research it on the Web.

❸ Record Your Reactions

Jot down your thoughts and impressions, both while and after you read. Consider using these formats.

JOURNAL
Capture your thoughts as you read.

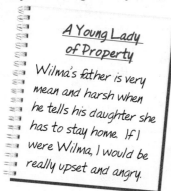

A Young Lady of Property

Wilma's father is very mean and harsh when he tells his daughter she has to stay home. If I were Wilma, I would be really upset and angry.

GRAPHIC ORGANIZER
After reading, create a graphic organizer to help you understand characters and events.

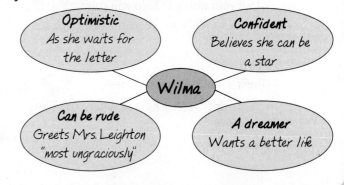

Optimistic — As she waits for the letter

Confident — Believes she can be a star

Wilma

Can be rude — Greets Mrs. Leighton "most ungraciously"

A dreamer — Wants a better life

Becoming an Active Reader

A science fiction story, a biography of an athlete, a news article about a faraway country—every kind of text offers a world of ideas for you to explore. Active reading skills and strategies can help you tap into those ideas. Most of the skills and strategies you will practice throughout this book are already familiar to you. Which ones do you recognize?

SKILLS AND STRATEGIES FOR ACTIVE READING

Preview
Get your bearings before you read.

- Scan the title, graphics, and subheadings.
- Skim the first paragraph to get a sense of what the text is about.

Set a Purpose
Think about *why* you are reading a text.

- Ask: Am I reading to learn, to be entertained, or for another reason?
- Decide how this purpose affects your reading. Pay close attention or simply enjoy?

Connect
Take the text personally.

- Think about whether any situations described remind you of experiences in your own life.
- Ask: If I were this character, how would I feel?

Use Prior Knowledge
Recall what you already know about a topic.

- Jot down any facts, descriptions, and impressions before you read.
- Use your notes to help you connect what you know to what you're learning.

Predict
Guess what will happen next.

- Note details that hint at where the story is going.
- Read on to find out if you guessed correctly.

Visualize
Picture in your mind what is being described.

- Note descriptions of characters and settings.
- Use these details to help you form a clear mental image.

Monitor
Check your understanding as you read.

- **Question** what is happening and why.
- Reread difficult parts or ask for help to **clarify** your understanding.
- **Evaluate** yourself as a reader. Ask: How well am I understanding the text?

Make Inferences
Make logical guesses based on details in the text and your own experiences.

- Record important details about characters, settings, and events.
- Ask: How can what I know help me "read between the lines"? (This chart shows how one student made an inference about a character in the story on the next page.)

Details in "Shells"	What I Know	My Inference
Both of Michael's parents died six months ago.	It takes time for people to deal with loss.	Michael's anger and sadness won't last forever.

This story is about a boy named Michael who goes to live with his aunt Esther after his parents die. Will Michael ever break out of his lonely shell and overcome his anger toward Esther? As you read this excerpt, use the **Close Read** questions to practice the skills and strategies you just learned.

from

Shells

Short story by **Cynthia Rylant**

"I can't make you happy, Michael. You just refuse to be happy here. And you punish me every day for it."

"*Punish* you?" Michael gawked at her. "I don't punish you! I don't care about you! I don't care what you eat or how you dress or where you
5 go or what you think. Can't you just leave me alone?"

He slammed down the glass, scraped his chair back from the table and ran out the door.

"Michael!" yelled Esther.

They had been living together, the two of them, for six months.
10 Michael's parents had died and only Esther could take him in—or, only she had offered to. Michael's other relatives could not imagine dealing with a fourteen-year-old boy. They wanted peaceful lives.

Esther lived in a condominium in a wealthy section of Detroit. Most of the area's residents were older (like her) and afraid of the world they
15 lived in (like her). They stayed indoors much of the time. They trusted few people.

Esther liked living alone. She had never married or had children. She had never lived anywhere but Detroit. She liked her condominium.

But she was fiercely loyal to her family, and when her only sister had
20 died, Esther insisted she be allowed to care for Michael. And Michael, afraid of going anywhere else, had accepted.

Oh, he was lonely. Even six months after their deaths, he still expected to see his parents—sitting on the couch as he walked into Esther's living room, waiting for the bathroom as he came out of the
25 shower, coming in the door late at night. He still smelled his father's Old Spice somewhere, his mother's talc.

Sometimes he was so sure one of them was somewhere around him that he thought maybe he was going crazy. His heart hurt him. He wondered if he would ever get better.

Close Read

1. **Set a Purpose** People often read short stories for enjoyment. Here, you also have another purpose—to practice active reading skills and strategies. Have a notebook ready in which you can record your observations.

2. **Monitor** Reread the boxed text. Why did Esther insist on taking care of Michael?

30 And though he denied it, he did hate Esther. She was so different from his mother and father. Prejudiced—she admired only those who were white and Presbyterian. Selfish—she wouldn't allow him to use her phone. Complaining—she always had a headache or a backache or a stomachache.

35 He didn't want to, but he hated her. And he didn't know what to do except lie about it.

Michael hadn't made any friends at his new school, and his teachers barely noticed him. He came home alone every day and usually found Esther on the phone. She kept in close touch with several other women
40 in nearby condominiums.

Esther told her friends she didn't understand Michael. She said she knew he must grieve for his parents, but why punish her? She said she thought she might send him away if he couldn't be nicer. She said she didn't deserve this.

45 But when Michael came in the door, she always quickly changed the subject.

One day after school Michael came home with a hermit crab. He had gone into a pet store, looking for some small, living thing, and hermit crabs were selling for just a few dollars. He'd bought
50 one, and a bowl.

Esther, for a change, was not on the phone when he arrived home. She was having tea and a crescent roll and seemed cheerful. Michael wanted badly to show someone what he had bought. So he showed her.

Esther surprised him. She picked up the shell and poked the long,
55 shiny nail of her little finger at the crab's claws.

"Where is he?" she asked.

Michael showed her the crab's eyes peering through the small opening of the shell.

"Well, for heaven's sake, come out of there!" she said to the crab,
60 and she turned the shell upside down and shook it.

"Aunt Esther!" Michael grabbed for the shell.

"All right, all right." She turned it right side up. "Well," she said, "what does he do?"

Michael grinned and shrugged his shoulders.
65 "I don't know," he answered. "Just grows, I guess."

His aunt looked at him.

"An attraction to a crab is something I cannot identify with. However, it's fine with me if you keep him, as long as I can be assured that he won't grow out of that bowl." She gave him a hard stare.
70 "He won't," Michael answered. "I promise." . . .

Close Read

3. **Make Inferences** Why do you think Michael treats his aunt the way he does? Explain how the details in lines 22–34 help you to understand his behavior at the beginning of the story.

4. **Visualize** Reread lines 51–64 and try to picture the scene in your mind. Cite specific details that helped you to see the characters, the setting, and the action.

5. **Predict** Do you think Michael and his aunt will ever find a way to get along? Try to guess what will happen to their relationship.

Strategies That Work: Reading

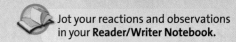 Jot your reactions and observations in your **Reader/Writer Notebook**.

❶ Read Independently

The best way to become a better reader is to read as much as you can, every chance you get.

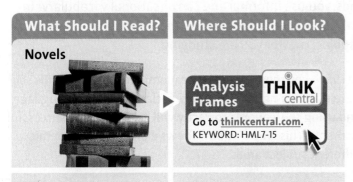

What Should I Read?	Where Should I Look?
Novels	**Analysis Frames** **THINK** central Go to thinkcentral.com. KEYWORD: HML7-15
Magazines Newspapers Web sites	Every time you check your favorite Web site or leaf through the daily newspaper, you are reading. Pick up whatever interests you, and keep reading.

❷ Use Graphic Organizers

Recording your observations as you read can help you better understand a selection. Try creating a two-column chart. In one column, record details or quotations from the selection. In the other, write your thoughts and impressions.

"Shells"	My Thoughts
Esther likes living by herself, and she never had children of her own.	No wonder Esther is frustrated with Michael. She can't seem to make him feel better, _and_ she's not used to taking care of someone else.

❸ Build Your Vocabulary

Creating a personal word list in your **Reader/Writer Notebook** can help you better understand not only a specific selection but also other readings throughout your life. Use these tips to get started:

- **List difficult words.** Consider listing vocabulary words from the selections, as well as other challenging terms you encounter.
- **Go beyond the definitions.** To help you remember each word and its meaning, list synonyms and antonyms, or write a sentence using the word.
- **Try them out.** Using new words in your writing and discussions is one of the best ways to build your vocabulary.

Word	Meaning
gawked (v.) "Shells," line 3	**Definition**: stared at long and hard in amazement **Synonym**: gaped **Antonym**: glanced **Sentence**: As they entered the lobby, the family _gawked_ at the magnificent hotel.

What Is Academic Vocabulary?

COMMON CORE

Included in this workshop:
L 4a–d, L 6

When you stop to think about it, words can be the most reliable and flexible tools you have. Whether you're texting your friends, organizing a community project, or updating your blog, you have thousands of words at your disposal. However, the kinds of words you use can change, depending on your purpose. With family and friends, you use informal and conversational vocabulary. In school, though, you rely on **academic vocabulary,** the language you use to talk and write about the subject matter you are studying.

Analyze, feature, identify—you may encounter academic vocabulary words such as these in *all* subject areas, including science, math, social studies, and language arts. Understanding and using these words correctly will help you to be successful in school and on assessments. This web diagram shows examples of academic vocabulary words in different subject areas.

SOCIAL STUDIES
How can a person belong to more than one **cultural** group?

LANGUAGE ARTS
What makes conflict the driving **feature** of a plot?

WORLD HISTORY
In what ways did the steam engine have a major **impact** on world history?

ACADEMIC VOCABULARY
The language that you use to think, talk, and write about different subject areas you are studying

BIOLOGY
How might the **structure** of a cell affect its function?

ALGEBRA
Describe how you would use equations to **solve** percent problems.

PHYSICAL SCIENCE
Identify the common forms of energy.

Use the following chart to become familiar with some of the academic vocabulary terms in this book. As you read, look for the activities labeled "Academic Vocabulary in Writing" and "Academic Vocabulary in Speaking." These activities provide opportunities to use academic language in your writing and discussions.

Word	Definition	Example
analyze	to separate, or break into parts and examine	**Analyze** the data in the bar graph.
area	a division of experience, activity, or knowledge	In what **area** did Sally Ride specialize?
aware	having knowledge of	Are you **aware** of your rights as a citizen of the United States?
conduct	to direct the course of something	To test their ideas, scientists **conduct** experiments.
cultural	the attitudes and behavior that characterize a group	The oral tradition was part of the **cultural** life of ancient African societies.
demonstrate	to show clearly	**Demonstrate** how to extract and observe DNA.
describe	to tell or write about in detail	**Describe** the narrator in "The Scholarship Jacket."
feature	a special quality or characteristic of something	Look at each **feature** of the Ming dynasty that is shown on the graphic.
identify	to point out characteristics	**Identify** the two systems of plants.
impact	the direct effect or impression of one thing on another	Images on TV and in newspapers had an **impact** on the civil rights movement.
objective	something worked toward	Your **objective** is to compare and order decimals.
react	to act in response to something	How did you **react** to the ending of "Charles"?
structure	something constructed or built	An ancient Egyptian pyramid is a **structure** shaped like a triangle.
theme	a message about life or human nature	One **theme** of the TV drama is that a mob can control individuals.
vary	to modify or alter	Genetics is a form of biology that explains why certain traits can **vary**.

Academic Vocabulary in Action

The terms below are examples of academic vocabulary. Knowing the meanings of these terms is essential for completing the activities and lessons in this book as well as mastering test items.

cultural *(adjective)*

Defining the Word

Anything dealing with the traits of a group of people is *cultural*. The word *cultural* is used often in social studies to describe the habits of groups of people. In addition, the word often appears in literature in describing the background of stories, poems, plays, speeches, and essays.

Using the Word

Now that you know the definition of *cultural*, practice using the word.

- Use a chart like the one shown to identify words you have learned about in different subject areas.
- Write a brief definition.
- Check a dictionary or glossary to make sure your definition is correct.

Subject Area	Word	Definition
social studies	cultural	the attitudes and behavior that characterize a group

conduct *(verb)*

Defining the Word

The word *conduct* means "to direct the course of something." A dam builder can conduct how water will flow, a scientist can conduct an experiment, and a band leader can conduct the playing of musicians.

Using the Word

Once you understand the meaning of a word root, you will be able to understand the meanings of other words that are formed in similar ways. The word *conduct* comes from combining the Latin roots *con* and *ducure*, which means, "to lead together."

- In a chart like this one, make a list of other words you know that are formed in a similar way.
- Look up each word in a dictionary and write down its meaning.
- Write a sentence using each word.

Word	Definition	Sentence
conductor	person who conducts	The subway train conductor slowed down the train to a full stop.

Strategies That Work: Vocabulary

 Record new vocabulary words in your **Reader/Writer Notebook.**

❶ Use Context Clues

The most important part of building your vocabulary is recognizing unfamiliar words as you read. When you encounter an unfamiliar word, look at the **context**, or the words, phrases, or sentences that surround that word. Often, the context can give you important clues to the word's meaning, as in the following example:

> One feature of the fable is the simple way in which it is told. Another trait of the fable is its purpose—to teach a lesson.

Even if you do not know what *feature* means, you can figure out from the surrounding context that it means "trait."

❷ Clarify Word Definitions

If you cannot rely on a word's context to help you understand its meaning, consult a dictionary. A dictionary entry will also provide a word's pronunciation, parts of speech, origin, and additional meanings. When you are reading a textbook or manual, you may find definitions for unfamiliar words in a glossary at the back of the book.

> **fossil** (fŏs′əl) *n.*: the remains of a living thing, preserved in soil or rock.

❸ Keep a Word List

List new academic terms in your **Reader/Writer Notebook.** Add to your list each time you take on a new reading assignment. In addition to listing the word and its definition, you might draw a symbol or picture to show you what the word represents or provide examples to remind you of what the word means. Challenge yourself to use words from the list in your writing and discussions. The more frequently you use the words, the easier they will be to remember.

Interactive Vocabulary **THINK** central
Go to **thinkcentral.com.**
KEYWORD: HML7-19

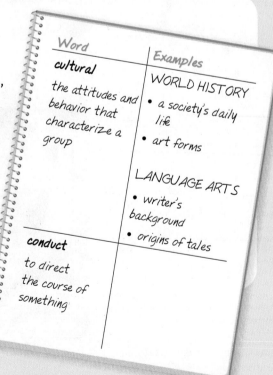

Word	Examples
cultural the attitudes and behavior that characterize a group	WORLD HISTORY • a society's daily life • art forms LANGUAGE ARTS • writer's background • origins of tales
conduct to direct the course of something	

For a complete list of terms in this book, see the **Glossary of Academic Vocabulary** *on pages R115–R116.*

Expressing Ideas in Writing

Writing is a way of sharing your ideas with others and learning more about what you really think. Whether you're writing a diary entry for your eyes alone or creating a Web site intended for millions of visitors, the power of words is in your hands.

⋯ COMMON CORE

Included in this workshop:
W 4, W 5

Consider Your Options

All writers must make some important choices *before* they start giving shape to their ideas. You might want to describe a hilarious incident, write a letter of complaint about a damaged CD, or post a movie review to an online database. No matter what your topic is, you should begin by considering your **purpose, audience,** and **format.**

PURPOSE	**AUDIENCE**	**FORMAT**
Why am I writing?	**Who are my readers?**	**Which format will best suit my purpose and audience?**
• to entertain	• classmates	• essay • journal entry
• to inform or explain	• teachers	• letter • research paper
• to argue or persuade	• friends	• poem
• to describe	• myself	• short story • script
• to express thoughts and feelings	• community members	• review • power presentation
	• Web users	• speech • Web site
	• customer service at a company	

Continue the Process

There is no single right way to write. Every writer does it a little differently. The **Writing Workshops** in this book will help you discover the process that works best for you. First, though, familiarize yourself with the basic process. Then you can move forward according to your own working style.

THE WRITING PROCESS

PLANNING/PREWRITING

Explore your ideas and decide what you want to write about. Once you have considered the options on the preceding page, try some of these strategies: **freewriting, brainstorming,** and **questioning.** See page 23 for more strategies.

▶ **WHAT DOES IT LOOK LIKE?**

> The Cay
>
> It must be terrifying to be stranded on an island. This scenario is often shown as being exciting (on TV, at least). Maybe I will write about what it takes to keep going in that situation.

DRAFTING

Turn your ideas into a rough draft. If you are doing some informal or personal writing, you might **draft to discover**—jump in without a formal outline to guide you. If you are writing an essay for school, you may want to **draft from an outline.** If you are writing a short story, create a **story map.**

▶ **WHAT DOES IT LOOK LIKE?**

> I. Survival depends on both physical and emotional strength.
>   A. Phillip has a serious physical problem—can't see
>   B. Needs to get his emotions under control

REVISING

Review your draft. Look for ways to improve the development, organization, and style. Make sure your writing is clear and **coherent,** or easy to follow.
- Use a **rubric** to make sure you are on track (page 22).
- Have a classmate review your draft.
- Consider trying a new approach if something simply is not working.
- **Proofread** for errors in spelling and grammar.

▶ **ASK A PEER READER**

> It's all about survival. Phillip in The Cay is in a terrible position. Luckily, he has the qualities he needs to pull through.
>
> **Suggestion:** Could you make the first sentence clearer? Also, it is too informal. Try: "What does it take to survive when your life is threatened?"

EDITING AND PUBLISHING
- Edit your draft to correct any distracting errors.
- Use the **Proofreader's Checklist** to help you catch common mistakes.
- Let the world know your idea. Where you publish will depend on your purpose, audience, and format.

▶ **PROOFREADER'S CHECKLIST**
✓ Revise sentence fragments and run-on sentences.
✓ Fix mistakes in subject-verb agreement and pronoun agreement.
✓ Capitalize and use punctuation marks correctly.
✓ Correct misspellings.

Scoring Rubric

Score	COMMON CORE TRAITS
6	• **Development** Includes a meaningful, memorable introduction; develops ideas with varied, relevant evidence; ends powerfully • **Organization** Is effectively and logically organized; uses varied transitions to create cohesion (flow) and link ideas • **Language** Uses precise language in original ways; effectively maintains an appropriate style; shows a strong command of grammar, mechanics, and spelling
5	• **Development** Has an effective introduction; develops ideas with relevant evidence; has a strong concluding section • **Organization** Is logically organized; uses transitions to create cohesion and link ideas • **Language** Uses precise language; maintains an appropriate style; has a few errors in grammar, mechanics, and spelling
4	• **Development** Has an introduction, but it could be more interesting; lacks support for one or two ideas; has an adequate concluding section • **Organization** Is logically organized, with one or two exceptions; could use a few more transitions • **Language** Generally uses precise language; has one or two lapses in style; includes a few distracting errors in grammar, mechanics, and spelling
3	• **Development** Has a superficial introduction that lacks interest; includes some unsupported ideas or irrelevant evidence; has a weak ending • **Organization** Has some flaws in organization; needs more transitions • **Language** Uses words correctly, though language is unoriginal; has frequent lapses in style; has some critical errors in grammar, mechanics, and spelling
2	• **Development** Has a weak, uninteresting introduction; does not support most ideas; ends abruptly • **Organization** Has a weak organization; lacks transitions throughout • **Language** Uses vague language and misuses some words; has an inappropriate style in many places; contains many distracting errors in grammar, mechanics, and spelling
1	• **Development** Lacks an introduction, support for ideas, and a concluding section • **Organization** Has no organization or transitions; is confusing and disconnected • **Language** Uses many words incorrectly; has an inappropriate style; has major problems with grammar, mechanics, and spelling

Strategies That Work: Writing

 Jot down your writing ideas, plans, and notes in your **Reader/Writer Notebook.**

❶ Use Prewriting Strategies

Try different strategies to help you get a strong start.

- **Freewrite.** Jot down whatever pops into your head.
- **Picture it.** Use a graphic organizer to capture your ideas.
- **Brainstorm with classmates.** Generate topics and supporting details with others.
- **Observe your surroundings.** Venture into the world with your notebook. Write notes about interesting people, events, and places.
- **Question yourself.** "What if I were president?" The answer to a silly or serious "what if" question could be your topic.

❷ Get Friendly Feedback

You can ask other writers for help at any stage of the writing process. Keep these guidelines in mind.

When You're the Writer	When You're the Reader
• Be clear about the feedback you want. Should readers comment on your ideas or proofread for errors? • Listen politely to readers' comments and suggestions. • Ask your readers to clarify suggestions that you find confusing. • Be willing to think about your writing in new ways.	• Be respectful and positive. • Support your opinions with relevant observations, and give suggestions for improvement. • Ask questions to learn more about the writer's goals and ideas. • Don't rewrite the work yourself.

❸ Pay Attention to Details

Even minor mistakes, such as errors in grammar, punctuation, and spelling, can keep readers from taking your ideas seriously.

Use these spelling tips to make sure your writing is polished and correct.

- Review spelling rules on pages R72–R74.
- Avoid misusing commonly confused words, such as accept and except. (See page R75 for more examples.)
- Use the spell-check feature in your word-processing program or a dictionary.
- Read your draft backwards to catch mistakes your eye might miss while scanning over sentences you are very familiar with.

When Phillip wakes up, he is all alone on the island ~~accept~~ except for a member of the ship's crew and a cat. Soon, Phillip becomes blind. Overcoming that is a huge ~~obstical~~ obstacle for him.

Writing Online

THINK central

Go to **thinkcentral.com.**
KEYWORD: HML7N-23

Weaving a Story

PLOT, CONFLICT, AND SETTING

- In Fiction
- In Nonfiction
- In Poetry
- In Drama
- In Media

Share What You Know

What makes a STORY unforgettable?

Whether it's a spellbinding mystery, a heartwarming true story, or a tale from your grandmother's past, an unforgettable story has a certain "something" that sets it apart from other tales. The story might have a riveting plot, a mysterious setting, or a powerful ending, but whatever that certain something is, an unforgettable story stays with you long after you've read or heard it.

ACTIVITY Think of an unforgettable story that you've read or heard. It might be a classic piece of fiction, such as **The Black Stallion,** or a family story that has been passed down for generations. With a group of classmates, discuss the following questions:

- What makes the story unforgettable?

- What do your reasons have in common?

- After your discussion, how would you answer the original question: What makes a story unforgettable?

Find It Online!

THINK central

Go to thinkcentral.com for the interactive version of this unit.

THE BLACK STALLION
Shipwrecked with a wild stallion!

Walter Farley

Preview Unit Goals

TEXT ANALYSIS
- Identify stages of plot; analyze plot development
- Analyze how setting shapes plot
- Identify conflict, flashback, and foreshadowing
- Analyze the structure an author uses to organize a text, including chronological order

READING
- Use reading strategies, including connecting and predicting

WRITING AND LANGUAGE
- Write an argument
- Spell possessives correctly
- Recognize and correct misplaced modifiers

SPEAKING AND LISTENING
- Create a persuasive podcast

VOCABULARY
- Understand and use prefixes, suffixes, and word roots
- Understand analogies

ACADEMIC VOCABULARY
- contemporary
- element
- identify
- influence
- structure

MEDIA AND VIEWING
- Identify and analyze visual and sound elements in film
- Analyze film techniques that establish plot and setting

Media Smart DVD-ROM

Unforgettable Stories in Movies

Experience pulse-racing action in a scene from the time-travel movie *Back to the Future.* Page 154

Plot, Setting, and Character

What makes you willing to spend two hours at the movie theater or a week reading a book? Is it the thrill of action-packed events or a connection to the characters? Is it a fascination with the setting, such as a faraway galaxy? Plot, conflict, setting, and characters all play a role in holding your interest in a story.

Part 1: What Drives a Story?

The idea for a story might begin with an observation or a thought that interests a writer. To build a story from that idea, a writer creates a plot structure using the elements of fiction listed here.

- **Setting** is the time and place of the action. The time might be the historical era, the season, or the time of day. The place might be a country, a neighborhood, or a room. In many stories, setting influences the plot and affects the characters' feelings.

- **Characters** are the people, animals, or imaginary creatures that take part in a story. The characters' behavior affects what happens.

- **Plot** is the series of events in a story. The plot usually centers on a **conflict,** a struggle between different forces. Conflict fuels the action, moving the plot forward. A conflict can be external or internal.

COMMON CORE

Included in this workshop:
RL 1 Cite several pieces of textual evidence to support analysis of what the text says explicitly. **RL 3** Analyze how different elements of a story interact.

TYPE OF CONFLICT	EXAMPLE
 *External Conflict* is a struggle between a character and an outside force. This force might be another character, a group of characters, or nature.	A sea captain attempts to guide his boat to shore in the middle of a deadly storm. ▶ **(sea captain vs. nature)** *Other Examples* • A boxer faces an opponent. • A girl has a fight with friends.
 *Internal Conflict* is a struggle within a character's mind. This kind of conflict happens when a character must deal with opposing thoughts or feelings.	A girl strongly disagrees with her friends, but she wants them to like her. Should she speak her mind or stay silent? ▶ **(girl vs. herself)** *Other Examples* • Admit needing help or do it alone? • Take a risk or play it safe?

MODEL 1: SETTING

This author draws you into the story by providing specific details about the setting. How might the setting influence what happens?

from The Clay Marble

Novel by **Minfong Ho**

The last rays of afternoon sun were filtering through the forest as we approached the Border. Gradually the trees thinned out and the path widened. Several trails merged into ours. It seemed as if all the paths out of Cambodia were converging on this one spot on the Thai border.

5   I could barely contain my excitement. I imagined mountains of rice lining the horizon, and piles of tools and fishnets everywhere. Perhaps there would even be mounds of sweet moist coconut cakes and banana fritters. "Hurry," I urged my brother.

Yet, as we finally emerged from the forest, all we could see was a vast
10 barren plain dotted with shrubs and scraggly trees, flat and desolate.

Close Read

1. What details about the setting do you find in lines 1–4? One detail has been boxed.

2. Describe what the narrator expects to see when she crosses the border. Then describe what she actually sees. How might the actual setting affect the narrator and the story?

MODEL 2: CONFLICT

Here, a girl watches from the deck of a ship as her brother is left on a deserted island. What do you learn about the conflict in this excerpt?

from Island of the Blue Dolphins

Novel by **Scott O'Dell**

Against my will, I screamed.
Chief Matasaip grasped my arm.
"We cannot wait for Ramo," he said. "If we do, the ship will be driven on the rocks."
5   "We must!" I shouted. "We must!"
"The ship will come back for him on another day," Matasaip said. "He will be safe. There is food for him to eat and water to drink and places to sleep."
"No," I cried.
10 Matasaip's face was like stone. He was not listening.

Close Read

1. Describe the conflict the girl experiences.

2. Is the girl's conflict internal or external? Explain how you know.

Part 2: Plot Development

No matter who the characters are, where the action takes place, or what conflicts occur, a story has a plot. Usually, a story begins by introducing a main character who has a conflict. The story then develops around this conflict. Important events move the story forward, often explaining past or present actions, and **foreshadowing,** or hinting at, future actions. As the story moves on, the character must find a solution to the conflict. Once the problem is solved, the story ends. This process is known as **plot development.**

A typical plot has five stages of action. By understanding these stages, you will know what to look for in a story as you follow it closely. For example, at the beginning—or **exposition**—of a story, pay attention to the details that tell you about the characters, the setting, and any potential conflicts.

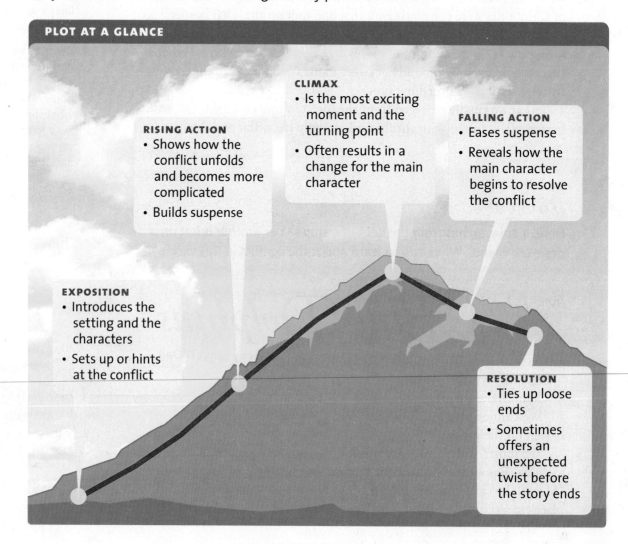

PLOT AT A GLANCE

CLIMAX
- Is the most exciting moment and the turning point
- Often results in a change for the main character

RISING ACTION
- Shows how the conflict unfolds and becomes more complicated
- Builds suspense

FALLING ACTION
- Eases suspense
- Reveals how the main character begins to resolve the conflict

EXPOSITION
- Introduces the setting and the characters
- Sets up or hints at the conflict

RESOLUTION
- Ties up loose ends
- Sometimes offers an unexpected twist before the story ends

MODEL 1: EXPOSITION

What do you learn about the setting and the conflict in the exposition of this story?

from
Last Cover
Short story by **Paul Annixter**

I'm not sure I can tell you what you want to know about my brother; but everything about the pet fox is important, so I'll tell all that from the beginning.

It goes back to a winter afternoon after I'd hunted the woods all
5 day for a sign of our lost pet. I remember the way my mother looked up as I came into the kitchen. Without my speaking, she knew what had happened. For six hours I had walked, reading signs, looking for a delicate print in the damp soil or even a hair that might have told of a red fox passing that way—but I had found nothing.

Close Read

1. What can you tell about the setting in which the main character lives? Find specific details that describe the setting.

2. Review the boxed details. Describe the conflict that the main character faces. What does this conflict suggest the story will be about?

MODEL 2: RISING ACTION

At the beginning of this story, lonely Mr. Peters is granted three wishes. He uses his first wish to ask for a wife. In the rising action, what do you learn about the conflict that results from this wish?

from
THE THIRD WISH
Short story by **Joan Aiken**

One evening he was returning home along the river path when he saw Leita in front of him, down by the water. A swan had sailed up to the verge and she had her arms round its neck and the swan's head rested against her cheek. She was weeping, and as he came nearer he
5 saw that tears were rolling, too, from the swan's eyes.

"Leita, what is it?" he asked, very troubled.

"This is my sister," she answered. "I can't bear being separated from her."

Now he understood that Leita was really a swan from the forest, and
10 this made him very sad because when a human being marries a bird it always leads to sorrow.

Close Read

1. Reread the boxed text. What conflict is Mr. Peters facing?

2. During the rising action, the plot moves toward the climax. What future decision or action might this situation hint at, or foreshadow?

Part 3: Analyze the Text

In this story, an elegant dinner party turns dangerous when an uninvited "guest" makes an appearance. As you read, use what you've just learned about plot, conflict, and setting to analyze the story.

The Dinner Party

Short story by
Mona Gardner

The country is India. A large dinner party is being given in an up-country station by a colonial official[1] and his wife. The guests are army officers and government attachés[2] and their wives, and an American naturalist.[3]

5   At one side of the long table a spirited discussion springs up between a young girl and a colonel. The girl insists women have long outgrown the jumping-on-a-chair-at-the-sight-of-a-mouse era, that they are not as fluttery as their grandmothers. The colonel says they are, explaining that women haven't the actual nerve control of men. The other men at
10 the table agree with him.

"A woman's unfailing reaction in any crisis," the colonel says, "is to scream. And while a man may feel like it, yet he has that ounce more of control than a woman has. And that last ounce is what counts!"

The American scientist does not join in the argument, but sits
15 watching the faces of the other guests. As he looks, he sees a strange expression come over the face of the hostess. She is staring straight ahead, the muscles of her face contracting slightly. With a small gesture she summons the native boy standing behind her chair. She whispers to him. The boy's eyes widen: he turns quickly and leaves the room.

---

1. **colonial official:** a person holding a position in the British government ruling India.
2. **attachés** (ăt′ə-shāz′): people who assist an ambassador.
3. **naturalist:** a person who studies living things by observing them directly.

Close Read
Exposition (Lines 1–13)

1. What do you learn about the setting in the exposition?

2. Explain what the young girl and the colonel are arguing about in lines 5–13. What might this topic foreshadow?

Close Read
Rising Action (Lines 14–36)

3. Find two details in lines 14–19 that might foreshadow future events in the story. One detail has been boxed.

20 No one else sees this, nor the boy when he puts a bowl of milk on the verandah[4] outside the glass doors.

    The American comes to with a start. In India, milk in a bowl means only one thing. It is bait for a snake. He realizes there is a cobra in the room.

25   He looks up at the rafters[5]—the likeliest place—and sees they are bare. Three corners of the room, which he can see by shifting only slightly, are empty. In the fourth corner a group of servants stand, waiting until the next course can be served. The American realizes there is only one place left—under the table.

30   His first impulse is to jump back and warn the others. But he knows the commotion will frighten the cobra and it will strike. He speaks quickly, the quality of his voice so arresting that it sobers everyone.

    "I want to know just what control everyone at this table has. I will count three hundred—that's five minutes—and not one of you is to
35 move a single muscle. The persons who move will forfeit 50 rupees.[6] Now! Ready!"

    The 20 people sit like stone images while he counts. He is saying ". . . two hundred and eighty . . ." when, out of the corner of his eye, he sees the cobra emerge and make for the bowl of milk. Four or five
40 screams ring out as he jumps to slam shut the verandah doors.

    "You certainly were right, Colonel!" the host says. "A man has just shown us an example of real control."

    "Just a minute," the American says, turning to his hostess, "there's one thing I'd like to know. Mrs. Wynnes, how did you know that cobra was
45 in the room?"

    A faint smile lights up the woman's face as she replies. "Because it was lying across my foot."

---

4. **verandah:** a long porch, usually roofed, along the side of a building.

5. **rafters:** wooden beams that support a roof.

6. **rupees** (rōō-pēz′)**:** Indian units of money.

4. Reread lines 22–24. What is the main conflict? Explain whether it is internal or external.

Close Read
Climax (Lines 37–40)

5. What happens at the climax, or the most exciting moment?

Close Read
Falling Action and Resolution (Lines 41–47)

6. At what point in the falling action does the tension begin to ease? Explain.

7. What surprise is revealed in the resolution? How does this explain Mrs. Wynnes's earlier reaction?

Seventh Grade

Short Story by Gary Soto

VIDEO TRAILER **THINK** central   KEYWORD: HML7-34

How do you make a good
IMPRESSION?

COMMON CORE

RL1 Cite several pieces of textual evidence to support what the text says explicitly.
RL3 Analyze how particular elements of a story interact.

All of us have times when we're eager to make a good impression—to win the approval of parents, teachers, or friends. But influencing how others see us isn't always easy. In "Seventh Grade," a boy finds that trying to make a good impression can lead to some embarrassing moments.

LIST IT What tips have you heard about how to make a good impression? Create a list of the suggestions you think are most effective.

How to Make a
Good Impression
1. Stand up straight.
2.
3.

TEXT ANALYSIS: PLOT

A **plot** is what happens in a story, and usually develops in five stages.

- The **exposition** introduces the characters, the setting, and often the conflict, or struggle between forces.
- The **rising action** moves the plot forward and shows how the conflict becomes more complicated.
- The **climax** is the moment of greatest interest.
- The **falling action** and **resolution** reveal the outcome.

In each stage of plot development, events may explain past or present actions or hint at future actions. As you read "Seventh Grade," notice how the characters, events, and setting contribute to the plot as it advances toward the climax.

READING STRATEGY: CONNECT

You can better understand the characters of almost any story by relating your knowledge and experiences to theirs. This is called **connecting,** and it helps you enter into the story. As you read the selection, use a chart like the one shown to connect what is happening in "Seventh Grade" to your life.

What's Happening in the Story	Connection to My Life
Victor is daydreaming about traveling to France.	I daydream about the world outside my neighborhood too.

VOCABULARY IN CONTEXT

The boldfaced words help tell the story of a day in the life of a seventh grader. After reading the sentences, write the definitions of the boldfaced words with which you are familiar.

1. A student may **quiver** when tests are handed back.
2. Feel free to **linger** after class if you have a question.
3. Sam loves to eat; he is rather **portly.**
4. The athlete's **ferocity** was praised.
5. She smiled **sheepishly** as she admitted to staying up late.
6. The class recited poems in **unison.**

 Complete the activities in your **Reader/Writer Notebook.**

Gary Soto
born 1952

A Neighborhood's Influence
Gary Soto fills his fiction and poetry for young adults with lively details of his upbringing in a Mexican-American neighborhood. Soto wants his work to help others appreciate his old neighborhood's values. But, he says, "I am really writing about the feelings and experiences of most American kids: having a pet, going to the park for a family cookout … getting a bee sting!"

The Power of Reading
Soto has said that as a child he never thought about being a writer. Today, though, he meets with young people to encourage their curiosity about reading and writing. The award-winning author explains, "I believe in literature and the depth it adds to all our lives."

BACKGROUND TO THE STORY
Fresno, California
"Seventh Grade" is set in Fresno, California, where Gary Soto grew up. Fresno is located southeast of San Francisco. Its dry, hot summers and cool, humid winters are excellent for growing grapes. A large number of Latinos, whose families are originally from Spanish-speaking countries, are employed in Fresno's vineyards.

Author Online
THINK central
Go to **thinkcentral.com.**
KEYWORD: HML7-35

35

Seventh Grade

Gary Soto

On the first day of school, Victor stood in line half an hour before he came to a wobbly card table. He was handed a packet of papers and a computer card on which he listed his one elective, French. He already spoke Spanish and English, but he thought some day he might travel to France, where it was cool; not like Fresno, where summer days reached 110 degrees in the shade. There were rivers in France, and huge churches, and fair-skinned people everywhere, the way there were brown people all around Victor. **A**

Besides, Teresa, a girl he had liked since they were in catechism classes[1] at Saint Theresa's, was taking French, too. With any luck they would be in the same class. Teresa is going to be my girl this year, he promised himself as he left the gym full of students in their new fall clothes. She was cute. And good in math, too, Victor thought as he walked down the hall to his homeroom. He ran into his friend, Michael Torres, by the water fountain that never turned off.

Analyze Visuals ▶

What might you **infer** about the girl from her expression?

A PLOT: EXPOSITION
What background information do you learn about Victor in the first paragraph?

---

1. **catechism** (kăt′ĭ-kĭz′əm) **classes:** formal classes in religious instruction.

They shook hands, *raza*-style,[2] and jerked their heads at one another in a *saludo de vato*.[3] "How come you're making a face?" asked Victor. **B**

"I ain't making a face, *ese*.[4] This *is* my face." Michael said his face had changed during the summer. He had read a GQ[5] magazine that his older
20 brother had borrowed from the Book Mobile and noticed that the male models all had the same look on their faces. They would stand, one arm around a beautiful woman, and *scowl*. They would sit at a pool, their rippled stomachs dark with shadow, and *scowl*. They would sit at dinner tables, cool drinks in their hands, and *scowl*.

"I think it works," Michael said. He scowled and let his upper lip **quiver.** His teeth showed along with the **ferocity** of his soul. "Belinda Reyes walked by a while ago and looked at me," he said.

Victor didn't say anything, though he thought his friend looked pretty strange. They talked about recent movies, baseball, their parents, and the
30 horrors of picking grapes in order to buy their fall clothes. Picking grapes was like living in Siberia,[6] except hot and more boring.

"What classes are you taking?" Michael said, scowling.

"French. How 'bout you?"

"Spanish. I ain't so good at it, even if I'm Mexican."

"I'm not either, but I'm better at it than math, that's for sure."

A tinny, three-beat bell propelled students to their homerooms. The two friends socked each other in the arm and went their ways, Victor thinking, man, that's weird. Michael thinks making a face makes him handsome.

On the way to his homeroom, Victor tried a scowl. He felt foolish,
40 until out of the corner of his eye he saw a girl looking at him. Umm, he thought, maybe it does work. He scowled with greater conviction. **C**

In homeroom, roll was taken, emergency cards were passed out, and they were given a bulletin to take home to their parents. The principal, Mr. Belton, spoke over the crackling loudspeaker, welcoming the students to a new year, new experiences, and new friendships. The students squirmed in their chairs and ignored him. They were anxious to go to first period. Victor sat calmly, thinking of Teresa, who sat two rows away, reading a paperback novel. This would be his lucky year. She was in his homeroom, and would probably be in his English and math classes. And,
50 of course, French.

The bell rang for first period, and the students herded noisily through the door. Only Teresa **lingered,** talking with the homeroom teacher.

B CONNECT
How do you greet your friends when you see them in the hall?

quiver (kwĭv'ər) *v.* to shake with a slight, rapid movement

ferocity (fə-rŏs'ĭ-tē) *n.* fierceness; extreme intensity

C PLOT: EXPOSITION
Reread lines 25–27 and lines 39–41. When the boys scowl, they see girls look at them. What might the girls be thinking?

linger (lĭng'gər) *v.* to continue to stay; delay leaving

---

2. *raza* (rä'sä)-**style** *Spanish*: in the manner that Mexican Americans greet each other.

3. *saludo de vato* (sä-lōō'dō dĕ bä'tō) *Spanish*: greeting between Mexican-American friends.

4. *ese* (ĕ'sĕ) *Spanish*: a slang term used in addressing someone, as in "Hey, man."

5. *GQ*: *Gentleman's Quarterly*, a magazine of men's styles and fashions.

6. **Siberia**: a cold, isolated region of northern Russia.

"So you think I should talk to Mrs. Gaines?" she asked the teacher. "She would know about ballet?"

"She would be a good bet," the teacher said. Then added, "Or the gym teacher, Mrs. Garza."

Victor lingered, keeping his head down and staring at his desk. He wanted to leave when she did so he could bump into her and say something clever.

He watched her on the sly. As she turned to leave, he stood up and hurried to the door, where he managed to catch her eye. She smiled and said, "Hi, Victor."

He smiled back and said, "Yeah, that's me." His brown face blushed. Why hadn't he said, "Hi, Teresa," or "How was your summer?" or something nice?

As Teresa walked down the hall, Victor walked the other way, looking back, admiring how gracefully she walked, one foot in front of the other. So much for being in the same class, he thought. As he trudged to English, he practiced scowling.

In English they reviewed the parts of speech. Mr. Lucas, a **portly** man, waddled down the aisle, asking, "What is a noun?"

"A person, place, or thing," said the class in **unison.**

"Yes, now somebody give me an example of a person—you, Victor Rodriguez."

"Teresa," Victor said automatically. Some of the girls giggled. They knew he had a crush on Teresa. He felt himself blushing again.

"Correct," Mr. Lucas said. "Now provide me with a place."

Mr. Lucas called on a freckled kid who answered, "Teresa's house with a kitchen full of big brothers."

After English, Victor had math, his weakest subject. He sat in the back by the window, hoping he would not be called on. Victor understood most of the problems, but some of the stuff looked like the teacher made it up as she went along. It was confusing, like the inside of a watch. ◆

After math he had a fifteen-minute break, then social studies, and, finally, lunch. He bought a tuna casserole with buttered rolls, some fruit cocktail, and milk. He sat with Michael, who practiced scowling between bites.

Girls walked by and looked at him.

portly (pôrt′lē) *adj.* stout or overweight

unison (yōō′nĭ-sən) *n.* harmony or agreement; as with one voice

◆ **GRAMMAR IN CONTEXT**
Look at the sentences in lines 87–90. Notice that every sentence has a subject (*Victor, He, Victor, It*) and a complete predicate that tells whom or what the sentence is about.

"See what I mean, Vic?" Michael scowled. "They love it."

"Yeah, I guess so."

They ate slowly, Victor scanning the horizon for a glimpse of Teresa. He didn't see her. She must have brought lunch, he thought, and is eating outside. Victor scraped his plate and left Michael, who was busy scowling
100 at a girl two tables away. **D**

The small, triangle-shaped campus bustled with students talking about their new classes. Everyone was in a sunny mood. Victor hurried to the bag lunch area, where he sat down and opened his math book. He moved his lips as if he were reading, but his mind was somewhere else. He raised his eyes slowly and looked around. No Teresa.

He lowered his eyes, pretending to study, then looked slowly to the left. No Teresa. He turned a page in the book and stared at some math problems that scared him because he knew he would have to do them eventually. He looked to the right. Still no sign of her. He stretched
110 out lazily in an attempt to disguise his snooping. **E**

Then he saw her. She was sitting with a girlfriend under a plum tree. Victor moved to a table near her and daydreamed about taking her to a movie. When the bell sounded, Teresa looked up, and their eyes met. She smiled sweetly and gathered her books. Her next class was French, same as Victor's.

D PLOT: RISING ACTION
What obstacles are getting in the way of Victor making Teresa "his girl"?

E CONNECT
What experiences have you had that help you understand how Victor might be feeling as he looks for Teresa?

They were among the last students to arrive in class, so all the good desks in the back had already been taken. Victor was forced to sit near the front, a few desks away from Teresa, while Mr. Bueller wrote French words on the chalkboard. The bell rang, and Mr. Bueller wiped his hands, turned to the class, and said, *"Bonjour."*[7]

"*Bonjour,*" braved a few students.

"*Bonjour,*" Victor whispered. He wondered if Teresa heard him. **F**

Mr. Bueller said that if the students studied hard, at the end of the year they could go to France and be understood by the populace.

One kid raised his hand and asked, "What's 'populace'?"

"The people, the people of France."

Mr. Bueller asked if anyone knew French. Victor raised his hand, wanting to impress Teresa. The teacher beamed and said, *"Très bien. Parlez-vous français?"*[8]

Victor didn't know what to say. The teacher wet his lips and asked something else in French. The room grew silent. Victor felt all eyes staring at him. He tried to bluff his way out by making noises that sounded French.

"La me vave me con le grandma," he said uncertainly. **G**

Mr. Bueller, wrinkling his face in curiosity, asked him to speak up.

Great rosebushes of red bloomed on Victor's cheeks. A river of nervous sweat ran down his palms. He felt awful. Teresa sat a few desks away, no doubt thinking he was a fool. Without looking at Mr. Bueller, Victor mumbled, "Frenchie oh wewe gee in September."

Mr. Bueller asked Victor to repeat what he said.

"Frenchie oh wewe gee in September," Victor repeated.

Mr. Bueller understood that the boy didn't know French and turned away. He walked to the blackboard and pointed to the words on the board with his steel-edged ruler.

"*Le bateau,*" he sang.

"*Le bateau,*" the students repeated.

"*Le bateau est sur l'eau,*"[9] he sang.

"*Le bateau est sur l'eau.*"

Victor was too weak from failure to join the class. He stared at the board and wished he had taken Spanish, not French. Better yet, he wished he could start his life over. He had never been so embarrassed. He bit his thumb until he tore off a sliver of skin.

The bell sounded for fifth period, and Victor shot out of the room, avoiding the stares of the other kids, but had to return for his math book. He looked **sheepishly** at the teacher, who was erasing the board, then

F PLOT: RISING ACTION
Why does the tension increase now that Victor and Teresa are in the same class together?

G CONNECT
Think of a time when you said you knew something that you really didn't. **Compare and contrast** how it made you feel with how Victor is feeling now.

Language Coach
Oral Fluency The word *thumb* ends with two consonants together, *mb*. The *b* is silent in this word, but the *m* is spoken. Reread line 151 aloud, being sure the *b* in *thumb* remains silent.

sheepishly (shē'pĭsh-lē) *adv.* with a bashful or embarrassed look

---

7. *Bonjour* (bôn'zhōōr) *French:* Good day.

8. *Très bien. Parlez-vous français?* (trĕ byăn pär'lā vōō frän'sĕ) *French:* Very good. Do you speak French?

9. *Le bateau est sur l'eau* (lə bä'tō ĕ sür lō) *French:* The boat is on the water.

widened his eyes in terror at Teresa who stood in front of him. "I didn't know you knew French," she said. "That was good." **H**

Mr. Bueller looked at Victor, and Victor looked back. Oh please, don't say anything, Victor pleaded with his eyes. I'll wash your car, mow your lawn, walk your dog—anything! I'll be your best student, and I'll clean
160 your erasers after school.

Mr. Bueller shuffled through the papers on his desk. He smiled and hummed as he sat down to work. He remembered his college years when he dated a girlfriend in borrowed cars. She thought he was rich because each time he picked her up he had a different car. It was fun until he had spent all his money on her and had to write home to his parents because he was broke. **I**

Victor couldn't stand to look at Teresa. He was sweaty with shame. "Yeah, well, I picked up a few things from movies and books and stuff like that." They left the class together. Teresa asked him if he would help
170 her with her French.

"Sure, anytime," Victor said.

"I won't be bothering you, will I?"

"Oh no, I like being bothered."

"Bonjour," Teresa said, leaving him outside her next class. She smiled and pushed wisps of hair from her face.

"Yeah, right, *bonjour*," Victor said. He turned and headed to his class. The rosebushes of shame on his face became bouquets of love. Teresa is a great girl, he thought. And Mr. Bueller is a good guy.

He raced to metal shop. After metal shop there was biology, and after
180 biology a long sprint to the public library, where he checked out three French textbooks.

He was going to like seventh grade. **J**

H PLOT: CLIMAX
Why is this the moment of greatest interest in the story?

I PLOT: FALLING ACTION
How do Mr. Bueller's actions affect the plot at this point?

J PLOT: RESOLUTION
How has Victor's life changed by the end of the day?

Comprehension

1. **Recall** What is the main reason Victor wants to take French?

2. **Recall** How does Victor respond when Teresa talks to him after homeroom?

3. **Summarize** Explain the events that happen after Victor tells Mr. Bueller that he speaks French.

COMMON CORE

RL 1 Cite several pieces of textual evidence to support what the text says explicitly.
RL 3 Analyze how particular elements of a story interact.

Text Analysis

4. **Connect** Review the chart you created as you read. How do the connections you made help you understand the characters and events that take place in the story? Note specific examples.

5. **Compare and Contrast** Compare and contrast Michael's efforts to impress girls with Victor's efforts to impress Teresa. Give examples from the story. How do their efforts give the story tension—and humor?

6. **Identify Plot Stages** The plot of "Seventh Grade" centers on Victor's attempts to impress Teresa. Look back at the story and make a list of the important events. Then use a diagram like the one shown, and fill in what happens at each stage of the plot.

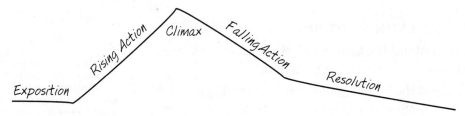

7. **Analyze Plot Development** The French teacher, Mr. Bueller, realizes that Victor is faking his knowledge of French. Identify the event from Mr. Bueller's past that leads him to keep the truth to himself. In what way does his decision help advance the plot?

Extension and Challenge

8. **Readers' Circle** In a group, discuss what Teresa might be thinking at each stage of the plot. Draw a diagram like the one shown in question 6, and note on it the thoughts and feelings your group identifies for her.

9. **Creative Project: Writing** Imagine that Victor and Michael work as personalities on a radio talk show. A boy calls in to ask for their advice about how to impress girls. Write the response each boy would give.

How do you make a good IMPRESSION?

In the story, Victor is finally able to impress Teresa. Do you think it matters that this impression is based on something that isn't true?

Vocabulary in Context

▲ VOCABULARY PRACTICE

Choose the word in each group that is most nearly opposite in meaning to the boldfaced word.

1. **ferocity:** (a) fear, (b) bravery, (c) gentleness
2. **quiver:** (a) tremble, (b) vibrate, (c) stiffen
3. **sheepishly:** (a) shyly, (b) boldly, (c) easily
4. **linger:** (a) struggle, (b) hurry, (c) prolong
5. **portly:** (a) fluid, (b) heavy, (c) thin
6. **unison:** (a) separation, (b) company, (c) time

ACADEMIC VOCABULARY IN WRITING

- contemporary - element - identify - influence - structure

Write a paragraph in which you **identify** three things Victor does because of his "crush" on Teresa. Describe what you think *you* might have done in the same three situations. Use at least one of the Academic Vocabulary words in your response.

VOCABULARY STRATEGY: THE LATIN ROOT *uni*

The vocabulary word *unison* contains the Latin root *uni,* which means "one." *Uni* is combined with base words and other roots in a number of English words. To understand the meaning of a word containing *uni,* use context clues—the words and sentences around the word—as well as your knowledge of the root.

PRACTICE Choose the word from the web that best completes each sentence. Be ready to explain how *uni* helps give meaning to each word.

1. The _____, a creature with one horn, exists only in fairy tales.
2. The clown rode in circles, balanced unsteadily on a _____.
3. Each team member stood out from the crowd in his bright purple _____.
4. The colonists banded together to form a new _____.
5. She claims her ring is _____, but I've seen others like it.

⋮ **COMMON CORE**

L 4b Use common, grade-appropriate Latin roots as clues to the meaning of a word.
L 6 Acquire and use accurately grade-appropriate general academic words.

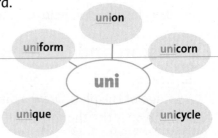

Interactive Vocabulary THINK central

Go to thinkcentral.com.
KEYWORD: HML7-44

Language

◆ **GRAMMAR IN CONTEXT:** Use Complete Sentences

COMMON CORE

L1 Demonstrate command of the conventions of standard English grammar and usage when writing. **W 3** Write narratives to develop imagined experiences.

Refer to the Grammar note on page 39. Every **complete sentence** has a subject and a predicate. The complete subject includes all the words that tell whom or what the sentence is about. The complete predicate includes the verb and all the words that go with it. If a sentence is missing a subject, a predicate, or both, then it is a **sentence fragment.** The missing part(s) must be added in order to make the sentence complete.

   Original: I had French class today. In Mr. Bueller's room.
                   (*"In Mr. Bueller's room" is a sentence fragment because it is missing a subject and a predicate.*)

   Revised: I had French class today. It was in Mr. Bueller's room.
                   (*This is now a complete sentence because it contains the subject "It" and the predicate "was in Mr. Bueller's room."*)

PRACTICE Decide whether the following sentence fragments (in bold) are missing a subject, a predicate, or both. Then insert the missing parts to make a complete sentence.

1. I went to homeroom. **Then to English class.**
2. **Saw Teresa in the hall.** She walked the other way.
3. After English class, I had math. **My weakest subject.**
4. Teresa and I get along well. **In most ways.**

For more help with sentence fragments, see page R64 in the ***Grammar Handbook.***

READING-WRITING CONNECTION

 Increase your understanding of "Seventh Grade" by responding to the prompt. Then use the **revising tip** to improve your writing.

WRITING PROMPT	REVISING TIP
Extended Constructed Response: Journal Entry What would Victor write in a journal about his first day of seventh grade? Write a **two- or three-paragraph journal entry** from Victor's point of view.	Review your journal entry. Follow the lesson above to help you turn any sentence fragments into complete sentences.

Interactive Revision **THINK** central

Go to **thinkcentral.com.**
KEYWORD: HML7-45

The Last Dog
Short Story by Katherine Paterson

Why are pets good
COMPANIONS?

COMMON CORE

RL 1 Cite several pieces of textual evidence to support what the text says explicitly. **RL 3** Analyze how particular elements of a story interact (e.g., how setting shapes the plot). **L 4** Clarify the meaning of multiple-meaning words. **L 4d** Verify the meaning of a word.

For many of us, pets are an important part of our lives. We feed them and care for them and often consider them to be a part of the family, but what do we get in return? Some would say that pets reward us with their companionship—their affection, loyalty, and good company. In "The Last Dog," a boy's powerful bond with a puppy helps teach him an important lesson.

LIST IT In a small group, make a list of reasons pets are good companions. To get started, use a list like the one shown. Then share your list with other groups.

Why Are Pets
Good Companions?
1. Pets are fun to
   play with.
2.
3.
4.

● TEXT ANALYSIS: SETTING

Setting is where and when a story happens. Sometimes the setting is a small part of a story. At other times, the setting has a major effect on the plot events. In the story you are about to read, look for details to help you understand the setting and its influence on plot development. Look for:

• details about scenery and weather

• details about buildings, clothing, culture, and technology

As you read, note these and other details about where and when the story takes place.

● READING SKILL: IDENTIFY SEQUENCE IN PLOT

A plot is made up of many events. The **sequence,** or order, of the events is important to understanding the story. These words and phrases are often clues to the sequence of events:

first   then   later   in the past

While events are often presented in the order in which they occur, sometimes the action is interrupted to present a scene from an earlier time. This is called a **flashback,** and it may include important new information.

As you read, keep track of the sequence by recording important events on a sequence chart like the one shown.

▲ VOCABULARY IN CONTEXT

Katherine Paterson uses the following words in her story about a futuristic world. In a three-column chart, define the words you know in the first column. In the second column, list the words you do not know. In the last column, provide dictionary definitions of all the words. Then use each word in a sentence.

WORD LIST		
copious	foray	posterity
disembodied	foresighted	reproof
evasive	languish	

Complete the activities in your **Reader/Writer Notebook.**

Meet the Author

Katherine Paterson
born 1932

"A Weird Little Kid"
Sometimes an outsider has an interesting way of looking at things. Katherine Paterson is convinced that as the child of U.S. missionaries in China, she learned valuable lessons about life. But being an outsider wasn't always easy. After returning to the United States at the age of five, Paterson and her family moved 18 times. She remembers feeling "small, poor, and foreign" on the playground. She was, in her own words, "a weird little kid," but she states today that "there are few things, apparently, more helpful to a writer than having once been a weird little kid."

BACKGROUND TO THE STORY
Science Fiction
In a work of science fiction, a writer combines real scientific information with elements from his or her imagination to create an altered universe. Science fiction stories typically take place in the distant future—in outer space or on a changed Earth. Plots often center on challenges characters face in these unusual settings.

Author Online
THINK central

Go to **thinkcentral.com.**
KEYWORD: HML7-47

THE LAST DOG

KATHERINE PATERSON

Analyze Visuals ▶

How would you describe the **setting** shown in this painting?

Brock approached the customs gate. Although he did not reach for the scanner, a feeling it might have labeled "excitement" made him tremble. His fingers shook as he punched in his number on the inquiry board. "This is highly irregular, Brock 095670038," the **disembodied** voice said. "What is your reason for external travel?"

Brock took a deep breath. "Scientific research," he replied. He didn't need to be told that his behavior was "irregular." He'd never heard of anyone doing research outside the dome—actual rather than virtual research. "I— I've been cleared by my podmaster and the Research Team. . . ."

10 "Estimated time of return?" So, he wasn't to be questioned further. "Uh, 1800 hours."

"Are you wearing the prescribed dry suit with helmet and gloves?"

"Affirmative."[1]

"You should be equipped with seven hundred fifty milliliters of liquid and food tablets for one day travel."

"Affirmative." Brock patted the sides of the dry suit to be sure. **Ⓐ**

"Remember to drink sparingly. Water supply is limited." Brock nodded. He tried to lick his parched lips, but his whole mouth felt dry. "Is that understood?"

20 "Affirmative." Was he hoping customs would stop him? If he was, they didn't seem to be helping him. Well, this was what he wanted, wasn't it? To go outside the dome.

"Turn on the universal locator, Brock 095670038, and proceed to gate."

Why weren't they questioning him further? Were they eager for him to go? Ever since he'd said out loud in group speak that he wanted to go outside the dome, people had treated him strangely—that session with the podmaster and then the interview with the representative

disembodied
(dĭs′ĕm-bŏ′dĕd)
adj. separated from or lacking a body
disembody *v.*

Ⓐ SETTING
Reread lines 1–16. What does the unusual technology in the dome suggest about the time in which the story takes place?

---

1. **affirmative** (ə-fûr′mə-tĭv): formal or scientific word for *yes.*

from Research. Did they think he was a deviant?[2] Deviants sometimes disappeared. The word was passed around that they had "gone outside," but no one really knew. No deviant had ever returned.

The gate slid open. Before he was quite ready for it, Brock found himself outside the protection of the dome. He blinked. The sun—at least it was what was called "the sun" in virtual lessons—was too bright for his eyes even inside the tinted helmet. He took a deep breath, one last backward look at the dome, which, with the alien sun gleaming on it, was even harder to look at than the distant star, and started across an expanse of brown soil [was it?] to what he recognized from holograms as a line of purplish mountains in the distance.  **B**

It was, he pulled the scanner from his outside pouch and checked it, "hot." Oh, that was what he was feeling. Hot. He remembered "hot" from a virtual lesson he'd had once on deserts. He wanted to take off the dry suit, but he had been told since he could remember that naked skin would suffer irreparable burning outside the protection of the dome. He adjusted the control as he walked so that the unfamiliar perspiration would evaporate. He fumbled a bit before he found the temperature adjustment function. He put it on twenty degrees centigrade[3] and immediately felt more comfortable. No one he really knew had ever left the dome (stories of deviants exiting the dome being hard to verify), but there was all this equipment in case someone decided to venture out. He tried to ask the clerk who outfitted him, but the woman was **evasive.** The equipment was old, she said. People used to go out, but the outside environment was threatening, so hardly anyone (she looked at him carefully now), hardly anyone ever used it now.

Was Brock, then, the only normal person still curious about the outside? Or had all those who had dared to venture out perished, discouraging further **forays?** Perhaps he *was* a deviant for wanting to see the mountains for himself. When he'd mentioned it to others, they had laughed, but there was a hollow sound to the laughter.

If he never returned, he'd have no one to blame but himself. He knew that. While his podfellows played virtual games, he'd wandered into a subsection of the historical virtuals called "ancient fictions." Things happened in these fictions more—well, more densely than they did in the virtuals. The people he met there—it was hard to describe—but somehow they were more *actual* than dome dwellers. They had strange names like Huck Finn and M. C. Higgins the Great.[4] They were even a little scary. It was their insides. Their insides were very loud. But even

VISUAL VOCABULARY

hologram *n.* a three-dimensional picture made by laser light

B SEQUENCE IN PLOT
What happens after Brock goes through the customs gate? As you read, use your chart to record the events described.

evasive (ĭ-vā′sĭv) *adj.* tending or trying to avoid

foray (fôr′ā′) *n.* a trip into an unknown area

---

2. **deviant** (dē′vē-ənt): a person who does not follow customary or accepted behavior.

3. **twenty degrees centigrade:** a temperature equivalent to 68 degrees Fahrenheit.

4. **Huck Finn and M. C. Higgins the Great:** the main characters in two books that are often read by young adults.

though the people in the ancient fictions frightened him a bit, he couldn't get enough of them. When no one was paying attention, he went back again and again to visit them. They had made him wonder about that
70 other world—that world outside the dome. **C**

Perhaps, once he had realized the danger the ancient fictions posed, he should have left them alone, but he couldn't help himself. They had made him feel hollow, hungry for something no food pellet or even virtual experience could satisfy. And now he was in that world they spoke of and the mountains of it were in plain view. **D**

He headed for the purple curves. Within a short distance from the dome, the land was clear and barren, but after he had been walking for an hour or so he began to pass rusting hulks and occasional ruins of what might have been the dwellings of ancient peoples that no one
80 in later years had cleared away for recycling or vaporization.[5]

He checked the emotional scanner for an unfamiliar sensation. "Loneliness," it registered. He rather liked having names for these new sensations. It made him feel a bit "proud," was it? The scanner was rather interesting. He wondered when people had stopped using them. He hadn't known they existed until, in that pod meeting, he had voiced his desire to go outside.

The podmaster had looked at him with a raised eyebrow and a sniff. "Next thing you'll be asking for a scanner," he said.

"What's a scanner?" Brock asked.
90 The podmaster requisitioned one from storage, but at the same time, he must have alerted Research, because it was the representative from Research who had brought him the scanner and questioned him about his expressed desire for an Actual Adventure—a journey outside the dome.

"What has prompted this, uh—unusual ambition?" the representative had asked, his eyes not on Brock but on the scanner in his hand. Brock had hesitated, distracted by the man's fidgeting with the strange instrument. "I—I'm interested in scientific research," Brock said at last. **E**

So here he was out of the pod, alone for the first time in his life. Perhaps, though, he should have asked one of his podfellows to come along. Or
100 even the pod robopet. But the other fellows all laughed when he spoke of going outside, their eyes darting back and forth. Nothing on the outside, they said, could equal the newest Virtual Adventure. He suddenly realized that ever since he started interfacing[6] with the ancient fictions, his fellows had given him that look. They did think he was odd—not quite the same as a regular podfellow. Brock didn't really vibe with the pod robopet.

C SETTING
Reread lines 54–70. What do these details tell you about the place where the story is set?

D SETTING
Why does Brock leave the dome?

E SEQUENCE IN PLOT
Reread lines 81–97. What information revealed in the **flashback** helps you better understand Brock and his present actions?

---

5. **vaporization** (vā'pər-ĭ-zā'shən): the process of making a thing disappear by changing it into a fog or mist.

6. **interfacing** (ĭn'tər-fā'sĭng): making connections.

It was one of the more modern ones, and when they'd programmed its artificial intelligence they'd somehow made it too smart. The robopet in the children's pod last year was older, stupider, and more "fun" to have around.

110   He'd badly underestimated the distance to the mountains. The time was well past noon, and he had at least three kilometers to go. Should he signal late return or turn about now? He didn't have much more than one day's scant supply of water and food tablets. But he was closer to the hills than to the dome. He felt a thrill ["excitement"] and pressed on.

    There were actual trees growing on the first hill. Not the great giants of virtual history lessons, more scrubby and bent. But they were trees, he was sure of it. The podmaster had said that trees had been extinct for hundreds of years. Brock reached up and pulled off a leaf. It was green and had veins. In some ways it looked like his own hand. He put the leaf in 120 his pack to study later. He didn't want anyone accusing him of losing his scientific objectivity.[7] Only deviants did that. Farther up the hill he heard an unfamiliar burbling sound. No, he knew that sound. It was water running. He'd heard it once when the liquid dispenser had malfunctioned. There'd been a near panic in the dome over it. He checked the scanner. There was no caution signal, so he hurried toward the sound. **F**

    It was a—a "brook"—he was sure of it! Virtual lessons had taught that there were such things outside in the past but that they had long ago grown poisonous, then in the warming climate had dried up. But here was a running brook, not even a four-hour journey from his dome. His 130 first impulse was to take off his protective glove and dip a finger in it, but he drew back. He had been well conditioned to avoid danger. He sat down clumsily on the bank. Yes, this must be grass. There were even some tiny flowers mixed in the grass. Would the atmosphere poison him if he unscrewed his helmet to take a sniff? He punched the scanner to read conditions, but the characters on the scanner panel danced about uncertainly until, at length, the disembodied voice said "conditions unreadable." He'd better not risk it. **G**

    He pushed the buttons now for liquid and pellets. A tube appeared in his mouth. It dropped a pellet on his tongue. From the tube he sucked 140 liquid enough to swallow his meal. What was it they called outside nourishment in the history virtuals? *Pecnec*? Something like that. He was having a *pecnec* in the *woods* by a *brook*. A hasty consulting of the scanner revealed that what he was feeling was "pleasure." He was very glad he hadn't come with an anxious podfellow or, worse, an advanced robopet that would, no doubt, be yanking at his suit already, urging him back toward the dome.

---

7. **scientific objectivity:** a way of looking upon a situation and remaining true to scientific facts.

Language Coach

Prefixes A prefix is a word part added to the beginning of a word to form a new word. In line 110, the prefix *under* is added to the word *estimated*. *Estimated* means that he made a careful guess. What, then, does *underestimated* mean?

F **SETTING**
Compare and contrast the setting outside the dome with the natural setting where you live. How familiar does the setting outside the dome seem to you?

G **SETTING**
Reread lines 126–137. Notice how Brock reacts to nature. In what ways has the setting inside the dome influenced Brock's reactions?

It was then, in the middle of post-*pecnec* satisfaction, that he heard the new sound. Like that programmed into a robopet, yet different. He struggled to his feet. The dry suit from storage was certainly awkward when you wanted to stand up or sit down. Nothing on the scanner indicated danger, so he went into the scrubby woods toward the sound. And stopped abruptly.

Something was lying under the shadow of a tree. Something about a meter long. It was furred and quite still. The sound was not coming from it. And then he saw the small dog—the puppy. He was sure it was a puppy, nosing the stiff body of what must once have been its mother, making the little crying sounds that he'd heard from the brook. Later, much later, he realized that he should have been wary. If the older dog had died of some extradomal disease, the puppy might have been a carrier. But at the time, all he could think of was the puppy, a small creature who had lost its mother.

He'd found out about mothers from the Virtuals. Mothers were extinct in the dome. Children were conceived and born in the lab and raised in units of twelve in the pods, presided over by a bank of computers and the podmaster. Nuclear families, as everyone knew, had been wasteful of time, energy, and space. There was an old proverb: The key to survival is efficiency. So though Brock could guess the puppy was "sad" (like that fictions person, Jo, whose podmate expired), he didn't know what missing a mother would feel like. And who would whimper for a test tube? ⓗ

Brock had never seen a dog, of course, but he'd seen plenty of dog breed descriptions on the science/history virtuals. Dogs had been abundant once. They filled the ancient fictions. They even had names

▲ **Analyze Visuals**
What do the details in the painting tell you about the **setting?**

COMMON CORE RL 3

ⓗ **SETTING**
Remember that setting is where and when a story happens, and that it can influence a story's plot. As you read about Brock's exploration of the world outside the dome, notice the sights and sounds that he discovers. Reread lines 147–167. In what way does this setting influence what happens next? Explain.

there—Lassie, Toto, Sounder. But now dogs were extinct, gone during the dark ages when the atmosphere had become warm and poisonous. The savages who had not had the intelligence or wealth to join the **foresighted** dome crafters had killed all animals wild or domesticated for food before they had eventually died out themselves. It was all in one of the very first virtual lessons. He had seen that one many times. He never confessed to anyone how, well, sad it made him feel.

But obviously, dogs were not quite extinct. Cautiously, he moved toward the small one.

180   "Alert. Alert. Scanning unknown object."

Brock pushed the off button. "Are you sure you want to turn off scanner?"

"Affirmative." He stuck the scanner into his pouch.

The puppy had lifted its head at the sound of his voice. It looked at him, head cocked, as though deciding whether to run or stay.

"It's all right, dog," Brock said soothingly. "I won't hurt you." He stayed still. He didn't want to frighten the little beast. If it ran, he wasn't sure he'd be able to catch it in his clumsy dry suit.

Slowly he extended his gloved hand. The dog backed away anxiously, but when Brock kept the hand extended, the puppy slowly crept toward him 190 and sniffed, making whimpering sounds. It wasn't old enough to be truly afraid, it seemed. The pup licked his glove tentatively, then backed away again. It was looking for food, and plasticine gloves weren't going to satisfy. ◆

Brock looked first at the dead mother whose source of nourishment must have long dried up, then around the landscape. What would a dog eat? A puppy on its own? He took off his glove and reached through his pouch into the inside pocket that held his pellet supply. Making every move slow and deliberate so as not to startle the dog, he held out a pellet. The dog came to his hand, licked it, then the pellet. It wrinkled its nose. Brock laughed. He didn't need the scanner now to tell him that what he 200 felt was "pleasure." He loved the feel of the rough tongue on his palm and the little furred face, questioning him.

"It's all right, fellow. You can eat it." ▯

As though understanding, the pup gulped down the pellet. Then looked around for more, not realizing that it had just bolted down a whole meal. When the dog saw there was no more coming, it ran over to the brook. Brock watched in horror as it put its head right down into the poisonous stream and lapped noisily.

"Don't!" Brock cried.

The puppy turned momentarily at the sound, then went back to 210 drinking, as though it was the most normal thing in the world. Well, it was, for the dog. Where else would a creature in the wild get liquid? If the streams were not all dried up, they must have learned to tolerate the water. But then, it was breathing the poisoned atmosphere, wasn't it?

foresighted (fôr'sī'tĭd) *adj.* having the ability to anticipate the future and prepare for it

◆ **GRAMMAR IN CONTEXT**
Look at lines 188–192. Notice that Paterson uses punctuation marks and the coordinating conjunctions *but* and *and* to make her sentences clear and easy to understand.

▯ **SEQUENCE IN PLOT**
What sequence of events leads to Brock's touching the puppy?

Why hadn't it hit Brock before? This was a fully organic creature on the outside *without any life support system*. What could that mean? Some amazing mutation[8] must have occurred, making it possible for at least some creatures to breathe the outside atmosphere and drink its poisoned water. Those who couldn't died, those who could survived and got stronger. Even the ancient scientist Darwin[9] knew that. And Brock had
220 come upon one of these magnificent mutants! ⓙ

The puppy whimpered and looked up at Brock with large, trusting eyes. How could he think of it as a mutant specimen? It was a puppy. One who had lost its mother. What would it eat? There was no sign of food for a carnivore.[10] Perhaps way back in the mountains some small mammals had also survived, keeping the food chain going, but the puppy would not live long enough to find its way there, much less know how to hunt with its mother gone. For the first time in his life something deep inside Brock reached out toward another creature. The thought of the puppy **languishing** here by the side of its dead parent until it, too . . .
230 "Your name is Brog, all right?" The ancient astronomers had named stars after themselves. He had discovered something just as wonderful. Didn't he have the right to name it sort of after himself while preserving the puppy's uniqueness? "Don't worry, Brog. I won't let you starve."

Which is why Brock appeared at the customs portal after dark, the front of his dry suit stained, carrying a wriggling *Canis familiaris*[11] of uncertain breed.

If there had been any way to smuggle the dog in, Brock would have. But he couldn't for the life of him figure out how. As it was, every alarm in the area went off when he stepped into the transitional cubicle.[12]
240 The disembodied voice of the monitor queried him:

"Welcome back, Brock 095670038. You're late."

"Affirmative."

"And you are carrying contraband."

"I pulled a leaf."

"Deposit same in quarantine bins."

"Affirmative."

"Sensors denote warm-blooded presence not on official roster."

"I found a dog," Brock mumbled.

ⓙ **SETTING**
Reread lines 209–220. How is finding the puppy changing what Brock has always believed about the outside?

languish (lăng'gwĭsh) *v.* to remain unattended or be neglected

---

8. **mutation** (myōō-tā'shən): a change within a creature's genes that results in a new trait or characteristic.

9. **Darwin:** Charles Darwin (1809–1882) was a British naturalist who founded the theory of evolution based on natural selection.

10. **carnivore** (kär'nə-vôr'): a flesh-eating animal.

11. *Canis familiaris* (kă'nĭs fə-mĭl-ē-âr'əs): the scientific name for the domesticated, or household, dog.

12. **transitional cubicle:** a small compartment where one is examined before moving from one environment into the next.

"Repeat."

250   "A dog."

"*Canis familiaris* is extinct."

"Well, maybe it's just a robopet that got out somehow."

"Correction. Robopets are bloodless. Leave dry suit for sterilization and proceed to quarantine inspection."

The officials in quarantine inspection, who rarely had anything to inspect, were at first nervous and then, as they watched the puppy happily licking Brock's face, interested despite themselves. An actual dog! None of them had ever seen one, of course, and Brock's dog was so much, well, more vital than a robopet. And although, on later reflection,

260 they knew they should have terminated or expelled it, they couldn't quite bring themselves to do so that night.

"It will have to go to Research," the chief inspector finally declared.

"Permission requested to hand carry the dog known as Brog to Research," Brock said. There was a bit of an argument about that. Several inspectors sought the honor, but the chief declared that Brock, having shed his dry suit and being already contaminated, should be placed with the dog in a hermetically sealed air car and transported to Research. **K**

The scientists in Research were predictably amazed to see a live *Canis familiaris.* But being scientists and more objective than the lower-grade

270 quarantine inspectors, they kept a safe distance both physically and psychically[13] from the creature. Only the oldest scientist, dressed in proper protective clothing, came into the laboratory with Brock and the dog.

---

13. **psychically** (sī′kĭk-lē): in a manner related to the mind or spirit.

▲ **Analyze Visuals**

Look at the boy's expression. What can you **infer** about his feelings toward the puppy?

K SEQUENCE IN PLOT

What events happen after Brock finds the puppy? As you read, record the sequence on your chart.

He scanned and poked and prodded the poor little fellow until it began to whimper in protest.

"Brog needs to rest," said Brock, interrupting the scientist in the midst of his inspection. "She's (for by this time gender had been indisputably established) had a hard day. And if there's some actual food available—she's not used to pellets."

"Of course, of course," said one of the researchers through the speaker
280 in the observation booth. "How thoughtless. Send someone out for a McLike burger without sauce. She may regard it as meat. Anyhow, it will seem more like food to her than a pellet, affirmative, Brock?"

The scientists, Brock soon realized, were looking to him for advice. He was, after all, the discoverer of the last dog. It gave him sudden scientific status. Brock had sense enough to take advantage of this. After Brog had swallowed the McLike burger in three quick gulps, Brock insisted that he be allowed to stay with Brog, so that he might interact and sleep with her. "She's not like us," he explained. "She's used to tumbling about and curling up with other warm bodies. In the old myths," he added, "puppies
290 separated from their litters cried all night long. She will need constant interaction with another warm-blooded creature or she might well die of," he loved using his new vocabulary, "'loneliness.'"

The scientists agreed. After all, research was rather like quarantine, and since Brock had touched the dog ungloved and unprotected, he might well have picked up some germ from her. It was better to keep them both isolated in the research lab where proper precautions would be taken.

For nearly a week, Brock lived with Brog in the research center, eating McLike burgers, playing "fetch," teaching Brog to "sit," "heel," "come"—all the commands he could cull from the ancient texts. The dog quickly
300 learned to obey Brock's commands, but it wasn't the automatic response of a robopet. Brog delighted in obedience. She wanted to please Brock, and those few times when she was too busy nosing about the lab and failed to obey instantly, those times when Brock's voice took on a sharp tone of **reproof,** the poor little thing put her tail between her legs, looked up at him with sorrowful eyes, begging to be forgiven. Brock was tempted to speak sharply to her even when there was no need, for the sight of her drooping ears and tail, her mournful eyes was so dear to him that he did what Travis Coates had done to Old Yeller.[14] He hugged her. There was no other way to explain it. He simply put his arms around her and held
310 her to his chest while she beat at him with her tail and licked his face raw. Out of the corner of his eye he was aware that one of the scientists was watching. Well, let him watch. Nothing was as wonderful as feeling this warmth toward another creature.

---

14. **Travis Coates . . . Old Yeller:** In the novel *Old Yeller*, Old Yeller is a stray dog who becomes friends with 14-year-old Travis.

○ COMMON CORE L 4d

Language Coach

Word Definitions
The word *indisputably* means that something is known for sure; it cannot be doubted. Reread lines 275–277. What do the scientists know *indisputably* about Brog? (Hint: *gender* means either male or female.)

reproof (rĭ-proof′) *n.* criticism for a fault

For the first week, the researchers seemed quite content to observe dog and boy from their glass-paneled observation booth and speak **copious** notes into their computers. Only the oldest of them would come into the lab and actually touch the alien creature, and he always wore a sterile protective suit with gloves. The others claimed it would interfere with objectivity if they got close to the dog, but they all seemed to behave 320 positively toward Brog. No mention was made to Brock of his own less than objective behavior. So Brock was astounded to awake in the middle of the night to the sounds of an argument. Someone had forgotten to turn off the communication system. **L**

"Cloning[15]—it's the only thing to do. If she's the last, we owe it to **posterity** to keep the line going."

"And how are we going to raise a pack of dogs in a dome? One is nearly eating and drinking us out of test tube and petri dish. We can't go on this way. As drastic as it may seem, we have to be realistic. Besides, no one has had the chance to do actual experiments since the dark ages. Haven't you 330 ever, just once, yearned to compare virtual research with actual?"

"What about the boy? He won't agree. Interfacing daily with the dog, he's become crippled by primal urges."

"Can you think what chaos might ensue if a flood of primordial emotions[16] were to surface in a controlled environment such as ours?" another asked. "Apparently, emotions are easily triggered by interactions with primitive beasts, like dogs."

"Shh. Not now. The speaker is—" The system clicked off. **M**

But Brock had already heard. He knew he had lost anything resembling scientific objectivity. He was no longer sure objectivity was a desirable 340 trait. He rather enjoyed being flooded by "primordial emotions." But he was more worried for Brog than for himself. It wasn't hard to figure out what the scientists meant by "actual experiments." Cloning would be bad enough. Ten dogs who looked just like Brog so no one would know how special, how truly unique Brog was. But experiments! They'd cut her open and examine her internal organs, the way scientists had in the dark ages. They'd prod her with electric impulses and put chips in her brain. They'd try to change her personality or modify her behavior. They'd certainly try to make her eat and drink less!

In the dark, he put his arm around Brog and drew her close. He loved 350 the terrible smell of her breath and the way she snored when she slept. They'd probably fix that, too.

The next day he played sick. Brog, faithful dog that she was, hung around him whimpering, licking his face. The scientists showed no

---

copious (kō'pē-əs) *adj.* more than enough; plentiful

L SEQUENCE IN PLOT
How long have Brock and Brog been living in the dome when the argument occurs?

posterity (pŏ-stĕr'ĭ-tē) *n.* future generations

M SEQUENCE IN PLOT
What are the scientists planning to do to Brog? As you read, note on your chart the events that follow.

---

15. **cloning:** the scientific process of creating several identical plants or animals from a single ancestor.

16. **primal urges . . . primordial** (prĭ-môr'dē-əl) **emotions:** feelings or desires that have existed from the beginning of humankind.

particular concern. They were too busy plotting what they might do with Brog.

Brock crept to the nearest terminal in the lab. It was already logged in. The scientists had been doing nothing but research on *Canis familiaris.* COMMON CANINE DISEASES. Brock scrolled down the list with descriptions. No, *distemper* wouldn't do. The first symptom was loss of appetite. He couldn't make Brog fake that. On and on it went—no, *heartworms* wouldn't do. What he needed was a disease that might affect *Homo sapiens*[17] as well as *Canis familiaris.* Here it was! "Rabies: A viral disease occurring in animals and humans, esp. in dogs and wolves. Transmitted by bite or scratch. The early stages of the disease are most dangerous, for an otherwise healthy and friendly appearing animal will suddenly bite without provocation."

Rabies was it! Somehow he would have to make Brog bite him. There was no antirabies serum in the dome, he felt sure. There were no animals in the dome. Why would they use precious space to store an unneeded medication? So they'd have to expel him as well as Brog for fear of spreading the disease. He shivered, then shook himself. No matter what lay on the outside, he could not stand to go back to the life he had lived in the dome before he met Brog. **N**

He crept back to bed, pulling the covers over Brog. When one of the scientists came into the observation booth, Brock pinched Brog's neck as hard as he could. Nothing. He pinched again, harder. Brog just snuggled closer, slobbering on his arm.

Disgusted, Brock got out of bed. Brog hopped down as well, rubbing against his leg. Pinching obviously was not going to do it. While the scientist on duty in the booth was bending over a computer terminal, Brock brought his foot down on Brog's paw. A tiny *yip* was all he got from that cruel effort—not enough sound even to make the man look up.

"Feeling better, Brock 095670038?" The oldest researcher had come into the lab.

"Affirmative," Brock answered.

"And how are you, puppy-wuppy?" The old man tickled Brog under her chin with his gloved hand. *If I were a dog, I'd bite someone like that,* thought Brock, but Brog, of course, simply licked the researcher's glove and wagged her tail.

That was when he got his great idea. He waited to execute it until the proper moment. For the first time, all the scientists had gathered in the lab, all of them in protective garb, some of them twitching nervously in their chairs. They were sitting in a circle around Brock and Brog, explaining what must be done.

N SETTING

How does the setting inside the dome help Brock make his decision?

---

17. *Homo sapiens* (hō′mō sā′pē-ənz): the scientific name for the species of human beings now on Earth.

"It has to be done for the sake of science," they began. Then they went on to, "For the sake of the dome community, which is always, as you well know, short on food, and particularly short on water." Brock listened to their arguments, nodding solemnly, pretending to agree. "It won't be as if she'll really be gone, you know. We've made virtuals of her—a special series
400 just for you to keep. You can virtually play with her whenever you like."

That was the cue. Brock turned and bit Brog on the tail so hard that the blood started. Brog, surprised and enraged, spun around and bit Brock on the nose.

There was a shocked silence. Every scientist leaned backward, body pressed hard against his or her chair back. Every eye was on the two of them.

"I—I don't know what got into me," Brock said. "I've been feeling very weird." The scientists continued to stare. "I was checking the historical records. . . ."

All of the scientists fled the room. Someone ran to a computer terminal.
410 When Brock offered to take Brog out of the dome and let her loose in the mountains, no one argued. Neither did they say, "Hurry back," or even, "Take care." No one came close as he loaded his pouch with water and food pellets. The customs gate monitor asked no questions. ◉

Out of sight of the dome, Brog was delirious with joy, jumping and running about in circles around Brock's boots. Why wasn't the

◉ **SEQUENCE IN PLOT**
How does Brock get the scientists to release him and Brog?

atmosphere choking Brog if it was as poisonous as the dome dwellers claimed? His heart beating rapidly, Brock unscrewed his helmet just enough to let in a little of the outside atmosphere. Nothing happened. In fact, he seemed to be breathing perfectly normally. He took off the
420 helmet entirely. He was still breathing freely. But his heart was beating so hard, he couldn't be sure. He waited for the choking sensation he had been warned of. It didn't occur. Could they be wrong? Could the outside world have healed itself? Perhaps—perhaps the reason the scanner had so much trouble reading the outside atmosphere was because it wasn't within the range of computerized expectations.

Could it be? Could it be that fear had kept the dome dwellers prisoner many years longer than a poisoned environment would have?

He unfastened the dry suit and slowly stepped out of it into the sunlight.

It was wonderful how much faster he could walk without the clumsy suit.
430 "Who knows?" Brock said to a frisking Brog. "Who knows, maybe out here you aren't the last dog. Your mother had to come from somewhere."

Brog barked happily in reply.

"And maybe, just maybe, where there are dogs, there are humans as well."

They stopped at the brook where they'd met, and both of them had a long drink. Brock no longer carried a scanner, but he knew what he felt was excitement. The water was delicious. 〰 **P**

(COMMON CORE **L 4**

Language Coach

Multiple-Meaning Words Multiple-meaning words have more than one meaning. The word *range* can mean a line of mountains, a geographic distance, or to be within certain limits. Which meaning of *range* is correct in line 425?

P **SETTING**
How are Brock's questions about the world outside the dome beginning to be answered?

Comprehension

1. **Recall** In the first half of the story, how does Brock know what emotions he is feeling?

2. **Clarify** Why does Brock fool the scientists into thinking he and Brog have rabies?

3. **Summarize** How does meeting Brog change Brock's life?

COMMON CORE

RL 1 Cite several pieces of textual evidence to support what the text says explicitly. **RL 3** Analyze how particular elements of a story interact (e.g., how setting shapes the plot). **W 7** Conduct short research projects to answer a question.

Text Analysis

4. **Make Inferences** What would you say is the **setting** of the story? Give details from the text about both the time and the place.

5. **Identify Sequence in Plot** Review the chart you created as you read. Identify which events in the plot occur in a **flashback.** What new information about the people in the dome do you learn in the flashbacks?

6. **Analyze Setting** One way to consider the importance of setting to a story's plot is to imagine the same story happening in a different time or place. Think about what might happen if you found a puppy. How would your experience be different from Brock's? Use a Venn diagram to **compare and contrast** which details might stay the same and which details might be different. Explain what your diagram suggests about the influence of setting on a story's plot.

If I Found a Puppy   When Brock Found a Puppy

7. **Draw Conclusions** Why do you think the people in the dome live the way they do? Think about their food, their fears, and their attitude about the outside world. Then consider how their history and their environment might be affecting them. Support your answer with details from the story.

Extension and Challenge

8. **SCIENCE CONNECTION** Read the article "'Spot' Goes High-Tech" on page 65. Then do research to find out what other kinds of tasks or functions robots are being asked to perform. Note at least three. In a small group, discuss how new technologies might have both a positive and a negative impact on our lives.

Why are pets good COMPANIONS?

Go back and review the list you created to answer the question on page 46. How do you think Brock might answer this question? Explain why you think Brog's companionship was important to Brock.

Vocabulary in Context

▲ VOCABULARY PRACTICE

For each item, choose the word that differs most in meaning from the other words.

1. (a) journey, (b) expedition, (c) foray, (d) climb
2. (a) perceptive, (b) foresighted, (c) careless, (d) prophetic
3. (a) evasive, (b) clever, (c) bright, (d) knowledgeable
4. (a) numerous, (b) copious, (c) plentiful, (d) thin
5. (a) trail, (b) ail, (c) languish, (d) suffer
6. (a) separated, (b) apart, (c) disembodied, (d) together
7. (a) ancestor, (b) posterity, (c) grandfather, (d) veteran
8. (a) blame, (b) reproof, (c) position, (d) criticism

copious
disembodied
evasive
foray
foresighted
languish
posterity
reproof

ACADEMIC VOCABULARY IN SPEAKING

• contemporary   • element   • identify   • influence   • structure

Which idea from "The Last Dog" most reminds you of life in **contemporary** society, or where you think society is heading? Discuss the positive and negative aspects of this idea with a small group. Use the Academic Vocabulary words in your discussion.

VOCABULARY STRATEGY: ANTONYMS AS CONTEXT CLUES

Context clues can often be found in the words and sentences that surround an unfamiliar word. These clues can help you figure out the meaning of the word. **Antonyms,** or words that mean the opposite of each other, can be one kind of context clue. For example, a sentence in "The Last Dog" talks of "actual rather than virtual research." The words *rather than* signal that *virtual* is an antonym of *actual*. Since you know *actual,* you can figure out *virtual*.

PRACTICE Identify the antonym of each boldfaced word. Then define the word.

1. Though he tried to **facilitate** the cleanup process, he complicated it instead.
2. Her costume was **ostentatious,** but her cousin's was quite plain.
3. You should praise your brother, rather than continually **disparaging** him.
4. Unlike Isabel, who had an **antipathy** to snakes, Luisa seemed to love them.
5. Jeremy was as **pugnacious** as his brother was peace loving.

COMMON CORE

L 4a Use context (e.g., a word's function in a sentence) as a clue to the meaning of a word. L 5b Use the relationship between particular words (e.g., antonym) to better understand each of the words.

Interactive Vocabulary **THINK** central

Go to thinkcentral.com.
KEYWORD: HML7-63

Language

◆ **GRAMMAR IN CONTEXT:** Use Correct Punctuation

A run-on sentence, sometimes simply called a run-on, is two or more sentences written as though they were a single sentence. Use one of these methods to correct a run-on:

- Insert an **end mark** and start a new sentence.
- Insert a **coordinating conjunction,** such as *and, but,* or *so,* after a **comma.**
- Change a comma to a **semicolon.**

> *Original:* Some people like having an animal companion, others may think a robot is just as good.

> *Revised:* Some people like having an animal companion, but others may think a robot is just as good.

PRACTICE Use the correct punctuation and coordinating conjuctions, as necessary, to rewrite the following run-on sentences.

1. Both types of pets make people feel needed people like feeling needed.

2. Animal pets really do need us, robot pets are just machines.

3. How can a metal dog take the place of a furry one, you can't hug a robot.

4. It might help to have a robotic dog it can't take the place of a real one.

*For more help with run-ons, see pages R64–R65 in the **Grammar Handbook.***

READING-WRITING CONNECTION

Explore the ideas presented in "The Last Dog" by responding to this prompt. Then use the **revising tip** to improve your writing.

WRITING PROMPT	REVISING TIP
Extended Constructed Response: Across Texts Look again at "'Spot' Goes High-Tech" on page 65. Both Brock and the elderly people in the article enjoy having the **companionship** of a pet, be it an animal pet or a robot. Is a robot pet as good as an animal pet? Using examples from both selections, write a **two- or three-paragraph response,** describing the benefits of each pet.	Review your response. If you have any run-on sentences, revise them by using the correct punctuation or by adding a coordinating conjunction and the correct punctuation.

Interactive Revision **THINK** central

Go to thinkcentral.com.
KEYWORD: HML7-64

COMMON CORE

L1 Demonstrate command of the conventions of grammar and usage. **L2** Demonstrate command of the conventions of punctuation. **W2** Write explanatory texts to examine a topic and convey ideas.

ONLINE ARTICLE Robotic pets, such as the ones in the dome, are not just futuristic fantasy. This news article describes a contemporary project that is testing whether robotic dogs can bring joy to senior citizens.

File   Edit   View   Tools   Help

Back   Forward   Stop   Refresh   Home   Search   Favorites   Mail   Print

E-mail This   Print This   Save This   Subscribe

'Spot' Goes High-Tech

Researchers Try Robotic Pets as Companions for the Elderly

Researchers in Indiana are trying to find out if robots —which no one has to feed or walk—can do the same job as flesh and blood animals.

Rosewalk Common is an assisted living community for seniors in Lafayette, Indiana. Rose Lawson, 90, has lived at Rosewalk for four years and recently joined other residents to meet "Aibo" (pronounced "I-bo"), a frisky, silver and black robotic dog.

Aibo made its way around a circle of seated residents, playing fetch, responding to spoken commands, sitting in laps to be petted—and winning friends.

"Do you like me? Do you like me?" Lawson asked Aibo. The robot responded with an electronic "Ohhh," winning a big smile from Lawson. . . .

Can Robots Make People Happier?

The robotic dogs were brought to Rosewalk by researchers at Indiana's Purdue University as part of a **project** to determine whether robots can make people happier.

Alan M. Beck, a professor at Purdue and director of the **Center for Human-Animal Bond** at the university's veterinary school, said one possible benefit may be better socialization.

"We find people who in nursing home settings might be socially isolated and don't routinely chat with each other have something to talk about together, to have fun, to have reminiscences," said Beck. . . .

Programmed to Generate Human Feelings

Robotic dogs are programmed to respond to commands, to wag their tails if told they are "good." All of this is supposed to lull humans into feeling . . . attached—to a robot.

The very concept of robots that seduce people into thinking they are real is just too much for sociologist Sherry Turkle, director of the **Initiative on Technology and Self** at the Massachusetts Institute of Technology.

"I think we should take it as a wake-up call and really say, 'Now, why are we giving robot pets to old people?' And the answer, I think, is that we really have been struggling to figure out how to give enough people to old people."

Assistant professor Nancy Edwards, of the Purdue School of Nursing, acknowledges the preference of human contact. But she still sees value in the Aibo study. "We know human interaction is best, we know human-animal [interaction] is probably second, but if these people are having no interaction, what we're saying is, will some interaction with a robot help in some way?"

"You can see smiling, laughing, remembering of good things, and talking among each other," said Beck. "This is more than just diversion. This is kind of a therapeutic event, where people really, I think, benefit from the experience."

Internet

Thank You, M'am
Short Story by Langston Hughes

Who sees the BEST in you?

COMMON CORE

RL1 Cite several pieces of textual evidence to support inferences drawn from the text. **RL3** Analyze how particular elements of a story interact.

Have you ever gone through a time when it seemed like you couldn't do anything right? If so, then you know how important it is to have someone have faith in you. When a friend, a family member, or a teacher believes you can do better, it can help you try harder instead of giving up. In "Thank You, M'am," a woman sees potential—or possibility—where others might see a problem.

QUICKWRITE Create a web of people you know who see the best in you. Then explain why you have included these people. In what ways do they show their belief in you?

Mr. Simpson

Who Sees My Best?

TEXT ANALYSIS: PLOT AND CONFLICT

In most stories, the plot centers on **conflict,** or the struggle between opposing forces. As the characters respond to the conflict, the plot develops and moves forward.

- An **external conflict** is a character's struggle against an outside force. For example, a character may struggle against nature or against another character.
- An **internal conflict** takes place inside the character. For example, a character may struggle between wanting something and knowing that taking it is wrong.

Stories often contain more than one conflict. As you read "Thank You, M'am," look for examples of both types of conflict.

● READING SKILL: MAKE INFERENCES

When you make an **inference,** you use your reason and experience to guess at what a writer doesn't say directly. Combining clues in a passage with your own knowledge helps you understand what characters are feeling and thinking. As you read "Thank You, M'am," make inferences to better understand the characters. Record your inferences on a chart like the one shown.

Detail About Character	What I Infer
Mrs. Jones holds Roger but lets him stoop to pick up her purse.	Mrs. Jones is trying to decide whether to trust Roger.

▲ VOCABULARY IN CONTEXT

The following words helped Langston Hughes write a story about a boy facing a serious conflict. To see how many words you already know, use them to complete the sentences.

> **WORD LIST**   barren   frail   mistrust   presentable

1. Don't _____ him; he will keep his promise.
2. Because he was _____, the hard work tired him.
3. The _____ room was a source of loneliness.
4. He wanted to look _____ for the assembly.

 Complete the activities in your **Reader/Writer Notebook.**

Meet the Author

Langston Hughes
1902–1967

A Fascinating Journey
As a child being raised by his grandmother in Lawrence, Kansas, Langston Hughes began a lifelong exploration of literature and blues music. He later went to Columbia University, worked in hotels, and traveled the world as a cook's assistant on freighters. Hughes was first recognized as a poet while working as a busboy. He left his poems at a table where the poet Vachel Lindsay was dining. Lindsay promoted the young poet's work, and Hughes's career was launched. Langston Hughes went on to become an influential writer of the 20th century.

The People's Poet
After being discovered, Hughes went on to write novels, short stories, and plays as well as poems. Hughes's work shows a special understanding of everyday people—people who may not be famous or rich but whose lives are inspiring and valuable nonetheless.

BACKGROUND TO THE STORY
Harlem
"Thank You, M'am" takes place in Harlem, a section of New York City. In the early 1900s, Harlem attracted many African-American writers. The stimulating community had a deep influence on their work.

Author Online
THINK central
Go to **thinkcentral.com.**
KEYWORD: HML7-67

Thank You, M'am

Langston Hughes

She was a large woman with a large purse that had everything in it but hammer and nails. It had a long strap, and she carried it slung across her shoulder. It was about eleven o'clock at night, and she was walking alone, when a boy ran up behind her and tried to snatch her purse. The strap broke with the single tug the boy gave it from behind. But the boy's weight and the weight of the purse combined caused him to lose his balance so, instead of taking off full blast as he had hoped, the boy fell on his back on the sidewalk, and his legs flew up. The large woman simply turned around and kicked him right square in his blue-jeaned sitter. Then she reached down, picked the boy up by his shirt front, and shook him until his teeth rattled. **A**

After that the woman said, "Pick up my pocketbook, boy, and give it here."

She still held him. But she bent down enough to permit him to stoop and pick up her purse. Then she said, "Now ain't you ashamed of yourself?"

Firmly gripped by his shirt front, the boy said, "Yes'm."

The woman said, "What did you want to do it for?"

The boy said, "I didn't aim to."

She said, "You a lie!"

By that time two or three people passed, stopped, turned to look, and some stood watching.

"If I turn you loose, will you run?" asked the woman.

A PLOT AND CONFLICT
Who is in conflict and why?

Analyze Visuals ▶

Look at the woman in the painting. What might you **infer** about her personality?

Faith Ringgold (1977), Alice Neel. Oil on canvas, 48″ × 36″. Private collection. © 2004 Estate of Alice Neel/Courtesy Robert Miller Gallery, New York/Philadelphia Museum of Art, Special Exhibition.

"Yes'm," said the boy.

"Then I won't turn you loose," said the woman. She did not release him.

"I'm very sorry, lady, I'm sorry," whispered the boy.

"Um-hum! And your face is dirty. I got a great mind to wash your face for you. Ain't you got nobody home to tell you to wash your face?"

"No'm," said the boy.

30 "Then it will get washed this evening," said the large woman starting up the street, dragging the frightened boy behind her. **B**

He looked as if he were fourteen or fifteen, **frail** and willow-wild, in tennis shoes and blue jeans.

The woman said, "You ought to be my son. I would teach you right from wrong. Least I can do right now is to wash your face. Are you hungry?"

"No'm," said the being-dragged boy. "I just want you to turn me loose."

"Was I bothering *you* when I turned that corner?" asked the woman.

"No'm."

"But you put yourself in contact with *me*," said the woman. "If you 40 think that that contact is not going to last awhile, you got another thought coming. When I get through with you, sir, you are going to remember Mrs. Luella Bates Washington Jones."

Sweat popped out on the boy's face and he began to struggle. Mrs. Jones stopped, jerked him around in front of her, put a half nelson about his neck, and continued to drag him up the street. When she got to her door, she dragged the boy inside, down a hall, and into a large kitchenette-furnished room at the rear of the house. She switched on the light and left the door open. The boy could hear other roomers laughing and talking in the large house. Some of their doors were open, too, so he 50 knew he and the woman were not alone. The woman still had him by the neck in the middle of her room. ◆

She said, "What is your name?"

"Roger," answered the boy.

"Then, Roger, you go to that sink and wash your face," said the woman, whereupon she turned him loose—at last. Roger looked at the door— looked at the woman—looked at the door—*and went to the sink.* **C**

"Let the water run until it gets warm," she said. "Here's a clean towel."

"You gonna take me to jail?" asked the boy, bending over the sink.

"Not with that face, I would not take you nowhere," said the woman.

60 "Here I am trying to get home to cook me a bite to eat and you snatch my pocketbook! Maybe you ain't been to your supper either, late as it be. Have you?"

"There's nobody home at my house," said the boy.

"Then we'll eat," said the woman. "I believe you're hungry—or been hungry—to try to snatch my pocketbook." **D**

B MAKE INFERENCES
Reread lines 18–31. From the details presented so far, what can you guess about the boy's background and personality? Add this information to your chart.

frail (frāl) *adj.* delicate; weak and fragile

◆ GRAMMAR IN CONTEXT
In the sentence in line 43, the word *boy's* is a **singular possessive** noun that tells whose face is being described. To show possession, an apostrophe followed by an *s* is attached to the word *boy.*

C PLOT AND CONFLICT
What is Roger's internal conflict?

D PLOT AND CONFLICT
What action does Mrs. Jones take as a result of her struggle with Roger?

"I wanted a pair of blue suede shoes," said the boy.

"Well, you didn't have to snatch *my* pocketbook to get some suede shoes," said Mrs. Luella Bates Washington Jones. "You could of asked me."

70 "M'am?"

The water dripping from his face, the boy looked at her. There was a long pause. A very long pause. After he had dried his face and not knowing what else to do dried it again, the boy turned around, wondering what next. The door was open. He could make a dash for it down the hall. He could run, run, run, run, *run!*

The woman was sitting on the day-bed.[1] After a while she said, "I were young once and I wanted things I could not get."

80 There was another long pause. The boy's mouth opened. Then he frowned, but not knowing he frowned.

The woman said, "Um-hum! You thought I was going to say *but,* didn't you? You thought I was going to say, *but I didn't snatch people's pocketbooks.* Well, I wasn't going to say that." Pause. Silence. "I have done things, too, which I would not tell you, son—neither tell God, if he didn't already know. So you set down while I fix us something to eat. You might run that comb through your hair so you will look **presentable.**"

90 In another corner of the room behind a screen was a gas plate and an icebox. Mrs. Jones got up and went behind the screen. The woman did not watch the boy to see if he was going to run now, nor did she watch her purse which she left behind her on the day-bed. But the boy took care to sit on the far side of the room where he thought she could easily see him out of the corner of her eye, if she wanted to. He did not trust the woman *not* to trust him. And he did not want to be **mistrusted** now.

"Do you need somebody to go to the store," asked the boy, "maybe to get some milk or something?"

"Don't believe I do," said the woman, "unless you just want sweet milk 100 yourself. I was going to make cocoa out of this canned milk I got here."

"That will be fine," said the boy.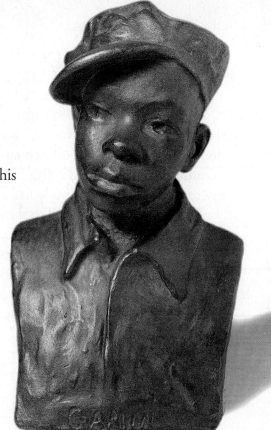

She heated some lima beans and ham she had in the icebox, made the cocoa, and set the table. The woman did not ask the boy anything about where he lived, or his folks, or anything else that would embarrass him. Instead, as they ate, she told him about her job in a hotel beauty shop that stayed open late, what the work was like, and how all kinds of women

Gamin (about 1929), Augusta Savage. Painted plaster, 9" × 5³⁄₄″ × 4³⁄₈″. Smithsonian American Art Museum, Gift of Benjamin and Olya Margolin.

presentable
(prĭ-zĕn′tə-bəl) *adj.*
fit to be seen
by people

mistrust (mĭs-trŭst′)
v. to think of without
confidence or trust

E MAKE INFERENCES
Why does Roger want
to go to the store for
Mrs. Jones? Add this
information to your
chart.

---

1. **day-bed:** a couch or sofa that can also serve as a bed.

came in and out, blondes, red-heads, and Spanish. Then she cut him a half of her ten-cent cake.

"Eat some more, son," she said.

110   When they were finished eating she got up and said, "Now, here, take this ten dollars and buy yourself some blue suede shoes. And next time, do not make the mistake of latching onto *my* pocketbook *nor nobody else's*— because shoes come by devilish like that will burn your feet. I got to get my rest now. But I wish you would behave yourself, son, from here on in."

She led him down the hall to the front door and opened it. "Goodnight! Behave yourself, boy!" she said, looking out into the street.

The boy wanted to say something else other than "Thank you, m'am" to Mrs. Luella Bates Washington Jones, but he couldn't do so as he turned at the **barren** stoop and looked back at the large woman in the door.

120 He barely managed to say "Thank you" before she shut the door. And he never saw her again. ◐ **F**

Language Coach

Syntax The way words are put together in a sentence is called syntax. In line 113, Mrs. Jones says "shoes come by devilish like that will burn your feet." What does she mean?

barren (băr′ən) *adj.* empty; lacking interest or charm

F MAKE INFERENCES
What else might Roger have wanted to say?

Connect: Poem

If I can stop one Heart from breaking

Emily Dickinson

If I can stop one Heart from breaking
I shall not live in vain
If I can ease one Life the Aching
Or cool one Pain

5 Or help one fainting Robin
Unto his Nest again
I shall not live in Vain.

Comprehension

1. **Recall** What happens when Roger tries to steal Mrs. Jones's purse?

2. **Clarify** What does Mrs. Jones say will happen to Roger if he gets the shoes through dishonest means?

3. **Summarize** What details do you learn about Roger and his life?

Text Analysis

4. **Identify Conflict in Plot** Using a chart like the one shown, go back through the story and record examples of **internal** and **external conflict.** Which conflict sets the plot in motion?

Conflict	Internal	External
Roger tries to steal Mrs. Jones's purse.		

5. **Make Inferences** Review the chart you created as you read. Use the inferences you made to answer the following question: Why does Mrs. Jones treat Roger the way she does? Give details from the story to support your answer.

6. **Analyze a Character** Reread lines 71–101, looking specifically at what Roger says and does. What might Roger's behavior suggest about his future potential? Give evidence to support your answer.

7. **Compare Literary Works** Reread Emily Dickinson's poem on page 72. Which lines remind you of the way Mrs. Jones might think? Explain why.

8. **Evaluate Theme** The theme of a story is a message about life or human nature that the writer shares with readers. What theme do you think Hughes communicates in "Thank You, M'am"? Explain your answer.

Extension and Challenge

9. **Readers' Circle** There's an African proverb that says, "It takes a village to raise a child." With your group, discuss how this proverb applies to "Thank You, M'am." Start by talking about whether the story supports or contradicts the statement.

Who sees the BEST in you?

Is it possible for someone you have just met to see the best in you? Support your answer with evidence from the story and from your own experience.

COMMON CORE

RL 1 Cite several pieces of textual evidence to support inferences drawn from the text. **RL 3** Analyze how particular elements of a story interact.

Vocabulary in Context

▲ VOCABULARY PRACTICE

Choose the letter of the word that means the same, or nearly the same, as the boldfaced word.

1. **presentable** clothing: (a) old-fashioned, (b) tattered, (c) proper, (d) sturdy
2. a **barren** house: (a) empty, (b) dark, (c) private, (d) lovely
3. **frail** patients: (a) unconscious, (b) friendly, (c) nervous, (d) weak
4. to **mistrust** someone's advice: (a) accept, (b) doubt, (c) seek, (d) believe

ACADEMIC VOCABULARY IN WRITING

> • contemporary • element • identify • influence • structure

Was Mrs. Jones a good **influence** on Roger? Write your response in a paragraph, using at least one of the Academic Vocabulary words.

VOCABULARY STRATEGY: PREFIXES THAT MEAN "NOT"

Many English prefixes come from Latin, Old English, and French languages. A **prefix** is a word part that appears at the beginning of a base word to form a new word, as in the vocabulary word *mistrust* (mis + trust). *Mis-*, which comes from Old English and Old French, is one of several prefixes that mean "not." Look at the chart to see other prefixes that mean "not" and to see what other meanings these prefixes may have. If you can identify the base word that a prefix is combined with, you can usually figure out the meaning of the new word.

○ **COMMON CORE**

L 4b Use common, grade-appropriate Latin affixes as clues to the meaning of a word.
L 6 Acquire and use accurately grade-appropriate general academic words.

PRACTICE One word in each sentence contains a prefix that can mean "not." Write the word and the word's definition.

1. Martin Luther King Jr. preached nonviolence.
2. Our school district has many unpaid teachers' aides.
3. It is probably inaccurate to say that the universe contains only one solar system.
4. The missile slipped behind the cloud and disappeared from sight.
5. It's common sense that animals should not be mistreated.

Prefix	Meanings
dis-	not; opposite of
in-	not; in
un-	not
mis-	not; incorrect or badly
non-	not; opposite of

Interactive Vocabulary **THINK** central

Go to **thinkcentral.com**.
KEYWORD: HML7-74

Language

COMMON CORE

L 2b Spell correctly. **W 2** Write explanatory texts to examine a topic and convey ideas.

◆ **GRAMMAR IN CONTEXT:** Spell Possessives Correctly

Refer to the Grammar note on page 70. The possessive form of a noun shows ownership or relationship. When forming a possessive noun, be sure to put the **apostrophe** in the correct place. To help keep your writing clear, follow these guidelines for spelling possessive nouns:

Singular nouns: Add an apostrophe and *s,* even if the word ends in *s* (*book's cover, waitress's tray, Louis's house*).

Plural nouns ending in *s:* Add an apostrophe (*songs' melodies, bees' honey*).

Plural nouns not ending in *s:* Add an apostrophe and *s* (*women's sports, people's health*).

> *Original:* In the beginning, Rogers' potential is not easy to see.
>
> *Revised:* In the beginning, Roger's potential is not easy to see.

PRACTICE Correct the spelling of the possessive nouns in the following sentences.

1. Mrs. Jones' treatment of Roger shows her sympathy toward him.
2. She proves that you cannot always prejudge childrens' actions.
3. She knows that many boy's actions do not reflect their true personalities.
4. Roger understands that it is wrong to take someone elses' money.

*For more help with apostrophes, see page R50 in the **Grammar Handbook.***

READING-WRITING CONNECTION

YOUR TURN Show your understanding of the characters in "Thank You, M'am" by responding to this prompt. Then use the **revising tip** to improve your writing.

WRITING PROMPT	REVISING TIP
Extended Constructed Response: Comparison Write **two or three paragraphs** comparing how Roger behaves on the street with how he behaves after spending some time with Mrs. Jones. Explain why Mrs. Jones's belief in his potential helps Roger show his best self.	Review your compare-and-contrast response. If you have used possessives, check your spelling to see that you have correctly placed the apostrophes.

Interactive Revision **THINK** central

Go to thinkcentral.com. KEYWORD: HML7-75

Rikki-tikki-tavi

Short Story by Rudyard Kipling

VIDEO TRAILER **THINK** central KEYWORD: HML7-76

What makes you BRAVE?

COMMON CORE

RL 3 Analyze how particular elements of a story interact.
L 5a Interpret figures of speech in context.

You see a small child stepping in front of a speeding car. . . . You get the chance to sing in front of a thousand people. . . . Your best friend needs help standing up to a bully. . . . All of these are occasions that might make you feel brave—full of energy and courage to meet a tough challenge. In the story you're about to read, you will see bravery in action.

PRESENT Think of a time when you felt brave. Create a picture of the occasion, including a caption explaining what was happening and why it made you brave. Share your picture with the class.

September 12, 2006   Belleville Herald   3

Local Teen Rescues Five Children

By Terry Jones Staff Reporter

A thirteen-year-old student from Oakdale Elementary School won praise from local community groups for her bravery this Tuesday when fire alarms in her building went off. Cathy Gutierrez was caring for two small brothers at the time and knew there were also young children in the apartment next door. At the sound of the alarms, Cathy rounded up the children, calmed them, and took them to the stairwell designated for evacuations by the Belleville Fire Department. Th

- **TEXT ANALYSIS: SUSPENSE AND FORESHADOWING**

    When you feel growing tension and excitement as you read or watch a movie, that feeling is called **suspense.** Sometimes writers build suspense by using **foreshadowing,** hints or clues about events that will happen later, as the plot develops. Foreshadowing can come from the setting details or from a character's unusual statement or strong warning. As you read "Rikki-tikki-tavi," notice how the author builds suspense and uses foreshadowing to make you want to keep reading.

    Review: **Plot and Conflict**

- **READING STRATEGY: PREDICT**

    A **prediction** is a reasonable guess about what will happen over the course of a story. Predicting helps you stay involved as you read. To make predictions, ask yourself:

    - What do I already know about the setting and plot?
    - On the basis of their words and actions, what might characters do in the future? What events might result?

    As you read, write predictions in a chart like the one shown.

Clues from the Story	Predictions
Teddy's mother takes Rikki-tikki home.	Rikki-tikki will become a part of Teddy's family.

    Review: **Cause and Effect**

- **VOCABULARY IN CONTEXT**

    Rudyard Kipling uses the following boldfaced words in telling his tale of bravery. Restate each sentence, using a different word or phrase for the boldfaced word.

    1. She made a **valiant** effort to overcome hardship.
    2. She tried to **revive** the unconscious woman.
    3. He **cunningly** outsmarted the other contestants.
    4. Do not **cower** in scary situations.
    5. The dog had a peculiar limping **gait.**
    6. The **fledgling** made its first trip outside the nest.
    7. We offered them **consolation** in their sorrow.
    8. Be careful not to **singe** the hair on your arms.

 Complete the activities in your **Reader/Writer Notebook.**

Meet the Author

Rudyard Kipling
1865–1936

A Man of Two Countries
When Rudyard Kipling was five, he left India, where he had been born, to go to school in England. India, however, would always be a powerful attraction for Kipling; he lived there again for a while as an adult, and many of his stories take place there. In works such as *The Jungle Book*, Kipling introduced a vivid cast of animal and human characters. Kipling's adventure stories gained worldwide popularity. In 1907, he received the Nobel Prize in literature.

BACKGROUND TO THE STORY
The Mongoose and the Cobra
The mongoose and the cobra are a pair of natural enemies—a pair that will fight to the death. The mongoose, a mammal growing to a length of only 16 inches, seems hardly a match for the poisonous cobra, a snake that averages six feet in length. But the mongoose's speed and agility make it a powerful fighter.

Life in Colonial India
This story is set in India during the late 1800s, when Great Britain ruled India. Many British families lived in bungalows—open, airy houses that permitted snakes to enter easily. In such an environment, mongooses were valuable assets.

Author Online

THINK central

Go to thinkcentral.com.
KEYWORD: HML7-77

Rikki-tikki-tavi

Rudyard Kipling

This is the story of the great war that Rikki-tikki-tavi fought single-handed, through the bathrooms of the big bungalow in Segowlee cantonment.[1] Darzee, the tailorbird, helped him, and Chuchundra,[2] the muskrat, who never comes out into the middle of the floor but always creeps round by the wall, gave him advice; but Rikki-tikki did the real fighting.

He was a mongoose, rather like a little cat in his fur and his tail but quite like a weasel in his head and his habits. His eyes and the end of his restless nose were pink; he could scratch himself anywhere he pleased
10 with any leg, front or back, that he chose to use; he could fluff up his tail till it looked like a bottle-brush, and his war cry as he scuttled through the long grass was: *Rikk-tikk-tikki-tikki-tchk!* **A**

One day, a high summer flood washed him out of the burrow where he lived with his father and mother and carried him, kicking and clucking, down a roadside ditch. He found a little wisp of grass floating there and clung to it till he lost his senses. When he **revived,** he was lying in the hot sun on the middle of a garden path, very draggled indeed, and a small boy was saying, "Here's a dead mongoose. Let's have a funeral."

"No," said his mother, "let's take him in and dry him. Perhaps he isn't
20 really dead."

Analyze Visuals ▸

What might you **infer** about the people who live in this house?

A PREDICT
Recall the information in the **Background** section on page 77. Whom will Rikki-tikki go to war with? Record this and other predictions in your chart as you read.

revive (rĭ-vīv′) *v.* to return to life or consciousness

---

1. **Segowlee** (sə-gou′lē) **cantonment:** area in India that was home to a British military base.

2. **Chuchundra** (chə-chŏŏn′drə).

Illustrations © 1997 by Jerry Pinkney.

They took him into the house, and a big man picked him up between his finger and thumb and said he was not dead but half choked; so they wrapped him in cotton wool and warmed him over a little fire, and he opened his eyes and sneezed. "Now," said the big man (he was an Englishman who had just moved into the bungalow), "don't frighten him, and we'll see what he'll do."

It is the hardest thing in the world to frighten a mongoose, because he is eaten up from nose to tail with curiosity. The motto of all the mongoose family is "Run and Find Out"; and Rikki-tikki was a true mongoose. He looked at the cotton wool, decided that it was not good to eat, ran all round
30 the table, sat up and put his fur in order, scratched himself, and jumped on the small boy's shoulder.

"Don't be frightened, Teddy," said his father. "That's his way of making friends."

"Ouch! He's tickling under my chin," said Teddy.

Rikki-tikki looked down between the boy's collar and neck, snuffed at his ear, and climbed down to the floor, where he sat rubbing his nose.

"Good gracious," said Teddy's mother, "and that's a wild creature! I suppose he's so tame because we've been kind to him."

"All mongooses are like that," said her husband. "If Teddy doesn't pick
40 him up by the tail or try to put him in a cage, he'll run in and out of the house all day long. Let's give him something to eat."

They gave him a little piece of raw meat. Rikki-tikki liked it immensely; and when it was finished, he went out into the veranda and sat in the sunshine and fluffed up his fur to make it dry to the roots. Then he felt better.

"There are more things to find out about in this house," he said to himself, "than all my family could find out in all their lives. I shall certainly stay and find out." **B**

He spent all that day roaming over the house. He nearly drowned himself
50 in the bathtubs, put his nose into the ink on a writing table, and burnt it on the end of the big man's cigar, for he climbed up in the big man's lap to see how writing was done. At nightfall he ran into Teddy's nursery to watch how kerosene lamps were lighted, and when Teddy went to bed, Rikki-tikki climbed up too; but he was a restless companion, because he had to get up and attend to every noise all through the night and find out what made it. Teddy's mother and father came in, the last thing, to look at their boy, and Rikki-tikki was awake on the pillow.

"I don't like that," said Teddy's mother; "he may bite the child."

"He'll do no such thing," said the father. "Teddy is safer with that little
60 beast than if he had a bloodhound to watch him. If a snake came into the nursery now—" **C**

But Teddy's mother wouldn't think of anything so awful.

VISUAL VOCABULARY

veranda *n.* a long, open porch, usually with a roof

B CAUSE AND EFFECT
How does Rikki-tikki come to live in the bungalow?

C SUSPENSE AND FORESHADOWING
What might the father's words be foreshadowing?

Early in the morning Rikki-tikki came to early breakfast in the veranda, riding on Teddy's shoulder, and they gave him banana and some boiled egg; and he sat on all their laps one after the other, because every well-brought-up mongoose always hopes to be a house mongoose some day and have rooms to run about in; and Rikki-tikki's mother (she used to live in the general's house at Segowlee) had carefully told Rikki what to do if ever he came across white men.

70　　Then Rikki-tikki went out into the garden to see what was to be seen. It was a large garden, only half-cultivated, with bushes, as big as summerhouses, of Marshal Niel roses, lime and orange trees, clumps of bamboos, and thickets of high grass. Rikki-tikki licked his lips. "This is a splendid hunting ground," he said, and his tail grew bottlebrushy at the thought of it; and he scuttled up and down the garden, snuffing here and there till he heard very sorrowful voices in a thorn bush. It was Darzee, the tailorbird, and his wife. They had made a beautiful nest by pulling two big leaves together and stitching them up the edges with fibers and had filled the hollow with cotton and downy fluff. The nest swayed to and fro,
80　as they sat on the rim and cried.

"What is the matter?" asked Rikki-tikki.

"We are very miserable," said Darzee. "One of our babies fell out of the nest yesterday, and Nag ate him."

"H'm!" said Rikki-tikki, "that is very sad—but I am a stranger here. Who is Nag?"

Darzee and his wife only **cowered** down in the nest without answering, for from the thick grass at the foot of the bush there came a low hiss—a horrid, cold sound that made Rikki-tikki jump back two clear
90　feet. Then inch by inch out of the grass rose up the head and spread hood[3] of Nag, the big black cobra, and he was five feet long from tongue to tail. When he had lifted one-third of himself clear of the ground, he stayed, balancing to and fro exactly as a dandelion tuft balances in the wind; and he looked at Rikki-tikki with the wicked snake's eyes that never change their expression, whatever the snake may be thinking of.

"Who is Nag?" said he. "*I* am Nag. The great god Brahm[4] put his mark upon all our people when
100　the first cobra spread his hood to keep the sun off Brahm as he slept. Look, and be afraid!"

---

3. **hood:** an expanded part on or near the head of an animal.

4. **Brahm** (bräm)**:** another name for Brahma, creator of the universe in the Hindu religion.

From 1858 to 1947, Britain ruled India. India gained its independence after decades of fighting for it.

cower (kou'ər) *v.* to crouch or shrink down in fear

◀ **Analyze Visuals**

Notice how the mongoose and the snake hold their bodies. Does either of these **characters** look particularly brave or scared?

He spread out his hood more than ever, and Rikki-tikki saw the spectacle mark on the back of it that looks exactly like the eye part of a hook-and-eye fastening. He was afraid for the minute, but it is impossible for a mongoose to stay frightened for any length of time; and though Rikki-tikki had never met a live cobra before, his mother had fed him on dead ones, and he knew that all a grown mongoose's business in life was to fight and eat snakes. Nag knew that too, and at the bottom of his cold heart, he was afraid.

"Well," said Rikki-tikki, and his tail began to fluff up again, "marks or
110 no marks, do you think it is right for you to eat **fledglings** out of a nest?"

Nag was thinking to himself and watching the least little movement in the grass behind Rikki-tikki. He knew that mongooses in the garden meant death sooner or later for him and his family; but he wanted to get Rikki-tikki off his guard. So he dropped his head a little, and put it on one side.

"Let us talk," he said. "You eat eggs. Why should not I eat birds?"

"Behind you! Look behind you!" sang Darzee.

Rikki-tikki knew better than to waste time in staring. He jumped up in the air as high as he could go, and just under him whizzed by the head of

fledgling (flĕj′lĭng) *n.* a young bird that has recently grown its flight feathers

Nagaina,[5] Nag's wicked wife. She had crept up behind him as he was
120 talking, to make an end of him; and he heard her savage hiss as the stroke
missed. He came down almost across her back, and if he had been an old
mongoose, he would have known that then was the time to break her back
with one bite; but he was afraid of the terrible lashing return stroke of the
cobra. He bit, indeed, but did not bite long enough; and he jumped clear
of the whisking tail, leaving Nagaina torn and angry. **D**

"Wicked, wicked Darzee!" said Nag, lashing up as high as he could
reach toward the nest in the thorn bush; but Darzee had built it out of
reach of snakes, and it only swayed to and fro.

Rikki-tikki felt his eyes growing red and hot (when a mongoose's eyes
130 grow red, he is angry), and he sat back on his tail and hind legs like a
little kangaroo and looked all around him and chattered with rage. But
Nag and Nagaina had disappeared into the grass. When a snake misses
its stroke, it never says anything or gives any sign of what it means to do
next. Rikki-tikki did not care to follow them, for he did not feel sure that
he could manage two snakes at once. So he trotted off to the gravel path
near the house and sat down to think. It was a serious matter for him. **E**

If you read the old books of natural history, you will find they say that
when the mongoose fights the snake and happens to get bitten, he runs
off and eats some herb that cures him. That is not true. The victory is only
140 a matter of quickness of eye and quickness of foot—snake's blow against
mongoose's jump—and as no eye can follow the motion of a snake's head
when it strikes, this makes things much more wonderful than any magic
herb. Rikki-tikki knew he was a young mongoose, and it made him all the
more pleased to think that he had managed to escape a blow from behind.

It gave him confidence in himself, and when Teddy came running down
the path, Rikki-tikki was ready to be petted. But just as Teddy was stooping,
something wriggled a little in the dust, and a tiny voice said, "Be careful.
I am Death!" It was Karait,[6] the dusty brown snakeling that lies for choice
on the dusty earth; and his bite is as dangerous as the cobra's. But he is so
150 small that nobody thinks of him, and so he does the more harm to people.

Rikki-tikki's eyes grew red again, and he danced up to Karait with the
peculiar rocking, swaying motion that he had inherited from his family.
It looks very funny, but it is so perfectly balanced a **gait** that you can fly
off from it at any angle you please; and in dealing with snakes this is an
advantage.

If Rikki-tikki had only known, he was doing a much more dangerous
thing than fighting Nag; for Karait is so small and can turn so quickly,

---

5. **Nagaina** (nä′gə-ē′nə).

6. **Karait** (kə-rīt′).

D SUSPENSE AND
FORESHADOWING
Reread lines 111–125.
Which details of
Nagaina's attack
on Rikki-tikki create
tension?

E PREDICT
As you read, check the
predictions you make.
Was the prediction
you made on page 78
correct?

gait (gāt) *n.* a manner
of walking or moving
on foot

that unless Rikki bit him close to the back of the head, he would get the return stroke in his eye or his lip. But Rikki did not know: his eyes were all red, and he rocked back and forth, looking for a good place to hold. Karait struck out. Rikki jumped sideways and tried to run in, but the wicked little dusty gray head lashed within a fraction of his shoulder, and he had to jump over the body, and the head followed his heels close. **F**

Teddy shouted to the house, "Oh, look here! Our mongoose is killing a snake"; and Rikki-tikki heard a scream from Teddy's mother. His father ran out with a stick, but by the time he came up, Karait had lunged out once too far, and Rikki-tikki had sprung, jumped on the snake's back, dropped his head far between his forelegs, bitten as high up the back as he could get hold, and rolled away.

That bite paralyzed Karait, and Rikki-tikki was just going to eat him up from the tail, after the custom of his family at dinner, when he remembered that a full meal makes a slow mongoose; and if he wanted all his strength and quickness ready, he must keep himself thin. He went away for a dust bath under the castor-oil bushes, while Teddy's father beat the dead Karait. "What is the use of that?" thought Rikki-tikki; "I have settled it all."

And then Teddy's mother picked him up from the dust and hugged him, crying that he had saved Teddy from death; and Teddy's father said that he was a providence,[7] and Teddy looked on with big scared eyes. Rikki-tikki was rather amused at all the fuss, which, of course, he did not understand. Teddy's mother might just as well have petted Teddy for playing in the dust. Rikki was thoroughly enjoying himself. **G**

That night at dinner, walking to and fro among the wineglasses on the table, he might have stuffed himself three times over with nice things; but he remembered Nag and Nagaina, and though it was very pleasant to be patted and petted by Teddy's mother and to sit on Teddy's shoulder, his eyes would get red from time to time, and he would go off into his long war cry of *"Rikk-tikk-tikki-tikki-tchk!"*

Teddy carried him off to bed and insisted on Rikki-tikki sleeping under his chin. Rikki-tikki was too well-bred to bite or scratch, but as soon as Teddy was asleep, he went off for his nightly walk around the house; and in the dark he ran up against Chuchundra, the muskrat, creeping around by the wall. Chuchundra is a brokenhearted little beast. He whimpers and cheeps all the night, trying to make up his mind to run into the middle of the room; but he never gets there.

"Don't kill me," said Chuchundra, almost weeping. "Rikki-tikki, don't kill me!"

"Do you think a snake killer kills muskrats?" said Rikki-tikki scornfully.

7. **providence:** blessing; something good given by God.

F SUSPENSE AND FORESHADOWING
Reread lines 156–163. What doesn't Rikki-tikki realize about Karait?

G PLOT AND CONFLICT
Which characters in this story have conflicts with the snakes in the garden?

"Those who kill snakes get killed by snakes," said Chuchundra, more sorrowfully than ever. "And how am I to be sure that Nag won't mistake 200 me for you some dark night?"

"There's not the least danger," said Rikki-tikki; "but Nag is in the garden, and I know you don't go there."

"My cousin Chua,[8] the rat, told me—" said Chuchundra, and then he stopped.

"Told you what?"

"H'sh! Nag is everywhere, Rikki-tikki. You should have talked to Chua in the garden."

"I didn't—so you must tell me. Quick, Chuchundra, or I'll bite you!"

Chuchundra sat down and cried till the tears rolled off his whiskers.
210 "I am a very poor man," he sobbed. "I never had spirit enough to run out into the middle of the room. H'sh! I mustn't tell you anything. Can't you *hear,* Rikki-tikki?"

Rikki-tikki listened. The house was as still as still, but he thought he could just catch the faintest *scratch-scratch* in the world—a noise as faint as that of a wasp walking on a windowpane—the dry scratch of a snake's scales on brickwork. **Ⓗ**

"That's Nag or Nagaina," he said to himself, "and he is crawling into the bathroom sluice.[9] You're right, Chuchundra; I should have talked to Chua."

He stole off to Teddy's bathroom, but there was nothing there, and 220 then to Teddy's mother's bathroom. At the bottom of the smooth plaster wall, there was a brick pulled out to make a sluice for the bath water, and as Rikki-tikki stole in by the masonry curb where the bath is put, he heard Nag and Nagaina whispering together outside in the moonlight.

"When the house is emptied of people," said Nagaina to her husband, "*he* will have to go away, and then the garden will be our own again. Go in quietly, and remember that the big man who killed Karait is the first one to bite. Then come out and tell me, and we will hunt for Rikki-tikki together."

"But are you sure that there is anything to be gained by killing the people?" said Nag.

230 "Everything. When there were no people in the bungalow, did we have any mongoose in the garden? So long as the bungalow is empty, we are king and queen of the garden; and remember that as soon as our eggs in the melon bed hatch (as they may tomorrow), our children will need room and quiet." **Ⓘ**

"I had not thought of that," said Nag. "I will go, but there is no need that we should hunt for Rikki-tikki afterward. I will kill the big man and his

8. **Chua** (chōō′ə).

9. **bathroom sluice** (slōōs): an opening in a wall through which the water in a bathtub can be drained outdoors.

COMMON CORE L 5a

Language Coach

Personification Giving human qualities to something that is not human is called personification. In lines 199–212, a mongoose and a muskrat have a discussion with each other, which is a human quality. What human quality does Chuchundra show in line 209?

Ⓗ SUSPENSE AND FORESHADOWING Reread lines 203–216. What details make the conversation between Chuchundra and Rikki-tikki suspenseful?

Ⓘ PREDICT Think about what Nag and Nagaina are planning to do. How do you think Rikki-tikki might respond?

wife, and the child if I can, and come away
quietly. Then the bungalow will be empty,
and Rikki-tikki will go."

240   Rikki-tikki tingled all over with rage
and hatred at this, and then Nag's head
came through the sluice, and his five feet
of cold body followed it. Angry as he was,
Rikki-tikki was very frightened as he saw
the size of the big cobra. Nag coiled himself
up, raised his head, and looked into the
bathroom in the dark, and Rikki could see
his eyes glitter.

    "Now, if I kill him here, Nagaina will

250 know; and if I fight him on the open floor,
the odds are in his favor. What am I to do?"
said Rikki-tikki-tavi.

    Nag waved to and fro, and then Rikki-
tikki heard him drinking from the biggest
water jar that was used to fill the bath.
"That is good," said the snake. "Now, when
Karait was killed, the big man had a stick.
He may have that stick still, but when he
comes in to bathe in the morning, he will

260 not have a stick. I shall wait here till he comes. Nagaina—do you hear
me?—I shall wait here in the cool till daytime."

    There was no answer from outside, so Rikki-tikki knew Nagaina had
gone away. Nag coiled himself down, coil by coil, around the bulge at the
bottom of the water jar, and Rikki-tikki stayed still as death. After an hour
he began to move, muscle by muscle, toward the jar. Nag was asleep, and
Rikki-tikki looked at his big back, wondering which would be the best
place for a good hold. "If I don't break his back at the first jump," said
Rikki, "he can still fight; and if he fights—O Rikki!" He looked at the
thickness of the neck below the hood, but that was too much for him;

270 and a bite near the tail would only make Nag savage. **J**

    "It must be the head," he said at last; "the head above the hood. And,
when I am once there, I must not let go."

    Then he jumped. The head was lying a little clear of the water jar,
under the curve of it; and, as his teeth met, Rikki braced his back against
the bulge of the red earthenware to hold down the head. This gave him
just one second's purchase,[10] and he made the most of it. Then he was
battered to and fro as a rat is shaken by a dog—to and fro on the floor, up

**J SUSPENSE AND
FORESHADOWING**

Why is the outcome of
Rikki-tikki's fight with
Nag uncertain?

---

10. **purchase:** an advantage, such as a firm hold, to be used when applying power.

and down, and round in great circles; but his eyes were red, and he held on as the body cart-whipped over the floor, upsetting the tin dipper and the soap dish and the flesh brush, and banged against the tin side of the bath. **K**

As he held, he closed his jaws tighter and tighter, for he made sure he would be banged to death; and, for the honor of his family, he preferred to be found with his teeth locked. He was dizzy, aching, and felt shaken to pieces when something went off like a thunderclap just behind him; a hot wind knocked him senseless, and red fire **singed** his fur. The big man had been awakened by the noise and had fired both barrels of a shotgun into Nag just behind the hood.

Rikki-tikki held on with his eyes shut, for now he was quite sure he was dead; but the head did not move, and the big man picked him up and said, "It's the mongoose again, Alice; the little chap has saved *our* lives now." **L**

Then Teddy's mother came in with a very white face and saw what was left of Nag, and Rikki-tikki dragged himself to Teddy's bedroom and spent half the rest of the night shaking himself tenderly to find out whether he really was broken into forty pieces, as he fancied.

When morning came, he was very stiff but well pleased with his doings. "Now I have Nagaina to settle with, and she will be worse than five Nags, and there's no knowing when the eggs she spoke of will hatch. Goodness! I must go and see Darzee," he said.

Without waiting for breakfast, Rikki-tikki ran to the thorn bush where Darzee was singing a song of triumph at the top of his voice. The news of Nag's death was all over the garden, for the sweeper had thrown the body on the rubbish heap.

"Oh, you stupid tuft of feathers!" said Rikki-tikki angrily. "Is this the time to sing?"

"Nag is dead—is dead—is dead!" sang Darzee. "The **valiant** Rikki-tikki caught him by the head and held fast. The big man brought the bang stick, and Nag fell in two pieces! He will never eat my babies again."

"All that's true enough; but where's Nagaina?" said Rikki-tikki, looking carefully round him.

"Nagaina came to the bathroom sluice and called for Nag," Darzee went on; "and Nag came out on the end of a stick—the sweeper picked him up on the end of a stick and threw him upon the rubbish heap. Let us sing about the great, the red-eyed Rikki-tikki!" And Darzee filled his throat and sang.

"If I could get up to your nest, I'd roll your babies out!" said Rikki-tikki. "You don't know when to do the right thing at the right time. You're

K PREDICT
Thinking about how the **plot** has unfolded so far, predict what will happen next.

singe (sĭnj) *v.* to burn lightly

L CAUSE AND EFFECT
What happens because of Rikki-tikki's tight hold on Nag?

valiant (văl'yent) *adj.* brave; courageous

safe enough in your nest there, but it's war for me down here. Stop singing a minute, Darzee."

"For the great, the beautiful Rikki-tikki's sake I will stop," said Darzee. "What is it, O Killer of the terrible Nag?"

"Where is Nagaina, for the third time?"

"On the rubbish heap by the stables, mourning for Nag. Great is Rikki-tikki with the white teeth."

"Bother my white teeth! Have you ever heard where she keeps her eggs?"

"In the melon bed, on the end nearest the wall, where the sun strikes nearly all day. She hid them there weeks ago."

"And you never thought it worthwhile to tell me? The end nearest the wall, you said?"

"Rikki-tikki, you are not going to eat her eggs?"

"Not 'eat' exactly, no. Darzee, if you have a grain of sense, you will fly off to the stables and pretend that your wing is broken and let Nagaina chase you away to this bush. I must get to the melon bed, and if I went there now, she'd see me." **Ⓜ**

Darzee was a featherbrained little fellow who could never hold more than one idea at a time in his head; and just because he knew that Nagaina's children were born in eggs like his own, he didn't think at first that it was fair to kill them. But his wife was a sensible bird, and she knew that cobra's eggs meant young cobras later on; so she flew off from the nest and left Darzee to keep the babies warm and continue his song about the death of Nag. Darzee was very like a man in some ways.

She fluttered in front of Nagaina by the rubbish heap and cried out, "Oh, my wing is broken! The boy in the house threw a stone at me and broke it." Then she fluttered more desperately than ever.

Nagaina lifted up her head and hissed, "You warned Rikki-tikki when I would have killed him. Indeed and truly, you've chosen a bad place to be lame in." And she moved toward Darzee's wife, slipping along over the dust.

"The boy broke it with a stone!" shrieked Darzee's wife.

"Well! It may be some **consolation** to you when you're dead to know that I shall settle accounts[11] with the boy. My husband lies on the rubbish heap this morning, but before night the boy in the house will lie very still. What is the use of running away? I am sure to catch you. Little fool, look at me!"

Darzee's wife knew better than to do *that,* for a bird who looks at a snake's eyes gets so frightened that she cannot move. Darzee's wife fluttered on, piping sorrowfully, and never leaving the ground, and Nagaina quickened her pace. **Ⓝ**

Rikki-tikki heard them going up the path from the stables, and he raced for the end of the melon patch near the wall. There, in the warm litter above

Ⓜ SUSPENSE AND FORESHADOWING
Why does Rikki-tikki's impatience with Darzee lend suspense to this scene?

consolation
(kŏn′sə-lā′shən) *n.* a comfort

Ⓝ PLOT AND CONFLICT
How do Darzee and his wife differ in their approach to the conflict with Nagaina?

---

11. **settle accounts:** even things out by getting revenge.

the melons, very **cunningly** hidden, he found twenty-five eggs, about the size of
360 a bantam's eggs[12] but with whitish skins instead of shells.

"I was not a day too soon," he said, for he could see the baby cobras curled up inside the skin, and he knew that the minute they were hatched they could each kill a man or a mongoose. He bit off the tops of the eggs as fast as he could, taking care to crush the young cobras, and turned over the litter from time to time to see
370 whether he had missed any. At last there were only three eggs left, and Rikki-tikki began to chuckle to himself when he heard Darzee's wife screaming.

"Rikki-tikki, I led Nagaina toward the house, and she has gone into the veranda and—oh, come quickly—she means killing!"

Rikki-tikki smashed two eggs and tumbled backward down the melon bed with the third egg in his mouth and scuttled to the veranda as hard as he could put foot to the ground. Teddy and his mother and father were there at early breakfast; but Rikki-tikki saw that they were
380 not eating anything. They sat stone still, and their faces were white. Nagaina was coiled up on the matting by Teddy's chair, within easy striking distance of Teddy's bare leg; and she was swaying to and fro, singing a song of triumph.

"Son of the big man that killed Nag," she hissed, "stay still. I am not ready yet. Wait a little. Keep very still, all you three! If you move, I strike, and if you do not move, I strike. Oh, foolish people who killed my Nag!"

Teddy's eyes were fixed on his father, and all his father could do was to whisper, "Sit still, Teddy. You mustn't move. Teddy, keep still." ⊙

Then Rikki-tikki came up and cried, "Turn round, Nagaina; turn
390 and fight!"

"All in good time," said she, without moving her eyes. "I will settle my account with you presently. Look at your friends, Rikki-tikki. They are still and white. They are afraid. They dare not move, and if you come a step nearer, I strike."

"Look at your eggs," said Rikki-tikki, "in the melon bed near the wall. Go and look, Nagaina!"

The big snake turned half round and saw the egg on the veranda. "Ah-h! Give it to me," she said.

cunningly (kŭn′ĭng-lē) *adv.* in a clever way that is meant to trick or deceive

⊙ **SUSPENSE AND FORESHADOWING**
At this point in the story, what questions are you waiting to have answered?

---

12. **bantam's eggs:** the eggs of a small hen.

Rikki-tikki put his paws one on each side of the egg, and his eyes were
400 blood-red. "What price for a snake's egg? For a young cobra? For a young
king cobra? For the last—the very last of the brood? The ants are eating
all the others down by the melon bed."

Nagaina spun clear round, forgetting everything for the sake of the one
egg; and Rikki-tikki saw Teddy's father shoot out a big hand, catch Teddy
by the shoulder, and drag him across the little table with the teacups, safe
and out of reach of Nagaina. **P**

"Tricked! Tricked! Tricked! *Rikk-tck-tck!*" chuckled Rikki-tikki. "The boy
is safe, and it was I—I—I that caught Nag by the hood last night in the
bathroom." Then he began to jump up and down, all four feet together,

P CAUSE AND EFFECT
Reread lines 395–406.
What does Rikki-tikki
do to save Teddy?

410 his head close to the floor. "He threw me to and fro, but he could not shake me off. He was dead before the big man blew him in two. I did it! *Rikki-tikki-tck-tck!* Come then, Nagaina. Come and fight with me. You shall not be a widow long."

Nagaina saw that she had lost her chance of killing Teddy, and the egg lay between Rikki-tikki's paws. "Give me the egg, Rikki-tikki. Give me the last of my eggs, and I will go away and never come back," she said, lowering her hood.

"Yes, you will go away, and you will never come back, for you will go to the rubbish heap with Nag. Fight, widow! The big man has gone for his 420 gun! Fight!"

Rikki-tikki was bounding all round Nagaina, keeping just out of reach of her stroke, his little eyes like hot coals. Nagaina gathered herself together and flung out at him. Rikki-tikki jumped up and backwards. Again and again and again she struck, and each time her head came with a whack on the matting of the veranda, and she gathered herself together like a watch spring. Then Rikki-tikki danced in a circle to get behind her, and Nagaina spun round to keep her head to his head, so that the rustle of her tail on the matting sounded like dry leaves blown along by the wind. ◆

He had forgotten the egg. It still lay on the veranda, and Nagaina came 430 nearer and nearer to it, till at last, while Rikki-tikki was drawing breath, she caught it in her mouth, turned to the veranda steps, and flew like an arrow down the path, with Rikki-tikki behind her. When the cobra runs for her life, she goes like a whiplash flicked across a horse's neck. Rikki-tikki knew that he must catch her, or all the trouble would begin again. ⓠ

She headed straight for the long grass by the thorn bush, and as he was running, Rikki-tikki heard Darzee still singing his foolish little song of triumph. But Darzee's wife was wiser. She flew off her nest as Nagaina came along and flapped her wings about Nagaina's head. If Darzee had helped, they might have turned her; but Nagaina only lowered her hood 440 and went on. Still, the instant's delay brought Rikki-tikki up to her, and as she plunged into the rat hole where she and Nag used to live, his little white teeth were clenched on her tail, and he went down with her—and very few mongooses, however wise and old they may be, care to follow a cobra into its hole. Ⓡ

It was dark in the hole; and Rikki-tikki never knew when it might open out and give Nagaina room to turn and strike at him. He held on savagely and stuck out his feet to act as brakes on the dark slope of the hot, moist earth.

Then the grass by the mouth of the hole stopped waving, and Darzee 450 said, "It is all over with Rikki-tikki! We must sing his death song. Valiant Rikki-tikki is dead! For Nagaina will surely kill him underground."

◆ **GRAMMAR IN CONTEXT**
Reread lines 421–428. Notice that Kipling uses the words *her, herself,* and *she* as he describes Nagaina's actions. Each of these words is a singular feminine pronoun that replaces or refers to the **antecedent** *Nagaina.*

ⓠ **SUSPENSE AND FORESHADOWING**
Reread lines 429–434. How does the suspense increase at this point?

Ⓡ **PREDICT**
What problem does Rikki-tikki now face? On the basis of the details you've learned, what do you predict?

So he sang a very mournful song that he made up on the spur of the minute;[13] and just as he got to the most touching part, the grass quivered again, and Rikki-tikki, covered with dirt, dragged himself out of the hole leg by leg, licking his whiskers. Darzee stopped with a little shout. Rikki-tikki shook some of the dust out of his fur and sneezed. "It is all over," he said. "The widow will never come out again." And the red ants that live between the grass stems heard him and began to troop down one after another to see if he had spoken the truth.

460   Rikki-tikki curled himself up in the grass and slept where he was— slept and slept till it was late in the afternoon, for he had done a hard day's work. **❺**

"Now," he said, when he awoke, "I will go back to the house. Tell the coppersmith, Darzee, and he will tell the garden that Nagaina is dead."

The coppersmith is a bird who makes a noise exactly like the beating of a little hammer on a copper pot; and the reason he is always making it is because he is the town crier to every Indian garden and tells all the news to everybody who cares to listen. As Rikki-tikki went up the path, he heard his "attention" notes like a tiny dinner gong, and then the steady
470   *"Ding-dong-tock!* Nag is dead—*dong!* Nagaina is dead! *Ding-dong-tock!"* That set all the birds in the garden singing and the frogs croaking, for Nag and Nagaina used to eat frogs as well as little birds.

When Rikki got to the house, Teddy and Teddy's mother (she looked very white still, for she had been fainting) and Teddy's father came out and almost cried over him; and that night he ate all that was given him till he could eat no more and went to bed on Teddy's shoulder, where Teddy's mother saw him when she came to look late at night.

"He saved our lives and Teddy's life," she said to her husband. "Just think, he saved all our lives."

480   Rikki-tikki woke up with a jump, for the mongooses are light sleepers.

"Oh, it's you," said he. "What are you bothering for? All the cobras are dead; and if they weren't, I'm here."

Rikki-tikki had a right to be proud of himself; but he did not grow too proud, and he kept that garden as a mongoose should keep it, with tooth and jump and spring and bite, till never a cobra dared show its head inside the walls. ✑

❺ PLOT AND CONFLICT
How is the conflict between Rikki-tikki and the cobras resolved?

Language Coach

Simile A simile is a comparison using the words *like* or *as*. Reread lines 465–466. A simile compares the sound of a bird to a hammer beating on a copper pot. Can you think of another simile that might describe that same sound?

---

13. **on the spur of the minute:** on a sudden impulse, without previous thought or planning.

Comprehension

1. **Recall** Why is Rikki-tikki grateful to Teddy's family?

2. **Recall** Why does Rikki-tikki destroy Nagaina's eggs?

3. **Represent** In a timeline, show the events in which Rikki acts bravely.

Text Analysis

4. **Predict** Check the predictions you wrote in your chart against what happened. Which details helped you guess correctly or misled you?

5. **Analyze Suspense and Foreshadowing** Go back through the story and write down clues that foreshadow Rikki-tikki's ultimate victory. Then write down details that led you to believe Rikki might be defeated. How did the combination of the two kinds of details help create suspense?

6. **Compare Literary Works** Both "Rikki-tikki-tavi" and "The Last Dog" have exciting plots, intriguing settings, and brave main characters. How else are the two stories similar? How are they different? To present your answer, add details to a Venn diagram like the one shown.

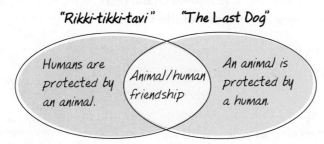

"Rikki-tikki-tavi"   "The Last Dog"

Humans are protected by an animal. / Animal/human friendship / An animal is protected by a human.

Extension and Challenge

7. **Creative Response: Drama** Plan an oral reading of a scene from the story. Some students can perform the parts of the characters and the narrator, while other students provide sound effects. Rehearse your performance and tape-record it for other classes.

8. **SOCIAL STUDIES CONNECTION** This story takes place in colonial India. With a partner, do research to find out more about India under British rule, from 1858 to 1947. What are two long-lasting effects that resulted from Britain's control of India? Present your findings to the class.

What makes you BRAVE?

Choose two characters from the story and explain why you think they behaved bravely. What would you do if you were in their position?

Vocabulary in Context

▲ **VOCABULARY PRACTICE**

Choose the vocabulary word that makes the most sense in each sentence.

1. After Rikki-tikki almost drowned, the family put him by the fire to _____ him.
2. The fire accidentally began to _____ his fur, and he quickly woke up.
3. Nag would not hesitate to eat a _____.
4. Though Darzee would _____ in fear at the sight of Nag, Rikki was not afraid.
5. He walked with a proud _____ that showed how brave he felt.
6. Rikki's killing Nag was a great _____ to the frightened family.
7. Rikki also _____ discovered Nagaina's eggs hidden among the melons.
8. Because of his _____ actions, everyone admired Rikki's courage.

consolation

cower

cunningly

fledgling

gait

revive

singe

valiant

ACADEMIC VOCABULARY IN WRITING

| • contemporary | • element | • identify | • influence | • structure |

What **elements** of Nagaina's personality make her a fearsome character? Write a short paragraph describing her, using at least one of the Academic Vocabulary words.

VOCABULARY STRATEGY: THE LATIN ROOTS *viv* AND *vit*

The vocabulary word *revive* contains the Latin root *viv*, which means "live." Another Latin root, *vit*, has the same meaning. *Viv* and *vit* occur in a number of English words. To understand the meaning of words with *viv* or *vit*, use context clues and your knowledge of what these roots mean.

PRACTICE Choose the word from the web that best completes each sentence. Then tell how *viv* or *vit* helps give meaning to each word.

1. People cannot _____ without food and water.
2. She was a _____ hostess who threw lively parties.
3. _____ can provide some of the substances our bodies need to be healthy.
4. He lost much of his _____ after the accident.
5. The artist used _____ colors in her painting.

COMMON CORE

L 4b Use common, grade-appropriate Latin roots as clues to the meaning of a word.
L 6 Acquire and use accurately grade-appropriate general academic words.

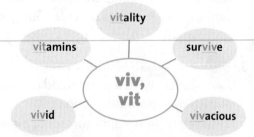

vitality

survive

vitamins

viv, vit

vivid

vivacious

Interactive Vocabulary

THINK central

Go to thinkcentral.com.
KEYWORD: HML7-94

Language

◆ **GRAMMAR IN CONTEXT:** Identify Antecedents and Maintain Agreement

You may recall that an **antecedent** is the noun or pronoun that a pronoun refers to. For example, in the following sentence, notice how the plural pronoun *their* refers to the plural antecedent *friends: My friends grabbed their bags.* Be especially careful when using antecedents like *each, someone,* and *no one.* These words should always be paired with singular pronouns. In the revised sentence, notice how the pronouns (in yellow) and the antecedent (in green) **agree in number.**

> *Original:* Someone had to take control. They would need to kill the snakes.
>
> *Revised:* Someone had to take control. He or she would need to kill the snakes.

PRACTICE Identify the antecedent in each sentence and correct the pronoun-antecedent error.

1. Each snake wants the garden for themselves.
2. No one in the family wants to have their life threatened by the snakes.
3. Rikki-tikki stands up to the snakes and gets rid of its eggs.
4. Each person has their own space again!

*For more help with pronoun-antecedent agreement, see pages R52–R53 in the **Grammar Handbook.***

READING-WRITING CONNECTION

YOUR TURN Deepen your understanding of "Rikki-tikki-tavi" by responding to this prompt. Then use the **revising tip** to improve your writing.

WRITING PROMPT	REVISING TIP
Extended Constructed Response: Scene Most of the characters, but not all, consider Rikki-tikki to be a hero. In **two or three paragraphs,** write a scene from the story from Nagaina's perspective. What does she think and feel about Rikki-tikki?	Review your response. Correct any pronouns that do not agree in number with their antecedents.

COMMON CORE

L 1 Demonstrate command of the conventions of standard English grammar and usage. **W 3** Write narratives to develop imagined experiences.

Interactive Revision THINK central

Go to **thinkcentral.com.** KEYWORD: HML7-95

Holes

Novel by Louis Sachar

COMMON CORE

RL 10 Read and comprehend literature.

Other Books by Louis Sachar

- *The Boy Who Lost His Face*
- *Dogs Don't Tell Jokes*
- *Sixth Grade Secrets*
- *Someday Angeline*

Meet Louis Sachar

Louis Sachar knows what it's like to be a kid. "When I write," he says, "I'm always putting myself in the shoes of the character and always reacting to how I would feel about something if I were that character." The fear of boring his readers inspires Sachar to keep his plots interesting.

Sachar worked at an elementary school while he was in college, and that gave him the idea to write books for young readers. He even used the names of his students in the first stories he wrote. He later went to law school, but found that he was more interested in writing than in practicing law.

Try an Adventure Novel

Holes is an example of an **adventure novel.** This type of fiction focuses on a main character who is usually on a mission and who faces many challenges and choices. Often, physical danger is involved. In *Holes,* the main character and his friend face overwhelming obstacles, but they do so with courage.

Reading Fluency Good readers read smoothly, accurately, and with feeling. To improve your reading fluency, read a passage several times. Your goal in silent reading is to make sense of the writer's words and ideas. When reading aloud, think about your purpose for reading and the type of text you are reading. Be sure to group words into meaningful phrases that sound like natural speech. You may need to adjust your speed and tone and how you emphasize certain words when reading fiction, nonfiction, or poetry.

Read a Great Book

Stanley Yelnats, the main character in *Holes,* gets teased in school, has no friends, and lives in a smelly apartment. He also has some unfortunate family history. Stanley is suffering from a curse dating back to the time of his great-great-grandfather, a "no-good-dirty-rotten-pig-stealing" character whose reputation continues to haunt Stanley. In an episode of bad luck, Stanley lands at Camp Green Lake, "a camp for bad boys." And so the adventure begins.

from

HOLES

There is no lake at Camp Green Lake. There once was a very large lake here, the largest lake in Texas. That was over a hundred years ago. Now it is just a dry, flat wasteland.

There used to be a town of Green Lake as well. The town shriveled and dried up along with the lake, and the people who lived there.

During the summer the daytime temperature hovers around ninety-five degrees in the shade—if you can find any shade. There's not much shade in a big dry lake.

The only trees are two old oaks on the eastern edge of the "lake."
10 A hammock is stretched between the two trees, and a log cabin stands behind that.

The campers are forbidden to lie in the hammock. It belongs to the Warden. The Warden owns the shade.

Out on the lake, rattlesnakes and scorpions find shade under rocks and in the holes dug by the campers.

Here's a good rule to remember about rattlesnakes and scorpions: If you don't bother them, they won't bother you.

Usually.

Being bitten by a scorpion or even a rattlesnake is not the worst
20 thing that can happen to you. You won't die.

Usually.

Sometimes a camper will try to be bitten by a scorpion, or even a small rattlesnake. Then he will get to spend a day or two recovering in his tent, instead of having to dig a hole out on the lake.

But you don't want to be bitten by a yellow-spotted lizard. That's the worst thing that can happen to you. You will die a slow and painful death.

Always.

If you get bitten by a yellow-spotted lizard, you might as well
30 go into the shade of the oak trees and lie in the hammock.

There is nothing anyone can do to you anymore.

The reader is probably asking: Why would anyone go to Camp Green Lake?

Most campers weren't given a choice. Camp Green Lake is a camp for bad boys.

If you take a bad boy and make him dig a hole every day in the hot sun, it will turn him into a good boy.

That was what some people thought.

Stanley Yelnats was given a choice. The judge said, "You may
40 go to jail, or you may go to Camp Green Lake."

Stanley was from a poor family. He had never been to camp before.

Stanley Yelnats was the only passenger on the bus, not counting the driver or the guard. The guard sat next to the driver with his seat turned around facing Stanley. A rifle lay across his lap.

Stanley was sitting about ten rows back, handcuffed to his armrest. His backpack lay on the seat next to him. It contained his toothbrush, toothpaste, and a box of stationery his mother had given him. He'd promised to write to her at least once a week.

He looked out the window, although there wasn't much to see—
50 mostly fields of hay and cotton. He was on a long bus ride to nowhere. The bus wasn't air-conditioned, and the hot, heavy air was almost as stifling as the handcuffs.

Stanley and his parents had tried to pretend that he was just going away to camp for a while, just like rich kids do. When Stanley was younger he used to play with stuffed animals, and

pretend the animals were at camp. Camp Fun and Games he called it. Sometimes he'd have them play soccer with a marble. Other times they'd run an obstacle course, or go bungee jumping off a table, tied to broken rubber bands. Now Stanley tried to pretend he was
60 going to Camp Fun and Games. Maybe he'd make some friends, he thought. At least he'd get to swim in the lake.

He didn't have any friends at home. He was overweight and the kids at his middle school often teased him about his size. Even his teachers sometimes made cruel comments without realizing it. On his last day of school, his math teacher, Mrs. Bell, taught ratios. As an example, she chose the heaviest kid in the class and the lightest kid in the class, and had them weigh themselves. Stanley weighed three times as much as the other boy. Mrs. Bell wrote the ratio on the board, 3:1, unaware of how much embarrassment she had caused
70 both of them.

Stanley was arrested later that day.

He looked at the guard who sat slumped in his seat and wondered if he had fallen asleep. The guard was wearing sunglasses, so Stanley couldn't see his eyes.

Stanley was not a bad kid. He was innocent of the crime for which he was convicted. He'd just been in the wrong place at the wrong time.

It was all because of his no-good-dirty-rotten-pig-stealing-great-great-grandfather!
80 He smiled. It was a family joke. Whenever anything went wrong, they always blamed Stanley's no-good-dirty-rotten-pig-stealing-great-great-grandfather.

Supposedly, he had a great-great-grandfather who had stolen a pig from a one-legged Gypsy, and she put a curse on him and all his descendants. Stanley and his parents didn't believe in curses, of course, but whenever anything went wrong, it felt good to be able to blame someone.

Things went wrong a lot. They always seemed to be in the wrong place at the wrong time.
90 He looked out the window at the vast emptiness. He watched the rise and fall of a telephone wire. In his mind he could hear his father's gruff voice softly singing to him.

"If only, if only," the woodpecker sighs,
"The bark on the tree was just a little bit softer."
While the wolf waits below, hungry and lonely,
He cries to the moo—oo—oon,
"If only, if only."

It was a song his father used to sing to him. The melody was sweet and sad, but Stanley's favorite part was when his father would howl the word "moon."

The bus hit a small bump and the guard sat up, instantly alert.

Stanley's father was an inventor. To be a successful inventor you need three things: intelligence, perseverance, and just a little bit of luck.

Stanley's father was smart and had a lot of perseverance. Once he started a project he would work on it for years, often going days without sleep. He just never had any luck.

Every time an experiment failed, Stanley could hear him cursing his dirty-rotten-pig-stealing-great-grandfather.

Stanley's father was also named Stanley Yelnats. Stanley's father's full name was Stanley Yelnats III. Our Stanley is Stanley Yelnats IV.

Everyone in his family had always liked the fact that "Stanley Yelnats" was spelled the same frontward and backward. So they kept naming their sons Stanley. Stanley was an only child, as was every other Stanley Yelnats before him.

All of them had something else in common. Despite their awful luck, they always remained hopeful. As Stanley's father liked to say, "I learn from failure."

But perhaps that was part of the curse as well. If Stanley and his father weren't always hopeful, then it wouldn't hurt so much every time their hopes were crushed.

"Not every Stanley Yelnats has been a failure," Stanley's mother often pointed out, whenever Stanley or his father became so discouraged that they actually started to believe in the curse. The first Stanley Yelnats, Stanley's great-grandfather, had made a fortune in the stock market. "He couldn't have been too unlucky."

At such times she neglected to mention the bad luck that befell the first Stanley Yelnats. He lost his entire fortune when he was moving from New York to California. His stagecoach was robbed by the outlaw Kissin' Kate Barlow.

130   If it weren't for that, Stanley's family would now be living in a mansion on a beach in California. Instead, they were crammed in a tiny apartment that smelled of burning rubber and foot odor.

If only, if only . . .

The apartment smelled the way it did because Stanley's father was trying to invent a way to recycle old sneakers. "The first person who finds a use for old sneakers," he said, "will be a very rich man."

It was this latest project that led to Stanley's arrest.

The bus ride became increasingly bumpy because the road was no longer paved.

140   Actually, Stanley had been impressed when he first found out that his great-grandfather was robbed by Kissin' Kate Barlow. True, he would have preferred living on the beach in California, but it was still kind of cool to have someone in your family robbed by a famous outlaw.

Kate Barlow didn't actually kiss Stanley's great-grandfather. That would have been really cool, but she only kissed the men she killed. Instead, she robbed him and left him stranded in the middle of the desert.

"He was *lucky* to have survived," Stanley's mother was quick

150 to point out.

The bus was slowing down. The guard grunted as he stretched his arms.

"Welcome to Camp Green Lake," said the driver.

Stanley looked out the dirty window. He couldn't see a lake.

And hardly anything was green. ✧

Keep Reading

Now you have a sense of the bad situation Stanley is in. Which part of the description of the camp surprised you most? To find out how Stanley will handle the situation, read the rest of the story. As the plot of *Holes* unfolds, Stanley experiences many challenges and obstacles, some because of the harsh setting and others because of some harsh people. Through it all, he learns a few things about himself.

from **Exploring the *Titanic***
Narrative Nonfiction by Robert D. Ballard

Video link at
thinkcentral.com

What can we learn from
DISASTERS?

COMMON CORE

RI 1 Cite several pieces of textual evidence to support what the text says explicitly.
RI 3 Analyze interactions between individuals, events, and ideas in a text (e.g., how ideas influence idividuals).
RI 5 Analyze the structure an author uses to organize a text.

Have you ever learned a lesson the hard way? Unfortunately, sometimes it takes a disaster to teach us to properly plan for danger. In the selection you're about to read, people on an "unsinkable" ship encounter terrible danger at sea—without enough lifeboats for everyone.

CHART IT When a disaster happens, we try to find out what went wrong so that we know how to be better prepared in the future. Using a chart like the one shown, list different types of disasters and things we can learn from them. Compare your chart with those of your classmates.

Disasters	What We Can Learn from Them
Fires	We can learn to build safer buildings.
	More fire drills will help people know what to do in emergencies.

EVACUATION ROUTE

● TEXT ANALYSIS: NARRATIVE NONFICTION

Narrative nonfiction uses literary elements, such as plot, setting, and conflict, to tell a story. Unlike fiction, though, narrative nonfiction tells a true story about events that really happened. To be accurate, narrative nonfiction relies on source material, such as quotations from real people, facts from reliable accounts, and photographs. As you read *Exploring the* Titanic, notice how literary elements and source material help create a compelling narrative.

Review: **Suspense and Foreshadowing**

● READING SKILL: USE CHRONOLOGICAL ORDER

When writers use **chronological order,** or time order, they present events in the order in which they happened. To help you recognize time order, look for

- calendar dates, such as *Wednesday, April 10, 1912*
- clock time, such as *shortly after noon* and *8:03 P.M.*
- words and phrases that show time order, such as *before, later, around lunchtime,* and *for the next ten months*

Use a timeline to track the events of the *Titanic*'s final day.

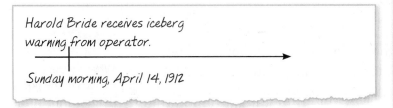

Harold Bride receives iceberg warning from operator.

Sunday morning, April 14, 1912

Review: **Make Inferences**

▲ VOCABULARY IN CONTEXT

The boldfaced words help tell the story of this disaster. Use context clues to give a definition for each word.

1. The elegant **accommodations** thrilled the passengers.
2. **Adjoining** rooms kept families together.
3. There were **moderate** prices for less luxurious rooms.
4. Travelers enjoyed the **novelty** of the ship's first voyage.
5. Some believed they had heard a **prophecy** of tragedy.
6. The crews worked **feverishly** to avoid a collision.
7. They were unable to prevent a **ghastly** disaster at sea.

Complete the activities in your **Reader/Writer Notebook.**

Meet the Author

Robert D. Ballard
born 1942

Underwater Explorer
Robert D. Ballard, a pioneer of deep-sea exploration, traces his interest in the ocean to childhood walks on the beach in San Diego. He was so fascinated by sea lore and by the crabs washed in by the tide that he decided to spend his life by the water. Ballard is trained as a marine geologist, a geophysicist (a mapper of land and oceans), and a Navy commander. After years of searching, he found one of the most important shipwrecks in history—the remains of the *Titanic*.

A World Beneath the Water
The oxygen-poor water at the bottom of the ocean keeps shipwrecks in excellent condition. "There's probably more history now preserved underwater than in all the museums of the world combined," Ballard has observed. To help excavate that history, Ballard organizes expeditions to areas rich in shipwrecks. He explores the depths with the help of robots and submersibles, or minisubmarines.

Mysteries Solved
Ballard's discovery solved many mysteries about the *Titanic*'s last hours. For instance, pieces on the ocean floor reveal that the ship broke in two before sinking.

Author Online **THINK** central

Go to **thinkcentral.com.**
KEYWORD: HML7-103

Exploring the TITANIC

Robert D. Ballard

The story of the *Titanic* began before anyone had even thought about building the great ship. In 1898, fourteen years before the *Titanic* sank, an American writer named Morgan Robertson wrote a book called *The Wreck of the* Titan.[1] In his story, the *Titan,* a passenger ship almost identical to the *Titanic,* and labeled "unsinkable," sails from England headed for New York. With many rich and famous passengers on board, the *Titan* hits an iceberg in the North Atlantic and sinks. Because there are not enough lifeboats, many lives are lost.

The story of the *Titan* predicted exactly what would happen to the
10 *Titanic* fourteen years later. It was an eerie **prophecy** of terrible things to come. Ⓐ

In 1907, nearly ten years after *The Wreck of the* Titan was written, two men began making plans to build a real titanic ship. At a London dinner party, as they relaxed over coffee and cigars, J. Bruce Ismay, president of the White Star Line of passenger ships, and Lord Pirrie, chairman of Harland & Wolff shipbuilders, discussed a plan to build three enormous

Analyze Visuals ▶

What do the words and images in the poster emphasize?

prophecy (prŏf′ĭ-sē) *n.* a prediction of the future

Ⓐ **CHRONOLOGICAL ORDER**

Why do you think Ballard begins his narrative with a reference to *The Wreck of the* Titan?

---

1. **Titan:** In Greek mythology, the Titans were a race of giants. The word *titanic* has come to be applied to any person or thing of great size or power.

Titanic, Olympic, White Star Line (1912), Montague B. Black. Christie's Images/Corbis.

ocean liners. Their goal was to give the White Star Line a competitive edge in the Atlantic passenger trade with several gigantic ships whose **accommodations** would be the last word in comfort and elegance.

20   The two men certainly dreamed on a grand scale.[2] When these floating palaces were finally built, they were so much bigger than other ships that new docks had to be built on each side of the Atlantic to service them. Four years after that London dinner party, the first of these huge liners, the *Olympic,* safely completed her maiden voyage.[3]

On May 31, 1911, the hull of the *Titanic* was launched at the Harland & Wolff shipyards in Belfast, Ireland, before a cheering crowd of 100,000. Bands played, and people came from miles around to see this great wonder of the sea. Twenty-two tons of soap, grease, and train oil were used to slide her into the water. In the words of one eyewitness,
30 she had "a rudder as big as an elm tree . . . propellers as big as a windmill. Everything was on a nightmare scale." **B**

For the next ten months the *Titanic* was outfitted and carefully prepared down to the last detail. The final size and richness of this new ship was astounding. She was 882 feet long, almost the length of four city blocks. With nine decks, she was as high as an eleven-story building.

Among her gigantic features, she had four huge funnels, each one big enough to drive two trains through. During construction an astonishing three million rivets had been hammered into her hull. Her three enormous anchors weighed a total of thirty-one tons—the weight of
40 twenty cars. And for her maiden voyage, she carried enough food to feed a small town for several months.

As her name boasted, the *Titanic* was indeed the biggest ship in the world. Nicknamed "the Millionaires' Special," she was also called "the Wonder Ship," "the Unsinkable Ship," and "the Last Word in Luxury" by newspapers around the world. **C**

The command of this great ocean liner was given to the senior captain of the White Star Line, Captain Edward J. Smith. This proud, white-bearded man was a natural leader and was popular with both crew members and passengers. Most important, after thirty-eight years' service
50 with the White Star Line, he had an excellent safety record. At the age of fifty-nine, Captain Smith was going to retire after this last trip, a perfect final tribute to a long and successful career.

On Wednesday, April 10, 1912, the *Titanic*'s passengers began to arrive in Southampton for the trip to New York. Ruth Becker was dazzled as she boarded the ship with her mother, her younger sister, and two-year-old brother, Richard. Ruth's father was a missionary in India. The rest of the

---

2. **on a grand scale:** in a large or impressive way.

3. **maiden voyage:** very first trip.

accommodations
(ə-kŏm'ə-dā'shənz)
n. rooms and food, especially in a hotel or on a ship or train

B NARRATIVE NONFICTION
What details help you picture the **setting** of the *Titanic*'s launch?

C NARRATIVE NONFICTION
What do the newspaper quotations add to your understanding?

Ruth Becker

Jack Thayer

Illustration © Onslow Auctions Limited/Mary Evans Picture Library.

family was sailing to New York to find medical help for young Richard, who had developed a serious illness in India. They had booked second-class tickets on the *Titanic*.

60   Twelve-year-old Ruth was delighted with the ship. As she pushed her little brother about the decks in a stroller, she was impressed with what she saw. "Everything was new. New!" she recalled. "Our cabin was just like a hotel room, it was so big. The dining room was beautiful—the linens, all the bright, polished silver you can imagine."

Meanwhile, seventeen-year-old Jack Thayer from Philadelphia was trying out the soft mattress on the large bed in his cabin. The first-class rooms his family had reserved for themselves and their maid had thick carpets, carved wooden panels on the walls, and marble sinks. As his parents were getting settled in their **adjoining** stateroom,[4] Jack decided
70 to explore this fantastic ship. **D**

On A Deck, he stepped into the Verandah and Palm Court and admired the white wicker furniture and the ivy growing up the trellised walls. On the lower decks, Jack discovered the squash court,[5] the swimming pool, and the Turkish bath[6] decorated like a room in a sultan's palace. In the gymnasium, the instructor was showing passengers the

---

4. **stateroom:** a private cabin on a ship.
5. **squash court:** a walled court or room for playing squash, in which a rubber ball is hit off the walls.
6. **Turkish bath:** steam bath.

▲ **Analyze Visuals**
The photographs of Ruth Becker and Jack Thayer are **source material.** How does seeing the faces of these young passengers affect the way you read the selection?

adjoining (ə-joi′nĭng) *adj.* next to or in contact with **adjoin** *v.*

D NARRATIVE NONFICTION
What details about the **setting** do you learn from firsthand observations of people on the ship?

Illustration by Steve Noon © Dorling Kindersley.

latest in exercise equipment, which included a mechanical camel you could ride on, stationary bicycles, and rowing machines.

Daylight shone through the huge glass dome over the Grand Staircase as Jack went down to join his parents in the first-class reception room.

80   There, with the ship's band playing in the background, his father pointed out some of the other first-class passengers. "He's supposed to be the world's richest man," said his father of Colonel John Jacob Astor, who was escorting the young Mrs. Astor. He also identified Mr. and Mrs. Straus, founders of Macy's of New York, the world's largest department store. Millionaire Benjamin Guggenheim was aboard, as were Jack's parents' friends from Philadelphia, Mr. and Mrs. George Widener and their son, Harry. Mr. Widener had made a fortune building streetcars. Mr. and Mrs. William Carter were also friends of the Thayers. Stowed in one of the holds below was a new Renault car that they were bringing

90   back from England.

J. Bruce Ismay, president of the White Star Line, moved about the room saying hello to people. He wanted to make sure that his wealthy passengers were comfortable, that they would feel relaxed and safe aboard his floating palace.

Language Coach

Oral Fluency   The first part of the word *Colonel* (in line 82) is spoken as if the middle *l* were an *r. Col* sounds like *cur.* The next part, *onel,* is spoken as if the *o* were silent. It sounds like *nel.* Read line 82 aloud, saying *Colonel* correctly.

First-class lounge

First-class cabin

◀ **Analyze Visuals**
Identify which parts of the ship are dedicated to the first-, second-, and third-class passengers. What differences do you note?

Indeed, when Ruth Becker's mother had asked one of the second-class staff about the safety of the ship, she had been told that there was absolutely nothing to worry about. The ship had watertight compartments that would allow her to float indefinitely. There was much talk among the passengers about the *Titanic* being unsinkable.

100   In 1912, people were divided into social classes according to background, wealth, and education. Because of these class lines, the *Titanic* was rather like a big floating layer cake. The bottom layer consisted of the lowly manual workers sweating away in the heat and grime of the boiler rooms and engine rooms. The next layer was the third-class passengers, people of many nationalities hoping to make a new start in America. After that came the second class—teachers, merchants, and professionals of **moderate** means like Ruth's family. Then, finally, there was the icing on the cake in first class: the rich and the aristocratic. The differences between these groups were enormous. While the wealthy brought their maids and valets[7]

110   and mountains of luggage, most members of the crew earned such tiny salaries that it would have taken them years to save the money for a single first-class ticket. **E**

moderate (mŏd′ər-ĭt) *adj.* not excessive or extreme; average

E **NARRATIVE NONFICTION**
Why is it important to understand the way social class influenced the people on the ship?

---

7. **valets** (vă-lāz′): gentlemen's personal servants.

At noon on Wednesday, April 10, the *Titanic* cast off. The whistles on her huge funnels were the biggest ever made. As she began her journey to the sea, they were heard for miles around.

Moving majestically down the River Test,[8] and watched by a crowd that had turned out for the occasion, the *Titanic* slowly passed two ships tied up to a dock. All of a sudden, the mooring ropes holding the passenger liner *New York* snapped with a series of sharp cracks like fireworks going 120 off. The enormous pull created by the *Titanic* moving past her had broken the *New York*'s ropes and was now drawing her stern toward the *Titanic*. Jack Thayer watched in horror as the two ships came closer and closer. "It looked as though there surely would be a collision," he later wrote. "Her stern could not have been more than a yard or two from our side. It almost hit us." At the last moment, some quick action by Captain Smith and a tugboat captain nearby allowed the *Titanic* to slide past with only inches to spare.

It was not a good sign. Did it mean that the *Titanic* might be too big a ship to handle safely? Those who knew about the sea thought that such 130 a close call at the beginning of a maiden voyage was a very bad omen. **F**

Jack Phillips, the first wireless operator on the *Titanic*, quickly jotted down the message coming in over his headphones. "It's another iceberg warning," he said wearily to his young assistant, Harold Bride. "You'd better take it up to the bridge." Both men had been at work for hours in the *Titanic*'s radio room, trying to get caught up in sending out a large number of personal messages. In 1912, passengers on ocean liners thought it was a real **novelty** to send postcard-style messages to friends at home from the middle of the Atlantic.

Bride picked up the iceberg message and stepped out onto the boat deck. 140 It was a sunny but cold Sunday morning, the fourth day of the *Titanic*'s maiden voyage. The ship was steaming at full speed across a calm sea. Harold Bride was quite pleased with himself at having landed a job on such a magnificent new ship. After all, he was only twenty-two years old and had just nine months' experience at operating a "wireless set," as a ship's radio was then called. As he entered the bridge area, he could see one of the crewmen standing behind the ship's wheel steering her course toward New York. **G**

Captain Smith was on duty in the bridge, so Bride handed the message to him. "It's from the *Caronia*,[9] sir. She's reporting icebergs and pack ice ahead." The captain thanked him, read the message, and then posted 150 it on the bulletin board for other officers on watch to read. On his way

---

8. **the River Test:** a river flowing into the English Channel at Southampton, the city in England from which the *Titanic* set sail.

9. *Caronia* (kə-rō′nē-ə).

An important technological advancement used on the *Titanic* was the wireless. A wireless telegraph is a machine used for transmitting and receiving messages.

F **SUSPENSE AND FORESHADOWING**
Reread lines 116–130. How does the author use foreshadowing to create suspense?

novelty (nŏv′əl-tē) *n.* something new, original, or unusual

G **CHRONOLOGICAL ORDER**
Reread lines 139–141. What day does Bride pick up the iceberg warning from the operator? Begin your timeline by recording this event. As you read on, record each major event that follows.

Harold Bride

The Titanic, Gordon Johnson. Oil on paper. © Margaret Johnson/SuperStock.

back to the radio room, Bride thought the captain had seemed quite unconcerned by the message. But then again, he had been told that it was not unusual to have ice floating in the sea lanes during an April crossing. Besides, what danger could a few pieces of ice present to an unsinkable ship?

Elsewhere on board, passengers relaxed on deck chairs, reading or taking naps. Some played cards, some wrote letters, while others chatted with friends. As it was Sunday, church services had been held in the morning, the first-class service led by Captain Smith. Jack Thayer spent most of the day walking about the decks getting some fresh air with his parents.

160   Two more ice warnings were received from nearby ships around lunch time. In the chaos of the radio room, Harold Bride only had time to take one of them to the bridge. The rest of the day passed quietly. Then, in the late afternoon, the temperature began to drop rapidly. Darkness approached as the bugle call announced dinner.

Jack Thayer's parents had been invited to a special dinner for Captain Smith, so Jack ate alone in the first-class dining room. After dinner, as he was having a cup of coffee, he was joined by Milton Long, another passenger going home to the States. Long was older than Jack, but in the easy-going atmosphere of shipboard travel, they struck up a conversation
170 and talked together for an hour or so. **H**

At 7:30 P.M., the radio room received three more warnings of ice about fifty miles ahead. One of them was from the steamer *Californian* reporting three large icebergs. Harold Bride took this message up to the bridge, and it was again politely received. Captain Smith was attending the dinner party being held for him when the warning was delivered. He never got

Language Coach

Prefixes A prefix is a word part added to the beginning of a word to form a new word. When *un-* is added to the word *sinkable,* it means "not sinkable." Reread the question in line 154. What did the captain think was the answer to this question?

H **CHRONOLOGICAL ORDER**
Reread lines 160–170. About how much time passes between these iceberg warnings and Jack's conversation?

to see it. Then, around 9:00 P.M., the captain excused himself and went up to the bridge. He and his officers talked about how difficult it was to spot icebergs on a calm, clear, moonless night like this with no wind to kick up white surf around them. Before going to bed, the captain ordered
180 the lookouts to keep a sharp watch for ice.

After trading travel stories with Milton Long, Jack Thayer put on his coat and walked around the deck. "It had become very much colder," he said later. "It was a brilliant, starry night. There was no moon, and I have never seen the stars shine brighter . . . sparkling like diamonds. . . . It was the kind of night that made one feel glad to be alive." At eleven o'clock, he went below to his cabin, put on his pajamas, and got ready for bed. **❶**

In the radio room, Harold Bride was exhausted. The two operators were expected to keep the radio working twenty-four hours a day, and Bride lay down to take a much-needed nap. Phillips was so busy with
190 the passenger messages that he actually brushed off the final ice warning of the night. It was from the *Californian*. Trapped in a field of ice, she had stopped for the night about nineteen miles north of the *Titanic*. She was so close that the message literally blasted in Phillips's ears. Annoyed by the loud interruption, he cut off the *Californian*'s radio operator with the words, "Shut up, shut up. I'm busy."

The radio room had received a total of seven ice warning messages in one day. It was quite clear that floating icebergs lay ahead of the *Titanic*. **❶**

High up in the crow's nest on the forward mast, Fred Fleet had passed a quiet watch. It was now 11:40 P.M., and he and his fellow lookout were
200 waiting to be relieved so they could head below, perhaps for a hot drink before hopping into their warm bunks. The sea was dead calm. The air was bitterly cold.

Suddenly, Fleet saw something. A huge, dark shape loomed out of the night directly ahead of the *Titanic*. An iceberg! He quickly sounded the alarm bell three times and picked up the telephone.

Illustration by Steve Noon © Dorling Kindersley.

❶ NARRATIVE NONFICTION
How does the inclusion of **primary source material**—Jack Thayer's firsthand observation—help you better understand what it must have been like on the ship that night?

❶ SUSPENSE AND FORESHADOWING
Reread lines 187–197. What details in these lines create a sense of worry and dread?

"What did you see?" asked the duty officer.

"Iceberg right ahead," replied Fleet.

Immediately, the officer on the bridge ordered the wheel turned as far as it would go. The engine room was told to reverse the engines, while
210 a button was pushed to close the doors to the watertight compartments in the bottom of the ship.

The lookouts in the crow's nest braced themselves for a collision. Slowly the ship started to turn. It looked as though they would miss it. But it was too late. They had avoided a head-on crash, but the iceberg had struck a glancing blow along the *Titanic's* starboard bow. Several tons of ice fell on the ship's decks as the iceberg brushed along the side of the ship and passed into the night. A few minutes later, the *Titanic* came to a stop. **K**

Many of the passengers didn't know the ship had hit anything. Because it was so cold, almost everyone was inside, and most people had already gone
220 to bed. Ruth Becker and her mother were awakened by the dead silence. They could no longer hear the soothing hum of the vibrating engines from below. Jack Thayer was about to step into bed when he felt himself sway ever so slightly. The engines stopped. He was startled by the sudden quiet.

Sensing trouble, Ruth's mother looked out of the door of their second-class cabin and asked a steward[10] what had happened. He told her that nothing was the matter, so Mrs. Becker went back to bed. But as she lay there, she couldn't help feeling that something was very wrong.

Jack heard running feet and voices in the hallway outside his first-class cabin. "I hurried into my heavy overcoat and drew on my slippers. All
230 excited, but not thinking anything serious had occurred, I called in to my father and mother that I was going up on deck to see the fun."

On deck, Jack watched some third-class passengers playing with the ice that had landed on the forward deck as the iceberg had brushed by. Some people were throwing chunks at each other, while a few skidded about playing football with pieces of ice.

Down in the very bottom of the ship, things were very different. When the iceberg had struck, there had been a noise like a big gun going off in one of the boiler rooms. A couple of stokers[11] had been immediately hit by a jet of icy water. The noise and the shock of cold water had sent them
240 running for safety. **L**

Twenty minutes after the crash, things looked very bad indeed to Captain Smith. He and the ship's builder, Thomas Andrews, had made a rapid tour below decks to inspect the damage. The mail room was filling up with water, and sacks of mail were floating about. Water was also pouring into some of the forward holds and two of the boiler rooms.

K **CHRONOLOGICAL ORDER**
What is the time order of the events that happen after Fleet spots the iceberg? Record the events on your timeline.

L **NARRATIVE NONFICTION**
In lines 218–240 the author describes how the passengers react after the collision. **Compare and contrast** the responses of the passengers and the workers in different areas of the ship.

10. **steward:** a worker on a ship who attends to the needs of the passengers.

11. **stokers:** workers who tended the boilers that powered steamships.

Captain Smith knew that the *Titanic*'s hull was divided into a number of watertight compartments. She had been designed so that she could still float if only the first four compartments were flooded, but not any more than that. But water was pouring into the first five compartments. And 250 when the water filled them, it would spill over into the next compartment. One by one all the remaining compartments would flood, and the ship would eventually sink. Andrews told the captain that the ship could last an hour, an hour and a half at the most. **M**

Harold Bride had just awakened in the radio room when Captain Smith stuck his head in the door. "Send the call for assistance," he ordered.

"What call should I send?" Phillips asked.

"The regulation international call for help. Just that." Then the captain was gone. Phillips began to send the Morse code[12] "CQD" distress call, flashing away and joking as he did it. After all, they knew the ship was 260 unsinkable.

Five minutes later, the captain was back. "What are you sending?" he asked.

"CQD," Phillips answered. Then Bride cut in and suggested that they try the new SOS[13] signal that was just coming into use. They began to send out the new international call for help—it was one of the first SOS calls ever sent out from a ship in distress.

Ruth and her family had stayed in their bunks for a good fifteen minutes or so after the room steward had told them nothing was wrong. But Ruth's mother couldn't stop worrying as she heard the sound of running feet and shouting voices in the hallway. Poking her head out 270 of the cabin, she found a steward and asked what the matter was.

"Put on your things and come at once," said the steward.

"Do we have time to dress?" she asked.

"No, madam. You have time for nothing. Put on your life jackets and come up to the top deck."

Ruth helped her mother dress the children quickly. But they only had time to throw their coats over their nightgowns and put on their shoes and stockings. In their rush, they forgot to put on their life jackets.

Just after midnight, Captain Smith ordered the lifeboats uncovered. The ship's squash court, which was thirty-two feet above the keel,[14] was 280 now completely flooded. Jack Thayer and his father came into the first-class lounge to try to find out exactly what the matter was. When Thomas Andrews, the ship's builder, passed by, Mr. Thayer asked him what was going on. He replied in a low voice that the ship had not much more than an hour to live. Jack and his father couldn't believe their ears. **N**

M NARRATIVE NONFICTION
What **conflict** do the people aboard the ship now face?

Language Coach

Idioms An idiom is a phrase that has a meaning different from its individual words. In line 262, Bride "cut in." This means he spoke while others were speaking. He did not actually cut anything. What other word or words could you use in place of the idiom *cut in*?

N MAKE INFERENCES
What can you infer about how Thomas Andrews, the ship's builder, might have felt as he passed through the passenger lounge?

---

12. **Morse code:** a system used in wireless telegraphy in which numbers and letters are represented by sets of long and short sounds or flashes of light.

13. **CQD . . . SOS:** standard international distress calls used by ships at sea.

14. **keel:** the main timber or steel piece that extends the whole length of the bottom of a ship.

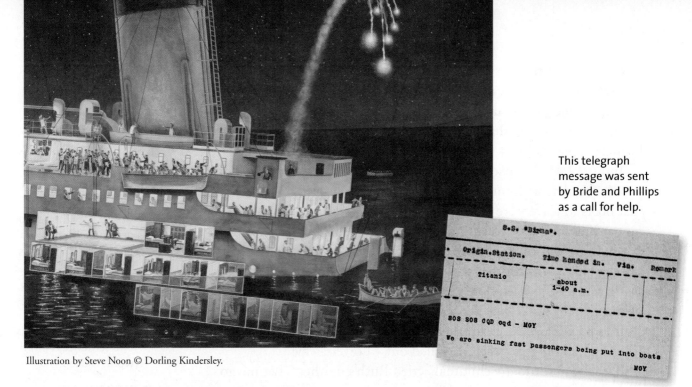
Illustration by Steve Noon © Dorling Kindersley.

This telegraph message was sent by Bride and Phillips as a call for help.

> S.S. "Birma".
>
> | Origin Station. | Time handed in. | Via. | Remark |
> |---|---|---|---|
> | Titanic | about 1-40 a.m. | | |
>
> SOS SOS CQD oqd - MGY
>
> We are sinking fast passengers being put into boats
>
> MGY

From the bridge of the *Titanic,* a ship's lights were observed not far away, possibly the *Californian's.* Captain Smith then ordered white distress rockets fired to get the attention of the nearby ship. They burst high in the air with a loud boom and a shower of stars. But the rockets made no difference. The mystery ship in the distance never answered.

290 In the radio room, Bride and Phillips now knew how serious the accident was and were **feverishly** sending out calls for help. A number of ships heard and responded to their calls, but most were too far away to come to the rescue in time. The closest ship they had been able to reach was the *Carpathia,*[15] about fifty-eight miles away. Immediately, the *Carpathia* reported that she was racing full steam to the rescue. But could she get there in time? ◉

Not far away, the radio operator of the *Californian* had gone to bed for the night and turned off his radio. Several officers and crewmen on the deck of the *Californian* saw rockets in the distance and reported them 300 to their captain. The captain told them to try to contact the ship with a Morse lamp. But they received no answer to their flashed calls. No one thought to wake up the radio operator. ℗

On board the *Titanic,* almost an hour after the crash, most of the passengers still did not realize the seriousness of the situation. But Captain Smith was a very worried man. He knew that the *Titanic* only carried lifeboats for barely half the estimated twenty-two hundred people on board. He would have to make sure his officers kept order to avoid any panic among the passengers. At 12:30 Captain Smith gave the orders

feverishly
(fē′vər-ĭsh-lē) *adv.* in a way marked by intense emotion or activity

◉ **SUSPENSE AND FORESHADOWING**
Given what you already know about the *Titanic,* what details help create suspense?

℗ **CHRONOLOGICAL ORDER**
Record the *Californian's* response on your timeline. At this point, how might disaster still have been minimized?

---

15. *Carpathia* (kär-pā′thē-ə).

to start loading the lifeboats—women and children first. Even though
the *Titanic* was by now quite noticeably down at the bow and listing[16]
slightly to one side, many passengers still didn't want to leave the huge,
brightly lit ship. The ship's band added to a kind of party feeling as the
musicians played lively tunes.

About 12:45 the first lifeboat was lowered. It could carry sixty-five
people, but left with only twenty-eight aboard. Indeed, many of the
first boats to leave were half empty. Ruth Becker noticed that there was
no panic among the crowds of passengers milling about on the decks.
"Everything was calm, everybody was orderly." But the night air was now
biting cold. Ruth's mother told her to go back to their cabin to get some
blankets. Ruth hurried down to the cabin and came back with several
blankets in her arms. The Beckers walked toward one of the lifeboats, and
a sailor picked up Ruth's brother and sister and placed them in the boat.

"That's all for this boat," he called out. "Lower away!"

"Please, those are my children!" cried Ruth's mother. "Let me go
with them!" **Q**

The sailor allowed Mrs. Becker to step into the lifeboat with her two
children. She then called back to Ruth to get into another lifeboat. Ruth
went to the next boat and asked the officer if she could get in. He said,
"Sure," picked her up, and dumped her in.

Boat No. 13 was so crowded that Ruth had to stand up. Foot by foot
it was lowered down the steep side of the massive ship. The new pulleys
shrieked as the ropes passed through them, creaking under the weight
of the boat and its load of sixty-four people. After landing in the water,
Ruth's lifeboat began to drift. Suddenly Ruth saw another lifeboat coming
down right on top of them! Fearing for their lives, the men in charge of
her boat shouted, "Stop!" to the sailors up on the deck. But the noise was
so great that nobody noticed. The second lifeboat kept coming down, so
close that they could actually touch the bottom of it. All of a sudden, one
of the men in Ruth's boat jumped up, pulled out a knife, and cut them
free of their lowering ropes. Ruth's boat pushed away from the *Titanic*
just as boat No. 15 hit the water inches away from them.

Below, in the third-class decks of the ship, there was much more
confusion and alarm. Most of these passengers had not yet been able
to get above decks. Some of those who did finally make it out had to
break down the barriers between third and first class. **R**

By 1:30 the bow was well down, and people were beginning to notice
the slant of the decks. In the radio room, Bride and Phillips were still
desperately sending out calls for help: "We are sinking fast . . . women
and children in boats. We cannot last much longer." The radio signal

310

320

330

340

◆ **GRAMMAR IN CONTEXT**
Reread lines 314–316. Notice how the author uses **transition words or phrases** to unify ideas. The phrase "About 12:45 the first" clarifies the order of events. The author connects the information in the next two sentences with the word "Indeed."

Q **NARRATIVE NONFICTION**
How does Ruth's mother's pleading with the sailor add to the **conflict?**

R **MAKE INFERENCES**
Given the lifeboat situation, what do delays in getting above decks mean for the third-class passengers?

16. **listing:** tilting; leaning.

Illustration by Steve Noon © Dorling Kindersley.

350 gradually got weaker and weaker as the ship's power faded out. Out on the decks, most passengers now began to move toward the stern[17] area, which was slowly lifting out of the water.

By 2:05 there were still over 1,500 people left on the sinking ship. All the lifeboats were now away, and a strange stillness took hold. People stood quietly on the upper decks, bunching together for warmth, trying to keep away from the side of the tilting ship.

Captain Smith now made his way to the radio room and told Harold Bride and Jack Phillips to save themselves. "Men, you have done your full duty," he told them. "You can do no more. Abandon your cabin. Now it's

360 every man for himself." Phillips kept working the radio, hanging on until the very last moment. Suddenly Bride heard water gurgling up the deck outside the radio room. Phillips heard it, too, and cried, "Come on, let's clear out."

Near the stern, Father Thomas Byles had heard confession and given absolution[18] to over one hundred passengers. Playing to the very end, the members of the ship's brave band finally had to put down their instruments and try to save themselves. In desperation, some of the passengers and crew began to jump overboard as the water crept up the slant of the deck. **S**

S **NARRATIVE NONFICTION**
Recall the **conflict** you identified on page 114. How do the various people on the ship respond to the conflict?

---

17. **stern:** the rear end of the ship.

18. **heard confession . . . absolution:** Father Byles had conducted a Roman Catholic religious ceremony in which a priest listens to people confess their sins and then declares them forgiven.

Jack Thayer stood with his friend Milton Long at the railing to keep
370 away from the crowds. He had become separated from his father in
the confusion on deck. Now Jack and his friend heard muffled thuds
and explosions deep within the ship. Suddenly the *Titanic* began to slide
into the water. The water rushed up at them. Thayer and Long quickly
said goodbye and good luck to each other. Then they both jumped.

As he hit the water, Jack Thayer was sucked down. "The cold was
terrific. The shock of the water took the breath out of my lungs. Down
and down I went, spinning in all directions." When he finally surfaced,
gasping for air and numbed by the water, the ship was about forty feet
away from him. His friend Milton Long was nowhere to be seen. Jack
380 would never see him again.

Jack Thayer was lucky. As he struggled in the water, his hand came
to rest on an overturned lifeboat. He grabbed hold and hung on, barely
managing to pull himself up out of the water. Harold Bride had been
washed overboard and now also clung to this same boat.

Both Jack and Harold witnessed the mighty ship's last desperate
moments. "We could see groups of . . . people aboard, clinging in clusters
or bunches, like swarming bees; only to fall in masses, pairs, or singly,
as the great part of the ship . . . rose into the sky. . . ." said Thayer.
"I looked upwards—we were right under the three enormous propellers.
390 For an instant, I thought they were sure to come right down on top of us.
Then . . . she slid quietly away from us into the sea."

Out in the safety of her lifeboat, Ruth Becker also witnessed the end
of the *Titanic*. "I could look back and see this ship, and the decks were
just lined with people looking over. Finally, as the *Titanic* sank faster,
the lights died out. You could just see the stern remaining in an upright
position for a couple of minutes. Then . . . it disappeared." **T**

Then, as Ruth recalled, "there fell upon the ear the most terrible noise
that human beings ever listened to—the cries of hundreds of people
struggling in the icy cold water, crying for help with a cry we knew could
400 not be answered." In Thayer's words, they became "a long continuous
wailing chant." Before long this **ghastly** wailing stopped, as the freezing
water took its toll.[19] **U**

Jack Thayer and Harold Bride and a number of other survivors clung
to their overturned lifeboat, inches away from an icy death in the North
Atlantic. Numb from the cold and not daring to move in case the boat
sank under their weight, they prayed and waited for help. Then, as the
first light of dawn crept on the horizon, a rocket was seen in the distance.
The *Carpathia* had come to their rescue. ❧

COMMON CORE RI 5

T CHRONOLOGICAL ORDER
When writers present events in the order in which they happened, they are using a structural pattern known as chronological order. Often, words such as *after, as, before, now,* and *then,* as well as dates and clock time, indicate time order. Reread lines 369–396. Which words indicate the order in which events happened?

ghastly (găst'lē) *adj.* terrifyingly horrible

U NARRATIVE NONFICTION
Reread lines 385–402 and decide which quotation is most memorable. Why do you think so?

---

19. **took its toll:** claimed passengers' lives.

Comprehension

1. **Recall** Why was Captain Smith given command of the *Titanic*?

2. **Recall** What kinds of accommodations did the ship have for first-class, second-class, and third-class passengers?

3. **Summarize** What safety precautions did Captain Smith and other crew members take before and after the collision?

Text Analysis

4. **Understand Chronological Order** Refer to the selection and the timeline you made to determine about how much time passed between the ship's hitting the iceberg and the survivors' being rescued.

5. **Make Inferences** Use a graphic organizer like the one shown to note how Harold Bride and Captain Smith reacted to the iceberg warnings. Explain why they might have reacted the way they did.

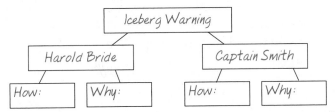

6. **Identify Events** Events are often related by cause and effect—that is, one event brings about another. Referring to your timeline, note which events caused others to happen.

7. **Evaluate Narrative Nonfiction** Ballard could have written the facts about the sinking of the *Titanic* as a piece of informational text. Instead, he wrote a piece of narrative nonfiction; he added **foreshadowing** and **suspense,** and he included the words and experiences of people on the ship. In your opinion, is Ballard's telling an effective way of involving readers in the story? Explain your answer.

Extension and Challenge

8. **Readers' Circle** The sinking of the *Titanic* has inspired many movies and books. In a group, discuss why this disaster lends itself to storytelling. Find details in the selection to support your views.

What can we learn from DISASTERS?

What lessons can you learn from the events Ballard describes in this excerpt from *Exploring the* Titanic?

○ COMMON CORE

RI 1 Cite several pieces of textual evidence to support what the text says explicitly. **RI 3** Analyze interactions between individuals, events, and ideas in a text (e.g., how ideas influence idividuals). **RI 5** Analyze the structure an author uses to organize a text.

Vocabulary in Context

▲ VOCABULARY PRACTICE

Choose the letter of the word that has the same, or nearly the same, meaning as the boldfaced word.

1. an exciting **novelty:** (a) innovation, (b) discussion, (c) solution, (d) occasion
2. working **feverishly:** (a) steadily, (b) carelessly, (c) frantically, (d) sickly
3. have **moderate** success: (a) huge, (b) average, (c) surprising, (d) little
4. elegant **accommodations:** (a) clothes, (b) lodging, (c) manners, (d) jewelry
5. a disturbing **prophecy:** (a) prediction, (b) crash, (c) party, (d) curse
6. a **ghastly** accident: (a) traffic, (b) slight, (c) terrible, (d) funny
7. in **adjoining** rooms: (a) carpeted, (b) decorated, (c) large, (d) connected

accommodations
adjoining
feverishly
ghastly
moderate
novelty
prophecy

ACADEMIC VOCABULARY IN WRITING

• contemporary   • element   • identify   • influence   • structure

What was it like to watch a great **structure** like the *Titanic* sink into the dark ocean? Write a paragraph describing what you would see from one of the lifeboats, as shown in the illustration on page 117. Use at least one Academic Vocabulary word in your paragraph.

VOCABULARY STRATEGY: ANALOGIES

An **analogy** shows a relationship between pairs of words. You can learn new words from analogies if you first figure out what kind of relationship exists between the words.

For example, *floor : house :: deck : ship* is a part-to-whole analogy. You can read this analogy aloud as "floor **is to** house **as** deck **is to** ship." The analogy is telling you that a floor is part of a house in the same way that a deck is part of a ship.

To complete an analogy, identify the relationship between the words in the first pair. The words in the second pair should relate to each other in the same way.

> **COMMON CORE**
>
> **L 5b** Use the relationship between particular words (e.g., analogy) to better understand each of the words. **L 6** Acquire and use accurately grade-appropriate general academic words.

PRACTICE Choose a word from the box to complete each analogy.

1. musician : band :: captain : _____
2. ounce : pound :: foot : _____
3. sleeve : nightgown :: collar : _____
4. branch : tree :: step : _____

staircase	yard
crew	overcoat

Interactive Vocabulary **THINK** central
Go to **thinkcentral.com**.
KEYWORD: HML7-120

Language

◆ GRAMMAR IN CONTEXT: Use Transitions for Coherence

COMMON CORE

L 3 Use knowledge of language and its conventions when writing. **W 1** Write arguments to support claims with clear reasons and relevant evidence.

Writing that has **coherence** flows clearly from one sentence to the next and from one paragraph to the next. To unify their ideas within and between paragraphs, writers use transitions. **Transitions** are words and phrases that show how the different parts of a written work are related. Different kinds of transitions show different relationships. Some transitions help clarify the **time order of events,** such as the words *then, later,* and *after.* Other words, such as *indeed, but,* and *also,* are used to **compare and contrast** or show similarities or differences between ideas. In your writing, be sure to choose transitions that connect your ideas.

> *Example:* The captain was going to retire after the ship reached New York.

> *Example:* She searched for lifejackets for the children. But there were none left.

PRACTICE Choose the correct transitions in the following sentences.

1. The wireless operator took the iceberg warning to the captain, who read it and (then, first) let the other officers read it.

2. He didn't seem very worried. (Also, Yet), he had a thoughtful look on his face.

3. An iceberg was spotted by the lookout (instead, before) he went off duty.

4. Most people did not hear the ship hitting the iceberg. (Instead, Always), the silence woke them up.

*For more help with transitions, see page R32 in the **Grammar Handbook.***

READING-WRITING CONNECTION

YOUR TURN Increase your understanding of the excerpt from *Exploring the Titanic* by responding to this prompt. Then use the **revising tip** to improve your writing.

WRITING PROMPT	REVISING TIP
Extended Constructed Response: Opinion What is your opinion of the behavior of the *Titanic*'s builder, captain, and crew before and during the **disaster**? Could more lives have been saved if they had responded differently? Write **two or three paragraphs,** giving your evaluation.	Review your response. Look for places where you can use transitions to connect or clarify your ideas.

Interactive Revision **THINK** central

Go to **thinkcentral.com.** KEYWORD: HML7-121

from **An American Childhood**

Memoir by Annie Dillard

When do you feel most
ALIVE?

○ COMMON CORE

RI 3 Analyze the interactions between individuals, events, and ideas in a text. **RI 5** Analyze the structure an author uses to organize a text. **L 5a** Interpret figures of speech in context.

We all have something that makes us appreciate the wonder and excitement of life. It might be a tense basketball game, a rocky roller-coaster ride, or the thrill of an unexpected snowstorm. The author Annie Dillard has said that nothing makes her feel alive like facing a tough challenge. This selection is about one of the most exciting challenges she ever faced.

QUICKWRITE When do you feel most alive? Reflect on this question in a journal entry. Other questions you might ask yourself are these: When do I feel the happiest? What makes me feel great about my life? When am I glad to be me? Explain your answers.

TEXT ANALYSIS: SETTING IN NONFICTION

In the memoir you're about to read, Annie Dillard tells a true story from her childhood. The **setting,** the time and place in which events occur, is the 1950s in suburban Pittsburgh, Pennsylvania, where Dillard grew up.

As you read, look for details that help you understand and picture where the selection takes place.

We were standing up to our boot tops in snow on a front yard on trafficked Reynolds Street . . .

Then look for ways the setting affects events.

READING SKILL: RECOGNIZE CAUSE AND EFFECT

Writers use a variety of structural patterns to help them write a narrative. For example, events are often related as **cause and effect**: one event brings about the other. The event that happens first is the cause; the one that follows is the effect. Often an effect becomes the cause of another effect, forming a chain of causes and effects. As you read "An American Childhood," record causes and effects in a chain like the one shown.

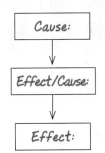

| Cause: |
| Effect/Cause: |
| Effect: |

Review: **Make Inferences**

▲ VOCABULARY IN CONTEXT

The following words help Annie Dillard relate her exciting experience. How many of them do you know? In your Reader/Writer Notebook, write a sentence for each of the vocabulary words. Use a dictionary or the definitions in the following selection pages to help you.

WORD LIST		
improvise	revert	spherical
perfunctorily	righteous	translucent
redundant	simultaneously	

Meet the Author

Annie Dillard
born 1945

Childhood Memories
Pulitzer Prize-winner Annie Dillard frequently writes about events in her life when she was growing up. Her parents shared with her and her sisters their favorite books and music and told stories and jokes. The young Dillard, full of curiosity, spent hours studying small pond creatures with her microscope. But despite a childhood filled with happy memories, as Dillard reached her late teens, she began to rebel and yearned to get away.

A Fulfilling Life
Dillard got her wish for a new adventure when she went away to college and began to focus on writing. Since then, she has written essays, a memoir, poetry, and a Western novel. Dillard spends a great deal of time alone in the wilderness, and she frequently writes about nature. One might think a nature writer would tend to be serious, but Dillard loves to laugh. She keeps an "index of jokes" and says that ". . . irony has the highest place. . ." in literature.

Author Online
THINK central
Go to thinkcentral.com.
KEYWORD: HML7-123

Complete the activities in your **Reader/Writer Notebook.**

An American Childhood

Annie Dillard

S ome boys taught me to play football. This was fine sport. You thought
up a new strategy for every play and whispered it to the others. You
went out for a pass, fooling everyone. Best, you got to throw yourself
mightily at someone's running legs. Either you brought him down or
you hit the ground flat out on your chin, with your arms empty before
you. It was all or nothing. If you hesitated in fear, you would miss and
get hurt: you would take a hard fall while the kid got away, or you would
get kicked in the face while the kid got away. But if you flung yourself
wholeheartedly at the back of his knees—if you gathered and joined body
10 and soul and pointed them diving fearlessly—then you likely wouldn't get
hurt, and you'd stop the ball. Your fate, and your team's score, depended
on your concentration and courage. Nothing girls did could compare
with it.

Boys welcomed me at baseball, too, for I had, through enthusiastic
practice, what was weirdly known as a boy's arm. In winter, in the snow,
there was neither baseball nor football, so the boys and I threw snowballs
at passing cars. I got in trouble throwing snowballs, and have seldom
been happier since. **Ⓐ**

**Analyze
Visuals ▶**

Why is it interesting to
see the snowballs flying
through the air but not
see who threw them?

Ⓐ CAUSE AND EFFECT
What effect does the
snow have on the
children's activities?
Begin creating your
chain here.

On one weekday morning after Christmas, six inches of new snow had
just fallen. We were standing up to our boot tops in snow on a front yard
on trafficked Reynolds Street, waiting for cars. The cars traveled Reynolds
Street slowly and evenly; they were targets all but wrapped in red ribbons,
cream puffs. We couldn't miss.

I was seven; the boys were eight, nine, and ten. The oldest two Fahey
boys were there—Mikey and Peter—polite blond boys who lived near
me on Lloyd Street, and who already had four brothers and sisters. My
parents approved Mikey and Peter Fahey. Chickie McBride was there,
a tough kid, and Billy Paul and Mackie Kean, too, from across Reynolds,
where the boys grew up dark and furious, grew up skinny, knowing, and
skilled. We had all drifted from our houses that morning looking for
action, and had found it here on Reynolds Street.

It was cloudy but cold. The cars' tires laid behind them on the snowy
street a complex trail of beige chunks like crenellated[1] castle walls. I had
stepped on some earlier; they squeaked. We could have wished for more
traffic. When a car came, we all popped it one. In the intervals between
cars we **reverted** to the natural solitude of children. **B**

I started making an iceball—a perfect iceball, from perfectly white
snow, perfectly **spherical,** and squeezed perfectly **translucent** so no
snow remained all the way through. (The Fahey boys and I considered
it unfair actually to throw an iceball at somebody, but it had been known
to happen.)

I had just embarked on the iceball project when we heard tire chains
come clanking from afar. A black Buick was moving toward us down
the street. We all spread out, banged together some regular snowballs,
took aim, and, when the Buick drew nigh, fired.

A soft snowball hit the driver's windshield right before the driver's face.
It made a smashed star with a hump in the middle.

Often, of course, we hit our target, but this time, the only time in
all of life, the car pulled over and stopped. Its wide black door opened;
a man got out of it, running. He didn't even close the car door.

He ran after us, and we ran away from him, up the snowy Reynolds
sidewalk. At the corner, I looked back; incredibly, he was still after us.
He was in city clothes: a suit and tie, street shoes. Any normal adult
would have quit, having sprung us into flight and made his point. This
man was gaining on us. He was a thin man, all action. All of a sudden,
we were running for our lives. **C**

Wordless, we split up. We were on our turf; we could lose ourselves
in the neighborhood backyards, everyone for himself. I paused and

COMMON CORE L 5a

Language Coach

Metaphors Writers use
metaphors to compare
two things without
using *like* or *as*. In
lines 21–23, cars are
compared to targets
and to cream puffs.
Reread these lines. Is
the writer saying it
was easy or difficult
to hit the cars with
snowballs?

revert (rǐ-vûrt′) *v.*
to return to a former
condition

B SETTING
How do you think the
tire tracks look on the
snowy street? Referring
to the footnote might
help you **visualize** the
scene.

spherical (sfîr′ǐ-kəl) *adj.*
having the shape of a
sphere or round ball

translucent
(trǎns-lōō′sənt) *adj.*
allowing light to pass
through

C CAUSE AND EFFECT
What happens when
the children hit the
Buick? Record the effect
in your chain.

---

1. **crenellated** (krěn′ə-lā′tǐd): notched at the top.

considered. Everyone had vanished except Mikey Fahey, who was just
rounding the corner of a yellow brick house. Poor Mikey—I trailed him.
The driver of the Buick sensibly picked the two of us to follow. The man
apparently had all day.

He chased Mikey and me around the yellow house and up a backyard
path we knew by heart: under a low tree, up a bank, through a hedge,
down some snowy steps, and across the grocery store's delivery driveway.
We smashed through a gap in another hedge, entered a scruffy backyard,
and ran around its back porch and tight between houses to Edgerton
Avenue; we ran across Edgerton to an alley and up our own sliding
woodpile to the Halls' front yard; he kept coming. We ran up Lloyd
Street and wound through mazy backyards toward the steep hilltop at
Willard and Lang. **D**

He chased us silently, block after block. He chased us silently over
picket fences, through thorny hedges, between houses, around garbage
cans, and across streets. Every time I glanced back, choking for breath,
I expected he would have quit. He must have been as breathless as we
were. His jacket strained over his body. It was an immense discovery,
pounding into my hot head with every sliding, joyous step, that this
ordinary adult evidently knew what I thought only children who trained
at football knew: that you have to fling yourself at what you're doing,
you have to point yourself, forget yourself, aim, dive. **E**

Mikey and I had nowhere to go, in our own neighborhood or out of
it, but away from this man who was chasing us. He impelled us forward;
we compelled him to follow our route. The air was cold; every breath tore
my throat. We kept running, block after block; we kept **improvising,**
backyard after backyard, running a frantic course and choosing it
simultaneously, failing always to find small places or hard places to slow
him down, and discovering always, exhilarated, dismayed, that only bare
speed could save us—for he would never give up, this man—and we were
losing speed.

He chased us through the backyard labyrinths of ten blocks before
he caught us by our jackets. He caught us and we all stopped. **F**

We three stood staggering, half blinded, coughing, in an obscure
hilltop backyard: a man in his twenties, a boy, a girl. He had released
our jackets, our pursuer, our captor, our hero: he knew we weren't going
anywhere. We all played by the rules. Mikey and I unzipped our jackets.
I pulled off my sopping mittens. Our tracks multiplied in the backyard's
new snow. We had been breaking new snow all morning. We didn't look
at each other. I was cherishing my excitement. The man's lower pant
legs were wet; his cuffs were full of snow, and there was a prow of snow
beneath them on his shoes and socks. Some trees bordered the little flat

D **SETTING**
Reread lines 63–71.
In what way does the
children's familiarity
with the neighborhood
help them?

E **MAKE INFERENCES**
Dillard uses the word
joyous to describe the
difficulty of the chase.
What does this choice
of words suggest
about her?

improvise (ĭm′prə-vīz′) *v.*
to make up on the spur
of the moment, without
preparation

simultaneously
(sī′məl-tā′nē-əs-lē)
adv. at the same time

F **CAUSE AND EFFECT**
What happens because
the children lose speed?
List the effect in your
chain.

backyard, some messy winter trees. There was no one around: a clearing in a grove, and we the only players.

It was a long time before he could speak. I had some difficulty at first recalling why we were there. My lips felt swollen; I couldn't see out of the sides of my eyes; I kept coughing.

"You stupid kids," he began **perfunctorily.**

We listened perfunctorily indeed, if we listened at all, for the chewing out was **redundant,** a mere formality, and beside the point. The point was that he had chased us passionately without giving up, and so he had 110 caught us. Now he came down to earth. I wanted the glory to last forever.

But how could the glory have lasted forever? We could have run through every backyard in North America until we got to Panama. But when he trapped us at the lip of the Panama Canal, what precisely could he have done to prolong the drama of the chase and cap its glory? I brooded about this for the next few years. He could only have fried Mikey Fahey and me in boiling oil, say, or dismembered us piecemeal, or staked us to anthills. None of which I really wanted, and none of which any adult was likely to do, even in the spirit of fun. He could only chew us out there in the Panamanian jungle, after months or years of 120 exalting pursuit. He could only begin, "You stupid kids," and continue in his ordinary Pittsburgh accent with his normal **righteous** anger and the usual common sense. **G**

If in that snowy backyard the driver of the black Buick had cut off our heads, Mikey's and mine, I would have died happy, for nothing has required so much of me since as being chased all over Pittsburgh in the middle of winter—running terrified, exhausted—by this sainted, skinny, furious redheaded man who wished to have a word with us. I don't know how he found his way back to his car. ∽

perfunctorily
(pər-fŭngk′tə-rĭ-lē)
adv. in a mechanical or unconcerned way

redundant (rĭ-dŭn′dənt)
adj. not needed; more than necessary

righteous (rī′chəs) *adj.* based on one's sense of what is right

G MAKE INFERENCES
Reread lines 111–122. Why does Dillard say that the man's response would have been the same even if he had finally caught them in Panama?

Comprehension

1. **Recall** Why did the man chase Dillard and her friend?

2. **Recall** What happened when he caught up with them?

3. **Represent** Reread the paragraph that begins at line 51 on page 126. Using details from the paragraph, sketch the scene.

COMMON CORE

RI 3 Analyze the interactions between individuals, events, and ideas in a text. **RI 5** Analyze the structure an author uses to organize a text. **W 7** Conduct short research projects to answer a question.

Text Analysis

4. **Recognize Cause and Effect** Look over the chain you created as you read. What was the most important effect in the story? Why?

5. **Make Inferences** What do you think the man who chased Dillard might be like? Use details from the selection to help you fill out a chart like the one shown.

The Man	Details	Inference
What work might the man do?		
What might he have been like as a kid?		
What might he be like now?		

6. **Evaluate Setting** Go through the selection and find passages that describe Dillard's neighborhood and the weather on the day of the chase. Which details are especially effective at conveying setting? Explain your answer.

7. **Analyze the Ending** Reread lines 111–128. Why do you think Dillard ended the piece this way, rather than just ending at line 110? Explain the information the last section provides and why Dillard included it.

Extension and Challenge

8. **Inquiry and Research** In the first paragraph, Dillard says that when she was growing up, nothing girls did could compare with playing football. Do research to find out how women's sports have changed and grown over the last 50 years. What team sport might Dillard play if she were growing up today? Share your findings with the class.

When do you feel most ALIVE?

Survey a small group of people to find out when they feel most alive. Also take the survey yourself. Then combine your findings with those of your classmates to create a master list of answers. What generalizations can you make about these experiences that thrill people?

Vocabulary in Context

▲ **VOCABULARY PRACTICE**

Show that you understand the vocabulary words by deciding if each
statement is true or false.

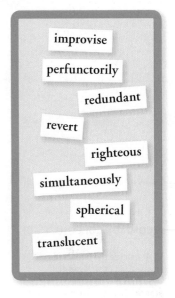

1. A **redundant** explanation is one that's already been given.
2. You can expect a **spherical** object to roll.
3. A tightly woven wool scarf is **translucent.**
4. If two events occur **simultaneously,** they happen one after the other.
5. If you clean your room **perfunctorily,** you do a very careful job.
6. If I **revert** to telling lies, I am going back to an old habit.
7. A speaker following carefully prepared notes will **improvise.**
8. A **righteous** person tends to act in a moral way.

ACADEMIC VOCABULARY IN SPEAKING

• contemporary • elements • identify • influence • structure

Annie Dillard could **identify** one event from her life that she will always
remember. Do you have an event you'll never forget? Describe it to a small
group, using one or more Academic Vocabulary words.

VOCABULARY STRATEGY: SUFFIXES THAT FORM ADJECTIVES

A **suffix** is a word part that appears at the end of a root or base word to form
a new word. Some suffixes, such as those in *righteous* and *spherical,* can be
added to nouns to form adjectives. If you can recognize the noun that a suffix
is attached to, you can often figure out the meaning of the adjective formed
from it. See the chart for the meanings of common suffixes derived from
Latin and Greek.

COMMON CORE

L 4b Use common, grade-
appropriate Greek or Latin
affixes as clues to the meaning
of a word. **L 6** Acquire and use
accurately grade-appropriate
general academic words.

Suffixes	Meanings
-ate, -ous, -eous, -ial, -ical	like; having to do with; showing

PRACTICE Identify the noun in each boldfaced word. Then define the
adjective.

1. The science experiment produced a **gaseous** cloud.
2. Their pet dog is gentle and **affectionate.**
3. Many famous people write **autobiographical** books or articles.
4. Pollution has a **ruinous** effect on our environment.
5. His **facial** features included a long, thin nose.

Interactive
Vocabulary

Go to thinkcentral.com.
KEYWORD: HML7-131

Casey at the Bat

Poem by Ernest Lawrence Thayer

Do sports FANS care too much?

COMMON CORE

RL 4 Analyze the impact of rhymes and other repetitions of sounds on a specific stanza. **RL 5** Analyze how a poem's form or structure contributes to its meaning.

Sports fans love their teams. They dress in the teams' colors, cheer wildly when great plays are made, and boo when things don't go their way. Is this a good thing, or do sports fans care too much about winning? In "Casey at the Bat," the fans expect only the best from their mighty hitter.

WEB IT Create an idea web of what can happen when fans care too much. List things you have read about or witnessed happening at sporting events.

Fights can break out.

What happens when fans care too much?

132

TEXT ANALYSIS: NARRATIVE POETRY

Like fiction, poetry can tell stories. Poems that do so are called **narrative poems.** A narrative poem, just like any other story, has elements of fiction such as characters, a plot, and a setting. It presents a conflict and might also include suspense.

As you read "Casey at the Bat," identify its setting, characters, and main plot events in a diagram like the one shown. Also note the suspense that builds as you read the story.

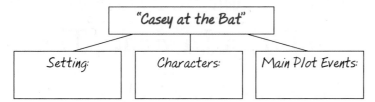

```
              "Casey at the Bat"
        ┌──────────┬──────────────┐
   Setting:    Characters:    Main Plot Events:
```

READING STRATEGY: READING POETRY

In addition to the elements that all stories have, narrative poems include poetic elements and structure that add meaning and interest. Much of the energy and excitement of "Casey at the Bat" comes from the poet's use of **sound devices,** such as repetition, rhyme, and rhythm.

- **Repetition** is the repeating of a sound, word, phrase, or line to emphasize something in a poem.

  For <u>Casey</u>, mighty <u>Casey</u>, was advancing to the bat.

- **Rhyme** is the repetition of sounds at the ends of words.

  It looked extremely rocky for the Mudville nine that <u>day</u>;
  The score stood two to four, with but an inning
      left to <u>play</u>.

- **Rhythm** is a pattern of stressed (´) and unstressed (ˇ) syllables in a line of poetry.

  Thĕn frŏm thĕ gláddĕnĕd múltĭtúde wĕnt úp ă
      jóyŏŭs yéll—

As you read the poem, pay attention to the sound devices. Reading the poem aloud may help you.

Review: **Make Inferences**

Complete the activities in your **Reader/Writer Notebook.**

Meet the Author

Ernest Lawrence Thayer
1863–1940

One-Hit Wonder
Although Ernest Lawrence Thayer wrote many poems for newspapers, he is remembered for just one: "Casey at the Bat." Thayer was educated at Harvard University. Being known among his classmates as a very funny person probably helped him become editor, and later president, of the university's humor magazine, the *Lampoon.*

Crowd Pleaser
After graduation, Thayer joined the staff of the *San Francisco Examiner,* where in 1887 he began writing a poem for each Sunday issue. "Casey at the Bat" was first printed in the paper in 1888. By the time of Thayer's death in 1940, "Casey at the Bat" had become an American favorite.

BACKGROUND TO THE POEM
America's Sport
Baseball began in the United States in the mid-1800s. Small towns and large cities formed teams and clubs. The first baseball game with set rules was played in 1846 between Cartwright's Knickerbockers and the New York Baseball Club. By the early 1900s, going to baseball games was a favorite pastime of people throughout the United States.

Author Online
THINK central
Go to **thinkcentral.com.**
KEYWORD: HML7-133

133

CASEY at the BAT

Ernest Lawrence Thayer

It looked extremely rocky for the Mudville nine that day;
The score stood two to four, with but an inning left to play.
So, when Cooney died at second, and Burrows did the same,
A pallor wreathed the features of the patrons of the game. **Ⓐ**

5　A straggling few got up to go, leaving there the rest,
With that hope which springs eternal within the human breast.
For they thought: "If only Casey could get a whack at that,"
They'd put even money now, with Casey at the bat.

But Flynn preceded Casey, and likewise so did Blake,
10　And the former was a pudd'n, and the latter was a fake.
So on that stricken multitude[1] a deathlike silence sat;
For there seemed but little chance of Casey's getting to the bat.

But Flynn let drive a "single," to the wonderment of all.
And the much-despised Blakey "tore the cover off the ball."
15　And when the dust had lifted, and they saw what had occurred,
There was Blakey safe at second, and Flynn a-huggin' third.

Then from the gladdened multitude went up a joyous yell—
It rumbled in the mountaintops, it rattled in the dell;[2]
It struck upon the hillside and rebounded on the flat;
20　For Casey, mighty Casey, was advancing to the bat. **Ⓑ**

Ⓐ NARRATIVE POETRY
What is the **setting** of this poem? How do you know?

Analyze Visuals ▶
Look at the picture. What can you **infer** about the baseball player's attitude?

Ⓑ READING POETRY
Reread line 20. Why do you think Casey's name is repeated?

---

1. **stricken multitude:** a crowd of people affected by great trouble.
2. **dell:** valley.

There was ease in Casey's manner as he stepped into his place,
There was pride in Casey's bearing and a smile on Casey's face;
And when responding to the cheers he lightly doffed his hat,
No stranger in the crowd could doubt 'twas Casey at the bat. **C**

25 Ten thousand eyes were on him as he rubbed his hands with dirt,
Five thousand tongues applauded when he wiped them on his shirt;
Then when the writhing pitcher ground the ball into his hip,
Defiance glanced in Casey's eye, a sneer curled Casey's lip.

And now the leather-covered sphere came hurtling through the air,
30 And Casey stood a-watching it in haughty grandeur[3] there.
Close by the sturdy batsman the ball unheeded sped;
"That ain't my style," said Casey. "Strike one," the umpire said. **D**

From the benches, filled with people, there went up a muffled roar,
Like the beating of the storm waves on the stern and distant shore.
35 "Kill him! Kill the umpire!" shouted someone on the stand;
And it's likely they'd have killed him had not Casey raised his hand. **E**

With a smile of honest charity great Casey's visage[4] shone;
He stilled the rising tumult, he made the game go on;
He signaled to the pitcher, and once more the spheroid[5] flew;
40 But Casey still ignored it, and the umpire said, "Strike two."

"Fraud!" cried the maddened thousands, and the echo answered "Fraud!"
But one scornful look from Casey and the audience was awed;
They saw his face grow stern and cold, they saw his muscles strain,
And they knew that Casey wouldn't let the ball go by again. **F**

45 The sneer is gone from Casey's lips, his teeth are clenched in hate,
He pounds with cruel vengeance his bat upon the plate;
And now the pitcher holds the ball, and now he lets it go,
And now the air is shattered by the force of Casey's blow.

Oh, somewhere in this favored land the sun is shining bright,
50 The band is playing somewhere, and somewhere hearts are light;
And somewhere men are laughing, and somewhere children shout,
But there is no joy in Mudville: Mighty Casey has struck out.

C MAKE INFERENCES
What inferences can you make about Casey from what you've read so far?

D READING POETRY
Describe the pattern of rhyme the poet uses in the poem.

E NARRATIVE POETRY
What is the **conflict** in this poem?

F READING POETRY
Reread lines 37–44. How does the poet's use of **rhyme** and **rhythm** increase the suspense in the poem?

---

3. **haughty grandeur:** proud majesty and splendor.

4. **visage** (vĭz′ĭj): face.

5. **spheroid** (sfîr′oid′): in this instance, another name for a baseball.

Comprehension

1. **Recall** What events occur to allow Casey a final turn at bat?

2. **Recall** How does Casey approach the last pitch?

3. **Represent** Review the poem and figure out what some of the game statistics are in the ninth inning. Include the score for each team and the number of hits and men left on base for "the Mudville nine."

	Score	Hits	Men Left on Base
Home			
Visitor			

Text Analysis

4. **Analyze Narrative Poetry** Review the notes about setting, characters, and plot that you included in your diagram as you read. Which of Casey's actions build suspense and lead to the **climax,** or moment of greatest interest in the poem's story?

5. **Analyze Repetition** A **stanza** is a group of lines that form a unit within a poem. Reread the last stanza and notice the word that is repeated in lines 50–51. What idea does the repeated word seem to emphasize?

6. **Evaluate the Poem** Why do you think this poem has remained popular for so many years?

Extension and Challenge

7. **Speaking and Listening** With a small group, practice reading the poem aloud in a way that captures the excitement and suspense of the game. Then discuss how the sound devices help you add drama to your oral reading.

8. **Inquiry and Research** Choose a famous baseball player—such as Babe Ruth or Hank Aaron—whose accomplishments have made history. Research the player to find out when he played and on which teams, his records, and what his fans and teammates had to say about him.

Babe Ruth
1895–1948

Do sports FANS care too much?

What are the best qualities of sports fans? Explain how such qualities can keep sports fans from caring too much about winning.

COMMON CORE

RL 4 Analyze the impact of rhymes and other repetitions of sounds on a specific stanza. **RL 5** Analyze how a poem's form or structure contributes to its meaning. **W 7** Conduct short research projects to answer a question.

The Monsters Are Due on Maple Street

Teleplay by Rod Serling

HISTORY Video link at thinkcentral.com

VIDEO TRAILER THINK central KEYWORD: HML7-138

What turns a crowd into a MOB?

COMMON CORE

RL 3 Analyze how particular elements of a drama interact. RL 5 Analyze how a drama's form contributes to its meaning.

People in a crowd often act differently than they do when they're alone. In a big group, people might laugh louder, feel braver, or get angrier. Sometimes a crowd can even become dangerous. When it does—as in the teleplay you're about to read—it becomes a mob.

DISCUSS With a small group, share stories you may have heard about crowds turning into mobs. Think about how some fans react after a favorite sports team wins a championship or about what can happen when frustrated people take the law into their own hands. Continue your discussion by creating a list of things that can turn a crowd into a mob.

> What Can Turn a Crowd into a Mob?
> 1. Feeling of victory
> 2.
> 3.
> 4.

● TEXT ANALYSIS: CONFLICT IN DRAMA

Like any story, a drama has a setting, characters, and a plot that centers on a **conflict**. Since drama is meant to be performed by actors, most of the story unfolds through action and **dialogue,** the conversation between characters. Dialogue usually advances the plot and reveals the conflict.

As you read "The Monsters Are Due on Maple Street," make notes about the story's conflict in a conflict map like the one shown.

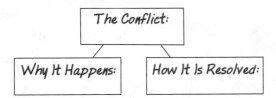

The Conflict:

Why It Happens: How It Is Resolved:

● READING STRATEGY: READING A TELEPLAY

One characteristic element of a drama is the stage directions. **Stage directions** are instructions for the actors, the director, and the reader. They often appear in italics within parentheses. In a **teleplay,** a drama written specifically for television, stage directions also include directions for the camera, such as the following:

The camera moves slowly across the various porches . . .

As you read this teleplay, use all of the stage directions to help you imagine the story as it might be presented on television.

▲ VOCABULARY IN CONTEXT

Rod Serling uses these words to help show the conflict unfolding. See how many of them you can match with their numbered definitions.

WORD LIST	assent	converging	optimistic
	antagonism	incriminate	revelation
	contorted		

1. hopeful; confident
2. hostility
3. something made known
4. agreement
5. to cause to appear guilty
6. twisted or pulled out of shape
7. moving toward one point

Complete the activities in your **Reader/Writer Notebook.**

Meet the Author

Rod Serling
1924–1975

Social Issues
During his extraordinary career, Rod Serling won six Emmy awards, the highest honors given to those in the television industry. Known to the public as a creator of exciting television shows, Serling was sometimes referred to by his friends and business associates as "the angry young man of television." Serling wanted to write teleplays about important social issues, but television executives often thought his topics were too controversial.

Science Fiction
Frustrated by this lack of support, Serling turned to writing science fiction and fantasy. He created an eerie series called *The Twilight Zone,* which became one of the most popular shows in television history during its 1959–1964 run. Because the teleplays for this series were not realistic, Serling had more freedom to deal with issues such as prejudice and intolerance. "The Monsters Are Due on Maple Street" first appeared in 1960 as an episode of *The Twilight Zone.*

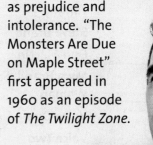

Author Online
Go to thinkcentral.com. KEYWORD: HML7-139

THINK central

THE MONSTERS
Are Due on Maple Street

Rod Serling

Empire of Lights (1954), René Magritte. Oil on canvas, 146 cm × 114 cm. Musée d'Art Moderne, Brussels. © 2008 C. Herscovici, Brussels/ Artists Rights Society (ARS), New York.

ACT 1

(*Fade in[1] on a shot of the night sky. The various heavenly bodies stand out in sharp, sparkling relief. The camera moves slowly across the heavens until it passes the horizon and stops on a sign that reads "Maple Street." It is daytime. Then we see the street below. It is a quiet, tree-lined, small-town American street. The houses have front porches on which people sit and swing on gliders, talking across from house to house. Steve Brand is polish-*
10 *ing his car, which is parked in front of his house. His neighbor,* Don Martin, *leans against the fender watching him. An ice-cream vendor riding a bicycle is just in the process of stopping to sell some ice cream to a couple of kids. Two women gossip on the front lawn. Another man is water-ing his lawn with a garden hose. As we see these various activities, we hear the* Narrator's *voice.*)

Narrator. Maple Street, U.S.A., late summer. A tree-lined little world of front-porch gliders,
20 hopscotch, the laughter of children, and the bell of an ice-cream vendor.

(*There is a pause, and the camera moves over to a shot of the ice-cream vendor and two small boys who are standing alongside just buying ice cream.*)

Narrator. At the sound of the roar and the flash of the light, it will be precisely six-forty-three P.M. on Maple Street.

(*At this moment* Tommy, *one of the two boys buy-ing ice cream from the vendor, looks up to listen*
30 *to a tremendous screeching roar from overhead. A flash of light plays on the faces of both boys and then moves down the street and disappears. Various people leave their porches or stop what they are doing to stare up at the sky. Steve Brand, the man who has been polishing his car, stands there transfixed, staring upwards. He looks at* Don Martin, *his neighbor from across the street.*)

---

1. **fade in:** cause the television image to appear gradually.

Steve. What was that? A meteor?

Don. That's what it looked like. I didn't hear
40 any crash though, did you?

Steve. Nope. I didn't hear anything except a roar.

Myra (*from her porch*). What was that?

Steve (*raising his voice and looking toward the porch*). Guess it was a meteor, honey. Came awful close, didn't it?

Myra. Too close for my money! Much too close.

(*The camera moves slowly across the various porches to people who stand there watching and
50 talking in low conversing tones.*)

Narrator. Maple Street. Six-forty-four P.M. on a late September evening. (*He pauses.*) Maple Street in the last calm and reflective moment (*pause*) before the monsters came!

(*The camera takes us across the porches again. A man is replacing a light bulb on a front porch. He gets off his stool to flick the switch and finds that nothing happens. Another man is working on an electric power mower. He plugs in the plug,*
60 *flicks the switch of the mower off and on, but noth-ing happens. Through a window we see a woman pushing her finger up and down on the dial hook of a telephone. Her voice sounds far away.*)

Woman. Operator, operator, something's wrong on the phone, operator! (*Myra Brand comes out on the porch and calls to* Steve.)

Myra (*calling*). Steve, the power's off. I had the soup on the stove, and the stove just stopped working.

70 **Woman.** Same thing over here. I can't get anybody on the phone either. The phone seems to be dead.

(*We look down again on the street. Small, mildly disturbed voices are heard coming from below.*)

Voice One. Electricity's off.

Voice Two. Phone won't work.

Voice Three. Can't get a thing on the radio.

Voice Four. My power mower won't move, won't work at all.

80 **Voice Five.** Radio's gone dead!

(Pete Van Horn, *a tall, thin man, is seen standing in front of his house.*)

Pete. I'll cut through the back yard to see if the power's still on, on Floral Street. I'll be right back!

(*He walks past the side of his house and disappears into the back yard. The camera pans*[2] *down slowly until we are looking at ten or eleven people standing around the street and overflowing to the* 90 *curb and sidewalk. In the background is* Steve Brand*'s car.*)

Steve. Doesn't make sense. Why should the power go off all of a sudden and the phone line?

Don. Maybe some kind of an electrical storm or something.

Charlie. That don't seem likely. Sky's just as blue as anything. Not a cloud. No lightning. No thunder. No nothing. How could it be a storm?

Woman. I can't get a thing on the radio. Not 100 even the portable.

(*The people again begin to murmur softly in wonderment.*)

Charlie. Well, why don't you go downtown and check with the police, though they'll probably think we're crazy or something. A little power failure and right away we get all flustered and everything—

Steve. It isn't just the power failure, Charlie. If it was, we'd still be able to get a broadcast 110 on the portable.

(*There is a murmur of reaction to this.* Steve *looks from face to face and then at his car.*)

Steve. I'll run downtown. We'll get this all straightened out.

(*He gets in the car and turns the key. Looking through the open car door, we see the crowd watching* Steve *from the other side. He starts the engine. It turns over sluggishly and then stops dead. He tries it again, and this time he can't get* 120 *it to turn over. Then very slowly he turns the key back to "off" and gets out of the car. The people stare at* Steve. *He stands for a moment by the car and then walks toward them.*)

---

2. **pans:** turns.

Steve. I don't understand it. It was working fine before—

Don. Out of gas?

Steve (*shakes his head*). I just had it filled.

Woman. What's it mean?

Charlie. It's just as if (*pause*) as if everything 130 had stopped. (*Then he turns toward* Steve.) We'd better walk downtown.

(*Another murmur of **assent** to this.*)

Steve. The two of us can go, Charlie. (*He turns to look back at the car.*) It couldn't be the meteor. A meteor couldn't do this.

(*He and* Charlie *exchange a look. Then they start to walk away from the group.* Tommy *comes into view. He is a serious-faced young boy in spectacles. He stands halfway between the group and the two* 140 *men, who start to walk down the sidewalk.*)

Tommy. Mr. Brand—you'd better not!

Steve. Why not?

Tommy. They don't want you to.

(Steve *and* Charlie *exchange a grin, and* Steve *looks back toward the boy.*)

Steve. *Who* doesn't want us to?

Tommy (*jerks his head in the general direction of the distant horizon*). Them!

Steve. Them?

150 **Charlie.** Who are them?

Tommy (*intently*). Whoever was in that thing that came by overhead.

(Steve *knits his brows for a moment, cocking his head questioningly. His voice is intense.*)

Steve. What?

Tommy. Whoever was in that thing that came over. I don't think they want us to leave here.

(Steve *leaves* Charlie, *walks over to the boy, and puts his hand on the boy's shoulder. He forces his* 160 *voice to remain gentle.*)

Steve. What do you mean? What are you talking about?

Tommy. They don't want us to leave. That's why they shut everything off.

Steve. What makes you say that? Whatever gave you that idea?

Woman (*from the crowd*). Now isn't that the craziest thing you ever heard?

Tommy (*persistent but a little frightened*). It's always that way, in every story I ever read about a ship landing from outer space.

Woman (*to the boy's mother, Sally, who stands on the fringe of the crowd*). From outer space yet! Sally, you better get that boy of yours up to bed. He's been reading too many comic books or seeing too many movies or something!

Sally. Tommy, come over here and stop that kind of talk.

Steve. Go ahead, Tommy. We'll be right back. And you'll see. That wasn't any ship or anything like it. That was just a . . . a meteor or something. Likely as not— (*He turns to the group, now trying very hard to sound more **optimistic** than he feels.*) No doubt it did have something to do with all this power failure and the rest of it. Meteors can do some crazy things. Like sunspots.

Don (*picking up the cue*). Sure. That's the kind of thing—like sunspots. They raise Cain[3] with radio reception all over the world. And this thing being so close—why, there's no telling the sort of stuff it can do. (*He wets his lips and smiles nervously.*) Go ahead, Charlie. You and Steve go into town and see if that isn't what's causing it all.

(Steve *and* Charlie *walk away from the group down the sidewalk as the people watch silently.* Tommy *stares at them, biting his lips, and finally calls out again.*)

Tommy. Mr. Brand!

(*The two men stop.* Tommy *takes a step toward them.*)

Tommy. Mr. Brand . . . please don't leave here.

(Steve *and* Charlie *stop once again and turn toward the boy. In the crowd there is a murmur of irritation and concern, as if the boy's words— even though they didn't make sense—were bringing up fears that shouldn't be brought up.* Tommy *is both frightened and defiant.*)

Tommy. You might not even be able to get to town. It was that way in the story. Nobody could leave. Nobody except—

Steve. Except who?

Tommy. Except the people they sent down ahead of them. They looked just like humans. And it wasn't until the ship landed that—

(*The boy suddenly stops, conscious of the people staring at him and his mother and of the sudden hush of the crowd.*)

Sally (*in a whisper, sensing the **antagonism** of the crowd*). Tommy, please son . . . honey, don't talk that way—

Man One. That kid shouldn't talk that way . . . and we shouldn't stand here listening to him. Why this is the craziest thing I ever heard of. The kid tells us a comic book plot, and here we stand listening—

(Steve *walks toward the camera and stops beside the boy.*)

Steve. Go ahead, Tommy. What kind of story was this? What about the people they sent out ahead?

Tommy. That was the way they prepared things for the landing. They sent four people. A mother and a father and two kids who looked just like humans . . . but they weren't.

(*There is another silence as* Steve *looks toward the crowd and then toward* Tommy. *He wears a tight grin.*)

Steve. Well, I guess what we'd better do then is to run a check on the neighborhood and see which ones of us are really human.

(*There is laughter at this, but it's a laughter that comes from a desperate attempt to lighten the*

---

3. **raise Cain:** cause trouble; create a disturbance. (In the Bible, Adam and Eve's son Cain becomes the first murderer when he kills his brother Abel.)

atmosphere. The people look at one another in the middle of their laughter.)

Charlie (*rubs his jaw nervously*). I wonder if Floral Street's got the same deal we got. (*He looks past the houses.*) Where is Pete Van Horn anyway? Isn't he back yet?

250 (*Suddenly there is the sound of a car's engine starting to turn over. We look across the street toward the driveway of* Les Goodman's *house. He is at the wheel trying to start the car.*)

Sally. Can you get started, Les?

(Les Goodman *gets out of the car, shaking his head.*)

Les. No dice.[4]

(*He walks toward the group. He stops suddenly as, behind him, the car engine starts up all by itself.* Les *whirls around to stare at the car. The car idles* 260 *roughly, smoke coming from the exhaust, the frame shaking gently.* Les's *eyes go wide, and he runs over to his car. The people stare at the car.*)

Man One. He got the car started somehow. He got *his* car started!

(*The people continue to stare, caught up by this* **revelation** *and wildly frightened.*)

Woman. How come his car just up and started like that?

Sally. All by itself. He wasn't anywheres near it. 270 It started all by itself.

(Don Martin *approaches the group and stops a few feet away to look toward* Les's *car.*)

Don. And he never did come out to look at that thing that flew overhead. He wasn't even interested. (*He turns to the group, his face taut and serious.*) Why? Why didn't he come out with the rest of us to look?

Charlie. He always was an oddball. Him and his whole family. Real oddball.

280 **Don.** What do you say we ask him?

(*The group starts toward the house. In this brief fraction of a moment, it takes the first step toward changing from a group into a mob. The group members begin to head purposefully across the street toward the house.* Steve *stands in front of them. For a moment their fear almost turns their walk into a wild stampede, but* Steve's *voice, loud, incisive, and commanding, makes them stop.*)

Steve. Wait a minute . . . wait a minute! Let's 290 not be a mob!

(*The people stop, pause for a moment, and then, much more quietly and slowly, start to walk across the street.* Les *stands alone facing the people.*)

Les. I just don't understand it. I tried to start it, and it wouldn't start. You saw me. All of you saw me.

(*And now, just as suddenly as the engine started, it stops, and there is a long silence that is gradually intruded upon by the frightened* 300 *murmuring of the people.*)

Les. I don't understand. I swear . . . I don't understand. What's happening?

Don. Maybe you better tell us. Nothing's working on this street. Nothing. No lights, no power, no radio, (*then meaningfully*) nothing except one car—yours!

(*The people's murmuring becomes a loud chant filling the air with accusations and demands for action. Two of the men pass* Don *and head* 310 *toward* Les, *who backs away from them against his car. He is cornered.*)

Les. Wait a minute now. You keep your distance —all of you. So I've got a car that starts by itself—well, that's a freak thing—I admit it. But does that make me a criminal or something? I don't know why the car works—it just does!

(*This stops the crowd momentarily, and* Les, *still backing away, goes toward his front porch. He goes up the steps and then stops, facing the mob.*)

---

4. **no dice:** no success.

Les. What's it all about, Steve?

Steve (*quietly*). We're all on a monster kick, Les. Seems that the general impression holds that maybe one family isn't what we think they are. Monsters from outer space or something. Different from us. Aliens from the vast beyond. (*He chuckles.*) You know anybody that might fit that description around here on Maple Street?

Les. What is this, a gag? (*He looks around the group again.*) This a practical joke or something?

330 (*Suddenly the car engine starts all by itself, runs for a moment, and stops. One woman begins to cry. The eyes of the crowd are cold and accusing.*)

Les. Now that's supposed to **incriminate** me, huh? The car engine goes on and off, and that really does it, doesn't it? (*He looks around at the faces of the people.*) I just don't understand it . . . any more than any of you do! (*He wets his lips, looking from face to face.*) Look, you all know me. We've lived here five years. Right in this 340 house. We're no different from any of the rest of you! We're no different at all. . . . Really . . . this whole thing is just . . . just weird—

Woman. Well, if that's the case, Les Goodman, explain why— (*She stops suddenly, clamping her mouth shut.*)

Les (*softly*). Explain what?

Steve (*interjecting*). Look, let's forget this—

Charlie (*overlapping him*). Go ahead, let her talk. What about it? Explain what?

350 **Woman** (*a little reluctantly*). Well . . . sometimes I go to bed late at night. A couple of times . . . a couple of times I'd come out here on the porch, and I'd see Mr. Goodman here in the wee hours of the morning standing out in front of his house . . . looking up at the sky. (*She looks around the circle of faces.*) That's right, looking up at the sky as if . . . as if he were waiting for something, (*pauses*) as if he were looking for something.

360 (*There's a murmur of reaction from the crowd again as* Les *backs away.*)

Les. She's crazy. Look, I can explain that. Please . . . I can really explain that. . . . She's making it up anyway. (*Then he shouts.*) I tell you she's making it up!

(*He takes a step toward the crowd, and they back away from him. He walks down the steps after them, and they continue to back away. Suddenly he is left completely alone, and he looks like a 370 man caught in the middle of a menacing circle as the scene slowly fades to black.*)

ACT

2 *Scene One*

(*Fade in on Maple Street at night. On the sidewalk, little knots of people stand around talking in low voices. At the end of each conversation they look toward Les Goodman's house. From the various houses, we can see candlelight but no electricity. The quiet that blankets the whole area is disturbed only by the almost whispered voices of the people standing around. In one group* Charlie *stands staring across at the Goodmans' house. Two men stand*
10 *across the street from it in almost sentrylike[5] poses.*)

Sally (*in a small, hesitant voice*). It just doesn't seem right, though, keeping watch on them. Why . . . he was right when he said he was one of our neighbors. Why, I've known Ethel Goodman ever since they moved in. We've been good friends—

Charlie. That don't prove a thing. Any guy who'd spend his time lookin' up at the sky early in the morning—well, there's something wrong
20 with that kind of person. There's something that ain't legitimate. Maybe under normal circumstances we could let it go by, but these aren't normal circumstances. Why, look at this street! Nothin' but candles. Why, it's like goin' back into the Dark Ages[6] or somethin'!

(Steve *walks down the steps of his porch, down the street to the Goodmans' house, and then stops at the foot of the steps.* Les *is standing there;* Ethel Goodman *behind him is very frightened.*)

30 **Les.** Just stay right where you are, Steve. We don't want any trouble, but this time if anybody sets foot on my porch—that's what they're going to get—trouble!

Steve. Look, Les—

Les. I've already explained to you people. I don't sleep very well at night sometimes. I get up and I take a walk and I look up at the sky. I look at the stars!

---

5. **sentrylike:** resembling those of guards.

6. **Dark Ages:** a period from about A.D. 400 to 1000, when learning and culture in Western Europe were decreasing.

Ethel. That's exactly what he does. Why, this whole thing, it's . . . it's some kind of madness or something.

Steve (*nods grimly*). That's exactly what it is—some kind of madness.

Charlie's Voice (*shrill, from across the street*). You best watch who you're seen with, Steve! Until we get this all straightened out, you ain't exactly above suspicion yourself.

Steve (*whirling around toward him*). Or you, Charlie. Or any of us, it seems. From age eight on up!

Woman. What I'd like to know is—what are we gonna do? Just stand around here all night?

Charlie. There's nothin' else we *can* do! (*He turns back, looking toward* Steve *and* Les *again.*) One of 'em'll tip their hand. They got to.

Steve (*raising his voice*). There's something you can do, Charlie. You can go home and keep your mouth shut. You can quit strutting around like a self-appointed judge and climb into bed and forget it.

Charlie. You sound real anxious to have that happen, Steve. I think we better keep our eye on you, too!

Don (*as if he were taking the bit in his teeth, takes a hesitant step to the front*). I think everything might as well come out now. (*He turns toward* Steve.) Your wife's done plenty of talking, Steve, about how odd you are!

Charlie (*picking this up, his eyes widening*). Go ahead, tell us what she's said.

(Steve *walks toward them from across the street.*)

Steve. Go ahead, what's my wife said? Let's get it all out. Let's pick out every idiosyncrasy[7] of every single man, woman, and child on the street. And then we might as well set up some kind of citizens' court. How about a firing squad at dawn, Charlie, so we can get rid of all the suspects. Narrow them down. Make it easier for you.

Don. There's no need gettin' so upset, Steve. It's just that . . . well . . . Myra's talked about how there's been plenty of nights you spent hours down in your basement workin' on some kind of radio or something. Well, none of us have ever seen that radio—

(*By this time* Steve *has reached the group. He stands there defiantly.*)

Charlie. Go ahead, Steve. What kind of "radio set" you workin' on? I never seen it. Neither has anyone else. Who do you talk to on that radio set? And who talks to you?

Steve. I'm surprised at you, Charlie. How come you're so dense all of a sudden? (*He pauses.*) Who do I talk to? I talk to monsters from outer space. I talk to three-headed green men who fly over here in what look like meteors.

(Myra Brand *steps down from the porch, bites her lip, calls out.*)

Myra. Steve! Steve, please. (*Then looking around, frightened, she walks toward the group.*) It's just a ham radio[8] set, that's all. I bought him a book on it myself. It's just a ham radio set. A lot of people have them. I can show it to you. It's right down in the basement.

Steve (*whirls around toward her*). Show them nothing! If they want to look inside our house—let them go and get a search warrant.

Charlie. Look, buddy, you can't afford to—

Steve (*interrupting him*). Charlie, don't start telling me who's dangerous and who isn't and who's safe and who's a menace. (*He turns to the group and shouts.*) And you're with him, too—all of you! You're standing here all set

---

7. **idiosyncrasy** (ĭd′ē-ō-sĭng′krə-sē): personal way of acting; odd mannerism.

8. **ham radio**: a two-way radio with which an amateur broadcaster communicates with other amateurs.

to crucify—all set to find a scapegoat[9]—all desperate to point some kind of a finger at a neighbor! Well now, look, friends, the only thing that's gonna happen is that we'll eat each other up alive—

(*He stops abruptly as* Charlie *suddenly grabs his arm.*)

120 **Charlie** (*in a hushed voice*). That's not the only thing that can happen to us.

(*Down the street, a figure has suddenly materialized in the gloom. In the silence we hear the clickety-clack of slow, measured footsteps on concrete as the figure walks slowly toward them. One of the women lets out a stifled cry.* Sally *grabs her boy, as do a couple of other mothers.*)

Tommy (*shouting, frightened*). It's the monster! It's the monster!

130 (*Another woman lets out a wail, and the people fall back in a group staring toward the darkness and the approaching figure. The people stand in the shadows watching.* Don Martin *joins them, carrying a shotgun. He holds it up.*)

Don. We may need this.

Steve. A shotgun? (*He pulls it out of* Don's *hand.*) No! Will anybody think a thought around here! Will you people wise up. What good would a shotgun do against—

140 (*The dark figure continues to walk toward them as the people stand there, fearful, mothers clutching children, men standing in front of their wives.*)

Charlie (*pulling the gun from* Steve's *hands*). No more talk, Steve. You're going to talk us into a grave! You'd let whatever's out there walk right over us, wouldn't yuh? Well, some of us won't!

(Charlie *swings around, raises the gun, and suddenly pulls the trigger. The sound of the shot explodes in the stillness. The figure suddenly lets*
150 *out a small cry, stumbles forward onto his knees,*

and then falls forward on his face. Don, Charlie, *and* Steve *race forward to him.* Steve *is there first and turns the man over. The crowd gathers around them.*)

Steve (*slowly looks up*). It's Pete Van Horn.

Don (*in a hushed voice*). Pete Van Horn! He was just gonna go over to the next block to see if the power was on—

Woman. You killed him, Charlie. You shot
160 him dead!

Charlie (*looks around at the circle of faces, his eyes frightened, his face* **contorted**). But . . . but I didn't know who he was. I certainly didn't know who he was. He comes walkin' out of the darkness—how am I supposed to know who he was? (*He grabs* Steve.) Steve—you know why I shot! How was I supposed to know he wasn't a monster or something? (*He grabs* Don.) We're all scared of the same thing. I was just tryin'
170 to . . . tryin' to protect my home, that's all! Look, all of you, that's all I was tryin' to do. (*He looks down wildly at the body.*) I didn't know it was somebody we knew! I didn't know—

(*There's a sudden hush and then an intake of breath in the group. Across the street all the lights go on in one of the houses.*)

Woman (*in a hushed voice*). Charlie . . . Charlie . . . the lights just went on in your house. Why did the lights just go on?

180 **Don.** What about it, Charlie? How come you're the only one with lights now?

Les. That's what I'd like to know.

(*Pausing, they all stare toward* Charlie.)

Les. You were so quick to kill, Charlie, and you were so quick to tell us who we had to be careful of. Well, maybe you had to kill. Maybe Pete there was trying to tell us something. Maybe he'd found out something and came

---

9. **scapegoat:** a person or thing made to bear the blame for the mistakes of others.

back to tell us who there was amongst us we
190 should watch out for—

(Charlie *backs away from the group, his eyes wide
with fright.*)

Charlie. No . . . no . . . it's nothing of the sort!
I don't know why the lights are on. I swear
I don't. Somebody's pulling a gag or something.

(*He bumps against* Steve, *who grabs him and
whirls him around.*)

Steve. A gag? A gag? Charlie, there's a dead
man on the sidewalk, and you killed him!
200 Does this thing look like a gag to you?

(Charlie *breaks away and screams as he runs
toward his house.*)

Charlie. No! No! Please!

(*A man breaks away from the crowd to chase*
Charlie. *As the man tackles him and lands on top
of him, the other people start to run toward them.*
Charlie *gets up, breaks away from the other man's
grasp, and lands a couple of desperate punches that
push the man aside. Then he forces his way, fight-*
210 *ing, through the crowd and jumps up on
his front porch.* Charlie *is on his porch
as a rock thrown from the group smashes
a window beside him, the broken glass
flying past him. A couple of pieces cut him.
He stands there perspiring, rumpled, blood
running down from a cut on the cheek.
His wife breaks away from the group
to throw herself into his arms. He buries
his face against her. We can see the crowd*
220 **converging** *on the porch.*)

Voice One. It must have been him.

Voice Two. He's the one.

Voice Three. We got to get Charlie.

(*Another rock lands on the porch.*
Charlie *pushes his wife behind him,
facing the group.*)

Charlie. Look, look, I swear to you . . .
it isn't me . . . but I do know who

it is . . . I swear to you, I do know who it is.
230 I know who the monster is here. I know who
it is that doesn't belong. I swear to you I know.

Don (*pushing his way to the front of the crowd*).
All right, Charlie, let's hear it!

(Charlie's *eyes dart around wildly.*)

Charlie. It's . . . it's . . .

Man Two (*screaming*). Go ahead, Charlie.

Charlie. It's . . . it's the kid. It's Tommy.
He's the one!

(*There's a gasp from the crowd as we see* Sally
240 *holding the boy.* Tommy *at first doesn't understand and then, realizing the eyes are all on him,
buries his face against his mother.*)

Sally (*backs away*). That's crazy! He's only a boy.

Woman. But he knew! He was the only one!
He told us all about it. Well, how did he know?
How could he have known?

(*Various people take this up and repeat
the question.*)

Voice One. How could he know?

250 **Voice Two.** Who told him?

Voice Three. Make the kid answer.

(*The crowd starts to converge around the mother, who grabs* Tommy *and starts to run with him. The crowd starts to follow, at first walking fast, and then running after him. Suddenly Charlie's lights go off and the lights in other houses go on, then off.*)

Man One (*shouting*). It isn't the kid . . . it's Bob Weaver's house.

Woman. It isn't Bob Weaver's house, it's Don
260 Martin's place.

Charlie. I tell you it's the kid.

Don. It's Charlie. He's the one.

(*People shout, accuse, and scream as the lights go on and off. Then, slowly, in the middle of this nightmarish confusion of sight and sound, the camera starts to pull away until, once again, we have reached the opening shot looking at the Maple Street sign from high above.*)

Scene Two

(*The camera continues to move away while*
270 *gradually bringing into focus a field. We see the metal side of a spacecraft that sits shrouded in darkness. An open door throws out a beam of light from the illuminated interior. Two figures appear, silhouetted against the bright lights. We get only a vague feeling of form.*)

Figure One. Understand the procedure now? Just stop a few of their machines and radios and telephones and lawn mowers. . . . Throw them into darkness for a few hours, and then
280 just sit back and watch the pattern.

Figure Two. And this pattern is always the same?

Figure One. With few variations. They pick the most dangerous enemy they can find . . . and it's themselves. And all we need do is sit back . . . and watch.

Figure Two. Then I take it this place . . . this Maple Street . . . is not unique.

Figure One (*shaking his head*). By no means. Their world is full of Maple Streets. And we'll
290 go from one to the other and let them destroy themselves. One to the other . . . one to the other . . . one to the other—

Scene Three

(*The camera slowly moves up for a shot of the starry sky, and over this we hear the* Narrator's *voice.*)

Narrator. The tools of conquest do not necessarily come with bombs and explosions and fallout. There are weapons that are simply thoughts, attitudes, prejudices—to be found only in the minds of men. For the record,
300 prejudices can kill and suspicion can destroy. A thoughtless, frightened search for a scapegoat has a fallout all its own for the children . . . and the children yet unborn, (*a pause*) and the pity of it is . . . that these things cannot be confined to . . . The Twilight Zone!

(*Fade to black.*)

Comprehension

1. **Recall** When do the neighbors first sense something is wrong?

2. **Clarify** How is Pete Van Horn killed?

3. **Clarify** Why do the neighbors become suspicious of Tommy?

COMMON CORE

RL 3 Analyze how particular elements of a drama interact.
RL 5 Analyze how a drama's form contributes to its meaning.

Text Analysis

4. **Identify Conflict** Review the conflict map you created as you read. Then explain the main conflict in the story. What do the characters' reactions to the conflict and their dialogue reveal about them?

5. **Analyze the Teleplay** How did the stage directions help you understand the teleplay? Record your answers on a chart like the one shown.

Stage Direction	Its Effect
Fade in on a shot of the night sky.	It makes you focus on outer space.

6. **Analyze Foreshadowing** Foreshadowing is a technique a writer uses to hint at something that will occur later in a story. Reread lines 51–54 of Act 1. What is the purpose of the narrator's role here?

7. **Draw Conclusions** At various points in the teleplay, the **mob** thinks different people are the monsters in their midst. Make a list of these people, and consider the moments when the mob turns on them. What conclusions can you draw about how the mob picks its victims?

8. **Make Judgments** In your opinion, who are the monsters referred to in the title? Give reasons for your answer.

Extension and Challenge

9. **Creative Project: Drama** With a small group, review the information about Rod Serling on page 139. Then act out a part of the teleplay that your group thinks communicates a message about prejudice and fear. Remember to follow stage directions as you act out your scene. After your performance, explain why your group chose that particular scene.

What turns a crowd into a MOB?

Not all of the characters in this teleplay are equally quick to go along with the crowd. Identify a character who urges people to think calmly and reasonably, and write three paragraphs describing his or her efforts. Include a sentence that tells why the character isn't successful in preventing the crowd from becoming a mob.

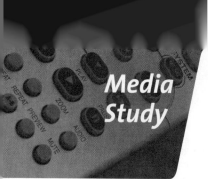
from **Back to the Future**
Film Clip on **Media Smart DVD-ROM**

What makes your
IMAGINATION soar?

COMMON CORE

RL 7 Analyze the effects of techniques unique to [a] medium (e.g., lighting, sound, color, or camera focus and angles in a film).

One of the keys to a good story is how it is told. Storytellers of all kinds know how satisfying a story can be when it taps into your sense of wonder and your willingness to believe in fantastic happenings and places. To explore how a movie can bring an unusual plot and setting to life, you'll watch a scene from a movie that has captured the imagination of millions of people.

Background

From Time to Time The movie *Back to the Future* is a science fiction adventure about time travel. Seventeen-year-old Marty McFly has a scientist friend, Dr. Emmett L. Brown, who has been experimenting with ways to travel across time. Doc, as Marty calls him, has invented a time machine that looks like a stylish, specially equipped car.

To escape sudden danger, Marty leaps into the car and speeds 30 years into the past—to 1955. He soon learns that having the power to control time comes with certain risks.

Media Literacy: Plot and Setting in Movies

Moviemakers tell stories by using visual and sound techniques. These techniques are used to help viewers follow the events of a plot. In addition, the techniques help to make the setting and the actions within it seem very real.

MOVIE TECHNIQUES	STRATEGIES FOR VIEWING	
Visual Techniques A movie director uses carefully chosen camera shots to support important elements of the plot. A **shot** is the continuous recording of a scene or image.	Watch for carefully chosen **camera shots.** • A **close-up shot** is a close view of a person or an object. It is often used to show a character's emotions or reactions. • A **reaction shot** shows a character responding in some way to what he or she sees. • A **low-angle shot,** in which the camera looks up at the subject, can help create the impression of height or distance.	
Editing The careful selection and arrangement of shots is called **editing.** Moviemakers put shots together in ways that help you follow the action of a story or show relationships between place and events.	• Single shots, when put together, can form a **sequence.** For example, a shot of someone tossing a ball, a shot of the same ball in mid-air, and then a shot of someone catching the ball fit together to form a complete action. • Look for shots that set up a cause-and-effect sequence. In movies with lots of actions, these shots add excitement.	
Sound Techniques Moviemakers use **sound** to make a setting or action believable. In addition, sound techniques can affect the audience's emotions as events unfold.	• Listen to the **sounds,** which in a movie consist of **music, sound effects,** and **dialogue.** • Be aware of what **sound effects** add to images. Seeing a flash of lightning is one thing, but hearing the clap of thunder helps viewers experience the setting and react to it.	

Viewing Guide for
Back to the Future

At this point in the movie, Marty has realized that his presence in the past has caused a disturbance in time. He has found Dr. Brown, who is 30 years younger, and convinced the inventor to help. If Marty can't leave the year 1955 within the next few minutes, his family will lose its place in the future. He and Doc make speedy preparations in the middle of a lightning storm. As they say their goodbyes, Marty feels he must take a moment to share some important information.

Watch the clip several times. Take as much time as you need to see the events unfold and to spot different visual and sound techniques. Use these questions to help you.

NOW VIEW

FIRST VIEWING: Comprehension

1. **Summarize** What has to happen for the time machine to leave 1955?

2. **Recall** What does Doc do with the information from Marty?

CLOSE VIEWING: Media Literacy

3. **Analyze Camera Shots** The director uses many **low-angle shots** to show Doc at work at the top of the clock tower. How do the low-angle shots help you believe Doc is in danger?

4. **Analyze Sound** Identify at least three **sound effects** that add excitement to the scene.

5. **Analyze Techniques** The clip from *Back to the Future* includes many shots of clocks—both old-fashioned and digital. Why do you think the director uses so many shots that focus on the time?

Write or Discuss

Evaluate the Film Clip In this lesson, you've explored several moviemaking techniques that are used to spark an audience's imagination. Consider the clip from *Back to the Future*. How close did you come to believing the amazing events? Give at least two reasons for your response. Think about

- how you reacted to the events at your first viewing
- how well the moviemakers use such techniques as camera shots and music and other sounds to create excitement

Produce Your Own Media

Storyboard a Race Against Time A **storyboard** is a device used to plan the shooting of a movie. A storyboard is made up of drawings and brief descriptions of what is happening in each shot of a scene. The drawings of a storyboard help moviemakers visualize how a finished scene might look before the scene is filmed. Create a storyboard for a part of the *Back to the Future* clip that you think shows a tense moment. Work with a partner to decide what part of the clip to present.

HERE'S HOW Here are two suggestions for making the storyboard:

- Show what happens in four to six individual frames.
- Show Marty and Doc's race against time. Include a shot or two that includes their quick actions.

STUDENT MODEL

Shot 1
Marty is speeding down the street.

Shot 2
The hand moves on the clock.

Shot 3
Lightning strikes the tower.

Shot 4
An electrical current moves down the cable.

Shot 5
Doc connects the cables in time.

Shot 6
The car and the current make contact!

COMMON CORE

RL 7 Analyze the effects of techniques unique to [a] medium (e.g., lighting, sound, color, or camera focus and angles in a film). SL 5 Include visual displays in presentations.

Media Tools

Go to thinkcentral.com.
KEYWORD: HML7-157

Tech Tip

Try using a computer drawing program to make the frames for the storyboard.

The Unnatural Course of Time
Movie Review

Use with the *Back to the Future* Media Study, page 154.

COMMON CORE

RI 1 Cite several pieces of textual evidence to support analysis of what the text says explicitly.
RI 6 Determine an author's point of view in a text and analyze how the author distinguishes his opinion.

What's the Connection?

Did you enjoy the film clip from *Back to the Future?* Find out what Daniel Briney thought of the entire film by reading his movie review, "The Unnatural Course of Time."

Standards Focus: Analyze a Writer's Position

If someone were to say, "That was a great movie! Go see it!" you might ask, "What's it about?" and "What makes it so good?"

When you run across a movie review, read to find out the reviewer's opinion of the film. But don't stop there. Read on to learn specific reasons and evidence for the reviewer's opinion. Then you can decide whether you might agree.

You can usually find the writer's opinion, or **position**, stated in the first paragraph. In the following review, Daniel Briney uses the first paragraph to express his position on the film. He writes

> *Back to the Future* is a thoughtful, beautifully crafted fantasy that maintains a joyous momentum from beginning to end. The movie succeeds so magnificently in everything it sets out to do as to be an absolutely perfect motion picture.

Now you know Briney's position. As you read the rest of his review and learn more about his position, complete the chart.

Briney's Position	Specific Reasons and Evidence
The movie is "thoughtful."	"Fox's Marty McFly is a genuine kid, with genuine fears for his future."
The movie is a "beautifully crafted fantasy."	All the characters and events affect one another in important ways.
The movie "maintains a joyous momentum from beginning to end."	
The movie succeeds "magnificently in everything it sets out to do."	
The movie is "an absolutely perfect motion picture."	

The Unnatural Course of Time

Review by **Daniel Briney**

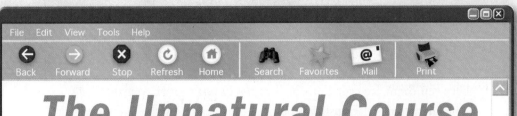

Back to the Future is a thoughtful, beautifully crafted fantasy that maintains a joyous momentum from beginning to end. The movie succeeds so magnificently in everything it sets out to do as to be an absolutely perfect motion picture. **A**

Its hero is Marty McFly (Michael J. Fox), an average American 17-year-old of the '80s—filled with youthful hopes for his future, and fearful that they may not come to pass. . . . One night,
10 an encounter with his friend Dr. Emmett L. Brown's (Christopher Lloyd) time machine throws Marty into a struggle for his very existence. . . . He's deposited in the year 1955, where his home town Hill Valley is cleaner and brighter, Doc Brown is a younger man only beginning to probe the fourth dimension, and Marty's own parents are high school students with their whole lives before them. . . . But by coming to the past, Marty has accidentally altered something with profound ramifications for his future: his parents' first meeting. A photo of Marty and his siblings, whose images are fading away one by one, is an ominous sign of what this turn of events means. Of course, if his parents never meet and fall in love, he can never
20 be born. . . . Marty has exactly a week to somehow bring them together, or be erased for all time. **B**

Fox's Marty McFly is a genuine kid, with genuine fears for his future— and as we are introduced to the other members of his family, failures all, his otherwise-normal teenage anxieties take on a greater urgency. . . . It's in this context that his friendship with Doc Brown makes such perfect sense.

Fox and Lloyd both turn in outstanding performances here—the personalities of these two and the excellent comic and dramatic chemistry

F **OCUS ON FORM**
"The Unnatural Course of Time" is a **movie review,** a short essay in which a writer presents and supports his or her opinions about a movie.

A **ANALYZE A WRITER'S POSITION**
Judging by his opening paragraph, what do you expect Daniel Briney to discuss in the rest of the review?

B **MOVIE REVIEW**
A movie review usually gives a short description of the movie's main plot and conflict. Briefly summarize Briney's description of *Back to the Future.*

COMMON CORE RI 6

C **ANALYZE A WRITER'S POSITION**

Remember that a writer's position is supported by reasons and evidence. In a film review, the writer will provide evidence from the film to support a position. Reread lines 22–28. What observations does Briney make to support his opinion that the film is "an absolutely perfect motion picture"? Add these to your chart.

D **ANALYZE A WRITER'S POSITION**

Part of Briney's position is that the film maintains momentum. Reread lines 49–54. What does Briney say in this paragraph that supports this idea? Add your answer to your chart. What words and phrases support this idea? Record them in your chart.

between them are crucial to *Back to the Future's* great appeal. . . . **C**
The characters' relationship is best communicated by the major conflict
30 that erupts between them: that of future knowledge. Doc is adamant
that *no one* should be allowed information about his own future, lest
that knowledge endanger the same future—just as Marty's has been
endangered. Marty faces a heart-rending decision over whether to heed
the scientist's warnings or ignore them. . . . And even if there were an
easy way to tell him, Doc won't listen. . . . In this, one of the movie's
most touching scenes, Doc rebuffs his friend's attempt to save him:

DOC: Marty, I'm going to be really sad to see you go. You've made
a real difference in my life; you've given me something to shoot for.
Just *knowing* that I'm going to be around to see *1985,* that I'm going
40 to succeed in *this,* that I'm going to have a chance to travel through time
. . . It's going to be really hard waiting thirty years before I can talk
to you about everything that's happened in the past few days. I'm really
going to miss you, Marty.

MARTY: I'm really going to miss you. (*a beat*) Doc, *about* the future . . .

DOC: *No!* Marty, we've already agreed that having information about
the future can be extremely dangerous! Even if your intentions are *good,*
it can backfire drastically. Marty, whatever you have to tell me, I'll find
out through the natural course of *time.*

Of course, the film deserves a great deal of praise for its action
50 sequences, most of which feature the bizarrely modified, impossibly cool
DeLorean time machine. There is a great deal of excitement in Marty's . . .
pursuit through the town square by an enraged bully, and a superbly
realized, adrenaline-fueled climax in which Doc Brown dangles
precipitously from the courthouse clock tower. . . . **D**

But it is *Back to the Future's* ultimate message—that we can change our
lives for the better—that is at the very heart of its enormous success. . . .

Back to the Future is a unique coming-of-age story that hits every mark
in spectacular fashion and leaves us not only thoroughly entertained, but
heartened. We don't need to believe in real-life time machines for it to
60 successfully remind us that all things are possible—and that we are our
own second chances.

Comprehension

1. **Recall** What does Daniel Briney say is the main message of *Back to the Future?*

2. **Summarize** In his movie review, Briney includes a touching scene between Doc and Marty. Summarize what happens in this scene.

Text Analysis

● 3. **Examine a Movie Review** Reread the notes next to the movie review. Besides providing a writer's opinions of a movie and support for those opinions, what else does a movie review usually provide? Tell why you think this might be helpful to a reader.

● 4. **Analyze a Writer's Position** Review the chart you completed. Does Briney support each part of his position? Explain.

COMMON CORE

RI 1 Cite several pieces of textual evidence to support analysis of what the text says explicitly. **RI 6** Determine an author's point of view in a text and analyze how the author distinguishes his opinion. **W 2a** Organize ideas using comparison/contrast.

Read for Information: Compare and Contrast

WRITING PROMPT

In the review you just read, Daniel Briney describes the clock-tower scene as "a superbly realized, adrenaline-fueled climax" (lines 52–53). Do you agree with his opinion of this scene? In a paragraph, compare and contrast your opinion of this scene with Briney's.

To answer this prompt, first decide on your own opinion of the clock-tower scene by jotting it down. Then follow these steps:

1. Use a Venn diagram to record your opinion and Daniel Briney's.

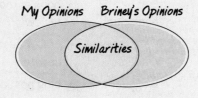

2. Look at your diagram to see whether there are more similarities or more differences.

3. In a sentence, tell whether your opinion and Briney's are very similar or quite different. Then support the sentence by pointing out the specific similarities and differences.

4. If your opinion of the clock-tower scene is very different from Briney's, consider explaining the reasons for your opinion.

Writing Workshop
ARGUMENT

Supporting an Opinion

Why do some stories grab you and never let go? This unit is filled with great stories told in fiction, nonfiction, poetry, drama, and even movies. In this workshop, you will choose one of these stories or another personal favorite. You will craft a skilled argument that answers the question: What makes this story such a page-turner?

 Complete the workshop activities in your **Reader/Writer Notebook.**

WRITE WITH A PURPOSE

WRITING TASK

Pick a story that's memorable to you. Which element is most responsible for making the story so unforgettable? Write an **argument** that persuades readers to agree with your viewpoint.

Idea Starters
- the ending of "The Dinner Party"
- Victor's conflict in "Seventh Grade"
- the science-fiction setting in "The Last Dog"
- the suspenseful plot in the movie *Back to the Future*

THE ESSENTIALS

Here are some common purposes, audiences, and formats for writing an argument.

PURPOSES	AUDIENCES	FORMATS
• to convince readers to agree with your position • to better understand your reactions to stories	• classmates and teacher • book club • newspaper readers • blog readers and other Web users	• essay for class • book or movie review • oral discussion or debate • blog posting or online review • podcast

COMMON CORE TRAITS

1. DEVELOPMENT OF IDEAS

- includes an engaging **introduction** that states a **claim,** or position
- provides **logical reasons** and **relevant evidence** to support the claim
- acknowledges and addresses **opposing claims**
- offers a **concluding section** that supports the claim

2. ORGANIZATION OF IDEAS

- **organizes** reasons and evidence in a **logical way**
- uses **transitions** to create cohesion and show the relationships among claims, reasons, and evidence

3. LANGUAGE FACILITY AND CONVENTIONS

- maintains a **formal style**
- uses **modifiers** correctly
- reflects correct **grammar, mechanics,** and **spelling**

Writing Online

THINK central

Go to **thinkcentral.com.**
KEYWORD: HML7N-988

Planning/Prewriting

COMMON CORE

W 1a–e Write arguments to support claims with clear reasons and relevant evidence. **W 5** Develop and strengthen writing by planning. **W 9a (RL 1)** Draw evidence from literary texts to support analysis; cite textual evidence.

Getting Started

CHOOSE A GREAT STORY

Recall the stories you have read in this unit or outside of school. Which ones have made a lasting impression on you? Jot down their titles. For each story, think about the element—plot, setting, or conflict, for example—that most affected your response. Ask yourself: Why is that element so important to the story? Scan your list, and choose a story about which you have the strongest opinion.

▶ WHAT DOES IT LOOK LIKE?

Favorite Stories	What's So Great About Them?
• "Seventh Grade"	• Victor has conflicts that are easy to relate to; the stuff he goes through is funny, too.
• "The Dinner Party"	• Loved the surprise ending!
• Stargirl	• Deals with conflicts that have to do with fitting in. I can relate.

FORMULATE A CLAIM

A solid argument is based on a **claim** that you can prove with **reasons** and **evidence.** Your claim should guide your argument; every detail you include in your writing should support this statement. If you find that your claim can't be supported well, then you should rework it or try a new approach.

▶ WHAT DOES IT LOOK LIKE?

Claim: The most important ingredient in Gary Soto's "Seventh Grade" is a conflict that every middle-schooler can relate to: trying to impress someone you like without making a fool of yourself.

THINK ABOUT AUDIENCE AND PURPOSE

Even this early in the writing process, you should consider your **audience**—the specific group of people you are trying to persuade. They may not share your opinion, so the **purpose** of your argument is to convince them you are right. As you plan, draft, and later revise, you will have to consider what words and details will persuade your audience to accept your claim.

▶ ASK YOURSELF:

- Do I expect my audience to agree with my claim?
- What other opinions might readers have?
- What details can I include to persuade my audience to agree with my claim?
- How much do my readers already know about my chosen story?

Planning/Prewriting *continued*

Getting Started

IDENTIFY SUPPORT

A strong argument includes solid **reasons** that tell why you believe what you do. Each reason should be backed up with specific **evidence** that is **relevant,** or closely related to that reason. Try to include a variety of evidence.

- **anecdotes**—brief, personal stories
- **quotations**—direct statements from the literary text
- **examples**—instances of an idea or situation
- **informal polls**—surveys of people that result in **statistics** to support your points

▶ WHAT DOES IT LOOK LIKE?

Reason
Most middle-school readers can relate to Victor's conflicts, which makes the story all the more memorable.

Supporting Evidence
Victor says, "La me vave me con le grandma," pretending he can speak French. I can relate to this humiliating situation. When my family traveled to Mexico, I kept saying "Cama see ohma" because I thought that was what other people were saying. (anecdote)

CONSIDER OPPOSING CLAIMS

You've probably heard people say, "There are two sides to every argument." You may not want to acknowledge that other people have different opinions; if you do, however, your audience will take your ideas more seriously. You have to address **opposing claims** directly and counter them point-by-point. When you do this, you will earn respect for your claim by showing that it can stand on its own against differing opinions.

▶ TIP

Complete these sentences to help you determine how to respond to other viewpoints.

- My audience is likely to think that _____ is the most important element in this story.

- I disagree with this viewpoint because _____ .

- My audience should consider my claim instead because _____ .

PEER REVIEW Share your working claim with a classmate who is familiar with the story you chose. Ask: What reasons and evidence can I include to address alternate viewpoints?

 YOUR TURN In your *Reader/Writer Notebook,* outline your writing plan. Record your claim, reasons, and evidence. Finally, write one opposing claim readers could have, and note how you will respond.

Drafting

The following chart shows how to draft a clear and concise argument.

COMMON CORE

W 1c Use words, phrases, and clauses to create cohesion and clarify the relationships among claim(s), reasons, and evidence. **W 4** Produce clear and coherent writing appropriate to task, purpose, and audience.

Organizing Your Argument

INTRODUCTION

- Introduce your topic to your **audience** with an engaging **question** or a relevant **anecdote.**
- Identify the **title** and **author** of the **literary text** you will be discussing.
- State your **claim** with confidence.

▼

BODY

- Present your **reasons** and **evidence** in the most **logical** order. You could start with your most important or compelling reason, or else end with it.
- Use **transitions** to clarify the relationships among your claim, reasons, and evidence.
- Acknowledge at least one **opposing claim.** Respond with reasons and evidence that show your claim is stronger than the opposing viewpoint.
- Establish and maintain a **formal style** by using an assured tone (attitude) and by avoiding overly casual language.

▼

CONCLUDING SECTION

- Restate your **claim** in different words.
- End with a powerful **quotation, question,** or **insight** that follows from your argument.

GRAMMAR IN CONTEXT: USING TRANSITIONS

Transitions are words and phrases that link your claim, reasons, and evidence so that your argument is **cohesive**—smooth and easy to follow. Examples of transitions that create cohesion include *one reason, another reason, however, furthermore, for example,* and *although.*

Type of Transition	Example
Word ▶	Gary Soto uses humor to describe some all-too-familiar conflicts. **Consequently**, many seventh-grade readers are likely to remember this story.
Phrase ▶	Readers are drawn to stories about characters with problems similar to their own. **For this reason**, most teens will love Soto's story.

YOUR TURN Develop a first draft of your argument, following the plan outlined in the chart above. Make sure you include several transitions to show the relationships among your ideas.

Revising

In the revising stage, you evaluate the development, organization, and style of your argument. Use this chart to help you revise and rewrite the parts of your argument that need improvement.

ARGUMENT

Ask Yourself	Tips	Revision Strategies
1. Does my introduction capture my audience's attention? Does it clearly state my claim?	▶ Put **parentheses** around the phrases or sentences that will grab your audience's attention. **Underline** your claim.	▶ **Add** an attention-grabbing anecdote or question. If necessary, **add** a claim or **revise** your existing one to state your opinion more clearly.
2. Does my introduction identify the title and author of the story? Does it provide necessary background information?	▶ **Bracket** the title and author of the story. **Highlight** any background information about the text.	▶ **Add** the title and author of the work. **Add** background information for readers who are unfamiliar with the story.
3. Do I include at least two logical reasons to support my claim? Do I include relevant evidence to back up each reason?	▶ Put an *R* above each reason you give. **Put an *E*** above sentences that provide evidence to support the reasons.	▶ **Add** reasons if your argument lacks enough support. **Replace** weak evidence with quotations, anecdotes, or examples that are more relevant to your reasons.
4. Do I acknowledge and respond to opposing or alternate claims?	▶ **Place a star** beside any opposing claims. **Circle** your response to each.	▶ **Add** a mention of an opposing claim. **Include** a response to counter that alternate claim.
5. Does my concluding section restate my claim? Does it offer a question or an anecdote for readers to consider?	▶ **Underline** your restated claim. **Highlight** the question or anecdote that persuades readers to consider your opinion.	▶ **Add** a restatement of your claim. **Add** a question or anecdote to emphasize the strength of your viewpoint.
6. Have I established and maintained a formal style?	▶ **Circle** any slang or other informal language.	▶ **Revise** to use precise language suited to your audience and purpose.

YOUR TURN

PEER REVIEW Have a peer review your draft. Ask each question in the chart to decide which parts need reworking or a new approach.

ANALYZE A STUDENT DRAFT

Read this student's draft and the comments about it as a model for revising your own argument.

COMMON CORE

W 1b Support claim(s) with relevant evidence. **W 5** Strengthen writing by revising, editing, rewriting, or trying a new approach, focusing on how well purpose and audience have been addressed.

Humiliation and "Seventh Grade"

by Christopher Fong, Randolph Intermediate School

❶   What do we seventh-graders have in common? Many of us wake up tired, race to school before the bell, try to keep up in class, and hang out with friends at lunch. Admit it, though. There's something else that unites us. For many of us, it's hard to get through a single day without embarrassing ourselves. In Gary Soto's short story "Seventh Grade," Victor has many humiliating conflicts as he tries to impress a girl he likes. These conflicts are most responsible for making Soto's story so unforgettable.

❷   Victor's conflicts are the most important ingredient in the story because they are easy to relate to. After all, who hasn't tried to impress someone and ended up looking like a complete moron? Most of my closest friends— myself included—have been in similar situations, usually because we tried to look cooler or smarter in order to impress someone. The story is hilarious because most of us can relate to Victor's embarrassment.

> Christopher grabs his audience's attention with a **relevant question.**

> He clearly states his **claim** and prepares his readers for the reasons and evidence that follow.

> Christopher includes an **anecdote** to support one reason. He could strengthen his point by including a quotation from the story that relates to his anecdote.

LEARN HOW Use Quotations as Evidence Christopher offers his strongest reason first—that Victor's conflicts are the most important element because they are so easy to relate to. While Christopher includes a personal anecdote to support this reason, he does not incorporate a relevant quotation from the story to strengthen his point. Notice how Christopher's revision helps the audience better understand one conflict Victor faces, as well as the character's resulting humiliation.

CHRISTOPHER'S REVISION TO PARAGRAPH ❷

Victor's conflicts are the most important ingredient in the story because they are easy to relate to. After all, who hasn't tried to impress someone and ended up looking like a complete moron?

For instance, in the story, Victor raises his hand in class and pretends to know French. He then has to fake his way out of this conflict by making up an answer that sounds French. As Victor admits to himself, "He … wished he could start his life over. He had never been so embarrassed."

❸   There is another reason that may not be so obvious but helps the reader to understand that the humorous conflicts are the most important element in "Seventh Grade." If Gary Soto had not included these conflicts in the first place, the story would be boring. The story would be reduced to a snapshot of a seventh-grade student going through the motions of an uneventful day.

> This reason is not clearly stated. To make his ideas more precise, Christopher needs to **eliminate wordiness.**

❹   Some might argue that the happy ending for readers is what makes "Seventh Grade" memorable. At the end of the story, Victor's teacher Mr. Bueller saves his student from extreme humiliation. This prompts Teresa to be really impressed by Victor, who happily concludes that he is "going to like seventh grade." Yet we all know that happy endings like these don't always occur in real life. Instead, this story is comforting for another reason—it reminds us that we're not alone in dealing with life's many humiliations. Whether we are trying too hard to impress someone or wishing we could take back a dumb comment, we could probably find others who have made similar mistakes. Who among us hasn't been in situations as embarrassing as those Victor faces? Isn't that universal conflict why Soto's story "speaks" to us?

> Christopher acknowledges an **opposing claim** and counters it with a sensible reason.

LEARN HOW **Eliminate Wordiness** In his third paragraph, Christopher introduces another reason to support his claim. However, he uses more words than are necessary to communicate his point. This **wordiness** weakens the impact of his argument. His audience has to wade through unnecessary words to make sense of his ideas. Notice how Christopher tightens his argument and makes it more concise.

CHRISTOPHER'S REVISION TO PARAGRAPH ❸

~~There is~~ another reason ^proves^ ~~that may not be so obvious but helps the reader to understand~~ that the humorous conflicts are the most important element in "Seventh Grade."

YOUR TURN Rework your essay using the revision strategies you've learned, as well as the feedback you've received from your peers and your teacher. If some parts of your argument remain confusing even after revision, try a fresh approach to win over your audience.

COMMON CORE

W 5 Strengthen writing by revising and editing. **L 1c** Correct misplaced and dangling modifiers. **L 2b** Spell correctly. **L 3a** Recognize and eliminate wordiness.

Editing and Publishing

As you edit, look for errors in grammar that make your argument sound awkward or confusing. Also, check that you haven't incorrectly used any commonly confused words, such as *to/too, affect/effect,* and *their/there/they're.* A spell-checker won't tell you whether you've used the correct word.

GRAMMAR IN CONTEXT: MISPLACED AND DANGLING MODIFIERS

When you write an argument, make sure to place modifiers as near as possible to the words or phrases they describe. Otherwise, you may introduce grammatical problems that can prevent your audience from tracking your ideas. Here are two common problems with modifiers:

Type of Modifier Problem	Example	Revision
A **misplaced modifier** modifies the wrong word in a sentence.	▶ People stared at Victor as they passed him in the hall **strangely.**	▶ People stared at Victor strangely as they passed him in the hall.
A **dangling modifier** does not clearly modify another word or word group in a sentence.	▶ **While trying to impress Teresa,** the situation got even more embarrassing.	▶ While trying to impress Teresa, Victor became more and more embarrassed.

As Christopher edited his argument, he identified a misplaced modifier. He corrected his error with the following revision:

> Some might argue that the happy ending for readers is what makes "Seventh Grade" memorable.

PUBLISH YOUR WRITING

Share your argument with an audience and make your viewpoint known.
- E-mail your essay to other students who have read the story you chose.
- As a class, create a blog on which students write arguments about literature. Edit your essay into a brief online posting that you upload for other readers to discuss and debate.
- Adapt your essay into a persuasive podcast that others can download.

YOUR TURN Proofread your essay carefully to eliminate any errors in grammar and spelling. Make sure your modifiers are properly placed. Read for wordiness and redundancy, and revise as needed.

Scoring Rubric

Use the rubric below to evaluate your argument from the Writing Workshop or your response to the on-demand writing task on the next page.

ARGUMENT

SCORE	COMMON CORE TRAITS
6	• **Development** Confidently asserts a clear claim; supports the claim with logical reasons and relevant evidence; effectively addresses opposing claims; ends with a strong, memorable concluding section • **Organization** Arranges reasons and evidence in a persuasive, logical order; uses transitions to create cohesion and link ideas • **Language** Consistently maintains a formal style; shows a strong command of conventions (grammar, mechanics, and spelling)
5	• **Development** Competently states a claim; offers mostly logical reasons and relevant evidence; addresses opposing claims; ends with a strong concluding section • **Organization** Organizes reasons and evidence logically; uses transitions to link ideas • **Language** Maintains a formal style; has a few errors in conventions
4	• **Development** States a claim; needs more evidence for reasons; does not thoroughly address opposing claims; has an adequate concluding section • **Organization** Has a logical organization; could use a few more transitions • **Language** Mostly maintains a formal style; includes a few distracting errors in conventions
3	• **Development** Has a claim that does not clearly state a position; provides some reasons that lack logic or evidence; mentions other viewpoints, but does not respond to them; has a concluding section that repeats ideas • **Organization** Reflects some flaws in organization; needs more transitions • **Language** Often lapses into an informal style; has several distracting errors in conventions
2	• **Development** Has a weak claim; offers illogical reasons and little evidence; ignores other viewpoints; introduces unrelated ideas in the concluding section • **Organization** Has organizational flaws; lacks transitions throughout • **Language** Uses an informal style; has many distracting errors in conventions
1	• **Development** Lacks a claim; offers little, if any, support; ignores opposing viewpoints; has no concluding section • **Organization** Has no organization or transitions • **Language** Uses an inappropriate style; has major problems with conventions

Preparing for Timed Writing

COMMON CORE

W 10 Write routinely over shorter time frames for a range of tasks, purposes, and audiences.

---

1. ANALYZE THE TASK   5 MIN

Read the task carefully. Then read it again, underlining words that tell the topic, the audience, and the purpose. Circle the type of writing you are being asked to do.

> **WRITING TASK**
>
> *Audience*   *Topic*
>
> Write an (argument) to convince frequent movie-goers why a particular movie is the best
> of the year. Make sure you provide reasons and evidence to support your claim. → *Purpose*

---

2. PLAN YOUR RESPONSE   10 MIN

Think about movies you've seen this year, and choose your favorite. Then, jot down your claim. Ask yourself: Why is this movie so compelling? The answer will help you formulate your reasons. For each reason, identify specific scenes or examples that you could use as evidence. Lastly, think about what other viewers could say in criticizing your choice. Record these details in a chart like the one shown.

Reasons	Evidence
Possible Opposing Claims	

---

3. RESPOND TO THE TASK   20 MIN

As you write your argument, keep these guidelines in mind:
- In the introduction, grab readers' attention with an interesting quotation, example, or anecdote. Then, clearly state your claim.
- In the body, support your argument with logical reasons and relevant evidence.
- Be sure to acknowledge an opposing claim and respond to it.
- In the concluding section, offer a thought-provoking question to ponder.

---

4. IMPROVE YOUR RESPONSE   5–10 MIN

Revising Compare your draft to the task. Is your argument clearly organized? Do logical reasons prove your claim? Is each piece of evidence relevant to the reason it supports?

Proofreading After you correct any errors in grammar, spelling, punctuation, and capitalization, make sure your work is neat and legible.

Checking Your Final Copy Read your essay once more to find any errors you missed.

Creating a Persuasive Podcast

Thanks to modern technology, it has become much easier to share your opinion with a wide audience. You might post your persuasive writing on a blog, create a documentary that you upload to a video-sharing site, or produce a podcast for people to download. A **podcast** is a short broadcast that uses images and sound to communicate information. Podcasts can be transmitted and stored on portable media devices. In this workshop, you will reformat your argument as a podcast.

 Complete the workshop activities in your **Reader/Writer Notebook**.

PRODUCE WITH A PURPOSE	COMMON CORE TRAITS
TASK Adapt your argument into a **persuasive podcast.** Use voice-over narration, as well as images and video, to entertain and persuade your audience.	**A SUCCESSFUL PODCAST . . .** • presents a focused, coherent argument • uses sound features, such as voice-over narration; also includes easy-to-read text and graphics • has an inviting and appropriate design • flows smoothly from one visual or audio effect to another • uses media to clarify and emphasize reasons and evidence

COMMON CORE

W 6 Use technology to produce writing and collaborate with others. **SL 4** Present claims and findings; use adequate volume and clear pronunciation. **SL 5** Include multimedia to clarify claims and findings. **SL 6** Adapt speech to a variety of contexts and tasks.

Planning Your Podcast

Your written essay used words to convey meaning. In your podcast, you will use graphics, images, music, and other audio features to make your point.

• **Focus Your Argument** Outline the most important points in your argument. Consider which parts of your writing could work as voice-over narration, and include that text in your outline. Then, consider any audio features and visuals that might support what you are saying.

• **Collect Multimedia Elements** Search for items that could add interest to your argument and help your audience understand your ideas. Consider including music or images with appropriate themes. Collect sound effects and any voice-over narration that you want to use. Be sure to respect copyright laws and use only music and images for which you have permission.

• **Shoot Video Clips** Have your friends act out short scenes from the story that you used as evidence in your argument. Another option is to film other students presenting opposing claims, or alternate arguments. You could then disprove those other viewpoints.

Media Tools

THINK central

Go to thinkcentral.com.
KEYWORD: HML7N-998

Producing a Podcast

Use these tips to create the content of your podcast and then produce it.

- **Chart Your Podcast** In a three-column chart, match the script of your argument with your visual and audio effects.

Voice-over Narration	Graphic Features	Audio Features
The story is hilarious because most of us can relate to Victor's embarrassment.	Video clip of student (Victor) raising his hand and then looking embarrassed in front of girl student and teacher.	Mr. Bueller: Does anyone know French? Victor: La me vave me con le grandma.

- **Produce Your Podcast** Use your chart to assemble all your components. Use podcasting software to guide your production. (Ask your teacher or librarian for help finding a free podcasting service.)

- **Edit Your Podcast** Review your material. Use this checklist as your guide:

  √ Check the timing. Is the pace of the narration too fast to understand or too slow to hold your audience's interest? Do pictures and sound effects match the narration of the argument?

  √ Are the tone and formality of the narration appropriate for your audience and your purpose? Is everything pronounced clearly?

  √ Review your audio and visual effects. Do they add to the presentation or distract from it? Are the audio effects at an adequate volume?

- **Upload the Final Product** Ask your school's technology specialist to help you get your podcast up and running. Advertise your podcast among your friends so they can download it.

YOUR TURN Plan and produce an entertaining podcast that presents your argument. Use the guidelines on these pages to help you. Once you've posted your podcast, ask a peer to download it and critique it.

Assessment Practice

DIRECTIONS Read this selection and answer the questions that follow.

Papa's Parrot   *by Cynthia Rylant*

1   Though his father was fat and merely owned a candy and nut shop, Henry Tillian liked his papa. Harry stopped liking candy and nuts when he was around seven, but, in spite of this, he and Mr. Tillian had remained friends and were still friends in the year Harry turned twelve.

2   For years, after school, Harry had always stopped in to see his father at work. Many of Harry's friends stopped there, too, to spend a few cents choosing penny candy from the giant bins or to sample Mr. Tillian's latest batch of roasted peanuts. Mr. Tillian looked forward to seeing his son and his son's friends every day. He liked the company.

3   When Harry entered junior high school, though, he didn't come by the candy and nut shop as often. Nor did his friends. They were older and they had more spending money. They went to a burger place. They played video games. They shopped for records. None of them were much interested in candy and nuts anymore.

4   A new group of children came to Mr. Tillian's shop now. But not Harry Tillian and his friends.

5   The year Harry turned twelve was also the year Mr. Tillian got a parrot. He went to a pet store one day and bought one for more money than he could really afford. He brought the parrot to his shop, set its cage near a sign for maple clusters and named it Rocky.

6   Harry thought this was the strangest thing his father had ever done, and he told him so, but Mr. Tillian just ignored him.

7   Rocky was good company for Mr. Tillian. When business was slow, Mr. Tillian would turn on a small color television he had sitting in a corner, and he and Rocky would watch the soap operas. Rocky liked to scream when the romantic music came on, and Mr. Tillian would yell at him to shut up, but they seemed to enjoy themselves.

8   The more Mr. Tillian grew to like his parrot, and the more he talked to it instead of to people, the more embarrassed Harry became. Harry would stroll past the shop, on his way somewhere else, and he'd take a quick look inside to see what his dad was doing. Mr. Tillian was always talking to the bird. So Harry kept walking.

9   At home things were different. Harry and his father joked with each other at the dinner table as they always had—Mr. Tillian teasing Harry

about his smelly socks; Harry teasing Mr. Tillian about his blubbery stomach. At home things seemed all right.

10   But one day, Mr. Tillian became ill. He had been at work, unpacking boxes of caramels, when he had grabbed his chest and fallen over on top of the candy. A customer had found him, and he was taken to the hospital in an ambulance.

11   Mr. Tillian couldn't leave the hospital. He lay in bed, tubes in his arms, and he worried about his shop. New shipments of candy and nuts would be arriving. Rocky would be hungry. Who would take care of things?

12   Harry said he would. Harry told his father that he would go to the store every day after school and unpack boxes. He would sort out all the candy and nuts. He would even feed Rocky.

13   So, the next morning, while Mr. Tillian lay in his hospital bed, Harry took the shop key to school with him. After school he left his friends and walked to the empty shop alone. In all the days of his life, Harry had never seen the shop closed after school. Harry didn't even remember what the CLOSED sign looked like. The key stuck in the lock three times, and inside he had to search all the walls for the light switch.

14   The shop was as his father had left it. Even the caramels were still spilled on the floor. Harry bent down and picked them up one by one, dropping them back in the boxes. The bird in its cage watched him silently.

15   Harry opened the new boxes his father hadn't gotten to. Peppermints. Jawbreakers. Toffee creams. Strawberry kisses. Harry traveled from bin to bin, putting the candies where they belonged.

16   "Hello!"

17   Harry jumped, spilled a box of jawbreakers.

18   "Hello, Rocky!"

19   Harry stared at the parrot. He had forgotten it was there. The bird had been so quiet, and Harry had been thinking only of the candy.

20   "Hello," Harry said.

21   "Hello, Rocky!" answered the parrot.

22   Harry walked slowly over to the cage. The parrot's food cup was empty. It's water was dirty. The bottom of the cage was a mess.

23   Harry carried the cage into the back room.

24   "Hello, Rocky!"

25   "Is that all you can say, you dumb bird?" Harry mumbled. The bird said nothing else.

GO ON ➡

26   Harry cleaned the bottom of the cage, refilled the food and water cups, then put the cage back in its place and resumed sorting the candy.

27   "Where's Harry?"

28   Harry looked up.

29   "Where's Harry?"

30   Harry stared at the parrot.

31   "Where's Harry?"

32   Chills ran down Harry's back. What could the bird mean? It was like something from *The Twilight Zone.*

33   "Where's Harry?"

34   Harry swallowed and said, "I'm here. I'm here, you stupid bird."

35   "You stupid bird!" said the parrot.

36   Well, at least he's got one thing straight, thought Harry.

37   "Miss him! Miss him! Where's Harry? You stupid bird!"

38   Harry stood with a handful of peppermints.

39   *"What?"* he asked.

40   "Where's Harry?" said the parrot.

41   "I'm *here,* you stupid bird! I'm here!" Harry yelled. He threw the peppermints at the cage, and the bird screamed and clung to its perch.

42   Harry sobbed, "I'm here." The tears were coming.

43   Harry leaned over the glass counter.

44   "Papa." Harry buried his face in his arms.

45   "Where's Harry?" repeated the bird.

46   Harry signed and wiped his face on his sleeve. He watched the parrot. He understood now: someone had been saying, for a long time, "Where's Harry? Miss him."

47   Harry finished his unpacking, then swept the floor of the shop. He checked the furnace so the bird wouldn't get cold. Then he left to go visit his papa.

Reading Comprehension

Use "Papa's Parrot" to answer questions 1–10.

1. Most of the story takes place at the —

    A. Tillian home   **C.** hospital

    B. candy shop   **D.** pet store

2. When does the conflict in the story begin?

    A. Harry's father buys a parrot.

    B. Rocky screams at the television.

    C. Harry turns twelve years old.

    D. Rocky says, "Where's Harry?"

3. The author probably starts the story when Harry is seven to show that —

   A. Harry liked visiting his father at the shop for many years

   B. Mr. Tillian became less talkative at that time

   C. Harry's friends did not like the shop

   D. Rocky changed Harry's feelings about the shop

4. Mr. Tillian's conflict is that —

   A. his parrot argues with him

   B. he does not like birds

   C. his store is losing money

   D. he misses his son's company

5. When does Mr. Tillian buy the parrot?

   A. When Harry and his school friends visit the nut shop

   B. When he first buys the candy and nut shop

   C. After he gets sick and has to go to the hospital

   D. After Harry stops visiting the shop every day

6. Harry's conflict is caused by his —

   A. embarrassment about his father

   B. dislike of candy

   C. unhappiness with his friends

   D. desire to work after school

7. The climax of the story occurs when —

   A. Harry and his friends stop visiting the store

   B. Mr. Tillian buys a parrot to keep himself company

   C. the parrot watches television with Mr. Tillian

   D. Harry realizes that his father has been lonely

SHORT CONSTRUCTED RESPONSE
Write two or three sentences to answer each question.

   8. Why are Harry's friends less interested in the shop after they turn twelve?

   9. Why can Harry and his father joke together at home but not at the store?

Write a paragraph to answer this question.

10. Discuss how the parrot brings about the climax of the story. What does Harry learn about his father when he takes care of the shop and Rocky?

GO ON ➡

Vocabulary

> Use your knowledge of context clues and the Latin word root definitions to answer the following questions.

1. The Latin word *ambulare* means "to go about." Which word from the story comes from *ambulare*?

   A. Ambulance

   B. Business

   C. Caramels

   D. Customer

2. The Latin word *hospes* means "guest." Which word from the story comes from *hospes*?

   A. Company

   B. Friends

   C. Home

   D. Hospital

3. The Latin word *fornax* means "oven." Which word from the story comes from *fornax*?

   A. Afford

   B. Food

   C. Forward

   D. Furnace

> Use context clues and your knowledge of prefixes and suffixes to answer the following questions.

4. What does the prefix *a-* mean in the word *around* in paragraph 1?

   A. In

   B. Not

   C. Under

   D. Without

5. What does the prefix *un-* mean in the word *unpacking* in paragraph 10?

   A. Again

   B. Away

   C. The opposite of

   D. Not done

6. Which suffix could change the word *music* in paragraph 7 into a word that means "skilled in music"?

   A. *-able*

   B. *-al*

   C. *-eous*

   D. *-ial*

7. Which suffix could change the word *room* in paragraph 23 into a word that means "having plenty of room"?

   A. *-ate*

   B. *-ial*

   C. *-ly*

   D. *-y*

Revising and Editing

DIRECTIONS Read this passage and answer the questions that follow.

(1) Nature can do some amazing things, sometimes, people even get to watch.
(2) In 1995, a new island formed as part of the Tonga Islands. (3) An active
volcano erupted at Metis Shoal this eruption caused a heavy flow of lava.
(4) After all the lava had bubbled up, it had built a new island. (5) Fortunately,
someone used their video camera to record this event. (6) According to many
scientists accounts, Metis Shoal had erupted before with similar results.
(7) The volcano produced new islands when they erupted in 1968 and 1979.

1. What is the BEST way to revise sentence 1?

   A. Nature can do some amazing things,
      sometimes people. Even get to watch.

   B. Nature can do some amazing things
      sometimes people even get to watch.

   C. Nature can do some amazing things
      sometimes, people; even get to watch.

   D. Nature can do some amazing things;
      sometimes, people even get to watch.

2. What is the BEST way to revise sentence 3?

   A. An active volcano erupted at Metis
      Shoal, and this eruption caused a
      heavy flow of lava.

   B. An active volcano erupted at Metis
      Shoal this eruption. Caused a heavy
      flow of lava.

   C. An active volcano erupted but at Metis
      Shoal this eruption caused a heavy
      flow of lava.

   D. An active volcano; erupted at Metis
      Shoal this eruption caused a heavy
      flow of lava.

3. What change, if any, should be made in
   sentence 5?

   A. Change *their* to **her**

   B. Change *Fortunately* to **Afterwards**

   C. Change *event* to **events'**

   D. Make no change

4. What change, if any, should be made in
   sentence 6?

   A. Change *many* to **lots of**

   B. Change *scientists* to **scientists'**

   C. Change *before* to **later**

   D. Make no change

5. What change, if any, should be made in
   sentence 7?

   A. Change *islands* to **islands'**

   B. Change *when* to **before**

   C. Change *they* to **it**

   D. Make no change

More Great Reads

Ideas for Independent Reading

Which questions from Unit 1 made an impression on you?
Continue exploring them with these books.

COMMON CORE

RL 10 Read and comprehend literature.

How do you make a good impression?

The Ghost in the Tokaido Inn
by Dorothy Hoobler

What do you long to be? Seikei wants to be a samurai, but he knows that as a merchant's son, the chances are slim. Will Seikei achieve his life's dream? Read this award-winning book and find out.

The Great Turkey Walk
by Kathleen Karr

It is 1860. Fifteen-year-old Simon likes and respects his teacher. One day she tells him it's time he left her class to venture out into the real world. But what will become of him in the rough world of this frontier setting?

No Man's Land
by Susan Bartoletti

Fourteen-year-old Thrasher lies about his age, joins the Confederate Army, and begins his courageous adventure. Along the way, Thrasher comes to know that enemies are people too.

Who sees the best in you?

Bearstone
by Will Hobbs

A troubled Native American teen is sent to work on a ranch in the mountains of Colorado. There the elderly owner provides the steadying influence the boy needs, but complications arise.

Good Night, Mr. Tom
by Michelle Magorian

Young Willie is among thousands of children evacuated from London because of the bombing raids at the brink of World War II. When a wise old man named Mr. Tom adopts him, Willie learns to trust his world again.

Nobody's Daughter
by Susan Pfeffer

Eleven-year-old Emily is packed off to an orphanage but dreams of finding her sister, who has been adopted. Harsh reality greets her in the form of Miss Browne, the director. Whom can she turn to?

What makes you brave?

North by Night
by Katherine Ayres

This story centers on the 1850 Fugitive Slave Act. Through her letters and journal entries, 16-year-old Lucinda tells of her family's attempts to turn their Ohio farm into an Underground Railroad station.

The Dark Is Rising
by Susan Cooper

Eleven-year-old Will Stanton struggles to overcome the powers of the Dark. Will must search for the six magical signs needed in the great battle between the Dark and the Light. Can he find them in time?

The Clay Marble
By Minfong Ho

After fleeing war-torn Cambodia in 1980, Dara, her older brother, and her mother find sanctuary on the Thailand border in a refugee camp. Then fighting erupts, and Dara is separated from her family.

Get Novel Wise

THINK central

Go to **thinkcentral.com**.
KEYWORD: HML7-180

Personality Tests

ANALYZING CHARACTER AND POINT OF VIEW

- In Fiction
- In Nonfiction
- In Poetry

Share What You Know

What makes a great CHARACTER?

An eccentric inventor, an orphaned boy, and a spider—hard to imagine what these three characters have in common, isn't it? But once you know their names—Willy Wonka, Harry Potter, and Charlotte—the connection becomes clearer. All three are examples of great characters—figments of authors' imaginations that are so lifelike they seem to pop off the page and into our own world.

ACTIVITY With a partner, brainstorm a list of great characters from stories, TV shows, and movies. Then discuss the following questions:

- Why did you choose these characters? Next to each name, jot down what makes him or her (or it!) great.

- What similarities do you notice about your reasons for selecting these characters?

- On the basis of your discussion, what advice would you give a first-time author about how to create great characters?

Find It Online! **THINK** central
Go to thinkcentral.com for the interactive version of this unit.

COMMON CORE

Preview Unit Goals

TEXT ANALYSIS	• Analyze how elements of a story interact, including plot, character, and setting • Analyze how authors develop point of view, including first person, limited third person, and omniscient
READING	• Make inferences, draw conclusions, and synthesize • Provide an objective summary of a text
WRITING AND LANGUAGE	• Write a comparison-contrast essay • Write a summary • Correctly use present, past, and future verb tenses • Correctly use appositive phrases
SPEAKING AND LISTENING	• Participate in a panel discussion
VOCABULARY	• Use context as a clue to the meaning of words • Use reference aids to verify the meaning of words
ACADEMIC VOCABULARY	• analyze • aware • develop • react • respond

Text Analysis Workshop

Character and Point of View

Bossy and loud, sensitive and shy, athletic and adventurous—what qualities make you admire one person and dislike another? When you meet characters in literature, you are likely to form strong impressions, just as you do with people in real life. By looking closely at character and point of view, you can understand your reactions to the people you meet on the page.

COMMON CORE

Included in this workshop:
RL 3 Analyze how particular elements of a story interact.
RL 6 Analyze how an author develops the points of view in a text.

Part 1: Point of View

Imagine watching three videotapes of a soccer game. One was taken from the sidelines; you can see all the players in action. The second was taped by someone running alongside one player. The third was taken *by* a player; you can see the game through her eyes. In literature, the **narrator** holds the camera—that is, tells the story. A writer's choice of narrator is referred to as **point of view.**

Just how much can point of view affect a story? Find out by contrasting these examples from comical retellings of the "Cinderella" tale.

FIRST-PERSON POINT OF VIEW

The Narrator

- is a character in the story
- uses the pronouns *I* and *me* to refer to himself or herself
- describes his or her own thoughts, feelings, and impressions
- does not know what other characters are thinking and feeling

Example

Cinderella was the last girl in the world I would want to marry. I mean, who wears glass slippers to a ball? I only picked up that lost slipper because it was a safety hazard. And it seemed like a princely thing to do.

THIRD-PERSON POINT OF VIEW

The Narrator

- is not a character in the story
- is called **limited** if he or she tells the thoughts and feelings of only one character
- is called **omniscient,** or all-knowing, if he or she reveals the thoughts and feelings of all the characters

Examples

Limited: Cinderella ran down the steps, losing a slipper along the way. The prince thought to himself, "She's going to break an ankle."

Omniscient: Cinderella hated to lose her slipper but knew she was running out of time. Watching her, the prince shook his head and thought, "There's an accident waiting to happen!"

MODEL 1: FIRST-PERSON POINT OF VIEW

This story is told by a teenage boy. What do you learn about him from what he says and thinks?

from AN HOUR WITH ABUELO

Short story by **Judith Ortiz Cofer**

My grandfather is in a nursing home in Brooklyn, and my mother wants me to spend some time with him, since the doctors say that he doesn't have too long to go now. *I* don't have much time left of my summer vacation, and there's a stack of books next to my bed I've
5 got to read if I'm going to get into the AP English class I want. I'm going stupid in some of my classes, and Mr. Williams, the principal at Central, said that if I passed some reading tests, he'd let me move up.

Besides, I hate the place, the old people's home, especially the way it smells like industrial-strength ammonia and other stuff I won't
10 mention, since it turns my stomach.

Close Read

1. Copy any sentence, then circle the pronouns that show the first-person point of view.

2. Describe two things you learn about the narrator from what he tells you about himself.

MODEL 2: THIRD-PERSON POINT OF VIEW

In a story told from the third-person limited point of view, the narrator reveals the thoughts of one character. Here, the character is a dog named Buck.

from THE CALL OF THE *Wild*

Novel by **Jack London**

Dazed, suffering intolerable pain from throat and tongue, with the life half throttled out of him, Buck attempted to face his tormentors. But he was thrown down and choked repeatedly, till they succeeded in filing the heavy brass collar from off his neck. Then the rope was
5 removed, and he was flung into a cagelike crate.

There he lay for the remainder of the weary night, nursing his wrath and wounded pride. He could not understand what it all meant. What did they want with him, these strange men? Why were they keeping him pent up in this narrow crate? He did not know why,
10 but he felt oppressed. . . .

Close Read

1. Find two places where the narrator reveals Buck's thoughts. One example has been boxed.

2. What more might an omniscient narrator be able to tell you?

Part 2: Methods of Characterization

As you read, you get to know the characters. You meet the **main characters,** the most important ones, as well as the less important **minor characters.** Each character has a motivation, or the reason behind his or her actions. A character has **traits,** which are qualities such as bravery or sloppiness. A character's motivation and traits often drive the plot as the character reacts to events in the story.

Writers use four **methods of characterization** to bring their characters to life. What do you learn about Cinderella's fairy godmother from each example?

METHOD OF CHARACTERIZATION	EXAMPLE
PHYSICAL APPEARANCE **A narrator's description can tell you about a character. Ask:** • What does the character look like? • What are his or her expressions, gestures, or body language?	▶ The fairy godmother was wearing greasy overalls with a rusty garden fork sticking out of one back pocket. She brushed some dirt off her hands and smiled.
 **THOUGHTS, SPEECH, AND ACTIONS** **A character's words and actions can reveal his or her personality. Ask:** • What does the character think, say, or do? • How does he or she treat others? • What kinds of things are important to him or her?	▶ The fairy godmother thought to herself, "I'd better get to work! I have only eight hours to get Cinderella ready for the ball. And from what I've seen of her, I'll need every second of it."
 **OTHER CHARACTERS** **Other characters' reactions to a character can also serve as clues. Ask:** • What do others think and say about the character? • How do they treat him or her?	▶ Cinderella's wicked stepsister shrieked when she saw the fairy godmother. "What is this disgusting woman doing in my home? Have her removed at once!"
 **NARRATOR'S COMMENTS** **Sometimes the narrator tells you directly about a character. Ask:** • What does the narrator say about the character? • Does the narrator respect the character or criticize him or her?	▶ The fairy godmother knew how to handle wicked people! In fact, she was frighteningly clever.

METHOD 1: PHYSICAL APPEARANCE

In this novel, a girl finds herself abandoned with her younger siblings in a car outside a shopping mall. What do you learn about their mother from this one brief glimpse?

from
Homecoming
Novel by **Cynthia Voigt**

The woman put her sad moon-face in at the window of the car. "You be good," she said. "You hear me? You little ones, mind what Dicey tells you. You hear?"

"Yes, Momma," they said.

5 "That's all right then." She slung her purse over her shoulder and walked away, her stride made uneven by broken sandal thongs, thin elbows showing through holes in the oversized sweater, her jeans faded and baggy. When she had disappeared into the crowd of Saturday morning shoppers entering the side doors of the mall, the three younger

10 children leaned forward onto the front seat.

Close Read

1. Find three details that describe the mother's appearance. One example has been boxed for you.

2. What do you learn about the mother from the narrator's description?

METHOD 2: THOUGHTS, SPEECH, AND ACTIONS

Here, a girl at her piano lesson notices an umbrella that was left behind by Eugenie, an older student she admires and envies.

from
The White Umbrella
Short story by **Gish Jen**

I stared at the umbrella. I wanted to open it, twirl it around by its slender silver handle; I wanted to dangle it from my wrist on the way to school the way the other girls did. I wondered what Miss Crosman would say if I offered to bring it to Eugenie at school tomorrow. She

5 would be impressed with my consideration for others; Eugenie would be pleased to have it back; and I would have possession of the umbrella for an entire night. I looked at it again, toying with the idea of asking for one for Christmas. I knew, however, how my mother would react.

"Things," she would say. "What's the matter with a raincoat? All you

10 want is things, just like an American."

Close Read

1. The boxed text suggests that the girl wants to fit in at school. What do her other thoughts tell you about her?

2. What do the girl's thoughts in lines 7–10 reveal about her relationship with her mother?

METHOD 3: OTHER CHARACTERS

In this excerpt, a girl named Cassie walks into her classroom and faces her classmates and her teacher. As you read, observe how the other characters react to Cassie. Does she seem to be well liked?

from

ROLL OF THUNDER, HEAR MY CRY

Novel by
Mildred Taylor

I hurried to the rear of the building, turned to the right, and slid into a third-row bench occupied by Gracey Pearson and Alma Scott.
"You can't sit here," objected Gracey. "I'm saving it for Mary Lou."
I glanced back at Mary Lou Wellever depositing her lunch pail on
5 a shelf in the back of the room and said, "Not any more you ain't."
Miss Daisy Crocker, yellow and buckeyed, glared down at me from the middle of the room with a look that said, "Soooooooo, it's you, Cassie Logan."

Close Read

1. Does Gracey Pearson like Cassie? Explain.

2. Reread the boxed sentence about Miss Crocker, Cassie's teacher. How does Miss Crocker feel about Cassie?

3. What impression do you get of Cassie from other characters' reactions to her?

METHOD 4: NARRATOR'S COMMENTS

Here, the narrator tells you directly about a character named Mack. What do you learn about Mack from the narrator's comments?

from

Kitty and Mack:
A Love Story

Short story by
Walter Dean Myers

He was eighteen and one newspaper article about him said that he could be in the major leagues by the time he was nineteen. That's how good he was. Naturally the baseball coach loved him. That was the thing about Mack, the people who liked him usually liked him because
5 he was a star. Mack had an attitude problem. He thought he could just show up and everybody was supposed to fall down and go crazy or something.
He was pretty smart, too, but he made this big show of not caring about grades.

Close Read

1. On the basis of the narrator's comments, how would you describe Mack?

2. Do you think the narrator admires Mack? Support your opinion with evidence.

Part 3: Analyze the Text

In this story, a girl named Katie spends her birthday visiting her dying mother in the hospital. Among her presents is one from her mother. It's a box—a beautiful, empty box. Katie is upset by the present and by her mother's last words to her: "It's you." As you read, use what you have learned to analyze both Katie and her mother.

from

BIRTHDAY BOX

Short story by **Jane Yolen**

... For about a year I cried at anniversaries, like Mama's birthday or mine, at Thanksgiving, on Mother's Day. I stopped writing. I stopped reading except for school assignments. I was pretty mean to my half brothers and totally rotten to my stepmother and Dad. I felt empty and
5 angry, and they all left me pretty much alone.

And then one night, right after my first birthday without Mama, I woke up remembering how she had said, "It's you." Not, "It's for you," just "It's you." Now Mama had been a high school English teacher and a writer herself. She'd had poems published in little magazines. She didn't
10 use words carelessly. In the end she could hardly use any words at all. So—I asked myself in that dark room—why had she said, "It's you"? Why were they the very last words she had ever said to me, forced out with her last breath?

I turned on the bedside light and got out of bed. The room was full
15 of shadows, not all of them real.

Pulling the desk chair over to my closet, I climbed up and felt along the top shelf, and against the back wall, there was the birthday box, just where I had thrown it the day I had moved in with my dad.

I pulled it down and opened it. It was as empty as the day I had put
20 it away.

"It's you," I whispered to the box.

And then suddenly I knew.

Mama had meant *I* was the box, solid and sturdy, maybe even beautiful or at least interesting on the outside. But I had to fill up the
25 box to make it all it could be. And I had to fill me up as well. She had guessed what might happen to me, had told me in a subtle way. In the two words she could manage.

I stopped crying and got some paper out of the desk drawer. I got out my fountain pen. I started writing, and I haven't stopped since.

Close Read

1. From what point of view is this story told? Explain how you can tell.

2. Reread the boxed paragraph. How does Katie react to her mother's death?

3. What do you learn about Katie's mother from what Katie tells you in lines 6–13?

4. Reread lines 23–27. Given what you know about the characters, why do you think Katie's mother would have chosen to deliver her message in this way?

5. How would you describe the character of Katie? Support your answer.

Zebra

 HISTORY. Video link at **thinkcentral.com**

Short Story by Chaim Potok

VIDEO TRAILER KEYWORD: HML7-190

What has the power to
HEAL?

COMMON CORE

RL 3 Analyze how particular elements of a story interact.

You never know what kind of wounds will cause the greatest damage. An argument with a friend can cause as much pain as a broken leg. Likewise, a physical injury can also scar the spirit. In "Zebra," you will read about a boy your age who needs to heal both his body and his mind.

LIST IT With a partner, create two lists. In the first, list three to five ways people cope with physical injuries or disabilities. In the second, identify at least three ways that people deal with emotional pain.

● TEXT ANALYSIS: CHARACTER AND PLOT

People who appear in stories are called **characters.** A story usually focuses on one or two **main characters** who change during the story. You learn about these characters from

- their thoughts, words, speech patterns, and actions
- the narrator's descriptions
- the thoughts, words, and actions of other characters

Quite often, what a character says and does will affect what happens in a story. As you read, look for ways that a character's **motivation,** or the reason a character behaves or acts in a certain way, affects the events of a story.

● READING STRATEGY: MONITOR

To be sure you're understanding what you're reading, it helps to check or **monitor** your reading. As you read, use a chart like this one to record your questions and answers.

My Questions	Answers
What actually happened to Zebra?	

Review: **Make Inferences**

▲ VOCABULARY IN CONTEXT

Chaim Potok uses the boldfaced words to help tell a story of pain and healing. To see how many you know, substitute a different word or phrase for each one.

1. He tried not to **grimace** in pain.
2. It was hard to unwrap the **intricate** bandage.
3. She is a firm **disciplinarian.**
4. The animal looked **gaunt** and underfed.
5. They skipped **jauntily** down the path.
6. He **winced** when he got a flu shot.
7. A cast might **chafe** your skin.
8. We saw the **contour** of the jagged mountain.
9. She appeared **somber** when she heard the bad news.
10. They applauded our team **exuberantly.**

Complete the activities in your **Reader/Writer Notebook.**

Meet the Author

Chaim Potok
1929–2002

Early Days
While growing up in New York City, Chaim Potok lived the strict life of a Hasidic Jew. His parents wanted him to be a religious scholar. But by the time he was 16, Potok had started reading literature other than traditional Jewish texts. The more he read, the more he struggled between religious learning and the call to become a creative artist.

Coming to Terms
Potok eventually left the Hasidic community for the Conservative movement of Judaism. He became a rabbi and published his first novel in 1967. Much of Potok's writing centers on characters who try to live in both the spiritual world and the secular world of everyday life.

BACKGROUND TO THE STORY

Vietnam War One of the characters in this story is a veteran of the Vietnam War. U.S. troops fought in Vietnam from 1965 until 1973. Approximately 58,000 Americans died there, and more than 300,000 were wounded. In 1982, the Vietnam Veterans Memorial was unveiled in Washington, D.C., to honor the men and women who served in the war. A black granite wall bears the names of those who died.

Author Online
THINK central
Go to **thinkcentral.com.**
KEYWORD: HML7-191

Zebra

Chaim Potok

He couldn't remember when he began to be called by that name. Perhaps they started to call him Zebra when he first began running. Or maybe he began running when they started to call him Zebra.

He loved the name and he loved to run.

When he was very young, his parents took him to a zoo, where he saw zebras for the first time. They were odd-looking creatures, like stubby horses, short-legged, thick-necked, with dark and white stripes.

Then one day he went with his parents to a movie about Africa, and he saw zebras, hundreds of them, thundering across a grassy plain, dust 10 rising in boiling brown clouds. **A**

Analyze Visuals ▶

Examine the photograph. What images can you identify?

A CHARACTER AND PLOT
What do you know about the character Zebra so far?

Was he already running before he saw that movie, or did he begin to run afterward? No one seemed able to remember.

He would go running through the neighborhood for the sheer joy of feeling the wind on his face. People said that when he ran he arched his head up and back, and his face kind of flattened out. One of his teachers told him it was clever to run that way, his balance was better. But the truth was he ran that way, his head thrown back, because he loved to feel the wind rushing across his neck.

Each time, after only a few minutes of running, his legs would begin
20 to feel wondrously light. He would run past the school and the homes on the street beyond the church. All the neighbors knew him and would wave and call out, "Go, Zebra!" And sometimes one or two of their dogs would run with him awhile, barking.

He would imagine himself a zebra on the African plain. Running. **B**

There was a hill on Franklin Avenue, a steep hill. By the time he reached that hill, he would feel his legs so light it was as if he had no legs at all and was flying. He would begin to descend the hill, certain as he ran that he needed only to give himself the slightest push and off he would go, and instead of a zebra he would become the bird he had once seen
30 in a movie about Alaska, he would swiftly change into an eagle, soaring higher and higher, as light as the gentlest breeze, the cool wind caressing his arms and legs and neck.

Then, a year ago, racing down Franklin Avenue, he had given himself that push and had begun to turn into an eagle, when a huge rushing shadow appeared in his line of vision and crashed into him and plunged him into a darkness from which he emerged very, very slowly. . . . **C**

"Never, never, *never* run down that hill so fast that you can't stop at the corner," his mother had warned him again and again.

His schoolmates and friends kept calling him Zebra even after they all
40 knew that the doctors had told him he would never be able to run like that again. **D**

His leg would heal in time, the doctors said, and perhaps in a year or so the brace would come off. But they were not at all certain about his hand. From time to time his injured hand, which he still wore in a sling, would begin to hurt. The doctors said they could find no cause for the pain.

One morning, during Mr. Morgan's geography class, Zebra's hand began to hurt badly. He sat staring out the window at the sky. Mr. Morgan, a stiff-mannered person in his early fifties, given to smart suits and dapper bow ties, called on him to respond to a question. Zebra stumbled about
50 in vain for the answer. Mr. Morgan told him to pay attention to the geography inside the classroom and not to the geography outside.

B CHARACTER AND PLOT
Reread lines 13–24. How does Zebra feel about running?

C MONITOR
Reread lines 33–36. What might the "huge rushing shadow" be?

D MAKE INFERENCES
What happened to Zebra a year ago? What details tell you this?

"In this class, young man, you will concentrate your attention upon the earth, not upon the sky," Mr. Morgan said.

Later, in the schoolyard during the midmorning recess, Zebra stood near the tall fence, looking out at the street and listening to the noises behind him.

His schoolmates were racing about, playing **exuberantly,** shouting and laughing with full voices. Their joyous sounds went ringing through the quiet street.

60 Most times Zebra would stand alongside the basketball court or behind the wire screen at home plate and watch the games. That day, because his hand hurt so badly, he stood alone behind the chain-link fence of the schoolyard. ⓔ

That's how he happened to see the man. And that's how the man happened to see him.

One minute the side street on which the school stood was strangely empty, without people or traffic, without even any of the dogs that often roamed about the neighborhood—vacant and silent, as if it were already in the full heat of summer. The red-brick ranch house that belonged to 70 Mr. Morgan, and the white clapboard two-story house in which Mrs. English lived, and the other homes on the street, with their columned front porches and their back patios, and the tall oaks—all stood curiously still in the warm golden light of the mid-morning sun.

Then a man emerged from wide and busy Franklin Avenue at the far end of the street.

Zebra saw the man stop at the corner and stand looking at a public trash can. He watched as the man poked his hand into the can and fished about but seemed to find nothing he wanted. He withdrew the hand and, raising it to shield his eyes from the sunlight, glanced at the street sign on 80 the lamppost.

He started to walk up the street in the direction of the school.

He was tall and wiry, and looked to be about forty years old. In his right hand he carried a bulging brown plastic bag. He wore a khaki army jacket, a blue denim shirt, blue jeans, and brown cowboy boots. His **gaunt** face and muscular neck were reddened by exposure to the sun. Long brown hair spilled out below his dark-blue farmer's cap. On the front of the cap, in large orange letters, were the words LAND ROVER.[1]

He walked with his eyes on the sidewalk and the curb, as if looking for something, and he went right past Zebra without noticing him.

90 Zebra's hand hurt very much. He was about to turn away when he saw the man stop and look around and peer up at the red-brick wall of

---

1. **Land Rover:** British automaker known for producing four-wheel-drive vehicles.

exuberantly
(ĭg-zoo′bər-ənt-lē) *adv.*
in a manner showing
enthusiasm or joy

ⓔ **CHARACTER AND PLOT**
What is Zebra's **motivation** for standing alone and watching the other students run and play?

Language Coach

Personification Giving human qualities to something that is not human is called personification. Lines 69–73 provide a description of the houses that "all stood curiously still." What effect does the writer create by describing the houses in this humanlike way?

gaunt (gônt) *adj.* thin and bony

the school. The man set down the bag and took off his cap and stuffed it into a pocket of his jacket. From one of his jeans pockets he removed a handkerchief, with which he then wiped his face. He shoved the handkerchief back into the pocket and put the cap back on his head. **F**

Then he turned and saw Zebra.

He picked up the bag and started down the street to where Zebra was standing. When the man was about ten feet away, Zebra noticed that the left sleeve of his jacket was empty.

100 The man came up to Zebra and said in a low, friendly, shy voice, "Hello."

Zebra answered with a cautious "Hello," trying not to look at the empty sleeve, which had been tucked into the man's jacket pocket.

The man asked, with a distinct Southern accent, "What's your name, son?"

Zebra said, "Adam."

"What kind of school is this here school, Adam?"

"It's a good school," Zebra answered.

"How long before you-all begin your summer vacation?"

110 "Three days," Zebra said.

"Anything special happen here during the summer?"

"During the summer? Nothing goes on here. There are no classes."

"What do you-all do during the summer?"

"Some of us go to camp. Some of us hang around. We find things to do."

Zebra's hand had begun to tingle and throb. Why was the man asking all those questions? Zebra thought maybe he shouldn't be talking to him at all. He seemed vaguely menacing in that army jacket, the dark-blue cap with the words LAND ROVER on it in orange letters, and the empty sleeve.

120 Yet there was kindness in his gray eyes and ruddy features.

The man gazed past Zebra at the students playing in the yard. "Adam, do you think your school would be interested in having someone teach an art class during the summer?"

That took Zebra by surprise. "An *art* class?"

"Drawing, sculpting, things like that."

Zebra was trying *very hard* not to look at the man's empty sleeve. "I don't know. . . ." **G**

"Where's the school office, Adam?"

"On Washington Avenue. Go to the end of the street and turn right."

130 "Thanks," the man said. He hesitated a moment. Then he asked, in a quiet voice, "What happened to you, Adam?"

"A car hit me," Zebra said. "It was my fault."

The man seemed to **wince.**

F CHARACTER AND PLOT
Reread lines 74–95. What are your first impressions of this new character?

G MONITOR
What are your own questions about the man at this point? Record them in your monitoring chart.

wince (wĭns) *v.* to draw back, as in pain or distress

For a flash of a second, Zebra thought to ask the man what had happened to *him*. The words were on his tongue. But he kept himself from saying anything.

The man started back up the street, carrying the brown plastic bag. Zebra suddenly called, "Hey, mister."

The man stopped and turned. "My name is John Wilson," he said softly.

140   "Mr. Wilson, when you go into the school office, you'll see signs on two doors. One says 'Dr. Winter,' and the other says 'Mrs. English.' Ask for Mrs. English."

Dr. Winter, the principal, was a **disciplinarian** and a grump. Mrs. English, the assistant principal, was generous and kind. Dr. Winter would probably tell the man to call his secretary for an appointment. Mrs. English might invite him into her office and offer him a cup of coffee and listen to what he had to say.

▲ **Analyze Visuals**
What might you **infer** from this figure's body language?

disciplinarian
(dĭs'ə-plə-nâr'ē-ən) *n.* someone who enforces strict discipline, or rules

The man hesitated, looking at Zebra.

"Appreciate the advice," he said. ⓗ

150 Zebra watched him walk to the corner.

Under the lamppost was a trash can. Zebra saw the man set down the plastic bag and stick his hand into the can and haul out a battered umbrella.

The man tried to open the umbrella, but its metal ribs were broken. The black fabric dangled flat and limp from the pole. He put the umbrella into the plastic bag and headed for the entrance to the school.

A moment later, Zebra heard the whistle that signaled the end of recess. He followed his classmates at a distance, careful to avoid anyone's bumping against his hand.

160 He sat through his algebra class, copying the problems on the blackboard while holding down his notebook with his left elbow. The sling **chafed** his neck and felt warm and clumsy on his bare arm. There were sharp pains now in the two curled fingers of his hand.

Right after the class he went downstairs to the office of Mrs. Walsh, a cheerful, gray-haired woman in a white nurse's uniform.

She said, "I'm sorry I can't do very much for you, Adam, except give you two Tylenols."

He swallowed the Tylenols down with water.

On his way back up to the second floor, he saw the man with the dark-
170 blue cap emerge from the school office with Mrs. English. He stopped on the stairs and watched as the man and Mrs. English stood talking together. Mrs. English nodded and smiled and shook the man's hand.

The man walked down the corridor, carrying the plastic bag, and left the school building.

Zebra went slowly to his next class.

The class was taught by Mrs. English, who came hurrying into the room some minutes after the bell had rung.

"I apologize for being late," she said, sounding a little out of breath. "There was an important matter I had to attend to."

180 Mrs. English was a tall, gracious woman in her forties. It was common knowledge that early in her life she had been a journalist on a Chicago newspaper and had written short stories, which she could not get published. Soon after her marriage to a doctor, she had become a teacher.

This was the only class Mrs. English taught.

Ten students from the upper school—seventh and eighth grades—were chosen every year for this class. They met for an hour three times a week

ⓗ **CHARACTER AND PLOT**
What might be Zebra's **motivation** for giving Mr. Wilson advice?

chafe (chāf) *v.* to irritate by rubbing

Language Coach
Idioms Notice the phrase *out of breath* in line 178. It is an idiom, an expression that has a different meaning from its individual words. The phrase *out of breath* means "breathing with difficulty" or "gasping." What other situations might cause someone to feel this way?

and told one another stories. Each story would be discussed and analyzed by Mrs. English and the class.

Mrs. English called it a class in the *imagination*.

190 Zebra was grateful he did not have to take notes in this class. He had only to listen to the stories.

That day, Andrea, the freckle-faced, redheaded girl with very thick glasses who sat next to Zebra, told about a woman scientist who discovered a method of healing trees that had been blasted apart by lightning.

Mark, who had something wrong with his upper lip, told in his quavery[2] voice about a selfish space cadet who stepped into a time machine and met his future self, who turned out to be a hateful person, and how the cadet then returned to the present and changed himself.

Kevin talked in blurred, high-pitched tones and often related parts
200 of his stories with his hands. Mrs. English would quietly repeat many of his sentences. Today he told about an explorer who set out on a journey through a valley filled with yellow stones and surrounded by red mountains, where he encountered an army of green shadows that had been at war for hundreds of years with an army of purple shadows. The explorer showed them how to make peace. **I**

When it was Zebra's turn, he told a story about a bird that one day crashed against a closed windowpane and broke a wing. A boy tried to heal the wing but couldn't. The bird died, and the boy buried it under a tree on his lawn.

210 When he had finished, there was silence. Everyone in the class was looking at him.

"You always tell such sad stories," Andrea said.

The bell rang. Mrs. English dismissed the class.

In the hallway, Andrea said to Zebra, "You know, you are a very gloomy life form."

"Andrea, get off my case," Zebra said. **J**

He went out to the schoolyard for the midafternoon recess. On the other side of the chain-link fence was the man in the dark-blue cap. Zebra went over to him.

220 "Hello again, Adam," the man said. "I've been waiting for you."

"Hello," said Zebra.

"Thanks much for suggesting I talk to Mrs. English."

"You're welcome."

"Adam, you at all interested in art?"

"No."

I MAKE INFERENCES
What do all the students in Mrs. English's class have in common with Zebra? Cite details to support your answer.

J CHARACTER AND PLOT
What does Andrea's comment tell you about Zebra?

---

2. **quavery** (kwā′vər-ē): quivering or trembling.

"You ever try your hand at it?"

"I've made drawings for class. I don't like it."

"Well, just in case you change your mind, I'm giving an art class in your school during the summer."

230 "I'm going to camp in August," Zebra said.

"There's the big long month of July."

"I don't think so," Zebra said.

"Well, okay, suit yourself. I'd like to give you something, a little thank-you gift."

He reached into an inside pocket and drew out a small pad and a pen. He placed the pad against the fence.

"Adam, you want to help me out a little bit here? Put your fingers through the fence and grab hold of the pad."

Extending the fingers of his right hand, Zebra held the pad to the fence
240 and watched as the man began to work with the pen. He felt the pad move slightly.

"I need you to hold it real still," the man said.

He was standing bent over, very close to Zebra. The words LAND ROVER on his cap shone in the afternoon sunlight. As he worked, he glanced often at Zebra. His tongue kept pushing up against the insides of his cheeks, making tiny hills rise and fall on his
250 face. Wrinkles formed **intricate** spidery webs in the skin below his gray eyes. On his smooth forehead, in the blue and purple shadows beneath the peak of his cap, lay glistening beads of sweat. And his hand—how dirty it was, the fingers and palm smudged with black ink and encrusted with colors.

Then Zebra glanced down and noticed the plastic bag near the man's
260 feet. It lay partly open. Zebra was able to see a large pink armless doll, a dull metallic object that looked like a dented frying pan, old newspapers, strings of cord, crumpled pieces of red and blue cloth, and the broken umbrella.

intricate (ĭn'trĭ-kĭt) *adj.* arranged in a complex way; elaborate

Analyze Visuals ▼

How does the sketch in this photo **compare** with your mental image of Zebra?

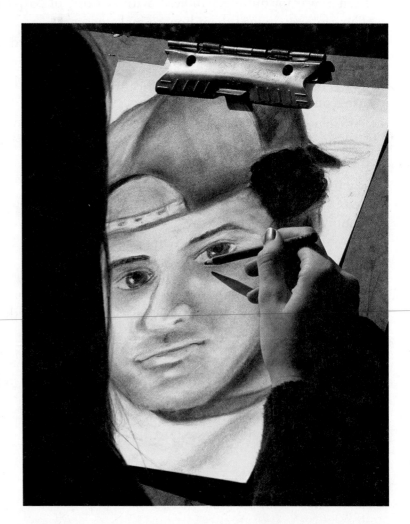

"One more minute is all I need," the man said.

He stepped back, looked at the pad, and nodded slowly. He put the pen back into his pocket and tore the top page from the pad. He rolled up the page and pushed it through the fence. Then he took the pad 270 from Zebra.

"See you around, Adam," the man said, picking up the plastic bag.

Zebra unrolled the sheet of paper and saw a line drawing, a perfect image of his face. K

He was looking at himself as if in a mirror. His long straight nose and thin lips and sad eyes and gaunt face; his dark hair and smallish ears and the scar on his forehead where he had hurt himself years before while roller skating.

In the lower right-hand corner of the page the man had written: "To Adam, with thanks. John Wilson."

280 Zebra raised his eyes from the drawing. The man was walking away.

Zebra called out, "Mr. Wilson, all my friends call me Zebra."

The man turned, looking surprised.

"From my last name," Adam said. "Zebrin. Adam Martin Zebrin. They call me Zebra."

"Is that right?" the man said, starting back toward the fence. "Well, in that case you want to give me back that piece of paper."

He took the pad and pen from his pocket, placed the page on the pad, and, with Zebra holding the pad to the fence, did something to the page and then handed it back.

290 "You take real good care of yourself, Zebra," the man said.

He went off toward Franklin Avenue.

Zebra looked at the drawing. The man had crossed out Adam and over it had drawn an animal with a stubby neck and short legs and a striped body.

A zebra!

Its legs were in full gallop. It seemed as if it would gallop right off the page.

A strong breeze rippled across the drawing, causing it to flutter like a flag in Zebra's hand. He looked out at the street.

300 The man was walking slowly in the shadows of the tall oaks. Zebra had the odd sensation that all the houses on the street had turned toward the man and were watching him as he walked along. How strange that was: the windows and porches and columns and front doors following intently the slow walk of that tall, one-armed man—until he turned into Franklin Avenue and was gone.

K **MAKE INFERENCES**
Why do you think Mr. Wilson drew the picture of Zebra?

The whistle blew, and Zebra went inside. Seated at his desk, he slipped the drawing carefully into one of his notebooks.

From time to time he glanced at it.

Just before the bell signaled the end of the school day, he looked at it again.

310   Now *that* was strange!

He thought he remembered that the zebra had been drawn directly over his name: the head over the A and the tail over the M. Didn't it seem now to have moved a little beyond the A?

Probably he was running a fever again. He would run mysterious fevers off and on for about three weeks after each operation on his hand. Fevers sometimes did that to him: excited his imagination.

He lived four blocks from the school. The school bus dropped him off at his corner. In his schoolbag he carried his books and the notebook with the drawing.

320   His mother offered him a snack, but he said he wasn't hungry. Up in his room, he looked again at the drawing and was astonished to discover that the zebra had reached the edge of his name and appeared poised to leap off.

It *had* to be a fever that was causing him to see the zebra that way. And sure enough, when his mother took his temperature, the thermometer registered 102.6 degrees.

She gave him his medicine, but it didn't seem to have much effect, because when he woke at night and switched on his desk light and peered at the drawing, he saw the little zebra galloping across the page, along the **contours** of his face, over the hills and valleys of his eyes and nose and
330   mouth, and he heard the tiny clickings of its hooves as cloudlets of dust rose in its wake.

He knew he was asleep. He knew it was the fever working upon his imagination.

But it was so real.

The little zebra running . . .

When he woke in the morning the fever was gone, and the zebra was quietly in its place over ADAM.

Language Coach

Idioms In line 314 appears the phrase *running a fever*, which means having a body temperature that is higher than normal. In what ways might running a fever affect someone?

contour (kŏn′tŏŏr′) *n.* the outline of a figure or body

Later, as he entered the school, he noticed a large sign on the bulletin board in the hallway:

340   ## SUMMER ART CLASS

The well-known American artist Mr. John Wilson will conduct an art class during the summer for students in 7th and 8th grades. For details, speak to Mrs. English. There will be no tuition fee for this class.

During the morning, between classes, Zebra ran into Mrs. English in the second-floor hallway.

"Mrs. English, about the summer art class . . . is it okay to ask where—um—where Mr. Wilson is from?"

"He is from a small town in Virginia. Are you thinking of signing
350 up for his class?"

"I can't draw," Zebra said.

"Drawing is something you can learn."

"Mrs. English, is it okay to ask how did Mr. Wilson—um—get hurt?"

The school corridors were always crowded between classes. Zebra and Mrs. English formed a little island in the bustling, student-jammed hallway.

"Mr. Wilson was wounded in the war in Vietnam," Mrs. English said. "I would urge you to join his class. You will get to use your imagination."

For the next hour, Zebra sat impatiently through Mr. Morgan's geography class, and afterward he went up to the teacher.

360   "Mr. Morgan, could I—um—ask where is Vietnam?"

Mr. Morgan smoothed down the jacket of his beige summer suit, touched his bow tie, rolled down a wall map, picked up his pointer, and cleared his throat.

"Vietnam is this long, narrow country in southeast Asia, bordered by China, Laos, and Cambodia.[3] It is a land of valleys in the north, coastal plains in the center, and marshes in the south. There are barren mountains and tropical rain forests. Its chief crops are rice, rubber, fruits, and vegetables. The population numbers close to seventy million people. Between 1962 and 1973, America fought a terrible war there to
370 prevent the south from falling into the hands of the communist north. We lost the war."

"Thank you."

"I am impressed by your suddenly awakened interest in geography, young man, though I must remind you that your class is studying the Mediterranean," said Mr. Morgan. **L**

During the afternoon recess, Zebra was watching a heated basketball game, when he looked across the yard and saw John Wilson walk by, carrying a laden plastic bag. Some while later, he came back along the street, empty-handed.

380 **O**ver supper that evening, Zebra told his parents he was thinking of taking a summer art class offered by the school.

His father said, "Well, I think that's a fine idea."

"Wait a minute. I'm not so sure," his mother said.

SOCIAL STUDIES
CONNECTION

In 1976 North Vietnam and South Vietnam were reunited into one country, the Socialist Republic of Vietnam.

L CHARACTER AND PLOT
What might be **motivating** Zebra to find out more about John Wilson?

---

3. **Laos** (lous) . . . **Cambodia** (kăm-bō′dē-ə): countries in southeast Asia.

"It'll get him off the streets," his father said. "He'll become a Matisse[4] instead of a lawyer like his dad. Right, Adam?"

"Just you be very careful," his mother said to Adam. "Don't do anything that might injure your hand."

"How can drawing hurt his left hand, for heaven's sake?" said his father.

That night, Zebra lay in bed looking at his hand. It was a dread and
390 a mystery to him, his own hand. The fingers were all there, but like dead leaves that never fell, the ring and little fingers were rigid and curled, the others barely moved. The doctors said it would take time to bring them back to life. So many broken bones. So many torn muscles and tendons. So many injured nerves. The dark shadow had sprung upon him so suddenly. How stupid, stupid, *stupid* he had been!

He couldn't sleep. He went over to his desk and looked at John Wilson's drawing. The galloping little zebra stood very still over ADAM.

Early the following afternoon, on the last day of school, Zebra went to Mrs. English's office and signed up for John Wilson's summer art class.
400 "The class will meet every weekday from ten in the morning until one," said Mrs. English. "Starting Monday."

Zebra noticed the three plastic bags in a corner of the office.

"Mrs. English, is it okay to ask what Mr. Wilson—um—did in Vietnam?"

"He told me he was a helicopter pilot," Mrs. English said. "Oh, I neglected to mention that you are to bring an unlined notebook and a pencil to the class." **M**

"That's all? A notebook and a pencil?"

Mrs. English smiled. "And your imagination."

When Zebra entered the art class the next Monday morning, he
410 found about fifteen students there—including Andrea from his class with Mrs. English.

The walls of the room were bare. Everything had been removed for the summer. Zebra noticed two plastic bags on the floor beneath the blackboard.

He sat down at the desk next to Andrea's.

She wore blue jeans and a yellow summer blouse with blue stripes. Her long red hair was tied behind her head with a dark-blue ribbon. She gazed at Zebra through her thick glasses, leaned over, and said, "Are you going to make gloomy drawings, too?"

Just then John Wilson walked in, carrying a plastic bag, which he put
420 down on the floor next to the two others.

He stood alongside the front desk, wearing a light-blue long-sleeved shirt and jeans. The left shirtsleeve had been folded back and pinned to the shirt.

4. **Matisse** (mə-tēs′) (1869–1954): a French painter who was one of the best-known artists of the 20th century.

Language Coach

Metaphors In lines 389–390, the phrase *it was a dread and a mystery* is a metaphor, which is a comparison of two basically unlike things. In this comparison, Zebra's hand is something he is fearful of and curious about. What other way might the writer have described Zebra's feelings about his hand?

M CHARACTER AND PLOT
What does Mrs. English tell Zebra about Mr. Wilson?

The dark-blue cap with the words LAND ROVER sat **jauntily** on his head.

"Good morning to you-all," he said, with a shy smile. "Mighty glad you're here. We're going to do two things this summer. We're going to make paper into faces and garbage into people. I can see by your expressions that you don't know what I'm talking about, right? Well, I'm about to show you."

He asked everyone to draw the face of someone sitting nearby.

430 Zebra hesitated, looked around, then made a drawing of Andrea. Andrea carefully drew Zebra.

He showed Andrea his drawing.

"It's awful." She **grimaced.** "I look like a mouse."

Her drawing of him was good. But was his face really so sad?

John Wilson went from desk to desk, peering intently at the drawings. He paused a long moment over Zebra's drawing. Then he spent more than an hour demonstrating with chalk on the blackboard how they should not be thinking *eyes* or *lips* or *hands* while drawing, but should think only *lines* and *curves* and *shapes*; how they should be looking at

440 where everything was situated in relation to the edge of the paper; and how they should not be looking *directly* at the edges of what they were drawing but at the space *outside* the edges.

jauntily (jôn′tə-lē) *adv.* in a light and carefree way

grimace (grĭm′ĭs) *v.* to twist one's face to show pain or disgust

🅝 **CHARACTER AND PLOT**
How does Andrea's drawing affect Zebra?

Zebra stared in wonder at how fast John Wilson's hand raced across the blackboard, and at the empty sleeve rising and falling lightly against the shirt.

"You-all are going to learn how to *see* in a new way," John Wilson said. They made another drawing of the same face.

"Now I look like a horse," Andrea said. "Are you going to add stripes?"

"You are one big pain, Andrea," Zebra said.

450 Shortly before noon, John Wilson laid out on his desk the contents of the plastic bags: a clutter of junked broken objects, including the doll and the umbrella.

Using strips of cloth, some lengths of string, crumpled newspaper, his pen, and his one hand, he swiftly transformed the battered doll into a red-nosed, umbrella-carrying clown, with baggy pants, a tattered coat, a derby hat, and a **somber** smile. Turning over the battered frying pan, he made it into a pedestal, on which he placed the clown.

"That's a sculpture," John Wilson said, with his shy smile. "Garbage into people."

460 The class burst into applause. The clown on the frying pan looked as if it might take a bow.

"You-all will be doing that, too, before we're done," John Wilson said. "Now I would like you to sign and date your drawings and give them to me."

When they returned the next morning the drawings were on a wall.

Gradually, in the days that followed, the walls began to fill with drawings. Sculptures made by the students were looked at with care, discussed by John Wilson and the class, and then placed on shelves along the walls: a miniature bicycle made of wire; a parrot made of an

470 old sofa cushion; a cowboy made of rope and string; a fat lady made of a dented metal pitcher; a zebra made of glued-together scraps of cardboard.

"I like your zebra," Andrea said.

"Thanks," Zebra said. "I like your parrot."

One morning John Wilson asked the class members to make a contour drawing of their right or left hand. Zebra felt himself sweating and trembling as he worked. �“

"That's real nice," John Wilson said, when he saw Andrea's drawing. He gazed at the drawing made by Zebra.

480 "You-all were looking at your hand," he said. "You ought to have been looking at the edge of your hand and at the space outside."

Zebra drew his hand again. Strange and ugly, the two fingers lay rigid and curled. But astonishingly, it looked like a hand this time.

somber (sŏm′bər) *adj.* serious; gloomy

🔲 **MONITOR**
Reread lines 475–477. Why might Zebra be reacting in this way?

One day, a few minutes before the end of class, John Wilson gave everyone an assignment: draw or make something at home, something very special that each person *felt deeply* about. And bring it to class.

Zebra remembered seeing a book titled *Incredible Cross-Sections* on a shelf in the family room at home. He found the book and took it into his room.

490   There was a color drawing of a rescue helicopter on one of the Contents pages. On pages 30 and 31, the helicopter was shown in pieces, its complicated insides displayed in detailed drawings. Rotor blades, control rods, electronics equipment, radar scanner, tail rotor, engine, lifeline, winch—all its many parts.

Zebra sat at his desk, gazing intently at the space outside the edges of the helicopter on the Contents page.

He made an outline drawing and brought it to class the next morning.

John Wilson looked at it. Was there a stiffening of his muscular neck, a sudden tensing of the hand that held the drawing? 🅟

🅟 MONITOR
What questions do you have about John Wilson's reaction?

500   He took the drawing and tacked it to the wall.

The next day he gave them all the same home assignment: draw or make something they *felt very deeply* about.

That afternoon, Zebra went rummaging through the trash bin in his kitchen and the garbage cans that stood near the back door of his home. He found some sardine cans, a broken eggbeater, pieces of cardboard, chipped buttons, bent bobby pins, and other odds and ends.

With the help of epoxy glue, he began to make of those bits of garbage a kind of helicopter. For support, he used his desktop, the floor, his knees, the elbow of his left arm, at one point even his chin. Struggling with the
510 last piece—a button he wanted to position as a wheel—he realized that without thinking he had been using his left hand, and the two curled fingers had straightened slightly to his needs. **Q**

His heart beat thunderously. There had been so many hope-filled moments before, all of them ending in bitter disappointment. He would say nothing. Let the therapist or the doctors tell him. . . .

The following morning, he brought the helicopter to the class.

"Eeewwww, what is *that*?" Andrea grimaced.

"Something to eat you with," Zebra said.

"Get human, Zebra. Mr. Wilson will have a laughing fit over that."
520 But John Wilson didn't laugh. He held the helicopter in his hand a long moment, turning it this way and that, nodded at Zebra, and placed it on a windowsill, where it shimmered in the summer sunlight.

The next day, John Wilson informed everyone that three students would be leaving the class at the end of July. He asked each of those students to make a drawing for him that he would get to keep. Something to remember them by. All their other drawings and sculptures they could take home.

Zebra lay awake a long time that night, staring into the darkness of his room. He could think of nothing to draw for John Wilson.
530 In the morning, he sat gazing out the classroom window at the sky and at the helicopter on the sill.

"What are you going to draw for him?" Andrea asked.

Zebra shrugged and said he didn't know.

"Use your imagination," she said. Then she said, "Wait, what am I seeing here? Are you able to move those fingers?"

"I think so."

"You *think* so?"

"The doctors said there was some improvement."

Her eyes glistened behind the thick lenses. She seemed genuinely happy. **R**

Q CHARACTER AND PLOT
What effect is John Wilson's art class having on Zebra?

R CHARACTER AND PLOT
How have Andrea's feelings toward Zebra changed?

540   He sat looking out the window. Dark birds wheeled and soared. There was the sound of traffic. The helicopter sat on the windowsill, its eggbeater rotor blades ready to move to full throttle.

   Later that day, Zebra sat at his desk at home, working on a drawing. He held the large sheet of paper in place by pressing down on it with the palm and fingers of his left hand. He drew a landscape: hills and valleys, forests and flatlands, rivers and plateaus. Oddly, it all seemed to resemble a face.

   Racing together over that landscape were a helicopter and a zebra.

   It was all he could think to draw. It was not a very good drawing. He signed it: "To John Wilson, with thanks. Zebra." **⑤**

550   The next morning, John Wilson looked at the drawing and asked Zebra to write on top of the name "John Wilson" the name "Leon."

   "He was an old buddy of mine, an artist. We were in Vietnam together. Would've been a much better artist than I'll ever be."

   Zebra wrote in the new name.

   "Thank you kindly," John Wilson said, taking the drawing. "Zebra, you have yourself a good time in camp and a good life. It was real nice knowing you."

   He shook Zebra's hand. How strong his fingers felt!

   "I think I'm going to miss you a little," Andrea said to Zebra
560 after the class.

   "I'll only be away a month."

   "Can I help you carry some of those drawings?"

   "Sure. I'll carry the helicopter."

Zebra went off to a camp in the Adirondack Mountains.[5] He hiked and read and watched others playing ball. In the arts and crafts program he made some good drawings and even got to learn a little bit about watercolors. He put together clowns and airplanes and helicopters out of discarded cardboard and wood and clothing. From time to time his hand hurt, but the fingers seemed slowly to be coming back to life. ◆

570   "Patience, young man," the doctors told him when he returned to the city. "You're getting there."

   One or two additional operations were still necessary. But there was no urgency. And he no longer needed the leg brace.

On the first day of school, one of the secretaries found him in the hallway and told him to report to Mrs. English.

   "Did you have a good summer?" Mrs. English asked.

   "It was okay," Zebra said.

⑤ CHARACTER AND PLOT
Why does Zebra thank John Wilson?

◆ GRAMMAR IN CONTEXT
In lines 564–567, notice the consistent way the writer uses **past tense verbs.**

---

5. **Adirondack** (ăd'ə-rŏn'dăk') **Mountains:** mountains covering a large area of northeast New York State.

"This came for you in the mail."

She handed him a large brown envelope. It was addressed to Adam
580 Zebrin, Eighth Grade, at the school. The sender was John Wilson, with
a return address in Virginia.

"Adam, I admit I'm very curious to see what's inside," Mrs. English said.
She helped Zebra open the envelope.

Between two pieces of cardboard were a letter and a large color photograph.

The photograph showed John Wilson down on his right knee before a
glistening dark wall. He wore his army jacket and blue jeans and boots,
and the cap with the words LAND ROVER. Leaning against the wall to his
right was Zebra's drawing of the helicopter and the zebra racing together
across a facelike landscape. The drawing was enclosed in a narrow frame.
590 The wall behind John Wilson seemed to glitter with a strange
black light. **T**

Zebra read the letter and showed it to Mrs. English.

T MONITOR
What are your questions about the story at this point?

> *Dear Zebra,*
>
> *One of the people whose names are on this wall was among
> my very closest friends. He was an artist named Leon Kellner.
> Each year I visit him and leave a gift—something very special that
> someone creates and gives me. I leave it near his name for a few
> hours, and then I take it to my studio in Virginia, where I keep
> a collection of those gifts. All year long I work in my studio, but*
600 *come summer I go looking for another gift to give him.*
>
> *Thank you for your gift.*
>
> *Your friend,*
John Wilson
>
> *P.S. I hope your hand is healing.*

Mrs. English stood staring awhile at the letter. She turned away
and touched her eyes. Then she went to a shelf on the wall behind her,
took down a large book, leafed through it quickly, found what she was
searching for, and held it out for Zebra to see.

Zebra found himself looking at the glistening black wall of the
610 Vietnam Memorial in Washington, D.C. And at the names on it,
the thousands of names. . . .

Later, in the schoolyard during recess, Zebra stood alone at the chain-link
fence and gazed down the street toward Franklin Avenue. He thought
how strange it was that all the houses on this street had seemed to turn
toward John Wilson that day, the windows and porches and columns
and doors, as if saluting him.

Had that been only his imagination?

◀ **Analyze Visuals**

Look carefully at this photograph. How do you think it was taken? What feelings was the photographer trying to show?

Maybe, Zebra thought, just maybe he could go for a walk to Franklin Avenue on Saturday or Sunday. He had not walked along Franklin
620 Avenue since the accident; had not gone down that steep hill. Yes, he would walk carefully down that hill to the corner and walk back up and past the school and then the four blocks home.

Andrea came over to him.

"We didn't get picked for the story class with Mrs. English," she said. "I won't have to listen to any more of your gloomy stories."

Zebra said nothing.

"You know, I think I'll walk home today instead of taking the school bus," Andrea said.

"Actually, I think I'll walk, too," Zebra said. "I was thinking maybe
630 I could pick up some really neat stuff in the street."

"You are becoming a pleasant life form," Andrea said. ◞ Ⓤ

Ⓤ **CHARACTER AND PLOT**
Reread lines 618–631. Why is it important for Zebra to walk along Franklin Avenue again?

The Rider

Naomi Shihab Nye

A boy told me
if he rollerskated fast enough
his loneliness couldn't catch up to him,

the best reason I ever heard
5 for trying to be a champion.

What I wonder tonight
pedaling hard down King William Street
is if it translates to bicycles.

A victory! To leave your loneliness
10 panting behind you on some street corner
while you float free into a cloud of sudden azaleas,
luminous pink petals that have never felt loneliness,
no matter how slowly they fell.

Comprehension

COMMON CORE

RL 3 Analyze how particular elements of a story interact.

1. **Recall** How does Zebra get his name?

2. **Recall** What does John Wilson do with Zebra's drawing?

3. **Represent** On the basis of the description in the story, sketch Zebra's drawing of a helicopter and a zebra racing together over a landscape.

Text Analysis

4. **Monitor** Review the chart you filled in as you read. Which questions and answers were most helpful for understanding the story?

5. **Analyze Character** How does Zebra change, or grow, from the beginning of the story to the end? Complete a chart like this one with details from the narrator's descriptions and from Zebra's and other characters' thoughts, words, and actions. Also, consider any character's motivation, or reason for certain actions.

Characters	Motivation	Explanation
Zebra		
John Wilson		

6. **Evaluate Characters** A **static character** doesn't change throughout a story. A **dynamic character** changes as a result of events in a story. Do you think John Wilson is a static or dynamic character? Support your answer with examples from the story.

7. **Compare Literary Works** Consider the character Zebra and the speaker in "The Rider" on page 212. How are they alike? How are they different?

Extension and Challenge

8. **SOCIAL STUDIES CONNECTION** What challenges did Vietnam veterans like John Wilson face when they came home? Research what aid and resources were available to them as they sought help in the healing process. Share your findings with the class.

What has the power to HEAL?

For over a year, Zebra deals with both physical and emotional pain. Review the two lists you made in response to the question on page 190. After reading this story, do you think you have discovered other ways in which people can heal? Explain.

Vocabulary in Context

▲ VOCABULARY PRACTICE

For each set, choose the word that differs most in meaning from the other words. Refer to a dictionary if you need help.

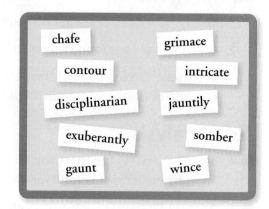

1. (a) elaborate, (b) ornate, (c) intricate, (d) plain
2. (a) joyously, (b) glumly, (c) delightedly, (d) exuberantly
3. (a) thick, (b) fat, (c) gaunt, (d) full
4. (a) smile, (b) grimace, (c) grin, (d) laugh
5. (a) somber, (b) dreary, (c) angry, (d) depressing
6. (a) cringe, (b) flinch, (c) approach, (d) wince
7. (a) disciplinarian, (b) counselor, (c) advisor, (d) guide
8. (a) jauntily, (b) slowly, (c) lightheartedly, (d) cheerfully
9. (a) outline, (b) contour, (c) color, (d) shape
10. (a) scrape, (b) chafe, (c) rub, (d) bless

ACADEMIC VOCABULARY IN WRITING

• analyze   • aware   • develop   • react   • respond

How do the characters **develop** in "Zebra"? Explain the changes that Zebra goes through in the story. Be sure to include one of the Academic Vocabulary words in your explanation.

VOCABULARY STRATEGY: SIMILES AS CONTEXT CLUES

Writers sometimes use **similes** to compare two things (using the words *like* or *as*) that are not alike. In this story, Zebra's fingers are said to be "rigid and curled," "**like** dead leaves that never fell." This simile helps you see his fingers in a new way.

Similes can also provide **context clues,** surrounding words or phrases, to help you figure out the meaning of unknown words. If you can visualize dead leaves, you can understand the meaning of *rigid*.

COMMON CORE

L 4a Use context as a clue to the meaning of a word.
L 5 Demonstrate understanding of figurative language.

PRACTICE Use the simile in each sentence as a context clue to help you define the boldfaced word.

1. Teresa felt as **emancipated** as a prisoner recently released from jail.
2. Like a dam bursting, the **impasse** between the enemies was finally broken.
3. The sight of his destroyed home made him **recoil** like a snake.
4. The clues to the robbery were as **enigmatic** as unidentified ruins found in a desert.
5. Tom was as **tenacious** in business as a survivor hanging on to a lifeboat.

Interactive Vocabulary THINK central

Go to thinkcentral.com.
KEYWORD: HML7-214

Language

◆ **GRAMMAR IN CONTEXT:** Use Correct Verb Tense

Review the **Grammar in Context** note on page 209. **Verb tense** indicates the time that an action takes place. The three basic verb tenses are **present, past,** and **future.** In your writing, be sure to use the same verb tense when describing actions that happen at the same time. Only make a change in verb tense if actions are happening at different times.

Original: I am grateful for your encouragement. I looked forward to seeing you again. (Am *is present tense, and* looked *is past tense.*)

Revised: I am grateful for your encouragement. I look forward to seeing you again. (*Since both actions are happening in the present, both verbs should be present tense.*)

PRACTICE Choose the correct verb tense to complete the sentence.

1. I feel good when I work on my art. It (reflected, reflects) my creativity.
2. Art inspires me. It (helps, helped) me to focus my energy.
3. After the accident, I never thought my hand would get better. Now I (knew, know) I'll be fine.
4. I will always remember you and (will try, tried) to keep in touch.

*For more help with verb tenses, see pages R56–R57 in the **Grammar Handbook.***

READING-WRITING CONNECTION

YOUR TURN

Increase your understanding of "Zebra" by responding to this prompt. Then use the **revising tip** to improve your writing.

WRITING PROMPT	REVISING TIP
Extended Constructed Response: Letter Write a **two- or three-paragraph letter** that Zebra might send in response to John Wilson's letter. It should include a description of how the art class and their friendship helped heal his hand and spirits.	Review your response. Are the tenses of your verbs consistent? If not, revise your writing.

Interactive Revision **THINK** central

Go to **thinkcentral.com**.
KEYWORD: HML7-215

The Legacy of the Vietnam War

- Book Excerpt, page 217
- Letter, page 220
- Timeline, page 222

Use with "Zebra," page 192.

What's the Connection?

In "Zebra" you read about a veteran of the Vietnam War. In the following selections, you will learn more about the war and the Vietnam Veterans Memorial.

Standards Focus: Summarize

COMMON CORE

RI 2 Determine central ideas in a text and analyze their development over the course of the text; provide an objective summary of the text.

Have you ever seen a news report about something, such as digital music, and then read about that topic in a book? Even though they were on the same subject, it is likely that the news report and the book each had a different **main idea,** the most important thing that a writer wants you to know about a topic.

As you read the book excerpt and the letter, you will identify the main ideas and the **supporting details,** which are examples or facts that help you understand the main ideas. After finishing these selections, write a **summary** of each of them, a brief retelling in your own words. Use a chart like the one shown to record the information and write each summary. Follow these steps:

- Break down the selections into parts, such as paragraphs or sections.
- Jot down the main idea and supporting details in each part. Think about the overall meaning—the writer's message.
- For the summary, write a topic sentence explaining the overall meaning of the text. Then provide the most significant details.

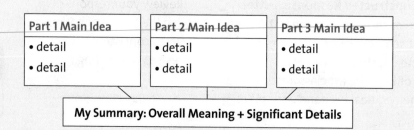

Part 1 Main Idea	Part 2 Main Idea	Part 3 Main Idea
• detail • detail	• detail • detail	• detail • detail

My Summary: Overall Meaning + Significant Details

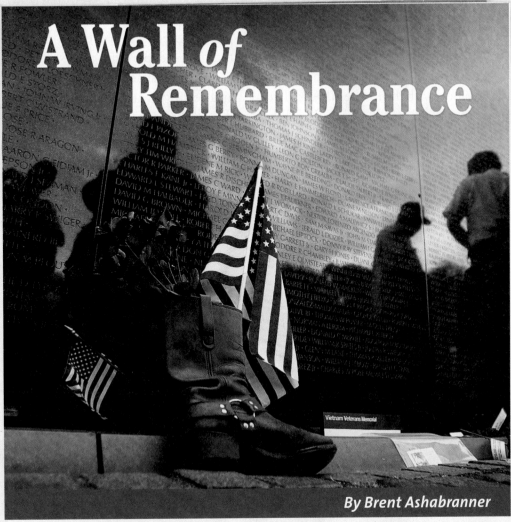

A Wall *of* Remembrance

By Brent Ashabranner

FOCUS ON FORM
This is an **excerpt** from a nonfiction book about a historical event. The purpose of a nonfiction book is to provide interesting information. Unlike a news article, it does not need to focus on current events.

The outpouring of messages and mementos left at the Vietnam Veterans Memorial is unique; no other national memorial has evoked such a response. On special days the tokens of love and remembrance are many, on rainy or snowy days perhaps only a few, but I have never been to the memorial when there were none.

I am sometimes puzzled by the mementos left, sometimes deeply touched, always reminded that behind the names on the memorial there were and are mothers, fathers, wives, children, grandchildren, friends, and sweethearts who still love and miss those who did not return from Vietnam. What is the meaning of a tattered dollar bill beneath panel 24E? An empty red glass beneath panel 14W? A can of sardines, a teddy bear, Tinker Toys, a soccer ball beneath other panels? Only the person who brought the remembrance can know what it means to him or her and what it would have meant to a special name on the wall.

A **SUMMARIZE**
Choose a phrase or sentence from lines 1–45 that sums up the most important idea of this section. On your chart, record that phrase or sentence and the main idea.

B **BOOK EXCERPT**
Reread Ashabranner's thoughts about the wall. Then reread **Focus on Form** on page 217. What makes the wall such a good topic for a book excerpt?

Notes and letters left at the memorial are different. You understand, at least in part, the emotion behind them. And I remember a card left at the wall by a woman whose husband's name was on one of the black granite panels. She had put the card there on what would have been their 40 silver wedding anniversary—twenty-five years. It reminded me of how long the Vietnam War had been over—and of how long the important memories are part of our lives. **A**

I long ago decided it was all right to read the messages left at the memorial. They are expressions of private grief and love, but I think 50 that the people who leave them do not mind sharing their thoughts and feelings with others; perhaps they want to share them. **B**

More than 55,000 remembrances of all kinds have been left at the wall since it was dedicated, and that number does not include tens of thousands of flowers, wreaths, and other flo-60 ral arrangements. Organic material is not saved, but National Park Service rangers collect all other items left at the memorial. The remembrances are gathered up at the end of each day and sent to a warehouse known as

the Museum Resource Center. At the center every item collected gets a bar code and is placed in a 70 plastic bag.

David Guynes, former director of the center, once said to me: "There are so many questions, so many mysteries, in these memorabilia. So many stories are in them, so much feeling, emotion, heartache. What can be learned about America and Americans from these things 80 they have brought? Altogether, these materials make up a very important part of the story of the Vietnam War. This is the material of social history." **C**

Duery Felton, curator of the National Vietnam Veterans Collection at the Museum Resource Center, told me that the number of memorabilia and messages be-90 ing left at the wall is increasing on special days. During one three-day period in 1997—Memorial Day, the day before, and the day after—park rangers collected 2,300 items that had been left at the wall.

And yet, in a certain sense, each of the thousands of things left at the memorial is unique. The rea-son, of course, is that the person 100 who left it and the person whose name is on the wall had a relation-ship that was theirs alone. **D**

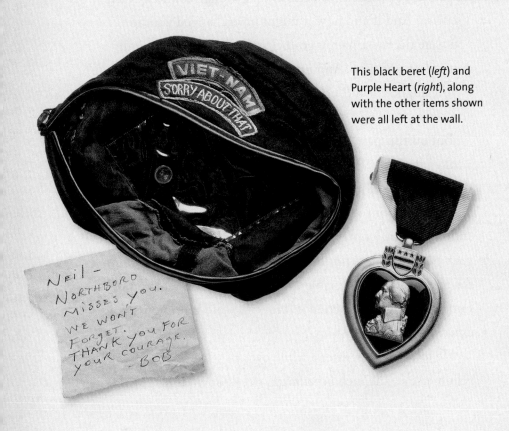

This black beret (*left*) and Purple Heart (*right*), along with the other items shown were all left at the wall.

C SUMMARIZE
Reread lines 54–70. Identify a phrase or sentence that gives the main idea of the section. Then do the same with lines 71–84.

COMMON CORE RI 2

D SUMMARIZE
Keep in mind that a **summary** is a brief retelling in your own words. In a summary that you prepare for evaluation, the **main idea** and **supporting details** must be stated as clearly as possible. For the book excerpt, review the main ideas and details you've recorded so far in your chart. Considering the entire book excerpt, what are your thoughts about its overall meaning? Start your summary with a topic sentence and include any details you think are significant.

A Mother's Words

Mrs. Eleanor Wimbish of Glen Burnie, Maryland, is the mother of William R. Stocks, who died in the Vietnam War. For years she left letters to her son under his name on the Vietnam Veterans Memorial in Washington, D. C. **E**

E SUMMARIZE
Carefully read the headline and introductory text at the top of this page. These will help you understand the main ideas of Eleanor Wimbish's letter.

Dear Bill,

Today is February 13, 1984. I came to this black wall again to see and touch your name, and as I do I wonder if anyone ever stops to realize that next to your name, on this black wall, is your mother's heart. A heart broken 15 years ago today, when you lost your life in Vietnam.

And as I look at your name, William R. Stocks, I think of how many, many times I used to wonder how scared and homesick you must have been in that strange country called
10 Vietnam. And if and how it might have changed you, for you were the most happy-go-lucky kid in the world, hardly ever sad or unhappy. And until the day I die, I will see you as you laughed at me, even when I was very mad at you, and the next thing I knew, we were laughing together.

But on this past New Year's Day, I had my answer. I talked by phone to a friend of yours from Michigan, who spent your last Christmas and the last four months of your life with you. Jim told me how you died, for he was there and saw the helicopter crash. He told me how you had flown
20 your quota and had not been scheduled to fly that day. How the regular pilot was unable to fly and had been replaced by someone with less experience. How they did not know the exact cause of the crash. . . .

He told me how, after a while over there, instead of a yellow streak, the men got a mean streak down their backs.

Each day the streak got bigger and the men became meaner. Everyone but you, Bill. He said how you stayed the same, happy-go-lucky guy that you were when you arrived in Vietnam. How your warmth and friendliness drew the
30 guys to you. How your lieutenant gave you the nickname of "Spanky," and soon your group, Jim included, were all known as "Spanky's gang." How when you died it made it so much harder on them for you were their moral support. And he said how you of all people should never have been the one to die. **F**

How it hurts to write this. But I must face it and then put it to rest. I know after Jim talked to me, he must have relived it all over again and suffered so. Before I hung up the phone I told Jim I loved him. Loved him for just being your
40 close friend, and for being there with you when you died. How lucky you were to have him for a friend, and how lucky he was to have had you. . . .

They tell me the letters I write to you and leave here at this memorial are waking others up to the fact that there is still much pain left, after all these years, from the Vietnam War. **G**

But this I know. I would rather have had you for 21 years, and all the pain that goes with losing you, than never to have had you at all.

Mom

F SUMMARIZE
Reread lines 24–35. What **supporting details** does this paragraph reveal about Bill's personality and his influence on others? Use your own words or brief quotations to answer.

G SUMMARIZE
This paragraph contains one of the main ideas of the letter. What is it?

Timeline: U.S. Involvement in Vietnam

The seeds of the Vietnam War were planted in 1858 when France attacked Vietnam for control of the government. After decades of frustration under foreign rule, many Vietnamese began supporting the Communist movement against the French. Meanwhile, the United States struggled against the spread of communism worldwide.

USA	VIETNAM
1950 The United States sends economic aid to the French forces in Vietnam.	**1954** The French are defeated. Vietnam divides into Communist North and non-Communist South. **1957** Communist rebels (the Viet Cong) fight for control of South Vietnam.
1965 Antiwar protests become widespread. **1968** U.S. citizens begin to think the war cannot be won.	**1965** The United States bombs North Vietnam. The first U.S. combat troops arrive in South Vietnam. **1968** The number of U.S. troops in Vietnam reaches its peak. The North Vietnamese and the Viet Cong launch the Tet offensive, a series of surprise attacks.
1970 Four students are killed at an antiwar demonstration in Ohio.	**1973** All U.S. troops leave Vietnam. **1975** South Vietnam surrenders to the Communists. The U.S. Embassy in Vietnam is evacuated. **1978** Thousands of refugees flee Vietnam to escape poverty and punishment for aiding the United States during the war.
1982 The Vietnam Veterans Memorial is dedicated in Washington, D.C.	**1986** The Vietnamese government begins economic restructuring.
1995 The United States and Vietnam restore full diplomatic relations.	

The decades covered in the timeline: 1950s, 1960s, 1970s, 1980s, 1990s.

Comprehension

1. **Recall** When did the last U.S. combat troops leave Vietnam?

2. **Clarify** What kind of person was Bill Stocks?

3. **Clarify** In general, how would you describe the remembrances people leave at the Wall?

Text Analysis

4. **Analyze** In the book excerpt, the objects left along the Vietnam Veterans War Memorial are described as "expressions of private grief and love." Why do you think the writer lists specific examples?

5. **Identify Main Idea** Think about the main idea of Eleanor Wimbish's letter. Describe this main idea to a friend or relative.

COMMON CORE

RI 2 Determine central ideas in a text and analyze their development over the course of the text; provide an objective summary of the text. **W 2** Write informative/explanatory texts to examine a topic and convey ideas.

Read for Information: Evaluate a Summary

WRITING PROMPT

Write a one-paragraph evaluation of a classmate's summary of the letter.

Exchange your summary of the letter with a classmate's. Read it carefully. Then review it as you check "Yes" or "No" to answer the checklist questions. Finally, write your one-paragraph evaluation, basing it on your checklist responses.

- Is the summary presented in a clear, well-organized manner?
- Is the summary brief?
- Does the summary touch upon the main ideas and supporting details of the selection?
- Does the summary convey the overall meaning of the selection?

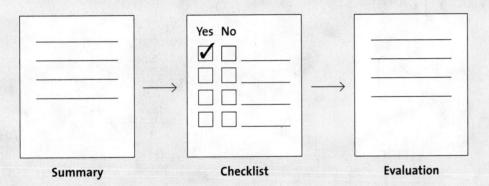

Summary   Checklist   Evaluation

The Scholarship Jacket
Short Story by Marta Salinas

What stands in the way of your
DREAMS?

COMMON CORE

RL 1 Cite textual evidence to support inferences drawn from the text. **RL 6** Analyze how an author develops and contrasts the points of view of characters or narrators in a text.

Your dream may be to go to camp, to be a star on the basketball court, to be class president, or to go to college someday. Whatever it is, hard work and luck can help you fulfill that dream. But, like the narrator of "The Scholarship Jacket," you may encounter obstacles that block your progress.

QUICKWRITE With a small group of classmates, discuss your dream for the future. What obstacles might you encounter while working to make your dream come true? Then, in your journal, write one or two ways to overcome each obstacle.

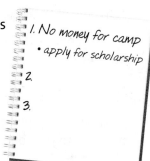

1. No money for camp
   • apply for scholarship
2.
3.

TEXT ANALYSIS: FIRST-PERSON POINT OF VIEW

When you listen to a friend talk, you can learn a great deal about him or her. Your friend's personality, experiences, and opinions all come through. The same is true when you read a story from one character's point of view. When a story is told from the **first-person point of view,** the narrator

- is a character in the story
- tells the story using the pronouns *I, me, we,* and *us*
- tells the story as he or she experiences it

As you read "The Scholarship Jacket," notice how the information you receive is limited to what the narrator sees, hears, thinks, and feels.

READING SKILL: MAKE INFERENCES

One way to get the most out of what you read is to make logical guesses, or **inferences,** about things that are not directly stated. Base your inferences on details in the story and on your own knowledge and experiences. As you read "The Scholarship Jacket," record each inference you make in an equation like the one shown.

Details from the Text	My Experiences	Inference
Martha couldn't play sports because of cost. **+**	I couldn't go to playoffs because of expense. **=**	Martha's grandparents don't have extra money.

▲ VOCABULARY IN CONTEXT

These words help tell the story of a girl facing obstacles. Write the word that best completes each sentence.

WORD	agile	dismay	falsify
LIST	despair	eavesdrop	vile

1. She unhappily swallowed the _____ medicine.
2. He would often _____ on his parents' conversations.
3. He tried not to _____ over the terrible news.
4. She climbed the tree in a very _____ manner.
5. There was a look of _____ when she received the news.
6. Don't _____ the records to hide the truth.

Complete the activities in your **Reader/Writer Notebook.**

Meet the Author

Marta Salinas
born 1949

California Native
Marta Salinas was born in Coalinga, California, and received a degree in creative writing from the University of California at Irvine. "The Scholarship Jacket" is one of several short stories Salinas has published in journals and collections.

BACKGROUND TO THE STORY
Texas History
The main character in "The Scholarship Jacket" is a Mexican-American girl who lives in Texas. The history of *Tejanos,* or Texas Mexicans, dates back more than 200 years. As early as 1731, Tejanos established a ranch community in what was then northeastern Mexico. About 100 years later, Mexico invited immigrants from the United States to settle in the region. The Tejanos and the immigrants eventually joined forces to fight for their independence from Mexico, and in 1845, Texas became part of the United States. Mexicans continued migrating to Texas, but they often faced discrimination. Today, over seven million residents of Texas are Mexican Americans.

Author Online **THINK** central

Go to **thinkcentral.com**.
KEYWORD: HML7-225

The Scholarship Jacket

Marta Salinas

The small Texas school that I went to had a tradition carried out every year during the eighth-grade graduation: a beautiful gold and green jacket (the school colors) was awarded to the class valedictorian, the student who had maintained the highest grades for eight years. The scholarship jacket had a big gold S on the left front side and your name written in gold letters on the pocket.

My oldest sister, Rosie, had won the jacket a few years back, and I fully expected to also. I was fourteen and in the eighth grade. I had been a straight A student since the first grade and this last year had looked
10 forward very much to owning that jacket. My father was a farm laborer who couldn't earn enough money to feed eight children, so when I was six I was given to my grandparents to raise. We couldn't participate in sports at school because there were registration fees, uniform costs, and trips out of town; so, even though our family was quite **agile** and athletic there would never be a school sports jacket for us. This one, the scholarship jacket, was our only chance. **A**

In May, close to graduation, spring fever had struck as usual with a vengeance.[1] No one paid any attention in class; instead we stared out the windows and at each other, wanting to speed up the last few weeks of

---

1. **with a vengeance** (věnʹjəns): to an extreme degree.

agile (ăjʹəl) *adj.* quick and light in movement

A **FIRST-PERSON POINT OF VIEW**
Who is the narrator? What have you learned from her so far?

Bernadita (1922), Robert Henri. Oil on canvas, 24 ¹/₈″ × 20 ¹/₈″. Gift of the San Diego Wednesday Club. © San Diego Museum of Art (1926:138).

ROBERT HENRI

20 school. I **despaired** every time I looked in the mirror. Pencil thin, not
a curve anywhere. I was called "beanpole" and "string bean," and I knew
that's what I looked like. A flat chest, no hips, and a brain; that's what
I had. That really wasn't much for a fourteen-year-old to work with,
I thought, as I absent-mindedly wandered from my history class to the
gym. Another hour of sweating in basketball and displaying my toothpick
legs was coming up. Then I remembered my P.E. shorts were still in a bag
under my desk where I'd forgotten them. I had to walk all the way back
and get them. Coach Thompson was a real bear if someone wasn't dressed
for P.E. She had said I was a good forward and even tried to talk Grandma
30 into letting me join the team once. Of course Grandma said no.

I was almost back at my classroom door when I heard voices raised
in anger as if in some sort of argument. I stopped. I didn't mean
to **eavesdrop,** I just hesitated, not knowing what to do. I needed those
shorts and I was going to be late, but I didn't want to interrupt an
argument between my teachers. I recognized the voices: Mr. Schmidt,
my history teacher, and Mr. Boone, my math teacher. They seemed to
be arguing about me. I couldn't believe it. I still remember the feeling
of shock that rooted me flat against the wall as if I were trying to blend
in with the graffiti written there.
40 "I refuse to do it! I don't care who her father is, her grades don't even
begin to compare to Martha's. I won't lie or **falsify** records. Martha has
a straight A-plus average and you know it." That was Mr. Schmidt and
he sounded very angry. Mr. Boone's voice sounded calm and quiet.
"Look. Joann's father is not only on the Board, he owns the only store
in town: we could say it was a close tie and—"
The pounding in my ears drowned out the rest of the words, only a
word here and there filtered through. ". . . Martha is Mexican . . . resign
. . . won't do it . . . ." Mr. Schmidt came rushing out and luckily for me
went down the opposite way toward the auditorium, so he didn't see me.
50 Shaking, I waited a few minutes and then went in and grabbed my bag and
fled from the room. Mr. Boone looked up when I came in but didn't say
anything. To this day I don't remember if I got in trouble in P.E. for being
late or how I made it through the rest of the afternoon. I went home very
sad and cried into my pillow that night so Grandmother wouldn't hear me.
It seemed a cruel coincidence that I had overheard that conversation. **B**
The next day when the principal called me into his office I knew what
it would be about. He looked uncomfortable and unhappy. I decided I
wasn't going to make it any easier for him, so I looked him straight in the
eyes. He looked away and fidgeted with the papers on his desk. **C**
60 "Martha," he said, "there's been a change in policy this year regarding
the scholarship jacket. As you know, it has always been free." He cleared

despair (dǐ-spâr') v.
to lose hope

Language Coach
Metaphors Writers use
metaphors to compare
two things without
using *like* or *as.* In line
28, "Coach Thompson
was a real bear" is a
metaphor. How might
the coach react to
someone who is late?

eavesdrop (ēvz'drŏp')
v. to listen secretly to a
private conversation
of others

falsify (fôl'sə-fī') v. to
make false by adding
to or changing

B **FIRST-PERSON**
POINT OF VIEW
Reread lines 46–55.
How does the argument
between Mr. Schmidt
and Mr. Boone make
Martha feel?

C **MAKE INFERENCES**
Why is the principal
unhappy?

his throat and continued. "This year the Board has decided to charge fifteen dollars, which still won't cover the complete cost of the jacket."

I stared at him in shock, and a small sound of **dismay** escaped my throat. I hadn't expected this. He still avoided looking in my eyes.

"So if you are unable to pay the fifteen dollars for the jacket it will be given to the next one in line." I didn't need to ask who that was.

Standing with all the dignity I could muster, I said, "I'll speak to my grandfather about it, sir, and let you know tomorrow." I cried on the walk home from the bus stop. The dirt road was a quarter mile from the highway, so by the time I got home, my eyes were red and puffy.

"Where's Grandpa?" I asked Grandma, looking down at the floor so she wouldn't ask me why I'd been crying. She was sewing on a quilt as usual and didn't look up.

"I think he's out back working in the bean field."

I went outside and looked out at the fields. There he was. I could see him walking between the rows, his body bent over the little plants, hoe in hand. I walked slowly out to him, trying to think how I could best ask him for the money. There was a cool breeze blowing and a sweet smell of mesquite[2] fruit in the air, but I didn't appreciate it. I kicked at a dirt clod. I wanted that jacket so much. It was more than just being a valedictorian and giving a little thank you speech for the jacket on graduation night. It represented eight years of hard work and expectation. I knew I had to be honest with Grandpa; it was my only chance. He saw my shadow and looked up.

He waited for me to speak. I cleared my throat nervously and clasped my hands behind my back so he wouldn't see them shaking. "Grandpa, I have a big favor to ask you," I said in Spanish, the only language he knew. He still waited silently. I tried again. "Grandpa, this year the principal said the scholarship jacket is not going to be free. It's going to cost fifteen dollars, and I have to take the money in tomorrow, otherwise it'll be given to someone else." The last words came out in an eager rush. Grandpa straightened up tiredly and leaned his chin on the hoe handle. He looked out over the field that was filled with the tiny green bean plants. I waited, desperately hoping he'd say I could have the money. **D**

He turned to me and asked quietly, "What does a scholarship jacket mean?"

I answered quickly; maybe there was a chance. "It means you've earned it by having the highest grades for eight years and that's why they're giving it to you." Too late I realized the significance of my words.

dismay (dĭs-mā′) *n.* distress caused by trouble or something unexpected

COMMON CORE RL 6

D **FIRST-PERSON POINT OF VIEW**
Notice how the author develops the **first-person narration** by drawing in readers, causing them to connect to the narrator and to identify with the conflicts he or she faces. Reread lines 76–95. Based on the first-person narration, what are your own thoughts about Martha as she takes her problem to her grandfather?

---

2. **sweet smell of mesquite** (mĕ-skēt′): Mesquite, a small tree or shrub native to hot, dry regions of North America, has small flowers and large super-rich pods that give off a sweet smell.

Portrait of Patience Escalier (1888), Vincent van Gogh. Oil on canvas.
Private collection. © Lefevre Fine Art Ltd., London/Bridgeman Art Library.

◀ **Analyze Visuals**

How does the man shown **compare** with your image of Martha's grandfather?

Grandpa knew that I understood it was not a matter of money. It wasn't that. He went back to hoeing the weeds that sprang up between the delicate little bean plants. It was a time-consuming job; sometimes the small shoots were right next to each other. Finally he spoke again as I turned to leave, crying.

"Then if you pay for it, Marta, it's not a scholarship jacket, is it? Tell your principal I will not pay the fifteen dollars." **E**

    I walked back to the house and locked myself in the bathroom for a long time. I was angry with Grandfather even though I knew he was
110 right, and I was angry with the Board, whoever they were. Why did they have to change the rules just when it was my turn to win the jacket? Those were the days of belief and innocence.

E MAKE INFERENCES
Why won't Martha's grandfather pay the money for the jacket?

I t was a very sad and withdrawn girl who dragged into the principal's office the next day. This time he did look me in the eyes.

    "What did your grandfather say?"

    I sat very straight in my chair.

    "He said to tell you he won't pay the fifteen dollars."

    The principal muttered something I couldn't understand under his breath and walked over to the window. He stood looking out

120 at something outside. He looked bigger than usual when he stood up; he was a tall, gaunt man with gray hair, and I watched the back of his head while I waited for him to speak. **F**

"Why?" he finally asked. "Your grandfather has the money. He owns a two-hundred acre ranch."

I looked at him, forcing my eyes to stay dry. "I know, sir, but he said if I had to pay for it, then it wouldn't be a scholarship jacket." I stood up to leave. "I guess you'll just have to give it to Joann." I hadn't meant to say that, it had just slipped out. I was almost to the door when he stopped me.

"Martha—wait."

130 I turned and looked at him, waiting. What did he want now? I could feel my heart pounding loudly in my chest and see my blouse fluttering where my breasts should have been. Something bitter and **vile** tasting was coming up in my mouth; I was afraid I was going to be sick. I didn't need any sympathy speeches. He sighed loudly and went back to his big desk. He watched me, biting his lip.

"Okay. We'll make an exception in your case. I'll tell the Board, you'll get your jacket." **G**

I could hardly believe my ears. I spoke in a trembling rush. "Oh, thank you, sir!" Suddenly I felt great. I didn't know about adrenalin[3] in those 140 days, but I knew something was pumping through me, making me feel as tall as the sky. I wanted to yell, jump, run the mile, do something. I ran out so I could cry in the hall where there was no one to see me.

At the end of the day, Mr. Schmidt winked at me and said, "I hear you're getting the scholarship jacket this year."

His face looked as happy and innocent as a baby's, but I knew better. Without answering I gave him a quick hug and ran to the bus. I cried on the walk home again, but this time because I was so happy. I couldn't wait to tell Grandpa and ran straight to the field. I joined him in the row where he was working, and without saying anything I crouched down and 150 started pulling up the weeds with my hands. Grandpa worked alongside me for a few minutes, and he didn't ask what had happened. After I had a little pile of weeds between the rows, I stood up and faced him.

"The principal said he's making an exception for me, Grandpa, and I'm getting the jacket after all. That's after I told him what you said."

Grandpa didn't say anything; he just gave me a pat on the shoulder and a smile. He pulled out the crumpled red handkerchief that he always carried in his back pocket and wiped the sweat off his forehead.

"Better go see if your grandmother needs any help with supper."

I gave him a big grin. He didn't fool me. I skipped and ran back 160 to the house whistling some silly tune. ❧

---

3. **adrenalin** (ə-drĕn′ə-lĭn): a hormone that speeds up the heartbeat and increases bodily energy. The body produces adrenalin when a person experiences emotions such as excitement or fear.

F FIRST-PERSON POINT OF VIEW
Reread lines 118–122. How does the first-person point of view limit your understanding of what the principal is thinking?

vile (vīl) *adj.* disgusting; unpleasant

G MAKE INFERENCES
Why do you think the principal changed his mind?

Language Coach

Word Definitions Find the phrase *making an exception* in line 153. The word *exception* means "an exclusion or a leaving out." In your own words, explain what the principal is doing for Martha.

Comprehension

COMMON CORE

RL1 Cite textual evidence to
support inferences drawn from the
text. RL6 Analyze how an author
develops and contrasts the points
of view of characters or narrators
in a text.

1. **Recall** Why does Martha call the scholarship jacket "our only chance"?

2. **Clarify** What do Mr. Boone and Mr. Schmidt argue about?

3. **Summarize** Tell why the scholarship jacket is so important to Martha. Cite evidence from the story.

Text Analysis

4. **Make Inferences** Review the inferences that you recorded in equations. Have any of your inferences changed after reading the story? If so, write a revised inference next to the equation. Explain your reasons.

5. **Interpret** Reread lines 47–48. During the teachers' argument, one of the teachers says, "Martha is Mexican." What could he mean by this?

6. **Analyze Character** Martha is the main character in the story. Use a web to describe how the minor characters interact with Martha and what effect they have on the story.

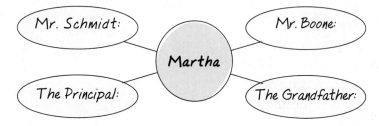

7. **Draw Conclusions** Martha's grandfather says little, but his words and actions mean much to Martha. What does Martha learn from him? Explain how you came to this conclusion.

8. **Contrast Points of View** The story of "The Scholarship Jacket" is told from the first-person point of view. Think about how the story might change if you knew everyone's thoughts and feelings. In what ways would the story be different? Would such a change affect the overall theme? Explain.

Extension and Challenge

9. **Speech** Write a thank-you speech for Martha to give when she receives her scholarship jacket. In the speech, mention the challenges Martha had to overcome in order to achieve this award.

What stands in the way of your DREAMS?

Review the list of obstacles you devised for the **QUICKWRITE** on page 224. Were any of the obstacles as difficult as the one Martha faced? Explain.

Vocabulary in Context

▲ VOCABULARY PRACTICE

Answer each question to show your understanding of the vocabulary words.

1. Which is a way to **falsify**—forging a signature or correcting an error?
2. Would an **agile** person be more likely to sing well or run quickly?
3. If I began to **despair,** would I more likely mingle with others or keep to myself?
4. Which is the more **vile** material—rotting garbage or rose petals?
5. Would losing one's glasses or having lunch with friends more likely cause **dismay?**
6. If you were going to **eavesdrop,** would you talk on the phone or listen behind a door?

ACADEMIC VOCABULARY IN WRITING

• analyze   • aware   • develop   • react   • respond

In "The Scholarship Jacket," a minor character experiences a change. In a brief paragraph, **analyze** the principal. Describe what the story reveals about his appearance and actions. Use at least one of the Academic Vocabulary words in your description.

VOCABULARY STRATEGY: CONTEXT CLUES

Sometimes writers tell you directly what difficult words mean. This kind of context clue, a **definition,** usually follows the difficult word. It is set off by commas or dashes or by expressions like *that is.* Look for a definition of *valedictorian* on page 226 of this story.

COMMON CORE

L 4a Use context as a clue to the meaning of a word.

PRACTICE Define the boldfaced words. Identify context clues that helped you understand the meaning of the word.

1. Loretta is a **polyglot**—that is, someone who knows several languages.
2. The hurricane began as an **amorphous** mass—a shapeless group of clouds.
3. When I **disparaged** him, he put me down in the same way.
4. She was not simply happy to receive the gift; she was **euphoric.**
5. The sleep clinic treats **somnambulists,** people who walk in their sleep.

A Retrieved Reformation

Short Story by O. Henry

VIDEO TRAILER **THINK** central KEYWORD: HML7-234

Who deserves a second CHANCE?

COMMON CORE

RL 6 Analyze how an author develops and contrasts the points of view of characters or narrators in a text.

Everybody makes mistakes—sometimes bad ones. But some people, if they're lucky, are given a chance to redeem themselves. In "A Retrieved Reformation," a man has the opportunity to change his scheming ways. Will he take it?

DISCUSS With a small group, think of one or two individuals who could have used a second chance. Perhaps it's a coach who had a losing season. Maybe it's someone who betrayed a friend's secret. What criteria could be used to determine whether that person deserves another chance?

REPLAY

● TEXT ANALYSIS: THIRD-PERSON POINT OF VIEW

A **third-person point of view** in a story is expressed by a narrator who tells the story using pronouns *he, she, it,* and *they*. This point of view can be omniscient or limited. In the **third-person omniscient point of view**, the narrator tells what all the characters in the story are thinking and doing. In the **third-person limited point of view**, the narrator tells the thoughts and feelings of only one character.

As you read "A Retrieved Reformation," notice when you have more information than the characters do.

● READING STRATEGY: PREDICT

One way to make reading a story even more interesting is to **predict** what will happen next. As you read "A Retrieved Reformation," record your predictions in a chart like the one shown.

My Prediction	Reason for Prediction
Jimmy will keep cracking safes.	

Review: **Make Inferences**

▲ VOCABULARY IN CONTEXT

The boldfaced words help tell the story of a man who is given another chance. Figure out the meaning of each word by using the context clues in each of the phrases.

1. **saunter** casually through the park
2. might **balk** and change his mind at the last minute
3. friendly neighbors chatting **genially**
4. an upright, **virtuous** individual
5. **compulsory** attendance with no excuses allowed
6. slipped away like an **elusive** butterfly
7. tried to **rehabilitate** the injured man
8. honored to have such an **eminent** guest
9. a suitcase in the corner **unperceived** by anyone
10. promised **retribution** if the offender was caught

Complete the activities in your **Reader/Writer Notebook.**

O. Henry
1862–1910

An Early Reader
How could one of the most famous short story writers of all time die with only 23 cents in his pocket? That is what happened to William Sydney Porter, better known as O. Henry. Porter's adventures began in the home of his aunt, who raised him. She encouraged the young boy's love of reading, writing, and drawing caricatures, which are comically exaggerated representations of people. The sense of humor seen in his drawings often appears in his writing.

No Ordinary Life
Porter continued writing and illustrating throughout his adult life in addition to working as a pharmacist, ranch hand, cook, and bank teller. Several years after leaving his position at the First National Bank of Austin, Texas, he was convicted of stealing money from the bank. He published several short stories from jail, using the pen name O. Henry in order to conceal his criminal record.

A Real Character
Porter's vast experiences serve as the inspiration for most of his stories. The main character in "A Retrieved Reformation" is based on a safecracker (someone who breaks into safes) whom Porter met in prison.

Author Online
THINK central
Go to **thinkcentral.com**.
KEYWORD: HML7-235

A Retrieved Reformation

O. Henry

Analyze Visuals ▶

What do the details in the painting help you **infer** about this man?

A guard came to the prison shoe shop, where Jimmy Valentine was assiduously stitching uppers,[1] and escorted him to the front office. There the warden handed Jimmy his pardon, which had been signed that morning by the governor. Jimmy took it in a tired kind of way. He had served nearly ten months of a four-year sentence. He had expected to stay only about three months, at the longest. When a man with as many friends on the outside as Jimmy Valentine had is received in the "stir"[2] it is hardly worthwhile to cut his hair. Ⓐ

"Now, Valentine," said the warden, "you'll go out in the morning.
10 Brace up, and make a man of yourself. You're not a bad fellow at heart. Stop cracking safes, and live straight."

"Me?" said Jimmy, in surprise. "Why, I never cracked a safe in my life."

"Oh, no," laughed the warden. "Of course not. Let's see, now. How was it you happened to get sent up on that Springfield job? Was it because you wouldn't prove an alibi for fear of compromising somebody in extremely high-toned society? Or was it simply a case of a mean old jury that had it in for you? It's always one or the other with you innocent victims."

COMMON CORE   RL 6

Ⓐ **THIRD-PERSON POINT OF VIEW**
Writers sometimes use the omniscient point of view to make general comments about life. Reread lines 6–8. What does this comment mean?

---

1. **assiduously** (ə-sĭj′o͞o-əs-lē) **stitching uppers:** carefully and industriously sewing together the top portions of shoes.

2. **"stir":** a slang term for prison.

Detail of *Tides of Memory* (1936), Norman Rockwell. Oil on board, 18¾″ × 15¼″.

"Me?" said Jimmy, still blankly **virtuous.** "Why, warden, I never was in Springfield in my life!"

20 "Take him back, Cronin," smiled the warden, "and fix him up with outgoing clothes. Unlock him at seven in the morning, and let him come to the bull-pen. Better think over my advice, Valentine."

At a quarter past seven on the next morning Jimmy stood in the warden's outer office. He had on a suit of the villainously fitting, ready-made clothes and a pair of the stiff, squeaky shoes that the state furnishes to its discharged **compulsory** guests.

The clerk handed him a railroad ticket and the five-dollar bill with which the law expected him to **rehabilitate** himself into good citizenship and prosperity. The warden gave him a cigar, and shook hands. Valentine, 30 9762, was chronicled[3] on the books "Pardoned by Governor," and Mr. James Valentine walked out into the sunshine.

Disregarding the song of the birds, the waving green trees, and the smell of the flowers, Jimmy headed straight for a restaurant. There he tasted the first sweet joys of liberty in the shape of a broiled chicken and a bottle of white wine—followed by a cigar a grade better than the one the warden had given him. From there he proceeded leisurely to the depot. He tossed a quarter into the hat of a blind man sitting by the door, and boarded his train. Three hours set him down in a little town near the state line. He went to the café of one Mike Dolan and shook hands with 40 Mike, who was alone behind the bar.

"Sorry we couldn't make it sooner, Jimmy, me boy," said Mike. "But we had that protest from Springfield to buck against, and the governor nearly **balked.** Feeling all right?"

"Fine," said Jimmy. "Got my key?"

He got his key and went upstairs, unlocking the door of a room at the rear. Everything was just as he had left it. There on the floor was still Ben Price's collar-button that had been torn from that **eminent** detective's shirt-band when they had overpowered Jimmy to arrest him.

Pulling out from the wall a folding-bed, Jimmy slid back a panel in the 50 wall and dragged out a dust-covered suitcase. He opened this and gazed fondly at the finest set of burglar's tools in the East. It was a complete set, made of specially tempered steel, the latest designs in drills, punches, braces and bits, jimmies, clamps, and augers, with two or three novelties invented by Jimmy himself, in which he took pride. Over nine hundred dollars they had cost him to have made at _____, a place where they make such things for the profession.

virtuous
(vûr′chŌŌ-əs) *adj.*
morally good; honorable

compulsory
(kəm-pŭl′sə-rē) *adj.*
forced; required

rehabilitate
(rē′hə-bĭl′ĭ-tāt′) *v.* to restore to useful life, as through therapy and education

Language Coach

Homonyms Words with the same spelling but different meanings are called homonyms. In line 38, *boarded* means "entered or gone aboard (a ship, an airplane, and so on)." What other meaning for *boarded* do you know? (Hint: it is related to wood.)

balk (bôk) *v.* to refuse to move or act

eminent (ĕm′ə-nənt) *adj.* famous; well-respected

---

3. **chronicled** (krŏn′ĭ-kəld): written down in a record book or ledger book.

In half an hour Jimmy went downstairs and through the café. He was now dressed in tasteful and well-fitting clothes, and carried his dusted and cleaned suitcase in his hand. **B**

60   "Got anything on?" asked Mike Dolan, **genially.**

"Me?" said Jimmy, in a puzzled tone. "I don't understand. I'm representing the New York Amalgamated Short Snap Biscuit Cracker and Frazzled Wheat Company."

This statement delighted Mike to such an extent that Jimmy had to take a seltzer-and-milk on the spot. He never touched "hard" drinks.

A week after the release of Valentine, 9762, there was a neat job of safe-burglary done in Richmond, Indiana, with no clue to the author. A scant eight hundred dollars was all that was secured. Two weeks after that a patented, improved, burglar-proof safe in Logansport was
70 opened like a cheese to the tune of fifteen hundred dollars, currency; securities and silver untouched. That began to interest the rogue catchers.[4] Then an old-fashioned bank safe in Jefferson City became active and threw out of its crater an eruption of banknotes amounting to five thousand dollars. The losses were now high enough to bring the matter up into Ben Price's class of work. By comparing notes, a remarkable similarity in the methods of the burglaries was noticed. Ben Price investigated the scenes of the robberies, and was heard to remark: "That's Dandy Jim Valentine's autograph. He's resumed business. Look at that combination knob—jerked out as easy as pulling up a radish in wet weather. He's got
80 the only clamps that can do it. And look how clean those tumblers were punched out! Jimmy never has to drill but one hole. Yes, I guess I want Mr. Valentine. He'll do his bit next time without any short-time or clemency foolishness."[5]

Ben Price knew Jimmy's habits. He had learned them while working up the Springfield case. Long jumps, quick get-aways, no confederates,[6] and a taste for good society—these ways had helped Mr. Valentine to become noted as a successful dodger of **retribution.** It was given out that Ben Price had taken up the trail of the **elusive** cracksman, and other people with burglar-proof safes felt more at ease. **C**

90   One afternoon Jimmy Valentine and his suitcase climbed out of the mailhack in Elmore, a little town five miles off the railroad down in the blackjack country of Arkansas. Jimmy, looking like an athletic young senior just home from college, went down the board sidewalk toward the hotel.

---

4. **rogue** (rōg) **catchers:** people who chase after criminals.

5. **He'll do his bit . . . foolishness:** He'll serve his full term in prison without anyone shortening the length of it or pardoning him.

6. **confederates** (kən-fĕd'ər-ĭts): accomplices or associates in crime.

B PREDICT
On the basis of Jimmy's actions in this paragraph, what do you predict he will do?

genially (jēn'yəl-lē) *adv.* in a pleasant, friendly manner

retribution (rĕt'rə-byōō'shən) *n.* punishment for bad behavior

elusive (ĭ-lōō'sĭv) *adj.* tending to elude capture

C THIRD-PERSON POINT OF VIEW
Reread lines 84–89. What information does the narrator share with you that the main character, Jimmy, doesn't know?

A young lady crossed the street, passed him at the corner, and entered a door over which was the sign "The Elmore Bank." Jimmy Valentine looked into her eyes, forgot what he was, and became another man. She lowered her eyes and colored slightly. Young men of Jimmy's style and looks were scarce in Elmore.

100 Jimmy collared a boy that was loafing on the steps of the bank as if he were one of the stockholders, and began to ask him questions about the town, feeding him dimes at intervals. By and by the young lady came out, looking royally unconscious of the young man with the suitcase, and went her way.

"Isn't that young lady Miss Polly Simpson?" asked Jimmy, with specious guile.[7]

"Naw," said the boy. "She's Annabel Adams. Her pa owns this bank. What'd you come to Elmore for? Is that a gold watch-chain? I'm going to get a bulldog. Got any more dimes?" **D**

110 Jimmy went to the Planters' Hotel, registered as Ralph D. Spencer, and engaged a room. He leaned on the desk and declared his platform to the clerk. He said he had come to Elmore to look for a location to go into business. How was the shoe business, now, in the town? He had thought of the shoe business. Was there an opening? **E**

The clerk was impressed by the clothes and manner of Jimmy. He, himself, was something of a pattern of fashion to the thinly gilded youth of Elmore, but he now perceived his shortcomings. While trying to figure out Jimmy's manner of tying his four-in-hand[8] he cordially gave information.

120 Yes, there ought to be a good opening in the shoe line. There wasn't an exclusive shoe store in the place. The dry-goods and general stores handled them. Business in all lines was fairly good. Hoped Mr. Spencer would decide to locate in Elmore. He would find it a pleasant town to live in, and the people 130 very sociable.

D PREDICT
What do you think will happen now that Jimmy and the bank owner's daughter have noticed each other?

E MAKE INFERENCES
Reread lines 110–114. Why does Jimmy change his name and say he's going into the shoe business?

7. **specious guile** (spē′shəs gīl): innocent charm masking real slyness.

8. **four-in-hand:** a necktie tied in the usual way, that is, in a slipknot with the ends left hanging.

Eleanor (1907), Frank Weston Benson. Oil on canvas, 64.13 cm × 76.83 cm. The Hayden Collection–Charles Henry Hayden Fund. © Museum of Fine Arts, Boston (08.326).

Mr. Spencer thought he would stop over in the town a few days and look over the situation. No, the clerk needn't call the boy. He would carry up his suitcase, himself; it was rather heavy.

Mr. Ralph Spencer, the phoenix[9] that arose from Jimmy Valentine's ashes—ashes left by the flame of a sudden and alterative attack of love—remained in Elmore, and prospered. He opened a shoe store and secured a good run of trade. **F**

Socially he was also a success and made many friends. And he accomplished the wish of his heart. He met Miss Annabel Adams, and became more and more captivated by her charms.

F THIRD-PERSON POINT OF VIEW
Who in the story knows that Ralph Spencer is also Jimmy Valentine?

At the end of a year the situation of Mr. Ralph Spencer was this: he had won the respect of the community, his shoe store was flourishing, and he and Annabel were engaged to be married in two weeks. Mr. Adams, the typical, plodding, country banker, approved of Spencer. Annabel's pride in him almost equaled her affection. He was as much at home in the family of Mr. Adams and that of Annabel's married sister as if he were already a member.

One day Jimmy sat down in his room and wrote this letter, which he mailed to the safe address of one of his old friends in St. Louis:

Dear Old Pal:

*I want you to be at Sullivan's place, in Little Rock, next Wednesday night, at nine o'clock. I want you to wind up some little matters for me. And, also, I want to make you a present of my kit of tools. I know you'll be glad to get them—you couldn't duplicate the lot for a thousand dollars. Say, Billy, I've quit the old business— a year ago. I've got a nice store. I'm making an honest living, and I'm going to marry the finest girl on earth two weeks from now. It's the only life, Billy—the straight one. I wouldn't touch a dollar of another man's money now for a million. After I get married I'm going to sell out and go West, where there won't be so much danger of having old scores brought up against me. I tell you, Billy, she's an angel. She believes in me; and I wouldn't do another crooked thing for the whole world. Be sure to be at Sully's, for I must see you. I'll bring along the tools with me. **G**

Your old friend,
Jimmy

Language Coach

Idioms An idiom is a phrase that has a different meaning from its individual words. In line 152, the phrase *wind up* means "to close or bring to a finish." Why do you think Jimmy chooses to use this phrase instead of being more specific?

G PREDICT
Do you think Jimmy will ever crack another safe? Why or why not?

---

9. **phoenix** (fē'nĭks): a mythological bird that lived for 500 years and then burned itself to death, only to rise from its own ashes to live another long life.

Hill, Main Street, Gloucester (1916), John Sloan. Oil on canvas, 25¾″ × 39⅞″. Littlejohn Collection, The Parrish Art Museum, Southampton, New York, 1961.3.208.

On the Monday night after Jimmy wrote this letter, Ben Price jogged unobtrusively into Elmore in a livery buggy.[10] He lounged about town in his quiet way until he found out what he wanted to know. From the
170 drugstore across the street from Spencer's shoe store he got a good look at Ralph D. Spencer.

"Going to marry the banker's daughter are you, Jimmy?" said Ben to himself, softly. "Well, I don't know!"

The next morning Jimmy took breakfast at the Adamses. He was going to Little Rock that day to order his wedding suit and buy something nice for Annabel. That would be the first time he had left town since he came to Elmore. It had been more than a year now since those last professional "jobs," and he thought he could safely venture out. ⓗ

After breakfast quite a family party went down together—Mr. Adams,
180 Annabel, Jimmy, and Annabel's married sister with her two little girls,

Analyze Visuals ▲

What **mood** do the colors in the painting suggest?

ⓗ **THIRD-PERSON POINT OF VIEW**
What do you know that Jimmy doesn't know at this point?

---

10. **livery** (lĭv′ə-rē) **buggy:** a hired horse and carriage.

aged five and nine. They came by the hotel where Jimmy still boarded, and he ran up to his room and brought along his suitcase. Then they went on to the bank. There stood Jimmy's horse and buggy and Dolph Gibson, who was going to drive him over to the railroad station.

All went inside the high, carved oak railings into the banking room—Jimmy included, for Mr. Adams's future son-in-law was welcome anywhere. The clerks were pleased to be greeted by the good-looking, agreeable young man who was going to marry Miss Annabel. Jimmy set his suitcase down. Annabel, whose heart was bubbling with happiness 190 and lively youth, put on Jimmy's hat and picked up the suitcase. ◆

"Wouldn't I make a nice drummer?"[11] said Annabel. "My! Ralph, how heavy it is. Feels like it was full of gold bricks."

"Lot of nickel-plated shoehorns in there," said Jimmy, coolly, "that I'm going to return. Thought I'd save express charges by taking them up. I'm getting awfully economical."

The Elmore Bank had just put in a new safe and vault. Mr. Adams was very proud of it, and insisted on an inspection by everyone. The vault was a small one, but it had a new patented door. It fastened with three solid steel bolts thrown simultaneously with a single handle, and had a time 200 lock. Mr. Adams beamingly explained its workings to Mr. Spencer, who showed a courteous but not too intelligent interest. The two children, May and Agatha, were delighted by the shining metal and funny clock and knobs. ▯

While they were thus engaged Ben Price **sauntered** in and leaned on his elbow, looking casually inside between the railings. He told the teller that he didn't want anything; he was just waiting for a man he knew.

Suddenly there was a scream or two from the women, and a commotion. **Unperceived** by the elders, May, the nine-year-old girl, in a spirit of play, had shut Agatha in the vault. She had then shot the bolts 210 and turned the knob of the combination as she had seen Mr. Adams do.

The old banker sprang to the handle and tugged at it for a moment. "The door can't be opened," he groaned. "The clock hasn't been wound nor the combination set."

Agatha's mother screamed again, hysterically.

"Hush!" said Mr. Adams, raising his trembling hand. "All be quiet for a moment. Agatha!" he called as loudly as he could. "Listen to me." During the following silence they could just hear the faint sound of the child wildly shrieking in the dark vault in a panic of terror.

"My precious darling!" wailed the mother. "She will die of fright! 220 Open the door! Oh, break it open! Can't you men do something?"

◆ GRAMMAR IN CONTEXT
Reread lines 189–190. O. Henry uses an **appositive phrase** in describing a character's feelings.

▯ MAKE INFERENCES
Why does "Mr. Spencer" show a "courteous but not too intelligent interest" in the new safe and vault?

saunter (sôn'tər) v. to stroll in a casual manner

unperceived
(ŭn-pər-sēvd') adj. not seen or noticed

---

11. **drummer:** an old-fashioned word for traveling salesman.

"There isn't a man nearer than Little Rock who can open that door," said Mr. Adams, in a shaky voice. "My God! Spencer, what shall we do? That child—she can't stand it long in there. There isn't enough air, and, besides, she'll go into convulsions from fright." **J**

Agatha's mother, frantic now, beat the door of the vault with her hands. Somebody wildly suggested dynamite. Annabel turned to Jimmy, her large eyes full of anguish, but not yet despairing. To a woman nothing seems quite impossible to the powers of the man she worships.

"Can't you do something, Ralph—try, won't you?"

230 He looked at her with a queer, soft smile on his lips and in his keen eyes.

"Annabel," he said, "give me that rose you are wearing, will you?"

Hardly believing that she had heard him aright, she unpinned the bud from the bosom of her dress, and placed it in his hand. Jimmy stuffed it into his vest pocket, threw off his coat and pulled up his shirt sleeves. With that act Ralph D. Spencer passed away and Jimmy Valentine took his place. **K**

"Get away from the door, all of you," he commanded, shortly.

He set his suitcase on the table, and opened it out flat. From that time on he seemed to be unconscious of the presence of anyone else. He laid
240 out the shining, queer implements swiftly and orderly, whistling softly to himself as he always did when at work. In a deep silence and immovable, the others watched him as if under a spell.

In a minute Jimmy's pet drill was biting smoothly into the steel door. In ten minutes—breaking his own burglarious record—he threw back the bolts and opened the door.

Agatha, almost collapsed, but safe, was gathered into her mother's arms.

Jimmy Valentine put on his coat, and walked outside the railings toward the front door. As he went he thought he heard a faraway voice that he once knew call "Ralph!" But he never hesitated. At the door a
250 big man stood somewhat in his way.

"Hello, Ben!" said Jimmy, still with his strange smile. "Got around at last, have you? Well, let's go. I don't know that it makes much difference, now."

And then Ben Price acted rather strangely.

"Guess you're mistaken, Mr. Spencer," he said. "Don't believe I recognize you. Your buggy's waiting for you, ain't it?"

And Ben Price turned and strolled down the street. ❧ **L**

J PREDICT
On the basis of everything you know about Jimmy, what do you think he will do?

K MAKE INFERENCES
What is Jimmy preparing to do? How does he expect it to affect his relationship with Annabel?

L MAKE INFERENCES
Why does Ben Price let Jimmy go free?

Comprehension

1. **Recall** What successes does Jimmy achieve in Elmore?

2. **Recall** How does Ben Price react when Jimmy cracks the safe?

3. **Summarize** How has Jimmy changed?

Text Analysis

● 4. **Make Inferences** Reread lines 95–99. What happens when Jimmy and Annabel first meet?

● 5. **Predict** Review the prediction chart you made as you read. How close were your predictions to what actually happens to Jimmy?

● 6. **Analyze Third-Person Point of View** Skim the story from lines 196–236. Use a graphic organizer like the one shown to note the information the reader knows that Jimmy does not.

I Know

Jimmy Knows

● 7. **Contrast Points of View** "A Retrieved Reformation" is told from the third-person omniscient point of view. Rewrite lines 247–256 by revealing only what Ben Price sees, thinks, and feels. How does using the third-person limited point of view affect the story?

Extension and Challenge

8. **Speaking and Listening** Do you agree with Ben Price's decision to let Jimmy go free? Hold a classroom trial to decide Jimmy's fate. Choose who will be Jimmy's defense lawyer, the prosecutor, the judge, the witnesses, the jury, the audience, and the court reporter. The defense will argue that Jimmy be granted a second chance, and the prosecution will argue that he be sent back to prison. The closing arguments should be presented to the classroom jury. Your arguments must be supported with evidence from the text.

Who deserves a second CHANCE?

Consider your first responses to the question on page 234. Now that you have read this story, does Jimmy Valentine's situation fit any of your criteria for deserving a second chance? Give a reason for your response.

COMMON CORE

RL 6 Analyze how an author develops and contrasts the points of view of characters or narrators in a text.

Vocabulary in Context

▲ VOCABULARY PRACTICE

Synonyms are words that have the same meaning, and **antonyms** are words that have the opposite meaning. Decide whether the words in each pair are synonyms or antonyms.

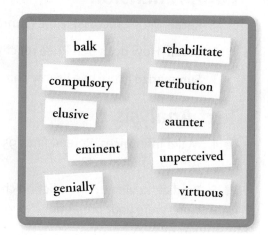

1. compulsory—voluntary
2. elusive—slippery
3. virtuous—honorable
4. saunter—stroll
5. balk—agree

6. retribution—punishment
7. eminent—unknown
8. rehabilitate—restore
9. unperceived—unnoticed
10. genially—disagreeably

ACADEMIC VOCABULARY IN WRITING

- analyze • aware • develop • react • respond

How do you think people **respond** to individuals who have served time in prison? How should we respond? Write an opinion. Be sure to include at least one of the Academic Vocabulary words in your opinion.

VOCABULARY STRATEGY: WORDS WITH MULTIPLE MEANINGS

Many English words have more than one meaning. For example, you might know that *compromising* can mean "giving in by both sides to reach an agreement." But you might not be familiar with its meaning in this story (line 15), "putting someone into a bad position or situation."

If a word does not make sense to you, try to find **context clues**. Look at the words around it for clues to other possible meanings. For further help, check a dictionary, which will give you the definition and tell you the part of speech. For example, which of these meanings of *balk* would you expect to find in a baseball article?

> **balk** (bôk) *v.* **1.** to refuse to move or act: *The horse balked at jumping the fence.* **2.** to make an illegal motion as a pitcher, especially to start a throw and not finish it.

PRACTICE Define the boldfaced words by using context clues or a dictionary.

1. Shipping is one of the city's **key** industries.
2. He floated down the stream with the **current.**
3. Several town officials helped to **frame** the new law.
4. The stars stood out in sharp **relief** against the sky.
5. What numbers must you multiply to figure out the **volume** of a room?

COMMON CORE

L 4d Verify the preliminary determination of the meaning of a word or phrase.

Interactive Vocabulary **THINK** central

Go to **thinkcentral.com**.
KEYWORD: HML7-246

Language

◆ **GRAMMAR IN CONTEXT:** Use Appositive Phrases

COMMON CORE

L 1a Explain the function of phrases in specific sentences.
W 2 Write informative/ explanatory texts to examine a topic and convey ideas.

Review the **Grammar in Context** note on page 243. An **appositive** is a noun or pronoun that identifies or renames another noun or pronoun. An **appositive phrase** is made up of an appositive and its modifiers. You can make your writing more clear by using an appositive or appositive phrase to combine two sentences into one.

> *Original:* Jimmy was released from prison. Jimmy was a notorious safecracker.

> *Revised:* Jimmy, a notorious safecracker, was released from prison. (A notorious safecracker *is an appositive phrase that identifies Jimmy.*)

Place commas before and after an appositive phrase when it adds extra, nonessential information about the noun or pronoun that precedes it, as in the example above.

PRACTICE In each item, combine the two sentences by changing the second sentence to an appositive phrase.

1. Cameron practices every day. He is a champion skateboarder.
2. Ashley has a large vocabulary. She is a master at languages.
3. The man wants to become a citizen. He is an immigrant.
4. The woman keeps asking questions. The woman is a TV reporter.

*For more help with appositives, see page R61 of the **Grammar Handbook.***

READING-WRITING CONNECTION

YOUR TURN

Increase your understanding of "A Retrieved Reformation" by responding to this prompt. Then use the **revising tip** to improve your writing.

WRITING PROMPT	REVISING TIP
Short Constructed Response: Comparison Jimmy Valentine and Ben Price both make surprising decisions at the end of "A Retrieved Reformation." Using details and examples from the text, write **one paragraph** in which you compare the two characters.	Review your response. Are sentences with appositive phrases correct? If not, revise your writing.

Interactive Revision THINK central

Go to thinkcentral.com.
KEYWORD: HML7-247

The Three-Century Woman
Short Story by Richard Peck

Charles
Short Story by Shirley Jackson

Why do people MISBEHAVE?

COMMON CORE

RL 3 Analyze how particular elements of a story interact.

No one's behavior is always perfect. When we misbehave, sometimes we do so for a reason—although that doesn't mean it's a good one. In the stories you are about to read, an elderly woman and a young boy misbehave at important milestones in their lives.

LIST IT Make a list of ways you've seen people misbehave. Did someone make a face in a yearbook picture? Did someone disrupt a serious ceremony? After making your list, discuss with classmates why you think those individuals may have acted as they did.

● TEXT ANALYSIS: CHARACTER MOTIVATION

Some of the most distinctive details in a story are those that reveal a character's traits and **motivations,** or the reasons behind his or her behavior. These details can drive a plot, as a character creates or reacts to events. To figure out a character's motivation, consider story details like these:

- the narrator's direct comments about a character's motivation
- a character's actions and thoughts
- what matters to a character

As you read the following two stories, note what the characters say and do and how their motivations affect the events of the plot.

● READING STRATEGY: SET A PURPOSE FOR READING

To **set a purpose** for reading, you choose specific reasons to read. As you read "The Three-Century Woman" and "Charles," find similarities and differences between the two main characters. Fill in the chart after you finish each story.

	Great-Grandma	Laurie
What does each character think, say, and do?		
How do other characters react to each character?		
How would you describe each character's motivation?		

Review: **Make Inferences**

▲ VOCABULARY IN CONTEXT

The listed words help reveal the characters' personalities. For each word, choose the numbered term closest in meaning.

WORD	cynically	insolently	renounce
LIST	incredulously	raucous	venerable

1. noisy
2. disrespectfully
3. sarcastically
4. skeptically
5. well-respected
6. give up

Complete the activities in your **Reader/Writer Notebook.**

Meet the Authors

Richard Peck
born 1934

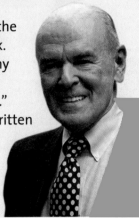

Inspired Teacher
Teaching high school English brought out the writer in Richard Peck. As he says, "I found my future readers right there in the roll book." Although Peck has written novels for adults, he is best known and loved for his young-adult fiction.

Shirley Jackson
1919–1965

Rebel with a Cause
From an early age, Shirley Jackson rebelled against what she considered her wealthy family's selfish lifestyle. Instead of taking part in social events, she would disappear into her journals. After she married, Jackson moved to a small town in Vermont and adopted a much different way of life. She wrote many novels, essays, and short stories. Jackson's friends and critics described the reclusive author as the "Madame of Mystery," referring to the dark humor and strange twists found in her stories. Sadly, Jackson died at 45 from a heart attack.

Authors Online
Go to **thinkcentral.com.** KEYWORD: HML7-249

The Three-Century *Woman*

Richard Peck

I guess if you live long enough," my mom said to Aunt Gloria, "you get your fifteen minutes of fame."

Mom was on the car phone to Aunt Gloria. The minute Mom rolls out of the garage, she's on her car phone. It's state of the art and better than her car.

We were heading for Whispering Oaks to see my Great-Grandmother Breckenridge, who's lived there since I was a little girl. They call it an Elder Care Facility. Needless to say, I hated going.

The reason for Great-Grandma's fame is that she was born in 1899.
10 Now it's January 2001. If you're one of those people who claim the new century begins in 2001, not 2000, even you have to agree that Great-Grandma Breckenridge has lived in three centuries. This is her claim to fame.

We waited for a light to change along by Northbrook Mall, and I gazed fondly over at it. Except for the Multiplex, it was closed because of New Year's Day. I have a severe mall habit. But I'm fourteen, and the mall is the place without homework. Aunt Gloria's voice filled the car. **Ⓐ**

"If you take my advice," she told Mom, "you'll keep those Whispering Oaks people from letting the media in to interview Grandma. Interview
20 her my foot! Honestly. She doesn't even know where she is, let alone how many centuries she's lived in. The poor old soul. Leave her in peace. She's already got one foot in the—"

"Gloria, your trouble is you have no sense of history." Mom gunned across the intersection. "You got a C in History."

"I was sick a lot that year," Aunt Gloria said.

"Sick of history," Mom murmured.

Analyze Visuals ▶

What can you **infer** about the personality of the woman in the red hat on the basis of her appearance?

Ⓐ CHARACTER MOTIVATION
Reread lines 14–17. What do you learn about the narrator here?

Red Hat (2003), Deidre Scherer. Fabric and thread. © Deidre Scherer.

"I heard that," Aunt Gloria said.

They bickered on, but I tuned them out. Then when we turned in at Whispering Pines, a sound truck from IBC-TV was blocking the drive.

30 "Good grief," Mom murmured. "TV."

"I told you," Aunt Gloria said, but Mom switched her off. She parked in a frozen rut.

"I'll wait in the car," I said. "I have homework."

"Get out of the car," Mom said.

If you get so old you have to be put away, Whispering Oaks isn't that bad. It smells all right, and a Christmas tree glittered in the lobby. A real tree. On the other hand, you have to push a red button to unlock the front door. I guess it's to keep the inmates from escaping, though Great-Grandma Breckenridge wasn't going anywhere and hadn't for 40 twenty years.

When we got to her wing, the hall was full of camera crews and a woman from the suburban newspaper with a notepad.

Mom sighed. It was like that first day of school when you think you'll be okay until the teachers learn your name. Stepping over a cable, we stopped at Great-Grandma's door, and they were on to us.

"Who are you people to Mrs. Breckenridge?" the newspaperwoman said. "I want names."

These people were seriously pushy. And the TV guy was wearing more makeup than Mom. It dawned on me that they couldn't get into Great-
50 Grandma's room without her permission. Mom turned on them. **B**

"Listen, you're not going to be interviewing my grandmother," she said in a quiet bark. "I'll be glad to tell you anything you want to know about her, but you're not going in there. She's got nothing to say, and . . . she needs a lot of rest."

"Is it Alzheimer's?"[1] the newswoman asked. "Because we're thinking Alzheimer's."

"Think what you want," Mom said. "But this is as far as you get. And you people with the camera and the light, you're not going in there either. You'd scare her to death, and then I'd sue the pants off you." **C**

60 They pulled back.

But a voice came wavering out of Great-Grandma's room. Quite an eerie, echoing voice.

"Let them in!" the voice said.

Language Coach

Homonyms Words that have the same spelling and sound but have different meanings are called homonyms. In line 41, the word *wing* means "a structure connected to the side of a main building." What other meaning do you know for *wing*?

B **CHARACTER MOTIVATION**
Reread lines 41–50. The narrator characterizes the news people as "seriously pushy." Which of their actions or words led to this description?

C **CHARACTER MOTIVATION**
Reread lines 51–59. What do you learn about the narrator's mother from how she talks to the reporters?

---

1. **Alzheimer's** (älts'hī-mərz): a disease of the brain that causes confusion and may lead to total loss of memory.

It had to be Great-Grandma Breckenridge. Her roommate had died. "Good grief," Mom murmured, and the press surged forward.

Mom and I went in first, and our eyes popped. Great-Grandma was usually flat out in the bed, dozing, with her teeth in a glass and a book in her hand. Today she was bright-eyed and propped up. She wore a fuzzy pink bed jacket. A matching bow was stuck in what remained of her hair.

70 "Oh for pity's sake," Mom murmured. "They've got her done up like a Barbie doll."

Great-Grandma peered from the bed at Mom. "And who are you?" she asked.

"I'm Ann," Mom said carefully. "This is Megan," she said, meaning me.

"That's right," Great-Grandma said. "At least you know who you are. Plenty around this place don't."

The guy with the camera on his shoulder barged in. The other guy turned on a blinding light.

Great-Grandma blinked. In the glare we noticed she wore a trace of
80 lipstick. The TV anchor elbowed the woman reporter aside and stuck a mike in Great-Grandma's face. Her claw hand came out from under the covers and tapped it.

"Is this thing on?" she inquired.

"Yes, ma'am," the TV anchor said in his broadcasting voice. "Don't you worry about all this modern technology. We don't understand half of it ourselves." He gave her his big, five-thirty news smile and settled on the edge of her bed. There was room for him. She was tiny. **D**

"We're here to congratulate you for having lived in three centuries— for being a Three-Century Woman! A great achievement."
90 Great-Grandma waved a casual claw. "Nothing to it," she said. "You sure this mike's on? Let's do this in one take."

The cameraman snorted and moved in for a closer shot. Mom stood still as a statue, wondering what was going to come out of Great-Grandma's mouth next. **E**

"Mrs. Breckenridge," the anchor said, "to what do you attribute your long life?"

"I was only married once," Great-Grandma said. "And he died young."

The anchor stared. "Ah. And anything else?"

"Yes. I don't look back. I live in the present."
100 The camera panned around the room. This was all the present she had, and it didn't look like much.

"You live for the present," the anchor said, looking for an angle, "even now?"

D CHARACTER MOTIVATION
Why is the TV anchor being so friendly?

E MAKE INFERENCES
Reread lines 77–94. How do you think Megan feels about the reporters?

Great-Grandma nodded. "Something's always happening. Last night I fell off the bed pan."

Mom groaned.

The cameraman pulled in for a tighter shot. The anchor seemed to search his mind. You could tell he thought he was a great interviewer, though he had no sense of humor. A tiny smile played around Great-
110 Grandma's wrinkled lips.

"But you've lived through amazing times, Mrs. Breckenridge. And you never think back about them?" **F**

Great-Grandma stroked her chin and considered. "You mean you want to hear something interesting? Like how I lived through the San Francisco earthquake—the big one of oh-six?"

Beside me, Mom stirred. We were crowded over by the dead lady's bed. "You survived the 1906 San Francisco earthquake?" the anchor said.

Great-Grandma gazed at the ceiling, lost in thought.

"I'd have been about seven years old. My folks and I were staying at
120 that big hotel. You know the one. I slept in a cot at the foot of their bed. In the middle of the night, that room gave a shake, and the chiffonier walked right across the floor. You know what chiffonier is?"

"A chest of drawers?" the anchor said.

"Close enough," Great-Grandma said. "And the pictures flapped on the walls. We had to walk down twelve flights because the elevators didn't work. When we got outside, the streets were ankle-deep in broken glass. You never saw such a mess in your life."

Mom nudged me and hissed: "She's never been to San Francisco. She's never been west of Denver. I've heard her say so."

130 "Incredible!" the anchor said.

"Truth's stranger than fiction," Great-Grandma said, smoothing her sheet.

"And you never think back about it?"

Great-Grandma shrugged her little fuzzy pink shoulders. "I've been through too much. I don't have time to remember it all. I was on the Hindenburg when it blew up, you know."

Mom moaned, and the cameraman was practically standing on his head for a close-up.

"The Hindenburg?"

"That big gas bag the Germans built to fly over the Atlantic Ocean.
140 It was called a zeppelin. Biggest thing you ever saw—five city blocks long. It was in May of 1937, before your time. You wouldn't remember. My husband and I were coming back from Europe on it. No, wait a minute."

Great-Grandma cocked her head and pondered for the camera.

F MAKE INFERENCES
Why do you think the reporter wants Great-Grandma to talk about her memories?

SOCIAL STUDIES CONNECTION

On April 18, 1906, an earthquake devastated San Francisco, California. It is still considered one of the worst natural disasters in the history of the United States.

"My husband was dead by then. It was some other man. Anyway, the two of us were coming back on the Hindenburg. It was smooth as silk. You didn't know you were moving. When we flew in over New York, they stopped the ball game at Yankee Stadium to see us passing overhead."

Great-Grandma paused, caught up in memories.

"And then the Hindenburg exploded," the anchor said, prompting her.

150 She nodded. "We had no complaints about the trip till then. The luggage was all stacked, and we were coming in at Lakehurst, New Jersey. I was wearing my beige coat—beige or off-white, I forget. Then whoosh! The gondola[2] heated up like an oven, and people peeled out of the windows. We hit the ground and bounced. When we hit again, the door fell off, and I walked out and kept going. When they caught up with me in the parking lot, they wanted to put me in the hospital. I looked down and thought I was wearing a lace dress. The fire had about burned up my coat. And I lost a shoe."

"Fantastic!" the anchor breathed. "What detail!" Behind him the
160 woman reporter was scribbling away on her pad.

"Never," Mom muttered. "Never in her life."

"Ma'am, you are living history!" the anchor said. "In your sensational span of years you've survived two great disasters!"

"Three." Great-Grandma patted the bow on her head. "I told you I'd been married."

"And before we leave this **venerable** lady," the anchor said, flashing a smile for the camera, "we'll ask Mrs. Breckenridge if she has any predictions for this new twenty-first century ahead of us here in the Dawn of the Millennium."

170 "Three or four predictions," Great-Grandma said, and paused again, stretching out her airtime. "Number one, taxes will be higher. Number two, it's going to be harder to find a place to park. And number three, a whole lot of people are going to live as long as I have, so get ready for us."

"And with those wise words,"
180 the anchor said, easing off the bed, "we leave Mrs. Breck—"

venerable
(vĕn'ər-ə-bəl) *adj.*
deserving respect because of age, character, or importance

---

2. **gondola** (gŏn'dl-ə): a car that hangs under an airship and contains equipment and controls.

"And one more prediction," she said. "TV's on the way out. Your network ratings are already in the basement. It's all websites now. Son, I predict you'll be looking for work."

And that was it. The light went dead. The anchor, looking shaken, followed his crew out the door. When TV's done with you, they're done with you. "Is that a wrap?" Great-Grandma asked.

But now the woman from the suburban paper was moving in on her. "Just a few more questions, Mrs. Breckenridge."

190 "Where you from?" Great-Grandma blinked pink-eyed at her.

"*The Glenview Weekly Shopper.*"

"You bring a still photographer with you?" Great-Grandma asked.

"Well, no."

"And you never learned shorthand either, did you?"

"Well . . . no."

"Honey, I only deal with professionals. There's the door."

So then it was just Mom and Great-Grandma and I in the room. Mom planted a hand on her hip. "Grandma. Number one, you've never been to San Francisco. And number two, you never *saw* one of 200 those zeppelin things."

Great-Grandma shrugged. "No, but I can read." She nodded to the pile of books on her nightstand with her spectacles folded on top. "You can pick up all that stuff in books."

"And number three," Mom said. "Your husband didn't die young. I can *remember* Grandpa Breckenridge."

"It was that TV dude in the five-hundred-dollar suit who set me off," Great-Grandma said. "He dyes his hair, did you notice? He made me mad, and it put my nose out of joint.[3] He didn't notice I'm still here. He thought I was nothing but my memories. So I gave him some."

210 Now Mom and I stood beside her bed.

"I'll tell you something else," Great-Grandma said. "And it's no lie."

We waited, holding our breath to hear. Great-Grandma Breckenridge was pointing her little old bent finger right at me. "You, Megan," she said. "Once upon a time, I was your age. How scary is that?"

Then she hunched up her little pink shoulders and winked at me. She grinned and I grinned. She was just this little withered-up leaf of a lady in the bed. But I felt like giving her a kiss on her little wrinkled cheek, so I did.

"I'll come to see you more often," I told her. **G**

"Call first," she said. "I might be busy." Then she dozed. ༽

3. **put my nose out of joint:** got me into a bad mood.

VISUAL VOCABULARY

spectacles
(spĕk'tə-kəls) *n.*
eyeglasses

G CHARACTER MOTIVATION
Which actions, thoughts, or words reveal that Megan has changed her opinion of Great-Grandma?

Comprehension

1. **Recall** Where does Great-Grandma live?

2. **Recall** Why are the reporters interviewing Great-Grandma?

COMMON CORE

RL 3 Analyze how particular elements of a story interact.

Text Analysis

3. **Examine the Main Character** How would you describe Great-Grandma to someone who hasn't read "The Three-Century Woman"?

4. **Analyze Character Motivation** What character trait might be Great-Grandma's motivation for making up the stories?

5. **Make Inferences** Why do you think the narrator's mother doesn't reveal what she knows about Great-Grandma to the reporters?

6. **Evaluate the Main Character** In line 99, Great-Grandma says, "I don't look back. I live in the present." Is this true? Support your opinion with examples from the story.

7. **Make Judgments** Skim "The Three-Century Woman" and look for examples where each of the characters misbehaves. Who misbehaves the most in this story?

Comparing Characters

8. **Set a Purpose for Reading** Now that you know more about Great-Grandma, start filling in your chart. Add information that helps you understand Great-Grandma's character.

	Great-Grandma	Laurie
What does each character think, say, and do?	She makes up stories for the news anchor.	
How do other characters react to each character?		
How would you describe each character's motivation?		

CHARLES

Shirley Jackson

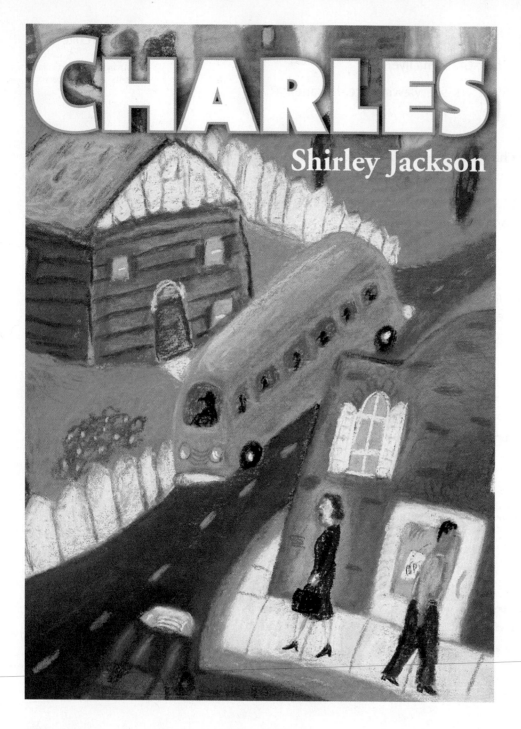

◀ **Analyze Visuals**

Make an **inference** about what kind of people live in this neighborhood. What details support your inference?

renounce (rĭ-nouns′) *v.* to give up

A CHARACTER MOTIVATION
What does the narrator imply about how and why Laurie's personality has changed recently?

The day my son Laurie started kindergarten he **renounced** corduroy overalls with bibs and began wearing blue jeans with a belt; I watched him go off the first morning with the older girl next door, seeing clearly that an era of my life was ended, my sweet-voiced nursery-school tot replaced by a long-trousered, swaggering character who forgot to stop at the corner and wave goodbye to me. **A**

He came home the same way, the front door slamming open, his cap on the floor, and the voice suddenly become **raucous** shouting, "Isn't anybody *here?*"

10   At lunch he spoke **insolently** to his father, spilled his baby sister's milk, and remarked that his teacher said we were not to take the name of the Lord in vain.

"How *was* school today?" I asked, elaborately casual.

"All right," he said.

"Did you learn anything?" his father asked.

Laurie regarded his father coldly. "I didn't learn nothing," he said.

"Anything," I said. "Didn't learn anything."

"The teacher spanked a boy, though," Laurie said, addressing his bread and butter. "For being fresh," he added, with his mouth full.

20   "What did he do?" I asked. "Who was it?"

Laurie thought. "It was Charles," he said. "He was fresh. The teacher spanked him and made him stand in a corner. He was awfully fresh."

"What did he do?" I asked again, but Laurie slid off his chair, took a cookie, and left, while his father was still saying, "See here, young man."

The next day Laurie remarked at lunch, as soon as he sat down, "Well, Charles was bad again today." He grinned enormously and said, "Today Charles hit the teacher."

"Good heavens," I said, mindful of the Lord's name, "I suppose he got spanked again?"

30   "He sure did," Laurie said. "Look up," he said to his father.

"What?" his father said, looking up.

"Look down," Laurie said. "Look at my thumb. Gee, you're dumb." He began to laugh insanely. **B**

"Why did Charles hit the teacher?" I asked quickly.

"Because she tried to make him color with red crayons," Laurie said. "Charles wanted to color with green crayons so he hit the teacher and she spanked him and said nobody play with Charles but everybody did."

The third day—it was Wednesday of the first week—Charles bounced a see-saw onto the head of a little girl and made her bleed, and the teacher

40   made him stay inside all during recess. Thursday Charles had to stand in a corner during story-time because he kept pounding his feet on the floor. Friday Charles was deprived of blackboard privileges because he threw chalk.

On Saturday I remarked to my husband, "Do you think kindergarten is too unsettling for Laurie? All this toughness, and bad grammar, and this Charles boy sounds like such a bad influence."

"It'll be all right," my husband said reassuringly. "Bound to be people like Charles in the world. Might as well meet them now as later."

raucous (rô′kəs) *adj.* loud and harsh sounding

insolently (ĭn′sə-lənt-lē) *adv.* boldly and insultingly

COMMON CORE RL 3

B **CHARACTER MOTIVATION**
Sometimes a character's **motivation** is directly stated in the story. Other times you must make inferences that are based on story information. Reread lines 7–33. Describe how Laurie treats his parents. How might Charles's behavior be affecting Laurie's actions in the story?

On Monday Laurie came home late, full of news. "Charles," he shouted as he came up the hill; I was waiting anxiously on the front steps.
50 "Charles," Laurie yelled all the way up the hill, "Charles was bad again."

"Come right in," I said, as soon as he came close enough. "Lunch is waiting."

"You know what Charles did?" he demanded, following me through the door. "Charles yelled so in school they sent a boy in from first grade to tell the teacher she had to make Charles keep quiet, and so Charles had to stay after school. And so all the children stayed to watch him."

"What did he do?" I asked.

"He just sat there," Laurie said, climbing into his chair at the table. "Hi, Pop, y'old dust mop."

60 "Charles had to stay after school today," I told my husband. "Everyone stayed with him."

"What does this Charles look like?" my husband asked Laurie. "What's his other name?"

"He's bigger than me," Laurie said. "And he doesn't have any rubbers[1] and he doesn't ever wear a jacket."

Monday night was the first Parent-Teachers meeting, and only the fact that the baby had a cold kept me from going; I wanted passionately to meet Charles's mother. On Tuesday Laurie remarked suddenly, "Our teacher had a friend come to see her in school today." **C**

70 "Charles's mother?" my husband and I asked simultaneously.

"Naaah," Laurie said scornfully. "It was a man who came and made us do exercises, we had to touch our toes. Look." He climbed down from his chair and squatted down and touched his toes. "Like this," he said. He got solemnly back into his chair and said, picking up his fork, "Charles didn't even do exercises."

"That's fine," I said heartily. "Didn't Charles want to do exercises?"

"Naaah," Laurie said. "Charles was so fresh to the teacher's friend he wasn't *let* do exercises."

"Fresh again?" I said.

80 "He kicked the teacher's friend," Laurie said. "The teacher's friend told Charles to touch his toes like I just did and Charles kicked him."

"What are they going to do about Charles, do you suppose?" Laurie's father asked him.

Laurie shrugged elaborately. "Throw him out of school, I guess," he said.

Language Coach

Homophones Words that sound alike but have different meanings and spellings are called homophones. In line 53, the word *through* means "in one side and out the other side of." Turn to page 259. In line 42, what is a homophone for *through* that means "tossed"?

C **CHARACTER MOTIVATION**
Why do you think Laurie's mother wanted to meet Charles's mother?

---

1. **rubbers:** low-cut overshoes once commonly worn when it rained.

Wednesday and Thursday were routine; Charles yelled during story hour and hit a boy in the stomach and made him cry. On Friday Charles stayed after school again and so did all the other children.

With the third week of kindergarten Charles was an institution in our family;[2] the baby was being a Charles when she cried all
90 afternoon; Laurie did a Charles when he filled his wagon full of mud and pulled it through the kitchen; even my husband, when he caught his elbow in the telephone cord and pulled the telephone and a bowl of flowers off the table, said, after the first minute, "Looks like Charles." **D**

During the third and fourth weeks it looked like a reformation in Charles; Laurie reported grimly at lunch on Thursday of the third week, "Charles was so good today the teacher gave him an apple."

"What?" I said, and my husband added warily, "You mean Charles?"

"Charles," Laurie said. "He gave the crayons around and he picked up the books afterward and the teacher said he was her helper."
100 "What happened?" I asked **incredulously.**

"He was her helper, that's all," Laurie said, and shrugged.

"Can this be true, about Charles?" I asked my husband that night. "Can something like this happen?"

"Wait and see," my husband said **cynically.** "When you've got a Charles to deal with, this may mean he's only plotting." He seemed to be wrong. For over a week Charles was the teacher's helper; each day he handed things out and he picked things up; no one had to stay after school.

"The PTA meeting's next week again," I told my husband one evening. "I'm going to find Charles's mother there."
110 "Ask her what happened to Charles," my husband said. "I'd like to know."

"I'd like to know myself," I said.

On Friday of that week things were back to normal. "You know what Charles did today?" Laurie demanded at the lunch table, in a voice slightly awed. "He told a little girl to say a word and she said it and the teacher washed her mouth out with soap and Charles laughed."

"What word?" his father asked unwisely, and Laurie said, "I'll have to whisper it to you, it's so bad." He got down off his chair and went around to his father. His father bent his head down and Laurie whispered joyfully. His father's eyes widened.
120 "Did Charles tell the little girl to say *that?*" he asked respectfully.

"She said it *twice,*" Laurie said. "Charles told her to say it *twice.*" **E**

"What happened to Charles?" my husband asked.

"Nothing," Laurie said. "He was passing out the crayons."

---

2. **an institution in our family:** something that has become a significant part of family life.

D CHARACTER MOTIVATION
Reread lines 88–93. Why does Laurie's family call certain actions "being a Charles"?

incredulously
(ĭn-krĕj′ə-ləs-lē) *adv.* in a way that shows doubt or disbelief

cynically (sĭn′ĭ-kəl-lē) *adv.* in a way that shows mistrust in the motives of others

E MAKE INFERENCES
Reread lines 112–121, paying close attention to how Laurie describes Charles's antics. How does Laurie seem to feel about Charles?

Monday morning Charles abandoned the little girl and said the evil word himself three or four times, getting his mouth washed out with soap each time. He also threw chalk.

My husband came to the door with me that evening as I set out for the PTA meeting. "Invite her over for a cup of tea after the meeting," he said. "I want to get a look at her."

130 "If only she's there," I said prayerfully.

"She'll be there," my husband said. "I don't see how they could hold a PTA meeting without Charles's mother."

At the meeting I sat restlessly, scanning each comfortable matronly face, trying to determine which one hid the secret of Charles. None of them looked to me haggard enough. No one stood up in the meeting and apologized for the way her son had been acting. No one mentioned Charles.

After the meeting I identified and sought out Laurie's kindergarten teacher. She had a plate with a cup of tea and a piece of chocolate cake; I had a plate with a cup of tea and a piece of marshmallow cake.

140 We maneuvered up to one another cautiously, and smiled.

"I've been so anxious to meet you," I said. "I'm Laurie's mother."

"We're all so interested in Laurie," she said.

"Well, he certainly likes kindergarten," I said. "He talks about it all the time."

"We had a little trouble adjusting, the first week or so," she said primly, "but now he's a fine little helper. With occasional lapses, of course."

"Laurie usually adjusts very quickly," I said. "I suppose this time it's Charles's influence."

"Charles?"

150 "Yes," I said, laughing, "you must have your hands full in that kindergarten, with Charles."

"Charles?" she said. "We don't have any Charles in the kindergarten." ∾ **F**

Language Coach

Etymology The history of a word is its etymology. The word *kindergarten* in line 137 originates from the German language. *Kinder* is the German word for "children"; *garten* is the German word for "garden." What do you think is the meaning of the combined word *kindergarten*?

F **MAKE INFERENCES**
Who is Charles?

Comprehension

1. **Recall** Who is the narrator of the story?

2. **Recall** Reread lines 25–45. Why does Laurie's mother think kindergarten is "unsettling" for Laurie?

3. **Clarify** According to Laurie, do the other students tend to side with Charles or the teacher?

Text Analysis

● 4. **Examine Character Motivation** Why does Laurie blame Charles for what were really his actions?

● 5. **Make Inferences** Why doesn't Laurie's mother realize that he is Charles?

● 6. **Analyze Character Motivation** Why do you think Laurie misbehaves? Support your opinion with details from the story.

Comparing Characters

● 7. **Set a Purpose for Reading** Now that you have read the second short story, finish filling in your chart. Add the final questions and answer them.

	Great-Grandma	Laurie
What does each character think, say, and do?	She makes up stories for the news anchor.	
How do other characters react to each character?		
How would you describe each character's motivation?		
In what ways are the characters similar? In what ways are they different?		

Why do people MISBEHAVE?

Refer to the list you made of people's misbehavior. If you made a list of the top five misbehaving people, would any of the characters from "The Three-Century Woman" or "Charles" make your list? Give reasons for your choices.

RL 3 Analyze how particular elements of a story interact.

COMMON CORE

Vocabulary in Context

▲ **VOCABULARY PRACTICE**

Show that you understand the boldfaced words. Decide if each statement is *true* or *false*.

1. At a **raucous** party, most guests sit quietly and talk.
2. You will most likely get in trouble if you speak **insolently** to the principal.
3. A **venerable** individual is usually between the ages of 9 and 12.
4. Dressing **cynically** is a good way to be safe on a long hike.
5. If you **renounce** your bad habits, you plan to continue them.
6. People respond **incredulously** to things they do not believe.

ACADEMIC VOCABULARY IN WRITING

> • analyze • aware • develop • react • respond

Should Laurie's parents have been more **aware** of what was really happening at school? Write an explanation for their behavior. Include at least one of the Academic Vocabulary words in your opinion.

VOCABULARY STRATEGY: THE LATIN ROOT *cred*

The Latin root *cred* means "believe." This root is combined with various prefixes and suffixes to form a number of English words. For example, you already know that the vocabulary word *incredulously* means "in a way that shows doubt or disbelief." To understand the meaning of other words with *cred*, use context clues and your knowledge of what this root means.

○ **COMMON CORE**

L 4b Use Latin roots as clues to the meaning of a word.

PRACTICE Choose a word from the web that best completes each sentence.

1. If the witness is not _____ , the jury will not believe her.
2. The opposition tried to _____ the candidate by making false statements about him.
3. Many banks offer customers a _____ , which allows them to buy things without using cash.
4. When you come to the job interview, please bring all your _____ with you.
5. She gossips so much that it is hard to put any _____ in what she says.

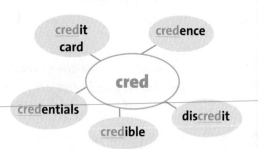

Interactive Vocabulary **THINK** central

Go to thinkcentral.com.
KEYWORD: HML7-264

Writing for Assessment

1. READ THE PROMPT

In writing assessments, you will often be asked to compare and contrast two works that are similar in some way, such as two short stories with similar **characters.**

In four or five paragraphs, compare and contrast Great-Grandma from "The Three-Century Woman" and Laurie from "Charles." Identify the characters' similarities and differences, citing details from the two stories to support your ideas. Then state whether you think the characters are more alike than they are different.

◀ **STRATEGIES IN ACTION**

1. I have to **tell** the **similarities and differences** between the characters.
2. I need to **give examples** that show how the characters are **alike** and how they are **different**.
3. I need to **decide** whether the characters are more alike than they are different.

2. PLAN YOUR WRITING

Using your chart, identify the ways in which the characters are alike and the ways they are different. Then think about how to best present these similarities and differences.

- Write a position statement that presents your main idea.
- Review the stories to find quotations and details that support the similarities and the differences you have identified.
- Create an outline to organize your ideas. This sample outline shows one way to organize your paragraphs.

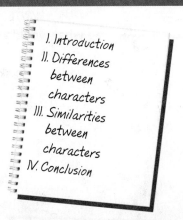

I. Introduction
II. Differences between characters
III. Similarities between characters
IV. Conclusion

3. DRAFT YOUR RESPONSE

Introduction Introduce the characters you are comparing, the titles of the stories in which the characters appear, and your reason for comparing the characters. Also include your position statement.

Body Present the characters' similarities and differences, using your outline as a guide. Make clear whether you think the similarities or differences are more important.

Conclusion State whether you think the characters are more alike than different. Leave your readers with a final thought about the two characters.

Revision Make sure each point of your comparison is supported by an example .

Encounter with Martin Luther King Jr.

Autobiography by Maya Angelou

HISTORY Video link at
thinkcentral.com

What if you could meet your HERO?

COMMON CORE

RI 3 Analyze the interactions between individuals, events, and ideas in a text.

You see them on TV, read about them in magazines and newspapers, and even watch movies that tell the stories of their accomplishments. But for most of us, meeting our famous heroes in person is something that only happens in daydreams. In this selection, Maya Angelou recounts an unforgettable private meeting with her larger-than-life hero, Martin Luther King Jr.

QUICKWRITE If a hero of yours walked into your home tomorrow, what would you say to him or her? In your journal, note whom you would like to meet in this way. Then write five questions you would ask if you had the chance.

TEXT ANALYSIS: CHARACTERIZATION IN NONFICTION

To help her readers understand what Martin Luther King Jr. was like, Maya Angelou uses methods of **characterization** that fiction writers use. She reveals King's personality by

- making direct statements about his personality
- describing his appearance and actions
- showing how others acted toward him
- sharing what he said and what others said about him

As you read the selection, notice the ways in which Angelou conveys what King was like in person.

READING STRATEGY: CONNECT

Whenever you find similarities between your life and someone else's, you are connecting with that person. You can **connect** with what you are reading by comparing the events described with experiences you are familiar with. As you read, keep a **log** to record connections between you and Angelou.

Angelou	Me
Angelou was so surprised to see King that she didn't shake his hand right away.	When I saw my teacher at the grocery store, I was so surprised that I didn't say hello right away.

VOCABULARY IN CONTEXT

The boldfaced words help Angelou convey the African-American experience in the 1960s. To see how many of them you know, restate each sentence, using a different word or words for the boldfaced term.

1. He did not allow his bitterness to **fester** and ruin his life.
2. For King, nonviolence was the key to winning the **fray.**
3. She is **punctual** and in her seat before the bell rings.
4. His kindness helped to **redeem** her from sadness.
5. For some, a **shanty** was the only affordable housing.

 Complete the activities in your **Reader/Writer Notebook.**

Encounter with
Martin
Luther
King Jr.

Maya Angelou

I returned from lunch. In the outer office Millie Jordan was working over a table of papers. Hazel was busy on the telephone. I walked into my office and a man sitting at my desk, with his back turned, spun around, stood up and smiled. Martin Luther King said, "Good afternoon, Miss Angelou. You are right on time."

The surprise was so total that it took me a moment to react to his outstretched hand.

I had worked two months for the SCLC, sent out tens of thousands of letters and invitations signed by Rev. King, made hundreds of statements in his name, but I had never seen him up close. He was shorter than I expected and so young. He had an easy friendliness, which was unsettling. Looking at him in my office, alone, was like seeing a lion sitting down at my dining-room table eating a plate of mustard greens. **A**

"We're so grateful for the job you all are doing up here. It's a confirmation for us down on the firing line."[1]

1. **a confirmation . . . line:** proof to us in the middle of the struggle that we are doing the right thing.

Analyze Visuals ▶

What might you **infer** about the expression on King's face?

A CHARACTERIZATION
Reread lines 10–13. What do you learn about King from Angelou's description of him?

I was finally able to say how glad I was to meet him.

"Come on, take your seat back and tell me about yourself."

I settled gratefully into the chair and he sat on the arm of the old sofa across the room.

20 "Stanley says you're a Southern girl. Where are you from?" His voice had lost the church way of talking and he had become just a young man asking a question of a young woman. I looked at him and thought about the good-looking . . . school athlete, who was invariably the boyfriend of the . . . cheerleader. **B**

I said, "Stamps, Arkansas. Twenty-five miles from Texarkana."

He knew Texarkana and Pine Bluff, and, of course, Little Rock. He asked me the size and population of Stamps and if my people were farmers. I said no and started to explain about Mamma and my crippled uncle who raised me. As I talked he nodded as if he knew them 30 personally. When I described the dirt roads and **shanties** and the little schoolhouse on top of the hill, he smiled in recognition. When I mentioned my brother Bailey, he asked what he was doing now.

The question stopped me. He was friendly and understanding, but if I told him my brother was in prison, I couldn't be sure how long his

B CHARACTERIZATION
Reread lines 20–24.
What change does the author notice in King's speech pattern? What does this suggest about King?

shanty (shăn'tē) *n.* a rundown house; a shack

understanding would last. I could lose my job. Even more important, I might lose his respect. Birds of a feather and all that, but I took a chance and told him Bailey was in Sing Sing.[2]

He dropped his head and looked at his hands.

"It wasn't a crime against a human being." I had to explain. I loved
40 my brother and although he was in jail, I wanted Martin Luther King to think he was an uncommon criminal. "He was a fence. Selling stolen goods. That's all." **C**

He looked up. "How old is he?"

"Thirty-three and very bright. Bailey is not a bad person. Really."

"I understand. Disappointment drives our young men to some desperate lengths." Sympathy and sadness kept his voice low. "That's why we must fight and win. We must save the Baileys of the world. And Maya, never stop loving him. Never give up on him. Never deny him. And remember, he is freer than those who hold him behind bars." **D**

50 Redemptive[3] suffering had always been the part of Martin's argument which I found difficult to accept. I had seen distress **fester** souls and bend

C CONNECT
Have you ever felt the need to explain or defend the actions of someone you love? Why do you think Angelou might have done this?

D CHARACTERIZATION
Reread lines 45–49. What does King's statement suggest about him?

fester (fĕs′tər) v. to become an increasing source of irritation or poisoning

2. **Sing Sing:** a prison in New York State.

3. **redemptive:** earning freedom or salvation.

peoples' bodies out of shape, but I had yet to see anyone **redeemed** from pain, by pain.

There was a knock at the door and Stanley Levison entered.

"Good afternoon, Maya. Hello, Martin. We're about ready."

Martin stood and the personal tenderness disappeared. He became the fighting preacher, armed and ready for the public **fray**.

He came over to my desk. "Please accept my thanks. And remember, we are not alone. There are a lot of good people in this nation. White
60 people who love right and are willing to stand up and be counted." His voice had changed back to the mellifluous Baptist cadence[4] raised for the common good. **E**

We shook hands and I wondered if his statement on the existence of good whites had been made for Stanley's benefit.

At the door, he turned. "But we cannot relax, because for every fair-minded white American, there is a Bull Connor[5] waiting with his shotgun and attack dogs."

I was sitting, mulling over the experience, when Hazel and Millie walked in smiling.
70 "Caught you that time, didn't we?"

I asked her if she had set up the surprise. She had not. She said when Martin came in he asked to meet me. He was told that I was due back from lunch and that I was fanatically **punctual.** He offered to play a joke by waiting alone in my office.

Millie chuckled. "He's got a sense of humor. You never hear about that, do you?"

Hazel said, "It makes him more human somehow. I like a serious man to be able to laugh. Rounds out the personality." **F**

Martin King had been a hero and a leader to me since the time when
80 Godfrey and I heard him speak and had been carried to glory on his wings of hope. However, the personal sadness he showed when I spoke of my brother put my heart in his keeping forever, and made me thrust away the small constant worry which my mother had given me as a part of an early parting gift: Black folks can't change because white folks won't change. ❧ **G**

redeem (rĭ-dēm′) *v.* to set free

fray (frā) *n.* a fight; a heated dispute

E CHARACTERIZATION
Reread lines 56–62. Describe the shift in King's attitude. What can you **infer** about why he is different in private than he is in public?

punctual
(pŭngk′chōō-əl) *adj.* on time; prompt

F CHARACTERIZATION
What do you learn about King through Millie's and Hazel's words?

G CONNECT
Think about how Angelou feels toward King. Who has touched your heart or mind in a similar way?

---

4. **mellifluous** (mə-lĭf′lōō-əs) **Baptist cadence** (kād′ns): the smooth rhythms of speech characteristic of Baptist preachers.

5. **Bull Connor:** an official in Birmingham, Alabama, best known for ordering police officers to use fire hoses and police dogs to break up a civil rights demonstration in 1963.

Comprehension

1. **Recall** What joke does King play on Maya Angelou?

2. **Recall** Why is Angelou afraid to tell King about her brother?

3. **Clarify** Why did King want to meet Angelou?

COMMON CORE

RI 3 Analyze the interactions between individuals, events, and ideas in a text.

Text Analysis

4. **Examine Connections** Review the notes you made in your log. What events were you able to connect with? Note which connection surprised you the most.

5. **Interpret Meaning** Reread lines 12–13. When Angelou enters her office and sees King, she describes her hero as a "lion sitting down at my dining-room table eating a plate of mustard greens." What does she mean by this?

6. **Analyze Characterization** What three words or phrases would you use to describe King's personality? Write them in a chart like the one shown. Below each word or phrase, cite several details from the selection to support it.

7. **Make Inferences** Reread the last paragraph. Why do you think King's comments about Angelou's brother helped Angelou stop worrying so much, or, in her words, "thrust away the small constant worry" she had felt since her mother left her?

8. **Draw Conclusions** Which side of King, the "fighting preacher" or the tender young man, do you think meant the most to Angelou? Give examples from the text to support your answer.

Extension and Challenge

9. **SOCIAL STUDIES CONNECTION** Read the workplace document from Martin Luther King Jr. on page 275. Why were King and the SCLC concerned about the African-American vote in the South? What was the result of their efforts? Research the Voting Rights Act of 1965 to find the answers. Also note how the law changed voting practices

What if you could meet your HERO?

Recall the questions you would ask your hero. Since reading Maya Angelou's account, would you change any of your questions? Why or why not?

Vocabulary in Context

▲ VOCABULARY PRACTICE

Choose the letter of the term that is most closely related to the boldfaced word.

1. **shanty:** (a) mansion, (b) abode, (c) hut
2. **fester:** (a) improve, (b) disturb, (c) go away
3. **redeem:** (a) rescue, (b) enslave, (c) preserve
4. **fray:** (a) conflict, (b) converse, (c) sew
5. **punctual:** (a) lazy, (b) on time, (c) late

ACADEMIC VOCABULARY IN WRITING

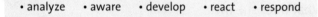

• analyze • aware • develop • react • respond

Think of a social problem of today. If King were alive today, how would he **react** to this problem? Write a brief statement of the issue and of how you think King would deal with it. Use at least one of the Academic Vocabulary words in your statement.

VOCABULARY STRATEGY: USING REFERENCE AIDS

To express ideas clearly and accurately, you need to choose just the right words. Reference aids, or resources of information, can improve your writing by providing synonyms for words you already know. Synonyms are words with similar meanings. For example, a synonym for *shanty* is *shack*. To find a synonym for a word, look in a reference aid.

• A **thesaurus** is a reference book of synonyms. Also, many word-processing programs contain an electronic thesaurus tool.

   shanty *noun* hovel, hut, lean-to, shack

• A **dictionary** lists synonyms after the definitions of some words.

   shanty (shăn′tē) *n., pl.* **-ties** a rundown house: *The shanty collapsed after years of neglect.* **syn** HOVEL, HUT, LEAN-TO, SHACK

COMMON CORE

L 4c Consult general and specialized reference materials, both print and digital, to clarify meaning.

PRACTICE Use a reference aid to find a synonym for each word. Note the synonym and the reference aid you used to find it. Then use each synonym in a sentence that matches its shade of meaning.

1. abolish
2. extricate
3. monopolize
4. voracious

Interactive Vocabulary THINK central

Go to **thinkcentral.com**.
KEYWORD: HML7-274

MEMORANDUM Following is a memo that Dr. King sent to the people organizing the opening-day rallies for the Crusade for Citizenship, a drive to register African Americans to vote. Notice the phrases that reflect Dr. King's fairness and leadership.

FROM: M. L. King Jr., President
TO: Speakers, Local Contacts, Participants in S. C. L. C.
RE: Crusade for Citizenship Mass Meeting, February 12, 1958

UNITY OF EMPHASIS

At our executive committee meeting on Thursday, Jan. 30, 1958, many expressed the hope that all persons would leave the Mass Meetings with a clear picture of the aims and purposes of the Southern Christian Leadership Conference, with a firm determination to register and vote, and with a sense of being part of a southwide "crusade."

To help achieve this unity of aim and direction, we are urging you to make certain that the following points are clearly and simply made from the platform by some responsible person during the mass meeting:

1. The Crusade for Citizenship is a southwide movement. These meetings express this. The list should be read. It should be clear that this is the opening step in a long and hard, but necessary and glorious struggle.

2. The Crusade has two aims:
   (a) to double the number of Negroes who vote in the South
   (b) and thus, to help liberate all Southerners, Negro and white, to extend democracy in our great nation. When Negroes can vote, white people will have greater economic and political freedom. The South can have a real two party system— a necessity for real democracy.

3. The Crusade will place emphasis on preparing spiritually and tactically for registration prior to the 1958 and 1960 elections.

4. The Crusade is non-partisan. Its major purpose is to get men and women to realize that voting is a "moral" and "political" duty to God, to the nation, to themselves, and to their children; then to help them learn how to register and to want to vote. The Crusade will not engage in partisan politics. We urge people to vote: we do not want to influence them to vote for any particular party. We believe in the people. When they are aroused to vote, they will vote intelligently. No one need tell them where their political interest lies. This is morally the right approach.

5. The right to vote is related to all other rights. When Negroes have won and fully exercise their right to vote many changes can then occur:
   (a) segregated buses will disappear
   (b) wages will be increased
   (c) police brutality will be a thing of the past
   (d) men who believe in justice will be sent to congress
   (e) "mob violence" will fade away
   (f) justice will be established in the courts.

These things will come about because the mayors, city councilmen, police commissioners, the governors, congressmen and even the President will know that they must do the right things or be turned out of office when the people go to the ballot box. . . .

Dirk the Protector
Memoir by Gary Paulsen

What do you need to SURVIVE?

COMMON CORE

RI 3 Analyze the interactions between individuals, events, and ideas in a text.
RI 6 Determine an author's point of view in a text.

Hunger, fear, injury, turmoil—it's amazing what people can withstand when they must. But there's a limit. Every human being needs certain things to survive. In "Dirk the Protector," a chance encounter provides a young Gary Paulsen with what he needs to survive life alone on the streets.

LIST IT What if you woke up tomorrow and all the adults had vanished? Brainstorm a list of items you would need to survive. Remember that no one would know how to operate electrical plants, manufacture products in factories, or purify drinking water. You may use the list that is shown to get started. When you're finished, compare your list with those of your classmates.

Items to Survive a World Without Adults
1. Flashlight
2. Gallons of purified water
3.
4.

● TEXT ANALYSIS: POINT OF VIEW IN A MEMOIR

In a **memoir,** the writer gives a true account of experiences in his or her life. Because the writer has participated in the events, he or she writes from the **first-person point of view,** using the pronoun *I.* However, that doesn't mean the writer states everything directly. As you read "Dirk the Protector," note when Gary Paulsen says something openly about himself and when he only hints at his true meaning.

● READING SKILL: IDENTIFY CAUSE AND EFFECT

To fully understand what you read, you need to know why things happen. Often, a writer tells you that one event (the **cause**) made another event (the **effect**) happen. In this example, Paulsen directly states that troubles with his parents caused him to leave home:

For a time in my life I became a street kid. It would be nice to put it another way but what with the drinking at home and the difficulties it caused with my parents I couldn't live in the house.

Other times you have to infer cause-and-effect relationships on the basis of clues in the text and your knowledge. As you read "Dirk the Protector," note other cause-and-effect relationships and record them in a diagram like this one.

Cause	Effect
Trouble with parents at home.	Paulsen moves into basement.

▲ VOCABULARY IN CONTEXT

In your *Reader/Writer Notebook,* write a sentence for each of the vocabulary words. Use a dictionary or the definitions in the following selection pages to help you.

WORD	cohort	forerunner	predatory
LIST	conventional	hustle	puny
	decoy	impasse	

Complete the activities in your **Reader/Writer Notebook.**

Meet the Author

Gary Paulsen
born 1939

A Young Survivor

Gary Paulsen was born to a family that faced many problems. As a boy, Paulsen often had to work and take care of himself. While delivering newspapers one cold evening, he went into a library to warm up. The librarian offered him a book and a library card. Paulsen recalls, "The most astonishing thing happened. This silly little card with my name on it gave me an identity." In the library, it did not matter what he wore, who liked him, or how much money he had.

Reader and Writer

Paulsen still reads a lot, and he is a very hardworking writer. He has published more than 150 books for children, young adults, and adults. His childhood experiences and outdoor adventures are frequent subjects in his writing.

Devoted to Dogs

"Dirk the Protector" is from Paulsen's memoir *My Life in Dog Years*. He gives the reader a peek into his own life by sharing memories of his dogs. Paulsen has said, "I've always thought of dogs as people.... They have personalities and likes and dislikes and humor and anger and great heart and spirit."

Author Online **THINK** central

Go to thinkcentral.com.
KEYWORD: HML7-277

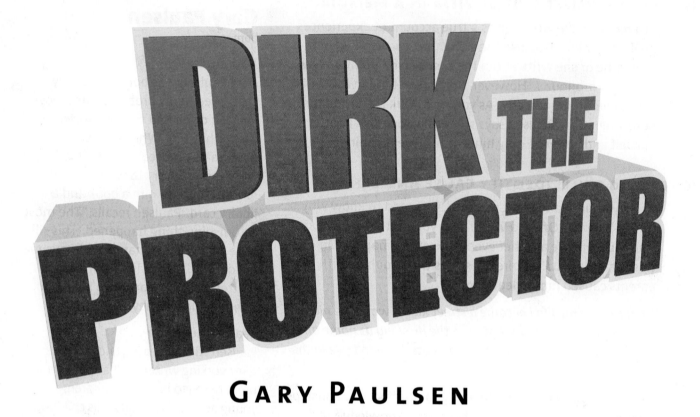

DIRK THE PROTECTOR

GARY PAULSEN

For a time in my life I became a street kid. It would be nice to put it another way but what with the drinking at home and the difficulties it caused with my parents I couldn't live in the house.

I made a place for myself in the basement by the furnace and hunted and fished in the woods around the small town. But I had other needs as well—clothes, food, school supplies—and they required money.

I was not afraid of work and spent most of my summers working on farms for two, three and finally five dollars a day. This gave me enough for school clothes, though never for enough clothes or the right kind; I was never cool or in. But during the school year I couldn't leave town to work the farms. I looked for odd jobs but most of them were taken by the boys who stayed in town through the summer. All the **conventional** jobs like working in the markets or at the drugstore were gone and all I could find was setting pins in the small bowling alley over the Four Clover Bar. Ⓐ

It had just six alleys and they were busy all the time—there were leagues each night from seven to eleven—but the pay for truly brutal

Analyze Visuals ▶
Examine this painting.
What can you **infer**
about the boy's life?

conventional
(kən-vĕn'shə-nəl) *adj.*
usual; traditional

Ⓐ **CAUSE AND EFFECT**
What causes Paulsen
to take the job at the
bowling alley? Keep
reading to find an effect
of working this job.

Boy with Orange, Murray Kimber.
© Murray Kimber/Illustrationworks.com.

work was only seven cents a line. There weren't many boys willing to do the work but with so few alleys, it was still very hard to earn much money. A dollar a night was not uncommon and three was outstanding.

20   To make up the difference I started selling newspapers in the bars at night. This kept me up and out late, and I often came home at midnight. But it added to my income so that I could stay above water.[1]

Unfortunately it also put me in the streets at a time when there was what might be called a rough element. There weren't gangs then, not exactly, but there were groups of boys who more or less hung out together and got into trouble. They were the **forerunners** of the gangs we have now, but with some singular differences. They did not have firearms—but many carried switchblade knives.

These groups were **predatory**, and they hunted the streets at night.

30   I became their favorite target in this dark world. Had the town been larger I might have hidden from them, or found different routes. But there was only a small uptown section and it was impossible for me to avoid them. They would catch me walking a dark street and surround me and with threats and blows steal what money I had earned that night.

I tried fighting back but there were usually several of them. I couldn't win. Because I was from "the wrong side of the tracks"[2] I didn't think I could go to the authorities. It all seemed hopeless. **B**

And then I met Dirk.

40   The bowling alley was on a second floor and had a window in back of the pit area. When all the lanes were going, the heat from the pin lights made the temperature close to a hundred degrees. Outside the window a ladder led to the roof. One fall evening, instead of leaving work through the front door, I made my way out the window and up the ladder onto the roof. I hoped to find a new way home to escape the boys who waited for me. That night one of the league bowlers had bowled a perfect game—300—and in celebration had bought the pit boys hamburgers and Cokes. I had put the burger and Coke in a bag to take back to my basement. The bag had grease stains and smelled of toasted buns, and my mouth watered as I moved from the roof of the bowling

50   alley to the flat roof over the hardware store, then down a fire escape that led to a dark alcove[3] off an alley.

There was a black space beneath the stairs and as I reached the bottom and my foot hit the ground I heard a low growl. It was not loud, more a rumble that seemed to come from the earth and so full of menace that it stopped me cold, my foot frozen in midair.

---

1. **stay above water**: survive.

2. **"the wrong side of the tracks"**: the less desirable part of town.

3. **alcove** (ăl'kōv'): a small hollow space in a wall.

I raised my foot and the growl stopped.

I lowered my foot and the growl came again. My foot went up and it stopped.

I stood there, trying to peer through the steps of the fire escape. For a time
60 I couldn't see more than a dark shape crouched back in the gloom. There was a head and a back, and as my eyes became accustomed to the dark I could see that it had scraggly, scruffy hair and two eyes that glowed yellow. **C**

We were at an **impasse.** I didn't want to climb up the ladder again but if I stepped to the ground it seemed likely I would be bitten. I hung there for a full minute before I thought of the hamburger. I could use it as a **decoy** and get away.

The problem was the hamburger smelled so good and I was so hungry.

I decided to give the beast under the stairs half a burger. I opened the sack, unwrapped the tinfoil and threw half the sandwich under the steps,
70 then jumped down and ran for the end of the alley. I was just getting my stride, legs and arms pumping, pulling air with a heaving chest, when I rounded the corner and ran smack into the latest group of boys who were terrorizing me.

There were four of them, led by a thug—he and two of the others would ultimately land in prison—named, absurdly, "Happy" Santun.

Happy was built like an upright freezer and had just about half the intelligence but this time it was easy. I'd run right into him.

"Well—lookit here. He came to us this time. . . ."

Over the months I had developed a policy of flee or die—run as fast
80 as I could to avoid the pain, and to hang on to my hard-earned money. Sometimes it worked, but most often they caught me.

This time, they already had me. I could have handed over the money, taken a few hits and been done with it, but something in me snapped and I hit Happy in the face with every ounce of strength in my **puny** body.

He brushed off the blow easily and I went down in a welter of blows and kicks from all four of them. I curled into a ball to protect what I could. I'd done this before, many times, and knew that they would stop sometime—although I suspected that because I'd hit Happy it might take longer than usual for them to get bored hitting me. **D**
90 Instead there was some commotion that I didn't understand and the kicks stopped coming. There was a snarling growl that seemed to come from the bowels of the earth, followed by the sound of ripping cloth, screams, and then the fading slap of footsteps running away.

For another minute I remained curled up, then opened my eyes to find that I was alone.

But when I rolled over I saw the dog.

C CAUSE AND EFFECT
Reread lines 52–62.
Make an **inference** about what kind of beast is under the stairs. What's causing the beast to growl?

impasse (ĭm′păs′) *n.* a situation in which no progress can be made; a deadlock

decoy (dē′koi′) *n.* a person or thing used to distract others or lead them in a different direction

puny (pyo͞o′nē) *adj.* weak and small

D POINT OF VIEW
Reread lines 79–89. As Paulsen describes the attack, what else does the reader learn about him?

*I*t was the one that had been beneath the stairs. Brindled, patches of hair gone, one ear folded over and the other standing straight and notched from fighting. He didn't seem to be any particular breed. Just big and rangy, right on the edge of ugly, though I would come to think of him as beautiful. He was Airedale crossed with hound crossed with alligator.

Alley dog. Big, tough, mean alley dog. As I watched he spit cloth— it looked like blue jeans—out of his mouth.

"You bit Happy, and sent them running?" I asked.

He growled, and I wasn't sure if it was with menace, but he didn't bare his teeth and didn't seem to want to attack me. Indeed, he had saved me.

"Why?" I asked. "What did I do to deserve . . . oh, the hamburger."

I swear, he pointedly looked at the bag with the second half of hamburger in it.

"You want more?"

He kept staring at the bag and I thought, Well, he sure as heck deserves it. I opened the sack and gave him the rest of it, which disappeared down his throat as if a hole had opened into the universe.

He looked at the bag.

"That's it," I said, brushing my hands together. "The whole thing."

A low growl.

"You can rip my head off—there still isn't any more hamburger." I removed the Coke and handed him the bag, which he took, held on the ground with one foot and deftly ripped open with his teeth. ◆

"See? Nothing." I was up by this time and I started to walk away. "Thanks for the help . . ."

He followed me. Not close, perhaps eight feet back, but matching my speed. It was now nearly midnight and I was tired and sore from setting pins and from the kicks that had landed on my back and sides.

"I don't have anything to eat at home but crackers and peanut butter and jelly," I told him. I kept some food in the basement of the apartment building, where I slept near the furnace.

He kept following and, truth be known, I didn't mind. I was still half scared of him but the memory of him spitting out bits of Happy's pants and the sound of the boys running off made me smile. When I arrived at the apartment house I held the main door open and he walked right in. I opened the basement door and he followed me down the steps into the furnace room.

I turned the light on and could see that my earlier judgment had been correct. He was scarred from fighting, skinny and flat sided and with patches of hair gone. His nails were worn down from scratching concrete.

"Dirk," I said. "I'll call you Dirk." I had been trying to read a detective novel and there was a tough guy in it named Dirk. "You look like somebody named Dirk."

E CAUSE AND EFFECT Reread lines 105–110. What is the cause- and-effect relationship Paulsen explains here?

GRAMMAR IN CONTEXT In line 118, Paulson properly places the **adjective clause,** *which he took.* The clause modifies the word *bag* and is set off by commas.

140 And so we sat that first night. I had two boxes of Ritz crackers I'd **hustled** somewhere, a jar of peanut butter and another one of grape jelly, and a knife from the kitchen upstairs. I would smear a cracker, hand it to him—he took each one with great care and gentleness—and then eat one myself. We did this, back and forth, until both boxes were empty and my stomach was 150 bulging; then I fell asleep on the old outdoor lounge I used for furniture.

The next day was a school day. I woke up and found Dirk under the basement stairs, watching me. When I opened the door he trotted up the steps and outside—growling at me as he went past—and I started off to school.

He followed me at a distance, then stopped across the street when I went 160 into the front of the school building. I thought I'd probably never see him again.

But he was waiting when I came out that afternoon, sitting across the street by a mailbox. I walked up to him.

"Hi, Dirk." I thought of petting him but when I reached a hand out he growled. "All right—no touching."

I turned and made my way toward the bowling alley. It was Friday and sometimes on Friday afternoon there were people who wanted to bowl 170 early and I could pick up a dollar or two setting pins.

Dirk followed about four feet back—closer than before—and as I made my way along Second Street and came around the corner by Ecker's Drugstore I ran into Happy. He had only two of his **cohorts** with him and I don't think they had intended to do me harm, but I surprised them and Happy took a swing at me.

Dirk took him right in the middle. I mean bit him in the center of his stomach, hard, before Happy's fist could get to me. Happy screamed and doubled over and Dirk went around and ripped into his rear and kept tearing at it even as Happy and his two companions fled down the street.

180 It was absolutely great. Maybe one of the great moments in my life. ⑨ I had a bodyguard.

Street Corner (1991), Daniel Bennett Schwartz. Oil on canvas, 91.4 cm × 71.1 cm. Private collection. © Bridgeman Art Library.

hustle (hŭs'əl) *v.* to gain by energetic effort

cohort (kō'hôrt') *n.* a companion or associate

⑨ POINT OF VIEW
On the basis of what you know about Paulsen, why does he say it was "one of the great moments in my life"?

It was as close to having a live nuclear weapon as you can get. I cannot say we became friends. I touched him only once, when he wasn't looking—I petted him on the head and received a growl and a lifted lip for it. But we became constant companions. Dirk moved into the basement with me, and I gave him a hamburger every day and hustled up dog food for him and many nights we sat down there eating Ritz crackers and he watched me working on stick model airplanes.

190 He followed me to school, waited for me, followed me to the bowling alley, waited for me. He was with me everywhere I went, always back three or four feet, always with a soft growl, and to my great satisfaction every time he saw Happy—every time—Dirk would try to remove some part of his body with as much violence as possible.

He caused Happy and his mob to change their habits. They not only stopped hunting me but went out of their way to avoid me, or more specifically, Dirk. In fact after that winter and spring they never bothered me again, even after Dirk was gone. **G**

D irk came to a wonderful end. I always thought of him as a street dog—surely nobody owned him—and in the summer when I was 200 hired to work on a farm four miles east of town I took him with me. We walked all the way out to the farm, Dirk four feet in back of me, and he would trot along beside the tractor when I plowed, now and then chasing the hundreds of seagulls that came for the worms the plow turned up.

The farmer, whose name was Olaf, was a bachelor and did not have a dog. I looked over once to see Dirk sitting next to Olaf while we ate some sandwiches and when Olaf reached out to pet him Dirk actually— this was the first time I'd seen it—wagged his tail.

He'd found a home.

I worked the whole summer there and when it came time to leave, 210 Dirk remained sitting in the yard as I walked down the driveway. The next summer I had bought an old Dodge for twenty-five dollars and I drove out to Olaf's to say hello and saw Dirk out in a field with perhaps two hundred sheep. He wasn't herding them, or chasing them, but was just standing there, watching the flock.

"You have him with the sheep?" I asked Olaf.

He nodded. "Last year I lost forty-three to coyotes," he said. "This year not a one. He likes to guard things, doesn't he?"

I thought of Dirk chasing Happy down the street, and later spitting out bits of his pants, and I smiled. "Yeah, he sure does." ◐

G CAUSE AND EFFECT
What is the long-term effect Dirk has on the young Paulsen's life?

Comprehension

1. **Recall** What keeps Paulsen out late at night?

2. **Recall** What does Paulsen do to take care of Dirk?

3. **Clarify** What are two challenges that Paulsen faces?

Text Analysis

4. **Analyze Point of View** On the left side of a two-column chart, list information you know about Paulsen because he states it directly. On the right, list the questions you have about Paulsen after reading the memoir.

What I Know About Paulsen	Questions I Have About Paulsen
He lived by himself in a basement.	Did his parents know he was there?

5. **Analyze Cause and Effect** Compare the cause-and-effect relationships you recorded with those recorded by another classmate. With that classmate, choose the one cause-and-effect relationship that you think influenced Paulsen's life the most, and explain why you think so.

6. **Analyze Character** Writers often give animals character traits that appear human. On the basis of the details Paulsen provides about Dirk, describe the dog's "personality."

7. **Compare and Contrast** Reread the first two paragraphs of "Dirk the Protector" and then the last three. How is Paulsen's life the same in the end, and how has it changed?

8. **Draw Conclusions** Dirk's protection ended the attacks against Paulsen. Why don't the attacks start up again after Dirk stays at the farm?

Extension and Challenge

9. **Survival Manual** Now that you've read "Dirk the Protector," think about the advice Paulsen might give you to enable you to survive in the world without the help of adults. Then create a survival manual based on your new list.

What do you need to SURVIVE?

How did reading "Dirk the Protector" affect your ideas about the necessities for survival? Review your list of items. Based on what you've read, would you change anything on your list? Explain.

COMMON CORE

RI 3 Analyze the interactions between individuals, events, and ideas in a text. RI 6 Determine an author's point of view in a text.

Vocabulary in Context

▲ **VOCABULARY PRACTICE**

Choose the vocabulary word that best completes each sentence.

1. The boy tried to get a(n) _____ job but could only find an unusual one.
2. He was frequently beaten up by members of a(n) _____ gang.
3. Unlike the big, strong gang members, he was _____.
4. He had to _____ all day for one solid meal.
5. There he met Dirk, and they stared each other down into a(n) _____.
6. The boy used his hamburger as a(n) _____ to distract the dog.
7. Dirk became the boy's protector and _____.
8. Is Dirk the _____ of other protectors in the boy's future?

cohort

conventional

decoy

forerunner

hustle

impasse

predatory

puny

ACADEMIC VOCABULARY IN WRITING

- analyze • aware • develop • react • respond

In a paragraph or two, **analyze** Paulsen's relationship to Dirk. Does it grow and change in ways you expected? Include at least one of the Academic Vocabulary words in your opinion.

VOCABULARY STRATEGY: IDIOMS

An **idiom** is an expression in which the overall meaning of the words in it is different from the meanings of the individual words. For example, in this story, Paulsen says that working at a certain job helped him "stay above water." *Stay above water* is an idiomatic expression because Paulsen was never in fear of drowning. We know Paulsen means that the job helped him survive.

Language is full of idioms. If you encounter an unfamiliar one, you can often use context clues to figure out its meaning. **Context clues** are words or phrases that surround an unfamiliar word and provide hints about the word's meaning. Otherwise, consult a dictionary.

COMMON CORE

L5 Demonstrate understanding of nuances in word meanings.

PRACTICE Identify the idiom in each sentence and give a definition for it.

1. They kicked around a few ideas about how to make scenery for the play.
2. She changed her tune once she found out the cost of the project.
3. I don't trust Jackson, but his friend seems on the level.
4. Will you take me under your wing if I decide to join the chorus?
5. Getting all this work done will be tough, but hang in there and we'll finish it.

Interactive Vocabulary THINK central

Go to thinkcentral.com.
KEYWORD: HML7-286

Language

◆ **GRAMMAR IN CONTEXT:** Use Adjective Clauses

Review the **Grammar in Context** note on page 282. A **clause** is a group of words that contains a subject and a verb. An **independent clause** expresses a complete thought and can stand alone as a sentence. A **dependent clause**, also known as a **subordinate clause**, cannot. **Adjective clauses** are dependent clauses that modify a noun or a pronoun. Adjective clauses tell what kind, which one, how many, or how much. Adjective clauses are introduced by the relative pronouns *who, whom, whose, that,* or *which*. When you use an adjective clause in your writing, place it close to the word it modifies. When using the word *which* to start an adjective clause, set off the clause with commas.

> *Original:* Dirk isn't easy to pet. Dirk doesn't like to be touched.
>
> *Revised:* Dirk, who doesn't like to be touched, isn't easy to pet.

PRACTICE In each item, combine the two sentences. Substitute the word or words in brackets with a relative pronoun to form an adjective clause. Be sure to use commas when appropriate.

1. Dirk is a dog. [Dirk] can protect people as well as animals.
2. The memoir describes meeting Dirk. [The memoir] was written by Gary Paulsen.
3. Money was hard to find. [Money] was what Paulsen needed.
4. Olaf is a farmer. [Olaf] adopts Dirk.

*For more help with adjective clauses, see page R62 of the **Grammar Handbook.***

READING-WRITING CONNECTION

YOUR TURN Increase your understanding of "Dirk the Protector" by responding to this prompt. Then use the **revising tip** to improve your writing.

WRITING PROMPT	REVISING TIP
Extended Constructed Response: Retelling In the memoir, we learn only as much about Dirk as Paulsen knows. If Dirk could talk, what kind of story might he tell? **In two or three paragraphs,** retell a part of the story from Dirk's point of view.	Review your response. If adjective clauses are used, is each adjective clause next to the word it modifies? If not, revise your writing.

Interactive Revision **THINK** central

Go to thinkcentral.com.
KEYWORD: HML7-287

COMMON CORE

L 1a Explain the function of phrases and clauses in general ad their function specific sentences. **W 3** Write narratives to develop real or imagined experiences or events.

It Was a Long Time Before
Poem by Leslie Marmon Silko

Abuelito Who
Poem by Sandra Cisneros

What do we learn from our ELDERS?

COMMON CORE

RL 3 Analyze how particular elements of a story or drama interact. **RL 5** Analyze how a poem's form or structure contributes to its meaning.

Between you, your parents, and your grandparents, the generations of your family may span a hundred years or more. As you move into the future, what will you take with you from the past? What will you take with you from the present? In the poems "It Was a Long Time Before" and "Abuelito Who," memories and more connect the generations.

LIST IT Think of someone in another generation who spends time with you. Brainstorm a list of the activities you do together. Reread the list; then write one way that person has affected your life or one thing that person has taught you.

TEXT ANALYSIS: CHARACTERIZATION IN POETRY

When poets describe people in their writing, they usually **characterize** them in fewer words than fiction writers do. An image, a phrase, or a telling detail—in a poet's hand, these can suggest an entire personality.

In "Abuelito Who," Sandra Cisneros characterizes her grandfather as someone "who throws coins like rain." This statement gives the reader the impression that the grandfather is generous. You might even be able to picture an elderly man making a ritual of tossing bright coins onto the floor for his grandchildren to scoop up. As you read "It Was a Long Time Before" and "Abuelito Who," pay attention to what else the poets' language suggests about the people in the poems.

READING STRATEGY: READING POETRY

Some poems contain complete sentences with standard punctuation. Other poems don't. But all poems are divided into **lines,** and where they are divided is important to the poems' meaning and rhythm. For example, read the following lines from "It Was a Long Time Before." The poet is telling the reader why she affectionately called her grandmother "Grandma A'mooh."

> *I had been hearing her say*
> > *"a'moo'ooh"*
> *which is the Laguna expression of endearment*
> *for a young child*
> *spoken with great feeling and love.*

Notice that all of these words, put together, create a sentence, but each line read separately has its own effect. Since "a'moo'ooh" appears on its own line, the reader lingers on it, letting its cultural and emotional importance sink in. As you read the two poems, pay attention to how each poet uses capital letters, line length, and word position to give meaning to each poem.

Complete the activities in your **Reader/Writer Notebook.**

Meet the Author

Leslie Marmon Silko
born 1948

Native American Storyteller
Leslie Marmon Silko was raised on the Laguna Pueblo reservation in New Mexico. As she grew up, female relatives taught her traditional Native American stories and legends. Today Silko considers herself part of the global community. She says, "I am writing to the world, not to the United States alone."

Sandra Cisneros
born 1954

Latina Writer
When Sandra Cisneros was a child, she and her family moved frequently between Chicago and her father's birthplace in Mexico. She often spoke English to her Mexican-American mother and Spanish to her father. For Cisneros, writing is a way to deal with the poverty, loneliness, and instability she faced in her childhood. She incorporates the Spanish language in her writing "to say things in English that have never been said before."

Authors Online

Go to **thinkcentral.com**. KEYWORD: HML7-289

It Was a Long Time Before

Leslie Marmon Silko

Rosita Johnson (1958), Lee Marmon. Laguna, New Mexico. © Lee Marmon.

It was a long time before
I learned that my Grandma A'mooh's
real name was Marie Anaya Marmon.
I thought her name really was "A'mooh."
5 I realize now it had happened when I was a baby
and she cared for me while my mother worked.
I had been hearing her say
        "a'moo'ooh"
which is the Laguna[1] expression of endearment
10 for a young child
spoken with great feeling and love. **Ⓐ**

Analyze Visuals ▲

What do the **details** in the photograph tell you about the woman?

Ⓐ CHARACTERIZATION IN POETRY
Why was Marie Anaya Marmon called Grandma A'mooh? Think about what the story of her name tells you about her.

---

1. **Laguna** (lə-gōo'nə): dialect of the Keres language spoken by the Laguna people, whose home is in rural New Mexico.

Her house was next to ours
and as I grew up
I spent a lot of time with her
15 because she was in her eighties
and they worried about her falling.
So I would go check up on her—which was really
an excuse to visit her.
After I had to go to school
20 I went to carry in the coal bucket
which she still insisted on filling.
I slept with her
in case she fell getting up in the night. **B**

She still washed her hair with yucca[2] roots
25 or "soap weed" as she called it. She said
it kept white hair like hers from yellowing.
She kept these yucca roots on her windowsill
and I remember I was afraid of them for a long time
because they looked like hairy twisted claws.

30 I watched her make red chili on the grinding stone
the old way, even though it had gotten difficult for her
to get down on her knees.
She used to tell me and my sisters
about the old days when they didn't have toothpaste
35 and cleaned their teeth with juniper[3] ash,
and how, instead of corn flakes, in the old days they ate
"maaht'zini"[4] crushed up with milk poured over it. **C**

Her last years they took her away to Albuquerque[5]
to live with her daughter, Aunt Bessie.
40 But there was no fire to start in the morning
and nobody dropping by.
She didn't have anyone to talk to all day
because Bessie worked.
She might have lived without watering morning glories
45 and without kids running through her kitchen
but she did not last long
without someone to talk to. **D**

B READING POETRY
Do the sentences in this poem follow standard patterns of grammar and punctuation? Where do the sentences begin and end?

C CHARACTERIZATION IN POETRY
Reread lines 24–37. What do the granddaughter's descriptions tell you about Grandma A'mooh?

D CHARACTERIZATION IN POETRY
Reread lines 38–47. From this description, what do you learn about Grandma A'mooh after her move to Albuquerque?

---

2. **yucca** (yŭk'ə): a plant that grows in warm regions, chiefly those of western North America. Yucca have long sword-shaped leaves, a woody base, and white flowers.

3. **juniper** (jōō'nə-pər): a pleasant-smelling evergreen shrub.

4. **maaht'zini** (mät-zē-nē): *Keres, one of numerous Pueblo languages:* thin, flaky bread made of finely ground blue corn flour.

5. **Albuquerque** (ăl'bə-kûr'kē): the largest city in New Mexico.

Abuelito *Who*

Sandra Cisneros

Abuelito[1] who throws coins like rain
and asks who loves him
who is dough and feathers
who is a watch and glass of water
5 whose hair is made of fur
is too sad to come downstairs today
who tells me in Spanish you are my diamond
who tells me in English you are my sky
whose little eyes are string
10 can't come out to play
sleeps in his little room all night and day
who used to laugh like the letter k
is sick
is a doorknob tied to a sour stick
15 is tired shut the door
doesn't live here anymore
is hiding underneath the bed
who talks to me inside my head
is blankets and spoons and big brown shoes
20 who snores up and down up and down up and down again
is the rain on the roof that falls like coins
asking who loves him
who loves him who? **E**

E READING POETRY
Reread line 2 and lines
22–23. How does the
phrase at the end of the
poem differ from the
phrase at the beginning?

---

1. **Abuelito** (ä-bwe-lē′tō) *Spanish:* an affectionate term for a grandfather.

Comprehension

1. **Recall** What language did each grandparent speak to his or her grandchildren?

2. **Recall** In "It Was a Long Time Before," why did Grandma A'mooh take care of her grandchild?

3. **Clarify** By the end of each poem, what has happened to each grandparent?

Text Analysis

4. **Make Inferences** In "It Was a Long Time Before," why did Grandma A'mooh still insist on filling the coal bucket?

● 5. **Recognize Characterization** Reread lines 3, 9, and 12 of "Abuelito Who." What do these descriptions tell you about Abuelito?

6. **Analyze Point of View** From what point of view is each of these poems written? How does the point of view affect the meaning of each poem?

● 7. **Examine Poetry** Note the differences in the ways each poet uses sentences and punctuation. How does the use of lines, sentences, and punctuation affect the way you read and understand the poems?

8. **Compare and Contrast** Using a Venn diagram like the one shown, compare and contrast Grandma A'mooh with Abuelito. To complete the diagram, draw on inferences you made about the characters as well as on details from the poems.

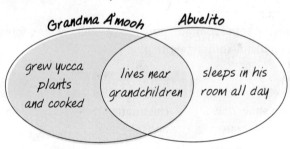

Grandma A'mooh / Abuelito

grew yucca plants and cooked — lives near grandchildren — sleeps in his room all day

COMMON CORE

RL 3 Analyze how particular elements of a story or drama interact. **RL 5** Analyze how a poem's form or structure contributes to its meaning.

Extension and Challenge

9. **SOCIAL STUDIES CONNECTION** Laguna Pueblo is one of many Pueblo communities located in New Mexico. Do some research to find out more about the Pueblo people. Look for information about their traditional culture and values and how they are reflected today.

What do we learn from our ELDERS?

Review the list you created for the activity on page 288. Now that you have read the poems, what new thoughts do you have about the person in your notes?

Writing Workshop
INFORMATIVE TEXT

Comparison-Contrast Essay

Exploring similarities and differences in any two literary texts can deepen your understanding of them. For example, you might explore how one character's conflict is similar to another's or how two stories express a theme differently. In this workshop, you will write a comparison-contrast essay.

 Complete the workshop activities in your **Reader/Writer Notebook.**

WRITE WITH A PURPOSE

WRITING TASK

Write a **comparison-contrast essay** for a specific audience in which you identify the similarities and differences between two literary texts.

Idea Starters
- characters who face a similar conflict
- stories with a common theme
- poems with a similar subject
- folk tales from different cultures

THE ESSENTIALS

Here are some common purposes, audiences, and formats for comparison-contrast writing.

PURPOSES	AUDIENCES	FORMATS
• to show how two literary texts are alike and different • to help your audience better understand two literary texts	• classmates and teacher • readers with an interest in either work • Web users • literature lovers	• essay for class • review for a book-selling Web site • your school's literary magazine • panel discussion • blog

COMMON CORE TRAITS

1. DEVELOPMENT OF IDEAS
- clearly introduces the **subjects being compared and contrasted**
- states the main idea in a clear **controlling idea**
- develops ideas with **evidence,** including **relevant details** and **quotations**
- has a **concluding section** that follows from and supports the ideas presented

2. ORGANIZATION OF IDEAS
- **organizes similarities** and **differences** in a **logical way**
- uses **transitions** to create **cohesion** and clarify relationships among ideas

3. LANGUAGE FACILITY AND CONVENTIONS
- maintains a **formal style** and **tone**
- uses **quotations** correctly
- employs **correct grammar, spelling,** and **punctuation**

Writing Online

THINK central

Go to **thinkcentral.com.**
KEYWORD: HML7N-294

Planning/Prewriting

COMMON CORE

W 2a–f Write informative/explanatory texts to examine and convey ideas, concepts, and information. **W 5** Develop and strengthen writing as needed by planning.

Getting Started

CHOOSE A TOPIC

For your comparison-contrast essay, think about stories, poems, or nonfiction pieces you have read recently. To choose a topic, list selections that interest you and record any similarities and differences that come to mind.

▶ **ASK YOURSELF:**

- Which selections have the most compelling similarities and differences?
- Which characters, conflicts, or themes in those selections could I focus on?

THINK ABOUT AUDIENCE AND PURPOSE

Even in the beginning stages of the writing process, remember to keep your **purpose** (why you are writing) in mind. Your main purpose is to explore similarities and differences in two literary texts so that you can better understand and appreciate those works. Be sure to consider the interests and knowledge of your **audience** (your readers), too.

▶ **ASK YOURSELF:**

- Who is my audience?
- What similarities and differences might my audience find interesting?
- Will I need to include and define any **domain-specific**, or specialized, **vocabulary** so my audience can follow my ideas?
- What **precise language** can I use to make sure my readers understand me?

IDENTIFY SIMILARITIES AND DIFFERENCES

Once you have decided on your subjects, use a chart to brainstorm all the similarities and differences you can identify. Y charts and Venn diagrams are good choices for comparing and contrasting. If you find that there are not many similarities or differences, you may need to try a new approach by choosing different subjects.

▶ **WHAT DOES IT LOOK LIKE?**

Martha
- earns the jacket
- asks Grandpa for help
- has support at home

Roger
- wants the shoes
- tries to steal money
- has no one at home

Both
- want an item of clothing
- get help from an older person

WRITE A CONTROLLING IDEA

To guide your writing, state the main idea of your comparison-contrast essay in a **controlling idea,** or thesis statement. Your controlling idea should point out the similarities and differences you are going to discuss.

▶ **WHAT DOES IT LOOK LIKE?**

Controlling idea: Martha and Roger both want special items of clothing, but for different reasons.

Planning/Prewriting *continued*

Getting Started

GATHER EVIDENCE

Look at the main points you have listed in your chart. What **relevant facts** and **concrete details** can you provide to back up the similarities and differences you noted in your controlling idea? List some specific facts and details that support your controlling idea.

▶ **WHAT DOES IT LOOK LIKE?**

Martha	Roger
• wants scholarship jacket	• wants blue suede shoes
• jacket is for being the best student	• these shoes are in style
• jacket represents hard work	• hasn't earned the shoes

PLAN YOUR ORGANIZATION

The body of a comparison-contrast essay is usually arranged by the subject-by-subject method or the point-by-point method. Choose the method that will best help you organize your ideas logically and clearly.

- **Subject-by-Subject Organization:** Presents all the points about one subject and then all the points about the other
- **Point-by-Point Organization:** Discusses one point at a time, as it applies to both subjects

▶ **WHAT DOES IT LOOK LIKE?**

Subject-by-Subject Method

Martha	Point 1: why she wants the special item Point 2: method she uses to get it Point 3: home life
Roger	Point 1: why he wants the special item Point 2: method he uses to get it Point 3: home life

Point-by-Point Method

Point 1: why the character wants the special item	Martha: Roger:
Point 2: method the character uses to get it	Martha: Roger:
Point 3: home life	Martha: Roger:

PEER REVIEW Share your controlling idea and main points with a peer who is familiar with the literary texts you are comparing and contrasting. Ask: What other facts or details should I include? If your ideas need stronger support, go back and rework them.

 YOUR TURN In your *Reader/Writer Notebook,* develop your writing plan. First, settle on your subjects. Then use a Y chart like the one on page 295 to list similarities and differences. Write a controlling idea and gather evidence to support it. Finally, select the organizational method you will use for your essay.

Drafting

The following chart shows how to structure a clear and coherent, or unified, comparison-contrast essay.

COMMON CORE

W 2b Develop the topic with quotations. **W 4** Produce clear and coherent writing appropriate to task, purpose, and audience. **W 9a (RL 1)** Cite textual evidence to support analysis. **L 2** Demonstrate command of standard English punctuation.

Organizing Your Comparison-Contrast Essay

INTRODUCTION

- Capture your audience's attention with an interesting **quotation, detail,** or **question.**
- Identify the titles and authors of the texts you are **comparing** and **contrasting**.
- Include a **controlling idea** that clearly introduces the main idea of your essay and sets up the **similarities** and **differences** you will discuss.

▼

BODY

- Use subject-by-subject or point-by-point organization and support each point with **relevant facts, concrete details, examples**, and **quotations**.
- Use **transitions** such as *both, like, however,* and *in contrast* to create cohesion.
- Maintain a **formal style** by using clear, unbiased language.

▼

CONCLUDING SELECTION

- Provide a **concluding section** that follows from and supports the ideas presented.
- Tell why your subjects are important to you and why your audience should care about them.

GRAMMAR IN CONTEXT: USING AND PUNCTUATING QUOTATIONS

To fully develop your topic, you will need to include quotations from both literary texts you are comparing and contrasting. As you write, make sure to put quotation marks around any text that is taken directly from another writer's work. If the quoted text is a complete sentence, capitalize the first letter of the sentence. If you are quoting only a word or phrase, weave the quotation into your sentence.

Type of Quote	Example
complete sentence	▶ The narrator says, "My oldest sister, Rosie, had won the jacket a few years back, and I fully expected to also."
word or phrase	▶ Martha describes herself as "a straight A student since the first grade."

YOUR TURN Develop a draft of your essay, following the structure above. Use correct punctuation and capitalization for any quotations you include.

Revising

When you revise, don't worry about every little grammatical detail. That will come later. Instead, focus on improving the content, organization, and style of your essay. Your goal is to determine if you have reached your audience and achieved your purpose. The strategies in this chart can help you revise and rewrite your draft.

COMPARISON-CONTRAST ESSAY

Ask Yourself	Tips	Revision Strategies
1. Does the introduction grab the audience's attention? Does it identify the subjects and include the controlling idea?	▶ **Put a box** around the sentence(s) that grabs your audience's attention. **Circle** the titles and authors. **Underline** the controlling idea.	▶ **Add** an interesting quotation, detail, or question. **Add** a sentence that states the controlling idea. **Add** the titles of the texts and the authors' names.
2. Does the essay discuss several similarities and differences?	▶ **Put a check mark** next to each example of comparison or contrast.	▶ **Add** examples of comparison or contrast.
3. Does the essay follow a logical and coherent organization, either subject-by-subject or point-by-point?	▶ **Write 1** above each point about the first subject and **2** above each point about the second subject.	▶ If necessary, **try** a new organizational approach.
4. Do relevant details, examples, and quotations support key points?	▶ **Highlight** supporting details, examples, and direct quotations.	▶ **Elaborate** on points that are not well supported by adding relevant details, examples, and direct quotations.
5. Do I maintain a formal style throughout the essay?	▶ **Draw** an arrow to words or phrases that are vague, biased, or informal.	▶ **Replace** text with language that is clear, unbiased, or more formal.
6. Does the concluding section restate the controlling idea and explain the importance of the subjects?	▶ **Bracket** the restatement of the controlling idea. **Circle** statements that tell why the subjects are meaningful.	▶ **Add** a sentence that restates the controlling idea. **Elaborate** to explain the subjects' relevance and meaning.

YOUR TURN **PEER REVIEW** With a peer, review your drafts. Answer each question from the chart to locate where and how your drafts could be revised or reworked. Ask for suggestions to help you better reach your intended audience.

ANALYZE A STUDENT DRAFT

Use this student's draft and the comments about it as a model for revising and reworking your own comparison-contrast essay.

COMMON CORE

W 2b Develop the topic with relevant details.
W 5 Develop and strengthen writing as needed by revising, editing, rewriting, or trying a new approach, focusing on how well purpose and audience have been addressed.

Martha and Roger: Different People, Different Lives
by Priya Mahapatra, Jefferson Middle School

❶ Did you ever long for a special item of clothing? In "The Scholarship Jacket" by Marta Salinas, Martha wants a jacket that her school awards for good grades. In "Thank You, M'am" by Langston Hughes, Roger wants a pair of blue suede shoes. The two characters are about the same age, and both are struggling to grow up in an unfair world. Martha and Roger are very different characters, however, because they have different reasons for what they want, different ways of trying to get it, and different lives at home.

❷ Martha and Roger want special items of clothing for different reasons. Martha wants the scholarship jacket because it is supposed to go to the best student in the school. At the beginning of the story, she reflects, "I had been a straight A student since the first grade and this last year had looked forward very much to owning that jacket." The jacket represents years of hard work. Martha turns to her grandfather to help her get the scholarship jacket. On the other hand, Roger hasn't earned the blue suede shoes. He just wants it desperately, probably because it's in style.

> Priya opens with an **interesting question.** She ends her introduction by clearly stating her **controlling idea.**

> Priya structures her ideas using the **point-by-point organization**—first examining both characters' reasons. However, she loses **focus** in the middle of the paragraph.

LEARN HOW **Maintain Focus** Priya begins her essay by comparing and contrasting Martha's and Roger's reasons for wanting a special item. However, in the middle of her essay, she mentions Martha's turning to her grandfather for help. This sentence introduces an unrelated detail that does not support the main idea of the paragraph. Priya fixed this error by deleting the unnecessary detail.

PRIYA'S REVISION TO PARAGRAPH ❷

Martha and Roger want special items of clothing for different reasons. Martha wants the scholarship jacket because it is supposed to go to the best student in the school. At the beginning of the story, she reflects, "I had been a straight A student since the first grade and this last year had looked forward very much to owning that jacket." The jacket represents years of hard work. ~~Martha turns to her grandfather to help her get the scholarship jacket.~~ On the other hand, Roger hasn't earned the blue suede shoes. He just wants them desperately, probably because they are in style.

❸   Martha and Roger also use different methods to get what they want. When the principal tells Martha that she has to pay for the jacket, she calmly says she will speak with her grandfather. Then she goes to her grandfather for help. She realizes, "I knew I had to be honest with Grandpa; it was my only chance." In contrast, Roger tries snatching a purse to solve his problem. When Mrs. Jones asks him why he did that, he lies. "I didn't aim to," he says.

❹   Another difference between Martha and Roger is their homes. Martha appears to have a good home. She knows she can turn to her grandpa for good advice. Unlike Martha, Roger appears to have no one at home. When Mrs. Jones asks, "Ain't you got nobody home to tell you to wash your face?" he says, "No'm." She also learns that Roger hasn't eaten any supper. He explains, "There's nobody home at my house."

❺   Martha and Roger have different reasons and methods for getting what they want. In addition, Martha gets help at home, while Roger finds help by luck.

> Priya uses **direct quotations** to support her main points.

> Priya signals similarities and differences with **transitions.**

> In her **concluding section,** Priya restates her main points, but she doesn't explain why her subjects are meaningful.

LEARN HOW **Strengthen Your Concluding Section** Priya does a good job of summing up her controlling idea in her concluding section, but she needs to go one step further. Look at the revision below. Notice that Priya added sentences that highlight why these stories matter to her. She shares with her audience a fresh insight that she gained from comparing and contrasting these characters.

PRIYA'S REVISION TO PARAGRAPH ❺

Martha and Roger have different reasons and methods for getting what they want. In addition, Martha gets help at home, while Roger finds help by luck. *Yet despite their differences, both characters end up getting excellent advice. Roger and Martha both get help and support from a caring older person. Both stories show the importance of having someone who cares.*

YOUR TURN Use the two "Learn How" lessons, as well as feedback from your teacher and peers, to revise your essay, rewriting when necessary. Be sure to keep your overall purpose and intended audience in mind as you revise.

Editing and Publishing

COMMON CORE **W 2f** Provide a concluding section that supports the information presented. **W 5** Develop and strengthen writing by revising and editing. **L 1** Demonstrate command of the conventions of standard English grammar when writing.

In the editing stage, you clean up any small errors in grammar, spelling, and punctuation that may distract your audience. Check to make sure that you are correctly punctuating the quotations you are including from both literary texts. You should also make sure you are using consistent verb tenses and complete sentences. No matter how strong your ideas are, if your sentences are filled with errors, then your audience may have difficulty following what you've written.

GRAMMAR IN CONTEXT: PRONOUN REFERENCES

Confusing pronoun references also can keep your audience from fully understanding your ideas. A **pronoun** is a word that is used in place of a noun or another pronoun. For example, in the following sentence, the pronoun reference is incorrect: *If a student needs to visit the school nurse, they must have a hall pass.* The sentence should read: *If a student needs to visit the school nurse, he or she must have a hall pass.*

When you use a pronoun such as *he, she, it,* or *they* in your writing, make sure it's clear what the pronoun refers to. The word or phrase that the pronoun refers to is called the pronoun's **antecedent.**

Confusing:	*On the other hand, Roger hasn't earned the blue suede shoes. He just wants it desperately, probably because it's in style.*
	[To what does *it* refer? The **pronoun** has no clear antecedent.]

Clear:	*On the other hand, Roger hasn't earned the blue suede shoes. He just wants* them *desperately, probably because* they are *in style.*
	[Priya edited this passage by inserting the pronouns *them* and *they*. The **antecedent** for these pronouns is *shoes*.]

PUBLISH YOUR WRITING

Share your comparison-contrast essay with an audience.
- Publish your essay in the school literary magazine.
- Adapt your essay for an in-class panel discussion comparing the texts.
- Post your essay on a blog or book-selling Web site.

YOUR TURN Edit your essay to correct any errors. Look closely at your pronoun references to make sure they are clear. Then publish your final essay where your audience is likely to see it.

Scoring Rubric

Use the rubric shown here to evaluate your comparison-contrast essay from the Writing Workshop or your response to the on-demand task on the next page.

COMPARISON-CONTRAST ESSAY

SCORE	COMMON CORE TRAITS
6	• **Development** Clearly introduces the subjects being compared and contrasted; states a strong controlling idea; supports similarities and differences with relevant evidence; ends strongly and insightfully • **Organization** Arranges ideas in a clear, logical order; effectively uses transitions to create cohesion and clarify relationships among ideas • **Language** Consistently maintains a formal style; uses precise language; shows a strong command of conventions
5	• **Development** Competently introduces the subjects being compared and contrasted; states a clear controlling idea; supports most similarities and differences with relevant evidence; ends with a strong concluding section • **Organization** Arranges ideas logically; uses transitions to create cohesion • **Language** Maintains a formal style; uses precise language; has a few errors in conventions
4	• **Development** Sufficiently introduces the subjects being compared and contrasted; states a controlling idea; could use more evidence to support similarities and differences; has a satisfactory concluding section • **Organization** Arranges ideas fairly logically; transitions may not make sense • **Language** Mostly maintains a formal style; needs more precise language at times; includes a few distracting errors in conventions
3	• **Development** States a controlling idea but lacks an engaging introduction; lacks enough relevant evidence; has an ordinary concluding section • **Organization** Has some organizational flaws; needs additional transitions • **Language** Frequently lapses into an informal style; uses some vague language; has some critical errors in conventions
2	• **Development** Has a weak introduction and controlling idea; lacks relevant evidence; has a weak concluding section • **Organization** Has organizational flaws; lacks transitions throughout • **Language** Uses informal style and vague language; has many conventions errors
1	• **Development** Has no introduction, controlling idea, and evidence; ends abruptly • **Organization** Has no organization or transitions • **Language** Uses an inappropriate style and vague words; has major problems with grammar, mechanics, and spelling

Preparing for Timed Writing

 COMMON CORE **W 10** Write routinely over shorter time frames for a range of tasks, purposes, and audiences.

1. ANALYZE THE TASK   5 MIN

Read the task carefully. Underline words that tell the type of writing, circle the topic, and double underline the purpose. Place a star by the audience.

> **WRITING TASK**
>
> In both Paulsen's "Dirk the Protector" on page 278 and Paterson's "The Last Dog" on page 48, a boy's life is changed by his relationship with a dog. Write a comparison-contrast essay in which you compare the two boys for a classmate who has not read the selections. Be sure to include similarities and differences you found between the boys' experiences.

2. PLAN YOUR RESPONSE   10 MIN

Think about the two boys and their experiences. Use a Venn diagram to list ways in which they are alike and different. Then underline the best points of comparison or contrast—those you can most easily support with relevant examples.

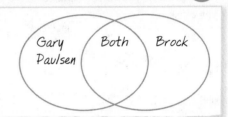

3. RESPOND TO THE TASK   20 MIN

Choose the organization you will use to structure your response: subject by subject or point by point. Follow these guidelines as you write:

- In the introduction, clearly identify the names of the authors and texts and present your topic in a controlling idea.
- In the body, discuss two or three of the most important similarities or differences. Be sure to include relevant details, examples, and quotations.
- In the body, use transitions to clarify relationships among ideas.
- Conclude by restating your controlling idea and telling why the subjects are important to you.

4. IMPROVE YOUR RESPONSE   5–10 MIN

Revising Check your draft. Have you addressed every aspect of the writing task? Did you choose an effective structure? Have you supported your ideas with evidence? **Proofreading** Find and correct any errors in grammar, spelling, and mechanics. Be sure that quotations are capitalized and punctuated correctly. **Checking Your Final Copy** Before you turn in your essay, read it through one more time to make sure that you have done your best work.

Participating in a Panel Discussion

Have you ever discussed a new movie with a group of friends—some of whom saw the movie and some of whom didn't? That kind of discussion, in which those who know about a subject share information with those who don't, is very similar to the way a panel discussion works.

 Complete the workshop activities in your **Reader/Writer Notebook**.

SPEAK WITH A PURPOSE	COMMON CORE TRAITS
TASK With a group of classmates, plan a **panel discussion** in which you compare and contrast two subjects. Then present your discussion to the class.	**A STRONG PANEL DISCUSSION . . .** • follows agreed-upon rules for collaborative discussion • demonstrates that participants are prepared • includes relevant observations and ideas • has participants who listen quietly while others speak • consists of participants who speak clearly at an adequate volume and use appropriate eye contact

COMMON CORE

SL 1a, c Engage in a collaborative discussion; come to discussions prepared; pose and respond to questions. **SL 4** Present claims and findings, emphasizing salient points in a focused, coherent manner; use eye contact and volume.

Plan the Discussion

Choose four classmates to form a panel. Then begin planning your discussion.

- **Decide on a topic.** Brainstorm topics together. Think of subjects that can be easily compared, such as two literary texts, two sports teams, or two popular local hangouts. You may need to take a vote on which topic to choose. Remember that your classmates are your audience. Make sure to choose a topic that will hold their interest.

- **Choose a moderator.** Select one panel member to moderate the discussion. The moderator's job is to keep the discussion moving by calling on panel members and by posing questions.

- **Agree on some basic rules.** Group members should speak clearly, listen without interrupting, and answer questions with relevant observations and ideas. Decide how your discussion will be structured. For example, set a time limit for how long each member will speak in response to each question asked by the moderator.

- **Plan and outline the discussion.** As a group, brainstorm questions for the moderator to ask panel members. Then spend some time preparing your thoughts, reading or researching as needed. Write two or three points of comparison or contrast that you would like to make during the discussion. List evidence that supports your ideas, such as facts, details, and examples.

THINK central

Speaking & Listening Online

Go to **thinkcentral.com**.
KEYWORD: HML7-304

Hold the Discussion

Have the moderator begin by identifying the topic and asking a question of the first panel member, such as "Which character has a better home life, Martha or Roger?" or "Which team has a stronger defense, Team A or Team B?"

- **Present your claims and findings.** Respond to questions posed by the moderator by stating your ideas in a clear and focused way. Draw on your preparation to support your claims with **salient**, or important, points.

- **Give others a chance to respond.** Listen while another speaker summarizes your ideas and adds his or her own thoughts. Consider taking notes on the other speaker's salient points.

- **Take questions from the audience.** Respond to questions and comments thoughtfully and bring the discussion back on topic as needed.

- **Wrap it up.** The moderator should summarize the discussion and thank the panelists and audience.

Get Your Message Across

These verbal and nonverbal techniques can add meaning to your words.

USE VERBAL TECHNIQUES

- **Pitch** Change the pitch (rise and fall) of your voice to add emphasis.
- **Rate** Speak slowly enough that your listeners can understand you. Speak more quickly to show excitement or emotion.
- **Volume** Speak loudly enough for the audience to hear. Use volume to emphasize important points.
- **Tone** Project confidence. Sound friendly and sure of yourself.

USE NONVERBAL TECHNIQUES

- **Eye contact** Use eye contact to keep listeners involved.
- **Facial expressions** Emphasize meaning with smiles, frowns, or raised eyebrows.
- **Gestures** Add emphasis with shrugs, nods, or hand movements.
- **Posture** Sit or stand straight to show confidence.

YOUR TURN

As a Speaker Use the tips in this workshop to present your claims clearly and confidently.

As a Listener Listen respectfully to other people's viewpoints. Listen carefully to be sure you understand all of the questions.

Assessment Practice

COMMON CORE

RL 1 Cite textual evidence to support inferences drawn from the text. **RL 3** Analyze how particular elements of a story interact. **RL 6** Analyze how an author develops and contrasts the points of view of different characters or narrators in a text. **L 4a** Use context as a clue to the meaning of a word. **L 4c** Consult general reference materials to clarify meaning. **L 1a** Explain the function of phrases.

DIRECTIONS Read these selections and answer the questions that follow.

Bob Lemmons is a cowboy who is able to capture a herd of mustangs single-handedly.

from The Man Who Was a Horse

by Julius Lester

1   He had been seeing the wild horses since he could remember. The first time had been at dusk one day. He had been playing near the corral when he happened to look toward the mesa and there, standing atop it, was a lone stallion. The wind blew against it and its mane and tail flowed in the breeze like tiny ribbons. The horse stood there for a long while; then, without warning, it suddenly wheeled and galloped away. Even now Bob remembered how seeing that horse had been like looking into a mirror. He'd never told anyone that, sensing that they would perhaps think him a little touched in the head. Many people thought it odd enough that he could bring in a herd of mustangs himself. But, after that, whenever he saw one mustang or a herd, he felt like he was looking at himself.

2   One day, several of the cowboys went out to capture a herd. The ranch was short of horses and no one ever thought of buying horses when there were so many wild ones. He had wanted to tell them that he would bring in the horses, but they would have laughed at him. Who'd ever heard of one man bringing in a herd? So he watched them ride out, saying nothing. A few days later they were back, tired and disgusted. They hadn't even been able to get close to a herd.

3   That evening Bob timidly suggested to Mr. Hunter that he be allowed to try. Everyone laughed. Bob reminded them that no one on the ranch could handle a horse like he could, that the horses came to him more than anyone else. The cowboys acknowledged that that was true, but it was impossible for one man to capture a herd. Bob said nothing else. Early the next morning he rode out alone, asking the cook to leave food in a saddlebag for him on the fence at the north pasture every day. Three weeks later the cowboys were sitting around the corral one evening and looked up to see a herd of mustangs galloping toward them, led by Bob. Despite their amazement, they moved quickly to open the gate and Bob led the horses in.

4   That had been some twenty years ago, and long after Bob left the Hunter Ranch he found that everywhere he went he was known.

from A Mother in Mannville

by Marjorie Kinnan Rawlings

1   When I took the cabin, I asked for a boy or man to come and chop wood for the fireplace. The first few days were warm, I found what wood I needed about the cabin, no one came, and I forgot the order.

2   I looked up from my typewriter one late afternoon, a little startled. A boy stood at the door, and my pointer dog, my companion, was at his side and had not barked to warn me. The boy was probably twelve years old, but undersized. He wore overalls and a torn shirt, and was barefooted.

3   He said, "I can chop some wood today."

4   I said, "But I have a boy coming from the orphanage."

5   "I'm the boy."

6   "You? But you're small."

7   "Size don't matter, chopping wood," he said. "Some of the big boys don't chop good. I've been chopping wood at the orphanage a long time."

8   I visualized mangled and inadequate branches for my fires. I was well into my work and not inclined to conversation. I was a little blunt.

9   "Very well. There's the ax. Go ahead and see what you can do."

10   I went back to work, closing the door. At first the sound of the boy dragging brush annoyed me. Then he began to chop. The blows were rhythmic and steady, and shortly I had forgotten him, the sound no more of an interruption than a consistent rain. I suppose an hour and a half passed, for when I stopped and stretched, and heard the boy's steps on the cabin stoop, the sun was dropping behind the farthest mountain, and the valleys were purple with something deeper than the asters.

11   The boy said, "I have to go to supper now. I can come again tomorrow evening."

12   I said, "I'll pay you now for what you've done," thinking I should probably have to insist on an older boy. "Ten cents an hour?"

13   "Anything is all right."

14   We went together back to the cabin. An astonishing amount of solid wood had been cut. There were cherry logs and heavy roots of rhododendron, and blocks from the waste pine and oak left from the building of the cabin.

15   "But you've done as much as a man," I said. "This is a splendid pile."

16   I looked at him, actually, for the first time. His hair was the color of the corn shocks and his eyes, very direct, were like the mountain sky when

rain is pending—gray, with a shadowing of that miraculous blue. As I spoke, a light came over him, as though the setting sun had touched him with the same suffused glory with which it touched the mountains. I gave him a quarter.

17   "You may come tomorrow," I said, "and thank you very much."

18   He looked at me, and at the coin, and seemed to want to speak, but could not, and turned away.

19   "I'll split kindling tomorrow," he said over his thin ragged shoulder. "You'll need kindling and medium wood and logs and backlogs."

20   At daylight I was half wakened by the sound of chopping. Again it was so even in texture that I went back to sleep. When I left my bed in the cool morning, the boy had come and gone, and a stack of kindling was neat against the cabin wall. He came again after school in the afternoon and worked until time to return to the orphanage. His name was Jerry; he was twelve years old, and he had been at the orphanage since he was four. I could picture him at four, with the same grave gray-blue eyes and the same—independence? No, the word that comes to me is "integrity."

Reading Comprehension

> **Use the excerpt from "The Man Who Was a Horse" to answer questions 1–4.**

1. From his thoughts in paragraph 1, you can infer that Bob —

   A. is as wild as a horse

   B. feels a kinship with horses

   C. loves to run through the hills

   D. has big ears and a long face

2. Because the story is told from the third-person limited point of view, we know that —

   A. all the cowboys think Bob is crazy

   B. wild horses are afraid of people

   C. Bob feels like a horse

   D. everyone trusts Bob

3. Which sentence from the story shows that Bob is a talented horseman?

   A. *He had been playing near the corral when he happened to look toward the mesa and there, standing atop it, was a lone stallion.*

   B. *But, after that, whenever he saw one mustang or a herd, he felt like he was looking at himself.*

   C. *He had wanted to tell them that he would bring in the horses, but they would have laughed at him.*

   D. *Bob reminded them that no one on the ranch could handle a horse like he could, that the horses came to him more than anyone else.*

4. In paragraph 3, Bob resolves his conflict by —

A. sitting around the corral

B. asking for the food in saddlebags

C. bringing in a wild herd alone

D. asking if he could go after a wild herd

Use the excerpt from "A Mother in Mannville" to answer questions 5–8.

5. The narrator of the story is —

A. a boy who lives in an orphanage

B. a writer who lives in a cabin

C. a voice outside the story

D. the mother of a young boy

6. Which sentence shows that this excerpt is told in the first person?

A. *The boy was probably twelve years old, but undersized.*

B. *He said, "I can chop some wood today."*

C. *I went back to work, closing the door.*

D. *An astonishing amount of solid wood had been cut.*

7. The narrator expects that she will need to hire another worker later because —

A. she is busy with her own work

B. the boy who shows up to work is so small

C. the boy from the orphanage is very quiet

D. it was getting too late in the day to work

8. A characteristic of Jerry's that affects the plot is his —

A. irritability

B. reliability

C. talkativeness

D. thoughtlessness

Use both selections to answer this question.

9. Which character trait do Bob and Jerry have in common?

A. Boldness

B. Dependability

C. Optimism

D. Recklessness

SHORT CONSTRUCTED RESPONSE
Write two or three sentences to answer this question.

10. Name two character traits of Bob Lemmons in "The Man Who Was a Horse." Give details from the story that reveal these traits.

Write a paragraph to answer this question.

11. Reread paragraphs 15–19 of "A Mother in Mannville." What can you infer about the boy from his reaction to the narrator's praise? Support your answer with details from the story.

GO ON ➡

Vocabulary

1. Read the dictionary entry for the word *blunt*.

blunt \blŭnt\ *adj.* **1.** having a dull edge; not sharp **2.** abrupt and frank in manner; gruff **3.** slow to understand **4.** lacking in feeling; insensitive

What is the definition of *blunt* as it is used in paragraph 8 in "A Mother in Mannville"?

A. Definition 1

B. Definition 2

C. Definition 3

D. Definition 4

2. Read the dictionary entry for the word *texture*.

texture \tĕks′ chər\ *n* **1.** the appearance of a fabric **2.** a grainy quality as opposed to a smooth quality **3.** the composition or structure of a substance **4.** a distinctive character

What is the definition of *texture* as it is used in paragraph 20 in "A Mother in Mannville"?

A. Definition 1

B. Definition 2

C. Definition 3

D. Definition 4

3. Which expression from "The Man Who Was a Horse" contains a simile?

A. *its mane and tail flowed in the breeze like tiny ribbons*

B. *Who'd ever heard of one man bringing in a herd?*

C. *no one on the ranch could handle a horse like he could*

D. *A few days later they were back, tired and disgusted.*

4. In paragraph 1 of "The Man Who Was a Horse," Bob remembers that "seeing that horse had been like looking into a mirror." This simile means that —

A. the horse looks like other horses

B. Bob looks like the horse

C. Bob and the horse are always together

D. Bob identifies with the horse

5. What does the following simile from paragraph 16 in "A Mother in Mannville" mean?

"his eyes, very direct, were like the mountain sky when rain is pending"

A. A nearby mountain was hiding some rain clouds.

B. The sky was about to pour rain on them.

C. The boy's eyes were a blue-grey color.

D. It was hard to see the boy's eyes.

Revising and Editing

DIRECTIONS Read this passage and answer the questions that follow.

(1) A hundred years ago, methods of transportation are very different. (2) It was tougher to get around during that era an important time period than it is now. (3) Traveling by surrey a horse-drawn carriage was usually slower than using streetcars or trains. (4) Transportation will improve greatly when the automobile and airplane were invented. (5) Planes and cars changed everything because they were much faster and more comfortable. (6) Today, these two modes of transportation automobile and airplane are now the most convenient of all.

1. What change, if any, should be made in sentence 1?

A. Add a comma after *methods* and *transportation*

B. Change *are* to **will be**

C. Change *are* to **were**

D. Make no change

2. What change, if any, should be made in sentence 2?

A. Change *was* to **is**

B. Add a comma after *era* and *period*

C. Add a comma after *time* and *period*

D. Make no change

3. What change, if any, should be made in sentence 3?

A. Add a comma after *surrey* and *carriage*

B. Add a comma after *carriage* and *streetcars*

C. Change *was* to **will be**

D. Make no change

4. What change, if any, should be made in sentence 4?

A. Change *will improve* to **improved**

B. Add a comma after *automobile* and *airplane*

C. Add a comma after *greatly* and *airplane*

D. Make no change

5. What change, if any, should be made in sentence 5?

A. Add a comma after *planes* and *cars*

B. Change *changed* to **will change**

C. Change *were* to **will be**

D. Make no change

6. What change, if any, should be made in sentence 6?

A. Add a comma after *transportation* and *airplane*

B. Add a comma after *automobile* and *convenient*

C. Change *are* to **were**

D. Make no change

Ideas for Independent Reading

Which questions from Unit 2 made an impression on you?
Continue exploring them with these books.

COMMON CORE

RL 10 Read and comprehend literature.

What has the power to heal?

Crazy Lady!
by Jane Leslie Conly

Does friendship have the power to heal? In this book, a woman's love for her son serves as a beacon of hope for a troubled youth.

Getting Near to Baby
by Audrey Couloumbis

Twelve-year-old Willa and Little Sister take to escaping to the roof of their aunt's house when their baby sister dies. Their mother, suffering from depression, can offer them nothing. Will time heal their wounds?

The Birthday Room
by Kevin Henkes

When Ben Hunter receives two unique gifts, he tells his mom that he'd prefer a trip to see his estranged uncle. Why would he choose an uncle he hasn't seen for ten years? Read this compelling story of one family's forgiveness.

What stands in the way of your dreams?

The Midwife's Apprentice
by Karen Cushman

Alyce is a homeless girl living in medieval England. The town's midwife offers to teach her the art of delivering babies. She learns a great deal, but will she be able to make herself independent?

Charlie Pippin
by Candy Dawson Boyd

Charlie's dad rarely shows her any affection. Now she's in trouble with the principal at school. Will father and daughter ever come to understand and appreciate each other?

Number the Stars
by Lois Lowry

Life in Copenhagen is very different now that Nazi soldiers have marched into town. When the Jews of Denmark are "relocated," ten-year-old Ellen moves in with her best friend's family so that her own life is spared.

Who deserves a second chance?

Spider Boy
by Ralph Fletcher

When Bobby Ballenger moves from the Midwest to New York, he has a difficult time adjusting. The cruelty of his classmates makes him long for his former friends. Will he face the bullies and earn a second chance?

Spinners
by Donna Jo Napoli and Richard Tchen

Napoli and Tchen retell a classic tale to give insights into the lives of Rumpelstiltskin and his daughter. Love, pride, avarice, and revenge are all a part of this delightful new version.

The Fire Pony
by Rodman Philbrick

Roy is happiest when he's with his older brother Joe, who has a fiery temper and a special gift for healing horses. All seems well when Joe rescues Roy from a foster home, but before long, Joe reveals a darker side.

Lessons to Learn

UNDERSTANDING THEME

- In Fiction
- In Poetry
- In Drama
- In Media

Share What You Know

What's the BIG IDEA?

"Things are not always what they seem." "There's no place like home." These are examples of themes, or messages about life and human nature that writers convey to their readers. Often, these ideas are what remain with you long after you've read the last page.

ACTIVITY Pick two or three of your all-time favorite books or movies. For each, reflect on what message the writer or director is trying to express about life and human nature. Get together with a small group and talk about your choices and your responses to these questions:

• What lessons do the characters learn?

• What message did you take away from the book or movie?

• How do you see this big idea, or message, apply to your own life?

Find It Online!

THINK central

Go to thinkcentral.com for the interactive version of this unit.

THE WONDERFUL WIZARD OF OZ

Preview Unit Goals

TEXT ANALYSIS	• Determine theme, including multiple themes • Compare and contrast themes and characters • Identify and interpret symbols • Analyze how theme is conveyed through dialogue and stage directions • Cite evidence to support analysis of inferences • Determine and analyze author's purpose
READING	• Use reading strategies, including monitoring and setting a purpose for reading • Identify and analyze cause and effect and sequence
WRITING AND LANGUAGE	• Write an imaginative short story • Choose among simple, compound, and complex sentences to show different relationships among ideas
SPEAKING AND LISTENING	• Create a class blog
VOCABULARY	• Understand and use denotation and connotation of words • Use general context clues to understand word meaning • Use Latin roots and affixes to determine word meanings
ACADEMIC VOCABULARY	• clause • context • cultural • symbol • theme
MEDIA AND VIEWING	• Compare and contrast a drama to its filmed version

Media Smart DVD-ROM

Big Ideas in Movies

View scenes from the timeless movie, *A Christmas Carol*, to see how filmmakers convey life lessons. Page 428

Understanding Theme

Everyone likes a story with a good plot, but there is more to a story than what happens to the characters. Often there is a deeper meaning, or theme. A **theme** is a message about life or human nature that a writer wants you to understand. A story usually has at least one theme. However, a story may have more than one theme or **multiple themes.**

Some popular themes, such as those about loyalty and friendship, appear in many different stories. They are called **recurring themes.**

Part 1: Themes in Literature

It's easy to confuse a story's theme with its topic. Here's a way to tell the difference: A topic can be summed up in a word or two, such as "taking risks." A theme, however, is a writer's message *about* a topic. It usually takes at least one complete sentence to express a theme—for example, "Life's biggest rewards come from taking risks."

Stories can mean different things to different people. Two people reading a story might describe its theme differently or find different themes.

COMMON CORE

Included in this workshop:
RL 1 Cite several pieces of textual evidence to support analysis of what the text says explicitly as well as inferences drawn from the text.
RL 2 Determine a theme and analyze its development over the course of the text.

EXAMPLES OF THEMES IN LITERATURE

Thank You, M'am

Unit 1
pages 68–72

PLOT SUMMARY

Mrs. Luella Bates Washington Jones catches Roger trying to steal her purse. She drags him to her home, makes him wash up, and feeds him. Then she gives him the ten dollars he was trying to steal.

TOPIC

• Second chances

POSSIBLE THEMES

• Everyone deserves a second chance.
• An act of kindness can make a difference in a person's life.

Casey at the Bat

Unit 1
pages 134–136

PLOT SUMMARY

When the hometown baseball hero Casey comes to bat, there are two outs and two men on base. Instead of winning the game with a home run, Casey strikes out, and his team loses.

TOPIC

• Baseball

POSSIBLE THEMES

• Even a hero can fail.
• Overconfidence can lead to failure.

MODEL 1: THEME IN A STORY

Fables often convey themes about human nature through the actions of animal characters. What lesson can readers learn from this fable?

The LION and the MOUSE

Fable by **Aesop**

A lion was idling in the sun, pretending to sleep, when he felt a tickle on his nose. He opened one eye and, with a swipe of his huge paw, caught a small mouse trying to run away. The lion roared angrily and tossed the mouse into the air. The mouse cried, "Please don't hurt
5   me! If only you will spare my life, I promise I will repay you." Surprised and amused by the little creature's earnest promise, the lion laughed and let the mouse go.

Time passed, and then one day the lion became ensnared in a trap. As he struggled to free himself, the ropes tightened around him until
10   he couldn't move. The little mouse was close by and heard the lion's roars. She came and set the lion free by gnawing through the ropes. "When you kindly spared my life," said the mouse, "you laughed at the idea that one day I would repay you."

Close Read

1. What does the lion decide to do after capturing the mouse? Explain how the mouse repays the lion.

2. What lesson can readers learn from the way the lion and the mouse treat each other?

MODEL 2: THEME IN A POEM

In this poem, the writer presents a strong message about family.

LiTTLE SiSTER

Poem by **Nikki Grimes**

little sister
holds on tight.
My hands hurt
from all that squeezing,
5   but I don't mind.
She thinks no one will bother her
when I'm around,
and they won't
if I can help it.
10   And even when I can't
I try
'cause she believes in me.

Close Read

1. How does the little sister rely on the speaker of the poem? Explain how the speaker feels about his or her sister.

2. Reread the boxed lines. Which statement best expresses the theme?

   a. When family members believe in you, it makes you stronger.

   b. Families should spend more time together.

Part 2: A Closer Look at Theme

Sometimes the theme of a story is stated directly by the narrator or a character. Most often, though, a theme is implied—hinted at but not stated directly. In such a case, you need to **infer** the theme by finding clues in the text. This chart tells you where to look for those clues. Use the questions shown to help you uncover the theme of any story you read.

CLUES TO THEME

TITLE

The title may reflect a story's topic, its theme, or both. Ask:
- What does each word in the title mean?
- What ideas does the title emphasize?

PLOT

A story's plot often revolves around a conflict that is important to the theme. Ask:
- What conflicts do the characters face?
- How are the conflicts resolved?

CHARACTERS

What characters do and learn can reflect a theme. Ask:
- What are the main characters like? (Analyze their speech, thoughts, and actions.)
- How do the characters respond to the conflicts?
- How do the characters change?
- What lessons do the characters learn?

SETTING

A setting (place and time) can suggest theme through its effects on the characters and on the events in the story. Ask:
- How does the setting influence the characters?
- How does the setting affect the conflicts?
- What might the setting represent? (For example, a historical setting, such as London in the mid-1800s when many people lived in poverty, may suggest a theme related to generosity or greed.)

Part 3: Analyze the Text

In this story, two brothers respond to a challenge by making very different choices. As you read, use the clues in the story to help you understand what the writer is saying about their choices.

THE TWO BROTHERS

Short story by **Leo Tolstoy**

T wo brothers set out on a journey together. At noon they lay down in a forest to rest. When they woke up they saw a stone lying next to them. There was something written on the stone, and they tried to make out what it was.

5   "Whoever finds this stone," they read, "let him go straight into the forest at sunrise. In the forest a river will appear; let him swim across the river to the other side. There he will find a she-bear and her cubs. Let him take the cubs from her and run up the mountain with them, without once looking back. On the top of the mountain

10   he will see a house, and in that house will he find happiness."

Close Read

1. The title of this story suggests that the two brothers are central to the theme. As you read, think about the differences in the brothers' outlooks on life.

2. What challenge do the brothers face? Predict how they might respond to the challenge.

When they had read what was written on the stone, the younger brother said:

"Let us go together. We can swim across the river, carry off the bear cubs, take them to the house on the mountain, and together find happiness."

"I am not going into the forest after bear cubs," said the elder brother, "and I advise you not to go. In the first place, no one can know whether what is written on this stone is the truth—perhaps it was written in jest. It is even possible that we have not read it correctly. In the second place, even if what is written here is the truth—suppose we go into the forest and night comes, and we cannot find the river. We shall be lost. And if we do find the river, how are we going to swim across it? It may be broad and swift. In the third place, even if we swim across the river, do you think it is an easy thing to take her cubs away from a she-bear? She will seize us, and, instead of finding happiness, we shall perish, and all for nothing. In the fourth place, even if we succeeded in carrying off the bear cubs, we could not run up a mountain without stopping to rest. And, most important of all, the stone does not tell us what kind of happiness we should find in that house. It may be that the happiness awaiting us there is not at all the sort of happiness we would want."

"In my opinion," said the younger brother, "you are wrong. What is written on the stone could not have been put there without reason. And it is all perfectly clear. In the first place, no harm will come to us if we try. In the second place, if we do not go, someone else will read the inscription on the stone and find happiness, and we shall have lost it all. In the third place: if you do not make an effort and try hard, nothing in the world will succeed. In the fourth place: I should not want it thought that I was afraid of anything."

The elder brother answered him by saying: "The proverb says: 'In seeking great happiness small pleasures may be lost.' And also: 'A bird in the hand is worth two in the bush.'"

Close Read

3. Reread the boxed text. The setting—the forest, the river, the bears, and the mountain—all represent danger to the elder brother. What does his reaction to the setting's challenges tell you about him?

4. Reread lines 16–39. How are the brothers' attitudes different? Describe each brother's outlook on life.

The younger brother replied: "I have heard: 'He who is afraid of the leaves must not go into the forest.' And also: 'Beneath a stone
45 no water flows.'"

Then the younger brother set off, and the elder remained behind.

No sooner had the younger brother gone into the forest than he found the river, swam across it, and there on the other side was the she-bear, fast asleep. He took her cubs, and ran up the
50 mountain without looking back. When he reached the top of the mountain the people came out to meet him with a carriage to take him into the city, where they made him their king.

He ruled for five years. In the sixth year, another king, who was stronger than he, waged war against him. The city was conquered,
55 and he was driven out.

Again the younger brother became a wanderer, and he arrived one day at the house of the elder brother. The elder brother was living in a village and had grown neither rich nor poor. The two brothers rejoiced at seeing each other, and at once began telling
60 of all that had happened to them.

"You see," said the elder brother, "I was right. Here I have lived quietly and well, while you, though you may have been a king, have seen a great deal of trouble."

"I do not regret having gone into the forest and up the mountain,"
65 replied the younger brother. "I may have nothing now, but I shall always have something to remember, while you have no memories at all."

Close Read

5. How do the brothers resolve their conflict?

6. Reread lines 61–66. How does each brother feel about the choice he made? Explain whether the brothers' attitudes have changed.

7. Consider what the writer might be saying about the choices people make. (Hint: Is there always a right or wrong choice?) Write a statement that expresses the theme of the story.

Amigo Brothers

Video link at
thinkcentral.com

Short Story by Piri Thomas

VIDEO TRAILER THINK central   KEYWORD: HML7-322

What happens when friends
COMPETE?

COMMON CORE

RL 2 Determine a theme.
RL 3 Analyze how particular
elements of a story interact.
L 4 Determine the meaning
of multiple-meaning words.

We face competition all the time, whether we are competing for someone's attention or for the best grade. And while some competitions are friendly and even fun, others can be brutal. In "Amigo Brothers," best friends Antonio and Felix find out if their deep friendship can survive an explosive competition.

QUICKWRITE Jot down a list of times when you competed with one or more friends. When you are done, review your list. Decide which of those experiences helped or hurt your friendship. Reflect on one of those experiences in a journal entry.

● TEXT ANALYSIS: THEME AND SETTING

A story's **theme** is a message about life or human nature that the writer wants readers to understand. The **setting,** or the time and place of the action, is often a key element of the theme. To determine how the setting influences the theme, note the following:

- details that give clues to time and place
- the way the setting affects the thoughts and actions of the characters
- the importance of the setting in the conflict and how the conflict is resolved

As you read "Amigo Brothers," keep these tips in mind in order to identify the story's theme.

● READING SKILL: COMPARE AND CONTRAST

Comparing and contrasting characters can help you better understand a story. When you **compare** two or more people or things, you look for ways they are similar. When you **contrast** them, you look for ways they are different. As you read "Amigo Brothers," note similarities and differences between Felix and Antonio in a Venn diagram like the one shown.

Felix   Both   Antonio

▲ VOCABULARY IN CONTEXT

The boldfaced terms help tell this story about **competition.** Restate each sentence, using a different word or words.

1. He received a **barrage** of criticism for his comments.
2. The report shows the **devastating** effects of the illness.
3. She considered the offer **pensively.**
4. The crowd burst into a **torrent** of laughter.
5. He can't stand her **perpetual** complaining.
6. We were surprised at their **unbridled** enthusiasm.
7. They worked hard to **dispel** my concerns.
8. It was a noisy classroom, where **bedlam** reigned.
9. His arms began to **flail** as he lost his balance.
10. She has remarkable **clarity** for a person her age.

Complete the activities in your **Reader/Writer Notebook.**

Meet the Author

Piri Thomas
born 1928

A Troubled Beginning
In the 1950s, Piri Thomas realized that he was getting into too much trouble with the law and needed to turn his life around. He said to himself, "Man, where am I at? I got a mind; let's see if I can use it." He says he then "jumped into books." For him, writing became a tool to discover who he really was and to portray his Puerto Rican and African-American heritage.

A Rich Heritage
Thomas's writings are all set where he grew up, in New York City. He writes about neighborhoods that are heavily populated with Puerto Ricans and African Americans, such as Spanish Harlem and the Lower East Side of Manhattan. Thomas's writing celebrates the strength and determination of the people in his community.

BACKGROUND TO THE STORY
Golden Gloves
In this story, Felix and Antonio compete to participate in a Golden Gloves tournament, a famous amateur boxing competition. Past winners who went on to fame and fortune include Sugar Ray Robinson, George Foreman, and Muhammad Ali.

Author Online
THiNK central
Go to **thinkcentral.com.**
KEYWORD: HML7-323

Amigo BROTHERS

PIRI THOMAS

Analyze Visuals ▶
What do the colors in this painting make you think of?

Antonio Cruz and Felix Vargas were both seventeen years old. They were so together in friendship that they felt themselves to be brothers. They had known each other since childhood, growing up on the lower east side of Manhattan in the same tenement building[1] on Fifth Street between Avenue A and Avenue B.

Antonio was fair, lean, and lanky, while Felix was dark, short, and husky. Antonio's hair was always falling over his eyes, while Felix wore his black hair in a natural Afro style.

Each youngster had a dream of someday becoming lightweight champion
10 of the world. Every chance they had the boys worked out, sometimes at the Boys Club on 10th Street and Avenue A and sometimes at the pro's gym on 14th Street. Early morning sunrises would find them running along the East River Drive, wrapped in sweatshirts, short towels around their necks, and handkerchiefs Apache style around their foreheads. **A**

While some youngsters were into street negatives, Antonio and Felix slept, ate, rapped, and dreamt positive. Between them, they had a collection of *Fight* magazines second to none, plus a scrapbook filled with torn tickets to every boxing match they had ever attended and some clippings of their own. If asked a question about any given fighter, they
20 would immediately zip out from their memory banks divisions,[2] weights, records of fights, knockouts, technical knockouts, and draws or losses.

Each had fought many bouts representing their community and had won two gold-plated medals plus a silver and bronze medallion. The difference was in their style. Antonio's lean form and long reach made him the better boxer, while Felix's short and muscular frame

A COMPARE AND CONTRAST
Reread lines 1–14 and use your Venn diagram to note similarities and differences between the two boys. Add more notes to your diagram as you continue reading.

---

1. **tenement building:** a rundown apartment building in which mostly poor families live.
2. **divisions:** weight groups into which boxers are separated.

The Boxers, Roger Coleman. Tempera. Private collection. Photo © The Bridgeman Art Library.

made him the better slugger. Whenever they had met in the ring for sparring sessions,[3] it had always been hot and heavy.

Now, after a series of elimination bouts,[4] they had been informed that they were to meet each other in the division finals that were scheduled
30 for the seventh of August, two weeks away—the winner to represent the Boys Club in the Golden Gloves Championship Tournament.

The two boys continued to run together along the East River Drive. But even when joking with each other, they both sensed a wall rising between them.

One morning less than a week before their bout, they met as usual for their daily workout. They fooled around with a few jabs at the air, slapped skin, and then took off, running lightly along the dirty East River's edge.

Antonio glanced at Felix, who kept his eyes purposely straight ahead,
40 pausing from time to time to do some fancy leg work while throwing one-twos followed by upper cuts to an imaginary jaw. Antonio then beat the air with a **barrage** of body blows and short **devastating** lefts with an overhand, jawbreaking right.

After a mile or so, Felix puffed and said, "Let's stop for awhile, bro. I think we both got something to say to each other."

Antonio nodded. It was not natural to be acting as though nothing unusual was happening when two ace boon buddies were going to be blasting each other within a few short days.

They rested their elbows on the railing separating them from the river.
50 Antonio wiped his face with his short towel. The sunrise was now creating day.

Felix leaned heavily on the river's railing and stared across to the shores of Brooklyn. Finally, he broke the silence.

"Man. I don't know how to come out with it."

Antonio helped. "It's about our fight, right?"

"Yeah, right." Felix's eyes squinted at the rising orange sun.

"I've been thinking about it too, *panín.*[5] In fact, since we found out it was going to be me and you, I've been awake at night, pulling punches[6] on you, trying not to hurt you."

"Same here. It ain't natural not to think about the fight. I mean,
60 we both are *cheverote*[7] fighters, and we both want to win. But only one of us can win. There ain't no draws in the eliminations."

SOCIAL STUDIES CONNECTION

Antonio and Felix grew up on the Lower East Side of Manhattan.

barrage (bə-räzh´) *n.*
a rapid, heavy attack

devastating
(dĕv´ə-stā´tĭng) *adj.*
very effective in causing pain or destruction
devastate *v.*

---

3. **sparring sessions:** practice boxing matches.

4. **elimination bouts:** matches to determine which boxers advance in a competition.

5. *panín* (pä-nēn´) *American Spanish:* pal; buddy.

6. **pulling punches:** holding back in delivering blows.

7. *cheverote* (chĕ-vĕ-rô´tĕ) *American Spanish:* great or fantastic.

Left Detail of *Moose*, (1956), Alice Neel. © Estate of Alice Neel. Courtesy Robert Miller Gallery, New York. *Right* Detail of *Call Me Joe* (1955), Alice Neel. Oil on canvas, 34" x 32". © Estate of Alice Neel. Courtesy Robert Miller Gallery, New York.

▲ **Analyze Visuals**

Compare and contrast these pictures with your own mental images of Felix and Antonio.

Felix tapped Antonio gently on the shoulder. "I don't mean to sound like I'm bragging, bro. But I wanna win, fair and square."

Antonio nodded quietly. "Yeah. We both know that in the ring the better man wins. Friend or no friend, brother or no . . ."

Felix finished it for him. "Brother. Tony, let's promise something right here. Okay?"

"If it's fair, *hermano*,[8] I'm for it." Antonio admired the courage of a tugboat pulling a barge five times its welterweight[9] size.

70 "It's fair, Tony. When we get into the ring, it's gotta be like we never met. We gotta be like two heavy strangers that want the same thing, and only one can have it. You understand, don'tcha?"

"*Sí,* I know." Tony smiled. "No pulling punches. We go all the way."

"Yeah, that's right. Listen, Tony. Don't you think it's a good idea if we don't see each other until the day of the fight? I'm going to stay with my Aunt Lucy in the Bronx.[10] I can use Gleason's Gym for working out. My manager says he got some sparring partners with more or less your style." **B**

COMMON CORE RL 2, RL 3

B THEME AND SETTING
The **setting** of a story is when and where it takes place. The setting can offer clues about a story's theme. What details offer clues to the setting? What does the setting have to do with the action in this story?

---

8. **hermano** (ĕr-mä′nô) *Spanish:* brother.

9. **welterweight:** one of boxing's weight divisions, with a maximum weight of 147 pounds.

10. **the Bronx:** a borough of New York City, north of Manhattan.

Tony scratched his nose **pensively.** "Yeah, it would be better for our heads." He held out his hand, palm upward. "Deal?"

80 "Deal." Felix lightly slapped open skin.

"Ready for some more running?" Tony asked lamely.

"Naw, bro. Let's cut it here. You go on. I kinda like to get things together in my head."

"You ain't worried, are you?" Tony asked. ◆

"No way, man." Felix laughed out loud. "I got too much smarts for that. I just think it's cooler if we split right here. After the fight, we can get it together again like nothing ever happened."

The *amigo*[11] brothers were not ashamed to hug each other tightly.

"Guess you're right. Watch yourself, Felix. I hear there's some
90 pretty heavy dudes up in the Bronx. *Suavecito,*[12] okay?"

"Okay. You watch yourself too, *sabe?*"[13]

Tony jogged away. Felix watched his friend disappear from view, throwing rights and lefts. Both fighters had a lot of psyching up to do before the big fight.

The days in training passed much too slowly. Although they kept out of each other's way, they were aware of each other's progress via the ghetto grapevine.[14]

The evening before the big fight, Tony made his way to the roof of his tenement. In the quiet early dark, he peered over the ledge.
100 Six stories below, the lights of the city blinked, and the sounds of cars mingled with the curses and the laughter of children in the street. He tried not to think of Felix, feeling he had succeeded in psyching his mind. But only in the ring would he really know. To spare Felix hurt, he would have to knock him out, early and quick.

Up in the South Bronx, Felix decided to take in a movie in an effort to keep Antonio's face away from his fists. The flick was *The Champion* with Kirk Douglas, the third time Felix was seeing it.

The champion was getting beat, his face being pounded into raw, wet hamburger. His eyes were cut, jagged, bleeding, one eye swollen,
110 the other almost shut. He was saved only by the sound of the bell.

Felix became the champ and Tony the challenger. **G**

The movie audience was going out of its head, roaring in blood lust at the butchery going on. The champ hunched his shoulders, grunting and sniffing red blood back into his broken nose. The challenger, confident that he had the championship in the bag, threw a left. The champ countered with a dynamite right that exploded into the challenger's brains.

---

11. *amigo* (ä-mē'gô) *Spanish:* friend.
12. *Suavecito* (swä-vě-sē'tô) *American Spanish:* Take it easy.
13. *sabe* (sä'bě) *Spanish:* you know.
14. **ghetto grapevine:** the chain of gossip that spreads through the neighborhood.

pensively (pĕn'sĭv-lē)
adv. thoughtfully

◆ **GRAMMAR IN CONTEXT**
Reread lines 80–84. Notice the placement of **the quotation marks.** What does Felix say in these lines?

G **THEME AND SETTING**
An **internal conflict** is a struggle within a character's mind. Setting can be important even to this type of conflict. Read lines 102–111. What is Antonio's internal conflict? How does the setting influence his struggle?

Felix's right arm felt the shock. Antonio's face, superimposed on the screen, was shattered and split apart by the awesome force of the killer blow. Felix saw himself in the ring, blasting Antonio against the ropes.
120 The champ had to be forcibly restrained. The challenger was allowed to crumble slowly to the canvas, a broken, bloody mess.

When Felix finally left the theatre, he had figured out how to psyche himself for tomorrow's fight. It was Felix the Champion vs. Antonio the Challenger.

He walked up some dark streets, deserted except for small pockets of wary-looking kids wearing gang colors. Despite the fact that he was Puerto Rican like them, they eyed him as a stranger to their turf. Felix did a last shuffle, bobbing and weaving, while letting loose a **torrent**
of blows that would demolish whatever got in its way. It seemed to
130 impress the brothers, who went about their own business.

COMMON CORE L4

Language Coach

Multiple Meanings
Many English words have more than one meaning. Reread line 119. The word *ring* often refers to the sound created by a bell. It is also an area set off by ropes in which boxing events are held. Use **context clues** to determine the meaning in line 119.

torrent (tôrʹənt) *n*. a violent, rushing stream

Still Open (1994), Douglas Safranek. Egg tempera on panel, 4 5/8' x 4'. © Museum of the City of New York (95.6).

◀**Analyze Visuals**

How does this picture **compare** with the description of the **setting** given in lines 98–101?

Finding no takers, Felix decided to split to his aunt's. Walking the streets had not relaxed him, neither had the fight flick. All it had done was to stir him up. He let himself quietly into his Aunt Lucy's apartment and went straight to bed, falling into a fitful sleep with sounds of the gong for Round One.

Antonio was passing some heavy time on his rooftop. How would the fight tomorrow affect his relationship with Felix? After all, fighting was like any other profession. Friendship had nothing to do with it. A gnawing doubt crept in. He cut negative thinking real quick by doing
140 some speedy fancy dance steps, bobbing and weaving like mercury. The night air was blurred with **perpetual** motions of left hooks and right crosses. Felix, his *amigo* brother, was not going to be Felix at all in the ring. Just an opponent with another face. Antonio went to sleep, hearing the opening bell for the first round. Like his friend in the South Bronx, he prayed for victory via a quick, clean knockout in the first round.

Large posters plastered all over the walls of local shops announced the fight between Antonio Cruz and Felix Vargas as the main bout.

The fight had created great interest in the neighborhood. Antonio and Felix were well liked and respected. Each had his own loyal following.
150 Betting fever was high and ranged from a bottle of Coke to cold, hard cash on the line.

Antonio's fans bet with **unbridled** faith in his boxing skills. On the other side, Felix's admirers bet on his dynamite-packed fists.

Felix had returned to his apartment early in the morning of August 7th and stayed there, hoping to avoid seeing Antonio. He turned the radio on to salsa music sounds and then tried to read while waiting for word from his manager.

The fight was scheduled to take place in Tompkins Square Park. It had been decided that the gymnasium of the Boys Club was not
160 large enough to hold all the people who were sure to attend. In Tompkins Square Park, everyone who wanted could view the fight, whether from ringside or window fire escapes or tenement rooftops.

The morning of the fight, Tompkins Square was a beehive of activity with numerous workers setting up the ring, the seats, and the guest speakers' stand. The scheduled bouts began shortly after noon, and the park had begun filling up even earlier.

The local junior high school across from Tompkins Square Park served as the dressing room for all the fighters. Each was given a separate class-room, with desktops, covered with mats, serving as resting tables. Antonio
170 thought he caught a glimpse of Felix waving to him from a room at the far end of the corridor. He waved back just in case it had been him. **D**

perpetual
(pər-pĕch′oo-əl) *adj.*
continual; unending

unbridled (ŭn-brīd′ld)
adj. lacking restraint
or control

D THEME AND
SETTING
What can you **infer**
about Antonio's attitude
toward Felix on the day
of the fight?

The fighters changed from their street clothes into fighting gear. Antonio wore white trunks, black socks, and black shoes. Felix wore sky blue trunks, red socks, and white boxing shoes. Each had dressing gowns to match their fighting trunks with their names neatly stitched on the back.

The loudspeakers blared into the open window of the school. There were speeches by dignitaries, community leaders, and great boxers of yesteryear. Some were well prepared, some improvised on the spot. They all carried the same message of great pleasure and honor at being 180 part of such a historic event. This great day was in the tradition of champions emerging from the streets of the lower east side.

Interwoven with the speeches were the sounds of the other boxing events. After the sixth bout, Felix was much relieved when his trainer, Charlie, said, "Time change. Quick knockout. This is it. We're on."

Waiting time was over. Felix was escorted from the classroom by a dozen fans in white T-shirts with the word FELIX across their fronts.

Antonio was escorted down a different stairwell and guided through a roped-off path.

As the two climbed into the ring, the crowd exploded with a roar. 190 Antonio and Felix both bowed gracefully and then raised their arms in acknowledgment.

Antonio tried to be cool, but even as the roar was in its first birth, he turned slowly to meet Felix's eyes looking directly into his. Felix nodded his head and Antonio responded. And both as one, just as quickly, turned away to face his own corner. **E**

Bong, bong, bong. The roar turned to stillness.

"Ladies and Gentlemen, *Señores y Señoras*."[15]

The announcer spoke slowly, pleased at his bilingual efforts.

"Now the moment we have all been waiting for—the main event between 200 two fine young Puerto Rican fighters, products of our lower east side."

"*Loisaida*,"[16] called out a member of the audience.

"In this corner, weighing 131 pounds, Felix Vargas. And in this corner, weighing 133 pounds, Antonio Cruz. The winner will represent the Boys Club in the tournament of champions, the Golden Gloves. There will be no draw. May the best man win."

The cheering of the crowd shook the windowpanes of the old buildings surrounding Tompkins Square Park. At the center of the ring, the referee was giving instructions to the youngsters.

"Keep your punches up. No low blows. No punching on the back 210 of the head. Keep your heads up. Understand. Let's have a clean fight. Now shake hands and come out fighting."

E THEME AND SETTING
Reread lines 192–195. How do you think the boys feel at this moment? How does the setting influence the way the boys feel?

---

15. *Señores y Señoras* (sĕ-nyô′rĕs ē sĕ-nyô′räs) *Spanish:* Ladies and Gentlemen.

16. *Loisaida* (loi-sī′dä) *American Spanish:* Lower East Side.

Both youngsters touched gloves and nodded. They turned and danced quickly to their corners. Their head towels and dressing gowns were lifted neatly from their shoulders by their trainers' nimble fingers. Antonio crossed himself. Felix did the same.

BONG! BONG! ROUND ONE. Felix and Antonio turned and faced each other squarely in a fighting pose. Felix wasted no time. He came in fast, head low, half hunched toward his right shoulder, and lashed out with a straight left. He missed a right cross as Antonio slipped the punch
220 and countered with one-two-three lefts that snapped Felix's head back, sending a mild shock coursing through him. If Felix had any small doubt about their friendship affecting their fight, it was being neatly **dispelled**.

Antonio danced, a joy to behold. His left hand was like a piston pumping jabs one right after another with seeming ease. Felix bobbed and weaved and never stopped boring in. He knew that at long range he was at a disadvantage. Antonio had too much reach on him. Only by coming in close could Felix hope to achieve the dreamed-of knockout. **F**

Antonio knew the dynamite that was stored in his *amigo* brother's fist. He ducked a short right and missed a left hook. Felix trapped him
230 against the ropes just long enough to pour some punishing rights and lefts to Antonio's hard midsection. Antonio slipped away from Felix, crashing two lefts to his head, which set Felix's right ear to ringing.

Bong! Both *amigos* froze a punch well on its way, sending up a roar of approval for good sportsmanship.

Felix walked briskly back to his corner. His right ear had not stopped ringing. Antonio gracefully danced his way toward his stool none the worse, except for glowing glove burns, showing angry red against the whiteness of his midribs.

"Watch that right, Tony." His trainer talked into his
240 ear. "Remember Felix always goes to the body. He'll want you to drop your hands for his overhand left or right. Got it?"

Antonio nodded, spraying water out between his teeth. He felt better as his sore midsection was being firmly rubbed.

Felix's corner was also busy.

"You gotta get in there, fella." Felix's trainer poured water over his curly Afro locks. "Get in there or he's gonna chop you up from way back."
250 *Bong! Bong!* Round two. Felix was off his stool and rushed Antonio like a bull, sending a hard right to his head. Beads of water exploded from Antonio's long hair.

dispel (dĭ-spĕl′) *v.*
to get rid of

F COMPARE AND CONTRAST
Reread lines 223–227. Compare and contrast the boys' boxing styles.

▼ **Analyze Visuals**
Describe the feeling this sculpture conveys.

Seated Fighter (1985), Joseph Sheppard. Bronze, height 21″.

Antonio, hurt, sent back a blurring barrage of lefts and rights that only meant pain to Felix, who returned with a short left to the head followed by a looping right to the body. Antonio countered[17] with his own flurry, forcing Felix to give ground. But not for long.

Felix bobbed and weaved, bobbed and weaved, occasionally punching his two gloves together.

260 Antonio waited for the rush that was sure to come. Felix closed in and feinted[18] with his left shoulder and threw his right instead. Lights suddenly exploded inside Felix's head as Antonio slipped the blow and hit him with a pistonlike left, catching him flush on the point of his chin.

Bedlam broke loose as Felix's legs momentarily buckled. He fought off a series of rights and lefts and came back with a strong right that taught Antonio respect.

Antonio danced in carefully. He knew Felix had the habit of playing possum when hurt, to sucker an opponent within reach of the powerful bombs he carried in each fist.

270 A right to the head slowed Antonio's pretty dancing. He answered with his own left at Felix's right eye that began puffing up within three seconds.

Antonio, a bit too eager, moved in too close, and Felix had him entangled into a rip-roaring, punching toe-to-toe slugfest that brought the whole Tompkins Square Park screaming to its feet.

Rights to the body. Lefts to the head. Neither fighter was giving an inch. Suddenly a short right caught Antonio squarely on the chin. His long legs turned to jelly, and his arms **flailed** out desperately. Felix, grunting like a bull, threw wild punches from every direction. Antonio, groggy, bobbed and weaved, evading most of the blows.
280 Suddenly his head cleared. His left flashed out hard and straight catching Felix on the bridge of his nose.

Felix lashed back with a haymaker,[19] right off the ghetto streets. At the same instant, his eye caught another left hook from Antonio. Felix swung out, trying to clear the pain. Only the frenzied screaming of those along ringside let him know that he had dropped Antonio. Fighting off the growing haze, Antonio struggled to his feet, got up, ducked, and threw a smashing right that dropped Felix flat on his back.

Felix got up as fast as he could in his own corner, groggy but still game.[20] He didn't even hear the count. In a fog, he heard the roaring of the crowd,
290 who seemed to have gone insane. His head cleared to hear the bell sound at the end of the round. He was very glad. His trainer sat him down on the stool.

bedlam (bĕd′ləm) *n.* a noisy confusion

flail (flāl) *v.* to wave wildly

---

17. **countered:** gave a blow after receiving or blocking his opponent's blow.

18. **feinted:** made a pretend attack to draw attention from his real purpose.

19. **haymaker:** a powerful blow.

20. **groggy but still game:** unsteady and shaky but willing to proceed.

In his corner, Antonio was doing what all fighters do when they are hurt. They sit and smile at everyone.

The referee signaled the ring doctor to check the fighters out. He did so and then gave his okay. The cold-water sponges brought **clarity** to both *amigo* brothers. They were rubbed until their circulation ran free.

Bong! Round three—the final round. Up to now it had been tick-tack-toe, pretty much even. But everyone knew there could be
300 no draw and that this round would decide the winner.

This time, to Felix's surprise, it was Antonio who came out fast, charging across the ring. Felix braced himself but couldn't ward off the barrage of punches. Antonio drove Felix hard against the ropes.

The crowd ate it up. Thus far the two had fought with *mucho corazón*.[21] Felix tapped his gloves and commenced his attack anew. Antonio, throwing boxer's caution to the winds, jumped in to meet him.

Both pounded away. Neither gave an inch, and neither fell to the canvas. Felix's left eye was tightly closed. Claret red blood poured from Antonio's nose. They fought toe-to-toe.

310 The sounds of their blows were loud in contrast to the silence of a crowd gone completely mute. The referee was stunned by their savagery.

Bong! Bong! Bong! The bell sounded over and over again. Felix and Antonio were past hearing. Their blows continued to pound on each other like hailstones.

Finally the referee and the two trainers pried Felix and Antonio apart. Cold water was poured over them to bring them back to their senses. **G**

They looked around and then rushed toward each other. A cry of alarm surged through Tompkins Square Park. Was this a fight to the death
320 instead of a boxing match?

The fear soon gave way to wave upon wave of cheering as the two *amigos* embraced.

No matter what the decision, they knew they would always be champions to each other.

Bong! Bong! Bong! "Ladies and Gentlemen. *Señores* and *Señoras*. The winner and representative to the Golden Gloves Tournament of Champions is . . ."

The announcer turned to point to the winner and found himself alone. Arm in arm, the champions had already left the ring. ∾

---

clarity (klăr′ĭ-tē) *n.* clearness of mind

G THEME AND SETTING
Reread lines 313–317. Why do such good friends keep fighting after the bell rings?

---

21. ***mucho corazón*** (mōō′chô kô-rä-sôn′) *Spanish:* a lot of heart; great courage.

Comprehension

1. **Recall** Why is this fight so important to Felix and Antonio?

2. **Recall** What happens at the end of the fight?

3. **Summarize** Describe how the two boys fight during the boxing match. What strengths does each boy demonstrate?

COMMON CORE

RL 2 Determine a theme.
RL 3 Analyze how particular elements of a story interact.
W 7 Conduct short research projects.

Text Analysis

4. **Make Inferences** Felix draws an **analogy,** or point-by-point comparison, between *The Champion* and his upcoming fight with Antonio. How does this analogy help Felix deal with his **internal conflict?**

5. **Compare and Contrast Characters** Look back at the Venn diagram you created as you read "Amigo Brothers." Which are more important, the similarities or the differences? Why?

6. **Draw Conclusions** What effect does the boxing competition have on Felix and Antonio's relationship? Support your answer with examples from the story.

7. **Identify Theme** Draw a chart like the one shown to help you identify clues that the writer provides about the theme of the story. What do you think the theme is?

Clues from Setting:		Possible Theme:
Clues from Characters:	→	
Clues from Conflicts:		

8. **Analyze Setting** How important is the setting to the theme of "Amigo Brothers"? Use examples from the story to support your response.

Extension and Challenge

9. **Creative Project: Music** Filmmakers often use music to enhance a movie's **theme.** Suppose you were asked to pick five songs for a film version of "Amigo Brothers." What would they be? Present your list to the class. Explain how each song reflects a theme of the selection.

10. **Inquiry and Research** Find out about the early life of a Golden Gloves champion who later became a professional boxer, such as Oscar de la Hoya or Muhammad Ali. How was the person you researched like Felix and Antonio? Present your findings to the class.

Oscar de la Hoya

What happens when friends COMPETE?

How would you act toward a friend during and after a competition?

Vocabulary in Context

▲ **VOCABULARY PRACTICE**

For each sentence, choose the vocabulary word that is similar in meaning to the boldfaced word or phrase.

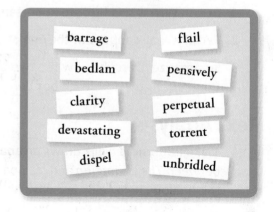

barrage   flail
bedlam   pensively
clarity   perpetual
devastating   torrent
dispel   unbridled

1. In the ring, both fighters threw blows that were **extremely good at causing pain.**
2. Felix was in **continual** motion on his feet.
3. Antonio's fans cheered with **uncontrolled** emotion.
4. The **noise** in the gym was so loud that Felix couldn't hear himself think.
5. The trainer sat **deep in thought.**
6. Antonio began to **wave his arms crazily** about.
7. Felix came at Antonio with a **concentrated attack** of punches.
8. Antonio responded with a **wild, never-ending stream** of blows.
9. At times, both fighters almost lost their **ability to think clearly.**
10. Felix was able to **get rid of** any doubts about his friend.

ACADEMIC VOCABULARY IN WRITING

• clause   • context   • cultural   • symbol   • theme

The setting in "Amigo Brothers" is very important to the **theme.** Write a paragraph in which you describe how the setting in the story influences the theme. Use one of the Academic Vocabulary words in your response.

○ **COMMON CORE**

L 4b Use common, grade-appropriate Latin roots as clues to the meaning of a word.
L 6 Acquire and use accurately grade-appropriate general academic words.

VOCABULARY STRATEGY: THE LATIN ROOT *pel*

The vocabulary word *dispel* contains the Latin root *pel,* which means "drive" or "push." This root, which is sometimes spelled *puls,* is found in many English words. To understand the meaning of words with *pel or puls,* use context clues and your knowledge of the root's meaning.

PRACTICE Choose the word from the web that best completes each sentence.

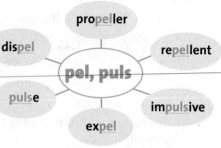

propeller
dispel   repellent
pel, puls
pulse   impulsive
expel

1. Use insect _____ before you hike through the woods.
2. A person who is _____ often doesn't think before acting.
3. She threatened to _____ any club member who missed more than two meetings.
4. A plane's _____ helps it move through the air.

Interactive Vocabulary   **THINK** central

Go to <u>thinkcentral.com</u>.
KEYWORD: HML7-336

Language

COMMON CORE

L 2 Demonstrate command of standard English punctuation.
W 3 Write narratives to develop imagined experiences.

◆ **GRAMMAR IN CONTEXT: Punctuate Dialogue Correctly**

Review the Grammar in Context note on page 328. Dialogue is a conversation between two or more speakers. If you don't punctuate it correctly, readers might be confused about who is speaking. To avoid confusion, use **quotation marks** at the beginning and end of a speaker's words. Place end marks, such as **periods**, inside closing quotation marks. Use **commas** to set off a speaker's words from the rest of a sentence. Notice the placement of the comma and quotation marks in the revised sentence.

> *Original:*   Antonio said Felix, you will always be my *amigo* brother.

> *Revised:*   Antonio said, "Felix, you will always be my amigo brother."

PRACTICE Fix the misplaced punctuation marks in the following dialogue and insert any missing marks.

1. Felix replied, Same here, bro. No way I would let anything come between us.
2. "So, I feel good about our decision", Antonio said.
3. Felix shrugged and said Yeah. Me, too.
4. "Brother, boxing will never mean more to me than our friendship does".

For more help with punctuating dialogue, see page R50 in the
Grammar Handbook.

READING-WRITING CONNECTION

YOUR TURN

Increase your understanding of "Amigo Brothers" by responding to this prompt. Then use the **revising tip** to improve your writing.

WRITING PROMPT	**REVISING TIP**
Extended Constructed Response: Dialogue What do you suppose Antonio and Felix talk about as they walk away from the boxing ring? Keep in mind the big question about **competition** on page 322 and what you know about the boys' friendship. Write their conversation as a **one-page dialogue**.	Review your dialogue. Add any missing commas and quotation marks.

Interactive Revision
THINK central

Go to **thinkcentral.com**.
KEYWORD: HML7-337

The War of the Wall

Short Story by Toni Cade Bambara

VIDEO TRAILER **THINK** central   KEYWORD: HML7-338

What makes a COMMUNITY?

Belonging to a community can give people feelings of identity and security. What things in the community help contribute to those feelings? In "The War of the Wall," an "outsider" comes to a town and challenges its residents' idea of what it means to be a community.

DISCUSS Think about the different communities, or groups, that you belong to, such as your school, your neighborhood, and your town. With a group of classmates, discuss how you would welcome someone new to your school or town.

TEXT ANALYSIS: MULTIPLE THEMES

A story usually has one main theme, but it may also have other themes. To determine the story's theme or themes,

- note the **setting** of the story and how it might relate to the plot and characters
- make inferences about **character** motivations and relationships
- note what **conflicts** arise and how they are resolved

A theme may be indicated through the lessons learned by the characters in a particular setting. As you read "War of the Wall," keep these tips in mind in order to identify the story's themes.

READING STRATEGY: MONITOR

Active readers check, or **monitor,** their understanding as they read. One way to monitor your understanding is to pause occasionally and ask yourself questions. Sometimes you'll need to reread to find the answer. Other times you'll want to read on, because your question might be answered later in the story. Either way, asking questions will help you focus on and better understand what you are reading.

As you read "The War of the Wall," record questions and answers about what is happening and why characters act the way they do. Use a chart like the one shown.

My Questions	Answers
What is the lady painting on the wall?	

VOCABULARY IN CONTEXT

The following phrases could be newspaper headlines for articles about the artist's painting in "The War of the Wall." Write a definition of each boldfaced word.

1. **Aroma** of Paint Was Promise of Future Beauty
2. Artist's **Masterpiece** Creates Sensation
3. Viewers in **Trance** over Splendid Work
4. Colors and Subject Matter **Beckon** to Wide Audience
5. **Inscription** on Mural Provides Dedication

 Complete the activities in your **Reader/Writer Notebook.**

Meet the Author

Toni Cade Bambara
1939–1995

Creative Beginnings

Born Miltona Mirkin Cade, Toni Cade Bambara announced at five years old that she was changing her name to Toni. Her mother, who supported all of Bambara's creative efforts, agreed. Bambara began writing as a child and never stopped. She went on to become an award-winning author, teacher, filmmaker, and a leading activist in the African-American community. Although set in a small town, "The War of the Wall" was inspired by Bambara's memories of growing up in the Harlem neighborhood of New York City.

BACKGROUND TO THE STORY

Murals

A mural is a large picture painted on an interior or exterior wall of a building. Many murals illustrate scenes from history or reflect the people of local communities. In the 1960s, African-American artists began a "wall of respect" movement. They painted murals as symbols of their respect for different groups. Walls of respect appeared everywhere from Eastern cities such as New York to Western cities such as Los Angeles. They were also painted in small Southern towns such as the one in which "The War of the Wall" takes place.

THE WAR OF THE WALL

TONI CADE BAMBARA

Me and Lou had no time for courtesies. We were late for school. So we just flat out told the painter lady to quit messing with the wall. It was our wall, and she had no right coming into our neighborhood painting on it. Stirring in the paint bucket and not even looking at us, she mumbled something about Mr. Eubanks, the barber, giving her permission. That had nothing to do with it as far as we were concerned. We've been pitching pennies against that wall since we were little kids. Old folks have been dragging their chairs out to sit in the shade of the wall for years. Big kids have been playing handball against

10 the wall since so-called integration[1] when the crazies 'cross town poured cement in our pool so we couldn't use it. I'd sprained my neck one time boosting my cousin Lou up to chisel Jimmy Lyons's name into the wall when we found out he was never coming home from the war in Vietnam to take us fishing. **Ⓐ**

"If you lean close," Lou said, leaning hipshot against her beat-up car, "you'll get a whiff of bubble gum and kids' sweat. And that'll tell you something—that this wall belongs to the kids of Taliaferro Street." I thought Lou sounded very convincing. But the painter lady paid us no mind. She just snapped the brim of her straw hat down and

20 hauled her bucket up the ladder.

"You're not even from around here," I hollered up after her. The license plates on her old piece of car said "New York." Lou dragged me away because I was about to grab hold of that ladder and shake it. And then we'd really be late for school.

When we came from school, the wall was slick with white. The painter lady was running string across the wall and taping it here and there. Me and Lou leaned against the gumball machine outside the pool hall and watched. She had strings up and down and back and forth. Then she began chalking them with a hunk of blue chalk.

---

1. **since so-called integration:** from the time in the 1960s when segregation, the separation of the races in public places, was outlawed. The narrator is being sarcastic, suggesting that integration has not been successful.

Detail of *Harlem Street Scene* (1942), Jacob Lawrence. Gouache on paper, 21″ × 20¾″. Private collection. © 2008 The Jacob and Gwendolyn Lawrence Foundation, Seattle/Artists Rights Society (ARS), New York.

Analyze Visuals ▶
Look closely at this picture. What details of **setting** does it include?

Ⓐ MULTIPLE THEMES
After reading the first few lines of this story, what do you think the main **conflict** will be? As you continue reading, think about what message this conflict might communicate.

30   The Morris twins crossed the street, hanging back at the curb next to the beat-up car. The twin with the red ribbons was hugging a jug of cloudy lemonade. The one with yellow ribbons was holding a plate of dinner away from her dress. The painter lady began snapping the strings. The blue chalk dust measured off halves and quarters up and down and sideways too. Lou was about to say how hip it all was, but I dropped my book satchel on his toes to remind him we were at war.

    Some good **aromas** were drifting our way from the plate leaking pot likker[2] onto the Morris girl's white socks. I could tell from where I stood that under the tinfoil was baked ham, collard greens, and candied yams.
40 And knowing Mrs. Morris, who sometimes bakes for my mama's restaurant, a slab of buttered cornbread was probably up under there too, sopping up some of the pot likker. Me and Lou rolled our eyes, wishing somebody would send us some dinner. But the painter lady didn't even turn around. She was pulling the strings down and prying bits of tape loose.

    Side Pocket came strolling out of the pool hall to see what Lou and me were studying so hard. He gave the painter lady the once-over, checking out her paint-spattered jeans, her chalky T-shirt, her floppy-brimmed straw hat. He hitched up his pants and glided over toward the painter lady, who kept right on with what she was doing.
50   "Whatcha got there, sweetheart?" he asked the twin with the plate.

    "Suppah," she said all soft and countrylike.

    "For her," the one with the jug added, jerking her chin toward the painter lady's back.

    Still she didn't turn around. She was rearing back on her heels, her hands jammed into her back pockets, her face squinched up like the **masterpiece** she had in mind was taking shape on the wall by magic. We could have been gophers crawled up into a rotten hollow for all she cared. She didn't even say hello to anybody. Lou was muttering something about how great her concentration was. I butt him with
60 my hip, and his elbow slid off the gum machine. **B**

    "Good evening," Side Pocket said in his best ain't-I-fine voice. But the painter lady was moving from the milk crate to the step stool to the ladder, moving up and down fast, scribbling all over the wall like a crazy person. We looked at Side Pocket. He looked at the twins. The twins looked at us. The painter lady was giving a show. It was like those old-timey music movies where the dancer taps on the tabletop and then starts jumping all over the furniture, kicking chairs over and not skipping a beat. She didn't even look where she was stepping. And for a minute there, hanging on the ladder to reach a far spot, she looked like she was going
70 to tip right over.

aroma (ə-rō′mə) *n.* a smell; odor

Language Coach

Homonyms Words that are spelled and pronounced the same but have different meanings are called homonyms. Reread lines 35–36 and 59–60. The word *hip* can mean "joint connecting the leg to the waist" or "stylish." Use context clues to figure out the meaning for each sentence.

masterpiece (măs′tər-pēs′) *n.* a great work of art

B MONITOR
Why do you think the **narrator** says, "We could have been gophers . . . for all she cared"? How is the narrator feeling?

---

2. **pot likker:** the broth or liquid in which meat or vegetables have been cooked.

"Ahh," Side Pocket cleared his throat and moved fast to catch the ladder. "These young ladies here have brought you some supper."

"Ma'am?" The twins stepped forward. Finally the painter turned around, her eyes "full of sky," as my grandmama would say. Then she stepped down like she was in a **trance.** She wiped her hands on her jeans as the Morris twins offered up the plate and the jug. She rolled back the tinfoil, then wagged her head as though something terrible was on the plate.

"Thank your mother very much," she said, sounding like her mouth was full of sky too. "I've brought my own dinner along." And then,
80 without even excusing herself, she went back up the ladder, drawing on the wall in a wild way. Side Pocket whistled one of those oh-brother breathy whistles and went back into the pool hall. The Morris twins shifted their weight from one foot to the other, then crossed the street and went home. Lou had to drag me away, I was so mad. We couldn't wait to get to the firehouse to tell my daddy all about this rude woman who'd stolen our wall.

All the way back to the block to help my mama out at the restaurant, me and Lou kept asking my daddy for ways to run the painter lady out of town. But my daddy was busy talking about the trip to the country
90 and telling Lou he could come too because Grandmama can always use an extra pair of hands on the farm.

Later that night, while me and Lou were in the back doing our chores, we found out that the painter lady was a liar. She came into the restaurant and leaned against the glass of the steam table, talking about how starved she was. I was scrubbing pots and Lou was chopping onions, but we could hear her through the service window. She was asking Mama was that a ham hock in the greens, and was that a neck bone in the pole beans, and were there any vegetables cooked without meat, especially pork.

"I don't care who your spiritual leader is," Mama said in that way of
100 hers. "If you eat in the community, sistuh, you gonna eat pig by-and-by, one way or t'other."

Me and Lou were cracking up in the kitchen, and several customers at the counter were clearing their throats, waiting for Mama to really fix her wagon[3] for not speaking to the elders when she came in. The painter lady took a stool at the counter and went right on with her questions. Was there cheese in the baked macaroni, she wanted to know? Were there eggs in the salad? Was it honey or sugar in the iced tea? Mama was fixing Pop Johnson's plate. And every time the painter lady asked a fool question, Mama would dump another spoonful of rice on the pile. She
110 was tapping her foot and heating up in a dangerous way. But Pop Johnson

trance (trăns) n. a condition of daydreaming or being unconscious of one's surroundings

---

3. **fix her wagon:** a slang expression meaning "put her in her place; bring about her downfall."

was happy as he could be. Me and Lou peeked through the service window, wondering what planet the painter lady came from. Who ever heard of baked macaroni without cheese, or potato salad without eggs? **C**

"Do you have any bread made with unbleached flour?" the painter lady asked Mama. There was a long pause, as though everybody in the restaurant was holding their breath, wondering if Mama would dump the next spoonful on the painter lady's head. She didn't. But when she set Pop Johnson's plate down, it came down with a bang.

When Mama finally took her order, the starving lady all of a sudden
120 couldn't make up her mind whether she wanted a vegetable plate or fish and a salad. She finally settled on the broiled trout and a tossed salad. But just when Mama reached for a plate to serve her, the painter lady leaned over the counter with her finger all up in the air.

"Excuse me," she said. "One more thing." Mama was holding the plate like a Frisbee, tapping that foot, one hand on her hip. "Can I get raw beets in that tossed salad?"

"You will get," Mama said, leaning her face close to the painter lady's, "whatever Lou back there tossed. Now sit down." And the painter lady sat back down on her stool and shut right up. **D**

130 All the way to the country, me and Lou tried to get Mama to open fire on the painter lady. But Mama said that seeing as how she was from the North, you couldn't expect her to have any manners. Then Mama said she was sorry she'd been so impatient with the woman because she seemed like a decent person and was simply trying to stick to a very strict diet. Me and Lou didn't want to hear that. Who did that lady think she was, coming into our neighborhood and taking over our wall? **E**

"Wellllll," Mama drawled, pulling into the filling station so Daddy could take the wheel, "it's hard on an artist, ya know. They can't always get people to look at their work. So she's just doing her work in the open, that's all."

140 Me and Lou definitely did not want to hear that. Why couldn't she set up an easel downtown or draw on the sidewalk in her own neighborhood? Mama told us to quit fussing so much; she was tired and wanted to rest. She climbed into the back seat and dropped down into the warm hollow Daddy had made in the pillow.

All weekend long, me and Lou tried to scheme up ways to recapture our wall. Daddy and Mama said they were sick of hearing about it. Grandmama turned up the TV to drown us out. On the late news was a story about the New York subways. When a train came roaring into the station all covered from top to bottom, windows too, with writings and drawings done with
150 spray paint, me and Lou slapped five. Mama said it was too bad kids in New York had nothing better to do than spray paint all over the trains. Daddy said that in the cities, even grown-ups wrote all over the trains and buildings too. Daddy called it "graffiti." Grandmama called it a shame.

C MULTIPLE THEMES
Reread lines 96–113. How is the painter different from the people who live in the community?

D MONITOR
What **questions** do you have about what is happening in this scene? Record them in your monitoring chart.

COMMON CORE RL 2

E MULTIPLE THEMES
Setting is the time and place where a story happens. Setting can influence a story in several ways. It can affect how characters act and it can even cause a conflict. Reread lines 130–136. What does the **setting** have to do with the **conflict** between the community and the painter?

W e couldn't wait to get out of school on Monday. We couldn't find any black spray paint anywhere. But in a junky hardware store downtown we found a can of white epoxy[4] paint, the kind you touch up old refrigerators with when they get splotchy and peely. We spent our whole allowance on it. And because it was too late to use our bus passes, we had to walk all the way home lugging our book satchels and gym shoes, and the bag with the epoxy.

When we reached the corner of Taliaferro and Fifth, it looked like a block party or something. Half the neighborhood was gathered on the sidewalk in front of the wall. I looked at Lou, he looked at me. We both looked at the bag with the epoxy and wondered how we were going to work our scheme. The painter lady's car was nowhere in sight. But there were too many people standing around to do anything. Side Pocket and his buddies were leaning on their cue sticks, hunching each other. Daddy was there with a lineman[5] he catches a ride with on Mondays. Mrs. Morris had her arms flung around the shoulders of the twins on either side of her. Mama was talking with some of her customers, many of them with napkins still at the throat. Mr. Eubanks came out of the barbershop, followed by a man in a striped poncho, half his face shaved, the other half full of foam.

"She really did it, didn't she?" Mr. Eubanks huffed out his chest. Lots of folks answered right quick that she surely did when they saw the straight razor in his hand. **F**

Mama **beckoned** us over. And then we saw it. The wall. Reds, greens, figures outlined in black. Swirls of purple and orange. Storms of blues and yellows. It was something. I recognized some of the faces right off. There was Martin Luther King, Jr. And there was a man with glasses on and his mouth open like he was laying down a heavy rap. Daddy came up alongside and reminded us that that was Minister Malcolm X. The serious woman with a rifle I knew was Harriet Tubman because my grandmama has pictures

F **MONITOR**
Reread lines 171–176. Why do people agree with Mr. Eubanks so quickly?

beckon (bĕk'ən) *v.* to summon or call, usually by a gesture or nod

---

4. **epoxy** (ĭ-pŏk'sē): a plastic used in glues and paints.
5. **lineman**: a person who repairs telephone or power lines.

of her all over the house. And I knew Mrs. Fannie Lou Hamer 'cause a signed photograph of her hangs in the restaurant next to the calendar.

Then I let my eyes follow what looked like a vine. It trailed past a man with a horn, a woman with a big white flower in her hair, a handsome dude in a tuxedo seated at a piano, and a man with a goatee holding a book. When I looked more closely, I realized that what had looked like
190 flowers were really faces. One face with yellow petals looked just like Frieda Morris. One with red petals looked just like Hattie Morris. I could hardly believe my eyes.

"Notice," Side Pocket said, stepping close to the wall with his cue stick like a classroom pointer. "These are the flags of liberation," he said in a voice I'd never heard him use before. We all stepped closer while he pointed and spoke. "Red, black and green," he said, his pointer falling on the leaflike flags of the vine. "Our liberation flag.[6] And here Ghana, there Tanzania. Guinea-Bissau, Angola, Mozambique."[7] Side Pocket sounded very tall, as though he'd been waiting all his life to give this lesson.

200 Mama tapped us on the shoulder and pointed to a high section of the wall. There was a fierce-looking man with his arms crossed against his chest guarding a bunch of children. His muscles bulged, and he looked a lot like my daddy. One kid was looking at a row of books. Lou hunched me 'cause the kid looked like me. The one that looked like Lou was spinning a globe on the tip of his finger like a basketball. There were other kids there with microscopes and compasses. And the more I looked, the more it looked like the fierce man was not so much guarding the kids as defending their right to do what they were doing. **G**

Then Lou gasped and dropped the paint bag and ran forward, running
210 his hands over a rainbow. He had to tiptoe and stretch to do it, it was so high. I couldn't breathe either. The painter lady had found the chisel marks and had painted Jimmy Lyons's name in a rainbow.

"Read the **inscription**, honey," Mrs. Morris said, urging little Frieda forward. She didn't have to urge much. Frieda marched right up, bent down, and in a loud voice that made everybody quit oohing and ahhing and listen, she read,

> *To the People of Taliaferro Street*
> *I Dedicate This Wall of Respect*
> *Painted in Memory of My Cousin*
> 220 *Jimmy Lyons* ❧

---

6. **Red, black and green . . . liberation flag:** a banner of red, black, and green horizontal stripes has been used in the United States as well as Africa to stand for the liberation, or freedom, sought by people of African heritage.

7. **Ghana . . . Tanzania. Guinea-Bissau, Angola, Mozambique** (mō'zəm-bēk'): countries in southern and western Africa.

SOCIAL STUDIES CONNECTION

Martin Luther King Jr., Malcolm X, Harriet Tubman, and Fannie Lou Hamer (shown here) were all African Americans who fought for freedom and equality.

G **MULTIPLE THEMES**
Reread lines 200–208. Here you see the story's main **characters** through the painter's eyes. How does this show that she understands the community?

inscription
(ĭn-skrĭp'shən) *n.* something written, carved, or engraved on a surface

Comprehension

1. **Recall** Why is the wall special to the narrator and Lou?

2. **Represent** Who is related to whom in this story? Use web diagrams to show the family relationships mentioned.

3. **Clarify** Why don't Lou and the narrator carry out their plan to recapture the wall?

Text Analysis

4. **Monitor** Review the chart you filled in as you read. Which questions and answers were most important for understanding the story? Why?

5. **Make Inferences** Reread lines 210–220. How do you think the two boys feel about having bought paint once they read the inscription on the wall? Explain.

6. **Analyze Characters** Mama's reaction to the painter seems to change over the course of the story. Her first impression of the painter seems to be negative. Why does she then defend the painter to the narrator and Lou?

7. **Identify Multiple Themes** Summarize what the characters learn about themselves and the painter. Then tell what you think is the main theme of the story. Then identify another theme in the story. Explain your answers.

8. **Evaluate** Was the painter an outsider or part of the community? Explain.

Extension and Challenge

9. **Readers' Circle** "The War of the Wall" is told from the **first-person point of view.** Everything we learn about the characters and plot comes from what the narrator chooses to tell us. For that reason, we don't know very much about the painter's thoughts and feelings. With a small group of classmates, talk about what the painter may have been thinking about the community. Support your responses with evidence from the story.

10. **SOCIAL STUDIES CONNECTION** Read the article "Back to the Wall" on page 349 about artist Judith Baca's mural restoration project. Identify similarities and differences between Los Angeles's Great Wall and the mural in the story. Think about the subject of each mural and the way each was created.

What makes a COMMUNITY?

Describe a community or group to which you belong.

COMMON CORE

RL 1 Cite several pieces of textual evidence to support analysis of what the text says explicitly as well as inferences drawn from the text. RL 2 Determine a theme; provide an objective summary of the text.

Vocabulary in Context

▲ **VOCABULARY PRACTICE**

Choose the letter of the situation that you would associate with each boldfaced vocabulary word.

1. **aroma:** (a) arguing with a friend, (b) writing a letter, (c) smelling a rose
2. **masterpiece:** (a) a game of catch, (b) a prize-winning play, (c) a stormy day
3. **trance:** (a) walking a dog, (b) snoring loudly, (c) not paying attention
4. **beckon:** (a) hailing a taxicab, (b) passing a test, (c) eating lunch
5. **inscription:** (a) military service, (b) words on a tombstone, (c) parts of a car

ACADEMIC VOCABULARY IN SPEAKING

> • clause   • context   • cultural   • symbol   • theme

The author of "War of the Wall" uses many **cultural** references, such as a wall where kids play handball and a pool hall, to make the neighborhood come to life. With a small group, discuss which references had the most impact on the story. Use at least one of the Academic Vocabulary words in your discussion.

VOCABULARY STRATEGY: DENOTATIONS AND CONNOTATIONS

A word's **denotation** is its literal meaning—that is, the meaning found in a dictionary definition. A word's **connotation** comes from the shades of meaning it has beyond its definition. For example, a stubborn person could also be described as *strong-willed* or *pig-headed*. But *strong-willed* connotes "independent in thinking and acting," while *pig-headed* connotes "inflexible." The context of a phrase, sentence, or paragraph can sometimes help you determine the connotation of a word.

··········
COMMON CORE

L 5c Distinguish among connotations of words with similar denotations. **L 6** Acquire and use accurately grade-appropriate general academic words.

PRACTICE Use the context in the following sentence pairs to determine the connotation of each boldfaced word.

1. There was a **gathering** of neighbors in the street to welcome the soldier.
2. An angry **mob** appeared in front of the courthouse to protest the verdict.

3. Her **slender** frame allows her to wear many different styles of clothing.
4. His **skinny** build prevented him from playing football.

5. People admired Joel for his **self-confidence**.
6. Mya is **arrogant** and thinks she's the only one who makes good decisions.

Interactive Vocabulary **THINK** central

Go to **thinkcentral.com**.
KEYWORD: HML7-348

MAGAZINE ARTICLE In "The War of the Wall," a woman paints a mural in a Southern town. In the following article, you'll read about the real-life artist Judith Baca and the people who helped her create and restore a large mural in Los Angeles, California.

Judith F. Baca, *Triumph of the Hearts* from *World Wall: A Vision of The Future Without Fear,* 1986–present. © SPARC/www.sparcmurals.com.

Back to the Wall

from *People Weekly*

Working in a city known more for freeways than museums, Judith Baca may be the quintessential Los Angeles artist, painting not on canvas but on concrete. Since 1974 she has overseen the creation of roughly 550 murals in public spaces, providing summer work for inner-city kids while she brings color and life to highway underpasses and parks. "I want it to continue," Baca, 58, says of her work. "I want future generations to see it."

One of her most famous pieces is the 13-foot-high, half-mile-long Great Wall, which depicts world and L.A. history on a flood-channel wall. Some 400 youths—many from poor, crime-ridden areas—worked on the mural, and 30 years later, some of their kids worked on its restoration. "People come first for Judy," says Priscilla Becker, 40, who, as a teen from a poor family, worked with Baca for three summers. Now CEO of a software company, Becker adds, "From Judy I learned that dreams are not just dreams."

Baca was teaching art in an inner-city park when she began planning murals to build bridges between rival gangs. She still wants her projects to meet the same goal. "All these people made the wall together," she says. "That's the story—what they made together."

What Do Fish Have to Do with Anything?

Short Story by Avi

What is the cure for
UNHAPPINESS?

COMMON CORE

RL 1 Cite several pieces of textual evidence to support inferences drawn from the text. **RL 2** Determine a theme. **RL 3** Analyze how particular elements of a story interact.

What helps you through sad times? Is it talking to another person? Is it listening to music by yourself? Everyone deals with unhappiness in his or her own way. In "What Do Fish Have to Do with Anything?" a young boy searches for a cure to the unhappiness he sees all around him.

QUICKWRITE With a partner or small group, brainstorm a list of strategies that can help people overcome unhappiness. You may use the list shown to get started. Then record the most effective strategies in your journal.

Dealing with Unhappiness
1. Focus on good things.
2. Write down feelings.
3.
4.
5.

● TEXT ANALYSIS: THEME AND SYMBOL

A symbol is a person, place, or thing that stands for something beyond itself. A dove is a well-known **symbol** for peace. To find symbols in a story, try the following:

- Look for people, places, things, or actions that the writer emphasizes or mentions over and over.
- Think about whether any repeated symbol might be a clue to identifying the overall **theme** of the story.
- Keep the title in mind, because it may contain clues.

As you read "What Do Fish Have to Do with Anything?" ask yourself what is being used as a symbol.

● READING SKILL: MAKE INFERENCES

An **inference** is a logical guess based on clues in the text plus your own knowledge. One clue that may help you understand the theme of a story is cultural context. The **cultural context** of a story refers to the social problems, traditions, and values that may have influenced the author and the writing. As you read the story, record each inference you make in an equation such as the one shown.

| Details or Evidence from Story | + | What I Know from Reading or Experience | = | Inference |

Review: **Compare and Contrast**

▲ VOCABULARY IN CONTEXT

Match each word in Column A with the word in Column B that is closest in meaning.

Column A
1. contemplate
2. inevitably
3. preoccupied
4. retort
5. threshold
6. urgency

Column B
a. unavoidably
b. distracted
c. reply
d. necessity
e. consider
f. entrance

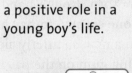

Complete the activities in your **Reader/Writer Notebook**.

Avi
born 1937

Early Challenges
Avi Wortis has written over 30 books for children and young adults, but he had to overcome a huge challenge to do so. As a boy, Avi had trouble spelling. But he loved reading—anything from comic books to histories. He later found out that he had a learning disability called dysgraphia, which caused him to reverse letters and misspell words. Although that affected his ability to write, Avi was determined to be a writer. He had no intention of giving up.

Success!
Today, Avi is one of the most well-known and respected writers for young adults and has the awards to prove it. His advice to readers: "Don't be satisfied with answers others give you. Don't assume that because everyone believes a thing, it is right or wrong. Reason things out for yourself. Work to get answers on your own." Avi includes this idea in "What Do Fish Have to Do with Anything?"

Homelessness
Avi's parents worked to promote civil rights and other social justice issues. As an adult, Avi has shared their concerns. His writing often addresses social problems. In this story, a homeless man plays a positive role in a young boy's life.

Author Online **THINK** central

Go to **thinkcentral.com**.
KEYWORD: HML7-351

351

WHAT DO FISH HAVE TO DO WITH ANYTHING? AVI

Every day at three o'clock Mrs. Markham waited for her son, Willie, to come out of school. They walked home together. If asked why she did it, Mrs. Markham would say, "Parents need to watch their children."

As they left the schoolyard, Mrs. Markham **inevitably** asked, "How was school?"

Willie would begin to talk, then stop. He was never sure his mother was listening. She seemed **preoccupied** with her own thoughts. She had been like that ever since his dad had abandoned them six months ago. No one knew where he'd gone. Willie had the feeling that his mother
10 was lost too. It made him feel lonely.

One Monday afternoon, as they approached the apartment building where they lived, she suddenly tugged at him. "Don't look that way," she said.

"Where?"

"At that man over there."

Willie stole a look over his shoulder. A man, whom Willie had never seen before, was sitting on a red plastic milk crate near the curb. His matted, streaky gray hair hung like a ragged curtain over his dirty face. His shoes were torn. Rough hands lay upon his knees. One hand was palm up. No one seemed to pay him any mind. Willie was certain he
20 had never seen a man so utterly alone. It was as if he were some spat-out piece of chewing gum on the pavement.

"What's the matter with him?" Willie asked his mother in a hushed voice.

Keeping her eyes straight ahead, Mrs. Markham said, "He's sick." She pulled Willie around. "Don't stare. It's rude."

"What kind of sick?"

inevitably
(ĭn-ĕv′ĭ-tə-blē) *adv.*
unavoidably; without fail

preoccupied
(prē-ŏk′yə-pīd′) *adj.* lost
in thought; distracted

Analyze Visuals ▶

What is the first thing you notice about this image? What sense does it give you about the person?

Gregory. Los Angeles, March 31st 1982 (1982), David Hockney. Composite Polaroid. 14¹/₂″ × 13¹/₄″. © David Hockney/The David Hockney No. 1 U.S. Trust.

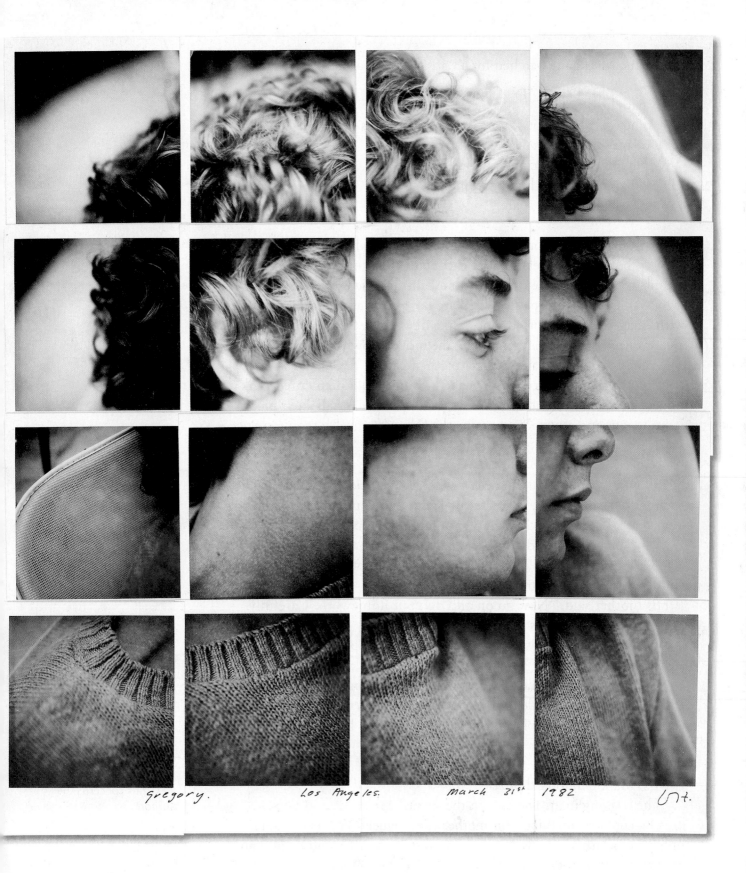

Gregory. Los Angeles. March 31st 1982

As Mrs. Markham searched for an answer, she began to walk faster.
"He's unhappy," she said.

"What's he doing?"

"Come on, Willie, you know perfectly well. He's begging."

30 "Do you think anyone gave him anything?"

"I don't know. Now, come on, don't look."

"Why don't you give him anything?"

"We have nothing to spare."

When they got home, Mrs. Markham removed a white cardboard box from the refrigerator. It contained pound cake. Using her thumb as a measure, she carefully cut a half-inch piece of cake and gave it to Willie on a clean plate. The plate lay on a plastic mat decorated with images of roses with diamondlike dewdrops. She also gave him a glass of milk and a folded napkin. She moved slowly.

40 Willie said, "Can I have a bigger piece of cake?"

Mrs. Markham picked up the cake box and ran a manicured pink fingernail along the nutrition information panel. "A half-inch piece is a portion, and a portion contains the following health requirements. Do you want to hear them?"

"No."

"It's on the box, so you can believe what it says. Scientists study people, then write these things. If you're smart enough you could become a scientist. Like this." Mrs. Markham tapped the box. "It pays well."

Willie ate his cake and drank the milk. When he was done he took 50 care to wipe the crumbs off his face as well as to blot his milk mustache with the napkin. His mother liked him to be neat.

His mother said, "Now go on and do your homework. Carefully. You're in sixth grade. It's important."

Willie gathered up his books that lay on the empty third chair. At the kitchen entrance he paused and looked back at his mother. She was staring sadly at the cake box, but he didn't think she was seeing it. Her unhappiness made him think of the man on the street.

"What *kind* of unhappiness do you think he has?" he suddenly asked.

"Who's that?"

60 "That man."

Mrs. Markham looked puzzled.

"The begging man. The one on the street." **A**

"Oh, could be anything," his mother said, vaguely. "A person can be unhappy for many reasons." She turned to stare out the window, as if an answer might be there.

A MAKE INFERENCES
Reread lines 54–62. Judging from Willie's questions, what problem or issue do you think concerns the author?

"Is unhappiness a sickness you can cure?"

"I wish you wouldn't ask such questions."

"Why?"

After a moment she said, "Questions that have no answers shouldn't
70 be asked."

"Can I go out?"

"Homework first."

Willie turned to go again.

"Money," Mrs. Markham suddenly said. "Money will cure a lot
of unhappiness. That's why that man was begging. A salesman once said
to me, 'Maybe you can't buy happiness, but you can rent a lot of it.'
You should remember that."

"How much money do we have?"

"Not enough."

80 "Is that why you're unhappy?"

"Willie, do your homework." **B**

Willie started to ask another question, but decided he would not get
an answer. He left the kitchen.

The apartment had three rooms. The walls were painted mint green.
Willie walked down the hallway to his room, which was at the front of
the building. By climbing up on the windowsill and pressing against the
glass he could see the sidewalk five stories below. The man was still there.

It was almost five when he went to tell his mother he had finished his
school assignments. He found her in her dim bedroom, sleeping. Since
90 she had begun working the night shift at a convenience store—two weeks
now—she took naps in the late afternoon.

For a while Willie stood on the **threshold,** hoping his mother would
wake up. When she didn't, he went to the front room and looked
down on the street again. The begging man had not moved.

Willie returned to his mother's room.

"I'm going out," he announced—softly.

Willie waited a decent interval[1] for his mother to waken. When she did
not, he made sure his keys were in his pocket. Then he left the apartment.

By standing just outside the building door, he could keep his eyes on
100 the man. It appeared as if he had still not moved. Willie wondered how
anyone could go without moving for so long in the chill October air.
Was staying still part of the man's sickness?

During the twenty minutes that Willie watched, no one who passed
looked in the beggar's direction. Willie wondered if they even saw the
man. Certainly no one put any money into his open hand.

B THEME AND SYMBOL
What might money symbolize to Mrs. Markham?

◆ GRAMMAR IN CONTEXT
In lines 85–86, notice that the sentence contains a **subordinate clause** that begins with the **relative pronoun** *which.* What noun does the clause relate to or give more information about?

threshold (thrĕsh′ōld′) *n.* a doorway or entrance

---

1. **interval:** amount of time.

A lady leading a dog by a leash went by. The dog strained in the direction of the man sitting on the crate. His tail wagged. The lady pulled the dog away. "Heel!" she commanded.

The dog—tail between his legs—scampered to the lady's side. Even so, 110 the dog twisted around to look back at the beggar.

Willie grinned. The dog had done exactly what Willie had done when his mother told him not to stare.

Pressing deep into his pocket, Willie found a nickel. It was warm and slippery. He wondered how much happiness you could rent for a nickel.

Squeezing the nickel between his fingers, Willie walked slowly toward the man. When he came before him, he stopped, suddenly nervous. The man, who appeared to be looking at the ground, did not move his eyes. He smelled bad.

"Here." Willie stretched forward and dropped the coin into the man's 120 open right hand. **C**

"God bless you," the man said hoarsely as he folded his fingers over the coin. His eyes, like high beams on a car, flashed up at Willie, then dropped.

Willie waited for a moment, then went back up to his room. From his window he looked down on the street. He thought he saw the coin in the man's hand, but was not sure.

A fter supper Mrs. Markham readied herself to go to work, then kissed Willie good night. As she did every night, she said, "If you have regular problems, call Mrs. Murphy downstairs. What's her number?"

"274-8676," Willie said.

130 "Extra bad problems, call Grandma."

"369-6754."

"Super special problems, you can call me."

"962-6743."

"Emergency, the police."

"911."

"Lay out your morning clothing."

"I will."

"Don't let anyone in the door."

"I won't."

140 "No television past nine."

"I know."

"But you can read late."

"You're the one who's going to be late," Willie reminded her.

"I'm leaving," Mrs. Markham said.

After she went, Willie stood for a long while in the hallway. The empty apartment felt like a cave that lay deep below the earth. That day in school Willie's teacher had told the class about a kind of fish that lived

Language Coach

Suffixes A word part added to the end of a word is called a suffix. Reread lines 111–112 and 121–122. The words *exactly* and *hoarsely* both end with the suffix *-ly*, which means "in a certain way." How would you define each word?

C MAKE INFERENCES Reread lines 113–120. From Willie's action, what can you infer about the author's feelings about poverty and homelessness?

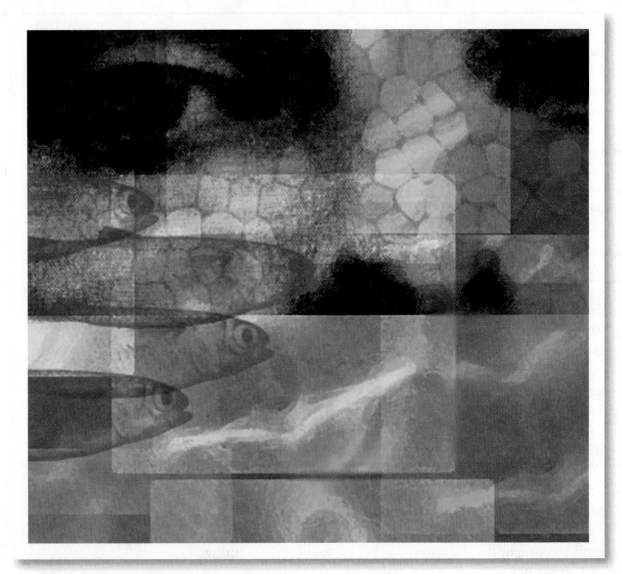

At the Aquarium (2003), Jim Macbeth. Digital collage. Photo © Jim Macbeth/SuperStock.

▲ **Analyze Visuals**

How do the details in this image connect with the story?

in caves. These fish could not see. They had no eyes. The teacher had said it was living in the dark cave that made them like that.

150   Willie had raised his hand and asked, "If they want to get out of the cave, can they?"

"I suppose."

"Would their eyes come back?"

"Good question," she said, but did not give an answer. **D**

Before he went to bed, Willie took another look out the window. In the pool of light cast by the street lamp, Willie saw the man.

On Tuesday morning when Willie went to school, the man was gone. But when he came home from school with his mother, he was there again.

"*Please* don't look at him," his mother whispered with some **urgency.**

160   During his snack, Willie said, "Why shouldn't I look?"

"What are you talking about?"

D THEME AND SYMBOL
Reread lines 145–154. What makes Willie think of the story about the fish with no eyes?

urgency (ûr′jən-sē) *n.* a condition of pressing importance; necessity

"That man. On the street. Begging."

"I told you. He's sick. It's better to act as if you never saw him. When people are that way they don't wish to be looked at."

"Why not?"

Mrs. Markham pondered for a little while. "People are ashamed of being unhappy."

Willie looked thoughtfully at his mother. "Are you sure he's unhappy?"

"You don't have to ask if people are unhappy. They tell you all the time."

170 "How?"

"The way they look."

"Is that part of the sickness?"

"Oh, Willie, I don't know. It's just the way they are."

Willie **contemplated** the half-inch slice of cake his mother had just given him. A year ago his parents seemed to be perfectly happy. For Willie, the world seemed easy, full of light. Then his father lost his job. He tried to get another but could not. For long hours he sat in dark rooms. Sometimes he drank. His parents began to argue a lot. One day, his father was gone.

180 For two weeks his mother kept to the dark. And wept.

Willie looked at his mother. "You're unhappy," he said. "Are *you* ashamed?"

Mrs. Markham sighed and closed her eyes. "I wish you wouldn't ask that."

"Why?"

"It hurts me."

"But are you ashamed?" Willie persisted.

He felt it was urgent that he know. So that he could do something. She only shook her head.

Willie said, "Do you think Dad might come back?"

190 She hesitated before saying, "Yes, I think so."

Willie wondered if that was what she really thought.

"Do you think Dad is unhappy?" Willie asked.

"Where do you get such questions?"

"They're in my mind."

"There's much in the mind that need not be paid attention to."

"Fish who live in caves have no eyes."

"What are you talking about?"

"My teacher said it's all that darkness. The fish forget how to see. So they lose their eyes." **E**

200 "I doubt she said that."

"She did."

"Willie, you have too much imagination."

contemplate
(kŏn′təm-plāt′) *v.*
to consider carefully and at length

Language Coach

Oral Fluency Reread lines 176 and 183. The letters *gh* are silent in *light* and *sighed*. Do you know any other words in which *gh* is silent?

E THEME AND SYMBOL
Reread lines 189–199. What is the connection between the questions Willie is asking his mother and the story about the fish?

After his mother went to work, Willie gazed down onto the street. The man was there. Willie thought of going down, but he knew he was not supposed to leave the building when his mother worked at night. He decided to speak to the man the next day.

That afternoon—Wednesday—Willie stood before the man. "I don't have any money," Willie said. "Can I still talk to you?"

The man lifted his face. It was a dirty face with very tired eyes. He needed a shave.

"My mother," Willie began, "said you were unhappy. Is that true?"

"Could be," the man said.

"What are you unhappy about?"

The man's eyes narrowed as he studied Willie intently. He said, "How come you want to know?"

◀ **Analyze Visuals**

Compare this man with how you picture the man in the story.

Willie shrugged.

"I think you should go home, kid."

"I am home." Willie gestured toward the apartment. "I live right here. Fifth floor. Where do you live?"

220   "Around."

"*Are* you unhappy?" Willie persisted.

The man ran a tongue over his lips. His Adam's apple bobbed. "A man has the right to remain silent," he said, and closed his eyes.

Willie remained standing on the pavement for a while before retreating back to his apartment. Once inside he looked down from the window. The man was still there. For a moment Willie was certain the man was looking at the apartment building and the floor where Willie lived.

The next day, Thursday—after dropping a nickel in the man's palm— Willie said, "I've never seen anyone look so unhappy as you do.

230 So I figure you must know a lot about it."

The man took a deep breath. "Well, yeah, maybe."

Willie said, "And I need to find a cure for it."

"A *what?*"

"A cure for unhappiness."

The man pursed his cracked lips and blew a silent whistle. Then he said, "Why?"

"My mother is unhappy."

"Why's that?"

"My dad went away."

240   "How come?"

"I think because he was unhappy. Now my mother's unhappy too— all the time. So if I found a cure for unhappiness, it would be a good thing, wouldn't it?"

"I suppose. Hey, you don't have anything to eat on you, do you?"

Willie shook his head, then said, "Would you like some cake?"

"What kind?"

"I don't know. Cake."

"Depends on the cake."

On Friday Willie said to the man, "I found out what kind of cake it is."

250   "Yeah?"

"Pound cake. But I don't know why it's called that."

"Long as it's cake it probably don't matter."

Neither spoke. Then Willie said, "In school my teacher said there are fish who live in caves and the caves are so dark the fish don't have eyes. What do you think? Do you believe that?"

"Sure."

"You do? How come?"

"Because you said so."

"You mean, just because someone *said* it you believe it?"

260 "Not someone. You." **F**

Willie was puzzled. "But, well, maybe it *isn't* true."

The man grunted. "Hey, do you believe it?"

Willie nodded.

"Well, you're not just anyone. You got eyes. You see. You ain't no fish."

"Oh." Willie was pleased.

"What's your name?" the man asked.

"Willie."

"That's a boy's name. What's your grown-up name?"

"William."

270 "And that means another thing."

"What?"

"I'll take some of that cake."

Willie started.[2] "You will?" he asked, surprised.

"Just said it, didn't I?"

Willie suddenly felt excited. It was as if the man had given him a gift. Willie wasn't sure what it was except that it was important and he was glad to have it. For a moment he just gazed at the man. He saw the lines on the man's face, the way his lips curved, the small scar on the side of his chin, the shape of his eyes, which he now saw were blue. **G**

280 "I'll get the cake," Willie cried and ran back to the apartment. He snatched the box from the refrigerator as well as a knife, then hurried back down to the street. "I'll cut you a piece," he said, and he opened the box.

"Hey, that don't look like a pound of cake," the man said.

Willie, alarmed, looked up.

"But like I told you, it don't matter."

Willie held his thumb against the cake to make sure the portion was the right size. With a poke of the knife he made a small mark for the proper width.

Just as he was about to cut, the man said, "Hold it!"

290 Willie looked up. "What?"

"What were you doing there with your thumb?"

"I was measuring the size. The right portion. A person is supposed to get only one portion."

"Where'd you learn that?"

"It says so on the box. You can see for yourself." He held out the box.

The man studied the box then handed it back to Willie. "That's just lies," he said.

"How do you know?"

"William, how can a box say how much a person needs?"

F COMPARE AND CONTRAST
Why do you think the man believes Willie but his own mother doesn't? How are the man and the mother different?

G MAKE INFERENCES
Reread lines 275–279. What "gift" has the man given Willie?

---

2. **started:** jumped or gave a sudden jerk in surprise.

Celia. Los Angeles, April 10th 1982, (1982) David Hockney. Composite Polaroid. 18″ × 30″. © David Hockney/The David Hockney No. 1 U.S. Trust.

300 "But it does. The scientists say so. They measured, so they know. Then they put it there."

"Lies," the man repeated.

Willie began to feel that this man knew many things. "Well, then, how much should I cut?" he asked.

The man said, "You have to look at me, then at the cake, and then you're going to have to decide for yourself."

"Oh." Willie looked at the cake. The piece was about three inches wide. Willie looked up at the man. After a moment he cut the cake into two pieces, each an inch and a half wide. He gave one piece to the man 310 and kept the other in the box.

"God bless you," the man said as he took the piece and laid it in his left hand. He began to break off pieces with his right hand and put them in his mouth one by one. Each piece was chewed thoughtfully. Willie watched him eat.

When the man was done, he licked the crumbs on his fingers.

"Now I'll give you something," the man said.

"What?" Willie said, surprised.

"The cure for unhappiness."

"You know it?" Willie asked, eyes wide.

320 The man nodded.

"What is it?"

"It's this: What a person needs is always more than they say."

"Who's *they?*" Willie asked.

The man pointed to the cake box. "The people on the box," he said.

In his mind Willie repeated what he had been told, then he gave the man the second piece of cake.

The man took it, saying, "Good man," and he ate it.

Willie grinned.

The next day was Saturday. Willie did not go to school. All morning
330 he kept looking down from his window for the man, but it was raining and he did not appear. Willie wondered where he was, but could not imagine it.

Willie's mother woke about noon. Willie sat with her while she ate her breakfast. "I found the cure for unhappiness," he announced.

"Did you?" his mother said. She was reading a memo from the convenience store's owner.

"It's 'What a person needs is always more than they say.'"

His mother put her papers down. "That's nonsense. Where did you hear that?"

◄ **Analyze Visuals**

Compare the image on page 362 with the one on page 353. What similarities and differences do you see?

340   "That man."

"What man?"

"On the street. The one who was begging. You said he was unhappy. So I asked him."

"Willie, I told you I didn't want you to even look at that man."

"He's a nice man. . . ."

"How do you know?"

"I've talked to him."

"When? How much?"

Willie shrank down. "I did, that's all."

350   "Willie, I forbid you to talk to him. Do you understand me? Do you? Answer me!" She was shrill.

"Yes," Willie said, but he'd already decided he would talk to the man one more time. He needed to explain why he could not talk to him anymore.

On Sunday, however, the man was not there. Nor was he there on Monday.

"That man is gone," Willie said to his mother as they walked home from school.

"I saw. I'm not blind."

"Where do you think he went?"

360   "I couldn't care less. But you might as well know, I arranged for him to be gone."

Willie stopped short. "What do you mean?"

"I called the police. We don't need a nuisance³ like that around here. Pestering kids."

"He wasn't pestering me."

"Of course he was."

"How do you know?"

"Willie, I have eyes. I can see."

Willie glared at his mother. "No, you can't. You're a fish. You live
370 in a cave." **H**

"Fish?" **retorted** Mrs. Markham. "What do fish have to do with anything? Willie, don't talk nonsense."

"My name isn't Willie. It's William. And I know how to keep from being unhappy. I do!" He was yelling now. "What a person needs is always more than they say! *Always!*" **I**

He turned on his heel and walked back toward the school. At the corner he glanced back. His mother was following. He kept going. She kept following. ❧

H **THEME AND SYMBOL**
Reread lines 356–370. Why does Willie compare his mother to the fish living in the cave?

retort (rĭ-tôrt′) *v.* to reply sharply

I **MAKE INFERENCES**
Reread lines 373–375. Why does Willie now insist that his name is William, not Willie?

---

3. **nuisance:** someone who is bothersome.

Comprehension

COMMON CORE

RL 1 Cite several pieces of textual evidence to support inferences drawn from the text. **RL 2** Determine a theme. **RL 3** Analyze how particular elements of a story interact.

1. **Recall** What do Willie and his class learn about a certain kind of fish that lives in caves?

2. **Recall** What does Willie's mother say is wrong with the homeless man?

3. **Retell** Use your own words to retell how the story ends.

Text Analysis

● 4. **Interpret Symbols** The type of fish with no eyes is mentioned many times in this story. What do you think it symbolizes? Now reread lines 34–48 and 286–310. What do you think the pound cake symbolizes?

● 5. **Make Inferences** Look over the equations you created as you read. What inferences did you draw about the cultural context in which the story was written?

● 6. **Compare and Contrast Characters** The two people in the story who have the greatest influence on Willie are his mom and the homeless man. Compare and contrast how these two characters try to help Willie.

● 7. **Analyze Theme** Use a chart to help you identify clues the writer provides about the theme of the story. What do you think the theme is?

8. **Evaluate** Willie's mother says, "Parents need to watch their children." Given what you know about her character, do you think she was right or wrong to call the police about the man?

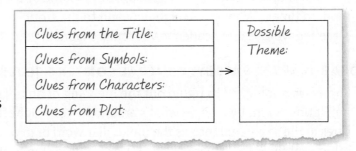

Clues from the Title:

Clues from Symbols:

Clues from Characters:

Clues from Plot:

→ Possible Theme:

Extension and Challenge

9. **SOCIAL STUDIES CONNECTION** Find out about organizations and volunteer programs in your community or a nearby city that help people who are homeless or living in poverty. Call or write to one of these organizations to ask for more information about what they do and how young people can help.

> **What is the cure for UNHAPPINESS?**
>
> Suppose Willie came to you for a cure for unhappiness. Using what you learned about Willie, what advice would you give him?

Vocabulary in Context

▲ **VOCABULARY PRACTICE**

Choose *true* or *false* for each statement.

1. If something happens **inevitably,** there is probably no way to avoid it.
2. A **preoccupied** person is one who lives in a house that was previously occupied.
3. A **threshold** can be found at the front of a house.
4. A person walking slowly communicates a feeling of **urgency.**
5. People who **contemplate** art tend to have little respect for culture.
6. If someone **retorts,** he or she is probably irritated or impatient.

contemplate

inevitably

preoccupied

retort

threshold

urgency

ACADEMIC VOCABULARY IN SPEAKING

> • clause   • context   • cultural   • symbol   • theme

The story "What Do Fish Have to Do with Anything?" takes place in a contemporary **context.** This means that the story seems to be happening in modern times. With a small group, discuss some of the clues that signal modern times. What clues might you add to the story if it were taking place today? Use one Academic Vocabulary word in your discussion.

VOCABULARY STRATEGY: GENERAL CONTEXT CLUES

Sometimes you need to figure out the meaning of an unfamiliar or ambiguous word by reading what's around it. You might find **context clues** in the same sentence as the unfamiliar word or in one or more other sentences in the paragraph. For example, a clue to the meaning of *preoccupied* in this story comes in the previous sentence, which says that Willie "was never sure his mother was listening." From this, we know she is often lost in thought, or preoccupied.

PRACTICE Use context clues to determine the definition of each boldfaced word. Then write its definition.

COMMON CORE

L 4a Use context (e.g., the overall meaning of a sentence or paragraph) as a clue to the meaning of a word.
L 6 Acquire and use accurately grade-appropriate general academic words.

1. Tossing about on their **skiff** in open waters, the passengers got drenched by the thunderstorm.
2. Lola actually made a mistake in counting the election results. She showed that she is **fallible** after all.
3. Mom could not **placate** Peter, no matter how hard she tried. He was determined to remain angry.
4. Wealthy **philanthropists** contribute large sums to charities.
5. Tobias became interested in **philately** once he saw my stamp collection.

Interactive Vocabulary **THiNK** central

Go to **thinkcentral.com.**
KEYWORD: HML7-366

Language

◆ **GRAMMAR IN CONTEXT: Use Relative Pronouns**

Review the Grammar in Context note on page 355. A **clause** is a group of words that contains a subject and a verb. A **subordinate clause** contains a subject and a verb but does not express a complete thought. Some subordinate clauses are introduced by **relative pronouns,** such as *who, whom, whose, that,* and *which*. These pronouns relate to or give more information about the words they modify. You can combine short sentences with related ideas by using relative pronouns.

> *Original:* Willie saw a man. The man was sitting on a milk crate.
>
> *Revised:* Willie saw a man who was sitting on a milk crate.

PRACTICE Use a relative pronoun to combine each pair of sentences. Underline each relative pronoun.

1. The apartment has three rooms. The rooms have green walls.
2. Mrs. Markham placed a slice of cake on a plate. The plate had images of roses.
3. Willie found a nickel. The nickel was slippery.
4. He gave the nickel to a man. The man was homeless.
5. Mrs. Markham read a memo. It was from the convenience store owner.

*For more help with relative pronouns, see page R54 in the **Grammar Handbook**.*

READING-WRITING CONNECTION

YOUR TURN Demonstrate your understanding of "What Do Fish Have to Do with Anything?" by responding to this prompt. Then use the **revising tip** to improve your writing.

WRITING PROMPT	REVISING TIP
Extended Constructed Response: Symbol On page 351, you learned that writers often use symbols to help them support ideas they want to share with their readers. Avi chose the fish with no eyes as his main symbol in this story. How does this symbol relate to the idea of unhappiness? Write a **two- or three-paragraph response.**	Review your essay. If you have used a lot of short sentences, use relative pronouns to combine some of them.

COMMON CORE

L 1a Explain the function of clauses in specific sentences.
W 2 Write explanatory texts to examine a topic and convey ideas.

Homeless
Problem-Solution Essay

Use with "What Do Fish Have to Do with Anything?" on page 352.

What's the Connection?

In the short story you just read, a mother instructs her son not to look at a homeless man who is begging. In the problem-solution essay you are about to read, Anna Quindlen notes that this is often the way people react to "the homeless," but she recommends a different response.

Standards Focus: Identify Author's Purpose

An **author's purpose** is his or her reason for creating a particular work. The purpose may be to entertain, to explain or inform, to express an opinion, or to persuade readers to do or believe something. An author may have more than one purpose for writing, but usually one is the most important. Sometimes the purpose is directly stated. Often, it is not stated. You may have to infer the purpose from the author's statements or from the theme of the work.

Here's how to identify Quindlen's purpose for writing:

• Notice which parts of the topic Quindlen focuses on.

• Write down direct statements about the way she thinks or feels about the topic.

• Note words and details she uses to describe the topic.

• Think about what these elements of her essay tell you about her purpose for writing.

As you read Quindlen's essay, use these tips to help you complete a chart like the one started here.

Direct Statements, Descriptive Words, and Other Details	What These Details Tell Me About Quindlen's Purpose
She introduces a homeless woman by name, emphasizing that this woman has a name and is a human being like any one of us.	She wants people to look at homeless people as individuals.
"I've never been very good at looking at the big picture, taking the global view."	

reprinted from **The New York Times**

Homeless

by Anna Quindlen

Her name was Ann, and we met in the Port Authority Bus Terminal several Januarys ago. I was doing a story on homeless people. She said I was wasting my time talking to her; she was just passing through, although she'd been passing through for more than two weeks. To prove to me that 10 this was true, she rummaged through a tote bag and a manila envelope and finally unfolded a sheet of typing paper and brought out her photographs.

They were not pictures of family, or friends, or even a dog or cat, its eyes brown-red in the flash-bulb's light. They were pictures of a house. It was like a thousand 20 houses in a hundred towns, not suburb, not city, but somewhere in between, with aluminum siding and a chainlink fence, a narrow driveway running up to a one-car

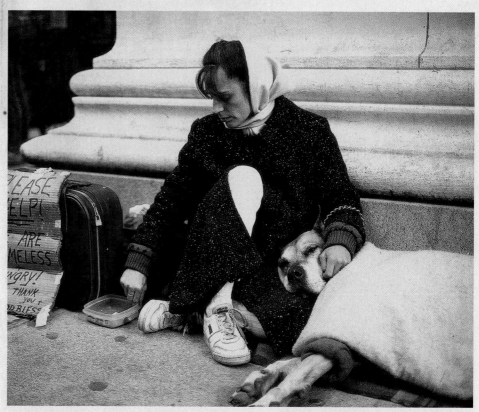

garage and a patch of backyard. The house was yellow. I looked on the back for a date or a name, but neither was there. There was no need for discussion. I knew what
30 she was trying to tell me, for it was something I had often felt. She was not adrift, alone, anonymous, although her bags and her raincoat with the grime shadowing its creases had made me believe she was. She had a house, or at least once upon a time had had one. Inside were curtains, a couch, a stove, potholders. You are where
40 you live. She was somebody.

I've never been very good at looking at the big picture, taking the global view, and I've always been a person with an overactive sense of place, the legacy[1] of an Irish grandfather. So it is natural that the thing that seems most wrong with the world to me right now is that there are so many people with no
50 homes. I'm not simply talking about shelter from the elements, or three square meals a day or a mailing address to which the welfare[2] people can send the check—although I know that all these are important for survival. I'm talking about a

---

1. **legacy** (lĕg′ə-sē): something handed down from an ancestor or from the past.
2. **welfare**: a program of financial aid provided by the government to people in need.

home, about precisely those kinds of feelings that have wound up in cross-stitch and French knots on
60 samplers[3] over the years. **A**

Home is where the heart is. There's no place like it. I love my home with a ferocity totally out of proportion to its appearance or location. I love dumb things about it: the hot-water heater, the plastic rack you drain dishes in, the roof over my head, which occasionally leaks. And yet it is precisely
70 those dumb things that make it what it is—a place of certainty, stability,[4] predictability, privacy, for me and for my family. It is where I live. What more can you say about a place than that? That is everything. **B**

Yet it is something that we have been edging away from gradually during my lifetime and the lifetimes of my parents and grand-
80 parents. There was a time when where you lived often was where you worked and where you grew the food you ate and even where you were buried. When that era passed, where you lived at least was where your parents had lived and where you would live with your children when you became
90 enfeebled.[5] Then, suddenly, where you lived was where you lived for three years, until you could move on to something else and something else again.

And so we have come to something else again, to children who do not understand what it means to go to their rooms because they have never had a room, to
100 men and women whose fantasy is a wall they can paint a color of their own choosing, to old people reduced to sitting on molded plastic chairs, their skin blue-white in the lights of a bus station, who pull pictures of houses out of their bags. Homes have stopped being homes. Now they are real estate. **C**

110 People find it curious that those without homes would rather sleep sitting up on benches or huddled in doorways than go to shelters. Certainly some prefer to do so because they are emotionally ill, because they have been locked in before and they are damned if they will be locked in again. Others are afraid of the violence and
120 trouble they may find there. But some seem to want something that is not available in shelters, and they will not compromise, not for a cot, or oatmeal, or a shower with special soap that kills the bugs. "One room," a woman with a baby who

A AUTHOR'S PURPOSE
What does Quindlen think is most wrong in the world right now? Name two facts she shares about herself to help readers understand her purpose in writing this essay.

B PROBLEM-SOLUTION ESSAY
Restate the point that Quindlen makes in this paragraph.

C AUTHOR'S PURPOSE
Reread lines 95–109. What does Quindlen say homes have become? What does she mean by this?

---

3. **in cross-stitch and French knots on samplers:** spelled out in fancy stitching and embroidered decorations.

4. **stability:** a condition of being reliable or permanent.

5. **enfeebled:** deprived of strength; made weak.

D **PROBLEM-SOLUTION ESSAY**
Reread lines 132–148. How does Quindlen think most people "work around" the problem of homelessness?

E **PROBLEM-SOLUTION ESSAY**
What does Quindlen recommend that readers do to start addressing the problem she has introduced?

was sleeping on her sister's floor, once told me, "painted blue." That was the crux[6] of it; not size or location, but pride of ownership. Painted blue.

This is a difficult problem, and some wise and compassionate people are working hard at it. But in the main I think we work around it, just as we walk around it when it is lying on the sidewalk or sitting in the bus terminal—the problem, that is. It has been customary to take people's pain and lessen our own participation in it by turning it into an issue, not a collection of human beings. We turn an adjective into a noun: the poor, not poor people; the homeless, not Ann or the man who lives in the box or the woman who sleeps on the subway grate. **D**

Sometimes I think we would be better off if we forgot about the broad strokes and concentrated on the details. Here is a woman without a bureau. There is a man with no mirror, no wall to hang it on. They are not the homeless. They are people who have no homes. No drawer that holds the spoons. No window to look out upon the world. My God. That is everything. **E**

---

6. **crux:** the most important point or element.

Comprehension

1. **Recall** In Quindlen's opinion, what was Ann trying to tell her by sharing her carefully protected pictures of a house? Explain.

2. **Recall** What do some homeless people want that they cannot get at a shelter? Explain.

Text Analysis

3. **Analyze Author's Purpose** Review the direct statements and details you noted in your chart. Then write a statement that describes Quindlen's main purpose in writing the essay.

4. **Evaluate a Problem-Solution Essay** A strong problem-solution essay does all of the following: gives a clear picture of the problem, explores its causes and effects, recommends a solution, and explains how to put the solution into effect. Would you say that this essay is a strong problem-solution essay? Why or why not?

COMMON CORE

RI 1 Cite several pieces of textual evidence to support analysis of inferences drawn from the text.
RI 6 Determine an author's point of view or purpose in a text.
RI 9 Analyze how two authors writing about the same topic shape their presentations.

Read for Information: Compare Ideas

WRITING PROMPT

Determine the theme of "What Do Fish Have to Do with Anything?" and the main purpose of "Homeless" and explain the differences in the ideas presented in these two selections.

To answer this prompt, first clarify the ideas presented in each selection. You might need to go back to the story to figure this out. Then follow these steps:

1. Review your chart to see what you have learned about Quindlen's purpose.

2. Then, keeping her purpose in mind, decide how it is different from the theme of the short story.

3. Look for evidence in "Homeless" and "What Do Fish Have to Do with Anything?" to support your conclusion.

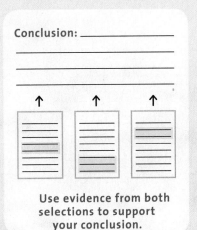

Conclusion: _____

Use evidence from both selections to support your conclusion.

A Crush
Short Story by Cynthia Rylant

What makes a GIFT special?

COMMON CORE

RL 1 Cite several pieces of textual evidence to support analysis of what the text says explicitly. **RL 2** Determine a theme. **RL 3** Analyze how particular elements of a story interact.

Everyone loves presents, right? Receiving a special gift is always a treat, but sometimes giving a gift can be even more rewarding. In the story "A Crush," simple but generous gifts bring about positive changes for both the recipients and the givers.

DISCUSS Gather in a small group to talk about gifts. Consider the following questions: What is the most special gift you have ever received? What is the most special gift you have ever given? How does gift giving make you feel? Do gifts have to cost a lot of money to be special? After your discussion, jot down one or two key points about gifts and giving.

● TEXT ANALYSIS: THEME AND CHARACTER

Paying attention to what **characters** say, do, think, and feel can help you identify a story's **theme,** or message about life. The following questions can guide you:

- What important statements are made by the characters or about the characters?

- What lessons do the characters learn?

- Do any characters change over the course of the story? If so, how do they change?

As you read "A Crush," keep these questions in mind to help you determine the story's theme.

● READING SKILL: IDENTIFY CAUSE AND EFFECT

Seeing how things are related can help you understand them. Events in a plot are often related to each other by **cause and effect.** Sometimes, an effect becomes the cause of another event, and so on until the end of the story. This is called a cause-and-effect chain. As you read "A Crush," record events in a chain graphic organizer like the one shown.

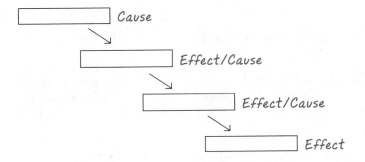

▲ VOCABULARY IN CONTEXT

The words in column A help tell Rylant's story about **giving.** For each word, choose the word or phrase in column B that is related in meaning.

Column A	Column B
1. cherish	a. overflow
2. usher	b. tall tale
3. improbable	c. Valentine card
4. excess	d. escort
5. taut	e. barely noticed
6. discreetly	f. strong knot

Complete the activities in your **Reader/Writer Notebook.**

Meet the Author

Cynthia Rylant
born 1954

Humble Beginnings
Award-winning author Cynthia Rylant grew up in the mountains of West Virginia. Rylant lived with her grandparents for four years while her mother was in nursing school. Her grandfather was a coal miner, and the family lived in a small house with no plumbing. When Rylant's mother finished school, she found an apartment for herself and her daughter. Rylant says she "felt rich" living there because the building had running water and an indoor bathroom.

BACKGROUND TO THE STORY
Inspiration
In Kent, Ohio, where Cynthia Rylant once lived, a man sometimes brought flowers to the waitresses at a little diner. He was Rylant's inspiration for one of the main characters in "A Crush." Next to the diner was a hardware store. "That's where my imagination found Dolores," said Rylant, referring to another character in the story. Rylant says she enjoys taking "people who don't get any attention in the world and making them really valuable in my fiction—making them absolutely shine with their beauty!"

Author Online
THINK central
Go to **thinkcentral.com.**
KEYWORD: HML7-375

A Crush

Cynthia Rylant

When the windows of Stan's Hardware started filling up with flowers, everyone in town knew something had happened. **Excess** flowers usually mean death, but since these were all real flowers bearing the aroma of nature instead of floral preservative, and since they stood bunched in clear Mason jars[1] instead of impaled on Styrofoam crosses,[2] everyone knew nobody had died. So they all figured somebody had a crush and kept quiet. **Ⓐ**

There wasn't really a Stan of Stan's Hardware. Dick Wilcox was the owner, and since he'd never liked his own name, he gave his store half 10 the name of his childhood hero, Stan Laurel[3] in the movies. Dick had been married for twenty-seven years. Once, his wife, Helen, had dropped a German chocolate cake on his head at a Lion's Club dance, so Dick and Helen were not likely candidates for the honest expression of the flowers in those clear Mason jars lining the windows of Stan's Hardware, and speculation had to move on to Dolores.

Dolores was the assistant manager at Stan's and had worked there for twenty years, since high school. She knew the store like a mother knows her baby, so Dick—who had trouble keeping up with things like prices and new brands of drywall compound[4]—tried to keep himself busy in 20 the back and give Dolores the run of the floor. This worked fine because the carpenters and plumbers and painters in town trusted Dolores and took her advice to heart. They also liked her tattoo.

---

1. **Mason jars:** glass jars with tight lids, used for canning or preserving foods.
2. **impaled on Styrofoam crosses:** pinned onto crosses made of a lightweight plastic material.
3. **Stan Laurel:** a comedian who with his partner, Oliver Hardy, made comedy films from the 1920s to the 1950s.
4. **drywall compound:** a mixture used to install or repair wallboard, of which the interior walls of many houses are made.

excess (ĭk-sĕs′) *adj.* too much or too many

Ⓐ CAUSE AND EFFECT The first paragraph of this story presents a cause-and-effect relationship. What is the effect of the windows' filling up with flowers?

Analyze Visuals ▶ Why do you think the artist used a "blurry" style for this image?

Bladen's Hardware (2002), Bill Firestone. © Bill Firestone.

Dolores was the only woman in town with a tattoo. On the days she went sleeveless, one could see it on the **taut** brown skin of her upper arm: "Howl at the Moon." The picture was of a baying coyote, which must have been a dark gray in its early days but which had faded to the color of the spackling paste[5] Dolores stocked in the third aisle. Nobody had gotten out of Dolores the true story behind the tattoo. Some of the men who came in liked to show off their own, and they'd roll up their

30 sleeves or pull open their shirts, exhibiting bald eagles and rattlesnakes and Confederate flags, and they'd try to coax out of Dolores the history of her coyote. All of the men had gotten their tattoos when they were in the service, drunk on weekend leave and full of the spitfire of young soldiers. Dolores had never been in the service, and she'd never seen weekend leave, and there wasn't a tattoo parlor anywhere near. They couldn't figure why or where any half-sober woman would have a howling coyote ground into the soft skin of her upper arm. But Dolores wasn't telling.

taut (tôt) *adj.* not loose or flabby

That the flowers in Stan's front window had anything to do with Dolores seemed completely **improbable.** As far as anyone knew,
40 Dolores had never been in love, nor had anyone ever been in love with her. Some believed it was the tattoo, of course, or the fine dark hair coating Dolores's upper lip which kept suitors away. Some felt it was because Dolores was just more of a man than most of the men in town, and fellows couldn't figure out how to court someone who knew more about the carburetor of a car or the back side of a washing machine than they did. Others thought Dolores simply didn't want love. This was a popular theory among the women in town who sold Avon and Mary Kay cosmetics. Whenever one of them ran into the hardware for a package of light bulbs or some batteries, she would mentally pluck every
50 one of the black hairs above Dolores's lip. Then she'd wash that grease out of Dolores's hair, give her a good blunt cut, dress her in a decent silk-blend blouse with a nice Liz Claiborne skirt from the Sports line, and, finally, tone down that swarthy, longshoreman look[6] of Dolores's with a concealing beige foundation,[7] some frosted peach lipstick, and a good gray liner for the eyes.

improbable (ĭm-prŏb'ə-bəl) *adj.* not likely

Dolores simply didn't want love, the Avon lady would think as she walked back to her car carrying her little bag of batteries. If she did, she'd fix herself up.

---

5. **spackling paste:** a substance used to repair holes or cracks in plaster.

6. **swarthy, longshoreman look:** darkly tanned skin, like that of a worker who unloads ships all day.

7. **concealing beige foundation:** a liquid makeup that covers skin flaws.

The man who was in love with Dolores and who brought her
zinnias and cornflowers and nasturtiums and marigolds and asters and
four-o'clocks in clear Mason jars did not know any of this. He did not
know that men showed Dolores their tattoos. He did not know that
Dolores understood how to use and to sell a belt sander.[8] He did not
know that Dolores needed some concealing beige foundation so she
could get someone to love her. The man who brought flowers to Dolores
on Wednesdays when the hardware opened its doors at 7:00 A.M. didn't
care who Dolores had ever been or what anyone had ever thought of her.
He loved her, and he wanted to bring her flowers. **B**

Ernie had lived in this town all of his life and had never before met
Dolores. He was thirty-three years old, and for thirty-one of those years
he had lived at home with his mother in a small dark house on the edge
of town near Beckwith's Orchards. Ernie had been a beautiful baby, with
a shock of shining black hair and large blue eyes and a round, wise face.
But as he had grown, it had become clearer and clearer that though he
was indeed a perfectly beautiful child, his mind had not developed with
the same perfection. Ernie would not be able to speak in sentences until
he was six years old. He would not be able to count the apples in a bowl
until he was eight. By the time he was ten, he could sing a simple song.
At age twelve, he understood what a joke was. And when he was twenty,
something he saw on television made him cry.

Ernie's mother kept him in the house with her because it was easier,
so Ernie knew nothing of the world except this house. They lived, the
two of them, in tiny dark rooms always illuminated by the glow of a
television set, Ernie's bags of Oreos and Nutter Butters littering the floor,
his baseball cards scattered across the sofa, his heavy winter coat thrown
over the arm of a chair so he could wear it whenever he wanted, and his
box of Burpee[9] seed packages sitting in the middle of the kitchen table.

These Ernie **cherished**. The seeds had been delivered to his home by
mistake. One day a woman wearing a brown uniform had pulled up in
a brown truck, walked quickly to the front porch of Ernie's house, set
a box down, and with a couple of toots of her horn, driven off again.
Ernie had watched her through the curtains and, when she was gone,
had ventured onto the porch and shyly, cautiously, picked up the box.
His mother checked it when he carried it inside. The box didn't have their
name on it, but the brown truck was gone, so whatever was in the box was
theirs to keep. Ernie pulled off the heavy tape, his fingers trembling, and
found inside the box more little packages of seeds than he could count. He
lifted them out, one by one, and examined the beautiful photographs of

B THEME AND
CHARACTER
How is the man who
loves Dolores different
from other people in
town?

cherish (chĕr′ĭsh) *v.*
to care for deeply

---

8. **belt sander:** a machine that uses a rough-textured moving belt to smooth surfaces.

9. **Burpee:** W. Atlee Burpee and Co. is the world's largest mail-order seed company.

"Gloria" Aster SEEDS

Cornflower SEEDS

Nasturtium SEEDS

flowers on each. His mother was not interested, had returned to the
100 television, but Ernie sat down at the kitchen table and quietly looked
at each package for a long time, his fingers running across the slick paper
and outlining the shapes of zinnias and cornflowers and nasturtiums and
marigolds and asters and four-o'clocks, his eyes drawing up their colors. **C**

Two months later Ernie's mother died. A neighbor found her at the
mailbox beside the road. People from the county courthouse came
out to get Ernie, and as they <u>ushered</u> him from the home he would never
see again, he picked up the box of seed packages from his kitchen table
and passed through the doorway.

Eventually Ernie was moved to a large white house near the main
110 street of town. This house was called a group home, because in it lived
a group of people who, like Ernie, could not live on their own. There
were six of them. Each had his own room. When Ernie was shown the
room that would be his, he put the box of Burpee seeds—which he had
kept with him since his mother's death—on the little table beside the bed,
and then he sat down on the bed and cried.

Ernie cried every day for nearly a month. And then he stopped. He dried
his tears, and he learned how to bake refrigerator biscuits and how to dust
mop and what to do if the indoor plants looked brown. **D**

Ernie loved watering the indoor plants, and it was this pleasure which
120 finally drew him outside. One of the young men who worked at the
group home—a college student named Jack—grew a large garden in
the back of the house. It was full of tomato vines and the large yellow
blossoms of healthy squash. During his first summer at the house,
Ernie would stand at the kitchen window, watching Jack and sometimes
a resident of the home move among the vegetables. Ernie was curious
but too afraid to go into the garden.

C THEME AND CHARACTER
Reread lines 96–103. Why do you think the seeds are so interesting to Ernie?

usher (ŭsh′ər) *v.* to guide in a certain direction

D CAUSE AND EFFECT
Reread lines 104–118. How does the death of Ernie's mother affect Ernie's life?

Then one day when Ernie was watching through the window, he noticed that Jack was ripping open several slick little packages and emptying them into the ground. Ernie panicked and ran to his room. But the box of Burpee seeds was still there on his table, untouched. He grabbed it, slid it under his bed, then went back through the house and out into the garden as if he had done this every day of his life.

He stood beside Jack, watching him empty seed packages into the soft black soil, and as the packages were emptied, Ernie asked for them, holding out his hand, his eyes on the photographs of red radishes and purple eggplant. Jack handed the empty packages over with a smile and with that gesture became Ernie's first friend.

Jack tried to explain to Ernie that the seeds would grow into vegetables, but Ernie could not believe this until he saw it come true. And when it did, he looked all the more intently at the packages of zinnias and cornflowers and the rest hidden beneath his bed. He thought more deeply about them, but he could not carry them to the garden. He could not let the garden have his seeds.

That was the first year in the large white house.

The second year, Ernie saw Dolores, and after that he thought of nothing else but her and of the photographs of flowers beneath his bed.

Jack had decided to take Ernie downtown for breakfast every Wednesday morning to ease him into the world outside that of the group home. They left very early, at 5:45 A.M., so there would be few people and almost no traffic to frighten Ernie and make him beg for his room. Jack and Ernie drove to the Big Boy restaurant which sat across the street from Stan's Hardware. There they ate eggs and bacon and French toast among those whose work demanded rising before the sun: bus drivers, policemen, nurses, mill workers. Their first time in the Big Boy, Ernie was too nervous to eat. The second time, he could eat, but he couldn't look up. The third time, he not only ate everything on his plate, but he lifted his head and he looked out the window of the Big Boy restaurant toward Stan's Hardware across the street. There he saw a dark-haired woman in jeans and a black T-shirt unlocking the front door of the building, and that was the moment Ernie started loving Dolores and thinking about giving up his seeds to the soft black soil of Jack's garden.

Love is such a mystery, and when it strikes the heart of one as mysterious as Ernie himself, it can hardly be spoken of. Ernie could not explain to Jack why he went directly to his room later that morning, pulled the box of Burpee seeds from under his bed, then grabbed Jack's hand in the kitchen and walked with him to the garden, where Ernie

Language Coach

Oral Fluency Notice the words *packages* in line 128 and *panicked* in line 129. In each word, *ck* is pronounced *k* as in *kangaroo*. Reread lines 127–129 aloud, pronouncing the words *packages* correctly.

had come to believe things would grow. Ernie handed the packets of seeds one by one to Jack, who stood in silent admiration of the lovely photographs before asking Ernie several times, "Are you sure you want to plant these?" Ernie was sure. It didn't take him very long, and when the seeds all lay under the moist black earth, Ernie carried his empty packages inside the house and spent the rest of the day spreading them across his bed in different arrangements. **E**

That was in June. For the next several Wednesdays at 7:00 A.M. Ernie watched every movement of the dark-haired woman behind the lighted windows of Stan's Hardware. Jack watched Ernie watch Dolores and **discreetly** said nothing.

When Ernie's flowers began growing in July, Ernie spent most of his time in the garden. He would watch the garden for hours, as if he expected it suddenly to move or to impress him with a quick trick. The fragile green stems of his flowers stood uncertainly in the soil, like baby colts on their first legs, but the young plants performed no magic for Ernie's eyes. They saved their shows for the middle of the night and next day surprised Ernie with tender small blooms in all the colors the photographs had promised.

The flowers grew fast and hardy, and one early Wednesday morning when they looked as big and bright as their pictures on the empty packages, Ernie pulled a glass canning jar off a dusty shelf in the basement of his house. He washed the jar, half filled it with water, then carried it to the garden, where he placed in it one of every kind of flower he had grown. He met Jack at the car and rode off to the Big Boy with the jar of flowers held tight between his small hands. Jack told him it was a beautiful bouquet.

When they reached the door of the Big Boy, Ernie stopped and pulled at Jack's arm, pointing to the building across the street. "OK," Jack said, and he led Ernie to the front door of Stan's Hardware. It was 6:00 A.M., and the building was still dark. Ernie set the clear Mason jar full of flowers under the sign that read "Closed," then he smiled at Jack and followed him back across the street to get breakfast.

When Dolores arrived at seven and picked up the jar of zinnias and cornflowers and nasturtiums and marigolds and asters and four-o'clocks, Ernie and Jack were watching her from a booth in the Big Boy. Each had a wide smile on his face as Dolores put her nose to the flowers. Ernie giggled. They watched the lights of the hardware store come up and saw Dolores place the clear Mason jar on the ledge of the front window. They drove home still smiling.

E THEME AND CHARACTER
Reread lines 162–173. Why does Ernie suddenly want to grow flowers after he sees Dolores?

discreetly (dĭ-skrēt'lē) *adv.* in a manner that shows caution and good judgment

VISUAL VOCABULARY

Mason jar *n.* a jar with a wide opening and a twist-on lid, used for canning and preserving foods

All the rest of that summer Ernie left a jar of flowers every Wednesday morning at the front door of Stan's Hardware. Neither Dick Wilcox nor Dolores could figure out why the flowers kept coming, and each of them assumed somebody had a crush on the other. But the flowers had an effect on them anyway. Dick started spending more time out on the floor making conversation with the customers, while Dolores stopped wearing T-shirts to work and instead wore crisp white blouses with the sleeves rolled back off her wrists. Occasionally she put on a bracelet. **F**

By summer's end Jack and Ernie had become very good friends, and when the flowers in the garden behind their house began to wither, and Ernie's face began to grow gray as he watched them, Jack brought home one bright day in late September a great long box. Ernie followed Jack as he carried it down to the basement and watched as Jack pulled a long glass tube from the box and attached this tube to the wall above a table. When Jack plugged in the tube's electric cord, a soft lavender light washed the room.

"Sunshine," said Jack. **G**

Then he went back to his car for a smaller box. He carried this down to the basement, where Ernie still stood staring at the strange light. Jack handed Ernie the small box, and when Ernie opened it, he found more little packages of seeds than he could count, with new kinds of photographs on the slick paper.

"Violets," Jack said, pointing to one of them.

Then he and Ernie went outside to get some dirt. ✖

F CAUSE AND EFFECT
Reread lines 207–214. What effect do the flowers have on Dick and Dolores?

G THEME AND CHARACTER
How is Jack's gift to Ernie like Ernie's gift to Dolores?

Detail of *Zinnias* (2001), Bill Firestone. © Bill Firestone.

Comprehension

1. **Recall** How is Ernie different from other people?

2. **Represent** Using stick figures with labels to represent characters, draw the scene in which Ernie first gets a crush on Dolores.

3. **Clarify** How does Jack help Ernie at the end of the story?

Text Analysis

4. **Make Inferences** Reflect on Jack's character. What gifts does he give Ernie in addition to seeds and a light?

5. **Analyze Character** Ernie changes a great deal from the time he receives the box of seeds to the end of the story. Note details about significant changes in his life and his behavior in a diagram such as the one shown. Using your notes, analyze how Ernie's behavior changes.

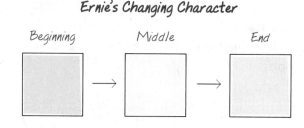

Ernie's Changing Character

Beginning → Middle → End

6. **Analyze Cause and Effect** Look at the cause-and-effect chain you created as you read. On the basis of your notes, which event would you say had the most significant effect on Ernie's life? Why?

7. **Identify Theme** Review the questions you asked yourself as you read (see page 375). What did the characters learn in this story? Restate the lesson or lessons as a theme.

8. **Evaluate Point of View** This story is told from a **third-person omniscient point of view,** in which the narrator is an invisible observer who can get into the minds of all the characters. Why is that the best point of view for the author to use in "A Crush"?

Extension and Challenge

9. **Creative Project: Newspaper Article** Newspapers often include stories about local events like those that take place in this story. Write a newspaper article about how Dolores's life changes because of the anonymous gifts of flowers. Remember to include a catchy headline for your article!

What makes a GIFT special?

How do you think Dolores might answer this question?

COMMON CORE

RL 1 Cite several pieces of textual evidence to support analysis of what the text says explicitly.
RL 2 Determine a theme.
RL 3 Analyze how particular elements of a story interact.

Vocabulary in Context

▲ **VOCABULARY PRACTICE**

Use context clues to identify the vocabulary word that best completes each sentence.

1. Dolores was a hard-working woman with _____ muscles.
2. For Ernie to fall in love with Dolores at one glance might seem _____.
3. Nevertheless, he began to _____ her from the first day he saw her.
4. Jack kindly helped to _____ Ernie into the world of gardening.
5. Ernie made a large bouquet of flowers, but he still had _____ flowers in his garden.
6. Not wanting to be noticed, Ernie _____ delivered the bouquet early in the morning.

> cherish
>
> discreetly
>
> excess
>
> improbable
>
> taut
>
> usher

ACADEMIC VOCABULARY IN WRITING

> • clause   • context   • cultural   • symbol   • theme

In "A Crush," the flowers become a **symbol** to Ernie, Dick, and Dolores. Write a paragraph about what the flowers mean to each person. Use at least one Academic Vocabulary word and one subordinating **clause** in your response.

VOCABULARY STRATEGY: FORMS OF THE PREFIX *in-*

As you have learned, the prefix *in-* often means "not." This prefix may have various spellings, depending on the letter that follows it.

- When added to words beginning with *b, m,* or *p,* it is spelled *im-,* as in the vocabulary word *improbable.*

- For words beginning with *l,* it is spelled *il-,* as in the word *illogical.*

- For words beginning with *r,* it is spelled *ir-,* as in the word *irreversible.*

Learning to recognize this prefix with its various spellings can help you figure out the meanings of many words.

PRACTICE Choose the word in each group that contains a correctly spelled prefix meaning "not." Then use the word in a sentence.

1. inproper, inperfect, impossible
2. irresponsible, irelevant, iregular
3. imcapable, imhospitable, intolerant
4. imature, imobile, immortal
5. iladvisable, illegal, inlogical
6. ireparable, irreplaceable, iresistible

COMMON CORE

L 4b Use common, grade-appropriate Greek or Latin affixes as clues to the meaning of a word. **L 6** Acquire and use accurately grade-appropriate general academic words.

Interactive Vocabulary **THINK** central

Go to **thinkcentral.com**.
KEYWORD: HML7-385

The Giver

Fantasy Novel by Lois Lowry

COMMON CORE

RL 10 Read and comprehend literature.

Other Books by Lois Lowry

- *Anastasia Krupnik*
- *Gathering Blue*
- *Messenger*
- *Number the Stars*
- *Rabble Starkey*
- *A Summer to Die*

Meet Lois Lowry

By the time she was three, Lois Lowry had already learned to read, so books played an important role in her childhood. "I was a solitary child who lived in the world of books and my own vivid imagination," she says. "That is how I write—I go back to the child I was and see things through those eyes."

Though she always loved reading and writing stories, Lowry didn't begin writing full-time until after she went to college, married, and raised her four children. She is now the author of over 30 books and has won many awards for her work.

Try a Fantasy Novel

Many of Lowry's books are a type of literature called **fantasy.** In a fantasy novel, you can travel to a different world where you'll find at least one element that is completely unreal and could exist only in the imagination. The setting might be strange, events might sound impossible, or you might read about characters with superhuman abilities.

Reading Fluency Good readers read smoothly, accurately, and with feeling. To improve your reading fluency, it helps to read a passage several times. Your goal in silent reading is to make sense of the writer's words and ideas. When reading aloud, think about your purpose for reading a text. Be sure to group words into meaningful phrases that sound like natural speech.

Read a Great Book

Lois Lowry puts her astonishing imagination to work in *The Giver*, a novel about a 12-year-old boy named Jonas, who lives in a world without fear of pain, hunger, poverty, or crime. Community leaders control everything, including what indviduals are allowed to say and do. Upon turning 12, children are given specific roles in the community, based on their abilities.

In the following section from the book, the day of assignments has arrived. Jonas anxiously awaits the decision of the Elders.

from  The Giver

Now Father sat beside Mother in the audience. Jonas could see them applauding dutifully as the Nines, one by one, wheeled their new bicycles, each with its gleaming nametag attached to the back, from the stage. . . .

Finally the Nines were all resettled in their seats, each having wheeled a bicycle outside where it would be waiting for its owner at the end of the day. Everyone always chuckled and made small jokes when the Nines rode home for the first time. "Want me to show you how to ride?" older friends would call. "I know you've never

10 been on a bike before!" But invariably the grinning Nines, who in technical violation of the rule had been practicing secretly for weeks, would mount and ride off in perfect balance, training wheels never touching the ground.

Then the Tens. Jonas never found the Ceremony of Ten particularly interesting—only time-consuming, as each child's hair was snipped neatly into its distinguishing cut: females lost their braids at Ten, and males, too, relinquished their long childish hair and took on the more manly short style which exposed their ears.

Laborers moved quickly to the stage with brooms and swept away

20 the mounds of discarded hair. Jonas could see the parents of the new Tens stir and murmur, and he knew that this evening, in many dwellings, they would be snipping and straightening the hastily done haircuts, trimming them into a neater line.

Elevens. It seemed a short time ago that Jonas had undergone the Ceremony of Eleven, but he remembered that it was not one of the more interesting ones. By Eleven, one was only waiting to be Twelve. It was simply a marking of time with no meaningful changes. There was new clothing: different undergarments for the females, whose bodies were beginning to change; and longer trousers for the males,
30 with a specially shaped pocket for the small calculator that they would use this year in school; but those were simply presented in wrapped packages without an accompanying speech.

Break for midday meal. Jonas realized he was hungry. He and his groupmates congregated by the tables in front of the Auditorium and took their packaged food. Yesterday there had been merriment at lunch, a lot of teasing, and energy. But today the group stood anxiously separate from the other children. Jonas watched the new Nines gravitate toward their waiting bicycles, each one admiring his or her nametag. He saw the Tens stroking their new shortened hair,
40 the females shaking their heads to feel the unaccustomed lightness without the heavy braids they had worn so long.

"I heard about a guy who was absolutely certain he was going to be assigned Engineer," Asher muttered as they ate, "and instead they gave him Sanitation Laborer. He went out the next day, jumped into the river, swam across, and joined the next community he came to. Nobody ever saw him again."

Jonas laughed. "Somebody made that story up, Ash," he said. "My father said he heard that story when *he* was a Twelve."

But Asher wasn't reassured. He was eyeing the river where it
50 was visible behind the Auditorium. "I can't even swim very well," he said. "My swimming instructor said that I don't have the right boyishness or something."

"Buoyancy," Jonas corrected him.

"Whatever. I don't have it. I sink."

"Anyway," Jonas pointed out, "have you ever once known of anyone—I mean really known for sure, Asher, not just heard a story about it—who joined another community?"

"No," Asher admitted reluctantly. "But you can. It says so in the rules. If you don't fit in, you can apply for Elsewhere and be released.
60 My mother says that once, about ten years ago, someone applied and

was gone the next day." Then he chuckled. "She told me that because I was driving her crazy. She threatened to apply for Elsewhere."

"She was joking."

"I know. But it was true, what she said, that someone did that once. She said that it was really true. Here today and gone tomorrow. Never seen again. Not even a Ceremony of Release."

Jonas shrugged. It didn't worry him. How could someone not fit in? The community was so meticulously ordered, the choices so carefully made.

70 Even the Matching of Spouses was given such weighty consideration that sometimes an adult who applied to receive a spouse waited months or even *years* before a Match was approved and announced. All of the factors—disposition, energy level, intelligence, and interests—had to correspond and to interact perfectly. Jonas's mother, for example, had a higher intelligence than his father, but his father had a calmer disposition. They balanced each other. Their match, which like all Matches had been monitored by the Committee of Elders for three years before they could apply for children, had always been a successful one.

80 Like the Matching of Spouses and the Naming and Placement of newchildren, the Assignments were scrupulously thought through by the Committee of Elders.

He was certain that his Assignment, whatever it was to be, and Asher's too, would be the right one for them. He only wished that the midday break would conclude, that the audience would reenter the Auditorium, and the suspense would end.

As if in answer to his unspoken wish, the signal came and the crowd began to move toward the doors.

Now Jonas's group had taken a new place in the Auditorium, 90 trading with the new Elevens, so that they sat in the very front, immediately before the stage.

They were arranged by their original numbers, the numbers they had been given at birth. The numbers were rarely used after the Naming. But each child knew his number, of course. Sometimes parents used them in irritation at a child's misbehavior, indicating that mischief made one unworthy of a name. Jonas always chuckled when he heard a parent, exasperated, call sharply to a whining toddler, "That's *enough*, Twenty-three!"

Jonas was Nineteen. He had been the nineteenth newchild born his year. It had meant that at his Naming, he had been already standing and bright-eyed, soon to walk and talk. It had given him a slight advantage the first year or two, a little more maturity than many of his groupmates who had been born in the later months of that year. But it evened out, as it always did, by Three.

After Three, the children progressed at much the same level, though by their first number one could always tell who was a few months older than others in his group. Technically, Jonas's full number was Eleven-nineteen, since there were other Nineteens, of course, in each age group. And today, now that the new Elevens had been advanced this morning, there were *two* Eleven-nineteens. At the midday break he had exchanged smiles with the new one, a shy female named Harriet.

But the duplication was only for these few hours. Very soon he would not be an Eleven but a Twelve, and age would no longer matter. He would be an adult, like his parents, though a new one and untrained still.

Asher was Four, and sat now in the row ahead of Jonas. He would receive his Assignment fourth.

Fiona, Eighteen, was on his left; on his other side sat Twenty, a male named Pierre whom Jonas didn't like much. Pierre was very serious, not much fun, and a worrier and tattletale, too. "Have you checked the rules, Jonas?" Pierre was always whispering solemnly. "I'm not sure that's within the rules." Usually it was some foolish thing that no one cared about—opening his tunic if it was a day with a breeze; taking a brief try on a friend's bicycle, just to experience the different feel of it.

The initial speech at the Ceremony of Twelve was made by the Chief Elder, the leader of the community who was elected every ten years. The speech was much the same each year: recollection of the time of childhood and the period of preparation, the coming responsibilities of adult life, the profound importance of Assignment, the seriousness of training to come.

Then the Chief Elder moved ahead in her speech.

"This is the time," she began, looking directly at them, "when we acknowledge differences. You Elevens have spent all your years till now learning to fit in, to standardize your behavior, to curb any impulse that might set you apart from the group.

"But today we honor your differences. They have determined your futures."

140 She began to describe this year's group and its variety of personalities, though she singled no one out by name. She mentioned that there was one who had singular skills at caretaking, another who loved newchildren, one with unusual scientific aptitude, and a fourth for whom physical labor was an obvious pleasure. Jonas shifted in his seat, trying to recognize each reference as one of his groupmates. The caretaking skills were no doubt those of Fiona, on his left; he remembered noticing the tenderness with which she had bathed the Old. Probably the one with scientific aptitude was Benjamin, the male who had devised new, important equipment

150 for the Rehabilitation Center.

He heard nothing that he recognized as himself, Jonas.

Finally the Chief Elder paid tribute to the hard work of her committee, which had performed the observations so meticulously all year. The Committee of Elders stood and was acknowledged by applause. Jonas noticed Asher yawn slightly, covering his mouth politely with his hand.

Then, at last, the Chief Elder called number One to the stage, and the Assignments began. ❧

Keep Reading

You've just gotten a sense of the community Jonas lives in. What details about the group seemed strange to you? To learn more about this strange community, read more of *The Giver*. You'll discover how Jonas is assigned to become the new Receiver of Memory for his community and begins training with a man known as The Giver. Once Jonas learns the truth about his society and how it compares to the larger world, he finds that he has some difficult choices to make.

Spring Harvest of Snow Peas
Poem by Maxine Hong Kingston

Eating Alone
Poem by Li-Young Lee

Can you be alone and
not LONELY?

Some people love to be alone. Others get bored or sad when no one else is around or feel lonely even when they are with other people. In the two poems you are about to read, the speakers share their thoughts and feelings about being alone.

DISCUSS What advice would you give to someone who is feeling lonely when alone? Work with a partner to list ways to overcome loneliness. Then share your insights with the class to come up with a master list of "loneliness busters."

1. Write in a journal.
2.
3.
4.
5.

TEXT ANALYSIS: RECURRING THEME

How many stories and poems have you read that conveyed the message "Love is all you need" or "Growing up is difficult"? You've probably come across these themes fairly often. When the same theme is presented in more than one piece of literature, it is called a **recurring theme.**

The two poems you are about to read have a common theme, but the poets express it differently. As you read each poem, pay attention to the following elements. They will help you find the poems' shared message.

- title
- subjects presented
- words and phrases that describe the speaker's feelings
- **images,** or words and phrases that help you know how things look, feel, smell, sound, or taste

READING STRATEGY: SET A PURPOSE FOR READING

Sometimes your purpose for reading might be to relax with a good book. At other times it might be to get information. In this lesson, your **purpose for reading** the two poems is to identify the recurring theme and compare the ways the poets communicate it.

After you've read "Spring Harvest of Snow Peas" and "Eating Alone," read the poems again. Then make a chart like the one shown. You will be asked to do more with this chart after you finish reading.

	"Spring Harvest of Snow Peas"	"Eating Alone"
What idea is described in the title?		
What subjects are presented?	garden, mother, food	garden, father, food
How is the speaker feeling?		
What important images can you find?		

Complete the activities in your **Reader/Writer Notebook.**

Meet the Authors

Maxine Hong Kingston
born 1940

Lifelong Poet
Maxine Hong Kingston grew up listening to her mother's bedtime stories and began writing poetry when she was in the fourth grade. She has since become one of the best-known Asian-American writers of nonfiction, fiction, and poetry. As the child of Chinese immigrants, Kingston often focuses her writing on her cultural heritage.

Li-Young Lee
born 1957

Master of Imagery
Li-Young Lee's first language was Chinese. He didn't speak English until he moved to the United States in 1964 with his parents. Yet Lee's artistic mastery of English is clear in his award-winning poetry, which has been praised for its imagery and the "brave honesty" of its language.

Authors Online

Go to **thinkcentral.com.** KEYWORD: HML7-393

THINK central

Detail of *Birds XII* (2003), Barbara Weldon. Oil, gold leaf, and wax on canvas, 60″ × 72″.

spring harvest
of snow peas

MAXINE HONG KINGSTON

They're taller than me.
I taste and eat as I pick along,
choose the flat big ones and baby ones,
and leave the bulging pods for shelling or seed.
5 The purple and lavender blossoms
and the blue blossoms wave above me
and touch my neck.
I stand on the ledge of the box, reach for more,
and remember my mother and father growing
10   snow peas[1] every season. **Ⓐ**
When she could hardly see anymore, my mother showed me
by feel how to plant 3 seeds per mound.
Every day, enough for dinner, and for leaving
15   at neighbors' doors.
The birds surround me and eat and sing. I am
      unequivocally happy.

Ⓐ THEME
Reread lines 1–10. How does the speaker seem to feel about being in the garden?

---

1. **snow peas:** peas of a type having a soft outer pod.

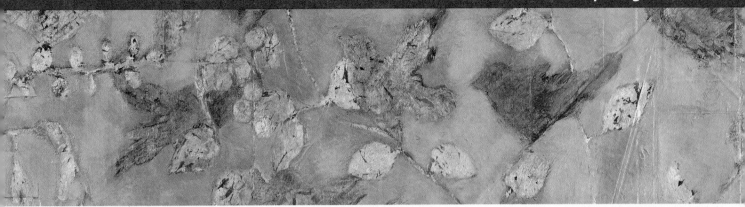

EATINGalone

LI-YOUNG LEE

Detail of *Birds III* (2002), Barbara Weldon. Oil, gold leaf, and wax on canvas, 40″ × 40″.

I've pulled the last of the year's young onions.
The garden is bare now. The ground is cold,
brown and old. What is left of the day flames
in the maples at the corner of my
5 eye. I turn, a cardinal vanishes.
By the cellar door, I wash the onions,
then drink from the icy metal spigot.

Once, years back, I walked beside my father
among the windfall pears. I can't recall
10 our words. We may have strolled in silence. But
I still see him bend that way—left hand braced
on knee, creaky—to lift and hold to my
eye a rotten pear. In it, a hornet
spun crazily, glazed in slow, glistening juice.

15 It was my father I saw this morning
waving to me from the trees. I almost
called to him, until I came close enough
to see the shovel, leaning where I had
left it, in the flickering, deep green shade. **B**

20 White rice steaming, almost done. Sweet green peas
fried in onions. Shrimp braised in sesame
oil and garlic. And my own loneliness.
What more could I, a young man, want.

B THEME
Reread lines 8–19.
Note what the speaker
remembers about
his father. Are they
positive memories?

Comprehension

1. **Recall** Where is the speaker in "Spring Harvest of Snow Peas"?

2. **Recall** What is one reason why the speaker in the second poem is eating alone?

Text Analysis

3. **Make Inferences** Reread lines 11–15 of "Spring Harvest of Snow Peas." What do you learn about the speaker's mother?

4. **Draw Conclusions** How do you think the speaker in "Eating Alone" feels about the meal he is fixing? Note the words or phrases that give you clues about his feelings.

5. **Identify Symbols** What does the food in each poem symbolize, or stand for beyond its usual meaning?

6. **Analyze** Note which season it is in each poem. How does the choice of season affect the meaning of each poem?

Comparing Themes

7. **Set a Purpose for Reading** Now that you've read both poems, finish filling in the chart. Then use the answers to the questions to help you identify the **recurring theme** in the poems.

	"Spring Harvest of Snow Peas"	"Eating Alone"
What idea is described in the title?		
What subjects are presented?	garden, mother, food	garden, father, food
How is the speaker feeling?		
What important images can you find?		
What theme do the poems have in common?		

COMMON CORE

RL 1 Cite textual evidence to support analysis of what the text says explicitly as well as inferences drawn from the text.
RL 2 Determine a theme and analyze its development.

Can you be alone and not LONELY?

How do you entertain yourself when you are alone?

Writing for Assessment

1. READ THE PROMPT

In writing assessments, you will often be asked to compare selections that share a **recurring theme.**

> While "Spring Harvest of Snow Peas" and "Eating Alone" share a recurring theme, Maxine Hong Kingston and Li-Young Lee express the theme differently. In four or five paragraphs, compare and contrast the ways the poets get the theme across. Support your response with details from the poems.

◀ **STRATEGIES IN ACTION**

1. I have to make sure I understand what **message** the poems share.
2. I need to identify the **similarities and differences** in the ways the poets express the message.
3. I should include **details** from the poems to show what I mean.

2. PLAN YOUR WRITING

Using the chart you filled out for the poems, note how each poet develops the theme. Write a position statement that expresses the main similarities and differences you find in the poets' methods. Then decide how you will set up your response.

- Do you want to focus on one poem first and then show how the other poem is similar and different, as shown in the sample outline?

- Do you want to compare each element—title, subject, feelings, and images—in a separate paragraph?

Once you have decided, put your ideas into outline form.

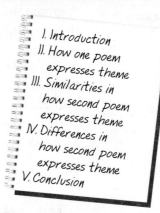

I. Introduction
II. How one poem expresses theme
III. Similarities in how second poem expresses theme
IV. Differences in how second poem expresses theme
V. Conclusion

3. DRAFT YOUR RESPONSE

Introduction Include the titles and poets' names for the poems you will be comparing. Next, briefly summarize each poet's experience. Then state the theme that the poems share. Also include your position statement.

Body Paragraphs If using an outline like the one shown, explain everything you want to about the first poem. Then start a new paragraph before you discuss how the second poem is similar or different.

Conclusion Wrap up your response with a restatement of your main idea and a thought about why the theme might appeal to different poets.

Revision Check to see whether adding transitions such as *similarly, unlike,* or *however* can help you make your comparisons and contrasts clearer.

A Christmas Carol

Video link at
thinkcentral.com

Novel by Charles Dickens
Dramatized by Frederick Gaines

How important is
MONEY?

COMMON CORE

RL 2 Determine a theme of a text and analyze its development over the course of the text. **RL 3** Analyze how particular elements of a drama interact. **RL 5** Analyze how a drama's form contributes to its meaning.

People say, "Money makes the world go round," "Show me the money," and "Time is money." But they also say, "You can't buy happiness." There are many sayings about what money can and can't do, about what it is and what it isn't. In *A Christmas Carol*, the main character's opinion about what it means to be wealthy changes drastically by the end of the play.

QUOTE IT Read over the four sayings quoted in the previous paragraph. In a chart, jot down your ideas about what each saying means. Then write your own saying on the last line, expressing your thoughts about money.

Saying	What It Means
1	
2	
3	
4	
My Saying:	

● TEXT ANALYSIS: THEME IN DRAMA

To identify the **theme** in a drama, notice the action and **dialogue** between characters. What characters do and say provides clues to the play's message. Characters' actions, the setting, and events are often explained in **stage directions,** which are set off in parentheses.

As you read *A Christmas Carol,* try to focus not only on what the characters say and do but also on how and why they say and do those things. Then ask yourself what message the playwright is sharing.

● READING SKILL: UNDERSTAND SEQUENCE IN PLOT

Knowing the order of events in a work of literature helps you better understand the work's theme. Events are not always presented in the order in which they happen. The reader may be taken backward or forward in time.

In a drama, clues about the order, or **sequence,** of events often appear in the stage directions. The titles of the scenes also provide clues about the sequence of events.

As you read *A Christmas Carol,* use a sequence wheel to help you keep track of the unusual sequence of events.

Key Events

Scrooge Before Spirits Visit 1. 2.

Past Shown by Spirit 1. 2.

Present Shown by Spirit 1. 2.

Possible Future Shown by Spirit 1.

Scrooge After Spirits Visit 1.

▲ VOCABULARY IN CONTEXT

The following words all help tell the story of a man who is too concerned with money. How many words can you match with their definition?

1. **accost**	a. abrupt or blunt in speaking
2. **anonymous**	b. made very angry
3. **brusque**	c. not having one's name known
4. **currency**	d. to approach and speak unpleasantly to
5. **incoherent**	e. money
6. **infuriated**	f. confused

Complete the activities in your **Reader/Writer Notebook.**

Charles Dickens
1812–1870

Unhappy Childhood
Charles Dickens's childhood in England provided material for many of his stories. When Dickens was 12 and living with his family in London, his father was put in prison for not paying his debts. Young Dickens had to leave school to work in a rat-infested factory to help earn money for his family. The hopelessness and shame he felt there affected him deeply.

BACKGROUND TO THE DRAMA
A Plea for the Poor
When Frederick Gaines wrote the play you are about to read, he based it on a novel by the same name that Charles Dickens first published in 1843. At that time, about one-third of the people in London were living in poverty and hunger. The city was dirty and overcrowded, and jobs and houses were in short supply. Many children were forced to work instead of staying in school. Charles Dickens wanted his novel *A Christmas Carol* to be "a plea for the poor." The book was instantly and widely popular, and as Dickens had hoped, it and his other writings did affect how his readers felt about the social conditions of their time.

Author Online
THINK central
Go to **thinkcentral.com.**
KEYWORD: HML7-399

A CHRISTMAS CAROL

Charles Dickens
dramatized by Fred Gaines

CHARACTERS

Carolers, Families, Dancers

First Boy

Second Boy

Third Boy

Girl with a doll

Ebenezer Scrooge

Bob Cratchit, Scrooge's clerk

Fred, Scrooge's nephew

Gentleman Visitor

Warder and Residents of the Poorhouse

Sparsit, Scrooge's servant

Cook

Charwoman

Jacob Marley

Priest

Leper

First Spirit, the Spirit of Christmas Past

Jack Walton

Ben Benjamin

Child Scrooge

Fan, Scrooge's sister

Fezziwig

Young Ebenezer

Dick Wilkins

Sweetheart of Young Ebenezer

Second Spirit, the Spirit of Christmas Present

Poorhouse Children

Mrs. Cratchit

Several Cratchit Children

Tiny Tim

Beggar Children, Hunger and Ignorance

Third Spirit, the Spirit of Christmas Yet to Come

Peter, a Cratchit child

Boy

Butcher

Coachman

PROLOGUE

The play begins amid a swirl of street life in Victorian London. Happy groups pass; brightly costumed carolers *and* families *call out to one another and sing "Joy to the World." Three* boys *and a girl are grouped about a glowing mound of coal. As the* carolers *leave the stage, the lights dim and the focus shifts to the mound of coals, bright against the dark. Slowly, the children begin to respond to the warmth. A piano plays softly*
10 *as the children talk.*

First Boy. I saw a horse in a window. (*pause*) A dapple . . . gray and white. And a saddle, too . . . red. And a strawberry mane down to here. All new. Golden stirrups. (*People pass by the children, muttering greetings to one another.*)

Second Boy. Christmas Eve.

Third Boy. Wish we could go.

First Boy. So do I.

Third Boy. I think I'd like it.

20 **First Boy.** Oh, wouldn't I . . . wouldn't I!

Second Boy. We're going up onto the roof. (*The* boys *look at him quizzically.*) My father has a glass. Telescope. A brass one. It opens up and it has twists on it and an eyepiece that you put up to look through. We can see all the way to the park with it.

Third Boy. Could I look through it?

Second Boy. Maybe . . . where would you look? (*The* third boy *points straight up.*) Why there?

30 **Third Boy.** I'd like to see the moon. (*The* boys *stand and look upward as the* girl *sings to her doll. One of the* boys *makes a snow angel on the ground.*)

Girl (*singing*).
Christ the King came down one day,
Into this world of ours,
And crying from a manger bed,
Began the Christmas hour.

(*speaking*)
40 Christ the King, my pretty one,
Sleep softly on my breast,
Christ the King, my gentle one,
Show us the way to rest.
(*She begins to sing the first verse again. As snow starts to fall on the* boy *making the snow angel, he stands up and reaches out to catch a single flake.*)

SCENE I

~ SCROOGE IN HIS SHOP ~

*The percussion[1] thunders. Scrooge hurls himself
through the descending snowflakes and sends
the children scattering. They retreat, watching.
Cratchit comes in. He takes some coal from the
mound and puts it into a small bucket; as he
carries it to a corner of the stage, the stage area
is transformed from street to office. Scrooge's
nephew Fred enters, talks with the children,
gives them coins, and sends them away with*
10 *a "Merry Christmas."*

Fred. A Merry Christmas, Uncle! God save you!

Scrooge. Bah! Humbug!

Fred. Christmas a humbug, Uncle? I hope that's
meant as a joke.

Scrooge. Well, it's not. Come, come, what is
it you want? Don't waste all the day, Nephew.

Fred. I only want to wish you a Merry
Christmas, Uncle. Don't be cross.

Scrooge. What else can I be when I live in such
20 a world of fools as this? Merry Christmas! Out
with Merry Christmas! What's Christmas to you
but a time for paying bills without money, a
time for finding yourself a year older and not an
hour richer. If I could work my will, every idiot
who goes about with "Merry Christmas" on his
lips should be boiled with his own pudding and
buried with a stake of holly through his heart.

Fred. Uncle!

Scrooge. Nephew, keep Christmas in your own
30 way and let me keep it in mine.

Fred. But you don't keep it.

Scrooge. Let me leave it alone then. Much good
may it do you. Much good it has ever done you.

Fred. There are many things from which I

might have derived good by which I have not
profited, I daresay, Christmas among the rest.
And though it has never put a scrap of gold
in my pocket, I believe it has done me good
and will do me good, and I say, God bless it!

40 **Scrooge.** Bah!

Fred. Don't be angry, Uncle. Come! Dine with
us tomorrow.

Scrooge. I'll dine alone, thank you.

Fred. But why?

Scrooge. Why? Why did you get married?

Fred. Why, because I fell in love with a
wonderful girl.

Scrooge. And I with solitude. Good afternoon.

Fred. Nay, Uncle, but you never came to
50 see me before I was married. Why give it as
a reason for not coming now?

Scrooge. Good afternoon.

Fred. I am sorry with all my heart to find you
so determined; but I have made the attempt in
homage to Christmas, and I'll keep that good
spirit to the last. So, a Merry Christmas, Uncle.

Scrooge. Good afternoon!

Fred. And a Happy New Year!

Scrooge. Good afternoon! (*Fred hesitates as
60 if to say something more. He sees that Scrooge
has gone to get a volume down from the shelf,
and so he starts to leave. As he leaves, the
doorbell rings.*) Bells. Is it necessary to always
have bells? (*The gentleman visitor enters,
causing the doorbell to ring again.*) Cratchit!

Cratchit. Yes, sir?

Scrooge. The bell, fool! See to it!

Cratchit. Yes, sir. (*He goes to the entrance.*)

---

1. **percussion:** noise made by loudly striking objects, such as drums or cymbals.

Scrooge (*muttering*). Merry Christmas . . .
Wolves howling and a Merry Christmas . . .

Cratchit. It's for you, sir.

Scrooge. Of course it's for me. You're not receiving callers, are you? Show them in.

Cratchit. Right this way, sir. (*The* gentleman visitor *approaches* Scrooge.)

Scrooge. Yes, yes?

Gentleman Visitor. Scrooge and Marley's, I believe. Have I the pleasure of addressing Mr. Scrooge or Mr. Marley?

Scrooge. Marley's dead. Seven years tonight. What is it you want?

Gentleman Visitor. I have no doubt that his liberality is well represented by his surviving partner. Here, sir, my card. (*He hands* Scrooge *his business card.*)

Scrooge. Liberality? No doubt of it? All right, all right, I can read. What is it you want? (*He returns to his work.*)

Gentleman Visitor. At this festive season of the year . . .

Scrooge. It's winter and cold. (*He continues his work and ignores the* gentleman visitor.)

Gentleman Visitor. Yes . . . yes, it is, and the more reason for my visit. At this time of the year it is more than usually desirable to make some slight provision for the poor and destitute[2] who suffer greatly from the cold. Many thousands are in want of common necessaries; hundreds of thousands are in want of common comforts, sir.

Scrooge. Are there no prisons?

Gentleman Visitor. Many, sir.

Scrooge. And the workhouse?[3] Is it still in operation?

Gentleman Visitor. It is; still, I wish I could say it was not.

Scrooge. The poor law is still in full vigor then?

Gentleman Visitor. Yes, sir.

Scrooge. I'm glad to hear it. From what you said, I was afraid someone had stopped its operation.

Gentleman Visitor. Under the impression that they scarcely furnish Christian cheer of mind or body to the multitude, a few of us are endeavoring to raise a fund to buy the poor some meat and drink and means of warmth. We choose this time because it is the time, of all others, when want is keenly felt and abundance rejoices.[4] May I put you down for something, sir?

Scrooge (*retreating into the darkness temporarily*). Nothing.

Gentleman Visitor. You wish to be **anonymous**?

Scrooge. I wish to be left alone. Since you ask me what I wish, sir, that is my answer. I don't make merry myself at Christmas, and I can't afford to make idle people merry. I help support the establishments I have mentioned . . . they cost enough . . . and those who are poorly off must go there.

Gentleman Visitor. Many can't go there, and many would rather die.

Scrooge. If they would rather die, they had better do it and decrease the surplus population. That is not my affair. My business is. It occupies me constantly. (*He talks both to the* gentleman visitor *and to himself while he thumbs through his books.*) Ask a man to give up life and means . . . fine thing. What is it, I want to know? Charity? . . . (*His nose deep in his books, he vaguely hears the dinner bell being rung in the workhouse; he*

---

2. **destitute:** people lacking the necessities of life.

3. **workhouse:** an establishment in which poor people are housed and required to do work.

4. **abundance rejoices:** those with wealth are happy.

looks up as if he has heard it but never focuses on the actual scene. The warder *of the poorhouse stands in a pool of light at the far left, slowly ringing a bell.*)

Warder. Dinner. All right. Line up. (*The poorly clad, dirty* residents of the poorhouse *line up and file by to get their evening dish of gruel,*[5] *wordlessly accepting it and going back to eat listlessly in the gloom.* Scrooge *returns to the business of his office.*
150 *The procession continues for a moment, then the image of the poorhouse is obscured by darkness. The dejected* gentleman visitor *exits.*)

Scrooge. Latch the door, Cratchit. Firmly, firmly. Draft as cold as Christmas blowing in here. Charity! (Cratchit *goes to the door, starts to close it, then sees the little* girl *with the doll. She seems to beckon to him; he moves slowly toward her, and they dance together for a moment.* Scrooge *continues to work. Suddenly* carolers *appear on the*
160 *platform, and a few phrases of their carol, "Angels We Have Heard on High," are heard.* Scrooge *looks up.*) Cratchit! (*As soon as* Scrooge *shouts, the* girl *and the* carolers *vanish and* Cratchit *begins to close up the shop.*) Cratchit!

Cratchit. Yes, sir.

Scrooge. Well, to work then!

Cratchit. It's evening, sir.

Scrooge. Is it?

Cratchit. Christmas evening, sir.

170 **Scrooge.** Oh, you'll want all day tomorrow off, I suppose.

Cratchit. If it's quite convenient, sir.

Scrooge. It's not convenient, and it's not fair. If I was to deduct half a crown[6] from your salary for it, you'd think yourself ill-used, wouldn't you? Still you expect me to pay a day's wage for a day of no work.

Cratchit. It's only once a year, sir.

Scrooge. Be here all the earlier the next morning.

Cratchit. I will, sir.

180 **Scrooge.** Then off, off.

Cratchit. Yes, sir! Merry Christmas, sir!

Scrooge. Bah! (*As soon as* Cratchit *opens the door, the sounds of the street begin, very bright and loud.* Cratchit *is caught up in a swell of people hurrying through the street. Children pull him along to the top of an ice slide, and he runs and slides down it, disappearing in darkness as the stage suddenly is left almost empty.* Scrooge *goes around the room blowing out the candles, talking to himself.*) Christmas
190 Eve. Carolers! Bah! There. Another day. (*He opens his door and peers out.*) Black, very black. Now where are they? (*The children are heard singing carols for a moment.*) Begging pennies for their songs, are they? Oh, boy! Here, boy! (*The little* girl *emerges from the shadows.* Scrooge *hands her a dark lantern, and she holds it while he lights it with an ember from the pile of coals.*)

---

5. **gruel:** a thin, watery food made by boiling ground grain in water or milk.

6. **half a crown:** until 1971, an amount of British money equal to one-eighth of a pound. The pound is the basic unit of British money.

SCENE 2
~ SCROOGE GOES HOME ~

Scrooge (*talking to the little girl*). Hold it quiet! There. Off now. That's it. High. Black as pitch. Light the street, that's it. You're a bright lad! Good to see that. Earn your supper, boy. You'll not go hungry this night. Home. You know the way, do you? Yes, that's the way. The house of Ebenezer Scrooge. (*As the two find their way to Scrooge's house, the audience sees and hears a brief image of a cathedral interior with a*

10 *living crèche[7] and a large choir singing "Amen!"; the image ends in a blackout. The lights come up immediately, and Scrooge is at his door.*) Hold the light up, boy, up. (*The girl with the lantern disappears.*) Where did he go? Boy? No matter. There's a penny saved. Lantern's gone out. No matter. A candle saved. Yes, here's the key. (*He turns with the key toward the door, and Marley's face swims out of the darkness. Scrooge watches, unable to speak. He fumbles for a match,*

20 *lights the lantern, and swings it toward the figure, which melts away. Pause. Scrooge fits the key in the lock and turns it as the door suddenly is opened from the inside by the porter, Sparsit. Scrooge is startled, then recovers.*) Sparsit?

Sparsit. Yes, sir?

Scrooge. Hurry, hurry. The door . . . close it.

Sparsit. Did you knock, sir?

Scrooge. Knock? What matter? Here, light me up the stairs.

30 **Sparsit.** Yes, sir. (*He leads Scrooge up the stairs. They pass the cook on the way. Scrooge brushes by her, stops, looks back, and she leans toward him.*)

Cook. Something to warm you, sir? Porridge?

Scrooge. Wha . . . ? No. No, nothing.

Cook (*waiting for her Christmas coin*). Merry Christmas, sir. (*Scrooge ignores the request and the cook disappears. Mumbling, Scrooge follows Sparsit.*)

Scrooge (*looking back after the cook is gone*). Fright a man nearly out of his life . . . Merry

40 Christmas . . . bah!

Sparsit. Your room, sir.

Scrooge. Hmmm? Oh, yes, yes. And good night.

Sparsit (*extending his hand for his coin*). Merry Christmas, sir.

Scrooge. Yes, yes . . . (*He sees the outstretched hand; he knows what Sparsit wants and is* **infuriated.**) Out! Out! (*He closes the door after Sparsit, turns toward his chamber, and discovers*

50 *the charwoman directly behind him.*)

Charwoman. Warm your bed for you, sir?

Scrooge. What? Out! Out!

Charwoman. Aye, sir. (*She starts for the door. Marley's voice is heard mumbling something unintelligible.*)

Scrooge. What's that?

Charwoman. Me, sir? Not a thing, sir.

Scrooge. Then, good night.

Charwoman. Good night. (*She exits, and*

60 Scrooge *pantomimes shutting the door behind her. The voice of* Marley *over an offstage microphone whispers and reverberates:[8] "Merry Christmas, Scrooge!" Silence. Scrooge hears the voice but cannot account for it. He climbs up to open a window and looks down. A cathedral choir singing "O Come, All Ye Faithful" is heard in the distance. Scrooge listens a moment, shuts the window,*

---

7. **a cathedral interior with a living crèche:** the inside of a large church in which real people pose for the Christmas manger scene.

8. **reverberates** (rĭ-vûr′bə-rāts′): echoes.

and prepares for bed. As soon as he has shut the sound out of his room, figures appear; they seem to *be coming down the main aisle of a church, bearing gifts to the living crèche. The orchestra plays "O Come, All Ye Faithful" as the procession files out. Scrooge, ready for bed, warms himself before the heap of coals. As he pulls his nightcap from a chair, a small hand-bell tumbles off onto the floor. Startled, he picks it up and rings it for reassurance; an echo answers it. He turns and sees the little* girl *on the street; she is swinging her doll, which produces the echo of his bell. Scrooge escapes to his bed; the* girl *is swallowed up in the darkness. The bell sounds grow to a din,* **incoherent** *as in a dream, then suddenly fall silent. Scrooge sits up in bed, listens, and hears the chains of* Marley *coming up the stairs. Scrooge reaches for the bell pull to summon* Sparsit. *The bell responds with a gong, and* Marley *appears. He and Scrooge face one another.*)

Scrooge. What do you want with me?

Marley (*in a ghostly, unreal voice*). Much.

Scrooge. Who are you?

Marley. Ask who I was.

Scrooge. Who were you?

Marley. In life, I was your partner, Jacob Marley.

Scrooge. He's dead.

Marley. Seven years this night, Ebenezer Scrooge.

Scrooge. Why do you come here?

Marley. I must. It is commanded me. I must wander the world and see what I can no longer share, what I would not share when I walked where you do.

Scrooge. And must go thus?

Marley. The chain? Look at it, Ebenezer, study it. Locks and vaults and golden coins. I forged it, each link, each day when I sat in these chairs, commanded these rooms. Greed, Ebenezer Scrooge, wealth. Feel them, know them. Yours was as heavy as this I wear seven years ago, and you have labored to build it since.

Scrooge. If you're here to lecture, I have no time for it. It is late; the night is cold. I want comfort now.

Marley. I have none to give. I know not how you see me this night. I did not ask it. I have sat invisible beside you many and many a day. I am commanded to bring you a chance, Ebenezer. Heed it!

Scrooge. Quickly then, quickly.

Marley. You will be haunted by three spirits.

Scrooge (*scoffing*). Is that the chance?

Marley. Mark it.

Scrooge. I do not choose to.

Marley (*ominously*). Then you will walk where I do, burdened by your riches, your greed.

Scrooge. Spirits mean nothing to me.

Marley (*slowly leaving*). Expect the first tomorrow, when the bell tolls one, the second on the next night at the same hour, the third upon the next night when the last stroke of twelve has ended. Look to see me no more. I must wander. Look that, for your own sake, you remember what has passed between us.

Scrooge. Jacob . . . Don't leave me! . . . Jacob! Jacob!

Marley. Adieu,[9] Ebenezer. (*At* Marley's *last words a funeral procession begins to move across the stage. A boy walks in front; a* priest *follows, swinging a censer;[10] sounds of mourning and the suggestion of church music are heard. Scrooge* calls out, *"Jacob, don't leave me!" as if talking in the midst of a bad dream. At the end of the procession is the little* girl, *swinging her doll and singing softly.*)

---

9. **adieu** (ə-dyo͞o′): farewell.

10. **censer:** a container in which incense is burned.

Girl.
Hushabye, don't you cry,
Go to sleep, little baby.
When you wake, you shall have
All the pretty little horses,
Blacks and bays, dapples and grays,
All the pretty little horses.

(*She stops singing and looks up at* Scrooge; *their*
150 *eyes meet, and she solemnly rings the doll in greeting.* Scrooge *pulls shut the bed curtains, and the
girl exits. The bell sounds are picked up by the bells
of a* leper[11] *who enters, dragging himself along.*)

Leper (*calling out*). Leper! Leper! Stay the way!
Leper! Leper! Keep away! (*He exits and the clock

begins to chime, ringing the hours.* Scrooge *sits
up in bed and begins to count the chimes.*)

Scrooge. Eight . . . nine . . . ten . . . eleven . . .
it can't be . . . twelve. Midnight? No. Not twelve.
160 It can't be. I haven't slept the whole day through.
Twelve? Yes, yes, twelve noon. (*He hurries to the
window and looks out.*) Black. Twelve midnight.
(*pause*) I must get up. A day wasted. I must get
down to the office. (*Two small chimes are heard.*)
Quarter past. But it just rang twelve. Fifteen
minutes haven't gone past, not so quickly.
(*Again two small chimes are heard.*) A quarter
to one. The spirit . . . It's to come at one. (*He
hurries to his bed as the chimes ring again.*) One.

---

11. **leper:** a person who has leprosy, a skin disease once
thought to be highly contagious.

SCENE 3

~ THE SPIRIT OF CHRISTMAS PAST ~

The hour is struck again by a large street clock, and the first spirit *appears. It is a figure dressed to look like the little girl's doll.*

Scrooge. Are you the spirit whose coming was foretold to me?

First Spirit. I am.

Scrooge. Who and what are you?

First Spirit. I am the Ghost of Christmas Past.

Scrooge. Long past?

10 **First Spirit.** Your past.

Scrooge. Why are you here?

First Spirit. Your welfare. Rise. Walk with me.

Scrooge. I am mortal still. I cannot pass through air.

First Spirit. My hand. (Scrooge *grasps the* spirit's *hand tightly, and the doll's bell rings softly. Scrooge remembers a scene from his past in which two boys greet each other in the street.*)

First Voice. Halloo, Jack!

20 **Second Voice.** Ben! Merry Christmas, Ben!

Scrooge. Jack Walton. Young Jack Walton. Spirits . . . ?

First Voice. Have a good holiday, Jack.

Scrooge. Yes, yes, I remember him. Both of them. Little Ben Benjamin. He used to . . .

First Voice. See you next term, Jack. Next . . . term . . .

Scrooge. They . . . they're off for the holidays and going home from school. It's Christmas 30 time . . . all of the children off home now . . . No . . . no, not all . . . there was one . . .

(*The* spirit *motions for* Scrooge *to turn, and he sees a young boy playing with a teddy bear and talking to it.*) Yes . . . reading . . . poor boy.

First Spirit. What, I wonder?

Scrooge. Reading? Oh, it was nothing. Fancy, all fancy and make-believe and take-me-away. All of it. Yes, nonsense.

Child Scrooge. Ali Baba.[12]

40 **Scrooge.** Yes . . . that was it . . .

Child Scrooge. Yes, and remember . . . and remember . . . remember Robinson Crusoe?[13]

Scrooge. And the parrot!

Child Scrooge. Yes, the parrot! I love him best.

Scrooge (*imitating the parrot*). With his stripy green body and yellow tail drooping along and couldn't sing—awk—but could talk, and a thing like a lettuce growing out the top of his head . . . and he used to sit on the very top of the tree—up there.

50 **Child Scrooge.** And Robinson Crusoe sailed around the island, and he thought he had escaped the island, and the parrot said, the parrot said . . .

Scrooge (*imitating the parrot*). Robinson Crusoe, where you been? Awk! Robinson Crusoe, where you been?

Child Scrooge. And Robinson Crusoe looked up in the tree and saw the parrot and knew he hadn't escaped and he was still there, still all alone there.

60 **Scrooge.** Poor Robinson Crusoe.

Child Scrooge (*sadly replacing the teddy bear*). Poor Robinson Crusoe.

Scrooge. Poor child. Poor child.

First Spirit. Why poor?

Scrooge. Fancy . . . fancy . . . (*He tries to mask his feelings by being* **brusque**.) It's his way, a child's

---

12. **Ali Baba:** in the *Arabian Nights*, a poor woodcutter who discovers a treasure.

13. **Robinson Crusoe:** a shipwrecked sailor who survives for years on a small island in the novel *Robinson Crusoe*.

way to . . . to lose being alone in . . . in dreams, dreams . . . Never matter if they are all nonsense, yes, nonsense. But he'll be all right, grow out of it. Yes. Yes, he did outgrow it, the nonsense. Became a man and left there, and he became, yes, he became a man and . . . yes, successful . . . rich! (*The sadness returns.*) Never matter . . . never matter. (Fan *runs in and goes to* Child Scrooge.) Fan!

Fan. Brother, dear brother! (*She kisses* Child Scrooge.)

Child Scrooge. Dear, dear Fan.

Fan. I've come to bring you home, home for good and ever. Come with me, come now. (*She takes his hand, and they start to run off, but* the spirit *stops them and signals for the light on them to fade. They look at the* spirit, *aware of their role in the* spirit's *"education" of* Scrooge.)

Scrooge. Let me watch them go? Let them be happy for a moment! (*The* spirit *says nothing.* Scrooge *turns away from them, and the light goes out.*) A delicate, delicate child. A breath might have withered her.

First Spirit. She died a woman and had, as I remember, children.

Scrooge. One child.

First Spirit. Your nephew.

Scrooge. Yes, yes, Fred, my nephew. (Scrooge *pauses, then tries to bluster through.*) Well? Well, all of us have that, haven't we? Childhoods? Sadnesses? But we grow and we become men, masters of ourselves. (*The* spirit *gestures for music to begin. It is heard first as from a great distance, then* Scrooge *becomes aware of it.*) I've no time for it, Spirit. Music and all of your Christmas folderol.[14] Yes, yes, I've learnt what you have to show me. (Fezziwig, Young Ebenezer, *and* Dick *appear, busily preparing for a party.*)

Fezziwig. Yo ho, there! Ebenezer! Dick!

Scrooge. Fezziwig! It's old Fezziwig that I 'prenticed[15] under.

First Spirit. Your master?

Scrooge. Oh, aye, and the best that any boy could have. There's Dick Wilkins! Bless me. He was very much attached to me was Dick. Poor Dick. Dear, dear.

Fezziwig. Yo ho, my boys! No more work tonight. Christmas Eve, Dick! Christmas, Ebenezer! Let's have the shutters up before a man can say Jack Robinson! (*The music continues. Chandeliers are pulled into position, and mistletoe, holly, and ivy are draped over everything by bustling servants. Dancers fill the stage for* Fezziwig's *wonderful Christmas party. In the midst of the dancing and the gaiety servants pass back and forth through the crowd with huge platters of food. At a pause in the music,* Young Ebenezer, *who is dancing, calls out.*)

Young Ebenezer. Mr. Fezziwig, sir, you're a wonderful master!

Scrooge and Young Ebenezer. A wonderful master!

Scrooge (*echoing the phrase*). A wonderful master! (*The music changes suddenly, and the* dancers *jerk into distorted postures and then begin to move in slow motion. The celebrants slowly exit, performing a macabre dance to discordant sounds.[16]*)

First Spirit. Just because he gave a party? It was very small.

Scrooge. Small!

First Spirit. He spent a few pounds of your "mortal" money, three, four at the most. Is that so much that he deserves this praise?

Scrooge. But it wasn't the money. He had the power to make us happy, to make our service light or burdensome. The happiness he gives

---

14. **folderol** (fŏl′-də-rŏl′): foolishness; nonsense.

15. **'prenticed:** short for *apprenticed,* here meaning "learned a trade while working."

16. **macabre** (mə-kä′brə) **dance to discordant sounds:** a bizarre, ghastly dance with unharmonious music.

140 is quite as great as if it cost a fortune. That's what . . . a good master is.

First Spirit. Yes?

Scrooge. No, no, nothing.

First Spirit. Something, I think.

Scrooge. I should like to be able to say a word or two to my clerk just now, that's all.

First Spirit. But this is all past. Your clerk, Cratchit, couldn't be here.

Scrooge. No, no, of course not, an idle thought.
150 Are we done?

First Spirit (*motioning for the waltz music to begin*). Nearly.

Scrooge (*hearing the waltz and remembering it*). Surely it's enough. Haven't you tormented me enough? (Young Ebenezer *is seen waltzing with his* Sweetheart.)

First Spirit. I only show the past, what it promised you. Look. Another promise.

Scrooge. Oh. Oh, yes. I had forgotten . . . her. Don't they dance beautifully? So young, so
160 young. I would have married her if only . . .

Sweetheart. Can you love me, Ebenezer? I bring no dowry[17] to my marriage, only me, only love. It is no **currency** that you can buy and sell with, but we can live with it. Can you? (*She pauses, then returns the ring* Scrooge *gave her as his pledge.*) I release you, Ebenezer, for the love of the man you once were. Will that man win me again, now that he is free?

Scrooge (*trying to speak to her*). If only you had
170 held me to it. You should not have let me go. I was young; I did love you.

Sweetheart (*speaking to* Young Ebenezer). We have never lied to one another. May you be happy in the life you have chosen. Good-bye. (*She runs out.* Young Ebenezer *slowly leaves.*)

Scrooge. No, no, it was not meant that way . . . !

First Spirit. You cannot change now what you would not change then. I am your mistakes, Ebenezer Scrooge, all of the things you could
180 have done and did not.

Scrooge. Then leave me! I have done them. I shall live with them. As I have, as I do; as I will.

First Spirit. There is another Christmas, seven years ago, when Marley died.

Scrooge. No! I will not see it. I will not! He died. I could not prevent it. I did not choose for him to die on Christmas Day.

First Spirit. And when his day was chosen, what did you do then?

190 **Scrooge.** I looked after his affairs.

First Spirit. His business.

Scrooge. Yes! His business! Mine! It was all that I had, all that I could do in this world. I have nothing to do with the world to come after.

First Spirit. Then I will leave you.

Scrooge. Not yet! Don't leave me here! Tell me what I must do! What of the other spirits?

First Spirit. They will come.

Scrooge. And you? What of you?

200 **First Spirit.** I am always with you. (*The little* girl *appears with her doll; she takes Scrooge's hand and gently leads him to bed. Numbed, he follows her. She leans against the foot of the bed, ringing the doll and singing. The* first spirit *exits as she sings.*)

Girl.
When you wake, you shall have
All the pretty little horses,
Blacks and bays, dapples and grays,
All the pretty little horses.

210 (*She rings the doll, and the ringing becomes the chiming of Scrooge's bell. The* girl *exits.* Scrooge *sits upright in bed as he hears the chimes.*)

Scrooge. A minute until one. No one here. No one's coming. (*A larger clock strikes one o'clock.*)

---

17. **dowry** (dou′rē): money or property brought by a bride to her husband when they marry.

SCENE 4

~ THE SPIRIT OF CHRISTMAS PRESENT ~

A light comes on. Scrooge *becomes aware of it and goes slowly to it. He sees the* second spirit, *the Spirit of Christmas Present, who looks like* Fezziwig.

Scrooge. Fezziwig!

Second Spirit. Hello, Scrooge.

Scrooge. But you can't be . . . not Fezziwig.

Second Spirit. Do you see me as him?

Scrooge. I do.

10 **Second Spirit.** And hear me as him?

Scrooge. I do.

Second Spirit. I wish I were the gentleman, so as not to disappoint you.

Scrooge. But you're not . . . ?

Second Spirit. No, Mr. Scrooge. You have never seen the like of me before. I am the Ghost of Christmas Present.

Scrooge. But . . .

Second Spirit. You see what you will see, Scrooge,
20 no more. Will you walk out with me this Christmas Eve?

Scrooge. But I am not yet dressed.

Second Spirit. Take my tails, dear boy, we're leaving.

Scrooge. Wait!

Second Spirit. What is it now?

Scrooge. Christmas Present, did you say?

Second Spirit. I did.

Scrooge. Then we are traveling here? In this
30 town? London? Just down there?

Second Spirit. Yes, yes, of course.

---

18. **bob:** a British slang term for shillings. (There were 20 shillings in a pound.)

Scrooge. Then we could walk? Your flying is . . . well, too sudden for an old man. Well?

Second Spirit. It's your Christmas, Scrooge; I am only the guide.

Scrooge (*puzzled*). Then we can walk? (*The* spirit *nods.*) Where are you guiding me to?

Second Spirit. Bob Cratchit's.

Scrooge. My clerk?

40 **Second Spirit.** You did want to talk to him? (Scrooge *pauses, uncertain how to answer.*) Don't worry, Scrooge, you won't have to.

Scrooge (*trying to change the subject, to cover his error*). Shouldn't be much of a trip. With fifteen bob[18] a week, how far off can it be?

Second Spirit. A world away, Scrooge, at least that far. (Scrooge *and the* spirit *start to step off a curb when a funeral procession enters with a child's coffin, followed by the* poorhouse
50 children, *who are singing. Seated on top of the coffin is the little* girl. *She and* Scrooge *look at one another.*) That is the way to it, Scrooge. (*The procession follows the coffin offstage;* Scrooge *and the* spirit *exit after the procession. As they leave, the lights focus on* Mrs. Cratchit *and her* children. Mrs. Cratchit *sings as she puts* Tiny Tim *and the other* children *to bed, all in one bed. She pulls a dark blanket over them.*)

Mrs. Cratchit (*singing*).

60 When you wake, you shall have
All the pretty little horses,
Blacks and bays, dapples and grays,
All the pretty little horses.
To sleep now, all of you. Christmas tomorrow.
(*She kisses them and goes to* Bob Cratchit, *who is by the hearth.*) How did our little Tiny Tim behave?

Bob Cratchit. As good as gold and better.
He told me, coming home, that he hoped the

people saw him in church because he was
70 a cripple and it might be pleasant to them
to remember upon Christmas Day who made
the lame to walk and the blind to see.

Mrs. Cratchit. He's a good boy. (*The* second spirit
and Scrooge *enter.* Mrs. Cratchit *feels a sudden
draft.*) Oh, the wind. (*She gets up to shut the door.*)

Second Spirit. Hurry. (*He nudges* Scrooge
in before Mrs. Cratchit *shuts the door.*)

Scrooge. Hardly hospitable is what I'd say.

Second Spirit. Oh, they'd say a great deal more,
80 Scrooge, if they could see you.

Scrooge. Oh, they should, should they?

Second Spirit. Oh yes, I'd think they might.

Scrooge. Well, I might have a word for
them . . .

Second Spirit. You're here to listen.

Scrooge. Oh. Oh yes, all right. By the fire?

Second Spirit. But not a word.

Bob Cratchit (*raising his glass*). My dear,
to Mr. Scrooge. I give you Mr. Scrooge, the
90 founder of the feast.

Mrs. Cratchit. The founder of the feast indeed!
I wish I had him here! I'd give him a piece
of my mind to feast upon, and I hope he'd
have a good appetite for it.

Bob Cratchit. My dear, Christmas Eve.

Mrs. Cratchit. It should be Christmas Eve,
I'm sure, when one drinks the health of such
an odious,[19] stingy, hard, unfeeling man as
Mr. Scrooge. You know he is, Robert! Nobody
100 knows it better than you do, poor dear.

Bob Cratchit. I only know one thing on
Christmas: that one must be charitable.

Mrs. Cratchit. I'll drink to his health for your
sake and the day's, not for his. Long life to
him! A Merry Christmas and a Happy New

---

19. **odious** (ō′dē-əs): causing or deserving strong dislike.

Year. He'll be very merry and very happy, I have no doubt.

Bob Cratchit. If he cannot be, we must be happy for him. A song is what is needed. Tim!

110 **Mrs. Cratchit.** Shush! I've just gotten him down, and he needs all the sleep he can get.

Bob Cratchit. If he's asleep on Christmas Eve, I'll be much mistaken. Tim! He must sing, dear; there is nothing else that might make him well.

Tiny Tim. Yes, Father?

Bob Cratchit. Are you awake?

Tiny Tim. Just a little.

Bob Cratchit. A song then! (*The* children *awaken and, led by* Tiny Tim, *sit up to sing "What Child*
120 *Is This?" As they sing,* Scrooge *speaks.*)

Scrooge. (*He holds up his hand; all stop singing and look at him.*) I . . . I have seen enough. (*When the* spirit *signals to the* children, *they leave the stage, singing the carol quietly.* Tiny Tim *remains, covered completely by the dark blanket, disappearing against the black.*) Tiny Tim . . . will he live?

Second Spirit. He is very ill. Even song cannot keep him whole through a cold winter.

130 **Scrooge.** But you haven't told me!

Second Spirit (*imitating* Scrooge). If he be like to die, he had better do it and decrease the surplus population. (Scrooge *turns away.*) Erase, Scrooge, those words from your thoughts. You are not the judge. Do not judge, then. It may be that in the sight of heaven you are more worthless and less fit to live than millions like this poor man's child. Oh God! To hear an insect on a leaf pronouncing that there is too much life among his hungry
140 brothers in the dust. Good-bye, Scrooge.

Scrooge. But is there no happiness in Christmas Present?

Second Spirit. There is.

Scrooge. Take me there.

Second Spirit. It is at the home of your nephew . . .

Scrooge. No!

Second Spirit (*disgusted with* Scrooge). Then there is none.

150 **Scrooge.** But that isn't enough . . . You must teach me!

Second Spirit. Would you have a teacher, Scrooge? Look at your own words.

Scrooge. But the first spirit gave me more . . . !

Second Spirit. He was Christmas Past. There was a lifetime he could choose from. I have only this day, one day, and you, Scrooge. I have nearly lived my fill of both. Christmas Present must be gone at midnight. That is near now.
160 (*He speaks to two* beggar children *who pause shyly at the far side of the stage. The* children *are thin and wan; they are barefoot and wear filthy rags.*) Come. (*They go to him.*)

Scrooge. Is this the last spirit who is to come to me?

Second Spirit. They are no spirits. They are real. Hunger, Ignorance. Not spirits, Scrooge, passing dreams. They are real. They walk your streets, look to you for comfort. And you
170 deny them. Deny them not too long, Scrooge. They will grow and multiply, and they will not remain children.

Scrooge. Have they no refuge, no resource?

Second Spirit (*again imitating* Scrooge). Are there no prisons? Are there no workhouses? (*tenderly to the* children) Come. It's Christmas Eve. (*He leads them offstage.*)

SCENE 5

~ THE SPIRIT OF CHRISTMAS YET TO COME ~

Scrooge *is entirely alone for a long moment. He is frightened by the darkness and feels it approaching him. Suddenly he stops, senses the presence of the* third spirit, *turns toward him, and sees him. The* spirit *is bent and cloaked. No physical features are distinguishable.*

Scrooge. You are the third. (*The* spirit *says nothing.*) The Ghost of Christmas Yet to Come. (*The* spirit *says nothing.*) Speak to me. Tell me

10 what is to happen—to me, to all of us. (*The* spirit *says nothing.*) Then show me what I must see. (*The* spirit *points. Light illumines the shadowy recesses of Scrooge's house.*) I know it. I know it too well, cold and cheerless. It is mine. (*The* cook *and the* charwoman *are dimly visible in Scrooge's house.*) What is . . . ? There are . . . thieves! There are thieves in my rooms! (*He starts forward to* **accost** *them, but the* spirit *beckons for him to stop.*) I cannot. You cannot tell me that

20 I must watch them and do nothing. I will not. It is mine still. (*He rushes into the house to claim his belongings and to protect them. The two women do not notice his presence.*)

Cook. He ain't about, is he? (*The* charwoman *laughs.*) Poor ol' Scrooge 'as met 'is end.[20] (*She laughs with the* charwoman.)

Charwoman. An' time for it, too; ain't been alive in deed for half his life.

Cook. But the Sparsit's nowhere, is he . . . ?

30 **Sparsit** (*emerging from the blackness*). Lookin' for someone, ladies? (*The* cook *shrieks, but the* charwoman *treats the matter more practically, anticipating competition from* Sparsit.)

Charwoman. There ain't enough but for the two of us!

Sparsit. More 'an enough . . . if you know where to look.

Cook. Hardly decent is what I'd say, hardly decent, the poor old fella hardly cold and

40 you're thievin' his wardrobe.

Sparsit. You're here out of love, are ya?

Charwoman. There's no time for that. (Sparsit *acknowledges* Scrooge *for the first time, gesturing toward him as if the living* Scrooge *were the corpse.* Scrooge *stands as if rooted to the spot, held there by the power of the* spirit.)

Sparsit. He ain't about to bother us, is he?

Charwoman. Ain't he a picture?

Cook. If he is, it ain't a happy one.

50 (*They laugh.*)

Sparsit. Ladies, shall we start? (*The three of them grin and advance on* Scrooge.) Cook?

Cook (*snatching the cuff links from the shirt* Scrooge *wears*). They're gold, ain't they?

Sparsit. The purest, madam.

Charwoman. I always had a fancy for that nightcap of his. My old man could use it. (*She takes the nightcap from* Scrooge's *head.* Sparsit *playfully removes* Scrooge's *outer garment, the coat*

60 *or cloak that he has worn in the previous scenes.*)

Sparsit. Bein' a man of more practical tastes, I'll go for the worsted[21] and hope the smell ain't permanent. (*The three laugh.*) Cook, we go round again.

Cook. Do you think that little bell he's always ringing at me is silver enough to sell? (*The three of them move toward the nightstand, and* Scrooge *cries out.*)

---

20. **'as met 'is end:** a dialect pronunciation of "has met his end."

21. **worsted:** a smooth woolen fabric.

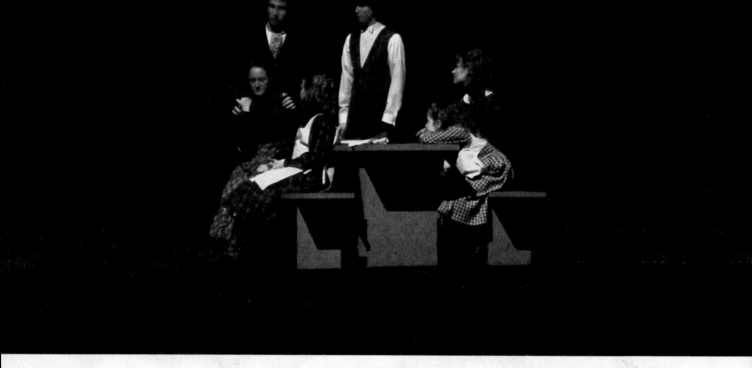

Scrooge. No more! No more! (*As the* spirit *directs* Scrooge's *attention to the tableau*[22] *of the three thieves standing poised over the silver bell,* Scrooge *bursts out of the house, clad only in his nightshirt.*) I cannot. I cannot. The room is . . . too like a cheerless place that is familiar. I won't see it. Let us go from here. Anywhere. (*The* spirit *directs his attention to the Cratchit house; the* children *are sitting together near* Mrs. Cratchit, *who is sewing a coat.* Peter *reads by the light of the coals.*)

Peter. "And he took a child and set him in the midst of them."

Mrs. Cratchit (*putting her hand to her face*). The light tires my eyes so. (*pause*) They're better now. It makes them tired to try to see by firelight, and I wouldn't show reddened eyes to your father when he comes home for the world. It must be near his time now.

Peter. Past it, I think, but he walks slower than he used to, these last few days, Mother.

Mrs. Cratchit. I have known him to walk with . . . I have known him to walk with Tiny Tim upon his shoulder very fast indeed. (*She catches herself, then hurries on.*) But he was very light to carry and his father loved him, so that it was no trouble, no trouble. (*She hears* Bob Cratchit *approaching.*) Smiles, everyone, smiles.

Bob Cratchit (*entering*). My dear, Peter . . . (*He greets the other* children *by their real names.*) How is it coming?

Mrs. Cratchit (*handing him the coat*). Nearly done.

---

22. **tableau** (tăb′lō′): a portion of a play where the actors momentarily freeze in their positions for dramatic effect.

Bob Cratchit. Yes, good, I'm sure that it will be done long before Sunday.

Mrs. Cratchit. Sunday! You went today then, Robert?

Bob Cratchit. Yes. It's . . . it's all ready. Two o'clock. And a nice place. It would have done you good to see how green it is. But you'll see it often. I promised him that, that I would walk there on Sunday . . . often.

Mrs. Cratchit. We mustn't hurt ourselves for it, Robert.

Bob Cratchit. No. No, he wouldn't have wanted that. Come now. You won't guess who I've seen. Scrooge's nephew, Fred. And he asked after us and said he was heartily sorry and to give his respect to my good wife. How he ever knew that, I don't know.

Mrs. Cratchit. Knew what, my dear?

Bob Cratchit. Why, that you were a good wife.

Peter. Everybody knows that.

Bob Cratchit. I hope that they do. "Heartily sorry," he said, "for your good wife, and if I can be of service to you in any way—" and he gave me his card—"that's where I live"—and Peter, I shouldn't be at all surprised if he got you a position.

Mrs. Cratchit. Only hear that, Peter!

Bob Cratchit. And then you'll be keeping company with some young girl and setting up for yourself.

Peter. Oh, go on.

Bob Cratchit. Well, it will happen, one day, but remember, when that day does come— as it must—we must none of us forget poor Tiny Tim and this first parting in our family.

Scrooge. He died! No, no! (*He steps back and the scene disappears; he moves away from the* spirit.)

SCENE 6

~ SCROOGE'S CONVERSION ~

Scrooge. Because he would not . . . no! You cannot tell me that he has died, for that Christmas
has not come! I will not let it come! I will be
there . . . It was me. Yes, yes, and I knew it and
couldn't look. I won't be able to help. I won't.
(*pause*) Spirit, hear me. I am not the man I was.
I will not be that man that I have been for so
many years. Why show me all of this if I am past
all hope? Assure me that I yet may change these
10 shadows you have shown me. Let the boy live!
I will honor Christmas in my heart and try to
keep it all the year. I will live in the Past, the
Present, and the Future. The spirits of all three
shall strive within me. I will not shut out the
lessons that they teach. Oh, tell me that I am
not too late! (*A single light focuses on the little* girl,
*dressed in a blue cloak like that of the Virgin Mary.
She looks up, and from above a dove is slowly
lowered in silence to her; she takes it and encloses*
20 *it within her cloak, covering it. As soon as she does
this, a large choir is heard singing "Gloria!" and the
bells begin to ring. Blackout. When the lights come
up again,* Scrooge *is in bed. The* third spirit *and
the figures in the church have disappeared.* Scrooge
awakens and looks around his room.) The curtains! They are mine and they are real. They are
not sold. They are here. I am here; the shadows
to come may be dispelled. They will be. I know
they will be. (*He dresses himself hurriedly.*) I don't
30 know what to do. I'm as light as a feather, merry
as a boy again. Merry Christmas! Merry Christmas! A Happy New Year to all the world! Hello
there! Whoop! Hallo! What day of the month
is it? How long did the spirits keep me? Never
mind. I don't care. (*He opens the window and
calls to a* boy *in the street below.*) What's today?

Boy. Eh?

Scrooge. What's the day, my fine fellow?

Boy. Today? Why, Christmas Day!

40 **Scrooge.** It's Christmas Day! I haven't missed
it! The spirits have done it all in one night.
They can do anything they like. Of course
they can. Of course they can save Tim. Hallo,
my fine fellow!

Boy. Hallo!

Scrooge. Do you know the poulterers[23] in the
next street at the corner?

Boy. I should hope I do.

Scrooge. An intelligent boy. A remarkable boy.
50 Do you know whether they've sold the prize
turkey that was hanging up there? Not the
little prize; the big one.

Boy. What, the one as big as me?

Scrooge. What a delightful boy! Yes, my bucko!

Boy. It's hanging there now.

Scrooge. It is? Go and buy it.

Boy. G'wan!

Scrooge. I'm in earnest! Go and buy it and
tell 'em to bring it here that I may give them
60 the direction where to take it. Come back
with the butcher and I'll give you a shilling.
Come back in less than two minutes and
I'll give you half a crown!

Boy. Right, guv! (*He exits.*)

Scrooge. I'll send it to Bob Cratchit's. He
shan't know who sends it. It's twice the size
of Tiny Tim and such a Christmas dinner it
will make. (Carolers *suddenly appear singing
"Hark! The Herald Angels Sing."* Scrooge *leans*

---

23. **poulterers** (pōl′tər-ərz): people who sell poultry, such as chickens and turkeys.

70 *out the window and joins them in the song.*)
I must dress, I must. It's Christmas Day! I must
be all in my best for such a day. Where is my
China silk shirt? (*The boy and the butcher run
in with the turkey.*) What? Back already? And
such a turkey. Why, you can't carry that all the
way to Cratchit's. Here, boy, here is your half
a crown and here an address in Camden Town.
See that it gets there. Here, money for the cab,
for the turkey, and for you, good man! (*The*
80 *boy and the butcher, delighted, catch the money
and run out. Scrooge sees the gentleman visitor
walking by the window.*) Halloo, sir!

Gentleman Visitor (*looking up sadly, less than
festive*). Hello, sir.

Scrooge. My dear sir, how do you do? I hope
you succeeded yesterday. It was very kind of
you to stop by to see me.

Gentleman Visitor (*in disbelief*). Mr. Scrooge?

Scrooge. Yes, that is my name, and I fear it may
90 not be pleasant to you. Allow me to ask your
pardon, and will you have the goodness to add
this (*throwing him a purse*) to your good work!

Gentleman Visitor. Lord bless me! My dear
Mr. Scrooge, are you serious?

Scrooge. If you please, not a penny less. A great
many back payments are included in it, I assure
you. Will you do me that favor?

Gentleman Visitor. My dear sir, I don't know
what I can say to such generosity . . .

100 **Scrooge.** Say nothing! Accept it. Come and see
me. Will you come and see me?

Gentleman Visitor. I will.

Scrooge. Thank 'ee. I am much obliged to you.
I thank you fifty times. God bless you and
Merry Christmas!

Gentleman Visitor. Merry Christmas to
you, sir!

Scrooge (*running downstairs, out of his house,
and onto the street*). Now which is the way
110 to that nephew's house. Girl! Girl!

Girl (*appearing immediately*). Yes, sir?

Scrooge. Can you find me a taxi, miss?

Girl. I can, sir. (*She rings her doll, and a
coachman appears.*)

Scrooge (*handing the coachman a card*).
Can you show me the way to this home?

Coachman. I can, sir.

Scrooge. Good man. Come up, girl. (*They
mount to the top of the taxi. This action may
120 be stylistically suggested.*) Would you be
an old man's guide to a Christmas dinner?

Girl. I would, sir, and God bless you!

Scrooge. Yes, God bless us every one! (*raising
his voice almost in song*) Driver, to Christmas!
(*They exit, all three singing "Joy to the World."
Blackout. The lights come up for the finale[24]
at Fred's house. The Cratchits are there with
Tiny Tim. All stop moving and talking when
they see Scrooge standing in the center,
130 embarrassed and humble.*) Well, I'm very glad
to be here at my nephew's house! (*He starts
to cry.*) Merry Christmas! Merry Christmas!

All (*softly*). Merry Christmas. (*They sing "Deck
the Halls," greeting one another and exchanging
gifts. Scrooge puts Tiny Tim on his shoulders.*)

Tiny Tim (*shouting as the carol ends*). God bless
us every one!

Scrooge (*to the audience*). Oh, yes! God bless
us every one!

---

24. **finale** (fə-năl′ē): conclusion.

ONLINE ARTICLE In the play *A Christmas Carol*, you read about a man named Scrooge, who was stingy with his money. In the following article, you'll read about why Charles Dickens wrote *A Christmas Carol* and how some real-life Scrooges took advantage of Dickens.

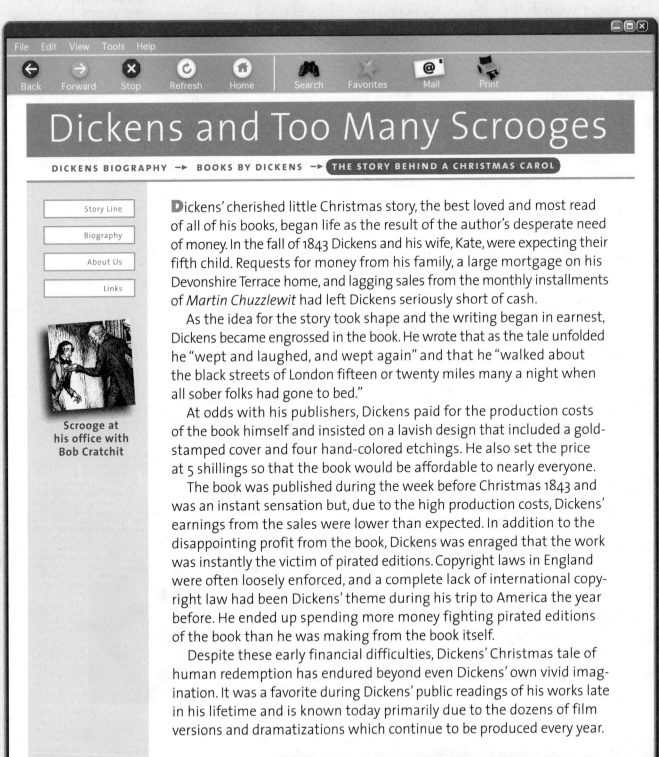

File   Edit   View   Tools   Help

Back   Forward   Stop   Refresh   Home   Search   Favorites   Mail   Print

Dickens and Too Many Scrooges

DICKENS BIOGRAPHY → BOOKS BY DICKENS → **THE STORY BEHIND A CHRISTMAS CAROL**

Story Line

Biography

About Us

Links

Scrooge at his office with Bob Cratchit

Dickens' cherished little Christmas story, the best loved and most read of all of his books, began life as the result of the author's desperate need of money. In the fall of 1843 Dickens and his wife, Kate, were expecting their fifth child. Requests for money from his family, a large mortgage on his Devonshire Terrace home, and lagging sales from the monthly installments of *Martin Chuzzlewit* had left Dickens seriously short of cash.

As the idea for the story took shape and the writing began in earnest, Dickens became engrossed in the book. He wrote that as the tale unfolded he "wept and laughed, and wept again" and that he "walked about the black streets of London fifteen or twenty miles many a night when all sober folks had gone to bed."

At odds with his publishers, Dickens paid for the production costs of the book himself and insisted on a lavish design that included a gold-stamped cover and four hand-colored etchings. He also set the price at 5 shillings so that the book would be affordable to nearly everyone.

The book was published during the week before Christmas 1843 and was an instant sensation but, due to the high production costs, Dickens' earnings from the sales were lower than expected. In addition to the disappointing profit from the book, Dickens was enraged that the work was instantly the victim of pirated editions. Copyright laws in England were often loosely enforced, and a complete lack of international copyright law had been Dickens' theme during his trip to America the year before. He ended up spending more money fighting pirated editions of the book than he was making from the book itself.

Despite these early financial difficulties, Dickens' Christmas tale of human redemption has endured beyond even Dickens' own vivid imagination. It was a favorite during Dickens' public readings of his works late in his lifetime and is known today primarily due to the dozens of film versions and dramatizations which continue to be produced every year.

Internet

Comprehension

1. **Recall** Who was Jacob Marley, and why does his spirit visit Scrooge?

2. **Recall** What does Scrooge do for the Cratchit family at the play's end?

3. **Clarify** How does Scrooge's view of money change from the beginning of the play to the end?

Text Analysis

4. **Understand Sequence in Plot** Review the sequence wheel you created as you read. Number the sections according to the order in which the time periods are presented in the play. Use your numbers to summarize the **sequence** of events in *A Christmas Carol*.

5. **Make Inferences About Dialogue** What does the Spirit of Christmas Past mean by saying, "I am always with you"? Explain your answer.

6. **Draw Conclusions** Why do you think Tiny Tim's death affects Scrooge so deeply?

7. **Interpret Symbols** In the play there are a number of things used as symbols, such as Marley's chains, the little girl with the doll, and a dove. Reread lines 102–108 in Scene 2, lines 200–212 in Scene 3, and lines 18–22 in Scene 6. Choose one symbol and interpret its meaning.

8. **Analyze Theme** Use a diagram like the one shown to describe the lesson each spirit teaches Scrooge. Based on these lessons, what do you think the **theme** of the play is?

Christmas Past—Lesson:	Christmas Present—Lesson:	Christmas Yet to Come—Lesson:

Theme:

Extension and Challenge

9. **Creative Project: Drama** With a small group, choose the scene or part of a scene that you feel best reflects Dickens's message. Act out the scene for the rest of the class. Then explain why your group chose it.

10. **SOCIAL STUDIES CONNECTION** What was it like to live in Victorian England (1837–1901)? Find out by researching one element of the time period: the Poor Law of 1834, workhouses, prisons, leprosy, how wealthy people lived, or how poor people lived. Present your research to the class.

How important is MONEY?

Do you think people can be happy without a lot of money?

COMMON CORE

RL 2 Determine a theme of a text and analyze its development over the course of the text.
RL 3 Analyze how particular elements of a drama interact.
RL 5 Analyze how a drama's form contributes to its meaning.

Language

◆ **GRAMMAR IN CONTEXT:** Use Complex Sentences

When you use different types of sentence structures, you make ideas clearer and add variety to your writing. One type of sentence structure is a complex sentence. A **complex sentence** consists of one **independent clause**, also known as a main clause, and one or more subordinate clauses. **Subordinate clauses** begin with subordinate conjunctions, such as *because, since, after, although, even though, however, when,* and *while.* Here is an example of a complex sentence with the independent clause highlighted in yellow and the subordinate clause highlighted in green. The subordinate conjunction is underlined.

> We can help people in need, <u>although</u> we don't have much money.

PRACTICE Rewrite the following paragraph. Use subordinating conjunctions to create at least two complex sentences. Then underline the independent clause and circle the subordinate clause in each sentence.

> I still like money. Reading the play has changed my mind a little. Money can be important. Helping people is even more important. Scrooge found this out. It took him a long time.

*For more help with independent and subordinate clauses, see pages R63–R64 in the **Grammar Handbook.***

READING-WRITING CONNECTION

Demonstrate your understanding of *A Christmas Carol* by responding to this prompt. Then use the **revising tip** to improve your writing.

WRITING PROMPT	REVISING TIP
Extended Constructed Response: Statement In lines 12–13 of Scene 6, Scrooge declares, "I will live in the Past, the Present, and the Future." In a **two- or three-paragraph response,** explain what Scrooge means by this statement. Also describe what steps he takes to accomplish his goal.	Review your essay. Make sure you use a variety of sentence structures, including complex sentences.

COMMON CORE

L 1b Choose complex sentences to signal differing relationships among ideas. **W 2** Write explanatory texts to examine a topic and convey ideas.

Interactive Revision

THINK central

Go to thinkcentral.com.
KEYWORD: HML7-427

from **A Christmas Carol**

Film Clip on **Media Smart** DVD-ROM

What's the MESSAGE?

COMMON CORE

RL 7 Compare and contrast a drama to its filmed version, analyzing the effects of techniques unique to each medium (e.g., lighting, sound, or camera focus in a film).

You've explored a play version of a timeless tale and have discovered its themes, or messages about life. Now experience the tale in a different way as you watch selected scenes from a classic movie version of *A Christmas Carol.*

Background

Classic Scrooge The images throughout this lesson are taken from two different movie versions of *A Christmas Carol.* Many stage plays, movies, cartoons, and television specials have been based on the story. This may be because the public enjoys revisiting the tale's timeless themes. An even bigger attraction may be the simple pleasure of seeing Scrooge's personality change.

You'll see four clips from a movie that was filmed many decades ago in black and white and yet remains a popular holiday classic.

Media Literacy: Theme in Movies

Characters need to grow up! As you know from your understanding of *A Christmas Carol* and the character Scrooge, themes are often conveyed through a character's growth and change. To discover a theme in a written story, you look at the words for clues. To identify the theme of a movie, you must focus on the images and sounds. Moviemakers—in particular, the director—use the following techniques to make sure you get the message.

THEME DELIVERY	STRATEGIES FOR VIEWING	
The Director's Plan A director makes basic decisions about how to transfer a well-known tale to the screen and what themes to portray.	• Be aware that a director usually presents the same **themes** that appeared in the original work. • Be prepared to find a theme expressed (or repeated) in the key scenes the director presents.	
The Director's Tools In presenting certain images important to the theme, a director uses film techniques to highlight the message.	• Study the **camera shots** that show more than one character. These shots bring an audience close enough to see the ways characters react to each other. • The **lighting** of characters can reveal a theme in an indirect way. For example, soft lighting can represent goodness or warm moments between characters. • Listen for verbal clues. A director can state a theme directly through **dialogue.** You can also listen to the narration of a **voice-over,** the voice of an unseen narrator who provides important information about the story.	
The Actor's Performance An actor can indicate a theme by showing changes in the behavior of his or her character.	• Notice an actor's **body movements.** An actor can portray a character's personality change by using different **gestures** or **facial expressions.** • Focus on the **tone of voice** of the actors. Think of how a voice can change to show surprise, anger, or weariness.	

Viewing Guide for
A Christmas Carol

Since you've read the play version of *A Christmas Carol*, you already know all that happens to Ebenezer Scrooge. Watch the four movie clips one at a time. Each clip focuses either on Scrooge or on others who are part of his life-changing experience. Try to spot the movie techniques and acting techniques that were carefully designed to deliver Charles Dickens's themes.

View each clip several times and take as much time as you need to observe the events that take place. Keep these questions in mind as you view.

NOW VIEW

FIRST VIEWING: Comprehension

1. **Recall** At what point does Scrooge declare, "I am not the man I was"?

2. **Summarize** What happens to Tiny Tim, according to the voice-over narration at the end?

CLOSE VIEWING: Media Literacy

3. **Compare Lighting Techniques** The lighting in Scrooge's office in clip 1 is dark and dreary. The lighting of Scrooge's home when he awakes in clip 3 is bright and cheerful. What comparison do you think the director is making between Scrooge's old way of looking at the world and his new way?

4. **Interpret Acting** Scrooge goes from being cold-hearted to being softhearted. Beyond his dialogue, how do you know he has changed? Respond by using a chart like the one shown.

Scrooge's Behavior

	Clip 1	Clip 2	Clip 3	Clip 4
Facial expression				
Body movements				
Tone of voice				

Write or Discuss

Compare Play and Film Versions You've read a play version of the Dickens tale and watched scenes from a movie version. What did you enjoy about reading the play as compared to watching the movie scenes? Use evidence from either version to support your answer. Think about

- the portrayal of the character Scrooge in both versions
- how well each version delivers Dickens's basic themes
- the details in the stage directions of the play and the visual representation of the scenes

Produce Your Own Media

Design a DVD Cover Imagine you're part of a team promoting a new, up-to-date version of *A Christmas Carol*. Create a DVD cover that presents the highlights of this retelling. Follow the instructions on the Design Guide to help you position words and pictures on the DVD cover.

HERE'S HOW Use the Design Guide and these tips as you create the cover:

- Think of a modern-day setting and a basic story line that make it clear that this version happens in a very different time and place.
- Brainstorm what images to use on the cover, where to place them, and what colors to use.
- Write a blurb—a brief description of the version to appear on the back of the cover. Be sure to include a statement that reflects a theme of the tale. Also create a critic's one-line comment about the movie.
- Share your DVD cover. See if classmates clearly understand the meaning of your text and images.

DESIGN GUIDE

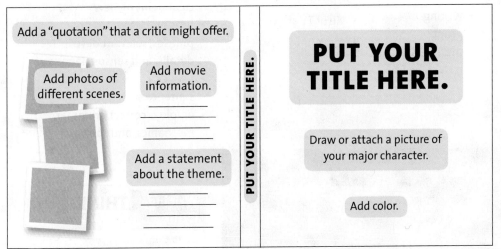

Add a "quotation" that a critic might offer.

Add photos of different scenes.

Add movie information.

Add a statement about the theme.

PUT YOUR TITLE HERE.

PUT YOUR TITLE HERE.

Draw or attach a picture of your major character.

Add color.

BACK COVER   FRONT COVER

COMMON CORE

RL 7 Compare and contrast a drama to its filmed version, analyzing the effects of techniques unique to each medium (e.g., lighting, sound, or camera focus in a film). **SL 5** Include visual displays in presentations.

Media Tools THINK central

Go to **thinkcentral.com**.
KEYWORD: HML7-431

Tech Tip

You can choose colored typefaces for your title and other text. Also, try arranging the elements in a unique way. For example, try your title at the bottom.

Writing Workshop

NARRATIVE

Short Story

Did the stories and characters in this unit surprise you, make you think, or remind you of something you know? Stories can entertain you and draw you into other worlds. In this workshop, you will learn how to write a short story about a real or imagined experience or event.

 Complete the workshop activities in your **Reader/Writer Notebook.**

WRITE WITH A PURPOSE

WRITING TASK

Write a **short story** in which you entertain your audience by showing a complex character facing and resolving a conflict or struggle.

Idea Starters
• a conflict that takes place in the distant future
• a new invention that causes problems for people
• an unexpected event that has surprising consequences
• a dangerous adventure

THE ESSENTIALS

Here are some common purposes, audiences, and formats for fictional writing.

PURPOSES	AUDIENCES	FORMATS
• to entertain readers	• classmates and teacher	• literary magazine
• to express thoughts about life or human nature	• parents	• writing contest
	• writing-group members	• blog posting
		• movie or TV show
	• Web readers	• CD recording

COMMON CORE TRAITS

1. DEVELOPMENT OF IDEAS

• introduces and develops **characters** and a **setting**
• introduces and develops a **central conflict**
• uses techniques such as **dialogue** and **description**
• resolves the conflict in a satisfying **conclusion**

2. ORGANIZATION IDEAS

• presents a **natural** and **logical sequence of events**
• uses **transitions** to convey sequence
• uses **pacing** to develop the plot

3. LANGUAGE FACILITY AND CONVENTIONS

• establishes and maintains a clear **point of view**
• uses **precise words** and **phrases, relevant descriptive details,** and **sensory language**
• uses effective and varied **sentence structures**
• employs **correct grammar, mechanics,** and **spelling**

Writing Online

Go to **thinkcentral.com.**
KEYWORD: HML7N-432

Planning/Prewriting

COMMON CORE

W 3a–e Write narratives to develop real or imagined experiences or events using effective technique, relevant descriptive details, and well-structured event sequences. **W 5** Develop and strengthen writing as needed by planning.

Getting Started

CHOOSE A STORY IDEA

A good story needs a main **character** facing a **conflict,** or problem. Here are two ways to choose a story idea:

- **Start with a character.** Build your story around an interesting or unusual person. That character might be a real person or someone you invent.
- **Start with a conflict.** Base your story on a problem or conflict you have heard about or experienced. Choose a conflict that's "ripped from the headlines," or make one up.

▶ **ASK YOURSELF:**

- Who are some interesting people I know or have read about?
- What kinds of conflicts have I read about in the news? What conflicts do people my age have? Which of these would make for an interesting story?
- Will my character's conflict be **external** (against an outside force, such as another character or a force of nature) or **internal** (within his or her mind)?

THINK ABOUT AUDIENCE AND PURPOSE

As you think about your story, keep your **purpose** and **audience** in mind. Your purpose is to entertain your readers and keep their interest.

▶ **ASK YOURSELF:**

- Who is my audience? What characters or conflicts will they enjoy reading about?
- How can I engage my readers so that they won't want to stop reading my story until they get to the end?

PLAN CHARACTERS AND SETTING

The star of your story will be a complex **main character,** one who seems like a real person. The supporting roles will be played by **minor characters.** You'll need to help your readers understand each character's personality, actions, and relationships with others.

You'll also need to develop a definite **setting:** where and when the story takes place. Use precise language and sensory details to describe the places, season, time period, or time of day. Such details help to create a mood and give readers more information about the characters' situations.

At this point, brainstorm as many descriptive details as you can about your characters and setting. Organize your details in a chart.

▶ **WHAT DOES IT LOOK LIKE?**

Main Character	Setting
• girl at camp	• camp in woods
• hangs out with a group of friends	• summertime
• slowpoke—friends call her "Turtle"	• late at night
• easily frightened	• crunch of footsteps on leaves
• overactive imagination	• sound of owl hooting
	• full moon
	• creepy shadows

Planning/Prewriting *continued*

Getting Started

PLAN YOUR PLOT

As you know, the **plot** is the series of events in a story. You can use a story map to plan what happens at each stage of your plot.

- **Exposition**—Introduces the characters and setting. Sets the stage for the conflict.
- **Rising Action**—Shows how the conflict becomes more complex as the main character faces obstacles. Creates suspense as the plot builds to the climax.
- **Climax**—Describes a turning point in the conflict—the conflict will be settled in one way or another.
- **Falling Action and Resolution**—Reveals the outcome of the climax and shows how the conflict is resolved. The main character is usually changed or learns a lesson.

▶ WHAT DOES IT LOOK LIKE?

> **Story Map**
>
> **Setting:** *the woods, near a campsite*
>
> **Characters:** *main—a girl walking by herself; minor—someone following her*
>
> **Conflict:** *A girl is being followed by a stranger.*
>
> **Exposition:** *The girl is walking alone in the woods, separated from her friends. She realizes she is lost and searches her pocket for something to help her.*
>
> **Rising action:** *She hears crunching and footsteps and sees a shadow behind her.*
>
> **Climax:** *The person catches up with the girl.*
>
> **Falling action/resolution:** *The person hands the girl her cell phone and leaves. She realizes the person wasn't going to harm her.*

CHOOSE A POINT OF VIEW

Decide who will tell your story and choose a point of view. The **point of view** is the perspective from which a story is told.

- **First Person**—The narrator is a character in the story and refers to himself or herself as *I*.
- **Third-Person Limited**—The narrator is outside the story and tells the thoughts and feelings of only one character.
- **Third-Person Omniscient**—The "all-knowing" narrator can tell what all the characters are thinking and feeling.

ASK YOURSELF:

- What would my story be like if my main character told it? What would my readers learn about the character by "hearing" his or her voice?
- What if the narrator were outside the story? What additional insights could this narrator provide about the events and characters?
- If I choose the third-person point of view, should the narrator know what every character is thinking, or just one?
- How will I establish my point of view and maintain it throughout my story?

PEER REVIEW Describe to a peer your main character and conflict. Ask: What more would you like to know about the character? What would be an interesting way to resolve the conflict?

YOUR TURN In your *Reader/Writer Notebook,* record your story ideas and details about your characters and setting. Then develop a story map like the one on this page. Share your plan with a peer and then revise it based on his or her feedback.

Drafting

COMMON CORE

W 4 Produce clear and coherent writing appropriate to task, purpose, and audience. **L 2** Demonstrate command of the conventions of standard English capitalization, punctuation, and spelling.

The following chart shows how to write a draft of an effective short story.

Developing Your Short Story

EXPOSITION

- Start with a **"hook"** to grab your audience's attention. For example, you might begin in the middle of an interesting conversation or an exciting scene.
- Introduce the **characters** and **setting,** and set the stage for the **central conflict**.
- Establish a **point of view** by introducing a narrator, or the voice that tells the story.

RISING ACTION AND CLIMAX

- Use **precise words** and **phrases** to describe the characters, setting, and events.
- Include complications, or obstacles, that show how the **conflict** becomes more complicated. **Pace** the events to create suspense and keep your audience interested in the plot.
- Sequence events so that they happen **naturally** and **logically**.
- Make sure events build to a **climax** or turning point.
- Use a variety of **transitional words, phrases,** and **clauses,** such as *before, meanwhile,* and *after* to help your audience understand changes in time or setting.

FALLING ACTION AND RESOLUTION

- Provide a **conclusion** that resolves the conflict.
- Tie up any **loose ends** that might leave your audience feeling confused.

GRAMMAR IN CONTEXT: PUNCTUATING DIALOGUE

Be sure to follow punctuation rules when you write **dialogue** for your story. Begin a new paragraph each time a different character starts speaking.

Rule	Examples
Use quotation marks to enclose both the character's words and the punctuation for those words.	*"What do you want?"* *"You left your cell phone by the pool."*
Use commas to set off dialogue tags that occur at the beginning, in the middle, or at the end of a sentence.	**My friend joked,** *"You're as slow as a turtle!"* *"Let's hurry,"* **Nina urged,** *"or we'll miss dinner."* *"Don't lose your phone,"* **warned my mother.**

YOUR TURN Develop a draft of your story, following the structure outlined in the chart above. As you write, make sure to punctuate dialogue correctly.

Revising

You can improve your story by adding details about your characters, including more dialogue, and making your plot more entertaining for your audience. The chart below will help you identify ways to revise and rework your draft.

SHORT STORY

Ask Yourself	Tips	Revision Strategies
1. **Is the plot compelling?** Does it develop a conflict through all stages of plot (exposition, rising action, climax, falling action, and resolution)?	**Circle** the sentences in which the conflict is introduced. **Place a check mark** next to the beginning of each plot stage.	If necessary, **add** sentences that develop the conflict or explain how it is resolved.
2. **Is the point of view maintained throughout the story?**	**Identify** pronouns that reveal the point of view from which the story is told. **Label** the story's point of view; then **circle** any parts that use the incorrect point of view.	If any parts are circled, **rewrite** them using the correct point of view.
3. **Are the characters realistic and interesting?** Do I describe the setting with vivid details?	**Underline** descriptive details about each character and the setting.	**Add** details and dialogue to develop characters. **Add** vivid sensory details to describe the setting.
4. **Does the pace keep the story moving?**	**Highlight** sentences that make the story seem slow.	**Rewrite** or **revise** parts that are highlighted. If necessary, **try** a new approach.
5. **Are the story events sequenced in a natural and logical order?**	**Number** the major plot events. **Underline** transitions such as *later*, *before the party*, and *after the game* that help readers follow the plot.	**Rearrange** events that are out of order. If you are lacking underlines, **add** transitional words, phrases, and clauses to help readers track the order of events.

PEER REVIEW Working with a classmate, review the chart above. Answer each question in this chart to decide how your drafts could be improved or reworked. Take notes so that you remember your partner's feedback when you are ready to revise your draft.

ANALYZE A STUDENT DRAFT

Read this student's draft; notice comments on its structure and suggestions for how it could be made even stronger.

COMMON CORE

W 3b Use narrative techniques, such as dialogue. **W 5** Develop and strengthen writing as needed by revising, editing, rewriting, or trying a new approach, focusing on how well purpose and audience have been addressed.

A Stranger in the Woods
by Ashley Hildebrandt, Horace Mann School

❶   I was walking in the forest. I was all alone walking back to my tent. All of my friends had gone ahead of me because I was too slow. I'd been walking for about an hour now, and I knew I was lost now, which isn't very unusual for me. I was instantly sure of what I needed to do. I reached into my pocket and realized it was empty. I frantically searched the ground around myself and walked with panic in my movements. I remembered then where I'd left it. I had left my only hope out by the lake. I then heard a soft crunching of leaves. It continued rhythmically edging closer and closer. As I listened carefully, I hesitantly decided to run to the left.

❷   I ran as fast as my legs could carry me until the only sound audible was my hard breathing and my feet gently destroying the leaves beneath me. I breathed a sigh of relief. An owl hoot-hooted. I caught a glimpse of the bright full moon. The soft crunching began again. A jolt of panic shot up my spine as I saw an approaching shadow. My heart and breathing paused, and I couldn't get my legs to move.

> The exposition establishes the **main character,** the **setting,** and the **conflict.** However, the opening lines are not likely to hook the reader. Ashley can improve her exposition by adding **dialogue.**

> Ashley further develops the conflict and begins to build **suspense.**

LEARN HOW **Use Dialogue to Create Interest** Ashley's repetitive sentence structures in the first few sentences are awkward and not likely to grab her reader's interest. By adding dialogue, shown in blue, she transports her reader to the scene of the action. The dialogue also keeps the reader from getting confused about why the main character is alone in the forest.

ASHLEY'S REVISION TO PARAGRAPH ❶

"Hey, Turtle! We'll never get back to camp walking this slow!"

"Yeah," giggled Nina, "my bathing suit is wet. I'm running back to camp."

"Me, too," agreed the rest of my friends. They disappeared, leaving me trudging along all alone.

~~I was walking in the forest. I was all alone walking back to my tent. All of my friends had gone ahead of me because I was too slow.~~ I'd been walking for about an hour now . . .

3   A man, now visible, moved closer, with death written all over his face. As I was building up the courage to scream, the man stopped only an arm's length away from me.

4   The man stared at me for what seemed like a lifetime and finally asked, "This yours?"

5   "Yes," I whispered.

6   He handed me the phone and walked off into the darkness of the woods and I stood staring after him. I walked right after him in order to thank him and after walking for a minute, I stood in front of five tents surrounded by my friends. I never thanked the stranger in the woods.

> The suspense builds as a man approaches. Ashley could add **sensory language** to help her audience picture the man.

> The **conflict is resolved** in a satisfying and surprising conclusion.

LEARN HOW Add Sensory Language In her draft, Ashley describes the man following the main character as having "death written all over his face." Since the man is simply returning the character's cell phone, this description does not fit the context of the story. How can Ashley create suspense but not mislead the reader? **Sensory details**—details that appeal to the five senses—will help. Such details will also help the reader visualize the man.

ASHLEY'S REVISION TO PARAGRAPH 3

         in the moonlight   *perspiration dripping from his red, puffy face.*

A man, now visible, moved closer, with ~~death written all over his face.~~

     felt a scream rising in my throat   *,dressed in workout gear,*

As I ~~was building up the courage to scream,~~ the man stopped only an arm's

length away from me.

 YOUR TURN Use the chart on page 436, feedback from your peers and teacher, and the two "Learn How" lessons to revise and rework your story. Evaluate how well you have achieved the traits of a good short story and whether you have succeeded in entertaining your audience. If necessary, try a new approach to better meet your purpose.

Editing and Publishing

COMMON CORE

W 3d Use sensory language. **W 5** Develop and strengthen writing by revising, editing, and rewriting. **L 1b** Choose among simple, compound, complex, compound-complex sentences. **L 2b** Spell correctly.

In the editing stage, you review your writing to make sure that it is free of grammar, usage, and punctuation errors. Be sure to also check closely for misspelled words. Even minor grammatical and spelling errors can keep readers from enjoying your story.

GRAMMAR IN CONTEXT: USING A VARIETY OF SENTENCE TYPES

A good story can lose its punch if the audience gets bored because of repetitive sentences. Effective writing includes a blend of simple, compound, complex, and compound-complex sentences. **Simple sentences** have only one independent clause. **Compound sentences** contain two or more independent clauses, usually joined by a conjunction (*and, but, or, nor, yet, for, so*). **Complex sentences** have one independent clause and one or more subordinate clauses. **Compound-complex sentences** have at least two independent clauses and one or more subordinate clauses.

In the last paragraph of her draft, Ashley uses the word *and* three times and has too many long compound sentences. To eliminate repetition, Ashley first highlighted the repeated word and then decided where to delete it to create more varied sentences.

He handed me the phone and walked off into the darkness of the woods.
~~and~~ I stood staring after him, and then I walked right after him in order to
thank him ~~and after walking~~ I had walked for a minute, I stood in front of five tents
surrounded by my friends.

[By breaking up several long sentences into a blend of types of sentences, Ashley made her resolution easier to read and therefore more effective.]

PUBLISH YOUR WRITING

Share your short story with an audience.

- Illustrate your story, bind it, and give it as a gift to a friend or family member.
- Post your story on a class blog and invite classmates to read and comment on it.
- Adapt your story into a short film. First write a script and cast the characters. Then shoot and edit the video before you arrange a "screening" to showcase your work.

YOUR TURN

Correct any errors in your story. As you are proofreading, make sure you have used a variety of sentence types. Then publish your final story for others to enjoy.

Scoring Rubric

Use the rubric below to evaluate your short story from the Writing Workshop or your response to the on-demand writing task on the next page.

SHORT STORY

SCORE	COMMON CORE TRAITS
6	• **Development** Effectively and engagingly introduces, develops, and resolves a conflict; develops characters and events with strong dialogue and description • **Organization** Effectively establishes a natural and logical sequence of events; uses effective pacing and transitions • **Language** Consistently maintains a clear point of view; ably uses precise words and sensory language; shows a strong command of conventions
5	• **Development** Introduces, develops, and resolves a conflict in an effective way; develops characters and events with dialogue and description • **Organization** Has a natural and logical sequence of events; uses mostly effective pacing and transitions • **Language** Maintains a clear point of view; weaves in precise words and sensory language; has a few errors in conventions
4	• **Development** Introduces, develops, and resolves a conflict; could use more dialogue or description to develop characters and events • **Organization** Has a generally logical sequence with some unnecessary events that cause ineffective pacing; uses some transitions don't make sense • **Language** Usually maintains a point of view; includes precise words and sensory language; includes a few distracting errors in conventions
3	• **Development** Introduces and resolves a conflict, but needs more development • **Organization** Has a confusing sequence due to unnecessary events; has a slow pace at times; needs more transitions to convey sequence • **Language** Has some lapses in point of view; could use more precise words and sensory language; has some major errors in conventions
2	• **Development** Introduces a conflict but does not develop or resolve it • **Organization** Has too many events that confuse the plot; has an uneven pace • **Language** Often changes point of view; lacks precise words and sensory language; has many errors in conventions
1	• **Development** Has no conflict; lacks dialogue and description • **Organization** Lacks sequence and transitions, which causes ineffective pacing • **Language** Has no clear point of view; does not include precise words or sensory language; has major problems with conventions

Preparing for Timed Writing

COMMON CORE

W 10 Write routinely over shorter time frames for a range of tasks, purposes, and audiences.

1. ANALYZE THE TASK — 5 MIN

Read the task carefully. Then read it again, underlining or circling the words that tell the type of writing, the topic, the purpose, and the audience.

WRITING TASK *Type of writing* *Purpose* *Audience*

Write a <u>short story</u> that will <u>entertain</u> your classmates with a plot focused on two best friends in conflict. Create believable characters and place them in a definite setting. Give specific details about events that lead to a resolution of the conflict.

Topic

2. PLAN YOUR RESPONSE — 10 MIN

Brainstorm experiences (real or imagined), characters, or places on which you could base a short story about two best friends in conflict. Which of these would make for the most compelling story? Decide on an idea. Then create a story map like the one shown here in which you develop key elements of the plot.

Conflict:
Characters:
Setting:
Events:
Resolution:

3. RESPOND TO THE TASK — 20 MIN

Use your story map as a guide, and keep the following points in mind as you write:

- Start writing, even if you're unsure about how to begin. You can always go back and rewrite the beginning of the story later.
- Describe the plot events in a logical order—from the introduction of the conflict to its resolution.
- Write from the same point of view throughout your story. You might have a first-person or a third-person narrator. Remember to keep the action moving.
- Use realistic dialogue, descriptive details, and sensory language to bring your characters to life.

4. IMPROVE YOUR RESPONSE — 5–10 MIN

Revising Check your draft against the task. Does your story explain the conflict? Is it well-paced? Are your characters and setting believable?

Proofreading Correct any errors in grammar, spelling, and punctuation.

Checking Your Final Copy Before you turn in your story, read through it once more to catch any errors you may have missed.

Technology Workshop

Creating a Class Blog

Whether you want to reach new readers, receive feedback on your writing, or share writing tips, a **blog,** or Web log, is a useful way to share stories and improve your writing.

 Complete the workshop activities in your **Reader/Writer Notebook.**

PRODUCE WITH A PURPOSE

TASK

Create a **blog** in which you and your classmates can share stories and comment on one another's writing. With a team of classmates, plan and build the blog. Then add posts, or messages, to spark discussion among your online community.

COMMON CORE TRAITS

A STRONG CLASS BLOG . . .

- uses the Internet as a way to produce and publish original stories on various topics
- has a structure that is easily navigated
- has a visually appealing home page with appropriate text and graphics
- has interactive discussion, with questions, responses, and comments
- is updated regularly

COMMON CORE

W 6 Use technology to produce and publish writing. **SL 1c** Pose questions and respond to others' questions and comments. **SL 2** Analyze the main ideas and supporting details presented in diverse media and formats (e.g., visually).

Plan and Produce the Blog

The following guidelines can help you create your blog:

- **Determine your discussion threads.** Include a separate **discussion thread**—chain of related posts—for each story. Clearly label each thread with the writer's name and the title of the story. In addition, think about other threads you might include, such as threads focusing on tips for overcoming writer's block or ideas for short stories. Take notes on all the team's ideas before voting to select the best ones.

- **Map out your home page.** Sketch your home page, visually representing how users will link to the different threads. Discuss and vote on what other information to include. For instance, you might explain the purpose of the blog or rules for participation.

- **Set an agenda.** Make a plan to complete all the team's goals by specific deadlines. Divide the work equally. One person might research Web sites that can host your blog. Another might create a logo for the home page. Make sure any graphics you plan to include are not copyrighted. In addition, each person should be responsible for posting his or her own story with a request for questions and comments.

- **Build the blog.** With the assistance of your school technology coordinator, assemble your blog on the Web site you chose.

Media Tools

Go to **thinkcentral.com.**
KEYWORD: HML7-442

Participate in an Online Discussion

Sharing your opinions in a blog is different from discussing stories in class. Here are some tips for participating in a meaningful online discussion:

- **Clearly state and support your position.** Identify your question or comment at the beginning of your post. Remember to refer to specific parts of the story. You can add links or cite other bloggers' posts to support what you say.

- **Make it brief.** Most bloggers don't want to scroll down indefinitely. Keep each post containing your feedback short and to the point.

- **Use a respectful tone.** Your audience can't see you face-to-face and observe your reactions to their ideas. That's why it's important to maintain a polite tone. Use these guidelines for your posts.

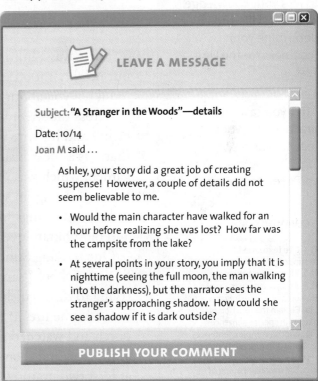

- Be positive and friendly when you talk about a writer's work.

- Use precise literary terms, such as *plot, suspense, conflict,* and *character.*

- Support your opinions with reasons.

- Give specific suggestions for improvement.

- Don't rewrite someone else's work. Let the writer make the final changes.

- Respond politely to readers' comments.

- Ask readers to clarify any confusing suggestions.

LEAVE A MESSAGE

Subject: "A Stranger in the Woods"—details

Date: 10/14

Joan M said …

Ashley, your story did a great job of creating suspense! However, a couple of details did not seem believable to me.

- Would the main character have walked for an hour before realizing she was lost? How far was the campsite from the lake?

- At several points in your story, you imply that it is nighttime (seeing the full moon, the man walking into the darkness), but the narrator sees the stranger's approaching shadow. How could she see a shadow if it is dark outside?

PUBLISH YOUR COMMENT

- **Keep the discussion focused.** Analyze and respond to the main ideas and supporting details in the posts. Reply to other posts by explaining how they helped to clarify or elaborate on the discussion or the story. Add relevant observations and new ideas to keep the discussion moving and on topic.

- **Invite other classmates into your blogosphere.** Motivate other classmates to interact and collaborate with you on your blog. Send them an e-mail with the link so that they can join in.

YOUR TURN Plan and produce a blog using the guidelines on these pages. Once you've launched your blog, read a new short story at least once per week and post your feedback.

Assessment Practice

DIRECTIONS Read the following selection and then answer the questions.

from The Hummingbird That Lived Through Winter

by William Saroyan

1   There was a hummingbird once which in the wintertime did not leave our neighborhood in Fresno, California.

2   I'll tell you about it.

3   Across the street lived old Dikran, who was almost blind. He was past eighty and his wife was only a few years younger. They had a little house that was as neat inside as it was ordinary outside—except for old Dikran's garden, which was the best thing of its kind in the world. Plants, bushes, trees, all strong, in sweet black moist earth whose guardian was old Dikran. All things from the sky loved this spot in our poor neighborhood, and old Dikran loved *them*.

4   One freezing Sunday, in the dead of winter, as I came home from Sunday School I saw old Dikran standing in the middle of the street trying to distinguish what was in his hand. Instead of going into our house to the fire, as I had wanted to do, I stood on the steps of the front porch and watched the old man. He would turn around and look upward at his trees and then back to the palm of his hand. He stood in the street at least two minutes and then at last he came to me. He held his hand out, and in Armenian he said, "What is this in my hand?"

5   I looked.

6   It is a hummingbird," I said half in English and half in Armenian. Hummingbird I said in English because I didn't know its name in Armenian.

7   "What is that?" old Dikran asked.

8   "The little bird," I said. "You know. The one that comes in the summer and stands in the air and then shoots away. The one with the wings that beat so fast you can't see them. It's in your hand. It's dying."

9   "Come with me," the old man said. "I can't see, and the old lady's at church. I can feel its heart beating. Is it in a bad way? Look again, once."

10   I looked again. It was a sad thing to behold. This wonderful little creature of summertime in the big rough hand of the old peasant. Here it

was in the cold of winter, absolutely helpless and pathetic, not suspended in a shaft of summer light, not the most alive thing in the world, but the most helpless and heartbreaking.

11   "It's dying," I said.

12   The old man lifted his hand to his mouth and blew warm breath on the little thing in his hand which he could not even see. "Stay now," he said in Armenian. "It is not long till summer. Stay, swift and lovely."

13   We went into the kitchen of his little house, and while he blew warm breath on the bird he told me what to do.

14   "Put a tablespoonful of honey over the gas fire and pour it into my hand, but be sure it is not too hot."

15   This was done.

16   After a moment the hummingbird began to show signs of fresh life. The warmth of the room, the vapor of the warm honey—and, well, the will and love of the old man. Soon the old man could feel the change in his hand, and after a moment or two the hummingbird began to take little dabs of the honey.

17   "It will live," the old man announced. "Stay and watch."

18   The transformation was incredible. The old man kept his hand generously open, and I expected the helpless bird to shoot upward out of his hand, suspend itself in space, and scare the life out of me—which is exactly what happened. The new life of the little bird was magnificent. It spun about in the little kitchen, going to the window, coming back to the heat, suspending, circling as if it were summertime and it had never felt better in its whole life.

19   The old man sat on the plain chair, blind but attentive. He listened carefully and tried to see, but of course he couldn't. He kept asking about the bird, how it seemed to be, whether it showed signs of weakening again, what its spirit was, and whether or not it appeared to be restless; and I kept describing the bird to him.

20   When the bird was restless and wanted to go, the old man said, "Open the window and let it go."

21   "Will it live?" I asked.

22   "It is alive now and wants to go," he said. "Open the window."

23   I opened the window, the hummingbird stirred about here and there, feeling the cold from the outside, suspended itself in the area of the open window, stirring this way and that, and then it was gone.

GO ON ➤

24   "Close the window," the old man said.

25   We talked a minute or two and then I went home.

26   The old man claimed the hummingbird lived through that winter, but I never knew for sure. I saw hummingbirds again when summer came, but I couldn't tell one from the other.

27   One day in the summer I asked the old man.

28   "Did it live?"

29   "The little bird?" he said.

30   "Yes," I said. "That we gave the honey to. You remember. The little bird that was dying in the winter. Did it live?"

31   "Look about you," the old man said. "Do you see the bird?"

32   "I see humming*birds*," I said.

33   "Each of them is our bird," the old man said. "Each of them, each of them," he said swiftly and gently.

Reading Comprehension

> **Use "The Hummingbird That Lived Through Winter" to answer questions 1–9.**

1. The setting in a garden affects the theme of the story by —

   A. emphasizing the certainty of death

   B. placing the story in Dikran's homeland

   C. giving the bird a place to escape to

   D. showing the abundance of nature

2. Seeing Dikran in the street causes the narrator to —

   A. worry that a car will hit Dikran

   B. run to his own house to get warm

   C. watch Dikran to see what he is doing

   D. look for birds suffering from the cold

3. Which action helps cause the hummingbird to revive?

   A. Keeping the bird inside all winter

   B. Asking questions about the bird

   C. Opening the window

   D. Feeding the bird warm honey

4. Compare and contrast the hummingbird's behavior. Which statement describes its change in behavior before and after Dikran took it inside?

   A. *It was a sad thing to behold.*

   B. *The transformation was incredible.*

   C. *I can feel its heart beating.*

   D. *I saw hummingbirds again. . . .*

5. Dikran lets the hummingbird go because he knows that —

   A. it will survive the winter now

   B. spring will come soon

   C. a wild creature needs to be free

   D. he can't take care of it

6. From the way he cares for the hummingbird, what can you infer that Dikran feels about nature?

   A. Nature is harsh and cruel at times.

   B. Nature does the right thing in the end.

   C. Some animals cannot survive in nature.

   D. Weaker animals are treated well by nature.

7. The most important way in which the narrator and Dikran are similar is the fact that they both —

   A. appreciate nature and life

   B. are from Armenia

   C. live in the same poor neighborhood

   D. know a lot about nature

8. Which statement best describes a theme of the story?

   A. The life force is powerful.

   B. Nature is very fragile.

   C. Elderly people deserve respect.

   D. Life is full of hardships.

9. Which lines from the story show how the character of the old man affects the theme?

   A. *Across the street lived old Dikran, who was almost blind.*

   B. *He stood in the street at least two minutes and then at last he came to me.*

   C. *The old man claimed the hummingbird lived through that winter, but I never knew for sure.*

   D. *"Each of them is our bird," the old man said. "Each of them, each of them," he said swiftly and gently.*

SHORT CONSTRUCTED RESPONSE
Write two or three sentences to answer this question.

10. Name two things Dikran does to cause the hummingbird to revive. Tell why each action helps the bird.

Write a paragraph to answer this question.

11. What theme does this story share with the poem "Spring Harvest of Snow Peas" on page 394? Compare and contrast how the authors express this theme.

GO ON

Vocabulary

1. What does the word *distinguish* mean in paragraph 4?

". . . I saw old Dikran standing in the middle of the street trying to <u>distinguish</u> what was in his hand."

A. Caress   **C.** Save

B. Hold   **D.** See

2. What does the word *pathetic* mean in paragraph 10?

"Here it was in the cold of winter, absolutely helpless and <u>pathetic</u>, not suspended in a shaft of summer light, not the most alive thing in the world, but the most helpless and heartbreaking."

A. Broken   **C.** Pitiful

B. Lost   **D.** Small

3. What does the word *suspend* mean in paragraph 18?

". . . I expected the helpless bird to shoot upward out of his hand, <u>suspend</u> itself in space, and scare the life out of me—which is exactly what happened. The new life of the little bird was magnificent."

A. Disappear from sight

B. Stop breathing for a short time

C. Hang in the air without falling

D. Spin out of control

4. In paragraph 3, the author uses the word *ordinary* to show that Dikran's house is —

"They had a little houses that was as neat inside as it was <u>ordinary</u> outside—except for old Dikran's garden, which was the best thing of its kind in the world."

A. Plain   **C.** Scary looking

B. Poor   **D.** Small

5. In paragraph 3, the author uses the word *sweet* to show that the soil in the garden is —

"Plants, bushes, trees—all strong, in <u>sweet</u> black moist earth whose guardian was old Dikran."

A. Cheap   **C.** Perfumed

B. Good   **D.** Tasty

6. In paragraph 10, the author uses the word *peasant* to show that Dikran is —

"This wonderful little creature of summertime in the big rough hand of the old <u>peasant</u>."

A. Coarse   **C.** Friendly

B. Crazy   **D.** Nervous

Revising and Editing

DIRECTIONS Read this passage and answer the questions that follow.

(1) Last summer, our family drove to Mexico. (2) Mexico is my mom's birthplace. (3) We saw the places where she played as a little girl and visited her home. (4) Her old neighborhood has narrow streets. (5) The streets curve past the houses. (6) My mom remembered her friends. (7) She couldn't find any of them. (8) She looked for her old grade school. (9) Like her friends, the school was gone. (10) Still, Mom was happy we went, so we'll probably go back again sometime.

1. What is the BEST way to combine sentences 1 and 2?

A. Last summer, our family drove to Mexico and my mom's birthplace is there.

B. Last summer, our family drove to Mexico, which is my mom's birthplace.

C. Last summer, our family drove to Mexico; Mexico is my mom's birthplace.

D. Our family drove to Mexico last summer, and Mexico is my mom's birthplace.

2. What is the BEST way to combine sentences 4 and 5?

A. Her old neighborhood has narrow streets, and the streets curve past the houses.

B. Her old neighborhood has narrow streets that curve past the houses.

C. Her old neighborhood has narrow streets, but the streets curve past the houses.

D. Her old neighborhood has narrow streets, and furthermore, these streets curve past the houses.

3. What is the BEST way to combine sentences 6 and 7?

A. My mom remembered her friends, she couldn't find any of them.

B. My mom remembered her friends, although she couldn't find any of them.

C. My mom remembered her friends, or she couldn't find any of them.

D. My mom remembered her friends, and she couldn't find any of them.

4. What is the BEST way to combine sentences 8 and 9?

A. She looked for her old grade school, and like her friends, the school was gone.

B. She looked for her old grade school, like her friends, the school was gone.

C. She looked for her old grade school, which like her friends, the school was gone.

D. She looked for her old grade school, although like her friends, the school was gone.

STOP

More Great Reads

Which questions from Unit 3 made an impression on you? Continue exploring them with these books.

COMMON CORE

RL 10 Read and comprehend literature.

What happens when friends compete?

Wolf Shadows
by Mary Casanova

As hunting season approaches, 12-year-old Seth finds himself disagreeing with his best friend, Matt, over the protection of wolves. On opening day, Matt wounds a wolf. Can Seth resolve his conflicting emotions before it's too late?

Friends and Enemies
by LouAnn Gaeddert

William and Jim are best friends. But when World War II breaks out, Jim refuses to support the war. Angered by his friend's stance, William joins classmates in attacking Jim. Will Jim ever forgive him?

End of the Race
by Dean Hughes

Two 12-year-olds find their friendship is tested when they represent their school in a track race. Jared feels he has to be the great athlete his dad was, while Davin, who is African American, considers their rivalry a racial conflict.

What is the cure for unhappiness?

Roll of Thunder, Hear My Cry
by Mildred D. Taylor

Cassie Logan, growing up in a loving family, has never had reason to suspect that anyone would wish her harm. All that changes when her community comes under constant threat from "night riders."

Because of Winn-Dixie
by Kate DiCamillo

If you were suddenly uprooted to a distant place, would you be able to adjust? India Opal Buloni's (pronounced "baloney") first summer in the little town of Naomi is action packed—all thanks to a big, ugly dog named Winn-Dixie.

Mick Harte Was Here
by Barbara Park

Can one ever feel happy after the death of a brother or sister? Thirteen-year-old Phoebe describes the stages of grief her family suffers after her brother Mick dies in an accident. Finally, she comes to terms with his death.

Can you be alone and not lonely?

Spider Boy
by Ralph Fletcher

When Bobby Ballenger moves from the Midwest to New York, he has a difficult time adjusting. The cruelty of his classmates makes him long for his former friends. Will he face the bullies and earn a second chance?

Spinners
by Donna Jo Napoli and Richard Tchen

Napoli and Tchen retell a classic tale to give insights into the lives of Rumpelstiltskin and his daughter. Love, pride, avarice, and revenge are all a part of this delightful new version.

The Fire Pony
by Rodman Philbrick

Roy is happiest when he's with his older brother Joe, who has a fiery temper and a special gift for healing horses. All seems well when Joe rescues Roy from a foster home, but before long, Joe reveals a darker side.

Get Novel Wise

THINK central

Go to **thinkcentral.com**.
KEYWORD: HML7-450

Finding a Voice

MOOD, TONE, AND STYLE

- In Fiction
- In Nonfiction
- In Poetry
- In Media

Share What You Know

What's your STYLE?

When we get ready for an important event, we usually start by figuring out what we are going to wear. Why do you think that is? What can our clothing and hairstyle say about us? By making choices about these things, each of us can create a personal style. In things such as writing, filmmaking, and art, style refers to the way a person expresses a message. Some people are even known for their unique style.

ACTIVITY Think of three people with distinct personal styles. They can be people you know and admire or people you have seen in movies or on television. Evaluate their styles by thinking about these questions:

- What made you notice each person?

- How do their styles differ?

- Which style is most similar to your own?

After answering these questions, write a description of your own style.

Find It Online! THINK central

Go to thinkcentral.com for the interactive version of this unit.

Preview Unit Goals

TEXT ANALYSIS	• Identify and analyze mood, tone, and irony • Identify and analyze elements of style, including word choice, sentence structure, imagery, and dialogue • Determine the meaning of words and phrases as they are used in a text, including figurative and connotative meanings
READING	• Use evidence to support what a text says explicitly • Make inferences • Identify characteristics of science fiction • Determine a writer's point of view
WRITING AND LANGUAGE	• Write a response to literature • Understand prepositions and prepositional phrases • Recognize misplaced and dangling modifiers
SPEAKING AND LISTENING	• Present a critique
VOCABULARY	• Understand synonyms • Use Latin and Greek roots as clues to the meaning of words
ACADEMIC VOCABULARY	• communicate • describe • illustrate • interpret • style
MEDIA AND VIEWING	• Analyze visual elements in media • Analyze main ideas in diverse media formats

Media Smart DVD-ROM

Style in Photographs

Discover how two master photographers create works of art with personality and eye appeal. Page 528

Text Analysis Workshop

Mood and Style

Think of a story as a homemade meal. You've learned about the basic ingredients: plot, characters, setting, and theme. What gives a writer's work a unique flavor? What makes you tear hungrily through one story, while another is hard to digest? The answer is the blend of spices, such as mood, imagery, and style.

Part 1: Mood and Imagery

COMMON CORE

Included in this workshop:
RL 3 Analyze how particular elements of a story interact.
RL 4 Determine the meaning of words and phrases as they are used in a text, including figurative and connotative meanings.

Mood is a feeling that a writer creates for readers. Imagine this scenario: You and a friend venture into a haunted house advertised as "spine-tinglingly scary." As you enter the shadowy house, your stomach tightens. You hear eerie howling. Suddenly, a high-pitched howl sends you running for the exit.

The mood of the haunted house was terrifying. As a reader, think of mood as the feeling the writer creates—the overall atmosphere. Often, you can identify the mood by looking at the writer's choice of words, particularly the use of **imagery**—words and phrases that appeal to a reader's senses of sight, sound, touch, smell, and taste.

MOOD	IMAGERY
Words to Describe Mood	**Words to Appeal to the Senses**
• cheerful • wondrous • peaceful • romantic • eerie • silly • somber • terrifying • thoughtful	• foggy • gritty • hissing • spaghetti as chewy as string • a shrill, ear-splitting fire alarm

Example
The highlighted words and phrases reveal the gloomy setting and create an eerie mood.

> A wind had sprung up, driving the dust of the weeks-dry road before it, when they entered the street on which they lived, and the leaves rustled ominously. Lightning flickered.
>
> —from "Rain, Rain, Go Away" by Isaac Asimov

Example
The highlighted words and details help you almost "see" the author's description.

> When he made a fist, his forearm tightened with muscles. His stomach was muscle, his legs muscle. His face was brown, like coffee laced with cream, and his hair black as a chunk of asphalt.
>
> —from *Taking Sides* by Gary Soto

MODEL 1: MOOD

Here, you see a New England autumn through the eyes of a girl from Barbados. Notice the words and details that are used to describe the setting. What mood do they help to create?

from
The Witch of Blackbird Pond

Novel by **Elizabeth George Speare**

. . . The October sun filled the world with mellow warmth. Before Kit's eyes a miracle took place, for which she was totally unprepared. She stood in the doorway of her uncle's house and held her breath with wonder. The maple tree in front of the doorstep burned like a gigantic
5 red torch. The oaks along the roadway glowed yellow and bronze. The fields stretched like a carpet of jewels, emerald and topaz and garnet. Everywhere she walked the color shouted and sang around her. The dried brown leaves crackled beneath her feet and gave off a delicious smoky fragrance. No one had ever told her about autumn in New
10 England. The excitement of it beat in her blood.

Close Read

1. Find two details that the writer uses to describe the setting. Then identify two details that tell you how Kit feels about her surroundings. One of each is boxed.

2. Judging by the details you found, how would you describe the mood?

MODEL 2: IMAGERY

When Roald Dahl was a boy, he spent a lot of time at the local candy shop. In this excerpt from his autobiography, Dahl uses imagery to describe the shop's owner, Mrs. Pratchett.

from
BOY: Tales of Childhood

Autobiography by **Roald Dahl**

But by far the most loathsome thing about Mrs. Pratchett was the filth that clung around her. Her apron was grey and greasy. Her blouse had bits of breakfast all over it, toast crumbs and tea stains and splotches of dried egg yolk. It was her hands, however, that disturbed us most.
5 They were disgusting. They were black with dirt and grime. They looked as though they had been putting lumps of coal on the fire all day long. And do not forget, please, that it was these very hands and fingers that she plunged into the sweet jars. . . .

Close Read

1. This excerpt includes words or phrases the writer chose to create a distinct feeling or impression. One example has been boxed. Find three more words or phrases.

2. Review the words you identified. How would you describe the overall mood that the imagery creates?

Part 2: What Is Style?

Mood and imagery can affect the way you feel about a work of literature. Style, though, is often what helps you recognize the writing of a particular author. In literature, **style** is the way something is written—not what is said, but *how* it's said. A writer's style can depend on **tone**, his or her attitude toward a subject. Style is made of such elements as sentence structure, word choice, and tone.

The celebrated author Gary Soto is known for his unique style of writing. Notice how three key elements help to create his one-of-a-kind style.

GARY SOTO'S STYLE

Soto sees himself as "someone who paints a vivid picture." He says, "Most of my writing is descriptive. You come away with clear pictures of the scene. . . ." Notice how Soto's style shines through in the examples from his novel *Taking Sides* and in one example from *A Summer Life*, a collection of essays about his childhood.

Word Choice

Style begins with **word choice,** a writer's use of words. With just a few descriptive verbs and adjectives, Soto puts you at the scene of a basketball practice.

Example

Shafts of afternoon sunlight glared on the polished gym floor.

Sentence Structure

Sentence structure refers to whether sentences are short and simple or long and complex. Notice how these sentences reflect the fast pace of a basketball game.

Example

Lincoln passed to James, who passed to Durkins, who took a shot and missed from the top of the key. But Lincoln pulled the ball down, chambered, and shot—*swish.*

Tone

Tone is how you imagine the writer "sounds." In one of Gary Soto's essays, notice his straightforward, good-natured tone.

Example

I began to think that mother was right when she said good manners were important. I began to say "yes," and not "uh-huh," and began to walk, not run when someone called. When my aunts kissed me on the cheek, I didn't turn away and make a sour face.

MODEL 1: STYLE IN SCIENCE FICTION

Many writers, including H. G. Wells, have crafted science fiction stories about time travel. Wells, who wrote *The Time Machine* in 1895, is known for his formal style and use of vivid imagery.

from

The Time Machine

Novel by **H. G. Wells**

. . . I made good my retreat to the narrow tunnel. But I had scarce entered this when my light was blown out, and in the blackness I could hear the Morlocks rustling like wind among leaves, and pattering like the rain, as they hurried after me.

5   In a moment I was clutched by several hands, and there was no mistaking that they were trying to haul me back. I struck another light, and waved it in their dazzled faces. You can scarce imagine how nauseatingly inhuman they looked—those pale, chinless faces and great, lidless, pinkish-grey eyes!—as they stared in their blindness
10   and bewilderment.

Close Read

1. Certain words and phrases, such as those in the boxed example, contribute to Wells's formal style. Find two more examples.

2. How would you describe the tone of this passage?

MODEL 2: STYLE IN SCIENCE FICTION

Here is an excerpt from another science fiction story, this one by a contemporary author with a much more informal style.

from

Future Tense

Short story by **Robert Lipsyte**

A half hour later, Mr. Smith called Gary out of Spanish. There was no expression on his regular features. He said, "I'm going to need some help with you."

Cold sweat covered Gary's body as Mr. Smith grabbed his arm and led
5   him to the new vice-principal. She read the composition while they waited. Gary got a good look at her for the first time. Ms. Jones was . . . just there. She looked as though she'd been manufactured to fit her name. Average. Standard. Typical. The cold sweat turned into goose pimples.

How could he have missed the clues? Smith and Jones were aliens!

Close Read

1. Look at the boxed phrases. How does Lipsyte's choice of words compare with Wells's?

2. What is the most striking difference between these two authors' styles? Consider word choice, sentence structure, and tone.

Part 3: Analyze the Text

A man goes out for a walk. What situation could be simpler? Both of the following excerpts begin with this setup. However, you will see how a story's mood, imagery, and style can make even the most similar situations seem very different.

from

One Ordinary Day, with Peanuts

Short story by **Shirley Jackson**

Mr. John Philip Johnson shut his front door behind him and went down his front steps into the bright morning with a feeling that all was well with the world on this best of all days, and wasn't the sun warm and good, and didn't his shoes feel comfortable after the resoling,
5 and he knew that he had undoubtedly chosen the very precise tie that belonged with the day and the sun and his comfortable feet, and, after all, wasn't the world just a wonderful place? In spite of the fact that he was a small man, and though the tie was perhaps a shade vivid, Mr. Johnson radiated a feeling of well-being as he went down the steps
10 and onto the dirty sidewalk, and he smiled at people who passed him, and some of them even smiled back. He stopped at the newsstand on the corner and bought his paper, saying, "*Good* morning" with real conviction to the man who sold him the paper and the two or three other people who were lucky enough to be buying papers when Mr.
15 Johnson skipped up. He remembered to fill his pockets with candy and peanuts, and then he set out to get himself uptown. He stopped in a flower shop and bought a carnation for his buttonhole, and stopped almost immediately afterward to give the carnation to a small child in a carriage, who looked at him dumbly, and then smiled, and Mr. Johnson
20 smiled, and the child's mother looked at Mr. Johnson for a minute and then smiled, too.

Close Read

1. What words and details in lines 1–7 help to create a cheerful mood?

2. Read the first sentence aloud. How would you describe its length and rhythm? Notice how the sentence structure reflects Mr. Johnson's carefree attitude.

3. Look at the boxed details. How do these phrases, which are all examples of imagery, contrast with the other details in the description of Mr. John Philip Johnson?

In this excerpt, Rip Van Winkle leaves his nagging wife and goes for a hike with his dog, Wolf. It won't take you long to notice the different "feeling" of this story. Read closely to find out what the author has done to create such a contrasting effect.

from

RIP VAN WINKLE

Short story by **Washington Irving**

. . . He looked down into a deep mountain glen, wild, lonely, and shagged, the bottom filled with fragments from the impending cliffs, and scarcely lighted by the reflected rays of the setting sun. For some time Rip lay musing[1] on this scene; evening was gradually advancing;
5   the mountains began to throw their long blue shadows over the valleys; he saw that it would be dark long before he could reach the village, and he heaved a heavy sigh when he thought of encountering the terrors of Dame Van Winkle.

   As he was about to descend, he heard a voice from a distance,
10   hallooing, "Rip Van Winkle! Rip Van Winkle!" He looked around, but could see nothing but a crow winging its solitary flight across the mountain. He thought his fancy[2] must have deceived him, and turned again to descend, when he heard the same cry ring through the still evening air; "Rip Van Winkle! Rip Van Winkle!"—at the
15   same time Wolf bristled up his back, and giving a low growl, skulked[3] to his master's side, looking fearfully down into the glen. Rip now felt a vague apprehension stealing over him; he looked anxiously in the same direction, and perceived a strange figure slowly toiling up the rocks, and bending under the weight of something he carried on his back.

---

1. **musing:** thinking or reflecting.
2. **fancy:** imagination.
3. **skulked:** moved fearfully.

Close Read

1. Examine the boxed words and details. What mood do they help to create?

2. Read lines 3–8 aloud and try to hear how the author "sounds" while describing Rip's thoughts. Is the author's tone serious or mocking? Explain.

3. Washington Irving is known for his use of formal words and phrases and long, complex sentences. Find two examples of each in this excerpt.

Dark They Were, and Golden-Eyed

HISTORY Video link at thinkcentral.com

Science Fiction by Ray Bradbury

VIDEO TRAILER THINK central   KEYWORD: HML7-460

Can where you are CHANGE who you are?

COMMON CORE

RL 1 Cite textual evidence to support inferences drawn from the text. **RL 3** Analyze how particular elements of a story interact. **RL 4** Determine the meaning of words and phrases as they are used in a text, including figurative and connotative meanings.

Your hobbies, interests, and habits often depend on the climate you are used to and the people and places you encounter every day. If you were to move away from everything you know, how much of who you are would change, and how much would stay the same? In "Dark They Were, and Golden-Eyed," a family moves to a very different environment and gets the chance to find out.

DISCUSS With a group, discuss your thoughts about the question at the top of the page. Take turns answering the question and explaining your reasons. Record the group's responses on a chart like the one shown.

Can Where You Are Change Who You Are?		
Name	Yes or No	Why or Why Not?

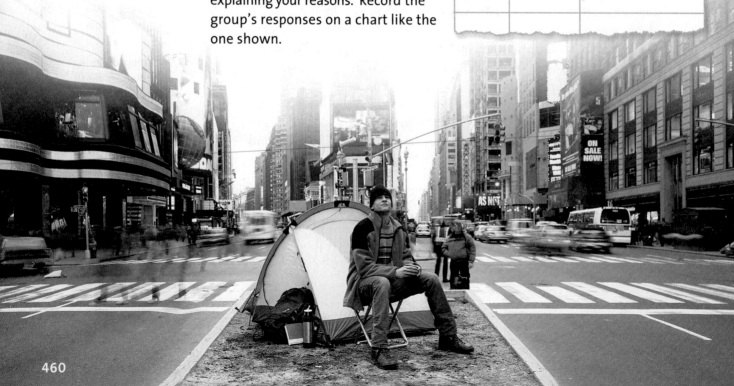

● TEXT ANALYSIS: MOOD

Has a story ever made you feel hopeful, nervous, or completely terrified? The feeling you get from a story is called the **mood.** Writers create a mood by

- carefully choosing words to describe the **plot, setting,** and **characters**
- showing what characters think and how they talk

Identifying mood can help you understand a story. As you read "Dark They Were, and Golden-Eyed," think about how it makes you feel, and what words affect you.

● READING STRATEGY: READING SCIENCE FICTION

In **science fiction,** writers often explore the future. They blend scientific facts and theories and familiar elements of real life with their own ideas.

Although science fiction writers portray future times and places, their themes often comment on the problems of today's world. As you read Ray Bradbury's story, use a chart to note characteristics of science fiction.

Characteristics of Science Fiction	Examples in the Story
scientific information	
familiar elements of life today	
imaginary worlds and situations	

Review: Make Inferences

▲ VOCABULARY IN CONTEXT

Bradbury's **word choice** affects the **mood** of his story. Match each numbered word or phrase with a vocabulary word.

WORD LIST		
convivial	forlorn	recede
dwindle	muse	subtly
flimsy	pendulum	

1. friendly
2. indirectly
3. hanging weight
4. decrease
5. become distant
6. daydream
7. lonely
8. breakable

Complete the activities in your **Reader/Writer Notebook.**

Ray Bradbury
born 1920

An Early Start
Ray Bradbury credits his mother for encouraging his imagination. She loved films and started taking her son to see them when he was only 3. By age 8, Bradbury had developed a love for both science fiction and the planet Mars. Bradbury wrote his first Martian stories when he was 12. Just before his 21st birthday, Bradbury sold his first story. That began a career filled with bestsellers, awards, and a lasting love of writing.

Man with a Mission Bradbury believes that one purpose of science fiction is to warn about negative things that might happen in the future if care is not taken in the present. Some of his writing reflects his worries about where our society is headed.

BACKGROUND TO THE STORY

Red Planet Mars has been the setting of many science fiction films and stories, including "Dark They Were, and Golden-Eyed." Films and stories about Mars rarely give a realistic description of the planet, but they often incorporate elements of actual scientific research and developments in space travel.

Author Online
THINK central
Go to **thinkcentral.com.**
KEYWORD: HML7-461

DARK THEY WERE, AND GOLDEN-EYED

RAY BRADBURY

The rocket metal cooled in the meadow winds. Its lid gave a bulging *pop*. From its clock interior stepped a man, a woman, and three children. The other passengers whispered away across the Martian meadow, leaving the man alone among his family.

The man felt his hair flutter and the tissues of his body draw tight as if he were standing at the center of a vacuum. His wife, before him, seemed almost to whirl away in smoke. The children, small seeds, might at any instant be sown to all the Martian climes.

The children looked up at him, as people look to the sun to tell what time of their life it is. His face was cold.

"What's wrong?" asked his wife.

"Let's get back on the rocket." ⒜

"Go back to Earth?"

"Yes! Listen!"

Analyze Visuals ▶

What can you **infer** about how the person in the painting might be feeling?

Ⓐ **MOOD**
How would you describe the man's first impression of Mars? Think about how his feelings affect the mood of the story.

Sugar Sphinx (1933), Salvador Dali. Oil on canvas.
© 2008 Artists Rights Society (ARS), New York.
© Salvador Dali. Gala-Salvador Dali Foundation.

The wind blew as if to flake away their identities. At any moment the Martian air might draw his soul from him, as marrow comes from a white bone. He felt submerged in a chemical that could dissolve his intellect and burn away his past.

They looked at Martian hills that time had worn with a crushing
20 pressure of years. They saw the old cities, lost in their meadows, lying like children's delicate bones among the blowing lakes of grass.

"Chin up, Harry," said his wife. "It's too late. We've come over sixty million miles."

The children with their yellow hair hollered at the deep dome of Martian sky. There was no answer but the racing hiss of wind through the stiff grass. **B**

He picked up the luggage in his cold hands. "Here we go," he said— a man standing on the edge of a sea, ready to wade in and be drowned.

They walked into town.

30 Their name was Bittering. Harry and his wife Cora; Dan, Laura, and David. They built a small white cottage and ate good breakfasts there, but the fear was never gone. It lay with Mr. Bittering and Mrs. Bittering, a third unbidden partner at every midnight talk, at every dawn awakening.

"I feel like a salt crystal," he said, "in a mountain stream, being washed away. We don't belong here. We're Earth people. This is Mars. It was meant for Martians. For heaven's sake, Cora, let's buy tickets for home!"

But she only shook her head. "One day the atom bomb will fix Earth. Then we'll be safe here."

"Safe and insane!"

40 *Tick-tock, seven o'clock* sang the voice-clock; *time to get up.* And they did.

Something made him check everything each morning—warm hearth, potted blood-geraniums—precisely as if he expected something to be amiss. The morning paper was toast-warm from the 6 A.M. Earth rocket. He broke its seal and tilted it at his breakfast place. He forced himself to be **convivial**. **C**

"Colonial days all over again," he declared. "Why, in ten years there'll be a million Earthmen on Mars. Big cities, everything! They said we'd fail. Said the Martians would resent our invasion. But did we find any Martians? Not a living soul! Oh, we found their empty cities, but no one
50 in them. Right?"

A river of wind submerged the house. When the windows ceased rattling Mr. Bittering swallowed and looked at the children.

"I don't know," said David. "Maybe there're Martians around we don't see. Sometimes nights I think I hear 'em. I hear the wind. The sand hits my window. I get scared. And I see those towns way up in the mountains where the Martians lived a long time ago. And I think I see things moving

---

B **MOOD**
Reread lines 15–26. On the basis of Bradbury's description of the **setting,** decide whether you have a positive or negative feeling about Mars. What words contribute to your feeling?

convivial
(kən-vĭv′ē-əl) *adj.* enjoying the company of others; sociable

C **READING SCIENCE FICTION**
Reread lines 40–45. What are three examples of how Bradbury brings present-day life into this futuristic **setting?** Jot down these examples in your chart.

around those towns, Papa. And I wonder if those Martians *mind* us living here. I wonder if they won't do something to us for coming here."

"Nonsense!" Mr. Bittering looked out the windows. "We're clean, decent
60 people." He looked at his children. "All dead cities have some kind of ghosts in them. Memories, I mean." He stared at the hills. "You see a staircase and you wonder what Martians looked like climbing it. You see Martian paintings and you wonder what the painter was like. You make a little ghost in your mind, a memory. It's quite natural. Imagination." He stopped. "You haven't been prowling up in those ruins, have you?"

"No, Papa." David looked at his shoes.

"See that you stay away from them. Pass the jam."

"Just the same," said little David, "I bet something happens."

Something happened that afternoon. Laura stumbled through
70 the settlement, crying. She dashed blindly onto the porch.

"Mother, Father—the war, Earth!" she sobbed. "A radio flash just came. Atom bombs[1] hit New York! All the space rockets blown up. No more rockets to Mars, ever!"

"Oh, Harry!" The mother held onto her husband and daughter.

"Are you sure, Laura?" asked the father quietly.

Laura wept. "We're stranded on Mars, forever and ever!"

For a long time there was only the sound of the wind in the late afternoon.

Alone, thought Bittering. Only a thousand of us here. No way back.
80 No way. No way. Sweat poured from his face and his hands and his body; he was drenched in the hotness of his fear. He wanted to strike Laura, cry, "No, you're lying! The rockets will come back!" Instead, he stroked Laura's head against him and said, "The rockets will get through someday."

"Father, what will we do?"

"Go about our business, of course. Raise crops and children. Wait. Keep things going until the war ends and the rockets come again."

The two boys stepped out onto the porch.

"Children," he said, sitting there, looking beyond them, "I've something
90 to tell you."

"We know," they said.

In the following days, Bittering wandered often through the garden to stand alone in his fear. As long as the rockets had spun a silver web

SCIENCE CONNECTION

Robotic equipment sent to Mars to gather data has shown that the planet has no signs of civilization, though there is some evidence of water on its surface.

D MOOD
Reread lines 79–84. Note that Bradbury uses sentence fragments to portray Bittering's thoughts. How does this help create a mood?

___

1. **atom bombs:** In 1945 the United States dropped atomic bombs over the cities of Hiroshima and Nagasaki, in Japan, killing over 100,000 people and injuring many thousands more.

across space, he had been able to accept Mars. For he had always told himself: Tomorrow, if I want, I can buy a ticket and go back to Earth.

But now: The web gone, the rockets lying in jigsaw heaps of molten girder and unsnaked wire. Earth people left to the strangeness of Mars, the cinnamon dusts and wine airs, to be baked like gingerbread shapes in Martian summers, put into harvested storage by Martian winters. 100 What would happen to him, the others? This was the moment Mars had waited for. Now it would eat them.

He got down on his knees in the flower bed, a spade in his nervous hands. Work, he thought, work and forget.

He glanced up from the garden to the Martian mountains. He thought of the proud old Martian names that had once been on those peaks. Earthmen, dropping from the sky, had gazed upon hills, rivers, Martian seats left nameless in spite of names. Once Martians had built cities, named cities; climbed mountains, named mountains; sailed seas, named seas. Mountains melted, seas drained, cities tumbled. In spite of this, the Earthmen had felt 110 a silent guilt at putting new names to these ancient hills and valleys. **E**

Nevertheless, man lives by symbol and label. The names were given.

Mr. Bittering felt very alone in his garden under the Martian sun, anachronism[2] bent here, planting Earth flowers in a wild soil.

Think. Keep thinking. Different things. Keep your mind free of Earth, the atom war, the lost rockets.

He perspired. He glanced about. No one watching. He removed his tie. Pretty bold, he thought. First your coat off, now your tie. He hung it neatly on a peach tree he had imported as a sapling from Massachusetts.

He returned to his philosophy of names and mountains. The Earthmen 120 had changed names. Now there were Hormel Valleys, Roosevelt[3] Seas, Ford Hills, Vanderbilt Plateaus, Rockefeller[4] Rivers, on Mars. It wasn't right. The American settlers had shown wisdom, using old Indian prairie names: Wisconsin, Minnesota, Idaho, Ohio, Utah, Milwaukee, Waukegan, Osseo. The old names, the old meanings.

Staring at the mountains wildly, he thought: Are you up there? All the dead ones, you Martians? Well, here we are, alone, cut off! Come down, move us out! We're helpless!

The wind blew a shower of peach blossoms.

He put out his sun-browned hand and gave a small cry. He touched 130 the blossoms and picked them up. He turned them, he touched them again and again. Then he shouted for his wife.

"Cora!"

She appeared at a window. He ran to her.

E READING SCIENCE FICTION
Reread lines 107–110. On the basis of these past accomplishments, consider the similarities between Martian and human civilizations. What comment about present-day human civilization might Bradbury be making through this comparison? Record the comment in your chart.

---

2. **anachronism** (ə-năk′rə-nĭz′əm): something placed outside of its proper time period.

3. **Roosevelt:** most likely refers to Franklin Delano Roosevelt, the 32nd president of the United States.

4. **Hormel...Ford...Vanderbilt...Rockefeller:** names of industrial and financial "giants" in American history.

Shellfish Flowers (1929), Max Ernst. Oil on canvas, 129 cm × 129 cm. Inv.: R 19 P. Photo Jean-Francois Tomasian. Musée National d'Art Moderne, Centre Georges Pompidou, Paris. © 2008 Artists Rights Society (ARS), New York/ADAGP, Paris.

◀ **Analyze Visuals**
Compare these flowers to the ones on Mars in the story. How are they similar?

"Cora, these blossoms!"

She handled them.

"Do you see? They're different. They've changed! They're not peach blossoms any more!"

"Look all right to me," she said.

"They're not. They're wrong! I can't tell how. An extra petal, a leaf, 140 something, the color, the smell!"

The children ran out in time to see their father hurrying about the garden, pulling up radishes, onions, and carrots from their beds.

"Cora, come look!"

They handled the onions, the radishes, the carrots among them.

"Do they look like carrots?"

"Yes . . . no." She hesitated. "I don't know."

"They're changed."

"Perhaps."

"You know they have! Onions but not onions, carrots but not carrots. 150 Taste: the same but different. Smell: not like it used to be." He felt his heart pounding, and he was afraid. He dug his fingers into the earth. "Cora, what's happening? What is it? We've got to get away from this." He ran across the garden. Each tree felt his touch. "The roses. The roses. They're turning green!" **F**

F READING SCIENCE FICTION
Think of what you know about plants. Do you think it's possible for plants to change like they do in this story, or is it purely imaginary?

DARK THEY WERE, AND GOLDEN-EYED **467**

And they stood looking at the green roses.

And two days later Dan came running. "Come see the cow. I was milking her and I saw it. Come on!"

They stood in the shed and looked at their one cow.

It was growing a third horn.

160 And the lawn in front of their house very quietly and slowly was coloring itself like spring violets. Seed from Earth but growing up a soft purple.

"We must get away," said Bittering. "We'll eat this stuff and then we'll change—who knows to what? I can't let it happen. There's only one thing to do. Burn this food!" **G**

"It's not poisoned."

"But it is. **Subtly,** very subtly. A little bit. A very little bit. We mustn't touch it."

He looked with dismay at their house. "Even the house. The wind's done something to it. The air's burned it. The fog at night. The boards,
170 all warped out of shape. It's not an Earthman's house any more."

"Oh, your imagination!"

He put on his coat and tie. "I'm going into town. We've got to do something now. I'll be back."

"Wait, Harry!" his wife cried. But he was gone.

In town, on the shadowy step of the grocery store, the men sat with their hands on their knees, conversing with great leisure and ease.

Mr. Bittering wanted to fire a pistol in the air.

What are you doing, you fools! he thought. Sitting here! You've heard the news—we're stranded on this planet. Well, move! Aren't you
180 frightened? Aren't you afraid? What are you going to do?

"Hello, Harry," said everyone.

"Look," he said to them. "You did hear the news, the other day, didn't you?"

They nodded and laughed. "Sure. Sure, Harry."

"What are you going to do about it?"

"Do, Harry, do? What *can* we do?"

"Build a rocket, that's what!"

"A rocket, Harry? To go back to all that trouble? Oh, Harry!"

"But you *must* want to go back. Have you noticed the peach blossoms,
190 the onions, the grass?"

"Why, yes, Harry, seems we did," said one of the men.

"Doesn't it scare you?"

"Can't recall that it did much, Harry." **H**

"Idiots!"

"Now, Harry."

G MOOD
When he sees that the plants and animals are changing, Mr. Bittering becomes afraid that he and his family will change too. What impact does this **plot** turn have on the mood of the story?

subtly (sŭt′lē) *adv.* not obviously; in a manner hard to notice or perceive

H MOOD
How do the **characters'** reactions to the situation make you feel?

Bittering wanted to cry. "You've got to work with me. If we stay here, we'll all change. The air. Don't you smell it? Something in the air. A Martian virus, maybe; some seed, or a pollen. Listen to me!"

They stared at him.

200 "Sam," he said to one of them.

"Yes, Harry?"

"Will you help me build a rocket?"

"Harry, I got a whole load of metal and some blueprints. You want to work in my metal shop on a rocket, you're welcome. I'll sell you that metal for five hundred dollars. You should be able to construct a right pretty rocket, if you work alone, in about thirty years."

Everyone laughed.

"Don't laugh."

Sam looked at him with quiet good humor.

210 "Sam," Bittering said. "Your eyes—"

"What about them, Harry?"

"Didn't they used to be gray?"

"Well now, I don't remember."

"They were, weren't they?"

"Why do you ask, Harry?"

"Because now they're kind of yellow-colored."

"Is that so, Harry?" Sam said, casually.

"And you're taller and thinner—"

"You might be right, Harry."

220 "Sam, you shouldn't have yellow eyes." **I**

"Harry, what color eyes have *you* got?" Sam said.

"My eyes? They're blue, of course."

"Here you are, Harry." Sam handed him a pocket mirror. "Take a look at yourself."

Mr. Bittering hesitated, and then raised the mirror to his face.

There were little, very dim flecks of new gold captured in the blue of his eyes.

"Now look what you've done," said Sam a moment later. "You've broken my mirror." **J**

230 Harry Bittering moved into the metal shop and began to build the rocket. Men stood in the open door and talked and joked without raising their voices. Once in a while they gave him a hand on lifting something. But mostly they just idled and watched him with their yellowing eyes.

"It's suppertime, Harry," they said.

His wife appeared with his supper in a wicker basket.

I READING SCIENCE FICTION
Are the changes in Sam's appearance realistic according to the laws of science, or is Bradbury using his imagination here?

J MAKE INFERENCES
Why did Sam's mirror break?

"I won't touch it," he said. "I'll eat only food from our Deepfreeze. Food that came from Earth. Nothing from our garden."

His wife stood watching him. "You can't build a rocket."

240 "I worked in a shop once, when I was twenty. I know metal. Once I get it started, the others will help," he said, not looking at her, laying out the blueprints.

"Harry, Harry," she said, helplessly.

"We've *got* to get away, Cora. We've got to!"

The nights were full of wind that blew down the empty moonlit sea meadows past the little white chess cities lying for their twelve-thousandth year in the shallows. In the Earthmen's settlement, the Bittering house shook with a feeling of change.

Lying abed, Mr. Bittering felt his bones shifted, shaped, melted like gold. 250 His wife, lying beside him, was dark from many sunny afternoons. Dark she was, and golden-eyed, burnt almost black by the sun, sleeping, and the children metallic in their beds, and the wind roaring **forlorn** and changing through the old peach trees, the violet grass, shaking out green rose petals. **K**

The fear would not be stopped. It had his throat and heart. It dripped in a wetness of the arm and the temple and the trembling palm.

A green star rose in the east.

A strange word emerged from Mr. Bittering's lips.

"Iorrt. Iorrt." He repeated it.

260 It was a Martian word. He knew no Martian.

In the middle of the night he arose and dialed a call through to Simpson, the archaeologist.

"Simpson, what does the word *Iorrt* mean?"

"Why that's the old Martian word for our planet Earth. Why?"

The Forest (1950), Alberto Giacometti. Bronze, painted, 22" x 24" x 19 1/4". Gift of Enid Haupt. National Gallery of Art, Washington, D.C. © National Gallery of Art, Washington, D.C. © 2008 Artists Rights Society (ARS), New York/ADAGP, Paris.

COMMON CORE RL 4

K MOOD
Reread lines 245–253. Notice the language Bradbury uses to describe the setting and characters. Writers use language that will help the reader sense the feeling of a scene. In addition, notice the sentence structure, such as "Dark she was . . ." What mood do these elements create?

forlorn (fər-lôrn´) *adj.* appearing lonely or sad

◀ **Analyze Visuals**
If this sculpture had been made specifically for this story, which figure would represent Harry?

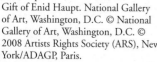

"No special reason."

270 The telephone slipped from his hand.

"Hello, hello, hello, hello," it kept saying while he sat gazing out at the green star. "Bittering? Harry, are you there?"

The days were full of metal sound. He laid the frame of the rocket with the reluctant help of three indifferent men. He grew very tired in an hour or so and had to sit down. ◆

"The altitude," laughed a man.

"Are you *eating,* Harry?" asked another.

"I'm eating," he said, angrily.

"From your Deepfreeze?"

280 "Yes!"

"You're getting thinner, Harry."

"I'm not!"

"And taller."

"Liar!"

His wife took him aside a few days later. "Harry, I've used up all the food in the Deepfreeze. There's nothing left. I'll have to make sandwiches using food grown on Mars."

He sat down heavily.

"You must eat," she said. "You're weak."

290 "Yes," he said.

He took a sandwich, opened it, looked at it, and began to nibble at it.

"And take the rest of the day off," she said. "It's hot. The children want to swim in the canals and hike. Please come along."

"I can't waste time. This is a crisis!"

"Just for an hour," she urged. "A swim'll do you good."

He rose, sweating. "All right, all right. Leave me alone. I'll come."

"Good for you, Harry."

The sun was hot, the day quiet. There was only an immense staring burn upon the land. They moved along the canal, the father, the mother,

300 the racing children in their swimsuits. They stopped and ate meat sandwiches. He saw their skin baking brown. And he saw the yellow eyes of his wife and his children, their eyes that were never yellow before. A few tremblings shook him, but were carried off in waves of pleasant heat as he lay in the sun. He was too tired to be afraid. ❶

"Cora, how long have your eyes been yellow?"

She was bewildered. "Always, I guess."

"They didn't change from brown in the last three months?"

She bit her lips. "No. Why do you ask?"

"Never mind."

◆ **GRAMMAR IN CONTEXT**
In lines 274–275, notice how Bradbury uses the prepositional phrase, *in an hour or so.* The verb that follows the phrase agrees with the subject, *He.*

❶ **MOOD**
Reread lines 301–304. Note how different Harry's attitude is now than it was before. What effect does this change have on you as a reader?

310   They sat there.

"The children's eyes," he said. "They're yellow, too."

"Sometimes growing children's eyes change color."

"Maybe *we're* children, too. At least to Mars. That's a thought." He laughed. "Think I'll swim."

They leaped into the canal water, and he let himself sink down and down to the bottom like a golden statue and lie there in green silence. All was water-quiet and deep, all was peace. He felt the steady, slow current drift him easily.

If I lie here long enough, he thought, the water will work and eat away 320 my flesh until the bones show like coral. Just my skeleton left. And then the water can build on that skeleton—green things, deep water things, red things, yellow things. Change. Change. Slow, deep, silent change. And isn't that what it is up *there*?

He saw the sky submerged above him, the sun made Martian by atmosphere and time and space.

Up there, a big river, he thought, a Martian river; all of us lying deep in it, in our pebble houses, in our sunken boulder houses, like crayfish hidden, and the water washing away our old bodies and lengthening the bones and—

330   He let himself drift up through the soft light.

Dan sat on the edge of the canal, regarding his father seriously.

"*Utha*," he said.

"What?" asked his father.

The boy smiled. "You know. *Utha's* the Martian word for 'father.'"

"Where did you learn it?"

"I don't know. Around. *Utha!*"

"What do you want?"

The boy hesitated. "I—I want to change my name."

"Change it?"

340   "Yes."

His mother swam over. "What's wrong with Dan for a name?"

Dan fidgeted. "The other day you called Dan, Dan, Dan. I didn't even hear. I said to myself, That's not my name. I've a new name I want to use."

Mr. Bittering held to the side of the canal, his body cold and his heart pounding slowly. "What is this new name?"

"Linnl. Isn't that a good name? Can I use it? Can't I, please?" Ⓜ

Mr. Bittering put his hand to his head. He thought of the silly rocket, himself working alone, himself alone even among his family, so alone.

350   He heard his wife say, "Why not?"

He heard himself say, "Yes, you can use it."

"Yaaa!" screamed the boy. "I'm Linnl, Linnl!"

Language Coach

Simile A simile is a comparison using *like* or *as*. Reread lines 315–316. The simile compares the sensation of Harry's sinking to the sinking of a golden statue. A golden statue would be quite heavy. Based on the comparison, does Harry sink quickly or slowly?

Ⓜ MAKE INFERENCES
Why does Dan want to change his name?

Racing down the meadowlands, he danced and shouted.

Mr. Bittering looked at his wife. "Why did we do that?"

"I don't know," she said. "It just seemed like a good idea."

They walked into the hills. They strolled on old mosaic paths, beside still pumping fountains. The paths were covered with a thin film of cool water all summer long. You kept your bare feet cool all the day, splashing as in a creek, wading.

360 They came to a small deserted Martian villa with a good view of the valley. It was on top of a hill. Blue marble halls, large murals, a swimming pool. It was refreshing in this hot summertime. The Martians hadn't believed in large cities.

"How nice," said Mrs. Bittering, "if we could move up here to this villa for the summer."

"Come on," he said. "We're going back to town. There's work to be done on the rocket."

But as he worked that night, the thought of the cool blue marble villa entered his mind. As the hours passed, the rocket seemed
370 less important.

In the flow of days and weeks, the rocket **receded** and **dwindled.** The old fever was gone. It frightened him to think he had let it slip this way. But somehow the heat, the air, the working conditions—

He heard the men murmuring on the porch of his metal shop.

"Everyone's going. You heard?"

"All going. That's right."

Bittering came out. "Going where?" He saw a couple of trucks, loaded with children and furniture, drive down the dusty street.

"Up to the villas," said the man.

380 "Yeah, Harry. I'm going. So is Sam. Aren't you Sam?"

"That's right, Harry. What about you?"

"I've got work to do here."

"Work! You can finish that rocket in the autumn, when it's cooler."

He took a breath. "I got the frame all set up."

"In the autumn is better." Their voices were lazy in the heat.

"Got to work," he said.

"Autumn," they reasoned. And they sounded so sensible, so right.

"Autumn would be best," he thought. "Plenty of time, then."

No! cried part of himself, deep down, put away, locked tight,
390 suffocating. No! No!

"In the autumn," he said.

"Come on, Harry," they all said.

"Yes," he said, feeling his flesh melt in the hot liquid air. "Yes, in the autumn. I'll begin work again then."

Detail from *Figures Crossing River on Gold Coins*, Andrew Judd. ©Andrew Judd/Masterfile.

▲ **Analyze Visuals**

What is the **mood** of this painting? Explain what elements help create this mood.

"I got a villa near the Tirra Canal," said someone.

"You mean the Roosevelt Canal, don't you?"

"Tirra. The old Martian name."

"But on the map—"

"Forget the map. It's Tirra now. Now I found a place in the Pillan
400 Mountains—"

"You mean the Rockefeller Range," said Bittering.

"I mean the Pillan Mountains," said Sam.

"Yes," said Bittering, buried in the hot, swarming air. "The Pillan Mountains."

Everyone worked at loading the truck in the hot, still afternoon of the next day.

Laura, Dan, and David carried packages. Or, as they preferred to be known, Ttil, Linnl, and Werr carried packages.

The furniture was abandoned in the little white cottage.

410 "It looked just fine in Boston," said the mother. "And here in the cottage. But up at the villa? No. We'll get it when we come back in the autumn."

Bittering himself was quiet.

"I've some ideas on furniture for the villa," he said after a time. "Big, lazy furniture."

"What about your encyclopedia? You're taking it along, surely?"

READING SCIENCE FICTION

Why is it significant that the people are changing the names of the landmarks and themselves?

Mr. Bittering glanced away. "I'll come and get it next week."

They turned to their daughter. "What about your New York dresses?"

The bewildered girl stared. "Why, I don't want them any more."

420 They shut off the gas, the water, they locked the doors and walked away. Father peered into the truck.

"Gosh, we're not taking much," he said. "Considering all we brought to Mars, this is only a handful!" **P**

He started the truck.

Looking at the small white cottage for a long moment, he was filled with a desire to rush to it, touch it, say good-bye to it, for he felt as if he were going away on a long journey, leaving something to which he could never quite return, never understand again.

Just then Sam and his family drove by in another truck.

430 "Hi, Bittering! Here we go!"

The truck swung down the ancient highway out of town. There were sixty others traveling in the same direction. The town filled with a silent, heavy dust from their passage. The canal waters lay blue in the sun, and a quiet wind moved in the strange trees.

"Good-bye, town!" said Mr. Bittering.

"Good-bye, good-bye," said the family, waving to it.

They did not look back again.

Summer burned the canals dry. Summer moved like flame upon the meadows. In the empty Earth settlement, the painted houses flaked

440 and peeled. Rubber tires upon which children had swung in back yards hung suspended like stopped clock **pendulums** in the blazing air.

At the metal shop, the rocket frame began to rust.

In the quiet autumn Mr. Bittering stood, very dark now, very golden-eyed, upon the slope above his villa, looking at the valley.

"It's time to go back," said Cora.

"Yes, but we're not going," he said quietly. "There's nothing there any more."

"Your books," she said. "Your fine clothes."

"Your *llles* and your fine *ior uele rre*," she said.

450 "The town's empty. No one's going back," he said. "There's no reason to, none at all."

The daughter wove tapestries and the sons played songs on ancient flutes and pipes, their laughter echoing in the marble villa.

Mr. Bittering gazed at the Earth settlement far away in the low valley. "Such odd, such ridiculous houses the Earth people built."

"They didn't know any better," his wife **mused**. "Such ugly people. I'm glad they've gone."

P MOOD
Reread lines 410–423. What effect does this **dialogue** have on the overall mood of the story?

pendulum (pĕn'jə-ləm) *n.* a weight hung so that it can swing freely, sometimes used in timing the workings of certain clocks

muse (myōōz) *v.* to say thoughtfully

They both looked at each other, startled by all they had just finished saying. They laughed.

460 "Where did they go?" he wondered. He glanced at his wife. She was golden and slender as his daughter. She looked at him, and he seemed almost as young as their eldest son. **Q**

"I don't know," she said.

"We'll go back to town maybe next year, or the year after, or the year after that," he said, calmly. "Now—I'm warm. How about taking a swim?"

They turned their backs to the valley. Arm in arm they walked silently down a path of clear-running spring water.

Five years later a rocket fell out of the sky. It lay steaming in the
470 valley. Men leaped out of it, shouting.

"We won the war on Earth! We're here to rescue you! Hey!"

But the American-built town of cottages, peach trees, and theaters was silent. They found a **flimsy** rocket frame rusting in an empty shop.

The rocket men searched the hills. The captain established headquarters in an abandoned bar. His lieutenant came back to report.

"The town's empty, but we found native life in the hills, sir. Dark people. Yellow eyes. Martians. Very friendly. We talked a bit, not much. They learn English fast. I'm sure our relations will be most friendly with them, sir."

"Dark, eh?" mused the captain. "How many?"

480 "Six, eight hundred, I'd say, living in those marble ruins in the hills, sir. Tall, healthy. Beautiful women."

"Did they tell you what became of the men and women who built this Earth settlement, Lieutenant?"

"They hadn't the foggiest notion of what happened to this town or its people."

"Strange. You think those Martians killed them?"

"They look surprisingly peaceful. Chances are a plague did this town in, sir."

"Perhaps. I suppose this is one of those mysteries we'll never solve.
490 One of those mysteries you read about." **R**

The captain looked at the room, the dusty windows, the blue mountains rising beyond, the canals moving in the light, and he heard the soft wind in the air. He shivered. Then, recovering, he tapped a large fresh map he had thumbtacked to the top of an empty table.

"Lots to be done, Lieutenant." His voice droned on and quietly on as the sun sank behind the blue hills. "New settlements. Mining sites, minerals to be looked for. Bacteriological specimens[5] taken. The work, all the work.

Q **READING SCIENCE FICTION**
Reread lines 460–462. Find details that tell you how the Bitterings have changed since they first arrived on Mars. Are they still human?

flimsy (flĭm′zē) *adj.* not solid or strong

R **MAKE INFERENCES**
What do you think will happen to the captain and the lieutenant?

---

5. **bacteriological specimens:** samples of different kinds of single-celled living things.

The Whole City (1935), Max Ernst. Oil on canvas, 60 cm × 81 cm. Kunsthaus, Zurich, Switzerland. © 2008 Artists Rights Society (ARS), New York/ADAGP, Paris.

And the old records were lost. We'll have a job of remapping to do, renaming the mountains and rivers and such. Calls for a little imagination.

500   "What do you think of naming those mountains the Lincoln Mountains, this canal the Washington Canal, those hills—we can name those hills for you, Lieutenant. Diplomacy. And you, for a favor, might name a town for me. Polishing the apple.[6] And why not make this the Einstein Valley, and farther over . . . are you *listening,* Lieutenant?"

The lieutenant snapped his gaze from the blue color and the quiet mist of the hills far beyond the town.

"What? Oh, *yes,* sir!" ❧

---

6. **polishing the apple:** acting in a way to get on the good side of another person.

NEWSPAPER ARTICLE As you read this interview, you'll find out how Ray Bradbury views himself as an author, how he writes stories like "Dark They Were, and Golden-Eyed," and what advice he has for beginning writers.

An Interview with
RAY BRADBURY

Q: You don't consider yourself a science fiction writer, even though others call you that. How do you see yourself?

A: I am a collector of metaphors. Any idea that strikes me I run with. . . .

I wrote *The October Country*, which is weird fantasy. There is no science fiction there. And *Halloween Tree*, which is a history of Halloween. And *Dandelion Wine*, which is my childhood in Illinois. *Something Wicked This Way Comes*, which is also my childhood plus fantasy. So when you look at the spread of things, there is only one novel that is science fiction. And that's *Fahrenheit 451*. In other words,

science fiction is the art of the possible, not the art of the impossible. As soon as you deal with things that can't happen you are writing fantasy.

Q: Walk me through your daily inspiration and writing process.

A: I just wake up with ideas every morning from my subconscious percolating. At 7 in the morning I lie in bed and I watch all the fragments of ideas swarming around in my head and these voices talk to me. And when they get to a certain point, I jump out of bed and run to the typewriter. So I'm not in control. Two hours later I have a new short story or an essay or part of a play. . . .

Q: What kind of advice would you give beginning writers?

A: Explode. Don't intellectualize. Get passionate about ideas. Cram your head full of images. Stay in the library. Stay off the Internet. Read all the great books. Read all the great poetry. See all the great films. Fill your life with metaphors. And then explode. And you're bound to do something good.

Comprehension

1. **Recall** Why do the Bitterings settle on Mars?

2. **Recall** Why do the rockets from Earth stop coming to Mars?

3. **Represent** Create a timeline of the main events of the story, including the physical changes Harry notices in the people and things around him.

Text Analysis

4. **Identify Mood** Before you read the story, you were asked to consider, as you read, how Bradbury's choice of words affected the way you felt. Now think of the story as a whole. What words would you use to describe the overall mood of the story? Cite examples of Bradbury's use of language to support your response.

5. **Analyze Science Fiction** Although this story was originally published in 1949, some of Bradbury's comments about life in the real world or about human nature still ring true. In portraying human life on Mars, what do you think Bradbury was saying about human nature?

6. **Analyze Character** Harry changes throughout the story. Using an organizer like the one shown, record his attitude and appearance at the beginning, middle, and end of the story.

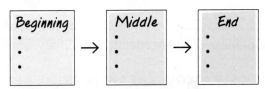

7. **Make Inferences** Who do you think will resist change the most, the captain or the lieutenant? Use examples from the story to support your answer.

8. **Evaluate Science Fiction** Reread Bradbury's first answer from the interview on page 478. Note that he does not consider himself a science fiction writer. In light of this information, do you think it is right to label "Dark They Were, and Golden-Eyed" as science fiction? Explain your answer, using support from the selection, the chart you created as you read, and the interview.

Extension and Challenge

9. **SCIENCE CONNECTION** Find out more about Mars by visiting the library in your school or neighborhood. What do we now know about the planet? What plans are scientists making to study it further? Focus your research on what interests you most. Report your findings to the class.

Can where you are CHANGE who you are?

Recall the chart you created on page 460. Now that you've read about the experience of the Bittering family, have you changed your mind about how a place might change you? Explain.

COMMON CORE

RL 1 Cite textual evidence to support inferences drawn from the text. **RL 3** Analyze how particular elements of a story interact. **RL 4** Determine the meaning of words and phrases as they are used in a text, including figurative and connotative meanings.

Vocabulary in Context

▲ VOCABULARY PRACTICE

Write the letter of the phrase that has a connection to each vocabulary word.

1. **pendulum:** (a) a grandfather clock, (b) a racing motorcycle, (c) a gossiping man
2. **forlorn:** (a) a heavy snowfall, (b) a bitter quarrel, (c) a lonely child
3. **dwindle:** (a) your supply of money, (b) your age, (c) your science textbook
4. **subtly:** (a) a fireworks show, (b) a gradually dimming light, (c) a long bus ride
5. **convivial:** (a) a dog and a squirrel, (b) a friendly crowd, (c) a curving staircase
6. **flimsy:** (a) a stuffed chair, (b) a weak argument, (c) a party in a yard
7. **recede:** (a) a plane flying away, (b) an arriving plane, (c) a plane parked at a gate
8. **muse:** (a) a noisy band, (b) a person considering choices, (c) a windy day

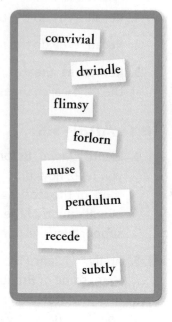

convivial
dwindle
flimsy
forlorn
muse
pendulum
recede
subtly

ACADEMIC VOCABULARY IN WRITING

> • communicate • describe • illustrate • interpret • style

In a paragraph, **describe** the series of changes that affect the Bitterings. Try to use one or more of the Academic Vocabulary words in your paragraph.

VOCABULARY STRATEGY: THE LATIN ROOT *pend*

The vocabulary word *pendulum* contains the Latin root *pend*, which means "hang." This root, which is sometimes spelled *pens*, is found in many English words. To understand the meaning of words with *pend or pens*, use context clues and your knowledge of the root's meaning.

⋮ **COMMON CORE**

L 4b Use Latin roots as clues to the meaning of a word.

PRACTICE Choose the word from the web that best completes each sentence. Then explain how the root *pend* relates to the meaning of the word.

1. She wears that _____ around her neck every day.
2. My choice is _____ on what you decide to do.
3. The book was so _____ that he couldn't stop reading it.
4. To hold up his pants, Dad prefers _____ to belts.
5. They could not shake off their feeling of _____ trouble.

suspenders
pendulum
suspenseful
pend, pens
dependent
impending
pendant

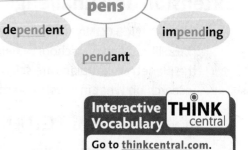

Interactive Vocabulary **THINK** central

Go to thinkcentral.com.
KEYWORD: HML7-480

Language

◆ **GRAMMAR IN CONTEXT: Understand Prepositions**

Review the **Grammar in Context** note on page 471. In all types of sentences, a verb must **agree in number** with its subject. **Number** refers to whether a word is singular or plural. A **prepositional phrase** is a group of words that begins with a preposition, such as *from, in, under,* or *with,* and ends with a noun or pronoun. Be especially careful when you form a sentence that has a **prepositional phrase** between the subject and the verb. In cases like these, the number of the subject is not changed by the phrase that follows the subject.

> *Original:* Harry, under the circumstances, struggle to cope.
>
> *Revised:* Harry, under the circumstances, struggles to cope.
> (*The subject* Harry *is singular so the verb should be too.*)

PRACTICE Choose the verb form that agrees in number with each subject.

1. Humans from around the world (wonder, wonders) about life on Mars.
2. Cora Bittering, with much patience, (try, tries) to understand her husband.
3. Harry, apart from the others, (resist, resists) the peculiar changes.
4. Eventually, Harry, along with the others, (move, moves) to the Martian villas.

For more help with subject-verb agreement, see pages R65–R67 in the **Grammar Handbook.**

READING-WRITING CONNECTION

Increase your understanding of "Dark They Were, and Golden-Eyed" by responding to this prompt. Then use the **revising tip** to improve your writing.

WRITING PROMPT	REVISING TIP
Short Constructed Response: Letter Bradbury originally named "Dark They Were, and Golden-Eyed" "The Naming of Names." Which title do you think is more appropriate? Using details and examples from the story, write a **one-paragraph letter** to the author to explain your choice.	Review your response. Do the subjects and verbs agree in number? If not, revise your writing.

COMMON CORE

L 1a Explain the function of phrases in specific sentences.
W 3 Write narratives to develop real or imagined experiences or events.

Interactive Revision **THINK** central

Go to **thinkcentral.com.**
KEYWORD: HML7-481

A Day's Wait

Short Story by Ernest Hemingway

Is it **BRAVE**
to suffer in silence?

COMMON CORE

RL 1 Cite textual evidence to support inferences drawn from the text. **RL 3** Analyze how particular elements of a story interact. **RL 4** Determine the meaning of words and phrases as they are used in a text.

Whether from an injury or a broken heart, everyone suffers at times. Some people try hard to keep their pain to themselves, while others believe it is better to share their thoughts and feelings with others. In "A Day's Wait," a young boy tries to be brave while suffering from an illness.

QUICKWRITE Do you consider it an act of bravery to face pain on your own, or does it take more courage for you to open up to other people? In a journal entry, explain your answers to these questions.

TEXT ANALYSIS: STYLE

Style is a writer's unique way of communicating ideas. It is often not only what writers say but how they say it that gives stories meaning and makes them memorable. To identify a writer's style, focus on these elements:

- **Word choice,** or the author's choice of language. Hemingway uses vivid verbs and precise nouns.

- **Sentence structure** and variety. In this story, Hemingway often uses long sentences for descriptions and short sentences when characters are talking.

- **Tone,** or the writer's attitude toward his or her subject. Hemingway's descriptions reveal his tone.

As you read "A Day's Wait," notice how these elements help create Hemingway's unique writing style.

READING SKILL: MAKE INFERENCES

Characters reveal much about themselves through **dialogue,** or conversations between characters. Dialogue can provide clues that help you **make inferences,** or logical guesses, about characters. You make an inference by combining a fact or clue with your own knowledge and experience.

As you read "A Day's Wait," make inferences about what characters say or don't say. Keep track of who's speaking by using a chart like the one shown.

Details About Character	What I Infer

VOCABULARY IN CONTEXT

How many of the boldfaced words do you know? Try to figure out the meaning of each.

1. People were there, but he felt **detached** from them.
2. There is a serious flu **epidemic** this winter.
3. He had **slack** muscles from lack of exercise.
4. It was **evidently** too much for him to deal with.
5. The man observed a **covey** of partridges.

 Complete the activities in your **Reader/Writer Notebook.**

Ernest Hemingway
1899–1961

An Adventurous Life

Ernest Hemingway lived a life full of adventure. He was one of a group of writers called the Lost Generation. These writers rejected what they saw as an American focus on acquiring many possessions. Along with being one of America's most famous writers, Hemingway was a fisherman, a hunter, and a fan of bullfighting. He participated in both world wars. Many of his works are based on his experiences in Europe and Cuba.

An Influential Style

Hemingway and other Lost Generation writers, including F. Scott Fitzgerald and Sherwood Anderson, expressed their ideas in writing styles that were new and different. Hemingway's writing style, particularly his method of writing dialogue, has influenced many other writers. He is one of the most often imitated writers of the 1900s.

BACKGROUND TO THE STORY

Fact Becomes Fiction Like much of Hemingway's writing, "A Day's Wait" is based on actual events in Hemingway's life. While Hemingway was living in France, his son came down with a high fever and reacted similarly to the boy in the story you will read.

Author Online
THINK central
Go to **thinkcentral.com**.
KEYWORD: HML7-483

A DAY'S WAIT

Ernest Hemingway

He came into the room to shut the windows while we were still in bed and I saw he looked ill. He was shivering, his face was white, and he walked slowly as though it ached to move.

"What's the matter, Schatz?"[1]

"I've got a headache."

"You better go back to bed."

"No. I'm all right."

"You go to bed. I'll see you when I'm dressed." **A**

But when I came downstairs he was dressed, sitting by the fire, looking
10 a very sick and miserable boy of nine years. When I put my hand on his forehead I knew he had a fever.

"You go up to bed," I said, "you're sick."

"I'm all right," he said.

When the doctor came he took the boy's temperature.

"What is it?" I asked him.

"One hundred and two."

1. **Schatz** (shäts): German term of affection meaning "my treasure," used here as a nickname.

Analyze Visuals ▶

Consider the expression on this boy's face. What **mood** does it convey?

A MAKE INFERENCES
Reread the **dialogue** in lines 4–8. Notice that Hemingway does not always tell the reader who is speaking. Use your chart to keep track of the different speakers.

Contemplation (1930), Alice Kent Stoddard. Oil on canvas.

Downstairs, the doctor left three different medicines in different-colored capsules with instructions for giving them. One was to bring down the fever, another a purgative,[2] the third to overcome an acid condition. The germs of influenza can only exist in an acid condition, he explained. He seemed to know all about influenza and said there was nothing to worry about if the fever did not go above one hundred and four degrees. This was a light **epidemic** of flu and there was no danger if you avoided pneumonia.

Back in the room I wrote the boy's temperature down and made a note of the time to give the various capsules.

"Do you want me to read to you?"

"All right. If you want to," said the boy. His face was very white and there were dark areas under his eyes. He lay still in the bed and seemed very **detached** from what was going on.

I read aloud from Howard Pyle's *Book of Pirates*,[3] but I could see he was not following what I was reading.

"How do you feel, Schatz?" I asked him.

"Just the same, so far," he said.

I sat at the foot of the bed and read to myself while I waited for it to be time to give another capsule. It would have been natural for him to go to sleep, but when I looked up he was looking at the foot of the bed, looking very strangely.

"Why don't you try to go to sleep? I'll wake you up for the medicine."

"I'd rather stay awake."

After a while he said to me, "You don't have to stay in here with me, Papa, if it bothers you." **B**

"It doesn't bother me."

"No, I mean you don't have to stay if it's going to bother you." **C**

I thought perhaps he was a little lightheaded and after giving him the prescribed capsules at eleven o'clock I went out for a while.

It was a bright, cold day, the ground covered with a sleet that had frozen so that it seemed as if all the bare trees, the bushes, the cut brush, and all the grass and the bare ground had been varnished with ice. I took the young Irish setter for a little walk up the road and along a frozen creek, but it was difficult to stand or walk on the glassy surface and the red dog slipped and slithered and I fell twice, hard, once dropping my gun and having it slide away over the ice. **D**

---

2. **purgative** (pûr′gə-tĭv): laxative.

3. **Howard Pyle's *Book of Pirates*:** a collection of tales about real and fictional pirates, very popular when it was published in the 1920s.

epidemic (ĕp′ĭ-dĕm′ĭk) *n.* an outbreak of a disease that spreads quickly among many people

detached (dĭ-tăcht′) *adj.* separated; disconnected **detach** *v.*

COMMON CORE RL 3, RL 4

B STYLE
Reread lines 35–42. One way to identify **style** is to look at a writer's word choice and sentence structure. Are the sentences short or simple? Are they long and complex with many details? What can you tell about Hemingway's style, based on these sentences?

C MAKE INFERENCES
Use your chart to track the speakers in the dialogue in lines 27–44.

D STYLE
Do the words Hemingway uses to describe the **setting** convey a positive or negative atmosphere? Explain.

◀ **Analyze Visuals**

How does this painting convey the passing of time?

covey (kŭv′ē) *n.* a small group or flock of birds, especially partridges or quail

    We flushed a <u>**covey**</u> of quail under a high clay bank with overhanging brush and I killed two as they went out of sight over the top of the bank. Some of the covey lit in trees, but most of them scattered into brush piles and it was necessary to jump on the ice-coated mounds of brush several times before they would flush. Coming out while you were poised unsteadily on the icy, springy brush, they made difficult shooting

60 and I killed two, missed five, and started back pleased to have found a covey close to the house and happy there were so many left to find on another day.

At the house they said the boy had refused to let anyone come into the room.

"You can't come in," he said. "You mustn't get what I have."

I went up to him and found him in exactly the position I had left him, white-faced, but with the tops of his cheeks flushed by the fever, staring still, as he had stared, at the foot of the bed.

I took his temperature.

70   "What is it?"

"Something like a hundred," I said. It was one hundred and two and four tenths.

"It was a hundred and two," he said.

"Who said so?"

"The doctor."

"Your temperature is all right," I said. "It's nothing to worry about."

"I don't worry," he said, "but I can't keep from thinking."

"Don't think," I said. "Just take it easy."

"I'm taking it easy," he said and looked straight ahead. He was

80   **evidently** holding tight onto himself about something.

"Take this with water."

"Do you think it will do any good?"

"Of course it will."

I sat down and opened the *Pirate* book and commenced to read, but I could see he was not following, so I stopped.

"About what time do you think I'm going to die?" he asked.

"What?"

"About how long will it be before I die?"

"You aren't going to die. What's the matter with you?"

90   "Oh, yes, I am. I heard him say a hundred and two."

"People don't die with a fever of one hundred and two. That's a silly way to talk."

"I know they do. At school in France the boys told me you can't live with forty-four degrees. I've got a hundred and two."

He had been waiting to die all day, ever since nine o'clock in the morning.

"You poor Schatz," I said. "Poor old Schatz. It's like miles and kilometers. You aren't going to die. That's a different thermometer. On that thermometer thirty-seven is normal. On this kind it's ninety-eight."

"Are you sure?"

100   "Absolutely," I said. "It's like miles and kilometers. You know, like how many kilometers we make when we do seventy miles in the car?"

"Oh," he said.

But his gaze at the foot of the bed relaxed slowly. The hold over himself relaxed too, finally, and the next day it was very **slack** and he cried very easily at little things that were of no importance. ∾

488   UNIT 4: MOOD, TONE, AND STYLE

Language Coach

Multiple-Meaning Words
Multiple-meaning words have more than one meaning. Reread lines 66–68. Here, the word *left* is the past tense of the word *leave*. What other meaning do you know for *left*?

evidently (ĕv′ĭ-dənt-lē) *adv.* obviously; clearly

SCIENCE CONNECTION

On the Celsius scale, water freezes at 0° and boils at 100°. On the Fahrenheit scale, water freezes at 32° and boils at 212°.

slack (slăk) *adj.* not firm or tight; loose

Comprehension

1. **Recall** Why does the boy think he is going to die?

2. **Clarify** Why does the father spend the afternoon hunting instead of staying with his worried son?

3. **Summarize** How does the story end?

Text Analysis

4. **Analyze Characterization** In what ways does the boy show concern for others? Does he reveal his concern through thoughts, words, or actions? Do the narrator's descriptions or other characters' thoughts, words, and actions help you see the boy's concern? Use a diagram like the one shown to record your support. Include line numbers when referring to parts of the story.

Boy's Thoughts, Words or Actions	→	What It Says About Him

5. **Draw Conclusions** Why does the boy cry so much the next day?

6. **Make Inferences** Do you think the boy's actions show bravery? Why or why not? Support your answer with examples from the story. Use a diagram like the one shown to record your support. Refer to the inferences you had recorded in your chart.

7. **Identify Style** Reread lines 65–83. Note Hemingway's **word choice**, **sentence structure**, and **tone.** Why is this passage a good example of Hemingway's style? Explain your answer, using evidence from the passage.

Extension and Challenge

8. **Creative Project: Drama** Most of this story is told through **dialogue** between the father and son. With a partner, choose one of their conversations to act out. Use details from the scene to accurately portray the characters. Practice on your own, and then present the dialogue to the class.

Is it BRAVE to suffer in silence?

Did Schatz's reaction to his illness in any way affect your opinions about bravery? What are your opinions now?

COMMON CORE

RL 1 Cite textual evidence to support inferences drawn from the text. **RL 3** Analyze how particular elements of a story interact. **RL 4** Determine the meaning of words and phrases as they are used in a text.

Vocabulary in Context

▲ VOCABULARY PRACTICE

Show that you understand the boldfaced words by deciding whether each statement is true or false.

1. If something is **evidently** true, it has been proven through a series of experiments.
2. A **covey** is a place where birds and small mammals go to spend the winter.
3. An **epidemic** generally affects a large number of people.
4. If you are **detached** from a situation, you are probably not very concerned about it.
5. Tightened muscles around someone's lips and jaw are typical of a **slack** expression.

ACADEMIC VOCABULARY IN WRITING

• communicate   • describe   • illustrate   • interpret   • style

Write a paragraph to explain what you liked—or didn't like—about Hemingway's **style**. Use at least two of the Academic Vocabulary words in your paragraph.

VOCABULARY STRATEGY: THE GREEK ROOT *therm*

The word *thermometer* contains the Greek root *therm*, which means "heat." This root is found in a number of English words. Use your understanding of the root's meaning, as well as context clues, to figure out the meanings of words formed from *therm*.

PRACTICE Choose a word from the web that best completes each sentence. If you need help, check a dictionary.

1. The _____ is the outermost shell of an atmosphere.
2. You can adjust the temperature of your home with a _____ .
3. _____ underwear keeps you warm in cold weather.
4. Exposure to extreme cold can lead to _____ .
5. _____ war would be a disaster for any part of the world.

COMMON CORE

L 4b Use Greek roots as clues to the meaning of a word.

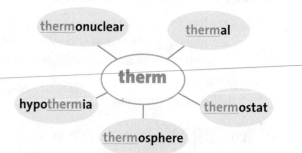

Interactive Vocabulary THINK central

Go to thinkcentral.com.
KEYWORD: HML7-490

Language

◆ **GRAMMAR IN CONTEXT:** Avoid Dangling Participles

A **participle** is a verb form that functions as an adjective. Participles usually modify nouns and pronouns. Most participles are present participle forms that end in *–ing* or past participle forms that end in *–ed* or *–en*.

Participial phrases are participles with all their modifiers and complements. When using a participle or participial phrase, place it close to the word it modifies. A **dangling participle** is one in which the modifier is not placed next to the word it modifies and creates confusion. You can make your sentences more clear by placing the phrase close to the word it modifies.

Original: Overhearing the conversation, fear seized Schatz.

Revised: Overhearing the conversation, Schatz was seized by fear.
(*The participial phrase modifies* Schatz.)

PRACTICE Rewrite each sentence, either by placing the participial phrase close to the word it modifies or by including a word (or words) for it to modify.

1. Peering through my fingers, the movie scene frightened me.
2. Drenched by the cold rain, the cabin was spotted by the drifter.
3. Buried in my file folder, I found your e-mail.
4. Driven to save lives, the building filled with firefighters.
5. Forgetting my keys, the lock couldn't open.

For more help with participles, see page R61 in the **Grammar Handbook.**

READING-WRITING CONNECTION

YOUR TURN Increase your understanding of "A Day's Wait" by responding to this prompt. Then use the **revising tip** to improve your writing.

WRITING PROMPT	REVISING TIP
Short Constructed Response: Evaluation Hemingway wrote, "A writer should create living people; people not characters." Does Hemingway create real people in "A Day's Wait"? Write a **one-paragraph response,** using the characters' thoughts, words, speech patterns, and actions to support your opinion.	Review your paragraph. If you find dangling participles, be sure to place the participle close to the word it modifies.

Interactive Revision **THINK** central

Go to **thinkcentral.com.**
KEYWORD: HML7-491

COMMON CORE

L 1c Place phrases within a sentence, recognizing and correcting misplaced and dangling modifiers. **W 1** Write arguments to support claims with clear reasons and relevant evidence.

How Hemingway Wrote
Informative Article

What's the Connection?

You've just read a short story by Ernest Hemingway, an author whose style is legendary. Now you will read an **informative article** that explains how Hemingway approached writing.

Standards Focus: Distinguish Fact from Opinion

An **opinion** is a statement of belief or feeling, such as "I think everyone should read Hemingway's stories." A **fact** is a statement that can be proved, such as "Hemingway wrote 51 stories." When you read informative articles, be careful not to mistake an opinion for a fact.

Articles can also contain **commonplace assertions,** strong statements or declarations that have no support or proof but are widely accepted as true. A commonplace assertion is different from a **factual claim,** which is a statement that can be proved by observation, an expert, and other reliable sources. For example, it would be possible for a team of scientists to conduct a study to explore the factual claim "Teens need at least eight hours of sleep each night."

As you read Bruce Rettman's article, list the facts in one column and Rettman's opinions in another. Use the tips on the chart to help you distinguish facts from opinions.

Use with "A Day's Wait," page 484.

COMMON CORE

RI 1 Cite textual evidence to support what the text says explicitly. **RI 3** Analyze the interactions between ideas in a text. **RI 6** Determine an author's point of view and how the author distinguishes his or her position from that of others.

FACT OR OPINION?

Is it a fact?	Is it an opinion?
Watch Out • Words and phrases often used to state facts: *the fact that, in fact, indeed, the truth is,* and *as a matter of fact* • The same words and phrases used to state facts *may* be used to disguise opinions or assertions as facts.	**Watch Out** Words and phrases often used to express opinions: *I think, I believe, perhaps,* and *maybe*
Can I prove it by • consulting a reliable source, such as a print or online encyclopedia? • interviewing a recognized expert in the field? • checking the statement against what I observe or know to be true? *If the answer is "yes,"* the statement is a **fact.**	**Ask yourself:** • Can this statement be debated? • Might people disagree with the statement? *If the answer is "yes,"* the statement is probably an **opinion.**

How Hemingway *Wrote*

by Bruce Rettman

Hemingway is shown here working on a story.

Ernest Hemingway said that the best writing advice he ever got came from the writing guidelines he received as a young reporter working for the *Kansas City Star.* These guidelines began as follows: "Use short sentences. Use short first paragraphs. Use vigorous English, not forgetting to strive for smoothness." Anyone who reads Hemingway's simple and direct sentences built on strong nouns and verbs—not "extravagant adjectives"—can see that he took those guidelines to heart. **B**

Hemingway's own advice for becoming a good writer is also informative. "When people talk, listen completely," said Hemingway to a young writer. "Don't be thinking what you're going to say. Most people never listen. Nor do they observe." In other words, Hemingway advises young writers to write from life, blending fact and fiction. The short story "A Day's Wait," for example, is based on an actual time when Hemingway's first child had a fever.

F OCUS ON FORM
"How Hemingway Wrote" is an **informative article**, a nonfiction article written to provide information or to explain something about a topic.

A INFORMATIVE ARTICLE
Now that you have read the title, what do you think this informative article will explain?

B DISTINGUISH FACT FROM OPINION
To check whether the statements in lines 1–16 are accurate, whom might you contact or what source might you consult?

So, are you getting a sense of how Hemingway approached writing? Well, there's still more to learn from Hemingway's manuscripts. I've studied them to learn how he wrote his stories. I've paid particular atten-

40 tion to his revisions to see how they changed the meaning of a story. What I've discovered is the surprising fact that his revisions were more often additions than cuts. He added details for clarity and depth. Like a painter, Hemingway added to his canvas until the picture was how he wanted it. From this observation

50 I would suggest that to approach writing as Hemingway did, you could start with the bare minimum and build, going back over your writing to see where details might add interest and clarity. **C**

There's another piece of information you need to have to begin to understand Hemingway's approach to writing. In

60 Hemingway's stories, dialogue is very important. For example, in "A Day's Wait," after the doctor takes the boy's temperature, the brief exchange that occurs between the doctor and the boy's father is what triggers the boy's day of suffering:

"What is it?" I asked him.
"One hundred and two."

70 At times Hemingway cut his description of a character's thoughts in order to rely more heavily on dialogue.

You might also want to keep in mind Hemingway's other bit of advice to a young writer: "Get in somebody else's head for a change. If I bawl you out, try to figure what I'm thinking about

80 as well as how you feel about it." In other words, try to see every event from all sides.

Now, perhaps, you are ready to start writing stories of your own. Of course, you have to have something to write about. Hemingway's life experiences were a rich source of material. He was a fisherman

90 and a hunter, went to bullfights, and experienced both World War I and World War II. He lived in Europe, Cuba, and different parts of the United States. I'm not suggesting that you need to do similar things. Just embrace life. Then, maybe, after a time—and if you follow all this advice—you

100 can be a successful writer like Hemingway. **D**

C DISTINGUISH FACT FROM OPINION
Is the last sentence in this paragraph a fact, an opinion, or an expert's opinion? Give reasons for your answer.

D DISTINGUISH FACT FROM OPINION
Which statement in this paragraph might people disagree about?

Comprehension

1. **Recall** Hemingway is known for writing what kinds of sentences?

2. **Clarify** What actual event in Hemingway's life helped inspire "A Day's Wait"?

Text Analysis

3. **Distinguish Fact from Opinion** Review the facts and opinions you identified in the informative article. Then choose one of each, and explain why you identified it as you did.

4. **Identify Topic Sentences** A **topic sentence** is one that tells what a paragraph is about. Not all paragraphs have a topic sentence, but when it is present, it is often the first or second sentence in the paragraph. Identify three topic sentences in this informative article.

5. **Evaluate an Informative Article** A strong informative article is easy to follow, interesting, and useful. Would you say that "How Hemingway Wrote" is a strong informative article? Explain.

COMMON CORE

RI 1 Cite textual evidence to support what the text says explicitly. **RI 3** Analyze the interactions between ideas in a text. **RI 6** Determine an author's point of view and how the author distinguishes his or her position from that of others. **W 2** Write informative/explanatory texts to examine a topic and convey ideas.

Read for Information: Create Instructions for Writers

WRITING PROMPT

In the informative article you just read, Bruce Rettman explains how to approach writing as Ernest Hemingway did. Now use these ideas to create a set of instructions for writers. To help explain your instructions, include examples from "A Day's Wait" or Rettman's article.

To answer this prompt, do as follows:

1. Scan Rettman's article to find six things a person can do to approach writing as Hemingway did.

2. Arrange the six directions in a logical order.

3. Illustrate at least two or three of these directions with examples from "A Day's Wait" or Rettman's article.

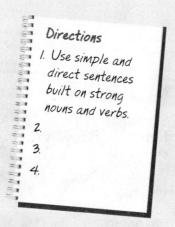

Directions
1. Use simple and direct sentences built on strong nouns and verbs.
2.
3.
4.

The People Could Fly

Video link at
thinkcentral.com

Folk Tale retold by Virginia Hamilton

Where do people find HOPE?

What is hope? Why do we need it? Where can we find it? How can we give hope to others? In her retelling of "The People Could Fly," Virginia Hamilton shares a story that gave people hope for freedom when little else did.

WEB IT With a partner, discuss the questions posed in the previous paragraph. Record ideas from your conversation in a word web like the one shown, adding to it as necessary.

What is hope?

Where can we find it?

Hope

Why do we need it?

How can we give hope to others?

TEXT ANALYSIS: STYLE IN FOLK TALES

The selection you are about to read is a **folk tale,** a story that has been passed from generation to generation by word of mouth. In writing the folk tale down, Virginia Hamilton chose to use a **style** that reflects how the story would sound if told aloud. That style includes

- nonstandard spellings that match how people might say certain words
- sentence structure that matches how people might talk

As you read, notice how Hamilton uses language to re-create the sounds and patterns of speech. It may help you to read parts of the story aloud, as it was originally meant to be told.

READING SKILL: SUMMARIZE

One way to check your understanding of what you are reading is to **summarize** it. A summary is a brief retelling, in your own words, of the main ideas of a story. When you summarize a story, include

- the characters, setting, conflict, and resolution
- key details, so that someone who has not read the story understands your summary

As you read "The People Could Fly," collect the information for a summary in a story map like the one shown.

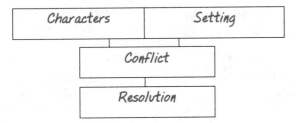

Characters	Setting
Conflict	
Resolution	

VOCABULARY IN CONTEXT

Try to figure out the meaning of each boldfaced word in the context of the numbered phrases.

1. **croon** a lullaby
2. **snagged** by a tree branch
3. slide and **shuffle** to the left
4. **glinty** diamond

Complete the activities in your **Reader/Writer Notebook.**

Meet the Author

Virginia Hamilton
1936–2002

A Storytelling Family
Virginia Hamilton grew up listening to her parents, grandparents, and others tell stories of their past. She has since realized that "they were passing along heritage and culture and a pride in their history."

From Listener to Writer Hamilton put these stories in writing and added some of her own, publishing more than 35 books. Many of her books, including *The People Could Fly*, deal with African-American history and culture.

BACKGROUND TO THE TALE

Slavery Between the 1500s and 1800s, about 12 million Africans were sent to North and South America as enslaved people. Colonists in the Americas wanted a cheap labor force to support their large-scale farming. People were kidnapped in Africa and sent overseas as enslaved people to be sold.

A Hopeful Community Despite the hardships they faced, enslaved people held on to a sense of community and tradition. They passed on stories, folk tales, and legends from generation to generation. The folk tale "The People Could Fly" is one example of these stories of hope and tradition.

Author Online **THINK** central

Go to thinkcentral.com.
KEYWORD: HML7-497

497

The People Could Fly

Virginia Hamilton

They say the people could fly. Say that long ago in Africa, some of
the people knew magic. And they would walk up on the air like
climbin' up on a gate. And they flew like blackbirds over the fields.
Black, shiny wings flappin' against the blue up there.

Then, many of the people were captured for Slavery. The ones that
could fly shed their wings. They couldn't take their wings across the
water on the slave ships. Too crowded, don't you know. **Ⓐ**

The folks were full of misery, then. Got sick with the up and down
of the sea. So they forgot about flyin' when they could no longer breathe
10 the sweet scent of Africa.

Say the people who could fly kept their power, although they shed their
wings. They kept their secret magic in the land of slavery. They looked
the same as the other people from Africa who had been coming over, who
had dark skin. Say you couldn't tell anymore one who could fly from one
who couldn't.

One such who could was an old man, call him Toby. And standin' tall,
yet afraid, was a young woman who once had wings. Call her Sarah. Now
Sarah carried a babe tied to her back. She trembled to be so hard worked
and scorned.

20 The slaves labored in the fields from sunup to sundown. The owner
of the slaves callin' himself their Master. Say he was a hard lump of clay.
A hard, **glinty** coal. A hard rock pile, wouldn't be moved. His Overseer[1]

glinty (glĭn′tē) *adj.*
sparkling

---

1. **Overseer:** a person who directs the work of others; a supervisor.
   During the time of slavery, the overseer was usually a white man.

on horseback pointed out the slaves who were slowin' down. So the one called Driver cracked his whip over the slow ones to make them move faster. That whip was a slice-open cut of pain. So they did move faster. Had to. **B**

Sarah hoed and chopped the row as the babe on her back slept.

Say the child grew hungry. That babe started up bawling too loud. Sarah couldn't stop to feed it. Couldn't stop to soothe and quiet it down. She let it cry. She didn't want to. She had no heart to **croon** to it.

30 "Keep that thing quiet," called the Overseer. He pointed his finger at the babe. The woman scrunched low. The Driver cracked his whip across the babe anyhow. The babe hollered like any hurt child, and the woman fell to the earth. **C**

The old man that was there, Toby, came and helped her to her feet.

"I must go soon," she told him.

"Soon," he said.

Sarah couldn't stand up straight any longer. She was too weak. The sun burned her face. The babe cried and cried, "Pity me, oh, pity me," say it sounded like. Sarah was so sad and starvin', she sat down in the row.

40 "Get up, you black cow," called the Overseer. He pointed his hand, and the Driver's whip snarled around Sarah's legs. Her sack dress tore into rags. Her legs bled onto the earth. She couldn't get up.

Toby was there where there was no one to help her and the babe.

"Now, before it's too late," panted Sarah. "Now, Father!"

"Yes, Daughter, the time is come," Toby answered. "Go, as you know how to go!"

He raised his arms, holding them out to her. *"Kum . . . yali, kum buba tambe,"* and more magic words, said so quickly, they sounded like whispers and sighs.

50 The young woman lifted one foot on the air. Then the other. She flew clumsily at first, with the child now held tightly in her arms. Then she felt the magic, the African mystery. Say she rose just as free as a bird. As light as a feather.

The Overseer rode after her, hollerin'. Sarah flew over the fences. She flew over the woods. Tall trees could not **snag** her. Nor could the Overseer. She flew like an eagle now, until she was gone from sight. No one dared speak about it. Couldn't believe it. But it was, because they that was there saw that it was.

60 Say the next day was dead hot in the fields. A young man slave fell from the heat. The Driver come and whipped him. Toby come over and spoke words to the fallen one. The words of ancient Africa once heard are never remembered completely. The young man forgot them as soon as he heard them. They went way inside him. He got up and rolled over on the air. He rode it awhile. And he flew away.

B SUMMARIZE
Note the **setting** and the names of the **characters** in your story map.

croon (krōōn) *v.* to sing softly

C SUMMARIZE
What is the **conflict**? Record it in your story map.

snag (snăg) *v.* to catch and tear

nother and another fell from the heat. Toby was there. He cried out to the fallen and reached his arms out to them. *"Kum kunka yali, kum . . . tambe!"* Whispers and sighs. And they too rose on the air. They rode the hot breezes. The ones flyin' were black and shinin' sticks, wheelin' above the head of the Overseer. They crossed the rows, the fields,

70 the fences, the streams, and were away.

"Seize the old man!" cried the Overseer.

"I heard him say the magic *words.* Seize him!"

The one callin' himself Master come runnin'. The Driver got his whip ready to curl around old Toby and tie him up. The slave owner took his hip gun from its place. He meant to kill old black Toby.

But Toby just laughed. Say he threw back his head and said, "Hee, hee! Don't you know who I am? Don't you know some of us in this field?" He said it to their faces. "We are ones who fly!"

And he sighed the ancient words that were a dark promise. He said

80 them all around to the others in the field under the whip, ". . . *buba yali . . . buba tambe . . ."*

There was a great outcryin'. The bent backs straighted up. Old and young who were called slaves and could fly joined hands. Say like they would ring-sing. But they didn't **shuffle** in a circle. They didn't sing. They rose on the air. They flew in a flock that was black against the heavenly blue. Black crows or black shadows. It didn't matter, they went so high. Way above the plantation, way over the slavery land. Say they flew away to *Free-dom.*

And the old man, old Toby, flew behind them, takin' care of them.

90 He wasn't cryin'. He wasn't laughin'. He was the seer. His gaze fell on the plantation where the slaves who could not fly waited. **E**

"Take us with you!" Their looks spoke it, but they were afraid to shout it. Toby couldn't take them with him. Hadn't the time to teach them to fly. They must wait for a chance to run.

"Goodie-bye!" the old man called Toby spoke to them, poor souls! And he was flyin' gone.

o they say. The Overseer told it. The one called Master said it was a lie, a trick of the light. The Driver kept his mouth shut.

The slaves who could not fly told about the people who could fly to their

100 children. When they were free. When they sat close before the fire in the free land, they told it. They did so love firelight and *Free-dom,* and tellin'.

They say that the children of the ones who could not fly told their children. And now, me, I have told it to you. **ᔆ**

Comprehension

1. **Recall** What special power did some of the people in Africa have?

2. **Recall** What does the Driver do to Sarah and her baby?

3. **Clarify** After Toby is gone, who tells the story of the people who could fly?

Text Analysis

4. **Summarize** Use the story map you created as you read to summarize the story. Compare your summary with that of a classmate.

5. **Draw Conclusions** Why do you think the people who first told this **folk tale** did not have all the slaves fly away?

6. **Evaluate Style in a Folk Tale** Reread lines 82–96. In a graphic like the one shown, note examples of Hamilton's style that appear in this section. Do you think this is an effective style for telling this story, or would you prefer to read it with standard spellings and complete sentences? Explain.

Hamilton's Style	
Spellings	Sentence Fragments
• _____	• _____
• _____	• _____
• _____	• _____

7. **Contrast Point of View** The narrator of this folk tale frequently uses the word *say* to mean "They say." The narrator is probably referring to the people who have told this tale from the period of slavery. How might this narrator be different from the previous tellers?

COMMON CORE

RL 2 Provide an objective summary of the text. **RL 3** Analyze how particular elements of a story interact. **RL 6** Analyze how an author develops and contrasts the points of view of different characters or narrators in a text.

Extension and Challenge

8. **SOCIAL STUDIES CONNECTION** The African-American **oral tradition** has its roots in Africa—particularly West Africa. Research to find out about griots (grē-ōz'), West African storytellers, and their role in the local culture.

Where do people find HOPE?

Revisit the **WEB IT** activity on page 496. This time, consider how either Toby or Sarah would answer the questions about hope. Use details from the folk tale and your own knowledge and experience to answer the questions as he or she would.

Vocabulary in Context

▲ **VOCABULARY PRACTICE**

Use **context clues** to choose a vocabulary word to complete each sentence.

1. Though they tried not to _____ them, people often ripped their clothes while doing hard labor in the fields.
2. The people had no money for jewelry or _____ things.
3. Folks would _____ with their heads down to keep the Overseer from noticing them.
4. At night, the mothers might _____ to their weeping children to comfort them.

croon

glinty

shuffle

snag

ACADEMIC VOCABULARY IN WRITING

> • communicate   • describe   • illustrate   • interpret   • style

In a brief follow-up to the folk tale, **describe** the place where Toby and the others escaped. Include at least one other Academic Vocabulary word in your description.

VOCABULARY STRATEGY: USING A THESAURUS

A **thesaurus**—a book or electronic tool used to find synonyms—can give writing flavor and variety. A thesaurus entry will tell you the spelling, part of speech, and meaning of a word and its synonyms. Common words like *sing* have many **synonyms,** or words with similar meanings. However, not all synonyms are interchangeable. In this story, for example, the verb *croon* gives a much more precise sense of the scene than the more common verb *sing* would convey.

PRACTICE Choose the synonym in parentheses that best replaces each boldfaced word. If you need help, consult a thesaurus or a dictionary.

1. His sleeves got **dirty** from the leaking printer ink. (smudged, dingy)
2. Little children often **frown** if they don't get their way. (glare, pout)
3. Al Capone was a **famous** criminal. (distinguished, notorious)
4. She was so hungry that she **ate** everything in sight. (devoured, dined on)
5. The frightened field mouse **ran** across the kitchen floor. (scampered, jogged)

COMMON CORE

L 4c Consult reference materials to determine or clarify [a word's] precise meaning. **L 5b** Use the relationship between particular words to better understand each of the words.

Interactive Vocabulary   **THINK** central

Go to **thinkcentral.com.**
KEYWORD: HML7-503

Out of the Dust

Novel in Verse by Karen Hesse

COMMON CORE

RL 10 Read and comprehend literature.

Other Books by Karen Hesse

- *Aleutian Sparrow*
- *Letters from Rifka*
- *A Light in the Storm*
- *The Music of Dolphins*
- *Phoenix Rising*
- *Stowaway*
- *A Time of Angels*
- *Witness*

Meet Karen Hesse

Karen Hesse has worked in a wide range of jobs, but at heart she's always been a writer. "I love writing," she says. "I can't wait to get to my keyboard every morning." She also loves books and has shared that passion with her two daughters.

Hesse had a troubled childhood, but she feels that it strengthened her writing. "My work reflects the bumps and knocks that I've experienced," she explains. "I write the kinds of books that I would've wanted as a child."

Try a Novel in Verse

Most novels are written in prose, the ordinary form of written language, but they can also be written as poetry. Hesse wrote *Out of the Dust* as a series of **free verse** poems, which are poems written without regular rhyme or rhythm. As personal journal entries, these poems provide a window into what the main character is thinking and feeling.

Reading Fluency Good readers read smoothly, accurately, and with feeling. To improve your reading fluency, read a passage several times. Your goal in silent reading is to make sense of the writer's words and ideas. When reading aloud, think about the type of text you are reading. You may need to adjust your speed and tone and how you emphasize certain words when reading fiction, nonfiction, or poetry.

Read a Great Book

Thirteen-year-old Billie Jo and her family of farmers are barely surviving the hardships of the Dust Bowl in Oklahoma in the 1930s. Drought and strong winds have ruined their crops. Dust covers everything, and money is scarce. Every day is a struggle. The only source of joy in Billie Jo's life is her talent for playing the piano.

from

Out of *the* Dust

Fields of Flashing Light

I heard the wind rise,
and stumbled from my bed,
down the stairs,
out the front door,
5 into the yard.
The night sky kept flashing,
lightning danced down on its spindly legs.

I sensed it before I knew it was coming.
I heard it,
10 smelled it,
tasted it.
Dust.

While Ma and Daddy slept,
the dust came,
15 tearing up fields where the winter wheat,
set for harvest in June,
stood helpless.
I watched the plants,
surviving after so much drought and so much wind,
20 I watched them fry,
or
flatten,
or blow away,
like bits of cast-off rags.

25 It wasn't until the dust turned toward the house,
like a fired locomotive,
and I fled,
barefoot and breathless, back inside,
it wasn't until the dust
30 hissed against the windows,
until it ratcheted the roof,
that Daddy woke.

He ran into the storm,
his overalls half-hooked over his union suit.
35 "Daddy!" I called. "You can't stop dust."

Ma told me to
cover the beds,
push the scatter rugs against the doors,

dampen the rags around the windows.
40 Wiping dust out of everything,
she made coffee and biscuits,
waiting for Daddy to come in.

Sometime after four,
rubbing low on her back,
45 Ma sank down into a chair at the kitchen table
and covered her face.
Daddy didn't come back for hours,
not
until the temperature dropped so low,
50 it brought snow.

Ma and I sighed, grateful,
staring out at the dirty flakes,
but our relief didn't last.
The wind snatched that snow right off the fields,
55 leaving behind a sea of dust,
waves and
waves and
waves of
dust,
60 rippling across our yard.

Daddy came in,
he sat across from Ma and blew his nose.
Mud streamed out.
He coughed and spit out
65 mud.
If he had cried,
his tears would have been mud too,
but he didn't cry.
And neither did Ma.

March 1934

Wild Boy of the Road

A boy came by the house today,
he asked for food.
He couldn't pay anything, but Ma set him down
and gave him biscuits
5 and milk.
He offered to work for his meal,
Ma sent him out to see Daddy.
The boy and Daddy came back late in the afternoon.
The boy walked two steps behind,
10 in Daddy's dust.
He wasn't more than sixteen.
Thin as a fence rail.
I wondered what
Livie Killian's brother looked like now.
15 I wondered about Livie herself.
Daddy asked if the boy wanted a bath,
a haircut,
a change of clothes before he moved on.
The boy nodded.
20 I never heard him say more than "Yes, sir" or
"No, sir" or
"Much obliged."

We watched him walk away
down the road,
25 in a pair of Daddy's mended overalls,
his legs like willow limbs,
his arms like reeds.
Ma rested her hands on her heavy stomach,
Daddy rested his chin on the top of my head.
30 "His mother is worrying about him," Ma said.
"His mother is wishing her boy would come home."

Lots of mothers wishing that these days,
while their sons walk to California,
where rain comes,
35 and the color green doesn't seem like such a miracle,
and hope rises daily, like sap in a stem.
And I think, some day I'm going to walk there too,
through New Mexico and Arizona and Nevada.
Some day I'll leave behind the wind, and the dust
40 and walk my way West
and make myself to home in that distant place
of green vines and promise.

July 1934

Keep Reading

This is just a small part of the story about the life of a family during the Great Depression and Dust Bowl of the 1930s. Which descriptions stand out most vividly in your mind? To find out more about Billie Jo and her family, read more of *Out of the Dust*. You'll read about Billie Jo's struggles, why she thinks about running away to a place "where rain comes," and how she finds hope for a better future.

Breaking the Ice

Essay by Dave Barry

What makes us LAUGH?

COMMON CORE

RI 4 Analyze the impact of specific word choice on meaning and tone. RI 6 Determine an author's point of view or purpose in a text.

There have probably been times when you told a joke and nobody laughed. Maybe you heard a joke that made other people laugh but that you didn't think was funny. How you react to a joke or tell a joke reflects your unique sense of humor. Some people are very good at finding humor in everyday situations and communicating it to others. The essay writer you are about to read has built a career out of making people laugh.

QUOTE IT "Laughter is the best medicine." "Laugh and the world laughs with you." "Laughter is the closest distance between two people." There are dozens of quotes about laughter. Now it is your turn to add to the list. Think of the kinds of things that make you laugh and how laughing makes you feel. Then write your own quote about laughter.

TEXT ANALYSIS: STYLE AND TONE

Have you ever been told, "Don't use that tone with me"? In literature, **tone** is a writer's attitude toward a topic. Tone is part of a writer's **style** and often can be described in one word, such as *sarcastic* or *sentimental*.

In Dave Barry's essay, he uses a unique tone to relate a humorous story about a dating experience. As you read, use these tips to help you identify the tone of the essay.

- Identify the topic. Ask: "What is the writer writing about?"
- Notice significant words and phrases. Do most of them convey a similar attitude?
- Notice images and descriptions. Are they exaggerated, silly, or frightening?
- Read parts of the essay aloud, focusing on the feelings behind the word. What do they tell you about the writer?

READING SKILL: IDENTIFY A WRITER'S POINT OF VIEW

In addition to making you laugh, a humorous essay conveys the **writer's point of view,** or opinion, about the topic. After you identify the essay's topic, **make inferences,** or logical guesses, about the writer's point of view. You make an inference by looking for clues in the essay and then combining them with your own knowledge and experience.

As you read, record words and phrases that reveal the writer's opinion in a chart like the one shown. Then jot down what you have learned about the writer's point of view from each example.

Topic of the Essay	
Words and phrases that reveal writer's point of view	What this tells me about the writer's point of view
"The most sensible way to ask a girl out is to walk directly up to her.... I never did this."	Barry thinks that dating in high school is not easy.

 Complete the activities in your **Reader/Writer Notebook.**

Meet the Author

Dave Barry
born 1947

Journalism's Funny Man
Pulitzer Prize-winning writer Dave Barry is best known for the columns he has written for the *Miami Herald* newspaper. These columns became so popular that they soon ran in more than 500 newspapers in the United States and abroad.

Inspired by Everyday Life
Barry's columns, including "Breaking the Ice," often exaggerate and poke fun at the daily life of his readers. As one reviewer put it, Barry has a gift for "squeezing every ounce of humor out of a perfectly ordinary experience." Barry is often inspired by his personal experiences—what can go wrong with house repairs, parenting teenagers, and, of course, careers in newspapers.

In college, Barry studied English and wrote for his college newspaper. His most recent work is a young-adult novel that he has co-authored with a long-time friend.

Author Online
Go to **thinkcentral.com**. KEYWORD: HML7-511

THINK central

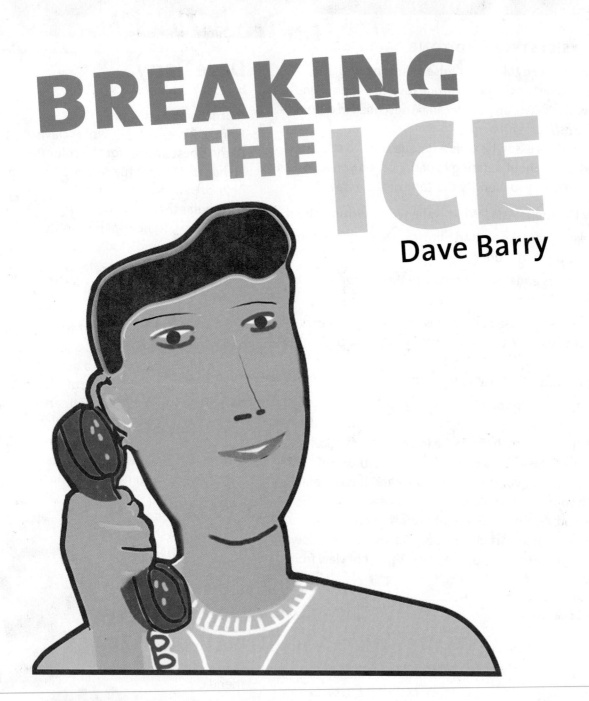

BREAKING THE ICE

Dave Barry

As a mature adult, I feel an obligation to help the younger generation, just as the mother fish guards her unhatched eggs, keeping her lonely vigil day after day, never leaving her post, not even to go to the bathroom, until her tiny babies emerge and she is able, at last, to eat them. "She may be your mom, but she's still a fish" is a wisdom nugget that I would pass along to any fish eggs reading this column.

But today I want to talk about dating. This subject was raised in a letter to me from a young person named Eric Knott, who writes:

▲ **Analyze Visuals**

As you look at this picture, **predict** what the essay will be about.

I have got a big problem. There's this girl in my English class
who is *really* good-looking. However, I don't think she knows
I exist. I want to ask her out, but I'm afraid she will say no, and
I will be the freak of the week. What should I do? **Ⓐ**

Eric, you have sent your question to the right mature adult, because
as a young person I spent a lot of time thinking about this very problem.
Starting in about eighth grade, my time was divided as follows:

Academic Pursuits: 2 percent.
Zits: 16 percent.
Trying to Figure Out How to Ask Girls Out: 82 percent.

The most sensible way to ask a girl out is to walk directly up to her
on foot and say, "So, you want to go out? Or what?" I never did this.
I knew, as Eric Knott knows, that there was always the possibility that
the girl would say no, thereby leaving me with no viable option[1] but
to leave Harold C. Crittenden Junior High School forever and go into
the woods and become a bark-eating hermit whose only companions
would be the gentle and understanding woodland creatures. **Ⓑ**
   "Hey, ZITFACE!" the woodland creatures would shriek in cute little
Chip 'n' Dale voices while raining acorns down upon my head. "You
wanna DATE? HAHAHAHAHAHA." **Ⓒ**
   So the first rule of dating is: Never risk direct contact with the girl
in question. Your role model should be the nuclear submarine, gliding
silently beneath the ocean surface, tracking an enemy target that does
not even begin to suspect that the submarine would like to date it. I spent
the vast majority of 1960 keeping a girl named Judy under surveillance,[2]
maintaining a minimum distance of 50 lockers to avoid the danger that
I might somehow get into a conversation with her, which could have led
to disaster:

   JUDY: Hi.
   ME: Hi.
   JUDY: Just in case you have ever thought about having a date with me,
   the answer is no.
   WOODLAND CREATURES: HAHAHAHAHAHA.

The only problem with the nuclear-submarine technique is that it's
difficult to get a date with a girl who has never, technically, been asked.
This is why you need Phil Grant. Phil was a friend of mine who had the

Ⓐ STYLE AND TONE
Reread lines 1–12. What
is the **topic** of the essay?

**Ⓑ WRITER'S POINT OF
VIEW**
Reread lines 21–25.
What are Barry's feelings
about high school
dating? Explain how he
conveys his opinion.

Ⓒ STYLE AND TONE
Reread lines 26–28.
What is Barry's attitude
toward his younger
self? Note how the **style**
of using capital letters
helps communicate
this attitude.

---

1. **viable option:** choice that has a possibility of working.

2. **surveillance** (sər-vā′ləns)**:** close observation.

ability to talk to girls. It was a mysterious superhuman power he had, comparable to X-ray vision. So, after several thousand hours of intense discussion and planning with me, Phil approached a girl he knew named Nancy, who approached a girl named Sandy, who was a direct personal friend of Judy's and who passed the word back to Phil via
50 Nancy that Judy would be willing to go on a date with me. This procedure protected me from direct humiliation. . . . **D**

Thus it was that, finally, Judy and I went on an actual date, to see a movie in White Plains, New York. If I were to sum up the romantic ambience[3] of this date in four words, those words would be: "My mother was driving." This made for an extremely quiet drive, because my mother, realizing that her presence was hideously embarrassing, had to pretend she wasn't there. If it had been legal, I think she would have got out and sprinted alongside the car, steering through the window. Judy and I, sitting in the backseat about 75 feet apart, were also silent, unable
60 to communicate without the assistance of Phil, Nancy, and Sandy. **E**

After what seemed like several years we got to the movie theater, where my mother went off to sit in the Parents and Lepers Section. The movie was called *North to Alaska,* but I can tell you nothing else about it because I spent the whole time wondering whether it would be necessary to amputate my right arm, which was not getting any blood flow as a result of being perched for two hours like a petrified snake on the back of Judy's seat exactly one molecule away from physical contact.

So it was definitely a fun first date, featuring all the relaxed spontaneity of a real-estate closing,[4] and in later years I did regain some feeling in
70 my arm. My point, Eric Knott, is that the key to successful dating is self-confidence. I bet that good-looking girl in your English class would LOVE to go out with you. But YOU have to make the first move. So just do it! Pick up that phone! Call Phil Grant. ✍ **F**

D STYLE AND TONE
Reread lines 44–51. Note Barry's description of Phil Grant's "superhuman" abilities. How would you describe the tone of this paragraph?

E STYLE AND TONE
Does Barry seem to enjoy the drive to the movie theater? Note words and phrases that give his description of the ride either a positive or a negative tone.

F WRITER'S POINT OF VIEW
Reread lines 68–73. Barry writes that self-confidence is "the key to successful dating." What other words or phrases in these lines reveal his point of view? Explain.

---

3. **ambience** (ăm′bē-əns): atmosphere; environment.
4. **spontaneity of a real-estate closing:** A real-estate closing is a meeting where a piece of property transfers from a seller to a buyer. Many required documents are signed, in a very formal, un-spontaneous way.

Comprehension

1. **Recall** How does Dave Barry ask Judy out on a date?

2. **Recall** Where do they go on their date?

3. **Clarify** Why is Barry uncomfortable on the date?

Text Analysis

4. **Identify Writer's Point of View** Refer to the chart you completed as you read the essay. What inference did you make about Barry's overall opinion of his topic? What experiences does he draw on to support his opinion?

5. **Examine Style and Tone** In his essay, Barry imitates an advice columnist, a writer who helps readers solve problems. Which examples of Barry's humorous **tone** tell you that this is not a typical advice column? Record the examples in a chart like the one shown and note why they are funny.

Examples of Humor	Why This Is Funny
"Your role model should be the nuclear submarine"	

6. **Analyze Style and Tone** On the basis of this example of Barry's style, how would you describe his sense of humor to someone who hasn't read anything by him?

Extension and Challenge

7. **Humorous Letter** Write a humorous letter of advice about a social situation that you might encounter. Begin by writing a question asking for advice, such as, "Who should pay for a meal on a first date?" or "How do I introduce my friends to my parents?" Then think of funny things that could happen, such as discovering that you are wearing different-colored socks when you go to meet your date. Remember that you can use exaggeration and vivid images to convey a humorous **tone.**

What makes us LAUGH?

Refer to the quote you wrote to reflect your own views about laughter. Does the quote fit Dave Barry's essay? Explain why or why not.

COMMON CORE

RI 4 Analyze the impact of specific word choice on meaning and tone. RI 6 Determine an author's point of view or purpose in a text.

One Perfect Rose
Song for an April Dusk

Poems by Dorothy Parker

Does everyone LOVE being in love?

○ COMMON CORE

RL 4 Determine the meaning of words or phrases as they are used in a text, including figurative and connotative meanings. **RL 5** Analyze how a poem's form or structure contributes to its meaning.

Love is a popular subject in songs, books, and movies. In fact, romance novels make up nearly half of all adult paperback fiction sales in the United States. But some people prefer things that aren't too "mushy," overly emotional, or sentimental. Dorothy Parker's poems give readers a sense of whether she would love being in love.

DISCUSS One of the most popular holidays for cards is Valentine's Day. Why do you think this is so? Talk about the reasons people send Valentine's Day cards. Also, talk about other holidays that are popular for sending cards.

TEXT ANALYSIS: IRONY AND SPEAKER

In the two poems you are about to read, the poet uses irony through the voice of the poems' speakers. **Irony** is a contrast between what is expected and what actually happens. Dorothy Parker creates irony in her poetry by

- starting with romantic images
- using form and language to set the poem's **tone,** creating what the reader thinks is Parker's attitude toward the subject
- revealing a different attitude at the end of the poem, taking the reader by surprise

Parker's ironic shifts in attitude add humor to her poems. This irony is expressed through a **speaker,** the voice that talks to the reader. As you read her poems, think about the expectation that women will always respond in the same way. Then notice how the speaker responds to romance.

READING STRATEGY: UNDERSTAND FORM IN POETRY

An important part of understanding poetry comes from understanding its form. A poem's **form** is the way it is laid out on the page. Traditional poems follow regular, or repeated, patterns.

- The length of each **line** in a poem helps create the poem's **rhythm** and meaning.
- Lines might be grouped into **stanzas,** which often express a single idea or **theme.**
- The pattern of lines and stanzas often creates a pattern of **rhyming** words.

Poets choose the form that best suits the intended message of a particular poem. Parker purposely chooses a traditional form for her ironic poems. As you read, make notes about the poems' lines, stanzas, and rhyming words. Use a chart like the one shown.

"One Perfect Rose"	
Line length	3 the same length, 1 shorter
Number of stanzas	
Rhyming words	

Complete the activities in your **Reader/Writer Notebook.**

Dorothy Parker
1893–1967

Harsh Humor
After being fired from *Vanity Fair* magazine in New York City for writing reviews that were considered too harsh, Dorothy Parker started writing poetry. With several other writers, she founded a literary group called the Algonquin Round Table. Parker and the rest of the group became known for their humorous and lively conversations.

A New Attitude As a young woman, Parker read the sentimental poetry that was popular in the Victorian era. When writing poetry of her own, Parker blended traditional poetic forms with the "challenge everything" attitude of her time. This new style was a hit. Her first book of poetry, *Enough Rope* (1926), was a bestseller.

Social Critic The 1920s are often symbolized by "flappers"— independent women who challenged what was considered a woman's proper role in society. Parker used her sharp humor to express her independent spirit and to help her comment on issues such as materialism and the limited roles available to women in the 1920s.

517

One PERFECT Rose

Dorothy Parker

A single flow'r he sent me, since we met.
　　All tenderly his messenger he chose;
Deep-hearted, pure, with scented dew still wet—
　　One perfect rose. **A**

5 I knew the language of the floweret;
　　"My fragile leaves," it said, "his heart enclose."
Love long has taken for his amulet[1]
　　One perfect rose.

Why is it no one ever sent me yet
10　　One perfect limousine, do you suppose?
Ah no, it's always just my luck to get
　　One perfect rose. **B**

A FORM IN POETRY
Notice which lines
rhyme in the first
stanza. Is the pattern
of rhyme the same in
stanzas 2 and 3?

B IRONY AND
SPEAKER
In which line does
the speaker's attitude
change?

---

1. **amulet:** an object worn as a magic charm.

Song for an APRIL DUSK

Dorothy Parker

Tell me tales of a lilied pool
    Asleep beneath the sun.
Tell me of woodlands deep and cool,
    When chuckling satyrs[1] run.
5 Tell me, in light and tinkling words,
    Of rippling, lilting streams.
Tell me of radiant-breasted birds,
    Who sing their amorous[2] dreams.
Tell of the doomed butterfly
10   That flings his hour away.
Fated to live and love and die
    Before the death of day. **C**

Tell me tales of the moon-pale sprites[3]
    Whose beauty none may know.
15 Tell me of secret, silver nights
    When great red stars are low.
Tell of the virgin Spring, the fair,
    Who roams the circling years.
Rain-drops strung in her fragrant hair,
20   Her eyes a-mist with tears.
Tell me of elves, who leap to kiss,
    Who trip the velvet sward.[4]
Tell me stories of things like this,
    And, boy, will I be bored! **D**

C FORM IN POETRY
Describe the **rhythm** of this poem. How does **repetition** add to the rhythm?

D IRONY AND SPEAKER
How does the last line change the meaning of the poem?

---

1. **satyrs** (sā′tərs): in Greek mythology, woodland spirits in the male form, but with the ears and tail of a horse or goat.

2. **amorous** (ăm′ər-es): filled with love.

3. **sprites:** elves or fairies.

4. **trip the velvet sward:** skip along a smooth lawn.

Comprehension

1. **Clarify** In "One Perfect Rose," what gift would the **speaker** prefer to receive?

2. **Summarize** What is the second poem about?

3. **Represent** Choose any pair of lines from "Song for an April Dusk" and illustrate them.

⋯ **COMMON CORE**

RL 4 Determine the meaning of words or phrases as they are used in a text, including figurative and connotative meanings. **RL 5** Analyze how a poem's form or structure contributes to its meaning.

Text Analysis

● 4. **Identify Irony and Speaker** For each poem, complete a chart like the one shown. Record what the first part of the poem leads you to expect, and what actually happens at the end.

Title: _____	
What We Expect	What Happens

● 5. **Analyze Poetic Form** Look back at the notes you made about the poet's use of **lines, stanzas,** and **rhyme.** Explain how Parker's use of traditional form reinforces the **irony** in her poetry.

● 6. **Analyze Irony and Speaker** Did the speaker's statements at the end of each poem change your understanding of the poem's meaning? Explain your response, using evidence from the poems. Note which ending you found to be more surprising.

7. **Evaluate Style** Parker is known as a witty and humorous writer. On the basis of these poems, do you think she deserves this reputation? Explain, using examples from the poems.

Extension and Challenge

8. **Creative Project: Poetry** Try writing a short, **ironic** poem about love. You may use Parker's poems as a model, if you wish, or follow a different form.

9. **Inquiry and Research** Research to find out who else was in Parker's literary group, the Algonquin Round Table. Investigate what the group did when they met and how long the group was together. Share your opinion as to how this group may have influenced Parker's writing and style.

Does everyone LOVE being in love?

Refer to your explanation for the popularity of Valentine's Day and other popular holiday cards. Now that you've read the Dorothy Parker poems, describe the type of card message she would be likely to appreciate.

Members of the Algonquin Round Table

maggie and milly and molly and may
who are you, little i
old age sticks

Poems by E. E. Cummings

VIDEO TRAILER **THINK** central KEYWORD: HML7-522

Are all things
CONNECTED?

COMMON CORE

RL 1 Cite textual evidence to support analysis of what the text says explicitly. **RL 4** Determine the meaning of words and phrases as they are used in a text. **RL 5** Analyze how a poem's form contributes to its meaning.

A snowflake always has six sides. An insect always has six legs. The moon you see at night is the same moon seen by people in Brazil. In a world of infinite variety, scientists, artists, and writers—including the poet whose work you are about to read—can reveal unexpected connections.

WEB IT Think of a plant or an animal, an object, and a very old or very young person that you share connections with. Use a word web to describe each connection. Then compare the connections you noted with those your classmates noted.

Me

My TomatoPlant

I water the plant and give it soil. The plant gives me tomatoes.

TEXT ANALYSIS: STYLE IN POETRY

Poet E. E. Cummings has one of the most recognizable **styles** in literature. As with many writers, his style is not in what he says, but in how he says it. To identify the poet's unique style, focus on the following elements:

- **Word Choice** Cummings often invented new words or used familiar words in an unfamiliar way.

- **Form** Cummings often created unusual line breaks in his poetry. Sometimes he even broke a line in the middle of a word. He also arranged the lines of some poems in order to create a visual pattern on the page.

- **Punctuation, Capitalization, and Word Position** Cummings used punctuation in new ways and rarely used capital letters. He sometimes eliminated the space between two words or positioned words alone on a line.

As you can see, Cummings broke many "rules." Watch for examples of his style as you read three of his poems.

READING STRATEGY: MONITOR

To get the most meaning out of what you are reading, it is good to occasionally check, or **monitor,** your understanding. One part of monitoring is to **clarify,** or pause to reflect on what you know so far and use clues in the selection to make inferences about meaning. When reading poetry, rephrasing lines in your own words can help make the meaning more clear.

   After you read each poem once, read it again. This time, pause to clarify the meaning of the lines as you go. For each poem, it may help you to create a chart like the one shown.

"maggie and milly and molly and may"		
Line Numbers	Poet's Words	My Words
5–6	"milly befriended a stranded star / whose rays five languid fingers were"	Milly discovered a starfish with five arms.

Complete the activities in your **Reader/Writer Notebook.**

E. E. Cummings
1894–1962

An American Original
Beginning at age eight, E. E. Cummings wrote a poem a day. While attending Harvard University, he switched from traditional to modern forms of poetry. He frequently traveled to Paris, where he was exposed to modern forms of literature and art.

A Lot of Style
Cummings crafted a writing style that would later make him famous. While the style of Cummings's poems was new and different, his subject matter and themes were often traditional. He frequently wrote about childhood, relationships, and nature. Cummings was also an accomplished visual artist whose work was frequently exhibited at galleries in New York City.

BACKGROUND TO THE POEMS
Breaking It Down
Cummings wrote during a period of literary and artistic experimentation. He was influenced by writers such as Gertrude Stein and artists such as Pablo Picasso. These writers and artists were trying to break down language and images into their most basic elements. Cummings frequently broke up his poems on the page, with the aim of making their appearance add to their meaning.

Author Online
THINK central
Go to **thinkcentral.com.**
KEYWORD: HML7-523

maggie and milly and molly and may

E. E. Cummings

maggie and milly and molly and may
went down to the beach(to play one day) **Ⓐ**

and maggie discovered a shell that sang
so sweetly she couldn't remember her troubles,and

5   milly befriended a stranded star
whose rays five languid[1] fingers were;

and molly was chased by a horrible thing
which raced sideways while blowing bubbles:and

may came home with a smooth round stone
10 as small as a world and as large as alone.

For whatever we lose(like a you or a me)
it's always ourselves we find in the sea **Ⓑ**

Ⓐ STYLE IN POETRY
In what ways are lines
1–2 both traditional
and unusual?

Ⓑ MONITOR
Clarify by restating
the meaning of the
last two lines.

---

1. **languid** (lăng′gwĭd): lacking energy; drooping.

Painting (1953), Joan Miró. Oil on canvas, 75 7/8" x 51". Collection Mr. and Mrs. Richard K. Weil, St. Louis, Missouri. © 2008 Successió Miró/Artists Rights Society (ARS), New York/AGAGP, Paris.

who are you,little i
E. E. Cummings

who are you,little i **C**

(five or six years old)
peering from some high

window;at the gold

5 of November sunset

(and feeling:that if day
has to become night

this is a beautiful way) **D**

C STYLE IN POETRY
What is the effect
of having unusual
line breaks?

D MONITOR
Clarify what the word
this refers to in line 8.

Painting (1953), Joan Miró. Oil on canvas, 75⅞" × 51". Collection Mr. and Mrs. Richard K. Weil, St. Louis, Missouri. © 2008 Successió Miró/Artists Rights Society (ARS), New York/AGAGP, Paris.

old
age
sticks

E. E. Cummings

old age sticks
up Keep
Off
signs)&

5   youth yanks them
down(old
age
cries No

Tres)&(pas)
10 youth laughs
(sing **E**
old age

E MONITOR
To **clarify,** rephrase what the poet says in lines 1–11.

scolds Forbid
den Stop
15 Must
n't Don't **F**

F STYLE IN POETRY
Note which words are **capitalized** in the poem. Why do you think Cummings chose to capitalize these words?

&)youth goes
right on
gr
20 owing old

Comprehension

1. **Recall** According to the poem "maggie and milly and molly and may," what do we find in the sea?

2. **Recall** What does little i see out the window?

3. **Clarify** In line 9 of "old age sticks," what familiar word is disguised by Cummings's style?

Text Analysis

4. **Monitor** Look back at the charts you created as you read. For each poem, choose one line or one set of lines and explain what clues helped you rephrase it as you did.

5. **Make Inferences** In the poem "who are you,little i," who do you think little i is in relation to the **speaker,** or voice that talks to the reader?

6. **Identify Irony** When what happens in a poem is different from what is expected, the poet has used **irony.** How is the ending of "old age sticks" ironic?

7. **Analyze Style** Reread the poems and identify three characteristics of Cummings's style that the poems all share. Using a chart like the one shown, note examples of each characteristic.

Style	Examples	Effects
Does not use capital letters		

Extension and Challenge

8. **SCIENCE CONNECTION** Cummings's poem "who are you,little i" mentions the connection between day and night. The poem "maggie and milly and molly and may" says "it's always ourselves we find in the sea." What other **connections** or cycles can you see in nature? Brainstorm ideas with a small group of your classmates.

9. **Speaking and Listening** How would Cummings's **punctuation** and **line breaks** affect a reading of his poetry? Prepare to read one of the poems for the class. Practice different ways of reading the poem until you feel your reading clearly expresses its meaning.

Are all things CONNECTED?

Refer to the word web you devised on page 522. How would you, after reading the poems, change your web to reflect the messages of the poems?

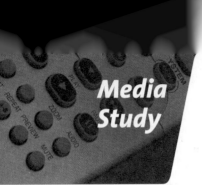

Style and Mood in Photographs
Image Collection on **Media ⬤ Smart** DVD-ROM

When is a PHOTO
more than a picture?

○ **COMMON CORE**

SL 2 Analyze the main ideas and supporting details presented in diverse media and formats, and explain how the ideas clarify a topic, text, or issue under study.

The saying "A picture is worth a thousand words" is perhaps the best way to describe the power of photography. Photographs create meaning beyond the images they contain. In this lesson, you'll discover how two imaginative photographers use their individual styles to make ordinary subjects extraordinary.

Background

Picture This! Imagine you've just received your first camera. What images would you shoot? Would you take pictures of family and friends or of places in your neighborhood? What would you do to make your photographs special?

The Sicilian photographer Ferdinando Scianna (fär'dĕ-nän'dō shä'nə) is known for capturing people and things in quiet moments. Instead of shooting a subject from the usual direct angle, he sometimes uses unusual points of view. Robert Doisneau (rō-bâr' dwä-no') is a famous French photographer. He is known for capturing everyday moments in the streets of Paris and for adding a humorous twist to his photographs.

Media Literacy: Style in Photography

Photographers not only take a picture; they create one. Before shooting a picture, photographers decide what they want to include in a frame. The **frame** is what the camera sees. When **composing,** or arranging a subject within a frame, photographers consider the effects of these elements:

- the position of a subject and its background
- the camera angles, such as low and high angles
- the lighting, which can change the way people or objects appear

Study the photographs closely to learn how Ferdinando Scianna experimented with the camera to create his unique style. To see larger versions of these photographs, please access the DVD.

STRATEGIES FOR INTERPRETING A PHOTOGRAPH

- Consider how photographs tell a story or convey a message. Once photographers find a subject, they experiment with the subject and its background. They may move closer to or farther away from a subject, depending on the message or mood they want to create. Look at the picture of the balconies. What is your impression of the building?

- Notice how Scianna composed the photographs, shooting from an unusual **angle** to create a dramatic effect. Where do you think the camera was placed?

- Observe the effects of **lighting.** Photographers experiment with lighting to create a **mood** or a dramatic effect, to draw attention to something, or to create a contrast between two or more things. For example, direct sunlight creates shadows that can make a person or object appear mysterious, threatening, or gloomy. What is the effect of the shadows in the second photograph?

- **Photograph Pair 1 :** "Milan" and "Coney Island" by Ferdinando Scianna
- **Photograph Pair 2:** "Musician in the Rain" and "The Cellist" by Robert Doisneau
- **Genre:** Photography

Viewing Guide for
Image Collection

The photographs shown on this page were taken by Robert Doisneau. Doisneau is known for his storytelling talents. His photographs celebrate the daily lives of children, artists, sailors, and others who are willing to tell their stories.

To help you explore the following questions, use the DVD to study larger sizes of the photographs.

NOW VIEW

FIRST VIEWING: Comprehension

1. **Summarize** What is happening in the photographs?

2. **Clarify** What do you think is unusual about the musician's position in "The Cellist"?

CLOSE VIEWING: Media Literacy

3. **Interpret Visual Techniques** Photographers can create a **mood** that will make viewers feel happy, sad, curious, or even confused. What mood does Doisneau create in these photographs?

4. **Analyze Style** What is the effect of placing an umbrella over the cello in the photograph entitled "Musician in the Rain"?

5. **Analyze Lighting** How do you think the meaning of the photographs would change if they had been taken on a sunny day? How would the meaning change if they had been taken at night?

6. **Analyze Composition** How would the meaning of "The Cellist" change if the photographer had taken a **close-up shot** of the cello player?

Write or Discuss

Analyze Style In this lesson, you've studied two very distinctive photographic styles. On the DVD, you'll find additional photographs taken by Scianna and Doisneau. Choose one photographer. In your own words, describe his style and its impact on you. As you prepare your response, consider the following:

- Whom or what do you see in each photograph?
- What mood do you think the photographs suggest?
- What elements of composition do you see in the photographs?
- How does the composition reflect the photographer's style?

Produce Your Own Media

Experiment with Photography Here's your opportunity to be the next Doisneau or Scianna. Take a few pictures that show your personal style.

HERE'S HOW The sample photograph was taken by a student in the stairwell of her high school. Notice how she experimented with light and shadow. The photograph was taken from an unusual angle to show the photographer's perspective. Before taking your photographs, follow these suggestions:

- Choose a subject that interests you.
- Determine what you want to keep in and leave out of each photograph.
- Experiment with the position of your subject, camera angles, and lighting.

STUDENT MODEL

COMMON CORE

SL 2 Analyze the main ideas and supporting details presented in diverse media and formats, and explain how the ideas clarify a topic, text, or issue under study.

Media Tools **THINK** central

Go to **thinkcentral.com**.
KEYWORD: HML7-531

Tech Tip

If you have access to photo-editing software, experiment with shades of color. See how different shades, including black and white tones, change the **mood** of your photographs.

Literary Analysis

In the stories in Unit 4, reality does some shifting, sliding, and squirming. To get a grip on it, you needed to figure out key details as you read. You'll do the same kind of work when you write a literary analysis. This type of essay requires you to **analyze,** or explain the meaning of, a literary text.

 Complete the workshop activities in your **Reader/Writer Notebook.**

WRITE WITH A PURPOSE

WRITING TASK

Write a **literary analysis** in which you examine one or two elements of a literary text, such as plot, characters, or theme. Develop an original interpretation of the text, using evidence that is supported consistently.

Idea Starters
- conflict in "The People Could Fly"
- character development in *The True Confessions of Charlotte Doyle*
- mood in "Dark They Were, and Golden-Eyed"

THE ESSENTIALS

Here are some common purposes, audiences, and formats for an analysis of literature.

PURPOSES	AUDIENCES	FORMATS
• to analyze a literary work in more depth • to help other readers understand and enjoy literature	• classmates and teacher • Web users • readers interested in literature • book-group members	• essay for class • blog post • magazine article • speech • critique in a book-review magazine • discussion

COMMON CORE TRAITS

1. DEVELOPMENT OF IDEAS
- presents an **engaging introduction** that identifies the title and author of the text
- develops a **controlling idea** that offers an **analysis** of one or two literary elements
- supports main points of analysis with **relevant concrete details** and **quotations** from the text
- provides a **concluding section** that supports the analysis

2. ORGANIZATION OF IDEAS
- **organizes** ideas in a logical way
- uses **appropriate transitions** to create cohesion and clarify relationships among ideas

3. LANGUAGE FACILITY AND CONVENTIONS
- maintains a **formal style**
- includes **precise language**
- uses **comparative forms** correctly
- employs correct **grammar, capitalization,** and **spelling**

Writing Online

THINK central

Go to **thinkcentral.com.**
KEYWORD: HML7N-532

Planning/Prewriting

 COMMON CORE **W 2a–f** Write informative/explanatory texts to examine a topic through the selection, organization, and analysis of relevant content. **W 5** Develop and strengthen writing by planning.

Getting Started

CHOOSE A LITERARY TEXT

Think of a literary text that profoundly affected you and that you would like to analyze in more depth. Review your *Reader/Writer Notebook* to recall your responses to texts you have read this year. Also consider the Idea Starters on page 532.

▶ **ASK YOURSELF:**

- Which story or selection did I enjoy most?
- How is a specific literary element—such as setting, plot, point of view, theme, or character—used in the text?
- What can I say about the text and its literary elements that would interest other readers?

THINK ABOUT AUDIENCE AND PURPOSE

Keep your audience and purpose in mind as you plan your analysis. Your **audience** includes your classmates and your teacher, who are knowledgeable and interested readers. Your primary **purpose** is to enhance their understanding and enjoyment of the text. You also want to convince your audience to accept your interpretation, using evidence to support your ideas.

▶ **ASK YOURSELF:**

- Who is my audience? What do I want this audience to know about the literary text?
- What elements might my audience find confusing or intriguing?
- What details, examples, and reasons will help convince my audience that my interpretation of the text is valid?
- What **domain-specific**, or specialized, **vocabulary** will my audience need to know to understand my analysis?

DEVELOP A CONTROLLING IDEA

Capture the main idea of your analysis in a **controlling idea,** or thesis statement. For example, if you plan to write about the changes a character undergoes throughout a story, then your controlling idea should briefly summarize those changes. In the rest of your analysis, you will explain those changes—and their causes—in further detail.

▶ **WHAT DOES IT LOOK LIKE?**

Controlling Idea: In *The True Confessions of Charlotte Doyle,* Charlotte's experiences with the captain and the sailors change her ideas about how to judge people and how she wants to live her life.

IDENTIFY YOUR KEY POINTS

Once you have developed a controlling idea, you need to determine the key points that will support it. It may help to skim or reread the literary text with your controlling idea in mind. Ask yourself: What facts, details, or examples in the work prove what I've stated in my controlling idea?

▶ **WHAT DOES IT LOOK LIKE?**

Key Point 1: Charlotte's views have been influenced by her father.

Key Point 2: Charlotte's view of the world affects her initial positive impression of Captain Jaggery.

Key Point 3: Charlotte's views of the captain change dramatically when she sees how he treats the crew.

Planning/Prewriting *continued*

Getting Started

COLLECT EVIDENCE

To be effective, your analysis must include **evidence—quotations, concrete details**, and **reasons** that support your key points. The evidence you provide must be **relevant**—in other words, it should develop and strongly support your controlling idea. Here are some kinds of evidence you might include:

WHAT DOES IT LOOK LIKE?

Direct quotations: sentences or phrases taken directly from the work, which you must place in quotation marks

> Captain Jaggery calls the crew "dirty beasts who demand the touch of the whip."

Concrete details: your own description of specific events, dialogue, and facts from the work that prove a point you want to make

> Mr. Doyle gave Charlotte a journal and expected her to write (with correct spelling) about the events of the voyage.

Reasons: statements that explain something in the text or reveal why you have reached a particular conclusion

> Charlotte's view of the captain begins to change when she sees how badly he treats the crew.

ORGANIZE YOUR IDEAS

In a literary analysis, you should organize your ideas in a logical and **cohesive,** or unified, way. For example, you can organize your key points in the order in which they occur in the story or in order of importance. Select the organizational strategy that works best for your analysis. Then create an informal outline.

WHAT DOES IT LOOK LIKE?

> 1. Influence of Charlotte's father
> - wants her to be well educated and "proper"
> - expects her to write about voyage in journal
> 2. Charlotte's initial view of Jaggery
> - seems like a proper Englishman
> - shares her father's views about girls' behavior

PEER REVIEW Share your controlling idea with a peer who is familiar with the text you plan to analyze. Then ask: What evidence would convince my audience to accept my controlling idea? Search for more quotations, details, and reasons, as necessary.

YOUR TURN In your *Reader/Writer Notebook*, develop your writing plan. Draft your controlling idea. Then list your key points, as shown on page 533. Reread the work, looking for a variety of relevant evidence to support your key points.

Drafting

COMMON CORE

W 4 Produce clear and coherent writing. **W 9a (RL 1, RL 3)** Cite textual evidence to support analysis; analyze how elements of a story interact. **L 1** Demonstrate command of English grammar and usage.

The following chart shows how to organize a clear and effective literary analysis.

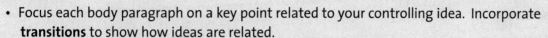
Organizing a Literary Analysis

INTRODUCTION

- To grab your readers' attention, begin with a **quotation** or a **surprising statement**.
- Remember to include the **exact title** of the literary work and the **author's name**.
- State your **controlling idea** clearly so that readers know what your essay will focus on.

▼

BODY

- Focus each body paragraph on a key point related to your controlling idea. Incorporate **transitions** to show how ideas are related.
- Use **precise language** to explain your key points and evidence. Avoid vague or empty words like *things* or *really*.
- Maintain a **formal style.** Avoid slang, and define domain-specific vocabulary as needed.

▼

CONCLUDING SECTION

- **Restate** your controlling idea, but use different words than you did in the introduction.
- Offer a **fresh insight** into the literary work that elaborates on your controlling idea and makes your audience want to read the work for themselves.

GRAMMAR IN CONTEXT: USING COMPARATIVES

When organizing evidence in order of importance, writers often use forms of comparison. The **comparative form** of an adjective or adverb compares two items. When using this form, add the ending *-er* or the word *more* to the adjective or adverb. The **superlative form** compares three or more items. In this case, add *-est* or the word *most*.

Comparative Form

> The sailors have an even great**er** influence on Charlotte than Captain Jaggery has.

> Charlotte survives, but **more** important is the bond she forms with the sailors.

Superlative Form

> The harsh**est** part of Charlotte's voyage occurs when Captain Jaggery kills two sailors.

> Charlotte's **most** impressive accomplishment is her changed attitude about people.

YOUR TURN

Develop a draft of your analysis by following the structure above. Use comparative and superlative modifiers to indicate which evidence is most important.

Revising

In the revision stage, you look closely to determine whether you've expressed your ideas in the most effective way for your purpose and audience. The information in this chart can help you revise, rewrite, and improve your draft.

LITERARY ANALYSIS

Ask Yourself	Tips	Revision Strategies
1. Does the introduction identify the author's name and the title of the work the analysis focuses on?	▶ **Highlight** the author and the title.	▶ **Add** a sentence or a phrase naming the author and the title.
2. Does the introduction have a controlling idea that explains the analysis?	▶ **Underline** the controlling idea.	▶ **Add** a sentence that clearly states the controlling idea and sets up the writer's analysis.
3. Do the key points presented in the body paragraphs support the controlling idea?	▶ **Bracket** the key point discussed in each paragraph of the body.	▶ If necessary, **revise** the body paragraphs to clearly explain the connection between each key point and the controlling idea.
4. Does the writer provide relevant evidence to support each key point?	▶ **Draw a box** around each supporting quotation, detail, or reason.	▶ If necessary, **add** quotations, concrete details, and reasons to support the key points.
5. Does the writer maintain a formal style?	▶ **Circle** contractions and informal language.	▶ **Reword** text to avoid contractions and **replace** informal language with precise, formal vocabulary.
6. Does the concluding section restate the controlling idea and offer a fresh insight into the literary text?	▶ **Highlight** the sentence that restates the controlling idea, and **draw** a wavy line under sentences that say something insightful about the text.	▶ If necessary, **reword** the controlling idea and **revise** or **rewrite** the concluding section to clarify why the text is significant.

YOUR TURN **PEER REVIEW** Exchange essays with a classmate. As you read your classmate's analysis, focus on the evidence he or she offers and judge whether that evidence clearly supports the controlling idea. If not, give concrete suggestions for improvement or reworking.

ANALYZE A STUDENT DRAFT

Read this student's draft and the comments about it as a model for revising your own literary analysis.

COMMON CORE

W 2b Develop the topic with relevant details. **W 5** Strengthen writing by revising, editing, rewriting, or trying a new approach. **W 9a (RL 1, RL 3)** Cite textual evidence to support analysis; analyze how elements of a story interact.

A Girl's Adventure
by Sophia Eckerle, Paradise Canyon Elementary School

❶ "Not every thirteen-year-old girl is accused of murder, brought to trial, and found guilty." This is the opening sentence of *The True Confessions Of Charlotte Doyle,* a novel by Avi. The novel takes place in 1832. It tells the story of Charlotte, who has finished her schooling in England and must sail home to America. She sails on the *Seahawk,* a rundown ship under the command of Captain Jaggery, a strange character. Charlotte's experiences with the captain and the sailors change her ideas about how to judge people and how she wants to live her life.

❷ As a wealthy and protective father, Mr. Doyle wants to shape Charlotte's future. He sends Charlotte to the expensive Barrington School for Better Girls in England. He has very high expectations for her and wants her to become an educated proper young lady. Before her journey, Mr. Doyle gave Charlotte a journal and expected her to write (with correct spelling) about the events of the voyage.

❸ At the start of the journey, Captain Jaggery is a proper Englishman— one a thirteen-year-old girl could look up to. Like Charlotte's father, the captain believes that a young girl should wear fancy dresses and devote herself to studying instead of parading around with the crew wearing men's clothes.

> In her introduction, Sophia mentions the **title of the work** and the **author's name.**

> Sophia states her **controlling idea** about the main character at the end of her first paragraph.

> She does not explain how the main idea of this paragraph **supports her controlling idea.**

LEARN HOW **Support Your Controlling Idea** Sophia supports her characterization of Jaggery with details, but she does not explain how this relates to her controlling idea. To fix the problem, she added details that describe the influences on Charlotte's view of the world.

SOPHIA'S REVISION TO PARAGRAPH ❸

Charlotte's views have been largely influenced by her father. Because of this, she sees

At the start of the journey, ~~Captain Jaggery is~~ *as* a proper Englishman— one a thirteen-year-old girl could look up to. ~~Like Charlotte's father, the captain believes that a young girl should wear fancy dresses and devote herself to studying instead of parading around with the crew wearing men's clothes.~~ *Charlotte is fooled into thinking the captain is trustworthy because of his meticulous clothes and manners.*

4   Charlotte's view of the captain begins to change when she sees how badly he treats the crew. He calls the crew "dirty beasts who demand the touch of the whip." Charlotte sees that this is not true.

5   When the men mutiny against him, the deterioration of Captain Jaggery's mind continues. He kills two of the sailors for an attempted uprising. Charlotte decides that the captain is mad. Changing her fancy clothes for the clothes of a common sailor, she joins the crew. She has learned that the sailors who treat her kindly are the ones to trust, not the cruel captain. His high rank and his nice clothes are not important. Jaggery retaliates by giving her the hardest work on the ship, destroying the barrier between the aristocrats and the working class that Charlotte joined. In this way, he contributes to Charlotte's changing attitudes.

6   Charlotte's father and Captain Jaggery influenced Charlotte's life and led to her adventures aboard the *Seahawk*. By the end of her ordeal, Charlotte was happy to run to the arms of her protective father.

> Sophia includes a **quotation** from the novel to illustrate a character's nature.

> She explains how the **details** of the story support her controlling idea.

> Sophia's concluding section does not return to her controlling idea or leave readers with any new insights.

LEARN HOW Strengthen Your Concluding Section In a literary analysis, a concluding section must restate the controlling idea in a different way and also should provide fresh insights into the work. In other words, the conclusion needs to leave readers with something to think about or a reason to be interested in the work. Sophia's original concluding section did little more than describe the end of the novel. Her revisions, shown in blue, strengthen her concluding section by clarifying her analysis.

SOPHIA'S REVISION TO PARAGRAPH 6

Charlotte's father and Captain Jaggery influenced the course of Charlotte's life, but perhaps the men on the ship influenced her more. Though at first happy to return to her father, Charlotte's experiences with the sailors forever changed the way she thought about the world. Read this exciting novel to appreciate all that Charlotte learns through her adventure and the surprising decision she makes about her future.

YOUR TURN   Use feedback from your peers and teacher, as well as the two "Learn How" lessons, to revise your essay. Evaluate how well you have achieved your purpose and provided an analysis that will intrigue your audience. If needed, try a new approach.

Editing and Publishing

 COMMON CORE **W 5** Strengthen writing by revising and editing.
L 2 Demonstrate command of the conventions of standard English capitalization, punctuation, and spelling when writing.

You've refined the development, style, and organization of your analysis. Now, in the proofreading stage, you must catch and correct errors in grammar, usage, spelling, and punctuation. These kinds of mistakes can distract your audience and make them less likely to accept your ideas.

GRAMMAR IN CONTEXT: CAPITALIZING CORRECTLY

In your literary analysis, you will mention the title of the text you are focusing on and the author's name. As you edit your draft, be sure you are following the rules of capitalization. For example, when you mention an author, capitalize the first name, the last name, and any initials.

> *Rudyard Kipling*   *Avi*   *Booker T. Washington*   *O. Henry*
>
> [Like all personal names, authors' names are capitalized.]

In the title of a text, always capitalize the first and last word and all of the important words in between. Do not capitalize articles (such as *a* and *the*), coordinating conjunctions (such as *and, or,* and *but*), or prepositions of fewer than five letters (such as *for, to,* and *of*), unless they begin or end the title.

> *"A Day's Wait"*   *Out of the Dust*
> *"It Was a Long Time Before"*   *"One Perfect Rose"*
>
> [In these titles, each word is capitalized except for the **preposition** *of* and the **articles** *a* and *the*.]

As Sophia edited her essay, she realized she had incorrectly capitalized the preposition *of* in the title of a novel.

> *This is the opening sentence of* The True Confessions Of Charlotte Doyle, *a novel by Avi.*

PUBLISH YOUR WRITING

Share your literary analysis with an audience.

- Submit your analysis to a magazine for young people.
- Publish your essay as a blog posting or on a book-review Web site.
- Adapt your essay into a critique that you deliver to your audience.

YOUR TURN Correct any errors in your analysis. Make sure you have correctly capitalized any titles and authors' names. Check for spelling and punctuation mistakes. Then publish your final essay for others to enjoy.

Scoring Rubric

Use the rubric below to evaluate your literary analysis from the Writing Workshop or your response to the on-demand writing task on the next page.

LITERARY ANALYSIS

SCORE	COMMON CORE TRAITS
6	• **Development** Has an engaging introduction; includes an insightful controlling idea; supports points with relevant evidence; ends powerfully • **Organization** Arranges ideas in an effective, logical order; uses appropriate transitions to create cohesion and link ideas • **Language** Consistently maintains a formal style; uses precise language; shows a strong command of conventions
5	• **Development** Has an effective introduction; provides an original controlling idea; supports points with evidence; has a strong concluding section • **Organization** Arranges ideas logically; uses transitions to link ideas • **Language** Maintains a formal style; uses precise language; has a few errors in conventions
4	• **Development** Has an introduction that could be more engaging; includes a controlling idea that states an analysis; could use some more evidence; has an adequate concluding section • **Organization** Arranges ideas logically; uses some ineffective transitions • **Language** Mostly maintains a formal style; needs more precise language at times; has a few distracting errors in conventions
3	• **Development** Has an adequate introduction; has a controlling idea that makes an obvious statement; lacks enough support; has an ordinary concluding section • **Organization** Has some flaws in organization; needs more transitions • **Language** Frequently lapses into an informal style; uses some vague words; has some major errors in conventions
2	• **Development** Has a weak introduction and controlling idea; lacks specific, relevant evidence; has a weak concluding section • **Organization** Has organizational flaws; lacks transitions throughout • **Language** Uses an informal style and vague words; has many distracting errors in conventions
1	• **Development** Has no controlling idea; lacks support; ends abruptly • **Organization** Has no organization or transitions • **Language** Uses an inappropriate style and vague words; has major problems with grammar, mechanics, and spelling

Preparing for Timed Writing

 COMMON CORE **W 10** Write routinely over shorter time frames for a range of tasks, purposes, and audiences.

1. ANALYZE THE TASK   5 MIN

Read the task carefully. Then read it again, underlining words that tell the topic, the type of writing, the audience, and the purpose.

WRITING TASK   *Topic*   *Type of writing*

Recall a <u>story with a character that you admired or liked</u>. Write a <u>literary analysis</u> in which you <u>describe and analyze the character</u> for your <u>classmates</u>. Include a clear controlling idea that tells why you like or admire the character, and support your controlling idea with relevant evidence from the story.   *Audience*

Purpose

2. PLAN YOUR RESPONSE   10 MIN

Think of a character you know well enough to write about. Write a one-sentence controlling idea that clearly explains why you admire the character. Then list several reasons you will use to support your controlling idea. Gather evidence to support each reason, including descriptions of the character's speech, actions, and thoughts, as well as quotations that reveal the character's admirable traits.

Reasons	Evidence

3. RESPOND TO THE TASK   20 MIN

Using the notes you just recorded, draft your analysis.
- In the introduction, present the author's name and the title of the work, and provide a clear controlling idea.
- Present each main point or reason in a separate paragraph, and provide relevant evidence. Include as many concrete details about your character as you can.
- In the concluding section, restate your controlling idea and offer a final insight.

4. IMPROVE YOUR RESPONSE   5–10 MIN

Revising Check your draft against the writing task. Did you offer a clear analysis? Did you support your controlling idea with concrete details and relevant evidence?
Proofreading Proofread your essay to correct errors in grammar, spelling, punctuation, and capitalization. Make your edits neatly, and erase any stray marks.
Checking Your Final Copy Before you turn in your analysis, read it one more time to catch any errors you may have missed.

Speaking & Listening Workshop

Presenting a Critique

How many times have you told your friends *exactly* what you think of movies, TV shows, or best-selling novels? When you present a critique of a literary text, you share your opinions in a more formal setting.

Complete the workshop activities in your **Reader/Writer Notebook.**

SPEAK WITH A PURPOSE	COMMON CORE TRAITS
TASK Adapt your literary analysis into an **oral literary critique.** Practice your critique, and then present it to your class.	**A STRONG ORAL CRITIQUE . . .** • stays focused on a controlling idea that offers an opinion • presents findings and evidence in a logical order • uses formal English to deliver the message • uses effective verbal techniques, such as speaking rate, volume, and enunciation • enhances the message with nonverbal techniques, such as eye contact and gestures

COMMON CORE

SL 4 Present claims and findings, emphasizing salient points in a focused, coherent manner; use eye contact, adequate volume, and clear pronunciation. **SL 6** Adapt speech, demonstrating command of formal English when appropriate.

Adapt Your Literary Analysis

In a critique, you have to go a step beyond the analysis you provided in your essay. To be successful, you have to **evaluate,** or judge, how well the author used the literary elements you discussed. Keep in mind these points as you plan and develop your critique:

- **Audience and Purpose** Your audience is your peers. Because you will be delivering your critique to the class, you should use the conventions of language appropriate for a formal presentation. Use correct formal English, avoid slang, and choose words that will be familiar to your audience. Your purpose is to keep your audience engaged as they listen.

- **Introduction** Include a quotation or a question that will grab your audience's attention. Revise your controlling idea to offer a **claim**, or opinion statement.

- **Evidence** Consider which descriptions, facts, details, and examples from the text are most **pertinent**, or relevant, to your claim. Write key points and evidence on note cards to help you present your findings in a focused, coherent way.

- **Transitions** Help your audience follow along by using plenty of transitional words and phrases. Phrases such as *one example of, a second example of,* and *further evidence of* will help your listeners keep track of your ideas.

- **Conclusion** Restate your claim in a memorable fashion. You might end by recommending the literary text to your listeners.

THINK central

Speaking & Listening Online

Go to thinkcentral.com.
KEYWORD: HML7-542

Deliver Your Speech

USE VERBAL TECHNIQUES

How you use your voice can be as important as what you say. Practice delivery techniques before you address your audience. Consider the tips in this chart.

Using Your Voice to Create Effects

TECHNIQUE	WHAT IT MEANS	TIPS
Enunciation	how clearly you pronounce words	• Practice your speech, noting words that you stumble over. • Use a dictionary to check pronunciations, or find replacement words in a thesaurus.
Volume	how loudly you speak	• To stress certain points, speak more loudly or softly. • Ask a partner whether your volume is varied enough and whether you can be heard clearly at all times.
Inflection	the tone of your voice, used to indicate feelings or opinions	• Emphasize important ideas by raising or lowering the pitch of your voice. • Ask a partner whether you sound convincing and reasonable.
Speaking Rate	how quickly you speak; also called *tempo*	• Speak slowly enough for your audience to keep up, but not so slowly that it sounds unnatural. • Use pauses to emphasize major points. • Stop and take a breath when necessary.

USE NONVERBAL TECHNIQUES

Use these nonverbal techniques to engage your audience:

- Stand up straight to show confidence.
- Make eye contact. During your speech, try to look at each person at least once.
- Use natural gestures to emphasize your points. For example, if you are describing a deep emotion felt by a story character, you might briefly touch your hand to your heart.
- Use appropriate facial expressions to reinforce your opinions.

YOUR TURN

As a Speaker Deliver your critique to a peer, using the tips on this page. Use feedback from your peer to revise your critique.

As a Listener Evaluate your peer's delivery. Listen to ensure you understand the claim and the details that support it. Note your peer's verbal and nonverbal techniques, and provide constructive, specific feedback.

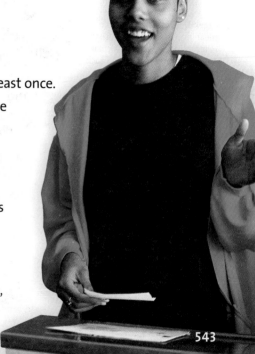

Assessment Practice

DIRECTIONS Read this selection and answer the questions that follow.

Mrs. Barrymore and her husband are servants at Baskerville Hall. Sherlock Holmes's friend, Dr. Watson, is describing the couple in a letter to the famous detective.

from The Hound of the Baskervilles *by Sir Arthur Conan Doyle*

1   Mrs. Barrymore is of interest to me. She is a heavy, solid person, very limited, intensely respectable, and inclined to be puritanical. You could hardly conceive a less emotional subject. Yet I have told you how, on the first night here, I heard her sobbing bitterly, and since then I have more than once observed traces of tears upon her face. Some deep sorrow gnaws ever at her heart. Sometimes I wonder if she has a guilty memory which haunts her, and sometimes I suspect Barrymore of being a domestic tyrant. I have always felt that there was something singular and questionable in this man's character, but the adventure of last night brings all my suspicions to a head.

2   And yet it may seem a small matter in itself. You are aware that I am not a very sound sleeper, and since I have been on guard in this house my slumbers have been lighter than ever. Last night, about two in the morning, I was aroused by a stealthy step passing my room. I rose, opened my door, and peeped out. A long black shadow was trailing down the corridor. It was thrown by a man who walked softly down the passage with a candle held in his hand. He was in shirt and trousers, with no covering to his feet. I could merely see the outline, but his height told me that it was Barrymore. He walked very slowly and circumspectly, and there was something indescribably guilty and furtive in his whole appearance.

3   I have told you that the corridor is broken by the balcony which runs round the hall, but that it is resumed upon the farther side. I waited until he had passed out of sight and then I followed him. When I came round the balcony he had reached the end of the farther corridor, and I could see from the glimmer of light through an open door that he had entered one of the rooms. Now, all these rooms are unfurnished and unoccupied, so that his expedition became more mysterious than ever. The light shone

steadily as if he were standing motionless. I crept down the passage as noiselessly as I could and peeped round the corner of the door.

4   Barrymore was crouching at the window with the candle held against the glass. His profile was half turned towards me, and his face seemed to be rigid with expectation as he stared out into the blackness of the moor. For some minutes he stood watching intently. Then he gave a deep groan and with an impatient gesture he put out the light. Instantly I made my way back to my room, and very shortly came the stealthy steps passing once more upon their return journey. Long afterwards when I had fallen into a light sleep I heard a key turn somewhere in a lock, but I could not tell whence the sound came. What it all means I cannot guess, but there is some secret business going on in this house of gloom which sooner or later we shall get to the bottom of. I do not trouble you with my theories, for you asked me to furnish you only with facts. I have had a long talk with Sir Henry this morning, and we have made a plan of campaign founded upon my observations of last night. I will not speak about it just now, but it should make my next report interesting reading.

GO ON ➤

Reading Comprehension

Use the excerpt from *The Hound of the Baskervilles* to answer questions 1–9.

1. Which word best describes the mood of this passage?

   A. Comforting

   B. Peaceful

   C. Suspenseful

   D. Thrilling

2. Which statement is the best summary of Dr. Watson's impression of Mrs. Barrymore?

   A. She is intensely moral, sometimes emotional, and not likeable at all.

   B. She is reliable, trustworthy, and yet unexpectedly severe and cold.

   C. She wants people to feel sorry for her, so she makes a show of crying at night.

   D. She gives an appearance of being under control, but something is upsetting her.

3. Which sentence contributes most clearly to the mood of this excerpt?

   A. *You could hardly conceive a less emotional subject.*

   B. *Last night, about two in the morning, I was aroused by a stealthy step passing my room.*

   C. *He was in shirt and trousers, with no covering to his feet.*

   D. *I do not trouble you with my theories, for you asked me to furnish you only with facts.*

4. How does Barrymore's "guilty and furtive" appearance affect the mood of the story?

   A. Creates a dark, frightening mood

   B. Makes the mood less scary

   C. Adds to the happy mood

   D. Produces a mood of silliness

5. The description of Barrymore's actions at the beginning of paragraph 4 affects the mood of the story by —

   A. providing relief

   B. increasing the tension

   C. making everything clear

   D. adding hope

6. The author's tone in the passage concerning Dr. Watson's investigation is —

   A. detached

   B. ironic

   C. suspicious

   D. vengeful

7. The author uses the imagery of a long, black shadow to create a mood of —

   A. anger

   B. liveliness

   C. mystery

   D. sorrow

8. The author's style is best described as —

    A. a formal, flowery style that relies on symbolic language

    B. a formal, conversational style that relies on descriptive observations

    C. an objective, journalistic style that relies on scientific facts

    D. an informal, folksy style that relies on natural speech patterns

9. Which statement is the best summary of Dr. Watson's actions on the morning after he sees Barrymore?

    A. Dr. Watson reports on what he saw to Sir Henry, and they come up with a plan of action.

    B. Dr. Watson hears a key turning in a lock, but he doesn't know where.

    C. Dr. Watson barely makes it back to his room before he hears steps coming back again.

    D. Dr. Watson hears someone weeping miserably in the house.

SHORT CONSTRUCTED RESPONSE
Write two or three sentences to answer this question.

10. Briefly summarize Dr. Watson's report to Sherlock Holmes. Identify the characters and the setting in your summary.

Write a paragraph to answer this question.

11. Reread the descriptions of Mr. and Mrs. Barrymore in the excerpt. Describe the author's style based on his words, sentences, and tone.

GO ON

547

Vocabulary

1. Which word has the same meaning as *conceive* in this sentence from paragraph 1?

"You could hardly <u>conceive</u> a less emotional subject."

    A. Imagine   **C.** Understand

    B. Plan   **D.** See

2. Which word has the same meaning as *gnaws* in this sentence from paragraph 1?

"Some deep sorrow <u>gnaws</u> ever at her heart."

    A. Angers   **C.** Strengthens

    B. Hovers   **D.** Worries

3. Which word has the same meaning as *intently* in this sentence from paragraph 4?

"For some minutes he stood watching <u>intently</u>."

    A. Angrily

    B. Carefully

    C. Intelligently

    D. Sadly

4. The Latin root *cline* means "lean." What does the word *inclined* mean in paragraph 1?

"She is a heavy, solid person, very limited, intensely respectable, and <u>inclined</u> to be puritanical."

    A. Tending to be a certain way

    B. Leaning over to the side

    C. Completely honest

    D. Extremely worried

5. The Greek word *theoros* means "spectator." What does the word *theories* mean in paragraph 4?

"I do not trouble you with my <u>theories</u>, for you asked me to furnish you only with facts."

    A. The acts that a person sees

    B. Games that people watch

    C. Guesses based on limited information

    D. Facts that really happen

Revising and Editing

DIRECTIONS Read this passage and answer the questions that follow.

(1) For thousands of years, bodies were preserved. (2) A process called embalming preserved them. (3) Mummification was an embalming process used by the Egyptians. (4) There were various embalming processes. (5) An embalmer would remove internal organs. (6) The embalmer would dry out the body and wrap it in linens. (7) The embalmer used herbs and salt for drying. (8) The embalmer placed linen inside the body. (9) Such careful preparations show how important burial was to the Egyptians.

1. What is the BEST way to combine sentences 1 and 2?

   A. Embalming for thousands of years were a process of preserving bodies.

   B. Embalming, a process for thousands of years, were preserving bodies.

   C. Embalming was a preserved bodies process for thousands of years.

   D. Embalming, a process of preserving bodies, was used for thousands of years.

2. What is the BEST way to combine sentences 3 and 4?

   A. Mummification, among the various embalming processes, were used by the Egyptians.

   B. Mummification, among the various embalming processes, was used by the Egyptians.

   C. Mummification, used by the Egyptians, were among the various embalming processes.

   D. Mummification was an embalming process, the Egyptians used various embalming processes.

3. What is the BEST way to combine sentences 5 and 6?

   A. An embalmer removed internal organs, dried out the body, and wrapped it in linens.

   B. Removing internal organs, the body was dried out and wrapped in linens.

   C. Removing internal organs, linens wrapped the dried out body.

   D. Removing internal organs, the dried out body was wrapped in linens.

4. What is the BEST way to combine sentences 7 and 8?

   A. Using herbs and salt for drying, linen was then placed inside the body.

   B. Using herbs and salt for drying, the body then had linen placed inside.

   C. Using herbs and salt for drying, the embalmer then placed linen inside the body.

   D. Using herbs and salt for drying, herbs, salt, and linen were then placed inside the body.

STOP

Ideas for Independent Reading

Which questions from Unit 4 made an impression on you?
Continue exploring them with these books.

Can where you are change who you are?

Skellig
by David Almond

What if you discovered an ailing being in an old garage in your new neighborhood? This happens to Michael, who shares his find with his neighbor, Mina, and the two embark on a secret mission to save Skellig.

Dragonwings
by Laurence Yep

In the early 1900s, a Chinese boy named Moon Shadow travels to San Francisco. There he joins his father, Windrider, whom he has never met. The two survive poverty, loneliness, and an earthquake as they work to fulfill a long-held dream.

Shabanu: Daughter of the Wind
by Suzanne Staples

Shabanu is the 11-year-old daughter of a nomadic family in Pakistan. When it becomes apparent that the family's only chance to survive is to pledge Shabanu in marriage, she has to make a decision. Where will she go?

Is it brave to suffer in silence?

Blackwater
by Eve Bunting

Thirteen-year-old Brodie feels he may have caused the accidental death of Pauline and Otis. It all started out innocently enough, but then there was a fall into the rushing current of the Blackwater River. Should Brodie tell what he knows?

The Window
by Michael Dorris

Rayona, who is part Native American and part African American, has suffered a childhood of neglect and secrets. When her father sends her to live with her grandmother in Kentucky, she finally finds some security and happiness.

The Voices of Silence
by Bel Mooney

When you live in a totalitarian society, keeping silent means staying alive. Does that make you brave? Thirteen-year-old Flora Popescu confronts this question as she comes of age in Communist Romania.

What makes us laugh?

Bud, Not Buddy
by Christopher Curtis

During the Great Depression, ten-year-old Bud escapes from a terrible foster home and hits the road in search of his real dad. The humorous way he tells about his travels across Michigan might make you laugh out loud.

Squashed
by Joan Bauer

Ellie's future prize-winning pumpkin needs to gain 200 pounds in time for the Rock River Pumpkin Weigh-In, and Ellie thinks she needs to lose 20 pounds. Ellie finds that one way to cope is through her sense of humor.

A Long Way from Chicago
by Richard Peck

Each summer Joey and his sister, Mary Alice, travel to downstate Illinois for a visit with Grandma Dowdel. This year, her tendency to stretch the truth and hatch wild schemes creates hilarious adventures.

Picture the Moment

APPRECIATING POETRY

Share What You Know

What is a POEM?

There are almost as many poems as there are people. Some poems are very formal, and others are more playful. Some rhyme, and some don't. Some are published in beautiful books, and others are written on sidewalks. But the thing that makes all poems alike is that each expresses the writer's imagination and feelings in a creative way.

ACTIVITY Think of the poems you've read in the past. Can you remember a particular one that you enjoyed? Now think about the lyrics of your favorite song. With a partner, share the name of the poem and song you chose. Then compare the poem and the song lyrics by considering the following questions:

• What is the most memorable line of the poem or song?

• Are the lines grouped in any particular way?

• Do any of the lines rhyme?

Discuss whether the song lyrics you chose should be considered a poem.

Find It Online!

THINK central

Go to thinkcentral.com for the interactive version of this unit.

Preview Unit Goals

TEXT ANALYSIS	• Analyze a poem's form and structure, including free verse, lyric poetry, narrative poetry, ballads, and haiku
	• Determine the figurative and connotative meanings of words and phrases in a text
	• Analyze the interaction of elements such as rhyme, repetition, and alliteration
READING	• Make inferences and connect ideas between texts
	• Analyze the structure an author uses to organize text
WRITING AND LANGUAGE	• Write an online feature article
	• Choose language to eliminate redundancy
	• Use commas to separate coordinate conjunctions
SPEAKING AND LISTENING	• Update an online feature article
VOCABULARY	• Identify the meaning of foreign words used in English
ACADEMIC VOCABULARY	• encounter • integrity • specific • tradition • vary

Appreciating Poetry

What makes a song unforgettable? Perhaps it's the rhythm of the music or the catchy lyrics. Poetry is memorable in the same way. Like musicians, poets use words, rhythm, and sounds to convey feelings and ideas. In this workshop, you will learn how poets use the structure and elements of poetry to express meaning.

Part 1: Structure and Form

How does a poem speak to you from the page? First, you may notice its shape. A poem's shape, or **form,** is the way its words and lines are laid out on the page. As the main unit in a poem, the **line** may or may not be a complete sentence, and it can vary in length.

In some poems, the lines are arranged in groups, called **stanzas**. A stanza's role in a poem is like that of a paragraph in prose. Each stanza is a separate emotion or idea, but it contributes to the overall meaning of the poem.

Some poems have a **conventional,** or **traditional,** form, which means they follow fixed rules, such as a set number of lines or a repeating pattern of rhythm or rhyme. Traditional forms include the limerick and haiku. Poems in **irregular,** or **open,** form may have rhyme, but their shapes and patterns may be unusual. **Free verse,** an open form, has a rhythm more like everyday speech, and it does not have regular patterns of rhyme.

Whether writing in traditional or open forms, poets use graphical elements to help convey meaning. **Graphical** elements include the position and appearance of words, capital letters, lines, and stanzas on the page.

Examine the structure and form of this traditional poem.

COMMON CORE

Included in this workshop:
RL 1 Cite textual evidence to support analysis of what the text says explicitly. **RL 4** Determine the meaning of words and phrases as they are used in a text, including figurative and connotative meanings; analyze the impact of rhymes and other repetitions of sounds on a specific verse or stanza of a poem. **RL 5** Analyze how a poem's form or structure contributes to its meaning.

A MINOR BIRD

Poem by **Robert Frost**

I have wished a bird would fly away,
And not sing by my house all day;

Have clapped my hands at him from the door
When it seemed as if I could bear no more.

5 The fault must partly have been in me.
The bird was not to blame for his key.

And of course there must be something wrong
In wanting to silence any song.

EXAMINE THE POEM

- Notice that this poem is made up of four two-line stanzas.

- Look at the four pairs of rhyming words.

- Read the poem aloud to hear its singsong rhythm.

- Note that each of the eight lines begins with a capital letter, even though there are only four complete sentences in the poem.

MODEL: STRUCTURE AND FORM

The following poem is written in free verse and sounds like everyday speech. Read it aloud to hear what the speaker is saying about his or her special hiding place. Notice how the poem's structure hints at its meaning.

UNDER THE BACK PORCH

Poem by **Virginia Hamilton**

Our house is two stories high
shaped like a white box.
There is a yard stretched around it
and in back
5   a wooden porch.

Under the back porch is my place.
I rest there.
I go there when I have to be alone.
It is always shaded and damp.
10   Sunlight only slants through the slats
in long strips of light,
and the smell of the damp
is moist green,
like the moss that grows here.

15   My sisters and brothers
can stand on the back porch
and never know
I am here
underneath.
20   It is my place.
All mine.

Close Read

1. Describe the focus of each stanza. (What do you "see"?) Look at the boxed details for clues.

2. Why do you think the speaker likes hiding under the back porch? Explain how the structure and form of the poem help you imagine the speaker's world.

3. Notice the last four lines of the poem. What effect does their short length help to create? (Hint: Think about where the speaker is at this point in the poem.)

Part 2: Poetic Devices

Poetry has the power to affect your emotions and transport you to new worlds, much as music and films do. Poets, however, rely on language alone to create sounds and images. With sound devices, poets can match the rhythm of ocean waves or the roar of a crowd. They use imagery and figurative language to appeal to your senses and create scenes as vivid as those that unfold on a movie screen. As you read a poem aloud, notice how the sounds and images capture your attention and help you understand the poem's meaning.

SOUND DEVICES

Sound devices give poems a musical quality, but they can also create a mood and emphasize important ideas or words. Here are a few of the sound devices poets use.

SOUND DEVICES	EXAMPLES
RHYME the repetition of sounds at the end of words, as in *me* and *see* **RHYTHM** the pattern of stressed (ˊ) and unstressed (˘) syllables in each line. (A poem with a repeating pattern has what is called a meter.)	Notice how the rhythm and rhyme in this poem help to create a playful, upbeat mood. They came to tell your faults to me, They named them over one by one; I laughed aloud when they were done, I knew them all so well before,— Oh, they were blind, too blind to see Your faults had made me love you more. — "Faults" by Sara Teasdale
REPETITION the use of a word, phrase, or line more than once **ALLITERATION** the repetition of consonant sounds at the beginning of words, such as the *c* in *curved crook*	The repeated phrases and the alliteration in the last line help to emphasize the moon's shape. How thin and sharp is the moon tonight! How thin and sharp and ghostly white Is the slim curved crook of the moon tonight! — "Winter Moon" by Langston Hughes

MODEL 1: RHYME AND RHYTHM

As you read this short poem aloud, notice how Emily Dickinson uses rhyme and rhythm to emphasize the most important words.

A word is dead
Poem by **Emily Dickinson**

A word is ‾dead‾
When it is ‾said,‾
Some say.

Í sǎy ĭt júst
5   Běgíns tǒ líve
That dáy.

Close Read

1. One pair of rhyming words is boxed. Find the other pair.

2. Stressed and unstressed syllables are marked in the second stanza. How does the rhythm in this stanza compare with that in the first stanza?

MODEL 2: OTHER SOUND DEVICES

This free-verse poem is filled with sound devices: repetition, rhyme, alliteration, and **onomatopoeia**—the use of words (made-up or real) whose sounds suggest their meanings. How do these sound devices help you experience the snow?

Cynthia in the Sn❄w
Poem by **Gwendolyn Brooks**

It SUSHES.
It hushes
The loudness in the road.
It flitter-twitters,
5   And laughs away from me.
It laughs a lovely whiteness,
And whitely whirs away,
To be
Some otherwhere,
10 Still white as milk or shirts.
So beautiful it hurts.

Close Read

1. What onomatopoeic words does the poet use to suggest the silencing effect of falling snow?

2. The use of alliteration in the boxed line helps to create a light, joyful mood. Find another example of alliteration.

3. Identify three pairs of rhymes. For one pair, explain what qualities of snow the rhyme helps to emphasize.

IMAGERY AND FIGURATIVE LANGUAGE

Imagery is language that appeals to the five senses—sight, hearing, smell, taste, and touch. "Cynthia in the Snow" focuses on the sense of hearing, but it also helps you see the snow as it "whitely whirs away." With a few vivid images, the poet draws you into the winter scene.

One way poets create imagery is through **figurative language.** Figurative language uses creative comparisons to help readers picture ordinary things in new ways. For example, the snow is not just white but "white as milk or shirts." Here are three types of figurative language.

TYPE	EXAMPLE
SIMILE a comparison between two unlike things, using the word *like* or *as*	**This simile compares a cat's coloring to spilled milk. The word *as* signals the comparison.** He's white As spilled milk, My cat who sleeps With his belly Turned toward The summer sky. —from "Ode to Mi Gato" by Gary Soto

METAPHOR
 	
 a comparison between two unlike things that does not contain the word *like* or *as*
	This metaphor compares fame to a bee. It conveys both the good and the bad side of fame.
	
	 Fame is a bee.
	    It has a song—
	 It has a sting—
	    Ah, too, it has a wing.
	
	 —by Emily Dickinson

PERSONIFICATION
 	
 a description of an object, an animal, a place, or an idea as if it were human or had human qualities
	Here, "proud words" are given human qualities.
	
	 Look out how you use proud words.
	 When you let proud words go, it is
	    not easy to call them back.
	 They wear long boots, hard boots; they
	    walk off proud; they can't hear you
	    calling—
	 Look out how you use proud words.
	
	 —"Primer Lesson" by Carl Sandburg

Part 3: Analyze the Text

In this poem, the speaker reflects on her mother's courage, a quality that she has missed since her mother died. Use what you've learned in this workshop to analyze the elements—structure, form, sound devices, figurative language, and imagery—that help to create a picture of a remarkable parent.

The COURAGE
That My Mother Had

Poem by **Edna St. Vincent Millay**

The courage that my mother had
Went with her, and is with her still:
Rock from New England quarried;[1]
Now granite in a granite hill.

5   The golden brooch[2] my mother wore
She left behind for me to wear;
I have no thing I treasure more:
Yet, it is something I could spare.

Oh, if instead she'd left to me
10 The thing she took into the grave!—
That courage like a rock, which she
Has no more need of, and I have.

---

1. **quarried:** dug up from the ground.
2. **brooch:** a piece of jewelry that can be fastened to clothing.

Close Read

1. Describe two characteristics that make this a traditional poem. Think about the number of lines in each stanza and the patterns of rhythm and rhyme.

2. One example of alliteration is boxed. Find another example.

3. Identify the simile in the third stanza. What does it suggest about the mother's personality?

4. Identify the focus of each stanza and describe what each one contributes to the overall meaning of the poem. Think about the speaker's view of herself and of her mother.

The Names

HISTORY Video link at
thinkcentral.com

Poem by Billy Collins

VIDEO TRAILER **THINK** central   KEYWORD: HML7-560

Why do we need
MEMORIALS?

COMMON CORE

RL 4 Determine the meaning of words and phrases as they are used in a text, including figurative and connotative meanings; analyze the impact of rhymes and other repetitions of sounds on a specific verse or stanza of a poem. **RL 5** Analyze how a poem's form or structure contributes to its meaning.

When tragedy strikes, people are often unsure about how to restore hope. Many people find that creating a memorial to remember and reflect on a loss provides great comfort. Read the memorial poem "The Names" to find out how, in a time of grief, one poet used his work to help others heal.

QUICKWRITE Consider your own experience with loss, or one that you've observed. Why do you think remembering a sad event might help the healing process? Reflect on this question in a journal entry.

POETIC FORM: FREE VERSE

Poetry written in an **open form** follows the poet's ideas instead of a fixed set of rules. **Free verse** is an open form of poetry with no regular pattern of rhyme, rhythm, or line length. When poets write free verse, they can create whatever line rhythms and rhymes they think will best communicate their ideas.

TEXT ANALYSIS: IMAGERY

Imagery consists of words and phrases that appeal to your senses of sight, hearing, smell, taste, and touch. Poets use imagery not only to vividly describe things, but also to communicate feelings and ideas. For example, look at the opening lines of "The Names":

Yesterday, I lay awake in the palm of the night.

A soft rain stole in, unhelped by any breeze,

The images "palm of the night" and "soft rain" appeal to your senses of sight and touch. These phrases also suggest a sense of troubled thoughtfulness and perhaps a feeling of change. As you read "The Names," use a word web to identify these and other examples of imagery.

READING SKILL: UNDERSTAND HISTORICAL CONTEXT

Many works of literature seem easier to understand once you know their historical context—the real events and situations that influenced them. Billy Collins wrote "The Names" as a tribute to the more than 3,000 people who died in the terrorist attacks of September 11, 2001. Before you read the poem, read the **Background** on this page. The information can help you better appreciate the imagery Collins uses.

 Complete the activities in your **Reader/Writer Notebook**.

Meet the Author

Billy Collins
born 1941

A Popular Poet
Poet Billy Collins is a spellbinding performer. His readings have helped spark a renewed hunger for poetry in America. Collins served as the U.S. poet laureate from 2001 to 2003.

BACKGROUND TO THE POEM
A City Grieves
Collins was born and raised in New York City. His hometown suffered heavy losses on September 11, 2001, when terrorists flew planes into the World Trade Center, causing its two towers to collapse. In the following days, signs, posters, and photographs showing the dead or missing were posted all over the city and the surrounding area. These postings often turned into memorials, with passersby adding notes, flowers, and mementos as it became clear that few of the missing had survived.

A Poem of Remembrance
When asked on the day of the attacks what poem was appropriate to the tragedy, Collins replied, "Any poem." Asked to explain, Collins stated that good poetry affirms life. Collins read "The Names" in a special session of Congress in New York City on September 6, 2002.

Author Online

THINK central

Go to **thinkcentral.com**.
KEYWORD: HML7-561

The NAMES

Billy Collins

Yesterday, I lay awake in the palm of the night.
A soft rain stole in, unhelped by any breeze,
And when I saw the silver glaze on the windows,
I started with A, with Ackerman, as it happened,
5 Then Baxter and Calabro,
Davis and Eberling, names falling into place
As droplets fell through the dark.

Names printed on the ceiling of the night.
Names slipping around a watery bend.
10 Twenty-six willows on the banks of a stream.

In the morning, I walked out barefoot
Among thousands of flowers
Heavy with dew like the eyes of tears,
And each had a name—
15 Fiori inscribed on a yellow petal
Then Gonzalez and Han, Ishikawa and Jenkins. **A**

Analyze Visuals ▲

The towers of light shown in the picture of the New York skyline are turned on each year on September 11. What do you think they **symbolize?**

A IMAGERY
Reread lines 11–16. Which images appeal to your senses of sight and touch? Record the images in your web. Then think about how they affect the poem's meaning.

Names written in the air
And stitched into the cloth of the day.
A name under a photograph taped to a mailbox.
20 Monogram[1] on a torn shirt,
I see you spelled out on storefront windows
And on the bright unfurled awnings of this city.
I say the syllables as I turn a corner—
Kelly and Lee,
25 Medina, Nardella, and O'Connor. **B**

When I peer into the woods,
I see a thick tangle where letters are hidden
As in a puzzle concocted for children.
Parker and Quigley in the twigs of an ash,
30 Rizzo, Schubert, Torres, and Upton,
Secrets in the boughs of an ancient maple.

Names written in the pale sky.
Names rising in the updraft[2] amid buildings.
Names silent in stone
35 Or cried out behind a door. **C**
Names blown over the earth and out to sea.

In the evening— weakening light, the last swallows.
A boy on a lake lifts his oars.
A woman by a window puts a match to a candle,
40 And the names are outlined on the rose clouds—
Vanacore and Wallace,
(let X stand, if it can, for the ones unfound)
Then Young and Ziminsky, the final jolt of Z.
Names etched on the head of a pin
45 One name spanning a bridge, another undergoing a tunnel.
A blue name needled into the skin. **D**

Names of citizens, workers, mothers and fathers,
The bright-eyed daughter, the quick son.
Alphabet of names in green rows in a field.
50 Names in the small tracks of birds.
Names lifted from a hat
Or balanced on the tip of the tongue.
Names wheeled into the dim warehouse of memory.
So many names, there is barely room on the walls of the heart.

---

1. **monogram:** the initials of one's name combined into a design.

2. **updraft:** an upward movement of air.

B HISTORICAL CONTEXT
Consider what you learned in the **Background** section on page 561. What can you **infer** about the people Collins is naming?

C FREE VERSE
Reread lines 34–35. Why do you think Collins broke this sentence fragment into two short lines instead of writing it as one line?

D IMAGERY
Reread lines 37–46. Identify images that strike you as particularly powerful. Note what senses they appeal to. What feelings do the images suggest?

Comprehension

1. **Recall** What does the letter *X* stand for in the poem?

2. **Recall** Describe three places where the poem's speaker sees the names.

3. **Clarify** Whom do the names in the poem belong to?

Text Analysis

● 4. **Understand Imagery** Look at the word web you created as you read. Which images from the poem do you consider especially effective? How do these images strengthen the meaning of the poem? Explain.

5. **Identify Theme** The theme of a poem is its basic message about life or human nature. Think about the subject of this poem, the key images, and the words that are emphasized or repeated. What do you think is the overall message about September 11, 2001, that Billy Collins wishes to convey in "The Names"? Collect your thoughts in a graphic like the one shown.

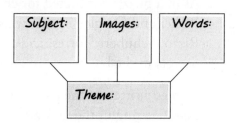

● 6. **Analyze Historical Context** Recall that Billy Collins read this memorial poem when Congress met in New York City nearly one year after the attacks. Choose three lines or sections of the poem and tell why they might have been meaningful to the people hearing them on that day.

● 7. **Evaluate Free Verse** Read the poem aloud as naturally as you can. Do you think this free verse poem is successful at communicating ideas and emotions? Explain why or why not.

Extension and Challenge

8.  **SOCIAL STUDIES CONNECTION** Read the article "Enemies Attack: A Nation Mourns" on page 565. Then reread "The Names." In what ways does the information in the article deepen your appreciation of the poem? Share your answer with a small group, being sure to point out at least two specific ways that knowing about the events of September 11 helped to broaden your understanding of the poem.

Why do we need MEMORIALS?

"The Names" is a memorial poem. Your local community may have different types of memorials to honor people. Choose one type that you think is effective and explain why you think it successfully honors a person or a group of people.

COMMON CORE

RL 4 Determine the meaning of words and phrases as they are used in a text, including figurative and connotative meanings; analyze the impact of rhymes and other repetitions of sounds on a specific verse or stanza of a poem. **RL 5** Analyze how a poem's form or structure contributes to its meaning.

ARTICLE Can the worst in humanity bring out the best in humanity? "The Names" reflects on the lives lost on September 11, 2001. Read this article to find out more about that day and the way people responded to the tragedy.

Enemies Attack: *A Nation Mourns*

Between 7:58 A.M. and 8:10 A.M. on September 11, 2001, four passenger planes left the Boston, Newark, and Washington, D.C., airports. In a matter of minutes, each of these planes was hijacked by terrorists. One of the worst attacks on the United States was underway.

Just seconds after 8:46 A.M., Eastern Standard Time, the first of these planes flew into Tower One of the World Trade Center in New York City; about fifteen minutes later, a second plane flew into Tower Two. Both towers collapsed less than two hours after the attacks. A third plane struck the Pentagon just outside of Washington, D.C. The fourth plane crashed in a Pennsylvania field. Its intended target remains unknown. In all, more than 3,000 civilians, firefighters, and police officers were killed that morning, and thousands were wounded.

The nation and most of the world responded with an outpouring of sympathy and good will. Immediately, volunteers in and around New York City and Washington, D.C., arranged services for the survivors and the rescuers. Around the country, people organized charities to aid the families of victims. Improvised memorials sprung up near the sites of the attacks and the victims' homes, and communities held vigils to pay tribute to the dead and comfort the grieving.

Newspapers published profiles of the deceased, revealing people of all ages and professions, from corporate executives to firefighters. The victims included immigrants from more than 80 nations.

Many of the spontaneous memorials that dotted the country in the weeks following the incident have since been replaced by permanent memorials. In Bucks County, Pennsylvania, a Garden of Reflection provides a peaceful place to pay respect. In Sherwood Island State Park in Connecticut, a Living Memorial granite monument and garden now stands. And where the World Trade Center once stood, several different memorials pay tribute to the victims and their families, as well as to the relief workers whose efforts to aid survivors endure as an example of the best in people.

the earth is a living thing
Poem by Lucille Clifton

Sleeping in the Forest
Poem by Mary Oliver

Gold
Poem by Pat Mora

What is our place in NATURE?

COMMON CORE

RL 1 Cite evidence to support inferences drawn from the text. **RL 4** Determine the meaning of words and phrases as they are used in a text, including figurative and connotative meanings. **RL 5** Analyze how a poem's form or structure contributes to its meaning.

When you left the house to go to school this morning, was the sky clear or cloudy? How did the air feel? Did you hear birds singing or see an insect darting by? Nature surrounds us, but sometimes we forget to notice.

SKETCH IT In a small group, discuss how you fit in with the natural world. In what ways does nature affect your life? Do you think people are part of nature or separate from it? Give concrete examples to support your opinion. Then make a sketch that shows your place in nature.

POETIC FORM: LYRIC POETRY

A **lyric poem** is a short poem in which a single speaker expresses personal thoughts and feelings. Lyric poems can be written in traditional or open forms. They cover many subjects, from love and death to everyday experiences, and—like those you're about to read—create a strong, unified impression.

TEXT ANALYSIS: FIGURATIVE LANGUAGE

Literal language reflects the dictionary definition of words. It forms a factual statement, such as "a tree sheds its leaves in autumn." **Figurative language** expesses an idea through a more imaginative use of words: "A tree mourns its lost leaves in autumn." Poets use figurative language to appeal to your senses and to suggest a mood.

Here are some types of figurative language poets use:

• **Personification** gives human qualities to an animal, an object, or an idea. (*whispering trees, angrily marching ants*)

• **Similes** compare two unlike things by using the word *like* or *as*. (*The stars flamed like torches.*)

• **Metaphors** compare two unlike things without using the word *like* or *as*. (*The stars were torches.*)

READING SKILL: MAKE INFERENCES

To understand poetry, you might have to **make inferences,** or logical guesses, about images and figurative language. Base these guesses on the details of the poem and your knowledge and experience. As you read, use a chart to record striking or puzzling lines or phrases from each poem. Then record your inferences.

Title: "Sleeping in the Forest"		
Lines and Phrases	What I Know from Reading or Experience	Inference
"I slept/as never before, a stone/on the riverbed"	The speaker sleeps like a stone. Stones lie still.	The speaker slept soundly, without moving.

 Complete the activities in your **Reader/Writer Notebook.**

Authors Online

Go to **thinkcentral.com**. KEYWORD: HML7-567

the earth
is a living thing

Lucille Clifton

is a black shuffling bear
ruffling its wild back and tossing
mountains into the sea

is a black hawk circling
5 the burying ground circling the bones
picked clean and discarded[1]

is a fish black blind in the belly of water
is a diamond blind in the black belly of coal **Ⓐ**

is a black and living thing
10 is a favorite child
of the universe
feel her rolling her hand
in its kinky hair
feel her brushing it clean **Ⓑ**

Ⓐ **FIGURATIVE LANGUAGE**
Reread the title and lines 1–8. To what four things is the earth being compared?

Ⓑ **FIGURATIVE LANGUAGE**
Reread lines 10–14. What relationship between the earth and the universe is suggested by this use of **personification**?

Analyze Visuals ▶

Compare the style of this art with the style of the art on page 571. Which is more realistic?

---

1. **discarded** (dĭ-skärd′ĕd): thrown away; gotten rid of.

Bear with Houses, Michael Wertz. Pastel. © Michael Wertz.

The Orchard (1997), Peter Davidson. Oil on paper, 37.5 cm × 44 cm. Private collection. Photo © Bridgeman Art Library.

Sleeping in the
FOREST

Mary Oliver

I thought the earth
remembered me, she
took me back so tenderly, arranging
her dark skirts, her pockets
5   full of lichens[1] and seeds. I slept **C**
as never before, a stone
on the riverbed, nothing
between me and the white fire of the stars
but my thoughts, and they floated
10   light as moths among the branches
of the perfect trees. All night
I heard the small kingdoms breathing
around me, the insects, and the birds
who do their work in the darkness. All night
15   I rose and fell, as if in water, grappling[2]
with a luminous doom. By morning
I had vanished at least a dozen times
into something better. **D** **E**

C **FIGURATIVE LANGUAGE**
Reread lines 1–5. What is being **personified?**

D **MAKE INFERENCES**
Reread the last sentence in the poem. What do you think the speaker means by "something better"?

E **LYRIC POETRY**
What thoughts and feelings is the speaker conveying in this poem?

---

1. **lichens** (lī′kəns): fungi that grow together with algae and form crustlike growths on rocks or tree trunks.

2. **grappling:** struggling.

G O L D

Pat Mora

Hacienda (2002), Vanessa Julian. Acrylic on matteboard, 23″ × 19″.
© Vanessa Julian.

When Sun paints the desert
with its gold,
I climb the hills.
Wind runs round boulders, ruffles
5 my hair. I sit on my favorite rock,
lizards for company, a rabbit,
ears stiff in the shade
of a saguaro.[1]
In the wind, we're all
10 eye to eye. **F**

Sparrow on saguaro watches
rabbit watch us in the gold
of sun setting.
Hawk sails on waves of light, sees
15 sparrow, rabbit, lizards, me,
our eyes shining,
watching red and purple
    sand rivers stream down the hills.

I stretch my arms wide as the sky
20 like hawk extends her wings
in all the gold light of this, home. **G**

F MAKE INFERENCES
Reread lines 1–10. What
can you **infer** about the
speaker's connection to
nature?

**G FIGURATIVE
LANGUAGE**
Reread lines 19–21.
What two **similes** are
used to describe the
speaker's arms?

---

1. **saguaro** (sə-gwär′ō): a tall, branching cactus found in
the southwestern United States and northern Mexico.

Comprehension

1. **Recall** What is the earth compared to in "the earth is a living thing"?

2. **Clarify** What are the "small kingdoms" that the speaker hears in "Sleeping in the Forest"?

3. **Represent** Where, and at what time of day, does the poem "Gold" take place? Make a drawing illustrating the setting described in lines 5–18.

Text Analysis

4. **Make Inferences** Review the charts you created as you read. Which inferences most helped you understand the poems? Explain your answers.

5. **Examine Figurative Language** What **similes, metaphors,** or examples of **personification** in these poems helped you see nature in a fresh way? Give three examples. For each one, tell what type of figurative language was used and why you found it to be effective.

6. **Interpret Meaning** Did the ending of "Sleeping in the Forest" surprise you? Reread lines 14–18, and describe the feeling you think they try to capture.

7. **Compare and Contrast** Use a Venn diagram to examine similarities and differences among the three poems. Think about the setting, the structure, and the mood, or feeling, of each poem. Then decide which two poems you think are most similar.

8. **Evaluate Lyric Poetry** Which of the poems do you think was most successful at communicating the speaker's thoughts and feelings? Include specific details from the poem to support your answer.

Extension and Challenge

9. **Speaking and Listening** Lyric poems are known for their strong, melodic rhythms. They often use repetition to emphasize emotional experiences. In a group, take turns reading each poem aloud. Which of the poems do you think has an especially appealing sound or rhythm? Discuss your answer.

What is our place in NATURE?

Now that you have read these poems, what do you think about your place in nature? Explain your answer.

COMMON CORE

RL 1 Cite evidence to support inferences drawn from the text. RL 4 Determine the meaning of words and phrases as they are used in a text, including figurative and connotative meanings. RL 5 Analyze how a poem's form or structure contributes to its meaning.

Language

◆ **GRAMMAR IN CONTEXT:** Use Correct Sentence Type

In order for your sentences to serve their correct purposes and reflect the emotions you intend, be sure to use the correct sentence type. A **declarative** sentence makes a statement and ends with a period. An **interrogative** sentence asks a question and ends with a question mark. An **imperative** sentence makes a request or gives a command (with the understood subject being *you*) and usually ends with a period. An **exclamatory** sentence shows strong feeling and ends with an exclamation point.

Original: How long has this mountain been here.
I can't believe its beauty.

Revised: How long has this mountain been here?
I can't believe its beauty!

PRACTICE Identify each sentence type and punctuate it correctly.

1. Its peak rises into the clouds like a skyscraper
2. How wonderful it looks
3. Can you hear how the wind whispers around it
4. Listen carefully

*For more help with sentence types, see page R60 in the **Grammar Handbook**.*

READING-WRITING CONNECTION

Explore the poems further by responding to this prompt. Then use the **revising tip** to improve your writing.

WRITING PROMPT	REVISING TIP
Extended Constructed Response: Analysis Reread "the earth is a living thing." Select three specific metaphors to explore further. Write **two or three paragraphs** explaining the view of nature that is suggested by each metaphor.	Have you used a variety of sentence types? Do they reflect the purpose and emotions that you intended? Are the sentences punctuated correctly?

Interactive Revision **THINK** central

Go to **thinkcentral.com**.
KEYWORD: HML7-573

⸬ **COMMON CORE**

L 1 Demonstrate command of the conventions of standard English grammar and usage.
L 2 Demonstrate command of the conventions of standard English punctuation when writing.
W 2 Write informative/ explanatory texts to examine a topic and convey ideas.

Scaffolding
Poem by Seamus Heaney

The World Is Not a Pleasant Place to Be
Poem by Nikki Giovanni

Annabel Lee
 HISTORY Video link at
thinkcentral.com

Poem by Edgar Allan Poe

VIDEO TRAILER **THINK** central KEYWORD: HML7-574

Whom do you feel
CLOSEST to?

COMMON CORE

RL 1 Cite evidence to support inferences drawn from the text.
RL 4 Determine the meaning of words and phrases as they are used in a text, including figurative and connotative meanings; analyze the impact of rhymes and other repetitions of sounds on a specific verse or stanza of a poem.
RL 5 Analyze how a poem's form or structure contributes to its meaning.

Think about a family member or friend you are close to. You have probably fought with each other as well as shared joy and comfort. Why is this? The poems you're about to read explore the mysteries of strong relationships.

QUICKWRITE Identify two or three relationships that are important to you. In your journal, write about what makes each a good relationship. What keeps your bonds strong when difficulties arise?

POETIC FORM: LINE AND STANZA

Poems are made up of **lines,** which may be of different lengths and which may or may not be complete sentences. In many poems, the lines are arranged in groups known as **stanzas.** Sometimes, as in this example from "The World Is Not a Pleasant Place to Be," you have to read the whole stanza to learn the speaker's complete thought:

> the world is not a pleasant place
> to be without
> someone to hold and be held by

TEXT ANALYSIS: RHYME SCHEME

Poets use **sound devices** to convey meaning and create emphasis. One sound device is **rhyme,** the repetition of sounds at the end of words. The **rhyme scheme** is the pattern of rhyme at the ends of lines in a poem. You can track the rhyme by assigning a letter to each line. The first line gets the letter *a*. Each following line that rhymes with it also gets an *a*. The first line that doesn't rhyme gets the letter *b*, as do the other lines that rhyme with that line. Each new rhyme gets a new letter.

And this was the reason that, long <u>ago</u>,	*a*
In this kingdom by the <u>sea</u>,	*b*
A wind blew out of a cloud by <u>night</u>	*c*
Chilling my Annabel <u>Lee</u>;	*b*

As you read "Scaffolding" and "Annabel Lee," use letters to identify each poem's rhyme scheme.

READING SKILL: UNDERSTAND SPEAKER

In poetry, the **speaker** is the voice that "talks" to the reader. To understand a poem, you have to learn who the speaker is and how he or she feels. Complete a chart like the one shown as you read each selection.

	Poem 1	Poem 2	Poem 3
Who is the speaker?			
How does he/she feel?			

Complete the activities in your **Reader/Writer Notebook.**

Seamus Heaney
born 1939

Celebrated Irishman Nobel Prize winner Seamus Heaney's poetry is celebrated throughout the world. Describing how he felt when he wrote his first successful poem, Heaney said, "I felt that I had let down a shaft into real life."

Nikki Giovanni
born 1943

Storyteller Poet Nikki Giovanni gained popularity as a poet after the release of an album of her readings, *Truth Is on Its Way.* She says that in her poetry, "I use a very natural rhythm; I want my writing to sound like I talk."

Edgar Allan Poe
1809–1849

Literary Giant Edgar Allan Poe has fascinated generations of readers with his haunting poetry and tales of horror. He and his adored young wife, Virginia, were poor and often sick. "Annabel Lee" is believed to be Poe's tribute to Virginia.

Authors Online

Go to **thinkcentral.com**. KEYWORD: HML7-575

THINK central

SCAFFOLDING

Seamus Heaney

Analyze
Visuals ▶

How does this painting
reflect the **title** of
the poem?

Masons,[1] when they start upon a building,
Are careful to test out the scaffolding;

Make sure that planks won't slip at busy points,
Secure all ladders, tighten bolted joints.[2] Ⓐ

5 And yet all this comes down when the job's done
Showing off walls of sure and solid stone.

So if, my dear, there sometimes seem to be
Old bridges breaking between you and me

Never fear. We may let the scaffolds fall
10 Confident that we have built our wall. Ⓑ

Ⓐ **LINE AND STANZA**
A stanza that consists
of two rhyming lines is
called a **couplet.** What
is being described in
this couplet?

Ⓑ **SPEAKER**
Reread lines 7–10.
Whom is the speaker
addressing? In your
chart, note how the
speaker feels about
this person.

---

1. **masons** (māˈsənz)**:** wallers who build with brick or stone.

2. **joints** (joints)**:** places where two parts or pieces join together.

Stages II, Paul Davis. Oil, 10″ × 8″.
Courtesy Coda Gallery. © Paul Davis.

THE WORLD IS NOT A PLEASANT PLACE TO BE

Nikki Giovanni

the world is not a pleasant place
to be without
someone to hold and be held by

a river would stop
5 its flow if only
a stream were there
to receive it

an ocean would never laugh
if clouds weren't there
10 to kiss her tears

the world is not
a pleasant place to be without
someone

Detail of *Family in the Park* (1999), Colin Bootman. Oil on canvas. Private collection. Photo © Bridgeman Art Library.

C **LINE AND STANZA**
Repetition is the repeating of a sound, word, phrase, or line to emphasize an idea. Notice how the last stanza echoes the first, but with small differences. What effect is created by these changes?

The Seashore (1900), William Henry Margetson. Oil on canvas. Private collection.
Photo © The Maas Gallery, London/Bridgeman Art Library.

Annabel Lee

Edgar Allan Poe

It was many and many a year ago,
  In a kingdom by the sea,
That a maiden there lived whom you may know
  By the name of Annabel Lee;—
5 And this maiden she lived with no other thought
  Than to love and be loved by me. **D**

She was a child and *I* was a child,
  In this kingdom by the sea,
But we loved with a love that was more than love—
10   I and my Annabel Lee—
With a love that the wingéd seraphs[1] of Heaven
  Coveted[2] her and me. **E**

D RHYME SCHEME
What rhyme scheme is used in the first stanza?

E SPEAKER
What is the speaker's relationship to Annabel Lee?

---

1. **seraphs** (sĕr′əfs): any of the highest order of angels.
2. **coveted** (kŭv′ĭ-tĭd): envied.

And this was the reason that, long ago,
    In this kingdom by the sea,
15 A wind blew out of a cloud by night
    Chilling my Annabel Lee;
So that her high-born kinsmen came
    And bore her away from me,
To shut her up in a sepulcher[3]
20   In this kingdom by the sea.

The angels, not half so happy in Heaven,
    Went envying her and me;
Yes! that was the reason (as all men know,
    In this kingdom by the sea)
25 That the wind came out of the cloud chilling
    And killing my Annabel Lee.

But our love it was stronger by far than the love
    Of those who were older than we—
    Of many far wiser than we—
30 And neither the angels in Heaven above
    Nor the demons down under the sea
Can ever dissever[4] my soul from the soul
    Of the beautiful Annabel Lee:— **F**

For the moon never beams without bringing me dreams
35   Of the beautiful Annabel Lee;
And the stars never rise but I feel the bright eyes
    Of the beautiful Annabel Lee;
And so, all the night-tide, I lie down by the side
Of my darling, my darling, my life and my bride
40   In her sepulcher there by the sea—
    In her tomb by the side of the sea. **G**

F LINE AND STANZA
Reread this stanza. Identify words and phrases that are repeated. What emphasis does this **repetition** create?

G LINE AND STANZA
The last two stanzas are among the longest in the poem. What ideas and emotions does the poet emphasize by ending the poem with long stanzas?

---

3. **sepulcher** (sĕp′əl-kər): a place for burial; tomb.
4. **dissever** (dĭ-sĕv′ər): separate; tear apart.

Comprehension

1. **Recall** Why does the speaker in "Scaffolding" say that the scaffolds in his relationship could be allowed to fall?

2. **Recall** In "The World Is Not a Pleasant Place to Be," what is the relationship between the ocean and the clouds?

3. **Clarify** What happened to Annabel Lee and the person who loved her?

Text Analysis

4. **Identify Rhyme Scheme** Determine the rhyme scheme in "Scaffolding." Why do you think Seamus Heaney might have chosen this rhyme scheme for a poem about a couple's relationship?

5. **Analyze Line and Stanza** Reread the first stanza of "The World Is Not a Pleasant Place to Be." How does the meaning of the first line change as you read the rest of the stanza? Find one other example of a line break that you think affects the meaning of the words in an important way.

6. **Draw Conclusions About Speakers** Review the chart you created as you read. Based on the details you recorded and your understanding of the poems, what conclusions can you draw about each speaker's attitude about relationships? Give evidence from the poems to support your conclusions.

7. **Make Judgments** Go back and reread "Annabel Lee." In a chart, note words and details that make the speaker seem romantic and those that make him seem grief stricken. Are his feelings and attitudes understandable? Support your opinion with examples from your chart.

Romantic	Grief Stricken
"...we loved with a love that was more than love—"	

Extension and Challenge

8. **Creative Project: Art** As you read the poems, which images seemed especially beautiful or powerful? Draw a sketch of one of these images, and explain how it helped draw you into the poem.

Whom do you feel CLOSEST to?

Which poem best characterizes one of your closest relationships? Compare the qualities described in the poem with the qualities you most admire in a relationship.

COMMON CORE

RL1 Cite evidence to support inferences drawn from the text. RL4 Determine the meaning of words and phrases as they are used in a text, including figurative and connotative meanings; analyze the impact of rhymes and other repetitions of sounds on a specific verse or stanza of a poem. RL5 Analyze how a poem's form or structure contributes to its meaning.

The Charge of the Light Brigade
Poem by Alfred, Lord Tennyson

The Highwayman
Poem by Alfred Noyes

VIDEO TRAILER **THINK** central KEYWORD: HML7-582

What is HONOR?

COMMON CORE

RL 1 Cite evidence to support inferences drawn from the text. **RL 4** Determine the meaning of words and phrases as they are used in a text, including figurative and connotative meanings; analyze the impact of rhymes and other repetitions of sounds on a specific verse or stanza of a poem. **RL 5** Analyze how a poem's form or structure contributes to its meaning.

When you think of honor, do you picture a person you respect, a noble sacrifice, or a good cause? In "The Charge of the Light Brigade" and "The Highwayman," the characters give up their lives for very different reasons. Are they and their causes equally honorable?

DISCUSS With a small group, discuss people who have acted honorably. On the basis of this conversation, how would you define honor? Be ready to share your definition with the class.

TEXT ANALYSIS: RHYTHM AND METER

Rhythm is the pattern of stressed and unstressed syllables in a line of poetry. Rhythm that follows a regular pattern from line to line is called **meter.**

When you "scan" a line of poetry, you analyze its rhythm, marking the syllables that are stressed (ˊ) and those that are unstressed (˘). This system is called scansion. Read these lines from "The Highwayman" out loud. Concentrate on the stressed and unstressed syllables.

The wind was a torrent of darkness among the gusty trees.

The moon was a ghostly galleon tossed upon cloudy seas.

As you read the following selections, notice each poem's rhythm and meter and the effect they create.

READING STRATEGY: READING A NARRATIVE POEM

"The Highwayman" and "The Charge of the Light Brigade" are **narrative poems,** which means they tell stories. Like novels and short stories, narrative poems have characters, a setting, and a plot. As you read each poem, keep track of these elements in a story map.

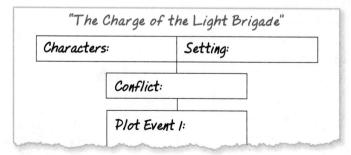

"The Charge of the Light Brigade"

Characters:	Setting:

Conflict:

Plot Event 1:

▲ VOCABULARY IN CONTEXT

The boldfaced vocabulary words can help you picture the scenes in these poems. Match each word in Column A to the word or phrase in Column B that is closest in meaning.

Column A   **Column B**

1. **cascade**   **a.** twist
2. **claret**   **b.** tan
3. **tawny**   **c.** waterfall
4. **writhe**   **d.** dark red

Complete the activities in your **Reader/Writer Notebook.**

Alfred, Lord Tennyson
1809–1892

Victorian Poet
Tennyson's best friend died in 1833, and the shock to Tennyson was severe. However, it was during this time of incredible grief that Tennyson wrote some of his best poetry. These poems were so popular that he was named poet laureate, or court poet, by Queen Victoria.

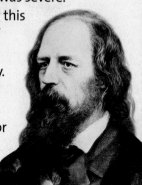

Alfred Noyes
1880–1958

Popular Poet
English poet Alfred Noyes wrote "The Highwayman" when he was only 24. Readers loved it, but critics didn't. Regardless of the critics, Noyes still earned his living from poetry.

BACKGROUND TO THE POEM

A Tragic Battle
"The Charge of the Light Brigade" was inspired by a real-life battle in the Crimean War between England and Russia (1854–1856). A group of British troops called the Light Brigade, armed only with swords, was ordered to charge a unit of Russian gunners. Though the British lost this battle, they eventually won the war.

Authors Online
THINK central
Go to **thinkcentral.com.** KEYWORD: HML7-583

THE CHARGE OF THE LIGHT BRIGADE

Alfred, Lord Tennyson

Half a league,[1] half a league,
Half a league onward,
All in the valley of Death
    Rode the six hundred.
5 "Forward, the Light Brigade!
Charge for the guns!" he said:
Into the valley of Death
    Rode the six hundred. **Ⓐ**

"Forward, the Light Brigade!"
10 Was there a man dismay'd?
Not tho' the soldier knew
    Some one had blunder'd:[2]
Theirs not to make reply,
Theirs not to reason why,
15 Theirs but to do and die:
Into the valley of Death
    Rode the six hundred.

Cannon to right of them,
Cannon to left of them,

Ⓐ RHYTHM AND METER
Reread lines 1–4, tapping your desk with each stressed syllable. How many stressed syllables are in each line?

Analyze Visuals ▶
How well do the **images** in this painting match the scene described in the poem? Explain your answer.

---

1. **league:** a distance of three miles.
2. **blunder'd:** made a mistake.

Detail of *The Charge of the Light Brigade.* © Getty Images.

20 Cannon in front of them
      Volley'd and thunder'd;
Storm'd at with shot and shell,
Boldly they rode and well,
Into the jaws of Death,
25 Into the mouth of Hell
      Rode the six hundred.

Flash'd all their sabers[3] bare,
Flash'd as they turn'd in air
Sabring the gunners there,
30 Charging an army, while
      All the world wonder'd:
Plunged in the battery[4] smoke,
Right thro' the line they broke;
Cossack and Russian
35 Reel'd from the saber-stroke,
      Shatter'd and sunder'd.[5]
Then they rode back, but not,
      Not the six hundred. **B**

Cannon to right of them,
40 Cannon to left of them,
Cannon behind them
      Volley'd and thunder'd;
Storm'd at with shot and shell,
While horse and hero fell,
45 They that had fought so well
Came thro' the jaws of Death.
Back from the mouth of Hell,
All that was left of them,
      Left of six hundred. **C**

50 When can their glory fade?
O, the wild charge they made!
      All the world wonder'd.
Honor the charge they made!
Honor the Light Brigade,
55   Noble six hundred!

B READING A NARRATIVE POEM
Since narrative poems have a plot, they also have a **climax,** or point of greatest excitement. What is the climax of this poem?

C RHYTHM AND METER
Reread lines 39–42 aloud. What is happening to the 600 soldiers? Explain how the meter of these lines matches the events being depicted.

---

3. **sabers:** heavy, slightly curved swords.

4. **battery:** related to guns and cannons used together.

5. **sunder'd:** broken apart; split into pieces.

Detail of *Equestrian Portrait of a Man with a Page* (1600s), Thomas de Keyser. Oil on canvas, 94.6 cm × 77.2 cm. Private collection. Photo © Bridgeman Art Library.

The Highwayman

Alfred Noyes

Part One

The wind was a torrent of darkness among the gusty trees.
The moon was a ghostly galleon[1] tossed upon cloudy seas.
The road was a ribbon of moonlight over the purple moor,[2]
And the highwayman came riding—
5   Riding—riding—
The highwayman came riding, up to the old inn-door.

He'd a French cocked-hat on his forehead, a bunch of lace at his chin,
A coat of the **claret** velvet, and breeches of brown doeskin.
They fitted with never a wrinkle. His boots were up to the thigh.
10 And he rode with a jeweled twinkle,
    His pistol butts a-twinkle.
His rapier hilt[3] a-twinkle, under the jeweled sky.

D READING A NARRATIVE POEM
What is the **setting** of this poem? Note the setting and the **characters** in your story map.

claret (klăr′ĭt) *adj.* dark red

---

1. **galleon** (găl′ē-ən): a large sailing ship.
2. **moor:** a wide, rolling open area, usually covered with low-growing shrubs.
3. **rapier** (rā′pē-ər) **hilt:** sword handle.

Over the cobbles[4] he clattered and clashed in the dark inn-yard.
He tapped with his whip on the shutters, but all was locked and barred.
15 He whistled a tune to the window, and who should be waiting there
But the landlord's black-eyed daughter,
   Bess, the landlord's daughter,
Plaiting[5] a dark red love-knot into her long black hair.

And dark in the dark old inn-yard a stable wicket[6] creaked
20 Where Tim the ostler[7] listened. His face was white and peaked.
His eyes were hollows of madness, his hair like moldy hay,
But he loved the landlord's daughter,
   The landlord's red-lipped daughter.
Dumb as a dog he listened, and he heard the robber say—

25 "One kiss, my bonny sweetheart, I'm after a prize tonight,
But I shall be back with the yellow gold before the morning light;
Yet, if they press me sharply, and harry me through the day,
Then look for me by moonlight,
   Watch for me by moonlight,
30 I'll come to thee by moonlight, though hell should bar the way."

He rose upright in the stirrups. He scarce could reach her hand,
But she loosened her hair in the casement.[8] His face burnt like a brand
As the black **cascade** of perfume came tumbling over his breast;
And he kissed its waves in the moonlight,
35   (O, sweet black waves in the moonlight!)
Then he tugged at his rein in the moonlight, and galloped away to
   the west.

Part Two
He did not come in the dawning. He did not come at noon;
And out of the **tawny** sunset, before the rise of the moon,
When the road was a gypsy's ribbon, looping the purple moor,
40 A redcoat troop came marching—
   Marching—marching—
King George's men came marching, up to the old inn-door.

SOCIAL STUDIES CONNECTION

With the cry of "Stand and deliver!" highwaymen halted and robbed the carriages of the upper class in 17th- and 18th-century England. Like Robin Hood, highwaymen were admired by ladies and celebrated by the poor, who often felt oppressed by the rich.

cascade (kă-skād') *n.* a waterfall or something that resembles a waterfall

tawny (tô'nē) *adj.* a warm, sandy shade of brownish orange

---

4. **cobbles:** rounded stones used for paving roads.

5. **plaiting:** braiding.

6. **wicket:** a small door or gate.

7. **ostler** (ŏs'-lər): a worker who takes care of horses at an inn.

8. **casement:** a window that opens outward on side hinges.

They said no word to the landlord. They drank his ale instead.
But they gagged his daughter, and bound her, to the foot of her
    narrow bed.
45 Two of them knelt at her casement, with muskets at their side!
There was death at every window;
    And hell at one dark window;
For Bess could see, through her casement, the road that *he* would ride.

They had tied her up to attention, with many a sniggering jest.
50 They had bound a musket beside her, with the muzzle beneath her breast!
"Now, keep good watch!" and they kissed her. She heard the doomed
        man say—
Look for me by moonlight;
    Watch for me by moonlight;
I'll come to thee by moonlight, though hell should bar the way! **E**

55 She twisted her hands behind her; but all the knots held good!
She **writhed** her hands till her fingers were wet with sweat or blood!
They stretched and strained in the darkness, and the hours crawled by
        like years,
Till, now, on the stroke of midnight,
    Cold, on the stroke of midnight,
60 The tip of one finger touched it! The trigger at least was hers!

The tip of one finger touched it. She strove no more for the rest.
Up, she stood up to attention, with the muzzle beneath her breast.
She would not risk their hearing; she would not strive again;
For the road lay bare in the moonlight;
65   Blank and bare in the moonlight;
And the blood of her veins, in the moonlight, throbbed to her
        love's refrain.

Tlot-tlot; tlot-tlot! Had they heard it? The horse hoofs ringing clear;
Tlot-tlot, tlot-tlot, in the distance? Were they deaf that they did not hear? **F**
Down the ribbon of moonlight, over the brow of the hill,
70 The highwayman came riding—
    Riding—riding—
The redcoats looked to their priming![9] She stood up, straight and still.

E READING A NARRATIVE POEM
How did the redcoats find out about Bess and the highwayman? Explain how you made this **inference.** Then note the main **conflict** in your story map.

writhe (rīth) v. to twist or move painfully

F RHYTHM AND METER
On a piece of paper, scan lines 67–68, noting the stressed and unstressed syllables in each line. Why is this meter perfectly suited to the action that's taking place?

---

9. **looked to their priming:** prepared their muskets by pouring in the gunpowder used to fire them.

Tlot-tlot, in the frosty silence! *Tlot-tlot,* in the echoing night!
Nearer he came and nearer. Her face was like a light.
75 Her eyes grew wide for a moment; she drew one last deep breath,
Then her finger moved in the moonlight,
   Her musket shattered the moonlight,
Shattered her breast in the moonlight and warned him—with her death. **G**

He turned. He spurred to the west; he did not know who stood
80 Bowed, with her head o'er the musket, drenched with her own blood!
Not till the dawn he heard it, his face grew grey to hear
How Bess, the landlord's daughter,
   The landlord's black-eyed daughter,
Had watched for her love in the moonlight, and died in the
         darkness there.

85 Back, he spurred like a madman, shouting a curse to the sky,
With the white road smoking behind him and his rapier brandished high.
Blood-red were his spurs in the golden noon; wine-red was his velvet coat;
When they shot him down on the highway,
   Down like a dog on the highway,
90 And he lay in his blood on the highway, with a bunch of lace at
         his throat. **H**

And still of a winter's night, they say, when the wind is in the trees,
When the moon is a ghostly galleon tossed upon cloudy seas,
When the road is a ribbon of moonlight over the purple moor,
A highwayman comes riding—
95   *Riding—riding—*
A highwayman comes riding, up to the old inn-door. ◆

Over the cobbles he clatters and clangs in the dark inn-yard.
He taps with his whip on the shutters, but all is locked and barred.
He whistles a tune to the window, and who should be waiting there
100 *But the landlord's black-eyed daughter,*
   Bess, the landlord's daughter,
Plaiting a dark red love-knot into her long black hair.

G READING A NARRATIVE POEM
What just happened? Note the event on your story map.

H MOOD
Reread lines 85–90. Note the images that stand out to you. What mood, or feeling, do they help create?

◆ GRAMMAR IN CONTEXT
Reread lines 91 to 96. These lines are written in the active voice; that is, the subject is performing the action. By using the active voice here, Alfred Noyes adds to the tension and excitement of "The Highwayman."

Comprehension

1. **Clarify** What is the outcome of the Light Brigade's charge?

2. **Recall** Where does Bess wait for the highwayman?

3. **Summarize** Explain how Bess and the highwayman each die.

Text Analysis

4. **Compare and Contrast Characters** For each poem, make a list of the **character traits** the soldiers display. Are the soldiers in the two poems similar or different? Explain your answer.

5. **Analyze a Ballad** "The Highwayman" is a special type of **narrative poem** called a ballad. Ballads have the same features as narrative poems, but they were originally meant to be sung or read aloud. What elements of "The Highwayman" make it an exciting poem to read aloud? Give examples.

6. **Reading a Narrative Poem** Review the **plot events** in the story map you created as you read "The Charge of the Light Brigade." Explain how the plot events and the setting work together to tell the story of the brigade.

7. **Identify Recurring Theme** A recurring theme is a message or insight about life that a variety of works share. Identify a recurring theme present in these two poems. Think about the characters' behavior and motives.

8. **Evaluate Rhythm and Meter** Choose a few lines from each poem and read them to yourself, emphasizing the stressed syllables. Write the lines in a chart like the one shown and mark the stressed and unstressed syllables. What effect does the rhythm have on each poem's story?

"The Charge of the Light Brigade"	
Lines from Poem	Effect
Half a league, half a league, Half a league onward,	sounds like a galloping horse

Extension and Challenge

9. **SOCIAL STUDIES CONNECTION** Research the true story behind the legendary Light Brigade. When and where did the battle described in the poem occur? How many soldiers lost their lives? Share your findings with the class.

What is HONOR?

Now that you have read these two poems, have your ideas about honor changed? Think about the characters in the poems and who you thought acted with honor: Bess, the highwayman, or the soldiers of the Light Brigade.

COMMON CORE

RL 1 Cite evidence to support inferences drawn from the text. **RL 4** Determine the meaning of words and phrases as they are used in a text, including figurative and connotative meanings; analyze the impact of rhymes and other repetitions of sounds on a specific verse or stanza of a poem. **RL 5** Analyze how a poem's form or structure contributes to its meaning.

Vocabulary in Context

▲ VOCABULARY PRACTICE

Choose the word from the list that best fits each sentence.

1. The hiker looked at the _____ glow of the setting sun and began to worry.
2. Not watching where he was walking, he tripped and fell, which made him _____ in pain.
3. A thin, _____-colored stream of blood trickled down his face.
4. He heard a _____ of water far in the distance and tried not to think about his growing thirst.

cascade

claret

tawny

writhe

ACADEMIC VOCABULARY IN WRITING

> • encounter • integrity • specific • tradition • vary

Which character or group of characters in these two poems most strongly appeals to your imagination? Write a paragraph in which you describe the character or characters, citing **specific** details from the poem. Use at least one Academic Vocabulary word in your response.

VOCABULARY STRATEGY: FOREIGN WORDS IN ENGLISH

The Latin and Greek languages influenced English as it developed, and words and terms from both of those languages appear in English even today. As speakers of English came in contact with different cultures, they adopted new words and terms from various languages. For example, the word *brigade* is a French word that refers to a military unit. Some words have the same spelling and meaning as they had in their original language, while others may have changed slightly over time. You can find the definitions of many foreign words or terms commonly used in English in a dictionary.

PRACTICE Look up the following words or terms in a dictionary, and then use each one in a sentence. At the end of each sentence, identify the original language of the word or term.

1. bona fide
2. e pluribus unum
3. fade
4. habeas corpus
5. nemesis
6. torrent

COMMON CORE

L 4c Consult reference materials to find the pronunciation of a word or determine or clarify its precise meaning. **L 6** Gather vocabulary knowledge when considering a word or phrase.

Interactive Vocabulary **THINK** central

Go to thinkcentral.com.
KEYWORD: HML7-592

Language

◆ **GRAMMAR IN CONTEXT: Use the Active Voice**

Review the Grammar in Context note on page 590. A verb can be in either the active voice or the passive voice. In a sentence that uses the **active voice**, the subject *performs* the verb's action. In a sentence that uses the **passive voice**, the subject of the sentence *receives* the verb's action.

> *Active:* The officers commanded the British soldiers.
> (*The subject* officers *performs the action of the verb* commanded.)

> *Passive:* The British soldiers were commanded by the officers.
> (*The subject* soldiers *receives the action of the verb phrase* were commanded.)

PRACTICE Rewrite each of these sentences by using the active voice.

1. The officers' commands were obeyed by the Light Brigade.
2. Sabers were the weapons used by the British soldiers.
3. Soldiers and horses alike were killed by the Russians.
4. The Light Brigade will be remembered by the world.

For more help with active and passive voice, see page R57 in the **Grammar Handbook**.

READING-WRITING CONNECTION

YOUR TURN

Increase your appreciation of "The Charge of the Light Brigade" and "The Highwayman" by responding to this prompt. Then use the **revising tip** to improve your writing.

WRITING PROMPT	REVISING TIP
Short Constructed Response: Dialogue Both Bess and the soldiers of the Light Brigade stand up to those who are more powerful than they are. Write a **half-page dialogue** between Bess and a soldier of the Light Brigade in which they discuss their ideas of honor.	Reread the dialogue you wrote. Is it concise and interesting? Add action and emphasis by rewriting sentences in the active voice rather than the passive voice. Refer to the Grammar in Context lesson to help you decide whether to use the active voice or the passive voice.

COMMON CORE

L1 Demonstrate command of the conventions of standard English grammar and usage. **L3** Use knowledge of language and its conventions when writing.

Two Haiku
Poems by Matsuo Bashō

Fireflies
Poem by Paul Fleischman

Fireflies in the Garden
Poem by Robert Frost

How do the SEASONS affect you?

COMMON CORE

RL 1 Cite evidence to support inferences drawn from the text. **RL 2** Determine a theme or central idea of a text. **RL 4** Determine the meaning of words and phrases as they are used in a text, including figurative and connotative meanings. **RL 5** Analyze how a poem's form or structure contributes to its meaning.

With shelters, cars, and climate controls of all kinds, it can sometimes be easy to overlook the dramatic changes that occur on the earth each year. But the seasons still determine the daily rhythms of our lives. As the poems you're about to read show, the changing seasons can even affect our emotions. How do the seasons make you feel?

SURVEY Conduct a survey of your classmates. Ask them for one or two words or phrases that they associate with each of the four seasons. Record their answers in a graphic organizer like the one shown. Review your data when you are done. What patterns do you see?

	Spring	Summer	Fall	Winter
Student 1				
Student 2				

POETIC FORM: HAIKU

Haiku is a form of poetry that originated hundreds of years ago in Japan. In haiku, poets seek to create a clear picture with few words. There are three key points to remember about traditional haiku.

- The entire poem consists of just 17 syllables arranged in three lines.
- The first and third lines each contain 5 syllables, and the second line has 7 syllables.
- Haiku centers on a symbol that instantly reminds its readers of a season.

The haiku by Bashō on page 596 are classics of the form.

TEXT ANALYSIS: SYMBOL AND THEME

A **symbol** is a person, place, object, or activity that stands for something beyond itself. For example, the U.S. flag in your classroom is a symbol of the United States.

- Some symbols are unique to certain cultures. In Japan, for example, plum blossoms symbolize early spring.
- Some symbols are understood across cultures. For instance, in most cultures, a heart represents love.

By using symbols, poets are able to communicate rich and complex ideas quickly. As you read the poems, identify the symbols and think about the ideas and themes they express.

READING STRATEGY: ASK QUESTIONS

Poets create images by using **sensory details**—words and phrases that appeal to the reader's senses of sight, touch, taste, smell, and hearing. To help you **interpret,** or understand the meaning of, sensory details, ask yourself:

- What image or picture do the details help me "see" or imagine?
- What ideas do the details suggest?

As you read each poem, record your answers in a chart.

Poem	Sensory Details	What I "See"
	1. flickering, glimmering	1. blinking lights
		2.

 Complete the activities in your **Reader/Writer Notebook.**

Meet the Authors

Matsuo Bashō
1644–1694

Japan's Master Poet
Matsuo Bashō pursued a career as a samurai before devoting himself to the poetry that he had loved in his youth. He created a new style that raised haiku to the level of serious literature.

Paul Fleischman
born 1952

A Musician of Words
Poet Paul Fleischman gives as much attention to the sound of his words as to their meaning. Fleischman grew up playing piano with his mother and listening to his father, an author, read aloud.

Robert Frost
1874–1963

A Legendary Poet
Robert Frost is one of the most beloved poets of the 20th century. As a young man, Frost ran a New Hampshire farm. The New England farmers Frost met were rich sources for his poetry. He won his first of four Pulitzer Prizes in 1924.

Authors Online
Go to **thinkcentral.com.** KEYWORD: HML7-595

THINK central

TWO HAIKU

Matsuo Bashō

Plum Garden, Kameido from *One Hundred Views of Famous Places in Edo* (1857),
Utagawa Hiroshige. Photo © Christie's Images/Corbis.

On sweet plum blossoms[1]
The sun rises suddenly.
Look, a mountain path! Ⓐ

Ⓐ **HAIKU**
Identify at least one
symbol in this poem.
Also note which season
the poem evokes.

A crow
has settled on a bare branch—
autumn evening. Ⓑ

Ⓑ **SYMBOL AND THEME**
What does the crow's
arrival **symbolize?**

---

1. When haiku is translated from the original Japanese into
English, the number of syllables per line sometimes changes
slightly.

Fireflies

Paul Fleischman

Light

Night
is our parchment[1]
5

fireflies
flitting

10 fireflies
glimmering

glowing
Insect calligraphers[2]
15 practicing penmanship

Six-legged scribblers
of vanishing messages,

20 Fine artists in flight
adding dabs of light

Signing the June nights
as if they were paintings

25
flickering
fireflies
fireflies.

Light
is the ink we use
Night

We're
fireflies
flickering

flashing

fireflies
gleaming **C**

Insect calligraphers

copying sentences
Six-legged scribblers

fleeting[3] graffiti
Fine artists in flight

bright brush strokes
Signing the June nights
as if they were paintings **D**
We're
fireflies
flickering
fireflies.

C ASK QUESTIONS
Reread lines 1–12. What words help you see the fireflies in your mind?

D ASK QUESTIONS
Reread lines 20–24. Notice that the fireflies are described as artists here. What kind of artists are they, and which sensory details help form this image?

---

1. **parchment:** fine-quality paper, usually made from the skin of goats or sheep.
2. **calligraphers** (kə-lĭg'rə-fərz): creators of beautiful, elaborate handwriting.
3. **fleeting:** passing swiftly; soon gone.

Fireflies
in the Garden

Robert Frost

Here come real stars to fill the upper skies,
And here on earth come emulating[1] flies,
That though they never equal stars in size,
(And they were never really stars at heart)
5 Achieve at times a very star-like start.
Only of course they can't sustain[2] the part. **E**

E SYMBOL AND THEME
Reread the poem and think about what the fireflies might symbolize.

---

1. **emulating:** imitating.

2. **sustain:** keep up; prolong.

Comprehension

1. **Recall** In the first haiku, what does the rising sun reveal? In the second haiku, where does the crow settle?

2. **Clarify** In "Fireflies," what is the "ink" the fireflies use?

3. **Summarize** In what ways are the fireflies in "Fireflies in the Garden" unlike the stars they try to copy?

Text Analysis

4. **Ask Interpretive Questions** Look back at the list of sensory details that you made as you read each poem. Choose one of the details and explain its meaning in the poem.

5. **Examine Haiku** Which haiku gives you a more hopeful feeling? Explain.

6. **Evaluate Sound Devices** In "Fireflies," Fleischman repeats many words and phrases. Which words does he repeat most often? What other example of **repetition** do you notice? Tell how this repetition reflects the subject of the poem.

7. **Analyze Symbol and Theme** In "Fireflies in the Garden," Robert Frost contrasts the stars in the "upper skies" with the fireflies "here on earth." Use a chart like the one shown to explore the comparison more closely. What theme or larger idea about life might Frost be trying to express by using the fireflies as a symbol?

Details About the Fireflies	My Thoughts
The flies copy the stars.	
The stars are in the sky, and the flies are on earth.	
The flies were "never really stars at heart."	
The flies can shine like stars, but they "can't sustain the part."	

Extension and Challenge

8. **Speaking and Listening** "Fireflies" is written for two voices. Work with a partner and prepare an oral reading of the poem. One of you should read the words in the left column while the other reads the words in the right. Perform your reading for the class. What images in the poem does reading aloud help to reinforce?

How do the SEASONS affect you?

Write a traditional haiku about one season of the year. Express how that season affects you. (You might look back at the words and phrases you collected in the survey on page 594 for ideas.)

COMMON CORE

RL 1 Cite evidence to support inferences drawn from the text. **RL 2** Determine a theme or central idea of a text. **RL 4** Determine the meaning of words and phrases as they are used in a text, including figurative and connotative meanings. **RL 5** Analyze how a poem's form or structure contributes to its meaning.

Stars with Wings
Science Article

What's the Connection?

The more you know about fireflies, the more easily you can spot the clever ways poet Paul Fleischman has imitated them in his poem "Fireflies." Take the time to learn about these creatures by reading the science article "Stars with Wings."

Use with "Fireflies" and "Fireflies in the Garden," pages 597–598.

COMMON CORE

RI 1 Cite textual evidence to support analysis of what the text says explicitly. **RI 5** Analyze the structure an author uses to organize a text, including how the major sections contribute to the development of ideas.

Standards Focus: Connect Ideas in Text

Whether you are reading poems about fireflies or the ingredients list on a cereal box, you are learning something new. What do you do when you want to know more about these or other topics? First, you gather facts, details, and ideas about the topic from the text you are reading or from a variety of sources. Then you **connect ideas,** or bring together information, to gain a better understanding of the topic.

When you read expository text, begin by reviewing the text features. **Text features** are like signs. They help you see the structure and purpose of an article, and they tell you the important ideas. For example, a title identifies the topic. You will usually find the writer's focus or main idea revealed in the first paragraph following the title or, as in "Stars with Wings," in the introductory question and paragraph. Headings and subheadings within the text signal the start of new ideas and identify them. Graphic aids give you visual information about the topic.

As you read the science article that follows, take notes about the scientific facts that teach you about fireflies. Use the text features to help you locate the facts and details. Use two-column notes, such as the ones started here, to record what you learn.

Text	Scientific Facts
Title: "Stars with Wings"	The article will be about fireflies.
Introductory question and paragraph:	Fireflies eat bugs that eat vegetable gardens.
Subheadings: 1. A Beetle, Actually 2.	1. Fireflies are not bugs or flies. They are beetles. 2.
Graphic aids:	

STARS with WINGS

by Therese Ciesinski

Who needs summer fireworks when you have a backyard display of lightning bugs?

Nature holds many wondrous sights, but few are as magical or close to home as a backyard busy with the luminous meanderings of fireflies. On sultry July evenings, adults ease back in lawn chairs while children race about and capture the pulsating glow of these lightning bugs in a glass jar. "I wonder how many amateur entomologists[1] first became interested in science and insects as the result of collecting fireflies," muses Greg Hoover, an entomologist at Pennsylvania State University in State College, Pennsylvania. Hoover, one of
10 the folks who helped the firefly species *Photuris pennsylvanica* (illustrated here) become the official insect of Pennsylvania, remembers fly-fishing one evening and watching fireflies arise from the woods and reeds along the water's edge. "It was really neat. It looked like the New York City skyline at night," he recalls. Call them fireflies or lightning bugs, these marvelous insects are more than just aesthetic wonders. They're also good for the garden, consuming slugs and other critters who hunger for your vegetables. Ⓐ

- **A Beetle, Actually** Ⓑ
  Neither bug nor fly, a firefly is a soft-bodied beetle belonging to the family Lampyridae, Latin for "shining fire." There are 124 species in
20 North America, mostly in the eastern states and provinces. Lightning bugs are usually brown or black with light-colored markings and grow about an inch in length.

---

1. **entomologists:** scientists who specialize in the study of insects.

• Light My Fire

A firefly lights up because of *bioluminescence,* a natural glow caused by the chemical reaction of oxygen and *luciferin* and *luciferase,* two substances in the insect's abdomen. Cells within the abdomen reflect and intensify the light. Some frogs love the bitter taste of lightning bugs and ingest so many that they begin to glow themselves.

• Cool Light

30　A glowing firefly held in the hand won't burn its captor, as the light is "cold." Bioluminescence is 100 percent efficient, giving off no heat. A typical lightbulb, by contrast, emits 10 percent of its energy as light and 90 percent as heat. . . .

• Hungry for Slugs

Juvenile lightning bugs are beneficial insects. The larvae[2] dine on snails, slugs, and aphids.[3] . . . At adulthood, some species don't eat at all; others eat only pollen and nectar.

• Grounded

The light-show portion of a firefly's life—about 3 to 8 weeks—is only a 40　small span of its existence. The life cycle begins when females lay eggs on swampy terrain. The larvae—nicknamed *glowworms* because they give off a faint light—hatch in late summer. After feeding for a few weeks, they burrow underground to escape the winter cold. Emerging in spring, the glowworms feed and later seal themselves within a cell of soil. After 2 weeks they emerge as adult, air-worthy lightning bugs.

• Time to Shine

Lightning bugs are most active in July and August. The light show begins at dusk and usually ends around midnight. In the daytime, you'll find fireflies clinging to tree trunks and branches. "Most people see them in 50　the day but don't realize what they are," says Hoover. "Fireflies like to hang out in crevices in tree bark."

• Water Lovers

Drought and the loss of wetlands impact firefly populations. The beetles need soggy places with low vegetation to breed and thrive. "Soil moisture determines the abundance of fireflies in any given year," Hoover says. "Gardeners may notice a decrease in the amount of fireflies after a drought." **G**

---

2. **larvae** (lär′vē): insects at a stage during which they are newly hatched and often wormlike.
3. **aphids** (ā′fĭdz): small, soft-bodied insects of the family Aphididae that have mouthparts specially adapted for feeding on sap from plants.

G SCIENCE ARTICLE
What do you think the **author's purpose** was for writing this article?

Comprehension

1. **Recall** What causes fireflies to light up?

2. **Clarify** Why is neither *firefly* nor *lightning bug* an accurate name?

Text Analysis

● **3. Identify Characteristics of a Science Article** What are three characteristics of a science article? Give an example of each one from "Stars with Wings."

● **4. Connect Ideas** Review the chart you completed while reading this science article. What scientific information did you learn about fireflies? Write a brief scientific description of fireflies, using the information you learned about them from the article.

COMMON CORE

RI 1 Cite textual evidence to support analysis of what the text says explicitly. **RI 5** Analyze the structure an author uses to organize a text, including how the major sections contribute to the development of ideas. **RI 9** Analyze how two or more authors writing about the same topic emphasize different evidence.

Read for Information: Connect Nonfiction and Poetry

WRITING PROMPT

When poets write about the natural world in their poems, they sometimes relate scientifically accurate details. However, poets might also use imaginative details to create images and express ideas or themes that convey a less literal truth. Explain which poem, "Fireflies" or "Fireflies in the Garden," uses more accurate details.

To answer this prompt, follow these steps:

1. Reread "Fireflies" and "Fireflies in the Garden." Note which lines appear to relate scientifically accurate details.

2. Review "Stars with Wings" and your notes on the article to find out whether the details are accurate. Note passages from the article that support or contradict the lines from the poems.

3. Write a paragraph explaining which poem is more accurate and a paragraph explaining which poem takes more liberties with the facts. Use quotations from the poems as well as the article to support your explanation.

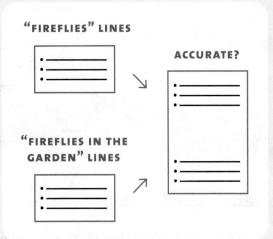

Jabberwocky

Poem by Lewis Carroll

Sarah Cynthia Sylvia Stout Would Not Take the Garbage Out

Poem by Shel Silverstein

Two Limericks

Poems by Edward Lear

When does NONSENSE make sense?

○ **COMMON CORE**

RL 3 Analyze how particular elements interact. **RL 4** Determine the meaning of words and phrases as they are used in a text, including figurative and connotative meanings; analyze the impact of rhymes and other repetitions of sounds on a specific verse or stanza of a poem. **RL 5** Analyze how a poem's form or structure contributes to its meaning.

Is there a strong feeling that you just can't put into words or a hilarious sight that is impossible to describe? What if you could invent a new word that would capture the idea exactly? A nonsense word, like some of those used in the poems that follow, might be just what you need.

BRAINSTORM With a partner, think of something you've never been able to describe clearly. It might be the bouncy movement a squirrel uses when it hops along a fence or the emotion you feel when a bully gets suspended. Invent a nonsense word that captures the idea perfectly, and then write a sentence that uses that word. Share your sentence with the rest of the class, and see if others can guess what it means.

"Ommymay, why do we alktay so unnyfay?"

POETIC FORM: HUMOROUS POETRY

Humorous poetry is written to make you laugh. To achieve a comic effect, poets often will use exaggeration, or **hyperbole**—that is, they describe things as much worse, better, smaller, or bigger than they really are. Sometimes, the comic effect comes from elements of fantasy that create a weird or mixed-up world. One form of humorous poetry is the **limerick,** a five-line poem characterized by a singsong rhythm.

TEXT ANALYSIS: SOUND DEVICES

Poets use **sound devices** to make their poems fun to read aloud, as well as musical and memorable. As you read, think about the effects the following sound devices add to the poems:

- **Rhyme** is the repetition of the sounds at the end of words. (bal*oney* and macar*oni*)
- **Repetition** is the use of a word or phrase more than once.
- **Onomatopoeia** is the use of words that sound like their meanings. (*buzz, whisper, squish*)
- **Alliteration** is the repetition of consonant sounds at the beginning of words. (*twenty tame tigers*)

READING STRATEGY: MONITOR

As you read these humorous poems, pause regularly to check, or **monitor,** how well you are understanding them.

- Reread confusing lines silently or aloud and discuss your ideas with classmates.
- To help you guess the meaning of an unfamiliar or made-up word, use **context clues,** or information in nearby lines.
- As you read each poem, use a chart like the one shown to record notes about language or ideas you clarify.

"Jabberwocky"	
Lines from Poem	My Notes
"'Twas brillig, and the slithy toves" (line 1)	"Brillig" might describe a time of day or the weather. "Slithy" reminds me of "slimy." "Toves" sounds like "toads."

 Complete the activities in your **Reader/Writer Notebook.**

Meet the Authors

Lewis Carroll
1832–1898

Math Magician Lewis Carroll was an Oxford University mathematician when he began making up children's stories. Before Carroll published his books *Alice's Adventures in Wonderland* and *Through the Looking Glass,* people believed children's books should instruct, not entertain. Carroll, however, offers readers pure delight.

Shel Silverstein
1932–1999

Cartoonist and Poet Shel Silverstein began his artistic career when he was a child. "I would much rather have been a good baseball player," he says. "But I couldn't play ball. . . . So I started to draw and write."

Edward Lear
1812–1888

Limerick Master The limerick is a type of poem that first appeared in England in the mid-1700s. Edward Lear became a master of the form and helped make limericks popular.

Authors Online

Go to **thinkcentral.com.** KEYWORD: HML7-605

THINK central

JABBERWOCKY
Lewis Carroll

'Twas brillig, and the slithy toves
Did gyre[1] and gimble in the wabe:
All mimsy were the borogoves,
And the mome raths outgrabe.

5 "Beware the Jabberwock, my son!
The jaws that bite, the claws that catch! **Ⓐ**
Beware the Jubjub bird, and shun
The frumious Bandersnatch!"

He took his vorpal sword in hand:
10 Long time the manxome foe he sought—
So rested he by the Tumtum tree,
And stood awhile in thought.

And, as in uffish thought he stood,
The Jabberwock, with eyes of flame,
15 Came whiffling through the tulgey wood,
And burbled as it came! **Ⓑ**

One, two! One, two! And through and through
The vorpal blade went snicker-snack!
He left it dead, and with its head
20 He went galumphing back.

"And hast thou slain the Jabberwock?
Come to my arms, my beamish boy!
O frabjous day! Callooh! Callay!"
He chortled in his joy.

25 'Twas brillig, and the slithy toves
Did gyre and gimble in the wabe:
All mimsy were the borogoves,
And the mome raths outgrabe.

---

1. **gyre** (jīr): whirl.

Ⓐ MONITOR
What do lines 5–6 tell you about the Jabberwock? Using **context clues,** explain what you think a Jabberwock is.

Ⓑ SOUND DEVICES
Which word in line 16 is an example of **onomatopoeia?** Say the word aloud.

Analyze Visuals ▶
What three **adjectives** best describe the beast on page 607?

Sarah Cynthia Sylvia Stout Would Not Take the Garbage Out

Shel Silverstein

Sarah Cynthia Sylvia Stout
Would not take the garbage out!
She'd scour the pots and scrape the pans,
Candy the yams and spice the hams,
5 And though her daddy would scream and shout,
She simply would not take the garbage out.
And so it piled up to the ceilings:
Coffee grounds, potato peelings,
Brown bananas, rotten peas,
10 Chunks of sour cottage cheese. **C**
It filled the can, it covered the floor,
It cracked the window and blocked the door

C SOUND DEVICES
Find two examples
of **alliteration** in lines
1–10. What do you
think the alliteration
adds to this disgusting
description?

With bacon rinds and chicken bones,
Drippy ends of ice cream cones,
15 Prune pits, peach pits, orange peel,
Gloppy glumps of cold oatmeal,
Pizza crusts and withered greens,
Soggy beans and tangerines,
Crusts of black burned buttered toast,
20 Gristly bits of beefy roasts . . .
The garbage rolled on down the hall,
It raised the roof, it broke the wall . . .
Greasy napkins, cookie crumbs,
Globs of gooey bubble gum,
25 Cellophane from green baloney,
Rubbery blubbery macaroni,
Peanut butter, caked and dry,
Curdled milk and crusts of pie,
Moldy melons, dried-up mustard,
30 Eggshells mixed with lemon custard,
Cold french fries and rancid meat,
Yellow lumps of Cream of Wheat. **D**
At last the garbage reached so high
That finally it touched the sky.
35 And all the neighbors moved away,
And none of her friends would come to play.
And finally Sarah Cynthia Stout said,
"OK, I'll take the garbage out!" **E**
But then, of course, it was too late . . .
40 The garbage reached across the state,
From New York to the Golden Gate.
And there, in the garbage she did hate,
Poor Sarah met an awful fate,
That I cannot right now relate
45 Because the hour is much too late.
But children, remember Sarah Stout
And always take the garbage out! **F**

D **HUMOROUS POETRY**
Silverstein lists 33 types of garbage in this poem. How does this add to the humor of the poem?

E **MONITOR**
Reread lines 33–38. Why does Sarah finally take the garbage out?

F **HUMOROUS POETRY**
Find an example of **hyperbole**, or exaggeration, and explain its effect on the poem.

TWO LIMERICKS

Edward Lear

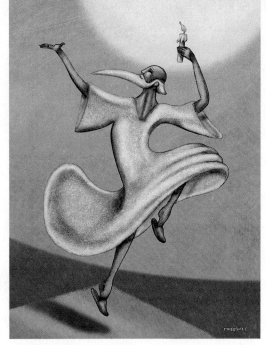

Old Man. Illustration by Alberto Ruggieri.

There was an old man with a light,
Who was dressed in a garment of white;
He held a small candle,
With never a handle,
5 And danced all the merry long night.

There was an old man who made bold,
To affirm[1] that the weather was cold;
So he ran up and down,
In his grandmother's gown,
5 Which was woollen, and not very old. **Ⓖ**

Ⓖ SOUND DEVICES
All true limericks
have the same **rhyme
scheme,** or pattern of
rhyming words. What
is the pattern?

---

1. **affirm** (ə-fûrm'): to declare or prove true.

Comprehension

1. **Recall** How does the Jabberwock die?

2. **Recall** What happens when Sarah finally agrees to take the garbage out?

3. **Recall** In the second limerick, why does the old man run around in his "grandmother's gown"?

Text Analysis

4. **Monitor** Review the information you recorded as you read "Jabberwocky." Does *frabjous* (line 23) mean "good" or "bad"? How can you tell?

5. **Identify Sensory Details** To create a vivid picture of the garbage in Sarah's house, Silverstein uses details that appeal to the five senses. Find four sensory details in the poem and explain which sense each appeals to.

6. **Analyze a Limerick** Limericks usually have a specific **rhythm,** or pattern of stressed and unstressed syllables. Reread the first limerick aloud. How many stressed syllables are in each line? Now read the second limerick. How similar is the rhythm to that in the first poem?

7. **Analyze Sound Devices** Reread "Sarah Cynthia Sylvia Stout Would Not Take the Garbage Out." As you read, look for several examples of rhyme, repetition, onomatopoeia, and alliteration. Record what you find on a chart and then explain why one of the devices adds to the humor of the poem.

Sound Devices in "Sarah Cynthia . . ."			
Rhyme	Repetition	Onomatopoeia	Alliteration
"Rubbery blubbery" (line 26)			

8. **Evaluate Humorous Poetry** Pick the poem you thought was the funniest one. Review the characteristics of humorous poetry discussed on page 605. Which characteristics helped to make your favorite poem so funny? Give examples to support your answer.

Extension and Challenge

9. **Inquiry and Research** The word *chortle* didn't exist until Carroll included it in "Jabberwocky." Using a dictionary or the Internet, find this word's definition. Do you think this former nonsense word makes sense?

When does NONSENSE make sense?

Try writing your own nonsense poem. Think about the nonsense word you made up for the activity on page 604. Write a short, funny poem that explains what your word means.

COMMON CORE

RL 3 Analyze how particular elements interact. **RL 4** Determine the meaning of words and phrases as they are used in a text, including figurative and connotative meanings; analyze the impact of rhymes and other repetitions of sounds on a specific verse or stanza of a poem. **RL 5** Analyze how a poem's form or structure contributes to its meaning.

The Delight Song of Tsoai-Talee
Poem by N. Scott Momaday

Four Skinny Trees
Vignette by Sandra Cisneros

How would you
DESCRIBE yourself?

⬡ **COMMON CORE**

RL 4 Determine the meaning of words and phrases as they are used in a text, including figurative and connotative meanings.

If someone were to ask you to describe yourself, what would you say? Often, we describe ourselves in comparison to something or someone. In the selections you're about to read, people compare themselves to the natural world.

WEB IT Comparing yourself to an element in nature, such as a blooming sunflower or a powerful tiger, can convey a vivid sense of who you are. Create a word web like the one shown. In it show what in nature you would compare yourself to, and why.

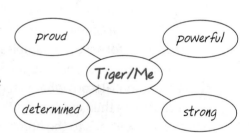

proud   powerful

Tiger/Me

determined   strong

● TEXT ANALYSIS: MOOD AND FIGURATIVE LANGUAGE

Have you ever described a story with a word like *mysterious, creepy, joyful,* or *cheerful*? Then you've described the **mood,** or the feeling that a writer creates for the reader. One way writers create mood is through **figurative language,** which is language used in imaginative ways to express ideas that are not literally true.

- A **metaphor** is a comparison between two unlike things. It does not use the word *like* or *as.* (*I am an antelope.*)
- **Personification** is a comparison that gives human qualities to an object, animal, or idea. (*My shoes punished the pavement*.)

In "The Delight Song of Tsoai-Talee," N. Scott Momaday uses metaphors; in "Four Skinny Trees," Sandra Cisneros uses personification. As you read, notice how the figurative language helps to set the mood of each piece.

Review: Repetition

● READING STRATEGY: SET A PURPOSE FOR READING

Every time you read, you read with a purpose. That purpose might be just to have fun, or it might be to learn information. In this lesson, your **purpose for reading** is to compare the moods of two pieces. To help you do this, look closely at the figurative language in each poem.

After you read "The Delight Song of Tsoai-Talee" and "Four Skinny Trees," read the selections again. You will then be asked to fill in a chart like the one shown.

Figurative Language in "The Delight Song of Tsoai-Talee" (metaphors)	Figurative Language in "Four Skinny Trees" (personification)
• •	• •
Mood:	Mood:

Complete the activities in your **Reader/Writer Notebook.**

N. Scott Momaday
born 1934

Rock Tree Boy Pulitzer Prize-winning poet N. Scott Momaday was born to Kiowa and Cherokee parents. He spent his childhood on Native American reservations throughout the Southwest. Momaday's Kiowa name, Tsoai-Talee, means "Rock Tree Boy" and refers to an 865-foot volcanic butte that is sacred to the Kiowa people.

Sandra Cisneros
born 1954

Writer on the Move Sandra Cisneros grew up as the only daughter in a large Mexican-American family. The family frequently moved back and forth between the United States and Mexico. "I didn't like school because we moved so much," she says. Despite her awkwardness in class, Cisneros read and wrote a great deal on her own. Around the time she published her first novel, *The House on Mango Street,* she was also teaching and counseling high school dropouts. The stories her students told her about their lives greatly influenced her writing.

Authors Online

THINK central

Go to **thinkcentral.com.** KEYWORD: HML7-613

The Delight Song of Tsoai-Talee

N. Scott Momaday

I am a feather on the bright sky
I am the blue horse that runs in the plain
I am the fish that rolls, shining, in the water
I am the shadow that follows a child
5 I am the evening light, the lustre of meadows
I am an eagle playing with the wind **Ⓐ**
I am a cluster of bright beads
I am the farthest star
I am the cold of the dawn
10 I am the roaring of the rain
I am the glitter on the crust of the snow
I am the long track of the moon in a lake
I am a flame of four colors
I am a deer standing away in the dusk
15 I am a field of sumac and the pomme blanche[1]
I am an angle of geese in the winter sky
I am the hunger of a young wolf
I am the whole dream of these things

You see, I am alive, I am alive
20 I stand in good relation to the earth
I stand in good relation to the gods
I stand in good relation to all that is beautiful
I stand in good relation to the daughter of Tsen-tainte[2]
You see, I am alive, I am alive **Ⓑ**

---

1. **pomme blanche** (pôm blänsh): a plant with heavy edible roots, also known as breadroot.
2. **Tsen-tainte:** a heroic and respected 19th-century Kiowa chief known for his bold raids on both white and Native American settlements.

Detail of *Four Directions* (1995), Jaune Quick-to-See Smith. Lithograph with linocut collage, 44.5″ × 30″. Photo provided by The Lawrence Lithography Workshop. Artwork © Jaune Quick-to-See Smith (an enrolled Flathead Salish, member of the Salish and Kootenal Nation Montana).

Analyze Visuals ▶

List the **images** you see in this collage. Which images portray aspects of nature?

Ⓐ MOOD AND FIGURATIVE LANGUAGE
Reread lines 1–6. Note the first several things that the poet compares himself to. What mood do these **metaphors** create?

Ⓑ REPETITION
Reread lines 19–24. Notice the **repetition** of certain phrases, such as "I stand" and "I am alive." What effect does this repetition create?

Four Skinny Trees

Sandra Cisneros

They are the only ones who understand me. I am the only one who understands them. Four skinny trees with skinny necks and pointy elbows like mine. Four who do not belong here but are here. Four raggedy excuses planted by the city. From our room we can hear them, but Nenny just sleeps and doesn't appreciate these things.

Their strength is secret. They send ferocious roots beneath the ground. They grow up and they grow down and grab the earth between their hairy toes and bite the sky with violent teeth and never quit their anger. This is how they keep. **C**

10   Let one forget his reason for being, they'd all droop like tulips in a glass, each with their arms around the other. Keep, keep, keep, trees say when I sleep. They teach.

When I am too sad and too skinny to keep keeping, when I am a tiny thing against so many bricks, then it is I look at trees. When there is nothing left to look at on this street. Four who grew despite concrete. Four who reach and do not forget to reach. Four whose only reason is to be and be. **D**

C MOOD AND FIGURATIVE LANGUAGE
Reread lines 1–9. What human qualities do the trees have? What emotion is **personified?**

D MOOD AND FIGURATIVE LANGUAGE
Reread lines 13–17. What words and phrases stand out to you? Consider the **mood** and meaning these words and phrases create.

Analyze Visuals ▶

What feeling or emotion do the colors of this image suggest to you?

Detail of *Houses, Trees, Bike,* Anne Lavina Dimeur.
© Anne Lavina Dimeur/Images.com.

Comprehension

1. **Recall** What animals does Tsoai-Talee compare himself to?

2. **Recall** In "Four Skinny Trees," when does the narrator look at the trees?

3. **Represent** In "Four Skinny Trees," what does the narrator's street look like? Make a sketch illustrating the scene.

Text Analysis

● 4. **Analyze Figurative Language** In "The Delight Song of Tsoai-Talee," what three **metaphors** are especially vivid or imaginative? Explain the feeling you think each metaphor creates.

5. **Interpret Meaning** Reread "The Delight Song of Tsoai-Talee," N. Scott Momaday's biography on page 613, and footnote 2 on page 614. On the basis of this information, how do you interpret the meaning of lines 23–24?

6. **Make Inferences** Why do you think the trees in "Four Skinny Trees" are personified with qualities that could also describe the narrator?

● 7. **Analyze Mood** Is the overall mood of "Four Skinny Trees" sad, determined, hopeful, or something in between? Explain your opinion by citing three examples of **personification** that contribute to the mood.

● 8. **Set a Purpose for Reading** Now that you've read both selections and answered some questions about them, fill in a chart like the one shown.

Figurative Language in "The Delight Song of Tsoai-Talee" (metaphors)	Figurative Language in "Four Skinny Trees" (personification)
• "I am a feather on the bright sky" • •	• • •
Mood: joyful	Mood:

COMMON CORE

RL 4 Determine the meaning of words and phrases as they are used in a text, including figurative and connotative meanings.

How would you **DESCRIBE** yourself?

Look back at the element of nature you chose in the activity on page 612. Write a poem in which you compare yourself to that element of nature. Model your poem after one of those you read in this lesson.

Writing for Assessment

1. READ THE PROMPT

In writing assessments, you will often be asked to explore how writers use language to create a mood. In this essay, you will focus on figurative language.

> The poem "Tsoai-Talee" and the vignette "Four Skinny Trees" convey two very different moods. In four or five paragraphs, contrast the moods and explore how each author uses figurative language to help create that feeling. Support your ideas with details from both selections.

◀ **STRATEGY**

1. I have to describe the **feeling** each selection creates.

2. I need to tell the similarities and differences between the feelings.

3. I should **give examples** of the **figurative language** that creates the different moods.

2. PLAN YOUR WRITING

Referring to your chart, note the figurative language and mood you identified for each selection. Then follow these steps.

- Write a statement that identifies the moods and describes the kinds of figurative language used to create each one.

- Use your chart to collect evidence to support your statement.

- Decide on a logical way to present your ideas; then make an outline. One example of how you might organize your paragraphs is shown here.

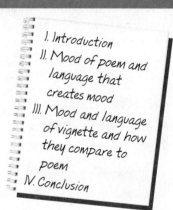

I. Introduction
II. Mood of poem and language that creates mood
III. Mood and language of vignette and how they compare to poem
IV. Conclusion

3. DRAFT YOUR RESPONSE

Introduction Introduce the selections and tell why you are comparing them. Include your statement of your main idea.

Body If you're using an outline similar to the one shown, explain how the language of the first selection creates a specific mood. Then start a new paragraph by telling how the second selection is similar or different.

Conclusion Leave your reader with a final thought about the way each author uses figurative language to create a specific mood.

Revision Make sure that the paragraphs after your introduction support the main idea you stated. If they don't, make changes to one or the other.

Writing Workshop
INFORMATIVE TEXT

Online Feature Article

Earlier in this unit, you read and analyzed various poems to understand their meaning, language, and form. In this workshop, you will explore a poem and analyze it in an **online feature article**—an informative piece of writing on an interesting topic or trend. You will use Web links to enrich your writing and add dimension to your analysis.

 Complete the workshop activities in your **Reader/Writer Notebook**.

WRITE WITH A PURPOSE

WRITING TASK

Write an **online feature article** in which you analyze a poem and explain its meaning. Use Web links to give your audience a better understanding of the work.

Idea Starters
- How does the form of Bashō's crow haiku affect its meaning?
- How is knowing the historical context of "The Names" by Billy Collins important to understanding the poem?
- What are the musical qualities of "Annabel Lee" by Edgar Allan Poe, and how do they influence your reading of the poem?

THE ESSENTIALS

Here are some common purposes, audiences, and formats for online writing about literature.

PURPOSES	AUDIENCES	FORMATS
• to help readers understand a poem • to develop and maintain an online readership	• classmates and teacher • book club members • Web users • online communities	• essay for class • literary magazine • wiki article • podcast • encyclopedia article

COMMON CORE TRAITS

1. DEVELOPMENT OF IDEAS
- clearly introduces a poem and states a **controlling idea**
- supports the topic with **evidence,** such as **relevant facts, details** and **quotations**
- provides a **concluding section** that supports the information

2. ORGANIZATION OF IDEAS
- **logically organizes** information
- includes **formatting, links, graphics,** and **multimedia**
- uses **appropriate transitions**

3. LANGUAGE FACILITY AND CONVENTIONS
- uses **precise language** and **domain-specific vocabulary**
- maintains a **formal style**
- reflects **correct grammar, mechanics,** and **spelling**

Writing Online

THINK central

Go to **thinkcentral.com**.
KEYWORD: HML7N-620

Planning/Prewriting

COMMON CORE

W 2a–f Write informative/explanatory texts to examine a topic. **W 5** Develop and strengthen writing by planning. **W 6** Use technology to produce and publish writing. **W 9a (RL 1)** Draw evidence from texts to support analysis.

Getting Started

CHOOSE A POEM

Your article should analyze a poem and explain its meaning to your audience. Ask yourself what you like most about the work. It could be the theme, images, or form that appeals to you. Another focus might be the connections between the work and the poet's background. Brainstorm possible topics with classmates. Then try to frame each topic as a **research question**. (See the Idea Starters on the previous page for samples.)

▶ **TIPS FOR FINDING A TOPIC:**

- Read similar poems online or in print.
- Review your class notes about the work or related topics.
- Visit blogs and Web sites your teacher recommends to see what others have written about the author and poem.
- Look online for images (photos, drawings, paintings) that reflect the work.

THINK ABOUT AUDIENCE AND PURPOSE

As you review the poem, think about your **purpose** and **audience**. Who is most likely to read and appreciate your article? What do you want your audience to learn? How you answer these questions will influence what you write and where you publish your final product.

▶ **ASK YOURSELF:**

- Who would be most interested in my analysis?
- What does my audience already know?
- What **background information** should I provide?
- What **domain-specific,** or specialized, terms will I need to define for my audience?
- What site might publish or host my article?

FIND SOURCES

When writing about a poem, start with your own response. Does the work bring back memories or remind you of your own life? What does the poem mean? What parts of the poem aren't clear to you? As you develop your ideas, look for sources in your library and on the Web. Consider what other people have said about the author or about the work. Since your article will be online, search for useful links to incorporate. Keep a record of all your sources.

See pages 1010–1027 for more information on locating and evaluating potential sources.

▶ **WHAT DOES IT LOOK LIKE?**

Sources	Comments
Book: <u>Haiku: Poetry</u> by Jackie Hardy	haiku from the past right up to the present; writers from around the world
Book: <u>Bashō's Haiku</u> by David Barnhill	information about Bashō's life; many poems in translation
Web site: http://ngmnationalgeographic.com/geopedia/Matsuo_Basho	helpful background information and bibliographies that I could use to find other sources

Planning/Prewriting *continued*

Getting Started

DRAFT A CONTROLLING IDEA

Draft a controlling idea that sums up the meaning of the poem. Think of the **controlling idea,** or thesis statement, as the most important thing you want your audience to understand about the poem. As you develop your article, include information you've learned and your own observations to support your controlling idea. Keep in mind that you may need to fine-tune your controlling idea as you start to analyze your poem in more depth.

▶ **WHAT DOES IT LOOK LIKE?**

> Even though haiku poems look simple, they can communicate a lot. Bashō's crow poem is an example of this.

CREATE A STORYBOARD

Before you write your article, create a **storyboard,** or plan for how you want to organize the information you have gathered. Your storyboard should show the sequence of ideas you wish to present, with only two or three paragraphs of text on each page. Plan where you want to include **multimedia** components, such as audio or video clips. Use **titles** and **headings** to make it easier for readers to find their way through your online article.

▶ **WHAT DOES IT LOOK LIKE?**

> **A Closer Look at a Poem by Bashō**
>
> **Sidebar**
> Introduction
> Interpretations
> Concluding
> Section
> Works Cited
>
> **Introduction**
>
> Photo
>
> Next

PEER REVIEW Trade storyboards with a classmate. Ask: Can you follow my article easily? What navigational changes should I make? What links or interactive elements could I include to support my controlling idea?

 YOUR TURN In your *Reader/Writer Notebook*, list research questions about poems you've read. Which question and poem interests you the most? Do online research to learn more about this poem and poet. Then draft a controlling idea that summarizes the poem's meaning. Create a storyboard, or outline, for your online article.

Drafting

COMMON CORE

W 4 Produce clear and coherent writing appropriate to task, purpose, and audience. **L 3a** Eliminate wordiness and redundancy.

The following chart shows a structure for developing a clear and well-organized online feature article.

Organizing Your Online Feature Article

INTRODUCTION

- Introduce your poem with an **interesting question**, **quotation**, or **statement**. Your introduction should grab your audience's attention and make them want to read on.
- Include important **background information** and the **controlling idea** you drafted earlier.
- Establish a **formal writing style** by using **precise language** and avoiding contractions and slang.

▼

BODY

- Include well-organized evidence—**details** and **quotations** from the poem, **facts, definitions, and multimedia**—to support your ideas.
- Use **transitions** to connect ideas to each other and to your controlling idea.
- Use **headings** and **links** to help your audience navigate your article.
- Document any **sources** you use. See pages 1028–1043 for more information.

▼

CONCLUDING SECTION

- Summarize the main ideas of your article.

GRAMMAR IN CONTEXT: AVOID REDUNDANCY

Each sentence in your article should include a new idea. Sometimes, however, writers repeat the same idea in different words. To avoid this kind of redundancy, express each unique idea only once. If you find repeated information, choose the best wording of the idea and delete the rest. While writing his article, George made the following change:

Redundant	Concise
Matsuo Bashō was a master of saying a lot with very few words. In just a small space, he could communicate a lot of ideas.	Matsuo Bashō was a master of saying a lot with very few words.

YOUR TURN Draft your article, using your storyboard as a guide. While you write, keep an eye out for redundancy. Upload your text to an approved online forum and add supporting multimedia.

Revising

As you revise your online article, check for unclear writing, poorly organized information, and weak or missing transitions. You may need to rewrite parts of your article or try a new approach to address your purpose and audience. The following chart will help you revise your article.

ONLINE FEATURE ARTICLE

Ask Yourself	Tips	Revision Strategies
1. Have I introduced my poem in an interesting way? Is my controlling idea clear?	▶ **Underline** the opening lines. **Circle** your controlling idea.	▶ **Add** a quote or question to grab your audience's attention. **Rework** your controlling idea to make it more precise.
2. Is my organization logical and easy to navigate?	▶ **Circle** headings, links, and menu options.	▶ **Group** related paragraphs under headings. **Add** menu links to let users jump between sections.
3. Does the information I provide support my main ideas?	▶ **Highlight** text or multimedia that seems out of place or that doesn't support your ideas.	▶ **Delete** information that does not support your main ideas. **Add** evidence to support ideas.
4. Have I maintained a formal writing style?	▶ **Bracket** phrases that are too conversational or use slang.	▶ **Replace** any slang. **Rewrite** sentences that are too casual.
5. Do I use transitions to create cohesion (a smooth flow) and show how ideas are related?	▶ **Draw a wavy line** under transitional words or phrases, such as *in addition to* or *another interpretation is*.	▶ **Add** transitions to link ideas and make sentences flow smoothly.
6. Does my concluding section support the information I presented?	▶ **Put a check mark** next to the section that best summarizes your controlling idea and article as a whole.	▶ **Rewrite** the concluding section to make sure it follows from the information you presented.

YOUR TURN **_PEER REVIEW_** Have a peer use this chart to evaluate your online article. Ask: Is the organization easy to follow? Do the multimedia and links aid understanding? Do you have any suggestions for improvement?

COMMON CORE

W 2a Include formatting, graphics, and multimedia to aid comprehension. **W 5** Develop and strengthen writing by revising, editing, rewriting, or trying a new approach. **SL 5** Include multimedia components to clarify findings and emphasize points.

ANALYZE A STUDENT DRAFT

As you read this draft, notice the comments about its strengths as well as the suggestions for how to improve it.

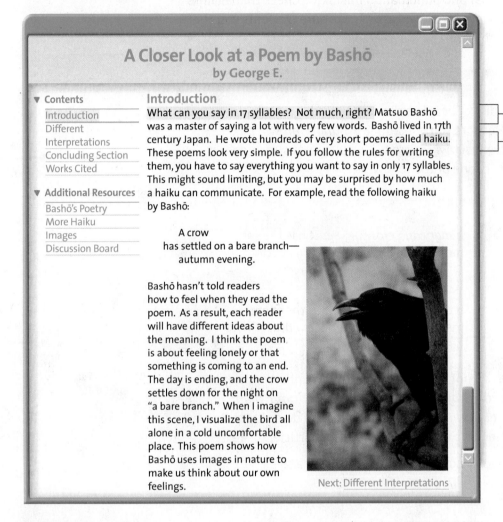

A Closer Look at a Poem by Bashō
by George E.

▼ Contents
Introduction
Different Interpretations
Concluding Section
Works Cited

▼ Additional Resources
Bashō's Poetry
More Haiku
Images
Discussion Board

Introduction

What can you say in 17 syllables? Not much, right? Matsuo Bashō was a master of saying a lot with very few words. Bashō lived in 17th century Japan. He wrote hundreds of very short poems called haiku. These poems look very simple. If you follow the rules for writing them, you have to say everything you want to say in only 17 syllables. This might sound limiting, but you may be surprised by how much a haiku can communicate. For example, read the following haiku by Bashō:

A crow
has settled on a bare branch—
autumn evening.

Bashō hasn't told readers how to feel when they read the poem. As a result, each reader will have different ideas about the meaning. I think the poem is about feeling lonely or that something is coming to an end. The day is ending, and the crow settles down for the night on "a bare branch." When I imagine this scene, I visualize the bird all alone in a cold uncomfortable place. This poem shows how Bashō uses images in nature to make us think about our own feelings.

Next: Different Interpretations

George grabs the attention of his audience by questioning them.

Links to external sites would give George's readers additional background and add interactivity.

The sidebar shows a **clear, easy-to-navigate organization.**

LEARN HOW **Link to External Sources** George's audience may not be familiar with Bashō or haiku poetry. He should link to **reliable**, or trustworthy, sites that will increase readers' understanding and provide background information.

> **GEORGE'S REVISION TO *INTRODUCTION***
> He wrote hundreds of very short poems called haiku.
> *link to a site with more background on the history of haiku*

YOUR TURN Use the feedback you received and the "Learn How" lesson to revise your article. Evaluate your use of multimedia and online text features. Consider trying a new approach if parts of your article aren't working.

Editing and Publishing

COMMON CORE

W 5 Develop and strengthen writing by editing. **L 2a** Use a comma to separate coordinate adjectives. **L 2b** Spell correctly.

In the editing stage, you re-read your article carefully. Correct any misspelled words and eliminate grammar and punctuation mistakes. Check that all links and multimedia elements work correctly. Lastly, make sure the fonts you chose are a good match for your content and are easy to read.

GRAMMAR IN CONTEXT: COMMAS AND COORDINATE ADJECTIVES

Coordinate adjectives modify or describe the same word. They require a comma between them. Here are some examples: *hungry, prowling beast; hot, bubbly sauce;* and *clever, squawking crow.* If you are not sure whether adjectives are coordinate, try one of the following:

Strategy	Example
Add *and* between each adjective in a phrase.	*hungry and prowling beast* has the same meaning as *hungry, prowling beast*
Reverse the order of adjectives.	*prowling, hungry beast* has the same meaning as *hungry, prowling beast*

Non-coordinate adjectives do not require commas. In the phrase *windy autumn night,* the adjective *windy* describes the phrase *autumn night.* The adjectives *windy* and *autumn* are non-coordinate and do not require a comma between them. Here is a revision from George's article.

> When I imagine this scene, I visualize the bird all alone in a cold‸ uncomfortable place.

PUBLISH YOUR WRITING

After you have finished editing and proofreading your article, publish it online. Then, invite readers to check out your work. Here are some ways to attract readers:

- E-mail your classmates. Tell them about your article and how to find it.
- Link your article to teacher-approved Web sites.
- Create an interactive Web page as part of your school or class main Web site.

YOUR TURN Proofread your article and correct any mistakes. Make sure to separate coordinate adjectives with commas. Then, publish your online article in an appropriate online forum.

Scoring Rubric

Use this rubric to evaluate your online feature article.

ONLINE FEATURE ARTICLE

SCORE	COMMON CORE TRAITS
6	• **Development** Effectively introduces a poem; clearly states an interesting controlling idea; offers varied and relevant evidence; ends powerfully • **Organization** Is effectively and logically organized; includes helpful text features and multimedia; uses varied transitions throughout • **Language** Ably uses precise words; maintains a formal style; shows a strong command of conventions
5	• **Development** Competently introduces a poem; states a clear controlling idea; offers relevant evidence; has a strong concluding section • **Organization** Is logically organized; includes text features and multimedia; effectively uses transitions • **Language** Uses precise words; generally maintains a formal style; has a few errors
4	• **Development** Introduces a poem; states a controlling idea; offers mostly relevant evidence; has an adequate concluding section • **Organization** Is mostly logically organized; could use some more text features or multimedia; needs more transitions • **Language** Uses some vague words; mostly maintains a formal style; includes a few distracting errors in conventions
3	• **Development** States a controlling idea, but the introduction could be more interesting; lacks enough evidence; has a somewhat weak concluding section • **Organization** Has some flaws in organization; needs more text features; uses multimedia that does not relate to the purpose; lacks many transitions • **Language** Needs more precise words; has frequent lapses in style; has some critical errors in conventions
2	• **Development** Has a weak controlling idea and lacks support; ends unexpectedly • **Organization** Has organizational flaws; lacks text features to guide readers; uses too much multimedia or not enough; lacks transitions throughout • **Language** Lacks precise words or uses them incorrectly; uses an informal style; has many errors in conventions
1	• **Development** Lacks a controlling idea, development, and a concluding section • **Organization** Has no organization or transitions; uses distracting multimedia • **Language** Uses vague words; has an inappropriate style; has major problems in conventions

Updating an Online Feature Article

As the author of an online feature article, your job is to keep your work updated. For example, you might add information, replace dead (broken) links, or even reorganize the article to make it easier for readers to navigate. In this workshop, you will learn how to effectively update, improve, and enhance your online article. As a result, your audience will know they can count on you as a source of reliable, up-to-date content.

 Complete the workshop activities in your **Reader/Writer Notebook.**

PRODUCE WITH A PURPOSE

TASK

Update your online feature article to provide new information on your topic, fix any navigation problems, and replace dead links.

COMMON CORE TRAITS

A SUCCESSFUL UPDATE . . .

- replaces dead links and out-of-date information
- responds to readers' feedback and comments promptly and respectfully
- adds or revises content to address new information about the topic
- improves the design or navigation
- attracts new readers and holds the interest of returning readers

COMMON CORE

W 6 Use technology to produce and publish writing and to collaborate with others, including linking to and citing sources. **SL 1c** Pose questions and respond to others' questions and comments. **SL 5** Include multimedia components.

Maintaining Your Article

After publishing your article, visit the host site as often as you can and spend a few minutes maintaining your work. Use these guidelines to help you:

- **Update Your Links** Check each link to make sure the Web address, or URL, is still working and connects to the information you intended. If you find any incorrect or dead links, update the URLs, find suitable replacements, or remove the links.

- **Respond to Comments** If you have provided a way for readers to give feedback on your article, make sure to read everything that's posted. Respond to comments or requests for information thoughtfully. Remove inappropriate comments as soon as possible.

- **Add a *Last Updated* Date** Include a line that tells when you last updated your article. You want your readers know how recent the information in your article is—and that you try to keep it up-to-date.

Media Tools

THINK central

Go to **thinkcentral.com.**
KEYWORD: HML7N-628

Modifying and Improving Your Article

Part of updating an online article is modifying it based on feedback from your readers and new information about your topic. Improving your article can increase its appeal to new readers and encourage former readers to return. You might modify your article for many reasons, such as:

- **To Add Content** Information may become outdated, or new material may be available. Add content by revising your article or including new links. Consider a *Recent News* or *Updates* section to keep your content fresh.

- **To Address User Feedback** Readers may comment on the accuracy of your facts, the design of your site, or its navigational features. Be prepared to revise your work, or even try a new approach, to address reader feedback.

- **To Redesign Your Article** Make your article as visually attractive and reader-friendly as possible. To accomplish this goal, consider reorganizing the menu or navigational features. You might add images or multimedia, or change fonts and backgrounds. Any changes you make should suit your analysis, audience, and purpose.

- **To Increase Readership** When you change your article, consider posting a status update on your social networking site. Also, send e-mail updates to your target audience and post a link to your article on any related sites. This way, you can pull in new readers and encourage former readers to return. In addition to using the Web, tell your friends and family about your article. Ask them to help spread the news, too.

> **Juli123** (reader) said . . .
>
> I liked your article, but did you ever think of adding a reading of the poem as a sound clip? It would be nice to hear it.
>
> November 21, 7:35 p.m.
>
> **GeorgeE** (Site Administrator) said . . .
>
> That's a great idea, Juli. I'll see if I can upload a clip. Check back soon!
>
> November 22, 8:05 a.m.

NEWS FEED

 GeorgeE Hello Bashō fans. Take a peek at my feature article about Bashō's crow haiku. Recent updates include audio clips and more information about the poet.

 YOUR TURN Visit your online article often. Make sure each link still works. Update or replace ones that don't. Respectfully address any comments from your readers. Keep your information current and try new approaches to satisfy your readers—and keep them coming back.

Assessment Practice

DIRECTIONS Read these poems and answer the questions that follow.

Ode to enchanted light
by Pablo Neruda

Under the trees light
has dropped from the top of the sky,
light
like a green
5 latticework of branches,
shining
on every leaf,
drifting down like clean
white sand.

10 A cicada sends
its sawing song
high into the empty air.

The world is
a glass overflowing
15 with water.

Practice Test **THiNK**central

Take it at thinkcentral.com.
KEYWORD: HML7N-630

630 UNIT 5: APPRECIATING POETRY

Snow in the Suburbs

by Thomas Hardy

Every branch big with it,
Bent every twig with it;
Every fork like a white web-foot;
Every street and pavement mute:
5 Some flakes have lost their way, and grope back upward, when
Meeting those meandering down they turn and descend again.
The palings are glued together like a wall,
And there is no waft of wind with the fleecy fall.

A sparrow enters the tree,
10 Whereon immediately
A snow-lump thrice his own slight size
Descends on him and showers his head and eyes,
And overturns him,
And near inurns him,
15 And lights on a nether twig, when its brush
Starts off a volley of other lodging lumps with a rush.

The steps are a blanched slope,
Up which, with feeble hope,
A black cat comes, wide-eyed and thin;
20 And we take him in.

Reading Comprehension

Use **"Ode to enchanted light"** to answer questions 1–6.

1. The imagery in Neruda's poem appeals primarily to the senses of —
   A. taste and sight
   B. touch and taste
   C. sight and hearing
   D. smell and touch

2. Which one of the following lines contains alliteration?
   A. *latticework of branches* (line 5)
   B. *drifting down like clean* (line 8)
   C. *high into the empty air* (line 12)
   D. *a glass overflowing* (line 14)

3. Which one of the following images is an example of a simile?
   A. *light / has dropped from the top of the sky* (lines 1–2)
   B. *light / like a green / latticework of branches* (lines 3–5)
   C. *its sawing song* (line 11)
   D. *The world is / a glass overflowing / with water* (lines 13–15)

4. The image in "A cicada sends / its sawing song" appeals to the sense of —
   A. hearing
   B. smell
   C. sight
   D. taste

5. What does the author mean by saying "The world is / a glass overflowing / with water" in lines 13–15?
   A. The world is made of more water than land.
   B. The wonder and beauty of nature are endless.
   C. Very few people can understand what the world is made of.
   D. Everyone in the world should appreciate it.

6. The image in lines 13–15 suggests that the speaker is responding to the world with —
   A. disappointment
   B. confusion
   C. wonder
   D. fear

Use **"Snow in the Suburbs"** to answer questions 7–12.

7. The fork in line 3 represents —
   A. a spider's web
   B. an eating utensil
   C. streets and pavements
   D. a snow-covered tree branch

8. In line 4, personification is used to create an image of a —
   A. strong wind
   B. snow-covered tree
   C. beautiful snowdrift
   D. quiet setting

9. The repetition of beginning sounds in line 8 emphasizes —

    A. coldness

    B. danger

    C. softness

    D. speed

10. Which line describes a fence covered with snow?

    A. *Every branch big with it* (line 1)

    B. *The palings are glued together like a wall* (line 7)

    C. *A snow-lump thrice his own slight size* (line 11)

    D. *The steps are a blanched slope* (line 17)

11. Which statement describes the pattern of rhyme in this poem?

    A. Only the first four lines rhyme.

    B. Every other line rhymes.

    C. Every pair of lines rhymes.

    D. Many lines do not rhyme.

12. Which expression refers to objects as if they were people?

    A. *Some flakes have lost their way* (line 5)

    B. *A sparrow enters the tree* (line 9)

    C. *The steps are a blanched slope* (line 17)

    D. *A black cat comes, wide-eyed and thin* (line 19)

> **Use both selections to answer this question.**

13. The two poems suggest that natural elements such as light and snow can —

    A. flood natural habitats

    B. destroy animals' food sources

    C. comfort people who are sad

    D. transform a landscape

SHORT CONSTRUCTED RESPONSE
Write two or three sentences to answer each question.

14. What can you infer that Neruda is saying about light in "Ode to enchanted light"? Select images from the poem to support your answer.

15. What is repeated in lines 13–14 of "Snow in the Suburbs"? What is the effect of this repetition?

Write a paragraph to answer this question.

16. What inference can you make about each poet's response to nature in these poems? Support your answer with details from the poems.

GO ON ➡

Vocabulary

Use context clues to answer the following questions about some Spanish words that appear in English today.

1. What does the Spanish word *amigo* mean in the following sentence?

I meet my <u>amigo</u> Don after school every day—sometimes we do homework and other times we just hang out together.

   A. Brother   **C.** Friend

   B. Classmate   **D.** Worker

2. What does the Spanish word *salsa* mean in the following sentence?

People dipped their crackers and chips into a bowl of pepper and tomato <u>salsa</u> before eating them.

   A. Cookware   **C.** Sauce

   B. Popcorn   **D.** Water

3. What does the Spanish word *corral* mean in the following sentence?

The trainer led the first horse out of the barn and into the south <u>corral</u> so that it would not run away.

   A. Fenced enclosure

   B. Large barn

   C. Leather harness

   D. Open field

4. What does the Spanish word *oregano* mean in the following sentence?

The chef used <u>oregano</u>, pepper, and a little bit of dill to make the food taste special.

   A. Pie filling

   B. Seasoning

   C. Flavor

   D. Cream

5. What does the Spanish word *armada* mean in the following sentence?

The captain led the entire <u>armada</u> into the huge harbor to anchor them for the night.

   A. Group of warplanes

   B. Fleet of warships

   C. Platoon of foot soldiers

   D. Team of pilots

6. What does the Spanish word *mesa* mean in the following sentence?

A flock of sheep wandered around a high <u>mesa</u>, grazing lazily and lying in the sun.

   A. High mountain

   B. Flat, elevated area

   C. Group of animals

   D. Steep ridge

Revising and Editing

DIRECTIONS Read this passage and answer the questions that follow.

(1) The Declaration of Independence forever changed American history. (2) Did you know the colonists listed their complaints against King George in this important document? (3) Freedom from British rule was declared by them. (4) One year earlier, the colonists had tried to make peace with the king. (5) They outlined their specific pleas in a document known as the Olive Branch Petition. (6) The king's approval of this document was sought by Congress. (7) After he rejected the petition, the king declared the colonists rebels.

1. What is the BEST way to revise sentence 2 to make it declarative?

   A. The colonists listed their complaints against King George in this important document.

   B. The colonists listed their complaints against King George in this important document!

   C. Read this important document to find out how the colonists listed their complaints against King George.

   D. Didn't the colonists list their complaints against King George in this important document?

2. What is the BEST way to rewrite sentence 3 in the active voice?

   A. They declared freedom from British rule.

   B. Freedom from British rule was desired by the colonists.

   C. To gain freedom from British rule was desired by the colonists.

   D. Freedom from British rule was what was declared by them.

3. What is the BEST way to rewrite sentence 6 in the active voice?

   A. Getting this document approved by the king was wanted by Congress.

   B. An attempt to get this document approved was made by Congress.

   C. Getting approval of this document by the king was attempted by Congress.

   D. Congress sought the king's approval of this document.

4. What is the BEST way to revise sentence 7 to make it exclamatory?

   A. Did you know that after the king rejected the petition, he declared the colonists rebels?

   B. After he rejected the petition, the king declared the colonists rebels!

   C. The king rejected the petition and declared the colonists rebels.

   D. Find out how the king rejected the petition and declared the colonists rebels.

Ideas for Independent Reading

Which questions from Unit 5 made an impression on you? Continue exploring them with these books.

COMMON CORE

RL 10 Read and comprehend literature. **RI 10** Read and comprehend literary nonfiction.

Why do we need memorials?

The Glory Field
by Walter Dean Myers

The Glory Field chronicles milestones in African-American history from the 1700s to the present day through five generations of the Lewis family. Each generation draws strength from the Glory Field, a hallowed plot of land that represents their cherished heritage.

Bull Run
by Paul Fleischman

In this story, characters memorialize the first battle of the Civil War from 16 different perspectives. Together they add an intimate dimension to our nation's bloodiest conflict.

The Monument
by Gary Paulsen

Can the artist behind a monument change you more than the monument itself? When an artist comes to design a war memorial in Rocky's small Kansas town, he becomes Rocky's mentor and opens her eyes to broader horizons.

Whom do you feel closest to?

Our Only May Amelia
by Jennifer L. Holm

Can time and place have an effect on the strength of family ties? You will enjoy reading 12-year-old May Amelia's diary as she gives a candid account of the joys and pains of pioneer life in the late 1800s.

Pink and Say
by Patricia Polacco

Patricia Polacco tells the story of her great-grandfather during the Civil War. Learn why the friendship of an Ohio farm boy and a freed slave has become a story retold through three generations.

Heaven
by Angela Johnson

When deception backfires, who gets hurt? Fourteen-year-old Marley lives in Heaven, Ohio—a perfect, loving community. Then she learns that her parents are not her real parents and that all her life she's lived with deception.

How would you describe yourself?

Rules of the Road
by Joan Bauer

What measurements could you use to describe your character? *Rules of the Road* follows the independent Jenna Boller as she learns what's important in life.

Buddy Love: Now on Video
by Ilene Cooper

When 13-year-old Buddy Love views his life through a camcorder lens, he gains insight into the lives of his family and friends and into his own character. To his delight, he finds his life is infinitely exciting.

The Crane Wife
by Odds Bodkin

Why do people describe themselves in a certain way, hoping to impress others? In this tale of a poor sail maker who saves the life of a beautiful white crane, greed overcomes virtue, and the sail maker must learn a harsh lesson.

Get Novel Wise

THiNK central

Go to **thinkcentral.com**.
KEYWORD: HML7-636

Sharing Our Stories

MYTHS, LEGENDS, AND TALES

637

Share What You Know

What can STORIES teach us?

Many stories do more than simply entertain us. People often tell stories to explain something important or to share different approaches to common experiences. Stories can also express the cultural values of a group of people. Through sharing stories, one generation can teach its values, heritage, and traditions to the next generation.

ACTIVITY Are there any legendary figures in your family line? What stories get passed down from one generation to another or get repeated year after year? In a small group, discuss which family stories mean the most to you and your classmates. Consider the following questions:

• Who told you the story?

• What did you learn from the story?

• Have you told the story to anyone else?

Find It Online! THINK central
Go to thinkcentral.com for the interactive version of this unit.

COMMON CORE

Preview Unit Goals

TEXT ANALYSIS
- Cite textual evidence to support analysis of the characteristics of myths, epics, legends, folk tales, and tall tales
- Identify cultural values in myths and legends
- Determine and compare recurring themes
- Provide and evaluate a summary of an original text

READING
- Use reading strategies, including predicting, asking questions, monitoring, and creating sensory images

WRITING AND LANGUAGE
- Write a how-to explanation
- Choose among simple, compound, and complex sentences to show different relationships among ideas

SPEAKING AND LISTENING
- Give and follow oral instructions and directions

VOCABULARY
- Understand foreign words commonly used in English
- Use a dictionary to determine pronunciation and parts of speech
- Understand analogies
- Use a glossary

ACADEMIC VOCABULARY
- attribute
- status
- conduct
- task
- physical

Myths, Legends, Epics, and Tales

From ancient Greece to medieval England, every culture has its own stories—myths, legends, epics, and tales that have been handed down from one generation to the next. Part of an oral tradition, these tales continue to entertain and teach us hundreds of years after they were first told.

Part 1: Characteristics of Traditional Stories

In this unit, you will be reading all types of stories, including the ones shown here.

COMMON CORE

Included in this workshop:
RL 1 Cite textual evidence to support analysis of what the text says explicitly.
RL 3 Analyze how particular elements of a story interact.
RL 10 Comprehend literature.

TYPE OF TALE	CHARACTERISTICS
MYTH A traditional story that was created to explain mysteries of the universe	• Often explains how something connected with humans or nature came to be • Reveals the consequences of both good and bad behavior • Features gods or other beings who have supernatural powers as well as certain flaws
LEGEND A story passed down through many generations that is believed to be based on real people and events	• Tells about a hero or heroine who has unusual powers • Focuses on the hero's or heroine's struggle to defeat a powerful force • Highlights a positive quality or way of behaving
EPIC A long, narrative poem, often written in formal language, that tells about a series of quests undertaken by a great hero	• Follows a quest, or journey, of a hero who has incredible strength and courage • Focuses on the hero's character traits • Features hero's tasks such as battles in which the hero is tested
FABLE A brief story that teaches a lesson, or moral, about human nature	• Usually includes animal characters that stand for specific human qualities, such as kindness or dishonesty • Has a moral that is directly stated at the end or indirectly communicated through what happens in the fable
TALL TALE A humorously exaggerated story about impossible events	• Stars a hero or heroine who is larger than life—that is, bigger, stronger, and even louder than an ordinary person • Uses exaggeration to emphasize the abilities and achievements of the hero or heroine

MODEL 1: CHARACTERISTICS OF A FABLE

What human qualities do the fox and the crow display in this fable?

THE FOX AND THE CROW

Fable by **Aesop**

A crow was sitting on a branch of a tree with a piece of cheese in her beak when a fox observed her and set his wits to work to discover some way of getting the cheese. Coming and standing under the tree, he looked up and said, "What a noble bird I see above me! Her beauty is without
5 equal, the hue of her plumage exquisite. If only her voice is as sweet as her looks are fair, she ought without doubt to be Queen of the Birds."
The crow was hugely flattered by this, and, just to show the fox that she could sing, she gave a loud caw. Down came the cheese, of course, and the fox, snatching it up, said, "You have a voice, madam, I see.
10 What you want are wits."
Flattery is the best persuasion.

Close Read

1. Reread the boxed details. What human qualities does each animal stand for?

2. The moral is directly stated in line 11. In your own words, restate the moral. How does the interaction between the fox and the crow illustrate the moral?

MODEL 2: CHARACTERISTICS OF A TALL TALE

Bess Call is the extraordinary heroine of this tall tale. Here, a stranger from England laughs when "big as life" Bess challenges him to a wrestling match. Will the stranger pay the price?

from

Bess Call

Tall tale retold
by **Robert D. San Souci**

"Humph!" said Bess. "I'll show you a *'real match'*—and no waitin', neither." She rolled up her sleeves and stomped out into the yard.
Back and forth they tussled, making more noise than a boatload of calves on the Hudson. First one, and then the other seemed to get the
5 upper hand, only to find that the edge had slipped over to his or her opponent. The cloud of dust they kicked up covered the sun so that people as far away as Clinton and Cayuga counties reached for their umbrellas thinking unseasonable rain was about to fall.
Their struggles sent them rolling across the yard right up to the fence
10 that separated the farmyard from the road. There Bess took hold of the Englishman one last time and tossed him body, boots, and britches over the fence, where he landed in a muddy ditch.

Close Read

1. In what way is Bess larger than life?

2. One example of humorous exaggeration is boxed. Find another example.

Part 2: Cultural Values in Traditional Stories

One reason for the lasting popularity of many traditional stories is their universal quality. You don't have to be an expert on ancient Greece to understand the moral of an Aesop fable, or know about daily life in 19th-century New York to be amused by "Bess Call."

You can usually appreciate a particular story without knowing much about the culture or society from which it originally came. But by noticing certain details, you can often draw conclusions about the **cultural values**—the ideals and beliefs—that were honored and upheld by that society or culture. For example, does the story stress the importance of obedience, or does it celebrate those who bend the rules?

Consider the legend of John Henry, a railroad worker and "steel drivin' man" whose job was to drill holes using a hammer and a steel spike. His story was popular among men who worked long days building railroad tracks across the United States after the Civil War. By closely examining the excerpt and asking yourself a few questions, you can learn a great deal about those workers and their concerns.

from

JOHN HENRY

Legend retold by **Mary Pope Osborne**

"I got the best steel driver in the country. His name is John Henry, and he can beat *two* dozen men working together."

"That's impossible," the salesman said. "But if you can prove your hand driller is faster than my steam driller, I'll give you this machine
5   for free."

The boss called to John Henry, "This fellow doubts which of you can drill faster. How about a big contest?"

As John Henry stared at the steam drill, he saw a picture of the future. He saw machines taking over the jobs of the country's finest workers.
10   He saw himself and his friends out of work and begging beside the road. He saw men robbed of their dignity and robbed of their families.

"I'd rather die with my hammer in my hand than let that steam drill run me down," he yelled back. And his boss and friends all cheered.

QUESTIONS TO ASK

Who are the heroes and villains in the story?
The hero is a railroad worker; the villain is a machine.

What attitudes and behaviors are rewarded and admired?
John Henry is rewarded with cheers for taking on the machine. Other workers admire his strength and bravery.

What can you infer about the fears of the country's workers during this time period?
Workers were worried about losing their jobs to machines.

MODEL 1: CULTURAL VALUES IN A MYTH

The Mexican myth of Quetzalcoatl explains how unhappiness came into the world. In this excerpt, the people—the Toltecs—are still happy.

from

Quetzalcoatl

Mexican myth retold by **Amy Cruse**

But the king-god Quetzalcoatl knew that if his people were to be really happy they must not spend their days in the idle enjoyment of all this loveliness and plenty. They must work, and learn to take a pride in working as well as they possibly could. So he taught them many
5   useful arts—painting and weaving and carving and working in metals. He taught them how to fashion the gold and silver and precious stones which were found in great abundance throughout the country into beautiful vessels and ornaments, and how to make marvelous many-tinted garments and hangings from the feathers of birds. Every one was
10   eager to work, and because each man did his share, there was plenty of leisure for all. No one was in want and no one was unhappy. It seemed as if, for these fortunate Toltecs, the Golden Age had really come.

Close Read

1. What attitudes toward work do you notice in this excerpt? Find specific details to support your answer.

2. Reread lines 4–9. What kinds of skills and products did the people who created this myth value?

MODEL 2: CULTURAL VALUES IN A LEGEND

In this legend, a monster bear called Nyagwahe threatens the peace among the five Iroquois nations. Swift Runner, a weak boy and an unlikely hero, kills the bear. Here, he returns to his village, victorious.

from

Racing the **Great Bear**

Iroquois legend retold by **Joseph Bruchac**

Then Swift Runner led his people back to the village. He carried with him the teeth of the Nyagwahe, and those who saw what he carried rejoiced. The trails were safe again, and the Great Peace would not be broken. Swift Runner went to his grandmother's lodge and embraced her.
5   "Grandson," she said, "you are now the man I knew you would grow up to be. Remember to use your power to help the people."
So it was that Swift Runner ran with the great bear and won the race. Throughout his long life, he used the teeth of the Nyagwahe to heal the sick, and he worked always to keep the Great Peace.

Close Read

1. What traits does Swift Runner's grandmother display in the boxed text? Draw a conclusion about the attitude the Iroquois people have toward their elders.

2. Reread lines 6–9. What traits or qualities are admired in the Iroquois culture? Support your answer.

Part 3: Analyze the Text

The myths of ancient Greece were first told more than 3,000 years ago. Yet people today still enjoy reading about the powers of mighty gods and goddesses and the daring adventures of heroes. Modern readers can even learn something from these characters' costly mistakes.

In this unit, you will read several Greek myths. Get your first taste of Greek mythology by reading this famous story of unrequited love. What characteristics of a myth do you notice in "Echo"? Through this tale, what do you learn about ancient Greek values?

Greek myth retold by **Alice Low**

Echo, a beautiful mountain nymph,[1] was a great talker and always had to have the last word. She was a favorite of Artemis, goddess of the hunt. Together they hunted in the woods, swam in mountain pools, and caught fish for meals. But Echo's delightful life was destroyed,
5   all because she tried to protect her friends from Hera's[2] wrath.

One day Hera came spying on a group of nymphs in the woods. She suspected that her husband, Zeus, was in love with one of them and hoped to find out which one he favored.

Echo did not know which nymph was Zeus's favorite, and so she
10 started a conversation with Hera in order to let all the other nymphs escape. "Isn't it lovely here?" she said.

"Yes, indeed," Hera replied, "but I am very busy right now and have no time for talk."

Close Read

1. The ancient Greeks believed that their gods acted like ordinary people and even experienced human emotions. Consider Hera's feelings and actions in the boxed lines. In what ways is she like a human being?

---

1. **nymph:** in Greek mythology, a godlike being that appears as a beautiful young woman in a natural setting.
2. **Hera's:** belonging to Hera, the wife of Zeus, the supreme ruler of Mount Olympus and all the gods and goddesses who live there.

"It seems to me you are busy talking," said Echo, "which is the
nicest way to be busy, don't you agree?" She went on and on, and
every time Hera tried to get away from her, Echo asked another
question. By the time Hera got away and ran to the nymphs' pool,
all the nymphs had fled.

"This is *your* doing," said Hera to Echo. "*You* kept talking to let them
escape. And I shall punish you for that. You shall never be able to speak
first, but shall only be able to repeat what others say. You shall always
have the last word."

Soon after that, Echo fell in love with a handsome young hunter
named Narcissus.[3] She followed him through the woods, hoping to
make him notice her. But she could not speak first and had to wait for
him to speak to her.

One day her chance came. Narcissus became separated from his
friends and called out, "Is anyone here?"

"Here," called Echo.

Narcissus could not see her, for she was behind a bush. He shouted,
"Come," thinking she was one of his companions, and she called back,
"Come."

"Let us be together," called Narcissus, for he still could not see anybody.

"Let us be together," called Echo, and she ran up to him with her
arms open, ready to embrace him. But Narcissus said cruelly, "Do not
touch me. I would rather perish than let you have power over me."

"Have power over me," said Echo pleadingly, but Narcissus bounded
away, leaving Echo alone and ashamed. Afterward she lived in a cave,
and finally, because of her great grief, she shrank to nothing. The only
thing left of her was her voice, which echoed through the mountains,
repeating the words of anyone who called.

Close Read

2. Why does Hera punish Echo?

3. Think about Echo's behavior and actions, as well as her resulting punishment. What can you infer about the kinds of behavior that the Greeks hoped to discourage by telling this myth?

4. Some myths attempt to explain how something in the world came to be. What natural phenomenon is explained by this myth?

---

3. **Narcissus:** a handsome but vain boy known for his cruel rejection of the many nymphs who fell in love with him.

Prometheus
Greek Myth Retold by Bernard Evslin

Orpheus and Eurydice
Greek Myth Retold by Olivia Coolidge

VIDEO TRAILER THINK central | KEYWORD: HML7-646

Do you THINK before you act?

Have you ever made a decision you wished you could take back? If so, then you know that your actions sometimes have consequences, or effects, that you didn't bargain for. You're not alone. As you'll see in the Greek myths you're about to read, people have been acting without thinking since ancient times.

QUICKWRITE Think of a risky decision you might make, such as choosing not to study for a test or choosing to make friends with a person outside your group. What are the possible **consequences** of the decision, both negative and positive? Write a short paragraph explaining whether you would be willing to face these consequences.

TEXT ANALYSIS: CHARACTERISTICS OF MYTHS

Since ancient times, people have passed down **myths,** or stories that explain mysteries of the universe. Most myths share these characteristics:

- They tell how something came to be, or they reveal the effects of human behavior.
- They feature gods or other beings with supernatural powers. These beings often show such human qualities as anger.

Many famous myths, like the ones you're about to read, were first told in Greece over 3,000 years ago. As you read, note what the myths explain and how the gods act.

READING STRATEGY: ASK QUESTIONS

The unusual characters, places, and situations in these myths may sometimes distract or confuse you. As you read, try **monitoring,** or checking, your understanding. One way to do this is by asking yourself **questions** about what's going on. If you can't answer, clarify your understanding by reading more slowly, going back, or reading on. Note your questions and the answers in a chart like the one shown.

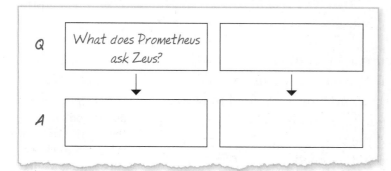

Q | What does Prometheus ask Zeus?

A |

VOCABULARY IN CONTEXT

In the selections, the boldfaced words help tell what happens when the gods are disobeyed. Restate each sentence, using a different word or words for the boldfaced terms.

1. The gods were **infinitely** more powerful than the humans.
2. He had little **aptitude** for following orders.
3. He swore **vengeance** against his enemies.
4. After her son was banished, she was **inconsolable.**
5. She wanted to **ascend** the mountain where the gods lived.

 Complete the activities in your **Reader/Writer Notebook.**

Meet the Authors

Bernard Evslin
1922–1993

Drawn to Myths
In the mid-1960s, Bernard Evslin found his calling retelling myths and legends. His 1986 book *Hercules* won the Washington Irving Children's Book Choice Award.

Olivia Coolidge
1908–2006

Bridging Past and Present
As a child, Olivia Coolidge and her sister made up fairy tales to tell each other. As an adult, Coolidge became a famous reteller of Greek tales and myths.

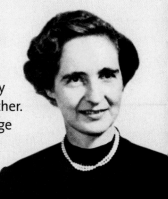

BACKGROUND TO THE MYTHS
Zeus, Prometheus, and Hades
The Greek gods were not all equal in power or status. Prometheus was a part of a family of giants, the Titans. Zeus defeated them and became ruler of all gods. He ordered Prometheus to create humans. Hades, who appears in "Orpheus and Eurydice," was the ruler of the underworld. He, too, answered to Zeus.

Authors Online
Go to **thinkcentral.com.** KEYWORD: HML7-647

PROMETHEUS

Retold by **Bernard Evslin**

Prometheus was a young Titan, no great admirer of Zeus. Although he knew the great lord of the sky hated explicit questions, he did not hesitate to beard[1] him when there was something he wanted to know.

One morning he came to Zeus and said, "O Thunderer, I do not understand your design. You have caused the race of man[2] to appear on earth, but you keep him in ignorance and darkness."

"Perhaps you had better leave the race of man to me," said Zeus. "What you call ignorance is innocence. What you call darkness is the shadow of my decree. Man is happy now. And he is so framed that he 10 will remain happy unless someone persuades him that he is unhappy. Let us not speak of this again."

But Prometheus said, "Look at him. Look below. He crouches in caves. He is at the mercy of beast and weather. He eats his meat raw. If you mean something by this, enlighten me with your wisdom. Tell me why you refuse to give man the gift of fire." Ⓐ

Analyze Visuals ▶

Notice the expression on the god's face and the position of his arms. What can you **infer** about the emotion he might be feeling?

Ⓐ **GREEK MYTHS**
Based on the conversation between the two gods, what aspect of the natural world do you think this myth will explain? Make a **prediction**.

---

1. **beard:** to confront or defy.
2. **man:** In older translations, the expression *man* was commonly used to refer to all people.

Detail from *Prometheus Carrying Fire,* Jan Cossiers. Prado, Madrid. © Art Resource, New York.

Zeus answered, "Do you not know, Prometheus, that every gift brings a penalty? This is the way the Fates[3] weave destiny—by which gods also must abide. Man does not have fire, true, nor the crafts which fire teaches. On the other hand, he does not know disease, warfare, old age, or that inward pest called worry. He is happy, I say, happy without fire. And so he shall remain."

"Happy as beasts are happy," said Prometheus. "Of what use to make a separate race called man and endow[4] him with little fur, some wit, and a curious charm of unpredictability? If he must live like this, why separate him from the beasts at all?"

"He has another quality," said Zeus, "the capacity for worship. An **aptitude** for admiring our power, being puzzled by our riddles and amazed by our caprice.[5] That is why he was made."

"Would not fire, and the graces he can put on with fire, make him more interesting?"

"More interesting, perhaps, but **infinitely** more dangerous. For there is this in man too: a vaunting pride that needs little sustenance[6] to make it swell to giant size. Improve his lot, and he will forget that which makes him pleasing—his sense of worship, his humility. He will grow big and poisoned with pride and fancy himself a god, and before we know it, we shall see him storming Olympus. Enough, Prometheus! I have been patient with you, but do not try me too far. Go now and trouble me no more with your speculations."

Prometheus was not satisfied. All that night he lay awake making plans. Then he left his couch at dawn and, standing tiptoe on Olympus, stretched his arm to the eastern horizon where the first faint flames of the sun were flickering. In his hand he held a reed filled with a dry fiber; he thrust it into the sunrise until a spark smoldered. Then he put the reed in his tunic and came down from the mountain. **B**

At first men were frightened by the gift. It was so hot, so quick; it bit sharply when you touched it and for pure spite made the shadows dance. They thanked Prometheus and asked him to take it away. But he took the haunch of a newly killed deer and held it over the fire. And when the meat began to sear and sputter, filling the cave with its rich smells, the people felt themselves melting with hunger and flung themselves on the meat and devoured it greedily, burning their tongues.

"This that I have brought you is called 'fire,'" Prometheus said. "It is an ill-natured spirit, a little brother of the sun, but if you handle

aptitude (ăp′tĭ-tōōd′) *n.* natural ability

infinitely (ĭn′fə-nĭt-lē) *adv.* extremely; greatly

SOCIAL STUDIES CONNECTION

Many settings in Greek myths are real places in Greece.

B **ASK QUESTIONS**
Make sure you understand the **conflict** between Prometheus and Zeus. What questions do you have about what has already happened and about what will happen next?

---

3. **the Fates:** in Greek mythology, the three goddesses who decide the course of people's lives.

4. **endow** (ĕn-dou′): to provide with a quality or talent

5. **caprice** (kə-prēs′): the quality of acting without planning or thinking beforehand.

6. **vaunting pride that needs little sustenance:** boastful pride that needs little support.

it carefully, it can change your whole life. It is very greedy; you must feed it twigs, but only until it becomes a proper size. Then you must stop, or it will eat everything in sight—and you too. If it escapes, use this magic: water. It fears the water spirit, and if you touch it with water, it will fly away until you need it again."

He left the fire burning in the first cave, with children staring at it
60 wide-eyed, and then went to every cave in the land.

Then one day Zeus looked down from the mountain and was amazed. Everything had changed. Man had come out of his cave. Zeus saw woodmen's huts, farmhouses, villages, walled towns, even a castle or two. He saw men cooking their food, carrying torches to light their way at night. He saw forges[7] blazing, men beating out ploughs, keels, swords, spears. They were making ships and raising white wings of sails and daring to use the fury of the winds for their journeys. They were wearing helmets, riding out in chariots to do battle, like the gods themselves. **C**

Zeus was full of rage. He seized his largest thunderbolt. "So they want
70 fire," he said to himself. "I'll give them fire—more than they can use. I'll turn their miserable little ball of earth into a cinder." But then another thought came to him, and he lowered his arm. "No," he said to himself, "I shall have **vengeance**—and entertainment too. Let them destroy themselves with their new skills. This will make a long, twisted game, interesting to watch. I'll attend to them later. My first business is with Prometheus."

He called his giant guards and had them seize Prometheus, drag him off to the Caucasus,[8] and there bind him to a mountain peak with great chains specially forged by Hephaestus[9]—chains which even a Titan in
80 agony could not break. And when the friend of man was bound to the mountain, Zeus sent two vultures to hover about him forever, tearing at his belly and eating his liver. **D**

Men knew a terrible thing was happening on the mountain, but they did not know what. But the wind shrieked like a giant in torment and sometimes like fierce birds.

Many centuries he lay there—until another hero was born brave enough to defy the gods. He climbed to the peak in the Caucasus and struck the shackles from Prometheus and killed the vultures. His name was Heracles.[10] ❧

C GREEK MYTHS
According to this myth, what event allowed people to build homes, farm, and go to war?

vengeance (vĕn'jəns) *n.* the infliction of punishment in return for an offense

D ASK QUESTIONS
What does Zeus do to Prometheus, and why? To **clarify** the answer, think about the conflict between the two gods. Then reread lines 77–82.

---

7. **forges** (fôr'jĭz): places where metal is heated and hammered into shape.

8. **Caucasus** (kô'kə-səs): a mountainous region in southeastern Europe.

9. **Hephaestus** (hĭ-fĕs'təs): the Greek god of fire and metalworking.

10. **Heracles** (hĕr'ə-klēz'): another name for Hercules, a son of Zeus who was famous for his great strength and courage.

Orpheus
and
Eurydice

Retold by
Olivia Coolidge

In the legend of Orpheus the Greek love of music found its fullest expression. Orpheus, it is said, could make such heavenly songs that when he sat down to sing, the trees would crowd around to shade him. The ivy and vine stretched out their tendrils. Great oaks would bend their spreading branches over his head. The very rocks would edge down the mountainsides. Wild beasts crouched harmless by him, and nymphs[1] and woodland gods would listen to him enchanted. **Ⓔ**

Orpheus himself, however, had eyes for no one but the nymph, Eurydice.[2] His love for her was his inspiration, and his power sprang from
10 the passionate longing that he knew in his own heart. All nature rejoiced with him on his bridal day, but on that very morning, as Eurydice went down to the riverside with her maidens to gather flowers for a bridal garland, she was bitten in the foot by a snake, and she died in spite of all attempts to save her.

Analyze Visuals ▶

Describe the listeners' expressions. How can you **connect** this ancient scene to your own experience with music?

Ⓔ GREEK MYTHS
Note what quality makes Orpheus special. According to the first sentence, how much did the Greeks value this quality?

---

1. **nymphs** (nĭmfs): divine beings represented as beautiful maidens who live in natural places such as trees.
2. **Eurydice** (yŏŏ-rĭd′ĭ-sē).

Orpheus in the Underworld (1863), Louis Jacquesson de la Chevreuse. Oil on canvas, 115 cm × 145 cm. Musée des Augustins. Toulouse, France. © akg-images.

Orpheus was **inconsolable.** All day long he mourned his bride, while birds, beasts, and the earth itself sorrowed with him. When at last the shadows of the sun grew long, Orpheus took his lyre and made his way to the yawning cave which leads down into the underworld, where the soul of dead Eurydice had gone.

20   Even grey Charon, the ferryman of the Styx,[3] forgot to ask his passenger for the price of crossing. The dog, Cerberus, the three-headed monster who guards Hades' gate, stopped full in his tracks and listened motionless until Orpheus had passed. As he entered the land of Hades, the pale ghosts came after him like great, uncounted flocks of silent birds. All the land lay hushed as that marvelous voice resounded across the mud and marshes of its dreadful rivers. In the daffodil fields of Elysium[4] the happy dead sat silent among their flowers. In the farthest corners of the place of punishment, the hissing flames stood still. Accursed Sisyphus,[5] who toils eternally to push a mighty rock uphill, sat down and knew not

30 he was resting. Tantalus,[6] who strains forever after visions of cool water, forgot his thirst and ceased to clutch at the empty air.

    The pillared hall of Hades opened before the hero's song. The ranks of long-dead heroes who sit at Hades' board looked up and turned their eyes away from the pitiless form of Hades and his pale, unhappy queen. Grim and unmoving sat the dark king of the dead on his ebony throne, yet the tears shone on his rigid cheeks in the light of his ghastly torches. Even his hard heart, which knew all misery and cared nothing for it, was touched by the love and longing of the music. **F**

40   At last the minstrel came to an end, and a long sigh like wind in pine trees was heard from the assembled ghosts. Then the king spoke, and his deep voice echoed through his silent land. "Go back to the light of day," he said. "Go quickly while my monsters are stilled by your song. Climb up the steep road to daylight, and never once turn back. The spirit of Eurydice shall follow, but if you look around at her, she will return to me."

    Orpheus turned and strode from the hall of Hades, and the flocks of following ghosts made way for him to pass. In vain he searched their ranks for a sight of his lost Eurydice. In vain he listened for the faintest sound behind. The barge of Charon sank to the very gunwales[7] beneath

inconsolable
(ĭn′kən-sō′lə-bəl) *adj.*
impossible or difficult
to comfort

VISUAL VOCABULARY

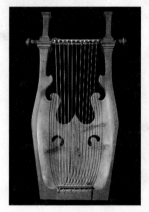

lyre (līr) *n.* an ancient stringed instrument resembling a small harp

F **ASK QUESTIONS**
What **questions** do you have about what the underworld is like? Reviewing what you've read, along with the footnotes, might help you find answers.

---

3. **Styx** (stĭks): in Greek mythology, the river across which the souls of the dead are transported.

4. **Elysium** (ĭ-lĭz′ē-əm): the home of the blessed, or those who were judged to have lived well, after death.

5. **Sisyphus** (sĭs′ə-fəs): a cruel king of Corinth condemned forever to roll a huge stone up a hill, only to have it fall down again.

6. **Tantalus** (tăn′tə-ləs): a king who, for his crimes, was condemned to stand in water that receded when he tried to drink.

7. **gunwales** (gŭn′əlz): the upper edge of the side of a vessel.

50 his weight, but no following passenger pressed it lower down. The way
from the land of Hades to the upper world is long and hard, far easier
to descend than climb. It was dark and misty, full of strange shapes and
noises, yet in many places merely black and silent as the tomb. Here
Orpheus would stop and listen, but nothing moved behind him. For all
he could hear, he was utterly alone. Then he would wonder if the pitiless
Hades were deceiving him. Suppose he came up to the light again and
Eurydice was not there! Once he had charmed the ferryman and the
dreadful monsters, but now they had heard his song. The second time his
spell would be less powerful; he could never go again. Perhaps he had lost
60 Eurydice by his readiness to believe. **G**

Every step he took, some instinct told him that he was going farther
from his bride. He toiled up the path in reluctance and despair, stopping,
listening, sighing, taking a few slow steps, until the dark thinned out
into greyness. Up ahead a speck of light showed clearly the entrance
to the cavern.

At that final moment Orpheus could bear no more. To go out into
the light of day without his love seemed to him impossible. Before he
had quite **ascended,** there was still a moment in which he could go back.
Quick in the greyness he turned and saw a dim shade at his heels, as

COMMON CORE L 5b

Language Coach

Antonyms Antonyms
are words with opposite
meanings. You can
sometimes figure out the
meaning of an unfamiliar
word in a sentence when
its antonym appears in
the same sentence. Read
lines 50–52. The word
descend is an antonym
for *climb.* Can you tell
what *descend* means?

G GREEK MYTHS
Recall the rule Hades
gave to Orpheus.
Predict whether
Orpheus will obey it.

ascend (ə-sĕnd´) *v.* to go
or move upward; rise

Orpheus Leading Eurydice from the Underworld (1861), Jean Baptiste Camille Corot. Oil on canvas,
112.3 cm × 137.1 cm. © Museum of Fine Arts, Houston. © Bridgeman Art Library.

70 indistinct as the grey mist behind her. But still he could see the look of sadness on her face as he sprung forward saying, "Eurydice!" and threw his arms about her. The shade dissolved in the circle of his arms like smoke. A little whisper seemed to say, "Farewell," as she scattered into mist and was gone. **H**

The unfortunate lover hastened back again down the steep, dark path. But all was in vain. This time the ghostly ferryman was deaf to his prayers. The very wildness of his mood made it impossible for him to attain the beauty of his former music. At last, his despair was so great that he could not even sing at all. For seven days he sat huddled together
80 on the grey mud banks, listening to the wailing of the terrible river. The flitting ghosts shrank back in a wide circle from the living man, but he paid them no attention. Only he sat with his eyes on Charon, his ears ringing with the dreadful noise of Styx.

Orpheus arose at last and stumbled back along the steep road he knew so well by now. When he came up to earth again, his song was pitiful but more beautiful than ever. Even the nightingale who mourned all night long would hush her voice to listen as Orpheus sat in some hidden place singing of his lost Eurydice. Men and women he could bear no longer, and when they came to hear him, he drove them away. At last the women
90 of Thrace, maddened by Dionysus[8] and infuriated by Orpheus' contempt, fell upon him and killed him. It is said that as the body was swept down the river Hebrus, the dead lips still moved faintly and the rocks echoed for the last time, "Eurydice." But the poet's eager spirit was already far down the familiar path.

In the daffodil meadows he met the shade of Eurydice, and there they walk together, or where the path is narrow, the shade of Orpheus goes ahead and looks back at his love. ◗ **I**

H ASK QUESTIONS
Reread lines 66–74. What is the "dim shade" at Orpheus' heels? Why does the shade disappear? If you're not sure, try rereading lines 41–45 and then rereading this passage to **clarify** your understanding.

I ASK QUESTIONS
How are Orpheus and Eurydice reunited? If you have any **questions**, review this page.

---

8. **women of Thrace** (thrās), **maddened by Dionysus** (dī′ə-nī′səs): Thrace was a Balkan region colonized by the Greeks; Dionysus was the god of wine.

Orpheus (1618), Marcello Provenzale. © Massimo Listri/Corbis.

Orpheus with his lute[1] made trees,
And the mountain tops that freeze,
   Bow themselves when he did sing:
To his music plants and flowers
5 Ever sprung; as sun and showers
   There had made a lasting spring.

Every thing that heard him play,
Even the billows[2] of the sea,
   Hung their heads, and then lay by.
10 In sweet music is such art,
Killing care and grief of heart
   Fall asleep, or hearing, die.

Song of Orpheus

William Shakespeare

---

1. **lute:** a small, stringed musical instrument with a pear-shaped body.

2. **billows:** huge waves.

Comprehension

1. **Recall** When Prometheus gives humans fire, what is their first reaction?

2. **Recall** Why does Zeus decide not to punish the humans for having fire?

3. **Clarify** Why does Hades at first agree to return Eurydice to Orpheus?

COMMON CORE

RL 1 Cite textual evidence to support analysis of what the text says explicitly. **RL 10** Read and comprehend literature. **W 7** Conduct short research projects to answer a question.

Text Analysis

4. **Ask Questions** Review the chart you created as you read. Are there questions you are unsure how to answer? Compare your chart with a classmate's. Together, go over the story to answer any remaining questions.

5. **Compare Literary Works** Compare "Orpheus and Eurydice" to William Shakespeare's "Song of Orpheus" on page 657. Identify the part of the myth the poem describes. Which literary work, the myth or the poem, better helps you visualize the scene? Explain your answer with details from the selection you choose.

6. **Analyze Characteristics of Greek Myths** Review lines 39–60 of "Prometheus." Why is this passage important in terms of explaining where fire comes from? Give specific details from the passage to support your answer.

7. **Draw Conclusions** What kind of behavior do you think these myths were meant to encourage? Make a chart and go back through the stories, noting which behaviors are rewarded and which are punished. Then give your conclusions about what kind of behavior the Greeks hoped to encourage in people by telling these myths.

Rewarded	Punished

Extension and Challenge

8. **Inquiry and Research** Zeus and Hades were part of a group of 12 gods who ruled from Mount Olympus. Do research to find out more about the Olympians. Then create a poster that lists all 12 of these gods and goddesses and tells what they were known for.

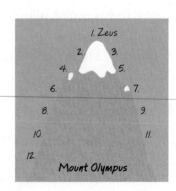

Do you THINK before you act?

Imagine you could ask Prometheus or Orpheus this question. Choose one of these characters and write the answer you think he would give on the basis of his experiences.

Vocabulary in Context

▲ **VOCABULARY PRACTICE**

Decide whether the words in each pair are synonyms (words that mean the same) or antonyms (words that mean the opposite).

1. aptitude/talent
2. ascend/descend
3. inconsolable/comforted
4. infinitely/barely
5. vengeance/mercy

aptitude
ascend
inconsolable
infinitely
vengeance

ACADEMIC VOCABULARY IN WRITING

> • attribute • conduct • physical • status • task

In these myths, the gods often disapprove of the way people **conduct** themselves. Write a paragraph describing how the gods react to the humans' behavior. Use at least two of the Academic Vocabulary words in your response.

VOCABULARY STRATEGY: FOREIGN WORDS IN ENGLISH

The English language is constantly adopting foreign words and phrases, especially Greek and Latin. Some words may keep their original meanings, but others may change. For example, the first line of the Greek myth "Prometheus" describes Prometheus as "a young Titan." In Greek mythology, the Titans were a family of giants. Today, the word *titan* means "a person or thing that has great power or influence." A dictionary will have the definitions and histories of many foreign words and phrases that are commonly used in English.

COMMON CORE

L 4c Consult general reference materials (e.g., dictionaries).
L 6 Acquire and use accurately grade-appropriate general academic words.

PRACTICE Create a chart like the one shown. Use a dictionary to fill in the chart for each word.

Foreign Word	Original Language	Original Meaning	Meaning in English
alfresco	Latin	in the fresh air, outdoors	in the fresh air

1. alibi
2. de facto
3. apogee

4. ad nauseam
5. mea culpa
6. hoi polloi

Interactive Vocabulary **THINK** central

Go to **thinkcentral.com**.
KEYWORD: HML7-659

Icarus and Daedalus
Greek Myth Retold by Josephine Preston Peabody

Phaëthon, Son of Apollo
Greek Myth Retold by Olivia Coolidge

Should people always REACH for the stars?

COMMON CORE

RL 1 Cite textual evidence to support analysis of what the text says explicitly. **RL 2** Determine a theme.

Parents, teachers, and others we admire often proclaim that the only limitations placed on what we can achieve are those we place on ourselves. But should we always "reach for the stars" and follow our dream, or should we first consider whether the dream is practical or achievable? The characters in the following selections may provide an answer.

CHART IT In the first column of a chart, list dreams or goals that people often mention. In the second column, list the limits that others sometimes put on those dreams. Then tell whether you think the dream is still worth pursuing.

Dream	Limits	Worth Pursuing?
be an actor	not much money at first and few actors are successful	

● TEXT ANALYSIS: CULTURAL VALUES IN MYTHS

Myths of every culture reveal the values of the society in which they were created. These **cultural values** are considered standards of behavior. In ancient Greece, people told stories that celebrated these values: obedience to elders, knowing one's place, and respect and obedience to the gods.

As you read, notice what happens to each character and decide what values the myth teaches.

● READING SKILL: DRAW CONCLUSIONS ABOUT MULTIPLE THEMES

A **theme** is a message about life or human nature that the writer wants readers to understand. Myths often have **multiple themes**. When themes are not directly stated, you have to draw conclusions to help you identify them. To determine theme, note the consequences of a character's actions, lessons learned by the main character, and the cultural values that are taught.

As you read, use a chart like the one shown to help you draw conclusions about the themes.

	Icarus and Daedalus	Phaëthon, Son of Apollo
Consequences of a character's actions		
Lessons learned		
Cultural values taught		

▲ VOCABULARY IN CONTEXT

Use context clues in the following sentences to write a definition for each boldfaced word.

1. He had to **veer** to the left to avoid a collision.
2. She tried to **dissuade** him from taking such a risk.
3. They made a **rash** decision to ignore the gods' warnings.
4. The boy has a **cunning** plan to outsmart his opponents.
5. The pathway ended in a **precipitous** drop.
6. Being so high up made the climber's head **reel**.
7. They showed no **deference** to the decision makers.
8. He worked to **sustain** his speed.

 Complete the activities in your **Reader/Writer Notebook**.

Meet the Authors

Josephine Preston Peabody
1874–1922

A Born Writer
Josephine Preston Peabody's interest in myths and legends frequently influenced her writing, which included poetry and nonfiction. She published *Old Greek Folk Stories Told Anew* in 1897.

Olivia Coolidge
1908–2006

A Lover of the Classics
Olivia Coolidge grew up in England, where she learned to share her family's love of history and the classics. She is now one of the best-loved retellers of Greek myths.

BACKGROUND TO THE MYTHS
Divine Connections
In Greek myths, gods and goddesses frequently have human offspring. Many human, or mortal, heroes are related in some way to the gods.

The Story of the Sun God
Apollo, who was also called Phoebus Apollo, was the god of the sun. Daily, he pulled the sun into and out of the sky while riding in his chariot.

Authors Online
Go to **thinkcentral.com**. KEYWORD: HML7-661

THINK central

ICARUS and DAEDALUS

Retold by Josephine Preston Peabody

A mong all those mortals who grew so wise that they learned the
secrets of the gods, none was more **cunning** than Daedalus.[1]

He once built, for King Minos of Crete,[2] a wonderful Labyrinth[3]
of winding ways so cunningly tangled up and twisted around that, once
inside, you could never find your way out again without a magic clue.
But the king's favor **veered** with the wind, and one day he had his master
architect imprisoned in a tower. Daedalus managed to escape from his
cell; but it seemed impossible to leave the island, since every ship that
came or went was well guarded by order of the king.

cunning (kŭn′ĭng) *adj.*
skillful, clever

veer (vîr) *v.* to change
direction; to shift

Analyze Visuals ▶

What might the red
shape inside the figure
symbolize? Explain
your thoughts.

---

1. **Daedalus** (dĕd′l-əs).

2. **Crete:** an island in the Mediterranean Sea, southeast of Greece.

3. **Labyrinth** (lăb′ə-rĭnth′)**:** a maze—that is, a complicated network of paths built to
cause confusion.

The Fall of Icarus, (1944), Henri Matisse.
Stencil print after a gouache and paper collage.
Published in the illustrated book *Jazz,* Editions
Tériade,1947. © 2008 Succession H. Matisse,
Paris/Artists Rights Society (ARS), New York.

10   At length, watching the sea-gulls in the air—the only creatures that
were sure of liberty—he thought of a plan for himself and his young
son Icarus,[4] who was captive with him. **Ⓐ**

Little by little, he gathered a store of feathers great and small. He
fastened these together with thread, molded them in with wax, and so
fashioned two great wings like those of a bird. When they were done,
Daedalus fitted them to his own shoulders, and after one or two efforts,
he found that by waving his arms he could winnow the air and cleave it,[5]
as a swimmer does the sea. He held himself aloft, wavered this way and
that with the wind, and at last, like a great fledgling,[6] he learned to fly.

20   Without delay, he fell to work on a pair of wings for the boy Icarus,
and taught him carefully how to use them, bidding him beware of rash
adventures among the stars. "Remember," said the father, "never to fly
very low or very high, for the fogs about the earth would weigh you
down, but the blaze of the sun will surely melt your feathers apart if you
go too near."

For Icarus, these cautions went in at one ear and out by the other.
Who could remember to be careful when he was to fly for the first time?
Are birds careful? Not they! And not an idea remained in the boy's head
but the one joy of escape. **Ⓑ**

30   The day came, and the fair wind that was to set them free. The father
bird put on his wings, and, while the light urged them to be gone, he
waited to see that all was well with Icarus, for the two could not fly hand
in hand. Up they rose, the boy after his father. The hateful ground of
Crete sank beneath them; and the country folk, who caught a glimpse
of them when they were high above the treetops, took it for a vision of
the gods—Apollo, perhaps, with Cupid after him.

At first there was a terror in the joy. The wide vacancy of the air dazed
them—a glance downward made their brains **reel.**

But when a great wind filled their wings, and Icarus felt himself
40 **sustained,** like a halcyon bird[7] in the hollow of a wave, like a child
uplifted by his mother, he forgot everything in the world but joy. He
forgot Crete and the other islands that he had passed over: he saw but
vaguely that winged thing in the distance before him that was his father
Daedalus. He longed for one draft of flight to quench the thirst of his
captivity: he stretched out his arms to the sky and made towards the
highest heavens.

Ⓐ **CULTURAL VALUES**
A character in a myth
often represents one
human trait, such as
goodness. What trait
does Daedalus display?

Ⓑ **DRAW
CONCLUSIONS**
What lesson can be
learned from Icarus's
actions?

reel (rēl) *v.* to feel
unsteady or dizzy

sustain (sə-stān') *v.*
to keep up; to support

---

4. **Icarus** (ĭk'ər-əs).

5. **winnow the air and cleave it:** fan the air, as if with wings, and cut through it.

6. **fledgling:** a young bird.

7. **halcyon** (hăl'sē-ən) **bird:** a bird that, according to legend, built a nest on the sea and thus calmed
   the water.

Falling Figure (Icarus) (1944), Henri Matisse. Color lithograph after a paper cut-out and gouache. Published on the back cover of the deluxe art review *Verve*. © 2008 Succession H. Matisse, Paris/ Artists Rights Society (ARS), New York.

Alas for him! Warmer and warmer grew the air. Those arms, that had seemed to uphold him, relaxed. His wings wavered, drooped. He fluttered his young hands vainly—he was falling—and in that
50 terror he remembered. The heat of the sun had melted the wax from his wings; the feathers were falling, one by one, like snowflakes; and there was none to help.

He fell like a leaf tossed down the wind, down, down, with one cry that overtook Daedalus far away. When he returned, and sought high and low for his poor boy, he saw nothing but the birdlike feathers afloat on the water, and he knew that Icarus was drowned. **C**

The nearest island he named Icaria, in memory of the child; but he, in heavy grief, went to the temple of Apollo in Sicily, and there hung up his wings as an offering. Never again did he attempt to fly. **D**

C DRAW CONCLUSIONS
What were the consequences of Daedalus teaching his son to fly?

D CULTURAL VALUES
Explain what this myth suggests about respecting the warnings of elders.

Phaëthon, Son of Apollo

Retold by Olivia Coolidge

Though Apollo always honored the memory of Daphne,[1] she was not his only love. Another was a mortal, Clymene,[2] by whom he had a son named Phaëthon.[3] Phaëthon grew up with his mother, who, since she was mortal, could not dwell in the halls of Olympus or in the palace of the sun. She lived not far from the East in the land of Ethiopia, and as her son grew up, she would point to the place where Eos,[4] goddess of the dawn, lighted up the sky and tell him that there his father dwelt. Phaëthon loved to boast of his divine father as he saw the golden chariot riding high through the air. He would remind his comrades of other
10 sons of gods and mortal women who, by virtue of their great deeds, had themselves become gods at last. He must always be first in everything, and in most things this was easy, since he was in truth stronger, swifter, and more daring than the others. Even if he were not victorious, Phaëthon always claimed to be first in honor. He could never bear to be beaten, even if he must risk his life in some **rash** way to win. ⓔ

Analyze Visuals ▶

Is the **mood,** or feeling, of this painting one of tension, exhilaration, or something else? Identify shapes that contribute to the mood.

rash (răsh) *adj.* reckless and careless

ⓔ **CULTURAL VALUES**
Reread lines 8–15. What can you **infer** about Phaëthon's personality?

---

1. **Daphne** (dăf′nē): a wood nymph who did not return Apollo's love. She disappeared, and a laurel tree grew in her place.
2. **Clymene** (klĭ′mə-nē).
3. **Phaëthon** (fā′ə-thŏn′).
4. **Eos** (ē′ŏs′).

Study of *Almanach Der Blaue Reiter* (1911), Wassily Kandinsky. Watercolor, gouache, and black ink. Inv. AM 1994–70. Photo by Philippe Migeat. Musée National d'Art Moderne, Centre Georges Pompidou, Paris. © 2008 Artists Rights Society (ARS), New York/ADAGP, Paris.

Most of the princes of Ethiopia willingly paid Phaëthon honor, since they admired him greatly for his fire and beauty. There was one boy, however, Epaphos,[5] who was rumored to be a child of Zeus himself. Since this was not certainly proved, Phaëthon chose to disbelieve it and to demand from Epaphos the **deference** that he obtained from all others. Epaphos was proud too, and one day he lost his temper with Phaëthon and turned on him, saying, "You are a fool to believe all that your mother tells you. You are all swelled up with false ideas about your father."

Crimson with rage, the lad rushed home to his mother and demanded that she prove to him the truth of the story that she had often told. "Give me some proof," he implored her, "with which I can answer this insult of Epaphos. It is a matter of life and death to me, for if I cannot, I shall die of shame." **F**

"I swear to you," replied his mother solemnly, "by the bright orb of the sun itself that you are his son. If I swear falsely, may I never look on the sun again, but die before the next time he mounts the heavens. More than this I cannot do, but you, my child, can go to the eastern palace of Phoebus Apollo—it lies not far away—and there speak with the god himself."

The son of Clymene leaped up with joy at his mother's words. The palace of Apollo was indeed not far. It stood just below the eastern horizon, its tall pillars glistening with bronze and gold. Above these it was white with gleaming ivory, and the great doors were flashing silver, embossed with pictures of earth, sky, and sea, and the gods that dwelt therein. Up the steep hill and the bright steps climbed Phaëthon, passing ◆ unafraid through the silver doors, and stood in the presence of the sun. Here at last he was forced to turn away his face, for Phoebus sat in state on his golden throne. It gleamed with emeralds and precious stones, while on the head of the god was a brilliant diamond crown upon which no eye could look undazzled.

Phaëthon hid his face, but the god had recognized his son, and he spoke kindly, asking him why he had come. Then Phaëthon plucked up courage and said, "I come to ask you if you are indeed my father. If you are so, I beg you to give me some proof of it so that all may recognize me as Phoebus' son."

The god smiled, being well pleased with his son's beauty and daring. He took off his crown so that Phaëthon could look at him, and coming down from his throne, he put his arms around the boy, and said, "You are indeed my son and Clymene's, and worthy to be called so. Ask of me whatever thing you wish to prove your origin to men, and you shall have it."

Phaëthon swayed for a moment and was dizzy with excitement at the touch of the god. His heart leaped; the blood rushed into his face. Now

5. **Epaphos** (ĕp′ə-fəs).

he felt that he was truly divine, unlike other men, and he did not wish to be counted with men any more. He looked up for a moment at his radiant father. "Let me drive the chariot of the sun across the heavens 60 for one day," he said.

Apollo frowned and shook his head. "I cannot break my promise, but I will **dissuade** you if I can," he answered. "How can you drive my chariot, whose horses need a strong hand on the reins? The climb is too steep for you. The immense height will make you dizzy. The swift streams of air in the upper heaven will sweep you off your course. Even the immortal gods could not drive my chariot. How then can you? Be wise and make some other choice."

The pride of Phaëthon was stubborn, for he thought the god was merely trying to frighten him. Besides, if he could guide the sun's chariot, 70 would he not have proved his right to be divine rather than mortal? For that he would risk his life. Indeed, once he had seen Apollo's splendor, he did not wish to go back and live among men. Therefore, he insisted on his right until Apollo had to give way. **G**

When the father saw that nothing else would satisfy the boy, he bade the Hours[6] bring forth his chariot and yoke the horses. The chariot was of gold and had two gold-rimmed wheels with spokes of silver. In it there was room for one man to stand and hold the reins. Around the front and sides of it ran a rail, but the back was open. At the end of a long pole there were yokes for the four horses. The pole was of gold and shone with 80 precious jewels: the golden topaz, the bright diamond, the green emerald, and the flashing ruby. While the Hours were yoking the swift, pawing horses, rosy-fingered Dawn hastened to the gates of heaven to draw them open. Meanwhile Apollo anointed his son's face with a magic ointment, that he might be able to bear the heat of the fire-breathing horses and the golden chariot. At last Phaëthon mounted the chariot and grasped the reins, the barriers were let down, and the horses shot up into the air.

At first the fiery horses sped forward up the accustomed trail, but behind them the chariot was too light without the weight of the immortal god. It bounded from side to side and was dashed up and down. Phaëthon was 90 too frightened and too dizzy to pull the reins, nor would he have known anyway whether he was on the usual path. As soon as the horses felt that there was no hand controlling them, they soared up, up with fiery speed into the heavens till the earth grew pale and cold beneath them. Phaëthon shut his eyes, trembling at the dizzy, **precipitous** height. Then the horses dropped down, more swiftly than a falling stone, flinging themselves madly from side to side in panic because they were masterless. Phaëthon dropped the reins entirely and clung with all his might to the chariot rail.

---

6. **the Hours:** attendants of Apollo that represented the various hours of the day.

dissuade (dĭ-swād′) *v.* to persuade not to do something

G CULTURAL VALUES
Reread lines 61–73. What does Apollo request of Phaëthon? What is Phaëthon's reaction? Make a **prediction** about whether Phaëthon's decision will turn out to be a wise one.

Language Coach

Suffixes A suffix at the end of a word creates a new word. To determine the meaning of the new word, separate the suffix from the base word. In line 96, *masterless* has the suffix *-less*, which means "without." What does *masterless* mean?

precipitous (prĭ-sĭp′ĭ-təs) *adj.* very steep

The Cavalier, Wassily Kandinsky. Staedtische Galerie im Lenbachhaus, Munich, Germany. © 2008 Artists Rights Society (ARS), New York/ADAGP, Paris. Photo © Giraudon/Art Resource, New York.

◀ **Analyze Visuals**

Is this painting a good representation of Phaëthon's ride? Why or why not?

Meanwhile as they came near the earth, it dried up and cracked apart. Meadows were reduced to white ashes, cornfields smoked and shriveled, 100 cities perished in flame. Far and wide on the wooded mountains the forests were ablaze, and even the snow-clad Alps were bare and dry. Rivers steamed and dried to dust. The great North African plain was scorched until it became the desert that it is today. Even the sea shrank back to pools and caves, until dried fishes were left baking upon the white-hot sands. At last the great earth mother called upon Zeus to save her from utter destruction, and Zeus hurled a mighty thunderbolt at the unhappy Phaëthon, who was still crouched in the chariot, clinging desperately to the rail. The dart cast him out, and he fell flaming in a long trail through the air. The chariot broke in pieces at the mighty blow, 110 and the maddened horses rushed snorting back to the stable of their master, Apollo. **H**

Unhappy Clymene and her daughters wandered over the whole earth seeking the body of the boy they loved so well. When they found him, they took him and buried him. Over his grave they wept and could not be comforted. At last the gods in pity for their grief changed them into poplar trees, which weep with tears of amber in memory of Phaëthon. ◦ **I**

H DRAW CONCLUSIONS
What are the consequences of Phaëthon's actions?

I CULTURAL VALUES
What happens to Phaëthon? Draw a **conclusion** about why the Greeks kept his story alive.

Comprehension

1. **Recall** Why does Daedalus tell Icarus not to fly too high?

2. **Recall** Why does Phaëthon go to Apollo's palace?

3. **Represent** Make a sketch of Phaëthon in Apollo's chariot. Cite at least three details from the selection that you've shown in your sketch.

COMMON CORE

RL 1 Cite textual evidence to support analysis of what the text says explicitly. **RL 2** Determine a theme.

Text Analysis

4. **Analyze Greek Gods** What human qualities do the gods in "Phaëthon" display? In your answer, include concrete details about the gods.

5. **Draw Conclusions** On the basis of the myths you have read, what conclusions can you draw about the attitude of ancient Greeks toward human nature? Use examples from the text to support your answer.

6. **Evaluate a Character** Was Icarus believable to you? Explain whether you think his thoughts and actions are similar to those of a real person. Also tell whether you think people today can relate to someone like Icarus.

7. **Make Inferences** How do you think Daedalus eventually felt about his decision to fly away from Crete? Cite details from the myth in your answer.

8. **Identify Cultural Values** The chart shown lists some of the main values held by the ancient Greeks. Complete a chart like it by citing the line numbers of passages that communicate each value. What other values do you think these myths convey? Add one to your chart, and cite passages to support it.

Values	"Icarus and Daedalus"	"Phaëthon"
Obey your elders.	lines 20–29	
Know your place.		
Respect and obey the gods.		

9. **Identify Multiple Themes** Review the chart you created as you read. Describe what you think is the main theme for each myth. Then identify another theme for each story.

Extension and Challenge

10. **Creative Project: Music** The ancient Greeks often told their myths through songs. Create your own song or rap telling the story of Icarus or Phaëthon. Be sure to base your piece on real details from the myth. Present your piece to the class.

Should people always REACH for the stars?

When do you think a person should not pursue a dream?

Vocabulary in Context

▲ VOCABULARY PRACTICE

For each item, choose the word that differs most in meaning from the other words. Refer to a dictionary if you need help.

1. (a) cunning, (b) clever, (c) resourceful, (d) wicked
2. (a) discourage, (b) prevent, (c) infuriate, (d) dissuade
3. (a) cooperate, (b) sustain, (c) support, (d) uphold
4. (a) steep, (b) sharp, (c) precipitous, (d) wide
5. (a) rash, (b) hasty, (c) impulsive, (d) distressed
6. (a) shift, (b) veer, (c) stare, (d) swerve
7. (a) esteem, (b) honor, (c) deference, (d) tolerance
8. (a) reel, (b) sway, (c) whisper, (d) totter

cunning
deference
dissuade
precipitous
rash
reel
sustain
veer

ACADEMIC VOCABULARY IN SPEAKING

> • attribute • conduct • physical • status • task

Phaëthon thought **status** was important. Discuss the positive and negative aspects of status with a small group. Use at least two of the Academic Vocabulary words in your discussion.

VOCABULARY STRATEGY: USING A DICTIONARY

A dictionary will tell you not only a word's definition, but also the way to pronounce it and divide it into syllables. Many words are spelled the same but have different etymologies (histories) and meanings. They may also have different pronunciations and syllabications. These words are called **homographs**. If you see a word used in a way that is unfamiliar to you, check the dictionary to see if the word is a homograph. A dictionary can tell you which homograph is appropriate for the meaning you want to convey.

> **des·ert**[1] (dez´ ərt) **n.** a dry, sandy region with little rainfall: *a desert island.*
>
> **de·sert**[2] (di-zûrt´) **v.** to withdraw from, in spite of responsibility: *deserted the troop before the battle.*

PRACTICE Use a dictionary to find two homographs for each word. Then write a sentence for each meaning. Also, show how each homograph would be divided into syllables. Read your sentences aloud to a partner to make sure you are pronouncing the homograph correctly.

1. minute   3. content   5. refuse
2. console   4. live   6. wind

COMMON CORE

L 4c Consult general reference materials (e.g., dictionaries) to find the pronunciation of a word or clarify its precise meaning.
L 4d Verify the preliminary determination of the meaning of a word.

Interactive Vocabulary **THINK** central

Go to **thinkcentral.com**.
KEYWORD: HML7-672

Language

◆ **GRAMMAR IN CONTEXT:** Use Simple And Compound Sentences

Review the Grammar in Context note on page 668. An **independent clause** is a group of words that contains a subject and a verb and can stand alone as a sentence. A **simple sentence** contains one independent clause, and a **compound sentence** contains two or more independent clauses joined either by a comma and a coordinating conjunction or by a semicolon. Use both types of sentences in your writing to give it clarity and style.

> **Simple:** Icarus flew too close to the sun. (*A simple sentence contains one independent clause.*)
>
> **Compound:** Icarus flew too close to the sun, and he fell to his death. (*Two independent clauses joined with a comma and a coordinating conjunction form a compound sentence.*)

PRACTICE The paragraph below has only simple sentences. Combine some sentences to form at least two compound sentences.

   I told Icarus not to fly too high or low. He didn't listen to me. The sun's heat melted the glue in his wings. The wing's feathers fell one by one. He wanted to fly high into the sky. His need for freedom cost him his life. Now I am left without my son.

*For more help with independent clauses, see page R62 in the **Grammar Handbook**. For more help with simple and compound sentences, see pages R63–R64 in the **Grammar Handbook**.*

READING-WRITING CONNECTION

YOUR TURN

Deepen your understanding of these myths by responding to the prompt. Then use the **revising tip** to improve your writing.

WRITING PROMPT	REVISING TIP
Extended Constructed Response: Evaluation Which of the two myths was better at making you see and feel the terrible descent from the sky? Write **two or three paragraphs** evaluating the description in each myth. Then explain which description was more effective and why.	Review your essay. Did you use compound as well as simple sentences? If not, revise your essay by combining some of the sentences.

COMMON CORE

L 1b Choose among simple, compound sentences to signal differing relationships among ideas. **W 2** Write explanatory texts to examine a topic and convey ideas.

Interactive Revision — **THINK** central

Go to **thinkcentral.com**. KEYWORD: HML7-673

from **Beowulf**

Epic Poem by the Beowulf Poet
Epic Translated by Burton Raffel

VIDEO TRAILER **THINK** central   KEYWORD: HML7-674

What are you willing to
FIGHT for?

⋯ **COMMON CORE**

RL 1 Cite textual evidence to
support analysis of what the
text says explicitly. **RL 3** Analyze
how particular elements of a
story interact. **RL 10** Read and
comprehend literature.

Have you ever had to face those who didn't agree with you in order
to stand up for something you believe in? Sometimes, supporting an
idea or taking an unpopular stance calls for courage. Courage often
means overcoming your own fears before taking a bold action. In
the epic poem *Beowulf*, you'll read about Beowulf the warrior, who is
clear about what he's fighting for, and why.

QUICKWRITE Often, we have to find enough inner strength to do
things that are challenging. Where do you find strength when you
are feeling insecure or afraid? Think of a specific example to write
about in your journal. In a paragraph, describe a time when you felt
discouraged. Describe your experience and the specific things that
inspired you.

TEXT ANALYSIS: CHARACTERISTICS OF THE EPIC

An **epic** is a long, narrative poem, often written in formal language that tells about a series of **quests,** or journeys, undertaken by a great hero. In ancient epics, such as *Beowulf,* the epic hero is a warrior who embodies the values cherished by the culture. Characteristics of the epic include:

- superhuman strength, courage, and loyalty
- encounters with strange creatures in exotic or fantastic lands
- **hero's tasks,** dangerous battles in which the hero is tested

As you read this excerpt from *Beowulf,* look for these characteristics of an epic.

READING STRATEGY: PARAPHRASE

Do you ever retell one of your favorite parts of a book or movie? When you restate information in your own words, you are **paraphrasing**. A good paraphrase includes all of the main ideas and supporting details that appear in the original source of information. The paraphrase will be just as long as or longer than the original. Putting a story into your own words can help you understand the plot and characters. As you read *Beowulf,* use a chart like the one shown to paraphrase parts of the poem that may be difficult to understand, such as the following lines.

Original: I drove five giants into chains, chased
All of the race from the earth.

Paraphrase: Beowulf fought five giants and imprisoned them all. Eventually he killed off the entire race.

Passage from Poem	Paraphrase

Complete the activities in your **Reader/Writer Notebook.**

The Beowulf Poet

For centuries, the poem *Beowulf* was originally sung or chanted aloud by poet-singers. For this reason, it is not known who originally wrote the poem. However, scholars do know where the poem was written. In the fifth century, nomadic tribes fled to England due to the bloody wars in northern Europe. It was from among this new group of Anglo-Saxons in England that the manuscript emerged, somewhere between the seventh and the tenth centuries A.D. The only surviving copy of *Beowulf* is thought to date from the year 1000 and is on display in the British Library in London.

BACKGROUND TO THE EPIC

Events described in the poem *Beowulf* take place in Scandinavia. In the story, Beowulf the warrior crosses the sea to defeat the monster Grendel, who has been terrorizing the Danes. In this excerpt, Beowulf has arrived at the court of Hrothgar, King of the Danes, to convince the king that he should be the warrior chosen to fight Grendel. He gives his credentials, meaning he lists his past accomplishments, in order to convince King Hrothgar of his readiness for battle.

BEOWULF

Translated by **Burton Raffel**

"Hail, Hrothgar!
Higlac is my cousin[1] and my king; the days
Of my youth have been filled with glory. Now Grendel's
Name has echoed in our land: Sailors
Have brought us stories of Herot,[2] the best
Of all mead halls,[3] deserted and useless when the moon
Hangs in skies the sun had lit,
Light and life fleeing together. **A**
My people have said, the wisest, most knowing

10 And best of them, that my duty was to go to the Danes'
Great King. They have seen my strength for themselves,
Have watched me rise from the darkness of war,

A PARAPHRASE
Reread lines 1–8.
Paraphrase these lines in
your chart. Remember
to include all the details
in your own words.

Analyze Visuals ▶

What do the dark tones
of this picture convey
about the mood in the
scene?

---

1. **cousin:** any relative. Higlac is Beowulf's uncle and his king

2. **Herot:** the great mead-hall built by King Hrothgar for his men.

3. **mead halls:** Mead is a drink made from honey, water, yeast, and malt. The hall was a central gathering
   place where warriors could feast, listen to a bard's stories, and sleep in safety.

Dripping with my enemies' blood. I drove
Five great giants into chains, chased
All of that race from the earth. I swam
In the blackness of night, hunting monsters
Out of the ocean, and killing them one
By one; death was my errand and the fate
They had earned. Now Grendel and I are called
20   Together, and I've come. Grant me, then,
Lord and protector of this noble place,
A single request! I have come so far,
Oh shelterer of warriors and your people's loved friend,
That this one favor you should not refuse me—
That I, alone and with the help of my men,
May purge all evil from this hall. I have heard, **B**
Too, that the monster's scorn of men
Is so great that he needs no weapons and fears none.
Nor will I. My lord Higlac
30   Might think less of me if I let my sword
Go where my feet were afraid to, if I hid
Behind some broad linden shield:⁴ My hands
Alone shall fight for me, struggle for life
Against the monster. God must decide
Who will be given to deaths cold grip. ✺ **C**

COMMON CORE   RL 3

B EPIC
The characteristics of
an epic poem include a
hero with superhuman
strength and courage,
encounters with strange
creatures, and **hero's
tasks** in which the hero
is tested against another
warrior or monster.
Reread lines 16–26.
How many of these
characteristics can you
find? Give examples.

C PARAPHRASE
Reread lines 29–35. How
does Beowulf's claim
in these lines show his
bravery? Paraphrase
these lines and add
them to your chart

4. **linden shield:** shield made from wood of the linden tree

Comprehension

1. **Recall** Who is Hrogthar?

2. **Clarify** Why has Beowulf come to see Hrothgar?

3. **Clarify** How does Beowulf try to convince Hrothgar that he is the one for the job?

COMMON CORE

RL 1 Cite textual evidence to support analysis of what the text says explicitly. **RL 3** Analyze how particular elements of a story interact. **RL 10** Read and comprehend literature.

Text Analysis

4. **Examine Epic Characteristics** Review the list of characteristics of the epic on page 675. Use a chart like the one shown to list Beowulf's traits that show he was an epic hero. Give examples from the poem.

Beowulf's Traits	Examples from Poem
superhuman courage	"dripping with my enemies' blood"

5. **Understand Paraphrasing** Now that you have read the whole excerpt, review the paraphrases you wrote in your chart as you read. Did you capture the correct meaning in each case? If not, revise your paraphrases.

Extension and Challenge

6. **Reader's Circle** If you were to film this excerpt as an action movie, what would the monster Grendel look like? Discuss your thoughts, giving details about the monster's physical appearance.

What are you willing to FIGHT for?

Beowulf chose to sail to another land to confront a monster and help those in danger. Would you willingly put yourself in harm's way in order to help people you did not know? Discuss your thoughts with a classmate.

Is there a job you were BORN to do?

COMMON CORE

RL 1 Cite textual evidence to support analysis of what the text says explicitly. **RL 3** Analyze how particular elements of a story interact.

Some people believe that we all have a destiny, a predetermined life that we can't change even if we want to. Others think that life is what we make of it. In the legend you're about to read, a kingdom waits to find out which boy is destined to be its king.

DISCUSS With a small group of classmates, discuss whether people are born to do some particular thing. Think of your feelings about your own future, and also consider individuals who have changed history through their dedication to a job or a goal. Be ready to share with the class whether you believe people choose their own destiny or are born to it.

● TEXT ANALYSIS: CHARACTERISTICS OF LEGENDS

A **legend** is a story about heroes or heroines that is handed down from the past. Legends often are based on real people and events. However, as the stories pass through the generations, the characters, setting, and events become more imaginary and less factual. For example, Arthurian legends are probably based on a real-life chieftain who lived in Britain around A.D. 500. In the course of many retellings, the legends' setting changed to the time of knights, 900 years later.

Because of the courage, honor, and fairness King Arthur displayed, he became a model for others to follow. As you read, notice the conflict young Arthur faces and how he proves his goodness.

● READING SKILL: IDENTIFY CHRONOLOGICAL ORDER

In a legend, events are often presented in **chronological order,** or the order in which they take place. As you read, look for words and phrases that provide clues to this order, such as *when, eventually, this time,* and *in the days that followed.* Mark the sequence of events on a timeline.

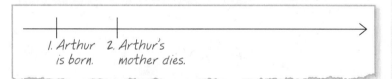

1. Arthur is born.   2. Arthur's mother dies.

▲ VOCABULARY IN CONTEXT

The words in Column A help re-create the world of medieval England. See how many you know by matching each word to the item in Column B that comes closest to its meaning.

Column A	Column B
1. grievous	a. respect
2. homage	b. cringing
3. reclaim	c. boss
4. dismount	d. recover
5. flinching	e. climb down
6. upstart	f. unhappiness
7. melancholy	g. socially climbing
8. taskmaster	h. severe

 Complete the activities in your **Reader/Writer Notebook.**

Meet the Author

Robert D. San Souci
born 1946

Always a Fan

One of the first books Robert D. San Souci ever read was a book about King Arthur, and he remembers being fascinated by dragons and knights. In addition to *Young Arthur,* San Souci has written three other books about the Arthurian legend: *Young Guinevere, Young Lancelot,* and *Young Merlin.* San Souci has also retold the tales and legends of groups ranging from the Alaska Natives to the native Australians.

BACKGROUND TO THE LEGEND
Pretenders and Kings
The Arthur legends paint a vivid picture of the intrigues of medieval life. In the Middle Ages, a king's oldest son was considered the heir to his father's throne. When the enemies of a king wished to take over his kingdom, they might try to kill his son.

Arthurian Legends and Merlin
In the Arthur legends, a magician named Merlin plays an important role. Legends often include unreal or magical people and relate events that could never happen in real life. Some legends also contain magical objects that confer special powers or privileges on their bearers.

Author Online
THINK central

Go to **thinkcentral.com.**
KEYWORD: HML7-681

Young *Arthur*

Retold by Robert D. San Souci

K ing Uther[1] heard the baby's wail and leaped to his feet. There was a sharp rap at the chamber door, and a servant entered grinning happily. "You have a son," he told the king. Uther's joy knew no bounds. When he was ushered into Queen Igerna's[2] bedchamber, Uther looked lovingly at mother and son. "The boy's name shall be Arthur," he declared, "and he shall be a great king. For Merlin [the magician] has foretold that he will one day rule the greatest kingdom under heaven."

But Uther's happiness did not last. His beloved queen died soon after Arthur's birth, and sadness sapped the king's spirit. He lost interest 10 in ruling, and Merlin was unable to rouse him from his **melancholy.**

---

1. **Uther** (yo͞o′thər).

2. **Igerna** (ē-gĕr′nə).

Analyze Visuals ▶

Examine the main **character** in this illustration. What kind of personality do you think he might have?

melancholy (mĕl′ən-kŏl′ē) *n.* sadness; depression

Illustration by Walter Crane in *King Arthur's Knights* by Henry Gilbert, 1911. © Edwin Wallace/Mary Evans Picture Library.

"Unrest grows throughout the land," Merlin warned. "Your old foes are rising in rebellion. Give the babe into my keeping, for you have enemies even at court." **A**

Anxious for his son's safety, Uther agreed. So Merlin, disguised as a beggar, took the infant Arthur to Sir Ector and his lady, who lived some distance from the court and all its dangers. He told them nothing about the child, save that his name was Arthur. The couple had recently lost their infant son and welcomed Arthur as their own. Soon rebellion divided the kingdom. Uther, **reclaiming** his old spirit, rallied his
20 knights and barons. With Merlin always beside him, he drove back his enemies.

But as Uther celebrated his victory in the town of Verulum,[3] traitors poisoned the town's wells. The king and his loyal followers were stricken. Merlin alone escaped. Though he tried his healing arts on Uther, he was forced to confess, "Sire, there is no remedy."

"Then," said the dying monarch, "I declare that my son shall be king of all this realm after me. God's blessing and mine be upon him." With these words, Uther died.

When the rebels entered Verulum, only Merlin was alive.
30 "Tell us where Uther's son is hidden," they demanded, "so that we can slay him and end Uther's line."

But Merlin vanished before their eyes.

Young Arthur was raised as a son in Sir Ector's house. He learned to read and write alongside his foster brother, Kay, who was four years older. By the time he was fifteen, Arthur was a tall, handsome, quick-witted lad. Though he had great strength, he also had a gentle manner.

Kay, who had recently been knighted, decided to train Arthur in the knightly arts himself. But Kay was vain and jealous of the favor Arthur found with their father, so he was a harsh **taskmaster.** Arthur came
40 away from his lessons in swordsmanship with many bruises and cuts. When he complained, Kay replied, "A knight must be thick-skinned and ready to bear even **grievous** wounds without **flinching**." Yet if Arthur so much as pricked his brother, Kay would bellow loudly for the physician. **B**

Eventually Kay appointed Arthur his apprentice. This was an honor the younger boy would happily have forgone. However, seeing that Sir Ector wished it so, Arthur sighed and agreed. But he felt in his heart that he already was a knight, though no lord had dubbed him such.

A CHRONOLOGICAL ORDER
What events have happened so far? Mark the events in order on your timeline.

reclaim (rĭ-klām') v. to get back; recover

taskmaster (tăsk'măs'tər) n. a person who sets tasks for others to do

grievous (grē'vəs) adj. painful; serious

flinching (flĭn'chĭng) n. drawing back from difficulty or danger **flinch** v.

B LEGENDS
Which of the characters you've met so far represent admirable characteristics and which represent undesirable ones?

---

3. **Verulum** (vĕr'ŏŏ-ləm).

Both Arthur and Kay knew it was vital to learn the arts of war. The
50 kingdom was still at the mercy of **upstart** lords who ruled by fire and sword.

The story of Uther's lost son, the true heir to the throne, would have
been forgotten but for Merlin. One Christmas Eve, the long-absent
magician reappeared and summoned the bishops, lords, and common
folk to London's square. There he drove a broadsword halfway into a
huge stone. Written on the blade in blazing gold letters were the words:
"Whoso pulleth out the sword from this stone is born the rightful King
of England." **C**

In the days that followed, knights and barons, cowherds and bakers,
an endless parade of would-be kings eagerly pulled at the sword. But
60 none could loosen it, let alone draw it forth.

When they accused Merlin of trickery, he said, "The rightful king
has not yet come. God will make him known at the proper time."

Now it happened that a great tournament[4] was held in London.
Among those who came were Sir Ector, Sir Kay, and young Arthur, who
served Kay. So eager was the boy to see the jousts[5] that he forgot to pack
Kay's sword. There was great upset when the mistake was discovered.

"Woe to you, boy," snarled Kay, "if your error costs me the victory
I would otherwise win today!"

Even Sir Ector scolded Arthur and ordered, "Go back directly and
70 fetch the missing sword."

Angry at his carelessness and impatient to see the contests, Arthur
started homeward. Then he suddenly reined in his horse.

In the deserted city square was a massive stone with a sword plunged
into its center. "Surely that sword is as good as the one left at home,"
he said. "I will borrow it. When Kay is finished, I will return it to this
curious monument."

So saying, he **dismounted,** scrambled up the stone, took the sword
handle, and tugged. The sword did not move. Impatient to return to the
tournament, he pulled again. This time, the sword slid easily out of the
80 stone. In his haste, he did not notice the words upon the blade. Shoving
the weapon into his belt, he remounted and raced to where Sir Kay
waited his turn upon the field.

The moment he saw the golden words upon the blade, Kay began
to tremble with excitement. When Arthur asked what was amiss, Kay
shouted, "Go! Get away! You have caused enough trouble." **D**

But Arthur was curious. So he followed as Kay ran to Sir Ector. "Look,
Father!" cried Kay. "Here is the sword of the stone. Therefore, it is I who
must be king of all this land!"

---

4. **tournament:** a medieval sporting event in which groups of armored men fought against each other.

5. **jousts:** competitions or combats between two knights on horseback, using lances.

upstart (ŭp'stärt') *adj.*
suddenly risen to wealth
or power

C CHRONOLOGICAL
ORDER
What phrase tells you
when Merlin put the
sword in the stone?
Mark the event on
your timeline.

Language Coach
Oral Fluency Notice
the words *broadsword* in
line 54 and *sword* in line
56. The letter *w* in each
word is silent. In both
words, *sw* is pronounced
like *s*, as in *sore.*

dismount (dĭs-mount')
v. to get down or off

D LEGENDS
Why does Kay tell Arthur
to get away?

When Sir Ector and the others saw the sword and read the golden
90 inscription, they began to shout, "The sword from the stone! The
king's sword!"

Hearing only this much, Arthur thought that he had stolen a king's
weapon. As people hurried excitedly toward Kay, Arthur spurred his horse
away, certain he had committed a great crime.

Looking back, he saw Kay and Sir Ector ride off, surrounded by the
greatest lords of the realm. Were they taking Kay to trial? he wondered.
Had he brought ruin upon Sir Ector's household?

"A true knight would not run away," he said to himself, "and I am a
true knight in my heart." Fearful, but determined to do what was right,
100 the boy wheeled his horse around.

The great square was now filled with people. Just how terrible a crime
had he committed?

Upon the stone stood Kay, holding the sword. The crowd shouted each
time he held the blade aloft. Then silence fell over the throng: Merlin had
appeared at the edge of the square. People stood aside to let the magician
approach the stone.

"Are you the one who pulled the sword from the stone?" Merlin asked.

"I am holding it, am I not?" Kay replied.

"The rightful king could pull it free a hundred times," said Merlin.
110 "Slip the sword into the groove and pull it out again."

With a shrug, Kay reinserted the sword. But when he tried to jerk it
free, it would not budge.

Suddenly all eyes turned toward Arthur, who was pushing his way
through the crowd, bellowing at the top of his lungs. "It wasn't Kay's
fault! I brought him the sword!" Merlin peered closely at Arthur. Then
he smiled and said, "Climb up and draw the sword from the stone."
Uncertainly Arthur clambered up beside Kay. Grasping the pommel,
he easily pulled the sword out. **E**

Then Merlin cried, "This is Arthur, son of Uther Pendragon,[6] Britain's
120 destined king."

An astonished Sir Ector knelt to pay the boy **homage,** followed by
Kay and many others. But all around, there was growing confusion and
dispute. Some cried, "It is the will of heaven! Long live the king!" while
others cried, "It is Merlin's plot to put a beardless boy, a puppet, on the
throne, and so rule the land."

[But] The cries of "Long Live King Arthur!" soon carried the day. ❧ **F**

6. **Pendragon** (pĕn-drăg′ən).

COMMON CORE RL 3

E LEGENDS
A **legend** is a story
handed down from the
past about a specific
person, usually someone
of heroic stature. Like an
epic, a legend may also
feature a **hero's task,** a
trial in which the hero is
tested against another
warrior or monster.
What hero's task does
Arthur perform?

VISUAL
VOCABULARY

pommel (pŭm′əl) *n.*
a knob on the handle
of a sword

homage (hŏm′ĭj) *n.*
a display of loyalty
and respect

**F CHRONOLOGICAL
ORDER**
After Sir Ector pays
Arthur homage, who
else does? Mark the
final events of the story
on your timeline.

Comprehension

1. **Recall** Why do Uther's enemies want to slay Arthur?

2. **Clarify** Why does Arthur remove the sword from the stone the first time?

3. **Paraphrase** What is written on the sword?

Text Analysis

● 4. **Identify Chronological Order** Review the story to make sure you included all its major events on your timeline. Then use your timeline to write a summary of the story.

● 5. **Examine Characteristics of Legends** Most legends feature a hero or heroine who faces a struggle or conflict. This character often has unusual powers and admirable traits. Note Arthur's conflict, special power, and good traits in a graphic like the one shown.

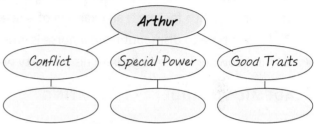

6. **Interpret Theme** Legends communicate their themes not only through the actions of heroes and the consequences the heroes face, but also through the actions of minor characters. Identify the qualities that Kay represents. Then tell whether Kay's behavior pays off in the end. What message about life are readers supposed to learn from Kay's example?

7. **Evaluate a Legend** The story of Arthur has captivated people for generations. What explanation do you have for this? Tell whether you think the legend deserves such wide popularity, and defend your opinion with concrete details from the story.

Extension and Challenge

8. **SOCIAL STUDIES CONNECTION** What was life like in Britain during the early Middle Ages? Read "Who Was King Arthur?" on page 689, and then do research on the Internet. Display your answers to the following questions on a poster:

- How was society organized?
- Who were the Britons fighting?
- What religion was practiced?

Is there a job you were BORN to do?

What ideas about destiny, or fate, are reflected in this legend? Are they different from or similar to the ideas your group discussed as part of the activity on page 680?

COMMON CORE

RL1 Cite textual evidence to support analysis of what the text says explicitly. **RL2** Provide an objective summary of the text. **RL3** Analyze how particular elements of a story interact.

Vocabulary in Context

▲ VOCABULARY PRACTICE

Show that you understand the vocabulary words by telling whether each statement is true or false.

1. I am **flinching** when I reach out to hug someone.
2. A sad look or a sigh is often a sign of **melancholy.**
3. It is hard to pay **homage** to someone you don't respect.
4. A **grievous** wound is generally easy to recover from.
5. An **upstart** politician is probably serving a second or third term in office.
6. A foreman in a factory is an example of a **taskmaster.**
7. A good time to **dismount** from a horse is when you are galloping on it.
8. A landowner trying to **reclaim** his property wants to get it back.

dismount

flinching

grievous

homage

melancholy

reclaim

taskmaster

upstart

ACADEMIC VOCABULARY IN WRITING

> • attribute   • conduct   • physical   • status   • task

Write a paragraph in which you describe at least one **attribute**, or characteristic, of a hero. Draw upon what you learned about Arthur from the selection. Use at least two Academic Vocabulary words in your response.

VOCABULARY STRATEGY: ANALOGIES

An **analogy** compares similar aspects of two or more different things. Sometimes an analogy is expressed as a problem, using two pairs of words. The relationship between the first pair of words is the same as that between the second pair of words. One relationship that is often expressed as an analogy is whole to part. In the following example, the first word represents the whole of something, and the second word represents a part of that whole.

COMMON CORE

L 5b Use the relationship of particular words (e.g., analogy) to better understand each of the words. **L 6** Acquire and use accurately grade-appropriate general academic words.

team : athlete : : cast : actor

(means "is to")   (means "as")

The relationship is expressed as *Team is to athlete as cast is to actor.*

PRACTICE Read each of the following analogy problems. Choose the word in parentheses that best completes each whole-to-part relationship.

1. hand : finger : : wheel : (bolt, spoke, metal)
2. clock : dial : : faculty : (teacher, parent, school)
3. encyclopedia : volume : : flower : (tree, stem, vase)
4. family : child : : state : (country, city, continent)
5. house : kitchen : : Africa : (Europe, France, Nigeria)

Interactive Vocabulary **THINK** central

Go to **thinkcentral.com**.
KEYWORD: HML7-688

Who Was King Arthur? by Jerry Dunn

King Arthur and his queen, Guinevere, ruled their kingdom in peace from their castle, Camelot. . . . Camelot represents a lost time of innocence and high adventure during the Dark Ages—the period from A.D. 476 to about A.D. 1000. . . .

But did Arthur and his peaceful Camelot ever really exist? Historians say that around A.D. 410, after the Romans left Britain, fierce invaders called Saxons came from Europe, conquering much of England. In the western part of the country, a local chieftain fought the Saxons. He won a great victory at Badon Hill around A.D. 500. According to some scholars, this real-life brave warrior was Arthur.

His triumph brought 12 years of peace. Could this golden age have been Camelot? Some experts say the real Camelot may have been Cadbury Castle in southern England. Here archaeologists found ruins of a fortified tower and what may have been a great hall of timber, all dating from Arthur's time. Other places around England also lay claim to the noble king. For instance Arthur may have fought his last battle in southwestern England at a place called Camlan.

We may never know all the facts about Arthur. Perhaps it doesn't matter. The legend of King Arthur holds its own timeless truths. This is why people have been reciting stories of King Arthur and his Round Table for at least a thousand years.

THE DARK AGES

- Disorder reigned in most of Europe between A.D. 476 and A.D. 1000, the period called the Dark Ages.
- King Arthur and his knights never wore full suits of armor. They lived in the sixth century; full plate armor didn't show up for another 900 years.
- People who lived in what is now England did not speak English. They probably spoke Latin or British, a language from which Welsh developed.
- Disease, poor diet, and frequent wars meant that most people could not expect to live beyond age 30.
- Only monks and some noblemen learned how to read.

from **Sir Gawain and the Green Knight**
Medieval Legend Retold by Michael Morpurgo

Is CHIVALRY dead?

COMMON CORE

RL 1 Cite textual evidence to support analysis of what the text says explicitly as well as inferences drawn from the text.
RL 10 Read and comprehend literature.

In the ninth century, chivalry was a set of rules that gave knights guidance about how to engage in battle, how to serve rulers, and how to behave toward women. Today *chivalry* refers to the personal qualities that were important to knights: bravery, honor, courtesy, and service. In this legend, an act of chivalry gets one knight into a terrible predicament.

SURVEY In our rough-and-tumble modern world, does chivalry still exist? Conduct a survey to find out how often your peers witness people acting chivalrously. Use your results to discuss what modern people are doing well and what they could do better.

	Often	Seldom	Never
Sacrificing for Others			
Keeping Promises			
Being Polite			

TEXT ANALYSIS: CULTURAL VALUES IN LEGENDS

Most popular movies focus on a hero—a person who is unusually brave. Long before people filmed stories or wrote them down, a hero was often the basis for a legend.

In a legend, the hero's main traits usually reflect the **cultural values** of the society, or the standards of behavior the society wants to promote. In medieval Arthurian legends, knights and their code of chivalry represent these ideals, which may also be themes in the story:

- Be loyal to those you serve and be courteous to all.
- Always be truthful and keep your word.
- Face danger with courage and show mercy to the weak.

As you read, look for examples of chivalry.

READING STRATEGY: PREDICT

Predicting is making a reasonable guess about what will happen next in a story. To predict, follow these steps:

- Ask yourself, "What do I know about the characters and plot?"
- Combine your answers with your own experience, and make a logical guess about what might happen next.
- Adjust your prediction as new information is presented.

As you read, track your predictions on a chart.

Text Evidence	Prediction	What Happens
King Arthur wishes for a challenge.		

VOCABULARY IN CONTEXT

The words listed help describe a knight and his challenge. In your *Reader/Writer Notebook,* write a sentence for each of the vocabulary words. Use a dictionary or the definitions in the following selection pages to help you.

WORD LIST	cumbersome	integrity	sever
	daunting	lanky	unperturbed
	demeaning	revere	

Complete the activities in your **Reader/Writer Notebook.**

Michael Morpurgo
born 1943

Storyteller with Heart
When Michael Morpurgo became a teacher, one of his favorite parts of the job was making up stories for his students. Their interest convinced him that he could become a writer. Now the British author has published over 50 books. In his spare time, Morpurgo runs three farms in England, where kids from the city can stay. In 2003, he was named the third Children's Laureate of England.

BACKGROUND TO THE LEGEND
The Chivalric Code
In the Middle Ages, young men from well-to-do families often became knights. As knights, they served a family of a higher social rank. Knights were expected to be extremely courteous and brave, as well as loyal to their lords.

Knights of the Round Table
Stories of Arthur were first told before the age of chivalry, but during the Middle Ages, the stories changed. Arthur and his followers began to be pictured as knights who lived in an ideal kingdom called Camelot. An English writer, Sir Thomas Malory, wrote about the Round Table, where the knights sat in perfect equality.

Author Online THINK central
Go to thinkcentral.com.
KEYWORD: HML7-691

Sir Gawain and the Green Knight

Retold by **Michael Morpurgo**

I t was Christmas time at Camelot, that time of the year when all King Arthur's Knights gathered to celebrate the birth of their Lord and Savior, Jesus Christ. For fifteen joyous days, after holy Mass each morning there was nothing but feasting and dancing and singing, and hunting and jousting too. Jousting was the favorite sport, each Knight striving to unseat the mighty Sir Lancelot—but rarely succeeding of course. And all was done in fun, in a spirit of great comradeship, for they were happy to be all together once more at this blessed time. During the year, these lords were often parted from one another, and from their ladies, as they rode
10 out through the kingdom on their dangerous missions. So this was a time when love and friendship were renewed, a time to celebrate with their young King all their achievements and their great and good purpose: to bring peace to the land, and make of it a kingdom as near to a heaven on earth as had never before been achieved in Britain, or in any other land, come to that. **Ⓐ**

Detail from illustration © Juan Wijngaard (1981) from
Sir Gawain and the Green Knight by Selina Hastings.
Reproduced by permission of Walker Books, Ltd., London.

Analyze Visuals ▶

How does the knight in this painting **compare** with your image of a knight?

Ⓐ CULTURAL VALUES
Reread lines 10–15. On the basis of this description, what can you **infer** about the kind of behavior people admired during the Middle Ages?

On New Year's Eve, after evening Mass had been said in the chapel and generous New Year's gifts exchanged, the High King and Guinevere,[1] his Queen, came at last into the great hall where all the lords and ladies were waiting to dine. No one could begin the feasting until they came,
20 of course, so as you can imagine, the lords and ladies cheered them to the rafters when they saw them. Guinevere had never looked so gloriously beautiful as she did that evening, and there were gasps of admiration from around the hall.

With Arthur on one side of her and Gawain[2] on the other, Guinevere sat down at the high table, which was set on a splendid dais draped all about with silk and richly hung with the finest tapestries from Toulouse[3] and Turkestan.[4] Then, with drummers drumming and pipers piping, the servants came in carrying the food on great silver plates, piling each table high with roasted meat, capons and venison and pork, and fish
30 fresh-baked in sea salt, and baskets of crusty bread, and steaming soups too. Truly there was enough to feed five thousand, but there were only five hundred there to eat it. As they poured out the wine and ale, filling every goblet to the brim, the scents of the feast that lay before them filled the air with succulence,[5] and their nostrils too, so that, their appetites whetted, they were all longing now to begin. But the High King and his Queen sat there, not touching their food, or their drink either. Everyone knew that if they did not begin, then out of respect nor could anyone else. And everyone knew also why it was that the king was refusing to let the feast begin.

40 The great hall fell silent as Arthur rose to his feet. "You know the custom," he began. "I will not take one mouthful, or one sip of wine, until I am told of some new and stirring tale, some wonderfully outlandish adventure, some extraordinary feat of arms so far unheard of. And it must be true too. I don't want you to go making it up just so you can get at the food—some of you are good at the tall stories." They laughed at that, but as they looked around, it became clear that none of them had a tale to tell. "What?" cried the High King. "What? Not one of you? Well then, I see we must all go hungry. Such a pity. Isn't it strange how food you cannot eat always smells so wonderful? It needn't be a story,
50 of course. It could be some new happening, some weird and wondrous event. If I can't have a story, then you'd better hope, as I do, that maybe

1. **Guinevere** (gwĭn′ə-vîr′).

2. **Gawain** (gə-wān′).

3. **Toulouse** (too̅-loo̅z′).

4. **Turkestan** (tûr′kĭ-stăn′): During the Middle Ages, trade occurred between Britain and many countries in Asia. Tapestries from the historical region Turkestan were prized objects that only the wealthy could afford.

5. **succulence:** juiciness and tastiness.

some stranger will come striding in here right now and challenge us face to face. That would do. I'd be happy with that. Then we could all begin our feasting before the food gets cold." And with that, he sat down. **B**

At that very same moment, just as the High King had finished speaking, they heard a sudden roaring of wind, the rattle of doors and windows shaking, and then outside, the clatter of a horse's hooves on stone. The great doors burst open, and into the hall rode the most awesome stranger anyone there had ever set eyes on. For a start, he was 60 a giant of a man, taller by two heads than any knight there, but not **lanky** and long, not at all. No, shoulder to shoulder he was as broad as any three men stood side by side, and his legs were massive—like tree trunks they were. And you could see the man's arms were about as thick and strong as his legs. But that wasn't all. This giant was green, green from head to toe. Yes, bright green, I tell you, as green as beech leaves in summer when the sun shines through. And when I say the man was green, I don't just mean his clothes. I mean him. His face. Green. His hands. Green. The hair that hung down to his shoulders. Green. Only his eyes, horror of horrors, glowed red, blood red and glaring from under his 70 heavy eyebrows, which were as green as the rest of him. Everyone in that hall simply gaped at him, at his hugeness and his greenness, and at his grimness too, for the man had a thunderous scowl on his face that struck terror into every heart.

Grim he may have been, but the giant was gorgeous too—if such an apparition can ever be said to be gorgeous. He wore a tunic of green velvet with buttons of gleaming gold. Stirrups and spurs were all of gold, both encrusted with the brightest emeralds of the deepest green. And his horse! His warhorse was a monster of a creature—he had to be, just to carry this giant. The horse was green too, green from nose to hoof, from 80 mane to tail. He was pawing at the ground, tossing his head, foaming at his bit; at least the foam was white. And he looked just as bad-tempered as his master. They suited each other, those two. **C**

Yet fierce though he seemed, the Knight in green wore no war helmet and no armor either. He held no shield before him, and carried no spear, not even a sword at his side. Instead, the hand clutching the reins held a sprig of holly—green naturally—which might have been laughable had everyone not already noticed what he was carrying in his other hand. It was an ax, but it was no ordinary battle-ax. This weapon was a real head cruncher, yet the handle was most delicately carved—bright green 90 of course, as was the cord that looped about it and the tassels that hung from it. Only the huge blade itself was not green. Curved like a crescent moon at the cutting edge, it was made of polished steel—a hideous

B PREDICT
Reread lines 40–54. Why does Arthur refuse to let the feast begin? Predict what will happen next.

lanky (lăng′kē) *adj.* tall and thin

C CULTURAL VALUES
Recall what you've learned about knights and chivalry. Does the Green Knight seem like a chivalrous type? As you read, note how chivalry influences his behavior and the reactions of others.

widow maker if ever there was one. Even
the dogs, usually so fierce with any stranger,
shrank back whining under the tables, their
tails between their legs.

There came no cheery New Year greeting
from this green man, not even a ghost of a
smile. In a thunderous, booming voice as
100 terrifying as the man himself, he said, "So,
who's in charge here?" No one answered him.
"Well, come on. Speak up. Which of you is
the King? It's him I've come to talk to, no
one else." But as he rode around the hall, his
blazing eyes scanning the lords and ladies
on every side, no one spoke up. And you
can understand why. Many of the knights
sitting there in that hushed hall had come
across all kinds of astounding and alarming
110 looking creatures on their quests[6]—dragons
and monsters, goblins and ghouls—but
never anything quite like this. Most sat there
stunned to silence. Others kept quiet out of
respect for their High King, wanting to hear
how he would reply.

No one doubted for a moment that he
would have the courage to speak up, and
so he did. Indeed, as he rose to his feet, he
was smiling broadly. After all, hadn't he just
120 been hoping for such a happening as this?
"Welcome to Camelot, Sir Knight," he began.
"I am the King you are looking for, I think.
My name is Arthur. Believe me, you could
not have arrived at a better moment. So please
dismount and join our New Year's feasting,
and afterward you can tell us perhaps why you
have come here to our court."

The knight in green rode toward the dais and spoke directly to the
High King, but more courteously now. "My thanks, great King. But I
130 will not stay, or keep you from your feasting. I will speak my purpose
plainly. I cannot tell you how honored I am to meet you at last, the great
Arthur, High King of all Britain. I have heard, as all the world has heard,

CULTURAL VALUES
Reread lines 116–127.
What can you **infer** about
how people in the Middle
Ages believed guests
should be treated?

---

6. **quests:** adventurous journeys made by knights.

how you have made of this place the most wondrous kingdom on earth,
and gathered around you the most worthy, courageous, and chivalrous
knights that ever lived. Looking around me, I begin to wonder whether
you deserve this glowing reputation at all. I mean no offense, great King.
As you can see from the sprig of holly I carry, I came in peace. If it were
otherwise, I'd be armed for a fight, would I not? But you see no armor on
me, no helmet, no sword or spear, because it is not war I come for, but
140 sport—well, a sport of sorts, anyway." **E**

E **PREDICT**
As you read, check your
predictions against what
actually happens. Did
the prediction you made
on page 695 come true?

"If it's jousting you're looking for," the High King replied as politely as his irritation would allow, "or wrestling maybe, then **daunting** though you may look, Sir Knight, you'll find no lack of sport here, I assure you."

"But I joust and wrestle only with men," replied the Green Knight. "I see here nothing but beardless boys. It would be no contest. None of you would stand a chance against me. No, I have in mind something much more testing of a man's courage, and much more interesting for everyone. But I cannot imagine there will be anyone here brave enough to take me on."

150   "We'll see about that," the High King cried, his face flushing with sudden anger at the stranger's insulting tone. "Just get on with it for goodness' sake and tell us what game it is you want to play. Our soup is getting cold."

The Green Knight laughed. "Why don't we just call it a New Year's game," he said. "I don't think any of you will ever have played it before, and nor have I. We'll soon see what stuff your Knights of the Round Table are made of, whether you're all you're cracked up to be." So saying, he held high his great ax. "Here is my battle-ax," he went on. "Is there anyone here in this hall brave enough to take it, I wonder? Whoever does will have

160 one chance, and one chance only, to strike my head from my shoulders. I shall not resist or fight back. I shall not even flinch, I promise."

"Is that the game?" the High King asked, as incredulous as everyone else in the hall.

"Not quite," replied the Green Knight. "Here's how the game goes. If any Knight has the courage to take up the challenge, then he will have to promise, on his honor, that in a year and a day from now he will submit himself to . . . let's call it a return match, shall we? Then it will be my turn to strike the same single blow, and it will be one of you who has to kneel there, bare his neck, and take it—without resisting, without

170 flinching. Well, who dares?" 🄵

If there was a hushed silence when he first came into the hall, the place was now as still as death as he glared all around, waiting for someone to speak up. But even the bravest of the Knights lowered their eyes. This was one challenge they all wanted to avoid if they could. The Green Knight ◆ wheeled his great warhorse and clattered around the hall, looking down at them, a supercilious sneer on his lips. "I thought so, I thought so," he said, his mocking laughter ringing in the air. "Where's your courage now? Where's that spotless honor, that perfect chivalry I've heard so much about? Is there no one here who has the stomach to take me on?" Still no

180 one spoke. "Chickens, the lot of you. Worse than chickens too. At least

daunting (dôn′tĭng) *adj.* frightening; intimidating
daunt *v.*

🄵 **PREDICT**
Use what you know about the **plot** and **characters** to predict what you think will happen next.

◆ **GRAMMAR IN CONTEXT**
In line 174, *if they could* is a dependent clause. It has been added to an independent clause to form a complex sentence.

chickens cluck. I can see I'm in the wrong place. This can't be the court of King Arthur. It's a court of cowards." Ⓖ

Stung to fury now, the High King had had enough. "Cease your insults!" he shouted. "None of us here is frightened of you. We're just speechless at the sheer stupidity of such a ridiculous duel. It's obvious that with an ax like that, whoever strikes the first blow is bound to be the winner. But since you insist upon it and are so brash and rude, I shall take up your challenge myself. So get down off that horse, hand me your ax, and I'll give you what you asked for." And with that, King Arthur
190 sprang down from the dais and strode across the hall toward the Green Knight, who dismounted and at once handed over his ax. "Make yourself ready, then," cried the High King, swinging the ax above his head, testing his grip, feeling the weight and balance of the weapon. The Green Knight looked on. He stood head and shoulders above the King, dwarfing him utterly. **Unperturbed** by the swishing ax, the Green Knight turned down the neck of his tunic and made himself ready.

At that moment, Gawain stood up. "No!" he cried. And leaving the table, he hurried across the hall to his uncle's aid. He bowed low before him. "Let me take your place, Uncle. Give me this fight, please, I beg
200 you. I shall teach this green and haughty man that in a fight there are no Knights braver than your own. It is true that I am no braver than any other man here, I know that, but I am your nephew. Make this an uncle's gift to his nephew. Because the truth is, good Uncle, that if I do lose my life, I would not be much missed compared to you. You are our King, and this is too silly, too **demeaning** a venture for you. Lose you and we lose the kingdom. Lose me and there will always be others to come in my place." Ⓗ

"For goodness' sake, make up your minds," said the Green Knight, shaking his head, "I do not have all day."
210 Ignoring the man's boorishness, Gawain knelt before the King. "Let me prove myself worthy, Uncle, worthy of being your Knight and your nephew too." There was much applause at this and many loud voices raised in support of Sir Gawain's plea. After thinking for a while, the High King lifted his hand for silence, and taking Gawain's hand, helped him to his feet. "As you wish, Nephew," he said. "There's nothing I'd like better than to separate this man's great green head from his great green shoulders, but I willingly give the task to you. Strike boldly, Nephew. If you do, I really cannot see, short of a miracle, how you will ever have to face him again in a year and a day. Here's the ax. You'll find it a bit
220 heavy and **cumbersome,** but it'll do the job."

Ⓖ **CULTURAL VALUES**
On the basis of what you've read so far, is the Green Knight chivalrous? Explain why or why not.

unperturbed
(ŭn′pər-tûrbd′) *adj.* not troubled or distressed

demeaning
(dĭ-mē′nĭng) *adj.* lowering one's dignity or standing **demean** *v.*

Ⓗ **CULTURAL VALUES**
How does Gawain demonstrate that he is chivalrous? Explain.

cumbersome
(kŭm′bər-səm) *adj.* awkward; hard to manage

Gawain took the ax from him, gripped it firmly and turned now to face the Green Knight, who stood towering above him, his hands on his hips. To everyone there they looked like David and Goliath—and all were hoping and praying for the same unlikely outcome. "So," said the giant Knight, "so we have a champion at last. Let's get on with it. But before we do I must know your name and make sure we both understand and agree on the rules of the game." **I**

"My name is Sir Gawain, and I already know the rules of your foolish game," came the blunt reply.

230 "Good Sir Gawain, I'm glad it is you," said the Green Knight then, altogether more polite now than he had been so far. "I'll be honored to take the first blow from a knight as noble and worthy as yourself, for you are known and **revered** throughout all Britain as a man of not only the greatest courage, but also the greatest **integrity**. Believe me, you will need both, and in full measure, for what I have in store for you. And just so there can be no misunderstanding, you must promise on your honor, and in the hearing of everyone in this hall, that a year and a day from now you will seek me out and find me so that I can pay you back in kind for whatever you do to me today."

240 "I promise you willingly, on my honor as a Knight of the Round Table," Gawain replied. "But how shall I be able to find you? I don't even know your name or from what part of the country you come. Just tell me, and I'll be there—you have my word." **J**

"Afterward I shall tell you all you need to know," said the Green Knight. "Once you have done your worst, I'll tell you exactly where to come and who I am." And with a smile that sent shivers even into brave Gawain's heart, the Green Knight went on, "I'll be looking forward to you calling on me in a year and a day. I'll be looking forward to it very much indeed."

250 With the smile still on his face, the Green Knight went down on one knee before Gawain and bared his neck. "Do the best you can, Sir Gawain," he said. "Remember, you have only one chance."

"Make your peace with your Maker," Gawain replied, running his finger along the blade.

Then, grasping the handle tight and putting his left foot forward, he took a deep breath and raised the great ax high above his head, the blade flashing blood red in the flames of the fire. Down it came and sliced right through the Green Knight's neck, cutting clean through bone and flesh and skin, **severing** the terrible head entirely and sending

260 it rolling hideously across the floor toward the lords and ladies at their

I **PREDICT**
Reread lines 223–224. How do King Arthur and the others in the hall think the match will turn out? Make your own prediction about the outcome.

revere (rĭ-vîr´) v. to honor or worship

integrity (ĭn-tĕg´rĭ-tē) n. honesty or sincerity

J **CULTURAL VALUES**
Do you think that others in the hall believe Gawain will keep his promise? Why or why not?

sever (sĕv´ər) v. to cut off or apart

table. And the blood was not green, as you might have imagined, but bright red like any man's, and it spurted freely from head and body alike.

But instead of toppling over, as everyone expected, that grotesque headless body rose up onto his feet and strode across the floor to where his head lay bleeding, the eyes closed in death. Snatching the baleful[7] head up by the hair, he went straight to his horse, set one foot in the stirrup, and swung himself up easily into his saddle as if nothing at all had happened. Suddenly those eyes opened and glared most horribly around the hall. Everyone was struck dumb with terror.

270   But worse was still to come, for then the mouth began to speak. "Well struck, Sir Gawain. Now I'm afraid you have your side of the bargain to keep, a promise you made freely and openly, in front of everyone here and in front of your King too. You must seek me out and find me at the Green Chapel, a year and a day from now. There I shall repay you, a blow for a blow, as we agreed. I am known everywhere as

---

7. **baleful:** foretelling evil.

COMMON CORE RL 10

K CULTURAL VALUES
A **legend** is a story handed down from the past about a specific person, usually someone of heroic stature. Like an epic, a legend may also feature a **quest**, a journey that the hero takes in order to achieve a goal. What quest must Gawain undertake?

the Knight of the Green Chapel. Look into the sky as you go and follow where your eyes and your ears lead you. I shall be waiting. Be sure you come, Sir Gawain, or the world will know you forever as a coward."

He said nothing more, not one goodbye, but turning his horse about, 280 set spurs to his side and galloped from that hall, sparks flying from the horse's hooves as he went. Where he had come from no one knew. Where he went to no one knew. But as you can well imagine, I think, all were glad to see him gone. **L**

It was some time before anyone in the hall found voice to speak, and then it was the High King himself who at last broke the silence. He was as amazed and horrified as everyone else by what they had just witnessed, but he did not like to see his queen and his court so downhearted on this festive evening. "Come on now. Let's not be upset," he said. "After all, this was just such a marvel as we were waiting for, was it not? And 290 marvels like this are as much a part of new year at Camelot as carols and feasting. Like it or not, and I agree it wasn't a very appetizing spectacle, you have to admit we've never seen anything quite like it before, have we? And best of all it means we can now begin our feasting. So hang up your ax, Gawain, somewhere where we can all see it and be reminded of your courage, and come and join us. Let's eat, my friends. Let's drink. Let's be merry." And so they were—all but Gawain, whose thoughts, as ours must now do, ran on ahead of him to New Year's Day a year hence, to the dreaded day when he would meet that Green Knight once again at the Green Chapel. ∿ **M**

Eventually, Sir Gawain did indeed set out to find the Green Chapel and fulfill his promise. On his journey, he encountered three temptations that tested his character. By the time he stood before the Green Knight, he had proven himself a worthy, though not perfect, knight. For this reason, the Green Knight injures Gawain slightly but does not take his life.

L PREDICT
Did the prediction you made on page 700 come true? Describe what happened after Gawain struck the Green Knight.

M CULTURAL VALUES
What reasons does King Arthur have for choosing this moment to invite his knights to the feast?

Comprehension

1. **Clarify** What has to happen before the feast can begin?

2. **Recall** Whom does the Green Knight come looking for?

3. **Represent** What does the scene in the great hall look like before the Green Knight appears? Make a drawing illustrating the description.

Text Analysis

4. **Predict** Review the chart of predictions you made as you read. What events were the most difficult to predict? Why?

5. **Make Inferences About Culture** What details in this legend reflect what people ate, what they wore, and how they celebrated? Tell what you infer about how the wealthy lived during the Middle Ages.

6. **Analyze Suspense** The growing tension, or excitement, that you feel as you read is called suspense. Which passages in this legend were especially suspenseful? Give the line numbers of at least two passages. Then explain your choices.

7. **Draw Conclusions About Cultural Values** People following the code of chivalry were expected to demonstrate the qualities shown in the web. Make a similar web and expand it by giving examples from the legend for each type of behavior. What conclusion can you draw about which of these qualities was most important to the people of the Middle Ages?

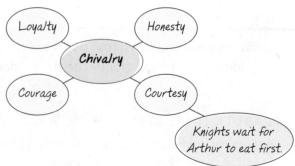

8. **Compare and Contrast Legends** How does the king Arthur portrayed by Michael Morpurgo compare with the young Arthur portrayed by Robert D. San Souci in the legend on page 682? Think about characters' attitude toward others, their confidence in themselves, and the courage they display. Decide whether the young Arthur is more similar to or more different from the adult he becomes.

Extension and Challenge

9. **Reader's Circle** Which character is the true hero of this legend? Discuss your thoughts, giving details from the legend to support your opinion.

Is CHIVALRY dead?

Do you think a society can survive without chivalry?

COMMON CORE

RL 1 Cite textual evidence to support analysis of what the text says explicitly as well as inferences drawn from the text. RL 10 Read and comprehend literature.

Vocabulary in Context

▲ **VOCABULARY PRACTICE**

Answer the questions to show your understanding of the vocabulary words.

1. Would a large package or one pair of socks more likely be **cumbersome?**
2. In which sport, basketball or football, might it be more important to be **lanky?**
3. If Ann is **unperturbed,** is she sitting calmly or shouting angrily?
4. Would being criticized publicly or being elected class president be more **demeaning?**
5. Would it show respect or disrespect to **revere** a person?
6. Is a telegram sent to **sever** a business deal meant to continue it or cut it off?
7. Who might be a better role model for **integrity,** an honest politician or a popular singer?
8. Which is more **daunting,** climbing a peak or resting in the backyard?

> cumbersome
> daunting
> demeaning
> integrity
> lanky
> revere
> sever
> unperturbed

ACADEMIC VOCABULARY IN SPEAKING

> • attribute   • conduct   • physical   • status   • task

What are some situations that might call for a hero's **task** today? Discuss your ideas with a small group. Use the Academic Vocabulary words in your discussion.

VOCABULARY STRATEGY: USING A GLOSSARY

A **glossary** is a list of specialized terms and their definitions. It is usually found at the back of a book. A glossary sometimes includes pronunciations and syllabication. Many textbooks contain glossaries. This textbook has four glossaries: an Academic Vocabulary Glossary, a Glossary of Literary and Nonfiction Terms, a Glossary of Reading and Informational Terms, and a Glossary of Vocabulary Words in English and Spanish. You will find glossaries useful when

• you cannot find a definition or context clue for a key term
• you are studying for a test
• you do not have a dictionary available

PRACTICE Use the three glossaries beginning on page R100 to answer the following questions.

1. In which glossary would you find the pronunciation for *aptitude?*
2. A question at the end of a selection asks you to clarify a paragraph in a selection. In which glossary will you find the meaning of *clarify?* How do you clarify information?

COMMON CORE

L 4c Consult general reference materials (e.g., glossaries) to find the pronunciation of a word or determine its precise meaning.
L 6 Acquire and use accurately grade-appropriate general academic words.

Interactive Vocabulary **THINK** central
Go to thinkcentral.com.
KEYWORD: HML7-704

Language

◆ **GRAMMAR IN CONTEXT:** Add Variety with Complex Sentences

Review the Grammar in Context note on page 698. A **dependent clause,** also known as a subordinate clause, is a group of words that contains a subject and a verb but cannot stand alone as a sentence. Dependent clauses begin with words such as *because, even though, if, that, when, while,* and *who.* When a dependent clause and an independent clause, or main clause, are combined, they form a **complex sentence.** Use complex sentences to help clarify the relationships between your ideas and to add variety to your writing.

> *Complex:* Gawain accepts the Green Knight's challenge because Gawain is brave. (*A dependent clause is joined to an independent clause with the subordinating conjunction because.*)

PRACTICE The paragraph below has only simple sentences. Combine some sentences to form at least two complex sentences.

> Gawain faces the Green Knight. Gawain is frightened. Gawain must face the Green Knight again in a year. Gawain promised he would. Gawain proves to be a good nephew. He sacrifices himself for his uncle.

READING-WRITING CONNECTION

YOUR TURN

Explore this legend further by responding to the prompt. Then use the **revising tip** to improve your writing.

WRITING PROMPT	REVISING TIP
Short Constructed Response: Explanation Why do you think Gawain accepted the Green Knight's challenge? Write a **one-paragraph explanation** of his motivation.	Review your paragraph. Did you use complex as well as simple sentences? If not, revise your paragraph by combining some of the sentences.

Interactive Revision **THINK** central

Go to **thinkcentral.com.**
KEYWORD: HML7-705

COMMON CORE

L 1b Choose complex sentences to signal differing relationships among ideas. **W 2** Write explanatory texts to examine a topic and convey ideas.

Crispin: The Cross of Lead

COMMON CORE

RL 10 Read and comprehend literature.

Historical Novel by Avi

Meet Avi

Avi notes that reading helped him to become a professional writer: "The more you read, the better your writing can be," he has said. By this measure, it's no surprise Avi is an award-winning writer. He earned a college degree in history and an advanced degree in drama. While working in the New York Public Library's theater collection, he decided to go back to school for an advanced degree in library science.

Avi first wrote plays, but while raising his children, he began writing books for young people. Since then, he has written over 50 books and won many important awards.

Other Books by Avi

- *Bright Shadow*
- *The Fighting Ground*
- *The Man Who Was Poe*
- *Midnight Magic*
- *Nothing but the Truth*
- *S.O.R. Losers*
- *The True Confessions of Charlotte Doyle*
- *Wolf Rider*

Try a Historical Novel

Have you ever wondered what it was like to live in the Middle Ages? Until inventors create a time machine, reading **historical fiction,** or stories that are set in the past, is one of the best ways to find out. Historical fiction can make the past come alive by mixing references to actual people, places, and events with fictional characters and dialogue and other creative details.

Reading Fluency Good readers read smoothly, accurately, and with feeling. To improve your reading fluency, read a passage several times. Your goal in silent reading is to make sense of the writer's words and ideas. When reading aloud, think about the type of text you are reading. You may need to adjust your speed and tone and how you emphasize certain words when reading fiction, nonfiction, or poetry.

Read a Great Book

This story is set in England in the year 1377, when nobles ruled the land and their agricultural workers, the serfs, had almost no rights at all. You are about to read a passage about a young serf named Crispin who is on his way home from his mother's funeral. He is attacked by a group of men for reasons he does not yet understand. He narrowly escapes and hides in the woods overnight, then goes to the village priest for advice on what he should do.

from

CRISPIN
THE CROSS OF LEAD

Near the altar the priest genuflected. I did the same. Then we knelt, facing each other. "Speak low," he said. "There's always Judas lurking. Are you hungry?"

"Yes, Father," I murmured.

From behind the tattered altar cloth he produced a loaf of barley bread and gave it to me. "I was hoping you would come," he said.

I took the heavy bread and began to devour it.

"Where have you been?" he asked.

"In the forest."

10 "Did you know they've been searching for you?"

My mouth full, I nodded.

"Aycliffe claims you stole money from the manor."

"Father," I said, "in all my life, I've never even been there."

"I don't doubt you," the priest said, gently putting his hand to my face to keep me calm. "Most people in the village don't believe the accusation, either. But why does Aycliffe put your name to the crime?"

I told the priest what had happened when I ran from my mother's burial—my fall, my waking to witness the meeting in the clearing, Aycliffe's attempt to kill me.

20 "He said none of this," the priest said.

"It's true."

"What was the thing the steward read?" the priest asked. "He never mentioned that either."

"I don't know," I said. Then I asked, "Who was the man he met?"

"Sir Richard du Brey," the priest said. "He's brought word that Lord Furnival—God keep him well—has returned from the wars. He's ill and expected to die."

"The stranger said Aycliffe must act immediately."

"About what?"

30 I shrugged. "He said, 'Are you not her kin? Do you not see the consequences if you don't?' To which Aycliffe replied, 'A great danger to us all.' Then the man said, 'Precisely. There could be those who will see it so and act accordingly. You'll be placed in danger, too.' It made no sense to me," I said.

The priest pondered the words in silence.

"Father," I said, "what will happen if I'm caught?"

The priest put his hand on my shoulder. "The steward," he said, "has declared you a wolf's head."

"A wolf's head!" I gasped, horrified.

40 "Do you understand what it means?"

"That . . . I'm considered not human," I said, my voice faltering. "That anyone may . . . kill me. Is that why they pulled down our house?"

"I suppose."

"But . . . *why?*"

The priest sat back and gave himself over to thought. In the dim light I studied his face. He seemed distraught, as if the pain of the whole world had settled in his soul.

"Father," I ventured, "is it something about my mother?"

He bowed his head. When he looked up it was to gaze at me. "Asta's son, unless you flee, you won't live long."

"But how can I leave?" I said. "I'm bound to the land. They'll never give me permission to go."

He sighed, reached forward, and placed the side of his frail hand aside my face. "Asta's son, listen to me with the greatest care. When I baptized you, you were named . . . Crispin."

"I was?" I cried.

"It was done in secret. What's more, your mother begged me not to tell you or anyone. She chose to simply call you 'Son.'"

"But . . . why?" I asked.

He took a deep breath and then said, "Did she tell you anything about your father?"

Once again the priest took me by surprise. "My *father?* Only that he died before I was born. In the Great Mortality," I reminded him. "But what has that to do with my name? Or any of this?"

"Dearest boy," the priest said wearily, "I beg you to find your way to some town or city with its own liberties. If you can stay there for a year and a day, you'll gain your freedom."

"Freedom?" I said. "What has that to do with me?"

"You could live by your own choices. As . . . a highborn lord . . . or a king."

"Father," I said, "that's impossible for me. I am what I am. I know nothing but Stromford."

"Even so, you must go. There are cities enough: Canterbury, Great Wexly, Winchester. Even London."

"What . . . what are these places like?"

"They have many souls living there, far more than here. Too many to count. But I assure you they are Christians."

"Father," I said, "I don't even know where these cities are."

"I'm not so certain myself," he admitted. "Follow the roads. Ask for help as you go. God will guide you."

"Is there no other way?"

"You could find an abbey and offer yourself to the church. But it's a grave step, and you're hardly prepared. In any case, you don't have the fees. If I had them, they would be yours. No, the most important thing is for you to get away."

"There's something about my mother that you are keeping from me, is there not?" I said.

He made no reply.

"Father . . ." I pressed, "was God angry at her . . . and me?"

He shook his head. "It's not for men to know what God does or does not will. What I do know is that you *must* leave."

Frustrated, I rose up, only to have the priest hold me back. "Your way will be long and difficult," he said. "If you can remain hidden in the forest for another day, I'll find some food to sustain you for a while. And perhaps someone will know the best way to go."

"As you say."

"Your obedience speaks well for you. Come back tomorrow night prepared to leave. Meet me at Goodwife Peregrine's house. I'll ask her to give you some things to protect you on your way."

I started off again.

"And," he added, as if coming to a decision, "when you come . . . I'll tell you about your father."

I turned back. "Why can't you tell me now?"

"Better—safer—to learn such things just before you go. That and my blessing are all I can give."

"Was he a sinner?" I demanded. "Did he commit some crime? Should I be ashamed of him?"

"I'll tell you all I know when you come to Peregrine's. Make sure it's dark so you'll not be seen."

I took his hand, kissed it, then started off, only to have him draw me back again.

"Can you read?"

"No more than my mother."

"But she could."

"Father, you're greatly mistaken."

"She could write, too."

I shook my head in puzzlement. "These things you say: a name. Reading. Writing. My father . . . Why would my mother keep such things from me?"

The priest became very still. Then, from his pocket, he removed my mother's cross of lead, the one with which she so oft prayed, which was in her hands when she died. I had forgotten about it. He held it up.

"Your mother's."

"I know," I said sullenly.

"Do you know what's on it?"

"Some writing, I think."

"I saw your mother write those words."

I looked at him in disbelief. "But—"

"Tomorrow," he said, cutting me off and folding my fingers over the cross, "I'll explain. Just remember, God mends all. Now go," he said. "And stay well hidden." ∾

Keep Reading

Crispin's life has just changed dramatically. What do you think is unusual about this boy? Why is he on the run? As you read the rest of Avi's book, you'll find that *Crispin: The Cross of Lead* is a suspenseful story from the start, and the action never slows down. You'll be transported to England in the Middle Ages and experience its sights, smells, and sounds as you follow Crispin on his adventures.

A Medieval Mystery

• Book Reviews

Use with *Crispin: The Cross of Lead*, page 707.

COMMON CORE

RI 1 Cite textual evidence to support analysis of what the text says explicitly.
RI 6 Analyze how the author distinguishes his or her position from that of others.

What's the Connection?

Even after reading the scene from *Crispin: The Cross of Lead*, you might not be sure whether you'd like to read the whole book. To reach a decision, read two book reviews of this historical novel.

Standards Focus: Identify Opinions

After you finish a book, how do you pick out the next one? Do you seek out others by the same author, set in the same time period, or of the same genre? One way to find a book you'll love as much as or more than the one before is to read book reviews.

Book reviewers try to provide enough details of a story's setting, characters, and plot to give their readers a sense of what the book offers without giving away the ending. Along the way, and then most strongly toward the end of the review, they sum up their opinions of these elements to explain why they recommend the book—or don't.

As you read the book reviews that follow, keep track in a chart like the one shown the opinions each reviewer provides.

Opinions About	Review by Rebecca Barnhouse	Review by Cheri Estes
Setting (time and place)	Details about the past are portrayed "accurately and compellingly."	
Character		
Plot		
Other Story Elements		

Book Review

Serf on the Run

by Rebecca Barnhouse

Crispin: The Cross of Lead
by Avi 261 pages

In 1377 England, mysteries surround thirteen-year-old Crispin, a serf from a rural village who never knows his own name until his mother dies. Nor does he know just who his mother really was—why she was an outcast or how she learned to read and write. Shortly after her burial, Crispin finds himself pursued by men who mean to kill him for reasons he does not understand. He escapes, only to be captured by a huge juggler named Bear. Bear teaches Crispin to sing and play the recorder, and slowly they begin to get to know one another. When they perform in villages and towns, however, they discover that the hunt for Crispin is still in full swing. For Crispin, this situation makes the question of Bear's trustworthiness vital, for Bear has secrets of his own. **A**

The suspense stays taut until the very end of the book, when Crispin uncovers his identity and then must decide how to act on that information. His journey to selfhood recalls Alice's in Karen Cushman's *The Midwife's Apprentice.* Like Alice, Crispin casts off his timidity to make a place for himself within a society that would discard him. As does Cushman, Avi renders the sights, sounds, and smells of medieval England accurately and compellingly. He shows the pervasiveness of the church in medieval society and, in a subplot, weaves in details about John Ball and the Peasants' Rebellion. Exciting and true to the past, this novel is historical fiction at its finest. **B**

F **OCUS ON FORM**
The two selections you are about to read are **book reviews,** short pieces of writing in which a writer describes the main elements of a book and summarizes his or her opinions of the book.

A **BOOK REVIEW**
What details of character, setting, and plot does Rebecca Barnhouse provide?

B **IDENTIFY OPINIONS**
Find the sentences in which Barnhouse states her opinions of *Crispin: The Cross of Lead.* In your own words, write her opinions in the appropriate place in your chart.

BOOK REVIEW

Crispin: The Cross of Lead

by Avi   261 pages

Medieval Adventures   Cheri Estes

As with Karen Cushman's *The Midwife's Apprentice,* the power of a name is apparent in this novel set in 14th-century England. "Asta's son" is all the destitute, illiterate hero has ever been called, but after his mother dies, he learns that his given name is Crispin, and that he is
10 in mortal danger. The local priest is murdered before he can tell him more about his background, and Aycliffe, the evil village steward for Lord Furnival, declares that the boy is a "wolf's head," less than human, and that he should be killed on sight. On the run, with nothing to sustain him but his faith in God,
20 Crispin meets "Bear," a roving entertainer who has ties to an underground movement to improve living conditions for the common people. They make

their way to Great Wexly, where Bear has clandestine meetings and Crispin hopes to escape from Aycliffe and his soldiers, who stalk him at every turn.
30 Suspense heightens when the boy learns that the recently deceased Lord Furnival was his father and that Aycliffe is dead set on preventing him from claiming his title. To trap his prey, the villain captures Bear, and Crispin risks his life to save him. **C**

   Avi has done an excellent job
40 of integrating background and historical information, of pacing the plot so that the book is a page-turner from beginning to end, and of creating characters for whom readers will have great empathy. The result is a meticulously crafted story, full of adventure, mystery, and action. **D**

C BOOK REVIEW
What do you learn about the book's setting, characters, and plot from Estes's review?

D IDENTIFY OPINIONS
What are Estes's opinions of the setting, plot, and characters of *Crispin: The Cross of Lead?* Add these to your chart. Be sure to put quotation marks around any direct quotations you use.

Comprehension

1. **Recall** Which characters are mentioned in Barnhouse's review? Which are mentioned in Estes's review?

2. **Recall** To what other novel do both reviewers compare *Crispin: The Cross of Lead?*

3. **Summarize** Summarize the reasons each reviewer gives for recommending *Crispin: The Cross of Lead.*

Text Analysis

4. **Compare Opinions** Review the chart you created as you read. Which of Barnhouse's and Estes's opinions are similar to each other's? Which, if any, are different?

5. **Evaluate Book Reviews** A good book review gives details of the story without spoiling the story's suspense. Which of these reviews does a better job of this? Explain.

COMMON CORE

RI 1 Cite textual evidence to support analysis of what the text says explicitly. **RI 6** Analyze how the author distinguishes his or her position from that of others. **W 2** Write explanatory texts to examine a topic.

Read for Information: Evaluate a Summary

> **WRITING PROMPT**
>
> Look at the summaries you wrote in response to Question 3. Now that you have written a summary of each reviewer's opinions, you can evaluate your own or a classmate's summary by comparing it to the original text.

To answer this prompt, follow these steps:

1. Underline the main ideas in the summaries. Are the main ideas the same as the ones in the reviews?

2. Circle the details that are included. Are they the most important details?

3. Reread each summary. Does the summary show that the writer has an understanding of the overall meaning of each review?

4. Write a short essay that describes how each summary compares to the original review.

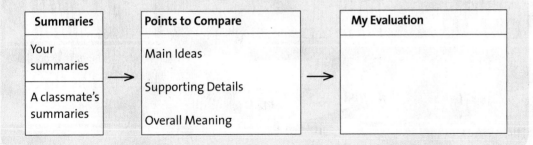

Summaries		Points to Compare		My Evaluation
Your summaries	→	Main Ideas	→	
A classmate's summaries		Supporting Details		
		Overall Meaning		

Brer Possum's Dilemma

African-American Folk Tale Retold by Jackie Torrence

Waters of Gold

Chinese Folk Tale Retold by Laurence Yep

What can we LEARN from stories?

COMMON CORE

RL 2 Determine a theme of a text and analyze its development; provide an objective summary of the text.

You've probably been lectured to many times about things you should and shouldn't do. The problem is, it's easy to forget what you hear in a lecture. But what if you happen to learn lessons while being entertained by interesting, even unforgettable, characters? Those lessons may be the ones you carry with you for the rest of your life.

LIST IT On a sheet of notebook paper, list three or four of your favorite stories of all time. What lessons did they teach? Add the lessons to your list, and compare the list to those of your classmates.

Title	Lesson
The Giver	Knowledge comes from experience.

● TEXT ANALYSIS: CHARACTERISTICS OF FOLK TALES

Folk tales are stories that have been handed down through generations by being told out loud. Every culture has its own folk tales, but the stories often share certain characteristics.

- Each character usually represents a specific trait, or quality.
- The plot often centers on events that occur in a set of three.
- Many folk tales teach a lesson, or **moral.**

As you read the selections, pay attention to the way the characters and plot work together to teach a lesson.

● READING STRATEGY: SUMMARIZE

When you **summarize**, you briefly retell the story's main points in your own words. To help you summarize, use a graphic organizer to record key information as you read each selection.

Title and Culture:	Author:	Setting:
Characters:		
Events:		
Lesson or Moral:		

Review: **Predict**

▲ VOCABULARY IN CONTEXT

Choose the word that completes each sentence.

WORD	commence	jostling	prime
LIST	humor	perilously	smugly

1. Don't get ahead in life by _____ others out of the way.
2. Sometimes it's better to _____ someone than to argue with him.
3. For the best results, _____ each day with a good attitude.
4. By wanting it all, she came _____ close to losing what she had.
5. Safety should be a _____ concern for all parents.
6. If you accept praise _____, you won't see much of it.

 Complete the activities in your **Reader/Writer Notebook.**

Meet the Authors

Jackie Torrence
1944–2004

The Story Lady
Jackie Torrence was working as a librarian when one day her boss came looking for help: the library's storyteller hadn't shown up, and children were waiting. Torrence reluctantly took over. She became famous for retelling African-American folk tales, many of which were handed down by her grandfather. Torrence said that "long before TV or radio, all cultures used storytelling to instill values and heritage."

Laurence Yep
born 1948

Folk Tale Collector
In addition to being an award-winning writer of books for young people, Laurence Yep researches and collects Chinese folk tales. ("Waters of Gold" came to the United States with Chinese immigrants who settled in California.) He feels that these stories have a "raw power" and mystery that appeal to all ages.

Authors Online
Go to **thinkcentral.com**. KEYWORD: HML7-717

THINK central

Brer Possum's Dilemma

Retold by
Jackie Torrence

Back in the days when the animals could talk, there lived ol' Brer Possum. He was a fine feller. Why, he never liked to see no critters in trouble. He was always helpin' out, a-doin' somethin' for others.

Ever' night, ol' Brer Possum climbed into a persimmon tree, hung by his tail, and slept all night long. And each mornin', he climbed outa the tree and walked down the road to sun 'imself.

One mornin', as he walked, he come to a big hole in the middle of the road. Now, ol' Brer Possum was kind and gentle, but he was also nosy, so he went over to the hole and looked in. All at once, he stepped
10 back, 'cause layin' in the bottom of that hole was ol' Brer Snake with a brick on his back.

Brer Possum said to 'imself, "I best git on outa here, 'cause ol' Brer Snake is mean and evil and lowdown, and if I git to stayin' around 'im, he jist might git to bitin' me."

So Brer Possum went on down the road.

But Brer Snake had seen Brer Possum, and he **commenced** to callin' for 'im.

"Help me, Brer Possum."

Brer Possum stopped and turned around. He said to 'imself, "That's ol'
20 Brer Snake a-callin' me. What do you reckon he wants?"

Well, ol' Brer Possum was kindhearted, so he went back down the road to the hole, stood at the edge, and looked down at Brer Snake.

"Was that you a-callin' me? What do you want?" Ⓐ

---

commence (kə-mĕns′) *v.*
to start or begin

Ⓐ **FOLK TALES**
The characters in folk tales may be humans or animals with human characteristics. What human characteristics does Brer Possum have?

Brer Snake looked up and said, "I've been down here in this hole for a mighty long time with this brick on my back. Won't you help git it offa me?"

Brer Possum thought.

"Now listen here, Brer Snake. I knows you. You's mean and evil and lowdown, and if'n I was to git down in that hole and git to liftin' that
30 brick offa your back, you wouldn't do nothin' but bite me."

Ol' Brer Snake just hissed.

"Maybe not. Maybe not. Maaaaaaaybe not." **B**

Brer Possum said, "I ain't sure 'bout you at all. I jist don't know. You're a-goin' to have to let me think about it."

So ol' Brer Possum thought—he thought high, and he thought low— and jist as he was thinkin', he looked up into a tree and saw a dead limb a-hangin' down. He climbed into the tree, broke off the limb, and with that ol' stick, pushed that brick offa Brer Snake's back. Then he took off down the road.

40 Brer Possum thought he was away from ol' Brer Snake when all at once he heard somethin'.

"Help me, Brer Possum."

Brer Possum said, "Oh, no, that's him agin."

But bein' so kindhearted, Brer Possum turned around, went back to the hole, and stood at the edge.

"Brer Snake, was that you a-callin' me? What do you want now?"

Ol' Brer Snake looked up outa the hole and hissed.

"I've been down here for a mighty long time, and I've gotten a little weak, and the sides of this ol' hole are too slick for me to climb. Do you
50 think you can lift me outa here?"

Brer Possum thought.

"Now, you jist wait a minute. If'n I was to git down into that hole and lift you outa there, you wouldn't do nothin' but bite me."

Brer Snake hissed.

"Maybe not. Maybe not. Maaaaaaaybe not."

Brer Possum said, "I jist don't know. You're a-goin' to have to give me time to think about this."

So ol' Brer Possum thought.

And as he thought, he jist happened to look down there in that hole
60 and see that ol' dead limb. So he pushed the limb underneath ol' Brer Snake and he lifted 'im outa the hole, way up into the air, and throwed 'im into the high grass.

Brer Possum took off a-runnin' down the road. **C**

Well, he thought he was away from ol' Brer Snake when all at once he heard somethin'.

B PREDICT
The characters disagree about what will happen if Brer Possum helps Brer Snake. From what you know about the characters so far, what do you predict will happen?

Language Coach

Homophones
Homophones are words that sound the same but have different spellings and meanings. In line 49, the word *weak*, which means "frail, not strong," is a homophone of *week*, which means "seven days," and *hole* is a homophone of *whole*, which means "all, entire."

C SUMMARIZE
In your graphic organizer, briefly note the events described so far.

"Help me, Brer Possum."

Brer Possum thought, "That's him agin."

But bein' so kindhearted, he turned around, went back to the hole, and stood there a-lookin' for Brer Snake. Brer Snake crawled outa the high grass just as slow as he could, stretched 'imself out across the road, rared up, and looked at ol' Brer Possum.

Then he hissed. "I've been down there in that ol' hole for a mighty long time, and I've gotten a little cold 'cause the sun didn't shine. Do you think you could put me in your pocket and git me warm?"

Brer Possum said, "Now you listen here, Brer Snake. I knows you. You's mean and evil and lowdown, and if'n I put you in my pocket you wouldn't do nothin' but bite me."

Brer Snake hissed.

"Maybe not. Maybe not. Maaaaaaaybe not."

"No, sireee, Brer Snake. I knows you. I jist ain't a-goin' to do it."

But jist as Brer Possum was talkin' to Brer Snake, he happened to git a real good look at 'im. He was a-layin' there lookin' so pitiful, and Brer Possum's great big heart began to feel sorry for ol' Brer Snake.

"All right," said Brer Possum. "You must be cold. So jist this once I'm a-goin' to put you in my pocket." **D**

So ol' Brer Snake coiled up jist as little as he could, and Brer Possum picked 'im up and put 'im in his pocket.

Brer Snake laid quiet and still—so quiet and still that Brer Possum even forgot that he was a-carryin' 'im around. But all of a sudden, Brer Snake commenced to crawlin' out, and he turned and faced Brer Possum and hissed.

"I'm a-goin' to bite you."

But Brer Possum said, "Now wait a minute. Why are you a-goin' to bite me? I done took that brick offa your back, I got you outa that hole, and I put you in my pocket to git you warm. Why are you a-goin' to bite me?"

Brer Snake hissed.

"You knowed I was a snake before you put me in your pocket."

And when you're mindin' your own business and you spot trouble, don't never trouble trouble 'til trouble troubles you. ༄ **E**

COMMON CORE RL 2

D FOLK TALES
Some folk tales, like some myths, are also circle stories. The plot in a **circle story** is developed by using a particular sequence or pattern over and over. The story often ends at the same place it started. What patterns are developing in this folk tale?

E FOLK TALES
Reread lines 99–100. Sometimes you may have to infer the **moral** of a folk tale, but in this case the moral is stated directly. Rephrase it in your own words.

Waters *of* Gold

Retold by Laurence Yep

Many years ago, there lived a woman whom everyone called Auntie Lily. She was Auntie by blood to half the county and Auntie to the other half by friendship. As she liked to say, "There's a bit of Heaven in each of us." As a result, she was always helping people out.

Because of her many kind acts, she knew so many people that she couldn't go ten steps without meeting someone who wanted to chat. So it would take her half the day to go to the village well and back to her home. **F**

Eventually, though, she helped so many people that she had no more 10 money. She had to sell her fields and even her house to her neighbor, a rich old woman. "If you'd helped yourself instead of others, you wouldn't have to do this," the neighbor said **smugly.** "Where are all those other people when you need them?"

"That isn't why I helped them," Auntie Lily said firmly. She wound up having to pay rent for the house she had once owned. She supported herself by her embroidery; but since her eyes were going bad, she could not do very much.

One day an old beggar entered the village. He was a ragbag of a man— a trash heap, a walking pig wallow. It was impossible to tell what color 20 or what shape his clothes had once been, and his hair was as muddy and matted as a bird's nest. As he shuffled through the village gates, he called out, "Water for my feet. Please, water for my feet. One little bowl of water—that's all I ask."

F FOLK TALES
What **trait** do you think Auntie Lily represents?

smugly (smŭg'lē) *adv.* in a self-satisfied way

Analyze Visuals ▶
Compare the village in this picture to the village described in the story. In what ways are they similar?

Orchard (2000), Chen Jia Qi. Watercolor. Red Lantern Folk Art, Mukashi Collection. © The Mukashi Collection/SuperStock.

Everyone ignored him, pretending to concentrate on their chores instead. One man went on replacing the shaft of his hoe. A woman swept her courtyard. Another woman fed her hens.

The beggar went to each in turn, but they all showed their backs to him.

After calling out a little while longer, the beggar went to the nearest 30 home, which happened to belong to the rich old woman. When he banged at her door, he left the dirty outline of his knuckles on the clean wood. And when the rich woman opened her door, his smell nearly took her breath away.

Now it so happened that she had been chopping vegetables when the beggar had knocked. When the beggar repeated his request, she raised her cleaver menacingly. "What good would one bowl of water be? You'd need a whole river to wash you clean. Go away."

"A thousand pardons," the old beggar said, and shambled on to the next house.

40 Though Auntie Lily had to hold her nose, she asked politely, "Yes?"

"I'd like a bowl of water to wash my feet." And the beggar pointed one grimy finger toward them.

Her rich neighbor had stayed in her doorway to watch the beggar. She scolded Auntie Lily now. "It's all your fault those beggars come into the village. They know they can count on a free meal."

It was an old debate between them, so Auntie Lily simply said, "Any of us can have bad luck."

"Garbage," the rich old woman declared, "is garbage. They must have done something bad, or Heaven wouldn't have let them become beggars."

50 Auntie Lily turned to the beggar. "I may be joining you on the road someday. Wait here."

Much to the neighbor's distress, Auntie Lily went inside and poured water from a large jar in her kitchen into a bucket. Carrying it in both hands, she brought it outside to the beggar and set it down.

The beggar stood on one leg, just like a crane, while he washed one callused, leathery sole over the bucket. "You can put mud on any other part of me, but if my feet are clean, then I feel clean."

As he fussily continued to cleanse his feet, Auntie Lily asked kindly, "Are you hungry? I don't have much, but what I have I'm willing to 60 share." **G**

The beggar shook his head. "I've stayed longer in this village than I have in any other. Heaven is my roof, and the whole world my house."

Auntie Lily stared at him, wondering what she would look like after a few years on the road. "Are you very tired? Have you been on the road for very long?"

G SUMMARIZE
What happens when Auntie Lily and the rich woman encounter the beggar? Record the events in your graphic organizer.

"No, the road is on me," the beggar said, and held up his hands from his dirty sides. "But thank you. You're the first person to ask. And you're the first person to give me some water. So place the bucket of water by your bed tonight and do not look into it till tomorrow morning."

70 As the beggar shuffled out of the village again, Auntie Lily stared down doubtfully at the bucket of what was now muddy water. Then, even though she felt foolish, she picked it up again.

"You're not really going to take that scummy water inside?" laughed the rich neighbor. "It'll probably breed mosquitoes."

"It seemed important to him," she answered. "I'll **humor** him."

"Humoring people," snapped the neighbor, "has got you one step from begging yourself."

However, Auntie Lily carried the bucket inside anyway. Setting it down near her sleeping mat, she covered the mouth of the bucket with an old, 80 cracked plate so she wouldn't peek into it by mistake, and then she got so caught up in embroidering a pair of slippers that she forgot all about the beggar and his bucket of water.

She sewed until twilight, when it was too dark to use her needle. Then, because she had no money for oil or candles, she went to sleep.

The next morning Auntie Lily rose and stretched the aches out of her back. She sighed. "The older I get, the harder it is to get up in the morning."

Detail from *Spring in the Old Village* (2001), Chen Jia Qi. Watercolor. Red Lantern Folk Art, Mukashi Collection. © The Mukashi Collection/SuperStock.

H PREDICT
Reread lines 66–69. From what the beggar has said about Auntie Lily, what kind of thing do you predict will happen if she follows his instructions?

humor (hyōō′mər) *v.* to give in to the wishes of

She was always saying something like that, but she had never stayed on her sleeping mat—even when she was sick. Thinking of all that day's chores, she decided to water the herbs she had growing on one side of her house.

Her eyes fell upon the beggar's bucket with its covering plate. "No sense using fresh water when that will do as well. After all, dirt's dirt to a plant."

Squatting down, she picked up the bucket and was surprised at how heavy it was. "I must have filled it fuller than I thought," she grunted.

She staggered out of the house and over to the side where rows of little green herbs grew. "Here you go," she said to her plants. "Drink deep."

Taking off the plate, she upended the bucket; but instead of muddy brown water, there was a flash of reflected light and a clinking sound as gold coins rained down upon her plants.

Auntie Lily set the bucket down hastily and crouched, not trusting her weak eyes. However, where some of her herbs had been, there was now a small mound of gold coins. She squinted in disbelief and rubbed her aching eyes and stared again; but the gold was still there.

She turned to the bucket. There was even more gold inside. Scooping up coins by the handful, she freed her little plants and made sure that the stalks weren't too bent.

Then she sat gazing at her bucket full of gold until a farmer walked by. "Tell me I'm not dreaming," she called to him.

The farmer yawned and came over with his hoe over his shoulder. "I wish I were dreaming, because that would mean I'm still in bed instead of having to go off to work."

Auntie Lily gathered up a handful of gold coins and let it fall in a tinkling, golden shower back into the bucket. "And this is real?"

The farmer's jaw dropped. He picked up one coin with his free hand and bit into it.[1] He flipped it back in with the other coins. "It's as real as me, Auntie. But where did you ever get that?"

So Auntie Lily told him. And as others woke up and stepped outside, Auntie told them as well, for she still could not believe her luck and wanted them to confirm that the gold was truly gold. In no time at all, there was a small crowd around her. ⑴

If the bucket had been filled with ordinary copper cash, that would have been more money than any of them had ever seen. In their wildest dreams, they had never expected to see that much gold. Auntie Lily stared at the bucket uncomfortably. "I keep thinking it's going to disappear the next moment."

Language Coach

Suffixes A word part added to the end of a word is called a suffix. Reread lines 119–121 and 125–126. The words *truly* and *uncomfortably* both end with the suffix *-ly*, which means "in a certain way." How would you define each word?

⑴ **SUMMARIZE**
In your own words, explain what happens to Auntie Lily.

---

1. **bit into it:** Gold is soft, so biting it is a way of testing its authenticity.

The farmer, who had been standing there all this time, shook his head. "If it hasn't disappeared by now, I don't think it will. What are you going 130 to do with it, Auntie?"

Auntie Lily stared at the bucket, and suddenly she came to a decision. Stretching out a hand, she picked up a gold coin. "I'm going to buy back my house, and I'm going to get back my land."

The farmer knew the fields. "Those old things? You could buy a valley full of **prime** land with half that bucket. And a palace with the other half."

"I want what I sweated for." Asking the farmer to guard her bucket, Auntie Lily closed her hand around the gold coin. Then, as the crowd parted before her, she made her way over to her neighbor. **J**

140 Now the rich old woman liked to sleep late; but all the noise had woken her up, so she was just getting dressed when Auntie knocked. The old woman yanked her door open as she buttoned the last button of her coat. "Who started the riot? Can't a person get a good night's sleep?"

With some satisfaction, Auntie Lily held up the gold coin. "Will this buy back my house and land?"

"Where did you get that?" the old woman demanded.

"Will it buy them back?" Auntie Lily repeated.

The rich old woman snatched the coin out of Auntie Lily's hand and bit into it just as the farmer had. "It's real," the old woman said 150 in astonishment.

"Will it?" Auntie asked again.

"Yes, yes, yes," the old woman said crabbily. "But where did you ever get that much gold?"

When Auntie Lily told her the story and showed her the bucket of gold, the rich old woman stood moving her mouth like a fish out of water. Clasping her hands together, she shut her eyes and moaned in genuine pain. "And I sent him away. What a fool I am. What a fool." And the old woman beat her head with her fists.

That very afternoon, the beggar—the ragbag, the trash heap, the 160 walking pig wallow—shuffled once more through the village gates with feet as dirty as before. As he went, he croaked, "Water for my feet. Please, water for my feet. One little bowl of water—that's all I ask." **K**

This time, people dropped whatever they were doing when they heard his plea. Hoes, brooms, and pots were flung down, hens and pigs were kicked out of the way as everyone hurried to fill a bucket with water. There was a small riot by the village well as everyone fought to get water at the same time. Still others rushed out with buckets filled from the jars in their houses.

prime (prīm) *adj.* first in quality or value

J FOLK TALES
Reread lines 131–139. What does Auntie Lily's decision about how to spend her money say about her?

K PREDICT
How do you predict the townspeople will behave now that the beggar has returned?

"Here, use my water," one man shouted, holding up a tub.

170   A woman shoved in front of him with a bucket in her arms. "No, no, use mine. It's purer."

They surrounded the old beggar, pleading with him to use their water, and in the process of **jostling** one another, they splashed a good deal of water on one another and came **perilously** close to drowning the beggar. The rich old woman, Auntie Lily's neighbor, charged to the rescue.

"Out of the way, you vultures," the rich old woman roared. "You're going to trample him." Using her elbows, her feet, and in one case even her teeth, the old woman fought her way through the mob.

No longer caring if she soiled her hands, the old woman seized the
180 beggar by the arm. "This way, you poor, misunderstood creature."

Fighting off her neighbors with one hand and keeping her grip on the beggar with the other, the old woman hauled him inside her house. Barring the door against the rest of the village, she ignored all the fists and feet thumping on her door and all the shouts.

"I really wasn't myself yesterday, because I had been up the night before tending a sick friend. This is what I meant to do." She fetched a fresh new towel and an even newer bucket and forced the beggar to wash his feet.

When he was done, he handed her the now filthy towel. "Dirt's dirt,
190 and garbage is garbage," he said.

However, the greedy old woman didn't recognize her own words. She was too busy trying to remember what else Auntie Lily had done. "Won't you have something to eat? Have you traveled very far? Are you tired?" she asked, all in the same breath.

The old beggar went to the door and waited patiently while she unbarred it. As he shuffled outside, he instructed her to leave the bucket of water by her bed but not to look into it until the morning.

That night, the greedy old woman couldn't sleep as she imagined the heap of shiny gold that would be waiting for her tomorrow. She waited
200 impatiently for the sun to rise and got up as soon as she heard the first rooster crow.

Hurrying to the bucket, she plunged her hands inside expecting to bring up handfuls of gold. Instead, she gave a cry as dozens of little things bit her, for the bucket was filled not with gold but with snakes, lizards, and ants. **L**

The greedy old woman fell sick—some said from her bites, some claimed from sheer frustration. Auntie Lily herself came to nurse her neighbor. "Take this to heart: Kindness comes with no price."

The old woman was so ashamed that she did, indeed, take the lesson to
210 heart. Though she remained sick, she was kind to whoever came to her door.

jostling (jŏs′lĭng) *n.* roughly bumping, pushing, or shoving **jostle** *v.*

perilously (pĕr′ə-ləs-lē) *adv.* dangerously

L FOLK TALES
Why do you think the old woman gets this result when she tries to behave like Auntie Lily?

Detail from *Sunny Spring* (1999), Zhang Min. Watercolor. Red Lantern Folk Art, Mukashi Collection. © The Mukashi Collection/SuperStock.

One day, a leper[2] came into the village. Everyone hid for fear of the terrible disease. Doors slammed and shutters banged down over windows, and soon the village seemed deserted.

Only Auntie Lily and her neighbor stepped out of their houses. "Are you hungry?" Auntie Lily asked.

"Are you thirsty?" the neighbor asked. "I'll make you a cup of tea."

The leper thanked Auntie Lily and then turned to the neighbor as if to express his gratitude as well; but he stopped and studied her. "You're looking poorly, my dear woman. Can I help?"

220   With a tired smile, the rich old woman explained what had happened. When she was finished, the leper stood thoughtfully for a moment. "You're not the same woman as before: You're as kind as Auntie Lily, and you aren't greedy anymore. So take this humble gift from my brother, the old beggar."

With that, the leper limped out of the village; and as he left, the illness fell away from the old woman like an old, discarded cloak. But though the old woman was healthy again, she stayed as kind as Auntie Lily and used her own money as well and wisely as Auntie Lily used the waters of gold. ❧ Ⓜ

Ⓜ **FOLK TALES**
What **moral** does this story convey?

---

2. **leper:** a person suffering from the infectious disease of leprosy, which can result in bodily deformities.

Comprehension

1. **Recall** Where does Brer Possum meet Brer Snake?

2. **Clarify** Why doesn't Brer Possum want to help Brer Snake at first?

3. **Recall** At the beginning of "Waters of Gold," why does the old woman own Auntie Lily's land?

Text Analysis

● 4. **Summarize** Review the graphic organizer you created for each tale. Then summarize one of the folk tales in your own words.

● 5. **Identify Characteristics of Folk Tales** Use a chart like the one shown to identify how each selection demonstrates the main characteristics of a folk tale.

	"Brer Possum"	"Waters of Gold"
Characters Who Represent a Trait	Brer Snake: Sneaky	
Events That Occur in Sets of Three		
A Moral		

6. **Compare and Contrast Characters** The characters in folk tales are often thought of as standing for good or evil. Consider the "good" characters in these two tales. Explain how they are alike and how they differ.

7. **Make Judgments** Which story's lesson is more useful in your everyday life? Explain your choice.

Extension and Challenge

8. **Reader's Circle** Jackie Torrence inherited "Brer Possum's Dilemma" from her great-grandfather, who had been enslaved. "Waters of Gold" was told by Chinese immigrant communities during the Great Depression. In a group, choose one of the stories and discuss how it might reflect the culture that created it. Questions to consider include the following:

- What do you think life was like for the original tellers of the tale?
- What traits does the story suggest are valuable?
- What traits does the story seem to warn readers about?
- Why might these traits have been significant to the original storytellers and their audiences? Why are they significant to you?

> ## What can we LEARN from stories?
>
> What lesson from a story has had the greatest impact on you?

COMMON CORE

RL 2 Determine a theme of a text and analyze its development; provide an objective summary of the text.

Vocabulary in Context

▲ VOCABULARY PRACTICE

Choose the letter of the item you would associate with each vocabulary word as it is used in these selections.

1. **smugly:** (a) carrying a heavy load, (b) looking pleased with oneself, (c) riding an old bike
2. **prime:** (a) an excellent meal, (b) a small family, (c) a necessary decision
3. **commence:** (a) the opening scene, (b) a large rectangle, (c) a long meeting
4. **jostling:** (a) children laughing, (b) dogs barking, (c) crowds pushing
5. **perilously:** (a) singing in a choir, (b) walking on a tightrope, (c) having lunch
6. **humor:** (a) give in, (b) get angry, (c) get better

commence
humor
jostling
perilously
prime
smugly

ACADEMIC VOCABULARY IN SPEAKING

• attribute   • conduct   • physical   • status   • task

Would you have reacted negatively to the **physical** characteristics of the beggar in "Waters of Gold"? Discuss your ideas with a small group. Use the Academic Vocabulary words in your discussion.

VOCABULARY STRATEGY: GENERAL CONTEXT CLUES

Context clues can appear in surrounding words, sentences, and even paragraphs. In the following example, the second sentence is a clue to the word *shambled*. From the second sentence, you can tell that *shambled* means "walk in a shuffling manner."

> The beggar slowly *shambled* from house to house asking for food. His feet hurt, so he walked in a shuffling manner.

PRACTICE Read the following pairs of sentences. Use context clues to determine the definition of each boldfaced word. Then write its definition.

1. Samantha was the only one in her class to receive an award of **distinction**. At the awards ceremony, the principal mentioned Samantha's outstanding academic achievements and her performance on the soccer team.
2. Harry had an expression of extreme **anguish** on his face. "Something horrible has happened!" he gasped.
3. Shane just can't make up his mind. He often **wavers** between choices for hours without ever making a decision.

COMMON CORE

L 4a Use context (e.g., the overall meaning of a sentence or paragraph) as a clue to the meaning of a word. **L 6** Acquire and use accurately grade-appropriate general academic words.

Interactive Vocabulary **THINK** central

Go to **thinkcentral.com**.
KEYWORD: HML7-731

Sally Ann Thunder Ann Whirlwind

HISTORY Video link at
thinkcentral.com

American Tall Tale Retold by Mary Pope Osborne

What makes a good
COUPLE?

COMMON CORE

RL 1 Cite textual evidence to
support analysis of what the
text says explicitly. **RL 3** Analyze
how particular elements of a
story interact. **RL 10** Read and
comprehend literature.

You know who they are. Couples who just seem so right together
that they radiate happiness when they walk down the street. Their
compatibility might come from having similar personalities or
interests, or even from respecting each other's differences. In this
selection, a character who is larger than life meets her match.

WEB IT In a small group, create an idea web. Fill it with examples
of compatible couples in books and movies, as well as those you
know from your own life. Then expand the web by including your
ideas about what makes the good couples good.

Good Couples

aunt
and uncle

laugh at
everything

● TEXT ANALYSIS: CHARACTERISTICS OF TALL TALES

A **tall tale** is a humorously exaggerated story about impossible events. Like other folk tales, tall tales were originally passed along by being told out loud. Tall tales share these characteristics:

- They use exaggeration to make difficult situations seem incredible or funny.
- The hero or heroine is often bigger, stronger, and even louder than an ordinary person.
- The setting is usually the American frontier.

As you read, notice how these characteristics apply to "Sally Ann Thunder Ann Whirlwind."

● READING STRATEGY: VISUALIZE

Tall tales are often so exaggerated, funny, and action packed that you might be able to **visualize,** or picture, them as cartoons. To try this, look for descriptive details that appeal to your senses of touch, sound, and especially sight. Then picture the characters and action in your mind. Use a chart like the one shown to record descriptive words and phrases in "Sally Ann Thunder Ann Whirlwind."

Character or Event	Descriptive Words or Phrases

▲ VOCABULARY IN CONTEXT

The words listed help add humor to the tall tale. In your *Reader/Writer Notebook*, write a sentence for each of the vocabulary words. Use a dictionary or the definitions in the following selection pages to help you.

WORD	forage	oblige
LIST	gigantic	varmint

Meet the Author

Mary Pope Osborne
born 1949

Female Heroes
As a child, Mary Pope Osborne says, she was "terrified of little things, like insects and worms and big dogs" and that "it was always a struggle to get over those fears." Now she creates stories with the kind of fearless female heroes that she thinks would have made her "less of a frightened child."

BACKGROUND TO THE TALL TALE
An American Tradition
In trying to claim new lands for building and farming, American settlers faced great challenges. Workers tested their endurance through chopping lumber and building railroads. Pioneers faced wild animals and brutal weather, as well as other difficulties. One way of coping with the difficulties life threw their way was to tell tall tales.

Bigger and Better
The heroes and heroines of these tall tales were people like the settlers, but they were larger than life and able to handle any hardship that came along. Paul Bunyan and Pecos Bill are two fictional heroes that came out of this tradition. Others, like Davy Crockett, were real people whose adventures were told so many times that they became legendary.

Author Online
THINK central
Go to thinkcentral.com.
KEYWORD: HML7-733

 Complete the activities in your **Reader/Writer Notebook.**

733

SALLY ANN THUNDER ANN Whirlwind

Retold by Mary Pope Osborne

One early spring day, when the leaves of the white oaks were about as big as a mouse's ear, Davy Crockett set out alone through the forest to do some bear hunting. Suddenly it started raining real hard, and he felt **obliged** to stop for shelter under a tree. As he shook the rain out of his coonskin cap, he got sleepy, so he laid back into the crotch of the tree, and pretty soon he was snoring.

Davy slept so hard, he didn't wake up until nearly sundown. And when he did, he discovered that somehow or another in all that sleeping his head had gotten stuck in the crotch of the tree, and he couldn't get it out.

Well, Davy roared loud enough to make the tree lose all its little mouse-ear leaves. He twisted and turned and carried on for over an hour, but still that tree wouldn't let go. Just as he was about to give himself up for a goner, he heard a girl say, "What's the matter, stranger?"

Man Leaning on Tree, © 1991 by Michael McCurdy. From *American Tall Tales* by Mary Pope Osborne. Used by permission of Alfred A. Knopf, an imprint of Random House Children's Books, a division of Random House, Inc.

Analyze Visuals ▶

Examine the woman in the painting. What can you **infer** about her personality?

oblige (ə-blīj′) *v.* to force; require

Even from his awkward position, he could see that she was extra-ordinary— tall as a hickory sapling, with arms as big as a keelboat tiller's. **A**

"My head's stuck, sweetie," he said. "And if you help me get it free, I'll give you a pretty little comb."

"Don't call me sweetie," she said. "And don't worry about giving me
20 no pretty little comb, neither. I'll free your old coconut, but just because I want to."

Then this extraordinary girl did something that made Davy's hair stand on end. She reached in a bag and took out a bunch of rattlesnakes. She tied all the wriggly critters together to make a long rope, and as she tied, she kept talking. "I'm not a shy little colt," she said. "And I'm not a little singing nightingale, neither. I can tote a steamboat on my back, outscream a panther, and jump over my own shadow. I can double up crocodiles any day, and I like to wear a hornets' nest for my Sunday bonnet."

30 As the girl looped the ends of her snake rope to the top of the branch that was trapping Davy, she kept bragging: "I'm a streak of lightning set up edgeways and buttered with quicksilver. I can outgrin, outsnort, outrun, outlift, outsneeze, outsleep, outlie any **varmint** from Maine to Louisiana. Furthermore, *sweetie,* I can blow out the moonlight and sing a wolf to sleep." Then she pulled on the other end of the snake rope so hard, it seemed as if she might tear the world apart. **B**

The right-hand fork of that big tree bent just about double. Then Davy slid his head out as easy as you please. For a minute he was so dizzy, he couldn't tell up from down. But when he got everything going straight
40 again, he took a good look at that girl. "What's your name, ma'am?"

"Sally Ann Thunder Ann Whirlwind," she said. "But if you mind your manners, you can call me Sally."

From then on Davy Crockett was crazy in love with Sally Ann Thunder Ann Whirlwind. He asked everyone he knew about her, and everything he heard caused another one of Cupid's arrows to jab him in the gizzard.

"Oh, I know Sally!" the preacher said. "She can dance a rock to pieces and ride a panther bareback!"

"Sally's a good ole friend of mine," the blacksmith said. "Once I seen her crack a walnut with her front teeth."

50 "Sally's so very special," said the schoolmarm. "She likes to whip across the Salt River, using her apron for a sail and her left leg for a rudder!"

Sally Ann Thunder Ann Whirlwind had a reputation for being funny, too. Her best friend, Lucy, told Davy, "Sally can laugh the bark off a pine tree. She likes to whistle out one side of her mouth while she eats with the other side and grins with the middle!" **C**

A VISUALIZE
Reread lines 14–16. What words and phrases help you picture Sally in your mind?

Language Coach

Prefixes A word part added to the beginning of a word is called a prefix. In lines 32–33, the words *outgrin, outsnort, outrun, outlift, outsneeze, outsleep,* and *outlie* all begin with the prefix *out-,* which means "in a way that goes beyond." How would you define each word?

varmint (vär'mĭnt) *n.* a troublesome person or wild animal

B TALL TALES
Reread lines 30–36. Notice the **metaphor** Sally uses to describe herself, as well as her other figures of speech. What is she saying about herself?

C TALL TALES
Reread the people's descriptions of Sally, starting with what the preacher says in lines 46–47. Which of her qualities have been exaggerated for humor or emphasis?

According to her friends, Sally could tame about anything in the world, too. They all told Davy about the time she was churning butter and heard something scratching outside. Suddenly the door swung open, and in walked the Great King Bear of the Mud Forest. He'd come to steal one of her smoked hams. Well, before the King Bear could say boo, Sally grabbed a warm dumpling from the pot and stuffed it in his mouth.

The dumpling tasted so good, the King Bear's eyes winked with tears. But then he started to think that Sally might taste pretty good, too. So opening and closing his big old mouth, he backed her right into a corner.

Sally was plenty scared, with her knees a-knocking and her heart a-hammering. But just as the King Bear blew his hot breath in her face, she gathered the courage to say, "Would you like to dance?"

Woman and Bear, © 1991 by Michael McCurdy. From *American Tall Tales* by Mary Pope Osborne. Used by permission of Alfred A. Knopf, an imprint of Random House Children's Books, a division of Random House, Inc.

As everybody knows, no bear can resist an invitation to a square dance, so of course the old fellow forgot all about eating Sally and
70 said, "Love to." **D**

Then he bowed real pretty, and the two got to kicking and whooping and swinging each other through the air, as Sally sang:

> *We are on our way to Baltimore,*
> *With two behind, and two before:*
> *Around, around, around we go,*
> *Where oats, peas, beans, and barley grow!*

And while she was singing, Sally tied a string from the bear's ankle to her butter churn, so that all the time the old feller was kicking up his legs and dancing around the room, he was also churning her butter! **E**
80 And folks loved to tell the story about Sally's encounter with another stinky varmint—only this one was a *human* varmint. It seems that Mike Fink, the riverboat man, decided to scare the toenails off Sally because he was sick and tired of hearing Davy Crockett talk about how great she was.

One evening Mike crept into an old alligator skin and met Sally just as she was taking off to **forage** in the woods for berries. He spread open his

D **VISUALIZE**
Reread lines 65–70. Notice the details that help you visualize Sally as she talks with the bear. Which details help you picture this scene as a cartoon?

E **TALL TALES**
Reread lines 77–79. What can you **infer** about Sally's intelligence from her actions? How is Sally's intelligence exaggerated?

forage (fôr′ĭj) *v.*
to search around for food or other supplies

Woman Beating Up Man © 1991 by Michael McCurdy. From *American Tall Tales* by Mary Pope Osborne. Used by permission of Alfred A. Knopf, an imprint of Random House Children's Books, a division of Random House, Inc.

gigantic mouth and made such a howl that he nearly scared himself to death. But Sally paid no more attention to that fool than she would have to a barking puppy dog.

However, when Mike put out his claws to embrace her, her anger rose higher than a Mississippi flood. She threw a flash of eye lightning at him, turning the dark to daylight. Then she pulled out a little toothpick and with a single swing sent the alligator head flying fifty feet! And then to finish him off good, she rolled up her sleeves and knocked Mike Fink clear across the woods and into a muddy swamp. **F**

When the fool came to, Davy Crockett was standing over him. "What in the world happened to you, Mikey?" he asked.

"Well, I—I think I must-a been hit by some kind of wild alligator!" Mike stammered, rubbing his sore head.

Davy smiled, knowing full well it was Sally Ann Thunder Ann Whirlwind just finished giving Mike Fink the only punishment he'd ever known.

That incident caused Cupid's final arrow to jab Davy's gizzard. "Sally's the whole steamboat," he said, meaning she was something great. The next day he put on his best raccoon hat and sallied forth[1] to see her.

When he got within three miles of her cabin, he began to holler her name. His voice was so loud, it whirled through the woods like a hurricane.

Sally looked out and saw the wind a-blowing and the trees a-bending. She heard her name a-thundering through the woods, and her heart began to thump. By now she'd begun to feel that Davy Crockett was the whole steamboat, too. So she put on her best hat—an eagle's nest with a wildcat's tail for a feather—and ran outside. **G**

Just as she stepped out the door, Davy Crockett burst from the woods and jumped onto her porch as fast as a frog. "Sally, darlin'!" he cried. "I think my heart is bustin'! Want to be my wife?"

"Oh, my stars and possum dogs, why not?" she said.

From that day on, Davy Crockett had a hard time acting tough around Sally Ann Thunder Ann Whirlwind. His fightin' and hollerin' had no more effect on her than dropping feathers on a barn floor. At least that's what *she'd* tell *you*. He might say something else. ∿

gigantic (jĭ-găn′tĭk) *adj.* extremely large

F VISUALIZE
Reread lines 89–94. Pay attention to the descriptive details in this passage. What do they help you see?

G TALL TALES
Reread lines 108–112. Describe Sally's "best hat." Why is the hat so appropriate for a tall-tale heroine like Sally?

---

1. **sallied forth:** set out.

Comprehension

COMMON CORE

RL1 Cite textual evidence to support analysis of what the text says explicitly. RL3 Analyze how particular elements of a story interact. RL10 Read and comprehend literature.

1. **Recall** How does Davy Crockett meet Sally?

2. **Clarify** Why does Sally tie a string to the bear's ankle?

3. **Summarize** What happens when Mike Fink tries to scare Sally?

Text Analysis

● 4. **Identify Characteristics of Tall Tales** In what ways is Sally a typical tall-tale character? Cite examples from the story.

● 5. **Visualize** Look at the visualizing chart you made as you read. Choose the character and event you can picture most clearly and sketch him, her, or it. Explain how the sketch reflects the notes in your chart.

6. **Evaluate Characters** Use a diagram to track the events that help Davy discover how compatible he and Sally are. For each event, note what Davy discovers about Sally. Are the characters a good couple? Why?

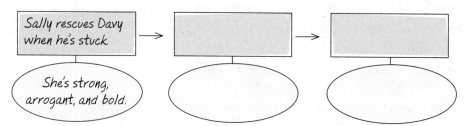

7. **Draw Conclusions** What would make Sally such an appealing character to early American settlers? Explain your answer.

Extension and Challenge

8. **Creative Project: Drama** In groups of two or three, select one of Sally's adventures and write it as a play. Act it out in front of the class. Pay close attention to the vivid and exaggerated details in each incident and find ways to include these details in your performance.

9. **SOCIAL STUDIES CONNECTION** Davy Crockett and Mike Fink are examples of real people whose adventures were turned into tall tales. Research one or two of their real-life accomplishments. Do their real roles in the American West resemble the roles they play in "Sally Ann Thunder Ann Whirlwind"?

What makes a good COUPLE?

Think about couples you know or couples who are famous. Who do you think is the ideal couple?

Vocabulary in Context

▲ **VOCABULARY PRACTICE**

Choose the word from the list that best fits the context of each sentence.

1. We saw an ugly-looking _____ digging around in our yard.
2. It seemed to be trying to _____ for acorns.
3. Its tail was extremely long, and its snout was _____ too.
4. Please _____ him and laugh at his jokes.

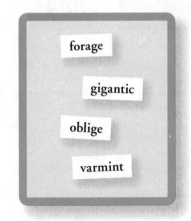

forage

gigantic

oblige

varmint

ACADEMIC VOCABULARY IN WRITING

> • attribute • conduct • physical • status • task

Write a paragraph in which you describe three things that Sally Ann can do because of her **physical** strength. Use at least one Academic Vocabulary word in your response.

VOCABULARY STRATEGY: DICTIONARY ENTRIES

Dictionaries often list several definitions for a word, including the part of speech that goes with each definition. The **part of speech** helps you use the word correctly by showing how it functions in a sentence. Part-of-speech labels are abbreviated and italicized in a dictionary entry. Here are the part-of-speech abbreviations that are commonly used in a dictionary, and a sample entry showing their placement in a dictionary entry.

COMMON CORE

L 4c Consult general reference materials (e. g., dictionaries) to find a word or determine or clarify its part of speech.
L 6 Acquire and use accurately grade-appropriate general academic words.

n. = noun   *adj.* = adjective   *prep.* = preposition
pron. = pronoun *adv.* = adverb   *interj.* = interjection
v. = verb   *conj.* = conjunction

> Part of Speech Being Defined

for•age (fôr´ ij, for´-) ***n.*** **1.** Food for domestic animals; fodder. **2.** The act of searching for food or provisions. ***v.*** **-aged, -aging, -ages**. **1.** To wander in search of food or provisions. **2.** To make a raid, as for food: soldiers foraging near an abandoned farm.

PRACTICE Each word listed is followed by a part of speech in parentheses. Look up each word in a dictionary and write a sentence that shows how it would be used as that part of speech.

1. offer (noun)   3. shelter (verb)   5. muddy (adjective)
2. official (noun)   4. streak (verb)   6. daily (adverb)

Interactive Vocabulary

THINK central

Go to **thinkcentral.com**.
KEYWORD: HML7-741

Two Ways to Count to Ten
Liberian Fable Retold by Frances Carpenter

The Race Between Toad and Donkey
Jamaican Fable Retold by Roger D. Abrahams

Would you rather be CLEVER or strong?

COMMON CORE

RL 1 Cite pieces of textual evidence to support analysis of what the text says explicitly as well as inferences drawn from the text. **RL 2** Determine a theme of a text and analyze its development.

In every society, athletes come together to try to outrun, outthrow, and outjump one another. When it comes to sports, strength and speed seem to be the point of the game. Can sheer brainpower ever be enough to win such contests? The fables you're about to read explore this question.

QUICKWRITE Put yourself in the place of a professional athlete. What would you say it takes to win a championship? Spend a few minutes writing down what you think an athlete might say. Would the manager or coach of the team have the same answer?

TEXT ANALYSIS: RECURRING THEME

Throughout the world, people speak different languages and have different customs—yet some feelings and experiences are remarkably similar. As a result, certain ideas are explored over and over again in a variety of stories. The selections you're about to read offer a similar **theme,** or message about life. To identify this theme, pay attention to

- the characters and what traits they represent
- the contests
- who wins the contests
- how they win

When a theme appears in two or more works, it's called a **recurring theme.** You can often find recurring themes in **fables,** which are brief stories that teach a lesson. As you read these two fables, notice that while they share the same theme, their stories are not identical. Each expresses the theme in its own way.

READING STRATEGY: SET A PURPOSE FOR READING

When you **set a purpose for reading,** you choose specific reasons for reading one or more works. Your purpose for reading "Two Ways to Count to Ten" and "The Race Between Toad and Donkey" is to identify the recurring theme and to find similarities and differences in how the fables express it. As you read the first fable, begin filling in a chart like the one shown.

	"Two Ways to Count to Ten"	"The Race Between Toad and Donkey"
Who are the characters?		
What is the contest and who declares it?		
Who wins the contest? How?		
What do the characters learn?		

Complete the activities in your **Reader/Writer Notebook.**

Frances Carpenter
1890–1972

World Traveler
When Frances Carpenter was young, she and her family traversed the world. Africa, where her geographer father traveled for work, was one of their destinations. Carpenter used the information gained on these trips in her writing.

Roger D. Abrahams
born 1933

Legendary Folklorist
Professor Roger D. Abrahams is one of the most respected scholars in the world of folklore. He has written many books about the folk tales and legends of Africans and African Americans.

Living Traditions
One place Abrahams collected folk tales is Jamaica. This island nation in the West Indies is home to a rich cultural tradition. Many Jamaicans are descendants of enslaved Africans who were taken to the island to work on plantations. The Africans brought their music, stories, and way of life with them. Jamaican life continues to reflect an African influence.

Authors Online
Go to **thinkcentral.com.** KEYWORD: HML7-743

TWO WAYS TO COUNT TO TEN

Retold by
Frances Carpenter

"Old Tanko has come! The Teller of Good Tales is here!"
The news spread quickly through the Liberian village and in the faraway back country. Men, women, and children came running to the Palaver House, the big "talky-talk" hut which had room for them all. **A**

Everyone in that village knew Old Tanko, the Teller of Good Tales. Everyone there enjoyed his exciting stories. Whenever he wandered into their cluster of grass-roofed huts, they made him welcome.

"Ai, I'll sing you a story," Tanko said that day when he had finished the bowl of soup they set before him. "It will be a strange tale from the long
10 ago." He arranged his white robe and settled himself cross-legged on the earth floor.

The old man placed a very small gourd drum in his lap. And with his bony brown fingers, he began to tap lightly, lightly upon it.

"I had this tale from my grandfather," he began. "He, too, was a great teller of tales."

"What will the tale say to us, Tanko?" The headman of the village was speaking. He had squatted down on the ground, close to the old man.

"It will say there is more than one way to count to ten. It will also tell how, if you can guess the right way, you can even get yourself a king's
20 daughter for your wife."

The people in the talky-talk house nodded to one another. They smiled. It was as if they were thinking, "This will be another good tale." But no one spoke. In silence, they waited for Old Tanko to tell his story.

A THEME
What is the **setting** of this fable?

Analyze Visuals ▶

The animals in this tale are **personified,** or given human characteristics. What human traits are suggested by this picture of the antelope?

The little drum on the old man's knees soon began to whisper. "Tap! Tap! Tap-tap-tap!" And Tanko in his soft singing voice told this strange tale.

In the long, long ago, animals were not so different, one from the other. Oh, they had different shapes, just as they do today. But they lived together in friendship and peace. Like people, those of one animal tribe sometimes took their wives from those of a different tribe. Like you and me, in those times beasts could talk. And, like people, they had a king to rule over them.

In the place of this story, the leopard was king. Rich he was, beyond telling. Mighty was he in his power over the other beasts. All the animals obeyed him.

"Whom shall I name to rule after me when I shall die?" King Leopard said one day to his pretty daughter. "I must find one who is wise enough so that he can rule well. Yes, my dear daughter, I must seek out the cleverest beast in our jungle land. I shall make him a prince. He shall have you for his bride. And to me he shall be a son."

King Leopard was pleased with his idea, and he planned a great feast. His royal drums carried word of it far and wide through the jungle. And all the animals came.

There were good things to eat. There was plenty to drink. The drums beat. And the guests at King Leopard's feast danced for three days.

At last the king called them to make a huge circle. Stepping into its center, he called his pretty daughter to come to his side. Then he spoke in a loud voice.

"Listen to my words, friends!" he cried. "Someday I must die. Someday another king must rule in my place. I will choose him now from among you, so that he will be ready."

There was a murmur of wonder all through the crowd. The King had to order them to be quiet.

"I shall seek the cleverest among you, for your king must be wise. I shall name him Prince. He shall be to me a son and to my dear daughter a husband. He shall share all my riches. And when I die he shall be your king."

Shouts came from the eager guests at the King's feast. No doubt each animal hoped that the good fortune would be his.

Then King Leopard held up his hunting spear. "Look at this, my people! Watch!" And he flung the spear far up into the air.

"With this spear will I test you," he went on. "He who would be our prince must throw the spear toward the sky. He must send it so high that he can count to ten before it drops down to earth again." **B**

SOCIAL STUDIES CONNECTION

Liberia, a country on the west coast of Africa, is home to rain forests filled with elephants, chimpanzees, bush oxen, and antelopes. Leopards, once common there, are in danger of disappearing.

Language Coach

Oral Fluency Reread lines 45–46 and 62–63. The words *center* and *count* both begin with the letter *c*, but it is not pronounced the same. Pronounce the *c* in *center* like *s* in *sit* and the *c* in *count* like *k* in *kind*.

B THEME
Why is King Leopard setting up a contest? In your chart, write down how the contest works.

There was a buzz of talk among all the animals then. This would not be so hard to do, they thought.

One after another, they came forward to try their skill. Each jungle beast danced before King Leopard and his pretty daughter. Each one sang a song that told how well he would rule, if he were chosen.

First to try his luck was the elephant. He was so big that he could push all the other beasts out of his way.

"I must be first," he said to himself. "This task is too easy. Almost any one of us can do it."

The elephant danced clumsily. He was very big and his body was heavy. Then, with his trunk in the air, he trumpeted all the fine deeds he would perform if he were prince. **C**

The great beast threw King Leopard's spear up into the air.

"One! Two! Three!" he began counting. But he spoke slowly, as he did everything else. An elephant cannot easily hurry, you know.

Before the elephant had said, "Four!" the King's spear had dropped to earth. The proud beast hung his head so low that the tip of his trunk dragged on the ground. He knew he had failed.

Next came the bush ox. His wide gray horns swept the other beasts to the side.

"I'll throw the spear up to the sun," the huge animal sang while he danced. "I'll be a strong husband for King Leopard's daughter." **D**

The bush ox picked the spear up in his mouth. With a mighty toss of his great head, he flung it far, far above his spreading horns.

"One! Two! Three! Four!" the bush ox counted more quickly than the elephant. But he, too, was slow. Before he could say "Five," the spear was down on the ground. He went off, ashamed, into the deep jungle.

The chimpanzee was third. He jumped up and down in a merry dance, and King Leopard's daughter laughed at his antics. He beat his hairy chest with his two fists, and he sang of how much he would like to be king in the leopard's place.

The young ape rose up straight on his hind legs. He held the spear in one hand, just like a man. With a twist of his long arm, he threw it up toward the sky.

"One-two-three-four-five-six-seven!" He chattered as fast as he could. The watching animals held their breaths. Surely, with such a quick tongue, the chimpanzee would make the count.

But he did not! He had not even said, "Eight!" before he had caught the spear once more in his hand.

One by one, other animals tried to count to ten while the spear was still up in the air. One by one, they all failed.

C THEME
In fables, animal characters often represent human traits. What trait might the elephant represent?

D THEME
Why does the bush ox think he would make a good husband?

"It seems I must look somewhere else for a prince to rule when I am gone," King Leopard spoke sadly.

Then out from the crowd stepped an antelope.

Beside the elephant, the bush ox, and even the chimpanzee, the young deerlike antelope seemed puny and weak. His legs were long, yet so 110 slender that it was almost a wonder that they would hold up his body. But the antelope spoke bravely.

"Let me try to throw your spear, O King," he cried. "I would like well to marry your pretty daughter."

"Ho! Ho!" The other animals burst into laughter. How could such a weak creature fling the King's spear high enough to say more than two or three words? However could he hope to count up to ten? **E**

But the antelope would not be turned aside.

"I wish to try," he insisted. And King Leopard nodded his head. He had promised a fair trial for all who wished to take part in this contest.

120 "Who can say what any creature can do until he has tried?" The King spoke to the crowd. "The antelope may throw the spear." So the other beasts were moved back to give him room. **F**

When the antelope, on his slender legs, danced before the King, the leopard's daughter cried out with pleasure. No one could deny that his steps were more graceful than those of the elephant, or of the bush ox, or the chimpanzee.

Then the antelope threw the spear. With a toss of his head, he flung it far up into the air. Before it could fall to earth, the clever beast called out two words. "Five! Ten!" he cried. "I have counted to ten. King Leopard 130 did not say how the count should be made."

The leopard laughed then. He nodded his royal head.

"No, I did not say how the count was to be made," he agreed. "And as everyone knows, one can count by fives as well as by ones. The antelope has won the contest. He has proved he is the cleverest of you all. He shall wed my dear daughter. He shall be king when I am gone."

The other animals stared stupidly at the winner. They did not understand yet what had happened. But they could see that the antelope had outwitted the King.

At the wedding feast that King Leopard gave for his daughter, they all 140 cheered for the antelope, their new prince.

Old Tanko put his drum down in his lap.

"Remember this tale, friends," he said to the crowd in the talky-talk hut. "Do not forget that it is not always the biggest nor the strongest, but sometimes the cleverest who wins the prize." ∾

E THEME
Why do the other animals laugh at the antelope?

F THEME
Reread lines 118–122. What do you learn about King Leopard based on his treatment of the antelope?

Comprehension

1. **Recall** To whom does Old Tanko tell the fable?

2. **Clarify** Why does King Leopard want a clever husband for his daughter? Describe the contest he creates to find the husband.

3. **Summarize** Summarize what happens when each of the following animals competes: the elephant, the bush ox, the chimpanzee, and the antelope.

Text Analysis

4. **Identify Characteristics of Fables** Which character in the fable do you think represents wisdom, or good judgment? Which character represents cleverness, or quick, original thinking? Cite evidence from the fable to support your answer.

5. **Analyze Theme** Sometimes the theme of a selection must be inferred. Other times, as with this selection, the theme is directly stated. What lines state the theme? Restate the theme in your own words.

6. **Make Judgments** Was King Leopard's contest a good way to find the next king? Explain why.

Comparing Recurring Themes

7. **Set a Purpose for Reading** Finish filling in the chart column under "Two Ways to Count to Ten." Add information that helped you understand how the fable expresses its theme.

	"Two Ways to Count to Ten"	"The Race Between Toad and Donkey"
Who are the characters?	Old Tanko, King Leopard, King Leopard's daughter, the elephant, the bush ox, the chimpanzee, and the antelope	
What is the contest and who declares it?		
Who wins the contest? How?		
What do the characters learn?		

COMMON CORE

RL 1 Cite pieces of textual evidence to support analysis of what the text says explicitly as well as inferences drawn from the text. **RL 2** Determine a theme of a text and analyze its development.

The Race Between Toad and Donkey

Retold by
Roger D. Abrahams

One day, Master King decided to have a race and he would give a big prize to whoever won. Both Toad and Donkey decided to enter, but Toad got Donkey angry with all his boasting about how he'd win.

Now, the race was to be for twenty miles. So when Donkey looked at Toad he wondered out loud how any animal so small and powerless could hope to keep up with him. "I have very long legs, you know, as well as long ears and tail. Just measure our legs, and you'll see why you can't possibly hope to win this race." But Toad was stubborn—and he was smart, too—and he said that he was going to win the race. That just got
10 Donkey more vexed. **A**

Analyze Visuals ▶
On the basis of this image, which character would you **infer** is the cleverer of the two? Why?

Ⓐ THEME
Note the character who will compete with Donkey. Why does Donkey think he'll win the race?

So Donkey told the king that he was ready to start, but the king said that he had to make the rules first. At each mile every racer had to sing out to indicate he had gotten that far—for the king wanted to know what was happening in the race, you know.

Now Toad is a smart little fellow, and he said to the king that he needed a little time to take care of business, so would he let him have a day or two. And the king said to the two of them, "You must come here first thing tomorrow." Donkey objected, for he knew that Toad was a very trickifying creature, but the king wouldn't listen. **B**

20 Now the toad had twenty children, and they all looked exactly alike. And while Donkey was sleeping, Toad took his twenty children along the racing ground, and at every milepost Toad left one of them. He told them that they must listen for Mr. Donkey, and whenever they heard him cry out, they should do so too. And Toad hid one of his children there behind each of those mileposts. **C**

So the race began the next day. Donkey looked around, and he was so sure in his heart that he was going to beat Toad that he sucked his teeth, *Tche*, to show everyone there how little he thought of Toad. "That little bit of a fellow Toad can't keep up with me. I'll even have a little time to 30 eat some grass along the way. *Tche*."

So he just went a little way down the road and he stopped and ate some grass. He poked his head through the fence where he saw some good-looking sweet-potato tops and had a taste of some gungo peas. He took more than an hour to get to the first milepost. And as he got there, he bawled out, "Ha, ha, I'm better than Toad." And the first child heard this, and he called, like all toads do:

Jin-ko-ro-ro, Jin-kok-kok-kok.

The sound really surprised Donkey, who of course thought he had gotten there first. Then he thought, "I delayed too long eating that grass. I must 40 run quicker this next mile." So he set off with greater speed, this time stopping only for a minute to drink some water along the way. And as he got to the next post, he bawled out:

Ha! Ha! Ha! I'm better than Toad.

And then the second child called out:

Jin-ko-ro-ro, Jin-kok-kok-kok.

B THEME
Why does Donkey object to Toad's request for more time?

C THEME
How does Toad plan to win the race? As you read, notice how Toad's plan affects Donkey.

Language Coach

Antonyms Antonyms are words that have opposite meanings. Reread line 26 and lines 31–32. Which word in line 31 is the antonym for the word *began* in line 26?

And Donkey said, "Lord, Toad can really move, for sure. Never mind, there are a lot more miles." So he started, and when he reached the third milepost, he bawled:

Ha! Ha! Ha! I'm better than Toad.

50 And the third child sang:

Jin-ko-ro-ro, Jin-kok-kok-kok.

Now Donkey got very angry when he heard Toad answer him, and he started to smash the toad, but Toad, being a little fellow, hid himself in the grass.

Donkey was then determined to get to the next milepost before Toad, and he took his tail and he switched it like a horsewhip and he began to gallop. And he got to the fourth milepost and he bawled:

Ha! Ha! Ha! I'm better than Toad.

And out came the answer from the fourth child.

60 When he heard that, he stood there and began to tremble, and he said, "My goodness, what am I going to do? I'm going to have to run so fast I really kick that hard, hard dirt." And he galloped off faster than he ever had before, until he reached the fifth milepost. And now he was very tired, and out of breath. He just barely had enough wind to bawl:

Ha! Ha! Ha! I'm better than Toad.

And then he heard:

Jin-ko-ro-ro, Jin-kok-kok-kok.

This time he was really angry, and he raced on harder than ever. But at each milepost he bawled out the same thing, and at each he heard the 70 same answer. And Donkey got so sad in his mind that he just gave up after a while, sad because he knew he had lost that race.

So through Toad's smartness, Donkey can never be a racer again. **D**

Jack Mandora me no choose one.[1]

SOCIAL STUDIES CONNECTION

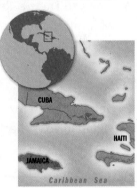

Many Jamaicans speak Creole, which combines elements of English, Spanish, French, and a variety of African languages.

D THEME
Restate the lesson or theme of the fable in your own words.

---

1. **Jack Mandora me no choose one:** Traditionally, Jamaican storytellers make this statement at the end of a tale. In Creole, it means "Don't blame me for the story I've just told."

Comprehension

1. **Recall** What are the rules of the race between Toad and Donkey?

2. **Clarify** What do Toad's children do to help him?

Text Analysis

3. **Identify Characteristics of Fables** What human abilities or traits does Donkey represent? What traits does Toad represent? Give examples from the story to support your answers.

4. **Make Judgments** In your view, did Toad win the contest fairly? Explain.

● 5. **Analyze Theme** Recall the theme you identified for this fable. Then think of another fable or story in which this same message appears. Why do you think this theme is repeated in different fables or stories?

Comparing Recurring Themes

● 6. **Set a Purpose for Reading** Now that you have read both fables, finish filling in your chart. Then state the recurring theme the selections share.

	"Two Ways to Count to Ten"	"The Race Between Toad and Donkey"
Who are the characters?	Old Tanko, King Leopard, King Leopard's daughter, the elephant, the bush ox, the chimpanzee, and the antelope	Master King, Toad, Donkey, Toad's 20 children
What is the contest and who declares it?		
Who wins the contest? How?		
What do the characters learn?		
What's the recurring theme?		

Would you rather be CLEVER or strong?

Have you ever won a championship using your wits?

RL 1 Cite pieces of textual evidence to support analysis of what the text says explicitly as well as inferences drawn from the text. RL 2 Determine a theme of a text and analyze its development.

COMMON CORE

Writing for Assessment

1. READ THE PROMPT

In writing assessments, you will often be asked to compare and contrast two works that are similar in some way, such as the two fables with a similar theme.

> While the fables "Two Ways to Count to Ten" and "The Race Between Toad and Donkey" communicate the same recurring theme, they express this theme in different ways. In four or five paragraphs, compare and contrast the ways in which the fables convey their message. Cite details from the fables to support your response.

◀ **STRATEGIES IN ACTION**

1. I have to make sure I understand the **message** both fables share.
2. I need to identify the **similarities and differences** in how the fables express the message.
3. I should give examples from the fables to help explain my ideas.

2. PLAN YOUR WRITING

Using your chart, identify the ways each fable conveys the theme. Then think about how you will set up your response.

- Do you want to focus on each fable in a separate paragraph and then write a paragraph comparing them, as shown in the sample outline?

- Do you want to compare each element—characters, contests, and theme—in a separate paragraph and then point out the differences between the stories in another paragraph?

Once you have decided, outline the order of your paragraphs.

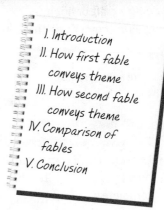

I. Introduction
II. How first fable conveys theme
III. How second fable conveys theme
IV. Comparison of fables
V. Conclusion

3. DRAFT YOUR RESPONSE

Introduction Introduce the fables and tell what recurring theme they share. Then state your main idea, which should include an overview of the similarities and differences in the ways the fables convey the theme.

Body Use your chart and outline as guides to the key points of your comparison. If you're using an outline that's similar to the sample, make sure you discuss the characters, contests, and theme for each selection.

Conclusion Wrap up with a restatement of your main idea and a reminder about how different stories can have the same theme.

Revision Make sure your sentences vary in structure.

Writing Workshop

INFORMATIVE TEXT

"How-To" Explanation

In this unit, you have read myths and tales that offer explanations about the world, human nature, and social customs. In this workshop, you will create a very different type of explanation—a "how-to" text that explains, using precise language, the process of doing or making something.

 Complete the workshop activities in your **Reader/Writer Notebook**.

WRITE WITH A PURPOSE

WRITING TASK

Write a **"how-to" explanation** in which you use relevant details and precise language to explain to an audience how to do or make something.

Idea Starters
- preparing a sandwich or making a special recipe
- playing a game
- doing a craft or hobby
- repairing something that is broken

THE ESSENTIALS

Here are some common purposes, audiences, and formats for a "how-to" explanation.

PURPOSES	AUDIENCES	FORMATS
• to explain how to complete a specific task or process	• classmates and teacher	• essay for class
	• friends	• instruction manual
	• parents	• user guide
• to inform people why it's important to know how to do the task	• consumers	• commercial
	• Web users	• magazine article
	• travelers	• blog

COMMON CORE TRAITS

1. DEVELOPMENT OF IDEAS
- clearly introduces the **topic** and tells why the reader should learn the process
- develops the topic with **relevant facts** and **concrete details**
- provides a **concluding section** that follows from the information presented

2. ORGANIZATION OF IDEAS
- presents the steps of the process in **chronological order**
- uses appropriate time-order **transitions** to link ideas and create **cohesion**

3. LANGUAGE FACILITY AND CONVENTIONS
- uses **precise language** and **domain-specific vocabulary**
- establishes and maintains a **formal style**
- uses effective **sentence types** and **structures**
- employs **correct grammar, spelling,** and **punctuation**

Writing Online

THINK central

Go to **thinkcentral.com**.
KEYWORD: HML7N-756

Planning/Prewriting

 COMMON CORE

W 2a–f Write informative/explanatory texts to examine a topic and convey ideas, concepts, and information.
W 5 Develop and strengthen writing as needed by planning.

Getting Started

CHOOSE A TOPIC

Brainstorm a list of things that you can make or do well. For each one, think about the process involved and whether you can break it down into steps. Avoid anything that requires more than seven steps. Your topic should be something you know well enough to explain clearly and completely. Choose a topic that will be fun for you to write about and for your audience to read about.

▶ **WHAT DOES IT LOOK LIKE?**

Topic	Can I do it? How well?	Is it interesting or unusual?
Skateboarding*	Yes. I've won trophies.	Yes, it's a lot of fun.
Baking bread	Kind of. I only made it twice.	Yes. Fresh bread is great.
Tying my shoes	Yes. I've been doing it since I was four.	No. Most everyone over four does it.

Notes: Skateboarding is interesting and I know it well—but it's too complicated to explain in seven steps. Maybe I can focus on one part of skating or fixing a skateboard.

THINK ABOUT AUDIENCE AND PURPOSE

After you've chosen a specific topic that you can explain clearly, think about your main **purpose**—to provide your **audience** with instructions necessary to complete a process. Ask yourself why people should learn the task you are explaining and how you can describe the process as clearly and precisely as possible.

▶ **ASK YOURSELF:**

- Who is my audience?
- Why should my audience know about my topic? How can I hold their interest?
- What steps are most important? What steps are unnecessary?
- What **domain-specific,** or specialized, **vocabulary** will my audience need to know?

MAP OUT THE STEPS

Brainstorm a list of steps in the process. Put the steps in **chronological order,** the order in which they should happen. This will help readers follow your explanation. Creating a flow chart is a good way to organize the order of the steps.

Imagine yourself completing the process. As you think about each step, write it in the flow chart. Delete any steps that seem unnecessary for the audience. Add any other steps that they might need.

▶ **WHAT DOES IT LOOK LIKE?**

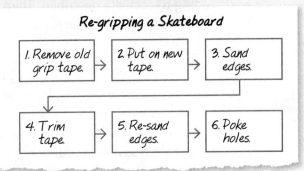

Re-gripping a Skateboard

1. Remove old grip tape. → 2. Put on new tape. → 3. Sand edges.
4. Trim tape. → 5. Re-sand edges. → 6. Poke holes.

Planning/Prewriting *continued*

Getting Started

LIST REQUIRED MATERIALS

After you identify the steps in the process, make a list of everything the reader needs to complete each step. Think about the task from the perspective of someone who has never done it before. Don't leave anything out. Something that seems obvious to you might not be obvious to someone doing the task for the first time.

▶ **WHAT DOES IT LOOK LIKE?**

> Materials for Re-gripping a Board
> • new grip tape
> • sandpaper
> • single-edge razor blade
> • screwdriver
> • protective gloves

FOCUS ON RELEVANT DETAILS

Your readers need to know more than just what the steps are. You must tell them how to complete each step using **precise language** that clearly explains what to do. Look at the steps in your flow chart, and write down details to include with each step. Be very specific, or concrete, when you discuss materials, and use consistent terms each time you refer to the same material or tool.

Keep in mind that your readers may be unfamiliar with terms that are important to your explanation. Define any **domain-specific vocabulary** so that your audience will know exactly what you are referring to.

▶ **WHAT DOES IT LOOK LIKE?**

> **1st step: Remove old grip tape.**
>
> Detail: Use a single-edge razor blade.
> Be gentle as you slide the blade under the old tape.
>
> Detail: Wear work gloves to protect your fingers.
>
> Detail: Be careful not to damage the wood under the tape.

PEER REVIEW Have a peer read your flow chart before you start to write. Tell that person to imagine doing the activity described. Then ask: Are any steps confusing, incomplete, or missing? Do any steps need to be reworked? Do I need to explain what any terms mean?

 YOUR TURN In your *Reader/Writer Notebook,* plan your "how-to" explanation. Record the steps of your process in a flow chart. Keeping your purpose and audience in mind, write down relevant details that should be included in your steps and in your materials list. If the process isn't working well, revisit and rework your topic and steps.

COMMON CORE

W 2c Use appropriate transitions. **W 4** Produce clear and coherent writing appropriate to task, purpose, and audience. **L 1** Demonstrate command of the conventions of standard English grammar and usage when writing.

Drafting

The following chart shows a structure for drafting a cohesive, or easy-to-follow, "how-to" explanation.

Organizing Your "How-To" Explanation

INTRODUCTION

- Grab the attention of your audience with a **question** or an interesting **fact**.
- Clearly **introduce** your topic and state why readers should learn about the process.

▼

BODY

- List the **materials** needed to complete the process.
- Present the steps of the process in **chronological order**. Describe each step in a paragraph, with details explaining how to complete it.
- Maintain a **formal style** by avoiding casual language and slang.
- Include **formatting** (such as headings), **graphics,** and **multimedia** to help readers better understand the steps in the process.

▼

CONCLUDING SECTION

- Briefly **summarize** the process.
- **Restate** why readers should learn the process you have described.

GRAMMAR IN CONTEXT: USING TRANSITIONS

Transitions are words and phrases that clarify how ideas and concepts are related to one another. Using transitions creates cohesion, or makes your writing easy to follow. Transitions that show chronological sequence and spatial organization are particularly useful in "how-to" explanations.

Type of Transition	Examples
Chronological: answers the question *In what order?*	*after, as, before, during, earlier, first, finally, immediately, later, next, second, soon, then, while*
Spatial: answers the question *Where?*	*above, across, along, behind, beside, in front of, in the middle, near, next to, on the right/left, over, there, under*

YOUR TURN Prepare a first draft of your "how-to" explanation. Follow the plan outlined in the chart above. Remember to use transitions to create clarity and cohesion in your explanation.

Revising

Revising gives you a chance to make sure that your audience can understand your "how-to" explanation easily. Use the following chart to revise, rewrite, and improve your draft. If you find that your explanation is difficult to follow, you may need to try a new approach.

"HOW-TO" EXPLANATION

Ask Yourself	Tips	Revision Strategies
1. Does the introduction clearly state the topic? Does it give a reason why readers should learn the process?	▶ **Put brackets** around the statement of the topic. **Put a star** next to the statement of the reason.	▶ **Add** a sentence that clearly indicates the topic of the essay. If needed, **add** a more powerful reason for learning the process.
2. Does the body list all the materials needed?	▶ **Circle** each of the materials needed to complete the task.	▶ **Add** any materials you may have left out.
3. Are steps presented in chronological order? Is each step in a separate paragraph?	▶ In the margin, **number** each step in the process.	▶ **Rearrange** steps to appear in correct sequence and in separate paragraphs.
4. Do appropriate transitions link ideas?	▶ **Draw an arrow** next to all the transitions.	▶ **Add** more transitions as needed to make your explanation clearer and more cohesive.
5. Is each step described in detail, using precise language?	▶ **Underline** concrete details. **Highlight** examples of precise language.	▶ If necessary, **elaborate** by adding more details and precise words. **Define** any domain-specific vocabulary that readers may not know.
6. Does the concluding section summarize the process and restate the reason for completing it?	▶ **Draw a wavy line** under the summary. **Put a plus sign** beside the sentence that restates the reason.	▶ If needed, **add** a summary of the steps. **Add** a sentence that restates why the reader should learn the process.

YOUR TURN **PEER REVIEW** Exchange your "how-to" explanation with a partner's. Review your drafts together and answer the questions in the chart. Determine if any parts of the drafts need reworking or a new approach.

W 2b Develop the topic with relevant information. **W 5** Develop and strengthen writing as needed by revising, editing, rewriting, or trying a new approach, focusing on how well purpose and audience have been addressed.

COMMON CORE

ANALYZE A STUDENT DRAFT

Read this student's draft and the comments about it. Use them as a model for revising your own "how-to" explanation.

Re-gripping a Skateboard
by George Oswald, Colonel Mitchell Paige Middle School

1   Anyone who skateboards a lot will eventually need to re-grip a skateboard. This simple yet important task will help prevent riders from accidentally slipping off the skateboard. There are six steps to this task.

2   Before starting, you will need to get new grip tape, a piece of medium sandpaper, a single-edge razor blade, and a flat screwdriver. The first step is to take off the old grip tape. Gently slide the razor blade under the edge of the old tape. Be careful not to cut the wood while digging under the grip tape. Slowly peel the tape back until you can pull it off with your bare hands. Wear protective work gloves when using the blade.

3   Next, put the new grip tape on the skateboard. As you put the tape on, start on one side of the board, and work your way to the other side. Do this slowly and carefully, and make sure there are no air bubbles.

> This **introduction** clearly states why someone would want this information.

> George lists the **required materials** before he presents the steps, but he doesn't include everything the reader needs.

LEARN HOW   **List the Required Materials**   George lists the materials needed at the beginning of the second paragraph. However, he does not include protective gloves. Although he later states that you must wear gloves when using the razor blade, he doesn't mention them until after they are needed. This is important information because readers might dig the razor blade under the tape with their bare hands. When revising, George added the gloves to the materials list. He also inserted a paragraph break before his description of the first step, so that each step in the process would be in a separate paragraph.

GEORGE'S REVISION TO PARAGRAPH 2

the following:

Before starting, you will need to get ∧ new grip tape, a piece of medium

, and a pair of protective work gloves. Whenever you use the blade, be sure to wear the gloves.

sandpaper, a single-edge razor blade, ~~and~~ a flat screwdriver. ¶ The first step is to take off the old grip tape. Gently slide the razor blade under the edge of the old tape. Be careful not to cut the wood while digging under the grip tape. Slowly peel the tape back until you can pull it off with your bare hands. ~~Wear protective work gloves when using the blade.~~

④ Once the new tape is on, sand the edges of the board. Slowly work your way around the entire board. When you're finished, there should be a clean, crisp white crease around the whole board.

⑤ Now trim the excess grip tape. Grasp the razor blade firmly and start cutting along the white crease. The edge will come out much neater if you cut long sections in one smooth motion rather than stopping after each little cut.

⑥ Then, to give your board a much cleaner look, lightly re-sand the edges of the grip tape. This step is optional, but I highly recommend it.

⑦ Finally, use the screwdriver to poke holes through the tape where needed. The easiest way to find the holes in your deck is to flip the board over and poke through the holes from the back side.

⑧ With only some new grip tape, sandpaper, and a few simple tools, you can add a brand-new surface to your skateboard. It will give you better control, it will look great, too.

> George presents steps in **chronological order,** and he uses **transitions** to create cohesion.

> **Precise language** and **details** help readers picture each step.

> More **precise language** is needed to describe the holes, or readers will be left with questions about this step.

LEARN HOW Use Precise Language George does a good job of including some **precise language** and **details** in these paragraphs, such as "clean, crisp white crease" and "grasp the razor blade firmly." However, the final step probably leaves most readers with questions. How big should the holes be? How can you tell where holes are needed? When George revised his explanation, he added precise words to help answer these questions.

GEORGE'S REVISION TO PARAGRAPH ⑦

Finally, use the screwdriver to poke holes through the tape where
your trucks belong. The holes are already in your deck you just need to find them.
~~needed.~~ The easiest way to find the holes ~~in your deck~~ is to flip the board over and poke through the holes from the back side.

I like to neaten up the holes by cutting around the edges with the razor blade, but it's up to you whether to do this or not. I do think it helps the screws fit more snugly in the holes.

YOUR TURN Use feedback from your peers and your teacher as well as the two "Learn How" lessons to revise your essay. Evaluate how well your "how-to" explanation fulfills its purpose. Add precise language to help your audience understand your explanation.

COMMON CORE

W 2d Use precise language. **W 5** Develop and strengthen writing by revising and editing. **L 1** Demonstrate command of grammar and usage. **L 2** Demonstrate command of capitalization, punctuation, and spelling.

Editing and Publishing

The editing stage gives you a chance to make sure that your essay contains no mistakes in grammar, usage, spelling, and punctuation. You don't want simple errors to interfere with your audience's understanding of your "how-to" explanation.

GRAMMAR IN CONTEXT: CORRECTING RUN-ON SENTENCES

A **run-on sentence** is two or more sentences written as if they were one sentence. Some run-ons contain no punctuation between the independent clauses. Others use commas where conjunctions or stronger punctuation is needed. When proofreading his essay, George realized that his final sentence was a run-on. He revised it by adding a conjunction.

> *and*
> *It will give you better control,ʌ it will look great, too.*

There are two other ways George could have corrected the run-on. He could have divided it into two separate sentences, or he could have separated the two independent clauses with a semicolon.

> *It will give you better control. It will look great, too.*
>
> [In this revision, the run-on has been divided into two sentences by changing the comma to a period.]

> *It will give you better control; it will look great, too.*
>
> [In this revision, the comma has been changed to a semicolon.]

PUBLISH YOUR WRITING

Share your "how-to" explanation with a wider audience.

- Make copies of your essay for all your classmates who might be interested.
- Post your explanation on a Web site or message board that people interested in the process might visit.
- Use your essay as the script for an actual demonstration that you videotape or present to an audience.

YOUR TURN
Correct any errors in your "how-to" explanation by carefully proofreading it. Look for errors in capitalization, punctuation, and spelling. Revise any run-on sentences. Then publish your final version where it is most likely to reach your audience.

Scoring Rubric

Use the rubric below to evaluate your "how-to" explanation from the Writing Workshop or your response to the on-demand task on the next page.

"HOW-TO" EXPLANATION

SCORE	COMMON CORE TRAITS
6	• **Development** Introduces a topic in a clear and engaging way; provides relevant facts, details, and information about each step in the process; ends with a strong concluding section that follows from the explanation • **Organization** Organizes process steps in a clear, chronological order; effectively uses appropriate transitions to link ideas and create cohesion • **Language** Consistently maintains a formal style; ably uses precise language; shows a strong command of conventions
5	• **Development** Clearly introduces a topic; provides relevant facts, details, and information about most steps in the process; ends with a concluding section that follows from the explanation • **Organization** Arranges steps chronologically; uses appropriate transitions • **Language** Maintains a formal style; uses precise language; has a few errors in conventions
4	• **Development** Sufficiently introduces a topic; could use more facts, details, and information to explain some steps; has an adequate concluding section • **Organization** Arranges most steps chronologically; uses some transitions • **Language** Mostly maintains a formal style; needs more precise language at times; includes a few distracting errors in conventions
3	• **Development** Introduces a topic and concludes the explanation in an ordinary way; lacks enough facts, details, and information in most steps • **Organization** Has some organizational flaws; needs transitions to link ideas • **Language** Frequently lapses into an informal style; uses some vague words; has some critical errors in conventions
2	• **Development** Has a weak introduction of the topic and concluding section; lacks facts, details, and information in all steps • **Organization** Has organizational flaws; lacks transitions throughout • **Language** Uses informal style and vague words; has many errors in conventions
1	• **Development** Lacks an introduction, concluding section, and explanation of steps • **Organization** Has no organization or transitions • **Language** Uses an inappropriate style and vague words; has major problems with grammar, mechanics, and spelling

Preparing for Timed Writing

COMMON CORE **W 10** Write routinely over shorter time frames for a range of tasks, purposes, and audiences.

1. ANALYZE THE TASK   5 MIN

Read the task carefully. Then read it again, underlining the words that tell the type of writing, the topic, and the purpose. Circle the audience.

> **WRITING TASK** *Type of writing*   *Purpose*   *Topic*
>
> Write a "how-to" explanation that explains a multi-step process or activity to your classmates. In your essay, clearly state why someone would want to know how to complete the process or activity, and present the steps in chronological order. Be sure to list all necessary materials.

2. PLAN YOUR RESPONSE   10 MIN

Think of something you know how to do very well. Make sure that you can explain it as a process that involves several steps. Jot down the steps required, in the order in which they should be completed. Make a flow chart to help you organize the steps.

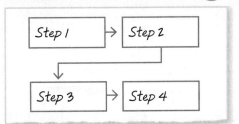

3. RESPOND TO THE TASK   20 MIN

Using the notes you've just made, draft your "how-to" explanation. As you write, keep the following points in mind:

- In the introduction, state the topic clearly. Write an attention-grabbing opener, and tell readers why they should learn this process.
- In the body, provide a complete list of materials, and present the steps in chronological order. Present each step in a separate paragraph.
- In the concluding section, summarize the process and the reason for completing it.

4. IMPROVE YOUR RESPONSE   5–10 MIN

Revising Review your explanation. Did you explain why readers would want to do what you are describing? Did you provide precisely worded steps in the proper order? Did you list all the necessary materials? Did you define any domain-specific vocabulary?

Proofreading Correct any errors in grammar, spelling, punctuation, and capitalization. Make sure your edits are neat. Erase any stray marks.

Checking Your Final Copy Before you turn in your explanation, read it one more time to catch any errors you may have missed.

Giving and Following Oral Instructions

People give and receive simple instructions every day. For example, you have probably given directions to your house or asked for directions to a friend's house. In order to effectively follow and give oral instructions of any kind, it's useful to practice purposeful speaking and listening.

 Complete the workshop activities in your **Reader/Writer Notebook**.

SPEAK WITH A PURPOSE

TASK

Adapt your "how-to" explanation as a set of **oral instructions** that teach your classmates to perform a useful task or process. Practice your presentation, and then give it to the class.

COMMON CORE TRAITS

EFFECTIVE ORAL INSTRUCTIONS . . .

- state the topic and purpose in a way that captures listeners' interest
- present steps in chronological order
- use precise language and offer tips for completing the task successfully
- are presented to attentive listeners who pose questions to clarify instructions
- are supported by multimedia components and visual displays

COMMON CORE

SL 1a Come to discussions prepared. SL 1c Pose questions and respond to others' questions and comments. SL 5 Include multimedia components and visual displays in presentations to clarify claims and findings and emphasize salient points.

Give Oral Instructions

Follow these guidelines as you adapt and deliver your oral instructions:

- **Prepare with note cards.** To prepare for your presentation, read your essay and write key words and phrases on index cards that you can refer to during your speech. You might create one card for your introduction, a card for each step in the process, and one card for your conclusion.

- **Speak clearly and naturally.** To help your audience follow along, speak at a slower rate and at a louder volume than you do in normal conversation.

- **Use gestures and visual displays.** Use "body language" to emphasize key ideas. For example, use your hands to show what it looks like to perform steps in the process. Use multimedia components and visual displays to clarify the process or emphasize salient, or important, points.

- **Pay attention to your audience.** If someone looks confused, you might need to pause to define a term or even repeat a whole step. Ask if your listeners have questions or comments. If so, respond with relevant observations or ideas. Remember to stay focused on the process under discussion.

Speaking & Listening Online

Go to **thinkcentral.com**.
KEYWORD: HML7-766

Follow Oral Instructions

These guidelines will help you listen effectively to oral instructions:

- **Know why you are listening.** Is your purpose to learn how to perform a new task or to better understand the steps in a process you already know? If you are familiar with the process being described, listen for new information or tips that will increase your knowledge. If the process is completely new to you, you'll need to pay close attention to everything the speaker says.

- **Limit distractions.** Decide that you are going to focus on the speaker for the next few minutes. Put aside distracting thoughts as you listen.

- **Listen for the steps in a process.** Listen for transitions that tell you the order of steps. Examples include such words as *first*, *next*, *then*, and *last*.

- **Take notes.** If the process includes many steps, take notes to help you remember them. Here's an example of what your notes might look like:

> *How to Re-grip a Skateboard*
> **Materials:** *grip tape, sandpaper, single-edge razor blade, flat screwdriver, work gloves*
> **Step 1:** *Remove old grip tape.*
> *— Wear gloves.*
> *— Slide razor blade under old tape (don't cut wood).*
> *— Peel tape off.*

- **Picture each step.** Imagine yourself completing each step in order.

- **Pose questions.** Make sure you understand all the instructions. Ask the speaker to elaborate on his or her explanation if any step is unclear.

- **Restate the instructions.** You may want to repeat the steps back to the speaker to make sure you understand them correctly.

- **Complete the process on your own.** If you've listened carefully and posed questions to clarify any points of confusion, you should be able to do the process yourself. Use your notes to guide you.

YOUR TURN

As a Speaker Present your oral instructions to a friend, using your note cards. As you speak, be prepared to respond to questions and comments if your friend becomes confused. When you are finished, ask your friend to evaluate your delivery.

As a Listener Use effective listening skills as your partner presents his or her oral instructions. Focus and reflect on what he or she is saying and listen for key transition words. Pose questions to check your understanding. Then attempt to complete the process yourself.

Assessment Practice

DIRECTIONS Read these selections and answer the questions that follow.

King Midas had pleased the god Dionysus, and so Dionysus promised to give Midas anything he wished. Midas wished that everything he touched would turn to gold.

from The King Who Wished for Gold *retold by Anne Rockwell*

1   As soon as he reached his palace, the king ordered a grand and extravagant feast to be set before him. All kinds of rare and expensive delicacies were prepared because Midas thought, After all, if I am so rich, why should I spare any expense?

2   And then he sat down to eat.

3   But the piece of bread he picked up hardened in his hand and turned to gold. Slices of meat became slabs of glimmering gold. He picked up his cup of wine, and slippery liquid gold gagged him so that he could not drink.

4   Poor King Midas realized that for all his newfound wealth he would soon starve to death if he could not eat or drink. Suddenly he hated the gift that he had wanted so much. He lifted his hands toward the sky and said, "Please, Lord Dionysus, forgive me for making such a foolish wish. I beg you, set me free from my own greed and stupidity!"

5   Dionysus was full of pity for the situation Midas had created for himself. Because he was a kindly and forgiving god, he immediately canceled the charm that had made everything King Midas touched turn to gold.

6   But he said to him, "Just to be sure that no trace of this charm remains, I want you to go and wash yourself at the source of the River Sardis. Where the spring spouts forth in clouds of spray, scrub your entire body and hair and beard until you wash all the gold away."

7   King Midas did as the god had told him. Dionysus had been right, for sprinkles of gold spangled the stream when he washed himself in it. To this day, gold flows through that river—the very gold that King Midas washed from himself.

8   From then on, King Midas was content with his rose garden and never again wished for gold and great wealth.

ASSESS
Taking this practice test will help you assess your knowledge of these skills and determine your readiness for the Unit Test.

REVIEW
After you take the practice test, your teacher can help you identify any standards you need to review.

COMMON CORE

RL 2 Determine a theme of a text. **RL 3** Analyze how particular elements of a story interact. **L 1b** Choose among compound, complex sentences to signal differing relationships among ideas. **L 4c** Consult general reference materials (e.g., dictionaries) to clarify [a word's] precise meaning.

from The Three Wishes   *by Ricardo E. Algería*

1   Many years ago, there lived a woodsman and his wife. They were very poor but very happy in their little house in the forest. Poor as they were, they were always ready to share what little they had with anyone who came to their door. They loved each other very much and were quite content with their life together. Each evening, before eating, they gave thanks to God for their happiness.

2   One day, while the husband was working far off in the woods, an old man came to the little house and said that he had lost his way in the forest and had eaten nothing for many days. The woodsman's wife had little to eat herself, but, as was her custom, she gave a large portion of it to the old man. After he had eaten everything she gave him, he told the woman that he had been sent to test her and that, as a reward for the kindness she and her husband showed to all who came to their house, they would be granted a special grace. This pleased the woman, and she asked what the special grace was.

3   The old man answered, "Beginning immediately, any three wishes you or your husband may wish will come true."

4   When she heard these words, the woman was overjoyed and exclaimed, "Oh, if my husband were only here to hear what you say!"

5   The last word had scarcely left her lips when the woodsman appeared in the little house with the ax still in his hands. The first wish had come true.

6   The woodsman couldn't understand it at all. How did it happen that he, who had been cutting wood in the forest, found himself here in his house? His wife explained it all as she embraced him. The woodsman just stood there, thinking over what his wife had said. He looked at the old man who stood quietly, too, saying nothing.

7   Suddenly he realized that his wife, without stopping to think, had used one of the three wishes, and he became very annoyed when he remembered all of the useful things she might have asked for with the first wish. For the first time, he became angry with his wife. The desire for riches had turned his head, and he scolded his wife, shouting at her, among other things, "It doesn't seem possible that you could be so stupid! You've wasted one of our wishes, and now we have only two left! May you grow ears of a donkey!"

8   He had no sooner said the words than his wife's ears began to grow, and they continued to grow until they changed into the pointed, furry ears of a donkey!

9   When the woman put her hand up and felt them, she knew what had happened and began to cry. Her husband was very ashamed and sorry, indeed, for what he had done in his temper, and he went to his wife to comfort her.

10   The old man, who had stood by silently, now came to them and said, "Until now, you have known happiness together and have never quarreled with each other. Nevertheless, the mere knowledge that you could have riches and power has changed you both. Remember, you have only one wish left. What do you want? Riches? Beautiful clothes? Servants? Power?"

11   The woodsman tightened his arm about his wife, looked at the old man, and said, "We want only the happiness and joy we knew before my wife grew donkey's ears."

12   No sooner had he said these words than the donkey ears disappeared. The woodsman and his wife fell upon their knees to ask forgiveness for having acted, if only for a moment, out of covetousness and greed. Then they gave thanks for all their happiness.

Reading Comprehension

> **Use "The King Who Wished for Gold" to answer questions 1–4.**

1. After Midas sits down to eat, —

  A. Dionysus sends him to the river

  B. he wishes to be wealthy

  C. no one attends his feast

  D. food turns to gold in his hands

2. Dionysus' behavior is characteristic of a Greek myth when he —

  A. shows supernatural power

  B. becomes extremely angry

  C. proves that he is an immortal

  D. knows that Midas is a fool

3. The aspect of the natural world that this myth explains is —

  A. how gold came to be in the river

  B. why rose gardens became popular

  C. why rivers have springs

  D. how thunder forms in the sky

4. Which words in paragraphs 1–3 are clues to the order of events in this myth?

  A. After all, became

  B. Ordered, turned

  C. Before, but

  D. As soon as, then

Use "The Three Wishes" to answer questions 5–8.

5. What is one theme of this tale?

  A. The key to happiness is being content with what you have.

  B. Things that glitter are not really gold.

  C. Wanting gold causes all the trouble in this world.

  D. It doesn't pay to be selfish.

6. What is another theme of this tale?

  A. Work hard and you will succeed.

  B. Sharing with others can bring an unexpected reward.

  C. Nobody wants to have unattractive features.

  D. Working in the woods does not make a good career.

7. The quality that the woodsman stands for in this tale is —

  A. foolishness

  B. honesty

  C. laziness

  D. simplicity

8. After the wife grows donkey ears, the —

  A. old man grants three wishes

  B. woodsman comforts his sad wife

  C. wife shares her food with a stranger

  D. old man knocks on the door

Use both selections to answer questions 9–10.

9. Which value is most likely prized by the cultures that gave us these two stories?

  A. Respect your elders.

  B. Be kind to strangers.

  C. Appreciate what you have.

  D. Work steadily toward a goal.

10. What theme is repeated in both selections?

  A. Poor people should be happy with what they already have.

  B. Greed causes trouble, whether you are rich or poor.

  C. Sharing one's wealth enriches everyone.

  D. Wealth can bring happiness if it is handled correctly.

SHORT CONSTRUCTED RESPONSE
Write two or three sentences to answer this question.

11. On the basis of "The King Who Wished for Gold," what human traits do you think the ancient Greeks valued?

Write a paragraph to answer this question.

12. What lessons do King Midas and the couple in "The Three Wishes" learn about happiness and wealth?

GO ON

Vocabulary

Use your knowledge of dictionaries to
answer the following questions.

1. Read the dictionary entry for the word
spare.

> **spare** \spâr\ *v.* **1.** to treat leniently or
> mercifully **2.** to hold back; withhold **3.** to
> give out of one's own supply *adj.* **1.** extra
> **2.** free to other use; unoccupied **3.** thin or
> lean

Which definition represents the meaning
of *spare* in the following sentence?

King Midas didn't want to <u>spare</u> any
expense, so he ordered an expensive feast.

  A. Definition *v.* 1

  B. Definition *v.* 2

  C. Definition *adj.* 1

  D. Definition *adj.* 2

2. Read the dictionary entry for the word
spring.

> **spring** \sprĭng\ *v.* **1.** to move upward or
> forward quickly **2.** to arise from a source
> *n.* **1.** an elastic device that keeps its shape
> after being compressed **2.** a natural flow
> of water

Which definition represents the meaning
of *spring* in the following sentence?

King Midas washed himself carefully in a
<u>spring</u>.

  A. Definition *v.* 1   **C.** Definition *n.* 1

  B. Definition *v.* 2   **D.** Definition *n.* 2

3. Read the dictionary entries for words
spelled "fell."

> **fell**[1] \fĕl\ *v.* to cut or knock down
> **fell**[2] \fĕl\ *adj.* **1.** of an inhumanly cruel
> nature; fierce **2.** capable of destroying
> **fell**[3] \fĕl\ *n.* the hide of an animal; pelt

Which entry word represents the meaning
of *fell* in the following sentence?

In "The Three Wishes," the woodsman's
job is to <u>fell</u> trees.

  A. Entry word *fell[1]*

  B. Entry word *fell[2]*

  C. Entry word *fell[3]*

  D. None of these

Revising and Editing

DIRECTIONS Read this passage and answer the questions that follow.

(1) One of the most famous magicians was Harry Houdini. (2) Houdini's original name was Erich Weisz. (3) Houdini was born in Hungary in 1874. (4) He later moved to America. (5) Houdini did not get very far in his education. (6) But he loved to read. (7) One day, he read a book by Robert-Houdin, a famous magician. (8) He decided he would be a magician too. (9) He named himself "Houdini" after Robert-Houdin.

1. What is the BEST way to combine sentences 1 and 2 into a complex sentence?

   A. One of the most famous magicians was Harry Houdini; Houdini's original name was Erich Weisz.

   B. Harry Houdini's original name was Erich Weisz, and he was one of the most famous magicians.

   C. One of the most famous magicians was Harry Houdini, whose original name was Erich Weisz.

   D. Harry Houdini was one of the most famous magicians, and his original name was Erich Weisz.

2. What is the BEST way to combine sentences 3 and 4 into a compound sentence?

   A. Houdini, who was born in Hungary in 1874, later moved to America.

   B. After he was born in Hungary in 1874, Houdini moved to America.

   C. Although he was born in Hungary in 1874, Houdini later moved to America.

   D. Houdini was born in Hungary in 1874; he later moved to America.

3. What is the BEST way to combine sentences 5 and 6 into a complex sentence?

   A. Although Houdini did not get very far in his education, he loved to read.

   B. Houdini did not get very far in his education, and he loved to read.

   C. Houdini did not get very far in his education, so he loved to read.

   D. He loved to read; however, Houdini did not get very far in his education.

4. What is the BEST way to combine sentences 8 and 9 into a compound sentence?

   A. Although he decided he would be a magician too, he named himself "Houdini" after Robert-Houdin.

   B. He decided he would be a magician too, because he named himself "Houdini" after Robert-Houdin.

   C. He named himself "Houdini" after Robert-Houdin, even though he decided he would be a magician too.

   D. He decided he would be a magician too, and he named himself "Houdini" after Robert-Houdin.

STOP

More Great Reads

Ideas for Independent Reading

Which questions from Unit 6 made an impression on you? Continue exploring them with these books.

COMMON CORE

RL 10 Read and comprehend literature. **RI 10** Read and comprehend literary nonfiction.

Do you think before you act?

Nothing but the Truth
by Avi

In this "documentary novel," 13-year-old Philip Malloy faces dire consequences when he defends his right to freedom of speech. The story is presented through fictional memos, letters, diary entries, and official school documents.

When JFK Was My Father
by Amy Gordon

When 13-year-old Georgia Hughes's family life is changed drastically, she creates a fantasy family in which President Kennedy is her father. What will she do when the time comes to consider reality and leave her fantasies behind?

Honus and Me
by Dan Gutman

Are you willing to risk a guilty conscience? Twelve-year-old Joe Stoshack discovers a baseball card worth half a million dollars—in someone else's attic. As he wrestles with his conscience, will he decide to keep the card?

Should people always reach for the stars?

Purely Rosie Pearl
by Patricia Cochrane

Two young girls—one an optimist and one a pessimist—help each other endure the hardships of the Great Depression. Is either philosophy right, or is the answer somewhere in between?

Through My Eyes
by Ruby Bridges

Could you be optimistic about your future in the face of awful experiences? Learn how Ruby Bridges kept her dreams alive as the only African-American first grader in a newly desegregated school in 1960.

Jazmin's Notebook
by Nikki Grimes

Fourteen-year-old Jazmin has been passed along from one foster home to another. When she is finally given a chance to realize her dream of becoming a writer, will she achieve her goal despite the obstacles?

Is there a job you were born to do?

Zack
by William Bell

During a tough year at his new school, Zack discovers that a distant relative of his was a former enslaved person who fought in the American Revolution. What he finds when he researches his family history will surprise you.

Promises to the Dead
by Mary Downing Hahn

Twelve-year-old Jesse promises Lydia, a dying runaway enslaved person, that he will bring her young son Perry to relatives in Baltimore. Along the way, Jesse learns young Perry's true heritage and has to reevaluate everything he's ever known.

Trouble River
by Betsy Byars

Dewey Martin, a 12-year-old boy living in the 1800s, is left behind to tend the family farm while his parents go to Hunter City. Fearing an Indian raid, Dewey, his grandmother, and their dog, Charlie, set off on a small raft on the uncharted Trouble River—the only escape!

Writing a Life

BIOGRAPHY AND AUTOBIOGRAPHY

- In Nonfiction
- In Media
- In Drama
- In Poetry

Share What You Know

How do we share
OUR STORIES?

Have you ever put together a photo album or scrapbook to help you tell others about an important event in your life? If someone looked through the book without you there to explain it, what would they learn about you? Sharing stories from our lives can help us better understand each other.

ACTIVITY Using words, pictures, or a mix of both, tell your class about a great day you had. As you share your story and listen to the stories told by your classmates, think about the following questions:

• In what ways are other stories similar to yours?

• In what ways are they different?

• What does each story teach you about the person telling it?

• What do your classmates learn about you from your story?

Find It Online!
THINK central
Go to **thinkcentral.com** for the interactive version of this unit.

Preview Unit Goals

TEXT ANALYSIS
- Identify purpose and characteristics of biography, autobiography, personal essay, historical drama, and diary
- Compare and contrast a fictional portrayal of a character and a historical account of the same period
- Analyze the interactions between individuals, events, and ideas in a text

READING
- Identify chronological order
- Make inferences and draw conclusions
- Summarize

WRITING AND LANGUAGE
- Write a personal narrative
- Use correct capitalization
- Use conjunctive adverbs

SPEAKING AND LISTENING
- Conduct an interview
- Present an anecdote

VOCABULARY
- Understand and use Latin and Anglo-Saxon roots
- Understand Anglo-Saxon affixes

ACADEMIC VOCABULARY
- demonstrate
- goal
- impact
- link
- undertake

MEDIA AND VIEWING
- Analyze a documentary
- Analyze main ideas in diverse media formats

Media Smart DVD-ROM

Life Stories on Film

Explore how a documentary captures the life and times of baseball legend Jackie Robinson. Page 852

Text Analysis Workshop

Biography and Autobiography

We are all curious about other people—about what they do, why they do it, and how they feel. The purpose of biographies and autobiographies is to satisfy our curiosity, to inform us about the effect people have on the world, and even to entertain us.

COMMON CORE

Included in this workshop:
RL 9 Compare and contrast a fictional portrayal of a time, place, or character and a historical account of the same period as a means of understanding how authors of fiction use or alter history. **RI 1** Cite textual evidence to support analysis of what the text says explicitly. **RI 3** Analyze the interactions between individuals, events, and ideas in a text.

Part 1: Understanding the Basics

A **biography** is a story of a person's life told by someone else and written from the third-person point of view. The writer, or **biographer,** usually gets information about the subject by doing detailed research using a number of sources. Sometimes, the biographer might even interview the subject directly.

An **autobiography** is also the story of a person's life, but it is told by that person and is written from the first-person point of view. Although most of the information is from the subject's mind and memories, he or she may still consult others for help in remembering details about his or her life.

Usually, when people talk about biographies or autobiographies, they are referring to whole books about people's lives. However, biographical and autobiographical writing also includes other forms, such as a **diary** or **journal.** These are daily records of a writer's thoughts, experiences, or feelings. Additional forms are shown in the chart.

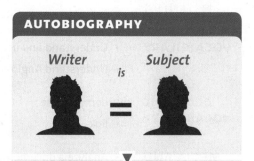

BIOGRAPHY	AUTOBIOGRAPHY
Writer *is not* Subject ≠	Writer *is* Subject =
SOURCES	**SOURCES**
• letters to and from the subject	• memories
• interviews with the subject and/or others	• thoughts and feelings
• books about the subject	• family, friends, or associates
• diaries or journals	• memorabilia
FORMS	**FORMS**
• biographical books	• autobiographical books
• encyclopedia entries	• diaries and journals
• feature articles in newspapers and magazines or on Web sites	• personal essays
	• memoirs

MODEL 1: BIOGRAPHY

This excerpt is from a biography about Wilbur and Orville Wright, two brothers who invented and flew the first machine-powered airplane.

from
THE WRIGHT BROTHERS

Biography by **Russell Freedman**

Orville was more impulsive, "bubbling over with ideas," according to his niece. Among family and friends, he had a reputation as a tease and a practical joker. Among strangers, however, he seemed uncomfortably shy. He would clam up and fade silently into the background.

5   Orville's greatest pleasure was to take something apart, see how it worked, and put it back together. Wilbur was more of a visionary, fascinated by the big picture rather than its individual parts. He was the one who first dreamed of building an airplane. . . .

Close Read

1. What clues tell you that this is a biography rather than an autobiography?

2. How were Wilbur and Orville different? Cite details to support your answer. Also note who provided the author with some of these details.

MODEL 2: AUTOBIOGRAPHY

Now read this excerpt from the autobiography of a Japanese-American author. What do you learn about her thoughts and feelings?

from
THE INVISIBLE THREAD

Autobiography by **Yoshiko Uchida**

I was born in California, recited the Pledge of Allegiance to the flag each morning at school, and loved my country as much as any other American—maybe even more.

    Still, there was a large part of me that was Japanese simply because
5 Mama and Papa had passed on to me so much of their own Japanese spirit and soul. Their own values of loyalty, honor, self-discipline, love, and respect for one's parents, teachers, and superiors were all very much a part of me.

    There was also my name, which teachers couldn't seem to pronounce
10 properly even when I shortened my first name to Yoshi. And there was my Japanese face, which closed more and more doors to me as I grew older.

How wonderful it would be, I used to think, if I had blond hair and blue eyes like Marian and Solveig.

Close Read

1. What clues in the boxed sentences signal that this is an autobiography?

2. Name two things you learn about Uchida from her description of her own thoughts and feelings.

Part 2: Reading Biographies and Autobiographies

From which book would you learn more—a biography or an autobiography? You might think that an autobiography is the better source. After all, who knows more about a person's experiences than that person? But each form has strengths and limitations. Here is how you can distinguish one form from the other.

BIOGRAPHY

When you read a biography, you . . .

- get information from a variety of sources
- discover how other people view the subject
- might get a more objective picture of the subject's life

Eleanor Roosevelt
by William Jay Jacobs
pages 786–797

AUTOBIOGRAPHY

When you read an autobiography, you . . .

- get the subject's interpretation of events, written from a subjective point of view
- learn the subject's private thoughts and feelings
- hear the subject's voice and get a sense of his or her personality

The Noble Experiment
by Jackie Robinson as told to Alfred Duckett
pages 834–843

Part 3: Reading Fictional Adaptations

Remarkable people, particularly historical figures, inspire all kinds of stories. Some are true but some are a blend of fact and fiction. **Fictional adaptations** are stories and plays about real people and events and may be based on biographies, autobiographies, and diaries. Writers of fictional adaptations combine factual details with imaginary ones, usually to create a compelling story. You can distinguish between fictional adaptations and autobiographical forms by understanding a few basic differences.

AUTOBIOGRAPHIES AND DIARIES

- written by the actual person
- writer's primary purpose is to inform
- writer presents fairly accurate details but with own point of view

FICTIONAL ADAPTATIONS

- written by a writer or playwright
- writer's purpose is to inform and entertain
- writer may include imaginary characters and events to boost dramatic effects

MODEL 1: READING A BIOGRAPHY

The actor Christopher Reeve was famous for his 1978 movie role as Superman. This article was published in 1982.

from

Feature article in *Current Biography*

$\boxed{\text{Another outstanding quality}}$ is that he [Reeve] brings the same energy and enthusiasm to his recreations that he does to acting: he owns both a $350,000 private plane and a glider; he is an $\boxed{\text{accomplished}}$ sailor who, upon completing *Superman*, gathered a six-man crew and sailed
5 a boat from Connecticut to Bermuda; and he has played classical piano since adolescence, usually practicing ninety minutes every day, and also composes music. His hobbies, moreover, include skiing, ice-skating, and playing tennis. But nothing takes precedence over his work, as Aljean Harmetz told readers of the *New York Times* (August 20, 1979), "He
10 thrives on acting. . . ." According to her, Reeve admitted: ". . . [I am] still at the stage where I'm taking care of myself, my career, first."

Close Read

1. Look at the $\boxed{\text{boxed}}$ details. How would you describe the author's attitude toward Reeve?

2. What source does the author use for quotes by and about Reeve?

3. Based on this article, how would you describe Reeve?

MODEL 2: READING AN AUTOBIOGRAPHY

In 1995, a fall from a horse left Reeve paralyzed from the neck down, and he died in 2004. In this essay, Reeve reminds people not to let fear take over their lives. Reeve conquered his own fears when he participated in research for spinal cord injuries.

from

LIVING WITHOUT FEAR

Personal essay by **Christopher Reeve**

Of course, the greater difficulty lies in being fearless in surrendering and in giving. I don't want to sound too noble, but I really have been able to say, All right, I've had some setbacks, but look at the other people who have benefited.
5 I recommend you do the same thing because being fearless is not always going to get you exactly where you expect to go. It might take you in a completely different direction. It might not give you what you want, but it can satisfy you to know you did something for the world, for the planet, or even just for your family or your neighbors. And that's enough.

Close Read

1. Describe Reeve's personality at this point in his life. In your opinion, has his attitude toward life changed or stayed the same?

2. What picture do you get of Reeve's life as a whole? Explain how this picture would be different if you had only read one of these excerpts.

Part 4: Analyze the Text

In 1955, a 42-year-old African-American woman in Montgomery, Alabama, refused to give up her seat on a public bus. Her action sparked a citywide bus boycott and helped break down the barriers of racial segregation in the South. Her name was Rosa Parks.

The first excerpt is from a biography of Parks; the second is from her autobiography. What do you learn about Parks from each excerpt?

from

ROSA PARKS

Biography by **Mary Hull**

The driver [J. F. Blake] repeated his order: "Look, woman, I told you I wanted the seat. Are you going to stand up?"

In a firm, steady voice, Parks questioned him. "Why should I have to get up and stand? Why should we have to be pushed around?"
5 The driver slammed on the brakes and pulled the bus over to the curb. He walked back to her seat and stood over her. He asked her if she was going to move, and Parks said, "No." He told her he would call the police if she did not move. "Go ahead. You may do that," Parks answered. Blake left the bus angrily and went for the police. Several
10 passengers—all of them black—followed, reluctant to become involved in an incident that invited trouble with whites. While everyone else aboard the bus waited to see what would happen next, Parks looked out the window at Montgomery.

Parks had a right to be scared, for she recognized the driver. Twelve
15 years earlier, she had refused to enter a bus through the rear door and had been evicted from the bus by this same driver. Although Parks had seen him before while waiting at bus stops, she never boarded a bus if she knew he was driving. In all these years she had never forgotten his face. That evening, Parks had not looked at the driver when she boarded,
20 but when he stood over her, there was no mistaking who he was.

Parks's mother and grandparents had always taught her not to regard herself as inferior to whites because she was black, but she admitted that until that fateful December day on the bus "every part of my life pointed to the white superiority and negro inferiority." She was uncertain about
25 what exactly had provoked her not to move on the bus driver's order, but her feet certainly hurt, her shoulders ached, and suddenly everything became too much. "I had had enough," Parks later said. She was tired of giving in. "I wanted to be treated like a human being."

Close Read

1. How can you tell that this excerpt is from a biography? Cite details to support your answer.

2. Consider how the author describes Parks's words and actions in lines 3–13. How does the author seem to feel about Parks?

3. What do you learn about Parks's upbringing from this biography?

4. One of the sources for this biography was Rosa Parks's own autobiography. As a result, the author was able to include details about Parks's thoughts and feelings. One example is boxed. Find one more.

Now read this excerpt from the beginning of Parks's autobiography. Pay attention to how Parks describes the incident on the bus. Also notice what she reveals about her thoughts and feelings at that time in her life.

from
Rosa Parks:
My Story

Autobiography by **Rosa Parks**
(with Jim Haskins)

One evening in early December 1955 I was sitting in the front seat of the colored section of a bus in Montgomery, Alabama. The white people were sitting in the white section. More white people got on, and they filled up all the seats in the white section. When that happened, we black people
5 were supposed to give up our seats to the whites. But I didn't move. The white driver said, "Let me have those front seats." I didn't get up. I was tired of giving in to white people.
    "I'm going to have you arrested," the driver said.
    "You may do that," I answered.
10   Two white policemen came. I asked one of them, "Why do you all push us around?"
    He answered, "I don't know, but the law is the law and you're under arrest."

    For half of my life there were laws and customs in the South that kept African Americans segregated from Caucasians and allowed white
15 people to treat black people without any respect. I never thought this was fair, and from the time I was a child, I tried to protest against disrespectful treatment. But it was very hard to do anything about segregation and racism when white people had the power of the law behind them.
20   Somehow we had to change the laws. And we had to get enough white people on our side to be able to succeed. I had no idea when I refused to give up my seat on that Montgomery bus that my small action would help put an end to the segregation laws in the South. I only knew that I was tired of being pushed around. I was a regular
25 person, just as good as anybody else.

Close Read

1. Reread the boxed sentences. Would you say that this autobiography was written in the 1950s, or later? Explain.

2. How can you tell that the author of the biography used Parks's autobiography as a source? Cite similar details in both excerpts to support your answer.

3. By revealing her thoughts and beliefs in lines 13–25, Parks gives readers a real sense of her personality. How would you describe her? In your opinion, do you get this same sense from reading the biography about her? Support your answer.

Eleanor Roosevelt

Video link at
thinkcentral.com

Biography by William Jay Jacobs

What is your
DUTY to others?

○ COMMON CORE

RI 1 Cite textual evidence to support analysis of what the text says explicitly. **RI 3** Analyze the interactions between individuals, events, and ideas in a text. **RI 5** Analyze the structure an author uses to organize a text.

There are probably times when you wish you didn't owe anything to anyone. However, like most people, you have responsibilities to many different people. Family members, teachers, classmates, and the teams and other groups you belong to all need you in one way or another. In "Eleanor Roosevelt," you'll learn how a famous first lady's commitment to her duties changed history.

QUICKWRITE Make a list of your duties to others. Which of these do you think will most influence the adult you will become? Explore that question in a journal entry, considering career possibilities and other life choices you will be making.

TEXT ANALYSIS: BIOGRAPHY

A **biography** is the story of a person's life told by another person, a biographer. Biographers often reveal their personal opinions of their subject. However, they also balance their opinions with facts and details that

- provide information about the person's life
- reveal important aspects of his or her personality
- show us what others thought of the person
- explain the importance of his or her life and work

As you read "Eleanor Roosevelt," think about the purpose and characteristics of a biography about a historical figure.

READING SKILL: IDENTIFY CHRONOLOGICAL ORDER

A biography usually presents events in **chronological order,** or the order in which they happened. Words and phrases such as *then, next, within 18 months, meanwhile, by spring,* and *the first few years* may signal the order of events in this type of work.

A timeline can help you to summarize events or actions by presenting the important details of a written work at a glance. As you read "Eleanor Roosevelt," keep track of the order of events on a timeline like the one shown.

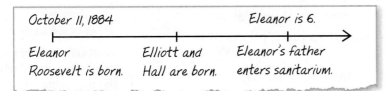

October 11, 1884 — Eleanor Roosevelt is born. | Elliott and Hall are born. | Eleanor is 6. Eleanor's father enters sanitarium.

▲ VOCABULARY IN CONTEXT

These headlines describe important moments in Eleanor Roosevelt's life. Use context clues to figure out the meaning of each boldfaced word.

1. Woman from **Prominent** Family Leads by Example
2. First Lady Is **Compassionate** Toward Others
3. **Impoverished** Families Going Hungry in America
4. **Migrant** Workers Search for Jobs
5. Roosevelt Feels **Grave** Obligation to Help
6. Women **Dominate** at Home-Front Meeting
7. **Wavering** Members Convinced to Support War Effort
8. Country **Brooding** at Death of President

 Complete the activities in your **Reader/Writer Notebook.**

Meet the Author

William Jay Jacobs
1933–2004

The Biographer As an author who wrote more than 30 biographies, William Jay Jacobs said that he was "able to reach a very special audience: young people searching for models. . . ."

A Strong Role Model Jacobs admired Eleanor Roosevelt for her strength of character. He noted, "The more I learned about Eleanor Roosevelt, the more I saw her as a woman of courage. She turned her pain to strength."

BACKGROUND TO THE BIOGRAPHY

Hard Times Eleanor Roosevelt was first lady of the United States from 1933 to 1945. Her husband, Franklin D. Roosevelt, took office during the Great Depression, a worldwide economic crisis that lasted through most of the 1930s. Millions of Americans were unemployed, penniless, and suffering.

Help on the Way To encourage recovery, the Roosevelt administration introduced programs—such as Social Security and a minimum wage—that still provide relief today. Many of the First Lady's ideas were incorporated into her husband's New Deal programs.

Author Online
THINK central
Go to **thinkcentral.com.**
KEYWORD: HML7-785

Eleanor Roosevelt

William Jay Jacobs

E leanor Roosevelt was the wife of President Franklin Delano
Roosevelt. But Eleanor was much more than just a president's
wife, an echo of her husband's career.

Sad and lonely as a child, Eleanor was called "Granny" by her
mother because of her seriousness. People teased her about her looks
and called her the "ugly duckling.". . .

Yet despite all of the disappointments, the bitterness, the misery she
experienced, Eleanor Roosevelt refused to give up. Instead she turned
her unhappiness and pain to strength. She devoted her life to helping
10 others. Today she is remembered as one of America's greatest women. **A**

Eleanor was born in a fine townhouse in Manhattan. Her family
also owned an elegant mansion along the Hudson River, where they
spent weekends and summers. As a child Eleanor went to fashionable
parties. A servant took care of her and taught her to speak French.
Her mother, the beautiful Anna Hall Roosevelt, wore magnificent jewels
and fine clothing. Her father, Elliott Roosevelt, had his own hunting
lodge and liked to sail and to play tennis and polo. Elliott, who loved
Eleanor dearly, was the younger brother of Theodore Roosevelt, who
in 1901 became president of the United States. The Roosevelt family,
20 one of America's oldest, wealthiest families, was respected and admired.

Analyze Visuals ▶

What can you **infer** about
Eleanor Roosevelt from
this 1957 photograph
taken at her home?

A BIOGRAPHY
Why might Jacobs have
chosen to begin with
an overview of Mrs.
Roosevelt's life?

To the outside world it might have seemed that Eleanor had everything that any child could want—everything that could make her happy. But she was not happy. Instead her childhood was very sad.

Almost from the day of her birth, October 11, 1884, people noticed that she was an unattractive child. As she grew older, she could not help but notice her mother's extraordinary beauty, as well as the beauty of her aunts and cousins. Eleanor was plain looking, ordinary, even, as some called her, homely. For a time she had to wear a bulky brace on her back to straighten her crooked spine. **B**

When Eleanor was born, her parents had wanted a boy. They were scarcely able to hide their disappointment. Later, with the arrival of two boys, Elliott and Hall, Eleanor watched her mother hold the boys on her lap and lovingly stroke their hair, while for Eleanor there seemed only coolness, distance.

Feeling unwanted, Eleanor became shy and withdrawn. She also developed many fears. She was afraid of the dark, afraid of animals, afraid of other children, afraid of being scolded, afraid of strangers, afraid that people would not like her. She was a frightened, lonely little girl.

The one joy in the early years of her life was her father, who always seemed to care for her, love her. He used to dance with her, to pick her up and throw her into the air while she laughed and laughed. He called her "little golden hair" or "darling little Nell."

Then, when she was six, her father left. An alcoholic, he went to live in a sanitarium[1] in Virginia in an attempt to deal with his drinking problem. Eleanor missed him greatly.

Next her mother became ill with painful headaches. Sometimes for hours at a time Eleanor would sit holding her mother's head in her lap and stroking her forehead. Nothing else seemed to relieve the pain. At those times Eleanor often remembered how her mother had teased her about her looks and called her "Granny." But even at the age of seven Eleanor was glad to be helping someone, glad to be needed—and noticed.

The next year, when Eleanor was eight, her mother, the beautiful Anna, died. Afterward her brother Elliott suddenly caught diphtheria[2] and he, too, died. Eleanor and her baby brother, Hall, were taken to live with their grandmother in Manhattan.

A few months later another tragedy struck. Elliott Roosevelt, Eleanor's father, also died. Within eighteen months Eleanor had lost her mother, a brother, and her dear father. **C**

B CHRONOLOGICAL ORDER
Jacobs begins his use of chronological order with Eleanor's birth date. Start adding events to your timeline.

C CHRONOLOGICAL ORDER
Reread lines 52–58. What words and phrases in these paragraphs help you understand the order of events and the passage of time?

---

1. **sanitarium** (săn′ĭ-târ′ē-əm): an institution for the care of people with a specific disease or with other health problems.

2. **diphtheria** (dĭf-thîr′ē-ə): a serious infectious disease.

Eleanor Roosevelt with her father, Elliott Roosevelt

For the rest of her life Eleanor carried with her the letters that her
60 father had written to her from the sanitarium. In them he had told her
to be brave, to become well educated, and to grow up into a woman
he could be proud of, a woman who helped people who were suffering.

Only ten years old when her father died, Eleanor decided even then
to live the kind of life he had described—a life that would have made
him proud of her. **D**

Few things in life came easily for Eleanor, but the first few years after
her father's death proved exceptionally hard. Grandmother Hall's
dark and gloomy townhouse had no place for children to play. The family
ate meals in silence. Every morning Eleanor and Hall were expected to
70 take cold baths for their health. Eleanor had to work at better posture
by walking with her arms behind her back, clamped over a walking stick.

Instead of making new friends, Eleanor often sat alone in her room
and read. For many months after her father's death she pretended that
he was still alive. She made him the hero of stories she wrote for school.
Sometimes, alone and unhappy, she just cried.

Some of her few moments of happiness came from visiting her uncle,
Theodore Roosevelt, in Oyster Bay, Long Island. A visit with Uncle Ted meant
playing games and romping outdoors with the many Roosevelt children.

Once Uncle Ted threw her into the water to teach her how to swim,
80 but when she started to sink, he had to rescue her. Often he would read

COMMON CORE RI 3

D BIOGRAPHY
In a **biography**, the story
of a person's life, the
biographer includes
facts and details that
reveal important
aspects of a subject's
personality. Often, a
biographer gives details
about a subject's early
life to show the major
forces that shaped
what the person would
become. Reread lines
59–65. According to
Jacobs, how did Eleanor's
father influence her
goals and values?

to the children old Norse[3] tales and poetry. It was at Sagamore Hill, Uncle Ted's home, that Eleanor first learned how much fun it could be to read books aloud.

For most of the time Eleanor's life was grim. Although her parents had left plenty of money for her upbringing, she had only two dresses to wear to school. Once she spilled ink on one of them, and since the other was in the wash, she had to wear the 90 dress with large ink stains on it to school the next day. It was not that Grandmother Hall was stingy. Rather, she was old and often confused. Nor did she show much warmth or love for Eleanor and her brother. Usually she just neglected them.

Just before Eleanor turned fifteen, Grandmother Hall decided to send her to boarding school in England. The school she chose was Allenswood, a private academy for girls located on the outskirts of London.

100 It was at Allenswood that Eleanor, still thinking of herself as an "ugly duckling," first dared to believe that one day she might be able to become a swan.

At Allenswood she worked to toughen herself physically. Every day she did exercises in the morning and took a cold shower. Although she did not like competitive team sports, as a matter of self-discipline she tried out for field hockey. Not only did she make the team but, because she played so hard, also won the respect of her teammates.

110 They called her by her family nickname, "Totty," and showed their affection for her by putting books and flowers in her room, as was the custom at Allenswood. Never before had she experienced the pleasure of having schoolmates actually admire her rather than tease her.

At Allenswood, too, she began to look after her health. She finally broke the habit of chewing her fingernails. She learned to eat nutritious foods, to get plenty of sleep, and to take a brisk walk every morning, no matter how miserable the weather.

Under the guidance of the school's headmistress, Mademoiselle Souvestre (or "Sou"), she learned to ask searching questions and think 120 for herself instead of just giving back on tests what teachers had said.

▲ **Analyze Visuals**
What **mood** does this photograph of a teenage Eleanor Roosevelt convey?

---

3. **Norse** (nôrs): coming from ancient Scandinavia, the area that is now Norway, Sweden, and Denmark.

She also learned to speak French fluently, a skill she polished by traveling in France, living for a time with a French family. Mademoiselle Souvestre arranged for her to have a new red dress. Wearing it, after all of the old, worn dresses Grandmother Hall had given her, made her feel very proud.

Eleanor was growing up, and the joy of young womanhood had begun to transform her personality.

In 1902, nearly eighteen years old, she left Allenswood, not returning for her fourth year there. Grandmother Hall insisted that, instead, she must be introduced to society as a debutante—to go to dances and parties and begin
130 to take her place in the social world with other wealthy young women.

Away from Allenswood, Eleanor's old uncertainty about her looks came back again. She saw herself as too tall, too thin, too plain. She worried about her buckteeth, which she thought made her look horselike. The old teasing began again, especially on the part of Uncle Ted's daughter, "Princess" Alice Roosevelt, who seemed to take pleasure in making Eleanor feel uncomfortable.

Eleanor, as always, did as she was told. She went to all of the parties and dances. But she also began working with poor children at the Rivington Street Settlement House[4] on New York's Lower East Side.
140 She taught the girls gymnastic exercises. She took children to museums and to musical performances. She tried to get the parents interested in politics in order to get better schools and cleaner, safer streets. **E**

Meanwhile Eleanor's life reached a turning point. She fell in love! The young man was her fifth cousin, Franklin Delano Roosevelt. Eleanor and Franklin had known each other since childhood. Franklin recalled how once he had carried her piggyback in the nursery. When she was fourteen, he had danced with her at a party. Then, shortly after her return from Allenswood, they had met by chance on a train. They talked and almost at once realized how much they liked each other.
150 For a time they met secretly. Then they attended parties together. Franklin—tall, strong, handsome—saw her as a person he could trust. He knew that she would not try to **dominate** him. **F**

But did he really love her? Would he always? She wrote to him, quoting a poem she knew: "Unless you can swear, *'For life, for death!'* . . . Oh, never call it loving!"

Franklin promised that his love was indeed "for life," and Eleanor agreed to marry him. It was the autumn of 1903. He was twenty-one. She was nineteen.

On March 17, 1905, Eleanor and Franklin were married. "Uncle Ted,"
160 by then president of the United States, was there to "give the bride away."

---

4. **settlement house:** a place in a poor, neglected neighborhood where services are provided for residents.

Language Coach

Etymology The history of a word is its etymology. Many words we commonly use include **affixes,** or word parts that are attached either to the beginning **(prefix)** or end **(suffix)** of base words to create new words. These affixes often come from older languages. The Anglo-Saxon suffix *-hood* means "state, quality, or group." Reread lines 125–126, which include the word *womanhood.* In your own words, tell what you think *womanhood* means.

E BIOGRAPHY
Reread lines 131–142. Note that Jacobs chooses details that reveal various aspects of Eleanor's personality. What are some of her strengths and weaknesses?

F CHRONOLOGICAL ORDER
Reread lines 143–152. What words and phrases help you understand the order in which Eleanor and Franklin's relationship progressed?

dominate (dŏm′ə-nāt′) *v.* to have control over

It was sometimes said that the dynamic, energetic Theodore Roosevelt had to be "the bride at every wedding and the corpse at every funeral." And it was certainly true that day. Wherever the president went, the guests followed at his heels.

Before long Eleanor and Franklin found themselves standing all alone, deserted. Franklin seemed annoyed, but Eleanor didn't mind. She had found the ceremony deeply moving. And she stood next to her husband in a glow of idealism—very serious, very **grave,** very much in love. In May 1906 the couple's first child was born. During the next nine years
170 Eleanor gave birth to five more babies, one of whom died in infancy. Still timid, shy, afraid of making mistakes, she found herself so busy that there was little time to think of her own drawbacks.

Still, looking back later on the early years of her marriage, Eleanor knew that she should have been a stronger person, especially in the handling of Franklin's mother, or, as they both called her, "Mammá." Too often Mammá made the decisions about such things as where they would live, how their home would be furnished, how the children would be disciplined. Eleanor and Franklin let her pay for things they could not afford—extra servants, vacations, doctor bills, clothing. She offered, and they accepted.

180 Before long, trouble developed in the relationship between Eleanor and Franklin. Serious, shy, easily embarrassed, Eleanor could not share Franklin's interests in golf and tennis. He enjoyed light talk and flirting with women. She could not be lighthearted. So she stayed on the sidelines. Instead of losing her temper, she bottled up her anger and did not talk to him at all. As he used to say, she "clammed up." Her silence only made things worse, because it puzzled him. Faced with her coldness, her **brooding** silence, he only grew angrier and more distant.

Meanwhile Franklin's career in politics advanced rapidly. In 1910 he was elected to the New York State Senate. In 1913 President Wilson
190 appointed him Assistant Secretary of the Navy—a powerful position in the national government, which required the Roosevelts to move to Washington, D.C. **G**

In 1917 the United States entered World War I as an active combatant. Like many socially **prominent** women, Eleanor threw herself into the war effort. Sometimes she worked fifteen and sixteen hours a day. She made sandwiches for soldiers passing through the nation's capital. She knitted sweaters. She used Franklin's influence to get the Red Cross to build a recreation room for soldiers who had been shell-shocked[5] in combat. . . .

In 1920 the Democratic Party chose Franklin as its candidate for
200 vice-president of the United States. Even though the Republicans won

grave (grāv) *adj.* solemn and dignified

brooding (broo'dĭng) *adj.* full of worry; troubled **brood** *v.*

G CHRONOLOGICAL ORDER
The word *meanwhile* indicates that something else happened at the same time. In what ways are the early years of their marriage different for Eleanor and Franklin?

prominent (prŏm'ə-nənt) *adj.* well-known; widely recognized

---

5. **shell-shocked:** affected with a nervous or mental disorder resulting from the strain of battle.

the election, Roosevelt became a well-known figure in national politics. All the time, Eleanor stood by his side, smiling, doing what was expected of her as a candidate's wife.

She did what was expected—and much more—in the summer of 1921 when disaster struck the Roosevelt family. While on vacation Franklin suddenly fell ill with infantile paralysis—polio—the horrible disease that each year used to kill or cripple thousands of children, and many adults as well. When Franklin became a victim of polio, nobody knew what caused the disease or how to cure it.

210 Franklin lived, but the lower part of his body remained paralyzed. For the rest of his life he never again had the use of his legs. He had to be lifted and carried from place to place. He had to wear heavy steel braces from his waist to the heels of his shoes.

His mother, as well as many of his advisers, urged him to give up politics, to live the life of a country gentleman on the Roosevelt estate at Hyde Park, New York. This time, Eleanor, calm and strong, stood up for her ideas. She argued that he should not be treated like a sick person, tucked away in the country, inactive, just waiting for death to come.

Franklin agreed. Slowly he recovered his health. His energy returned.
220 In 1928 he was elected governor of New York. Then, just four years later, he was elected president of the United States. **H**

H BIOGRAPHY
Why was Franklin's illness a turning point for Eleanor?

President Franklin Delano Roosevelt and First Lady Eleanor Roosevelt, April 17, 1938

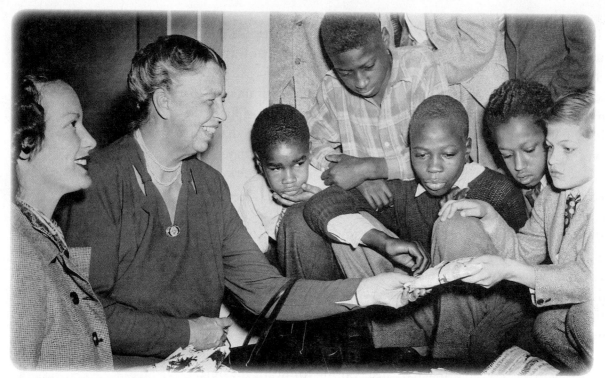
By visiting places such as this school for underprivileged boys, Eleanor Roosevelt raised public awareness of social problems.

Meanwhile Eleanor had changed. To keep Franklin in the public eye while he was recovering, she had gotten involved in politics herself. It was, she thought, her "duty." From childhood she had been taught "to do the thing that has to be done, the way it has to be done, when it has to be done."

With the help of Franklin's adviser Louis Howe, she made fund-raising speeches for the Democratic Party all around New York State. She helped in the work of the League of Women Voters, the Consumer's League, and the Foreign Policy Association. After becoming interested 230 in the problems of working women, she gave time to the Women's Trade Union League (WTUL).[6]

It was through the WTUL that she met a group of remarkable women—women doing exciting work that made a difference in the world. They taught Eleanor about life in the slums. They awakened her hopes that something could be done to improve the condition of the poor. She dropped out of the "fashionable" society of her wealthy friends and joined the world of reform—social change.

For hours at a time Eleanor and her reformer friends talked with Franklin. They showed him the need for new laws: laws to get children 240 out of the factories and into schools; laws to cut down the long hours that women worked; laws to get fair wages for all workers.

Language Coach

Idioms An idiom is a phrase that has a meaning that is different from that of its individual words. The phrase *in the public eye* means "frequently seen in public and in the media." With that meaning in mind, why do you think Eleanor's actions were so important?

---

6. **Women's Trade Union League:** an organization founded in 1903 to promote laws to protect the rights of women working in factories and to help establish labor unions for women.

*B*y the time that Franklin was sworn in as president, the nation was facing its deepest depression. One out of every four Americans was out of work, out of hope. At mealtimes people stood in lines in front of soup kitchens for something to eat. Mrs. Roosevelt herself knew of once-prosperous families who found themselves reduced to eating stale bread from thrift shops or traveling to parts of town where they were not known to beg for money from house to house.

250 Eleanor worked in the charity kitchens, ladling out soup. She visited slums. She crisscrossed the country learning about the suffering of coal miners, shipyard workers, **migrant** farm workers, students, housewives— Americans caught up in the paralysis of the Great Depression. Since Franklin himself remained crippled, she became his eyes and ears, informing him of what the American people were really thinking and feeling.

Eleanor also was the president's conscience, personally urging on him some of the most **compassionate,** forward-looking laws of his presidency, including, for example, the National Youth Administration (NYA), which provided money to allow **impoverished** young people to stay in school.

260 She lectured widely, wrote a regularly syndicated[7] newspaper column, "My Day," and spoke frequently on the radio. She fought for equal pay for women in industry. Like no other First Lady up to that time, she became a link between the president and the American public.

Above all she fought against racial and religious prejudice. When Eleanor learned that the DAR (Daughters of the American Revolution) would not allow the great black singer Marian Anderson to perform in their auditorium in Washington, D.C., she resigned from the organization. Then she arranged to have Miss Anderson sing in front of the Lincoln Memorial.

Similarly, when she entered a hall where, as often happened in those days, blacks and whites were seated in separate sections, she made it 270 a point to sit with the blacks. Her example marked an important step in making the rights of blacks a matter of national priority.

On December 7, 1941, Japanese forces launched a surprise attack on the American naval base at Pearl Harbor, Hawaii, as well as on other American installations in the Pacific. The United States entered World War II, fighting not only against Japan but against the brutal dictators who then controlled Germany and Italy.

Eleanor helped the Red Cross raise money. She gave blood, sold war bonds. But she also did the unexpected. In 1943, for example, she visited barracks and hospitals on islands throughout the South Pacific. When 280 she visited a hospital, she stopped at every bed. To each soldier she said something special, something that a mother might say. Often, after she left, even battle-hardened men had tears in their eyes. Admiral Nimitz,

migrant (mī′grənt) *adj.* moving from place to place

compassionate (kəm-păsh′ə-nĭt) *adj.* wanting to help those who suffer

impoverished (ĭm-pŏv′ər-ĭsht) *adj.* very poor **impoverish** *v.*

SOCIAL STUDIES CONNECTION

At the Lincoln Memorial, Marian Anderson performed in front of 75,000 people. Later, in 1943, Anderson performed at Constitution Hall, where she had been denied the opportunity to sing.

---

7. **syndicated** (sĭn′dĭ-kāt′ĭd): sold to many newspapers for publication.

who originally thought such visits would be a nuisance, became one of her strongest admirers. Nobody else, he said, had done so much to help raise the spirits of the men. **❶**

By spring 1945 the end of the war in Europe seemed near. Then, on April 12, a phone call brought Eleanor the news that Franklin Roosevelt, who had gone to Warm Springs, Georgia, for a rest, was dead.

As Eleanor later declared, "I think that sometimes I acted as his
290 conscience. I urged him to take the harder path when he would have preferred the easier way. In that sense, I acted on occasion as a spur, even though the spurring was not always wanted or welcome.

"Of course," said Eleanor, "I loved him, and I miss him."

After Franklin's funeral, every day that Eleanor was home at Hyde Park, without fail, she placed flowers on his grave. Then she would stand very still beside him there.

With Franklin dead, Eleanor Roosevelt might have dropped out of the public eye, might have been remembered in the history books only as a footnote to the president's program of social reforms. Instead she
300 found new strengths within herself, new ways to live a useful, interesting life—and to help others. Now, moreover, her successes were her own, not the result of being the president's wife. **❶**

I n December 1945 President Harry S. Truman invited her to be one of the American delegates going to London to begin the work of the United Nations. Eleanor hesitated, but the president insisted. He said that the nation needed her; it was her duty. After that, Eleanor agreed.

In the beginning some of her fellow delegates from the United States considered her unqualified for the position, but after seeing her in action, they changed their minds.
310 It was Eleanor Roosevelt who, almost single-handedly, pushed through the United Nations General Assembly a resolution giving refugees from World War II the right *not* to return to their native lands if they did not wish to. The Russians angrily objected, but Eleanor's reasoning convinced **wavering** delegates. In a passionate speech defending the rights of the refugees she declared, "We [must] consider first the rights of man and what makes men more free—not governments, but man!"

Next Mrs. Roosevelt helped draft the United Nations Declaration of Human Rights. The Soviets wanted the declaration to list the duties people owed to their countries. Again Eleanor insisted that the United
320 Nations should stand for individual freedom—the rights of people to free speech, freedom of religion, and such human needs as health care and education. In December 1948, with the Soviet Union and its allies refusing to vote, the Declaration of Human Rights won approval of the UN General Assembly by a vote of forty-eight to zero.

❶ BIOGRAPHY
What does Admiral Nimitz's change in attitude suggest about the quality of the First Lady's work?

❶ BIOGRAPHY
Reread lines 297–302. What words and phrases does Jacobs use that give important details about Eleanor?

wavering (wā′vər-ĭng) *adj.* hesitating between two choices **waver** *v.*

As a delegate to the United Nations, Eleanor Roosevelt defended people's rights and freedoms.

Even after retiring from her post at the UN, Mrs. Roosevelt continued to travel. In places around the world she dined with presidents and kings. But she also visited tenement slums[8] in Bombay, India; factories in Yugoslavia; farms in Lebanon and Israel. **K**

Everywhere she met people who were eager to greet her. Although 330 as a child she had been brought up to be formal and distant, she had grown to feel at ease with people. They wanted to touch her, to hug her, to kiss her.

Eleanor's doctor had been telling her to slow down, but that was hard for her. She continued to write her newspaper column, "My Day," and to appear on television. She still began working at seven-thirty in the morning and often continued until well past midnight. Not only did she write and speak, she taught retarded children and raised money for health care of the poor.

As author Clare Boothe Luce put it, "Mrs. Roosevelt has done more good deeds on a bigger scale for a longer time than any woman who 340 ever appeared on our public scene. No woman has ever so comforted the distressed or so distressed the comfortable."

Gradually, however, she was forced to withdraw from some of her activities, to spend more time at home.

On November 7, 1962, at the age of seventy-eight, Eleanor died in her sleep. She was buried in the rose garden at Hyde Park, alongside her husband.

Adlai Stevenson, the American ambassador to the United Nations, remembered her as "the First Lady of the World," as the person—male or female—most effective in working for the cause of human rights. As Stevenson 350 declared, "She would rather light a candle than curse the darkness." **L**

And perhaps, in sum, that is what the struggle for human rights is all about. ❧

K CHRONOLOGICAL ORDER
Reread lines 303–328. Note the accomplishments that Mrs. Roosevelt achieved after her husband's death. What words and phrases help you figure out the order of the events?

L BIOGRAPHY
Reread lines 338–350. Why might Jacobs quote two famous people and their thoughts about Mrs. Roosevelt in these last paragraphs?

---

8. **tenement** (tĕn′ə-mənt) **slums:** parts of a city where poor people live in crowded, shabby buildings.

Comprehension

1. **Recall** Tell how Eleanor felt about herself as a young girl.

2. **Summarize** What are some examples of ways Mrs. Roosevelt helped society?

3. **Clarify** How did Mrs. Roosevelt act as her husband's "eyes and ears" when he was president?

COMMON CORE

RI 1 Cite textual evidence to support analysis of what the text says explicitly. **RI 3** Analyze the interactions between individuals, events, and ideas in a text. **RI 5** Analyze the structure an author uses to organize a text.

Text Analysis

4. **Examine Chronological Order** Review the timeline you made. What period do you think contains the most important events in Eleanor Roosevelt's life?

5. **Make Inferences** Reread the quotation by Clare Boothe Luce in lines 338–341. Who were the "comfortable" people, and how did Mrs. Roosevelt "distress" them?

6. **Analyze Cause and Effect** How do you think Eleanor's childhood affected the choices she made later in life? Create a chart to show the effects of these experiences, or causes. Some causes will have more than one effect.

Cause	Effect	Effect
Eleanor's father told her to help people who were suffering.	She worked with poor children.	
Eleanor was teased and made fun of.		

7. **Make Judgments** Adlai Stevenson referred to Mrs. Roosevelt as the "First Lady of the World." Do you agree with this statement? Explain.

8. **Evaluate Biography** Review the bulleted list at the top of page 785. In your opinion, did Jacobs achieve his purpose as a biographer? Provide examples from the text that support your opinion.

Extension and Challenge

9. **SOCIAL STUDIES CONNECTION** In addition to arranging for Marian Anderson to sing at the Lincoln Memorial, Mrs. Roosevelt supported civil rights in other ways. Research to find two more examples of how the First Lady promoted women's rights or racial equality.

What is your DUTY to others?

On page 794, Jacobs writes that Eleanor Roosevelt was taught "to do the thing that has to be done, the way it has to be done, when it has to be done." Think about how this view had an impact on her life. Then reread the journal entry you wrote for page 784. Compare your generation's attitude toward duty to Eleanor Roosevelt's attitude.

Vocabulary in Context

▲ **VOCABULARY PRACTICE**

Note the letter of the item you might associate with each boldfaced word.

1. **prominent:** (a) an unexplored cave, (b) a well-known lawyer, (c) a narrow valley
2. **brooding:** (a) an unhappy person, (b) a late-model car, (c) a small garden
3. **migrant:** (a) a successful business, (b) a bad headache, (c) a traveling worker
4. **grave:** (a) a loud party, (b) a serious illness, (c) a reunion between two brothers
5. **impoverished:** (a) a brick sidewalk, (b) a large grocery store, (c) a poor family
6. **wavering:** (a) a nosy neighbor, (b) a tough decision, (c) the beginning of winter
7. **dominate:** (a) a poorly planned event, (b) an undefeated team, (c) a serious drought
8. **compassionate:** (a) two children playing, (b) an angry crowd, (c) a kind nurse

ACADEMIC VOCABULARY IN WRITING

- demonstrate   - goal   - impact   - link   - undertake

In a paragraph, **link** Eleanor Roosevelt's childhood traits to those she displayed as an adult. Try to use one or more of the Academic Vocabulary words in your paragraph.

VOCABULARY STRATEGY: WORDS WITH ANGLO-SAXON ROOTS

Many word parts we use today come from the Anglo-Saxon language, an early form of English called Old English. For example, the word *forecast* is made up of the Anglo-Saxon word *fore-*, which means "in front, before, ahead of time," and *cast,* which means "to throw or calculate." To understand the meaning of words with *cast,* you can often use context clues and your knowledge of the root's meaning.

◌ **COMMON CORE**

L 4b Use common grade-appropriate roots as clues to the meaning of a word.

PRACTICE Choose a word from the web that best completes each sentence. Use context clues or, if necessary, a dictionary.

1. After losing the big game, the _____ team left the field.
2. The reality-show contestant felt like a _____ when she was eliminated from the competition.
3. Because of the weather _____, we looked forward to a snow day.
4. On the deserted island, the _____ had no contact with anyone.
5. In order to hear the concert, you must download the _____ .

Interactive **THINK** Vocabulary central

Go to **thinkcentral.com.**
KEYWORD: HML7-799

A First Lady Speaks Out

- Letter, page 801
- Autobiography, page 802

Use with "Eleanor Roosevelt," page 786.

COMMON CORE

RI 1 Cite evidence to support inferences drawn from the text.
RI 2 Determine two or more central ideas in a text.
RI 3 Analyze the interactions between individuals, events, and ideas in a text.

What's the Connection?

In "Eleanor Roosevelt," you read William Jay Jacobs's description of Eleanor's life growing up and then as the wife of the president. Now you will have the chance to hear from Mrs. Roosevelt herself as you read a letter she wrote to the Daughters of the American Revolution (DAR) and part of her autobiography.

Standards Focus: Synthesize

Have you ever formed an idea about someone from what one person told you? If so, perhaps your opinion changed once you met him or her for yourself.

When you put together information from more than one source, you **synthesize.** As a result, you gain a better understanding of a subject.

After you read the following letter and autobiography excerpt, you will synthesize the information about Eleanor Roosevelt. Take a moment to think about the impression of the First Lady you formed from Jacobs's biography. Then, as you learn more about her from the following selections, notice whether your idea of Mrs. Roosevelt changes. Doing the following can help:

- Summarize what you learned about Mrs. Roosevelt from reading the biography of her.

- Jot down any additional information you gather about her as you read her letter and autobiography. Feel free to note your own impressions or opinions of her as well.

Record your notes in a chart like the one shown.

Source	Strengths, Weaknesses, Accomplishments, and Other Information
"Eleanor Roosevelt"	She was a sad and lonely child. She devoted her life to helping others.
Letter to the DAR	
Autobiography	

Letter to the President General of the Daughters of the American Revolution

Eleanor Roosevelt

Eleanor Roosevelt wrote this letter after the Daughters of the American Revolution barred Marian Anderson's performance at Constitution Hall in Washington, D.C. Mrs. Roosevelt further protested their actions by organizing a performance for Marian Anderson in front of 75,000 people at the Lincoln Memorial.

THE WHITE HOUSE
WASHINGTON

February 28, 1939

My dear Mrs. Henry M. Robert Jr.:

I am afraid that I have never been a very useful member of the Daughters of the American Revolution, so I know it will make very little difference to you whether I resign, or whether I continue to be a member of your organization.

However, I am in complete disagreement with the attitude taken in refusing Constitution Hall to a great artist. You have set an example which seems to me unfortunate, and I feel obliged to send in to you my resignation. You had an opportunity to lead in an enlightened way and it seems to me that your organization has failed. [A]

I realize that many people will not agree with me, but feeling as I do this seems to me the only proper procedure to follow. [B]

Very sincerely yours,

Eleanor Roosevelt

FOCUS ON FORM
A **letter** is a handwritten or printed text addressed to a particular person or organization and usually sent by mail. Letters from historical figures help you better understand their private thoughts, feelings, opinions, and daily concerns.

[A] SYNTHESIZE
What event prompted Mrs. Roosevelt to write this letter? In your chart, note what you learn about her from her response to this event.

[B] LETTER
From Mrs. Roosevelt's closing remark, what do you learn about her personality? Add this to your chart.

~ F R O M ~
# THE AUTOBIOGRAPHY OF ELEANOR ROOSEVELT

by Eleanor Roosevelt

In the beginning, because I felt, as only a young girl can feel it, all the pain of being an ugly duckling, I was not only timid, I was afraid. Afraid of almost everything, I think: of mice, of the dark, of imaginary dangers, of my own inadequacy. My chief objective, as a girl, was to do my duty. This had been drilled into me as far back as I could remember. Not my duty as I saw it, but my duty as laid down for me by other people. It never occurred to me to revolt. Anyhow, my one overwhelming need in those days was to be approved, to be loved, and I did whatever was required of me, hoping it would bring me nearer to the approval and
10 love I so much wanted. **C**

As a young woman, my sense of duty remained as strict and rigid as it had been when I was a girl, but it had changed its focus. My husband and my children became the center of my life, and their needs were my new duty. I am afraid now that I approached this new obligation much as I had my childhood duties. I was still timid, still afraid of doing something wrong, of making mistakes, of not living up to the standards required by my mother-in-law, of failing to do what was expected of me.

As a result, I was so hidebound by duty that I became too critical, too much of a disciplinarian. I was so concerned with bringing up my
20 children properly that I was not wise enough just to love them. Now, looking back, I think I would rather spoil a child a little and have more fun out of it. **D**

C SYNTHESIZE
In "Eleanor Roosevelt," you learned that Eleanor was a lonely child. In your chart, write down additional information about her childhood that you learn from her autobiography.

D SYNTHESIZE
What new information and insights does Mrs. Roosevelt share about her adulthood? Add these to your chart.

Comprehension

1. **Recall** Why does Mrs. Roosevelt write to Mrs. Henry M. Robert Jr.?

2. **Recall** As a child, why was Eleanor so concerned with doing her duty?

Text Analysis

3. **Identify Primary Sources** A primary source on Mrs. Roosevelt could be anything she wrote that provides information about her. It could also be a photograph of her or something written about her by someone who knew her. Are the autobiography and letter you just read primary sources on Eleanor Roosevelt? Explain why or why not.

4. **Draw Conclusions from a Letter** What do you learn about Mrs. Roosevelt's character from her letter to Mrs. Henry M. Robert Jr.? Use evidence from the letter to support your answer.

5. **Synthesize** Review the notes in your chart. How did Eleanor's attitude toward duty change over the course of her life? Support your answer.

COMMON CORE

RI 1 Cite evidence to support inferences drawn from the text.
RI 2 Determine two or more central ideas in a text.
RI 3 Analyze the interactions between individuals, events, and ideas in a text. **W 2** Write informative/explanatory texts to examine a topic and convey ideas.

Read for Information: Draw Conclusions

> **WRITING PROMPT**
>
> In a paragraph, state and support a conclusion about one of these topics:
> • the way Eleanor Roosevelt changed over time
> • the kind of person Eleanor Roosevelt was
> • what motivates people to do great things

As you may recall, a **conclusion** is a judgment or belief about something. Following the numbered steps can help you reach and support a conclusion about one of the three topics given above.

1. Review your notes about Mrs. Roosevelt. What do they lead you to conclude? Jot down a conclusion for each topic. Then pick one you think you can best support.

2. Reread the three selections to find details that support your conclusion. If you can't find much support, consider revising your conclusion or picking a different one.

3. Once you have a conclusion you can support well, state it in a topic sentence. Then present the reasons and evidence that support this conclusion.

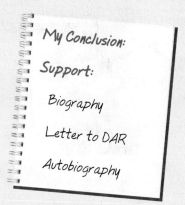

My Conclusion:

Support:

Biography

Letter to DAR

Autobiography

Names/Nombres

Personal Essay by Julia Alvarez

VIDEO TRAILER **THINK** central KEYWORD: HML7-804

What does your NAME really mean?

Parents may choose a name for their child because its original meaning is important to them. They might name a new baby after a relative or a famous person. Sometimes parents select a name just because they like the way it sounds. But when it comes to nicknames, adults don't always have control. In "Names/Nombres," author Julia Alvarez writes about how her many nicknames affected her.

WEB IT Create an idea web with your name in the middle. Write down all the names and nicknames you have had throughout your life. Who uses each name and what does that name mean to you?

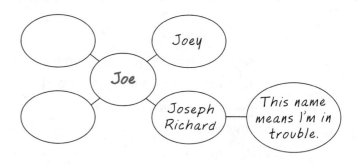

Betsy Malone
"Hollywood"
Drama Club, Choir,
Pep Club

Sam Mathews
"Sam the Man"
Soccer Captain,
Dance Committee,
Newspaper Staff

Anna Carter
"Brain"
Valedictorian, Student
Council, Chess Club,
Debate Team

TEXT ANALYSIS: PERSONAL ESSAY

A **personal essay** is a form of nonfiction whose purpose is to express the writer's thoughts and feelings about one subject. The time and place in which a writer lives can influence a the **writer's message,** or main point. To understand the message, pay close attention to the characteristics of a personal essay, which include the writer's

- use of **anecdotes,** or short accounts of events
- choice of words that give the essay an informal, personal style
- descriptions of thoughts and feelings

As you read "Names/Nombres," pay attention to the anecdotes, thoughts, and feelings Alvarez shares about her name.

READING STRATEGY: CONNECT

Think about the many conversations you have had with your friends. You probably find it easy to relate to what they say. Similarly, you can **connect** with what you read by comparing the events described to your own experiences. Connecting can help you better understand other people's writing and your own world.

As you read "Names/Nombres," keep a log to record any connections that you have with the essay.

Julia	Me
Her parents call her "Hoo-lee-tah."	My family calls me "Little Joe."

VOCABULARY IN CONTEXT

The boldfaced words help Julia Alvarez convey her feelings and experiences. Use context clues to figure out what each word means.

1. She noted **ironically** that rain made her think of her former home.
2. Leaving one home for another was exciting but **chaotic.**
3. His **convoluted** answers to my simple questions were frustrating.
4. We wanted to **specify** our choices on the questionnaire.
5. The students wanted to **merge** into their new culture.

 Complete the activities in your **Reader/Writer Notebook.**

Meet the Author

Julia Alvarez
born 1950

A Tale of Two Countries
Although Julia Alvarez was born in New York City, she lived in the Dominican Republic until she was ten. When the family returned to New York in 1960 to escape the Dominican dictatorship, Alvarez felt out of place—a foreigner with a different language, name, and way of life.

A World of Words
Alvarez's first years back in New York were tough, but she soon found a way to cope. She started to write stories and poetry. "I could save what I didn't want to lose—memories and smells and sounds, things too precious to put anywhere else," she explained. Alvarez's writings continue to draw on her early memories and immigrant experiences.

BACKGROUND TO THE ESSAY
A Troubled History
The Dominican Republic is a nation that covers about two-thirds of the island of Hispaniola in the Caribbean Sea. A dictator, General Rafael Trujillo, ruled the nation from 1930 to 1961. Many Dominicans came to the United States—especially New York City—during this violent, unsettling period in Dominican history.

NAMES/
NOMBRES

Julia Alvarez

When we arrived in New York City, our names changed almost immediately. At Immigration, the officer asked my father, *Mister Elbures,* if he had anything to declare.[1] My father shook his head no, and we were waved through. I was too afraid we wouldn't be let in if I corrected the man's pronunciation, but I said our name to myself, opening my mouth wide for the organ blast of the *a,* trilling my tongue[2] for the drumroll of the *r, All-vah-rrr-es!* How could anyone get *Elbures* out of that orchestra of sound? Ⓐ

At the hotel my mother was *Missus Alburest,* and I was *little girl,* 10 as in, "Hey, little girl, stop riding the elevator up and down. It's *not* a toy."

When we moved into our new apartment building, the super[3] called my father *Mister Alberase,* and the neighbors who became mother's friends pronounced her name *Jew-lee-ah* instead of *Hoo-lee-ah.* I, her namesake, was known as *Hoo-lee-tah* at home. But at school I was *Judy* or *Judith,* and once an English teacher mistook me for *Juliet.*

---

1. **At Immigration . . . declare:** Immigration is the place where government officials check the documents of people entering a country. People must acknowledge, or declare, certain goods or moneys that they are carrying.

2. **trilling my tongue:** rapidly vibrating the tongue against the roof of the mouth, as in pronouncing a Spanish *r.*

3. **super:** superintendent, or building manager.

Analyze Visuals ▶

What **mood** do the colors, images, and brushstrokes create in this painting?

Ⓐ **PERSONAL ESSAY**
Reread lines 1–8. Consider Alvarez's choice of words and her thoughts at Immigration. Do you think Julia is proud of her last name?

West 17th Street, New York City
(20th century), Patti Mollica.
© Patti Mollica/SuperStock.

It took a while to get used to my new names. I wondered if I shouldn't correct my teachers and new friends. But my mother argued that it didn't matter. "You know what your friend Shakespeare said, 'A rose by any other name would smell as sweet.'"[4] My family had gotten into the habit of
20 calling any literary figure "my friend" because I had begun to write poems and stories in English class.

By the time I was in high school, I was a popular kid, and it showed in my name. Friends called me *Jules* or *Hey Jude*,[5] and once a group of troublemaking friends my mother forbade me to hang out with called me *Alcatraz*.[6] I was *Hoo-lee-tah* only to Mami and Papi and uncles and aunts who came over to eat *sancocho*[7] on Sunday afternoons—old world folk whom I would just as soon go back to where they came from and leave me to pursue whatever mischief I wanted to in America. JUDY ALCATRAZ: the name on the wanted poster would read. Who would ever trace her to me? **B**

30 My older sister had the hardest time getting an American name for herself because *Mauricia* did not translate into English. **Ironically,** although she had the most foreign-sounding name, she and I were the Americans in the family. We had been born in New York City when our parents had first tried immigration and then gone back "home," too homesick to stay. My mother often told the story of how she had almost changed my sister's name in the hospital.

After the delivery, Mami and some other new mothers were cooing over their new baby sons and daughters and exchanging names and weights and delivery stories. My mother was embarrassed among the Sallys and
40 Janes and Georges and Johns to reveal the rich, noisy name of *Mauricia*, so when her turn came to brag, she gave her baby's name as *Maureen*.

"Why'd ya give her an Irish name with so many pretty Spanish names to choose from?" one of the women asked her.

My mother blushed and admitted her baby's real name to the group. Her mother-in-law had recently died, she apologized, and her husband had insisted that the first daughter be named after his mother, *Mauran*. My mother thought it the ugliest name she had ever heard, and she talked my father into what she believed was an improvement, a combination of *Mauran* and her own mother's name, *Felicia*. ◆
50 "Her name is Mao-ree-shee-ah," my mother said to the group.

"Why, that's a beautiful name," the new mothers cried. "*Moor-ee-sha, Moor-ee-sha*," they cooed into the pink blanket. *Moor-ee-sha* it was when

---

4. **'A rose . . . smell as sweet':** In Shakespeare's *Romeo and Juliet*, the main characters' families are enemies. But when Romeo and Juliet fall in love, Juliet uses almost these words to say that Romeo is precious to her no matter what his family name is.

5. *Hey Jude:* the title of a hit song by the Beatles in 1968.

6. *Alcatraz* (ăl′kə-trăz′): the name of an island in San Francisco Bay that was once the site of a prison.

7. *sancocho* (säng-kô′chô) *Spanish*: a traditional Caribbean stew of meat and vegetables.

COMMON CORE L 5a

Language Coach

Allusion An **allusion** is a reference to a well-known person, song, place, event, or literary work. Writers often use allusions to characterize situations or to highlight important ideas. Why might Alvarez's mother have made an allusion to a line from Shakespeare?

B CONNECT
You might have listed a nickname for the activity on page 804. Compare how this nickname makes you feel with how Julia's nicknames make her feel.

ironically (ī-rŏn′ĭk-lē) *adv.* in a way that is contrary to what is expected or intended

◆ **GRAMMAR IN CONTEXT**
In lines 47–49, notice the correct capitalization of common and proper nouns.

we returned to the States eleven years later. Sometimes, American tongues found even that mispronunciation tough to say and called her *Maria* or *Marsha* or *Maudy* from her nickname *Maury*. I pitied her. What an awful name to have to transport across borders! **C**

My little sister, Ana, had the easiest time of all. She was plain *Anne*—that is, only her name was plain, for she turned out to be the pale, blond "American beauty" in the family. The only Hispanic-seeming thing about
60 her was the affectionate nicknames her boyfriends sometimes gave her. *Anita,* or as one goofy guy used to sing to her to the tune of the banana advertisement, *Anita Banana.*

Later, during her college years in the late 60's, there was a push to pronounce Third World[8] names correctly. I remember calling her long distance at her group house and a roommate answering.

"Can I speak to Ana?" I asked, pronouncing her name the American way.

"Ana?" The man's voice hesitated. "Oh! You must mean *Ah-nah!*"

Our first few years in the States, though, ethnicity was not yet "in." Those were the blond, blue-eyed, bobby-sock years of junior high
70 and high school before the 60's ushered in peasant blouses, hoop earrings, *sarapes.*[9] My initial desire to be known by my correct Dominican name faded. I just wanted to be Judy and **merge** with the Sallys and Janes in my class. But, inevitably, my accent and coloring gave me away. "So where are you from, Judy?"

"New York," I told my classmates. After all, I had been born blocks away at Columbia Presbyterian Hospital.

"I mean, *originally.*"

"From the Caribbean," I answered vaguely, for if I **specified,** no one was quite sure what continent our island was located on.
80 "Really? I've been to Bermuda. We went last April for spring vacation. I got the worst sunburn! So, are you from Portoriko?"

"No," I shook my head. "From the Dominican Republic."

"Where's that?"

"South of Bermuda."

They were just being curious, I knew, but I burned with shame whenever they singled me out as a "foreigner," a rare, exotic friend.

"Say your name in Spanish, oh, please say it!" I had made mouths drop one day by rattling off my full name, which, according to Dominican custom, included my middle names, Mother's and Father's surnames[10]
90 for four generations back.

---

8. **Third World:** from the developing nations of Latin America, Africa, and Asia.

9. *sarapes* (sə-rä′pāz) *Spanish:* long, blanketlike shawls.

10. **surnames:** last names.

COMMON CORE RI 3

C **PERSONAL ESSAY**
In a **personal essay,** the writer expresses thoughts and feelings about a subject. Such thoughts are often influenced by a certain place and time period that have left their mark on a writer's memory. One characteristic of a personal essay is the use of the **anecdote,** a short account of events. By including the anecdote about her sister, what does Alvarez reveal about the effect of 1950s American attitudes on her family?

merge (mûrj) *v.* to blend together

specify (spĕs′ə-fī′) *v.* to make known or identify

SOCIAL STUDIES CONNECTION

The Dominican Republic

"Julia Altagracia María Teresa Álvarez Tavares Perello Espaillat Julia Pérez Rochet González." I pronounced it slowly, a name as **chaotic** with sounds as a Middle Eastern bazaar or market day in a South American village.

I suffered most whenever my extended family attended school occasions. For my graduation, they all came, the whole noisy, foreign-looking lot of fat aunts in their dark mourning dresses and hair nets, uncles with full, droopy mustaches and baby-blue or salmon-colored suits and white pointy shoes and fedora hats, the many little cousins who snuck in without tickets. They sat in the first row in order to better understand
100 the Americans' fast-spoken English. But how could they listen when they were constantly speaking among themselves in florid-sounding phrases, rococo consonants, rich, rhyming vowels? Their loud voices carried.

Introducing them to my friends was a further trial to me. These relatives had such complicated names and there were so many of them, and their relationships to myself were so **convoluted.** There was my Tía Josefina, who was not really an aunt but a much older cousin. And her daughter, Aída Margarita, who was adopted, *una hija de crianza.*[11] My uncle of affection, Tío José, brought my *madrina* Tía Amelia and her *comadre* Tía Pilar.[12] My friends rarely had more than their nuclear family[13] to introduce,
110 youthful, glamorous-looking couples ("Mom and Dad") who skied and played tennis and took their kids for spring vacations to Bermuda. **D**

After the commencement ceremony, my family waited outside in the parking lot while my friends and I signed yearbooks with nicknames which recalled our high school good times: "Beans" and "Pepperoni" and "Alcatraz." We hugged and cried and promised to keep in touch.

Sometimes if our goodbyes went on too long, I heard my father's voice calling out across the parking lot. "*Hoo-lee-tah! Vámonos!*"[14] **E**

Back home, my *tíos* and *tías* and *primas*, Mami and Papi, and *mis hermanas* had a party for me with *sancocho* and a store-bought *pudín,*
120 inscribed with *Happy Graduation, Julie.*[15] There were many gifts—that was a plus to a large family! I got several wallets and a suitcase with my initials and a graduation charm from my godmother and money from my uncles. The biggest gift was a portable typewriter from my parents for writing my stories and poems.

Someday, the family predicted, my name would be well-known throughout the United States. I laughed to myself, wondering which one I would go by. ❧

chaotic (kā-ŏt′ĭk) *adj.* confused; disordered

convoluted (kŏn′və-lōō′tĭd) *adj.* difficult to understand; complicated

D CONNECT
Think about how Julia feels when she introduces her family to her friends. What situation have you experienced or read about that can help you understand her feelings?

E PERSONAL ESSAY
Reread lines 112–117. Do you think Julia likes her nickname by the time she graduates from high school? Tell what clues helped you answer this question.

---

11. *una hija de crianza* (ōō′nä ē′hä dě krē-än′sä) *Spanish:* a child raised as if one's own.

12. **My uncle of affection . . . Tía Pilar:** My favorite uncle, Uncle José, brought my godmother Aunt Amelia and her close friend Aunt Pilar.

13. **nuclear family:** a family unit consisting of a mother, a father, and their children.

14. *Vámonos* (bä′mä-nôs) *Spanish:* Let's go.

15. **Back home . . . Julie:** Back home, my uncles and aunts and cousins, Mami and Papi, and my sisters had a party for me with a stew and a store-bought pudding, inscribed with *Happy Graduation, Julie.*

Comprehension

1. **Clarify** Why does Julia say it is a "trial" to introduce her family?

2. **Summarize** Explain what happens in the hospital when Mauricia is born.

3. **Represent** Review "Names/Nombres" to find all of Julia's names and nicknames. Arrange her names into three categories: (1) those used by her family and friends, (2) those used by strangers, and (3) those used by both.

Text Analysis

● 4. **Examine Connections** Review the notes you made in your log while reading. What can you learn from Alvarez about your own experiences?

5. **Make Inferences** Reread lines 1–15. Why do you think Alvarez chooses to refer to the mispronunciation of her and her family's names as a changing of their names?

● 6. **Interpret a Personal Essay** Make a graphic like the one shown. Under each characteristic of a personal essay, note clues that reveal Alvarez's **theme** or message about names and identities. What is the writer's theme in "Names/Nombres"? Use the clues to explain your reasoning.

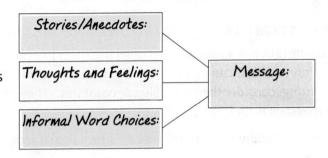

Extension and Challenge

7. **Creative Project: Drama** With a partner, role-play a conversation between Eleanor Roosevelt and Julia Alvarez about their experiences with nicknames. Start by reviewing "Eleanor Roosevelt" and "Names/Nombres" to find the nicknames each woman had. Then have them discuss what they think of their nicknames, how their names influenced them, and what advice they have about nicknames.

8. 🌐 **SOCIAL STUDIES CONNECTION** Julia Alvarez divided her childhood between the United States and the Dominican Republic. Write three questions about the Dominican Republic and research to find the answers. Share the information with the class.

What does your NAME really mean?

Review the nicknames you listed for page 804. What do you think about the nicknames now, in the light of the writer's message?

COMMON CORE

RI 2 Determine two or more central ideas in a text and analyze their development over the course of the text. RI 3 Analyze the interactions between individuals, events, and ideas in a text.

Vocabulary in Context

▲ **VOCABULARY PRACTICE**

Decide whether the words in each pair are synonyms (words that have the same meaning) or antonyms (words that have opposite meanings).

1. chaotic/ orderly
2. ironically/predictably
3. specify/identify
4. merge/join
5. convoluted/simple

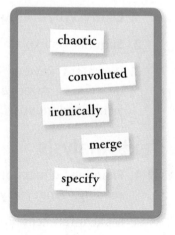

ACADEMIC VOCABULARY IN WRITING

> • demonstrate   • goal   • impact   • link   • undertake

Julia Alvarez's American friends influenced her thoughts and feelings. What **impact** might she have had on them? Write a brief response to this question, using one or more of the Academic Vocabulary words.

VOCABULARY STRATEGY: CONNOTATIONS AND MEANING

A word's **connotation** is a combination of all the feelings and images the word suggests. Connotations can be positive, negative, or neutral. When choosing words in writing, consider their possible connotations. They can affect the way your message is understood.

COMMON CORE

L 5c Distinguish among the connotations of words with similar denotations.

- **Positive connotation:** What a *striking* costume. (an attractive, eye-catching costume)
- **Neutral connotation:** What a *presentable* costume.
- **Negative connotation:** What a *garish* costume. (an overdone, unattractive costume)

PRACTICE For each of the following words, tell whether the connotation is positive or negative. Then write a sentence using the word correctly. You may need to use a dictionary.

1. cottage
2. cheap
3. mysterious
4. sincere
5. reckless
6. peculiar
7. funny
8. casual
9. modern
10. strong-willed

Language

◆ **GRAMMAR IN CONTEXT:** Capitalize Correctly

Review the **Grammar in Context** note on page 808. A **common noun** is a general name for a person, a place, a thing, or an idea *(sister, country, park)* and is usually not capitalized. A **proper noun** is the name of a particular person, place, thing, or idea *(Kathy, Spain, Central Park)* and is always capitalized. Words that indicate family relationships are only capitalized when they are used as names or before names.

Original: When Julia first arrived in new york, she was known by many different names.

Revised: When Julia first arrived in New York, she was known by many different names. *(New York* is a proper noun.)

PRACTICE Correct the capitalization in each of the following sentences.

1. Julia was known as *Hoo-lee-tah* only to her parents and Aunts and Uncles.
2. Mauricia, Julia's Sister, also had many nicknames.
3. Julia knew she had to listen to mother's advice.
4. Julia probably wanted uncle José and aunt Amelia to call her Judy.

For more help with capitalization, see page R51 in the **Grammar Handbook.**

READING-WRITING CONNECTION

YOUR TURN   Now that you've read "Names/Nombres," explore the importance of names by responding to this prompt. Then use the **revising tip** to improve your writing.

WRITING PROMPT	REVISING TIP
Extended Constructed Response: Explanation Julia Alvarez has had many different names in her life, but she hasn't always felt the same way about them. Write a **two- or three-paragraph explanation** of how her attitude about having different names changes from the beginning to the end of the essay.	Review your explantion. If you missed capitalizing any proper nouns, be sure to correct them.

COMMON CORE

L 2 Demonstrate command of the conventions of standard English capitalization when writing. **W 2** Write informative/explanatory texts to examine a topic and convey ideas.

Interactive Revision   **THINK** central

Go to **thinkcentral.com.**
KEYWORD: HML7-813

from **It's Not About the Bike**

Autobiography by Lance Armstrong
with Sally Jenkins

from **23 Days in July**

Nonfiction Account by John Wilcockson

VIDEO TRAILER **THINK** central   KEYWORD: HML7-814

What is a WINNER?

COMMON CORE

RI 1 Cite textual evidence to support inferences drawn from the text. **RI 2** Determine two or more central ideas in a text. **RI 6** Determine an author's point of view or purpose in a text.

You might normally associate a winner with a contest, a game, or a sport. But can you also be a winner when you're not competing with other people? If so, how? In the selections you're about to read, you will find out how Lance Armstrong faced two very different challenges and came out a winner in both.

SKETCH IT Do you remember a time in your life when you felt like a winner? Maybe you won a spelling bee or achieved something that no one else ever had. Perhaps you faced a fear or a challenge. Create a sketch of the moment and include a title that describes what is happening. Share your sketch with the class.

● TEXT ANALYSIS: AUTHOR'S PURPOSE AND THEME

In literary works, the writer's goal is to convey a **theme,** or central idea about life or human nature. A reader examines the title, characters, language, and lessons learned. In an expository text, such as a magazine article, the **author's purpose** is to express thoughts or feelings, inform or explain, persuade, or entertain on a particular topic. To determine an author's purpose, you examine

• subject and tone • details and words • effect on the reader

As you read the excerpt from *It's Not About the Bike,* look for clues about the theme conveyed by Armstrong. As you read the excerpt from "23 Days in July," look for clues to help you determine the author's purpose.

● READING SKILL: MAKE INFERENCES

To understand what you read, it helps to **make inferences,** or make logical guesses based on new clues and what you already know. As you read, make equations to record your inferences about Lance Armstrong.

Clue + What I Know = Inference

▲ VOCABULARY IN CONTEXT

From the following words about Armstrong's victories, choose the word that best completes each sentence.

WORD	culminate	prestigious	stance
LIST	perception	recessed	terse

1. The athlete's comeback will _____ in a prized medal.
2. His _____, with his feet firmly planted, was one that showed determination.
3. She gave _____, one-word answers to some of his questions.
4. The winner received a _____ award befitting a hero.
5. Special features on the bicycle are _____ in order to aid the cyclist.
6. His nurse spoke with wisdom and _____.

Complete the activities in your **Reader/Writer Notebook.**

Lance Armstrong
born 1971

Against All Odds
Lance Armstrong was a rising star in the world of professional cycling when his life was turned upside down. In 1996, he was diagnosed with cancer and given less than a 50 percent chance of survival. He underwent difficult chemotherapy treatments that made him very ill and did not guarantee success. However, Armstrong returned to professional bicycling and won his first Tour de France in 1999. He went on to win again in 2000, 2001, 2002, 2003, and 2004. John Wilcockson captured the moments of the history-making sixth Tour de France win of 2004 in *23 Days in July.*

Then in 2005, Armstrong did the unbelievable once again—he won a seventh Tour de France. After his 2005 win, he announced that he would devote his time and energy to a different kind of challenge: cancer research.

BACKGROUND TO THE AUTOBIOGRAPHY
The Tour de France
The Tour de France is a 3-week bicycling race that covers about 2,500 miles in France and other European countries.

Author Online THINK central
Go to **thinkcentral.com.**
KEYWORD: HML7-815

815

It's **NOT** About the Bike

Lance Armstrong

After his cancer diagnosis, Lance Armstrong launched a relentless attack against his disease with the help of the doctors and nurses at Indiana University Medical Center in Indianapolis. The photo on the right shows Armstrong after chemotherapy treatment.

There are angels on this earth and they come in subtle forms, and I decided LaTrice Haney was one of them. Outwardly, she looked like just another efficient, clipboard-and-syringe-wielding[1] nurse in a starched outfit. She worked extremely long days and nights, and on her off hours she went home to her husband, Randy, a truck driver, and their two children, Taylor, aged seven, and Morgan, four. But if she was tired, she never seemed it. She struck me as a woman utterly lacking in ordinary resentments, sure of her responsibilities and blessings and unwavering in her administering of care, and if that wasn't angelic
10 behavior, I didn't know what was.

Often I'd be alone in the late afternoons and evenings except for LaTrice, and if I had the strength, we'd talk seriously. With most people I was shy and **terse,** but I found myself talking to LaTrice, maybe because she was so gentle-spoken and expressive herself. LaTrice was only in her late 20s, a pretty young woman with a coffee-and-cream complexion, but she had self-possession and **perception** beyond her years. While other people our age were out nightclubbing, she was already the head nurse for the oncology research unit.[2] I wondered why she did it. "My satisfaction is to make it a little easier for people," she said.

20 She asked me about cycling, and I found myself telling her about the bike with a sense of pleasure I hadn't realized I possessed. "How did you start riding?" she asked me. I told her about my first bikes, and the early sense of liberation, and that cycling was all I had done since I was 16. I talked about my various teammates over the years, about their humor and selflessness, and I talked about my mother, and what she had meant to me. **Ⓐ**

I told her what cycling had given me, the tours of Europe and the extraordinary education, and the wealth. I showed her a picture of

terse (tûrs) *adj.* speaking little; communicating in few words

perception (pər-sĕp′shən) *n.* insight; ability to understand people and situations

Ⓐ AUTHOR'S PURPOSE AND THEME
Reread lines 1–25 and take note of the title. Based on this information, what do you think might be the theme of this excerpt?

---

1. **syringe-wielding** (sə-rĭnj′ wēl′dĭng): holding and using an instrument for giving patients injections.
2. **oncology** (ŏn-kŏl′ə-jē) **research unit:** in a hospital or clinic, the division or section dedicated to the study of cancer.

my house, with pride, and invited her to come visit, and I showed her snapshots of my cycling career. She leafed through images of me racing
30 across the backdrops of France, Italy, and Spain, and she'd point to a picture and ask, "Where are you here?" **B**

I confided that I was worried about my sponsor, Cofidis,[3] and explained the difficulty I was having with them. I told her I felt pressured. "I need to stay in shape, I need to stay in shape," I said over and over again.

"Lance, listen to your body," she said gently. "I know your mind wants to run away. I know it's saying to you, 'Hey, let's go ride.' But listen to your body. Let it rest."

I described my bike, the elegant high performance of the ultralight tubing and aerodynamic wheels. I told her how much each piece cost, and
40 weighed, and what its purpose was. I explained how a bike could be broken down so I could practically carry it in my pocket, and that I knew every part and bit of it so intimately that I could adjust it in a matter of moments.

I explained that a bike has to fit your body, and that at times I felt melded to it. The lighter the frame, the more responsive it is, and my racing bike weighed just 18 pounds. Wheels exert centrifugal force[4] on the bike itself, I told her. The more centrifugal force, the more momentum. It was the essential building block of speed. "There are 32 spokes in a wheel," I said. Quick-release levers allow you to pop the wheel out and change it quickly, and my crew could fix a flat tire in less than 10 seconds.
50   "Don't you get tired of leaning over like that?" she asked.

Yes, I said, until my back ached like it was broken, but that was the price of speed. The handlebars are only as wide as the rider's shoulders, I explained, and they curve downward in half-moons so you can assume an aerodynamic **stance** on the bike.

"Why do you ride on those little seats?" she asked.

The seat is narrow, contoured to the anatomy, and the reason is that when you are on it for six hours at a time, you don't want anything to chafe your legs. Better a hard seat than the torture of saddle sores. Even the clothes have a purpose. They are flimsy for a reason: to mold
60 to the body because you have to wear them in weather that ranges from hot to hail. Basically, they're a second skin. The shorts have a chamois padded[5] seat, and the stitches are **recessed** to avoid rash. **C**

When I had nothing left to tell LaTrice about the bike, I told her about the wind. I described how it felt in my face and in my hair. I told her about being in the open air, with the views of soaring Alps, and the

---

stance (stăns) *n.* posture; position

recessed (rē'sĕst') *adj.* set-in or set back   **recess** *v.*

---

3. **Cofidis:** the sponsor of the French cycling team that Armstrong then rode for.

4. **centrifugal** (sĕn-trĭf′yə-gəl) **force:** the force that seems to cause a revolving object to move away from the point it revolves around.

5. **chamois** (shăm′ē) **padded:** padded with soft leather made from the skin of goats, sheep, or deer.

glimmer of valley lakes in the distance. Sometimes the wind blew as if it were my personal friend, sometimes as if it were my bitter enemy, sometimes as if it were the hand of God pushing me along. I described the full sail of a mountain descent, gliding on two wheels only an inch wide. **D**

70 "You're just out there, free," I said.

"You love it," she said.

"Yeah?" I said.

"Oh, I see it in your eyes," she said.

I understood that LaTrice was an angel one evening late in my last cycle of chemo.[6] I lay on my side, dozing on and off, watching the steady, clear drip-drip of the chemo as it slid into my veins. LaTrice sat with me, keeping me company, even though I was barely able to talk.

"What do you think, LaTrice?" I asked, whispering. "Am I going to pull through this?"

80 "Yeah," she said. "Yeah, you are."

"I hope you're right," I said, and closed my eyes again.

LaTrice leaned over to me.

"Lance," she said softly, "I hope someday to be just a figment of your imagination.[7] I'm not here to be in your life for the rest of your life. After you leave here, I hope I never see you ever again. When you're cured, hey, let me see you in the papers, on TV, but not back here. I hope to help you at the time you need me, and then I hope I'll be gone. You'll say, 'Who was that nurse back in Indiana? Did I dream her?'" **E**

It is one of the single loveliest things anyone has ever said to me.

90 And I will always remember every blessed word. ◌

D MAKE INFERENCES
Reread lines 63–69. What can you infer about why Lance rides his bike?

E AUTHOR'S PURPOSE AND THEME
Reread lines 83–88. What does this quote suggest about the theme?

6. **chemo** (kē'mō): short for *chemotherapy*.

7. **figment of your imagination:** something not real; a fantasized or made-up image.

Lance Armstrong and LaTrice Haney

23 DAYS IN JULY

JOHN WILCOCKSON

Although Armstrong went on to win a seventh Tour de France in 2005, the 2004 race was especially meaningful since no other cyclist had ever won a sixth Tour.

Paris is looking magnificent. Her golden domes and eagles and gilded gates are all glowing in the late-afternoon sunshine. The dark-green plane trees along the Champs-Élysées have been newly trimmed. Rainbows shimmer in the spray from the crystal fountains of the Place de la Concorde.[1] And across the Seine River, the thousand-foot-high Eiffel Tower stands starkly regal against an opaque blue sky.

Another Tour de France has just ended, this one **culminating** in a historical sixth consecutive victory for a long-jawed young man from the lone star state of Texas. He stands now on the top step of the podium, at the finish line on the Champs-Élysées. Dressed in a golden tunic, Lance Armstrong holds a yellow LiveStrong[2] cap over his heart as a full-blooded rendition of the "Star Spangled Banner" rings out, resounding proudly over the russet-brown cobblestones of these Elysian Fields. . . .[3]

At the foot of the yellow steps of the canopied, most **prestigious** viewing stand, Armstrong's coach Chris Carmichael reminds me: "I told you back in March, it wasn't even going to be close. You gotta know the intensity of this guy. Nobody has got his intensity. Nobody. It's just phenomenal." **F**

---

1. **Champs-Élysées** (shän-zā-lē-zā′) ... **Place de la Concorde** (pläs′ də lä kôn-kôrd′): a famous boulevard and a large plaza in Paris.
2. **LiveStrong:** livestrong.org is the official Web site for the Lance Armstrong Foundation.
3. **Elysian** (ĭ-lĭzh′ən) **Fields:** the English translation of *Champs-Élysées.* In Greek mythology, the Elysian Fields were where good people went after death.

Analyze Visuals ▶

Look back at the picture of Lance Armstrong on page 817. What comes to mind as you **contrast** the two pictures?

culminate
(kŭl′mə-nāt′) *v.* to reach the highest point or degree

prestigious (prĕ-stē′jəs) *adj.* having a high reputation

F AUTHOR'S PURPOSE AND THEME
Consider what Chris Carmichael says about Armstrong. What might be the writer's purpose in including the quote?

Armstrong said on the eve of this day, "Winning in '99 was a complete
20 shock and surprise for me. Not that I've gotten used to winning the Tour
de France, but I do know what it means and I know what it feels like to
ride into the Champs-Élysées. . . . This one is very, very special for me.
They're all special, but this one is something that in '99 I never believed
possible. I never thought I'd win a second one, or a third, or however
many. This one is incredibly special. I'm humbled by it. A lot of people
just one month ago thought it wouldn't be possible for me to do it. We
tried to stay calm, the team tried to stay calm . . . and we were confident
that we had a good chance." **G**

I think back to December, and remember something Armstrong told
30 me in Austin: "I'm doing three or four hours of exercise every day right
now. Yesterday I was in DC, so I got up early—I'd just come back from
Europe and had jetlag[4]—and I went down to the gym for an hour and
a half . . . yes, lifting weights. It was pouring with freezing rain outside,
so I went back to the room, and rode my bike for an hour on the rollers.
It's not easy to ride rollers. I hate that."

But he doesn't hate this: homage from a half-million people lining
the most glorious boulevard in the world. When he and his U.S. Postal
team are introduced by race announcer Daniel Mangeas, as the last team
to start their lap of honor around the Champs-Élysées, the modern
40 "anthem" of the British rock group Queen thumps into the balmy Paris air:

**G AUTHOR'S
PURPOSE AND
THEME**
Reread lines 19–28.
What effect is the writer
creating by including
this quote?

---

4. **jet lag:** tiredness and other effects that may be caused by a long flight through several time zones.

Armstrong, in yellow, takes a victory lap with his teammates along the Champs-Élysées in Paris.

"We are the champions, my friend. . . . We are the champions. We are the champions. We are the champions . . . of the world."

Girlfriends perch on boyfriends' shoulders to get a better view. Banners unfurl, one saying, "The eyes of Texas are upon you." Thousands of fans from all over the United States line the barriers, most dressed in yellow. Two guys from Texas in the crowd say, "We did it. And next year we'll come again!" . . .

50 Now they're playing another song over the loudspeakers. Its words float down the boulevard backed by the thumping guitar chords of the champion's gal: "All I want to *do* . . . is have some fun . . ." And Lance *is* having fun. The celebrations will continue all night, maybe for the rest of his life. A life that almost ended in 1996. Six Tour de France wins have come along since then, since his chemo nurse LaTrice gave him that silver cross.

"I really love this event," Armstrong says. "I think it's an epic sport. It's something I will sit around the TV and watch in ten years, and in twenty years." He will always be a fan of the Tour, but right now he's the champion. *Le patron.*[5]

It's after 7 p.m. and the crowds are starting to leave. One of the last to go is a friendly, middle-aged American. He rolls up his Texas flag, 60 grabs his wife's hand, and, before he walks down the stone steps into the Metro,[6] proclaims to the world, "He's the man!" ☙

MAKE INFERENCES
Why are the fans dressed in yellow?

---

5. *le patron* (lə pä-trôn) *French:* the boss.
6. **Metro:** the Paris subway.

Comprehension

1. **Recall** In the excerpt from *It's Not About the Bike*, why is Armstrong in the hospital?

2. **Clarify** Why does Armstrong call his head nurse, LaTrice, an "angel"?

3. **Clarify** Reread lines 22–25 in the excerpt from "23 Days in July." Armstrong says winning the 2004 Tour de France was "incredibly special" to him. Why was it so special?

Text Analysis

4. **Make Inferences** Review the inference equations that you made while reading. Which, if any, of your inferences have changed? Explain your reasons for either changing an inference or keeping an original inference.

5. **Compare and Contrast** The autobiography *It's Not About the Bike* shows the private side of Lance Armstrong. On the other hand, John Wilcockson's account portrays Armstrong in public. Use a Y chart like the one shown to compare and contrast the private and public man.

Private
He describes himself as shy.

Public

Similarities

6. **Examine Author's Purpose and Theme** Explain the difference between the theme of *It's Not About the Bike* and the author's purpose in "23 Days in July." Use evidence from the text to support your answer.

7. **Draw Conclusions** In 1996, Armstrong beat cancer. In 2004, he became a six-time winner of the Tour de France. Considering what you learned from the selections that you just read, what qualities helped Armstrong win such big victories?

Extension and Challenge

8. **Inquiry and Research** Research the Tour de France and create a tourist's guide to the race. Provide the reader with some historical information, explain the rules of the race, and include a map of the upcoming race.

Tour de France 2005

What is a WINNER?

Take another look at the winner sketch you created for the activity on page 814. Take a look at the victory photograph of Lance Armstrong on page 821. Think about the details you've learned about Armstrong's struggles. What does your sketch have in common with the photograph?

COMMON CORE

RI 1 Cite textual evidence to support inferences drawn from the text. RI 2 Determine two or more central ideas in a text. RI 6 Determine an author's point of view or purpose in a text. RI 9 Analyze how two or more authors writing about the same topic shape their presentations of key information.

Vocabulary in Context

▲ VOCABULARY PRACTICE

For each item, choose the word that differs most in meaning from the other words. Refer to a dictionary if you need help.

1. chatty, talkative, terse, gossipy
2. culminate, top, begin, crown
3. awkward, hidden, recessed, inset
4. pose, posture, worry, stance
5. intuition, ignorance, understanding, perception
6. prestigious, notable, honorable, unworthy

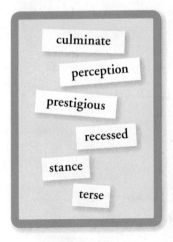

ACADEMIC VOCABULARY IN WRITING

| • demonstrate | • goal | • impact | • link | • undertake |

Lance Armstrong as portrayed in the first selection is pursuing a very different **goal** from the Lance Armstrong of the second selection. Write a brief description of these goals. Try to use one or more of the Academic Vocabulary words in your description.

VOCABULARY STRATEGY: ANGLO-SAXON AFFIXES

Many words we commonly use come from Anglo-Saxon (Old English). Some of these Anglo-Saxon words are used today as **affixes**—word parts that can be attached to the beginning (**prefix**) or end (**suffix**) of base words to create new words. The chart shows Anglo-Saxon prefixes and suffixes and their meanings. Understanding the meaning of the affixes can help you determine the meanings of unfamiliar words that contain these word parts.

PRACTICE Add either an Anglo-Saxon prefix or suffix from the chart to the base word in each sentence. Use a dictionary to check your answers.

⊙ **COMMON CORE**

L 4b Use grade-appropriate affixes as clues to the meaning of a word.

Prefix	Meaning
over-	above; too much
under-	below; less than
Suffix	**Meaning**
-most	most, nearest to
-hood	state, quality, or group

1. She thought the project would take longer than it did, so she accidentally _____estimated the time it would take to complete it.
2. We're planning to make welcoming speeches at the neighbor_____ block party next week.
3. A biography often includes details about a person's child_____.
4. Wear extra layers for the trip by putting a sweatshirt over your _____shirt.
5. A diary entry can express a subject's inner_____ feelings.

Interactive Vocabulary **THINK** central

Go to **thinkcentral.com**.
KEYWORD: HML7-825

Malcolm X: By Any Means Necessary

COMMON CORE

RI 10 Read and comprehend nonfiction.

Biography by Walter Dean Myers

Meet Walter Dean Myers

Walter Dean Myers knows what it's like to rise above difficult circumstances. His mother died before he was two years old, and his father, who was very poor, had to give Walter away. Walter's foster mother, Florence Dean, taught him to read, and books soon became a welcome escape for Walter. One of his teachers suggested that he write down his thoughts in the form of poems and stories. Walter began writing then and has never stopped producing novels, short stories, poems, and nonfiction books.

Other Books by Walter Dean Myers

Nonfiction
- *Bad Boy: A Memoir*
- *The Greatest: Muhammad Ali*

Fiction
- *Crystal*
- *The Glory Field*
- *Monster*
- *Scorpions*
- *Somewhere in the Darkness*

Try a Biography

A **biography** is a story of a person's life that is written by someone else. Most biographies are about famous people who changed history or made an impact in other ways. Biographies are often told in chronological order. The introduction and conclusion of a biography usually highlight the lasting importance of the person.

Reading Fluency Good readers read smoothly, accurately, and with feeling. To improve your reading fluency, read a passage several times. Your goal in silent reading is to make sense of the writer's words and ideas. When reading aloud, think about your purpose for reading a text. Be sure to group words into meaningful phrases that sound like natural speech.

Read a Great Book

Malcolm X was an important figure in the struggle for equal rights for African Americans. The following section from Myers's award-winning biography provides an overview of Malcolm X's life and legacy. You'll read about how Malcolm's experiences shaped him into a leader of the 20th century.

from

Malcolm X:
By Any Means Necessary

Walter Dean My

Who was Malcolm X, and what is his legacy?

Malcolm's life seems so varied, he did so many things over the far too short thirty-nine years of his life, that it almost appears that there was not one Malcolm at all, but four distinct people. But in looking at Malcolm's life, in examining the expectations against what he actually did, we see a blending of the four Malcolms into one dynamic personality that is distinctively American in its character. For only a black man living in America could have gone through what Malcolm went through.

10   The first Malcolm was Malcolm the child, who lived in Nebraska and Michigan. He lived much like a million other black boys born in the United States. He was loved by two parents, Earl and Louise Little. From them he learned about morality, and decency, and the need to do well in school. His parents gave him a legacy of love, but also a legacy of pride.

Malcolm saw his father, a Baptist minister, at the meetings of the Universal Negro Improvement Association, saw him speaking about the black race, and about the possibility of justice. From what the young Malcolm saw, from what he experienced as a young child,

20   one might have expected him, upon reaching maturity, to become a religious man and an activist for justice, as was his father.

Even when Earl Little was killed, Louise Little tried to hold the family together. Malcolm started school and did well. His mother saw to it that he did his assignments, and there was no doubt that Malcolm was bright. Bright children often understand their gifts, and it is possible that Malcolm understood his early on. He said in his autobiography that he had not given a lot of thought to what he wanted to do with those gifts when he was asked by a teacher in the eighth grade. A lawyer, he ventured.

30 Malcolm had not known exactly what he wanted to do with his talents, but he understood that the talents he possessed were valued in his schoolmates. The teacher said to him that it was not practical for him to be a lawyer, because he was black. The teacher probably thought of himself as being a realist. There is no use misleading Malcolm, he probably thought. Where does a black teenaged boy go, to what does he turn if he is not allowed the same avenues of value as his white friends?

The second Malcolm answers that question. The black teenager goes among his own people, and searches among the values of his
40 peers for those he can use. So Malcolm bought the zoot suit, with the gold chain dangling against the pants leg. He bought the wide-brimmed hat and learned the hip jargon of the street, the same way teenagers today buy the gold chains and sneakers that cost enough to feed a family for a week. Malcolm was a human being, and human beings need to be able to look into the mirror and see something that pleases them. . . .

Malcolm said that he wanted to be a lawyer, to use his mind. He was told that no, he couldn't do that because he was black. Perhaps it wouldn't have made any difference what the teacher had said. As
50 was the case with so many black teenagers, Malcolm's family, now with only the mother to support it, would not have been able to afford college for him.

Malcolm toughened himself. Malcolm used his mind. If he couldn't use it to study law, he would use it in street hustles. He used it in making money the way people in the inner cities who don't have "downtown" jobs make money. Eventually he used it to commit burglaries. Some societies never learn that to make a person socially responsible you must first include him or her in your

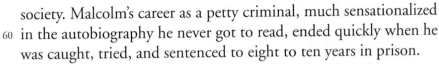

society. Malcolm's career as a petty criminal, much sensationalized
60 in the autobiography he never got to read, ended quickly when he
was caught, tried, and sentenced to eight to ten years in prison.

The second Malcolm, the one using his wits to survive on
the streets, skirting both sides of the law, might have continued
after he was released if it were not for the Nation of Islam. Elijah
Muhammad claimed that he lifted Malcolm up and saved him
from a life of degradation. Nothing was more truthful. The
Nation of Islam, with its strict moral codes, its religion, its
understanding, forgiveness, and even celebration of black men
who had fallen by the wayside, was the garden from which the
70 third Malcolm emerged.

Here now was Malcolm the religious man, the activist, the
thinker, the man who stood up for his people, who confronted the
forces of injustice in America at a time when black people were
being beaten in the streets, were being publicly humiliated and even
killed. Here was a Malcolm who offered himself as the voice of the
defeated, the manliness of a people who badly needed manliness.

And he was a worker. He organized and preached. He cajoled
and threatened. He attacked racism with the biting tone of the
absolute cynic, vowing to attain freedom by any means necessary
80 and with any sacrifice. He understood, as few other leaders did, that
there were people like himself in the streets, and in the prisons, who
had contributions to make. He included people in the struggle for
human rights in America who had never before been included. This
was the third Malcolm.

Malcolm grew. He grew away from the Nation of Islam, and
away from the separatist philosophy of that organization. The
Nation of Islam had returned to him the wings that had been taken
from him because of his color, and Malcolm, the fourth Malcolm,
found himself able to fly.

90 What one would have expected, or at least hoped for, on meeting
the wide-eyed boy in the Pleasant Grove Elementary School, was
that he would one day touch the edge of greatness. It is what we
wish for all children. The fourth Malcolm—the one with his head
slightly bowed as he listened to Jomo Kenyatta, the great African
leader, the one learning firsthand about the liberation of the African

continent so that he could liberate his own—had touched the edge of that greatness.

Malcolm's life was about growth, about the intensely changing man that moved from thievery to honesty, from being a racial separatist to searching for true brotherhood, and from atheism to Islam.

But his life was also about the return to the idealism of his childhood. The world of the child, before he or she is exposed to racism, before he or she is conditioned to react to the hurts inflicted on him or her, is one of acceptance and love. Malcolm had grown, and in that growing had learned to accept those people, regardless of race or nationality, who accepted and loved him.

Malcolm spoke for the voiceless, for the people from whom not even some black leaders wanted to hear. He spoke for the jobless, and for the homeless. He spoke for the young men whose hard bodies, bodies that could perform miracles on inner-city basketball courts, were not wanted in America's offices. He spoke for the millions of black Americans who saw themselves as a minority in a world in which most of the inhabitants were people of color like themselves. He spoke for the men and women who had to turn too many other cheeks, had to fight off too many insults with nothing but smiles.

Malcolm had walked in their shoes, and they knew it when they heard him speak. . . .

Malcolm, . . . having experienced the same hunger, the same frustrations, even the same jails as poor blacks did, understood something else as well: that all the goals of the mainstream civil rights movement, the civil rights laws, school integration, voting rights, none of these would have meaning if African-Americans still thought of themselves as a racially crippled people, if they still walked with their heads down because they were black.

In the last year of his life, having grown away from the Nation of Islam, and having made a spiritual pilgrimage to Mecca, Malcolm was moving both to a new and an old place. He was moving more solidly into Pan-Africanism, the territory that his father had explored over forty years before.

Malcolm's message is remembered by many people who find comfort and inspiration in it today. One of them is the African-

American poet Wopashitwe Mondo Eyen we Langa, who wrote the poem "Great Bateleur." A bateleur is a reddish-brown eagle found in Africa. It is notable for its acrobatic flying style and its ferocious cry as it dives to capture its prey.

from **Great Bateleur**
(In Tribute to Malcolm)

We were those who begged, Malcolm
140 *who could not find courage*
nor faith in ourselves
who could not peer into reflecting pools
nor look each other in the face
and see the beauty that was ours
but for you, Malcolm
but for you, Great Bateleur
Eagle of Africa
still your spirit flies.

150 Perhaps history will tell us that there were no wrong strategies in the civil rights movement of the sixties. That all factors involved, the pray-ins, the legal cases, the marches, the militancy, were all vital to the time, that each had its place. Undoubtedly, too, as current needs color memories of distant events, we will bring different concepts from that period of American history, and voices. One voice that we will not forget is that of El Hajj Malik el Shabazz, the man we called Malcolm. ☙

Keep Reading

Which part of this overview of Malcolm X's dramatic life sparked your curiosity? In other parts of Myers's biography, you'll read more about the hard times Malcolm faces as a child, how he gets into trouble with the law, why he makes some people angry while inspiring others, and the tragic way his life comes to an end.

The Noble Experiment

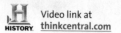

Video link at thinkcentral.com

From the Autobiography *I Never Had It Made* by Jackie Robinson
As Told to Alfred Duckett

When is there
DIGNITY in silence?

COMMON CORE

RI 1 Cite textual evidence to support analysis of what the text says explicitly. **RI 2** Determine two or more central ideas in a text and analyze their development over the course of the text; provide an objective summary of the text. **RI 3** Analyze the interactions between individuals, events, and ideas in a text.

What do you do when someone yells at you? Some people choose to yell back. Some people explain themselves calmly. But there are times when silence is the most effective response. When does silence give you dignity, or make you worthy of respect? In the selection you're about to read, Jackie Robinson tells why he needed to find strength in silence.

DISCUSS With a group, decide the best response to each scenario listed. Should you yell back, explain calmly, or simply stay silent?

Scenario	Response
The principal accuses you of something you didn't do.	
A younger sibling calls you names to make you angry.	
The referee makes a call you think is unfair.	
A friend yells at you for calling a play against him.	

● TEXT ANALYSIS: AUTOBIOGRAPHY

An **autobiography** is the story of a person's life as written by that person. The writer

- uses the first-person point of view
- often introduces people who influenced him or her
- shares thoughts and feelings about his or her experiences

Autobiographies not only help you understand a person, but they also help you understand the society in which the person lived. As you read "The Noble Experiment," note what you learn about Jackie Robinson and his times.

● READING STRATEGY: SUMMARIZE

When you **summarize,** you briefly restate in your own words the main ideas and important details of something you've read. As you read "The Noble Experiment," note important people and events in a log. Later you can use the log to help you identify the main ideas and summarize the selections.

> Important Characters
> - Branch Rickey—Ohio Wesleyan baseball coach
> - Charley Thomas—Player for Ohio Wesleyan
> -
>
> Important Events
> -

▲ VOCABULARY IN CONTEXT

The listed words all help tell about a dramatic turning point in Jackie Robinson's life. In your *Reader/Writer Notebook*, write a sentence for each of the vocabulary words. Use a dictionary or the definitions in the following selection pages to help you.

WORD LIST		
camouflage	insinuation	speculate
capitalize	integrated	taunt
disillusionment	retaliate	
eloquence	shrewdly	

Complete the activities in your **Reader/Writer Notebook.**

Meet the Author

Jackie Robinson
1919–1972

National Hero
Jackie Robinson was the first man at the University of California, Los Angeles, to earn varsity letters in four sports. He then went on to play professional baseball in 1945 in the Negro Leagues. His talent and extraordinary character were quickly noticed.

In 1947, he joined the Brooklyn Dodgers. Robinson was honored as Rookie of the Year in 1947 and National League Most Valuable Player in 1949. He was inducted into the Baseball Hall of Fame in 1962. With the help of his wife, Rachel, Jackie paved the way for African-American athletes.

Cowriter and Fan
Robinson worked on his autobiography with Alfred Duckett, a writer and baseball fan. Active in the civil rights movement, Duckett was a speechwriter for Dr. Martin Luther King Jr.

BACKGROUND TO THE AUTOBIOGRAPHY
Segregated National Pastime
In the 1940s, African Americans faced many barriers. Segregation kept African Americans separate from whites in every part of society, including sports. In baseball the Negro League was completely separate from the all-white teams of the Major League. Jackie Robinson would help change that.

Author Online
THINK central
Go to **thinkcentral.com**.
KEYWORD: HML7-833

THE NOBLE EXPERIMENT

Jackie Robinson
As Told to Alfred Duckett

In 1910 Branch Rickey was a coach for Ohio Wesleyan. The team went to South Bend, Indiana, for a game. The hotel management registered the coach and team but refused to assign a room to a black player named Charley Thomas. In those days college ball had a few black players. Mr. Rickey took the manager aside and said he would move the entire team to another hotel unless the black athlete was accepted. The threat was a bluff because he knew the other hotels also would have refused accommodations to a black man. While the hotel manager was thinking about the threat, Mr. Rickey came up with a compromise. He suggested
10 a cot be put in his own room, which he would share with the unwanted guest. The hotel manager wasn't happy about the idea, but he gave in. **Ⓐ**

Years later Branch Rickey told the story of the misery of that black player to whom he had given a place to sleep. He remembered that Thomas couldn't sleep.

"He sat on that cot," Mr. Rickey said, "and was silent for a long time. Then he began to cry, tears he couldn't hold back. His whole body shook with emotion. I sat and watched him, not knowing what to do until he began tearing at one hand with the other—just as if he were trying to scratch the skin off his hands with his fingernails. I was alarmed. I asked
20 him what he was trying to do to himself.

"'It's my hands,' he sobbed. 'They're black. If only they were white, I'd be as good as anybody then, wouldn't I, Mr. Rickey? If only they were white.'"

"Charley," Mr. Rickey said, "the day will come when they won't have to be white."

Analyze Visuals ▶

What might you **infer** from the cover of this 1951 special edition comic book?

Ⓐ AUTOBIOGRAPHY
What does Robinson want the reader to know about the society in which Branch Rickey was coaching?

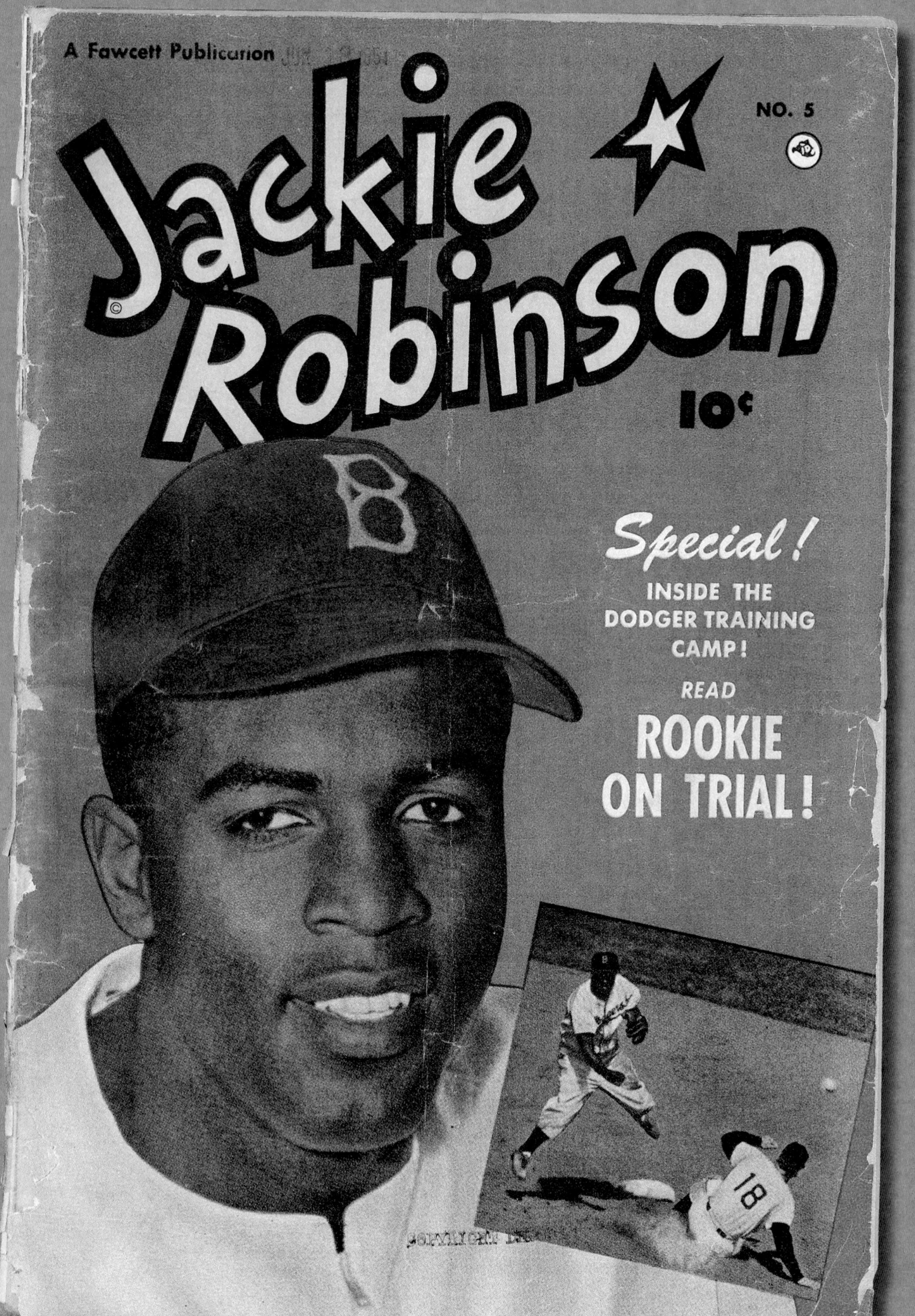

A Fawcett Publication

NO. 5

Jackie Robinson

10¢

Special!

INSIDE THE
DODGER TRAINING
CAMP!

READ

ROOKIE
ON TRIAL!

Thirty-five years later, while I was lying awake nights, frustrated, unable to see a future, Mr. Rickey, by now the president of the Dodgers, was also lying awake at night, trying to make up his mind about a new experiment.

He had never forgotten the agony of that black athlete. When he became a front-office executive in St. Louis, he had fought, behind the
30　scenes, against the custom that consigned black spectators to the Jim Crow section[1] of the Sportsman's Park, later to become Busch Memorial Stadium. His pleas to change the rules were in vain. Those in power argued that if blacks were allowed a free choice of seating, white business would suffer. **B**

Branch Rickey lost that fight, but when he became the boss of the Brooklyn Dodgers in 1943, he felt the time for equality in baseball had come. He knew that achieving it would be terribly difficult. There would be deep resentment, determined opposition, and perhaps even racial violence. He was convinced he was morally right, and he **shrewdly**
40　sensed that making the game a truly national one would have healthy financial results. He took his case before the startled directors of the club, and using persuasive **eloquence,** he won the first battle in what would be a long and bitter campaign. He was voted permission to make the Brooklyn club the pioneer in bringing blacks into baseball.

Winning his directors' approval was almost insignificant in contrast to the task which now lay ahead of the Dodger president. He made certain that word of his plans did not leak out, particularly to the press. Next, he had to find the ideal player for his project, which came to be called "Rickey's noble experiment." This player had to be one who could take
50　abuse, name-calling, rejection by fans and sportswriters and by fellow players not only on opposing teams but on his own. He had to be able to stand up in the face of merciless persecution and not **retaliate.** On the other hand, he had to be a contradiction in human terms; he still had to have spirit. He could not be an "Uncle Tom."[2] His ability to turn the other cheek had to be predicated[3] on his determination to gain acceptance. Once having proven his ability as player, teammate, and man, he had to be able to cast off humbleness and stand up as a full-fledged participant whose triumph did not carry the poison of bitterness. **C**

Unknown to most people and certainly to me, after launching a major
60　scouting program, Branch Rickey had picked me as that player. The Rickey talent hunt went beyond national borders. Cuba, Mexico, Puerto Rico, Venezuela, and other countries where dark-skinned people lived

1. **consigned . . . to the Jim Crow section:** directed African Americans to sit in a separate section.

2. **"Uncle Tom":** an offensive term for an African-American person seen as trying overly hard to please white people; originally from the novel *Uncle Tom's Cabin,* written in 1851 by Harriet Beecher Stowe.

3. **predicated** (prĕd′ĭ-kā′tĭd): based.

B **SUMMARIZE**
What are the important details about the people Jackie Robinson has introduced you to so far? Add the information to your log.

shrewdly (shrōōd′lē) *adv.* wisely; in a clever way

eloquence (ĕl′ə-kwəns) *n.* forceful, convincing speech or writing

retaliate (rĭ-tăl′ē-āt′) *v.* to get revenge; get even

C **AUTOBIOGRAPHY**
Why does Jackie Robinson choose to tell you so much about Branch Rickey's thoughts on the qualities the first major-league black baseball player will have to have?

Jackie Robinson in his Kansas City Monarchs uniform shortly before he met Branch Rickey, 1945

had been checked out. Mr. Rickey had learned that there were a number of black players, war veterans mainly, who had gone to these countries, despairing of finding an opportunity in their own country. The manhunt had to be **camouflaged.** If it became known he was looking for a black recruit for the Dodgers, all hell would have broken loose. The gimmick he used as a cover-up was to make the world believe that he was about to establish a new Negro league. In the spring of 1945 he called a press
70 conference and announced that the Dodgers were organizing the United States League, composed of all black teams. This, of course, made blacks and prointegration whites indignant. He was accused of trying to uphold the existing segregation and, at the same time, **capitalize** on black players. Cleverly, Mr. Rickey replied that his league would be better organized than the current ones. He said its main purpose, eventually, was to be absorbed into the majors. It is ironic that by coming very close to telling the truth, he was able to conceal that truth from the enemies of **integrated** baseball. Most people assumed that when he spoke of some distant goal of integration, Mr. Rickey was being a hypocrite on this issue
80 as so many of baseball's leaders had been. **D**

Black players were familiar with this kind of hypocrisy. When I was with the Monarchs, shortly before I met Mr. Rickey, Wendell Smith, then sports editor of the black weekly Pittsburgh *Courier,* had arranged for me and two other players from the Negro league to go to a tryout

camouflage
(kăm′ə-fläzh′) *v.* to disguise or portray falsely in order to conceal

capitalize (kăp′ĭ-tl-īz′) *v.* to take advantage of

integrated (ĭn′tĭ-grā′tĭd) *adj.* open to people of all races and groups **integrate** *v.*

D SUMMARIZE
What challenges will face Rickey and any African-American player he chooses?

with the Boston Red Sox. The tryout had been brought about because a Boston city councilman had frightened the Red Sox management. Councilman Isadore Muchneck threatened to push a bill through banning Sunday baseball unless the Red Sox hired black players. Sam Jethroe of the Cleveland Buckeyes, Marvin Williams of the Philadelphia Stars, and I had been grateful to Wendell for getting us a chance in the Red Sox tryout, and we put our best efforts into it. However, not for one minute did we believe the tryout was sincere. The Boston club officials praised our performance, let us fill out application cards, and said, "So long." We were fairly certain they wouldn't call us, and we had no intention of calling them.

Incidents like this made Wendell Smith as cynical as we were. He didn't accept Branch Rickey's new league as a genuine project, and he frankly told him so. During this conversation, the Dodger boss asked Wendell whether any of the three of us who had gone to Boston was really good major league material. Wendell said I was. I will be forever indebted to Wendell because, without his even knowing it, his recommendation was in the end partly responsible for my career. At the time, it started a thorough investigation of my background. **E**

In August 1945, at Comiskey Park in Chicago, I was approached by Clyde Sukeforth, the Dodger scout. Blacks have had to learn to protect themselves by being cynical but not cynical enough to slam the door on potential opportunities. We go through life walking a tightrope[4] to prevent too much **disillusionment.** I was out on the field when Sukeforth called my name and beckoned. He told me the Brown Dodgers were looking for top ballplayers, that Branch Rickey had heard about me and sent him to watch me throw from the hole. He had come at an unfortunate time. I had hurt my shoulder a couple of days before that, and I wouldn't be doing any throwing for at least a week.

Sukeforth said he'd like to talk with me anyhow. He asked me to come to see him after the game at the Stevens Hotel.

Here we go again, I thought. Another time-wasting experience. But Sukeforth looked like a sincere person, and I thought I might as well listen. I agreed to meet him that night. When we met, Sukeforth got right to the point. Mr. Rickey wanted to talk to me about the possibility of becoming a Brown Dodger. If I could get a few days off and go to Brooklyn, my fare and expenses would be paid. At first I said that I couldn't leave my team and go to Brooklyn just like that. Sukeforth wouldn't take no for an answer. He pointed out that I couldn't play for a few days anyhow because of my bum arm. Why should my team object?

---

4. **walking a tightrope:** maintaining a narrow balance.

E **AUTOBIOGRAPHY**
Reread lines 96–103. Notice that Robinson uses first-person pronouns such as *I* and *we*. To whom does the *we* refer?

disillusionment
(dĭs´ĭ-lo͞o´zhən-mənt) *n.* disappointment; loss of hope

VISUAL VOCABULARY

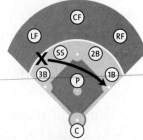

throw from the hole *v.* to throw from deep in the infield (**X**) to first base (**1B**)

Jackie Robinson and Branch Rickey on signing day

I continued to hold out and demanded to know what would happen if the Monarchs fired me. The Dodger scout replied quietly that he didn't believe that would happen.

I shrugged and said I'd make the trip. I figured I had nothing to lose.

130 **B**ranch Rickey was an impressive-looking man. He had a classic face, an air of command, a deep, booming voice, and a way of cutting through red tape and getting down to basics. He shook my hand vigorously and, after a brief conversation, sprang the first question.

"You got a girl?" he demanded.

It was a hell of a question. I had two reactions: why should he be concerned about my relationship with a girl; and, second, while I thought, hoped, and prayed I had a girl, the way things had been going, I was afraid she might have begun to consider me a hopeless case. I explained this to Mr. Rickey and Clyde. **F**

140 Mr. Rickey wanted to know all about Rachel. I told him of our hopes and plans.

"You know, you *have* a girl," he said heartily. "When we get through today, you may want to call her up because there are times when a man needs a woman by his side."

My heart began racing a little faster again as I sat there **speculating.** First he asked me if I really understood why he had sent for me. I told him what Clyde Sukeforth had told me.

F AUTOBIOGRAPHY
Reread lines 135–139. What can you **infer** about Jackie Robinson's personal life and feelings?

speculate
(spĕk′yə-lāt′) *v.* to view or consider different possibilities; to guess what might happen

"That's what he was supposed to tell you," Mr. Rickey said. "The truth is you are not a candidate for the Brooklyn Brown Dodgers. I've sent for you because I'm interested in you as a candidate for the Brooklyn National League Club. I think you can play in the major leagues. How do you feel about it?"

My reactions seemed like some kind of weird mixture churning in a blender. I was thrilled, scared, and excited. I was incredulous. Most of all, I was speechless.

"You think you can play for Montreal?" he demanded.

I got my tongue back. "Yes," I answered.

Montreal was the Brooklyn Dodgers' top farm club. The players who went there and made it had an excellent chance at the big time.

I was busy reorganizing my thoughts while Mr. Rickey and Clyde Sukeforth discussed me briefly, almost as if I weren't there. Mr. Rickey was questioning Clyde. Could I make the grade?

Abruptly, Mr. Rickey swung his swivel chair in my direction. He was a man who conducted himself with great drama. He pointed a finger at me.

"I know you're a good ballplayer," he barked. "What I don't know is whether you have the guts."

I knew it was all too good to be true. Here was a guy questioning my courage. That virtually amounted to him asking me if I was a coward. Mr. Rickey or no Mr. Rickey, that was an **insinuation** hard to take. I felt the heat coming up into my cheeks. **G**

Before I could react to what he had said, he leaned forward in his chair and explained.

I wasn't just another athlete being hired by a ball club. We were playing for big stakes. This was the reason Branch Rickey's search had been so exhaustive. The search had spanned the globe and narrowed down to a few candidates, then finally to me. When it looked as though I might be the number-one choice, the investigation of my life, my habits, my reputation, and my character had become an intensified study.

"I've investigated you thoroughly, Robinson," Mr. Rickey said.

One of the results of this thorough screening were reports from California athletic circles that I had been a "racial agitator"[5] at UCLA. Mr. Rickey had not accepted these criticisms on face value. He had demanded and received more information and came to the conclusion that if I had been white, people would have said, "Here's a guy who's a contender, a competitor."

After that he had some grim words of warning. "We can't fight our way through this, Robinson. We've got no army. There's virtually nobody on our side. No owners, no umpires, very few newspapermen. And I'm afraid

insinuation
(ĭn-sĭn′yoo-ā′shən) *n.*
a suggestion or hint intended to insult

COMMON CORE RI 3

G AUTOBIOGRAPHY
You may recall that in an **autobiography**—the story of a person's life as written by that person—the writer will share private thoughts and feelings. When a writer reveals details about a significant life event, what he or she shares can provide insights into a personality that a biography cannot. Reread lines 153–170. What words and phrases help you understand how Robinson felt during his interview with Branch Rickey?

---

5. **"racial agitator":** negative term used for someone who tries to stir up trouble between the races.

that many fans will be hostile. We'll be in a tough position. We can win
only if we can convince the world that I'm doing this because you're a
great ballplayer and a fine gentleman."

He had me transfixed as he spoke. I could feel his sincerity, and I began
to get a sense of how much this major step meant to him. Because of his
nature and his passion for justice, he had to do what he was doing. He
continued. The rumbling voice, the theatrical gestures were gone.
He was speaking from a deep, quiet strength.

"So there's more than just playing," he said. "I wish it meant only hits,
runs, and errors—only the things they put in the box score. Because you
know—yes, you would know, Robinson, that a baseball box score is a
democratic thing. It doesn't tell how big you are, what church you attend,
what color you are, or how your father voted in the last election. It just
tells what kind of baseball player you were on that particular day." **H**

H SUMMARIZE
What does Branch
Rickey really want to
find out about Jackie
Robinson during this
interview? Include these
details in your log.

Jackie Robinson crosses the plate after one of his many home-run hits for the Montreal Royals.

I interrupted. "But it's the box score that really counts—that and that alone, isn't it?"

"It's all that *ought* to count," he replied. "But it isn't. Maybe one of these days it *will* be all that counts. That is one of the reasons I've got you here, Robinson. If you're a good enough man, we can make this a start in the right direction. But let me tell you, it's going to take an awful lot of courage."

He was back to the crossroads question that made me start to get angry
210 minutes earlier. He asked it slowly and with great care.

"Have you got the guts to play the game no matter what happens?"

"I think I can play the game, Mr. Rickey," I said.

The next few minutes were tough. Branch Rickey had to make absolutely sure that I knew what I would face. Beanballs[6] would be thrown at me. I would be called the kind of names which would hurt and infuriate any man. I would be physically attacked. Could I take all of this and control my temper, remain steadfastly loyal to our ultimate aim?

He knew I would have terrible problems and wanted me to know the extent of them before I agreed to the plan. I was twenty-six years old,
220 and all my life—back to the age of eight when a little neighbor girl called me names—I had believed in payback, retaliation. The most luxurious possession, the richest treasure anybody has, is his personal dignity. I looked at Mr. Rickey guardedly, and in that second I was looking at him not as a partner in a great experiment, but as the enemy—a white man. I had a question, and it was the age-old one about whether or not you sell your birthright. ❶

"Mr. Rickey," I asked, "are you looking for a Negro who is afraid to fight back?"

I never will forget the way he exploded.
230 "Robinson," he said, "I'm looking for a ballplayer with guts enough not to fight back."

After that, Mr. Rickey continued his lecture on the kind of thing I'd be facing.

He not only told me about it, but he acted out the part of a white player charging into me, blaming me for the "accident" and calling me all kinds of foul racial names. He talked about my race, my parents, in language that was almost unendurable.

"They'll **taunt** and goad you," Mr. Rickey said. "They'll do anything to make you react. They'll try to provoke a race riot in the ballpark.
240 This is the way to prove to the public that a Negro should not be allowed in the major league. This is the way to frighten the fans and make them afraid to attend the games."

Language Coach

Slang When made-up words or ordinary words are used in a way other than what is expected, they are called slang. Reread line 211. The word *guts* means "forcefulness or courage." In the physical sense, any professional player would need *guts*. What kind of courage do you think Branch Rickey is referring to?

❶ **AUTOBIOGRAPHY**
Reread lines 218–226. What is most important to Jackie Robinson?

taunt (tônt) *v.* to make fun of

---

6. **beanballs:** pitches thrown purposely at a batter's head.

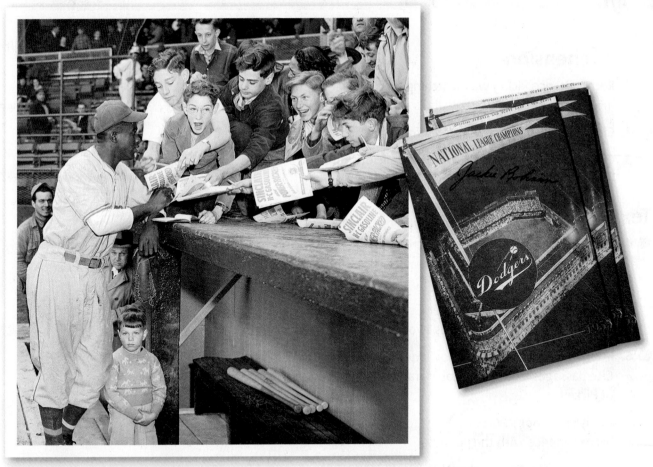

Jackie makes the big time with the Brooklyn Dodgers.

If hundreds of black people wanted to come to the ballpark to watch me play and Mr. Rickey tried to discourage them, would I understand that he was doing it because the emotional enthusiasm of my people could harm the experiment? That kind of enthusiasm would be as bad as the emotional opposition of prejudiced white fans.

Suppose I was at shortstop. Another player comes down from first, stealing, flying in with spikes high, and cuts me on the leg. As I feel
250 the blood running down my leg, the white player laughs in my face.

"How do you like that, boy?" he sneers. **J**

Could I turn the other cheek? I didn't know how I would do it. Yet I knew that I must. I had to do it for so many reasons. For black youth, for my mother, for Rae, for myself. I had already begun to feel I had to do it for Branch Rickey.

I was offered, and agreed to sign later, a contract with a $3,500 bonus and $600-a-month salary. I was officially a Montreal Royal. I must not tell anyone except Rae and my mother. ෴

J SUMMARIZE
How does Branch Rickey test Jackie Robinson to make sure he is strong enough to succeed with dignity?

Comprehension

1. **Recall** Branch Rickey was searching for a special person to help him integrate baseball. What qualities did he believe this player needed to have?

2. **Clarify** Why was Rickey's search for an African-American player kept secret?

3. **Clarify** Why was Jackie Robinson suspicious of Clyde Sukeforth's invitation to meet with Branch Rickey?

Text Analysis

4. **Summarize** Review the log you created while reading and cross out details that don't seem as important now. Use the remaining information to write a summary of the selection.

5. **Draw Conclusions** What general statement can you make in regard to the society Jackie Robinson writes about? Cite details to support your answer.

6. **Interpret Autobiography** How does Robinson feel about Branch Rickey? Cite passages from the autobiography that show Robinson's impressions of Rickey.

7. **Analyze Author's Purpose** Why do you think Robinson wanted to share his experience with the public?

8. **Evaluate Title** Do you think "The Noble Experiment" is an appropriate title for this selection? Why or why not?

Extension and Challenge

9. **SOCIAL STUDIES CONNECTION** The 1940s, when Jackie Robinson entered professional baseball, was a dramatic decade. Create a timeline of the era that gives the events in the autobiography and also those in the Eleanor Roosevelt biography beginning on page 786. Then research to find four other events that were happening in the world at the same time. Add these other events to your timeline.

1943

⟶

Branch Rickey becomes the boss of the Brooklyn Dodgers.

When is there DIGNITY in silence?

Refer to the Scenario chart on page 832. Now that you've read this biography, explain how your group's responses compare to Robinson's responses to unfairness.

COMMON CORE

RI 1 Cite textual evidence to support analysis of what the text says explicitly. **RI 2** Determine two or more central ideas in a text and analyze their development over the course of the text; provide an objective summary of the text. **RI 3** Analyze the interactions between individuals, events, and ideas in a text.

Vocabulary in Context

▲ VOCABULARY PRACTICE

Choose the word from the box that is the best substitute for each boldfaced word or term.

1. Branch Rickey **cleverly** devised a cover story to mislead the press.
2. He was accused of trying to **gain advantage** on African Americans.
3. The **lack of hope** African-American baseball players felt about joining the major leagues was based on past experience.
4. Robinson took time to **think** about the outcome of his actions.
5. The true goal of Rickey's plan was to have **desegregated** major leagues.
6. Some players on other teams would **make fun of** Robinson.
7. Robinson was not allowed to **get even.**
8. A sportswriter made a **suggestion** intended to insult Robinson.
9. The minister spoke with **great verbal skill** about the evils of prejudice.
10. Branch Rickey had to **conceal** his plan.

camouflage
capitalize
disillusionment
eloquence
insinuation
integrated
retaliate
shrewdly
speculate
taunt

ACADEMIC VOCABULARY IN WRITING

> • demonstrate   • goal   • impact   • link   • undertake

In their quest to change society's attitudes, Jackie Robinson and Branch Rickey would **undertake** a major challenge. Using one or more of the Academic Vocabulary words, write a brief paragraph about their personal traits.

VOCABULARY STRATEGY: THE LATIN ROOT *spec*

The vocabulary word *speculate* contains the Latin root *spec,* which means "to see" or "to look." This root, which may also be spelled *spect,* is found in many English words. To understand the meaning of words with *spec* or *spect,* you can often use context clues and your knowledge of the root's meaning.

PRACTICE Choose a word from the web that best completes each sentence. Use context clues or, if necessary, a dictionary.

1. The _____ fireworks show thrilled everyone.
2. Interview the witness to get a better _____ on the accident.
3. The health _____ makes sure that all local restaurants are clean.
4. The _____ of speaking before an audience makes me nervous.
5. The police officer carefully removed the blood _____ from the crime scene.

COMMON CORE

L 4b Use Latin roots as clues to the meaning of a word.

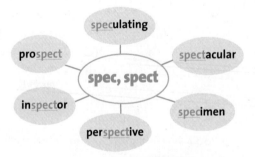

speculating
prospect
spectacular
spec, spect
inspector
specimen
perspective

Interactive Vocabulary **THINK** central

Go to **thinkcentral.com.**
KEYWORD: HML7-845

Use with "The Noble Experiment," page 834.

Jackie Robinson Makes Headlines
Newspaper Articles

What's the Connection?

You have just read Jackie Robinson's autobiography. Now read what newspaper reporters had to say about him during his career.

Standards Focus: Identify Treatment and Scope

Even when the same writing topic is assigned to everyone in your class, each student's paper will be different. This happens because you each make different decisions about how to cover the topic.

The way a topic is handled is called its **treatment.** Treatment includes the form the writer chooses to use, as well as the writer's purpose. Treatment also includes **tone,** or the writer's attitude toward the subject. For example, here are two ways to treat the same topic: movie ratings.

Movie Ratings	Form	Purpose	Tone
Treatment A	news article	to inform	serious
Treatment B	editorial	to persuade	lighthearted

Another thing that makes each piece of writing different is the writer's **scope**—what he or she focuses on. For example, even two serious articles about movie ratings can still be very different in scope. One might focus on how movie ratings have changed over the years. The other could focus on how inaccurate ratings hurt good movies. As you read the articles that follow, identify their treatment and scope by answering the questions in this chart. Doing so will help you to connect ideas within each selection and between them.

Element	Questions to Answer	"Montreal Signs Negro Shortstop"	"Robinson Steals Home in Fifth"
Treatment	What form does the writing take?	sports article	sports article
	What is the purpose?		
	What is the tone?		
Scope	What is the topic?		
	What aspects of the topic are covered in the article?		
	How much detail is provided?		

MONTREAL SIGNS NEGRO SHORTSTOP

Organized Baseball Opens Its Ranks to Negro Player

Jackie Robinson signs with the Montreal Royals. Looking on are Hector Racine, Royals president; Branch Rickey Jr.; and Romeo Gauvreau, Royals vice president.

Robinson Gets Bonus to Sign Ⓐ

MONTREAL, Oct. 23 (AP)— The first Negro player ever to be admitted to organized baseball, Jack Robinson, today put his signature on a contract calling not only for a player's salary, but also a bonus for signing.

Product of a three-year search and $25,000 hunt for Negro 10 diamond talent by the Dodgers, Robinson signed up in a history-making huddle with Hector Racine and Lieut. Col. Romeo Gauvreau, Royals' president and vice president respectively, and Branch Rickey Jr., who heads the Brooklyn farm system.

"Mr. Racine and my father," said young Rickey, "will undoubtedly 20 be severely criticized in some sections of the United States where racial prejudice is rampant. They are not inviting trouble, but they won't avoid it if it comes. Jack Robinson is a fine type of young man, intelligent and college bred, and I think he can take it, too."

Ⓕ OCUS ON FORM

The purpose of a newspaper article is to provide timely news about an event that has just taken place. Newspaper articles typically have the following elements:

- a **headline**, which is printed in large type and often sums up the article
- a **subtitle**, which adds a "teaser," a prompt to make you want to read
- a **dateline** at the beginning of the article to tell when and where the story was written
- **photographs**
- **captions**
- a **lead**, the attention-grabbing first few sentences
- **information** about *who, what, when, where, why,* and *how*

Ⓐ NEWSPAPER ARTICLE
What do you learn from the **subtitle** of this article that you don't learn from the **headline?**

Robinson, himself, had little to say. "Of course, I can't begin to tell 30 you how happy I am that I am the first member of my race in organized ball," he declared. "I realize how much it means to me, to my race and to baseball. I can only say I'll do my very best to come through in every manner."

Robinson is seen here as he takes a practice swing.

Implications Are Realized

With sports writers and photographers assembled, young Rickey and Racine made the announce- 40 ment here. Rickey Jr. went on to explain that both he and his father—who was not present— realized the implications and possible reactions in other quarters of the diamond world. **B**

"It may cost the Brooklyn organization a number of ball players," he said. "Some of them, particularly if they come from certain sections 50 of the South, will steer away from a club with colored players on its roster. Some players now with us may even quit, but they'll be back in baseball after they work a year or two in a cotton mill."

Rickey Sr.'s hunt for Negro talent has produced some twenty-five others he expects to sign to contracts for double-A ball, with the 60 intention of developing them into big leaguers.

On Aug. 29 Robinson was quietly taken to Brooklyn. Rickey Sr. told him what he had in mind, and the broad-shouldered Pasadena, Calif., Negro agreed to sign a contract by Nov. 1.

"Robinson is a good ball player and comes to us highly recom- 70 mended by our scouts," Racine said. "He will join us at our training camp in Florida next spring." **C**

Reprint from **The New York Times**

ROBINSON STEALS HOME IN FIFTH

by ROSCOE McGOWEN

Robinson slides home to win the ball game against Pittsburgh. **D**

PITTSBURGH, June 24— They're never too old to learn something. The 40-year-old Fritz Ostermueller learned tonight at Forbes Field, before 35,331 distressed witnesses, that it is unwise to wind up with Jackie Robinson on third base. **E**

The Negro flash stole home with two out in the fifth inning while Fritz was going through his full motion to pitch a third ball to Dixie Walker—and that run was enough to win the ball game, although the Brooks went on to outscore the Pirates, 4–2.

At the time Robinson committed his larceny the score was tied, both teams having scored twice in the second inning. Dixie Walker

D **NEWSPAPER ARTICLE**
Based on the **headline**, **photo**, and **caption**, what does the article focus on?

E **TREATMENT AND SCOPE**
Reread lines 2–8. What **tone** does a phrase like "They're never too old to learn something" convey?

opened the second with a long triple to left center and Pee Wee Reese, catching a three-and-one pitch on the fat part of his bat, walloped the ball far over the outer left field barrier for his eighth homer of the campaign.

The Box Score

PITTSBURGH

		ab.	r.	h.	po.	a.	e.
Rikard	rf	3	0	1	3	0	0
Wiet'nn	2b	4	0	0	3	1	0
Gustine	3b	4	0	0	0	2	0
Kiner	lf	3	1	1	1	0	0
Cox.	ss	3	1	2	2	3	0
Fletcher	1b	4	0	1	5	1	0
W'lake	cf	4	0	0	2	0	0
Howell	c	4	0	1	8	1	0
Oster'ler	p	3	0	1	3	1	0
Sullivan		1	0	0	0	0	0
Total		33	2	7	27	9	0

BROOKLYN

		ab.	r.	h.	po.	a.	e.
Stanky	2b	4	0	1	1	4	0
Gionfriddo	lf	4	1	0	3	0	0
Robinson	1b	4	1	1	11	0	0
Furillo	cf	4	0	2	2	0	1
Walker	rf	3	1	1	1	0	0
Reese	ss	4	1	1	3	3	0
Jorgens'n	3b	4	0	2	0	2	0
Hodges	c	3	0	0	5	0	0
Branca	p	4	0	0	1	1	0
Total		34	4	8	27	10	1

```
Brooklyn . . . . . 0   2   0   0   1   0   1   0   0   —   4
Pittsburgh . . . . 0   2   0   0   0   0   0   0   0   —   2
```

Runs batted in—Reese 2, Fletcher, Furillo
Two-base hit—Rikard. Three-base hit—Walker. Home run—Reese. Stolen bases—Furillo, Robinson, Gionfriddo. Double play—Stanky, Reese and Robinson. Left on bases—Brooklyn 7. Pittsburgh 7. Bases on balls— Off Branca 3. Ostermueller 4. Struck out—By Ostermueller 7. Branca 4. Umpires—Stewart, Ballanfant and Henline. Time of game—2:41. Attendance—35,331. **F**

Comprehension

1. **Recall** What was Jackie Robinson the first African-American person to do?

2. **Summarize** In the newspaper article "Montreal Signs Negro Shortstop," Branch Rickey Jr. says that he and his father realize what the reactions to signing Robinson may be. Summarize these possible reactions.

Text Analysis

3. **Analyze the Lead** Explain what a lead is. Identify the lead in either one of the two newspaper articles you just read. Then explain how that lead gets its readers' attention.

4. **Compare Treatment and Scope** Using the chart you completed, compare the treatment and scope of the two articles.

COMMON CORE

RI 1 Cite evidence to support analysis of what the text says explicitly. **RI 9** Analyze how two or more authors writing about the same topic shape their presentations by emphasizing different evidence or interpretations of facts. **W 2** Write explanatory texts to examine a topic and convey ideas, concepts, and information.

Read for Information: Evaluate Texts for Usefulness

WRITING PROMPT

Imagine you have chosen one of the following topics for a report:

- box scores and how they have changed over the years
- attitudes toward African-American athletes in the 1940s
- sports reporting

Explain which newspaper article you would use as a source of information for this topic and why. If both articles would be useful to you, be sure to explain what each would provide.

To answer this prompt, first identify the topic you would want to focus on. Then follow these steps:

1. Review the chart you filled in. What information does each article provide?

2. In a paragraph, identify the topic you picked, the article(s) you would use for a report on that topic, and a brief explanation as to why the article(s) would be useful to you.

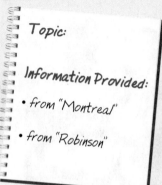

Topic:

Information Provided:

• from "Montreal"

• from "Robinson"

from Jackie Robinson
Documentary on **Media ◗ Smart** DVD-ROM

What makes a person a
TRAILBLAZER?

COMMON CORE

SL 2 Analyze the main ideas and supporting details presented in diverse media and formats and explain how the ideas clarify a topic, text, or issue under study.

Jackie Robinson did more than play baseball. He helped pave the way for racial equality in professional sports. You've read about the key moment in his remarkable career. Now watch a documentary that shows the obstacles Jackie Robinson overcame to pave a new path for baseball.

Background

Retiring Number 42 It's common for a professional team to retire the jersey number of an outstanding player. It's quite uncommon to retire a number throughout an entire league. This happened in 1997, when Jackie Robinson's number, 42, was retired to mark the 50th anniversary of breaking the color barrier in baseball. Many baseball greats were at the ceremony to pay tribute to this trailblazer.

This documentary from the A&E Channel's *Biography* series shows how Robinson's courage won him the respect of his teammates and earned him admiration nationwide.

Media Literacy: Documentary

A **documentary** is a nonfiction film or television production that tells about important people, historic places, or major events. The purpose of a documentary may be to inform, to explain, or to persuade. A documentary that is biographical presents the factual details of a person's life, focusing on major events. Most documentaries use interesting visuals and sounds and are edited to make the information easy to follow.

BASIC FEATURES	STRATEGIES FOR VIEWING	
Visuals To bring a subject to life, a documentary uses **photographs, film, interviews,** or **graphics.**	• Look for **footage** that helps you understand the subject. Footage can include photographs, letters, interviews, news reports, film clips, and even home video movies. Documentary filmmakers use footage to show key information or details about a person, a place, or an event and to give a sense of a particular time. • Pay attention to **interviews.** People who are interviewed can be experts on a topic, or people who are directly involved with the subject of the documentary.	
Sound Many documentaries include **voice-over narration,** which is the voice of an unseen speaker who is heard as the documentary plays. Other sounds include **music, sound effects,** and **dialogue.**	• Listen carefully to the **voice-over narrator.** The voice-over tells viewers why the subject is important and provides clues about how the information is organized. The voice-over may also summarize key scenes or events. • Follow **musical cues.** Music can be used simply to entertain viewers. It can also signal a change in the documentary's setting or changes in mood.	
Editing **Editing** is the process of selecting and arranging visuals and sounds in a way that makes sense and is interesting for viewers.	Pay attention to how the information is presented and **edited.** Most documentaries will show events from beginning to end in a chronological, or time-order, sequence.	

Media ● Smart DVD-ROM
- **Video Clip:** *Jackie Robinson*
- **Genre:** Documentary
- **Running Time:** 8 minutes

Viewing Guide for
Jackie Robinson

Today, all athletes have an equal chance to play in professional sports, but there was a time when Jackie Robinson was the only African-American athlete out in the field. As you view the documentary, pay attention to the comments of those who knew and worked with Robinson. They will help you understand why he is considered a hero by so many people.

To continue exploring the features of a documentary, answer the following questions.

NOW VIEW

FIRST VIEWING: Comprehension

1. **Recall** Who is the player who became Jackie Robinson's friend during Robinson's first year with the Dodgers?

2. **Clarify** The documentary ends with this quotation from Jackie Robinson: "A life is not important except in the impact it has on other lives." In your own words, explain what this means.

CLOSE VIEWING: Media Literacy

3. **Examine Musical Cues** Describe the music that is used during the footage of the 1947 World Series. What kind of **mood,** or feeling, does the music create?

4. **Analyze Interviews** Andrew Young, a civil rights leader, explains why he admires Jackie Robinson. Based on the interview, what do you think Young wants today's viewers to admire about Jackie Robinson?

5. **Evaluate Footage** The documentary uses such footage as interviews, photographs, and video. Which of these features helped you understand most about the impact of "The Noble Experiment"? Explain.

Write or Discuss

Analyze the Documentary The television documentary clip you've just viewed shows highlights of Jackie Robinson's life and baseball career. What new information did you learn about Jackie Robinson from the documentary? Think about

- the interviews with Rachel Robinson, Andrew Young, Branch Rickey, and Jackie Robinson himself
- the film footage that shows Jackie Robinson as a player, the Brooklyn fans, and the 1947 World Series
- the voice-over narration that provides details of key events in Robinson's life

Produce Your Own Media

Record an Interview Imagine you're creating a documentary about someone you think is an everyday hero. Make plans for an **interview.** If you don't have direct contact with a hero, create a list of jobs that you think involve heroism and courage. Then get permission to find and interview someone whose job you have listed.

HERE'S HOW Use the tips and the student model to help you prepare for and carry out an interview session.

- Do some research about your interview subject. Then contact the person and arrange an interview. Arrange to have an adult accompany you for this session.
- Make a list of questions you'd like to ask. Organize those questions into a key-word outline. For example, questions about the subject's childhood and education could be listed under the key word *Background*.
- During the interview, listen to the person's responses and ask follow-up questions. Refer to your key-word outline for question ideas.

STUDENT MODEL

> QUESTIONS
>
> Background
>> Where did you grow up?
>> Who was your hero when you were young?
>
> Earliest Success
>> What was the first project you really felt successful doing?
>> How did you feel about being given greater responsibility?
>
> Favorite Activities
>> What do you like to do most in your spare time?
>> Do you have a favorite book?

Media Tools

THINK central

Go to **thinkcentral.com**.
KEYWORD: HML7-855

Tech Tip

If available, use an audio or video recorder to tape the interview.

Clara Barton: Battlefield Nurse

Drama by Jeannette Covert Nolan

from The War Diary of Clara Barton

Diary Entry by Clara Barton

VIDEO TRAILER THINK central KEYWORD: HML7-856

How can we CHANGE what's wrong?

COMMON CORE

RL 9 Compare and contrast a fictional portrayal of a time, place, or character and a historical account of the same period as a means of understanding how authors of fiction use or alter history. **RI 1** Cite textual evidence to support analysis of what the text says explicitly.

It's not easy to change what is wrong or unfair. Those people who fought to end slavery, those who helped women get the right to vote, and those who protected children from harmful working conditions were considered troublemakers by many in their day. Yet their victories made the world a better place. In this play and diary entry, you'll learn about one such person.

DISCUSS List people who fought for change in order to make the world a better place. Discuss whether these people might have achieved the same results if they hadn't upset anyone.

TEXT ANALYSIS: HISTORY-RELATED WRITINGS

History-related writings are fiction or nonfiction texts that focus on people or events from history. History-related writing can take different forms. For example, a **historical drama**, a fictional form, is a play based on real events and people that takes place in the past. However, the dialogue and action are mostly created by the playwright. An example of a nonfiction form is the diary of a historical figure. A **diary** is a daily record of a writer's thoughts, experiences, and feelings. Diary entries can shed light on what life was like at the time the writer lived.

As you read *Clara Barton: Battlefield Nurse* and the excerpt from *The War Diary of Clara Barton,* look for details that tell you about Clara and the time in which she lived.

READING STRATEGY: COMPARE AND CONTRAST

When you **compare and contrast** two works on the same topic, but one is fictional and the other is factual, you should examine the similarities in how each work portrays the characters, their actions, the setting, and the events. By noting contrasts between the works, you can get a sense of how fiction writers blend factual details with imaginary ones to achieve a dramatic effect.

As you read the historical drama about Clara Barton and the diary entry written by her, use a chart like the one shown to compare and contrast details.

	Clara Barton: Battlefield Nurse	War Diary of Clara Barton
Characters/ Real-life people	Captain Neal	"dapper captain"
Actions	Blocks Clara's attempts to aid soldiers	
Setting		
Events		

Complete the activities in your **Reader/Writer Notebook.**

Jeannette Covert Nolan
1897–1974

History Lover

Bringing history to life was Jeanette Covert Nolan's specialty. Poets, spies, presidents—Nolan covered them all in more than 45 biographies, essays, and books of historical fiction. She also worked for a time as a reporter and as a teacher of writing for children and young adults.

Clara Barton
1821–1912

Humanitarian

Clara Barton accomplished many amazing feats in her day. She began teaching at age 15 and opened a free school in her 30s. During the Civil War, she worked on the battlefield, distributing supplies and nursing the wounded. After the war, Barton was inspired by the International Red Cross to organize the American National Red Cross. She served as its president for more than 20 years. For her life's work, she came to be known as the "angel of the battlefield."

Authors Online

Go to **thinkcentral.com.** KEYWORD: HML7-857

CLARA BARTON
Battlefield Nurse

Jeannette Covert Nolan

CHARACTERS

Captain Neal, of the U.S. Army
    Medical Corps

Sergeant Fisk

Pvt. Joe Brown ⎤
              ⎦— orderlies
Pvt. Carl Jenkins ⎦

Mrs. Almira Fales

Clara Barton

George, Clara's handyman

Courier

Messenger

Offstage Voice

Time: *The evening of December 13, 1862.*[1]

Setting: *A room in a small building on the grounds of Lacy House,*[2] *a plantation mansion in Falmouth, Virginia.*

At rise:[3] Captain Neal *sits at table, going through stacks of paper.* Sergeant Fisk *looks out window. Bursts of gunfire can be heard intermittently.*

---

1. **December 13, 1862:** the Battle of Fredericksburg, one of the early important battles of the American Civil War, was fought in and near Fredericksburg, Virginia, on December 13–15, 1862. Confederate troops defeated Union troops during this battle.

2. **Lacy House . . . Virginia:** During the Battle of Fredericksburg, a Union army hospital was established at Lacy House, a mansion not far from the fighting.

3. **At rise:** as the curtain rises.

Captain Neal (*suddenly*). What's this?

Fisk (*turning*). Sir?

10 **Captain Neal.** This packet of letters.

Fisk. Letters the men in Lacy House want sent to their families, sir. They're for the return mail tonight. A courier is coming from Washington, as you know.

Captain Neal (*irritably, breaking in*). How should I know? I arrived here only yesterday, and I don't have the hang of things yet. I begin to wonder if I ever will! (*leafs through letters*) They're all in the same handwriting.

Illustrations by Dove (David) McHargue

Fisk. Clara Barton's handwriting, sir. Those
men are among the worst wounded; they can't
write, can't hold a pen. They tell Miss Barton
what to say, and she writes it down for them.

Captain Neal (*with exasperation*). Miss Barton? I
might have guessed! That woman is a nuisance!

Fisk (*surprised*). Clara Barton, a nuisance, sir?

Captain Neal. An infernal nuisance! She has
no respect for rank or discipline, no official
capacity—no right to be here. Yet she behaves
30 as though she had invented the place!

Fisk. Well, sir, in a way she did. She's been in
Falmouth more than a week, working round
the clock, organizing the hospital, ever since
our troops started assembling.

Captain Neal. That's her usual procedure. If a
battle is anticipated, Miss Barton moves in with
the vanguard regiments.[4] Or if the skirmish
occurs without forewarning, she moves in
as soon as the news reaches Washington. In
40 either circumstance she rushes into the field,
establishes herself and assumes control of the
situation.

Fisk. She brought five wagonloads of supplies
with her, sir. Food, blankets, bandages,
medicines—

Captain Neal (*in scoffing tone*). She always
brings supplies.

Fisk. They say she buys them with her own
money.

50 **Captain Neal.** Yes, and with donations solicited
from her friends all over the country. She's
not timid. She'll stop at nothing. (*abruptly*)
Sergeant, are you married?

Fisk (*taken aback*). Married? (*proudly*) Why,
yes, sir.

---

4. **vanguard regiments:** the troops moving at the head of the army.

5. **Patent Office:** a government office that grants patents,
documents giving inventors exclusive rights to make, use, or sell
an invention.

Captain Neal. And how does your wife spend
her time?

Fisk. Why, minding the house and the kids, sir.

Captain Neal. As well she should! I'm sure your
60 wife wouldn't dream of neglecting her home
and family to make a spectacle of herself on a
battlefield, picking up the dead, nursing the
injured. Nor should mine!

Fisk. But Miss Barton isn't married, sir.

Captain Neal (*sharply*). What has that to do
with it? I know plenty of unmarried ladies
who are content to stay in their homes, where
they belong, and leave the rough tasks to men.

Fisk (*slightly puzzled*). They say Miss Barton
70 never was much of a homebody, sir. She had
a job in Washington before the war; she was a
clerk in the government Patent Office.[5]

Captain Neal (*interrupting*). And she ought
to be there now. Instead, she traipses down
to Falmouth, takes over the Lacy Plantation
House, (*pointing to door, left*) turns it into a
hospital—and proposes to manage it!

Fisk. Without any permission at all?

Captain Neal. Oh, she probably obtained
80 some sort of permission, but with or without permission, it wouldn't matter to Clara Barton. She never stands on ceremony. She just rushes in with her wagonloads of supplies, her handful of volunteer assistants—

Fisk (*more puzzled*). She accomplished a lot of good, sir.

Captain Neal. What's good about a woman on the field? It's against nature, against Army rules! (*impatiently*) She seems to bewitch people to
90 do her bidding. They seem to be in awe of her. But I am not! I officially represent the Medical Corps at this post now, and I will not be bluffed by a fussy little woman like— (Pvt. Joe Brown *enters up right, carrying huge covered basket. As he opens door, explosion of cannon is heard off.*)

Brown. Whew! That was a whopper! Those Confederate gunners—[6]

Captain Neal. Shut the door, soldier!

100 **Brown.** Yes, sir. (*shuts door and sets basket on floor*)

Captain Neal. Where have you been, Brown?

Brown. Out trading with neighborhood farmers for fresh milk and eggs. Fared right well, too.

Captain Neal. Did I say anything to you about fresh milk and eggs?

Brown. No, sir. Miss Barton did. She said I was to take some of that canned stuff from her stores and trade it for—

110 **Captain Neal** (*coldly*). Let me remind you, Brown, that you're a Medical Corps orderly, not Miss Barton's errand-boy.

Brown (*in confusion*). Yes, sir—no sir—(*pauses as another explosion is heard off*)

Captain Neal (*rising; anxiously*). Fisk, go see what's happening in Fredericksburg! Get me a report! (*as Fisk nods*) No, nevermind, I'll go myself! I have to know what's going on— (*exits quickly right*)

120 **Brown.** Air's pretty thick in here, eh, Sergeant?

Fisk (*nodding*). Pretty thick, Joe

Brown. The old man's sure got his dander up.

Fisk. I think he's worried.

Brown. Everybody's worried. The Johnny Rebs are giving us Yanks[7] the very devil.

Fisk. Captain Neal's brother is in the midst of it. His artillery battery[8] is in an exposed position that the Confederates have been shelling for hours.

130 **Brown.** Lieutenant Ralph Neal? I know him. He's just a boy.

Fisk (*sighing*). A boy of nineteen. (*pause*) How old are you, Joe?

Brown. Twenty—but a veteran. (*steps to window, looks out*) Every man out there is somebody's brother or son or sweetheart.

Fisk. And another thing—the Captain is at odds with Miss Barton.

Brown. What about?

140 **Fisk.** I think he resents the fact that she was here before he was, and he doesn't like playing second fiddle.

Brown. Jealous, eh?

Fisk. Maybe. He's certainly critical of everything.

---

6. **Confederate gunners:**
7. **Johnny Rebs . . . Yanks:** slang for Confederate soldiers (Rebels) and Union soldiers (Yankees).
8. **artillery battery:** an army unit responsible for cannons and other big guns.

Brown. But why? Miss Barton—why, Sergeant, she's an angel!

Fisk. Captain Neal isn't a bad fellow.

Brown. I'll take Miss Barton!

150 **Fisk** (*grinning*). You're one of those people she's bewitched, Joe.

Brown. I'm one she nursed back to health last year. There are hundreds of us; we owe our lives to her. (*Knock is heard at right door. Fisk opens it to* Mrs. Almira Fales, *dressed in traveling costume and carrying a small valise.*)

Mrs. Fales. I'm looking for Miss Barton. Do you know where she is?

Fisk. In the hospital, ma'am. Will you have a
160 seat? I'll call her for you. (*exits left*)

Mrs. Fales (*sitting on bench, puts valise on floor*). What's the news, young man?

Brown. Not very cheerful, ma'am. The day seems to be going badly for us.

Mrs. Fales. I feared so. Well, I suppose we can't win every engagement.

Brown. No, ma'am. Though that would be nice, wouldn't it? (*glancing appraisingly at her*) Traveling's kind of inconvenient in these times
170 for a lady.

Mrs. Fales. Oh, I travel whenever and wherever I please.

Brown. Are you some kin to Miss Barton?

Mrs. Fales. No. But I know Miss Barton—and admire her. (*smiling reminiscently*) Miss Barton and I met on the way to a battlefield. It was in August, at Bull Run.[9] You see, Mr.—

Brown. Brown—the name is Joe Brown, ma'am.

180 **Mrs. Fales.** You see, Mr. Brown, my sons are soldiers. I knew they were at Bull Run. Somehow I had the notion they'd been hurt, perhaps killed. There was no reliable information about the battle, no list of casualties. My husband and I were frantic. Finally I decided I would just go down there and find out about our boys. It was on the road I met Miss Barton. I had heard of her and the magnificent service she's performing.
190 I asked if I could work with her at Bull Run. She had a few men working with her, but we were the only women in the outfit. (*shaking her head*) And how we worked! The battle was over, the ground literally strewn with human wreckage—and not enough doctors from the Medical Corps.

Brown (*shaking head*). There never are enough, ma'am.

Mrs. Fales. We had several days and nights of
200 it, working at top speed in the most adverse conditions. At last we got the field cleared, the dead buried, and the wounded shipped by train to hospitals in the surrounding cities. I learned most about nursing from Miss Barton. She is an expert.

Brown (*fervently*). An angel!

Mrs. Fales. Yes, she seemed just that. Then, a week ago, when I heard she was in Falmouth, I made up my mind to come and help—if she'll
210 have me.

Brown (*enthusiastically*). Oh, I reckon she will, ma'am, and gladly. (*tentatively*) But—your sons?

Mrs. Fales. They survived Bull Run. So far they've been spared, thank goodness! (Captain Neal *enters right.* Brown *salutes.*)

Brown. Mrs. Fales is here to see Miss Barton, sir.

Captain Neal (*nodding gruffly*). Madam.

220 **Mrs. Fales.** How do you do, sir?

---

9. **Bull Run:** the site of a famous early Civil War battle, in which Confederate forces defeated Union forces and nearly 5000 men were killed, wounded, captured, or gone missing.

Captain Neal. Well, Brown, is this your rest period? Be off!

Brown (*clicking his heels*). Yes, sir. (*moves toward door*)

Captain Neal. What about your milk and eggs?

Brown. Oh, yes, sir! I almost forgot. (*Exits with basket.* Captain Neal *eyes* Mrs. Fales *curiously, then sits at table and busies himself with pen and paper.* Clara Barton *enters left.*)

230 **Mrs. Fales** (*rising*). Clara!

Clara. Almira Fales!

Mrs. Fales (*pleased*). So you remember me?

Clara (*warmly*). As if I ever could forget! (*clasping* Mrs. Fales' *hands*) Is it possible you've come to volunteer?

Mrs. Fales. Yes, I have.

Clara (*happily*). Oh, I'm so grateful! Do sit down. I'm so happy you're here.

Mrs. Fales (*sitting with* Clara *on the bench*).
240 You're looking well, Clara.

Clara. I am well. Always tired, but well. (*smiles*) My health seems to thrive on abuse.

Mrs. Fales. And still wearing that red bow in honor of your father.

Clara. In memory of him, now. My father died recently.

Mrs. Fales (*sadly*). Oh, I'm so sorry to hear that.

Clara. Thank you, Almira. (*sighing*) Red was his favorite color; it's mine, too.

250 **Mrs. Fales.** The badge of bravery. (*leans forward, intently*) You are so often in danger, Clara! Are you never afraid?

Clara. Afraid? Constantly! I just try to hide my fear—with a bright red ribbon.

George (*entering left, carrying wooden tool kit; gruffly*). Miss Barton, I've built those extra bunks you were talking about.

Clara. Thank you, George. I'd like you to meet Mrs. Fales, a good friend of mine, and
260 a good nurse. (*to* Mrs. Fales) George is my right-hand man.

George (*grinning cordially at* Mrs. Fales). You'll be welcome, ma'am. (*to* Clara) I made space for the poor chaps. Reckon we'll get 'em, too. The stretcher-bearers are out now.

Clara. I'll inspect the bunks. Will you come with me, Almira? (*They rise and exit left. George starts to follow, but* Captain Neal *stops him with a gesture.*)

270 **Captain Neal.** Are you a carpenter?

George (*with a laugh*). Carpenter, porter, chief cook, and bottle washer, jack-of-all-trades.

Captain Neal. I have some carpenter's chores for you to do, at your leisure.

George. Well, sir, I don't have much leisure— and I'd be obliged to ask Miss Barton.

Captain Neal (*sharply*). No, you would not! I am in charge here. Miss Barton has no connection with the Army—

280 **George.** She's tried to connect herself with the Army, sir, but those people in Washington won't let her do what she wants to do.

Captain Neal. Nor will I, here at Lacy House.

George. So you're one of 'em? Well, sir, you'll just have to get your own carpenter. I'm working for Miss Barton! (*exits quickly through door right*)

Clara (*reopening door left*). The bunks are fine, George. . . . Oh, George is gone?

290 **Captain Neal** (*dryly*). Yes, he's gone—quite suddenly,

Clara. Well, I must get Mrs. Fales settled.

Captain Neal. Just a moment, Miss Barton! Why is that lady in Falmouth?

Clara (*smiling*). I think you know why. Weren't you eavesdropping?

Captain Neal (*incensed*). Miss Barton, I do not intend to have Lacy House turned into an institution for interfering females!

300 **Clara.** Oh, Captain, how I wish there were more interfering females. They make such splendid nurses.

Captain Neal. Then they should enlist as nurses in the Army.

Clara. I thought of doing that, but those women are sent to work in city hospitals; they can never go into the field. I would like the Army to sponsor me as a field nurse, where I know I'm most effective.

310 **Captain Neal** (*sternly*). Where you have no authority to be. The Army does not approve of women in military encampments. The battlefield is not a place for women.

Clara. How silly! So many lives are sacrificed because of the Army's rigidity.

Voice (*offstage*). Miss Barton! Miss Barton is needed!

Clara. Excuse me, please, Captain. (*exits*)

Captain Neal. Miss Barton is needed! All

320 day, by everyone! But if I have my way, Miss Barton may soon find there are such things as rules and regulations.

Fisk. (*entering*). Excuse me, Captain, but there's heavy firing on our artillery positions.

Captain Neal (*anxiously*). How bad is it?

Fisk. A great many casualties, it would seem. (*goes to window and looks out*) The stretcher-bearers are busy with the wounded. (*Guns boom in distance.*)

330 **Jenkins** (*entering right*). Sergeant, where do we take these Graycoats?

Captain Neal. Graycoats?

Jenkins (*noticing* Captain Neal, *salutes him*). Yes, sir. The Confederate Johnnies. Are they to be put in the hospital with our boys?

Captain Neal. Who said they were to be brought to Lacy House?

Jenkins. Miss Barton, sir.

Captain Neal. The hospital is crowded!

340 **Jenkins.** Not too crowded, Miss Barton said.

Captain Neal. Go outside and wait there! (Jenkins *salutes and exits.*) Fisk, call Miss Barton.

Fisk. Yes, sir. (*exits*)

Captain Neal (*to himself*). Now she has gone too far. Much too far. (*After a moment,* Fisk *reenters, escorting* Clara.) I'll talk privately with Miss Barton, Sergeant. (Fisk *exits right.*) Miss Barton, since when have we adopted a policy of 350 rescuing our sworn enemies?

Clara (*calmly*). I have always done it, Captain.

Captain Neal. You have done it?

Clara. I have never withheld aid to any man lying on any battlefield, merely because his uniform was gray rather than blue. I never stop to ask him his race, politics, or religion, either. If he is a human being—suffering, I give him all the help I can.

Captain Neal (*angrily*). This is ridiculous. Do 360 you for an instant suppose that our men who fall on a Southern battlefield are shown such mercy?

Clara. Of course, I suppose that! I know it is true! And you must surely know it, too. I think the Confederates' ideas and convictions are wrong. But I am not so deluded as to think they aren't human!

Jenkins (*opening door; thrusting in his head*). Miss Barton, the Sergeant said you were in 370 here. Shall we take the Rebs into Lacy House? It's getting dark and raining a little.

Clara. Yes, Jenkins.

Captain Neal. Just a minute, orderly. We cannot accommodate those men.

Clara. We can accommodate them, Captain. And we must!

Captain Neal. Our facilities are limited.

Clara. George built more bunks—and he can build more, many more.

380 **Captain Neal.** By taking in these Confederates, we may be depriving men who fell inside our lines.

Jenkins. These men fell inside our lines, sir.

Clara. Indeed, Captain, should we have allowed them to lie there and die? How could we turn them away? (*to* Jenkins) Take them into Lacy House! (Jenkins *has been looking bewilderedly from* Clara *to* Captain Neal, *he exits.*)

390 **Captain Neal** (*furiously*). Miss Barton, this situation is intolerable! (Fisk *enters.*) Sergeant, didn't I tell you—

Fisk (*apologetically*). The mail, sir. The courier from Washington. (*stands aside*)

Courier (*entering, placing mail pouch on table*). Anything to go back, Captain?

Captain Neal. Yes. (*He picks up packet of letters that* Clara *has written for the soldiers, tosses it to* Courier, *who salutes and exits, followed by* Fisk. *Glancing briefly through contents of the mail pouch, he pounces upon one letter, opens and scans it hurriedly. Holding the letter,* Captain Neal *turns to* Clara.) Miss Barton, I am not a cruel man—

Clara. Oh, I'm sure of that. Merely short-sighted and old-fashioned in your prejudices. And obstinate. But I am obstinate,[10] myself.

Voice (*offstage*). Miss Barton! Miss Barton is needed!

Clara. Excuse me, Captain. (*starts toward door left*)

Captain Neal. Since the moment of my arrival in Falmouth, I have known there would be this crisis.

Clara (*turning back*). Crisis?

Captain Neal. Between us. I have seen it as inevitable that while you were here, some members of the small staff in Lacy House, perhaps most of them, would ignore me and look to you for direction—

Clara (*quietly*). Only because I was here first.

Captain Neal (*raising his voice*). You are everywhere first, Miss Barton! It is uncanny. (*more calmly, with an effort at controlling his temper*) Therefore, I have known that one of us must go. And I have not doubted which one it would be.

Clara (*matter-of-factly*). Is that your opinion? Mine is just the contrary, Captain. I don't see why we both can't remain, and on good terms, too. If there is a crisis between us, it is not of my making.

Captain Neal (*with sarcasm*). Oh, no?

Clara. I wish only to work with you—with anyone who serves the end of justice and mercy. Very often I've been thrown into contact with a man like you—prejudiced, suspicious of me and my methods, even my motives; but still we have worked together well enough. And sometimes we have become fast friends. I have many friends among the Medical Corps doctors. I don't see why you and I can't arrange some sort of compromise—

Captain Neal (*harshly*). It is too late for compromise.

Voice (*offstage*). Miss Barton!

Clara. Too late, Captain?

Captain Neal. This letter—

Brown (*opening door at left*). Miss Barton, that fellow with the malaria[11] has got a chill, a violent chill—

Captain Neal (*shouting*). Get out! Get out!

Clara (*above* Captain Neal's *shouting*). Give him a dose of quinine,[12] Brown. See that he swallows it. I'll come presently.

Brown. Yes, ma'am. (*closes door*)

Captain Neal. Miss Barton, I've received a letter from Washington. (*holding up letter*) From my superior officers. It is the reply to a telegram I dispatched last night—just twelve hours after my arrival. I am lucky to have a reply so promptly.

Clara (*uneasily*). And what does it say?

Captain Neal. The tone of this letter is unequivocal.[13] It states very definitely that you are to be relieved of all duty in the Falmouth area. At once. In plain words, Miss Barton, you are dismissed.

---

10. **obstinate:** stubborn.

11. **malaria:** a disease transmitted by mosquitoes.

12. **quinine:** a type of medicine.

13. **unequivocal:** clear; unquestionable.

Clara (*incredulously*). You wired to the War Department, complaining of me?

Captain Neal. I did.

Clara. You complained of my skill at nursing?

Captain Neal. Not that. You may be a very good nurse.

Clara (*vehemently*). I am a good nurse!

Captain Neal. I complained of you as a meddler.

480 **Clara** (*angrily*). In plain words, Captain, you let your dislike of me override your judgment regarding the welfare of this hospital.

Captain Neal (*emphatically*). There is nothing more to be said on the subject. You are relieved of all duty. I'll have a wagon made ready to convey you safely to the railroad station. Of course, the other lady, Mrs. Fales, will accompany you.

Clara (*angrily*). But I won't go! I can't desert the men, the wounded men in Lacy House. I know them—know them all by name!

490 **Captain Neal** (*firmly*). You will go, Miss Barton. Under the circumstances it would be most awkward for you to remain. Your dismissal is from Washington, and it is specific and urgent.

Clara. Who will do the work in my place? I've snatched back from death's door many patients whom your doctors and nurses had given up as lost.

Captain Neal (*sneeringly*). I'm not interested in a recital of your triumphs.

500 **Clara** (*angrily*). How absurdly, blindly biased you are, Captain!

Captain Neal (*with controlled anger*). Sergeant Fisk will fetch a wagon. You must have a bag, or something to pack?

Clara (*sadly, realizing her defeat*). Yes, I have a bag. (*starts toward left door, speaks over her shoulder*) I came with five wagon-loads of supplies. For days they were the only supplies available, and they're not yet exhausted. I

510 hope you will accept what's left—for the sake of the hospital. Lint, medicines, muslin sheets—such articles have value, even if I have none.

Captain Neal (*stiffly*). I will accept them, Miss Barton. (*As she exits, he paces up and down, muttering.*) A strange woman. Most women would have cried. She didn't. No tears. She has courage—the courage of a man!

Fisk (*entering from door right*). May I come
520 in, sir?

Captain Neal (*barking*). Why not? (*a slight pause, as sound of cannon is heard off*) You're to fetch a wagon and drive Miss Barton and the other lady to the railroad station. They're catching the night train.

Fisk (*regretfully*). I'm sorry, sir. Miss Barton was so set on staying.

Captain Neal (*wryly*). More eavesdropping!

530 **Fisk** (*meekly*). Well, I was just at the door, sir, I couldn't have avoided—

Captain Neal. No matter. Go fetch a wagon.

Fisk (*lingering*). It does seem too bad, when Miss Barton's so popular with everybody—

Captain Neal (*roaring*). Fetch a wagon!

Fisk. Yes, sir. (*turns toward door*
540 *right and collides with* Messenger, *who rushes in, breathless*)

Messenger. Captain Neal? I'm from General Burnside's headquarters. We are in full retreat across the bridge, sir, falling back on all fronts. The Rebels have swept everything before them. (*pausing, panting*) And your brother, sir—

Captain Neal. My brother!

550 **Messenger.** Lieutenant Neal—

Captain Neal. What about him? (*seizing* Messenger *by the sleeve*) What about Lieutenant Neal?

Messenger. Shot, sir.

Captain Neal. Killed?

Messenger. Wounded, sir.

Captain Neal (*tugging roughly at* Messenger's *sleeve*). Is it—serious?

Messenger. Yes, sir. Serious. But the doctor in
560 Fredericksburg did an emergency operation. They're bringing him to Lacy House, sir.

Captain Neal (*releasing* Messenger's *sleeve*). Fisk! Fisk!

Fisk (*at door*). Yes, sir. Just off to fetch the wagon, sir.

Captain Neal. Wagon! (*wildly*) Blast the wagon! Fetch Miss Barton! Get her in here! (*shouts*) Miss Barton! (Clara, *wearing her traveling cloak and bonnet, enters.*)

570 **Clara.** Did you call me?

Captain Neal (*rushing to her*). I did call you, Miss Barton. My brother— (*He buries his face in his hands.*)

Messenger. It's Lieutenant Neal, ma'am. Seriously wounded.

Clara. The Captain's brother? Oh, dreadful! But—not dead?

Messenger. No, ma'am. Not yet.

Clara. Well, with proper nursing I'm sure—

580 **Messenger.** That's what the doctor said. With you here, the doctor said—

Captain Neal (*looking up; emotionally*). Miss Barton, my brother is so young!

Clara (*quietly*). Most of them are, aren't they? (*They exchange looks, then slowly, she takes off her bonnet and throws it on to bench.*) The doctor seems to think that something can be done.

Captain Neal. Miss Barton, if you will do your best for my brother—

590 **Clara.** I'll give him the same care I give all the men neither more nor less.

Captain Neal. I understand, Miss Barton. I understand—and I could ask for nothing better.

Mrs. Fales (*entering left, in traveling costume, carrying her valise*). Well, Clara, I'm ready, if we must go.

Clara. We're not going.

Mrs. Fales (*puzzled*). Not going?

600 **Clara.** We're staying—at Captain Neal's request.

Mrs. Fales. But I thought he—

Clara. The Captain wants us to work with him—and he's in command, isn't he?

Mrs. Fales (*perplexed*). I don't know. And I don't believe he knows either! (*to herself*) A very snappish man!

Clara (*smiling*). Sh-h! We must get into our work uniforms. (*They exit.*)

Captain Neal (*to* Fisk *and* Messenger). Why 610 are you standing there gaping? I have a letter to write. A letter which must be sent tonight. To Washington. (*hesitantly, as if with effort*) A letter acknowledging that I've been in error, and recommending that Miss Clara Barton be permanently attached to the United States Army, as an Army nurse—in the field, or wherever she chooses to be. (Fisk *and* Messenger *exit right.* Captain Neal *sits at table and writes rapidly. Lights dim slightly; shot is* 620 *heard off.*)

Clara (*entering at left*). Captain, your brother is in the hospital, and conscious. Would you like to speak to him?

Captain Neal (*springing up*). Will he pull through? Do you think there's a chance?

Clara. I think there's a chance.

Captain Neal. And you'll help him? (Clara *nods.*) I do want to speak to him! (*pauses*) I'd like you to read this letter.

630 **Clara** (*dismayed*). The letter from Washington?

Captain Neal (*quickly*). No, no, it's not the one I received! It's a letter I'm just in process of writing and haven't quite finished. But since it concerns you—(*hands letter to her, then crosses to door left and exits*)

Clara. I do think the Captain's heart is in the right place. (*Sits on bench and reads letter silently. She smiles, still holding letter.*) Sometimes I have a vision, or what seems a 640 vision. I see my country whole and healed once more, North and South reunited, one people, never again to be divided by war and hatred. (*pauses*) I see beyond the present, far, far into a future when this humble work of mine has found boundless, universal support. I see the work growing, embracing all the civilized nations of the world through both war and peace. (*During her speech, room has gradually darkened. On rear wall, spotlight* 650 *shines on emblem of Red Cross.*)

Voice (*offstage*). Miss Barton!

Clara (*rousing, turning her head*). Yes?

Voice. Miss Barton is needed!

Clara (*rising, standing a moment under Red Cross emblem, then hurrying to exit*). Coming!

Clara Barton became the founder of the Red Cross.

A **ANALYZE HISTORY-RELATED WRITINGS** Remember that **history-related writings** focus on people and events from history. A **diary entry**, a daily record of a writer's thoughts, experiences, and feelings, is one type of history-related writing. A diary entry can provide genuine insights into a real-life figure's personality. In addition, a diary entry can help readers see a time and place through that figure's own eyes. Reread lines 17–32. How do these details seem different from details about wounded soldiers in the play?

No one has forgotten the heart-sickness which spread over the entire country as the busy wires flashed the dire tidings of the terrible destitution and suffering of the wounded of the Wilderness whom I attended as they lay in Fredericksburg. But you may never have known how many hundredfold of these ills were augmented[1] by the conduct of improper, heartless, unfaithful officers in the immediate command of the city and upon whose actions and indecisions depended entirely the care, food, shelter, comfort, and lives of that whole city of wounded men. One of the highest officers there has
10 since been convicted a traitor. And another, a little dapper captain[2] quartered with the owners of one of the finest mansions in the town, boasted that he had changed his opinion since entering the city the day before; that it was in fact a pretty hard thing for refined people like the people of Fredericksburg to be compelled to open their homes and admit these "dirty, lousy, common soldiers," and that he was not going to compel it.

This I heard him say, and waited until I saw him make his words good, till I saw, crowded into one old sunken hotel, lying helpless upon its bare, wet, bloody floors, five hundred fainting men hold
20 up their cold, bloodless, dingy hands, as I passed, and beg me in Heaven's name for a cracker to keep them from starving (and I had none); or to give them a cup that they might have something to drink water from, if they could get it (and I had no cup and could get none); till I saw two hundred six-mule army wagons in a line, ranged down the street to headquarters, and reaching so far out on the Wilderness road that I never found the end of it; every wagon crowded with wounded men, stopped, standing in the rain and mud, wrenched back and forth by the restless, hungry animals all night from four o'clock in the afternoon till eight next morning and
30 how much longer I, know not. The dark spot in the mud under many a wagon, told only too plainly where some Poo fellow's[3] life had dripped out in those dreadful hours. **A**

---

1. **augmented:** made greater; added to.
2. **dapper . . . quartered with:** neat and stylish captain who is staying with.
3. **Poo fellow's:** poor man's.

I remembered one man who would set it right, if he knew it, who possessed the power and who would believe me if I told him I commanded immediate conveyance back to Belle Plain. With difficulty I obtained it, and four stout horses with a light army wagon took me ten miles at an unbroken gallop, through field and swamp and stumps and mud to Belle Plain and a steam tug at once to Washington. Landing at dusk I sent for Henry Wilson, chairman of the Military Committee of
40 the Senate. A messenger brought him at eight, saddened and appalled like every other patriot in that fearful hour, at the weight of woe under which the Nation staggered, groaned, and wept. **B**

He listened to the story of suffering and faithlessness, and hurried from my presence, with lips compressed and face like ashes. At ten he stood in the War Department.[4] They could not credit his report. He must have been deceived by some frightened villain. No official report of unusual suffering had reached them. Nothing had been called for by the military authorities commanding Fredericksburg.

Mr. Wilson assured them that the officers in trust there were
50 not to be relied upon. They were faithless, overcome by the blandishments[5] of the wily inhabitants. Still the Department doubted. It was then that he proved that my confidence in his firmness was not misplaced, as, facing his doubters he replies: "One of two things will have to be done—either you will send some one to-night with the power to investigate and correct the abuses of our wounded men at Fredericksburg, or the Senate will send some one tomorrow."

This threat recalled their scattered senses.

At two o'clock in the morning the Quartermaster-General[6] and
60 staff galloped to the 6th Street wharf under orders; at ten they were in Fredericksburg. At noon the wounded men were fed from the food of the city and the houses were opened to the "*dirty, lousy soldiers*" of the Union Army.

Both railroad and canal were opened. In three days I returned with carloads of supplies.

No more jolting in army wagons! And every man who left Fredericksburg by boat or by car owes it to the firm decision of one man that his grating bones were not dragged ten miles across the country or left to bleach in the sands of that city. ∿

B COMPARE AND CONTRAST
In the play, you learned about Clara mainly through dialogue. How do you learn about Clara in her diary? Record the information in your chart.

Senator Henry Wilson became vice-president.

---

4. **War Department:** the department of the U.S. government now called the Department of Defense.

5. **blandishments:** coaxings.

6. **Quartermaster-General:** the staff officer in charge of supplies for the entire army.

Comprehension

1. **Recall** In Clara Barton's diary, why is she so upset with the officers in Fredericksburg?

2. **Clarify** According to Clara's diary, why didn't the officials at the War Department believe Mr. Wilson at first?

3. **Summarize** In the play, why does Captain Neal change his mind about Clara?

COMMON CORE

RL 9 Compare and contrast a fictional portrayal of a time, place, or character and a historical account of the same period as a means of understanding how authors of fiction use or alter history. **RI 1** Cite textual evidence to support analysis of what the text says explicitly.

Text Analysis

4. **Draw Conclusions** For the diary entry, use a diagram to track the actions that reveal each person's traits. What do their actions tell you about the "dapper captain," Clara, and Mr. Wilson?

Real-Life Person	His or Her Actions	My Conclusion
"dapper captain"		
Clara		
Mr. Wilson		

5. **Compare and Contrast** You have read a **historical drama** about Clara Barton and a **diary entry** that she wrote. In these writings, what is similar and what is different about the struggles Clara faces?

6. **Analyze History-Related Writings** Based on these history-related writings, what impressions do you have of the role of women in the mid-1800s?

7. **Evaluate** Review the chart you created as you read. In your opinion, does the play or the diary provide a more interesting picture of Clara? Explain.

Extension and Challenge

8. **Inquiry and Research** Do research on the Lacy House and the Battle of Fredericksburg to find out how accurate the play is to historical events. Present your findings, including any photos you can locate of the house or the surrounding area.

How can we CHANGE what's wrong?

Recall your list of fighters for change from page 856. Which person on that list has personal qualities that are similar to Clara Barton's? Explain.

Language

◆ **GRAMMAR IN CONTEXT: Using Conjunctive Adverbs**

A **conjunctive adverb** is used to express a relationship between two independent clauses. By using a conjunctive adverb, you can combine two sentences into one, and avoid choppy-sounding writing. Here are some commonly used conjunctive adverbs and their appropriate uses.

Comparison: similarly, likewise, still   **Contrast:** however, regardless, besides
Examples: for example, namely   **Summary:** as a result, therefore, finally

To punctuate sentences with conjunctive adverbs, be sure to use a semicolon after the first independent clause and a comma after the conjunctive adverb.

Original: Clara Barton was a leader. She became an organizer.

Revised: Clara Barton was a leader; therefore, she became an organizer.

PRACTICE Combine the two sentences in each item below by using an appropriate conjunctive adverb from the examples above.

1. Captain Neal resisted Clara's help. He changed his mind.
2. The captain worried about his brother. Clara worried about every soldier.
3. Clara was not without sympathy at Lacy House. Mrs. Almira Fales came to offer help.
4. The unfaithful officers would not respond to Clara. She turned to Senator Henry Wilson.
5. Senator Wilson made a powerful threat. The War Department took action.

For more help with sentence fragments, see page R64 in the ***Grammar Handbook.***

READING-WRITING CONNECTION

YOUR TURN Demonstrate your understanding of the Clara Barton selections by responding to this prompt. Then use the **revising tip** to improve your writing.

WRITING PROMPT	REVISING TIP
Short Constructed Response: Analysis If Clara Barton were alive today, which national or world issues might concern her? In **one paragraph,** describe one or two current problems Barton might work to change.	Review your analysis. If you have included a conjunctive adverb, be sure to check the punctuation.

COMMON CORE

L 1 Demonstrate command of the conventions of standard English grammar and usage when writing. **L 2** Demonstrate command of standard punctuation. **W 2** Write informative/explanatory texts to examine a topic and convey ideas, concepts, and information.

Interactive Revision **THINK** central

Go to **thinkcentral.com**.
KEYWORD: HML7-873

My Mother Enters the Work Force
Poem by Rita Dove

Washington Monument by Night
Poem by Carl Sandburg

Why should you keep
TRYING?

COMMON CORE

RL 1 Cite evidence to support inferences drawn from the text.
RL 4 Determine the meaning of words and phrases as they are used in a text, including figurative and connotative meanings.

Heroes are not necessarily people who are perfect or who never fail. Often they are the people who keep trying until they are successful. This quality is called perseverance, and the people in the poems you're about to read share it. Their successes can show us the value of trying over and over again.

WEB IT Create an **idea web** that shows some people you consider heroes. Expand the web by adding the challenges they have faced and the successes they have achieved.

My Heroes

She has dyslexia.

sister

She graduated from college.

● **TEXT ANALYSIS: FIGURATIVE LANGUAGE**

Poems often use **figurative language,** or words that mean something other than their "real" meaning. For example, in "Washington Monument by Night," Sandburg describes the monument this way:

A lean swimmer dives into night sky,

Sandburg does not really mean a person is leaping into the sky. Instead, he's using words in an imaginative way. The words create a dramatic effect and emphasize how the monument soars above everything else.

If you restate figurative language in your own words, or **paraphrase** it, you can often better understand a poem's main ideas. As you read each poem, paraphrase any examples of figurative language and jot them down.

● **READING STRATEGY: MAKE INFERENCES ABOUT THE SPEAKER**

The **speaker** of a poem is the voice who "talks" to the reader through the poem's words. The speaker and the poet aren't necessarily the same person. To **infer,** or guess, who the speaker is, notice the feelings, ideas, and experiences the speaker is sharing. As you read these poems, watch for clues that tell you who the speaker is and what he or she thinks of the subject of the poem. Use a chart like the one shown to record clues and inferences.

Clues for "Washington Monument"	My Inferences
Line 6: "It is cool to look at."	The speaker does not live in the distant past.

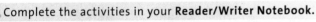

Complete the activities in your **Reader/Writer Notebook.**

Meet the Authors

Rita Dove
born 1952

People's Poet
Rita Dove served as poet laureate, or the representative poet, of the United States from 1993 to 1995. Her poems reflect experiences of the many whose stories haven't always been heard.

Carl Sandburg
1878–1967

People's Voice
Carl Sandburg, recognized as a poet who uses the language of the people, honored both the great heroes of U.S. history and the everyday heroes who make the country work.

BACKGROUND TO THE POEM
An Eight-Year Conflict
One of the poems you are about to read refers to the Revolutionary War, which lasted from 1775 to 1783. A low point for the American troops occurred during the winter of 1777 and 1778. Led by General George Washington, the ragtag soldiers camped out at Valley Forge, Pennsylvania. They had little food or warm clothing, and disease was widespread.

Authors Online
Go to **thinkcentral.com.** KEYWORD: HML7-875

875

MY MOTHER ENTERS THE
WORK FORCE

Rita Dove

The path to ABC Business School
was paid for by a lucky sign:
ALTERATIONS, QUALIFIED SEAMSTRESS INQUIRE WITHIN.
Tested on sleeves, hers
5   never puckered—puffed or sleek,
leg-o'-mutton or raglan—[1]
they barely needed the damp cloth
to steam them perfect. **A**

Those were the afternoons. Evenings
10   she took in piecework,[2] the treadle machine
with its locomotive whir
traveling the lit path of the needle
through quicksand taffeta
or velvet deep as a forest.
15   *And now and now* sang the treadle,
I know, I know. . . . **B**

And then it was day again, all morning
at the office machines, their clack and chatter
another journey—rougher,
20   that would go on forever
until she could break a hundred words
with no errors—ah, and then

no more postponed groceries,
and that blue pair of shoes!

A SPEAKER
The title of the poem gives a good clue about the speaker. Who is "telling" this poem?

B FIGURATIVE LANGUAGE
In your own words, restate what the speaker is describing in lines 9–16.

Analyze Visuals ▶

How does the woman in this painting **compare** with your mental image of the mother in the poem?

---

1. **leg-o'-mutton or raglan:** types of sleeves. A leg-of-mutton sleeve is wide at the top and narrow at the bottom. A raglan sleeve is cut so that it continues up to the collar.

2. **piecework:** work paid for according to the amount done, not the time it takes.

Alma Sewing (about 1935), Francis Criss. Oil on canvas, 33″ × 45″. High Museum of Art, Atlanta, Georgia.

Francis Criss

WASHINGTON MONUMENT
by Night
CARL SANDBURG

1

The stone goes straight.
A lean swimmer dives into night sky,
Into half-moon mist.

2

Two trees are coal black.
5 This is a great white ghost between.
It is cool to look at.
Strong men, strong women, come here. **C**

3

Eight years is a long time
To be fighting all the time.

4

10 The republic is a dream.
Nothing happens unless first a dream.

5

The wind bit hard at Valley Forge one Christmas.
Soldiers tied rags on their feet.
Red footprints wrote on the snow . . .
15 . . . and stone shoots into stars here
. . . into half-moon mist tonight.

6

Tongues wrangled dark at a man.
He buttoned his overcoat and stood alone.
In a snowstorm, red hollyberries, thoughts,
      he stood alone.

7

20 Women said: He is lonely
. . . fighting . . . fighting . . . eight years . . .

8

The name of an iron man goes over the world.
It takes a long time to forget an iron man. **D**

9

. . .   .
25 . . .   .

C FIGURATIVE LANGUAGE
In your chart, tell what surrounds the monument and what color the monument is.

D SPEAKER
Is the speaker someone who lived during Washington's time or someone who lives in the present time of the poem? Tell how you know.

Comprehension

1. **Recall** How does the mother in "My Mother Enters the Work Force" pay for business school?

2. **Clarify** How does the mother's life change in lines 21–24 of "My Mother Enters the Work Force"?

3. **Clarify** Who is the "man" in stanzas 6, 7, and 8 in "Washington Monument by Night"?

COMMON CORE

RL 1 Cite evidence to support inferences drawn from the text.
RL 4 Determine the meaning of words and phrases as they are used in a text, including figurative and connotative meanings.

Text Analysis

4. **Make Inferences About Speaker** What is the speaker's opinion of her mother in "My Mother Enters the Work Force"? Support your answer with words and phrases from the poem.

5. **Analyze Figurative Language** Compare the paraphrases you wrote with those of a partner. What do these suggest about the main ideas in each poem?

6. **Interpret** What does the last stanza in "Washington Monument by Night" suggest about the "iron man"?

7. **Compare and Contrast Character** Both the mother in "My Mother Enters the Work Force" and the man in "Washington Monument by Night" persevered in the face of huge obstacles. What other similarities do they share? What are their differences? Use a Venn diagram like the one shown to compare and contrast the two people.

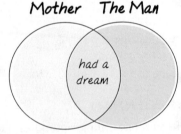

Mother   The Man

had a dream

8. **Evaluate Figurative Language** Is line 5 of "Washington Monument by Night" a good description of the Washington Monument? Refer to evidence in the poem and to the photograph on page 878 to support your opinion.

Extension and Challenge

9. **Creative Project: Art** Carl Sandburg's poem describes a monument to the man in the poem. Now sketch a monument in honor of the speaker's mother in "My Mother Enters the Work Force." List the materials you would use to make the monument. In a short dedication speech, explain your reasons for the monument's design, why you chose the colors you did, and how the materials reflect the mother's personality.

Why should you keep TRYING?

Review the idea web that you made for page 874. Write a journal entry that explains how you think each hero in your web would answer the question now. Then write a response for the mother in "My Mother Enters the Work Force" and the man in "Washington Monument by Night."

Writing Workshop
NARRATIVE

Personal Narrative

Although few people have a life story like Jackie Robinson's or Eleanor Roosevelt's, every life is filled with stories to share. You have them, too. In this workshop, you will use techniques such as dialogue, pacing, and description to turn one of these stories into a personal narrative.

 Complete the workshop activities in your **Reader/Writer Notebook.**

WRITE WITH A PURPOSE

WRITING TASK

Write a **personal narrative** that describes a special event in your life. Include relevant descriptive details and well-structured event sequences to help your audience understand what the event was like. Be sure to explain why the event was important to you.

Idea Starters
- learning a skill
- helping others
- winning a game
- going to a new place

THE ESSENTIALS

Here are some common purposes, audiences, and formats for personal narratives.

PURPOSES	AUDIENCES	FORMATS
• to share a meaningful experience • to entertain readers	• classmates and teacher • friends and family • community members • Web users	• essay for class • journal • speech • documentary • blog

COMMON CORE TRAITS

1. DEVELOPMENT OF IDEAS
- provides an **engaging introduction**
- uses techniques such as **dialogue** and **description** to develop the events
- provides a **conclusion** that reflects on events in the narrative

2. ORGANIZATION OF IDEAS
- uses appropriate **transitions** to convey a **logical sequence of events**
- uses effective **pacing** to develop the narrative

3. LANGUAGE FACILITY AND CONVENTIONS
- establishes and maintains a **point of view**
- includes **precise words** and **phrases, relevant descriptive details,** and **sensory language**
- uses **adjectives** and **proper nouns** correctly
- employs correct **grammar, mechanics,** and **spelling**

Writing Online

THINK central

Go to **thinkcentral.com**.
KEYWORD: HML7N-880

Planning/Prewriting

COMMON CORE

W 3a–e Write narratives to develop real or imagined experiences or events using effective technique, relevant descriptive details, and well-structured event sequences. **W 5** Develop and strengthen writing as needed by planning.

Getting Started

CHOOSE A TOPIC

For your personal narrative, make a list of memorable experiences that you might want to write about. Jot down ideas about each event—such as why it is meaningful to you, whether you recall many details about it, and whether you would feel comfortable sharing it with an audience. Put a star next to the event that you would most enjoy writing about.

▶ **WHAT DOES IT LOOK LIKE?**

Going to my grandmother's funeral
- It was meaningful because my whole family was sad.
- I was only four years old, so I don't recall many details.
- This story might be too sad to share with my class.

Picking bilberries in England*
- It was a funny and memorable event.
- I remember every detail of the experience.
- I'd love to share this story.

THINK ABOUT AUDIENCE AND PURPOSE

As you begin to think about planning your narrative, consider your **purpose**—to tell about a meaningful experience in your life. You may want to entertain your readers with a funny or scary story. How well you know your **audience** will help you determine how much background information to provide.

▶ **ASK YOURSELF:**

- Who will read my personal narrative?
- Why do I want to share my experience with this audience? For example, do I want to make them laugh or make them think?
- What background information will my audience need to understand my narrative?

LIST THE FACTS

Once you have chosen a particular experience, take notes on how it unfolded and how you felt about it. Record information that explains who was involved, what happened, when and where it happened, and why you're telling about it. This will help you organize an event sequence that unfolds naturally and logically.

As you plan your narrative, remember to think about **pacing.** Events in your narrative should move forward smoothly. Avoid lingering on unimportant details as they will distract your audience and slow your pace.

▶ **WHAT DOES IT LOOK LIKE?**

Subject: *Family vacation in England*

Who?	me, my sister, my mom, my dad
What?	picking bilberries on a hike
When?	when I was nine
Where?	Ennerdale Lake path, England
Why?	It's how I got my nickname; it was a funny and memorable experience.

Planning/Prewriting *continued*

Getting Started

GATHER DETAILS

Think about the experience you plan to write about. Recall as many relevant descriptive details as you can, including sensory images. You want readers to be able to visualize the setting of your narrative and follow key events. You also want to bring characters to life by including **dialogue,** or the exact words that they say. It's OK if you don't recall what everyone said word for word. Jot down a few memorable lines as you remember them.

▶ **WHAT DOES IT LOOK LIKE?**

Setting	the deck at Ennerdale View; the dirt road with four gates; the pastures filled with sheep; the bilberry patches
Events	Mom's announcing that we're going on yet another hike; meeting the man with the purple hands; finding the bilberries and devouring them; smearing bilberry juice on my cookie; getting a new nickname
Dialogue	Dad: "I don't know about taking a hike today. I think I will take a nap." Mom: "Honey, we are going on a hike."

ORDER THE KEY EVENTS

The sequence of events in your personal narrative should unfold naturally and logically. Your readers will easily follow your narrative if you use **chronological order,** or the order in which events happened. A flow chart can help you map out a logical sequence of events. List only the most important events in your flow chart. Later, as you draft your narrative, you can fill in more details.

▶ **WHAT DOES IT LOOK LIKE?**

"We're going on a hike," my mom announced.

↓

On the way to the path, a man with purple hands told us he'd been picking bilberries.

↓

We found a bilberry patch and began devouring berries.

↓

Everyone looked at me funny when I smeared bilberry juice on my cookie.

PEER REVIEW Explain the subject and purpose of your essay to a peer. Then ask what kinds of details would make your narrative vivid and memorable for readers.

 YOUR TURN

In your *Reader/Writer Notebook,* develop your writing plan. Follow the steps on page 881 to choose a topic and begin gathering facts. Use a flow chart to map out your sequence of events. Consider these tips:

- List all of the events that are important to your narrative.
- Include sensory details that will appeal to your readers' senses of sight, hearing, smell, taste, or touch.
- Write down any dialogue that you recall.

Drafting

The following chart shows how to organize your draft to create an effective personal narrative.

W 4 Produce clear and coherent writing in which the development, organization, and style are appropriate to task, purpose, and audience.
L 1 Demonstrate command of the conventions of standard English grammar and usage when writing.

Organizing a Personal Narrative

INTRODUCTION

- Start your narrative with a **question**, a **statement**, a **description**, or a **piece of dialogue** that captures the reader's attention.
- Engage and orient your reader by providing **context** and **background information**, as necessary.

▼

BODY

- Since you are telling your own story, use the **first-person point of view,** with pronouns such as *I, me, my, we, us,* and *our.*
- Organize the sequence of events in **chronological order.** Use **transitional words, phrases, and clauses,** such as *first, then,* and *finally* to make the order of events clear.
- Use effective **pacing** to keep events moving smoothly.
- Help re-create the experience for readers by using precise words and phrases and vivid **sensory details.**

▼

CONCLUDING SECTION

- Provide a **conclusion** that explains why the experience was important to you.

GRAMMAR IN CONTEXT: ADJECTIVES

To make your personal narrative come to life for your readers, you'll want to use vivid adjectives in your writing. **Adjectives** are words that describe, or modify, nouns. Adjectives indicate size, color, number, and other characteristics.

Example		*Explanation*
Tea became her **favorite** drink while she was in England.	▶	The adjective *favorite* modifies the noun *drink*.
My sister, **who ate all of the bilberries,** wasn't hungry for lunch.	▶	The adjective clause *who ate all of the bilberries* modifies the noun *sister*.
The color **of the ripe bilberry patch** was deep purple.	▶	The adjective phrase *of the ripe bilberry patch* modifies the noun *color*.

YOUR TURN Develop a draft of your essay, following the structure above. Make sure you use vivid adjectives and sensory details to help your audience visualize the experience.

Revising

If your writing has flaws in content, organization, pacing, and style, your readers will have trouble understanding it. The following chart can help you decide which parts of your writing need to be revised or rewritten, and where you should consider a new approach.

PERSONAL NARRATIVE

Ask Yourself	Tips	Revision Strategies
1. Does the introduction engage and orient readers and help set the scene?	▶ **Underline** the attention-grabbing opener.	▶ **Add** a memorable question, statement, or piece of dialogue to the opener. **Add** sensory details to describe the setting more precisely.
2. Is the point of view consistent throughout?	▶ **Identify** pronouns that show the first-person point of view. **Circle** any information not given from that point of view.	▶ If any sentences are circled, **delete** them. If necessary, **add** the same information told from the first-person point of view.
3. Does the essay provide the audience with essential background information?	▶ **Put a star** next to details that make clear the context, or background, of the narrative.	▶ **Add** information that will help the audience understand the events in the narrative.
4. Are events presented in chronological order? Do transitions help guide readers through the sequence of events?	▶ **Number** events to show the order in which they happened. **Draw an arrow** next to transitions that show sequence.	▶ If necessary, **rearrange** events to put them in chronological order. **Add** transitions to clarify the sequence.
5. Does the pacing keep events moving smoothly?	▶ **Bracket** unnecessary details that slow the pace.	▶ **Delete** unnecessary details to improve the pace of your narrative.
6. Has the writer described his or her thoughts and feelings to clarify why the experience is important?	▶ **Put an exclamation point** next to the statement that explains the author's feelings on why the experience is important.	▶ **Add** sentences that express relevant thoughts and feelings explaining why the experience matters.

YOUR TURN

PEER REVIEW Review your draft with a peer. Answer each question in this chart to locate where and how your drafts could be improved or reworked, or when you should try a new approach.

ANALYZE A STUDENT DRAFT

Read this student's draft and the comments about it as a model for revising your own personal narrative.

COMMON CORE

W 3a Engage and orient the reader by establishing a context. **W 5** Develop and strengthen writing as needed by revising, editing, rewriting, or trying a new approach, focusing on how well purpose and audience have been addressed.

Claire of Bilberry

by Claire Moreland-Ochoa, Lake Travis Middle School

1 "I don't know about taking a hike today," my dad hinted. "I think I will take a nap."

2 While my dad was taking a nap, Danielle and I had some tea outside. Tea was becoming my favorite drink at any time of the day because it was very cold in England. While we were sitting outside on the deck at Ennerdale View, my mom walked out and gave me the *worst* news of the day.

3 "Honey, we are going on a hike," she broke into a smile. I wanted to frown, but instead I kept a straight face and asked, "When are we leaving?"

4 "Now."

5 We soon came to a man with purple hands sitting on a bench. The rental car slowly halted beside him. My dad introduced himself and asked why the man had purple hands.

6 "Well, I have been picking bilberries all morning on the Ennerdale lake path," he said, sitting on a bench with a tin can in one of his hands. After a couple of words were said, we drove a little way and turned left.

7 Traveling down a narrow lane, the car turned onto a dirt road. We stopped at a gate. I climbed out and opened it. The car drove by. I closed the gate behind it, realizing that the gates are there to keep the sheep in. But there was not just one gate. There were four gates to open.

Claire opens with **dialogue** to pull readers into her narrative. However, some background information is needed to clarify the setting and better orient readers.

First-person pronouns show that Claire is telling her story from the **first-person point of view.**

Specific details and **sensory language** help readers picture the setting and the action.

LEARN HOW Establish Context Readers could follow Claire's narrative more easily if they knew from the start that the family is on vacation in England, has been there for a while, and might be getting bored. When Claire revised her essay, she added **background information** to the first paragraph.

CLAIRE'S REVISION TO PARAGRAPH 1

"I don't know about taking a hike today," my dad hinted. "I think I will take a nap." *Our family had been in western England on vacation for about two weeks. We were renting a house in the remote Lake District. Everyone but Mom was growing weary of our daily hikes through the forest.*

8 "What is it with England and gates?" I asked myself. After long minutes of taking pictures of sheep and hiking, we finally saw the first bilberry patch. Running up to the patch, I started picking the bilberries and shoveling them into my mouth, while thinking, "I am **so** hungry!" Soon the whole family was devouring bilberries. My mom filmed the process. The bilberries disappeared on this patch, and we moved on. One by one, the bilberry patches popped up on each side of us. One by one, the bilberry patches turned into just patches without the bilberries anymore.

9 Halfway through the hike my parents ordered me to stop eating and Danielle to stop picking. We fell back a little and pretended to stoop over and look at all kinds of things. Sometimes it was a bug we were looking at; other times it was a flower or a strange-looking plant. We never stopped to look at any of those. We just saw a nice bilberry patch and stopped to pick and eat them.

10 On the way back we stopped to have a shortbread cookie. I smeared bilberry juice on the top of mine and thought it was very good. Everyone's faces twisted up when they saw what I was doing to the poor cookie. When we were finally back in the car, I was relieved but satisfied with a full stomach of bilberries. From then on I had a nickname, "Claire of Bilberry."

> Claire uses **transitional words and phrases** to help readers follow the action. However, there seems to be a gap in the sequence of events at the start of this paragraph.

> The **conclusion** explains the significance of the experience—it's how Claire got her nickname.

LEARN HOW Clarify the Sequence of Events One of Claire's readers pointed out that the action moves from opening the gates to taking pictures and hiking without transition or explanation. When she revised her draft, Claire added details to fill in the missing events and make the sequence clear.

CLAIRE'S REVISION TO PARAGRAPH ❽

After the car passed through the fourth gate, we traveled to the end of the dirt road. There, at the edge of the forest, we located the path and started off on foot.

"What is it with England and gates?" I asked myself. After long minutes of taking pictures of sheep and hiking, we finally saw the first bilberry patch.

YOUR TURN Use feedback from your peers and your teacher as well as the two "Learn How" lessons to revise your personal narrative. Evaluate whether your narrative achieves its purpose. If needed, try a new approach.

COMMON CORE

W 3c Use transitions to convey sequence. **W 5** Strengthen writing by revising and editing. **L 2** Demonstrate command of standard English capitalization, punctuation, and spelling.

Editing and Publishing

The experience of reading a personal narrative can be spoiled if the writing is full of grammar, spelling, and punctuation errors. In the editing stage, you clean up your narrative so that your audience can fully enjoy the experience you have chosen to share with them.

GRAMMAR IN CONTEXT: PROPER NOUNS

In a personal narrative, you are likely to refer to specific people or places. When you do so, you are using proper nouns. A **proper noun** refers to a particular person, place, or thing. Proper nouns are always capitalized. Study the following examples from Claire's narrative.

> *"What is it with England and gates?" I asked myself.*

[*England* is a **proper noun**—it names the specific country Claire visited. Therefore, it begins with a capital letter.]

> *When we were finally back in the car, I was relieved but satisfied with a full stomach of bilberries. From then on I had a nickname, "Claire of Bilberry."*

[In the first sentence, *bilberries* is a **common noun** and is not capitalized. In the second sentence, Claire capitalizes *Bilberry* because it is part of her nickname.]

As Claire edited her essay, she capitalized *lake* in the following sentence because Ennerdale Lake is a specific body of water.

> *"Well, I have been picking bilberries all morning on the Ennerdale lake path,"* *he said, sitting on a bench with a tin can in one of his hands.*

PUBLISH YOUR WRITING

Share your personal narrative with an audience.

- Adapt your narrative into an interview with someone who was involved in the experience.
- Post your narrative as a blog entry along with photos from the experience.
- Use drawings to illustrate your narrative. Then present it as a gift to someone who shared the experience with you.
- Incorporate your narrative into a speech for school or for a community organization.

YOUR TURN Correct any errors in your narrative. Use proper nouns to refer to specific people and places, and make sure you capitalize them correctly. Then publish your personal narrative for your audience.

Scoring Rubric

Use the rubric below to evaluate your personal narrative from the Writing Workshop or your response to the on-demand task on the next page.

PERSONAL NARRATIVE

SCORE	COMMON CORE TRAITS
6	• **Development** Has an engaging introduction that orients readers; develops events with strong dialogue and description; provides a strong conclusion • **Organization** Establishes a natural and logical sequence of events; uses effective pacing and transitions to convey sequence • **Language** Consistently maintains a clear point of view; uses relevant descriptive details and vivid sensory language; shows a strong command of conventions
5	• **Development** Has an effective introduction; develops events with dialogue and description; provides a conclusion that sums up the narrative • **Organization** Has a logical sequence of events; uses mostly effective pacing and some transitions to signal shifts in time • **Language** Maintains a point of view; includes relevant descriptive details and some sensory language; has a few errors in conventions
4	• **Development** Has an introduction, but doesn't provide context; could use more dialogue or description to develop events; provides an adequate conclusion • **Organization** Has a logical sequence of events but needs more transitions • **Language** Mostly maintains a point of view; needs more descriptive details and sensory language; includes a few distracting errors in conventions
3	• **Development** Has an introduction, but needs more development; needs more dialogue and description; lacks a strong conclusion • **Organization** Has a confusing sequence; has a slow pace at times • **Language** Has some lapses in point of view; lacks effective descriptive details and sensory language; has some major errors in conventions
2	• **Development** Lacks an effective introduction and fails to develop events • **Organization** Includes events that distract from the narrative; has choppy pacing • **Language** Lacks a clear point of view; mostly lacks details and sensory language; has many errors in conventions
1	• **Development** Has no introduction; lacks dialogue and description; ends abruptly • **Organization** Has no transitions and an unclear sequence of events • **Language** Has no clear point of view, no effective details or sensory language; has major errors in conventions

Preparing for Timed Writing

COMMON CORE   **W 10**   Write routinely over shorter time frames for a range of tasks, purposes, and audiences.

1. ANALYZE THE TASK   5 MIN

Read the task carefully. Underline the words that tell the type of writing, circle the topic, and double underline the purpose.

> **WRITING TASK** *Type of writing*   *Topic* ↓
>
> Write a <u>personal narrative</u> that describes (a special event in your life.) Include details that help your audience understand what the event was like. Be sure to <u><u>explain why the event was important to you.</u></u>
>
>   *Purpose* ↗

2. PLAN YOUR RESPONSE   10 MIN

Think of some personal experiences that are important to you. Which of these experiences would you feel comfortable writing about? Once you have chosen a subject, write down who was involved, what happened, where it happened, when it happened, and why it's still meaningful to you. Use a sequence chart to list the events in chronological order.

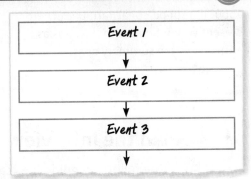

3. RESPOND TO THE TASK   20 MIN

Using the notes you've just made, draft your narrative. Follow these guidelines:

- In the introduction, use an interesting question, statement, description, or piece of dialogue to grab your audience's attention.
- In the body, use effective pacing as you relate the events in the order that they occurred. Make your narrative vivid with relevant descriptions and sensory details.
- In the conclusion, explain why the experience is meaningful to you.

4. IMPROVE YOUR RESPONSE   5–10 MIN

Revising Go back over key parts of the narrative. Did you describe the events? Did you use specific details? Did you explain the event's importance to you?
Proofreading Read your paper to correct any mistakes in grammar, spelling, punctuation, and capitalization. Make sure your writing is clear and legible.
Checking Your Final Copy Before you turn in your narrative, read it one more time to catch any errors you may have missed.

Conducting an Interview

You have probably seen, heard, or read interviews involving athletes, innovators, celebrities, politicians, or eyewitnesses to events in the news. Interviews can be formal or informal, personal or professional. The interviewer prepares questions in advance for the interviewee to answer about his or her life experiences.

 Complete the workshop activities in your **Reader/Writer Notebook.**

SPEAK WITH A PURPOSE	COMMON CORE TRAITS
TASK	**A STRONG INTERVIEW . . .**
Plan and conduct an **interview** with someone about his or her life or work. You might interview a person who shared the experience you wrote about in your personal narrative. Then present your interview to the class as either a written summary or an audio or video presentation.	• poses questions that thoroughly probe the subject of the interview • includes attentive listening by the interviewer • reveals the point of view of the person being interviewed • shows the interest and engagement of both the interviewer and the interviewee

COMMON CORE

SL 1a–c Engage effectively in a range of collaborative discussions with diverse partners. **SL 5** Include multimedia components and visual displays to clarify claims and findings and emphasize salient points.

Plan the Interview

The following guidelines can help you plan your interview:

• **Identify an interview subject.** Is there someone in your family, school, or community whom you would like to interview? For example, is there a senior citizen who took part in a historical event that interests you? Or, is there a topic or hobby that you would like to find out more about? Create a list of people who you think would make good interview subjects.

• **Contact your subject.** Contact the person you've identified by phone, e-mail, or letter. Identify yourself and explain your purpose. Ask the person whether he or she is willing to be interviewed by you. If so, set up a definite time and place. If you would like to audiotape or videotape the interview, be sure to ask the interviewee for permission first.

• **Write questions.** Keep in mind that the purpose of an interview is to gather information about someone or something. Read and research relevant materials to help you write thoughtful questions. Avoid questions that lead to simple yes or no answers. Instead, prepare questions that require thoughtful, informative answers. Write your questions on index cards and leave space to take notes during the interview.

Conduct the Interview

Here are some tips for participating in a meaningful interview:

- **Use an appropriate level of formality.** Interviews can be formal or informal. Interviewing a friend about a fun experience you shared is different from interviewing a scientist you contacted for a school assignment. Here are some differences between the two kinds of interview:

FORMAL INTERVIEW	INFORMAL INTERVIEW
• interviewee may be someone you don't know well, such as an expert on your chosen topic • usually takes place in a quiet setting, such as an empty classroom • focuses on the topic and questions that the interviewer has prepared in advance	• interviewee may be someone you know well, such as a friend or family member • may take place in a casual setting, such as the school cafeteria or your home • may stray from the original topic as the conversation flows naturally

- **Listen carefully.** Whether your interview is formal or informal, it's important to listen attentively when your subject is speaking. Your facial expressions and body language should show your interest in hearing what the person has to say. Take brief notes on the points you want to remember.

- **Ask follow-up questions.** If you do not understand the answer to a question, ask the interviewee to elaborate. Asking good follow-up questions is another way to show your interest and attention.

- **Say thanks.** Thank your subject for sharing time and information with you. Send the person a handwritten thank-you note as soon as possible.

Share the Interview

Use one of these methods to share your interview with a wider audience:

- **Create a written summary.** Review your notes or the transcript from your interview and select the most important and interesting ideas. Use these ideas to write a summary of what you learned from the interview.

- **Make a presentation with audio and/or video.** If you taped your interview, select the best and most salient, or important, clips to share. Edit and arrange them so they make sense together, and add an introduction that tells the purpose of the interview and clearly identifies your interviewee.

 YOUR TURN

As a Speaker Prepare for and conduct your interview using the techniques described on these pages.

As a Listener Listen carefully to the responses as you conduct your interview. Ask follow-up questions as appropriate.

Assessment Practice

DIRECTIONS Read the following selection and then answer the questions.

The world-famous pilot Amelia Earhart worked as a volunteer nurse in Toronto, Canada, during World War I. There, she developed her lifelong interest in flying.

from East to the Dawn: The Life of Amelia Earhart *by Susan Butler*

1   When Amelia had spare time, she headed for the stables, and it was through her riding that she got her first exposure to airplanes. She was riding a horse named Dynamite, whom she had "gentled" with a combination of horsemanship and apples, when she was joined by three air force officers. They were so impressed by how well she controlled her mount—famous for bucking off a colonel—that they asked her to go out to Armour Heights, an airfield at the edge of the city, to watch how they controlled their planes.

2   Amelia had seen planes before. She saw her first at a fair in Des Moines when she was ten, but "it was a thing of rusty wire and wood and looked not at all interesting." The chances are, it was the same first plane that Clarence Chamberlin, who also grew up to be a crack pilot, saw in his home town of Denison, Iowa, at about the same time—an old-style pusher, with the pilot sitting out front "on a sort of birdcage seat," and the propeller and engine in the rear. He too had been "frankly unimpressed . . . quite willing to let anyone take such fool chances who would."

3   But ten years had passed. These planes were a different generation; now they were beautiful: "They were full sized birds that slid on the hard-packed snow and rose into the air with an extra roar that echoed from the evergreens that banked the edge of the field." She stood close to them—so close that the propellers threw snow in her face, and "I felt a first urge to fly." She tried to get permission to go up, but failed—"not even a general's wife could do so—apparently the only thing she couldn't do." So she did "the next best thing" and got to know the fliers.

4   One day she had a chance to test her faith in planes, not by flying but by standing in the path of one. It was at a Toronto fair, and the pilots, war aces, were giving exhibitions of stunt flying. She and a girlfriend

Practice Test THINK central

Take it at thinkcentral.com.
KEYWORD: HML7N-892

892 UNIT 7: BIOGRAPHY AND AUTOBIOGRAPHY

were standing in the middle of a clearing off by themselves in order to see better. The pilot began diving at the crowd. She would never forget what happened next.

5   "He was bored. He had looped and rolled and spun and finished his little bag of tricks, and there was nothing left to do but watch the people on the ground running as he swooped close to them." Then he started diving at the two girls off in the clearing. "I remember the mingled fear and pleasure which surged over me as I watched that small plane at the top of its earthward swoop. Common sense told me that if something went wrong with the mechanism, or if the pilot lost control, he, the airplane and I would be rolled up in a ball together. I did not understand it at the time but I believe that little red airplane said something to me as it swished by." Her friend ran off. Amelia didn't; she was fascinated.

Reading Comprehension

Use the excerpt from *East to the Dawn: The Life of Amelia Earhart* to answer questions 1–9.

1. One clue that this is a biography and not an autobiography is the fact that the author —

   A. reveals the thoughts and feelings of the subject

   B. uses the word *she* to refer to Amelia Earhart

   C. reveals the thoughts and feelings of other people

   D. includes dialogue that was spoken by the subject

2. Which of these is the best summary of paragraph 1?

   A. Embarrassed that Earhart could tame a wild horse better than they could, three air force officers showed off their flying skills.

   B. Impressed with Earhart's ability to control a wild horse, three air force officers invited her to watch them fly.

   C. Earhart tamed a wild horse so that she might be invited to see the newest planes.

   D. Earhart was afraid of airplanes and decided to tame a wild horse to prove that she was brave.

3. Events in this excerpt are presented in —

   A. random order

   B. mostly chronological order

   C. the order of their importance to Earhart

   D. the order in which the author learned about them

4. Which words or phrases in the excerpt help you understand the order in which Earhart developed an interest in flying?

   A. *Spare time, first exposure, one day*

   B. *Chances, different generation, next best thing*

   C. *Stood close, in order to, also*

   D. *Before, ten years had passed, what happened next*

5. Which quotation from the excerpt gives you an important clue about Amelia Earhart's future?

   A. *She was riding a horse named Dynamite, whom she had "gentled" with a combination of horsemanship and apples. . . .*

   B. *Amelia had seen planes before. She saw her first at a fair in Des Moines when she was ten. . . .*

   C. *She stood close to them—so close that the propellers threw snow in her face, and "I felt a first urge to fly."*

   D. *She and a girlfriend were standing in the middle of a clearing off by themselves in order to see better.*

6. Which of these is the best summary of paragraph 3?

   A. Ten years after she first fell in love with airplanes, Amelia Earhart saw the beautiful new airplanes and enjoyed the way they roared off the field.

   B. The latest airplanes were beautiful, large machines that roared when they took off, kicked up snow with their propellers, and slid on snow when they landed.

   C. Although she was fascinated with the latest airplanes, Amelia Earhart knew she could never fly them because even a general's wife could not get permission to fly.

   D. Amelia Earhart loved watching the beautiful new planes and wanted to fly; when she was unable to get permission to go up in them, she befriended the fliers instead.

7. Which of these is the best summary of paragraph 5?

   A. The pilot was bored, so he started to do more tricks and scared the two young women in the field.

   B. The pilot lost control of the plane and it started to swoop down toward Earhart, who did not move.

   C. After the pilot had run out of stunts and started diving at people, he dove at the two girls; Earhart stood watching, spellbound, and her friend ran away.

   D. Earhart's friend ran away after the pilot of the stunt plane threatened the crowd at the fair, but Earhart froze in fear as the plane dove at her.

8. From her reaction to the diving plane, you can infer that Earhart has the qualities of —

   A. pride and defiance

   B. foolishness and immaturity

   C. level-headedness and reliability

   D. curiosity and courageousness

9. Which of the following presents the main events in this excerpt in chronological order?

   A. Earhart met air force pilots; she saw her first plane; she stood in the path of a diving plane.

   B. Earhart tamed a horse; she saw her first plane; she watched stunt flying.

   C. Earhart saw her first plane; she watched air force pilots; she stood in the path of a diving plane.

   D. Earhart tamed a horse; she went to a fair; she met war pilots.

SHORT CONSTRUCTED RESPONSE
Write two or three sentences to answer this question.

10. What can you infer about the biographer's opinion of Amelia Earhart?

Write a paragraph to answer this question.

11. What can you infer about Earhart's future from her statement in paragraph 5 that, "I did not understand it at the time but I believe that little red airplane said something to me as it swished by"?

Vocabulary

Use your knowledge of context clues and the Anglo-Saxon word root definitions to answer the following questions.

1. The Anglo-Saxon word *baelg* means "a bag." Which word from the story comes from *baelg*?

   A. Bag
   B. Birdcage
   C. Best
   D. Banked

2. The Anglo-Saxon word *wak* means "conscious, not sleeping." Which word from the story comes from *wak*?

   A. Surged
   B. Wire
   C. Watch
   D. Willing

3. The Anglo-Saxon word *eorthe* means "earth." Which word from the story comes from *eorthe*?

   A. Exhibitions
   B. Beautiful
   C. Exposure
   D. Earthward

Use context clues and your knowledge of prefixes and suffixes to answer the following questions.

4. What does the prefix *over-* mean in the word *overwhelmed* in this sentence?

   "Earhart was <u>overwhelmed</u> by the sight of the airplane diving and swooping."

   A. Less than
   B. Too much
   C. Full of
   D. Group

5. What does the prefix *under-* mean in the word *underneath* in this sentence?

   "As she stood <u>underneath</u> the plane, it seemed to dive directly at her."

   A. Above
   B. Less than
   C. Below
   D. Full of

6. What does the suffix *-ful* mean in the word *wonderful* in this sentence?

   "The diving airplane was a <u>wonderful</u> sight to Amelia."

   A. Full of
   B. State
   C. Less than
   D. Quality

Revising and Editing

DIRECTIONS Read this passage and answer the questions that follow.

(1) Women have always excelled in the field of aviation. (2) In 1912, harriet quimby became the first woman to fly across the English channel. (3) Nine years later, bessie coleman became the world's first licensed African-American aviator. (4) In 1935, amelia earhart became the first person to fly solo across the Pacific ocean. (5) Women reached another milestone in 1983. (6) Astronaut Sally Ride became the first U.S. woman in space. (7) Many articles tell of their achievements. (8) Books describe women's success.

1. The words that should be capitalized in sentence 2 are —

A. harriet, quimby

B. harriet, quimby, woman

C. channel

D. harriet, quimby, channel

2. The words that should be capitalized in sentence 3 are —

A. bessie, coleman

B. coleman, aviator

C. bessie, coleman, licensed

D. world's, first, licensed

3. The words that should be capitalized in sentence 4 are —

A. amelia, earhart, person

B. amelia, earhart, ocean

C. amelia

D. person, ocean

4. What is the BEST way to combine sentences 5 and 6 using a conjunctive adverb?

A. Women reached another milestone in 1983; namely, astronaut Sally Ride became the first U.S. woman in space.

B. Women reached another milestone in 1983, however, astronaut Sally Ride became the first U.S. woman in space.

C. Women reached another milestone in 1983, therefore; astronaut Sally Ride became the first U.S. woman in space.

D. Women reached another milestone in 1983; besides, astronaut Sally Ride became the first U.S. woman in space.

5. What is the BEST way to combine sentences 7 and 8 using a conjunctive adverb?

A. Many articles tell of their achievements, however; books depict women's success.

B. Many articles tell of their achievements; as a result, books depict women's success.

C. Many articles tell of their achievements; regardless, books depict women's success.

D. Many articles tell of their achievements; likewise, books depict women's success.

STOP

More Great Reads

Ideas for Independent Reading

Which questions from Unit 7 made an impression on you?
Continue exploring them with these books.

What is your duty to others?

Lyddie
by Katherine Paterson

When her family loses their farm, 14-year-old Lyddie Worthen risks everything and takes a job in a Massachusetts mill. Under the worst possible working conditions, she succeeds in overcoming adversity through the strength of her character.

Across Five Aprils
by Irene Hunt

This historical novel centers on the divided loyalties of the Creightons during the Civil War. Jethro is left behind to run the family farm, but he is not spared the horrors of war as experienced from the home front.

The Greatest: Muhammad Ali
by Walter Dean Myers

This biography traces the life of boxer Muhammad Ali from his childhood through his present-day struggles with Parkinson's disease. Along the way, he fights racism, stands up for his beliefs, and becomes a hero to millions.

When is there dignity in silence?

Touching Spirit Bear
by Ben Mikaelsen

Families have rules, schools have rules, and societies have rules. Fifteen-year-old Cole Matthews has always had trouble with those rules. Can he change his destructive path while living alone on a remote island?

On the Way Home
by Laura Ingalls Wilder

Finding strength in writing, Laura Ingalls Wilder captures in her diary the landscapes, cultures, and people she encounters as her family travels from South Dakota to Missouri in the late 1800s.

Homeless Bird
by Gloria Whelan

What is it like to live in a society where how you are treated depends on your gender? In modern-day India, 13-year-old Koly must marry a 16-year-old boy from a distant village. When he dies, Koly is alone in an unfamiliar city.

How can we change what's wrong?

Beyond the Burning Time
by Kathryn Lasky

What would it take to make you stand alone? In a New England village during colonial times, 12-year-old Mary Chase must defend her mother against the community's accusations of witchcraft.

The Golden Compass
by Philip Pullman

Fairy tales and legends allow you to imagine yourself saving the world. In the first book of a trilogy, the adventurer Lyra holds the future of the world and all of its inhabitants in her hands.

Under the Blood-Red Sun
by Graham Salisbury

Life is normal for 13-year-old Tomi Nakaji. Then, on December 7, 1941, Japanese planes bomb Pearl Harbor and Tomi's world turns into a nightmare.

Face the Facts

UNIT **8**

INFORMATION, ARGUMENT, AND PERSUASION

- In Nonfiction
- In Media

899

Share What You Know

Can you BELIEVE everything you read?

All around you are sources of information—newspapers, books, magazines, and the Internet, to name a few. You may also get information from television, radio, billboards, product labels, and people you know. But can you believe all of it? It is important to learn to evaluate the information you receive so that you can know what to believe and what not to believe.

ACTIVITY What do you know? How did you come to know it? Think about all the sources of information you encounter in a day. Make a list of the sources, and then answer the following questions:

• How useful is the information you get from each source?

• Which source do you depend on most often?

• Is the information from that source always accurate?

After answering these questions, write a paragraph encouraging people to use your favorite source for information.

Dog Enrolls in College

August 9   Dr. Zachary Lynch, veterinarian at Zach's General Store, thought that someone had made a mistake when he was asked to help conduct physicals for incoming freshmen at the local community

Two-Headed Turtle Talks Twice As Much

August 9   In recent weeks scientists have been observing the language habits of the recently discovered two-headed turtle. The turtle, which was found nesting on a small island off the coast of Bora Bora, seemed somewhat disoriented

Find It Online!

THINK central

Go to thinkcentral.com for the interactive version of this unit.

Preview Unit Goals

TEXT ANALYSIS
- Identify and use text features to locate and comprehend information
- Distinguish factual claims from opinions
- Analyze the structure an author uses to organize a text
- Understand elements of an argument
- Analyze persuasive techniques and rhetorical fallacies

WRITING AND LANGUAGE
- Write a persuasive essay
- Use commas and colons correctly
- Understand appositive phrases

SPEAKING AND LISTENING
- Deliver a persuasive speech

VOCABULARY
- Use word roots and prefixes to help determine the meanings of words
- Use context clues to understand idioms

ACADEMIC VOCABULARY
- area
- domain
- hypothesis
- objective
- resolve

MEDIA AND VIEWING
- Interpret explicit and implicit messages in media
- Interpret visual and sound techniques in media
- Evaluate how media influence and inform audiences

Media Smart DVD-ROM

Reading Before Believing

Become a savvy consumer of information by "reading" and analyzing news reports and TV ads. Pages 942 and 984

Reading for Information

In today's information age, knowledge is power. Facts and figures on just about any subject, from consumer products to Jupiter's moons, are at your fingertips. How do you find the information you're looking for in expository texts? What are the best ways to understand and remember what you read? By paying attention to the structure, purpose, and organization of informational texts, you will more fully comprehend what you read.

COMMON CORE

Included in this workshop:
RI 1 Cite textual evidence to support analysis of what the text says explicitly. **RI 2** Determine central ideas in a text; provide an objective summary. **RI 5** Analyze the structure an author uses to organize a text.

Part 1: Text Features and Graphic Aids

Flipping through a newspaper or surfing the Web for information can be an overwhelming experience. To help readers get their bearings and quickly see what a text is about, many writers use **text features,** or special design elements. Text features include headings, subheadings, boldfaced type, and captions. These elements all serve as road signs, guiding you through a text and pointing out key ideas.

Just as you would look at a road map before driving to a new place, you may find it helpful to **preview** a text before you start to read it. Notice how much you can tell about this textbook article by scanning the text features.

The **title** reveals the topic of the article—the Dust Bowl.

Graphic aids, such as this map, present detailed information in an easy-to-read format.

Captions clarify information in the graphic aid.

Headings state the main idea of each paragraph.

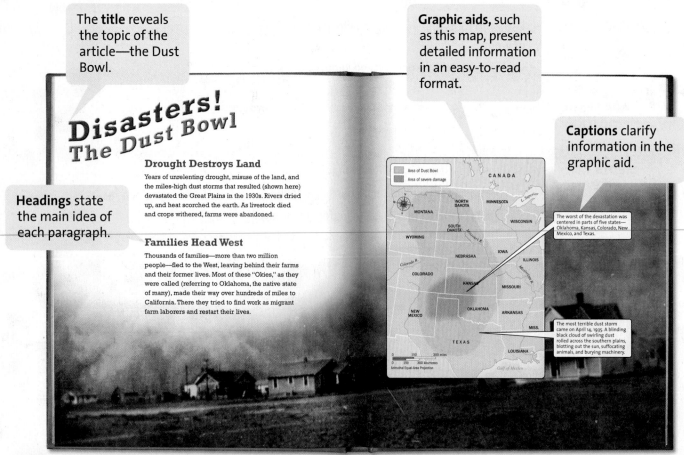

Disasters! The Dust Bowl

Drought Destroys Land

Years of unrelenting drought, misuse of the land, and the miles-high dust storms that resulted (shown here) devastated the Great Plains in the 1930s. Rivers dried up, and heat scorched the earth. As livestock died and crops withered, farms were abandoned.

Families Head West

Thousands of families—more than two million people—fled to the West, leaving behind their farms and their former lives. Most of these "Okies," as they were called (referring to Oklahoma, the native state of many), made their way over hundreds of miles to California. There they tried to find work as migrant farm laborers and restart their lives.

Area of Dust Bowl
Area of severe damage

CANADA

NORTH DAKOTA
MINNESOTA
MONTANA
WISCONSIN
SOUTH DAKOTA
WYOMING
IOWA
NEBRASKA
ILLINOIS
COLORADO
MISSOURI
KANSAS
NEW MEXICO
OKLAHOMA
ARKANSAS
MISS.
TEXAS
LOUISIANA
Gulf of Mexico

The worst of the devastation was centered in parts of five states—Oklahoma, Kansas, Colorado, New Mexico, and Texas.

The most terrible dust storm came on April 14, 1935. A blinding black cloud of swirling dust rolled across the southern plains, blotting out the sun, suffocating animals, and burying machinery.

MODEL: TEXT FEATURES

Quickly skim the text features of this article. After seeing these features, what information do you think the article will provide? Now read the passage closely and answer the questions.

from

EARTHQUAKES

Reference article in *Popular Science Almanac*

. . . Earth's crust isn't just one solid piece, like an eggshell. Instead, it's broken up into different pieces, called plates. . . .

5 . . . Plate movement is responsible for earthquakes as well as volcanoes. See, Earth's plates are constantly growing at one end, getting consumed at the other, shifting alongside other
10 plates, and pushing headlong into others. All of this causes a tremendous amount of pressure build-up. Rocks are rigid. Since they don't break easily, they resist this pressure for a long,
15 long time. But after a while, something's got to give. Rapid movement of massive blocks of rock releases the tension . . . at least for the time being.

The San Andreas Fault in California falls at the boundary of two tectonic plates. The slipping of these plates is often the cause of earthquakes in the region.

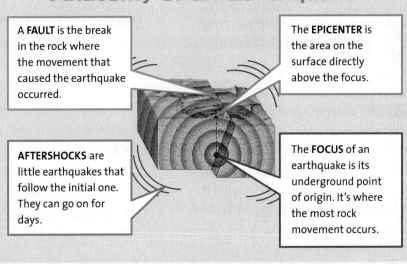

Anatomy of an Earthquake

A **FAULT** is the break in the rock where the movement that caused the earthquake occurred.

The **EPICENTER** is the area on the surface directly above the focus.

AFTERSHOCKS are little earthquakes that follow the initial one. They can go on for days.

The **FOCUS** of an earthquake is its underground point of origin. It's where the most rock movement occurs.

Close Read

1. An **almanac** is an annual reference book. Its purpose is to publish brief articles relating to a specific field. If you were doing a report on the parts of an earthquake, would this almanac article help you? Explain your answer.

2. Name two things you learn about earthquakes from the caption and the photograph.

3. Review the graphic aid at the bottom of this article. In your own words, describe the information it presents.

Part 2: Use Organizational Patterns

Text features may be the road signs guiding you through a text, but your final destination is an understanding of what you've read. The following strategies can help you reach that destination.

IDENTIFY THE MAIN IDEAS

Main ideas, or **central ideas,** are the most important ideas about a topic that a writer wants to communicate to readers. **Supporting details,** such as facts and examples, help to explain or elaborate on the main ideas. Most of the time, the main idea of a paragraph is directly stated in a **topic sentence,** which is usually located at the beginning or end of that paragraph. Consider this example from the article you just read.

> . . . Plate movement is responsible for earthquakes as well as volcanoes. See, Earth's plates are constantly growing at one end, getting consumed at the other, shifting alongside other plates, and pushing headlong into others. . . .

This **topic sentence** states the main idea of one paragraph in the article: the cause of earthquakes.

This **supporting detail** further explains what plate movement is and how it can cause earthquakes.

If the main idea is **implied**—suggested but not directly stated—you have to **infer** it by asking yourself: What do the supporting details add up to?

To clearly communicate their ideas, writers usually organize an entire text in a pattern. One of the most basic **patterns of organization** for an expository text is main idea and supporting details, in which a central idea about a topic is presented and then supported by details. There are many other organizational patterns that communicate a text's important ideas and details, including cause and effect and chronological order. You can use any of these organizational patterns as guides to help you form an overview of a text and **summarize** it, which is to briefly retell a text's main ideas in your own words.

TAKE NOTES

When you take notes, you zero in on the main ideas and supporting details and restate them in your own words. You can take notes by setting up a **graphic organizer** or an **outline** that you can follow easily. For example, to create a formal outline like this one, use Roman numerals to label the main ideas, capital letters to label the supporting points, and Arabic numerals to label supporting details.

Earthquakes

I. Caused by movement of plates (pieces of the earth's crust)

   A. Plates hit each other.

   B. Movement causes pressure on rocks.

   C. Tension is released when rock shifts.

II. Anatomy of an earthquake

   A. Focus is the point where rock shifts underground.

   B. Epicenter is the point on surface above focus.

Part 3: Analyze the Text

Read this article about the *Titanic*, the famous ship that sank in 1912. Preview the article and answer the first **Close Read** question. Then read the article more closely, using the other questions to help you take notes.

What's Eating the *Titanic*?

The world's most famous sunken wreck becomes a gift for deep-sea scientists.

Oceanographer Robert Ballard is returning to the *Titanic*, but it's not the same sunken ship he found in 1985. The deep ocean has been steadily destroying the once-great cruise liner, and scientists say the process is unlike any they've ever seen. "Even if we could stop it, I
5 wouldn't," says scientist Charles Pellegrino. "The *Titanic* is becoming something that belongs to biology."

The ship has attracted all kinds of hungry deep-sea life. Other critters (including tourists) are steadily chomping away at the ship too. Here's your guide to the wreck's undoing.

THE CULPRITS	THE DESTRUCTION	AN END IN SIGHT?
Mollusks and microorganisms that stirred up from the ocean floor when the ship first hit bottom	Worms munched on softer woods, while microorganisms ate some clothes and other fabrics. By the time scientists arrived to survey the ship, only the hard woods, such as mahogony, remained.	The worms moved on—the worst is done.
Bacteria from the ocean floor	Living off the sulfur in steel, bacteria also remove iron for housing and get rid of the rest. Bacteria have sucked over 1,000 tons of iron from the ship.	The bacterial colonies are growing, and half the steel could be gone by 2204.
The elements, such as water pressure, salt, and icebergs	Water pressure damaged parts of the ship when it sank. Salt slowly eats away at the hull, while gravel from icebergs overhead rains down on the deck.	Some suggest saving specific parts of the *Titanic* by bringing them on shore.
Tourists, pirates, and explorers attracted by profit and the popularity of *Titanic* TV specials	Small submarines are used to explore the site of the wreck. Careless piloting of these submarines has caused some damage to the hull and the deck.	The government has rules for protecting sunken ships, but it does not have the power to enforce them.

Close Read

1. Preview the title, the subtitle, and the headings in the chart. What do you think this article will be about?

2. The main idea of the first paragraph is listed in the outline shown. In your notebook, record two supporting details.

> I. Scientists see the *Titanic*'s destruction as an opportunity for study.
> A.
> B.

3. The second paragraph and the chart present another main idea listed by Roman numeral II. One supporting detail has been filled in. Complete the outline by adding other details.

> II. Many culprits are causing the destruction.
> A. Mollusks and microorganisms
>   1. Worms ate softer woods.
>   2. Microorganisms ate fabrics.
>   3. Worst damage is done.

What Do You Know About Sharks?
Magazine Article by Sharon Guynup

Can appearances DECEIVE?

COMMON CORE

RI 1 Cite textual evidence to support analysis of the what the text says explicitly. **RI 2** Determine central ideas in a text; provide an objective summary. **RI 4** Determine the meaning of phrases as they are used in a text, including figurative meanings. **RI 5** Analyze the structure an author uses to organize a text.

Cute doesn't always mean cuddly, and frightening doesn't always mean vicious. Appearances can deceive, as you will find out when you read "What Do You Know About Sharks?"

DISCUSS How much do you really know about sharks? Copy the chart shown here, and decide whether each statement is true or false. Then gather with others in a small group and share your answers. Does everyone agree on the "facts"?

Statement	True or False?
1. The great white is the largest shark.	
2. Most sharks are dangerous to humans.	
3. Sharks lived at the time of dinosaurs.	

TEXT ANALYSIS: TEXT FEATURES

Writers often organize text and highlight key ideas with design elements called **text features**. Common text features include

- titles
- subheadings
- sidebars
- graphic aids
- captions
- bulleted lists

As you read the article, identify the text features. Ask yourself how each one helps you understand expository text.

READING SKILL: OUTLINE

To find and remember the main or central ideas in a text, you can create an **outline**, a summary of an article's most important information. Begin by looking at the text features and topic sentences in a text. In "What Do You Know About Sharks?" each subhead introduces a new main idea.

Another guide to main ideas is a text's **organizational pattern**. For example, if a text presents a main idea as a cause and its effect, look for other causes and effects. Take notes in your outline on each main idea and label it with a Roman numeral. Place supporting details under each main idea and label each one with a capital letter.

> "What Do You Know About Sharks?"
>
> I. Sharks are vanishing
>
> A. Sharks need protection
>
> B. Without sharks, other species would overpopulate.

VOCABULARY IN CONTEXT

The boldfaced words helped Sharon Guynup share her knowledge of sharks and the sea. Use context clues to figure out what each word means.

1. Fish and whales are **aquatic** creatures.
2. The ocean is one kind of **ecosystem.**
3. A terrible disease can **decimate** a species.
4. The **carcass** of a half-eaten sea lion washed ashore.
5. Light will **diffuse** as it enters the water.
6. A life jacket increases a swimmer's **buoyancy.**

Complete the activities in your **Reader/Writer Notebook.**

Meet the Author

Sharon Guynup
born 1958

Animal Lover

Sharon Guynup (gĭ'nəp) has found a way to combine her two loves, writing and the environment. She completed a master's degree in journalism from New York University's Science and Environmental Reporting program and continues to write articles about animals and the environment. Her work has appeared in national science magazines, in newspapers, and on the Web. Guynup also produces *State of the Wild,* a yearly review of the condition of the world's wildlife and lands.

BACKGROUND TO THE ARTICLE

An Ocean of Knowledge

How do we know so much about sharks? People who study fish and how they live and grow in their environment are called ichthyologists (ĭk'thē-ŏl'ə-jĭsts). Their work in laboratories, in museums, at universities, and on research ships provides information about over 300 species of sharks. "What Do You Know About Sharks?" gives information about sharks in general, as well as facts about specific species.

Author Online

Go to **thinkcentral.com**. KEYWORD: HML7-907

THINK central

WHAT DO YOU KNOW ABOUT SHARKS? Ⓐ

SHARON GUYNUP

They're ferocious predators. They haunt us in nightmares. But the scariest thing about sharks may be that they're vanishing from the world's oceans. . . .

Why do sharks need protection? Sharks are top predators in the **aquatic** food chain—a web that interconnects all organisms, in which smaller creatures become food for larger predators. Without sharks, the ocean's delicate **ecosystem** would be disrupted. Species that sharks devour, like seals, for example, would overpopulate and in turn **decimate** other species, like
10 salmon. Read the following questions and answers to learn more about the world's most fear-inspiring fish.

Nurse Shark
Nurse sharks are sluggish bottom dwellers found in the Atlantic Ocean. They're usually not dangerous and are one of the few sharks that breathe by pumping water through their gills while lying motionless. They sometimes suck in prey as well.

Wobbegong Shark
Wobbegongs are found resting on the sea floor in shallow waters of the Indo-Pacific and the Red Sea. The barbels, or fringe of flesh around their mouths, are feelers that act as camouflage. ◆

What Are Sharks? B

Sharks are fish with skeletons made of rubbery cartilage (tough, flexible tissue) instead of bone. They're cold-blooded (unable to generate their own body heat), breathe through gills (respiratory organs), and have a two-chambered heart. Though most live in warm seas, the Greenland shark thrives in frigid Arctic seas. C

What's the Largest Shark? The Smallest?

Weighing in at 15 tons and stretching up to 14 meters (46 feet) long, the whale shark is the world's largest fish—bigger than a school bus! Nine hundred meters (2,953 feet) below the ocean surface lives the smallest shark: the dwarf shark. An adult measures only 25 centimeters (10 inches) long!

Are All Sharks Dangerous to People?

Most sharks are harmless. "Out of 375 shark species, only two dozen are in any way really dangerous to us," says Robert Hueter, director of the Center for Shark Research at Mote Marine Laboratory. Still, scientists don't know for sure why sharks sometimes attack humans. One theory: sharks may mistake the sound of swimming humans for that of injured fish—which are easy prey.

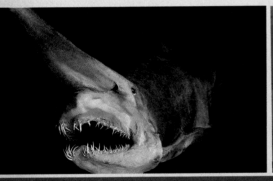

Goblin Shark
Goblin sharks feature needle-like teeth. They're rarely spotted—only 36 specimens have been counted—most found in waters deeper than 1,150 feet. Scientists think they inhabit seas from Europe to Australia.

Hammerhead Shark
Hammerheads inhabit shorelines and deep seas worldwide. The head, or cephalofoil, provides greater maneuverability—and enlarged nostrils and eyes at the ends of their "hammer" receive more information giving them a hunting advantage. D

B OUTLINE
Each orange question is a **subheading** that introduces a new main idea. State each main idea as a phrase and add it to your outline.

COMMON CORE RI 2

C OUTLINE
An outline shows the relationship between a text's main ideas and its supporting details. In an outline, you arrange the information by using Roman numerals to show the main ideas and capital letters to point out supporting details. If you need to add another level of details, use Arabic numerals to indicate those. What are the important details in this paragraph? Add them to your outline.

D TEXT FEATURES
Sidebars are set off from the main article—usually on the side or bottom of the page—and provide additional information. You can read sidebars at any time. What information does this sidebar give you?

E **TEXT FEATURES**
A **subheading** signals
the beginning of a new
topic within a text.
Preview the **subheadings**
on these pages. Which
section will tell you
where swimmers are
most at risk?

COMMON CORE RI 4

Language Coach

Similes The phrase "like
being crushed beneath
the weight of ten cars"
(lines 45–46) is a **simile**,
a comparison using the
words *like* and *as*. What
is the writer comparing
with this simile?

Which Shark Is the Most Dangerous to Humans? **E**

30 "In terms of fatal attacks, it's a tossup between the great
white, the tiger, and the bull shark," Hueter says. People fear
the massive great white the most because of its size—up to
6.4 meters (21 feet) long—and its large razor-like teeth, not
to mention the terror stirred up by *Jaws* flicks. But great whites
usually inhabit deep seas—not shallow waters where people
swim. Worldwide, fewer than 100 human attacks by all shark
species are reported each year.

Where Do Most Shark Attacks Happen?

Florida leads the world in shark bites, with 22 to 25 reported
incidents each year. But, claims Hueter, they're not repeated
40 shark attacks—usually a single bite. . . . "Most really bad
attacks occur off the coasts of California, Hawaii, Australia,
and South Africa," Hueter says.

Just How Powerful Is a Shark's Bite?

Scientists built a "shark-bite meter" that measures the jaw
strength of one species, the dusky shark. It exerts 18 tons of
pressure per square inch on a victim. That's like being crushed
beneath the weight of ten cars!

Whale Shark
The largest fish in the sea—whale
sharks—are very docile. They feed
on plankton, tiny drifting animals.
They swim with their enormous
mouths open, filtering food from the
water with 15,000 tiny teeth.

Leopard Shark
Leopard sharks are commonly
found near shore, often in large
schools along the Pacific coast from
Oregon to Mexico. They feed on
small fish and crustaceans and are
generally harmless.

What Do Sharks Eat?

Sharks chow down on what they can when they can—usually smaller animals from shrimp and fish to turtles and seabirds. Some, like the bull shark, consume large mammals like
50   sea lions or dolphins; others, like the whale shark, eat only plankton, tiny drifting animals. And tiger sharks devour just about anything—mammal **carcasses**, tin cans, plastic bags, coal, and even license plates have been found inside their stomachs! **F**

How Do Sharks Find Prey?

Sharks can hear a wide range of sounds but are attracted by bursts of sound—like those made by an injured fish—or occasionally humans romping in water. At close range, sharks also sense vibration with their lateral line, a sensory system that runs from head to tail on each side of a shark's body.
60   Inside the lateral line, which helps a shark maintain balance as well as detect sound, are canals filled with fluid and tiny "hair cells." Sound causes the liquid to vibrate, alerting the shark to the presence of another creature. This sense allows sharks to hunt even in total darkness.

Brushing and Flossing

Sharks continually lose their teeth, but some species grow new teeth as often as every week to replace worn or lost ones. During their lifetime, some species shed 30,000 teeth. Shark teeth vary according to what's on the menu:

    top: nurse shark teeth, which chew up shellfish

    middle: tiger shark teeth, which crunch everything from fish and birds to tin cans and other garbage

    bottom: mako shark teeth, which grind up squid and big fish like tuna and mackerel **G**

carcass (kär′kəs) *n.* the dead body of an animal

F OUTLINE
How many details about what sharks eat have you included in your outline? Remember that you can include as many lettered or Arabic-numbered details as you need.

G TEXT FEATURES
Graphic aids are visuals, such as graphs, photographs, and maps, that provide more information on a topic. What information do you get from looking at these photographs that you don't get from the text?

What's a "Feeding Frenzy"?

Sharks usually travel solo, but if one finds easy prey, an excited, competitive swarm of sharks may join in the feast, biting anything that lies in its path.

How Do Sharks Breathe?

A shark usually swims with its mouth open
70 to force oxygen-rich water to pass over a set of gills housed in a cavity behind its head—a process known as ramjet ventilation. Gill flaps called lamellae absorb and help **diffuse** oxygen into the shark's bloodstream. Lamellae also help sharks expel carbon dioxide, a gaseous waste product of breathing, from the bloodstream.

diffuse (dĭ-fyōōz′) *v.* to spread out or through

(H) TEXT FEATURES
A **caption** is the text that provides information about a graphic aid. How does this caption support your understanding of the photo and reinforce the article?

Shark Attack

This sea lion managed to survive a vicious shark attack. **H**

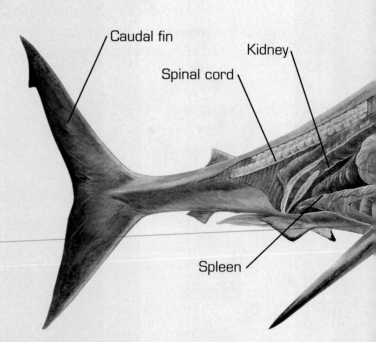

Caudal fin

Kidney

Spinal cord

Spleen

Top-Powerful Tail
Since its upper lobe is larger than the lower one, the great white's thrashing tail movements drive the shark forward and push its head down. This nosedive is countered by the fish's wedge-shaped head and its pectoral fins, which lift the front end.

Are Sharks Smart?

80 Experiments show that sharks recognize and remember shapes and patterns. Using shark snacks as rewards, scientists have taught lemon sharks to swim through mazes, ring bells, and press targets. "Although we learn new things about sharks every day, there's still a lot we don't know about them," says Hueter.

Great White Shark

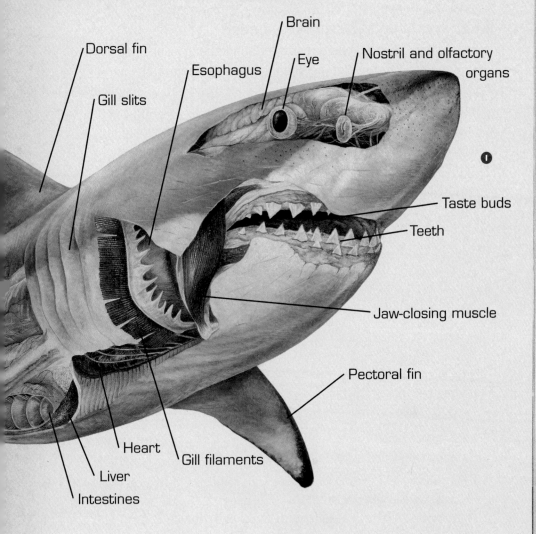

Brain
Dorsal fin
Esophagus
Eye
Nostril and olfactory organs
Gill slits
Taste buds
Teeth
Jaw-closing muscle
Pectoral fin
Heart
Gill filaments
Liver
Intestines

❶ TEXT FEATURES
Use the **labels** on the illustration to identify the spinal cord, kidney, and brain.

Sandpaper Skin
Rough and tough, shark skin is made of hard, platelike scales, like tiny teeth pointing backward.

Gills
Water flows in the mouth and over blood-rich gill filaments. Some dissolved oxygen passes into the bloodstream before the water flows out through gill slits.

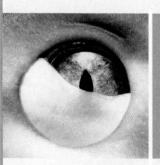

Shark Eyes

Sharks have good eyesight and can see colors. Their eyes are protected by a nictitating (nĭk′tĭ-tā′tĭng) membrane that moves up and down like an eyelid.

What Are Sharks' Natural Enemies?

Large sharks sometimes eat smaller sharks, and killer whales also dine on sharks. But the shark's greatest enemy is people. Humans kill sharks for food, use their skins for leather, make medicine from their liver oil, and use shark teeth for jewelry. Many sharks are killed senselessly for sport or get trapped and die in fishing nets. And it takes a long time for shark populations to rebound. Most shark species take ten years to reach reproductive age and produce small litters of less than a dozen pups.

90

Bite-Size Facts

- The first sharks appeared in the ancient oceans about 400 million years ago—200 million years before the dinosaurs!

- Sharks are carnivores (meat-eaters). Most gobble their prey whole or rip it into large, shark-size bites.

- Most sharks are found in the ocean but some, like the bull shark, also swim in lakes and rivers. Most shark attacks occur in warm waters—20° to 30°C (68° to 86°F).

- Sharks lack the inflatable swim bladder that allows bony fish to control <u>buoyancy</u>. Most sharks must swim endlessly. If they stop, they sink to the bottom and may drown from a lack of water flowing over the gills. **J**

buoyancy (boi′ən-sē)
n. the ability to remain afloat in liquid

J TEXT FEATURES
The Bite-Size Facts are organized in a **bulleted list.** Why do you think writers use bulleted lists to present information?

Comprehension

1. **Recall** What does the author think is the scariest thing about sharks?

2. **Clarify** What place do sharks hold in the aquatic food chain?

3. **Represent** Draw a simple illustration of a shark. Label its tail, dorsal fin, pectoral fins, and gill slits.

Text Analysis

● 4. **Understand Text Features** Locate the information about shark eyes on page 914. What do you learn from the photograph? What do the other text features add to your understanding of the photograph?

● 5. **Compare Outlines** Compare the outline you made while reading this article to one created by a classmate. Which main ideas and supporting details did you both have? Which were different?

6. **Analyze Author's Purpose** What do you think is the author's main purpose for writing "What Do You Know About Sharks?" Explain how the **text features** help Guynup achieve this purpose.

7. **Draw Conclusions** Why do sharks need to be protected? Make a chart like the one shown to list details and facts that you think support protecting sharks as well as those that support not protecting them. Use information from your outline or from the article. Which conclusion do you support?

Sharks Should Be Protected	Sharks Should Not Be Protected
The ecosystem would be disrupted without sharks.	

8. **Evaluate Objective Point of View** When writing from an objective point of view, the writer leaves out personal opinions and instead presents information in a straightforward way. How does the author's use of the objective point of view influence your response to the article?

Extension and Challenge

9. **Creative Project: Art** Work with a partner to create a poster illustrating **facts** about sharks. Include some of the important information about sharks that you put in your outline.

Can appearances DECEIVE?

Have you changed your opinion about sharks now that you have read this article? Think of another fish or an animal about which people may have strong opinions that don't match the facts. Compare that fish or animal's appearance with the facts that you know about it. Why do you think its appearance is deceptive?

COMMON CORE

RI 1 Cite textual evidence to support analysis of what the text says explicitly. RI 2 Determine central ideas in a text; provide an objective summary. RI 5 Analyze the structure an author uses to organize a text.

Vocabulary in Context

▲ VOCABULARY PRACTICE

Answer the questions to show your understanding of the vocabulary words.

1. Which is an example of an **ecosystem,** a desert or a gymnasium?
2. Which would be more likely to **decimate** a species, overhunting or rain?
3. If you wanted to **diffuse** air in a room, would you use a vacuum or a fan?
4. Which has **buoyancy,** a boulder or a raft?
5. If something is a **carcass,** is it alive or dead?
6. Would a person who liked **aquatic** things more likely own a fish tank or a cactus?

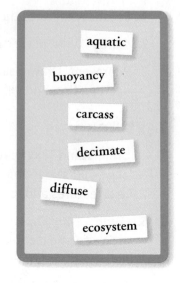

aquatic

buoyancy

carcass

decimate

diffuse

ecosystem

ACADEMIC VOCABULARY IN WRITING

> • area   • domain   • hypothesis   • objective   • resolve

Write a paragraph describing the **domain** of different types of sharks. Include facts from the article about where sharks can be found. Use at least one of the Academic Vocabulary words in your paragraph.

VOCABULARY STRATEGY: CONTENT-SPECIFIC WORDS

Whenever you study a specific subject or explore an area of interest, you are likely to encounter new words that are directly related to that subject. For example, in this article about sharks, you learned that the word *aquatic* refers to things that grow or live in the water. By learning content-specific words, you'll be better able to understand, discuss, and write about the subject yourself.

PRACTICE Match the word in the first column with its definition in the second column. Refer to a dictionary or science textbook if you need help.

1. tsunami
2. current
3. mollusks
4. marine
5. kelp
6. crustaceans

a. having to do with the sea or the things in it
b. animals with soft bodies and often hard shells
c. large brown seaweed
d. ocean stream that moves continuously in one direction
e. hard-shelled animals with jointed body and legs
f. destructive wave caused by an underwater earthquake

Interactive Vocabulary **THINK** central

Go to **thinkcentral.com.**
KEYWORD: HML7-916

Language

◆ **GRAMMAR IN CONTEXT:** Use Commas Correctly

Commas are used to make the meanings of sentences clear by setting off certain elements. One such element is an **appositive.** An appositive is a noun or pronoun that explains, identifies, or renames the noun or pronoun it follows. Sometimes the appositive has a modifier. This is called an **appositive phrase.**

Original: The tiger shark a ferocious predator will eat just about anything.

Revised: The tiger shark, a ferocious predator, will eat just about anything. *(Insert a comma before and after the appositive phrase "a ferocious predator.")*

PRACTICE   In the following sentences, add commas where necessary.

1. Great white sharks the most fearsome fish usually live in deep seas.
2. The whale shark the world's largest fish eats plankton.
3. Humans the shark's greatest enemy kill sharks for leather.
4. The nurse shark a slow bottom dweller is not usually dangerous.

For more help with punctuating appositive phrases, see page R61 in the **Grammar Handbook**.

READING-WRITING CONNECTION

YOUR TURN   Increase your understanding of "What Do You Know About Sharks?" by responding to this prompt. Then use the **revising tip** to improve your writing.

WRITING PROMPT	REVISING TIP
Short Constructed Response: Informational Text Rewrite the information in the caption for "Shark Eyes" on page 914 so that it is organized in a question-answer format. Use the organization of the article as a model. Include a subheading in the form of a question and provide a clear main idea and at least two details.	Be sure that you have placed a comma before and after appositives and appositive phrases. ▶ If the sentence ends with an appositive phrase, you need only place a comma before it and a period at its end.

COMMON CORE

L1 Demonstrate command of the conventions of standard English grammar and usage.
L2 Demonstrate command of the conventions of standard English punctuation. **W2** Write informative texts to examine a topic.

Interactive Revision   **THINK** central
Go to thinkcentral.com.
KEYWORD: HML7-917

Great White Sharks

 Video link at
thinkcentral.com

Magazine Article by Peter Benchley

Can you tell
FACT from fiction?

COMMON CORE

RI 6 Determine an author's point of view and analyze how the author distinguishes his position.
RI 8 Trace specific claims in a text.

Artists and writers often use what they know to be true about the world to create imaginary scenarios that can seem more real than life itself. But how do you know when a work of fiction is technically accurate and when it's not? Peter Benchley has made a name for himself by dealing in both facts and fiction about great white sharks.

LIST IT Choose a movie or a book you have enjoyed that features animals or natural events. For each movie or book, list some of the details that were included, explaining whether they're true or not.

Homeward Bound
1. Animals can find their way home across hundreds of miles.
2.
3.
4.

TEXT ANALYSIS: EVIDENCE IN INFORMATIONAL TEXT

Writers of informational text usually support their claims with evidence, such as **facts,** which are statements that can be proved. Be sure that you can tell the difference between factual claims and opinions or commonplace assertions.

- **A factual claim** is a statement that can be proved from evidence such as a fact, personal observation, reliable source, or an expert's opinion.
- **An opinion** is a statement of personal belief, feeling, or thought, which does not require proof or evidence.
- **A commonplace assertion** is a statement that many people assume to be true, but which is not necessarily so.

As you read, look for evidence that will help you distinguish factual claims from opinions and commonplace assertions.

READING SKILL: RECOGNIZE AUTHOR'S BIAS

Even nonfiction writers can reveal a bias toward their topics. **Bias** is the side of an issue that a writer favors. One way writers reveal their bias is through **loaded language**, words that are strongly positive or negative. As you read, record the loaded language in a chart and identify the author's bias.

Loaded Language	Possible Author's Bias
"most _wonderful_ of _natural-born killers_"	Benchley is impressed by sharks' survival instincts.

▲ VOCABULARY IN CONTEXT

The boldfaced words help Peter Benchley share facts and feelings about great white sharks. Use context clues to figure out the meaning of each word.

1. Humans **demonize** an innocent creature out of fear.
2. The tourist gave **anecdotal** evidence instead of hard facts.
3. We finally reached a **consensus** after a loud debate.
4. The evidence was subject to close **scrutiny.**
5. Most scary movies are based on our **visceral** fears.
6. The scientist interviewed two **prospective** assistants.
7. The test errors were caused by **inadvertence** to detail.
8. The trial was a **travesty** because the jury was biased.

Complete the activities in your **Reader/Writer Notebook.**

Meet the Author

Peter Benchley
1940–2006

The _Jaws_ Sensation
Peter Benchley is best known for his novel _Jaws,_ which is about the hunt for a great white shark that killed several people in a beach community. _Jaws_ stayed on the bestseller list for 40 weeks. In 1975, Steven Spielberg turned it into one of the top-grossing movies at the time. It was also nominated for an Academy Award for Best Picture. Benchley went on to write other novels and screenplays with the ocean as the setting, as well as nonfiction works about the ocean.

Regrets
In the 1970s, when Benchley wrote _Jaws,_ little was known about great white sharks. His description of them as vicious man-eaters frightened many people out of the water and triggered an aggressive shark hunt. Benchley, always fascinated by the ocean, spent a great deal of his life exploring it. He came to discover that much of what he wrote was incorrect. He was outspoken in his regrets for helping to create this hysteria. Benchley noted, "For every human being killed by a shark, roughly ten million sharks are killed by humans."

Author Online
THINK central
Go to **thinkcentral.com.**
KEYWORD: HML7-919

919

GREAT WHITE SHARKS

PETER BENCHLEY

Analyze Visuals ▶

What might you **infer** about the great white shark from this photograph?

Considering the knowledge accumulated about great whites in the past 25 years, I couldn't possibly write *Jaws* today—not in good conscience anyway. Back then, it was generally accepted that great whites were anthropophagous—they ate people by choice. Now we know that almost every attack on a human is an accident. The shark mistakes the human for its normal prey. **Ⓐ**

Back then, we thought that once a great white scented blood, it launched a feeding frenzy that inevitably led to death. Now
10 we know that nearly three-quarters of all bite victims survive, perhaps because the shark recognizes that it has made a mistake and doesn't return for a second bite.

Back then, we believed that great whites attacked boats. Now we know that their sensory systems detect movement, sound, and electrical fields, such as those caused by metal and motors, in water, and when they approach a boat, they're merely coming to investigate. Granted, investigation by a 3,000-pound animal can wreak havoc.[1] **Ⓑ**

Finally, back then, it was OK to **demonize** an animal,
20 especially a shark, because man had done so since the beginning of time, and, besides, sharks appeared to be infinite in number.

No longer. Today we know that these most wonderful of natural-born killers, these exquisite creatures of evolution, are not only *not* villains, they are victims in danger of—if not extinction quite yet—serious, perhaps even catastrophic, decline. Much of the evidence is **anecdotal.** Fishermen and naturalists are seeing fewer great whites, and in most places those they are seeing are younger and smaller. **Ⓒ**

---

1. **wreak havoc:** bring about great destruction.

COMMON CORE RI 8

Ⓐ EVIDENCE
Reread lines 1–7. A commonplace assertion is a statement that many people assume to be true but which is not necessarily so. What commonplace assertion does Benchley cite? What factual claim does he make to dispute it?

Ⓑ EVIDENCE
Reread lines 13–18. What commonplace assertion does Benchley cite? What factual claim does he make to dispute it?

demonize (dē′mə-nīz′) *v.* to give evil, demonic qualities to

anecdotal (ăn′ĭk-dōt′l) *adj.* based on observations rather than scientific analysis

Ⓒ RECOGNIZE AUTHOR'S BIAS
Reread lines 23–27. What examples of **loaded language** do you find here? Record them in your chart.

30　　Scientists estimate that, worldwide, populations of some species of sharks have dropped by 80 percent. Though precise numbers of white sharks aren't known, there is a growing **consensus** that they are not reproducing at a rate sufficient to maintain the population. What *is* known now is that great white sharks—scarce by nature and growing scarcer thanks to contact with man—are, for all their grace and power and manifest menace, remarkably fragile. . . . **D**

Nowadays more people are coming to respect and appreciate sharks for what they are: beautiful, graceful,
40　　efficient, and, above all, integral members of the ocean food chain. In large measure the change is due to television and the abundance of films documenting not only the glories from sharks but also the dangers to them from longlines, nets, and the odious practice of finning— slicing the fins off sharks to sell in Asian markets, then tossing the living
50　animals overboard to die. Gradually governments and individuals are learning that while a dead shark may bring ten or twenty or even fifty dollars to a single fisherman, a live shark can be worth thousands of dollars more in tourist revenue to a community. Divers will fly halfway around the world to see white sharks.

　　Immodestly I claim some credit
60　for the change in attitude. For while the *Jaws* phenomenon was blamed for distorting the public's view of sharks and causing sporadic outbreaks of macho mayhem,[2] it also generated a fascination with and, over time, an affection for sharks that had not existed before.

Shark finning in the
Pacific Ocean

This 17-foot great white shark
was caught in the Atlantic
Ocean. It weighed a record-
breaking 3,500 pounds.

---

2. **sporadic outbreaks of macho mayhem:** occasional wild flare-ups of people trying to show their superiority over sharks by attacking and killing them.

These days I receive more than a thousand letters a year from youngsters who were not alive when *Jaws* appeared, and all of
70 them, without exception, want to know more about sharks in general and great whites in particular.

A great white shark in South Africa jumps out of the water to attack a seal.

Great white sharks are among the true apex predators in the ocean. The largest predatory fish in the world, they have few natural enemies. And so, in balanced nature, there are not very many great whites, and the number grows or shrinks depending on availability of food. They breed late in life and pup relatively few. Again, nobody knows exactly how many, but seven or eight seems to be a safe average. The youngsters appear alive, four or five feet long, weighing 50–60 pounds,
80 fully armed and ready to rumble. Still, many don't survive the first year because other sharks, including great whites, will eat them. **E**

Of all the infuriating unknowns about great white sharks, none is more controversial than size. How big can they grow to be? Fishermen from Nova Scotia to South Australia, from Cape Town to Cape Cod claim to have encountered 25-footers, 30-footers, even 36-footers. Usually the proof offered is that the beast was "bigger than the boat." There have been reports of a 23-footer in the waters off Malta and a 21-foot, 7,000-pounder
90 off Cuba, but none has held up under **scrutiny.** The largest

E **EVIDENCE**
Reread lines 72–82. What factual claims does Benchley make about the quantity of great white sharks? Identify three resources that you could use to verify these statements.

scrutiny (skrōōt′n-ē) *n.* close examination or study

F EVIDENCE
Informational text often includes opinions as well as factual claims. A **factual claim** is a main idea that can be proved from evidence such as facts or expert sources. An **opinion** is a statement of personal belief. Reread lines 94–101. Which part of this statement is a factual claim? Which part is an opinion?

Language Coach

Word Definition The word *adage* in line 116 refers to a saying that is known to many people and has been accepted as true for a long time. Explain the meaning of the adage about a swimmer in lines 116–117.

visceral (vĭs′ər-əl) *adj.* instinctive

generally accepted catch—made by lasso, of all things—was a shark 19.5 feet long. The largest great white shark ever caught on rod and reel weighed 2,664 pounds.

According to British biologist Ian Fergusson, chairman of the Shark Trust, no great white shark longer than 19.5 feet has ever been validated, and in a widely circulated e-mail, he expressed irritation at "this stubborn reluctance by some elements of the media to accept the facts and even more of a reluctance to accept that a 16-foot, 4500-pound white shark is big, very big,
100 and should need no further exaggeration to impress even the most discerning of viewers when seen up close." **F**

I can attest that underwater, cruising toward you out of the gloom with the serene confidence of the invincible, a 12-foot great white looks like a locomotive with malice in mind. . . .

At the moment science accepts about 400 species of sharks, but the number changes as new species are discovered. Of all known species, only four attack human beings with any frequency: bull sharks, tiger sharks, oceanic whitetips, and great whites.
110 In Australia, between 1876 and 1999, 52 attacks by great whites were recorded, and of them 27 were fatal. In the Mediterranean Sea since 1900 there have been 23 reliably recorded encounters with great whites, including one in 1909 in which the remains of two adults and a child were found inside a single 15-foot-long female shark caught off Augusta, Sicily.

The old adage is true: A swimmer has a better chance of being struck by lightning than killed by a shark. And around the world many, many more people die every year from bee stings, snakebites, falling off ladders, or drowning in bathtubs
120 than from shark attack. None of which, to be sure, detracts from the ghastly, **visceral** horror of being eaten by a huge fish, but all of which should give some comfort to the recreational swimmer. . . .

More and more these days it is the naturalists and field operators, guides and dive masters who are contributing to the accumulation of practical knowledge about great whites. To cite just one example: Until recently scientists thought that the scars that mar nearly every

mature shark were acquired either from prey that fought back
130 or from ritual biting by **prospective** mates. Now there is
eyewitness testimony of aggressive social interaction[3] between
sharks and also of spectacular threat displays that take the
place of major—potentially fatal—encounters with other
white sharks.

prospective
(prə-spĕk′tĭv) *adj.* likely
to be or become

G **RECOGNIZE
AUTHOR'S BIAS**
Reread lines 130–134.
What does the word
spectacular reveal about
Benchley's attitude
toward sharks' behavior?

A caged diver in South Australia comes face to face with a great white shark.

So we are learning—bit by bit, anecdote by anecdote—more
and more about these magnificent predators. We must hope
that we're learning enough to save them before, through
ignorance and **inadvertence,** we destroy them.

Great white sharks have survived, virtually unchanged,
140 for millions of years. They are as perfectly in tune with their
environment as any living thing on the planet. For them to be
driven to extinction by man, a relative newcomer, would be
more than an ecological tragedy; it would be a moral **travesty.** **H**

inadvertence
(ĭn′əd-vûr′tns) *n.* a lack
of attention; carelessness

travesty (trăv′ĭ-stē) *n.*
a degraded or grotesque
likeness

H **RECOGNIZE
AUTHOR'S BIAS**
Identify the **loaded
language** in the last two
paragraphs. Why do
you think Benchley uses
loaded language here?

3. **aggressive social interaction:** contact that is combative even though there is no actual
intent to fight.

Comprehension

1. **Recall** How many years passed between the time the author wrote *Jaws* and the time he wrote the article?

2. **Clarify** Why are there naturally so few great white sharks?

Text Analysis

3. **Identify Evidence** Statistics are facts expressed in numbers, and they are often used as evidence. Reread lines 110–115 and identify the statistics. What factual claim made by the writer do they support?

4. **Distinguish Types of Evidence** The main idea, or factual claim, of this article is that people have the wrong impression of sharks. Use a chart like the one shown to list factual claims, opinions, and commonplace assertions that Benchley uses to support his main idea. Which type of evidence does he use the most?

Type of Evidence	Examples
Factual Claim	
Opinion	
Commonplace Assertion	

5. **Analyze Author's Bias** What is Benchley's attitude toward his subject? Refer to the chart you made while you were reading and identify Benchley's **loaded language**. Describe the bias you see in these examples.

6. **Analyze Stereotype** A stereotype, or an overgeneralization, is a form of **bias** that presents an idea or an image of someone or something that is too simple or that may not be wholly true. What stereotype of sharks does Benchley present? How does he attempt to change it?

Extension and Challenge

7. SCIENCE CONNECTION Review the article and choose three facts about great white sharks. For each fact, find two reliable sources, such as an encyclopedia, an atlas, or an almanac, that verify it. Present your findings to the class.

Can you tell FACT from fiction?

Write a fictional paragraph about nature in which you include facts that are real. Exchange paragraphs with a classmate. Can you accurately identify each other's facts?

COMMON CORE

RI 6 Determine an author's point of view and analyze how the author distinguishes his position.
RI 8 Trace specific claims in a text.

Vocabulary in Context

▲ VOCABULARY PRACTICE

Decide whether the words in each pair are synonyms (words with the same meaning) or antonyms (words with opposite meanings).

1. consensus/disagreement
2. inadvertence/inattention
3. visceral/analytical
4. demonize/praise
5. travesty/distortion
6. scrutiny/observation
7. anecdotal/scientific
8. prospective/unexpected

anecdotal
consensus
demonize
inadvertence
prospective
scrutiny
travesty
visceral

ACADEMIC VOCABULARY IN SPEAKING

• area • domain • hypothesis • objective • resolve

Benchley explains that observations about sharks have led to new theories about their behavior. In a small group of classmates, choose a **hypothesis** that is posed in the article, and design a process for testing it. Use the Academic Vocabulary words in your discussion.

VOCABULARY STRATEGY: PREFIXES AND THE LATIN ROOT *vert*

The vocabulary word *inadvertence* contains the Latin root *vert,* which means "turn." This root, sometimes spelled *vers(e),* is combined with various prefixes to form simple English words. To understand the meanings of words with *vert* or *vers(e),* use the meaning of the root and the prefixes it is used with.

PRACTICE Combine a prefix from the chart with *vert* or *vers(e)* to form words to complete each of these sentences. Note that some prefix spellings vary.

1. If you back up a car, you put it in _____.
2. A person who is very outgoing is known as a(n) _____.
3. If you don't want to watch a scary movie, you can _____ your eyes.
4. To cross a desert, you must _____ a lot of sand.

Prefixes Used with *vert, vers(e)*	Meaning
ab-, a-	away from
extra-, extro-	outside
re-	again; back
trans-, tra-	across

COMMON CORE

L 4b Use common grade-appropriate Greek or Latin affixes and roots as clues to the meaning of a word. **L 6** Acquire and use accurately grade-appropriate general academic words.

Interactive Vocabulary **THINK**central

Go to **thinkcentral.com**.
KEYWORD: HML7-927

Like Black Smoke:
The Black Death's Journey
Magazine Article by Diana Childress

A World Turned Upside Down:
How the Black Death Affected Europe
Magazine Article by Mary Morton Cowan

VIDEO TRAILER **THiNK** central KEYWORD: HML7-928

How do we fight
DISEASE?

COMMON CORE

RI 1 Cite textual evidence to
support analysis of what the
text says explicitly. **RI 5** Analyze
the structure an author uses to
organize a text. **RI 9** Analyze
how two authors writing about
the same topic shape their
presentations of key information.

Communities can do a lot to stay healthy and prevent disease. But
people didn't always know what we know now. The articles you are
about to read tell about a time during the Middle Ages when the
bubonic plague affected so many people that it changed a society.

LIST IT What can we do to encourage good health for ourselves and
others? List five guidelines that people can follow to prevent diseases
from spreading. Be ready to explain why you included each guideline.

● TEXT ANALYSIS: CAUSE-AND-EFFECT PATTERN OF ORGANIZATION

Nonfiction writers often use patterns of organization to help explain particular ideas. One commonly used pattern is **cause-and-effect organization**, which shows the relationship between an event and its cause or effect. Cause-and-effect organization

- can answer the questions "What happened?" and "Why did it happen?"
- uses signal words and phrases, such as *caused, because, led to, for this reason, as a result,* and *may be due to*

As you read these two articles, notice how the writers use cause-and-effect patterns to explain key points.

● READING STRATEGY: SET A PURPOSE FOR READING

In this lesson, your **purpose for reading** is to compare articles that use cause-and-effect organization. As you read, use a chart to note which topics are covered by each article. You will be asked to do more with this chart after you finish reading.

Topics Covered	"Like Black Smoke"	"A World Turned Upside Down"
Agricultural changes		
How disease spread		
Loss of life		
Trade routes		
Worker shortages		

Review: Interpret Graphic Aids

▲ VOCABULARY IN CONTEXT

The following words help provide information about the bubonic plague. Use the ones you know in a sentence. Look up the meaning of the others in a dictionary, and then write a sentence for each of those words.

WORD	artisan	cope	rampage
LIST	bacterium	disarray	recurrence
	chronicle	hierarchy	

Complete the activities in your **Reader/Writer Notebook.**

Meet the Authors

Diana Childress
born 1940

History Lover
Award-winning author Diana Childress has written numerous books and articles for young people, most of them based on her favorite subject—history.

Mary Morton Cowan
born 1939

Many Talents
Articles aren't the only thing Mary Morton Cowan writes for young people. She also writes folk tales, historical plays, photo essays, and puzzles.

BACKGROUND TO THE ARTICLES
Devastation in the Middle Ages
The Middle Ages lasted from about A.D. 500 to A.D. 1500. One of the most significant events of this time period was the spread of the bubonic plague, or the Black Death. Those who caught the disease suffered fever and painful swellings, called buboes, in the lymph glands. The buboes, from which the disease gets its name, were followed by black spots on the skin. Next came a severe, bloody cough, and after that—death. At the time, no one knew what caused the disease.

Authors Online
Go to **thinkcentral.com**. KEYWORD: HML7-929

929

Burying plague victims in coffins at Tournai in 1349. Flemish manuscript illumination, 14th century. The Granger Collection, New York.

Analyze Visuals ▶
What are the individuals in this image doing?

A SET A PURPOSE FOR READING
Read the title and scan the **subheadings.** What do you expect to learn from this article?

Like Black Smoke
The Black Death's Journey A
Diana Childress

"We see death coming into our midst like black smoke," wrote the poet Jeuan Gethin,[1] when plague invaded Wales in March 1349. This "rootless phantom which has no mercy" was especially frightening for those who witnessed it because they knew it was somehow contagious, but no one could halt or explain its relentless spread across Europe.

Eastern Beginnings

The earliest evidence of the Black Death lies in a cemetery in what was once a prosperous town near Lake Issyk-Kul[2] on the fabled Silk Road[3] in Central Asia. An unusually large number of graves there are dated 1338 and 1339. Three headstones mentioning the cause of death provide a clue about why
10 so many people died: the plague.

Did the Black Death originate near Issyk-Kul? No one knows for sure. Most medieval writers say that the plague began in the East. They name places like Cathay (China), India, and Turkey. Modern historians agree that

---

1. **Jeuan Gethin** (yā'ən gĕth'ĭn).
2. **Lake Issyk-Kul** (ĭ'sĭk-kŭl').
3. **Silk Road:** an important trade route on which both goods and ideas were exchanged between China and the countries of western Europe.

the epidemic started in Asia—more specifically, somewhere on the central steppes[4] or in the Himalayan lowlands on the border of India and China. In both regions, the plague **bacterium,** *Yersinia pestis,*[5] has long thrived among wild marmots, ground squirrels, and gerbils.

On the Move

How did the disease travel from wild rodents to humans? According to early accounts, before the Black Death broke out, earthquakes, floods, and
20 famines devastated Asia. One theory is that these disasters drove wild animals into villages and towns in search of food. Fleas then spread plague germs to rats. . . .

When rats died of the plague, their fleas hunted for new hosts. Since rats nested in the adobe (sun-dried brick) walls and thatched roofs of medieval houses, the next meal for these fleas often came from people. . . .

The disease spread more easily if an infected person's lungs started filling up with plague bacteria. Then, every cough and sneeze spewed germs into the air, spreading pneumonic plague[6]
30 directly to others.

If they are not among the lucky few who recover, people and rats soon die of the plague, but infected fleas can lurk in a rat's nest, barnyard manure, or bedding and
40 clothing for many months without eating. A medieval writer was not far wrong when he wrote that "even the houses or clothes of the victims could kill."

Fleas infect rats with *Yersinia pestis,* the plague bacterium. Rats spread the disease to humans. Once human lungs fill with plague bacteria, the germ becomes airborne every time a person coughs or sneezes.

. . . Cloth, grain, furs, and hides kept in rat-infested warehouses soon became delayed-action "plague bombs" waiting to go off. An account tells

---

4. **steppes:** treeless plains in southeastern Europe and in Asia.

5. *Yersinia pestis* (yər-sĭn′ē-ə pĕst′ĭs).

6. **pneumonic** (nŏŏ-mŏn′ĭk) **plague:** the most contagious and deadly form of the Black Death.

---

bacterium (băk-tîr′ē-əm) *n.* the singular form of *bacteria,* microscopically small living things that may cause disease

B **CAUSE AND EFFECT**
The question in line 18 introduces a cause-and-effect chain of events. What explanation does the author give for the plague's spread to villages and town?

C **CAUSE AND EFFECT**
Reread lines 23–25. Why did fleas move on from rats to humans for their next meal?

COMMON CORE RI 5

D **CAUSE AND EFFECT**
When a writer describes a relationship that has multiple causes, multiple events, or is a series of causes and effects, the explanations can become complicated. Notice that Childress helps to clarify a series of causes and effects by illustrating it. Use the illustration and the information in lines 26–49 to understand how people spread the disease. Once people have the plague bacterium, what happens when they cough or sneeze?

Multiple-Meaning Words A word with more than one meaning is known as a multiple-meaning word. Which meaning of the word *galleys* is used in line 60?
• large ships driven by sails and oars
• small, narrow kitchens, such as those in campers
• long, metal trays used to hold type for a printing press

50 how four soldiers learned the hard way about contaminated goods. Looting houses in a deserted town, they stole a fleece off a bed and later slept under it. They were dead by morning.

Commercial caravans, Mongol armies, and other wayfarers[7] "carried" the Black Death in their baggage as they crisscrossed Asia. By 1345, it had traveled from Issyk-Kul to Sarai and Astrakhan,[8] the major cities of the Golden Horde[9] (a part of the Mongol Empire that is today southwestern Russia).

From Asia to the Mediterranean

At the time, Italian merchants from Genoa and Venice had established trading posts at Kaffa, a city on the Crimean Peninsula that juts out into the Black Sea. Since the mid-1200s, their galleys had transported Asian

60 horses, furs, and slaves to Syria and Egypt and silks and spices to Italy. When plague began to spread to the Crimea, many of the Europeans tried to escape by sea, but the Black Death sailed with them.

---

7. **commercial caravans . . . wayfarers:** Commercial caravans are bands of merchants or traders traveling together for safety. Mongols had a large empire covering most of Asia and eastern Europe. Wayfarers are generally people who travel on foot.

8. **Sarai** (sä-rī′) . . . **Astrakhan** (ăs′trə-kăn′).

9. **Golden Horde:** a name for the Mongol army.

The following summer, plague broke out in Constantinople. From there, it crossed the Mediterranean region. That fall, ships brought the plague to Alexandria, Egypt, one arriving with only 45 of its original crew of 332 men still alive. Another fleet came to Messina, Sicily, its crew so ill that a **chronicle** reports that the men had "sickness clinging to their very bones."

70   The epidemic reached Genoa on New Year's Eve 1347 aboard three galleys laden with spices from the East. On discovering that many seamen were sick, the Genoese chased the ships from the port with "burning arrows and engines of war." Plague-ridden rats, however, had already jumped ship. The galleys sailed off along the coast of France, still hoping to find a place to sell their deadly merchandise.

Following the Trade Routes

Following 14th-century trade routes, the Black Death swept across Europe, North Africa, and the Middle East. After it assaulted the seaports, smaller boats carried it to neighboring towns and to river ports far inland. It could not be stopped. Although some towns refused entry to travelers from

80 infected areas, and people learned to mistrust "plague goods," few noticed the dead rats, and no one thought of the fleas. **F**

    Reports of plague in 1348 show how the circles of infection widened. In the east, it hit Cyprus, Aleppo, Damascus, Jerusalem, and even pilgrims

chronicle (krŏn′ĭ-kəl) *n.* a record of historical events in the order in which they took place

F CAUSE AND EFFECT
Reread lines 76–81. Why did the plague spread around the globe?

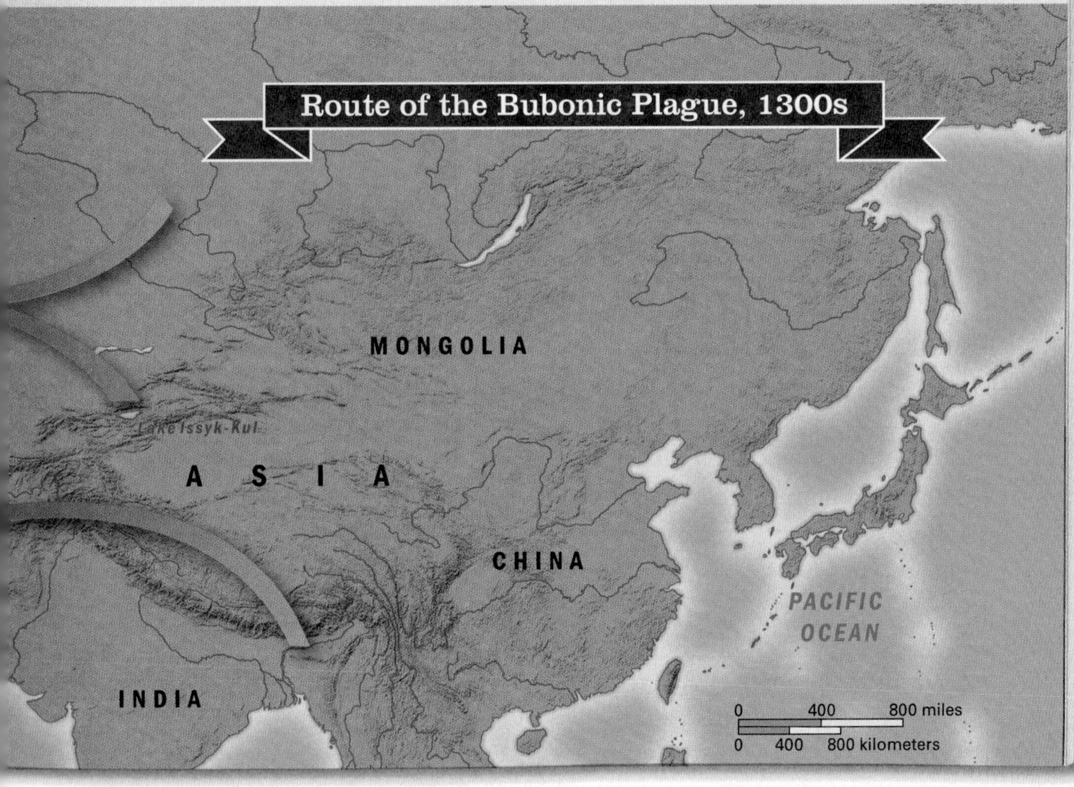

Route of the Bubonic Plague, 1300s

MONGOLIA

Lake Issyk-Kul

A S I A

CHINA

PACIFIC OCEAN

INDIA

0   400   800 miles
0   400   800 kilometers

visiting Mecca. From Genoa and Venice it crept down the Italian boot toward Florence and Rome. Going west, it struck Marseilles, Tunis, and Barcelona. By June, the epidemic was storming Paris, causing the French royal family to flee to Rouen,[10] where it soon followed. That summer, it overran Germany, Poland, and Hungary and crossed the channel to southern England.

90 Winter did not slow its progress. The weather was unusually mild and wet, perhaps warm enough for fleas living on house rats to remain active. Huddled indoors, people were also exposed to air contaminated both by those suffering from pneumonic plague and by the dust from rodent droppings. **G**

As the disease moved northward through England, citizens of Lincoln wrote wills at 30 times the normal annual rate. At first, the Scots avoided the plague, but when they assembled troops to invade England, pestilence[11] struck, perhaps imported by soldiers from France.

The Black Death landed in Scandinavia on a ship carrying wool from
100 London to Norway. The ship had run aground near Bergen because all the crew had died. From there, plague spread across Norway, into Sweden, and across the Baltic Sea to Russia.

The Journey Ends

In 1350, plague peaked in Scotland and Scandinavia, while in southern Spain, it killed King Alfonso XI of Castile. The following year, it stretched to Greenland, where it helped wipe out the Norwegian colony, and to Yemen, at the tip of the Arabian peninsula. In 1353, it closed in on Moscow, killing both the patriarch of the Russian church and the grand duke of Muscovy.

110 Finally, the Black Death petered out somewhere in Kiev, having come almost full circle back to Kaffa. During its long **rampage,** between one-third and one-half of the population of Europe, North Africa, and the Middle East died. No natural disaster before or since has caused such devastation of human life over such a large area. It was one of the greatest catastrophes in human history.

A priest blesses plague-infected monks. Illumination from *Omne Bonum* (about 1370), Jacobus Anglicus. Ms. Royal 6, E VI, fol. 301. © British Library/akg-images.

10. **Rouen** (rōō-än'): a city in France, about 84 miles northwest of Paris.
11. **pestilence** (pĕs'tə-ləns): any disease that spreads rapidly and causes many deaths.

G CAUSE AND EFFECT
What conditions might have caused the plague to spread in winter?

rampage (răm'pāj') *n.* a wild or violent outbreak

Comprehension

1. **Recall** Where do most historians think the Black Death started?

2. **Recall** How did boats spread the disease?

3. **Summarize** Summarize how the plague spread from rodents to people.

Text Analysis

4. **Identify Fact or Opinion** Reread the last statement in the article. Is this sentence a fact or an opinion? Explain why you think so.

5. **Understand Cause and Effect** During the rampage of the plague, why did people believe that "even the houses or clothes of the victims could kill" (lines 31–52)?

6. **Analyze Author's Purpose** What do you think are the main points Childress wants readers to learn from this article? Explain your reasoning.

7. **Evaluate Events** Create a timeline of the key events that contributed to the spread of the Black Death. Which event do you think was most critical? Support your choice with details from the article.

Comparing Articles

8. **Set a Purpose for Reading** Review what you recorded in your chart. Choose one of the topics and describe its cause-and-effect relationship with the plague.

Topics Covered	"Like Black Smoke"	"A World Turned Upside Down"
Agricultural changes		
How disease spread	X	
Loss of life		
Trade routes		
Worker shortages		

COMMON CORE

RI 1 Cite textual evidence to support analysis of what the text says explicitly. RI 5 Analyze the structure an author uses to organize a text.

Detail of *Triumph of Death* (1597), Jan Brueghel. Oil on canvas, 119 cm × 164 cm. Steiermärk. Landesmuseum Johanneum. © akg-images.

A WORLD TURNED UPSIDE DOWN: HOW THE BLACK DEATH AFFECTED EUROPE

Mary Morton Cowan

A SET A PURPOSE
FOR READING
Reread lines 1–4.
Paraphrase the main
idea that this article
will explore.

hierarchy (hī′ə-rär′kē)
n. an organization of
people according to rank

Substantial changes in population often have dramatic effects on society. The bubonic plague, which in just four years killed up to one-third of the people in Europe, almost literally turned Europe's social structure upside down. **A**

Life in the Middle Ages centered around a **hierarchy** called the feudal system. Noble lords lived in castles or manors, which were surrounded by acres of land. The nobles depended on peasants to farm their land. In turn, peasants received protection, shelter, and a small plot of land to plant their own crops. According to the Christian church, the feudal system was God's
10 plan, and no one questioned the authority of the church.

In the 300 years before the Black Death, the European population tripled. Additional land was cultivated, but food was still scarce. Some peasants left

◄ **Analyze Visuals**

What might the skeletons in this painting **symbolize**, or stand for?

for a better life in the city, where merchants and craftsmen were beginning to thrive. The now-crowded cities, however, could not handle the overflow of unskilled laborers.

After gunpowder was invented, the lords had found it harder to defend their castles. They also experienced some bad harvests, and many had to **cope** with the consequences of a war between France and England. Yet, they remained in control.

cope (kōp) *v.* to struggle with and act to overcome

20 Then, without warning, the Black Death swept through Western Europe, killing 25 million people. Some families were wiped out. Large estates were left without heirs. Survivors moved in and claimed any property they could find. Cities and towns lost people by the thousands. Monasteries,[1] which previously had as many as 150 monks, now had only seven or eight. In all, thousands of villages were abandoned. **B**

Agriculture was also in **disarray**. The tools and land were there, but suddenly the workers were missing. Food prices dropped, and there was even a surplus of food where once many had barely had enough to stay alive.

30 Because workers were scarce, peasants who survived the plague now had bargaining power for the first time. Resentment among the working class led to violence and revolt in the centuries that followed, as Europe teetered between the old feudal system and a new economic system.

B **CAUSE AND EFFECT**
Reread lines 20–25. What effects of the Black Death does the author describe?

disarray (dĭs'ə-rā') *n.* a state of disorder; confusion

---

1. **monasteries:** buildings where religious men called monks live, work, and pray together.

The shortage of skilled craftsmen caused an industrial crisis. Unlike agricultural workers, craftsmen require long apprenticeships, and now
40 there were few replacements when any skilled **artisan** died. Reduced production forced prices of saddles, farm tools, and other goods to soar. **C**

This depopulation crisis, however, encouraged technological developments. The most notable labor-
50 saving invention was the printing press, developed around 1450. One such press replaced hand-copying by hundreds of scribes.[2]

Survivors of the plague use a printing press to copy manuscript.

Illumination from *Chants royaux* (about 1500). Bibliothèque Nationale. © akg-images/VISIOARS.

The Black Death affected the entire medieval social structure. When the pestilence returned a few years later, people were even more terrified. Its unpredictable **recurrence** in the following decades was enough to keep Europeans in constant fear.

A mood of gloom swept
60 across Europe, and many began to question the authority of the church. In fact, they began to have doubts about their entire world view. Yet, it was this questioning that led to far-reaching reforms in religion, art, medicine, and science. Without a doubt, the Black
70 Death forever changed Europe's economic and social structure.

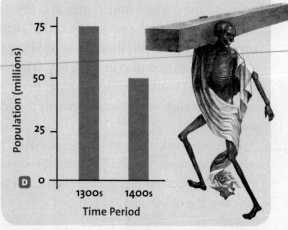

Population of Western Europe Before and After the Bubonic Plague

Detail of *Danse Macabre. Pope* (1500s), Bernt Notke. Oil on canvas, 160 cm × 750 cm. St. Nicholas' Church, Art Museum of Estonia, Tallinn, Estonia. © Bridgeman Art Library.

---

artisan (är′tĭ-zən) *n.* a person who is skilled in a trade

C CAUSE AND EEFFECT
Reread lines 30–45. What clue words help you recognize the pattern of organization?

recurrence (rĭ-kûr′əns) *n.* the act of happening again; return

D INTERPRET GRAPHIC AIDS
What was the population of western Europe in the early 1300s?

---

2. **scribes:** people whose job was to copy manuscripts.

Comprehension

1. **Recall** How long did it take for the bubonic plague to wipe out one-third of Europe's population?

2. **Recall** Why did the depopulation of Europe encourage technological developments?

3. **Summarize** What was life like in Europe in the Middle Ages before the Black Death swept through?

Text Analysis

4. **Identify Author's Main Idea** Writers choose the details that will best support the main idea they want to convey. What main idea is Cowan supporting in this article?

5. **Examine Cause and Effect** Why did food prices drop after the Black Death swept through western Europe?

6. **Analyze Graphic Aids** What information does the bar graph on page 938 give you that the text does not?

7. **Evaluate** Which topics were emphasized in each article? Which article do you think provided the most effective discussion concerning the spread of the disease? Support your opinion with details from the articles.

Comparing Articles

8. **Set a Purpose for Reading** Review your completed chart. Then use the information to help you compare the two articles.

Topics Covered	"Like Black Smoke"	"A World Turned Upside Down"
Agricultural changes		
How disease spread	X	
Loss of life		X
Trade routes		
Worker shortages		

How do we fight DISEASE?

Even today, doctors and scientists disagree about some of the causes of the bubonic plague, so they continue to research this and other historical diseases. Do you think it is important for medical researchers to continue to investigate historical diseases? Explain why or why not.

COMMON CORE

RI 1 Cite textual evidence to support analysis of what the text says explicitly. **RI 5** Analyze the structure an author uses to organize a text. **RI 9** Analyze how two authors writing about the same topic shape their presentations of key information by emphasizing different evidence.

Vocabulary in Context

▲ **VOCABULARY PRACTICE**

In each item, choose the word that differs most in meaning from the other words. Refer to a dictionary if you need help.

1. (a) record, (b) listing, (c) chronicle, (d) clock
2. (a) artisan, (b) police officer, (c) firefighter, (d) sanitation worker
3. (a) turmoil, (b) commotion, (c) caretaker, (d) disarray
4. (a) hierarchy, (b) anarchy, (c) chaos, (d) disorganization
5. (a) class, (b) frenzy, (c) rampage, (d) uproar
6. (a) bacterium, (b) germ, (c) pandemonium, (d) microorganism
7. (a) reappearance, (b) renounce, (c) repetition, (d) recurrence
8. (a) instruct, (b) teach, (c) cope, (d) educate

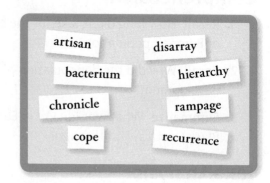

artisan   disarray

bacterium   hierarchy

chronicle   rampage

cope   recurrence

ACADEMIC VOCABULARY IN WRITING

• area   • domain   • hypothesis   • objective   • resolve

Pretend that you are a survivor of the Black Death. Using several Academic Vocabulary words, write about what has changed in your life and how you hope to resolve the problems you face. Base your story on information in the two articles.

VOCABULARY STRATEGY: SPECIALIZED VOCABULARY

Recognizing a word that is often associated with disease or its prevention or treatment can help you better understand issues related to health. Ancient Latin and Greek cultures made major contributions to the medical field, so many medical terms come from the Latin and Greek languages. For example, the word *antibiotic* comes from the Greek prefix *anti-* added to the Greek word *biotikus*.

COMMON CORE

L 6 Acquire and use accurately grade-appropriate general academic and domain-specific words.

PRACTICE Match the word in the first column with its definition in the second column. Refer to a dictionary or a science textbook if you need help.

1. virus   **a.** medicine for treating infections caused by bacteria
2. antibiotic   **b.** free from germs
3. pandemic   **c.** substance used to build immunity to a disease
4. inoculation   **d.** process of administering a vaccine
5. vaccine   **e.** decrease or disappearance of symptoms of a disease
6. remission   **f.** very small particle that can cause many types of disease
7. sterile   **g.** a very widespread or worldwide epidemic

Interactive Vocabulary **THINK** central

Go to **thinkcentral.com**.
KEYWORD: HML7-940

Writing for Assessment

1. READ THE PROMPT

In writing assessments, you might be asked to compare and contrast two informational texts that have a similar subject but differ in other ways.

> In three or four paragraphs, compare and contrast "Like Black Smoke" and "A World Turned Upside Down." Point out how each article makes use of cause-and-effect organization. Support your response with details from the two articles.

◀ **STRATEGIES IN ACTION**

1. I have to note **similarities** and **differences** between the two articles.

2. I must **tell** which **key points** each writer explains with **cause-and-effect** organization.

3. I should **give examples** from each article to prove my points.

2. PLAN YOUR WRITING

Review the chart you filled out on page 939. Use the chart to help you identify how the articles are alike and different. Write a position statement that conveys your main idea about how the articles compare. Then think about how to best present the similarities and differences.

- Review the articles to find examples and details that support the similarities and differences.

- Create an outline to organize your ideas. The sample outline shows one way to organize your paragraphs.

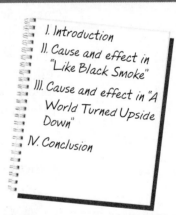

> I. Introduction
> II. Cause and effect in "Like Black Smoke"
> III. Cause and effect in "A World Turned Upside Down"
> IV. Conclusion

3. DRAFT YOUR RESPONSE

Introduction Introduce the topic mentioned in the prompt. Include your position statement.

Body Use your chart and outline as guides to writing the key points of your comparison. Support your points with details from the selections.

Conclusion Leave your readers with a final thought comparing how each writer used a cause-and-effect organizational pattern to share important information.

Revision Use words that make your ideas clear. Proofread your response.

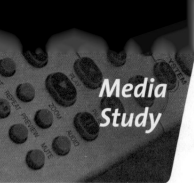
News Reports

TV Newscast Clip / Web News Report on **Media** ⬤ **Smart** DVD-ROM

What DECISIONS shape the news?

The news is a flow of information that doesn't stop. Today's fresh news reports compete for space with updated details of news that happened yesterday. What helps journalists choose what to publish each day? You'll examine two news forms to discover who decides what news is reported and why.

Background

Uneasy Seasons The hurricane seasons of 2004 and 2005 were difficult ones for millions of people who live along the Atlantic and Gulf coastal regions of the United States. In two of the most dangerous and destructive seasons on record, Florida, Louisiana, Mississippi, Texas, and other coastal states suffered major damage. The TV newscast in this lesson deals with Hurricane Charley, the first of four major hurricanes that battered Florida in 2004. The Web news report deals with Hurricane Frances.

Media Literacy: Newsworthiness

Newsworthiness is the importance of an event or action that makes it worthy of media reporting. Each day, journalists such as news editors decide which news stories will appear in newspapers, on newscasts, and online. Certain factors guide journalists in choosing a report and in shaping its details.

KEY FACTORS OF NEWSWORTHINESS

Timeliness is the quality of being current. The public is always eager for the latest news reports.

Proximity is the nearness of an event to a particular city, region, or country. Most people are more interested in stories that take place locally.

Widespread impact is said to belong to any event with a far-reaching effect. The more people the event could affect, the more likely it is to be newsworthy.

Uniqueness is a quality of news reports about very uncommon events or circumstances.

Human interest characterizes stories that cause readers or viewers to feel emotions such as happiness, anger, or sadness. People are interested in learning news about other people.

The **compelling images** and **sounds** of electronic journalism grab viewers' attention. With video, camera, and audio techniques, today's journalists can affect viewers' responses to worldwide events.

STRATEGIES FOR VIEWING

In general, the more factors of newsworthiness that a story has, the stronger its effect will be on the audience.

• Consider the **purposes** behind a report. The primary purpose of the news is to inform. Another purpose is to present the advertisements that pay for published or broadcast news.

• Be aware that dramatic wording is often in the **lead** (opening sentences) of a news story.

• Ask yourself: How do the images, text, and sounds in a news story work together to affect me? Think about the journalists' techniques—camera angles, music, sound effects, editing—that sway your emotions. (See pages R87 and R88 for details.)

NATIONAL NEWS
September 7, 2004

Florida and Georgia Recover after Frances

Three weeks after Hurricane Charley pounds Florida, the storm-weary state is hit hard by Frances

This trailer park home in Fort Pierce, Florida was destroyed.

📄 print this story

Dangerous winds blew at 115 miles per hour, ripping off roofs and smashing boats along Florida's east coast early Sunday. More than 13 inches of rain flooded some West Palm Beach streets up to four feet deep. By Tuesday, about 3 million people in Florida were without electricity as Hurricane Frances weakened to a tropical depression.

Viewing Guide for
News Reports

The ABC network news report was first broadcast shortly after Hurricane Charley had struck a Florida town called Punta Gorda. The Web news report was published three weeks later, when Florida was struck by Hurricane Frances.

Watch the TV newscast clip and read the Web report a few times. Keep in mind the time that each report was first published. This can help you figure out what factors of newsworthiness were operating at the time. Use these questions to help you.

NOW VIEW

FIRST VIEWING: **Comprehension**

1. **Recall** Describe conditions in Punta Gorda based on the images and sounds in the TV news report.

2. **Recall** According to the text in the Web news report, how much damage (in dollars) did Hurricane Frances cause?

CLOSE VIEWING: **Media Literacy**

3. **Analyze Newsworthiness** Review the key factors of newsworthiness on page 901. If you had been a reporter in Florida at the time of the hurricanes, which one of the factors would have been most important to you? Give a reason for your choice.

4. **Analyze Electronic Journalism** The TV newscast you watched relies on images, sounds, and some text to transmit information. The Web news report uses still camera images and no sounds, but much more text. Which format did the better job of conveying information? How did each news account affect your emotions? Cite specific techniques or elements in each to support your answer.

Write or Discuss

Compare Newsworthiness Now that you've examined two news reports about hurricanes, think about how the two are alike or different. Which of the key factors of newsworthiness do you think might have led journalists to publish each report? Briefly explain the reasons for your choices. Think about the factors that make a news event worth reporting.

- Timeliness
- Widespread impact
- Human interest
- Proximity
- Uniqueness
- Compelling images and sound

Produce Your Own Media

Make a Reporter's Guidebook Use recent news reports and photographs to present what you've learned about the key factors of newsworthiness. Begin by gathering three days' worth of newspaper clippings and Web news reports. (Be sure you have permission to take clippings and to make copies.) Skim the reports. Using sticky notes, label the stories (or photographs) with the factors you find, such as timeliness, widespread impact, and so on.

HERE'S HOW In a small group, follow these steps to assemble the guidebook:

- Use construction paper and paper fasteners to form the basic booklet. Choose a different color to represent each factor of newsworthiness.
- Start each section with a cover sheet that presents a key factor and its definition.
- Look over the clippings and photographs more carefully. Select the best examples for each section of the guide.
- Paste the clippings into the appropriate sections.

STUDENT MODEL

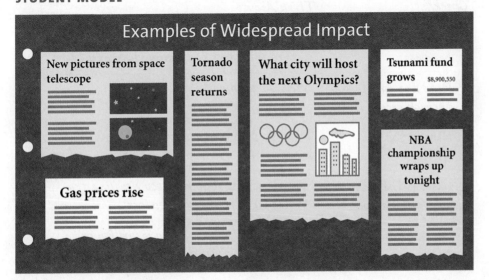

Examples of Widespread Impact

New pictures from space telescope

Tornado season returns

What city will host the next Olympics?

Tsunami fund grows $8,900,550

NBA championship wraps up tonight

Gas prices rise

Media Tools

Go to thinkcentral.com.
KEYWORD: HML7-945

Tech Tip

You can use a word-processing program to create cover sheets for the key factors.

Use with Media Study:
News Reports, page 942.

COMMON CORE

RI 5 Analyze the structure an author uses to organize a text, including how the major sections contribute to the whole.
RI 10 Read and comprehend literary nonfiction.

Preparing for Emergencies

- Informational Brochure
- Poster
- Supply List

What's the Connection?

The news reports you analyzed described two damaging storms. What should you do if a hurricane or other natural disaster threatens your town? A lot of information has been prepared to help you protect yourself from danger. Find out how to use these procedural documents to get ready for a disaster.

Standards Focus: Follow Directions

In an emergency situation, it is vital that you are able to follow directions, whether they come from a newscast, a brochure, or a poster.

Following directions requires you to follow steps in a particular order, pay attention to detail, and understand procedural information and graphics. Some directions are simple and logical, while others are more complicated and multi-dimensional. They may include written text, a diagram or other graphic, and a key or legend, as well as a step-by-step procedure. As a reader, you are expected to **synthesize,** or put together, information from all of these elements and then act on them.

As you read, use a checklist like this one to make sure you follow directions carefully and avoid mistakes. Place a check in each box after you have completed the task.

Checklist	Think About
☑ **Scan** the title and headings.	What process is being explained? Are there numbers or letters that show the steps?
☑ **Read** the directions through once.	What do you need to accomplish?
☑ **Reread** the instructions.	What steps should you follow? Where are you as you follow the instructions?
☐ **Examine** the diagram or other graphic.	How can you use it to help you visualize the written directions or other information?
☐ **Check** the key or legend.	What symbols are explained in the key on the graphic? Do you need to ask for help?

Disaster Strikes Are You Ready?

FOCUS ON FORM
The school evacuation plan on page 948 is a **procedural document,** an illustrated set of instructions or directions that explains a method for doing something. Procedural documents often include graphical components such as numbered steps, a bulleted list, a chart, and a key.

Gale warnings, tropical storms, hurricanes, tornadoes—wherever you live, you may be affected by severe weather conditions. The following information will help you prepare for threatening storms, including one of the most powerful, the hurricane.

Hurricanes are among the most dangerous of all storms, bringing high winds and waters to many coastal areas. Their destructive paths can take them far inland, too, where they produce tornadoes and floods. There are five categories of hurricanes, which are measured by their wind speed in miles per hour and their storm surge. A storm
10 surge is a rise in coastal water, topped by waves, which can range from 4 feet to over 20 feet.

To help people decide what they should do and where they should go, weather stations and government agencies broadcast information about the intensity of a storm. A hurricane is defined as an intense storm system with a pronounced rotation and a constant wind speed of 74 miles per hour or greater. Some hurricanes can generate winds as high as 300 miles per hour.

Depending on the path of a storm, its strength, and your location, you might have to seek immediate shelter or evacuate to a distant
20 location. Here are some terms that will help you decide if you are in a situation that calls for quick action. **A**

- **Hurricane Watch** Get prepared—hurricane conditions may threaten a coastal area within 24–36 hours.
- **Hurricane Warning** Put your action plans in place immediately to protect people and property—a hurricane is expected in a specific coastal area within 24 hours or less.

Before any weather emergency threatens your community, you should create a family emergency and evacuation plan and prepare
30 an emergency supply kit. Also find your school or community shelter location and become familiar with the community evacuation plan.

A FOLLOW DIRECTIONS
When following directions, remember to scan the heading and any bulleted or numbered text. What do these bulleted items tell you to do?

Emergency Procedures

In some weather-related emergencies, students will be directed outside
for dismissal. Sometimes the school will provide shelter for students,
staff, and community members.

Shelters can be an assembly area, a gym, interior hallways, or a specific
tornado shelter, depending on the type of emergency.

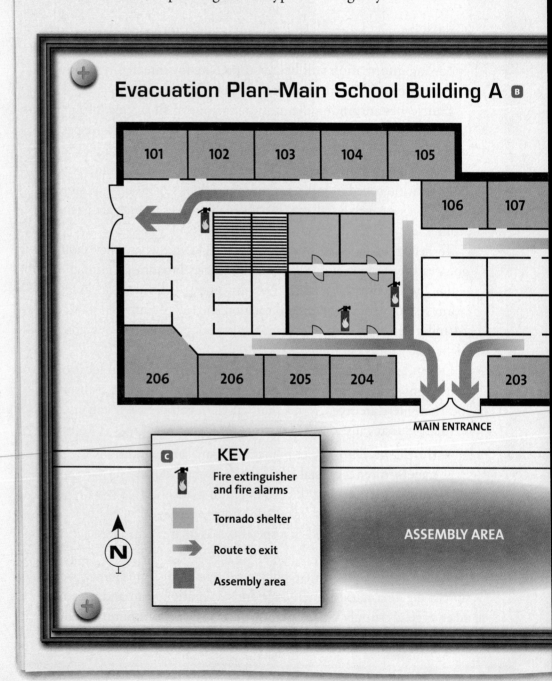

Evacuation Plan–Main School Building A B

MAIN ENTRANCE

C KEY

🧯 Fire extinguisher
and fire alarms

Tornado shelter

→ Route to exit

Assembly area

N

ASSEMBLY AREA

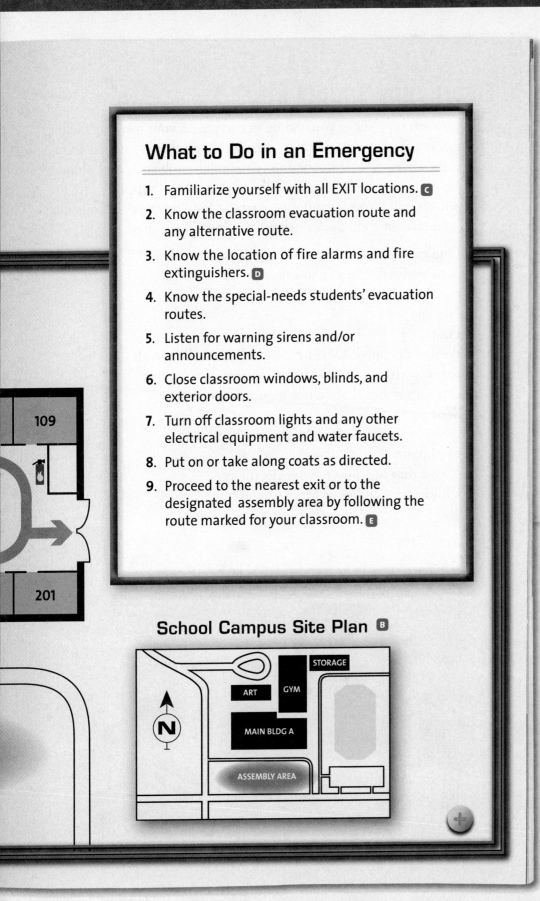

What to Do in an Emergency

1. Familiarize yourself with all EXIT locations. **C**

2. Know the classroom evacuation route and any alternative route.

3. Know the location of fire alarms and fire extinguishers. **D**

4. Know the special-needs students' evacuation routes.

5. Listen for warning sirens and/or announcements.

6. Close classroom windows, blinds, and exterior doors.

7. Turn off classroom lights and any other electrical equipment and water faucets.

8. Put on or take along coats as directed.

9. Proceed to the nearest exit or to the designated assembly area by following the route marked for your classroom. **E**

School Campus Site Plan **B**

109

201

STORAGE

ART GYM

N

MAIN BLDG A

ASSEMBLY AREA

C FOLLOW DIRECTIONS
Read step 1 in the numbered list and look at the school map. If you are in room 201, in which direction is the nearest exit? Be sure to read the compass rose.

COMMON CORE RI 10

D FOLLOW DIRECTIONS
Remember that with multi-dimensional directions, you must synthesize, or put together, information from the diagram, the written text, and the key. Read step 3, look at the key on page 948, and count how many fire extinguishers are in the school. If you are in room 106, where is the closest extinguisher?

E FOLLOW DIRECTIONS
In an emergency, what should you do to prepare the classroom? Refer to steps 1–9 to help you answer this question.

Emergency Supply Kit

Keep enough supplies in your home to survive on your own, or shelter in place, for at least three days. If possible, keep these materials in an easily accessible, separate container or special cupboard. You should indicate to your household members that these supplies are for emergencies only. Check expiration dates of food and update your kits when you change your clock during daylight-saving times.

- One gallon of drinking water per person per day
- Non-perishable, ready-to-eat canned foods and manual can opener
- First-aid kit
- Flashlight
- Battery-operated AM/FM radio, NOAA[1] all-hazards radio receiver, and extra batteries (you can also buy wind-up radios that do not require batteries)
- Whistle
- Personal hygiene items: soap, toothbrush and toothpaste, etc.
- Phone that does not rely on electricity
- Child-care supplies or other special care items

F

F PROCEDURAL DOCUMENT
What is the purpose of the photograph?

---

1. **NOAA:** the National Oceanic and Atmospheric Administration

Comprehension

1. **Recall** What is the difference between a hurricane watch and a hurricane warning?

2. **Recall** How many days' worth of supplies should be placed in an emergency supply kit?

Text Analysis

● 3. **Examine a Procedural Document** What information can you gather from the school diagram that you cannot find in the written text?

● 4. **Follow Directions** If you were in classroom 105 and you were directed to go to the tornado shelter, which route is marked for you to follow? Describe the route you would follow, starting with the direction you would take when you exit the classroom. Before you begin, reread the checklist on page 946 and look carefully at the evacuation plan.

COMMON CORE

RI 5 Analyze the structure an author uses to organize a text, including how the major sections contribute to the whole.
RI 10 Read and comprehend literary nonfiction. **SL 2** Analyze the main ideas and supporting details presented in diverse formats (e.g., visually).

Read for Information: Evaluate Graphics

WRITING PROMPT

How effective are the graphic elements of the Evacuation Plan and the Emergency Supply Kit? Evaluate the purpose, clarity, and usefulness of the graphics.

To answer the prompt, follow these steps:

1. Consider whether the graphics clearly illustrate necessary information. Do the graphics fulfill their purpose?

2. Consider whether the graphics are easy to read and understand.

3. Decide whether they would be useful for someone in an emergency.

4. In a paragraph or two, explain why the graphics are or are not effective. Focus on the purpose, clarity, and usefulness of each.

	School Map	Supply Kit Photo
Purpose		
Clarity		
Usefulness		

Argument and Persuasion

Have you ever tried to count the number of persuasive messages you see and hear each day? Letters to the editor, billboards, slogans on the back of your cereal box—persuasive messages are everywhere. In this workshop, you will learn how to analyze the arguments at the heart of these messages and recognize the techniques that are used to persuade you. Armed with this knowledge, you can make up your own mind about messages and ideas that matter.

Part 1: What Is an Argument?

COMMON CORE

Included in this workshop:
RI 4 Determine the meaning of words and phrases as they are used in a text; analyze the impact of word choice.
RI 5 Analyze the structure an author uses to organize a text.
RI 8 Trace and evaluate the argument and specific claims in a text, assessing whether the reasoning is sound.

When you hear the word *argument,* you might think of a fight between two people, complete with differences of opinion, angry shouting, and hurt feelings. In formal speaking and writing, however, an argument is not emotional. It is a claim supported by reasons and evidence.

A **claim** is a writer's position on a problem or an issue. A claim might be stated directly, as in this example: "Crunchy Puffs are an important part of a nutritious breakfast." Sometimes a writer's claim is implied, as in this slogan: "Juan for Student Council—Let the Good Times Roll." The slogan suggests that if Juan is elected, everyone at school will have more fun.

The strength of an argument depends not on the claim but on the **support,** or the reasons and evidence that are used to prove the claim. It is important to evaluate the adequacy, accuracy, and appropriateness of the evidence, which can include facts, statistics, and examples.

Look closely at the elements of an argument in this example.

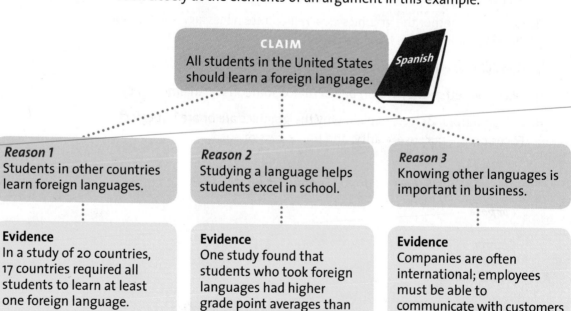

CLAIM
All students in the United States should learn a foreign language.

Spanish

Reason 1
Students in other countries learn foreign languages.

Reason 2
Studying a language helps students excel in school.

Reason 3
Knowing other languages is important in business.

Evidence
In a study of 20 countries, 17 countries required all students to learn at least one foreign language.

Evidence
One study found that students who took foreign languages had higher grade point averages than those who didn't.

Evidence
Companies are often international; employees must be able to communicate with customers and with each other.

MODEL: THE ELEMENTS OF AN ARGUMENT

A **policy speech** is a speech that recommends a plan of action or a set of guidelines or rules to address an issue. It often contains the same elements as a written argument. In the following excerpt from a policy speech, Melinda Gates makes a claim about malaria, a disease that affects many children in Africa. As you read her speech, try to identify her claim. What is she urging her audience to do or believe? What reasons and evidence help her make her case?

from Malaria Forum

Speech by **Melinda French Gates**

No child should die from malaria. No child. And the only way to end death from malaria is to end malaria.

It's fair to ask how is such a thing
5 possible? Is such a thing possible?

Here's how we see it. To eradicate malaria, you have to end transmission—and there are multiple points where you can intervene. Reduce the number of infected mosquitoes. Keep mosquitoes from biting people. Keep people who are bitten from getting infected. Keep
10 people who are infected from transmitting malaria back to mosquitoes.

Those are the intervention points. If we could find a tool that was one hundred percent effective, and if we could implement it completely at any one of these points, we would break the cycle of transmission and eradicate the disease.

15 This is just not possible today with the huge numbers of cases and the current tools. But it is possible—using the tools we have today, and addressing all the steps in a multi-pronged approach—to dramatically drive down the number of cases. Then, if we make the cases few enough, and the map of malaria small enough, we
20 could—theoretically—with a new vaccine, or a new medicine, or a new insecticide—identify and target one step in this cycle, totally stop transmission, and end the disease.

Close Read

1. Reread lines 1–7. What is Gates's claim about malaria?

2. In the [boxed] paragraph, Gates explains that one can interrupt the spread of malaria at multiple points. What evidence does she give to support this statement?

3. In the last paragraph, Gates explains why taking a multi-pronged approach would support her claim. In your own words, summarize this approach. Does she give evidence to support it?

Part 2: Persuasive Techniques and Rhetorical Fallacies

A writer will often use **persuasive techniques,** or methods intended to encourage you to accept his or her argument. Persuasive techniques use language to stir up people's emotions. The following appeals can be effective, but they are often used to disguise flaws in a weak argument.

Persuasive Technique	Definition	Example
Bandwagon Appeal	Suggests that a person should believe or do something because "everyone else" does it	"See the movie that everybody's talking about!"
Testimonial	Relies on endorsements from well-known people or satisfied customers	"As an Olympic athlete, I need a lot of energy. That's why I drink Quench-Ade."
Appeal to Pity, Fear, or Vanity	Uses strong feelings rather than facts to persuade	"Won't you give this abandoned puppy a home?" 
Loaded Language	Uses words with strongly positive or negative connotations	"Start your day with Morning Glory's refreshing, all-natural juice." 

In some cases, writers and speakers may use false or misleading statements known as **rhetorical fallacies** to persuade you to agree with them. Two examples of rhetorical fallacies are shown in the following chart.

Type of Fallacy	Definition	Example
Ad hominem	Attempts to discredit an idea by attacking the person's character rather than his or her argument	"My opponent cannot be trusted: Elect him, and city violence will surely increase."
Stereotyping	Makes a broad statement about people on the basis of their gender, ethnicity, race, or political, social, professional, or religious group	"All musicians think the same way." 

MODEL 1: PERSUASION IN TEXT

The author of this editorial argues that playing video games can have some significant harmful effects. What techniques does the author use to persuade you to adopt his position?

from

Break the Addiction!

Editorial by **Ethan Flemming**

Hours disappear, and you don't notice. You spend all your money buying more. You think it's an effective way to relieve stress but you end up cutting yourself off from family, friends, and reality.

What started in living rooms across the country as a few hours here
5 and there has become an alarming widespread problem—a population addicted to video games. In fact, the average eighth-grade boy spends 23 hours a week playing video games, while the average eighth-grade girl spends 12 hours.

You may think that video games are just harmless fun, but studies
10 tell a more disturbing story. Some studies have concluded that excessive playing can decrease attention spans, dull imaginations, and create serious social problems. At least 60 percent of games are violent, and most teenagers cite those as their favorites. Repeatedly seeing violent situations unfold on a TV screen can take its toll. After all, such games
15 glamorize violent behavior and paint an unrealistic picture of the world.

Close Read

1. What emotion is the author appealing to in this editorial? Explain how the author might want readers to react to his message.

2. One example of loaded language is boxed. What bias might the author be revealing with this word? Find two more examples of loaded language.

MODEL 2: PERSUASION IN ADVERTISING

If you've turned on the television or skimmed a magazine recently, you know that persuasive techniques are used to sell all kinds of products, from soap to video games. What techniques do you notice in this ad?

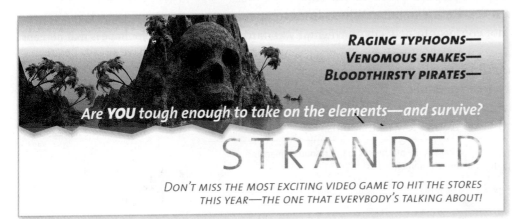

RAGING TYPHOONS—
VENOMOUS SNAKES—
BLOODTHIRSTY PIRATES—

*Are **YOU** tough enough to take on the elements—and survive?*

STRANDED

DON'T MISS THE MOST EXCITING VIDEO GAME TO HIT THE STORES
THIS YEAR—THE ONE THAT EVERYBODY'S TALKING ABOUT!

Close Read

1. Explain how this ad tries to appeal to your vanity.

2. Does this ad contain any rhetorical fallacies? Why or why not?

Part 3: Analyze the Text

In this essay, British scientist Jane Goodall shares her outlook on the future of the earth. Originally famous for studying the behaviors of chimpanzees in Africa, Goodall now travels around the world, speaking to people about the importance of protecting the environment. Read Goodall's essay, and then examine the public service ad that follows. What argument does each text present? What techniques does each use to persuade you?

THE PROMISE

Nonfiction article by **Jane Goodall**

As we begin the 21st century, it is easy to be overwhelmed by feelings of hopelessness. We humans have destroyed the balance of nature: forests are being destroyed, deserts are spreading, there is terrible pollution and poisoning of air, earth, water. Climate is changing, people are starving.
5 There are too many humans in some parts of the world, overconsumption in others. There is human cruelty to "man" and "beast" alike; there is violence and war. Yet I do have hope. Let me share my four reasons.

Firstly, we have at last begun to understand and face up to the problems that threaten the survival of the earth. And we are problem-
10 solving creatures. Our amazing brains have created modern technology, much of which has greatly benefited millions of people around the globe. Sadly, along with our tendency to overreproduce, it has also resulted in massive destruction and pollution of the natural world. But can we not use our awesome problem-solving ability to now find more
15 environmentally friendly ways to conduct our business? Good news—it's already happening as hundreds of industries and businesses adopt new "green" ethics.[1] And we must play our part—in our billions we must adopt less-harmful lifestyles. Refuse to buy products from companies, corporations, that do not conform to new environmental standards. We
20 *can* change the world.

Second, nature is amazingly resilient.[2] Given the chance, poisoned rivers can live again. Deforested land can be coaxed—or left—to blossom again. Animal species, on the verge of extinction, can sometimes be bred and saved from a few individuals.

---

1. **"green" ethics:** rules and guidelines that require businesses to use resources, machines, and procedures that are not harmful to the environment.

2. **resilient:** flexible.

Close Read

1. Reread the first paragraph. What is Goodall's claim?

2. In the boxed examples of loaded language, Goodall uses negative words to describe the world's problems. However, she also uses positive words to explain why she still has hope. Find four examples.

3. Goodall's first reason for hope is that humans have already begun to solve some of the problems affecting our environment. What evidence does she give to back up this reason?

25   My third reason for hope lies in the tremendous energy, enthusiasm, and commitment of young people around the world. Young people want to fight to right the wrongs, for it will be their world tomorrow—they will be the ones in leadership positions, and they themselves will be parents. . . .

    My fourth reason for hope lies in the indomitable[3] nature of the

30 human spirit. There are so many people who have dreamed seemingly unattainable dreams and, because they never gave up, achieved their goals against all the odds, or blazed a path along which others could follow.

    So let us move into the next millennium with hope—with faith in

35 ourselves, in our intelligence, in our indomitable spirit. Let us develop respect for all living things. Let us try to replace violence and intolerance with understanding and compassion and love.

---

3. **indomitable:** incapable of being defeated; unconquerable.

Close Read

4. Summarize the other reasons that Goodall gives to support her claim.

Close Read

1. Examine the text and the photographs at the top of this ad. What emotional appeal is being used?

2. Which words could be considered loaded language?

3. What claim is being made in this ad? (Think about what the ad is trying to convince you to do.)

Pro Athletes' Salaries Aren't Overly Exorbitant

Editorial by Mark Singletary

Do Professional Athletes Get Paid Too Much?

Editorial by Justin Hjelm

VIDEO TRAILER **THiNK** central KEYWORD: HML7-958

Are people paid FAIRLY?

COMMON CORE

RI 8 Trace and evaluate the argument and specific claims in a text, assessing whether the reasoning is sound and the evidence is relevant and sufficient to support the claims.

The president of the United States earns $400,000 a year. A Wall Street stock trader can earn even more, while a first-year New York City police officer earns less than $45,000. Is this fair? In the editorials that follow, two writers offer opposite opinions about the multimillion-dollar salaries today's professional athletes make.

DISCUSS With a group of classmates, examine this chart of average annual salaries. Talk about who you think deserves more, who could do with a little less, who is paid the right amount, and why.

AVERAGE ANNUAL SALARIES

Retail Salesperson $22,540	**Firefighter** $38,810
Kindergarten Teacher $43,530	**Registered Nurse** $52,810
Computer Programmer $65,170	**Airline Pilot** $129,230
Surgeon $182,690	**Major League Baseball Player** $2,376,580

Source: "November 2003 National Occupational Employment and Wage Estimates," U.S. Department of Labor: Bureau of Labor Statistics

● TEXT ANALYSIS: ARGUMENT

An **argument** expresses a position on an issue or problem and provides support for that position. Strong arguments have the following elements:

- a **claim,** which is the writer's main idea or position
- **support,** or reasons and evidence that back up the claim
- **counterarguments,** which are arguments made to address points that someone with an opposing view might raise

As you read, identify the elements in each argument.

● READING SKILL: EVALUATE REASONING

In a strong argument, the writer supports claims and assertions with sound reasoning and evidence. If the argument is based on **rhetorical fallacies**, which are false or misleading statements, then the argument is weakened.

One common rhetorical fallacy that writers use is stereotyping. A **stereotype** is a way of thinking about a group of people as if all members are alike and have no individual differences. It can lead to unfair judgments based on people's ethnic background, beliefs, practices, or physical appearance. "All teenagers love to listen to loud music" is a stereotype because not all teenagers do.

As you read, use a chart to record examples of stereotyping.

Example of Stereotyping	Explanation
"... the players are selfish ..." (line 10)	An unfair judgment based on the actions of a few

▲ VOCABULARY IN CONTEXT

The boldfaced words help these authors construct their arguments. To see how many you know, substitute a different word or phrase for each boldfaced term.

1. Star Player's **Compensation** Shoots Up to $15 Million
2. **Brevity** of Pitcher's Career Caused by Arm Injury
3. Umpire Call Challenged by **Dissenter**
4. Coach's **Entitlement** to Special Treatment Questioned
5. **Appalling** Brawl in Bleachers Injures 20
6. **Voracious** Fans Can't Get Enough of Home Team

Complete the activities in your **Reader/Writer Notebook.**

Meet the Authors

Mark Singletary
born 1952

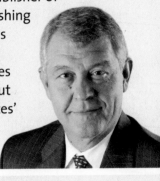

Veteran Publisher Mark Singletary is president and publisher of New Orleans Publishing Group, which prints business-related journals. What does Singletary say about professional athletes' salaries? "More power to 'em."

Justin Hjelm
born 1983

Student Journalist While attending Westmont College in California, Justin Hjelm (yĕlm) knew that the best way to make his views known was to write about them. Hjelm's editorial is an example of how students can make their voices heard.

BACKGROUND TO THE ARTICLES

Weighing In on Heavy Salaries
Frequently when athletes' salaries make the news, editorials start appearing in many publications. "Pro Athletes' Salaries Aren't Overly Exorbitant" appeared in *New Orleans CityBusiness.* "Do Professional Athletes Get Paid Too Much?" was published in Westmont College's campus newspaper, the *Horizon.*

Authors Online
Go to <u>thinkcentral.com</u>. KEYWORD: HML7-959

New Orleans City Business

A player signs autographs for die-hard fans before the 75th Major League Baseball All-Star Game.

Pro Athletes' Salaries Aren't Overly Exorbitant[1] Ⓐ

MARK SINGLETARY

I am going to try and make a point about the salaries that professional athletes get to play their games. I think I'm moving into a very solid "more power to 'em" position. I guess until recently I've thought the players were a bit selfish and their salaries would lead to the failure of professional sports.

10 Of course, the players are selfish and ultimately professional sports will fail or have to be restructured significantly. Who knows when that time will come? Ⓑ

But the players are no more selfish than the owners who pay the salaries. And the owners are no more selfish than the television and radio networks that pay outlandish sums to broadcast 20 the games.

All of us are looking for something. The games work best when those willing to pay match up evenly with what the others have to sell.

I've always thought of myself as the kind of guy who would give his left arm or eye or big toe to have a chance to play any of the major league sports. Now I think I can honestly 30 say that I would give up a lot, but

Ⓐ **ARGUMENT**
You can immediately identify the author's claim by reading the editorial's title. **Paraphrase** the title, or restate it in your own words.

Ⓑ **EVALUATE REASONING**
What **stereotype** does Singletary present in lines 10–13? Explain why his statement is unfair.

---

1. **exorbitant** (ĭg-zôr′bĭ-tənt): exceeding all bounds of custom or fairness.

not everything, to have the chance to play one big game.

Pause and reflection make me think now that it would still be awesome to train hard, make a major league roster and spend an entire season with the team, but at some point the fun might turn into work.

40 I would probably begin to think that if I was good enough to make the squad, then I would deserve to be paid the same as my teammates. And if by chance I would happen to be star quality and could reasonably assume that coming to see me play was a big deal, then I might end up asking for a little more than the average player gets.

Also, when I read the sports or business pages of the newspaper, I see 50 that television networks pay huge sums to broadcast my games. When I go to work, I realize that other companies want to name our stadium, promote our schedule and decorate our arena with their advertisements.

The historical argument for paying exorbitant salaries to athletes is the **brevity** of their careers. All of these athletes are a busted knee, concussion 60 or torn rotator cuff[2] away from the end of their career, and very few sports offer guaranteed contracts that go beyond the season when the injury occurs.

Our fans are important to the economic health of our ball club. My teammates and I are responsible for

finding and keeping fans. If I am a star, it can rightly be assumed the fans come to see me play.

70 When the fans come to see the stars perform, the value of the franchise[3] increases. I'm pretty smart and understand all this and how it relates to me. I also know what I make and how that relates to others that play my game.

So, it seems to me that even though I love the game, even though just playing the game is huge **compensation** and very, very 80 satisfying, I want things to be fair.

Fair is fair. And fair is that the athletes deserve what the fans are willing to pay.

The owners probably don't care what the athletes make, as long as they can pass the cost on to sponsors and ticket buyers. The intelligence in sports ownership is the ability to predict exactly where the fans and 90 sponsors lose interest.

Until that time, it seems fair to allocate as much as possible to the players that make the games entertaining. It's also the only way to win consistently in modern, major league sports. The smartest in all the groups are not only taking as much and passing along as much as possible, but they are also looking toward the 100 future to see when it all ends. **C**

So, everyone benefits right up until the time that no one benefits.

compensation
(kŏm′pən-sā′shən) *n.*
payment

brevity (brĕv′ĭ-tē) *n.*
shortness

C **ARGUMENT**
Reread lines 91–100, which contain Singletary's main **claim**, and his reasons for supporting it. Paraphrase, or restate, his claim.

---

2. **concussion ... rotator cuff:** A concussion is an injury to the brain caused by a fall or a blow to the head. A rotator cuff is the muscle and tendon that support the shoulder joint, a place of common injury among baseball pitchers.

3. **franchise:** a team that is a member of a professional sports league.

TheHorizon

WESTMONT COLLEGE   SANTA BARBARA, CALIFORNIA

DO PROFESSIONAL ATHLETES GET PAID TOO MUCH?

JUSTIN HJELM
Staff Reporter

◆ **GRAMMAR IN CONTEXT**
Notice that the sentence in lines 6–10 begins with an introductory phrase followed by a comma. The comma alerts readers to pause and helps them clearly understand the sentence.

D ARGUMENT
"Athletes have always made a lot of money"—that's the argument Hjelm anticipates in lines 6–21. What is his **counterargument?**

YES. When asked in the early twenties what justified him making more money than the President of the United States, Babe Ruth[1] replied "Well, I had a better year."

For nearly a century, superstar athletes have demanded and received salaries grossly out of proportion with the average income of their
10 times. What makes modern times different and more disturbing is that even the role players in professional sports are pulling in an exorbitant amount of money. ◆

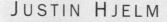

Fifty years ago, only the 40-home-run outfielder would make a huge salary. Now, however, the utility infielder who comes in as a defensive replacement three times a week makes
20 ten times more than the average working man. **D**

Nolan Ryan[2] broke ground in 1979, becoming the first athlete to receive a $1-million-a-year contract. It took over a century for baseball to reach this milestone income figure, and just 25 years later a $1 million contract offer is considered an insult.

---

1. **Babe Ruth:** a baseball player from 1914 to 1935, considered by many to be the best baseball player in the history of the sport.

2. **Nolan Ryan:** a baseball pitcher from 1966 to 1993 who held over 50 major-league records.

The contracts of professional athletes
30 have gone unchecked for too long,
and now athletes are among the
wealthiest people in our nation.

Athletes are paid far too much
for simply playing games. Essentially,
as anyone can tell you, sports
are entertainment. We pay to see
these athletes perform at the
highest level. **E**

It is a sad commentary on our
40 societal values that these entertainers
are raking in seven-figure salaries
while teachers, police officers, and fire
fighters make less than one percent
of the income of some athletes.
Entertainment is a necessary thing,
but it is not needed nearly as much as
countless other occupations are.

What kind of message are we
sending our children with these
50 backward values?

From the perspective of a young
person, sports seem like the better
and easier path. Would a child rather
play basketball and make millions
or go to school for years and end up
making $50,000 a year?

<u>Dissenters</u> will say that it is not
that cut and dried,[3] and they are
probably right. Making a professional
60 sporting league is exceptionally
difficult. But fewer and fewer kids
are realizing this.

One only needs to look as far as
the NBA draft[4] for proof of this.

Athlete: Babe Ruth
Sport: Baseball
Team: New York Yankees
Contract Year: 1921
Contracted Salary: $39,638
Salary Adjusted to 2004 Dollars: $418,303

Athlete: Jackie Robinson
Sport: Baseball
Team: Brooklyn Dodgers
Contract Year: 1947
Contracted Salary: $8,500
Salary Adjusted to 2004 Dollars: $72,002

Athlete: Bill Russell
Sport: Basketball
Team: Boston Celtics
Contract Year: 1956
Contracted Salary: $19,500
Salary Adjusted to 2004 Dollars: $135,425

Athlete: Nolan Ryan
Sport: Baseball
Team: Houston Astros
Contract Year: 1979
Contracted Salary: $1,100,000
Salary Adjusted to 2004 Dollars: $2,862,121

Language Coach

Slang Words that are
made up or words that
are used informally and
in a way other than
expected are called
slang. In line 41, the
phrase *raking in* is an
example of slang. Here,
it means "earning."

E ARGUMENT
Reread lines 33–38.
What is Hjelm's **claim**
about the salaries of
professional athletes?
As you continue to trace
Hjelm's argument, note
how he **supports** his
claim.

dissenter (dĭ-sĕn′tər)
n. one who disagrees or
holds a different opinion

---

3. **cut and dried:** simple
4. **NBA draft:** the process by which teams in the National Basketball Association select, or draft,
   players. Generally, the teams with the worst records from the preceding year get the top draft choices.

Athlete: **Kenny Anderson**
Sport: **Basketball**
Team: **Boston Celtics**
Contract Year: **1999**
Contracted Salary: **$5,845,000**
Salary Adjusted to 2004 Dollars: **$6,627,374**

Athlete: **Alex Rodriguez**
Sport: **Baseball**
Team: **New York Yankees**
Contract Year: **2004**
Contracted Salary: **$21,726,881**

A decade ago, a high school player skipping college was a rarity. In 1994, you could count the early entrants on one hand. Now, however, there are numerous high schoolers declaring for 70 the draft every year, some of whom do not even get drafted. These players forfeit their college eligibility and will struggle for years to make an NBA team. After that, without a college education, they struggle to find a decent job.

Also troubling are the egos of the athletes receiving these giant paychecks. They have no ability to 80 relate to the public. During the NBA lockout in 1998-99, players were crying poverty. **F**

Kenny Anderson, then a guard for the Boston Celtics, complained of not being able to afford the insurance on his eight cars. The sense of **entitlement** that these athletes have is **appalling.** They play a game that many would play for meal money and 90 get paid like royalty, and then have the gall to whine that they are not paid enough.

It's startling that people have blasé[5] attitudes about $100 million contracts. Eight-figure deals are not something to be yawned at, but with their current frequency, it is becoming that way. Athletes are paid far too much for what they do, 100 but I believe that society is more at fault for this than the athletes themselves are.

We simply put too much importance on entertainment, and with this statement I condemn myself and the rabidity[6] with which I follow sports. The once tightly controlled finances of the sporting world have been torn apart and the winds of greed and America's 110 **voracious** thirst for entertainment have scattered the pieces so that they can never be put together again.

F EVALUATE REASONING
Reread lines 77–82. What stereotype is Hjelm making about professional athletes? Explain.

entitlement
(ĕn-tīt′l-mənt) *n.* the state of having a right or claim to something

appalling (ə-pô′lĭng) *adj.* outrageous; terrible
appall *v.*

voracious (vô-rā′shəs) *adj.* possessing an insatiable desire; greedy

---

5. **blasé** (blä-zā′): unconcerned; uninterested.
6. **rabidity:** craziness or unreasonable extremeness.

Comprehension

1. **Recall** What does Singletary believe about the future of professional sports?

2. **Clarify** Why does Hjelm place some of the blame for athletes' high salaries on himself as a sports fan and on society as a whole?

Text Analysis

● 3. **Identify a Counterargument** Reread lines 10–20 of the first editorial. What counterargument does Singletary offer to oppose the notion that pro athletes are selfish?

● 4. **Trace an Argument** Think about the **claim** that Hjelm presents in "Do Professional Athletes Get Paid Too Much?" Complete the graphic by listing three reasons or examples Hjelm uses to **support** his claim.

Claim: "Athletes are paid far too much for simply playing games." (lines 33–34)

Support: Support: Support:

● 5. **Evaluate Reasoning** Choose one example of stereotyping that you noted as you read. What point was the writer trying to make? Suggest how Singletary or Hjelm could strengthen his argument by rewording this statement so that it does not rely on stereotyping.

Extension and Challenge

6. **Speaking and Listening** In class, set up a panel discussion about pro athletes' salaries. Assign classmates to a role: team owner, professional athlete, sports broadcaster, and fan. A moderator can take questions from the audience for the panelists, who can respond as their characters would.

7. **MATH CONNECTION** Using Babe Ruth's salary adjusted to 2004 dollars, how much more money did Alex Rodriguez make in 2004 than Babe Ruth did in 1921? What percentage increase is this? You can find these numbers in the sidebars on pages 963 and 964.

$$\% \text{ increase} = \frac{\text{amount of increase}}{\text{lower salary in 2004 dollars}}$$

Are people paid FAIRLY?

Think of a job or chore that you or a friend did recently. Do you think that you or your friend received a fair payment? Why or why not?

COMMON CORE

RI 8 Trace and evaluate the argument and specific claims in a text, assessing whether the reasoning is sound and the evidence is relevant and sufficient to support the claims.

Vocabulary in Context

▲ VOCABULARY PRACTICE

Decide whether each statement is true or false.

1. A **dissenter** is usually a person who goes along with what others think.
2. Someone with a **voracious** appetite for sports often goes to several games a week.
3. An **appalling** situation is one that shocks and depresses you.
4. If you do volunteer work, you don't expect **compensation** for your services.
5. The author of a 3,400-page book should be praised for her **brevity.**
6. Meek, humble people usually feel a strong sense of **entitlement.**

appalling
brevity
compensation
dissenter
entitlement
voracious

ACADEMIC VOCABULARY IN SPEAKING

> • area   • domain   • hypothesis   • objective   • resolve

With a small group, research some starting salaries for different careers that might interest you. Discuss with your classmates why one **area** of expertise deserves a higher salary than another. Use the Academic Vocabulary words in your discussion.

VOCABULARY STRATEGY: IDIOMS

Idioms are common expressions whose meaning is different from the meaning of the individual words in them. For example, the expression *cut and dried,* which appears on page 963, means "simple," not "sliced into pieces and dried."

PRACTICE Define the italicized idiom in each sentence.

1. To get along with Madeline, you need to learn to *hold your tongue.*
2. All those compliments are *going to Sam's head.*
3. After he lost his job, Mr. Murphy looked a bit *down at the heels.*
4. I can't quite *put my finger on* why she makes me so angry.
5. It is a good idea for business partners to *see eye to eye* on most things.
6. The rumor is that Jake *paid through the nose* for that car.

COMMON CORE

L 5 Demonstrate understanding of nuances in word meanings.
L 6 Acquire and use accurately grade-appropriate general academic words.

Interactive Vocabulary **THINK** central

Go to **thinkcentral.com.**
KEYWORD: HML7-966

Language

◆ **GRAMMAR IN CONTEXT:** Use Commas After Introductory Words

COMMON CORE

L 2 Demonstrate command of the conventions of standard English punctuation. **W 1** Write arguments.

Be sure to use commas correctly after **introductory words and phrases** and when listing **items in a series.** Place commas immediately after introductory words such as *Finally* and *Afterwards* and after introductory phrases that contain prepositional phrases. Also place a comma after every item in a series except the last one. (A series consists of three or more items.)

Original:	During their careers athletes face injuries stiff competition and a lot of pressure to prove themselves.
Revised:	During their careers, athletes face injuries, stiff competition, and a lot of pressure to prove themselves.

PRACTICE In each sentence, add commas where they are needed.

1. In recent years athletes' salaries have greatly increased.
2. Babe Ruth Jackie Robinson and Nolan Ryan deserved good salaries.
3. Within the sports community it is well known how much money owners make from sponsors.
4. The owners the networks and the sponsors are all making money.

For more help with punctuating introductory words and phrases and items in a series, see page R49 in the **Grammar Handbook**.

READING-WRITING CONNECTION

Demonstrate your understanding of these editorials by responding to the prompt. Then use the **revising tip** to improve your writing.

WRITING PROMPT	**REVISING TIP**
Short Constructed Response: Letter Write a **one-paragraph letter** to the editor of *New Orleans CityBusiness* or the *Horizon* in response to one of the selections. Explain whether you agree or disagree with the writer's opinion. Remember to keep your audience in mind as you write.	Review your letter. Did you remember to use commas after any introductory words or phrases? If not, add commas where they are needed.

Interactive Revision

THINK central

Go to **thinkcentral.com**.
KEYWORD: HML7-967

Why We Shouldn't Go to Mars

Magazine Article by Gregg Easterbrook

Do we have our PRIORITIES straight?

COMMON CORE

RI 6 Analyze how the author distinguishes his position from that of others. **RI 8** Trace and evaluate the argument and specific claims in a text, assessing whether the reasoning is sound. **RI 10** Read and comprehend literary nonfiction.

As a seventh grader, you may have many obligations to juggle—homework, sports or hobbies, time with friends and family, and maybe even an after-school job. Deciding on priorities, or what is most important, can be a difficult task. Setting priorities can be tough for nations and societies too. You're about to read one writer's ideas of what our national priorities should and should not be.

ROLE-PLAY With a group, create a panel discussion in which each student represents a different demand on one seventh grader's time. (The list of obligations in the paragraph above can give you ideas.) Each person should argue why his or her demand deserves to be a priority. Then decide as a group which two demands should be at the top of the priority list.

TEXT ANALYSIS: COUNTERARGUMENT

A strong counterargument is an important part of any argument. A **counterargument** anticipates what "the other side" might say and answers possible objections with reasons and evidence.

As this article's title suggests, author Gregg Easterbrook believes that sending astronauts to Mars is a mistake. Rather than ignoring those who disagree with him, Easterbrook states his opponents' views and then tells why he disagrees. As you read, search for examples of this technique.

READING SKILL: PARAPHRASE

Easterbrook supports his opinion with many scientific facts and figures that may not be easy to understand. A good way to make sure you understand Easterbrook's ideas is to **paraphrase** them, or restate them in your own words. A good paraphrase includes all of the main ideas and supporting details of the original source and is usually just as long, or longer. As you read, use a chart like the one shown to paraphrase parts of the article.

Passage from Article	Paraphrase
Space-exploration proponents deride as lack of vision the mention of technical barriers or the insistence that needs on Earth come first.	People in favor of exploring space criticize as backwards those who point out mechanical problems or who demand that problems on Earth be solved first.

▲ VOCABULARY IN CONTEXT

The boldfaced words help Easterbrook make his argument. See if you can match each vocabulary word in Column A to the word or phrase in Column B that is closest in meaning.

Column A
1. amenable
2. exhilarating
3. tantalizing
4. automated
5. proponent
6. rationality

Column B
a. tempting
b. agreeable
c. self-running
d. reasonableness
e. supporter
f. thrilling

Complete the activities in your **Reader/Writer Notebook**.

Gregg Easterbrook
born 1953

A Wide World of Writing
Before he became a full-time writer and editor, Gregg Easterbrook worked as a bus driver and a used-car salesman. Now a senior editor of *The New Republic*, Easterbrook has contributed to *Time*, *Newsweek*, and ESPN.

BACKGROUND TO THE ARTICLE

The Red Planet
The United States and the former Soviet Union began attempting flights to Mars in the early 1960s. In 1965, the first successful mission was completed when a U.S. spacecraft flew by Mars and sent 22 photos back to Earth. Since then, extensive space missions have revealed that Mars is rocky, cold, and sterile. Humans have never gone to Mars, and scientists still aren't sure if there has ever been life there.

Mission to Mars?
In 2004, President George W. Bush announced a new space exploration program. Gregg Easterbrook responded to this announcement by writing the article "Why We Shouldn't Go to Mars" for *Time* magazine.

Author Online
Go to **thinkcentral.com**. KEYWORD: HML7-969

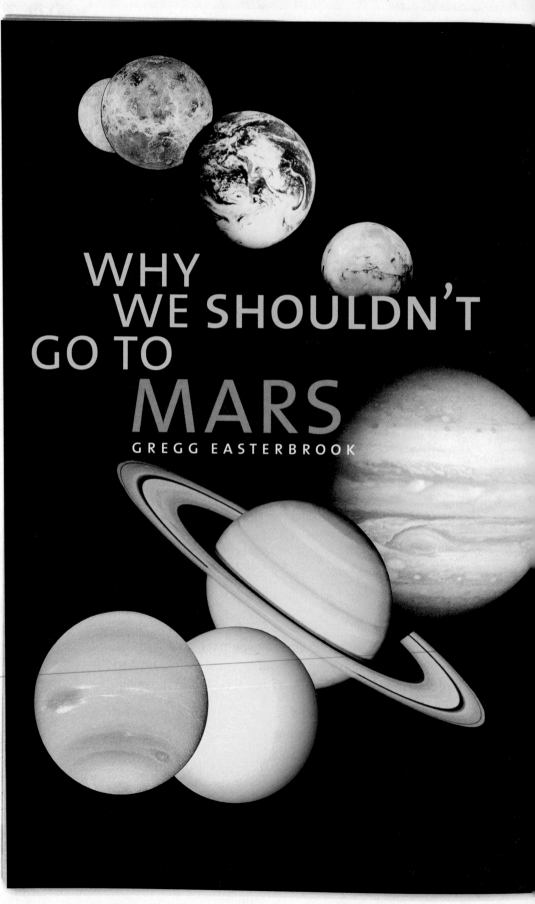

Analyze Visuals ▶

This picture of the planets combines photographs taken by different spacecraft. Pluto is not shown because no spacecraft has yet visited it. As a whole, what **mood** does this image convey?

WHY WE SHOULDN'T GO TO MARS

GREGG EASTERBROOK

"Two centuries ago, Meriwether Lewis and William Clark left St. Louis to explore the new lands acquired in the Louisiana Purchase,"[1] George W. Bush said, announcing his desire for a program to send men and women to Mars. "They made that journey in the spirit of discovery. . . . America has ventured forth into space for the same reasons."

Yet there are vital differences between Lewis and Clark's expedition and a Mars mission. First, Lewis and Clark were
10 headed to a place **amenable** to life; hundreds of thousands of people were already living there. Second, Lewis and Clark were *certain* to discover places and things of immediate value to the new nation. Third, the Lewis and Clark venture cost next to nothing by today's standards. In 1989 NASA estimated that a people-to-Mars program would cost $400 billion, which inflates to $600 billion today. The Hoover Dam cost $700 million in today's money, meaning that sending people to Mars might cost as much as building about 800 new Hoover Dams. A Mars mission may be the single
20 most expensive nonwartime undertaking in U.S. history. **Ⓐ**

The thought of travel to Mars is **exhilarating.** Surely men and women will someday walk upon that planet, and surely they will make wondrous discoveries about geology[2] and the history of the solar system, perhaps even about the very origin of life. Many times I have stared up at Mars in the evening sky—in the mountains, away from cities, you can almost see the red tint—and wondered what is there, or was there.

But the fact that a destination is **tantalizing** does not mean the journey makes sense, even considering the human
30 calling to explore. And Mars as a destination for people makes absolutely no sense with current technology.

---

1. **Louisiana Purchase:** an area extending from the Mississippi River to the Rocky Mountains, purchased from France in 1803.

2. **geology:** the scientific study of the history and structure of the earth.

amenable (ə-mē′nə-bəl) *adj.* open; agreeable

⋯⋯ **COMMON CORE** RI 8

Ⓐ COUNTERARGUMENT
In persuasive texts, writers may use **rhetorical fallacies**, or false or misleading statements. One type of rhetorical fallacy is a false analogy. **A false analogy** is a comparison that doesn't hold up because of an important difference between the two subjects. How does Easterbrook prove that likening a Mars mission to Lewis and Clark's expedition is a false analogy?

exhilarating (ĭg-zĭl′ə-rā′tĭng) *adj.* stimulating; making one feel thrilled or inspired **exhilarate** *v.*

tantalizing (tăn′tə-lī′zĭng) *adj.* tempting but out of reach **tantalize** *v.*

Left, NASA artist's concept of the Mars Exploration Rover, which landed on Mars in 2004; *right*, computer-generated image of the surface of Mars.

automated (ô'tə-mā'tĭd) *adj.* able to function with little or no assistance from people **automate** *v.*

B PARAPHRASE
Paraphrase the main reasons that Easterbrook gives in lines 32–42 for not sending a person to Mars. Add it to your chart.

Present systems for getting from Earth's surface to low-Earth orbit[3] are so fantastically expensive that merely launching the 1,000 tons or so of spacecraft and equipment a Mars mission would require could be accomplished only by cutting health-care benefits, education spending or other important programs—or by raising taxes. Absent some remarkable discovery, astronauts, geologists and biologists once on Mars could do little more than analyze rocks and feel awestruck
40 beholding the sky of another world. Yet rocks can be analyzed by **automated** probes without risk to human life, and at a tiny fraction of the cost of sending people. **B**

It is interesting to note that when President Bush unveiled his proposal, he listed these recent major achievements of space exploration: pictures of the rings of Saturn and the outer planets, evidence of water on Mars and the moons of Jupiter, discovery of more than 100 planets outside our solar system and study of the soil of Mars. All these accomplishments came from automated probes or automated space telescopes. Bush's
50 proposal, which calls for "reprogramming" some of NASA's present budget into the Mars effort, might actually lead to a reduction in such unmanned science—the one aspect of space exploration that's working really well.

Rather than spend hundreds of billions of dollars to hurl tons toward Mars using current technology, why not take

---

3. **low-Earth orbit:** a region roughly 200 to 500 miles above Earth, the easiest area to reach in space and the area from which scientists hope to launch future space missions.

Mars, the Red Planet

Language Coach

Suffixes Sometimes adding a suffix to a word may change its part of speech. *Reduce* is a verb meaning "to make less." In line 73, the suffix *-tion*, which means "the state of," has been added to *reduce* to form *reduction*. What part of speech is *reduction*? What does it mean?

a decade—or two decades, or however much time is required—researching new launch systems and advanced propulsion? If new launch systems could put weight into orbit affordably, and if advanced propulsion could speed
60 up that long, slow transit to Mars, then the dream of stepping onto the Red Planet might become reality. Mars will still be there when the technology is ready.

Space-exploration **proponents** deride as lack of vision the mention of technical barriers or the insistence that needs on Earth come first. Not so. The former is **rationality,** the latter the setting of priorities. If Mars proponents want to raise $600 billion privately and stage their own expedition, more power to them; many of the great expeditions of the past were privately mounted. If Mars proponents expect
70 taxpayers to foot their bill, then they must make their case against the many other competing needs for money. And against the needs for health care, education, poverty reduction, reinforcement of the military and reduction of the federal deficit,[4] the case for vast expenditures to go to Mars using current technology is very weak. **C**

The drive to explore is part of what makes us human, and exploration of the past has led to unexpected glories. Dreams must be tempered by realism, however. For the moment, going to Mars is hopelessly unrealistic.

---

4. **federal deficit:** a shortage of funds caused by the government's spending more than it collects in taxes.

proponent (prə-pō′nənt) *n.* a person who supports something

rationality (răsh′ə-năl′ĭ-tē) *n.* reasonableness

C COUNTERARGUMENT Easterbrook's opponents could claim that he has a "lack of vision" because he is against a Mars mission. Reread lines 63–75. What is his counterargument to this possible criticism?

Comprehension

1. **Recall** How does the cost of a Mars mission compare to the cost of the Hoover Dam?

2. **Clarify** What national issues does Easterbrook suggest are more important than sending U.S. astronauts to Mars?

COMMON CORE

RI 6 Analyze how the author distinguishes his position from that of others. RI 8 Trace and evaluate the argument and specific claims in a text, assessing whether the reasoning is sound. RI 10 Read and comprehend literary nonfiction.

Text Analysis

3. **Understand Paraphrasing** Review the paraphrases you wrote in your chart as you read. Did you capture the main reasons Easterbrook gives for believing that the government should not send people to Mars? If not, revise your paraphrases.

4. **Identify a Counterargument** Reread lines 43–53. Easterbrook's opponents argue that sending astronauts on missions is necessary in order to make achievements in space exploration. What counterargument does Easterbrook offer in response?

5. **Evaluate Support** Easterbrook supports his argument with evidence. Which pieces of evidence did you find most, or least, convincing? Pick at least two and list them in a chart. Then describe your reaction to the evidence.

Evidence	My Reaction
Lewis and Clark's expedition cost very little, while a Mars mission will cost $600 billion.	I think $600 billion seems like way too much money! We could put that money to better use.

Extension and Challenge

6. **Reader's Circle** When deciding how to spend taxpayers' money, Easterbrook says, "needs on Earth come first." Discuss whether you agree with Easterbrook's opinion about what our national priorities should be.

7. **SCIENCE CONNECTION** Do some research on past automated Mars missions. Consider the following questions:
   - What was the name of the spacecraft that first orbited Mars?
   - What year did a U.S. craft first land on the planet?
   - What do you think is the best thing that Mars probes have discovered?

Do we have our PRIORITIES straight?

Think about the things you need to accomplish next week. Write your goals in a numbered list. How do your priorities change as the week progresses?

Vocabulary in Context

▲ **VOCABULARY PRACTICE**

Choose the letter of the item most closely associated with each vocabulary word.

1. **tantalizing:** (a) an old pair of tennis shoes, (b) the smell of chocolate-chip cookies baking, (c) a statement about an overdue bill
2. **amenable:** (a) an easygoing person, (b) a dilapidated car, (c) a protest march
3. **automated:** (a) a soccer ball, (b) a robot, (c) a birthday party
4. **exhilarating:** (a) a brisk walk on a beach, (b) a large herd of cattle, (c) a low hedge
5. **proponent:** (a) part of an airplane, (b) leader of a voting drive, (c) carton of unworn gloves
6. **rationality:** (a) a new shopping center, (b) a letter from an old friend, (c) a well thought-out plan

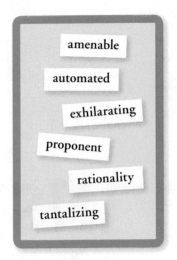

ACADEMIC VOCABULARY IN SPEAKING

• area	• domain	• hypothesis	• objective	• resolve

One **objective** of space exploration is to find out whether other planets will support human life. With a small group, discuss whether or not you think this is a worthwhile investment of time and money. Use the Academic Vocabulary words in your discussion.

⋯ **COMMON CORE**

L 4b Use Greek roots as clues to the meaning of a word.

VOCABULARY STRATEGY: THE GREEK ROOT *aut*

The vocabulary word *automated* contains the Greek root *aut*, which means "self." This root, and the related prefix *auto-*, is found in a number of English words. Use your understanding of the root's meaning, as well as context clues, to figure out the meanings of words formed from *aut*.

PRACTICE Choose a word from the web that best completes each sentence. If you need help, check a dictionary.

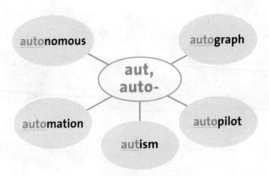

1. A genuine _____ by Abraham Lincoln is worth a lot of money.
2. How often are planes flown on _____?
3. Because of _____, many jobs can be done more quickly and with less effort.
4. Countries that are _____ are governed by their own people.
5. _____ limits its sufferers' ability to communicate with others.

Interactive Vocabulary

Go to **thinkcentral.com**.
KEYWORD: HML7-975

Remarks at the Dedication of the Aerospace Medical Health Center

Speech by John F. Kennedy

HISTORY Video link at
thinkcentral.com

VIDEO TRAILER **THINK**central KEYWORD: HML7-976

What
INSPIRES people?

COMMON CORE

RI 4 Analyze the impact of a specific word choice on meaning and tone. **RI 8** Trace and evaluate the argument and specific claims in a text.

Every once in a while, a leader emerges who can inspire people to break through their fear and think of new ways to make our society the best it can be. You're about to read a speech by one such leader—President John F. Kennedy.

QUICKWRITE Think about a time when someone convinced you to make a change or take an action. Write a journal entry telling why you felt inspired.

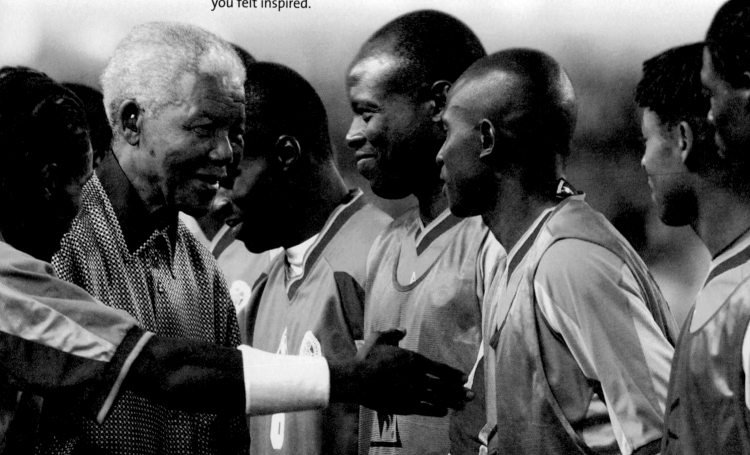

● TEXT ANALYSIS: ARGUMENT IN SPEECH

An effective written argument delivers a claim, support, and a counterargument. An argument in a policy speech has the same elements. A **policy speech** is a speech that recommends guidelines, rules, or a plan of action to address an issue. In his policy speech, President Kennedy develops his argument with **analogies**, or the comparison of things that are alike in some, but not all, ways.

As you read Kennedy's speech, identify his central argument, the method he uses to develop it, and the type of evidence he uses to support it.

● READING SKILL: IDENTIFY PERSUASIVE TECHNIQUES

After reading the speech silently, read it aloud. Listen closely for the persuasive techniques and sound devices listed in the following chart. Use a chart like this to note examples.

Persuasive Techniques and Devices	Examples from the Speech
evoking strong feelings (emotional appeal)	
appealing to the desire to belong (appeal by association)	
sound devices such as repetition and alliteration	first paragraph repeats "era"

▲ VOCABULARY IN CONTEXT

The boldfaced words helped Kennedy communicate the importance of space research. Restate each sentence using a different word or words for the boldfaced term.

1. It is a **partisan** law that only benefits the rich.
2. This is a noble **endeavor** that will eventually succeed.
3. The pilot observed the spacecraft on **radar.**
4. She experienced **disorientation** in the space lab.
5. Exercise helped the patient increase his **metabolism.**
6. He has a temporary **impairment** and needs to use crutches.
7. Cheap land was a great **impetus** for the new settlers.
8. Studying the chart is a **tedious** task.

Complete the activities in your **Reader/Writer Notebook.**

John F. Kennedy
1917–1963

U.S. President
John F. Kennedy, the 35th president of the United States, set out to lead the way into a future filled with scientific discoveries and improvements in society. Wanting to bring democracy and freedom to the world, Kennedy asked that all American citizens join him in this New Frontier.

A Race to Space
In 1957, the country then known as the Soviet Union launched *Sputnik I*, the first satellite to orbit the earth. After becoming president in 1961, Kennedy was determined to surpass the Soviets' knowledge of space. He said, "No nation which expects to be the leader of other nations can expect to stay behind in this race for space." Before Congress in 1961, Kennedy called for plans to send astronauts to the moon. The United States achieved this goal on July 20, 1969.

An Inspirational Speaker
A line from Kennedy's inaugural address is often quoted: "Ask not what your country can do for you—ask what you can do for your country." You are about to read the speech he made on November 21, 1963. The following day, November 22, 1963, John F. Kennedy was assassinated.

Author Online

THINK central

Go to **thinkcentral.com.**
KEYWORD: HML7-977

Remarks at the Dedication of the Aerospace Medical Health Center

President John F. Kennedy

Mr. Secretary, Governor, Mr. Vice President, Senator, Members of the
Congress, members of the military, ladies and gentlemen:

For more than 3 years I have spoken about the New Frontier. This is
not a **partisan** term, and it is not the exclusive property of Republicans or
Democrats. It refers, instead, to this Nation's place in history, to the fact
that we do stand on the edge of a great new era, filled with both crisis and
opportunity, an era to be characterized by achievement and by challenge.
It is an era which calls for action and for the best efforts of all those who
would test the unknown and the uncertain in every phase of human
10 **endeavor**. It is a time for pathfinders and pioneers. Ⓐ

I have come to Texas today to salute an outstanding group of pioneers,
the men who man the Brooks Air Force Base School of Aerospace Medicine
and the Aerospace Medical Center. It is fitting that San Antonio should be the
site of this center and this school as we gather to dedicate this complex of
buildings. For this city has long been the home of the pioneers in the air. It
was here that Sidney Brooks, whose memory we honor today, was born and
raised. It was here that Charles Lindbergh and Claire Chennault,[1] and a host
of others, who, in World War I and World War II and Korea, and even today
have helped demonstrate American mastery of the skies, trained at Kelly
20 Field and Randolph Field,[2] which form a major part of aviation history. And
in the new frontier of outer space, while headlines may be made by others in
other places, history is being made every day by the men and women of the
Aerospace Medical Center, without whom there could be no history.

Many Americans make the mistake of assuming that space research
has no values here on earth. Nothing could be further from the truth.
Just as the wartime development of **radar** gave us the transistor, and all
that it made possible, so research in space medicine holds the promise of

---

1. **Sidney Brooks ... Charles Lindbergh ... Claire Chennault** (shən´ôlt): Sidney Brooks was a young
   flyer killed in a training accident. Charles Lindbergh was the first transatlantic solo pilot, and Claire
   Chennault was an important figure in the development of air-war theories.
2. **Kelly Field and Randolph Field:** airfields in the San Antonio area where many military pilots were trained.

partisan (pär´tǐ-zən) *adj.*
relating to or in support
of one political party

endeavor (ĕn-dĕv´ər)
n. purposeful or serious
activity; enterprise

Ⓐ **PERSUASIVE
TECHNIQUES**
Reread lines 3–10.
Speech writers often
use **repetition** and
alliteration, or the
repetition of consonant
sounds at the beginning
of words, to create
memorable phrases.
Find an example of both.

radar (rā´där) *n.* a
method of detecting
distant objects through
the use of radio waves

substantial benefit for those of us
who are earthbound. For our effort in
30 space is not, as some have suggested,
a competitor for the natural resources
that we need to develop the earth. It is
a working partner and a coproducer of
these resources. And nothing makes
this clearer than the fact that medicine
in space is going to make our lives
healthier and happier here on earth.

I give you three examples: first,
medical space research may open up
40 new understanding of man's relation
to his environment. Examinations of
the astronaut's physical, and mental,
and emotional reactions can teach
us more about the differences between normal and abnormal, about the
causes and effects of **disorientation**, about changes in **metabolism** which
could result in extending the life span. When you study the effects on our
astronauts of exhaust gases which can contaminate their environment, and
you seek ways to alter these gases so as to reduce their toxicity, you are
working on problems similar to those we face in our great urban centers
50 which themselves are being corrupted by gases and which must be clear.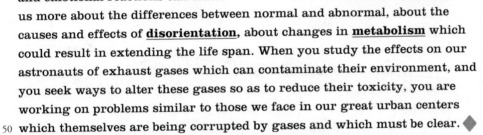

And second, medical space research may revolutionize the technology and
the techniques of modern medicine. Whatever new devices are created, for
example, to monitor our astronauts, to measure their heart activity, their
breathing, their brain waves, their eye motion, at great distances
and under difficult conditions, will also represent a major advance in general
medical instrumentation. Heart patients may even be able to wear
a light monitor which will sound a warning if their activity exceeds
certain limits. An instrument recently developed to record automatically
the impact of acceleration upon an astronaut's eyes will also be of help to small
60 children who are suffering miserably from eye defects, but are
unable to describe their **impairment**. And also by the use of instruments
similar to those used in Project Mercury, this Nation's private as well as public
nursing services are being improved, enabling one nurse now to give more
critically ill patients greater attention than they ever could in the past.

And third, medical space research may lead to new safeguards against
hazards common to many environments. Specifically, our astronauts will
need fundamentally new devices to protect them from the ill effects of

impetus (ĭm'pĭ təs) *n.* a driving force; a motivation

tedious (tē'dē-əs) *adj.* tiresome; boring

radiation which can have a profound influence upon medicine and man's relations to our present environment. **D**

70   Here at this center we have the laboratories, the talent, the resources to give new **impetus** to vital research in the life centers. I am not suggesting that the entire space program is justified alone by what is done in medicine. The space program stands on its own as a contribution to national strength. And last Saturday at Cape Canaveral I saw our new Saturn C-1 rocket booster,³ which, with its payload,⁴ when it rises in December of this year, will be, for the first time, the largest booster in the world, carrying into space the largest payload that any country in the world has ever sent into space.

I think the United States should be a leader. A country as rich and powerful as this which bears so many burdens and responsibilities, which

80 has so many opportunities, should be second to none. And in December, while I do not regard our mastery of space as anywhere near complete, while I recognize that there are still areas where we are behind—at least in one area, the size of the booster—this year I hope the United States will be ahead. And I am for it. We have a long way to go. Many weeks and months and years of long, **tedious** work lie ahead. There will be setbacks and frustrations and disappointments. There will be, as there always are, pressures in this country to do less in this area as in so many others, and temptations to do something else that is perhaps easier. But this research here must go on. This space effort must go on. The conquest of space must

90 and will go ahead. That much we know. That much we can say with confidence and conviction.

Frank O'Connor, the Irish writer, tells in one of his books how, as a boy, he and his friends would make their way across the countryside, and when they came to an orchard wall that seemed too high and too doubtful to try and too difficult to permit their voyage to continue, they took off their hats and tossed them over the wall—and then they had no choice but to follow them.

This Nation has tossed its cap over the wall of space, and we have no choice but to follow it. Whatever the difficulties, they will be overcome.

100 Whatever the hazards, they must be guarded against. With the vital help of this Aerospace Medical Center, with the help of all those who labor in the space endeavor, with the help and support of all Americans, we will climb this wall with safety and with speed—and we shall then explore the wonders on the other side. **E**

Thank you.

---

3. **booster:** a rocket used to launch a spacecraft.

4. **payload:** the load carried by a rocket or other vehicle.

Comprehension

1. **Recall** Who is in the audience that President Kennedy is speaking to?

2. **Clarify** Why does President Kennedy believe that the United States needs to be a leader?

3. **Summarize** According to President Kennedy, what are three ways that medical research in space can make life on Earth better?

Text Analysis

4. **Identify Audience** Reread lines 11–23. What does President Kennedy say to the audience members to make a strong connection with them?

5. **Identify a Counterargument** Reread lines 24–37. President Kennedy anticipates that his opponents will argue that research in space medicine competes for the natural resources we need to develop the earth. What counterargument does President Kennedy give?

6. **Examine Persuasive Techniques** Review the chart that you made while you read. Which persuasive technique do you think President Kennedy uses most successfully? Give an example of how he uses this technique to inspire people.

7. **Evaluate an Argument in a Speech** President Kennedy uses three **analogies** to develop the central argument in his speech. Do you think the structure of his argument is successful? Why or why not?

8. **Compare Opinions** Both Gregg Easterbrook, author of "Why We Shouldn't Go To Mars," and President Kennedy try to influence people's beliefs about funding space-related programs. Use a Y chart to compare and contrast Easterbrook's and President Kennedy's reasons for their differing opinions.

Easterbrook
A mission to Mars will not give us things we can use on Earth.

President Kennedy
Space exploration will make our lives better.

Similarities

9. Listen to an audio version of President Kennedy's speech. How do you think his delivery of the speech affects the impact of his words?

What INSPIRES people?

What could you do to inspire a friend? Describe how you could inspire someone with words, actions, or both.

COMMON CORE

RI 4 Analyze the impact of a specific word choice on meaning and tone. **RI 7** Compare and contrast a text to an audio version of the text (e.g., how the delivery of a speech affects the impact of the words). **RI 8** Trace and evaluate the argument and specific claims in a text.

Vocabulary in Context

▲ VOCABULARY PRACTICE

Choose the word from the list that best completes each sentence.

1. Sending people to the moon was a difficult _____ .
2. I would rather do anything else than that _____ job.
3. The wrestler used his _____ as an excuse to forfeit the match.
4. The senator was not reelected because of his _____ voting record.
5. The quest for advancement in medicine was a(n) _____ for space research.
6. The plane flew under the _____.
7. The astronaut's _____ grew worse as the rocket disappeared into space.
8. It is important to have a healthy _____ to live and grow.

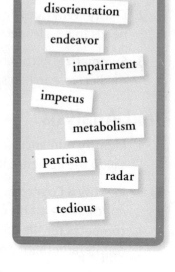

disorientation

endeavor

impairment

impetus

metabolism

partisan

radar

tedious

ACADEMIC VOCABULARY IN SPEAKING

• area   • domain   • hypothesis   • objective   • resolve

Easterbrook makes a convincing argument against space programs while President Kennedy makes a convincing argument for them. Imagine that you and your classmates have to make a decision about space travel based on these arguments. How would you **resolve** this issue? Discuss your ideas with a small group. Use the Academic Vocabulary words in your discussion.

VOCABULARY STRATEGY: ANALOGIES

Analogies are comparisons. In an analogy problem, a comparison is made using two groups of words. The relationship between the first pair of words is the same as the relationship between the second pair of words. Two relationships that are often expressed in analogies are **part to whole** and **whole to part**. The following examples show two ways that each relationship in an analogy can be expressed.

○ **COMMON CORE**

L 5b Use the relationship between particular words (e.g., analogy) to better understand each of the words. **L 6** Acquire and use accurately grade-appropriate general academic words.

Part to Whole

juror : jury : : soldier : army

(*Juror* is to *jury* as *soldier* is to *army*.)

Whole to Part

jury : juror : : army : soldier

(*Jury* is to *juror* as *army* is to *soldier*.)

PRACTICE Choose a word from the left column to complete each analogy problem. Then identify the relationship as part to whole or whole to part.

1. era
2. laboratory
3. yard
4. spacecraft
5. Texas

a. desk : classroom : : grass : _____
b. universe : Earth : : United States : _____
c. day : month : : year : _____
d. heart : body : : researcher : _____
e. engine : car : : booster : _____

Interactive Vocabulary **THINK** central

Go to **thinkcentral.com**.
KEYWORD: HML7-982

Language

◆ **GRAMMAR IN CONTEXT: Use Colons Correctly**

Colons have many uses. They indicate that a **list** follows *(I need to get the following groceries: bread, milk, and butter)*. They are used after a **formal greeting** in a business letter *(Dear Madam:)*. They also are used **between numerals** in expressions of time *(5:45)*. When using a colon to introduce a list, avoid placing the colon directly after a verb or a preposition.

> *Original:* Our new school provides: better opportunities, newer computers, and many activities.
>
> *Revised:* Our new school provides the following: better opportunities, newer computers, and many activities. *(Inserting the following makes use of the colon correct.)*

PRACTICE In the following sentences, insert or delete colons where needed.

1. Some of the activities include the following an art club and a school newspaper.
2. We will meet at 11 00 A.M. today to discuss more of these activities.
3. We should be proud of: the support we've received, the high quality of our students, and the new facilities.
4. Please join me at 1 30 P.M. tomorrow to celebrate our new school.

*For more help with using colons correctly, see page R50 in the **Grammar Handbook**.*

READING-WRITING CONNECTION

YOUR TURN Explore the ideas presented in President Kennedy's speech by responding to the prompt. Then use the **revising tip** to improve your writing.

WRITING PROMPT	REVISING TIP
Short Constructed Response: Letter Write a **one-paragraph letter** to a congressional representative or senator arguing your position on funding space research with tax dollars.	Review your letter. Did you list several reasons for your position? To make your reasons stand out, you may need a colon to introduce them.

Interactive Revision **THINK** central

Go to **thinkcentral.com**.
KEYWORD: HML7-983

COMMON CORE

L 2 Demonstrate command of the conventions of standard English punctuation. **W 1** Write arguments to support claims with clear reasons.

Persuasive Techniques in Commercials

TV Commercials on **Media ⬤ Smart** DVD-ROM

How do you SELL an idea?

COMMON CORE

SL 2 Analyze the main ideas and supporting details presented in diverse media and formats (e.g., visually).

From the latest gadgets to the trendiest pair of shoes, advertisers want you to buy their products. They will use many persuasive tools to get your attention. In this lesson, you'll watch two TV commercials that will help you explore the techniques advertisers use to **sell** practically everything.

Background

To Buy or Not to Buy Ads are everywhere. They're on trains, buses, buildings, and even stadium walls. Think about the logos, the symbols or names of companies, that appear on your clothes and shoes. Right now, you may be a walking advertisement.

Each year, companies spend billions of dollars on TV commercials that showcase products and services. The first TV commercial you'll view is for Mountain Dew, a popular soft drink. The second commercial is for Kibbles 'n Bits, a well-known brand of dog food.

Media Literacy: Persuasion in Advertising

Advertisers carefully design TV ads with a specific audience in mind. A **target audience** is one that sponsors want to persuade. Members of a target audience share certain features, such as age, gender, ethnic background, values, or lifestyle. An advertisement often contains both explicit and implicit messages. The **explicit message** is the purpose of the product being sold. The **implicit message** is the idea or image that the product is associated with. To deliver these messages, advertisers rely on certain **persuasive techniques,** which are methods used to convince a target audience to buy products. Here are some things to think about when you're analyzing TV commercials.

STRATEGIES FOR ANALYZING TV COMMERCIALS

Persuasive Techniques

- Notice how some ads use words to appeal to your sense of reason, while other ads appeal to your emotions. **Emotional appeals** create strong feelings, such as happiness, sadness, or excitement. For example, if a commercial makes you laugh, chances are you'll remember the product and the commercial.
- Watch for ads that tell viewers that everyone is using their product. The **bandwagon** technique appeals to people's desire to fit in or be accepted.
- Listen for **repetition.** Repeated words help viewers remember a product.

Visual Techniques

- Notice the use of **color.** Colors can create certain feelings about a product. For example, blue is often used to create a fresh or peaceful feeling.
- Think about how commercials are **edited.** Each shot is carefully selected and arranged to create a persuasive effect. The **pace,** or length of time each shot stays on the screen, is often designed to express excitement.

Sound Techniques

- Pay attention to the **music.** For example, an upbeat, popular song might be used to make a product seem exciting.
- Listen for **sound effects,** such as the screeching of tires, the sizzling of a burger, or the popping and fizzing of a soft drink. Sound effects are often used to make a product more appealing or to grab viewers' attention.
- Listen closely to what the voice in the commercial (called a **voice-over**) is saying. The details that viewers hear about a product are just as important as the carefully designed images.

Viewing Guide for
TV Commercials

The first TV commercial is a Mountain Dew ad that begins at the entrance of a parking lot. As you view the ad, pay attention to music and sound effects. The second commercial is entitled "Spike and Speck II." The ad follows two dogs on their way to dinner. Notice persuasive techniques that help make this commercial memorable.

To help you analyze how persuasive techniques are used in TV commercials, view each ad more than once and answer the following questions.

NOW VIEW

FIRST VIEWING: Comprehension

1. **Summarize** Describe what happens in each commercial.
2. **Recall** Describe the music and sound effects that are used in the Mountain Dew ad.

CLOSE VIEWING: Media Literacy

3. **Analyze Visual Techniques** The Mountain Dew ad uses fast-paced **editing**. What is the effect of using this technique?
4. **Analyze Sound Techniques** Music is often used to create an image for a product. For example, the use of classical music can create an image of elegance and class. What kind of image do you think the **music** creates in the Mountain Dew ad?
5. **Understand Explicit and Implicit Messages** What idea or image is associated with each ad? What are the implicit and explicit messages in each ad? Explain your answers.
6. **Evaluate Persuasive Techniques** Do you think the technique of **repetition** is effective in the Kibbles 'n Bits commercial? Why or why not? Think about the following:

   - how repetition may affect viewers' memories
   - the kind of emotional appeal advertisers might be making by using a repeated word or phrase.

Write or Discuss

Evaluating TV Commercials Consider how the commercials in this lesson inform and influence you. Which one do you think is more effective at grabbing your attention and helping you remember the product? As part of your response think about

- how the visual elements help the product stand out
- how the sound techniques trigger certain emotions
- how the persuasive techniques influence how you feel about the product

Produce Your Own Media

Designing a Print Ad Imagine that you are part of an advertising team whose job it is to create a magazine **print ad** for a major company. In small groups, choose one product from the list and create your own print ad.

- Turbo Racer (video game)
- Raisin Oatbran O's (healthy cereal)
- Zoom (running shoes)
- Dazzle (toothpaste)
- Pep (energy snack bar)
- Essence (bottled water)

HERE'S HOW Before you create your ad, consider where you will place the product and how much space it will take up on the page. To help you create the ad, think about the following suggestions:

- Determine who will be the target audience—for example, teens, athletes, parents, or young children.
- Use persuasive techniques that will make your ad more appealing.
- Use visual techniques, such as color, that will draw attention to your product.

STUDENT MODEL

Media Tools

THINK central

Go to thinkcentral.com.
KEYWORD: HML7-987

Tech Tip

Search the Internet for clip art and other images that can be used in your ad.

Writing Workshop

ARGUMENT

Persuasive Essay

The writers in this unit explored real-life issues and asserted firm **claims,** or positions. They supported their claims with reasons and evidence, and they also used persuasive techniques to sway their audiences. In this workshop, you will learn how to write a strong persuasive essay using these key elements.

 Complete the workshop activities in your **Reader/Writer Notebook.**

WRITE WITH A PURPOSE

WRITING TASK

Write a **persuasive essay** that asserts a strong claim on an issue. Support your claim with reasons and evidence that will convince your audience to act or think a certain way.

Idea Starters
- ways to improve your neighborhood or school
- request to family members for a privilege or activity
- social problems, such as discrimination
- school locker searches

THE ESSENTIALS

Here are some common purposes, audiences, and formats for writing persuasive essays.

PURPOSES	AUDIENCES	FORMATS
• to convince others to agree with your claim • to motivate others to take action	• classmates and teacher • parents • school community • neighbors • school or town officials • Web users	• essay for class • editorial in school or local newspaper • speech • committee proposal • blog

COMMON CORE TRAITS

1. DEVELOPMENT OF IDEAS

- includes an **introduction** that identifies an issue and states a **claim**
- provides **logical reasons** and **relevant evidence** to support the claim
- anticipates and acknowledges **opposing claims**
- offers a **concluding section** that follows from and supports the claim

2. ORGANIZATION OF IDEAS

- **organizes** reasons and evidence in a **logical way**
- uses **transitions** to create **cohesion** and link ideas

3. LANGUAGE FACILITY AND CONVENTIONS

- maintains a **formal style** and **tone**
- uses **rhetorical questions** correctly and effectively
- employs correct **grammar, mechanics,** and **spelling**

Writing Online

THINK central

Go to **thinkcentral.com.**
KEYWORD: HML7N-988

Planning/Prewriting

COMMON CORE

W 1A-E Write arguments to support claims with clear reasons and relevant evidence.
W 5 Develop and strengthen writing as needed by planning.

Getting Started

CHOOSE AN ISSUE

An **issue** is a subject, situation, or idea about which people disagree, such as the best way to raise money for a class trip or whether video games are harmful to children. Use the Idea Starters on page 988 to help you brainstorm issues that interest you. Select an issue that you feel strongly about, and then use a chart to list arguments on both sides. You want to make sure your issue is one on which people could actually disagree.

▶ **WHAT DOES IT LOOK LIKE?**

Issue: *Should kids be paid for chores?*

Pros	Cons
• They would have their own money to spend on what they wanted and would not have to keep asking their parents for money. • They would learn responsibility and develop a work ethic.	• They should do chores without being paid to help their family out. • Parents would have less control over what kids spend their money on.

THINK ABOUT AUDIENCE AND PURPOSE

As you begin thinking about your issue in more depth, keep your **purpose** and **audience** in mind. Your purpose is to convince your audience to agree with your position on a controversial issue. To be successful, you need to understand your audience's background and their perspective on the topic. Then you can choose the reasons and evidence that will be most convincing for them.

▶ **ASK YOURSELF:**

• Who will read my essay?
• What interest do my readers have in the issue?
• How do my readers currently feel about the issue? How do I know?
• What reasons might the readers have for opposing my claim, or position?
• What arguments can I use to counter the readers' opposing claims?

STATE YOUR CLAIM

Every issue has at least two sides—for it and against it. As a writer, you need to adopt a viewpoint on the issue and confidently state your position in a clear **claim.** Make sure your claim is a statement that you can prove or support with solid reasons and evidence. If you discover that your claim can't be supported easily, then you should rework it.

▶ **WHAT DOES IT LOOK LIKE?**

Issue	Viewpoint	Claim
chores	in favor of payment for chores	I strongly believe that kids should be paid for doing chores around the house.

Planning/Prewriting *continued*

Getting Started

GATHER SUPPORT FOR YOUR CLAIM

Strong **reasons** tell why you believe what you do. They are **logical,** or clearly and directly in support of your claim. Each of your reasons must then be supported by at least one of these kinds of **relevant,** or related, evidence:

- **ancedote**—a brief story that illustrates a point
- **example**—a specific instance that illustrates a general idea
- **expert opinion**—a statement made by an authority on a subject
- **fact**—a statement that can be proven true
- **statistic**—a fact given in number form

For any facts and statistics you gather, make sure they are **accurate,** or correct, and that they come from **credible,** or trustworthy, sources.

▶ WHAT DOES IT LOOK LIKE?

Reason	Evidence
Paying for chores teaches responsibility.	John Covey, author and father of ten, says that doing chores helps kids to grow up. (expert opinion)
Paying for chores ends conflict in the household.	story about my cousin Jeremy (anecdote)

ANTICIPATE READER CONCERNS

Some readers may be opposed to your viewpoint. Address their **alternate** or **opposing claims** and explain why your viewpoint is more valid. Return to the chart in which you listed the pros and cons of your issue. Depending on which position you took, the details in the other column are possible opposing claims. Think of arguments you could develop to counter these claims.

▶ WHAT DOES IT LOOK LIKE?

Opposing Claim: Kids should do chores without being paid to help their family out.

My response: That would be nice, but it's not realistic. Kids will always need money, and parents will always need help with chores. Paying kids to do chores is a good compromise.

PEER REVIEW Explain to a peer the claim you intend to assert and the audience you will be seeking to persuade. Describe your evidence and evaluate it for accuracy and credibility. If the evidence isn't as strong as you might like, ask: What new approach could I take to strengthen my claim?

YOUR TURN In your *Reader/Writer Notebook,* write your claim. Then complete a chart similar to the one on this page, identifying evidence for each of your reasons. Try to vary your types of evidence to appeal to different members of your audience. At the bottom of the chart, state possible opposing claims and outline your responses.

Drafting

The following chart shows how to organize your draft to create an effective persuasive essay.

W 1C Use words, phrases, and clauses to create cohesion and clarify the relationships among claim(s), reasons, and evidence. **W 4** Produce clear and coherent writing appropriate to task, purpose, and audience.

Organizing a Persuasive Essay

INTRODUCTION

- Grab the audience's attention with a **quotation** or a **statistic.**
- State your position in a strong **claim**.

▼

BODY

- Present your reasons in a **logical order,** such as order of importance.
- Support each reason with **accurate facts, relevant examples,** and **other types of evidence.**
- Address **opposing claims** to your argument and provide responses.
- Maintain a **formal style** by using a serious tone, a confident voice, and thoughtful, persuasive words.

▼

CONCLUDING SECTION

- Restate your **claim.**
- End with a **call to action**—tell readers what they should do if they agree with your position.

GRAMMAR IN CONTEXT: USING TRANSITIONS

When your claim, reasons, and evidence are tied together well, your essay is **coherent,** or smooth and easy to follow. Use **transitions**—words, phrases, and clauses that show the relationships among your ideas—to create a coherent argument.

Transitions That Create Cohesion	Examples
however if . . . then furthermore one reason consequently for example although so	*Kids should be paid for their chores. Some people disagree. They claim that chores are a normal family expectation and shouldn't be rewarded with money.* **However, if** *kids can't learn to manage their own money,* **then** *they may make poor spending choices as adults.* **Furthermore,** *kids would be more motivated to do the chores their parents nag them to do.*

YOUR TURN Develop a first draft of your essay. Include words, phrases, and clauses to connect your ideas and create a cohesive argument.

Revising

No one writes a perfect essay in the first draft. The revising stage gives you a chance to improve upon the content, organization, and style of your draft. Use the chart shown to help you revise and rewrite where necessary. Check that you achieve your purpose and persuade your audience.

PERSUASIVE ESSAY

Ask Yourself	Tips	Revision Strategies
1. Does the introduction grab the audience's attention?	▶ **Put stars** next to questions, anecdotes, or statements that would interest the audience.	▶ **Add** an attention-grabber to the beginning of the introduction.
2. Does the introduction have a strong claim?	▶ **Underline** the claim. Ask a peer to read it and identify the writer's position.	▶ **Add** a claim, or replace the claim with a stronger one.
3. Are there at least two logical reasons that support the claim? Does at least one piece of relevant evidence support each reason?	▶ **Highlight** the reasons that support the claim. **Circle** the evidence that supports each reason. **Draw an arrow** from the evidence to the reason.	▶ If necessary, **add** logical reasons that support the claim. **Add** relevant evidence to support each reason. **Elaborate** on pieces of evidence by adding details or explaining their meaning.
4. Are the reasons in the order that is most persuasive?	▶ **Number** the reasons in the margin, ranking them by their strength and persuasiveness.	▶ **Reorder** the ideas in a logical order, such as order of importance.
5. Does the argument acknowledge opposing claims and counter them?	▶ **Draw a wavy line** under the opposing claims and your responses to them.	▶ If necessary, **add** a sentence or two that addresses other viewpoints.
6. Does the concluding section restate the claim and include a call to action?	▶ **Put a check mark** next to the restatement. **Underline** the call to action.	▶ **Add** a restatement of the claim if it is missing. **Add** a call to action if there is none.

 YOUR TURN *PEER REVIEW* With a peer, go over the chart. Then review your drafts together. Answer each question in the chart to identify which parts of your drafts need reworking or a new approach.

W 5 Develop and strengthen writing as needed by revising, editing, rewriting, or trying a new approach, focusing on how well purpose and audience have been addressed.

···· COMMON CORE ····

ANALYZE A STUDENT DRAFT

Read this student's draft and the comments about it as a model for revising your own persuasive essay.

Kids Should Be Paid for Chores
by T. J. Wilson, Atlantic Middle School

① According to the Joint Council on Economic Education, teenagers between the ages of 13 and 17 will spend $89 billion in this country. Where will that staggering amount of money come from? Many teens are not allowed to work outside of the home; therefore, I strongly believe that kids should be paid for doing chores around the house. Kids all across the country constantly nag their parents for money to go to the movies, buy music, and purchase trendy clothes. Consequently, many parents complain about their kids always asking them for money.

② Constant friction results. Parents complain that kids don't help out around the house enough. Lots of times, kids get nagged until they clean up their rooms, put out the trash, cut the lawn, shovel the snow, and do many other chores. But conflicts result at home. Why can't kids and parents reach a compromise about money and chores? This would end the feuding and make everyone in the household happy. Parents would pay kids a small fee for doing chores without being reminded. Kids would no longer ask for money.

> T. J. grabs the attention of his audience by presenting a **statistic.**

> In his introduction, T. J. clearly states his **claim** on the issue.

> T. J. provides some **examples** to support his point about conflict. He could add an anecdote that shows how a real-life conflict was resolved.

LEARN HOW Use Anecdotes as Supporting Evidence T. J.'s second paragraph ends with the point that paying kids for chores could end feuding in the household. Instead of simply stating this outcome, he decided he could be more persuasive by showing it through an **anecdote,** a brief story that proves his point.

T. J.'S REVISION TO PARAGRAPH ②

This would end the feuding and make everyone in the household happy. ~~Parents would pay kids a small fee for doing chores without being reminded. Kids would no longer ask for money.~~

For example, my cousin Jeremy in Dallas constantly argued with his dad about mowing the lawn and walking the dog. Every time Jeremy asked for money, the accusations began again. Then they decided on a set fee for the chores: $20.00 a week for mowing and $7.00 a week for daily dog walks. Jeremy now eagerly does his chores, and he doesn't argue with his dad—even the dog is happy!

❸   This compromise teaches kids responsibility. John Covey, a father of ten and co-author of *The Seven Habits of Effective Families,* says there are two reasons to get children to do chores: "to get the job done and to help them grow." Teens learn to be responsible and develop a work ethic. When their chores are completed with no nagging, they'd be paid whatever their parents had agreed to pay them. Kids could spend the money on things they like or save money for expensive items.

T. J. cites an **expert opinion** to support his second reason in favor of paying kids to do chores.

❹   In an ideal world, kids would happily do chores, never ask for money, and parents would have the resources to pay for outside help or have the time to do all the work themselves. But for most families this is a fantasy. The real world demands a compromise on chores and money.

In this paragraph, T. J. presents a response to an **opposing claim**.

❺   Kids would stop begging for money. Parents would stop nagging kids to clean up their rooms or the kitchen. Both parents and kids would be getting what they want.

T. J.'s concluding section lacks a **call to action**.

LEARN HOW   Conclude with a Call to Action   In revising his essay, T. J. realized that, although his conclusion restates his most important ideas, it does not tell his audience exactly what he wants them to do. He added a **call to action** to make his concluding section stronger.

T. J.'S REVISION TO PARAGRAPH ❺

Do you want to   *Do you want your parents to*   *you about chores.*

~~Kids would~~ stop begging for money. ~~Parents would~~ stop nagging ~~kids to~~

> *Talk to your parents today. Propose a compromise of responsibility and payment for chores.*

~~clean up their rooms or the kitchen.~~ Both parents and kids would be getting what they want.

YOUR TURN   Use feedback from your peers and your teacher as well as the two "Learn How" lessons to revise your persuasive essay. Evaluate how well your essay convinces your audience to act on the issue through compelling reasons, strong evidence, and a rousing call to action.

Editing and Publishing

COMMON CORE

W 5 Develop and strengthen writing by revising, editing, rewriting, or trying a new approach. **L 2** Demonstrate command of the conventions of standard English capitalization, punctuation, and spelling.

In a persuasive essay, you want your audience to see you as an authority on your topic. Errors in grammar, spelling, and punctuation make you sound less authoritative. In the editing stage, you find and correct such errors so your audience can fully appreciate the persuasiveness of your argument.

GRAMMAR IN CONTEXT: PUNCTUATING RHETORICAL QUESTIONS

Rhetorical questions directly address the audience but do not demand answers. Instead, they are used to catch readers' attention and make them think. Still, they must be punctuated correctly with question marks.

Type of Question	Example
request for infomation	▶ *What time should we meet for lunch tomorrow?*
rhetorical question	▶ *How would you like to eat the same boring sandwich for lunch every single day?*

When T. J. edited his essay, he discovered that he had forgotten to use the correct punctuation marks for some rhetorical questions.

Do you want to stop begging for money? Do you want your parents to stop nagging you about chores? Talk to your parents today. Propose a compromise of responsibility and payment for chores. Both parents and kids would be getting what they want.

PUBLISH YOUR WRITING

Share your essay with an audience.
- Make copies of your essay for others with an interest in your issue.
- Develop your essay into an editorial for your school or local newspaper.
- Present your essay as the first entry in a class blog. Elicit others' opinions on the issue and your claim.
- Adapt your essay into a persuasive speech to present to an audience.

YOUR TURN Correct any errors in your essay by carefully proofreading it. Punctuate any rhetorical questions correctly. Then publish your final product where it is most likely to reach your intended audience.

Scoring Rubric

Use the rubric below to evaluate your persuasive essay from the Writing Workshop or your response to the on-demand task on the next page.

PERSUASIVE ESSAY

SCORE	◌ COMMON CORE TRAITS
6	• **Development** Effectively introduces the issue and asserts a claim; supports the claim with relevant reasons and evidence; addresses opposing claims; ends with a strong, memorable concluding section • **Organization** Arranges reasons and evidence in a logical order; uses transitions to create cohesion and link ideas • **Language** Consistently maintains a formal style; shows a strong command of conventions
5	• **Development** Competently introduces the issue and states a claim; offers logical reasons and evidence; acknowledges opposing claims; ends with a strong concluding section • **Organization** Cites reasons and evidence logically; uses transitions to link ideas • **Language** Maintains a formal style; has a few errors in conventions
4	• **Development** Introduces the issue and states a claim; offers mostly relevant support; needs to more thoroughly address opposing claims; has an adequate concluding section • **Organization** Has a logical organization; could use a few more transitions • **Language** Mostly maintains a formal style; includes a few distracting errors in conventions
3	• **Development** States a claim; provides some reasons, but needs more evidence; does not sufficiently address other viewpoints; has a somewhat weak concluding section • **Organization** Reflects some flaws in organization; needs more transitions • **Language** Often lapses into an informal style; has several errors in conventions
2	• **Development** Has a weak claim; offers some irrelevant reasons and needs more evidence; fails to acknowledge other viewpoints; has a weak concluding section • **Organization** Has organizational flaws; lacks transitions throughout • **Language** Uses an informal style; has many distracting errors in conventions
1	• **Development** Lacks a clear claim; offers little, if any, support; ignores opposing viewpoints; has no concluding section • **Organization** Has no organization and transitions • **Language** Lacks a formal style; has major problems with grammar, mechanics, and spelling

Preparing for Timed Writing

COMMON CORE

W 10 Write routinely over shorter time frames for a range of tasks, purposes, and audiences.

1. ANALYZE THE TASK   5 MIN

Read the task carefully. Then read it again, underlining the words that tell the type of writing, the topic, and the purpose.

> **WRITING TASK**
>
> *Topic*
>
> Your school is considering <u>adding a 15-minute period each morning for students to relax, talk, listen to music, and get a snack</u>. The school day would be lengthened to accommodate this break. <u>Write an essay</u> for your school paper <u>convincing readers to support this proposal.</u> Use logical reasons and relevant evidence.
>
> *Purpose ↗*   *Type of writing*

2. PLAN YOUR RESPONSE   10 MIN

Ask yourself: Why would it be a good idea to have a break in the middle of the morning? Your answers will be your reasons. Use a chart to list reasons and gather evidence, such as examples and anecdotes, to support each of your reasons. Also, note an opposing claim your readers might have. What reasons and evidence might address their concerns?

Reasons	Evidence
Possible Opposing Claim:	

3. RESPOND TO THE TASK   20 MIN

Once you have gathered your reasons and evidence, draft your essay. As you write, keep these guidelines in mind:

- In the introduction, grab your audience's attention and state your claim.
- In each body paragraph, provide a reason and the evidence that supports it.
- Acknowledge and address an opposing claim.
- Conclude by restating your claim and proposing some action that your audience should take.

4. IMPROVE YOUR RESPONSE   5–10 MIN

Revising Review key aspects of the essay. Do you state your claim clearly? Do you include convincing reasons, solid evidence, and a call to action?

Proofreading Neatly correct any errors in grammar, spelling, and mechanics.

Checking Your Final Copy Before you turn in your essay, read it once more to catch any errors you may have missed and to make any finishing touches.

Presenting a Persuasive Speech

If you have ever talked a friend or relative into agreeing with your opinion about something, then you have spoken persuasively. A persuasive speech shares the same purpose as a persuasive essay—you want to convince an audience through your words to agree with your **claim,** or position, on an issue.

 Complete the workshop activities in your **Reader/Writer Notebook.**

SPEAK WITH A PURPOSE	COMMON CORE TRAITS
TASK Adapt your written essay into a **persuasive speech.** Practice your speech, and then present it to your class. As you listen to other students' speeches, evaluate their delivery and the evidence they present.	**A STRONG PERSUASIVE SPEECH . . .** • clearly presents a claim and findings • emphasizes **salient**, or important, points with logical reasons and relevant evidence • is organized logically • anticipates and counters possible opposing claims • is strengthened by the speaker's eye contact, adequate volume, and clear pronunciation

COMMON CORE

SL 3 Delineate a speaker's argument and claims, evaluating the reasoning and evidence. **SL 4** Present claims and findings; use appropriate eye contact, volume, and pronunciation. **SL 5** Include visual displays to clarify claims. **SL 6** Demonstrate command of formal English.

Adapt Your Essay

A good persuasive speaker engages the audience. Use these strategies to grab listeners' attention and make them care about your issue:

- **Provide the big picture.** Present all sides of the issue as well as any terms and details that your audience will need to know.

- **Give logical reasons and relevant evidence.** Present reasons why your audience should agree with you, and support them with evidence (anecdotes, examples, expert opinions, facts, details, and statistics).

- **Present visuals and media displays.** Use handmade visuals or technology-based media displays to clarify claims and emphasize points.

- **Organize.** Use an organization that will help you fulfill your purpose.

  — If your audience opposes your claim, your purpose is to get them to consider it. First acknowledge their point of view, and then present your reasons and evidence in response.

  — If your audience agrees with your claim, your purpose is to get them to take action. First solidify their existing opinion by stating your claim and listing reasons and evidence. Then close with a clear call to action.

  — If your audience is unsure about your position, your purpose is to persuade them to agree with you. Present your reasons and evidence clearly, and be sure to address possible opposing claims.

Speaking & Listening Online

Go to **thinkcentral.com.**
KEYWORD: HML7-998

Deliver Your Persuasive Speech

A strong presenter can make any argument persuasive by effectively using verbal and nonverbal techniques such as those listed below.

- **Enunciation** Pronounce words carefully and clearly.
- **Tempo** Adjust the speed and rhythm of your speech. Be sure to pause to emphasize salient points.
- **Voice Modulation** Stress certain words and phrases by changing the volume of your voice.
- **Body Language** Show that you believe your position is a good one by using facial expressions that convey certainty. A confident posture can make you seem more **credible**, or believable.
- **Eye Contact** Keep your audience members involved by maintaining eye contact with them throughout your speech.
- **Formal English** Use language that is appropriate for a formal speech. Your audience will take you more seriously if you avoid overly casual phrases.

Evaluate a Persuasive Speech

Keep these tips in mind as you listen to other students' speeches:

- **Delineate**, or trace, the speaker's argument so that you can decide whether you agree with him or her. Start by asking yourself: What is the speaker's claim? If I accept this claim, what action does the speaker want me to take?
- Evaluate the findings that the speaker presents in support of the claim. Are the reasons provided **sound**, or logical? Is the evidence relevant and **sufficient**, or clear and varied enough to be persuasive?
- Evaluate the speaker's delivery. How well does he or she use verbal and nonverbal techniques to convey the information?
- Decide whether the speech is organized in an effective way. Are the reasons presented in the most persuasive order?
- Take brief notes on the speaker's main points. At the end of the speech, ask questions or make comments about the reasons and evidence the speaker has presented.

YOUR TURN

As a Speaker Give your presentation to a partner, incorporating the techniques described on this page.

As a Listener Listen to your partner's speech carefully. Ask questions about the reasons and evidence before summarizing the purpose and content of the speech. Evaluate the effectiveness of your partner's delivery.

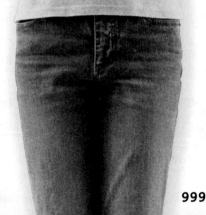

Assessment Practice

DIRECTIONS Read the following selections and then answer the questions.

Teen Reading Survey
by **SmartGirl.org** *online magazine*

Reading Habits: Respondent Behavior and Opinion

1   The survey showed that

• Many teens enjoy reading and often do read for pleasure; 43% of teens surveyed said that most often they read for the fun of it.

• There was a significant difference, however, between boys and girls; 50% of girls said they read for pleasure, while only 32% of boys did.

2   While teens appear to enjoy reading, they find that they often do not have the time to do so. Other reasons given for not reading or not reading more: they found reading boring and prefer watching television or movies; they lack good reading materials.

Survey Results

SmartGirl asked: Which statement below do you agree with most?

Statement	Total	Girls	Boys
I read constantly for my own satisfaction, and I love it.	26%	31%	18%
I don't have much time to read for pleasure, but I like to when I get a chance.	46%	49%	40%
I only read what I'm supposed to for school.	16%	12%	22%
I don't read books much at all.	7%	4%	11%
No answer	6%	4%	9%

SmartGirl asked: Most often, the reason I read is . . . (Please choose the best answer from this selection).

Statement	Total	Girls	Boys
Just for the fun of it	43%	50%	32%
Because I have to for school	19%	17%	22%
Because I get bored and have nothing else to do	12%	13%	11%
To learn new things on my own	12%	10%	15%
I don't really read much	5%	3%	8%
Because my parents encourage me to	4%	3%	4%

Take a Book Wherever You Go

by Joan Aiken

1   If you were going to sail round the world alone in a small boat, and could take only one of these things to amuse you, which would you choose: a big iced cake, a beautiful picture, a book, a pack of cards, a paintbox (and paper), a pair of knitting needles and wool, a musical box, a harmonica . . . ? It would be a hard choice. Myself, I wouldn't want the cake; I'd eat it too fast. Nor the cards; they might blow away. Nor the wool; in case it got wet. The harmonica would be better than the musical box, for one could make up one's own tunes. I wouldn't take the picture, for I could look at the sea. Nor the paintbox, because in the end I'd use up all the paper. So the last choice would be between the harmonica and the book. And I'm pretty sure I'd choose the book.

2   *One book!* I can hear someone say. But if you were sailing round the world, you'd have read it a hundred times before the trip was over. You'd know it by heart.

3   And I'd answer, Yes, I might read it a hundred times; yes, I might know it by heart. *That wouldn't matter.* You don't refuse to see your friend, or your mother, or your brother, because you have met them before. You don't leave home because you know what's there.

4   A book you love is like a friend. It is like home. You meet your friend a hundred times. On the hundred-and-first meeting you can still say, "Well, I never realized you knew that!" You go home every day; after ten years you can still say, "I never noticed how beautiful the light is, when it shines on that corner."

5   There is always something new to find in a book, however often you read it.

6   When you read a story you do something that no animal can, however well trained; only man can do it; you are stepping out of your own mind into someone else's. You are listening to the thoughts of another person. While doing this, you are making your own mind work. And making your own mind work is the most interesting thing there is to do.

7   So I'd sit in my boat and read that book over and over. First I'd think about the people in the story, why they acted the way they did. Then I might wonder why the writer wrote that particular story. Then I might

GO ON

carry on the story in my mind, after the end. Then I'd go back and read all my favorite bits and wonder why I liked them best. Then I'd read all the rest and look for things that I hadn't noticed before. Then I'd list the things I'd learned from the book. Then I'd try to imagine what the writer was like, from the way he's written his story. . . . It would be like having another person in the boat.

8   A book you love is a friend; it's a familiar place where you can go when you choose. It's something of your own, for no two people read the same book in the same way.

9   If every single person in the world had a book, just one book (they'd have to be able to read it, of course) we'd have a lot less trouble, I'm sure.

10   Just one book apiece. That shouldn't be too hard to manage.

11   How shall we start?

Reading Comprehension

> **Answer these questions about "Teen Reading Survey."**

1. The title "Teen Reading Survey" tells you that this selection will most likely —

  A. compare books and movies for teens

  B. analyze book sales in the teen market

  C. list teens' favorite interests and activities

  D. give statistics about teens' reading habits

2. Which statement from paragraphs 1 and 2 expresses the main idea of the survey results?

  A. *Many teens enjoy reading and often do read for pleasure.*

  B. *They lack good reading materials.*

  C. *50% of girls said they read for pleasure, while only 32% of boys did.*

  D. *They found reading boring and prefer watching television or movies.*

3. Which statement is a factual claim that you can support with evidence from the survey?

  A. Almost half of all teens do not read because few books are written for a teen audience.

  B. Schools don't require teens to read enough novels.

  C. Teens who enjoy reading are self-motivated readers.

  D. Parents are actively involved in getting their teens to read.

4. Based on the survey, which statement is an opinion?

  A. Close to half of teens surveyed think they have little time to read for pleasure.

  B. Boys should spend more time reading.

  C. Ten percent of girls read to learn new things on their own.

  D. More boys than girls read only what is required for school.

Answer these questions about "Take a Book Wherever You Go."

5. By choosing to take a book on her trip, the author is making which claim?

   A. A book is easy to carry on a trip.

   B. There are many kinds of books that appeal to different people.

   C. A book will provide the most satisfaction and pleasure.

   D. Books are inexpensive to replace.

6. Which reason does the author give to support her claim?

   A. Every time you read a book, you can discover something new.

   B. Reading a book would make the trip seem shorter.

   C. By reading, you could learn how to write your own book.

   D. You could learn a book so well that you could discuss it later with your friends.

7. Which statement is a factual claim?

   A. *It would be a hard choice.* (paragraph 1)

   B. *A book you love is like a friend.* (paragraph 4)

   C. *And making your own mind work is the most interesting thing there is to do.* (paragraph 6)

   D. *When you read a story you do something that no animal can.* (paragraph 6)

8. What counterargument does the author address in paragraphs 2 and 3?

   A. She would probably stop reading the book before she got to the end of it.

   B. She would have to read the book over and over again on such a long trip.

   C. The book would probably fall apart before the trip was done.

   D. She would regret her choice and wish she had the harmonica.

Answer this question about both selections.

9. Both selections convey the idea that reading is —

   A. an enjoyable activity

   B. necessary in order to succeed

   C. unlike any other activity

   D. like talking to a friend

SHORT CONSTRUCTED RESPONSE

10. Read the first subheading in "Teen Reading Survey." What two categories of reading habits are covered in the survey? Which chart covers each category?

11. Discuss the main idea of "Take a Book Wherever You Go." What details does the author use to support this idea?

GO ON

Vocabulary

1. In the first chart in "Teen Reading Survey," the idiom *at all* means —
   A. often
   B. to any extent
   C. considering everything
   D. to the degree expected

2. In the second chart in "Teen Reading Survey," the idiom *on my own* means —
   A. in a short time
   B. by one's own efforts
   C. at one's own house
   D. with guidance

3. In paragraph 1 of "Take a Book Wherever You Go," the idiom *in the end* means —
   A. eventually
   B. maybe
   C. somewhere
   D. soon

4. In paragraph 2 of "Take a Book Wherever You Go," the idiom *by heart* means —
   A. learned to read
   B. felt deeply
   C. memorized word for word
   D. understood meanings

5. The Latin word *videre* means "to look." In the title "Teen Reading Survey," what does the word *survey* mean?
   A. A careful inspection
   B. The determination of an area's boundaries
   C. A collection of data or viewpoints
   D. An outline of a subject

6. The Latin prefix *ad-* means "toward," and the Latin word *parere* means "to show." In paragraph 2 of "Teen Reading Survey," what does the word *appear* mean?
   A. Show up
   B. Exist
   C. Seem
   D. Intend

7. The Latin word *manus* means "hand." In paragraph 10 of "Take a Book Wherever You Go," what does the word *manage* mean?
   A. Continue to get along
   B. Direct business affairs
   C. Control the use of
   D. Succeed in accomplishing

Revising and Editing

DIRECTIONS Read this passage and answer the questions that follow.

Dear Student

(1) This Friday is the last day of school. (2) As a result we will be having a small party. (3) The party a hot dog lunch will be held in the cafeteria. (4) However, when school lets out at 335 P.M., please behave. (5) Do not run, push, or yell. (6) Students who violate these rules are subject to the following a call to parents a meeting with the principal or other disciplinary action.

1. Choose the correct way to punctuate the formal greeting.

  A. Dear Student!   **C.** Dear Student:

  B. Dear Student;   **D.** Dear Student.

2. Choose the correct way to add a comma to sentence 2.

  A. As a result we will be having a small, party.

  B. As a result we will, be having a small party.

  C. As a result we will be having a small party.

  D. As a result, we will be having a small party.

3. Choose the correct way to add commas to the appositive phrase in sentence 3.

  A. The party a hot, dog lunch, will be held in the cafeteria.

  B. The party, a hot dog lunch, will be held in the cafeteria.

  C. The party a hot dog lunch will be held, in the cafeteria.

  D. The party a hot dog lunch, will be held in the cafeteria.

4. Choose the correct place to insert a colon in sentence 4.

  A. 335 P.M.:   **C.** please:

  B. 3:35 P.M.   **D.** However:

5. Choose the correct way to add a colon and commas to sentence 6.

  A. Students who violate these rules are subject to the following: a call, to parents, a meeting with the principal or other disciplinary action.

  B. Students who violate these rules are subject to: the following a call to parents, a meeting with the principal, or other disciplinary action.

  C. Students who violate these rules are: subject to the following, a call to parents, a meeting with the principal, or other disciplinary action.

  D. Students who violate these rules are subject to the following: a call to parents, a meeting with the principal, or other disciplinary action.

1005

Ideas for Independent Reading

Which questions from Unit 8 made an impression on you?
Continue exploring them with these books.

COMMON CORE

RL 10 Read and comprehend literature. **RI 10** Read and comprehend literary nonfiction.

Can appearances deceive?

Buffalo Gals: Women of the Old West
by Brandon Marie Miller

This book makes history "come alive" through journal entries, letters, and songs. Learn about the many experiences of these strong, fearless women and the difficulties they faced as they took care of their children and homes.

The Contender
by Robert Lipsyte

An African-American high school dropout living in Harlem in the 1960s, during the civil rights movement, struggles to prove himself through the rigor and discipline of boxing. He wonders whether he has the heart of a contender— inside and outside the ring.

The Tulip Touch
by Anne Fine

Who might deceive you? Advertisers? Friends? When Natalie meets her neighbor, a girl named Tulip, she becomes a willing pawn in Tulip's wicked deceits. When the lies turn dangerous, can Natalie escape?

How do we fight disease?

Fever 1793
by Laurie Halse Anderson

In this novel, 14-year-old Mattie Cook's day in 18th-century Philadelphia begins with her coffeehouse chores and ends with an epidemic of yellow fever. Does Mattie become a statistic of this outbreak?

Lost in the War
by Nancy Antle

Events like war are often a kind of disease. Thirteen-year-old Lisa Grey is too young to remember her father, who was killed in Vietnam. But she relives the war every day through her mom, who suffers from posttraumatic stress disorder.

Snake Dreamer
by Priscilla Galloway

Disease can be physical or mental. Sixteen-year-old Dusa suffers from nightmares of writhing snakes. When her mother takes her to a sleep-disorder clinic in Greece, things become even more frightening.

What inspires people?

Walks Alone
by Brian Burks

It's how we overcome challenges that can make us heroes. It's 1879, and 15-year-old Walks Alone watches the massacre of her people during a raid. Her loss and the challenges that follow teach her courage and hope.

Passage to Freedom
by Ken Mochizuki

Japanese diplomat Chiune Sugihara watched Nazi forces invade Europe at the start of World War II. Jewish citizens were applying for visas in order to leave, but for many there were no visas. Inspired to help, Sugihara risked much to grant visas to as many as 10,000 Jews.

Bound for the North Star: True Stories of Fugitive Slaves
by Dennis Brindell Fradin

The former enslaved people described in these 12 stories of heroic escapes have inspired movies and books. These stories continue to inspire readers to fight against cruelty worldwide.

Get Novel Wise

THiNK central

Go to **thinkcentral.com**.
KEYWORD: HML7-1006

UNIT 9

Investigation and Discovery

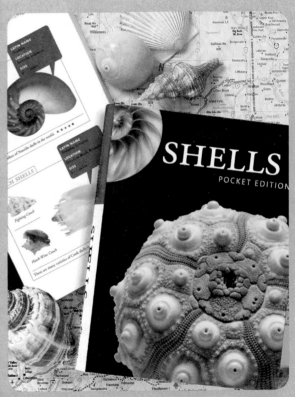

THE POWER OF RESEARCH

- Research Strategies
- Writing Research Papers

Share What You Know

How can I find ANSWERS?

You do research every day. You find out the weather report, movie times, and game scores. Maybe you also locate the lowest price for an item or the best Web site for keeping up with music. Every time you track down information, even in the phone book or on TV, you are doing research. However, some kinds of research require more effort, such as gathering information for a school report. In this unit, you'll learn to sharpen your skills to answer harder questions.

ACTIVITY List some research questions you answer at home, at school, and in other places. Tell where you get answers.

	Questions	Where I Find Answers
Home		
School		
Other places		

Preview Unit Goals

DEVELOPING RESEARCH SKILLS
- Plan research
- Develop relevant research questions
- Use library and media center resources
- Evaluate information and sources, including nonfiction books, periodicals, and Web sites
- Collect your own data

WRITING AND LANGUAGE
- Write a research paper
- Formulate a major research question
- Locate and evaluate sources
- Take notes
- Prepare a source list
- Summarize and paraphrase
- Quote directly and avoid plagiarism
- Present clear and accurate perspectives on the topic
- Document sources and prepare a Works Cited list
- Choose complex sentences to signal different relationships

SPEAKING AND LISTENING
- Create a Wiki

ACADEMIC VOCABULARY
- evaluate
- locate
- process
- focus
- primary

Writing and Research in a Digital Age

THINK central

KEYWORD: HML7-1009

From online news feeds and electronic archives to podcasts and digital notebooks, technology tools can help you tackle any research project. Find out how.

Where do I look for INFORMATION?

COMMON CORE

Included in this workshop:
W 6 Use technology, including the Internet, to link to and cite sources. **W 7** Conduct short research projects to answer a question. **W 8** Gather relevant information from multiple print and digital sources, using search terms effectively; assess the credibility and accuracy of each source. **SL 1c** Pose questions that elicit elaboration.

Finding answers isn't always easy, especially since many questions have more than one answer. This unit will help you answer research questions in efficient and reliable ways. You will learn how and where to look, as well as how to look critically at everything you find.

QUICKWRITE In this unit, you will follow a group of students as they look for information about different kinds of collections. Begin by putting yourself in the same situation. Imagine that your school puts on a collectors' show each year. You want to participate, but what will you display? Working alone or with a partner, list several types of collections that you would like to learn more about.

**Annual
Collectors' Show**

Saturday, May 7

Grant Middle School

2118 Catalpa Street

10:00 A.M. **to 4:00** P.M.

Planning Your Research

Good research begins with a reading and thinking stage. Don't just jump in. Stop and think about what you want to accomplish.

SET A GOAL

What do you want to learn from your research? Start by listing your general and specific goals.

> **General goal:** How can I figure out something I would like to collect?
>
> **Questions:**
> - **What especially interests me?** I like baseball, bugs, rocks, and camping.
> - **Do any of my interests lead to collections?** I could collect baseball cards, certain kinds of bugs, or different kinds of rocks.
>
> **Specific goal:** I want to learn more about collecting baseball cards.

GET AN OVERVIEW

After you set a goal, it's time to understand your topic better.

- **Talk to people.** Look for a person who knows about your topic. Talking to him or her may give you lots of ideas.
- **Use the Internet.** For example, if you type the words *baseball cards* into a search engine, you will probably get a few million hits. Look at the first ten entries or so. They may give you ideas for more specific terms to use.
- **Visit the library.** Is there a reference book or an encyclopedia article on your topic? These sources will give you an overview.
- **Talk with a librarian.** He or she may be able to suggest books, magazines, and online sources.

NARROW YOUR FOCUS

Big topics are harder to manage than smaller, more specific ones. Once you decide on a specific topic, you might brainstorm ways to narrow it. The result of your brainstorm might look like this.

Topic	More Specific	Even More Specific
baseball cards	baseball cards from a specific time period	baseball cards of a specific team or player

Research Tools

THINK central

Go to thinkcentral.com.
KEYWORD: HML7-1011

WRITE RESEARCH QUESTIONS

Let's say you have a narrow topic—for example, Seattle Mariners baseball cards. A good next step is to develop questions to guide your research.

Research questions are big questions about your topic. They can't be answered with just a yes or a no. They sum up what you want to know about your topic. Your research questions should be **relevant** (that means closely connected to an important part of your topic). They should also be **tightly drawn**—detailed and specific. After you write your research questions, highlight key terms in them.

- When did people first start collecting Seattle Mariners baseball cards?
- What determines the prices and values of these cards?
- What are some interesting stories about collectors and Mariners cards?

Use the questions and the terms to focus your research.

GET READY TO TAKE NOTES

As you get started on your research, the more organized you are, the better off you will be. When you do research for a class assignment, one of the best ways to take notes is by using note cards. You will learn more about note cards on pages 1032–1033.

For other kinds of research, you might use different note-taking tools, such as charts or lists. Think about the kinds of information you need and the format that would work best to keep you organized. For instance, you might create a chart of terms used by baseball card collectors.

Term	Meaning
Star cards	cards of the best-known players—can be expensive
Common cards	cards of lesser-known players—cheaper, but very important to collectors who want all the cards of a certain team
Insert cards	cards with special designs that are placed into some packs
Memorabilia cards	insert cards that either are autographed by the players or contain fragments of equipment used by the players, such as pieces of bats, jerseys, or caps

Using the Internet

When you use the World Wide Web, you are also using the Internet, a huge system of linked computers. The Web includes hundreds of millions of Web sites and billions of Web pages.

SEARCH THE WEB

Begin your search by going to one or more search engines. **Search engines** are Web sites that locate information based on titles, keywords, and content. There are many to choose from, and each yields different information.

USE KEYWORDS

A **keyword** is the term or phrase that you enter into a search engine. The best keywords are very specific, like those you highlighted on page 1012.

Suppose you want to learn more about collecting bracelets that people wear to show their support for a cause. Here's what may happen if you use a search engine.

YOU TYPE IN...	YOU GET...	THIS IS...
bracelet	4,120,000 results	too broad, but perhaps you see the word *awareness* a lot
+bracelet +awareness	324,000 results	still too broad, but now you see *nonprofit*, so you try *+bracelets +nonprofit*

ADVANCED SEARCHES

Some search engines let you make a search more specific by using the word *AND, NOT,* or *OR*. Other search engines let you use plus and minus signs. Here are some examples:

- *bracelet NOT charm* (This eliminates results about charm bracelets.)
- *+bracelet +nonprofit +"Lance Armstrong"* (This finds only pages that mention all three terms.)
- *bracelet AND "Race for the Cure"* (This finds only pages that mention both terms.)

LIBRARY CATALOG SEARCHES

Library search engines tend to be different from commercial search engines. A good way to get started searching on them is to explain your topic to a reference librarian and ask for help in identifying key terms.

TERMS FOR THE INTERNET

Here are terms that you will use when discussing the Internet:

- World Wide Web
- Web site
- keyword
- home page
- URL (uniform resource locator, also called a Web address)
- search engine
- menu
- hyperlink
- icon

TIP Use quotation marks to enclose words that go together as one term. For example, instead of *Lance Armstrong*, type in *"Lance Armstrong."*

EXAMINE SEARCH ENGINE RESULTS

One search can bring up millions of results. For example, a rock collector who types in *rocks* could get information on everything from Red Rocks Community College to a database of rock music downloads. A more manageable search might begin with *"rock collecting"* or *rock NOT music* or *+collecting +rocks +minerals*.

Follow these guidelines for examining the results that pop up:

1. Don't just click on the first result. The page that the search engine lists first may not be the most useful source for you.

2. Read the description of each page, including the Web address. The abbreviation at the end of the domain name in the Web address tells you about the page's source. For example, names of U.S. government domains end in *.gov*. Names of school sites contain *.edu*.

3. If a description seems to match your goal or keywords, click on it. If not, either go to the next description or think of ways to make your search terms better and try again.

TIP The most common ending in domain names is *.com*. Sites with *.com* in their names are generally personal sites or product sites. Domains with names that end in *.org* often belong to nonprofit organizations, including some libraries.

 YOUR TURN

Select Search Engine Results

Entering *"rock collecting"* in a search engine led to these results (and more than 30,000 others). Which ones would you click on? Why?

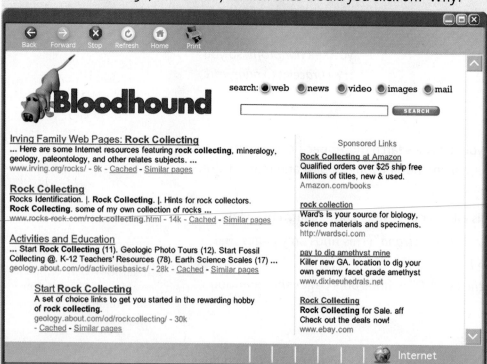

Close Read

1. What term was used in this search? How could you narrow the search even more?

2. Which of these results would you click on first? Why?

3. The "sponsored links" are paid for by businesses. They want to sell their products on the Web. Predict what you would find at one of the sponsored links on this page.

EXPLORE A WEB SITE

Web sites have many special features.

- **Home page** A home page is the "first" page of a Web site—a title page and table of contents all in one. It welcomes you to the site, provides general information, and helps you get where you want to go.

- **Menus** These can run across the top, along the sides, or across the bottom of pages. They tell you what pages or sections the site has and can keep you from getting lost as you explore the site. Many sites also include **hyperlinks** (underlined or boldfaced words) and **icons** (small pictures or symbols). Clicking on any of these takes you to other pages or to different sites.

- **Sponsor or creator** A site should tell you who created it.

- **Credits** Many sites include information about who created them and when they were last updated.

YOUR TURN

Navigate a Web Site

Look at the information on this Web page about collecting.

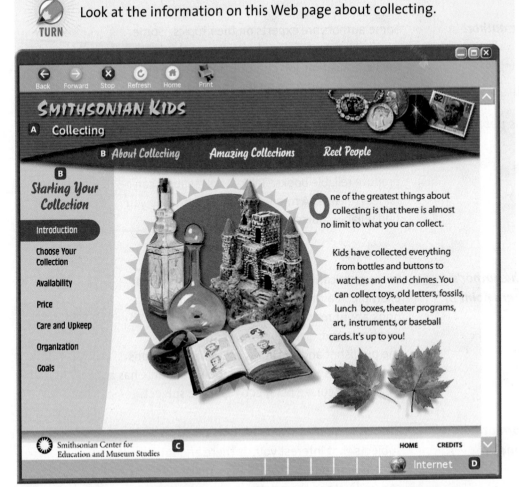

A Home page   **B** Menus   **C** Sponsor/creator   **D** Credits

Close Read

1. Where are the menus on this page?

2. What would you click on to get ideas about different kinds of collections?

3. Where would you click to find out who created this site and when it was last updated? Why is that information important?

Evaluating Information

To be sure the sources you choose are **valid**, or based on fact and recognized by authorities, you must evaluate them. Ask yourself whether the source has **adequate**, or enough, coverage of your topic. Then ask whether the source is **reliable**, or trustworthy. Next, ask whether it is **accurate**, or free from errors. Finally, consider whether the source is **appropriate**. Is it too childish, too scholarly, or just right? Apply these guidelines to all sources—books, magazines, newspapers, Web sites, and even interviews.

WHAT TO ASK	WHY IT MATTERS
What is the date of the information?	For some topics—especially in science, medicine, technology, and sports—up-to-the-minute information is especially important. Even when an event happened long ago, up-to-date sources often contain the latest findings and insights.
Who is the author?	Some authors are experts on their topics. Some aren't. Look for information on the author's other books, education, job or profession, and awards. Is he or she an authority on this topic?
Who is the publisher?	Some publishers are more reliable than others. They take care to ensure that the information they present is accurate and objective. University presses tend to produce reliable books. Tabloid newspapers can be far less reliable. A reference librarian can help you find reliable sources.
What is the author's or publisher's point of view?	Some publications are one-sided or **biased.** For example, if a model-train company publishes a book about model trains, its purpose may be to sell its own brand. Look for information about the publisher and the author. Draw conclusions about purpose and about whether the source has a clear and accurate perspective on the subject.
Is this information useful to me?	Check the menu or the table of contents for subjects that interest you. Is there enough information on your topic? Also, make sure you can understand the source. Is the language at a level that's right for you?

EVALUATE A WEB SITE

Publishing a book usually involves an author and editors. Many books are fact-checked and updated regularly. The Web is different. A personal Web site is usually the work of just one individual. Not all personal Web sites are unreliable, but be cautious. Ask yourself these questions:

- **Who created the site?** Is there a way to contact that person or group?

- **Why was the site created?** Is the site designed to give you information, to entertain you, or to sell you something? Some sites are created for more than one purpose.

- **Does the site contain problems?** Do you notice misspelled words, grammatical errors, or broken hyperlinks?

- **Does the author of the site seem knowledgeable about the topic?** Could you find more or better information in another source, such as an encyclopedia?

- **Is the information adequate, accurate, and appropriate?** The guidelines you read about on page 1016 apply to Web sites, too.

TIP Even reputable publishers and Web sites sometimes publish incorrect information. Use a variety of sources when you do research.

YOUR TURN

Examine a Web Site

This is an example of a personal Web site. What do you think is useful here? What problems do you see?

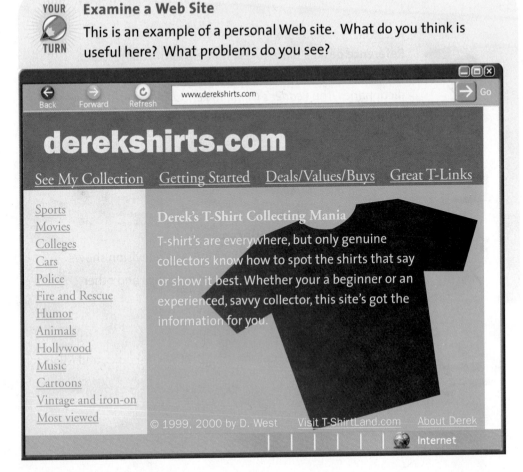

www.derekshirts.com   → Go
Back   Forward   Refresh

derekshirts.com

See My Collection   Getting Started   Deals/Values/Buys   Great T-Links

Sports
Movies
Colleges
Cars
Police
Fire and Rescue
Humor
Animals
Hollywood
Music
Cartoons
Vintage and iron-on
Most viewed

Derek's T-Shirt Collecting Mania

T-shirt's are everywhere, but only genuine collectors know how to spot the shirts that say or show it best. Whether your a beginner or an experienced, savvy collector, this site's got the information for you.

© 1999, 2000 by D. West   Visit T-ShirtLand.com   About Derek

Internet

Close Read

1. Who created this site?
2. What is the purpose of this site?
3. When was the site last updated? How do you know?
4. What problems do you notice?

TERMS FOR THE LIBRARY

You will use these terms when doing research in the library or media center:

- reference section
- primary source
- secondary source
- table of contents
- bibliography
- index
- catalog
- database

Libraries have sections for adults, for children, and often for young adults or teens. In addition, most libraries have several other areas:

- meeting and study rooms
- special sections (such as ones for business, local history, and genealogy)
- special resources (such as maps)
- computer terminals

LIBRARY AND MEDIA CENTER RESOURCES

BOOKS

Fiction: Works of fiction come from writers' imaginations, although the writers may base their works on real people and events. Novels and short stories are works of fiction.

Nonfiction: Nonfiction is writing that tells about real people, places, and events. Biographies, diaries, newspaper and magazine articles, essays, and true-life adventure stories are examples of nonfiction.

REFERENCE

Reference desk: a place to ask for help with your research

Reference materials: encyclopedias, almanacs, atlases, dictionaries, the *Reader's Guide to Periodical Literature*, and similar works, which usually cannot be checked out

NEWSPAPERS AND PERIODICALS

Magazines and newspapers: current issues, plus past issues in print or on microfilm

AUDIO AND VIDEO RESOURCES

DVDs: documentaries and other films and television shows

Audio resources: audio recordings of speeches and other events, audio books, and audio CDs

E-RESOURCES

Electronic collections: databases, CD-ROMs, e-books, and MP3s

THE LIBRARY CATALOG

An online library **catalog** is a complete index of a library's or library network's holdings. Some libraries also have a non-electronic version, called a card catalog. If you have questions about accessing the catalog, or if you want tips on more efficient searching, ask a reference librarian.

There are at least four ways to search a library catalog:

- **Author** Check to see whether you should type the first name first (for example, *Juan Gutierrez*) or the last name first (*Gutierrez, Juan*).

- **Title** You do not need to type in beginning words such as *A, An,* or *The*.

- **Subject** You may need to try a variety of words to get to your subject. For example, some systems may not respond to the subject word *seashells*. Instead, they may use *shells*.

- **Keyword** You can try various keywords, or you can ask a reference librarian for help.

YOUR TURN

Search a Library Catalog

To get to a catalog page, you might do a subject search for the term *shells*. That search would probably give you a list of subcategories, such as "Shells—Caribbean Sea" and "Shells in Art." The catalog page below is for the subcategory "Shells—Collection and Preservation."

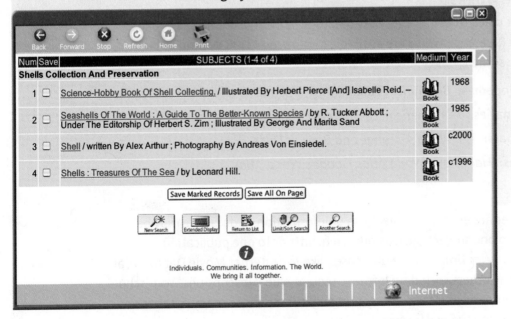

Close Read

1. Which book has information about both shells and collecting? How do you know?

2. Are these books or periodicals? How do you know?

Choosing and Evaluating Sources

The many different departments and resources in your local library can seem confusing. Be sure to ask a librarian for guidance in choosing adequate, accurate, appropriate sources.

PRIMARY AND SECONDARY SOURCES

All sources are either primary or secondary. This chart shows the difference.

PRIMARY SOURCES	SECONDARY SOURCES
Definition: firsthand accounts created by people who took part in or witnessed events	**Definition:** records of events created by people who were not directly involved in or present at the events
Examples: letters, diaries, photographs, autobiographies, interviews, speeches, birth certificates, census reports, first-person newspaper and magazine articles	**Examples:** textbooks, reference books, biographies, third-person newspaper and magazine articles

REFERENCE WORKS

The best place to get an overview of a topic is often a library's reference section. Reference works are available in print, on CD-ROM, and online. Here are some types of reference works:

- **Encyclopedias:** *Britannica Student Encyclopedia*
- **Dictionaries:** *The American Heritage Dictionary*
- **Almanacs:** *The World Almanac and Book of Facts*
- **Atlases:** *Hammond World Atlas, Goode's World Atlas*

DATABASES

Databases are electronic collections of information. A database may be specific to one subject, such as human health, or to one publication, such as the *Los Angeles Times*. Some databases, like the Internet Movie Database, are free. Many others, including InfoTrac, require paid subscriptions. Your school media center or your local library probably subscribes to many databases, which you can browse for free.

NONFICTION BOOKS

One of the best ways to get in-depth information about a topic is to check out a nonfiction book. Certain parts of a book can help you decide whether the book is right for your research.

1. Read the **title** and **subtitle** to get a general idea of the subject matter.

2. Check out the **copyright page** for the copyright date. The latest date is the one you should focus on. Is the book recent enough for your topic?

3. Read the **table of contents** for an overview. This page can also tell you whether the book contains a **bibliography** (a list of the sources used) or a list of **further reading.** Another useful feature in many books is a **glossary,** which is an alphabetical list of specialized terms, with definitions.

4. Look in the **index** for specific terms and topics that interest you. See how many pages include your topic. If the index lists just a page or two, the book may only mention your topic rather than explain it.

TIP Are there whole books written on your exact topic? Then your topic may be too broad.

YOUR TURN — Examine the Parts of a Book

Which parts of a book are shown here?

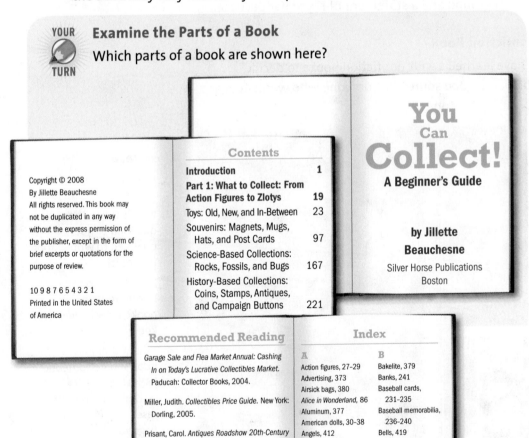

Copyright © 2008
By Jillette Beauchesne
All rights reserved. This book may not be duplicated in any way without the express permission of the publisher, except in the form of brief excerpts or quotations for the purpose of review.

10 9 8 7 6 5 4 3 2 1
Printed in the United States of America

Contents

You Can Collect!
A Beginner's Guide

by Jillette Beauchesne

Silver Horse Publications
Boston

Recommended Reading

Garage Sale and Flea Market Annual: Cashing In on Today's Lucrative Collectibles Market. Paducah: Collector Books, 2004.

Miller, Judith. *Collectibles Price Guide.* New York: Dorling, 2005.

Prisant, Carol. *Antiques Roadshow 20th-Century Collectibles.* New York: Workman, 2003.

Williams, Don. *Saving Stuff: How to Care for and Preserve Your Collectibles.* New York: Fireside, 2005.

Index

Close Read

1. How does the subtitle help you understand what the book is about?

2. Does this book contain information about collecting post cards? How about autographs? How do you know?

3. How up-to-date is this information? How do you know?

EVALUATE NONFICTION BOOKS

To be sure that the information in a nonfiction book is adequate, accurate, and appropriate for your purposes, ask these questions:

- **What is the most recent copyright date?** Check the **copyright notice,** which is usually on the back side of the title page. Have there been many updates and printings? That is often a sign that the book is reliable.

- **Is this a well-researched book?** Look for the author's sources. Is there a **bibliography,** a list of works the author consulted? Are there **footnotes, endnotes,** or **cross-references** that help you understand how the author got information? Is there an **appendix** of additional material, such as maps, tables, or charts?

- **What does the book say about the author?** Look for information about the author on the book jacket, at the beginning of the book, and at the end. Check the **preface** too. In this short introductory essay you may find clues to the author's background and a statement of his or her purpose.

YOUR TURN

Examine a Nonfiction Book

Use what you have learned about nonfiction books to decide whether this book is a good source for someone who wants to learn more about collecting buttons.

Collecting Campaign Buttons

Collecting Tips and Price Guide

Richard Danoff

Completely Updated for 2008!

4th Edition

Richard Danoff is the author of the best-selling *Know Your Collectibles*. He has written articles on collecting for many magazines and journals. He began collecting at age 10 with an "I Like Ike" button. Some parts of his collection have already been donated to the Smithsonian Institution and to other museums and libraries across the nation.

Close Read

1. What is this book about?

2. Why is the author qualified or not qualified to write about the topic?

3. How recent is the information in the book? How do you know?

4. What other parts of the book should someone look at to be sure it's suitable for his or her research? (Hint: See page 1021.)

NEWSPAPERS AND PERIODICALS

Newspapers are publications that contain news and advertising and that are published very frequently, in most cases daily or weekly. Newspapers and books have different purposes. Newspapers bring you brief information on current events, while most books deliver in-depth information on events of long-lasting importance. To learn more about the characteristics of a newspaper article, see page R14.

Publications that are issued on a regular basis of more than one day apart are called **periodicals.** Magazines are a common type of periodical.

- **Newspapers** *Seattle Times, Boston Globe, St. Louis Post-Dispatch*
- **Magazines** *Time, Teen Ink, Next Step, Skateboarder, Newsweek, Odyssey*

One of the best ways to search for articles on your topic is by using a database of newspaper and magazine articles, such as InfoTrac. The page below comes from InfoTrac Junior Edition, a database aimed at students in grades 5–12.

YOUR TURN

Finding a Newspaper or Magazine Article

A keyword search for *collecting autographs* brought up these results on InfoTrac Junior Edition. Clicking on the title of a document or on the "Check Out" link brings up the text of the entire article.

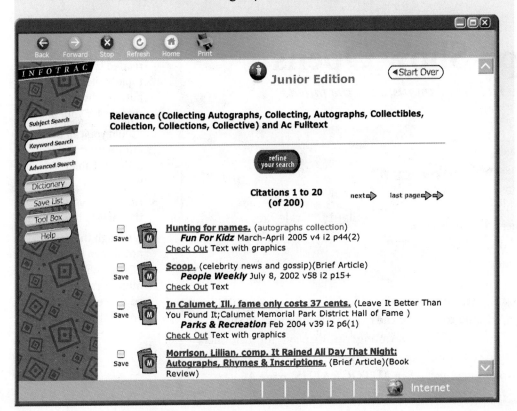

Close Read

1. If you were hunting for information on collecting autographs, which result would you click on first? Why?

2. These results are arranged by relevance, or how well they are related to the user's search terms. What does that tell you about the entries near the end of the list?

3. What could you click on to improve your search?

EVALUATE NEWSPAPERS AND PERIODICALS

Newspaper and magazine articles can be a good source of concise information. Your library may offer some of them in hard copies and many others online, on microfilm, or on microfiche. Once you find an article, you should evaluate it before you use it. Ask yourself these questions:

- **Is the source well-known and respected?** Most large-circulation newspapers and many national magazines are reliable. Avoid newspapers and magazines that cover mostly celebrity gossip, fad diets, UFOs, and similar topics.

- **When was it published?** Up-to-date is great, but not always best. For example, if you're researching the first moon landing, a newspaper article from 1969 could be your best source.

- **Who is the author?** Staff writers and contributing editors for major newspapers and magazines tend to be reliable. Some articles include notes about the authors' qualifications and previous publications.

- **Can the facts be verified?** Does the author give sources for the facts?

YOUR TURN

Examine a Newspaper Article

Ask questions to evaluate whether this article is adequate, accurate, and appropriate for a student seeking information on autograph collecting.

from the Springfield Courier

Autograph Show Opens

Exhibit features the rich, the famous, and the faded

BY TAISHA JACKSON, STAFF WRITER

The autographs of John F. Kennedy, Rosa Parks, and Tiger Woods will be on display for the next six weeks at the Ritter Museum's first-ever autograph show. Visitors will see those signatures and almost 1,200 others on letters, photographs, books, and documents.

Other highlights include a football signed by Joe Montana, a movie poster signed by Harrison Ford, and a very rare document with George Washington's signature.

Museum director Marcia Fiore calls this show a must for anyone interested

WHAT MAKES AN AUTOGRAPH VALUABLE?

Age/rareness

Popularity/"fickle factor"

Quality/condition

in collecting. "There's a ton of stuff here for the beginning collector," she adds.

Among the displays for beginners are a timeline of collecting history, tips **See AUTOGRAPHS, page A6**

Close Read

1. How well is this article related to the research topic "collecting autographs"? Give reasons for your answer.

2. Would you call the information in this article reliable? Why or why not?

3. How could you check the facts in this article?

4. Although they are not shown here, the newspaper's and museum's e-mail addresses appear at the end of the article. Why is this important?

Collecting Your Own Data

Although the library and the Internet are good resources, they are not the only places to get information. When you conduct an interview or learn by observation, you are doing original research.

INTERVIEWS

Interviews can be excellent means of gathering information. First, they provide primary-source information. Second, they can give you new insights into your topic or even whole new ways of looking at it.

You might interview someone who has in-depth knowledge of your topic. An interview can take place in person, or it can be conducted by telephone, e-mail, or letter. The most important part of an interview is preparing for it. Specific questions, prepared and thought through in advance, are a must.

See pages R81–R82: Interview

FIELD RESEARCH AND OBSERVATION

When you observe with a research goal in mind, you are doing **field research.** For example, if you want to know more about teddy bear collecting, you might do field research at a flea market that attracts teddy bear collectors. In that case, your field research might include creating a chart of available items and their prices. Or you might visit a museum if you want to learn about certain kinds of butterflies or about life during the European Middle Ages. Observations that you make and carefully record in these places are also field research.

Notes on Visit to Wharton County Flea Market, 5/21/2008

- *132 booths/tables/displays, only 4 with teddy bears*
- *military-themed bears: army, navy, marines, air force*
- *teddy bears with brand-name labels; also teddy bears that are sold along with children's books*
- *koala, panda, and other "bears"*
- *prices ranging from $1 to $1,500 (for a teddy bear from the 1950s)*
- *bears vary by clothing, ribbons, other accessories; some bears for holidays (Valentine's Day) or occasions (graduation)*

If you gather large amounts of data, you may want to create spreadsheets or databases to help you manage information or prepare your paper. See page R44 for details.

Research Tips and Strategies

Library Sleuth

Two basic systems are used to classify nonfiction books. Most high school and public libraries use the Dewey decimal system; university and research libraries generally use the Library of Congress system.

DEWEY DECIMAL SYSTEM

000–099	General works
100–199	Philosophy and psychology
200–299	Religion
300–399	Social sciences
400–499	Language
500–599	Natural sciences and mathematics
600–699	Technology (applied sciences)
700–799	Arts and recreation
800–899	Literature and rhetoric
900–999	Geography and history

LIBRARY OF CONGRESS SYSTEM

A	General works		L	Education
B	Philosophy, psychology, religion		M	Music
C	History		N	Fine arts
D	General and Old World history		P	Language and literature
E–F	American history		Q	Science
G	Geography, anthropology, recreation		R	Medicine
H	Social sciences		S	Agriculture
J	Political science		T	Technology
K	Law		U	Military science
			V	Naval science
			Z	Bibliography and library science

Web Watch

Knowing what search tools to use is crucial to finding information on the World Wide Web.

Search Engines

Search engines differ in speed, size of database, method of searching, and other variables. Never use only one search engine.

- Google
- Yahoo!
- Ask.com

Metasearch Engines

A metasearch tool can save you time by sending a search to multiple search engines simultaneously.

- TheInfo.com
- Dogpile
- Metacrawler

Directories

Directories are useful when you are researching a general topic, because they arrange resources into subject categories.

- AOL
- About.com
- Yahoo!

Virtual Libraries

At a virtual library, you can look up information in encyclopedias, directories, and indexes.
You can even e-mail a question to a librarian.

- Internet Public Library
- Librarians' Index to the Internet

Other Web Resources

Library catalogs: Library of Congress
Encyclopedias: Encyclopaedia Britannica Online
Newspaper archives: New York Times Index
Specialized databases: Medline

Writing and Research in a Digital Age
Discover a wealth of Web search tools and resources.

THINK central
KEYWORD: HML7-1026

Checklist for Evaluating Sources

☑ The information is relevant to the topic you are researching.

☑ The information is **valid** and up-to-date. (This point is especially important when researching time-sensitive fields such as science, medicine, and sports.)

☑ The information is from someone who is an **authority** on this topic.

☑ The information is from a trusted, **reliable** source that is updated or reviewed regularly.

☑ The author's or institution's purpose for writing is clear (whether the source is **objective** or biased).

☑ The information is written at the right level for your needs. For example, a children's book is probably too simplistic, while a scientific paper may be too complex.

☑ The information has the level of detail you need—neither too general nor too specific.

☑ The facts are **accurate** and can be verified in more than one source.

Sharing Your Research

At last you have established your research goal, located sources of information, evaluated the materials, and taken notes on what you learned. Now you have a chance to share the results with the people in your world—and even beyond. Here are some options:

- Use presentation software to create a power presentation for your classmates, friends, or family.

- Publish your research findings on a wiki.

- Develop a newsletter or brochure summarizing your information.

- Explain what you learned in an oral presentation to your classmates or to people in your community.

- Write up your research in a formal research paper. **See the following pages.** ▶

See pages 1044–1045: Creating a Wiki

Writing Workshop
INFORMATIVE TEXT

Research Paper

Now that you have explored a range of research skills, it's time to apply them. In this workshop, you will write a short research paper in which you show what you have learned about a topic and present your own ideas about it.

 Complete the workshop activities in your **Reader/Writer Notebook**.

WRITE WITH A PURPOSE

WRITING TASK

Write a **research paper** that presents information on a question that interests you.

Idea Starters

- What does it take to become a doctor?
- What was it like to be alive in the Middle Ages?
- How do television ads try to influence us?
- What is the future of the book as a form of communication?
- To what extent are pop singers good role models?

THE ESSENTIALS

Here are some common purposes, audiences, and formats for informative/explanatory writing.

PURPOSES	AUDIENCES	FORMATS
• to inform readers about a topic you have researched • to express ideas about a topic	• classmates and teacher • friends • co-workers • community members • Web users	• essay for class • feature article for a newspaper or newsletter • oral report • power presentation • wiki • documentary

COMMON CORE TRAITS

1. DEVELOPMENT OF IDEAS

- clearly introduces a topic and states a **controlling idea** that answers the **research question**
- supports the topic with **evidence,** such as **relevant facts, details,** and **quotations**
- draws information from **several sources**
- provides a **concluding section** that supports the information

2. ORGANIZATION OF IDEAS

- **logically organizes** ideas, concepts, and information
- includes **formatting, graphics,** and **multimedia** when useful
- uses **appropriate transitions** to connect ideas

3. LANGUAGE FACILITY AND CONVENTIONS

- uses **precise language** and **domain-specific vocabulary**
- maintains a **formal style**
- uses standard **format** for quoting or citing sources
- reflects **correct grammar, mechanics,** and **spelling**

Writing Online

THINK central

Go to thinkcentral.com.
KEYWORD: HML7N-1028

Planning/Prewriting

COMMON CORE — **W 2a–f** Write informative/explanatory texts to examine and convey ideas, concepts, and information. **W 5** Develop and strengthen writing as needed by planning. **W 7** Conduct short research projects to answer a question.

Getting Started

CHOOSE A TOPIC

For help in coming up with possible topics, use the Idea Starters on page 1028. You will be spending quite a bit of time researching and writing about your topic, so be sure to choose one that genuinely interests you. Also, think about whether you will be able to find information on the topic. You will need to draw on several reliable sources of information in your research paper.

▶ TIPS FOR FINDING A TOPIC

- Brainstorm a list of possible topics with a classmate.
- Consider hobbies, sports, art, music, and other interests you have.
- Think about historical events you have studied or writers whose work you have read in this unit.

NARROW YOUR FOCUS

Once you have selected a general topic, you need to decide how to focus on it. If a topic is too broad, you will not be able to cover it well in a short research paper. If it is too narrow, it may be hard to find good information about it. Use a graphic organizer, such as a cluster diagram, to help you narrow your topic.

TIP Check library catalogs and databases for information on a topic. If there's too little information, broaden your focus; if there's too much, you may need to limit your focus.

▶ WHAT DOES IT LOOK LIKE?

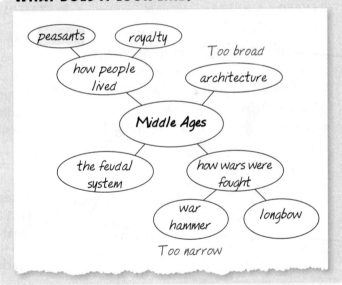

THINK ABOUT AUDIENCE AND PURPOSE

An essential step in planning your research paper is to identify your **audience** and your **purpose.** You will want to keep both in mind at all times as you gather information and develop the content of your paper.

▶ ASK YOURSELF:

- Who is my audience? What do I want these readers to learn about my topic?
- Is my audience familiar or unfamiliar with my topic? What background information will they need?
- What aspects of my topic would my audience find most interesting?

Planning/Prewriting *continued*

Getting Started

FORMULATE A RESEARCH QUESTION

Once you have a focused topic, you need to turn it into a major question that your research paper will answer. This question will keep you on track as you select sources and gather facts. It should be open-ended and not have a one-word answer. It's also helpful to develop more focused questions that are related to your major research question. These questions will help you find specific evidence to use in your paper.

▶ WHAT DOES IT LOOK LIKE?

Topic: peasants in the Middle Ages

Major Research Question: What was life like for a typical peasant in the Middle Ages?

Related Questions:
- What work did peasants do?
- Were they more like enslaved people or more like farmers?
- What were their homes like?
- What did they do besides work?

DEVELOP A RESEARCH PLAN

Create a plan that outlines your major research question, your purpose, your audience, several sources you might investigate, and your schedule. It's a good idea to have your teacher review and approve your plan before you get started on your research.

▶ TEMPLATE FOR A RESEARCH PLAN

Name: ....

Major Research Question: ....
....

Purpose: ....
Audience: ....
Possible Sources: ....
....

SCHEDULE
Research Due: ....
First Draft Due: ....
Final Draft Due: ....

Teacher Approval: ....

PEER REVIEW Have a classmate review your research plan. Ask if he or she thinks your major research question is clear, focused, and interesting. Then ask what other related questions a reader would want to be answered in your paper.

YOUR TURN List four or five topic ideas in your *Reader/Writer Notebook*. Think through each topic and pick the best one for your essay. Then narrow your topic and develop a major question to guide your research. With your purpose and audience in mind, prepare a research plan using the template above.

Researching

COMMON CORE

W 8 Gather relevant information from multiple sources; assess the credibility and accuracy of each source; quote or paraphrase the data and conclusions of others while avoiding plagiarism. **W 9b (RI 1)** Draw evidence from informational texts to support research.

Following Your Research Plan

LOCATE SOURCES

To find answers to your research questions, you'll need to gather information from a variety of sources. One of the best places to start is an encyclopedia, whether in print, online, or in CD-ROM form. You might begin by looking up a broad topic, such as "Middle Ages," to find a subsection on a narrower topic, such as "peasants."

Reading about your topic in an encyclopedia will give you ideas for specific **search terms,** or keywords, to use when you search on the Web or in a library catalog. Use a chart to keep track of the most promising sources you locate. Record the name of each source, where you found it, and brief comments on its usefulness.

See pages 1013–1015 and 1018–1019 for more information about research tools available to you.

▶ WHAT DOES IT LOOK LIKE?

Sources	Comments
General Encyclopedias "Middle Ages," <u>World Book Online</u> "Middle Ages," <u>World Book</u> (print)	interesting; good facts not a lot about peasants
Library Reference Books <u>Encyclopedia of the Middle Ages</u> (Ref 940.1 ENC) <u>Medieval Europe, 814–1350</u> (Ref 940.14 MED)	really hard to understand! good info; I can understand this
Other Library Materials <u>Life in the Middle Ages: The Serf</u> (J VIDEO 909.07 SERF) <u>Daily Life in Medieval Europe</u> (940.1 S617)	video from children's room terrific source; lots of facts, illustrations, explanation
Web Sites "The Middle Ages" "The Middle Ages: Life of a Medieval Peasant"	great; I bookmarked this easy to read; reliable?

EVALUATE EACH SOURCE

From your list of potential sources, you want to choose the most useful ones. But each source must also pass another test: it must be **credible,** or reliable and trustworthy. A source is credible if it is

- **relevant**—covers your specific topic
- **accurate**—contains information written or furnished by experts or well-informed writers
- **objective**—presents an unbiased viewpoint, or multiple viewpoints, on the topic

▶ ASK YOURSELF:

- What makes this source useful for my specific topic?
- What qualifies the author to write about this topic? If the author is not an expert, does he or she cite the work of experts?
- What, if any, signs of bias do I see—such as the intention to sell something or push certain ideas?

Researching *continued*

Following Your Research Plan

MAKE A SOURCE LIST

When doing research, it's important to keep track of the source for each fact you collect. You can record information about your sources in an electronic file or on index cards. Another option is to use special note-taking software that guides you through the research process. Your school librarian can tell you if this option is available.

Include the following details in your list of sources, making sure to number each source.

Online encyclopedia
- author (if given) and title of article
- name of publisher
- date of publication or posting (if given)
- medium of publication (Web)
- date you accessed the article

Print or CD-ROM encyclopedia
- author (if given) and title of article
- name and year of encyclopedia
- place of publication and publisher
- medium of publication (Print or CD-ROM)

World Wide Web site
- author (if given) and title of Web page or article
- name of site where page or article appears
- name of organization responsible for the site
- date created or posted (if given)
- medium (Web) and date accessed

Book
- author (or editor) and title
- place of publication and publisher
- year of publication
- library call number
- medium of publication (Print)

▶ WHAT DOES IT LOOK LIKE?

Online encyclopedia

> **Source #:** 1
> **Type:** Online encyclopedia
>
> Deliyannis, Deborah Mauskopf. "Middle Ages." *World Book Online Reference Center.* World Book. 2005. Web. 25 Feb. 2009.

Print encyclopedia

> **Source #:** 2
> **Type:** Print encyclopedia
>
> Lyon, Bryce. "Middle Ages." *The World Book Encyclopedia.* 2000 ed. Print.

World Wide Web site

> **Source #:** 3
> **Type:** Article on Web site
>
> "The Middle Ages: Homes." *Learner.org.* Annenberg/CPB. Web. 6 Mar. 2009.

Book

> **Source #:** 4
> **Type:** Book
>
> Singman, Jeffrey L. *Daily Life in Medieval Europe.* Westport, CT: Greenwood, 1999. 940.1 S617. Print.

Following Your Research Plan

TAKE NOTES

As you read your sources, look for information that answers your research questions. You can record each piece of information in an electronic file or on a separate index card. Include

- the source number (from your source list)
- a specific heading
- the fact or idea for your paper
- a page number, if one is available

▶ **WHAT DOES IT LOOK LIKE?**

Source #: 1 How long people lived
In the 900s, the average life span was just 30 years (online, no page number).
Comments/Questions: Why did they die so young?

RECORD INFORMATION ACCURATELY

There are three different methods you can use to capture a piece of information:

- **Quote**—copy the text exactly. You must put quotation marks around the words taken from your source.
- **Paraphrase**—restate the ideas in the text in your own words, including all of the main ideas and details in the same logical order as the original text. A paraphrase is about the same length as the original passage.
- **Summarize**—tell the main idea and the most significant details. A summary is shorter than the original passage.

TIP A good summary reflects the underlying meaning of the passage and omits less important details.

▶ **WHAT DOES IT LOOK LIKE?**

Original Source

Each house was a simple single-room, single-story, high-roofed structure. At the center of the room was an open-hearth fire on the packed-earth floor; it vented through a hole in the roof.

Hackett, Jeremiah, ed., Medieval Europe, 814–1350

Paraphrase

Source #: 5 Peasants' homes
A peasant's home was just one room with high walls, a roof, and a dirt floor. Each home had a fireplace in the middle and an opening in the roof to let the smoke out (158).

Summary

Source #: 5 Peasants' homes
A peasant's home was just a hut with a place for a fire in the middle (158).

Researching *continued*

Following Your Research Plan

AVOID PLAGIARISM

Plagiarism is the use of other people's words and ideas without an explanation of where the words and ideas came from. It is a way of taking credit for research and thinking that you didn't do—and that's dishonest. Here are some tips to help you avoid plagiarizing:

- **Summarize and paraphrase often when taking notes.** This will help you avoid lifting other people's words when you draft.
- **Don't rely heavily on one source.** The more you read from many authors, the more likely you are to see a bigger picture—and start developing your own ideas and opinions on the topic.
- **Put away all your sources when you draft.** At that time, use only your note cards or electronic notes.
- **Use brackets and ellipses within quotations.** Brackets ([ ]) tell your reader that you have added a word or phrase to a quotation to make it clearer, like this: "The fortunate peasant might have a cow [tied up near] the garden." Ellipses (. . .) tell your reader that you have left out some words from the quotation, like this: "grazing on the . . . grasses."

TIP When you use distinctive phrases that someone else wrote, you must credit the source. For example, if a source uses the phrase "the fortunate peasant" and you use that phrase without citing the source, you are plagiarizing.

▶ WHAT DOES IT LOOK LIKE?

Original Source

Children have weak immune systems, and the high incidence of disease and limited medical knowledge of the period meant that many children never reached adulthood. During the thirteenth century, about one child in six may have died in the first year, one in four by age five; perhaps two-thirds lived to age twenty.

Singman, Jeffrey L., Daily Life in Medieval Europe

Plagiarized

> In the thirteenth century, about one child in six may have died in the first year.

Correctly Documented

> Singman explains that during the 1200s, one child out of every six died before his or her first birthday (18).

Original Source

The fortunate peasant might have a cow tethered at the base of the garden grazing on the naturally growing grasses.

Hackett, Jeremiah, ed., Medieval Europe, 814–1350

Plagiarized

> The fortunate peasant might have a cow tied up at the edge of the garden.

Correctly Documented

> Only "the fortunate peasant" might have a cow (Hackett 159).

Following Your Research Plan

WRITE YOUR CONTROLLING IDEA

Ask yourself: What are the answers to my most important or interesting research questions? Use them to decide what main point you want to make about your topic. Record this main point in a **controlling idea,** or a thesis statement. Remember that your controlling idea doesn't have to be perfect right now. You can revise it later.

TIP Your controlling idea governs what information you will present to your readers and how the parts of your paper will be arranged.

▶ ### WHAT DOES IT LOOK LIKE?

Answers to Some of My Research Questions:
- Peasants didn't have a life of their own. They had to do what their lord wanted.
- They farmed—long, hard work!
- Their homes were small and basic and had farm animals in them (yuck).
- Peasants didn't live long.

Controlling Idea:
Peasants had to do what their lord wanted, worked hard, had bad homes, and didn't live long.

CREATE AN OUTLINE

Read through the notes you made in your file or on your note cards. Group notes with the same or similar headings. Then review your notes again. Look for three or four key ideas that stand out. These will become main entries in your outline. Write or type your outline, including several supporting facts or details under each main entry.

TIP When organizing notes in a word-processing file, highlight the note and then copy and paste it—or drag and drop it—next to other notes with the same or similar headings.

▶ ### WHAT DOES IT LOOK LIKE?

The Hard Lives of Peasants
I. What was life like during the Middle Ages?
  A. Movies make medieval life seem glamorous.
  B. However, peasants' lives were very difficult.
II. Each day was a struggle.
  A. Peasants had to grow or make everything.
  B. They had to do extra jobs for their lord.
  C. They could earn money but couldn't buy much.
  D. They had terrible homes.
  E. They didn't live long.
III. Peasants cared about crops, not castles.
  A. It was tough to be a peasant.
  B. People don't know what it was really like.

YOUR TURN Locate and evaluate sources related to your major research question. Then prepare a source list and take notes. Use your notes to draft a controlling idea and develop an outline. If necessary, narrow or broaden your major research question so that you can answer it thoroughly in your research paper.

Drafting

The following chart gives a framework for drafting a research paper.

Organizing Your Research Paper

INTRODUCTION

- Lead with a **quotation,** an **anecdote,** or a **question** that will get your readers' attention.
- Provide enough **details** for readers to understand the topic.
- State your **controlling idea**—the main idea of your paper—which you developed from your investigation of your research questions.
- Establish a **formal style** by avoiding contractions and choosing precise language.

▼

BODY

- Present each idea that **supports** your controlling idea in a separate paragraph. (These should be the main entries in your outline.)
- Support the main idea of each paragraph with **evidence** you have gathered and organized in your notes. If you find a "hole" in your evidence, go back to your notes or sources to find what you need.
- Include a variety of **facts, details,** and **quotations.** Introduce quotations with phrases such as "According to Jeffrey Singman" or "Singman believes."
- Arrange your main ideas in a systematic way. Use **transitions** to create cohesion (a smooth flow) and show how ideas or facts are related to each other.
- **Synthesize** information—that is, use prior knowledge and evidence from a variety of sources to draw original conclusions about your topic.
- Define **domain-specific,** or specialized, terms that may be unfamiliar.
- Consider using a **chart, graph,** or **diagram** to aid comprehension or emphasize an idea. Add a source line to show where you found specific facts or figures in the graphic.

▼

CONCLUDING SECTION

- Restate your controlling idea and **summarize** your main points.
- **Reflect** on the information you have shared, and leave readers with something to think about, such as an unanswered question or a reason why your topic is important.

▼

WORKS CITED LIST

- Include a **Works Cited list** as a separate page at the end of your draft.
- Use a **style guide,** such as the *Modern Language Association Handbook for Writers of Research Papers* or *The Chicago Manual of Style,* to make sure you are correct and consistent in citing sources.
- List sources in **alphabetical order** by the author's last name (or by the work's title if no author is given).
- Begin each entry on a **new line**; indent additional lines of an entry by one-half inch.

LEARN HOW **Cite Sources** As you draft your paper, you need to credit the sources of quotations and specific facts. Very basic facts found in nearly every source do not need to be documented—for example, the fact that peasants were the lowest class in medieval society. However, most facts require a citation in parentheses at the end of the sentence.

COMMON CORE

W 4 Produce clear and coherent writing. **W 8** Follow a standard format for citation. **L 2** Demonstrate a command of the conventions of standard English punctuation.

Guidelines for Citing Sources in a Research Paper

Source with one author—author's last name, page number (if any)	▶ Peasants "worked from sunrise to sunset" (Hackett 158).
Author or editor named in sentence—page number only	▶ All this work and all these costs made life hard. No wonder Hackett says that peasants "worked from sunrise to sunset" (158).
Author unknown—shortened title of the work, page number (if any)	▶ Peasants who survived had few comforts, because "most medieval homes were cold, damp, and dark" ("Middle Ages").
Multiple sources for one fact—first author's last name, page number (if any); second author's last name, page number; and so on	▶ A peasant's diet was simple: bread, beans, chicken, eggs, vegetables, and perhaps milk and cheese (Deliyannis; "Middle Ages"; Singman 70).

GRAMMAR IN CONTEXT: PUNCTUATING TITLES

When citing or listing sources, follow these rules for punctuating the titles of works.

Rule	*Example*
Underline or italicize titles of books, encyclopedias, movies, magazines, newspapers, CDs, TV and radio programs, and Web sites.	▶ One of the best books on this topic is Hackett's *Medieval Europe, 814–1350.*
Use **quotation marks** around titles of short stories, chapters in a book, encyclopedia articles, magazine or newspaper articles, and single Web pages.	▶ "The Middle Ages: Homes." *Learner.org.* Annenberg/CPB. Web. 6 Mar. 2009.

YOUR TURN Develop a first draft of your research paper. Remember to cite sources consistently. Make sure you use the correct punctuation for titles in both the body of your paper and your Works Cited list.

Revising

In this stage, you evaluate the content, structure, and style of your draft with your purpose and audience in mind. The chart below can help you revise, rewrite, or try a new approach.

RESEARCH PAPER

Ask Yourself	Tips	Revision Strategies
1. Does the introduction clearly state your controlling idea? Does it grab the reader's attention?	**Underline** the controlling idea. **Put brackets** around the "hook" used to grab the audience's attention.	**Add** or clarify your controlling idea. **Add** an attention-grabber.
2. Does each body paragraph develop a main point related to the controlling idea?	In the margin, **label** each paragraph with the main point it develops.	**Cut** unrelated ideas. **Rearrange** information into separate paragraphs where necessary.
3. Does the paper present supporting evidence for each main point?	**Highlight** the facts, examples, statistics, and quotations that support each main point.	**Add** supporting details from your notes, if necessary.
4. Is information properly paraphrased, summarized, or quoted?	**Circle** sentences that sound as if someone else wrote them. **Draw a wavy line** under the quoted information.	**Replace** circled sentences with your own words, or **add** quotation marks.
5. Does the conclusion restate the controlling idea and summarize the writer's findings?	**Put a check mark** next to the restatement. **Put a star** next to the summary.	**Add** a restatement. **Elaborate** on your findings.
6. Does the Works Cited list include at least three sources? Is each one correctly cited?	**Number** the sources listed. **Put a check mark** next to each one that is cited in the paper.	**Add** sources to the Works Cited list, if necessary. **Delete** from the list any sources that are not used in the paper.

YOUR TURN

PEER REVIEW Ask a peer to read your paper and suggest improvements using the chart on this page. In addition, ask: Does my paper answer my major research question? Are there any confusing sentences or passages that I need to clarify? Identify which parts of your draft, if any, need reworking or a new approach.

ANALYZE A STUDENT DRAFT

Read this student's draft and the comments about it.

COMMON CORE

W 2d Use precise language.
W 5 Strengthen writing by revising, editing, rewriting, or trying a new approach, focusing on how well purpose and audience have been addressed.

Latushkin 1

Alex Latushkin
Ms. Tokoyuni
English 7
March 12, 2010

A Short, Hard Life

❶   What was it like to be alive during the Middle Ages? Movies and television shows make the Middle Ages seem exciting. However, most Europeans of the time were peasants, and their lives were anything but glamorous. Peasants were at the bottom of the society, so they struggled to survive, had few comforts, and lived short lives.

❷   For the typical peasant, each day was a struggle. Peasants had to grow their own food and make everything they needed to live. They also had to grow grain for their lord, who owned the land. Farming was backbreaking work in the Middle Ages because peasants had only basic tools, such as plows and pitchforks, instead of machinery (Hackett 254). If crops failed for any reason, the peasants didn't have enough to eat.

> Alex's **introduction** includes a clear **controlling idea,** but he needs to do more to grab his readers' attention.

> Here Alex supports a main point with a **paraphrase** from one of his sources.

LEARN HOW **Write an Effective Introduction** Alex begins his paper with a question, which sparks the reader's curiosity. However, the next sentence is dull and not very descriptive. To enliven his hook and better engage his audience, Alex added precise words that create a vivid image in the reader's mind.

ALEX'S REVISION TO PARAGRAPH ❶

     What was it like to be alive during the Middle Ages? Movies and television *have led many people to imagine handsome young knights dodging swords, arrows, and axes as they storm a castle.*
shows ~~make the Middle Ages seem exciting.~~ However, most Europeans of the
          ^   *not knights,*
time were peasants, and their lives were anything but glamorous.
          ^

3   A peasant's struggle to survive did not end with growing crops. Peasants "had few rights and were almost completely at the mercy of their lords" (Deliyannis). Besides growing food for their lord, they had to do services for him. For example, they might have to build roads or cut wood for him. They even had to fight sometimes, although they did not have training or good weapons. Peasants also had to pay one-tenth of everything they produced to the church (Singman 100). All this work and all of these costs made life hard. No wonder Hackett says that peasants "worked from sunrise to sunset" (158).

> The first sentence here makes a **transition** from the previous paragraph. Other transitions link ideas within the paragraph.

4   Even though some peasants earned a little money through their labor, they still struggled. According to Singman, in England in the late 1200s, some peasants could earn about 1 d. (one English penny) per day (59). As this chart shows, that didn't buy very much.

Some Thirteenth-Century Prices	
1 loaf of bread . . . . 1/4 d.	1 ax . . . . .4 d.
1 dozen eggs. . . . . 1/2 d.	1 pound of candles. . . . . . .6 d.

Source: Singman 60.

> A **chart** of numerical data illustrates one of Alex's points in the text.

5   Peasants who survived had few comforts because "most medieval homes were cold, damp, and dark" ("Middle Ages"). A peasant's home was just a hut with a place for a fire in the middle (Hackett 158). Pigs and chickens might live in the house with the family. The floor was dirt or clay, and there was not much light or heat. People slept on sacks of straw on the floor. For furniture, there might have been a stool, a bench, and maybe a table (Singman 84–85). A peasant's diet was simple: bread, beans, chicken, eggs, vegetables (such as cabbage and onions), and perhaps milk and cheese (Deliyannis; "Middle Ages"; Singman 70). Only "the fortunate peasant" might have a cow (Hackett 159).

> Alex synthesizes facts from **multiple sources** and uses the correct formats for **parenthetical citations.**

Latushkin 3

6   Compared with today, people in the Middle Ages had short lives. They faced "malnutrition, poor hygiene, parasitic infections, and disease" (Hackett 158). Singman explains that during the 1200s, one child out of every six died before his or her first birthday (18). Many others died before they became adults. Deliyannis says the average life span was 30 years in the 900s. Old age was especially hard on peasants. Singman believes that many old peasants had to beg to survive (31). After a lifetime of hard work, it must have been terrible to beg for a crust of bread.

Alex smoothly integrates a **direct quotation** into this paragraph.

Here Alex shows his own **perspective** on what he has learned while maintaining an appropriately **formal style.**

7   Many films and television shows make life in the European Middle Ages seem exciting and glamorous. The peasants probably had a different view of things. Their lives were short and hard, and their crops meant far more to them than any castle did.

A thoughtful **concluding section** refers back to the introduction and summarizes the writing.

Latushkin 4

Works Cited

Deliyannis, Deborah Mauskopf. "Middle Ages." World Book
     Online Reference Center. World Book. 2005. Web. 25 Feb. 2009

Hackett, Jeremiah, ed. *Medieval Europe, 814–1350.* World Eras 4.
     Detroit: Gale, 2002. Print.

The Middle Ages: Homes. *Learner.org.* Annenberg/CPB. Web.
     6 Mar. 2009

Singman, Jeffrey L. *Daily Life in Medieval Europe.* Westport, CT:
     Greenwood, 1999. Print

LEARN HOW Format a Works Cited List It's important to cite all of your sources according to the guidelines your teacher gives you. In preparing his Works Cited list, Alex did not consistently follow these guidelines:

- End each entry with a period.
- Italicize the name of a Web site.
- Place quotation marks around the title of a Web page or article.

Notice Alex's revisions in blue.

YOUR TURN Use feedback from your peers and teacher as well as the two "Learn How" lessons to revise or rewrite parts of your research paper.

COMMON CORE

W 5 Strengthen writing by editing.
L 1b Choose among simple, compound, and complex sentences.
L 2 Demonstrate command of the conventions of standard English capitalization, punctuation, and spelling.

Editing and Publishing

In the editing stage, you proofread your paper to correct errors in grammar, spelling, and mechanics before sharing it with an audience. You should also review these guidelines to be sure your paper is correctly formatted:

- Leave one-inch margins at the top, bottom, and sides of each page (except for page numbers).
- On the first page, at the top left, type your name, your teacher's name, the class, and the date (as shown on page 1039).
- On each page, type your last name and the page number one-half inch from the top in the right corner.
- Double-space all text, including the Works Cited list.
- Indent paragraphs one-half inch from the left margin.

GRAMMAR IN CONTEXT: WRITING COMPLEX SENTENCES

As you edit your draft, you may find places where combining two simple sentences into a complex sentence could help you explain a point more clearly. A **complex sentence** has a main clause and a dependent clause that adds meaning to the main clause.

By joining two simple sentences to make a complex sentence, Alex clarified the contrast between two ideas. He correctly added a comma after the dependent clause.

> *Although*
> ^Many films and television shows make life in the European Middle Ages seem exciting and glamorous. The peasants probably had a different view of things. Their lives were short and hard, and their crops meant far more to them than any castle did.

PUBLISH YOUR WRITING

Here are some ways you might share your research paper with an audience:

- Make copies of your paper and distribute them to others who are likely to be interested in your topic, or e-mail electronic copies.
- Deliver an oral report to classmates or interested community members.
- Turn your paper into a **wiki,** a series of Web pages on which you and other classmates add and edit information about your topic.

YOUR TURN

Proofread your draft to correct errors and polish the text. Create complex sentences where it would help to clarify your points. Then publish your final research paper where it will reach your audience.

Scoring Rubric

Use the rubric below to evaluate your research paper.

RESEARCH PAPER

SCORE	COMMON CORE TRAITS
6	• **Development** Effectively introduces a topic; states an insightful, well-researched controlling idea; offers varied and relevant evidence; ends powerfully • **Organization** Logically organizes information; includes formatting, graphics, or multimedia to enhance the information; effectively uses varied transitions • **Language** Ably uses precise words; maintains a formal style; shows a strong command of conventions; correctly cites all sources
5	• **Development** Competently introduces a topic; states a well-researched and clear controlling idea; offers relevant evidence; has a strong concluding section • **Organization** Is logically organized; includes formatting, graphics, or multimedia; effectively uses transitions • **Language** Uses precise words; generally maintains a formal style; has a few errors in conventions; correctly cites sources
4	• **Development** Sufficiently introduces a topic; states a clear controlling idea; offers mostly relevant evidence; has an adequate concluding section • **Organization** Is mostly logically organized; could use some more formatting, graphics, or multimedia; needs more transitions • **Language** Uses some vague words; mostly maintains a formal style; includes a few distracting errors in conventions; incorrectly formats a few source citations
3	• **Development** States a controlling idea, but the introduction could be more engaging; lacks enough evidence; has a somewhat weak concluding section • **Organization** Has some flaws in organization; doesn't include enough formatting, graphics, or multimedia; lacks many transitions • **Language** Needs more precise words; has frequent lapses in style; has some critical errors in conventions; incorrectly formats some source citations
2	• **Development** Has a weak controlling idea; does not support ideas; ends abruptly • **Organization** Lacks organization, formatting, multimedia, and transitions • **Language** Lacks precise words or uses them incorrectly; uses an informal style; has many errors in conventions; does not cite all sources and cites many incorrectly
1	• **Development** Lacks a controlling idea, development, and a concluding section • **Organization** Has no organization, formatting, graphics, multimedia, or transitions • **Language** Uses vague words; has an inappropriate style; has major problems in conventions; plagiarizes or does not credit sources

Creating a Wiki

Producing a wiki is one way to creatively share the information you have gathered for a research project. A **wiki** is an interactive Web site made by people working together to collect, review, and discuss information on a topic.

 Complete the workshop activities in your **Reader/Writer Notebook.**

PRODUCE WITH A PURPOSE

TASK

Create a **wiki** that uses text, graphics, multimedia, and links to present information on a topic. Collaborate with a team of classmates to collect and organize information and then share it with others.

COMMON CORE TRAITS

A STRONG WIKI . . .

- focuses on an interesting topic
- includes group planning documents, such as a project schedule and a description of roles
- shows proof of collaboration, including peer editing and discussion threads
- has an appealing design that fits the topic, purpose, and audience
- presents information effectively, using text, graphics, multimedia, and links

COMMON CORE

W 6 Use technology to produce writing. **SL 1b, d** Follow rules for collegial discussions, track progress toward specific goals and deadlines, and define roles. Acknowledge information expressed by others and modify views. **SL 5** Include multimedia in presentations.

Set Up the Wiki

Before creating your wiki, develop a research topic and some related questions that you want to answer. Then use these tips to create your wiki:

- **Launch the project.** Meet with your team to decide how you will present your research. How many pages will you include? What information will appear on each page? Acknowledge other people's ideas and be willing to modify your own views to make compromises. Take notes on your discussion, and vote on any issues on which team members disagree.

- **Assign research tasks.** Assign different aspects of the research to each team member. For example, for a wiki on life in the Middle Ages, one person might investigate the lives of peasants. Another might focus on knights.

- **Select a moderator.** The moderator, or administrator, manages the Web pages and invites others to view and comment on your team's research. Other team members write and edit the information that will appear in the wiki.

- **Set up a schedule.** As a team, create a project plan that gives deadlines for the researching, writing, and editing stages.

- **Build your wiki.** With help from your school technology coordinator, choose a free Web site to host your wiki. Then create the basic structure of your site. Choose a title and upload your planning documents.

Media Tools

THINK central

Go to **thinkcentral.com**.
KEYWORD: HML7-1044

Develop the Wiki

Follow these guidelines to make your wiki worth visiting:

- **Do the research.** Using Web sites, books, and others sources, gather information on the topic assigned to you. See pages 1016–1017 and 1020–1024 for guidelines on evaluating sources.

- **Stay in touch with your team.** Use the wiki's communication tools, such as **discussion threads**—chains of related messages. Report on your progress, ask a question, or get feedback from team members.

- **Create your pages.** Present the information you found in your wiki. Consider using easy-to-read bulleted lists to format your findings. Don't forget to cite all your sources.

- **Add links.** Look for opportunities to link to other pages within your wiki or to other Web sites on the same topic.

- **Go graphic.** Use visuals and multimedia to clarify and emphasize the information on your pages. If you plan to include copyrighted items, ask permission from the person or organization that holds the rights to those items.

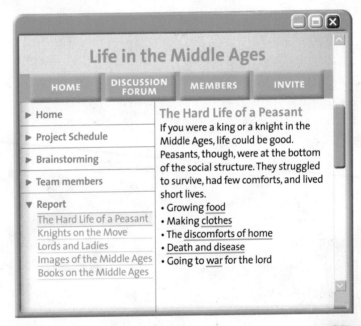

Life in the Middle Ages

| HOME | DISCUSSION FORUM | MEMBERS | INVITE |

▶ Home
▶ Project Schedule
▶ Brainstorming
▶ Team members
▼ Report
　The Hard Life of a Peasant
　Knights on the Move
　Lords and Ladies
　Images of the Middle Ages
　Books on the Middle Ages

The Hard Life of a Peasant
If you were a king or a knight in the Middle Ages, life could be good. Peasants, though, were at the bottom of the social structure. They struggled to survive, had few comforts, and lived short lives.
- Growing food
- Making clothes
- The discomforts of home
- Death and disease
- Going to war for the lord

- **Review and revise.** Ask a team member to read your pages and offer feedback on the information and how it is arranged. Make final changes to the pages you wrote.

- **Design your home page.** Create a visually appealing home page. Include an inviting statement summarizing the contents of your wiki, a catchy title, and graphics.

- **Invite your teacher and classmates to explore.** When you have put the finishing touches on your wiki, send an e-mail inviting others to read and respond to your research.

YOUR TURN Plan and produce a wiki using the guidelines on these pages. Visit your wiki often after you've launched it. Make an effort to respond to comments from users and update the information as needed.

Student Resource Bank

R1

Reading any text—short story, poem, magazine article, newspaper, Web page—requires the use of special strategies. For example, you might plot the events of a short story on a diagram, while you may use text features to spot main ideas in a magazine article. You also need to identify patterns of organization in the text. Using such strategies can help you read different texts with ease and also help you understand what you're reading.

COMMON CORE

Included in this handbook:
RI 1, RI 2, RI 3, RI 4, RI 5, RI 6, RI 8, RI 10

1 Reading Literary and Nonfiction Texts

Literary and **nonfiction texts** include short stories, novels, poems, dramas, biographies, autobiographies, and essays. To appreciate and analyze literary and nonfiction texts, you will need to understand the characteristics of each type of text.

1.1 READING A SHORT STORY
Strategies for Reading

- Read the **title.** As you read the story, you may notice that the title has a special meaning.

- Keep track of **events** as they happen. Plot the events on a diagram like this one.

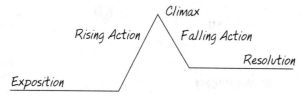

- From the details the writer provides, **visualize** the characters. **Predict** what they might do next.

- Look for specific adjectives that help you visualize the **setting**—the time and place in which events occur.

1.2 READING A POEM
Strategies for Reading

- Notice the **form** of the poem, or the number of its lines and their arrangement on the page.

- Read the poem aloud a few times. Listen for **rhymes** and **rhythms.**

- **Visualize** the images and comparisons.

- **Connect** with the poem by asking yourself what message the poet is trying to send.

- Create a word web or another **graphic organizer** to record your reactions and questions.

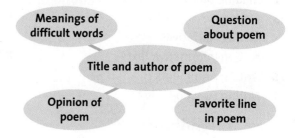

1.3 READING A PLAY
Strategies for Reading

- Read the stage directions to help you **visualize** the setting and characters.

- **Question** what the title means and why the playwright chose it.

- Identify the main conflict (struggle or problem) in the play. To **clarify** the conflict, make a chart that shows what the conflict is and how it is resolved.

- **Evaluate** the characters. What do they want? How do they change during the play? You may want to make a chart that lists each character's name, appearance, and traits.

1.4 READING LITERARY NONFICTION
Strategies for Reading

- If you are reading a biography, an autobiography, or another type of biographical writing, such as a diary, a memoir, or letters, use a family tree or word web to keep track of the people mentioned.

- When reading an essay, **evaluate** the writer's ideas. Is there a clear main or central idea? Does the writer use appropriate details to support a main idea?

❷ Reading Informational Texts: Text Features

An **informational text** is writing that provides factual information. Informational materials, such as chapters in textbooks and articles in magazines, encyclopedias, and newspapers, usually contain elements that help the reader recognize their purpose, organization, and central ideas. These elements are known as **text features.**

2.1 UNDERSTANDING TEXT FEATURES

Text features are design elements of a text that indicate its organizational structure or otherwise make its central ideas and information understandable. Text features include titles, headings, subheadings, boldface type, bulleted and numbered lists, and graphic aids, such as charts, graphs, illustrations, and photographs. Notice how the text features help you find key information on the textbook page shown.

Ⓐ The **title** identifies the topic.

Ⓑ A **subheading** indicates the start of a new topic or section and identifies the focus of that section.

Ⓒ **Questions** may be used to focus your understanding of the text.

Ⓓ A **bulleted list** shows items of equal importance.

Ⓔ **Graphic aids,** such as illustrations, photographs, charts, diagrams, maps, and timelines, often make ideas in the text clearer.

Ⓕ A **caption,** or the text that accompanies a graphic aid, gives information about the graphic aid that isn't necessarily obvious from the image itself.

PRACTICE AND APPLY

1. What is the first subhead following the title?

2. Reread the Essential Question. Identify one lasting contribution of Roman culture.

3. What activity does the mosaic portray? What do you learn from the caption?

Ⓓ ▶ TERMS & NAMES
mosaic
Stoicism
aqueduct

Ⓐ The Legacy of Rome

Build on What You Know Look at the buildings in your community. Do some have columns or domes? Are there bridges with arches? If so, these structures may have features that developed during the Roman Empire.

Ⓑ The Impact of Roman Culture

Ⓒ **ESSENTIAL QUESTION** What lasting contributions of Roman culture influenced later societies?

As Roman culture developed, it borrowed many aspects of Greek civilization. The Greeks, as you recall, were the dominant civilization in the Mediterranean before the Romans. The Romans conquered the Greeks but kept alive many of their ways. In addition, Roman artists, philosophers, and writers created their own styles that would influence many societies to follow.

Roman Art The Romans popularized an earlier type of floor art called mosaic. A **mosaic** is a picture made out of many small, colored tiles or pieces of glass. Examples of mosaics can still be found in churches and government buildings around the world.

Sculptural styles from the Roman era are also a regular sight in modern times. The Greeks were the first to create statues based on realistic forms. The Romans adopted this style. The Statue of Liberty in New York Harbor is one example of a modern statue whose style dates back to Greek and Roman times.

Ⓕ **Roman Mosaic**
This mosaic shows Roman fighters battling wild animals, a popular spectator sport among Romans. ▼

Ⓔ

67

2.2 USING TEXT FEATURES

You can use text features to locate information, to help you understand it, and to take notes. Just use the following strategies when you encounter informational text.

Strategies for Reading

- **Preview** the text by looking at the title, headings, and subheadings to get an idea of the main concepts and the way the text is organized.

- Before you begin reading the text more thoroughly, **skim** it—read it quickly—to get an overview.

- Read any **questions** that appear at the end of a lesson or chapter. Doing this will help you set a purpose for your reading.

- Turn subheadings into questions. Then use the text below the subheadings to answer the questions. Your answers will be a **summary** of the text.

- **Take notes** by turning headings and subheadings into main ideas, or central ideas. You might use a chart like the following.

The Legacy of Rome	Main heading
Impact of Roman culture	Notes: 1. borrowed from Greeks 2. created their own styles 3. example is mosaic

Subheading

- As you read to locate particular facts or details, **scan** the text. Look for key words and phrases as you move slowly down the page.

2.3 TURNING TEXT HEADINGS INTO OUTLINE ENTRIES

After you have read a selection at least once, you can use text features to take notes in outline form. The following outline shows how one student used text headings from the sample page on page R3. Study the outline and use the strategies that follow to create an outline based on text features.

I. Legacy of Rome
  A. Impact of Roman culture
    1. Roman Art
      a. mosaic
      b. sculpture
  B.
    1.
    2.

Main heading roman numeral entry

Subheading capital letter entry

Detail number entry

Strategies for Using Text Headings

- Preview the headings and subheadings in the text to get an idea of what different kinds there are and what their positions might be in an outline.

- Be consistent. Note that subheadings that are the same size and color should be used consistently in Roman-numeral or capital-letter entries in the outline. If you decide that a chapter heading should appear with a Roman numeral, then that's the level at which all other chapter headings should appear.

- Write the headings and subheadings that you will use as your Roman-numeral and capital-letter entries first. As you read, fill in numbered details from the text under the headings and subheadings in your outline.

PRACTICE AND APPLY

Reread "Like Black Smoke: The Black Death's Journey," pages 930–934. Use text features in the selection to take notes in outline form.

Preview the subheadings in the text to get an idea of the different kinds. Write the headings and subheadings you are using as your Roman-numeral and capital-letter entries first. Then fill in the details.

2.4 GRAPHIC AIDS

Information is communicated not only with words but also with graphic aids. **Graphic aids** are visual representations of verbal statements. They can be charts, webs, diagrams, graphs, photographs, or other visual representations of information. Graphic aids usually make complex information easier to understand. For that reason, graphic aids are often used to organize, simplify, and summarize information for easy reference.

Graphs

Graphs are used to illustrate statistical information. A **graph** is a drawing that shows the relative values of numerical quantities. Different kinds of graphs are used to show different numerical relationships.

Strategies for Reading

Ⓐ Read the title.

Ⓑ Find out what is being represented or measured.

Ⓒ In a circle graph, compare the sizes of the parts.

Ⓓ In a line graph, study the slant of the line. The steeper the line, the faster the rate of change.

Ⓔ In a bar graph, compare the lengths of the bars.

A **circle graph,** or **pie graph,** shows the relationships of parts to a whole. The entire circle equals 100 percent. The parts of the circle represent percentages of the whole.

MODEL: CIRCLE GRAPH

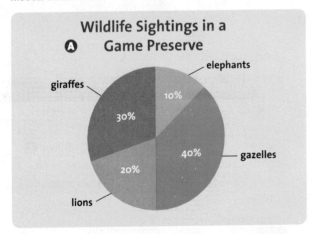

Line graphs show changes in numerical quantities over time and are effective in presenting trends such as world population growth. A line graph is made on a grid. Here, the vertical axis indicates quantity, and the horizontal axis shows years. Points on the graph indicate data. The line that connects the points highlights a trend or pattern.

MODEL: LINE GRAPH

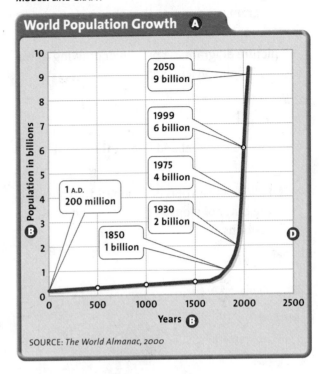

SOURCE: *The World Almanac, 2000*

In a **bar graph,** vertical or horizontal bars are used to show or compare categories of information, such as voting trends. The lengths of the bars indicate the quantities.

MODEL: BAR GRAPH

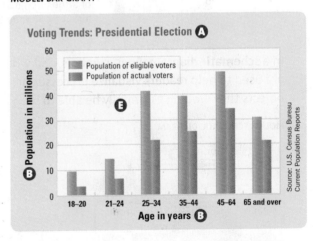

Source: U.S. Census Bureau Current Population Reports

WATCH OUT! Evaluate carefully the information presented in graphs. For example, circle graphs show major factors and differences well but tend to reduce the importance of smaller factors and differences.

Diagrams

A **diagram** is a drawing that shows how something works or how its parts relate to one another.

A **picture diagram** is a picture or drawing of the subject being discussed.

Strategies for Reading

Ⓐ Read the title.

Ⓑ Read each label and look at the part it identifies.

Ⓒ Follow any arrows or numbers that show the order of steps in a process, and read any captions.

MODEL: PICTURE DIAGRAM

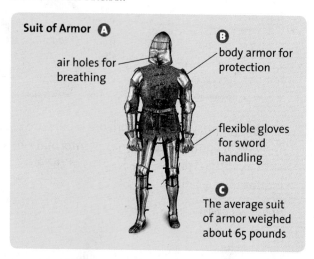

Suit of Armor Ⓐ

air holes for breathing

Ⓑ body armor for protection

flexible gloves for sword handling

Ⓒ The average suit of armor weighed about 65 pounds

In a **schematic diagram,** lines, symbols, and words are used to help readers visualize processes or objects they wouldn't normally be able to see.

MODEL: SCHEMATIC DIAGRAM

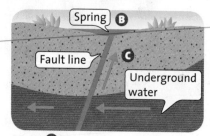

Spring Ⓑ

Fault line Ⓒ

Underground water

Oasis Ⓐ
An oasis is a fertile or green spot in the midst of a desert.

Charts and Tables

A **chart** presents information, shows a process, or makes comparisons, usually in rows or columns.

A **table** is a specific type of chart that presents a collection of facts in rows and columns and shows how the facts relate to one another.

Strategies for Reading

Ⓐ Read the title to learn what information the chart or table covers.

Ⓑ Study column headings and row labels to determine the categories of information presented.

Ⓒ Look down columns and across rows to find specific information.

MODEL: CHART

Size of Selected Civilizations Ⓐ		
Civilization	Ⓑ Dates	Size (est.) millions of sq. miles
Persia	559–330 B.C.	Ⓒ 2.0
Rome	27 B.C.–A.D. 476	3.40
Mongol	1206–1368	11.7
Aztec	1325–1521	0.2
United States	1776	3.7

MODEL: TABLE

The Beaufort Scale of Wind Strength Ⓐ		
Wind Ⓑ	Wind Speed	Effect of Wind
Calm (0)	Less than 1 kph	smoke rises straight up.
Light air (1)	1 to 5 kph	Smoke drifts. Ⓒ
Light breeze (2)	6 to 11 kph	Wind felt on face.
Gentle breeze (3)	12 to 19 kph	Leaves and twigs move.
Moderate breeze (4)	20 to 28 kph	Flags flap.
Fresh breeze (5)	29 to 38 kph	Small trees sway.
Strong breeze (6)	39 to 49 kph	Large branches move.
Moderate gale (7)	50 to 61 kph	Whole trees sway.
Fresh gale (8)	62 to 74 kph	Twigs break off trees.
Strong gale (9)	75 to 88 kph	Branches break off trees.
Whole gale (10)	89 to 102 kph	Trees uprooted.
Storm (11)	103 to 117 kph	Widespread damage.
Hurricane (12)	More than 117 kph	Destruction.

Maps

A **map** visually represents a geographic region, such as a state or country. It provides information about areas through lines, colors, shapes, and symbols. There are different kinds of maps.

- **Political maps** show political features, such as national borders.

- **Physical maps** show the landforms in areas.

- **Road or travel maps** show roads and highways.

- **Thematic maps** show information on a specific topic, such as climate, weather, or natural resources.

Strategies for Reading

Ⓐ Read the title to find out what kind of map it is.

Ⓑ Read the labels to get an overall sense of what the map shows.

Ⓒ Look at the **key** or **legend** to find out what the symbols and colors on the map stand for.

MODEL: PHYSICAL MAP

MODEL: THEMATIC MAP

PRACTICE AND APPLY

Use the graphic aids shown on pages R5–R7 to answer the following questions:

1. According to the circle graph, were there more elephants than lions at the game preserve?

2. How many years did it take to double the world population from 1 billion to 2 billion?

3. According to the bar graph, does the number of actual voters equal the number of eligible voters in any age group?

4. What important feature is part of the helmet of a suit of armor?

5. According to the diagram of an oasis, how does water get to the surface of the ground?

6. Which civilization controlled the largest amount of territory according to the chart?

7. Using the table, find the wind speed that is strong enough to make whole trees sway.

8. Are there mountains over 13,000 feet high in Brazil?

9. Using the key on the climate map of Brazil, determine whether the driest area is in the eastern or western part of the country.

❸ Reading Informational Texts: Patterns of Organization

Reading any type of writing is easier once you recognize how it is organized. Writers usually arrange ideas and information in ways that best help readers see how they are related. There are several common patterns of organization:

- main idea and supporting details
- chronological order
- cause-effect organization
- compare-and-contrast organization

3.1 MAIN IDEA AND SUPPORTING DETAILS

Main idea and supporting details is a basic pattern of organization in which a central idea about a topic is supported by details. The **main idea** is the most important idea about a topic that a particular text or paragraph conveys. **Supporting details** are words, phrases, or sentences that tell more about the main idea. The main idea may be directly stated at the beginning and then followed by supporting details, or it may be merely implied by the supporting details. It may also be stated after it has been implied by supporting details.

Sometimes you will come across a main idea that is a **factual claim**—a statement that can be verified by observation, a reliable source, or an expert's view. In some cases the main idea may be stated as a **commonplace assertion**—a statement that many people assume to be true, but is not necessarily so. In both cases, the details should support the statements.

Strategies for Reading

- To find a stated main idea in a paragraph, identify the paragraph's topic. The topic is what the paragraph is about and can usually be summed up in one or two words. The word, or synonyms of it, will usually appear throughout the paragraph. Headings and subheadings are also clues to the topics of paragraphs.
- Ask: What is the topic sentence? The topic sentence states the most important idea, message, or information the paragraph conveys

about this topic. It is often the first sentence in a paragraph; however, it may appear at the end.

- To find an implied main idea, ask yourself: Whom or what did I just read about? What do the details suggest about the topic?
- Formulate a sentence stating this idea and add it to the paragraph. Does your sentence convey the main idea?

Notice how the main idea is expressed in each of the following models.

MODEL: MAIN IDEA AS THE FIRST SENTENCE

When the nomads of Africa began using camels around 300 A.D., trade across the Sahara became easier. — **Main idea**

The donkeys, horses, and oxen that had been used previously could not travel far without stopping for food and water. Camels, on the other hand, could cover 25 miles in a day and often go for two weeks without water. — **Supporting details**

MODEL: MAIN IDEA AS THE LAST SENTENCE

The new trade routes passed through lands occupied by the Soninke people. These farming people referred to their chief as ghana. Soon the land came to be known as the kingdom of Ghana. The tribal chiefs taxed the goods that traveled across their territory. — **Supporting details**

By the eighth century, trade had made Ghana a rich kingdom. — **Main idea**

MODEL: IMPLIED MAIN IDEA

The West African savannas and forests south of the savanna were rich in gold. No salt was available there, though. In the Sahara, on the other hand, there was abundant salt but no gold. Traders brought salt south through the desert and traded it for gold mined from the forests. — **Implied main idea: Gold and salt were two important items that were traded in West Africa.**

Read each paragraph, and then do the following:

1. Identify the main idea in the paragraph, using one of the strategies discussed on the previous page.

2. Identify whether the main idea is stated or implied in the paragraph.

> Home is where the heart is. There's no place like it. I love my home with a ferocity totally out of proportion to its appearance or location. I love dumb things about it: the hot-water heater, the plastic rack you drain dishes in, the roof over my head, which occasionally leaks. And yet it is precisely those dumb things that make it what it is—a place of certainty, stability, predictability, privacy, for me and for my family. It is where I live. What more can you say about a place than that? That is everything.
>
> —Anna Quindlen, "Homeless"

> Some boys taught me to play football. This was fine sport. You thought up a new strategy for every play and whispered it to the others. You went out for a pass, fooling everyone. Best, you got to throw yourself mightily at someone's running legs. Either you brought him down or you hit the ground flat out on your chin, with your arms empty before you. It was all or nothing. If you hesitated in fear, you would miss and get hurt: you would take a hard fall while the kid got away, or you would get kicked in the face while the kid got away. But if you flung yourself wholeheartedly at the back of his knees—if you gathered and joined body and soul and pointed them diving fearlessly—then you likely wouldn't get hurt, and you'd stop the ball. Your fate, and your team's score, depended on your concentration and courage. Nothing girls did could compare with it.
>
> —Annie Dillard, *An American Childhood*

3.2 CHRONOLOGICAL ORDER

Chronological order is the arrangement of events in the order in which they happen. This type of organization is used in short stories and novels, historical writing, biographies, and autobiographies. To show the order of events, writers use order words such as *before, after, next,* and *later* and time words and phrases that identify specific times of day, days of the week, and dates, such as *the next morning, Tuesday,* and *on July 4, 1776.*

Strategies for Reading

- Look in the text for headings and subheadings that may indicate a chronological pattern of organization.

- Look for words and phrases that identify times, such as *in a year, three hours earlier, in 202 B.C.,* and *the next day.*

- Look for words that signal order, such as *first, afterward, then, during,* and *finally,* to see how events or steps are related.

- Note that a paragraph or passage in which ideas and information are arranged chronologically will have several words or phrases that indicate time order, not just one.

- Ask yourself: Are the events in the paragraph or passage presented in time order?

Notice the words and phrases that signal time order in the first two paragraphs of the following model.

MODEL

A Butterfly Gets Its Wings

How does a butterfly get its wings? During its life, the butterfly goes through different growth stages. There are four main stages altogether: 1) the egg, 2) the caterpillar, 3) the pupa, and 4) the adult. The ancient Greeks called this whole process *metamorphosis,* a word we still use today.

At first, the butterfly is a single slimy egg, no larger than a fingertip. The baby insect grows within the egg until it is ready to hatch. For most types of butterflies, this first stage lasts about 10 days. When the egg cracks open, a caterpillar crawls out.

Events

Order words and phrases

Time words and phrases

In the second stage, the caterpillar spends most of its time eating and growing. As the caterpillar becomes bigger, it sheds its spiky or fuzzy skin. This process is called *molting*. A caterpillar molts several times during its life. Once the caterpillar has shed its skin for the last time, it becomes a pupa.

In the third stage, the pupa immediately grows a hard shell called a *chrysalis*. Then, inside the chrysalis, the pupa goes through the changes that will make it a butterfly. The pupa's hormones turn its body into wings, antennas, and other butterfly parts. After all the changes are complete, the shell splits open. A butterfly is ready to make its entrance.

Finally, the adult butterfly breaks from the chrysalis. Its body, however, doesn't look quite right. It's all soft and wrinkly. As air and blood are pumped through the butterfly's body, it starts to look more like its usual self. In a short time, the butterfly is ready to try out its new wings. With a few flutters, it's off and away!

PRACTICE AND APPLY

Refer to the preceding model to do the following:

1. List at least six words in the last three paragraphs that indicate time or order.

2. What does the writer call the four main parts in the life of a butterfly?

3. In what form does a butterfly begin its life?

3.3 CAUSE-EFFECT ORGANIZATION

Cause-effect organization is a pattern of organization that shows causal relationships between events, ideas, and trends. Cause-effect relationships may be directly stated or merely implied by the order in which the information is presented. Writers often use the cause-effect pattern in historical and scientific writing. Cause-effect relationships may have several forms.

One cause with one effect

Cause ▶ Effect

One cause with multiple effects

Cause ▶ Effect
▶ Effect

Multiple causes with a single effect

Cause ▶
Cause ▶ Effect

A chain of causes and effects

Cause ▶ Effect (Cause) ▶ Effect

Strategies for Reading

- Look for headings and subheadings that indicate a cause-effect pattern of organization, such as "Effects of Food Allergies."

- To find the effect or effects, read to answer the question, What happened?

- To find the cause or causes, read to answer the question, Why did it happen?

- Look for words and phrases that help you identify specific relationships between events, such as *because, since, had the effect of, led to, as a result, resulted in, for that reason, due to, therefore, if . . . then,* and *consequently*.

- Look closely at each cause-effect relationship. Do not assume that because one event happened before another, the first event caused the second event.

- Use graphic organizers like the diagrams shown to record cause-effect relationships as you read.

Notice the words that signal causes and effects in the following model.

MODEL

How a Tsunami Forms

Tsunami is a word that brings fear to people who live near the sea. Also known in English as a tidal wave, a tsunami is a huge ocean wave caused by an underwater volcanic eruption or earthquake.

    Effect

    Signal words

An earthquake or the explosion of a volcano on the ocean floor creates massive waves of energy. These energy waves spread out in widening circles, like waves from a pebble dropped into a pond.

    Cause

    Cause

    Effect

As the tsunami nears the shore, it begins to scrape along the ocean bottom. This friction causes the waves in the front to slow down. As a result, the waves traveling behind begin piling up and growing higher. This increase in height can happen very quickly—by as much as 90 feet in 10 or 15 minutes.

The effects of a tsunami can include the death of many people and the destruction of ships, buildings, and land along the shore. An especially dangerous situation may occur when the first part of a tsunami to hit the shore is the trough, or low point, rather than the crest of a wave. This trough sucks all the water away from the shore and may attract curious people on the beach. Within a few minutes, however, the crest of the wave will hit and may drown the onlookers. The most destructive tsunami ever recorded struck the Indonesian island of Sumatra, in 2004. It left more than 200,000 people dead.

PRACTICE AND APPLY

1. Use the pattern of a chain of causes and effects, illustrated on page R10, to make a graphic organizer showing the causes and effects described in the text.

2. List three words that the writer uses to signal cause and effect in the last two paragraphs.

3.4 COMPARE-AND-CONTRAST ORGANIZATION

Compare-and-contrast organization is a pattern of organization that provides a way to look at similarities and differences in two or more subjects. A writer may use this pattern of organization to compare the important points or characteristics of two or more subjects. These points or characteristics are called **points of comparison.** The compare-and-contrast pattern of organization may be developed in either of two ways:

Point-by-point organization—The writer discusses one point of comparison for both subjects, then goes on to the next point.

Subject-by-subject organization—The writer covers all points of comparison for one subject and then all points of comparison for the next subject.

Strategies for Reading

- Look in the text for headings, subheadings, and sentences that may suggest a compare-and-contrast pattern of organization, such as "Plants Share Many Characteristics," to help you identify where similarities and differences are addressed.

- To find similarities, look for words and phrases such as *like, similarly, both, all, every, also,* and *in the same way.*

- To find differences, look for words and phrases such as *unlike, but, on the other hand, more, less, in contrast,* and *however.*

- Use a graphic organizer, such as a Venn diagram or a compare-and-contrast chart, to record points of comparison and similarities and differences.

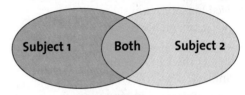

	Subject 1	Subject 2
Point 1		
Point 2		
Point 3		

Read the following models. As you read, use the signal words and phrases to identify the similarities and differences between the subjects and how the details are organized in each text.

MODEL 1

Living in Outer Space

Ten . . . nine . . . eight . . . The date is December 21, 1968.

Seven . . . six . . . five . . . Alongside a launch gantry at Cape Kennedy, Florida, a huge Saturn V rocket stands fueled and ready for blastoff, hydrogen vapor steaming from its rocket motors.

Four . . . three . . . two . . . At the top of the rocket sits the *Apollo 8* command module, the capsule that will ferry astronauts Frank Borman, James A. Lovell Jr., and William A. Anders to the moon and back.

One . . . zero . . . Liftoff! The Saturn's powerful engines roar to life, and another exciting chapter in the history of the United States space program begins.

Today, that same *Apollo 8* command module is one of the most popular attractions at the Henry Crown Space Center at the Museum of Science and Industry in Chicago. For six days in 1968, this cone-shaped capsule was home to the first humans to leave the security of Earth's orbit and venture out to visit another heavenly body.

Museum visitors, especially young people accustomed to space travel in the shuttle era, are often amazed at the cramped quarters within the capsule, and they wonder just how three adults lived for six days in such a compact environment. Space travel has come a long way since those pioneering days of the 1960s. Some of the main similarities and differences relate to living quarters and food.

Today's shuttle crews have both a flight deck and a lower crew-quarters deck in which to move around. The Apollo crews, however, were pretty much confined to their metal-and-fabric flight couches, although there was a little stretching room beneath the couches and around the hatch area that led to the Lunar Excursion Module.

Mealtime is a highlight of anyone's day, including every astronaut's. Early space travelers were limited to puréed foods squeezed out of toothpaste tubes and juices in plastic bags. Shuttle crews, on the other hand, enjoy a much more appetizing diet. It's still not exactly fine dining, but at least the food is served on trays, is eaten with utensils, and includes healthy snacks, like fresh fruit.

At the end of a working "day" in space, all astronauts are ready for some rest. In *Apollo,* the crew simply drifted off to sleep on their couches. Aboard the shuttle, crew members sleep in special sleep restraints. Some sleep horizontally, while others opt for a vertical snooze. In zero gravity, position doesn't matter!

The United States has continued to develop the space program. The lessons learned during the first three decades of space flight are making life in the alien environment beyond Earth's atmosphere much more pleasant for a new generation of space explorers.

Comparison words and phrases

Contrast words and phrases

Subjects

MODEL 2

To compare the two types of energy, we must first understand what energy is. Energy is the ability to do work. That doesn't just mean work as in homework or yard work. Energy comes in many forms, such as a rock falling off a cliff, a moving bicycle, or the stored energy in food. With all these forms, there are only two main types of energy, potential and kinetic. These are the energies of rest and motion.

Potential energy is the energy an object has stored up based on how high up it is or how much it weighs. For instance, suppose two kids weigh the same and climb a tree. If they are on different branches, the kid on the higher branch has more potential energy than the kid on the lower branch. However, if one kid weighs more than the other, and they both sit at the same height, the heavier kid has more potential energy than the lighter kid.

If the kids jump out of the tree, their potential energy becomes kinetic energy. This kind comes from the motion of an object. Kinetic energy increases with the speed of an object. When the kids jump, their speed increases as they fall. They have more kinetic energy when they are falling

Subjects

Comparison words and phrases

Contrast words and phrases

faster than they do when they first jump and are falling more slowly. Also, the more mass an object has, the more kinetic energy it has. Even if both kids jump at the exact same time, the one with more mass will always have more kinetic energy.

These two kids probably knew they were using a lot of energy, but they would probably be surprised to know how much work they had been doing.

PRACTICE AND APPLY

Refer to the preceding models to answer the following questions:

1. Which model is organized by subject? Which model is organized by points of comparison?

2. Identify two words or phrases in each model that signal a compare-and-contrast pattern of organization.

3. List two points that the writer of each model compares and contrasts.

4. Use a Venn diagram or a compare-and-contrast chart to identify two or more points of comparison and the similarities and differences shown in one of the two models.

3.5 PROBLEM-SOLUTION ORDER

Problem-solution order is a pattern of organization in which a problem is stated and analyzed and then one or more solutions are proposed and examined. This pattern of organization is often used in persuasive writing, such as editorials or proposals.

Strategies for Reading

- Look for an explanation of the problem in the first or second paragraph.

- Look for words, such as *problem* and *reason*, that may signal an explanation of the problem.

- To find the solution, ask: What suggestion does the writer offer to solve the problem?

- Look for words, such as *propose*, *conclude*, and *answer*, that may signal a solution.

MODEL

I love baseball, but I won't be going to any major-league games, and I won't be rooting for the local major-league team. The reason is simple. There is no local major-league team in North Dakota. There's none in South Dakota or in Montana or even in Wyoming. The closest major-league team is the Minnesota Twins, and that's over 240 miles away!

The problem is that getting a major-league team costs money. Any city that wants a team has to have enough money to build a stadium. The city also has to have a big enough population to support the team. Fargo is the biggest city in North Dakota, and it only has about 91,484 people. That's not enough to support a major-league franchise. Sports stadiums often hold more people than Fargo has!

Even though the towns around here aren't exactly huge, there are a lot of die-hard baseball fans like my friends and me. So here's my plan. Why couldn't a couple of towns get together to build a stadium and start a team? For example, Moorhead, Minnesota, is right next to Fargo. They already share the same airport, and the metropolitan area has about 174,367 people. That might be enough to support a team. If it's not, then maybe Grand Forks, or even Aberdeen, could join in too.

People might say that there would be a problem naming a team that is supported by cities in two or three different states. I think baseball fans would be so happy to have a team, they wouldn't really care what it was called.

If enough people wrote to the Fargo and Moorhead city governments, maybe the idea could be put on the ballot. Major-league baseball is supposed to be our national pastime. Shouldn't we be a part of it too?

PRACTICE AND APPLY

Reread the model and then answer the following questions:

1. According to the model, what is the cause of the problem?

2. What solution does the writer offer? What words are a clue?

❹ Reading Informational Texts: Forms

Magazines, newspapers, Web pages, and consumer, public, and workplace documents are all informational materials, but each one has its own purpose. To understand and analyze these texts, look at their structure, which includes text features and patterns of organization.

4.1 READING A NEWSPAPER ARTICLE

The purpose of a daily or weekly **newspaper** is to provide readers with timely news, opinions, and advertising. Because people often skim newspapers, publishers use images and other structural elements to capture readers' attention.

Strategies for Reading

Ⓐ "Teen Rap" is the name of a **column,** a type of article that appears regularly in a newspaper and is usually written by the same person.

Ⓑ Notice whether **graphic aids** or **quotations** attract your attention.

Ⓒ Read the **title** and other **headings** to find out more about its topic and organization.

Ⓓ Notice whether the article has a **byline,** a line naming the author.

Ⓔ A **caption** accompanying a graphic aid may provide information that adds to the meaning of the article.

PRACTICE AND APPLY

1. Why does this article meet the purpose of a newspaper?

2. How does the circle graphic relate to the title?

3. What does the photograph with its caption tell you?

4. What other kinds of information do you expect to find in a newspaper?

Ⓐ

Source: The *Boston Herald*   by Lauren Beckham Ⓓ

Ⓒ
The Difference a City Year Makes

Ⓑ What kind of person gets up at the break of dawn, spends all day tutoring teenagers, cleaning up former crack houses, or teaching kids to read and write—all in the name of community service?

The kind who joins City Year.

Hundreds of young adults come together in Boston for CYZYGY, City Year's Annual Convention of Idealism, to show community leaders, business people and—most importantly—other young adults that community service, though difficult, is rewarding to both those who give and those who receive.

CITY YEAR

Ⓑ **"Young people are coming together and giving back"**

When Anthony Samuels of Dorchester graduated from Melrose High School last year, he had a specific plan.

"I was ready to give back to my community," Samuels, 19, said. "When I learned about City Year, I jumped right in."

Samuels spends his days at the Umana

Two participants in a Winter Wonderland camp for young children displaced by Hurricane Katrina. Ⓔ

Barnes Middle School in East Boston, mentoring and tutoring at-risk boys in a remedial class.

"I could say that it was a challenge but that's what I needed," said the Dorchester teen. "And they needed me. I'm proud to be part of their accomplishments."

Samuels plans to attend Bunker Hill Community College next year and then pursue a bachelor's degree in child psychology. Meanwhile, he is looking forward to the CYZYGY conference.

"Hopefully in the next five years we'll have, instead of eight City Year sites, 15 to 20," he said. "CYZYGY will show Boston that young people are coming together and giving back."

4.2 READING A TEXTBOOK

Each textbook has its own structure based on the content in the book. Look at the table of contents to see how the book is organized and to identify special features, such as sidebars, charts, and graphs. Because a textbook's purpose is to educate people, each of its features will support the book's focus.

Strategies for Reading

Ⓐ Before you begin reading the lesson or chapter, read any **questions** that appear at the end of it. Then use the questions to set your purpose for reading.

Ⓑ **Read carefully** to understand and remember the ideas presented in the text. When you come to an unfamiliar word, first try to figure out its meaning from **context clues.** If necessary, use a **glossary** in the textbook or a dictionary. Avoid interrupting your reading by constantly looking up words in a dictionary.

*For more information on context clues and glossaries, see the **Vocabulary and Spelling Handbook,** pages R68 and R72.*

Ⓒ Use the book's special features, such as sidebars, to increase your understanding of the text. The purpose of a **sidebar** is to present additional information, usually set off in a box.

Ⓓ Take notes as you read. Use text features such as **maps** to help you understand the content. Use **subheadings** and boldfaced terms to help identify important topics. Record your notes in graphic organizers, such as cause-effect charts, to help clarify relationships among ideas.

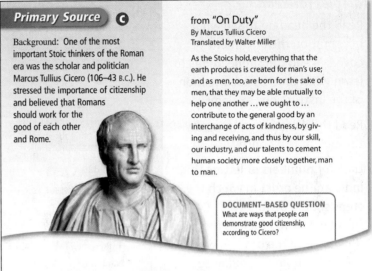

Primary Source **Ⓒ**

Background: One of the most important Stoic thinkers of the Roman era was the scholar and politician Marcus Tullius Cicero (106–43 B.C.). He stressed the importance of citizenship and believed that Romans should work for the good of each other and Rome.

from "On Duty"
By Marcus Tullius Cicero
Translated by Walter Miller

As the Stoics hold, everything that the earth produces is created for man's use; and as men, too, are born for the sake of men, that they may be able mutually to help one another…we ought to…contribute to the general good by an interchange of acts of kindness, by giving and receiving, and thus by our skill, our industry, and our talents to cement human society more closely together, man to man.

> **DOCUMENT–BASED QUESTION**
> What are ways that people can demonstrate good citizenship, according to Cicero?

Philosophy and Citizenship The Romans borrowed much of their **Ⓑ** philosophy from the Greeks. The philosophy of **Stoicism** was especially influential in Rome. It was developed by the Greek philosopher Zeno. Stoicism stressed the importance of virtue, duty, and endurance in life. These were all values that many Romans prized.

The beliefs of Stoicism helped create a strong sense of citizenship in Rome. Citizenship refers to the relationship individuals have with their country. As part of this relationship, a country provides protection and security for its citizens. In return, citizens are expected to take an active part in society in order to strengthen their country. Today, these aspects of Stoicism are viewed by many as necessary qualities for being a good citizen.

Ⓓ **Roman Language** Another lasting aspect of Roman culture was its language, known as Latin. Because the Romans conquered most of Europe, Latin is the basis for several European languages. These include Spanish, Italian, French, Portuguese, and Romanian. In addition, more than half of the words in English have a basis in Latin. What's more, Latin was the official language of the Roman Catholic Church into the 20th century.

Ⓐ **REVIEW** What influence did Latin have on the larger world?

PRACTICE AND APPLY

1. Compare the structure of the newspaper article on page R14 with the textbook page here. Identify some features they share.

2. How is the purpose of a textbook different from that of a newspaper?

4.3 READING A CONSUMER DOCUMENT

Consumer documents are printed materials that accompany products and services. Their purpose is to provide information about the use, care, operation or assembly of the products. Some common consumer documents are contracts, warranties, instructional manuals, and schedules. These materials are usually very carefully structured to make them easy to use.

Strategies for Reading

Ⓐ Read the heading to see what information the document covers. Read the **subheadings** to learn what process each section of the instructions explains.

Ⓑ Read the directions all the way through at least once.

Ⓒ Look for **numbers** or **letters** that indicate the order in which the steps should be followed. Or look for signal words such as *first* and *finally* to see the order in which the steps should be followed.

Ⓓ Words that appear in **all capital letters** are often names or labels that appear on the device you are being shown how to use. If there is an illustration or diagram, try to match the words in the instructions to words or symbols in the graphic aid.

Ⓔ Look for **verbs that describe actions** you should take, such as *plug, touch, enter,* and *press.*

Ⓕ Pay attention to **warnings** or **notes** that describe problems.

MICROWAVE INSTRUCTIONS

Ⓐ Before Operating

Ⓑ 1. Plug the power cord into a three-pronged electrical outlet.

Ⓒ 2. Display panel will light up and flash 00:00. Touch STOP/CLEAR pad.

3. Set the clock.

Ⓓ Touch STOP/CLEAR pad when the oven is first plugged in, or after the electrical power has been interrupted.

Ⓐ Setting the Clock

Procedure

Ⓔ 1. Touch TIMER CLOCK pad.

2. Enter the time of day. For example, if it is 10:30, touch the number pads 1030 and "10:30" will appear.

3. Press the TIMER CLOCK pad again to set the time.

Note You can select any time of the day from 1:00–12:59. To reset Clock, repeat steps 1 through 3 above. If incorrect time (for example, 8:61 or 13:00, etc.) is entered, "EE" will appear on display. Touch STOP/CLEAR pad and program correctly.

Canceling a Program

- To reset, or cancel, a cooking program as it is being entered, touch STOP/CLEAR pad once.

- To stop the oven while it is operating, touch STOP/CLEAR pad once. Do not open the door without pressing STOP/CLEAR pad.

- An entire cooking program (one stage or multiple stages) can be canceled after the oven has started cooking. This can be done by touching STOP/CLEAR pad twice.

Ⓕ Note See page 10 to create your own cooking programs.

Power Levels

Most foods can be cooked at full power (P-HI). However, for best results, some foods require a lower cooking power. Some foods such as tender cuts of meat can be cooked only with a lower power. Before setting any power level, the POWER LEVEL pad must be touched, followed by desired number.

1	2	3
4	5	6
7	8	9
POWER LEVEL	0	TIMER CLOCK
STOP CLEAR		START

Reread the microwave instructions and answer the questions.

1. Explain how to reset the clock after a power outage.

2. Restate how to solve the following problem: The clock was incorrectly set at 14:30.

3. Why do these instructions meet the purpose of a consumer document?

4. Compare how this information is organized with how the information in a textbook is organized (see page R15). What are the main differences in their structure?

4.4 READING A PUBLIC DOCUMENT

The purpose of **public documents** is to provide people with information that may interest them. These documents are often free and inform people of decisions and events. Public documents may be government documents, speeches, laws, signs, or rules and regulations. The structure of a public document often depends on the content of the document and the audience for which it is intended.

Strategies for Reading

A Read the **title** and take note of any **special features** that tell what information the document covers.

B Read the document carefully to find out what the document is asking or telling you to do.

C Look for the source of the document. Public documents are usually identified as coming from a particular agency or group. They are usually not commercial advertisements.

D Look for a contact person or group. You will need this information to find out more about the topic or to clear up anything you don't understand.

E Notice any graphic aids that may convey information. Symbols as well as shapes and colors may have certain purposes or meanings. For example, signs often rely on graphic aids to communicate messages clearly and briefly.

PUBLIC DOCUMENT

E **County Food Services**

A **Summer Fun and Food Program**

The Fun and Food Program (FFP) will begin the summer season with FREE healthy cold lunches to youth ages 1 through 18 at all county recreation centers. The program directors hope to provide **B** city children with at least one nutritious meal per day when school is not in session. The County Food Services Department has prepared a menu that is healthy and appealing. Following the lunch meals, various age-appropriate activities sponsored by the Department of Parks will be offered to those in attendance.

C The program is funded in part by the U.S. Department of Agriculture (USDA) and administered by the state through County Food Services.

The Fun and Food Program is open to all youth ages 1 through 18.* **E**

NOTE: Persons in a school or non-profit program who are 19 years and older can also participate.

D *For more information, contact the program office at (555) 564-1234, or check your local recreation center for a flier.

PRACTICE AND APPLY

Reread the document and answer the questions.

1. What is the purpose of the document?

2. Who should read the document?

3. What would you do if you had questions about the program?

4. How is the purpose of the public document different from the purpose of a workplace document?

4.5 READING A WORKPLACE DOCUMENT

Workplace documents are materials that are produced or used within a workplace. Their purpose is to aid in the functioning of a business. They may be documents created by a business to monitor itself, such as minutes of a meeting or a sales report. They may also be documents that explain company policies, organization, safety rules, and operating procedures. Because workplace documents include memos, business letters, job applications, and résumés, their structures will vary. Most of them, however, will use short sentences and text features, such as bullets, boldface type, and charts, to highlight key points.

Strategies for Reading

A Read the title and any subtitles to see what information the document covers.

B Determine who needs to read the document. Look for clues to see if it applies to you.

C Look for subheadings to identify main ideas and topics and to see how the document is organized.

D Read the document slowly and carefully, as it may contain details that should not be overlooked.

E Look for a contact person or group. You will need this information to clear up anything you don't understand.

F Take notes to help you remember what actions are required.

PRACTICE AND APPLY

Reread the document and answer the questions.

1. What is the document's purpose?

2. Who needs to read the document?

3. Who should be with the children on the playground?

4. If there is a fire, what should you do before opening the door?

5. What structural features make the document easy to read?

OPERATING PROCEDURES

"Little Folks" Play Group **A**

Middleton Park District

Notice to Volunteers
Safety Guidelines **B**

We're glad you have volunteered to help with our Saturday morning play group for children ages 2–5. To keep our space clean and safe and our children happy, we all must follow these safety rules.

Staffing **C**
- An adult must be in the playroom at all times.
- Children who go outside to the playground must be accompanied by an adult.

Emergencies **C**
- In case of emergency, dial 911 on the phone in the kitchen. **D**
- In case of fire, evacuate the children through the main door or the emergency exit. Before opening a door, touch it to see if it is hot. A fire extinguisher is located next to the emergency exit.

Cleanup **C**
- Make sure the playroom is clean at the end of the day. Put all toys in the toy chests.
- Wipe tabletops clean with a damp sponge.
- Turn off the lights as you leave.

This document was prepared by the Middleton Park District. If you have questions or concerns, contact the Program Coordinator. **E**

4.6 READING ELECTRONIC TEXT

Electronic text is any text that is in a form that a computer can store and display on a screen. Electronic text can be part of Web pages, CD-ROMs, search engines, and documents that you create with your computer software. Like books, Web pages often provide aids for finding information. However, each Web page is designed differently, and information is not in the same location on each page. It is important to know the functions of different parts of a Web page so that you can easily find the information you want.

Strategies for Reading

A Look at the **title** of a page to determine what topics it covers.

B For an online source, such as a Web page or search engine, note the **Web address,** known as a **URL** (Universal Resource Locator). You may want to make a note of it if you need to return to that page.

C Look for a **menu bar** along the top, bottom, or side of a Web page. Clicking on an item in a menu bar will take you to another part of the Web site.

D Notice any hyperlinks to related pages. **Hyperlinks** are often underlined or highlighted in a contrasting color. You can click on a hyperlink to get to another page—one that may or may not have been created by the same person or organization.

E For information that you want to keep for future reference, save documents on your computer or print them. For online sources, you can pull down the **Favorites** or **Bookmarks** menu and bookmark pages so that you can easily return to them or print the information you need. Printing the pages will allow you to highlight key ideas on a hard copy.

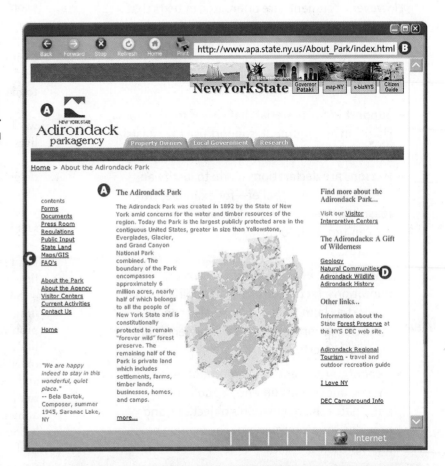

PRACTICE AND APPLY

1. What is the URL of the Web page shown?

2. What is the main purpose of this Web page?

3. Which links would you click on to find out about recreation in the park?

4. What would you do if you had questions that weren't answered by information on the site?

5. Compare the structure and purpose of this Web page with that of a textbook page.

5 Reading Persuasive Texts

5.1 ANALYZING AN ARGUMENT

An **argument** expresses a position on an issue or problem and supports it with reasons and evidence. Being able to analyze and evaluate arguments will help you distinguish between claims you should accept and those you should not. A sound argument should appeal strictly to reason. However, arguments are often used in texts that also contain other types of persuasive devices. An argument includes the following elements:

- A **claim** is the writer's position on an issue or problem.

- **Support** is any material that serves to prove a claim. In an argument, support usually consists of reasons and evidence.

- **Reasons** are declarations made to justify an action, decision, or belief—for example, "My reason for thinking we will be late is that we can't make it to the appointment in five minutes."

- **Evidence** can be the specific references, quotations, facts, examples, and opinions that support a claim. Evidence may also consist of statistics, reports of personal experience, or the views of experts.

- A **counterargument** is an argument made to oppose another argument. A good argument anticipates the opposition's objections and provides counterarguments to disprove or answer them.

Claim	I think I should be allowed to watch more TV.
Reason	TV can provide opportunities for learning and enjoyment.
Evidence	TV can take you to faraway places and can bring art, music, and science right into your home.
Counterargument	Some people think TV is really bad for kids, but those people are looking at only the worst part of TV, not the best.

Read the following editorial and use a chart like the one shown to identify the claim, reason, evidence, and counterargument.

Important Hours
by Gina Maraini

"The Golden Years." That is what some people call old age. They think it is a time of peace and relaxation. But many old people spend time alone. Some cannot get out of their homes because of illness. "What can I do?" you ask. You can do more than you think to make an important contribution to an older person's life. Even spending an hour a week can mean a lot to an older neighbor who lives alone.

Some kids might say that they can only do good for an older person if they have lots of time and lots of patience. It's easy to talk yourself out of volunteering your time by saying, "I only have an hour a week. What good would that do?" Never underestimate just how much good you can do even in a little bit of time.

Sometimes things happen that seem unimportant to a kid but can really be a problem to an old person. If a small object like a pen or pencil slides under furniture, an older person often is not able to stoop down and pick it up. But they feel embarrassed to ask for help. So, the pen stays there. Sometimes it gets forgotten about and becomes lost. You can help that older person find these things. And by helping, you are reminding that person that he or she is not forgotten about either.

Sometimes it is hard for an older person to reach up high. Putting things away, like groceries, becomes a problem. Often the older person gets tired and gives up. You can help to put groceries and other heavy objects away. And by doing that, you are helping that older person feel like he or she can still keep up with life's challenges.

One of the most important things you can do for a senior citizen who lives alone is to give that person someone to talk to. Old people, who have lived long lives and had many experiences, have stories to tell that you can learn a lot from. And it is important for you to say so, too. That way, you can show the older person that he or she is contributing to your life.

You can make a real contribution to an older person's life. Even if you only have an hour to spend, you can help an older person feel cared about and important. Find ways to reach out, whether through volunteer organizations or just by being aware of who is alone in your neighborhood. And always remember: as much as you give, you get back so much more, simply by knowing the difference that you have made.

5.2 RECOGNIZING PERSUASIVE TECHNIQUES

Persuasive texts typically rely on more than just the **logical appeal** of an argument to be convincing. They also rely on ethical and emotional appeals and other **persuasive techniques**—devices that can convince you to adopt a position or take an action.

Ethical appeals establish a writer's credibility and trustworthiness with an audience. When a writer links a claim to a widely accepted value, the writer not only gains moral support for that claim but also establishes a connection with readers. For example, with the following appeal, the writer reminds readers of a value they should accept and links a claim to it: "Most of us agree that we should protect our natural resources, but we don't invest a lot of time or money to preserve them."

The chart shown here explains several other means by which a writer may attempt to sway you to adopt his or her position. Learn to recognize these techniques, and you are less likely to be influenced by them.

Persuasive Technique	Example
Appeals by Association	
Bandwagon appeal Suggests that a person should believe or do something because "everyone else" does	Every day more buyers are enjoying the conveniences of catalog shopping.
Testimonial Relies on endorsements from well-known people or satisfied customers	Todd Marshall, star of stage and screen, buys his shoes at Fine Footwear. Shouldn't you?
Snob appeal Taps into people's desire to be special or part of an elite group	Be among the first to enjoy the upgraded facilities at Spring Lake Fitness Center.
Appeal to loyalty Relies on people's affiliation with a particular group	Say *Yes!* to your community—support the campaign to build a new library!
Emotional Appeals	
Appeals to pity, fear, or vanity Use strong feelings, rather than facts, to persuade	We need to keep the homeless shelter open—think how you would feel if you had no place to go.
Word Choice	
Glittering generality A generalization that includes a word or phrase with positive connotations, to promote a product, person, or idea.	Buying handmade jewelry from the Hang Up helps support small-town America.

Identify the persuasive techniques used in this model.

> **Vote for Velazquez!**
>
> Whom do you want to represent you in Congress—a dinosaur who's stuck in the past or someone who's courageously facing the future? Why settle for Jill Jolsen, who hasn't lifted a finger to help this community? Don't let her slick ads fool you. Instead, join the leaders in the community and many of your neighbors who have already put their support behind Victor Velazquez. Local businesswoman Janice Wu is behind Velazquez all the way—she says he will bring new jobs and fresh ideas that will really work. Don't miss this once-in-a-lifetime chance to change this town. Vote for Velazquez!

5.3 ANALYZING LOGIC AND REASONING

While persuasive techniques may sway you to side with a writer, they should not be enough to convince you that an argument is sound. To determine the soundness of an argument, you really need to examine the argument's claim and support and the logic or reasoning that links them. To do this, it is helpful to identify the writer's mode of reasoning.

The Inductive Mode of Reasoning

When a person uses specific evidence to arrive at a **general principle,** or generalization, that person is using **inductive reasoning.** Similarly, when a writer presents specific evidence first and then offers a generalization drawn from that evidence, the writer is making an **inductive argument.** Here is an example of inductive reasoning.

SPECIFIC FACTS

Fact 1 Turtles are the only reptiles that have a shell.

Fact 2 The green turtle, a sea turtle, can swim almost 20 miles an hour.

Fact 3 Snapping turtles have powerful, sharp-edged jaws and are aggressive when attacked.

GENERALIZATION

Turtles have a variety of protective strategies.

There are several types of inductive reasoning.

- **argument by cause and effect:** In this type of argument, the writer or speaker attempts to persuade by showing the causes that would lead to a desired or an undesired effect. **Example:** *If we don't see the movie today, we won't be able to see it on the weekend because the theatre will be too crowded.*

- **argument by analogy:** In this type of argument, the writer or speaker compares familiar events and things to those that are unfamiliar in an attempt to persuade the audience to accept the new situation. **Example:** *You'll like this new movie because it has a plot that is similar to others you've seen.*

- **argument by authority:** In this type of argument, the writer or speaker attempts to persuade by using an authoritative and reliable source as evidence. **Example:** *The movie critic gave the new movie three stars, so we should go see it.*

Strategies for Determining the Soundness of Inductive Arguments

Ask yourself the following questions to evaluate an inductive argument:

- **Is the evidence valid and sufficient support for the conclusion?** Inaccurate facts lead to inaccurate conclusions.

- **Does the conclusion follow logically from the evidence?** From the facts listed above, the conclusion that *all* turtles have a wide variety of protective strategies would be too broad a generalization.

- **Is the evidence drawn from a large enough sample?** Even though there are only three facts listed above, the sample is large enough to support the claim. If you wanted to support the conclusion that only turtles have a variety of protective strategies, the sample is not large enough.

The Deductive Mode of Reasoning

When a person uses a **general principle,** or generalization, to form a conclusion about a particular situation or problem, that person is using **deductive reasoning.** For example,

Being exposed to loud noise over a long period will damage a person's hearing.	General principle or generalization

I listen to my stereo at its highest setting for hours every day.	The situation being observed or considered

I will have some hearing loss.	Conclusion (also considered a deduction)

Similarly, a writer is making a **deductive argument** when he or she begins the argument with a claim that is based on a general principle and then presents evidence to support the claim. For example, a writer might begin a deductive argument with the claim "Many people have some hearing loss."

Strategies for Determining the Soundness of Deductive Arguments

Ask yourself the following questions to evaluate a deductive argument:

- **Is the general principle actually stated, or is it implied?** Note that writers often use deductive reasoning in arguments without stating the general principles. They assume that readers will recognize and agree with the principles. Be sure to identify the general principle for yourself.

- **Is the general principle sound?** Don't just assume the general principle is sound. Ask yourself whether it is really true.

- **Is the conclusion valid?** To be valid, a conclusion in a deductive argument must follow logically from the general principle and the specific situation.

The following chart shows two conclusions drawn from the same general principle.

All seventh-graders are going to the zoo next week.	
Accurate Deduction	**Inaccurate Deduction**
Laura is in the seventh grade; therefore, Laura is going to the zoo next week.	Laura is going to the zoo next week; therefore, Laura is in the seventh grade.

Laura may be going to the zoo with her family or friends.

PRACTICE AND APPLY

Identify whether inductive or deductive reasoning is used in the following paragraph. If the mode of reasoning used is inductive, tell whether the paragraph uses argument by cause and effect, analogy, or authority.

> In science class, I learned what different substances do for the human body. Protein aids growth and repairs muscles. Fruits and vegetables provide critical vitamins, and calcium strengthens bones. Carbohydrates supply energy to the body. Clearly, a balanced diet is important for good health.

Identifying Faulty Reasoning

Sometimes an argument at first appears to make sense but isn't valid because it is based on a fallacy. A **rhetorical fallacy** is a false or misleading statement. Learn to recognize these rhetorical fallacies.

TYPE OF FALLACY	DEFINITION	EXAMPLE
Circular reasoning	Supporting a statement by simply repeating it in different words	I'm tired because **I don't have any energy.**
Either/or fallacy	A statement that suggests that there are only two choices available in a situation that really offers more than two options	**Either** we raise taxes, **or** we close the parks.
Oversimplification	An explanation of a complex situation or problem as if it were much simpler than it is	Getting a good grade in Mrs. Raimi's class depends on **whether she likes you.**
Overgeneralization	A generalization that is too broad. You can often recognize overgeneralizations by the use of words such as *all, everyone, every time, anything, no one,* and *none.*	You **never** get me anything I want.
Hasty generalization	A conclusion drawn from too little evidence or from evidence that is biased	She left after fifteen minutes. **She must not like us.**
Stereotyping	A dangerous type of overgeneralization. Stereotypes are broad statements about people on the basis of their gender, ethnicity, race, or political, social, professional, or religious group.	**All rock stars** are self-centered.
Ad hominem or attacking the person	An attempt to discredit an idea by attacking the person or group associated with it. Candidates often engage in name-calling during political campaigns.	The **narrow-minded** senator opposes recycling.
Evading the issue	Responding to an objection with arguments and evidence that do not address its central point	Yes, I broke my campaign promise not to raise taxes, **but higher taxes have led to increases in police patrols and paved highways.**
False cause	The mistake of assuming that because one event occurred after another event in time, the first event caused the second one to occur	John didn't get his homework done because he had to take the dog for a walk.

Strategies and Practice for State and Standardized Tests

The test items in this section are modeled after test formats that are used on many state and standardized tests. The strategies presented here will help you prepare for these tests. This section offers general test-taking strategies and tips for answering multiple-choice items, as well as questions that are short constructed response and extended constructed response. It also includes guidelines and samples for essay writing. For each test, read the tips in the margin. Then apply the tips to the practice items. You can also apply the tips to Assessment Practice Tests in this book.

1 General Test-Taking Strategies

- Arrive on time and be prepared. Be sure to bring either sharpened pencils with erasers or pens—whichever you are told to bring.

- If you have any questions, ask them before the test begins. Make sure you understand the test procedures, the timing, and the rules.

- Read the test directions carefully. Look at the passages and questions to get an overview of what is expected.

- Tackle the questions one at a time rather than thinking about the whole test.

- Look for main ideas as you read passages. They are often stated at the beginning or the end of a paragraph. Sometimes the main idea is implied.

- Refer back to the reading selections as needed. For example, if a question asks about an author's attitude, you might have to reread a passage for clues.

- If you are not sure of your answer, make a logical guess. You can often arrive at the correct answer by reasoning and eliminating wrong answers.

- As you fill in answers on your answer sheet, make sure you match each test item to its numbered space on the answer sheet.

- Don't look for patterns in the positions of correct choices.

- Only change an answer if you are sure your original choice is incorrect. If you do change an answer, erase your original choice neatly and thoroughly.

- Check your answers and reread your essay.

② Critical Reading

As you advance through middle school and into high school, you will be exposed to different types of writing, both fiction and nonfiction. You will read novels, persuasive essays, poems, historical documents, and scientific or technical information. Tests will measure your ability to read and analyze these kinds of writings. Test selections can range in length from 100 words to 500 or 600 words.

> **Directions:** Read the selection and then answer the questions on the following page.

SELECTION

On Friday I had my last day at Happy Valley Elementary School. On Saturday the moving truck came and took all our stuff to Hoboken, New Jersey, and we left our house in Happy Valley forever. On Sunday, our first day in the new house, the temperature was one hundred degrees Fahrenheit— the beginning of the hottest heat wave ever recorded in Hoboken in the month of June for 120 years.

One hundred and twenty years ago was when our Hoboken house had been built. This is what my parents did. They gave up a modern house in Happy Valley, New Jersey—a house with a front yard, a backyard, and trees,
10 on a street with similar houses and similar trees—to move to a brick house with no front yard, practically no backyard, and no trees, on a street with guys sitting on the steps and spitting on the sidewalk, and cars and buses running right past our door. And the Hoboken house was in rotten condition and cost three times as much as we got for our Happy Valley house.

My parents said we were going to fix up the house and have an "urban lifestyle." This is what an urban lifestyle is: My bike was stolen the first hour we were in town. And it was one hundred degrees Fahrenheit. My mother said she didn't want me growing up in a suburb. She said life was real in cities. I went upstairs to sit in my crummy 120-year-old room.

20 My father climbed the stairs to my room. "Egad! It's hot as an oven in here, old pal," he said.

My father says things like "egad" and "odds bodkin." They have no meaning. I simply tolerate these weirdnesses, along with so many things my parents do.

"Sorry about your bike, old man," my father said.

He calls me *old man*, also *old chap*. There is no explanation for this.

"We'll get you another bike, I promise," he said. "But could you possibly wait until your birthday? There are a lot of expenses fixing up the new house."

This was great. I could have a bike for my birthday, instead of some other present, which I would have gotten if I was not to get a bike, which I would
30 not be getting if the one I already had hadn't been stolen, which it probably would not have been if we had not moved to Hoboken, which was not my idea in the first place. . . .

Tips: Reading Text

① Before you begin reading a passage, skim the questions that follow it to focus your reading.

② Look for key ideas as you read. Change is a key idea in this passage. It is expressed in the opening lines.

③ Pay attention to the connotation of words. The examples that the narrator uses to define an "urban lifestyle" give the expression a negative connotation.

④ Draw conclusions. The narrator isn't happy with the move, but he tells his father that everything is fine. He probably doesn't want to hurt his father's feelings.

Look for examples of logical fallacies in the following argument. Identify each one and explain why you identified it as such.

Dear Editors:

There has been a lot of talk about students' lack of concern for the appearance of our school. Nobody gets rid of his or her trash properly and everyone writes graffiti on the walls. But if the school seemed more worth caring about, students would take better care of it. Most of the school is very old. The halls are dark and the walls are dingy because the maintenance staff has been on strike for several weeks. The old-fashioned school board said that an entirely new building wasn't needed. So only a new gym was added. It is clean and bright because students have kept it that way. Either we build a new school, or it will be destroyed in three years.

5.4 EVALUATING PERSUASIVE TEXTS

Learning how to evaluate persuasive texts and identify bias will help you become more selective when doing research and also help you improve your own reasoning and arguing skills. **Bias** is an inclination for or against a particular opinion or viewpoint. A writer may reveal a strongly positive or negative bias on an issue by

• **presenting only one way** of looking at it

• **overlooking key information**

• **stacking more evidence on one side** of the argument than the other

• **using unfairly weighted evidence,** which is weak or unproven evidence that a writer treats as if it is more important than it really is

• **using loaded language,** which consists of words with strongly positive or negative connotations

EXAMPLE: *Barbara Larsen is the best choice for student council president because she has fresh ideas and fantastic people skills.* (*Fresh* and *fantastic* have very positive connotations.)

Propaganda is any form of communication that is so distorted that it conveys false or misleading information. Some politicians create and distribute propaganda. Many logical fallacies, such as name-calling, the either/or fallacy, and false causes, are often used in propaganda. The following example shows an oversimplification. The writer uses one fact to support a particular point of view but does not reveal another fact that does not support that viewpoint.

EXAMPLE: *Since the new park opened, vandalism in the area has increased by 10 percent. Clearly, the park has had a negative impact on the area.* (The writer does not include the fact that the vandalism was caused by people who were not drawn into the area by the park.)

*For more information on logical fallacies, see **Identifying Faulty Reasoning,** page R24.*

Strategies for Assessing Evidence

It is important to have a set of standards by which you can evaluate persuasive texts. Use the questions below to help you assess the adequacy, accuracy, and appropriateness of facts and opinions that are presented as evidence.

• **Are the facts accurate?** Facts can be proved by eyewitness accounts, authoritative sources such as encyclopedias and experts, or research.

• **Are the opinions well informed?** Any opinions offered should be supported by facts, be based on research or eyewitness accounts, or come from experts on the topic.

• **Is the evidence sufficient?** Thorough, or sufficient, evidence leaves no reasonable question unanswered. If a choice is offered to the reader, enough evidence for making the choice should be given. If taking a side is called for, all sides of the issue should be presented.

• **Is the evidence biased?** Be alert to evidence that contains loaded language or other signs of bias.

• **Is the evidence relevant?** The evidence needs to apply to the topic and come from people, groups, or organizations that have important knowledge of, or credentials relating to, the topic.

- **Is it important that the evidence be current?**
  Where timeliness is crucial, as in the areas of medicine and technology, the evidence should reflect the latest developments in the areas.

Read the argument below. Identify the facts, opinion, and elements of bias.

> Let your voice be heard. The Students' League is hosting a demonstration against U.S Representative Sharon Bullhorn on Saturday. Just last week, Representative Bullhorn voted against raising the minimum wage. Obviously Representative Bullhorn doesn't care about young people. If she did, she would have helped pass the much-needed minimum wage increase, so that preteens and teens could earn the money they deserve.

Strategies for Determining a Strong Argument

Make sure that all or most of the following statements are true:

- The argument presents a claim or thesis.

- The claim is connected to its support by a general principle that most readers would readily agree with. Valid general principle: *It is the job of a school to provide a well-rounded physical education program.* Invalid general principle: *It is the job of a school to produce healthy, physically fit people.*

- The reasons make sense.

- The reasons are presented in a logical and effective order.

- The claim and all reasons are adequately supported by sound evidence.

- The evidence is sufficient, accurate, and relevant.

- The logic is sound. There are no instances of faulty reasoning.

- The argument adequately anticipates and addresses reader concerns and counterclaims with counterarguments.

Use the preceding criteria to evaluate the strength of the following proposal.

MODEL

Summary of Proposal

I propose that our school install video cameras in halls, lunchrooms, and other public areas to monitor students' activities.

Need

The halls and public areas of our school are not well supervised because of a shortage of security staff. Last month, three students were hurt in fights on school property.

Proposed Solution

Installing video monitors in the halls and public areas of the school will create a safe environment for students at a reasonable cost.

There is good evidence that video monitoring works. Westview School has monitored its students for over a year. In that time there has not been one incident of fighting or damage to property.

People who are against video monitoring don't agree. They say that monitoring violates students' rights to privacy.

In my opinion, junior high students need to act like responsible adults. We need guidelines and monitoring to show us where the limits are and to help us learn to act responsibly on our own.

Not only does video monitoring work, but installing the equipment can lower supervisory costs in the long run. Only eight cameras would be needed, installed in the two main hallways, the lunchroom, and the auditorium. The total cost would be around $16,000. I believe the money can be found in the general school budget.

What idiot would not support video monitoring of students?

It would be a crime not to have video monitoring.

Most school officials only care about their jobs and not what's good for students. I say to those school officials who do care: Either install video cameras or wait for more students to be injured.

6 Adjusting Reading Rate to Purpose

You may need to change the way you read certain texts in order to understand what you read. To adjust the way you read, you first need to be aware of what you want to get out of what you are reading. Then you can adjust the speed at which you read in response to your purpose and the difficulty of the material.

Determine Your Purpose for Reading

You read different types of materials for different purposes. You may read a novel for enjoyment. You may read a textbook unit to learn a new concept or to master the content for a test. When you read for enjoyment, you naturally read at a pace that is comfortable for you. When you read for information, you need to read material more slowly and thoroughly. When you are being tested on material, you may think you have to read fast, especially if the test is being timed. However, you can actually increase your understanding of the material if you slow down.

Determine Your Reading Rate

The rate at which you read most comfortably is called your **independent reading level.** It is the rate that you use to read materials that you enjoy. To learn to adjust your reading rate to read materials for other purposes, you need to be aware of your independent reading level. You can figure out your reading level by following these steps:

1. Select a passage from a book or story you enjoy.
2. Have a friend or classmate time you as you begin reading the passage silently.
3. Read at the rate that is most comfortable for you.
4. Stop when your friend or classmate tells you one minute has passed.
5. Determine the number of words you read in that minute and write down the number.
6. Repeat the process at least two more times, using different passages.
7. Add the numbers and divide the sum by the number of times your friend timed you.

Reading Techniques for Informational Material

You can use the following techniques to adapt your reading for informational texts, to prepare for tests, and to better understand what you read:

- **Skimming** is reading quickly to get the general idea of a text. To skim, read only the title, headings, graphic aids, highlighted words, and first sentence of each paragraph. Also, read any introduction, conclusion, or summary. Skimming can be especially useful when taking a test. Before reading a passage, you can skim questions that follow it in order to find out what is expected and better focus on the important ideas in the text.

   When researching a topic, skimming can help you decide whether a source has information that is related to your topic.

- **Scanning** is reading quickly to find a specific piece of information, such as a fact or a definition. When you scan, your eyes sweep across a page, looking for key words that may lead you to the information you want. Use scanning to review for tests and to find answers to questions.

- **Changing pace** is speeding up or slowing down the rate at which you read parts of a particular text. When you come across familiar concepts, you might be able to speed up without misunderstanding them. When you encounter unfamiliar concepts or material presented in an unpredictable way, however, you may need to slow down to understand the information.

WATCH OUT! Reading too slowly can affect your ability to understand what you read. Make sure you aren't just reading one word at a time. Practice reading phrases.

PRACTICE AND APPLY

Find an article in a magazine or textbook. Skim the article. Then answer the following questions:

1. What did you notice about the organization of the article from skimming it?
2. What is the main idea of the article?

Through writing, you can explore and record your thoughts, feelings, and ideas for yourself alone or you can communicate them to an audience.

COMMON CORE

Included in this handbook:
W 1a–e, W 2a–f, W 3a–e, W 4, W 5, W 6

1 The Writing Process

The writing process consists of the following stages: prewriting, drafting, revising and editing, proofreading, and publishing. These are not stages that you must complete in a set order. Rather, you may return to an earlier stage at any time to improve your writing.

1.1 PREWRITING

In the prewriting stage, you explore what you want to write about, what your purpose for writing is, whom you are writing for, and what form you will use to express your ideas. Ask yourself the following questions to get started.

Topic	• Is my topic assigned, or can I choose it? • What would I be interested in writing about?
Purpose	• Am I writing to entertain, to inform, to persuade, or for some combination of these purposes? • What effect do I want to have on my readers?
Audience	• Who is the audience? • What might the audience members already know about my topic? • What about the topic might interest them?
Format	• Which format will work best? Essay? Poem? Speech? Short story? Article? Research paper?

Find Ideas for Writing

• Browse through magazines, newspapers, and Web sites.

• Start a file of articles you want to save for future reference.

• With a group, brainstorm as many ideas as you can. Compile your ideas into a list.

• Write down anything that comes into your head.

• Interview someone who is an expert on a particular topic.

• Use a cluster map to explore subordinate ideas that relate to a general topic.

Organize Ideas

Once you've chosen a topic, you will need to compile and organize your ideas. If you are writing a description, you may need to gather sensory details. For an essay or a research paper, you may need to record information from different sources. To record notes from sources you read or view, use any or all of these methods:

• **Summarize:** Briefly retell the main ideas of a piece of writing in your own words.

• **Paraphrase:** Restate all or almost all of the information in your own words.

• **Quote:** Record the author's exact words.

Depending on what form your writing takes, you may also need to arrange your ideas in a certain pattern.

*For more information, see the **Writing Handbook**, pages R34–R41.*

1.2 DRAFTING

In the drafting stage, you put your ideas on paper and allow them to develop and change as you write. You don't need to worry about correct grammar and spelling at this stage. There are two ways that you can draft:

Discovery drafting is a good approach when you are not quite sure what you think about your subject. You just start writing and let your feelings and ideas lead you in developing the topic.

Planned drafting may work better if you know that your ideas have to be arranged in a certain way, as in a research paper. Try making a writing plan or an informal outline before you begin drafting.

1.3 REVISING AND EDITING

The revising and editing stage allows you to polish your draft and make changes in its content, organization, and style. Ask yourself:

- Does my writing have a **main idea** or central focus? Is my controlling idea clear?

- Have I used **precise** nouns, verbs, and modifiers?

- Have I included **adequate detail** and **evidence?** Where might I include a telling detail, revealing statistic, or vivid example?

- Is my writing **unified?** Do all ideas and supporting details help explain my main idea?

- Is my writing **logical** and **coherent?** Do sentences connect to one another smoothly?

- Is my writing **balanced,** or do I include too many or not enough details in one part?

- Have I used a consistent **point of view?**

- Do I need to add **transitional words, phrases,** or sentences to explain relationships among ideas?

- Have I used a **variety of sentence types?** Are they well constructed? What sentences might I combine to improve the rhythm of my writing?

- Have I used a **tone** appropriate for my audience and purpose?

1.4 PROOFREADING

Check your paper for mistakes in grammar, usage, and mechanics. You may want to do this several times, looking for a different type of mistake each time. Use the following questions to help you correct errors:

- Have I corrected any errors in **subject-verb agreement** and **pronoun-antecedent agreement?**

- Have I double-checked for errors in **confusing word pairs,** such as *it's/its, than/then,* and *too/to?*

- Have I corrected any **run-on sentences** and **sentence fragments?**

- Have I followed rules for **correct capitalization?**

- Have I used **punctuation marks** correctly?

- Have I checked the **spellings of all unfamiliar words** in the dictionary?

TIP If possible, put your work away for at least a few hours before proofreading. This will make it easier to identify mistakes.

*For more information, see the **Grammar Handbook** and the **Vocabulary and Spelling Handbook**, pages R46–R75.*

Use the proofreading symbols in the chart to mark changes on your draft.

Proofreading Symbols	
∧ Add letters or words.	/ Make a capital letter lowercase.
⊙ Add a period.	⌗ Begin a new paragraph.
≡ Capitalize a letter.	⌐ Delete letters or words.
⊃ Close up space.	∩ Switch the positions of letters or words.
∧ Add a comma.	

1.5 PUBLISHING AND REFLECTING

Always consider sharing your finished writing with a wider audience.

Publishing Ideas

- Post your writing on a blog.

- Create a multimedia presentation and share it with classmates.

- Publish your writing in a school newspaper, local newspaper, or literary magazine.

- Present your work orally in a report, speech, reading, or dramatic performance.

Reflecting on Your Writing

Think about your writing process and whether you would like to add what you have written to your writing portfolio. Ask yourself:

- Which parts of the process did I find easiest? Which parts were more difficult?

- What was the biggest problem I faced during the writing process? How did I solve the problem?

- What changes have occurred in my writing style?

- Have I noticed any features in the writing of published authors or my peers that I can apply to my own work?

1.6 PEER RESPONSE

Peer response consists of the suggestions and comments you make about the writing of your peers and also the comments and suggestions they make about your writing. You can ask a peer reader for help at any time in the writing process.

Using Peer Response as a Writer

- Indicate whether you are more interested in feedback about your ideas or about your presentation of them.

- Ask questions that will help you get specific information about your writing. Open-ended questions that require more than yes-or-no answers are more likely to give you information you can use as you revise.

- Give your readers plenty of time to respond thoughtfully to your writing.

- Encourage your readers to be honest.

Being a Peer Reader

- Respect the writer's feelings.

- Offer positive reactions first.

- Make sure you understand what kind of feedback the writer is looking for, and then respond accordingly.

For more information on the writing process, see the **Introductory Unit,** *pages 20–23.*

2 Building Blocks of Good Writing

Whatever your purpose in writing, you need to capture your reader's interest and organize your thoughts clearly.

2.1 INTRODUCTIONS

An introduction should present a controlling idea and capture your reader's attention.

Kinds of Introductions

There are a number of ways to write an introduction. The one you choose depends on who the audience is and on your purpose for writing.

Make a Surprising Statement Beginning with a startling statement or an interesting fact can arouse your reader's curiosity about a subject, as in the following model.

> **MODEL**
>
> Bats may seem like a nuisance, but not as much as the many pounds of insects a colony of bats can eat in one night. Despite their ugly faces and all the scary stories about them, bats are very important and useful animals.

Provide a Description A vivid description sets a mood and brings a scene to life for your reader.

Here, details about wild geese swimming in an unfrozen river during the winter set the tone for an essay about water pollution.

> **MODEL**
>
> The temperature is 15 degrees. Drifts of snow hide picnic tables and swings. In the middle of the park, however, steam rises from a lake where Canada geese swim. It sounds beautiful, but the water is warm because it has been heated by a chemical plant upriver. In fact, the geese should have migrated south by now.

Ask a Question Beginning with a question can make your reader want to read on to find out the answer. The following introduction asks what two seemingly different things have in common.

> **MODEL**
>
> What do billiard balls and movie film have in common? It was in an effort to find a substitute for ivory billiard balls that John Hyatt created celluloid. This plastic substance was also used to make the first movies.

Relate an Anecdote Beginning with an anecdote, or brief story, can hook your reader and help you make a point in a dramatic way. The following anecdote introduces a humorous story about a childhood experience.

MODEL

When I was younger, my friends and I would rub balloons in our hair and make them stick to our clothes. Someone once said, "I get a charge out of this," not knowing that we were really generating static electricity.

Address the Reader Speaking directly to your reader establishes a friendly, informal tone and involves the reader in your topic.

MODEL

Learn the latest dances from a famous video choreographer. Come to the community center for a free dance lesson on Saturday night at 6 P.M.

Begin with a Controlling Idea A controlling idea expressing a main idea may be woven into both the beginning and the end of a piece of nonfiction writing.

MODEL

Unlike the strategically planned warfare in today's world, warfare in medieval times was unsophisticated and included many primitive weapons.

TIP To write the best introduction for your paper, you may want to try more than one of the methods and then decide which is the most effective for your purpose and audience.

2.2 PARAGRAPHS

A paragraph is made up of sentences that work together to develop an idea or accomplish a purpose. Whether or not it contains a topic sentence stating the main idea, a good paragraph must have unity and coherence.

Unity

A paragraph has unity when all the sentences support and develop one stated or implied idea. Use the following technique to create unity in your paragraphs:

Write a Topic Sentence A topic sentence states the main idea of the paragraph; all other sentences in the paragraph provide supporting details. A topic sentence is often the first sentence in a paragraph, as shown in the model that follows. However, it may also appear later in a paragraph or at the end, to summarize or reinforce the main idea.

MODEL

Flying a hot-air balloon looks fun, but it requires a good mathematician to fly one safely. Since a balloon is controlled by heating and cooling the air inside the balloon, the pilot must know the temperature of the air outside it and how high he or she plans to fly in order to calculate the maximum weight the balloon can carry. If the pilot doesn't do the math correctly, the balloon could crash.

TIP Paying attention to topic sentences when you read literature can help you craft your own topic sentences. Notice the use of strong topic sentences in "The Noble Experiment" on pages 834–843. For example, the fourth paragraph on page 836 begins, "Winning his directors' approval was almost insignificant in contrast to the task which now lay ahead of the Dodger president." The rest of the paragraph then explains that task in detail.

Coherence

A paragraph is coherent when all its sentences are related to one another and each flows logically to the next. The following techniques will help you achieve coherence in paragraphs:

- Present your ideas in the most logical order.
- Use pronouns, synonyms, and repeated words to connect ideas.
- Use transitional words to show relationships among ideas.

In the model shown here, the writer used several techniques to create a coherent paragraph.

MODEL

Before you buy a backpack, you should make sure it fits you and will last a long time. First, check the seams to be sure they are zigzag stitched and not single-row stitched. Next, check that the zippers are covered by flaps so your homework doesn't get wet when it rains. Finally, make sure that the bottom of the backpack rests comfortably on your hips.

2.3 TRANSITIONS

Transitions are words and phrases that show connections between details. Clear transitions help you to **unify important ideas.** In other words, they show how the different parts of your writing are related.

Kinds of Transitions

The types of transitions you choose depend on the ideas you want to convey.

Time or Sequence Some transitions help to clarify the sequence of events over time. When you are telling a story or describing a process, you can connect ideas with such transitional words as *first, second, always, then, next, later, soon, before, finally, after, earlier, afterward,* and *tomorrow.*

MODEL

Long before mountain bikes were made, bicycles were much less comfortable. The first cycle, which actually had four wheels, was made in 1645 and had to be walked. Later, two-wheeled cycles with pedals were called boneshakers because of their bumpy ride.

Spatial Order Transitional words and phrases such as *in front, behind, next to, along, nearest, lowest, above, below, underneath, on the left,* and *in the middle* can help your reader visualize a scene.

MODEL

The audience entered the theater from the back. The stage was in front, and fire exits were located to the right and left of the stage.

Degree of Importance Transitional words such as *mainly, strongest, weakest, first, second, most important, least important, worst,* and *best* may be used to rank ideas or to show degrees of importance.

MODEL

My strongest reason for going on the canoeing trip would be not hearing my little brother and sister squabbling over the TV. My weakest reason for going is that there is nothing better to do.

Compare and Contrast Words and phrases such as *similarly, likewise, also, like, as, neither . . . nor,* and *either . . . or* show similarity between details. *However, by contrast, yet, but, unlike, instead, whereas,* and *while* show difference. Note the use of transitions showing contrast in the model.

MODEL

While my local public library is a quieter place to study than home, I don't always get much done in the library. I'm so used to the cheerful chatter of my baby brother that, by contrast, the stillness of the library makes me sleepy.

TIP Both *but* and *however* can be used to join two independent clauses. When *but* is used as a coordinating conjunction, it is preceded by a comma. When *however* is used as a conjunctive adverb, it is preceded by a semicolon and followed by a comma.

EXAMPLE

A greenbottle fly is small, but its eyes contain many lenses.

You can try to quietly sneak up on a fly with a swatter; however, the fly, with its compound eyes, will still be able to see the motion of the swatter.

Cause-Effect When you are writing about a cause-effect relationship, use transitional words and phrases such as *since, because, thus, therefore, so, due to, for this reason,* and *as a result* to help explain that relationship and make your writing coherent.

MODEL

> Because we missed seven days of school as a result of snowstorms, the school year will be extended. Therefore, we will be in school until June 17.

2.4 CONCLUSIONS

A conclusion should leave readers with a strong final impression.

Kinds of Conclusions

Good conclusions sum up ideas in a variety of ways. Here are some techniques you might try.

Restate Your Controlling Idea A good way to conclude an essay is by restating your controlling idea, or thesis, in different words. The following conclusion restates the controlling idea introduced on page R31.

MODEL

> It may be hard to imagine that ladders, bows, and catapults were once used in battle; yet these primitive weapons accomplished the attackers' main goal—to get a castle's inhabitants to surrender.

Ask a Question Try asking a question that sums up what you have said and gives your reader something new to think about. This question concludes a piece of persuasive writing and suggests a course of action.

MODEL

> If tutoring a student in writing, reading, or math can help you do better in these subjects yourself, shouldn't you take advantage of the opportunities to tutor at Western Elementary School?

Make a Recommendation When you are persuading your audience to take a position on an issue, you can conclude by recommending a specific course of action.

MODEL

> Since learning a foreign language gives you a chance to expand your world view and make new friends, register for one of the introductory courses that start next fall.

Offer an Opinion Leave your reader with something to think about by offering your personal opinion on the topic. The following model offers an opinion about medieval warfare.

MODEL

> Even though the tools used in medieval times seem primitive today, warfare is serious and deadly business, no matter what century you're in.

End with the Last Event If you're telling a story, you may end with the last thing that happens. Here, the ending includes an important moment for the narrator.

MODEL

> As I raced down the basketball court in the final seconds of the game, I felt as alone as I did on all those nights practicing by myself in the driveway. My perfect lay-up drew yells from the crowd, but I was cheering for myself on the inside.

2.5 ELABORATION

Elaboration is the process of developing an idea by providing specific supporting details that are relevant and appropriate to the purpose and form of your writing.

Facts and Statistics A fact is a statement that can be verified, and a statistic is a fact expressed as a number. Make sure the facts and statistics you supply are from reliable, up-to-date sources.

MODEL

> Rhode Island is the smallest state in area; however, it is not the smallest in population. According to the U.S. Census Bureau, its population was estimated to be 1,080,632 in 2004. There are fewer people living in Alaska, Delaware, Montana, North Dakota, South Dakota, Vermont, and Wyoming.

Descriptions Describe how something looks, sounds, tastes, smells, or feels to make readers feel they are actually experiencing what you are describing. Which senses does the writer appeal to in the following model?

MODEL

I was nervous during my math test last week. Chewing on my pencil left my mouth feeling dry and flaky. My palms were sweating so much, they left stains on the pages. The ticking of the clock seemed like the beating of a drum inside my head.

Anecdotes From our earliest years, we are interested in hearing "stories." One way to illustrate a point powerfully is to relate an incident or tell a brief anecdote, as shown in the example.

MODEL

People who are afraid of heights tend to panic even in perfectly safe situations. When my friend Jill and I rode to the top floor of a shopping mall, I enjoyed the view from the glass-enclosed elevator, but Jill's face was pale and her hands trembled.

Examples An example can help make an abstract idea concrete or can serve to clarify a complex point for your reader.

MODEL

The origins of today's professional sporting events in the United States can be traced to countries all over the world. For example, hockey is believed to have been influenced by the Irish game of hurling, which included a stick and a square wooden block.

Quotations Choose quotations that clearly support your points, and be sure that you copy each quotation word for word. Remember always to credit the source.

MODEL

After the tragic events that come to pass in Rod Serling's teleplay *The Monsters Are Due on Maple Street,* the narrator says to the audience, "The tools of conquest do not necessarily come with bombs and explosions and fallout. There are weapons that are simply thoughts, attitudes, prejudices—to be found only in the minds of men. For the record, prejudices can kill and suspicion can destroy."

3 Writing Description

Descriptive writing allows you to paint word pictures about anything, from events of global importance to the most personal feelings. It is an essential part of almost every piece of writing.

> **RUBRIC: Standards for Writing**
>
> **Successful descriptive writing should**
> - have a clear focus and sense of purpose
> - use sensory details and precise words to create a vivid image, establish a mood, or express emotion
> - present details in a logical order

3.1 KEY TECHNIQUES

Consider Your Goals What do you want to accomplish with your description? Do you want to show why something is important to you? Do you want to make a person or scene more memorable? Do you want to explain an event?

Identify Your Audience Who will read your description? How familiar are they with your subject? What background information will they need? Which details will they find most interesting?

Think Figuratively What figures of speech might help make your description vivid and interesting? What simile or metaphor comes to mind? What imaginative comparisons can you make? What living thing does an inanimate object remind you of?

Gather Sensory Details Which sights, smells, tastes, sounds, and textures make your subject come alive? Which details stick in your mind when you observe or recall your subject? Which senses does it most strongly affect?

You might want to use a chart like the one shown here to collect sensory details about your subject.

Sights	Sounds	Textures	Smells	Tastes

Organize Your Details Details that are presented in a logical order help the reader form a mental picture of the subject. Descriptive details may be organized chronologically, spatially, by order of impression, or by order of importance.

3.2 OPTIONS FOR ORGANIZATION

Option 1: Spatial Order Choose one of these options to show the spatial order of elements in a scene you are describing.

*For more information, see **Transitions,** page R32.*

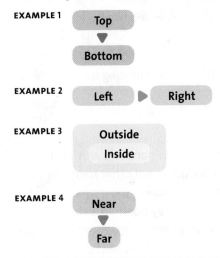

MODEL

The room was quiet—too quiet. To my left loomed the big white refrigerator. To my right squatted the gas stove, blue pilots glowing. Straight ahead sat the huge island. Cutting board, knife, and half-chopped carrot lay abandoned upon it now. Stepping cautiously to the right of the island, I came in view of the oven. That's where I froze. The oven door was open. A faint, white light pulsed and flickered high in one corner.

Option 2: Order of Impression Order of impression is the order in which you notice details.

MODEL

As she lost her balance on the slippery pebbles, her first thought was that she was going to sprain her ankle and be swept away by the surf. Her heart beat rapidly, but before she knew it, she was sitting in the sand while the warm surf rolled in, almost covering her. She realized that the water was not going to reach beyond her shoulders and that she was safe. Then, suddenly, she felt the tug of the water in the other direction as the undertow flowed back, sweeping the sand from under her as it went. As soon as the water had receded she scrambled to her feet.

TIP Use transitions that help readers understand the order of the impressions you are describing. Some useful transitions are *after, next, during, first, before, finally,* and *then.*

Option 3: Order of Importance You can use order of importance as the organizing structure for a description.

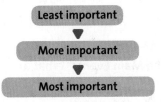

MODEL

I think our school should offer karate as part of the gym program. There are several reasons this is a good idea. First, karate is fun, and anyone can learn to do it. Many students who want to learn martial arts can't afford to because private lessons are so expensive. Karate is also a great form of exercise. It improves strength, coordination, and grace. The most important reason, though, is that learning karate makes students more confident and gives them skills that can help them throughout life.

*For more information, see **Transitions,** page R32.*

Option 4: Chronological Order You can use chronological order as the organizing structure for a description. See section 4.2 on page R36 for an example of how this is done.

④ Writing Narratives

Narrative writing tells a story. If you write a story from your imagination, it is a fictional narrative. A true story about actual events is a nonfictional narrative. Narrative writing can be found in short stories, novels, news articles, personal narratives, and biographies.

> **RUBRIC: Standards for Writing**
>
> **A successful narrative should**
> - develop a standard plot line, with a beginning, conflict, rising action, climax, and denouement
> - include complex major and minor characters and a definite setting
> - maintain a consistent point of view
> - capture reader attention with dialogue and suspense
> - include descriptions of movement, gestures, and expressions
> - have a logical organization and clear transitions

For more information, see **Writing Workshop: Short Story,** *pages 432–441.*

4.1 KEY TECHNIQUES

Identify the Main Events What are the most important events in your narrative? Is each event needed to tell the story?

Describe the Setting When do the events occur? Where do they take place? How can you use setting to create mood and to set the stage for the characters and their actions?

Depict Characters Vividly What do your characters look like? What do they think and say? How do they act? What details can show what they are like?

TIP Dialogue is an effective means of developing characters in a narrative. As you write dialogue, choose words that express your characters' personalities and that show how the characters feel about one another and about the events in the plot.

4.2 OPTIONS FOR ORGANIZATION

Option 1: Chronological Order One way to organize a piece of narrative writing is to arrange the events in chronological order, as shown.

EXAMPLE

Roger walked into the store where he had seen the fancy new bikes.

"Can I help you?" the salesperson asked. Roger pointed toward the bikes against a wall.

As his hand glided over the handle-bars on the bike, he barely heard the salesperson ask if he had money.

Roger ran for the door, knowing he had to find the old woman who had given him the money.

Introduction
Characters and setting

Event 1

Event 2

End
Perhaps showing the significance of the events

Option 2: Flashback In narrative writing, it is also possible to introduce events that happened before the beginning of the story. You may want to hook your reader's interest by opening a story with an exciting event. After your introduction, you can use a flashback to show how past events led up to the present situation or to provide background about a character or event. Use clue words such as *last summer, as a young girl, the previous school year,* and *his earliest memories* to let your reader know that you are interrupting the main action to describe earlier events.

Notice how the flashback interrupts the action in the model.

MODEL

At the trials for the first big meet of the school year, Shayna was eager to prove to the coach that she could be a leader on the track team. During warm-ups, her mind drifted back to her disastrous showing in the final meet last year, when she had dropped a baton in a relay race.

Option 3: Focus on Conflict When a fictional narrative focuses on a central conflict, the story's plot may be organized as in the following example.

EXAMPLE

A kind stranger gives Roger money he doesn't really deserve. Roger decides he will buy a bike with the money. In the store the bikes are lined up in a row, beautiful, shiny, and bright.

> Describe main characters and setting.

Roger is struggling with spending the stranger's money on a fancy bike that he really doesn't need.

> Present conflict.

- A salesperson walks up to Roger.
- Roger explains that he is looking at a 12-speed, super-lightweight bike.
- The salesperson tells Roger that the bike is very expensive and asks if he has enough money.

> Relate events that make conflict complex and cause characters to change.

Roger realizes that he shouldn't spend the money needlessly and runs out of the store in search of the stranger. He plans to return the money.

> Present resolution or outcome of conflict.

5 Writing Informative Texts

Expository writing informs and explains. You can use it to explain how to cook spaghetti, to explore the origins of the universe, or to compare two pieces of literature. There are many types of expository writing. Think about your topic and select the type that presents the information most clearly.

5.1 COMPARISON AND CONTRAST

Compare-and-contrast writing examines the similarities and differences between two or more subjects. You might, for example, compare and contrast two short stories, the main characters in a novel, or two movies.

RUBRIC: Standards for Writing

Successful compare-and-contrast writing should

- hook the reader's attention with a strong introduction
- clearly identify the subjects that are being compared and contrasted
- include specific, relevant details
- follow a clear plan of organization
- use language and details appropriate to the audience
- use transitional words and phrases to clarify similarities and differences

*For more information, see **Writing Workshop: Comparison-Contrast Essay**, pages 294–303, **Writing Workshop: Literary Analysis**, pages 532–541, **Writing Workshop: Online Feature Article**, pages 620–627, and **Writing Workshop: "How-to" Explanation**, pages 756–765.*

Options for Organization

Compare-and-contrast writing can be organized in different ways. The examples that follow demonstrate point-by-point organization and subject-by-subject organization.

Option 1: Point-by-Point Organization

EXAMPLE

I. Similarities in Appearance
> Point 1

Subject A. Domestic honeybees are about five-eighths of an inch long.

Subject B. Africanized bees, contrary to rumor, are about the same size.

II. Differences in Temperament
> Point 2

Subject A. Domestic honeybees are bred to be gentle.

Subject B. The Africanized bee is a "wild" bee that is quick-tempered around animals and people.

Option 2: Subject-by-Subject Organization

EXAMPLE

I. Domestic Honeybees   **Subject A**

   Point 1. Domestic honey-bees are about five-eighths of an inch long.

   Point 2. Domestic honeybees are bred to be gentle.

II. Africanized Bees   **Subject B**

   Point 1. Africanized bees are about five-eighths of an inch long.

   Point 2. The Africanized bee is a "wild" bee that is quick-tempered around animals and people.

*For more information, see **Writing Workshop: Comparison-Contrast Essay,** pages 294–303.*

5.2 CAUSE AND EFFECT

Cause-effect writing explains why something happened, why certain conditions exist, or what resulted from an action or a condition. You might use cause-effect writing to explain a character's actions, the progress of a disease, or the outcome of a war.

> **RUBRIC: Standards for Writing**
>
> **Successful cause-effect writing should**
>
> - hook the reader's attention with a strong introduction
> - clearly state the cause-and-effect relationship
> - show clear connections between causes and effects
> - present causes and effects in a logical order and use transitions effectively
> - use facts, examples, and other details to illustrate each cause and effect
> - use language and details appropriate to the audience

*For more information, see **Writing Workshop: "How-to" Explanation,** pages 756–765.*

Options for Organization

Your organization will depend on your topic and your purpose for writing.

Option 1: Effect-to-Cause Organization If you want to explain the causes of an event, such as the threat of Africanized bees to commercial beekeeping, you might first state the effect and then examine its causes.

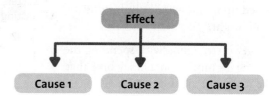

Option 2: Cause-to-Effect Organization If your focus is on explaining the effects of an event, such as the appearance of Africanized bees in the United States, you might first state the cause and then explain the effects.

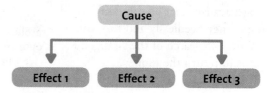

Option 3: Cause-Effect Chain Organization Sometimes you'll want to describe a chain of cause-and-effect relationships to explore a topic such as the myths about the Africanized honeybee.

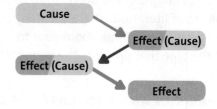

TIP Don't assume that a cause-effect relationship exists just because one event follows another. Look for evidence that the later event could not have happened if the first event had not caused it.

5.3 PROBLEM-SOLUTION

Problem-solution writing clearly states a problem, analyzes the problem, and proposes a solution to the problem. It can be used to identify and solve a conflict between characters, investigate global warming, or tell why the home team keeps losing.

RUBRIC: Standards for Writing

Successful problem-solution writing should

- hook the reader's attention with a strong introduction
- identify the problem and help the reader understand the issues involved
- analyze the causes and effects of the problem
- include quotations, facts, and statistics
- explore possible solutions to the problem and recommend the best one(s)
- use language, details, and a tone appropriate to the audience

Options for Organization

Your organization will depend on the goal of your problem-solution piece, your intended audience, and the specific problem you have chosen to address. The organizational methods that follow are effective for different kinds of problem-solution writing.

Option 1: Simple Problem-Solution

Option 2: Deciding Between Solutions

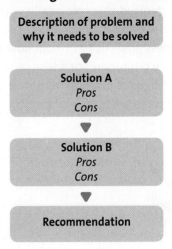

5.4 ANALYSIS

In writing an analysis, you explain how something works, how it is defined, or what its parts are.

RUBRIC: Standards for Writing

A successful analysis should

- hook the reader's attention with a strong introduction
- clearly define the subject and its parts
- use a specific organizing structure to provide a logical flow of information
- show connections among facts and ideas through transitional words and phrases
- use language and details appropriate for the audience

Options for Organization

Organize your details in a logical order appropriate to the kind of analysis you're writing. Use one of the options on the following page.

Option 1: Process Analysis A process analysis is usually organized chronologically, with steps or stages in the order in which they occur. You might use a process analysis to explain how to program a cell phone or prepare for a test, or to explain the different stages of development in an insect's life.

MODEL	
Insect metamorphosis	Introduce process.
Many insects grow through a four-step cycle.	Give background.
Step 1 egg Step 2 larva Step 3 pupa Step 4 adult	Explain steps.

Option 2: Definition Analysis You can organize the details of a definition analysis in order of importance or impression. Use a definition analysis to explain a quality (such as excellence), the characteristics of a limerick, or the characteristics of insects.

MODEL	
What is an insect?	
An insect is a small animal with an external skeleton, three body segments, and three pairs of legs.	Introduce term and definition.
Feature 1: external skeleton	Explain features.
Feature 2: three body segments	
Feature 3: three pairs of legs	

Option 3: Parts Analysis The following parts analysis explains the main parts of an insect.

MODEL	
An insect's body is divided into three main parts.	Introduce subject.
Part 1: The head includes eyes, mouth, and antennae.	Explain parts.
Part 2: The thorax has the legs and wings attached to it.	
Part 3: The abdomen contains organs for digesting food, eliminating waste, and reproducing.	

6 Writing Arguments

Persuasive writing allows you to use the power of language to inform and influence others. It includes speeches, persuasive essays, newspaper editorials, advertisements, and critical reviews.

> **RUBRIC: Standards for Writing**
> **Successful persuasive writing should**
> - hook the reader's attention with a strong introduction
> - state a clear position or claim in support of a proposition or proposal
> - support the proposition with clearly explained evidence
> - anticipate and answer reader concerns and counterarguments
> - conclude by summing up reasons or calling for action

*For more information, see **Writing Workshop: Persuasive Essay**, pages 988–997.*

6.1 KEY TECHNIQUES

Clarify Your Claim What do you believe about the issue? How can you express your opinion most clearly?

Know Your Audience Who will read your writing? What do they already know and believe about the issue? What objections to your position might they have? What additional information might they need? What tone and approach would be most effective?

Support Your Opinion Why do you feel the way you do about the issue? What facts, statistics, descriptions, specific examples, quotations, anecdotes, or expert opinions support your view? What reasons will convince your readers? What evidence can answer their objections?

Ways to Support Your Argument	
Statistics	facts that are stated in numbers
Examples	specific instances that explain points
Observations	events or situations you yourself have seen
Anecdotes	brief stories that illustrate points
Quotations	direct statements from authorities

*For more information, see **Identifying Faulty Reasoning**, page R24.*

Begin and End with a Bang How can you hook your readers and make a lasting impression? What memorable quotation, anecdote, or statistic will catch their attention at the beginning or stick in their minds at the end? What strong summary or call to action can you conclude with?

MODEL

Beginning

   If you want to spend an evening with your neighbors, seeing a live performance or shopping for homemade crafts, will you come to the community center? Probably not. It's too hot!

End

   Many people put hours and weeks into providing our town with entertainment. Often only a few people attend these events at the community center because the building is too hot on summer evenings. One "cool" solution would be to purchase an air-conditioning system.

6.2 OPTIONS FOR ORGANIZATION

In a two-sided persuasive essay, you want to show the weaknesses of other opinions as you explain the strengths of your own.

Option 1: Reasons for Your Opinion

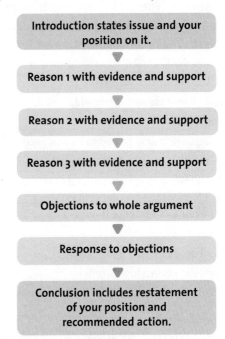

Option 2: Point-by-Point Basis

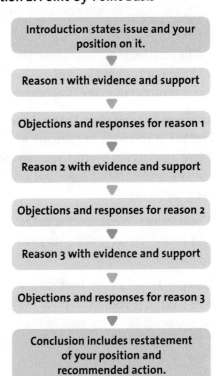

7 Writing Functional Texts

Business writing is writing done in a workplace to support the work of a company or business. You may need to do business writing to request information or complain about a product or service. Several types of formats, such as memos, letters, e-mails, and applications, have been developed to make communication easier.

> **RUBRIC: Standards for Writing**
>
> **Successful business writing should**
>
> - be courteous
> - use language that is geared to its audience
> - state the purpose clearly in the opening sentences or paragraph
> - have a formal tone and not contain slang, contractions, or sentence fragments
> - use precise words
> - present only essential information
> - present details in a logical order
> - conclude with a summary of important points

7.1 KEY TECHNIQUES OF WORKPLACE WRITING

Think About Your Purpose Why are you doing this writing? Do you want to order or complain about a product?

Identify Your Audience Who will read your writing? What background information will they need? What tone or language is appropriate?

Use a Pattern of Organization That Is Appropriate to the Content If you have to compare and contrast two products in a letter, you can use the same compare-and-contrast organization that you would use in an essay.

Support Your Points What specific details might clarify your ideas? What reasons do you have for your statements?

Finish Strongly How can you best sum up your statements? What is your main point? What action do you want the recipients to take?

Revise and Proofread Your Writing Just as you are graded on the quality of an essay you write for a class, you will be judged on the quality of your writing in the workplace.

7.2 MATCHING THE FORMAT TO THE OCCASION

E-mail messages, memos, and letters have similar purposes but are used in different situations. The chart shows how each format can be used.

Format	Occasion
Memo	Use to send correspondence **inside** the workplace only.
E-mail message	Use to send correspondence **inside or outside** the company.
Letter	Use to send correspondence **outside** the company.

TIP Memos are often sent as e-mail messages in the workplace. Remember that both require formal language and standard spelling, capitalization, and punctuation.

Technical writing is used for detailed instructions or descriptions of items and processes. It is important to a variety of fields, such as science, government, and industry. Technical writing is used to present information in such a way that the reader can use it to complete a task, such as performing an experiment, assembling an object, or using a tool.

At work, at school, or in everyday life you may have to use technical writing to leave instructions for another person.

> **RUBRIC: Standards for Writing**
>
> **Instructions should**
>
> - present only essential information
> - present steps in a logical order
> - include sentences that are short and simple
> - include definitions of unfamiliar terms if necessary
> - use transitions and/or numbered steps
> - use verbs that describe actions
> - use the present tense

7.3 KEY TECHNIQUES OF TECHNICAL WRITING

Think About Your Organization As you write, make sure you are presenting your information in a sensible order. For example, you would probably list any necessary tools and materials early on. Then you would present the steps in the order in which they should be followed.

Keep Your Audience in Mind Make sure you explain to readers unfamiliar with the activity or process what they need to know. Sometimes making a comparison to something the reader is familiar with can help. Graphics, such as pictures and maps, can also help make instructions easier to understand.

Use Transitions as Needed Transitions such as *first, next, after,* and *last* and numbered steps can make the order of steps clear and guide your reader from one step to the next.

Review Your Ending You can simply end with the last step, or you can end by describing the result or outcome of following the directions.

Evaluate Your Instructions Have a friend follow your instructions to make sure they are clear.

7.4 FORMATS

Business letters usually have a formal tone and a specific format as shown below. The key to writing a business letter is to get to the point as quickly as possible and to present your information clearly.

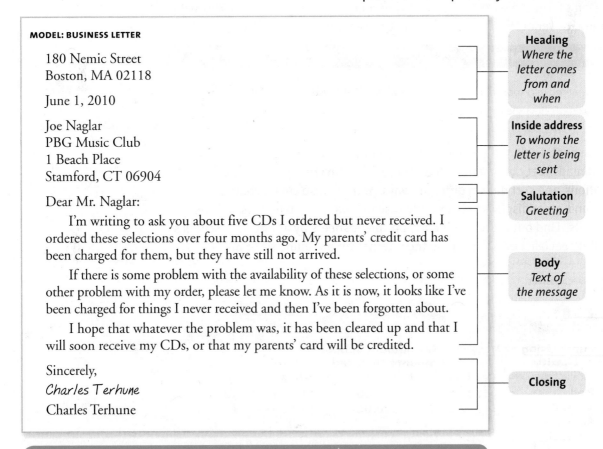

MODEL: BUSINESS LETTER

180 Nemic Street
Boston, MA 02118

June 1, 2010

Joe Naglar
PBG Music Club
1 Beach Place
Stamford, CT 06904

Dear Mr. Naglar:

    I'm writing to ask you about five CDs I ordered but never received. I ordered these selections over four months ago. My parents' credit card has been charged for them, but they have still not arrived.

    If there is some problem with the availability of these selections, or some other problem with my order, please let me know. As it is now, it looks like I've been charged for things I never received and then I've been forgotten about.

    I hope that whatever the problem was, it has been cleared up and that I will soon receive my CDs, or that my parents' card will be credited.

Sincerely,
Charles Terhune
Charles Terhune

Heading
Where the letter comes from and when

Inside address
To whom the letter is being sent

Salutation
Greeting

Body
Text of the message

Closing

PRACTICE AND APPLY

Draft a response to the letter. Then revise your letter as necessary according to the rubric at the beginning of page R42. Make sure you have included the necessary information and have written in an appropriate tone. Proofread your letter for grammatical errors and spelling mistakes. Follow the format of the model and use appropriate spacing between each part.

Memos are often used in workplaces as a way of sending information in a direct and concise manner. They can be used to announce or summarize meetings and to request actions or specific information.

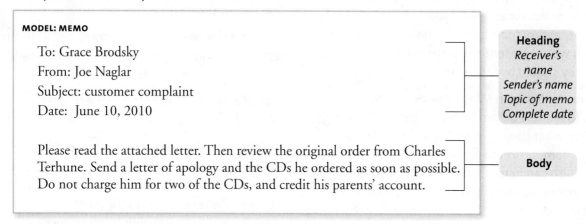

MODEL: MEMO

To: Grace Brodsky
From: Joe Naglar
Subject: customer complaint
Date: June 10, 2010

Please read the attached letter. Then review the original order from Charles Terhune. Send a letter of apology and the CDs he ordered as soon as possible. Do not charge him for two of the CDs, and credit his parents' account.

Heading
Receiver's name
Sender's name
Topic of memo
Complete date

Body

TIP Don't forget to write the topic of your memo in the subject line. This will help the receiver determine the importance of your memo.

PRACTICE AND APPLY

Write a memo in response to the memo shown here. Tell the receiver what actions you have taken. Follow the format of the model.

A spreadsheet displays data in rows and columns. When you type information into a spreadsheet document on a computer, you can create databases, make calculations, and sort data in different ways. You can also create charts, graphs, and other displays to insert into research papers, lab reports, or other documents. Find out more about creating spreadsheets by asking your school's computer specialist or by searching the Internet for an online tutorial.

MODEL: SPREADSHEET

	A	B	C	D	E
1	Fundraising at McLean Intermediate School				
2	Charity	Amounts Donated			
3		Grade 6	Grade 7	Grade 8	TOTALS
4	Red Cross	$136.50	$142.80	$111.44	$390.74
5	AmeriCares	$82.00	$80.08	$77.39	$239.47
6	Second Harvest Food Bank	$31.00	$44.00	$63.20	$138.20

PRACTICE AND APPLY

Use your school's spreadsheet software to create a database. For example, you might poll your classmates on their favorite foods or favorite movies. Arrange the information in a chart, with results listed from most popular to least popular.

MODEL: INSTRUCTIONS

How to Prove That Rusting Is a Chemical Reaction That Causes Heat

You can do a simple experiment that shows that rusting is a chemical reaction that produces heat.

You will need:

- a pad of steel wool
- vinegar
- a small bowl
- a thermometer
- a large glass jar with a lid

1. Place the thermometer in the jar and put the lid on the jar.
2. After five minutes, record the temperature while the thermometer is still in the jar.
3. Fill the small bowl with vinegar.
4. Soak the steel-wool pad in the vinegar for two minutes.
5. Remove the lid from the jar, and wrap the steel-wool pad around the bulb of the thermometer. Put the lid back on the jar.
6. After five more minutes, record the temperature again while the thermometer is still in the jar.

Notice that the temperature has risen a few degrees. The vinegar removes a coating from the steel wool. As a result the iron in the steel-wool pad starts to rust. The rusting is caused by the interaction of iron and oxygen. This chemical reaction releases heat, causing the temperature reading on the thermometer to rise.

PRACTICE AND APPLY

Think about something you might want someone else to do because you won't be at home, such as do laundry or prepare dinner. Use the rubric at the bottom of page R42 to write instructions. Be sure to include the following:

- an opening statement that describes what needs to be done
- a list of tools and materials needed to perform the task
- the steps needed to perform the task
- transition words and/or numbered steps if order is important
- any special notes or warnings about a tool or step in the process

Writing Online THINK central
Go to thinkcentral.com.
KEYWORD: HML7N-R45

Writing that has a lot of mistakes can confuse or even annoy a reader. A business letter with a punctuation error might lead to a miscommunication and delay a reply. Or a sentence fragment might lower your grade on an essay. Paying attention to grammar, punctuation, and capitalization rules can make your writing clearer and easier to read.

COMMON CORE

Included in this handbook:
L 1a–c, L 2a–b, L 3

Quick Reference: Parts of Speech

PART OF SPEECH	FUNCTION	EXAMPLES
Noun	names a person, a place, a thing, an idea, a quality, or an action	
Common	serves as a general name, or a name common to an entire group	poet, novel, love, journey
Proper	names a specific, one-of-a-kind person, place, or thing	Jackson, Pleasant Street, Statue of Liberty
Singular	refers to a single person, place, thing, or idea	shark, planet, flower, truth
Plural	refers to more than one person, place, thing, or idea	sharks, planets, flowers, truths
Concrete	names something that can be perceived by the senses	snake, path, Philadelphia, damage
Abstract	names something that cannot be perceived by the senses	intelligence, fear, joy, loneliness
Compound	expresses a single idea through a combination of two or more words	girlfriend, father-in-law, Christmas Eve
Collective	refers to a group of people or things	army, flock, class, species
Possessive	shows who or what owns something	Strafford's, Bess's, children's, witnesses'
Pronoun	takes the place of a noun or another pronoun	
Personal	refers to the person making a statement, the person(s) being addressed, or the person(s) or thing(s) the statement is about	I, me, my, mine, we, us, our, ours, you, your, yours, she, he, it, her, him, hers, his, its, they, them, their, theirs
Reflexive	follows a verb or preposition and refers to a preceding noun or pronoun	myself, yourself, herself, himself, itself, ourselves, yourselves, themselves
Intensive	emphasizes a noun or another pronoun	(same as reflexives)
Demonstrative	points to one or more specific persons or things	this, that, these, those
Interrogative	signals a question	who, whom, whose, which, what
Indefinite	refers to one or more persons or things not specifically mentioned	both, all, most, many, anyone, everybody, several, none, some
Relative	introduces an adjective clause by relating it to a word in the clause	who, whom, whose, which, that

PART OF SPEECH	FUNCTION	EXAMPLES
Verb	expresses an action, a condition, or a state of being	
Action	tells what the subject does or did, physically or mentally	run, reaches, listened, consider, decides, dreamed
Linking	connects the subject to something that identifies or describes it	am, is, are, was, were, sound, taste, appear, feel, become, remain, seem
Auxiliary	precedes the main verb in a verb phrase	be, have, do, can, could, will, would, may, might
Transitive	directs the action toward someone or something; always has an object	The storm **sank** the ship.
Intransitive	does not direct the action toward someone or something; does not have an object	The ship **sank.**
Adjective	modifies a noun or pronoun	**strong** women, **two** epics, **enough** time
Adverb	modifies a verb, an adjective, or another adverb	walked **out, really** funny, **far** away
Preposition	relates one word to another word	at, by, for, from, in, of, on, to, with
Conjunction	joins words or word groups	
Coordinating	joins words or word groups used the same way	and, but, or, for, so, yet, nor
Correlative	used as a pair to join words or word groups used the same way	both . . . and, either . . . or, neither . . . nor
Subordinating	introduces a clause that cannot stand by itself as a complete sentence	although, after, as, before, because, since, when, if, unless
Interjection	expresses emotion	wow, ouch, hurrah

Quick Reference: The Sentence and Its Parts

The diagrams that follow will give you a brief review of the essentials of a sentence and some of its parts.

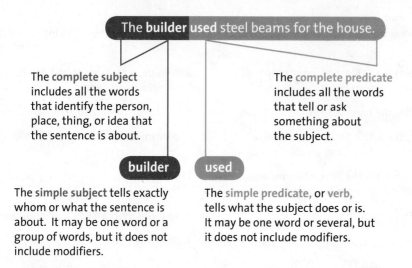

The **builder used** steel beams for the house.

The **complete subject** includes all the words that identify the person, place, thing, or idea that the sentence is about.

The **complete predicate** includes all the words that tell or ask something about the subject.

builder

used

The **simple subject** tells exactly whom or what the sentence is about. It may be one word or a group of words, but it does not include modifiers.

The **simple predicate,** or **verb,** tells what the subject does or is. It may be one word or several, but it does not include modifiers.

Every word in a sentence is part of a complete subject or a complete predicate.

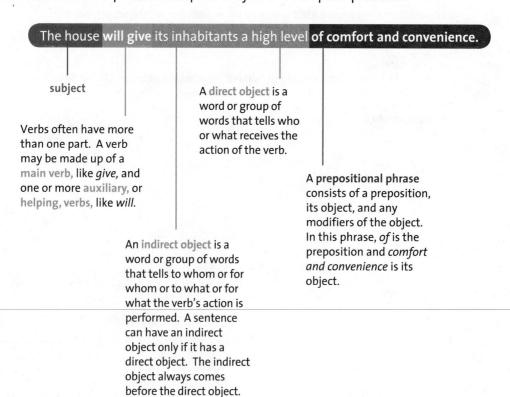

The house **will give** its inhabitants a high level **of comfort and convenience.**

subject

Verbs often have more than one part. A verb may be made up of a **main verb,** like *give,* and one or more **auxiliary,** or **helping, verbs,** like *will.*

A **direct object** is a word or group of words that tells who or what receives the action of the verb.

A **prepositional phrase** consists of a preposition, its object, and any modifiers of the object. In this phrase, *of* is the preposition and *comfort and convenience* is its object.

An **indirect object** is a word or group of words that tells to whom or for whom or to what or for what the verb's action is performed. A sentence can have an indirect object only if it has a direct object. The indirect object always comes before the direct object.

Quick Reference: Punctuation

MARK	FUNCTION	EXAMPLES
End Marks period, question mark, exclamation point	ends a sentence	We can start now. When would you like to leave? What a fantastic hit!
period	follows an initial or abbreviation **Exception:** postal abbreviations of states	Mrs. Dorothy Parker, McDougal Littell Inc., C. P. Cavafy, P.M., A.D., lb., oz., Blvd., Dr. NE (Nebraska), NV (Nevada)
period	follows a number or letter in an outline	I. Volcanoes A. Central-vent 1. Shield
Comma	separates part of a compound sentence	I had never disliked poetry, but now I really love it.
	separates items in a series	She is brave, loyal, and kind.
	separates adjectives of equal rank that modify the same noun	The slow, easy route is best.
	sets off a term of address	Maria, how can I help you? You must do something, soldier.
	sets off a parenthetical expression	Hard workers, as you know, don't quit. I'm not a quitter, believe me.
	sets off an introductory word, phrase, or dependent clause	Yes, I forgot my key. At the beginning of the day, I feel fresh. While she was out, I was here. Having finished my chores, I went out.
	sets off a nonessential phrase or clause	Ed Pawn, the captain of the chess team, won. Ed Pawn, who is the captain, won. The two leading runners, sprinting toward the finish line, finished in a tie.
	sets off parts of dates and addresses	Mail it by May 14, 2010, to the Hauptman Company, 321 Market Street, Memphis, Tennessee.
	follows the salutation and closing of a letter	Dear Jim, Sincerely yours,
	separates words to avoid confusion	By noon, time had run out. What the minister does, does matter. While cooking, Jim burned his hand.
Semicolon	separates items that contain commas in a series	We spent the first week of summer vacation in Chicago, Illinois; the second week in St. Louis, Missouri; and the third week in Albany, New York.
	separates parts of a compound sentence that are not joined by a coordinating conjunction	The last shall be first; the first shall be last. I read the Bible; however, I have not memorized it.
	separates parts of a compound sentence when the parts contain commas	After I ran out of money, I called my parents; but only my sister was home, unfortunately.

MARK	FUNCTION	EXAMPLES
Colon	introduces a list	Those we wrote were the following: Dana, John, and Will.
	introduces a long quotation	Abraham Lincoln wrote: "Four score and seven years ago, our fathers brought forth on this continent a new nation. . . ."
	follows the salutation of a business letter	To Whom It May Concern: Dear Leonard Atole:
	separates certain numbers	1:28 P.M., Genesis 2:5
Dash	indicates an abrupt break in thought	I was thinking of my mother—who is arriving tomorrow—just as you walked in.
Parentheses	enclose less important material	It was so unlike him (John is always on time) that I began to worry. The last World Series game (did you see it?) was fun.
Hyphen	joins parts of a compound adjective before a noun	The not-so-rich taxpayer won't stand for this!
	joins parts of a compound with *all-, ex-, self-,* or *-elect*	The ex-firefighter helped rescue him. Our president-elect is self-conscious.
	joins parts of a compound number (to ninety-nine)	Today, I turned twenty-one.
	joins parts of a fraction	My cup is one-third full.
	joins a prefix to a word beginning with a capital letter	Which Pre-Raphaelite painter do you like best? It snowed in mid-October.
	indicates that a word is divided at the end of a line	How could you have any reasonable expect-ations of getting a new computer?
Apostrophe	used with *s* to form the possessive of a noun or an indefinite pronoun	my friend's book, my friends' books, anyone's guess, somebody else's problem
	replaces one or more omitted letters in a contraction or numbers in a date	don't (omitted *o*), he'd (omitted *woul*), the class of '99 (omitted *19*)
	used with *s* to form the plural of a letter	I had two A's on my report card.
Quotation Marks	set off a speaker's exact words	Sara said, "I'm finally ready." "I'm ready," Sara said, "finally." Did Sara say, "I'm ready"? Sara said, "I'm ready!"
	set off the title of a story, an article, a short poem, an essay, a song, or a chapter	I like Paulsen's "Dirk the Protector" and Poe's "Annabel Lee." I like Ritchie Valens's "La Bamba."
Ellipses	replace material omitted from a quotation	"When in the course of human events . . . and to assume among the powers of the earth. . . ."
Italics	indicate the title of a book, a play, a magazine, a long poem, an opera, a film, or a TV series, or the name of a ship	*Holes, The Monsters Are Due on Maple Street, Newsweek,* the *Odyssey, Madame Butterfly, Gone with the Wind, Seinfeld, Titanic*
Brackets	indicate a word or phrase that has been added to a quotation to make it clearer	"Spreading awareness [of the hurricane's damage] is just as important as the work we will do."

Quick Reference: Capitalization

CATEGORY	EXAMPLES
People and Titles	
Names and initials of people	Amy Tan, W. H. Auden
Titles used before a name	Professor Holmes, Senator Long
Deities and members of religious groups	Jesus, Allah, Buddha, Zeus, Baptists, Roman Catholics
Names of ethnic and national groups	Hispanics, Jews, African Americans
Geographical Names	
Cities, states, countries, continents	Philadelphia, Kansas, Japan, Europe
Regions, bodies of water, mountains	the South, Lake Baikal, Mount Everest
Geographic features, parks	Great Basin, Yellowstone National Park
Streets and roads, planets	318 East Sutton Drive, Charles Court, Jupiter, Pluto
Organizations, Events, Etc.	
Companies, organizations, teams	Ford Motor Company, Boy Scouts of America, St. Louis Cardinals
Buildings, bridges, monuments	Empire State Building, Eads Bridge, Washington Monument
Documents, awards	Declaration of Independence, Stanley Cup
Special named events	Mardi Gras, World Series
Government bodies, historical periods and events	U.S. Senate, House of Representatives, Middle Ages, Vietnam War
Days and months, holidays	Thursday, March, Thanksgiving, Labor Day
Specific cars, boats, trains, planes	Porsche, *Carpathia, Southwest Chief,* Concorde
Proper Adjectives	
Adjectives formed from proper nouns	French cooking, Spanish omelet, Edwardian age, Western movie
First Words and the Pronoun *I*	
First word in a sentence or quotation	This is it. He said, "Let's go."
First word of sentence in parentheses that is not within another sentence	The spelling rules are covered in another section. (Consult that section for more information.)
First words in the salutation and closing of a letter	Dear Madam, Very truly yours,
First word in each line of most poetry Personal pronoun *I*	Then am I A happy fly If I live Or if I die.
First word, last word, and all important words in a title	*The Call of the Wild,* "Take Me Out to the Ball Game"

1 Nouns

A **noun** is a word used to name a person, a place, a thing, an idea, a quality, or an action. Nouns can be classified in several ways.

For more information on different types of nouns, see **Quick Reference: Parts of Speech**, *page R46.*

1.1 COMMON NOUNS

Common nouns are general names, common to entire groups.

1.2 PROPER NOUNS

Proper nouns name specific, one-of-a-kind people, places, and things.

Common	Proper
leader, park, forest, mountain	Sequoya, Sierra Nevada, Giant Forest, Mount Whitney

For more information, see **Quick Reference: Capitalization,** *page R51.*

1.3 SINGULAR AND PLURAL NOUNS

A noun may take a singular or a plural form, depending on whether it names a single person, place, thing, or idea or more than one. Make sure you use appropriate spellings when forming plurals.

Singular	Plural
tourist, city, mouse	tourists, cities, mice

For more information, see **Forming Plural Nouns,** *page R74.*

1.4 POSSESSIVE NOUNS

A **possessive noun** shows who or what owns something.

For more information, see **Forming Possessives,** *page R74.*

2 Pronouns

A **pronoun** is a word that is used in place of a noun or another pronoun. The word or word group to which the pronoun refers is called its **antecedent.**

2.1 PERSONAL PRONOUNS

Personal pronouns change their form to express person, number, gender, and case. The forms of these pronouns are shown in the following chart.

	Nominative	Objective	Possessive
Singular			
First person	I	me	my, mine
Second person	you	you	your, yours
Third person	she, he, it	her, him, it	her, hers, his, its
Plural			
First person	we	us	our, ours
Second person	you	you	your, yours
Third person	they	them	their, theirs

2.2 AGREEMENT WITH ANTECEDENT

Pronouns should agree with their antecedents in number, gender, and person.

If an antecedent is singular, use a singular pronoun.

> **EXAMPLE:** *Rachel wrote a **detective story**. It has a surprise ending.*

If an antecedent is plural, use a plural pronoun.

> **EXAMPLES:** *The **characters** have their motives for murder.*
>
> *Javier loves **mysteries** and reads them all the time.*

The gender of a pronoun must be the same as the gender of its antecedent.

> **EXAMPLE:** *The **man** has to use all his wits to stay alive and solve the crime.*

The person of the pronoun must be the same as the person of its antecedent. As the chart in Section 2.1 shows, a pronoun can be in first-person, second-person, or third-person form.

> **EXAMPLE:** *You want a story to grab your attention.*

Rewrite each sentence so that the underlined pronoun agrees with its antecedent.

1. The story "Dark They Were, and Golden-Eyed" tells about a man who travels to Mars and <u>its</u> life.

2. Harry has a feeling of dread, but he ignores <u>them</u>.

3. The colonists began to change, but <u>he</u> didn't notice anything odd.

4. Harry's fears were coming true, and <u>it</u> was hard to ignore.

5. When you finish this story, <u>we</u> might wonder if it could really happen.

2.3 PRONOUN FORMS

Personal pronouns change form to show how they function in sentences. The three forms are the subject form, the object form, and the possessive form. For examples of these pronouns, see the chart in Section 2.1.

A **subject pronoun** is used as a subject in a sentence.

EXAMPLE: A Christmas Carol *tells about Ebenezer Scrooge. He visits his past.*

Also use the subject form when the pronoun follows a linking verb.

EXAMPLE: *The first ghost was he.*

An **object pronoun** is used as a direct object, an indirect object, or the object of a preposition.

SUBJECT   OBJECT
He will lead them to us.
OBJECT OF PREPOSITION

A **possessive pronoun** shows ownership. The pronouns *mine, yours, hers, his, its, ours,* and *theirs* can be used in place of nouns.

EXAMPLE: *This money is mine.*

The pronouns *my, your, her, his, its, our,* and *their* are used before nouns.

EXAMPLE: *Scrooge thanked the spirits for their help.*

WATCH OUT! Many spelling errors can be avoided if you watch out for *its* and *their.* Don't confuse the possessive pronoun *its* with the contraction *it's,* meaning "it is" or "it has." The homonyms *they're* (a contraction of *they are*) and *there* ("in that place" or an expletive) are often mistakenly used for *their.*

TIP To decide which pronoun to use in a comparison, such as "He tells better tales than (I *or* me)," fill in the missing word(s): *He tells better tales than I tell.*

Write the correct pronoun form to complete each sentence.

1. Charles Dickens wrote *A Christmas Carol* when (he, him) was 31 years old.

2. This work of (him, his) was written in only a few weeks.

3. Dickens wrote other novels about Christmas. All of (their, his) dates of composition are from the 1840s.

4. (Them, They) have rather serious themes mixed with some humor.

5. When William Makepeace Thackeray, a fellow writer, reviewed *A Christmas Carol,* he said that (its, his) publication was a national benefit.

2.4 REFLEXIVE AND INTENSIVE PRONOUNS

These pronouns are formed by adding *-self* or *-selves* to certain personal pronouns. Their forms are the same, and they differ only in how they are used.

A **reflexive pronoun** follows a verb or preposition and reflects back on an earlier noun or pronoun.

EXAMPLES: *He likes himself too much.*

She is now herself again.

Intensive pronouns intensify or emphasize the nouns or pronouns to which they refer.

EXAMPLES: *They themselves will educate their children.*

You did it yourself.

WATCH OUT! Avoid using *hisself* or *theirselves*. Standard English does not include these forms.

> NONSTANDARD: *Alex dedicated hisself to learning the magician's secrets.*

> STANDARD: *Alex dedicated himself to learning the magician's secrets.*

2.5 DEMONSTRATIVE PRONOUNS

Demonstrative pronouns point out things and persons near and far.

	Singular	Plural
Near	this	these
Far	that	those

2.6 INDEFINITE PRONOUNS

Indefinite pronouns do not refer to specific persons or things and usually have no antecedents. The chart shows some commonly used indefinite pronouns.

Singular	Plural	Singular or Plural	
another	both	all	none
anybody	few	any	some
no one	many	more	most
neither			

TIP Indefinite pronouns that end in *one, body,* or *thing* are always singular.

> INCORRECT: *Did everybody play their part well?*

If the indefinite pronoun might refer to either a male or a female, *his or her* may be used to refer to it, or the sentence may be rewritten.

> CORRECT: *Did everybody play his or her part well?*
> *Did all the students play their parts well?*

2.7 INTERROGATIVE PRONOUNS

An **interrogative pronoun** tells a reader or listener that a question is coming. The interrogative pronouns are *who, whom, whose, which,* and *what.*

> EXAMPLES: *Who is going to rehearse with you?*
> *From whom did you receive the script?*

TIP *Who* is used as a subject; *whom,* as an object. To find out which pronoun you need to use in a question, change the question to a statement.

> QUESTION: *(Who/Whom) did you meet there?*
> STATEMENT: *You met (?) there.*

Since the verb has a subject (*you*), the needed word must be the object form, *whom.*

> EXAMPLE: *Whom did you meet there?*

WATCH OUT! A special problem arises when you use an interrupter, such as *do you think,* within a question.

> EXAMPLE: *(Who/Whom) do you think will win?*

If you eliminate the interrupter, it is clear that the word you need is *who.*

2.8 RELATIVE PRONOUNS

Relative pronouns relate, or connect, adjective clauses to the words they modify in sentences. The noun or pronoun that a relative clause modifies is the antecedent of the relative pronoun. Here are the relative pronouns and their uses.

	Subject	Object	Possessive
Person	who	whom	whose
Thing	which	which	whose
Thing/Person	that	that	whose

Often, short sentences with related ideas can be combined by using a relative pronoun to create a more effective sentence.

> SHORT SENTENCE: *Poe wrote "Annabel Lee."*

> RELATED SENTENCE: *"Annabel Lee" is a well-known poem in American literature.*

> COMBINED SENTENCE: *Poe wrote "Annabel Lee," which is a well-known poem in American literature.*

2.9 PRONOUN REFERENCE PROBLEMS

The referent of a pronoun should always be clear. Avoid problems by rewriting sentences.

An **indefinite reference** occurs when the pronoun *it, you,* or *they* does not clearly refer to a specific antecedent.

UNCLEAR: *My aunt hugged me in front of my friends, and it was embarrassing.*

CLEAR: *My aunt hugged me in front of my friends, and I was embarrassed.*

A **general reference** occurs when the pronoun *it, this, that, which,* or *such* is used to refer to a general idea rather than a specific antecedent.

UNCLEAR: *Jenna takes acting lessons. This has improved her chances of getting a part in the school play.*

CLEAR: *Jenna takes acting lessons. The lessons have improved her chances of getting a part in the school play.*

*Ambiguou*s means "having more than one possible meaning." An **ambiguous reference** occurs when a pronoun could refer to two or more antecedents.

UNCLEAR: *Tony talked to Fred and said that he could meet us later.*

CLEAR: *Tony talked to Fred and said that Fred could meet us later.*

3 Verbs

A **verb** is a word that expresses an action, a condition, or a state of being.

*For more information, see **Quick Reference: Parts of Speech,** page R47.*

3.1 ACTION VERBS

Action verbs express mental or physical activity.

EXAMPLE: *Mr. Cho slept with the window open.*

3.2 LINKING VERBS

Linking verbs join subjects with words or phrases that rename or describe them.

EXAMPLE: *When he awoke the next morning, his bed was wet from the rain.*

3.3 PRINCIPAL PARTS

Action and linking verbs typically have four principal parts, which are used to form verb tenses. The principal parts are the **present,** the **present participle,** the **past,** and the **past participle.**

Action verbs and some linking verbs also fall into two categories: regular and irregular. A **regular verb** is a verb that forms its past and past participle by adding *-ed* or *-d* to the present form.

Present	Present Participle	Past	Past Participle
jump	(is) jumping	jumped	(has) jumped
solve	(is) solving	solved	(has) solved
grab	(is) grabbing	grabbed	(has) grabbed
carry	(is) carrying	carried	(has) carried

An **irregular verb** is a verb that forms its past and past participle in some other way than by adding -ed or -d to the present form.

Present	Present Participle	Past	Past Participle
begin	(is) beginning	began	(has) begun
break	(is) breaking	broke	(has) broken
go	(is) going	went	(has) gone

3.4 VERB TENSE

The **tense** of a verb indicates the time of the action or the state of being. An action or state of being can occur in the present, the past, or the future. There are six tenses, each expressing a different range of time.

The **present tense** expresses an action or state that is happening at the present time, occurs regularly, or is constant or generally true. Use the present part.

NOW: *That snow looks deep.*

REGULAR: *It snows every day.*

GENERAL: *Snow falls.*

The **past tense** expresses an action that began and ended in the past. Use the past part.

EXAMPLE: *The storyteller finished his tale.*

The **future tense** expresses an action or state that will occur. Use *shall* or *will* with the present part.

EXAMPLE: *They will attend the next festival.*

The **present perfect tense** expresses an action or state that (1) was completed at an indefinite time in the past or (2) began in the past and continues into the present. Use *have* or *has* with the past participle.

EXAMPLE: *Poetry has inspired many readers.*

The **past perfect tense** expresses an action in the past that came before another action in the past. Use *had* with the past participle.

EXAMPLE: *He had built a fire before the dog ran away.*

The **future perfect tense** expresses an action in the future that will be completed before another action in the future. Use *shall have* or *will have* with the past participle.

EXAMPLE: *They will have read the novel before they see the movie version of the tale.*

TIP A past-tense form of an irregular verb is not used with an auxiliary verb, but a past-participle main irregular verb is always used with an auxiliary verb.

INCORRECT: *I have saw her somewhere before.* (*Saw* is the past-tense form of an irregular verb and shouldn't be used with *have*.)

CORRECT: *I have seen her somewhere before.*

INCORRECT: *I seen her somewhere before.* (*Seen* is the past participle of an irregular verb and shouldn't be used without an auxiliary verb.)

3.5 PROGRESSIVE FORMS

The progressive forms of the six tenses show ongoing actions. Use forms of *be* with the present participles of verbs.

PRESENT PROGRESSIVE: *She is rehearsing her lines.*

PAST PROGRESSIVE: *She was rehearsing her lines.*

FUTURE PROGRESSIVE: *She will be rehearsing her lines.*

PRESENT PERFECT PROGRESSIVE: *She has been rehearsing her lines.*

PAST PERFECT PROGRESSIVE: *She had been rehearsing her lines.*

FUTURE PERFECT PROGRESSIVE: *She will have been rehearsing her lines.*

WATCH OUT! Do not shift from tense to tense needlessly. Watch out for these special cases.

• In most compound sentences and in sentences with compound predicates, keep the tenses the same.

INCORRECT: *His boots freeze, and he shook with cold.*

CORRECT: *His boots freeze, and he shakes with cold.*

- If one past action happens before another, do shift tenses.

    INCORRECT: *They wished they started earlier.*
    CORRECT: *They wished they had started earlier.*

GRAMMAR PRACTICE

Rewrite each sentence, using a form of the verb in parentheses. Identify each form that you use.

1. Some medical developments (begin) with the space age—for example, laparoscopy and robotics.

2. Both of these areas (grow) and (advance) the field of surgery.

3. In the 1990s "robotic assistants" (help) in surgery.

4. People (come) to expect simpler procedures because of these new techniques.

5. Some day other procedures that avoid cutting into tissue (develop).

Rewrite each sentence to correct an error in tense.

1. I seen a movie about the cobra and its natural enemy, the mongoose.

2. Most snakes hide and avoided people.

3. The cobra raised its head when it seeks out its next victim.

4. Both the male and female protected their eggs and will attack an approaching intruder.

5. The venom of a cobra was deadly and kills a human being within a few hours.

3.6 ACTIVE AND PASSIVE VOICE

The voice of a verb tells whether its subject performs or receives the action expressed by the verb. When the subject performs the action, the verb is in the **active voice.** When the subject is the receiver of the action, the verb is in the **passive voice.**

Compare these two sentences:

ACTIVE: *Lois Lowry wrote* The Giver.
PASSIVE: The Giver *was written by Lois Lowry.*

To form the passive voice, use a form of *be* with the past participle of the verb.

WATCH OUT! Use the passive voice sparingly. It can make writing awkward and less direct.

    AWKWARD: The Giver *is a novel that was written by Lois Lowry.*
    BETTER: *Lois Lowry wrote the novel* The Giver.

There are occasions when you will choose to use the passive voice because

- you want to emphasize the receiver: *The king was shot.*

- the doer is unknown: *My books were stolen.*

- the doer is unimportant: *French is spoken here.*

4 Modifiers

Modifiers are words or groups of words that change or limit the meanings of other words. Adjectives and adverbs are common modifiers.

4.1 ADJECTIVES

Adjectives modify nouns and pronouns by telling which one, what kind, how many, or how much.

    WHICH ONE: *this, that, these, those*
    EXAMPLE: *That bird is a scarlet ibis.*

    WHAT KIND: *small, sick, courageous, black*
    EXAMPLE: *The sick bird sways on the branch.*

    HOW MANY: *some, few, ten, none, both, each*
    EXAMPLE: *Both brothers stared at the bird.*

    HOW MUCH: *more, less, enough*
    EXAMPLE: *The bird did not have enough strength to remain perched.*

4.2 PREDICATE ADJECTIVES

Most adjectives come before the nouns they modify, as in the examples above. A **predicate adjective,** however, follows a linking verb and describes the subject.

    EXAMPLE: *My friends are very intelligent.*

Be especially careful to use adjectives (not adverbs) after such linking verbs as *look, feel, grow, taste,* and *smell.*

    EXAMPLE: *The bread smells wonderful.*

4.3 ADVERBS

Adverbs modify verbs, adjectives, and other adverbs by telling where, when, how, or to what extent.

WHERE: *The children played outside.*

WHEN: *The author spoke yesterday.*

HOW: *We walked slowly behind the leader.*

TO WHAT EXTENT: *He worked very hard.*

Adverbs may occur in many places in sentences, both before and after the words they modify.

EXAMPLES: *Suddenly the wind shifted.*

The wind suddenly shifted.

The wind shifted suddenly.

4.4 ADJECTIVE OR ADVERB?

Many adverbs are formed by adding *-ly* to adjectives.

EXAMPLES: *sweet, sweetly; gentle, gently*

However, *-ly* added to a noun will usually yield an adjective.

EXAMPLES: *friend, friendly; woman, womanly*

4.5 COMPARISON OF MODIFIERS

Modifiers can be used to compare two or more things. The form of a modifier shows the degree of comparison. Both adjectives and adverbs have **comparative** and **superlative** forms.

The **comparative form** is used to compare two things, groups, or actions.

EXAMPLES: *His father's hands were stronger than his own.*

His father was more courageous than the other man.

The **superlative form** is used to compare more than two things, groups, or actions.

EXAMPLES: *His father's hands were the strongest in the family.*

His father was the most courageous of them all.

4.6 REGULAR COMPARISONS

Most one-syllable and some two-syllable adjectives and adverbs have comparatives and superlatives formed by adding *-er* and *-est*. All three-syllable and most two-syllable modifiers have comparatives and superlatives formed with *more* or *most*.

Modifier	Comparative	Superlative
small	smaller	smallest
thin	thinner	thinnest
sleepy	sleepier	sleepiest
useless	more useless	most useless
precisely	more precisely	most precisely

WATCH OUT! Note that spelling changes must sometimes be made to form the comparatives and superlatives of modifiers.

EXAMPLES: *friendly, friendlier* (Change *y* to *i* and add the ending.)

sad, sadder (Double the final consonant and add the ending.)

4.7 IRREGULAR COMPARISONS

Some commonly used modifiers have irregular comparative and superlative forms. They are listed in the following chart. You may wish to memorize them.

Modifier	Comparative	Superlative
good	better	best
bad	worse	worst
far	farther *or* further	farthest *or* furthest
little	less *or* lesser	least
many	more	most
well	better	best
much	more	most

4.8 PROBLEMS WITH MODIFIERS

Study the tips that follow to avoid common mistakes:

Farther* and *Further Use *farther* for distances; use *further* for everything else.

Double Comparisons Make a comparison by using *-er/-est* or by using *more/most*. Using *-er* with *more* or using *-est* with *most* is incorrect.

INCORRECT: *I like her more better than she likes me.*

CORRECT: *I like her better than she likes me.*

Illogical Comparisons An illogical or confusing comparison results when two unrelated things are compared or when something is compared with itself. The word *other* or the word *else* should be used when comparing an individual member to the rest of a group.

ILLOGICAL: *The narrator was more curious about the war than any student in his class.* (implies that the narrator isn't a student in the class)

LOGICAL: *The narrator was more curious about the war than any other student in his class.* (identifies that the narrator is a student)

Bad vs. Badly *Bad,* always an adjective, is used before a noun or after a linking verb. *Badly,* always an adverb, never modifies a noun. Be sure to use the right form after a linking verb.

INCORRECT: *Ed felt badly after his team lost.*

CORRECT: *Ed felt bad after his team lost.*

Good vs. Well *Good* is always an adjective. It is used before a noun or after a linking verb. *Well* is often an adverb meaning "expertly" or "properly." *Well* can also be used as an adjective after a linking verb when it means "in good health."

INCORRECT: *Helen writes very good.*

CORRECT: *Helen writes very well.*

CORRECT: *Yesterday I felt bad; today I feel well.*

Double Negatives If you add a negative word to a sentence that is already negative, the result will be an error known as a double negative. When using *not* or *-n't* with a verb, use *any-* words, such as *anybody* or *anything,* rather than *no-* words, such as *nobody* or *nothing,* later in the sentence.

INCORRECT: *We haven't seen nobody.*

CORRECT: *We haven't seen anybody.*

Using *hardly, barely,* or *scarcely* after a negative word is also incorrect.

INCORRECT: *They couldn't barely see two feet ahead.*

CORRECT: *They could barely see two feet ahead.*

Misplaced Modifiers Sometimes a modifier is placed so far away from the word it modifies that the intended meaning of the sentence is unclear. Prepositional phrases and participial phrases are often misplaced. Place modifiers as close as possible to the words they modify.

MISPLACED: *We found the child in the park who was missing.*

CLEARER: *We found the child who was missing in the park.* (The child was missing, not the park.)

Dangling Modifiers Sometimes a modifier doesn't appear to modify any word in a sentence. Most dangling modifiers are participial phrases or infinitive phrases.

DANGLING: *Looking out the window, his brother was seen driving by.*

CLEARER: *Looking out the window, Josh saw his brother driving by.*

GRAMMAR PRACTICE

Choose the correct word or words from each pair in parentheses.

1. When Ellis Island opened, it was the (larger, largest) port of entry to the United States.

2. In the 1980s, the facility underwent the (greatest, most greatest) restoration ever performed.

3. The restoration project (bad, badly) needed funds.

4. The project didn't have (no, any) funding until fundraising efforts began in 1982.

5. In 1990, the (grandly, grand) reopening was received (good, well).

GRAMMAR PRACTICE

Rewrite each sentence that contains a misplaced or dangling modifier. Write "correct" if the sentence is written correctly.

1. We traveled to Yellowstone Park with many tourists.

2. Driving our car, the mother bear growled.

3. We took pictures of the bears in the camper.

4. My brother and I went for a hike, but we got lost.

5. Taping our adventures, we had lots of film.

5 The Sentence and Its Parts

A **sentence** is a group of words used to express a complete thought. A complete sentence has a subject and a predicate.

For more information, see **Quick Reference: The Sentence and Its Parts,** *page R48.*

5.1 KINDS OF SENTENCES

There are four basic types of sentences.

Type	Definition	Example
Declarative	states a fact, a wish, an intent, or a feeling	Gary Soto understands youths.
Interrogative	asks a question	Did you read "Seventh Grade"?
Imperative	gives a command or direction	Read the story.
Exclamatory	expresses strong feeling or excitement	The story is great!

5.2 COMPOUND SUBJECTS AND PREDICATES

A compound subject consists of two or more subjects that share the same verb. They are typically joined by the coordinating conjunction *and* or *or.*

> **EXAMPLE:** *A short story or novel will keep you engaged.*

A compound predicate consists of two or more predicates that share the same subject. They too are usually joined by a coordinating conjunction: *and, but,* or *or.*

> **EXAMPLE:** *The class finished all the poetry but did not read the short stories.*

5.3 COMPLEMENTS

A **complement** is a word or group of words that completes the meaning of the sentence. Some sentences contain only a subject and a verb. Most sentences, however, require additional words placed after the verb to complete the meaning of the sentence. There are three kinds of complements: direct objects, indirect objects, and subject complements.

Direct objects are words or word groups that receive the action of action verbs. A direct object answers the question *what* or *whom.*

> **EXAMPLES:** *The students asked many questions.* (Asked what?)
>
> *The teacher quickly answered the students.* (Answered whom?)

Indirect objects tell to whom or what or for whom or what the actions of verbs are performed. Indirect objects come before direct objects. In the examples that follow, the indirect objects are highlighted.

> **EXAMPLES:** *My sister usually gave her friends good advice.* (Gave to whom?)
>
> *Her brother sent the store a heavy package.* (Sent to what?)

Subject complements come after linking verbs and identify or describe the subjects. A subject complement that names or identifies a subject is called a **predicate nominative.** Predicate nominatives include **predicate nouns** and **predicate pronouns.**

> **EXAMPLES:** *My friends are very hard workers.*
>
> *The best writer in the class is she.*

A subject complement that describes a subject is called a **predicate adjective.**

> **EXAMPLE:** *The pianist appeared very energetic.*

6 Phrases

A **phrase** is a group of related words that does not contain a subject and a predicate but functions in a sentence as a single part of speech.

6.1 PREPOSITIONAL PHRASES

A **prepositional phrase** is a phrase that consists of a preposition, its object, and any modifiers of the object. Prepositional phrases that modify nouns or pronouns are called **adjective phrases.** Prepositional phrases that modify verbs, adjectives, or adverbs are **adverb phrases.**

> **ADJECTIVE PHRASE:** *The central character of the story is a villain.*
>
> **ADVERB PHRASE:** *He reveals his nature in the first scene.*

6.2 APPOSITIVES AND APPOSITIVE PHRASES

An **appositive** is a noun or pronoun that identifies or renames another noun or pronoun. An **appositive phrase** includes an appositive and modifiers of it. An appositive usually follows the noun or pronoun it identifies.

An appositive can be either **essential** or **nonessential**. An **essential appositive** provides information that is needed to identify what is referred to by the preceding noun or pronoun.

> EXAMPLE: *The book is about the author Dave Barry.*

A **nonessential appositive** adds extra information about a noun or pronoun whose meaning is already clear. Nonessential appositives and appositive phrases are set off with commas.

> EXAMPLE: *The book, an autobiography, tells how he began writing.*

7 Verbals and Verbal Phrases

A **verbal** is a verb form that is used as a noun, an adjective, or an adverb. A **verbal phrase** consists of a verbal along with its modifiers and complements. There are three kinds of verbals: **infinitives, participles,** and **gerunds.**

7.1 INFINITIVES AND INFINITIVE PHRASES

An **infinitive** is a verb form that usually begins with *to* and functions as a noun, an adjective, or an adverb. An **infinitive phrase** consists of an infinitive plus its modifiers and complements.

> NOUN: *To know her is my only desire.* (subject)
> *I'm planning to walk with you.* (direct object)
> *Her goal was to promote women's rights.* (predicate nominative)
> ADJECTIVE: *We saw his need to be loved.* (adjective modifying *need*)
> ADVERB: *She wrote to voice her opinions.* (adverb modifying *wrote*)

Because *to,* the sign of the infinitive, precedes infinitives, it is usually easy to recognize them. However, sometimes *to* may be omitted.

> EXAMPLE: *Let no one dare [to] enter this shrine.*

7.2 PARTICIPLES AND PARTICIPIAL PHRASES

A **participle** is a verb form that functions as an adjective. Like adjectives, participles modify nouns and pronouns. Most participles are present-participle forms, ending in *-ing*, or past-participle forms ending in *-ed* or *-en*. In the examples below, the participles are highlighted.

> MODIFYING A NOUN: *The dying man had a smile on his face.*
> MODIFYING A PRONOUN: *Frustrated, everyone abandoned the cause.*

Participial phrases are participles with all their modifiers and complements.

> MODIFYING A NOUN: *The dogs searching for survivors are well trained.*
> MODIFYING A PRONOUN: *Having approved your proposal, we are ready to act.*

7.3 DANGLING AND MISPLACED PARTICIPLES

A participle or participial phrase should be placed as close as possible to the word that it modifies. Otherwise the meaning of the sentence may not be clear.

> MISPLACED: *The boys were looking for squirrels searching the trees.*
> CLEARER: *The boys searching the trees were looking for squirrels.*

A participle or participial phrase that does not clearly modify anything in a sentence is called a **dangling participle.** A dangling participle causes confusion because it appears to modify a word that it cannot sensibly modify. Correct a dangling participle by providing a word for the participle to modify.

> DANGLING: *Running like the wind, my hat fell off.* (The hat wasn't running.)
> CLEARER: *Running like the wind, I lost my hat.*

7.4 GERUNDS AND GERUND PHRASES

A **gerund** is a verb form ending in *-ing* that functions as a noun. Gerunds may perform any function nouns perform.

> SUBJECT: *Running is my favorite pastime.*
> DIRECT OBJECT: *I truly love running.*

INDIRECT OBJECT: *You should give running a try.*

SUBJECT COMPLEMENT: *My deepest passion is running.*

OBJECT OF PREPOSITION: *Her love of running keeps her strong.*

Gerund phrases are gerunds with all their modifiers and complements.

SUBJECT: *Wishing on a star never got me far.*

OBJECT OF PREPOSITION: *I will finish before leaving the office.*

APPOSITIVE: *Her avocation, flying airplanes, finally led to full-time employment.*

> **GRAMMAR PRACTICE**
>
> Rewrite each sentence, adding the type of phrase shown in parentheses.
>
> 1. I read Jackie Robinson's autobiography. (infinitive phrase)
> 2. I found several books and articles about him. (participial phrase)
> 3. Opposition to Robinson died down. (prepositional phrase)
> 4. Robinson played his entire major-league career with the same team. (appositive phrase)
> 5. Robinson went on to become one of the most popular Dodger players. (gerund phrase)

8 Clauses

A **clause** is a group of words that contains a subject and a predicate. There are two kinds of clauses: independent, or main, clauses and subordinate clauses.

8.1 MAIN AND SUBORDINATE CLAUSES

A **main (independent) clause** can stand alone as a sentence.

MAIN CLAUSE: *I read "Amigo Brothers."*

A sentence may contain more than one main clause.

EXAMPLE: *I finished dinner, and I read the story.*

In the preceding example, the coordinating conjunction *and* joins two main clauses.

For more information, see **Coordinating Conjunction,** page R47.

A **subordinate (dependent) clause** cannot stand alone as a sentence. It is subordinate to, or dependent on, a main clause.

EXAMPLE: *After I finished dinner, I read "Amigo Brothers."*

The highlighted clause cannot stand by itself. Note that a comma is added to the end of a dependent clause when it comes before a main clause.

8.2 ADJECTIVE CLAUSES

An **adjective clause** is a subordinate clause used as an adjective. It usually follows the noun or pronoun it modifies.

EXAMPLE: *Felix and Antonio are the boys who are the main characters in "Amigo Brothers."*

Adjective clauses are typically introduced by the relative pronouns *who, whom, whose, which,* and *that.*

For more information, see **Relative Pronouns,** page R54.

EXAMPLE: *The story, which takes place in New York, is about a boxing tournament.*

An adjective clause can be either essential or nonessential. An **essential adjective clause** provides information that is necessary to identify the preceding noun or pronoun.

EXAMPLE: *The boys had to make a decision that might change their lives.*

A **nonessential adjective clause** adds additional information about a noun or pronoun whose meaning is already clear. Nonessential clauses are set off with commas.

EXAMPLE: *The boys, who fought each other, wanted to remain friends.*

8.3 ADVERB CLAUSES

An **adverb clause** is a subordinate clause that is used to modify a verb, an adjective, or an adverb. It is introduced by a subordinating conjunction.

For examples of subordinating conjunctions, see **Noun Clauses,** page R63.

Adverb clauses typically occur at the beginning or end of sentences.

MODIFYING A VERB: *When we need you, we will call.*

MODIFYING AN ADVERB: *I'll stay here where there is shelter from the rain.*

MODIFYING AN ADJECTIVE: *Roman felt as good as he had ever felt.*

TIP An adverb clause should be followed by a comma when it comes before a main clause. When an adverb clause comes after a main clause, a comma may not be needed.

8.4 NOUN CLAUSES

A **noun clause** is a subordinate clause that is used as a noun. A noun clause may be used as a subject, a direct object, an indirect object, a predicate nominative, or the object of a preposition. Noun clauses are introduced either by pronouns, such as *that, what, who, whoever, which,* and *whose,* or by subordinating conjunctions, such as *how, when, where, why,* and *whether.*

For more subordinating conjunctions, see **Quick Reference: Parts of Speech,** *page R47.*

TIP Because the same words may introduce adjective and noun clauses, you need to consider how a clause functions within its sentence. To determine if a clause is a noun clause, try substituting *something* or *someone* for the clause. If you can do it, it is probably a noun clause.

EXAMPLES: *I know whose woods these are.* ("I know *something*." The clause is a noun clause, direct object of the verb *know*.)

Give a copy to whoever wants one. ("Give a copy to *someone*." The clause is a noun clause, object of the preposition *to*.)

GRAMMAR PRACTICE

Add descriptive details to each sentence by writing the type of clause indicated in parentheses.

1. Some students volunteer at animal shelters. (adjective clause)

2. They help take care of dogs and cats. (adverb clause)

3. The veterinarian tries to explain to the students. (noun clause)

4. Many people appreciate the students. (adjective clause)

5. I plan to work at the shelter. (adverb clause)

9 The Structure of Sentences

When classified by their structure, there are four kinds of sentences: simple, compound, complex, and compound-complex.

9.1 SIMPLE SENTENCES

A **simple sentence** is a sentence that has one main clause and no subordinate clauses.

EXAMPLES: *Sam ran to the theater.*

Max waited in front of the theater.

A simple sentence may contain a compound subject or a compound verb.

EXAMPLES: *Sam and Max went to the movie.* (compound subject)

They clapped and cheered at their favorite parts. (compound verb).

9.2 COMPOUND SENTENCES

A **compound sentence** consists of two or more main clauses. The clauses in compound sentences are joined with commas and coordinating conjunctions (*and, but, or, nor, yet, for, so*) or with semicolons. Like simple sentences, compound sentences do not contain any subordinate clauses.

EXAMPLES: *Sam likes action movies, but Max prefers comedies.*

The actor jumped from one building to another; he barely made the final leap.

WATCH OUT! Do not confuse compound sentences with simple sentences that have compound parts.

EXAMPLE: *The actor knew all the lines but didn't play the part well.*

(Here *but* joins parts of a compound predicate, not a compound sentence.)

9.3 COMPLEX SENTENCES

A **complex sentence** consists of one main clause and one or more subordinate clauses.

EXAMPLES: *One should not complain unless one has a better solution.*

Mr. Neiman, who is an artist, sketched pictures until the sun went down.

9.4 COMPOUND-COMPLEX SENTENCES

A **compound-complex sentence** contains two or more main clauses and one or more subordinate clauses. Compound-complex sentences are, simply, both compound and complex. If you start with a compound sentence, all you need to do to form a compound-complex sentence is add a subordinate clause.

COMPOUND: *All the students knew the answer, yet they were too shy to volunteer.*

COMPOUND-COMPLEX: *All the students knew the answer that their teacher expected, yet they were too shy to volunteer.*

9.5 PARALLEL STRUCTURE

When you write sentences, make sure that coordinate parts are equivalent, or **parallel,** in structure.

NOT PARALLEL: *Erin loved basketball and to play hockey.* (*Basketball* is a noun; *to play hockey* is a phrase.)

PARALLEL: *Erin loved basketball and hockey.* (*Basketball* and *hockey* are both nouns.)

NOT PARALLEL: *He wanted to rent an apartment, a new car, and traveling around the country.* (*To rent* is an infinitive, *car* is a noun, and *traveling* is a gerund.)

PARALLEL: *He wanted to rent an apartment, to drive a new car, and to travel around the country.* (*To rent, to drive,* and *to travel* are all infinitives.)

🔟 Writing Complete Sentences

Remember, a sentence is a group of words that expresses a complete thought. In writing that you wish to share with a reader, try to avoid both sentence fragments and run-on sentences.

10.1 CORRECTING FRAGMENTS

A **sentence fragment** is a group of words that is only part of a sentence. It does not express a complete thought and may be confusing to a reader or listener. A sentence fragment may be lacking a subject, a predicate, or both.

FRAGMENT: *Waited for the boat to arrive.* (no subject)

CORRECTED: *We waited for the boat to arrive.*

FRAGMENT: *People of various races, ages, and creeds.* (no predicate)

CORRECTED: *People of various races, ages, and creeds gathered together.*

FRAGMENT: *Near the old cottage.* (neither subject nor predicate)

CORRECTED: *The burial ground is near the old cottage.*

In your writing, fragments may be a result of haste or incorrect punctuation. Sometimes fixing a fragment will be a matter of attaching it to a preceding or following sentence.

FRAGMENT: *We saw the two girls. Waiting for the bus to arrive.*

CORRECTED: *We saw the two girls waiting for the bus to arrive.*

10.2 CORRECTING RUN-ON SENTENCES

A **run-on sentence** is made up of two or more sentences written as though they were one. Some run-ons have no punctuation within them. Others may have only commas where conjunctions or stronger punctuation marks are necessary. Use your judgment in correcting run-on sentences, as you have choices. You can change a run-on to two sentences if the thoughts are not closely connected. If the thoughts are closely related, you can keep the run-on as one sentence by adding a semicolon or a conjunction.

RUN-ON: *We found a place for the picnic by a small pond it was three miles from the village.*

MAKE TWO SENTENCES: *We found a place for the picnic by a small pond. It was three miles from the village.*

RUN-ON: *We found a place for the picnic by a small pond it was perfect.*

USE A SEMICOLON: *We found a place for the picnic by a small pond; it was perfect.*

ADD A CONJUNCTION: *We found a place for the picnic by a small pond, and it was perfect.*

WATCH OUT! When you form compound sentences, make sure you use appropriate punctuation: a comma before a coordinating conjunction, a semicolon when there is no coordinating conjunction, and a semicolon before a conjunctive adverb and a comma after it. A very common mistake is to use a comma alone instead of a comma and a conjunction. This error is called a **comma splice.**

INCORRECT: *He finished the job, he left the village.*

CORRECT: *He finished the job, and he left the village.*

⓫ Subject-Verb Agreement

The subject and verb in a clause must agree in number. Agreement means that if the subject is singular, the verb is also singular, and if the subject is plural, the verb is also plural.

11.1 BASIC AGREEMENT

Fortunately, agreement between subjects and verbs in English is simple. Most verbs show the difference between singular and plural only in the third person of the present tense. In the present tense, the third-person singular form ends in -s.

Present-Tense Verb Forms	
Singular	**Plural**
I sleep	we sleep
you sleep	you sleep
she, he, it sleeps	they sleep

11.2 AGREEMENT WITH *BE*

The verb *be* presents special problems in agreement, because this verb does not follow the usual verb patterns.

Forms of *Be*			
Present Tense		**Past Tense**	
Singular	**Plural**	**Singular**	**Plural**
I am	we are	I was	we were
you are	you are	you were	you were
she, he, it is	they are	she, he, it was	they were

11.3 WORDS BETWEEN SUBJECT AND VERB

A verb agrees only with its subject. When a prepositional phrase or other words come between a subject and a verb, ignore them when considering proper agreement. Identify the subject, and make sure the verb agrees with it.

EXAMPLES: *A story in the newspapers tells about the 1890s.*

Dad as well as Mom reads the paper daily.

11.4 AGREEMENT WITH COMPOUND SUBJECTS

Use plural verbs with most compound subjects joined by the word *and.*

EXAMPLE: *My father and his friends play chess everyday.*

To confirm that you need a plural verb, you could substitute the plural pronoun *they* for *my father and his friends.*

If a compound subject is thought of as a unit, use a singular verb. Test this by substituting the singular pronoun *it.*

EXAMPLE: *Peanut butter and jelly [it] is my brother's favorite sandwich.*

Use a singular verb with a compound subject that is preceded by *each*, *every*, or *many a*.

> **EXAMPLE:** *Each novel and short story seems grounded in personal experience.*

When the parts of a compound subject are joined by *or, nor,* or the correlative conjunctions *either . . . or* or *neither . . . nor,* make the verb agree with the noun or pronoun nearest the verb.

> **EXAMPLES:** *Cookies or ice cream is my favorite dessert.*
>
> *Either Cheryl or her friends are being invited.*
>
> *Neither ice storms nor snow is predicted today.*

11.5 PERSONAL PRONOUNS AS SUBJECTS

When using a personal pronoun as a subject, make sure to match it with the correct form of the verb *be*. (See the chart in Section 11.2.) Note especially that the pronoun *you* takes the forms *are* and *were*, regardless of whether it is singular or plural.

> **WATCH OUT!** *You is* and *you was* are nonstandard forms and should be avoided in writing and speaking. *We was* and *they was* are also forms to be avoided.
>
> **INCORRECT:** *You was a good student.*
>
> **CORRECT:** *You were a good student.*
>
> **INCORRECT:** *They was starting a new school.*
>
> **CORRECT:** *They were starting a new school.*

11.6 INDEFINITE PRONOUNS AS SUBJECTS

Some indefinite pronouns are always singular; some are always plural.

Singular Indefinite Pronouns			
another	either	neither	one
anybody	everybody	nobody	somebody
anyone	everyone	no one	someone
anything	everything	nothing	something
each	much		

> **EXAMPLES:** *Each of the writers was given an award.*
>
> *Somebody in the room upstairs is sleeping.*

Plural Indefinite Pronouns			
both	few	many	several

> **EXAMPLES:** *Many of the books in our library are not in circulation.*
>
> *Few have been returned recently.*

Still other indefinite pronouns may be either singular or plural.

Singular or Plural Indefinite Pronouns		
all	more	none
any	most	some

The number of the indefinite pronoun *any* or *none* often depends on the intended meaning.

> **EXAMPLES:** *Any of these topics has potential for a good article.* (any one topic)
>
> *Any of these topics have potential for good articles.* (all of the many topics)

The indefinite pronouns *all, some, more, most,* and *none* are singular when they refer to quantities or parts of things. They are plural when they refer to numbers of individual things. Context will usually give a clue.

> **EXAMPLES:** *All of the flour is gone.* (referring to a quantity)
>
> *All of the flowers are gone.* (referring to individual items)

11.7 INVERTED SENTENCES

A sentence in which the subject follows the verb is called an **inverted sentence.** A subject can follow a verb or part of a verb phrase in a question, a sentence beginning with *here* or *there*, or a sentence in which an adjective, an adverb, or a phrase is placed first.

> **EXAMPLES:** *There clearly are far too many cooks in this kitchen.*
>
> *What is the correct ingredient for this stew?*
>
> *Far from the embroiled cooks stands the master chef.*

TIP To check subject-verb agreement in some inverted sentences, place the subject before the verb. For example, change *There are many people* to *Many people are there.*

11.8 SENTENCES WITH PREDICATE NOMINATIVES

In a sentence containing a predicate noun (nominative), the verb should agree with the subject, not the predicate noun.

EXAMPLES: *The speeches of Martin Luther King Jr. are a landmark in American civil rights history.* (*Speeches* is the subject—not *landmark*—and it takes the plural verb *are.*)

One landmark in American civil rights history is the speeches of Martin Luther King Jr. (The subject is *landmark*—not *speeches*—and it takes the singular verb *is.*)

11.9 *DON'T* AND *DOESN'T* AS AUXILIARY VERBS

The auxiliary verb *doesn't* is used with singular subjects and with the personal pronouns *she, he,* and *it.* The auxiliary verb *don't* is used with plural subjects and with the personal pronouns *I, we, you,* and *they.*

SINGULAR: *She doesn't know Martin Luther King's famous "I Have a Dream" speech.*

Doesn't the young woman read very much?

PLURAL: *We don't have the speech memorized.*

Don't speakers usually memorize their speeches?

11.10 COLLECTIVE NOUNS AS SUBJECTS

Collective nouns are singular nouns that name groups of persons or things. *Team,* for example, is the collective name of a group of individuals. A collective noun takes a singular verb when the group acts as a single unit. It takes a plural verb when the members of the group act separately.

EXAMPLES: *Our team usually wins.* (The team as a whole wins.)

Our team vote differently on most issues. (The individual members vote.)

11.11 RELATIVE PRONOUNS AS SUBJECTS

When the relative pronoun *who, which,* or *that* is used as a subject in an adjective clause, the verb in the clause must agree in number with the antecedent of the pronoun.

SINGULAR: *I didn't read the **poem** about fireflies that was assigned.*

The antecedent of the relative pronoun *that* is the singular *poem*; therefore, *that* is singular and must take the singular verb *was.*

PLURAL: ***Mary Oliver and Pat Moran,** who are very different from each other, are both outstanding poets.*

The antecedent of the relative pronoun *who* is the plural compound subject *Mary Oliver and Pat Moran.* Therefore *who* is plural, and it takes the plural verb *are.*

GRAMMAR PRACTICE

Locate the subject of each verb in parentheses in the sentences below. Then choose the correct verb form.

1. In "Zebra" one (learn, learns) how John Wilson and Adam become friends.

2. John (tell, tells) Adam that he has an idea for a summer art class.

3. Many of Adam's classmates (think, thinks) that the summer art class will be fun.

4. Some (go, goes) to camp during the summer months, while others just (hang, hangs) around.

5. Among psychologists, many (believe, believes) that making art is good therapy.

6. Even you (has, have) a chance to be a good artist.

7. Does anyone else (want, wants) to take this class?

8. Objects in the attic, such as a broken umbrella, (is, are) good materials for making sculptures.

9. There (is, are) many beautiful objects made from old things.

10. Each of the students (leave, leaves) the class having learned something special.

The key to becoming an independent reader is to develop a tool kit of vocabulary strategies. By learning and practicing the strategies, you'll know what to do when you encounter unfamiliar words while reading. You'll also know how to refine the words you use for different situations—personal, school, and work.

Being a good speller is important when communicating your ideas in writing. Learning basic spelling rules and checking your spelling in a dictionary will help you spell words that you may not use frequently.

COMMON CORE

Included in this handbook:
L 4a–d, L 5a–c, L 6

1 Using Context Clues

The context of a word is made up of the punctuation marks, words, sentences, and paragraphs that surround the word. A word's context can give you important clues about its meaning.

1.1 GENERAL CONTEXT

Sometimes you need to determine the meaning of an unfamiliar word by reading all the information in a passage.

The sweater was of inferior quality. It was torn and had several buttons missing.

You can figure out from the context that *inferior* means "poor or low."

1.2 SPECIFIC CONTEXT CLUES

Sometimes writers help you understand the meanings of words by providing specific clues such as those shown in the chart.

1.3 IDIOMS, SLANG, AND FIGURATIVE LANGUAGE

An **idiom** is an expression whose overall meaning is different from the meaning of the individual words. **Slang** is informal language in which made-up words and ordinary words are used to mean something different from their meanings in formal English. **Figurative language** is language that communicates meaning beyond the literal meaning of the words. Use context clues to figure out the meanings of idioms, slang, and figurative language.

Button your lip about the party. (idiom; means "keep quiet")

That's a really bad jacket; I want one. (slang: means "good-looking, excellent")

My brother had tried to make dinner. The kitchen was a battleground of dirty dishes, stains, spills, and potato peels. (figurative language; battleground, dirty dishes, stains, spills, and potato peels represent a messy scene)

Specific Context Clues

Type of Clue	Key Words/ Phrases	Example
Definition or restatement of the meaning of the word	or, which is, that is, in other words, also known as, also called	Most chemicals are *toxic,* or **poisonous.**
Example following an unfamiliar word	such as, like, as if, for example, especially, including	**Amphibians,** such as **frogs and salamanders,** live in the pond by our house.
Comparison with a more familiar word or concept	as, like, also, similar to, in the same way, likewise	Like the rest of my *frugal* family, I always **save** most of the money I earn.
Contrast with a familiar word or experience	unlike, but, however, although, on the other hand, on the contrary	I wish I had more *ingenuity* in making money instead of simply relying on the **same old** baby-sitting jobs.
Cause-and-effect relationship in which one term is familiar	because, since, when, consequently, as a result, therefore	Because the chemicals are *flammable,* the scientists wear special **fire-resistant** clothing.

For more information, see **Vocabulary Strategy: Similes as Context Clues,** page 214, **Vocabulary Strategy: Context Clues,** pages 233 and 366, **Vocabulary Strategy: Idioms,** pages 286 and 966.

2 Analyzing Word Structure

Many words can be broken into smaller parts. These word parts include base words, roots, prefixes, and suffixes.

2.1 BASE WORDS

A **base word** is a word part that by itself is also a word. Other words or word parts can be added to base words to form new words.

2.2 ROOTS

A **root** is a word part that contains the core meaning of the word. Many English words contain roots that come from older languages such as Greek, Latin, Old English (Anglo-Saxon), and Norse. Knowing the meaning of the word's root can help you determine the word's meaning.

*For more information, see **Vocabulary Strategy: Word Roots**, pages 44, 94, 264, 336, 480, 490, 799, 845, 927, 940, and 975.*

Root	Meaning	Example
photo (Greek)	light	photography
therm (Greek)	heat	thermometer
cred (Latin)	believe	credit
mot (Latin)	move	motion
hēadfod (Old English)	head, top	headfirst

2.3 PREFIXES

A **prefix** is a word part attached to the beginning of a word. Most prefixes come from Greek, Latin, or Old English.

Prefix	Meaning	Example
mal-	bad or wrong	**mal**function
micro-	small or short	**micro**scope
semi-	half	**semi**circle

*For more information, see **Vocabulary Strategy: Prefixes**, pages 74, 385, and 927, **Vocabulary Strategy: Anglo-Saxon Affixes**, page 825.*

Interactive Vocabulary THINK central
Go to thinkcentral.com.
KEYWORD: HML7-R69

2.4 SUFFIXES

A **suffix** is a word part that appears at the end of a root or base word to form a new word. Some suffixes do not change word meaning. These suffixes are

- added to nouns to change the number of persons or objects
- added to verbs to change the tense
- added to modifiers to change the degree of comparison

Suffix	Meaning	Examples
-s, -es	to change the number of a noun	lock + s = locks
-d, -ed, -ing	to change verb tense	stew + ed = stewed
-er, -est	to indicate comparison in modifiers	mild + er = milder soft + est = softest

Other suffixes can be added to the root or base to change the word's meaning. These suffixes can also determine a word's part of speech.

Suffix	Meaning	Example
-er	one who does	teacher
-able	capable of	readable
-ly	in what manner	slowly

*For more information, see **Vocabulary Strategy: Suffixes That Form Adjectives**, page 131.*

2.5 CONTENT-AREA VOCABULARY

Knowing the meaning of Greek, Latin, and Anglo-Saxon word parts can help you figure out the meaning of content-area vocabulary.

Word Part	Meaning	Example
derm	skin	dermatologist
logy	study of	astrology
bio	life	biography
hydr	water	hydrant
hypo	below, beneath	hypodermic
vid/vis	to see	visual
fract	to break	fraction

Strategies for Understanding Unfamiliar Words

- Look for any prefixes or suffixes. Remove them so that you can concentrate on the base word or the root.

- See if you recognize any elements—prefix, suffix, root, or base—of the word. You may be able to guess its meaning by analyzing one or two elements.

- Think about the way the word is used in the sentence. Use the context and the word parts to make a logical guess about the word's meaning.

- Look in a dictionary to see whether you are correct.

PRACTICE AND APPLY

Use the strategies in this section and the vocabulary lessons in this book to help you figure out the meanings of the following content-area words.

forefathers	vision	microfilm
biology	fracture	import
auditory	ecology	hypothermia

3 Understanding Word Origins

3.1 ETYMOLOGIES

Etymologies show the origin and historical development of a word. When you study a word's history and origin, you can find out when, where, and how the word came to be.

> **ge•om•e•try** (jē-ŏm′i-trē) *n., pl.* **-tries** **1.** The mathematics of the properties, measurement, and relationships of points, lines, angles, surfaces, and solids. **2.** Arrangement. **3.** A physical arrangement suggesting geometric lines and shapes. [from Greek *geōmetriā,* from *geōmetrein,* to measure land].

3.2 WORD FAMILIES

Words that have the same root make up a word family and have related meanings. The following chart shows a common Greek and a common Latin root. Notice how the meanings of the example words are related to the meanings of their roots.

Latin Root	*sens:* "sense or feel"
English	**sensory** relating to the senses
	sensitive responsive to sensations
	sensation a perception or feeling

Greek Root	*ast(e)r:* "star"
English	**asteroid** a small object in outer space
	asterisk a star-shaped punctuation mark
	astronomy the study of outer space

3.3 FOREIGN WORDS

The English language includes words from diverse languages, such as French, Dutch, Spanish, Italian, and Chinese. Many words have stayed the way they were in their original languages.

French	Dutch	Spanish	Italian
ballet	boss	canyon	diva
vague	caboose	rodeo	cupola
mirage	dock	bronco	spaghetti

For more information, see **Vocabulary Strategy: Foreign Words in English,** *pages 592 and 659.*

4 Synonyms and Antonyms

4.1 SYNONYMS

A **synonym** is a word with a meaning similar to that of another word. You can find synonyms in a thesaurus or a dictionary. In a dictionary, synonyms are often given as part of the definition of the word. The following word pairs are synonyms:

satisfy/please	occasionally/sometimes
rob/steal	schedule/agenda

For more information, see **Vocabulary Strategy: Using a Thesaurus,** *page 503.*

4.2 ANTONYMS

An **antonym** is a word with a meaning opposite that of another word. The following word pairs are antonyms:

accurate/incorrect	similar/different
fresh/stale	unusual/ordinary

For more information, see **Vocabulary Strategy: Antonyms as Context Clues,** *page 63.*

5 Denotation and Connotation

5.1 DENOTATION

A word's dictionary meaning is called its **denotation.** For example, the denotation of the word *thin* is "having little flesh; spare; lean."

5.2 CONNOTATION

The images or feelings you connect to a word add a finer shade of meaning, called **connotation.** The connation of a word goes beyond its basic dictionary definition. Writers use connotations of words to communicate positive or negative feelings.

Positive	Negative
slender	scrawny
thrifty	cheap
young	immature

Make sure you understand the denotation and connotation of a word when you read it or use it.

*For more information, see **Vocabulary Strategy: Denotations and Connotations,** pages 348 and 812.*

6 Analogies

An **analogy** is a comparison based on similarities between some things. Analogies can be used to explain unfamiliar words, subjects, or ideas in terms of familiar ones. An **analogy problem** shows a relationship between pairs of words. The relationship between the first pair of words is the same as the relationship between the second pair. Two relationships that analogy problems can express are part to whole and whole to part.

Part to Whole

handle : mug : : hilt : _____
a. hammer   b. jewelry   c. plate   d. sword

Read this analogy as "handle **is to** mug as hilt **is to** ____."

What is the relationship between a *handle* and a *mug*? (A *handle* is the part designed for holding a *mug*.)

A *hilt* is part of which item? (A *hilt* is the handle of a *sword*.)

Whole to Part

horse : mane : : pheasant : _____
a. bird   b. feather   c. paw   d. animal

What is the relationship between a *horse* and a *mane*? (A *horse* has a *mane*, the long hair along the top and sides of its neck.)

Which item is part of a *pheasant*? (The bird called a *pheasant* has a *feather* covering.)

*For more information, see **Vocabulary Strategy: Analogies,** pages 120, 688, and 982.*

7 Homonyms, Homographs, and Homophones

7.1 HOMONYMS

Homonyms are words that have the same spelling and sound but have different meanings.

The snake shed its skin in the shed behind the house.

Shed can mean "to lose by natural process," but an identically spelled word means "a small structure."

If only one of the meanings of a homonym is familiar to you, use context clues to help you define the word if it is used in an unfamiliar way.

7.2 HOMOGRAPHS

Homographs are words that are spelled the same but have different meanings and origins. Some are also pronounced differently, as in these examples.

Please close the door. (clōz)
That was a close call. (clōs)

If you see a word used in a way that is unfamiliar to you, check a dictionary to see if it is a homograph.

*For more information, see **Vocabulary Strategy: Using a Dictionary,** page 672.*

7.3 HOMOPHONES

Homophones are words that sound alike but have different meanings and spellings. The following homophones are frequently misused:

it's/its	they're/their/there
to/too/two	stationary/stationery

Many misused homophones are pronouns and contractions. Whenever you are unsure whether to write *your* or *you're* and *who's* or *whose*, ask yourself if you mean *you are* and *who is/has*. If you do, write the contraction. For other homophones, such as *fair* and *fare*, use the meaning of the word to help you decide which one to use.

8 Words with Multiple Meanings

Some words have acquired additional meanings over time that are based on the original meaning.

> *I had to be replaced in the cast of the play because of the cast on my arm.*

The word *cast* has two meanings here, but both have the same origin. All of the meanings of *cast* are listed in one entry in the dictionary.

*For more information, see **Vocabulary Strategy: Words with Multiple Meanings**, page 246.*

9 Specialized Vocabulary

Specialized vocabulary refers to terms used in a particular field of study or work. For example, science and mathematics each has its own technical or specialized vocabulary. You can use context clues, dictionaries on specific subjects, atlases, or manuals to help you define these terms.

*For more information, see **Vocabulary Strategy: Content-Specific Words**, page 916, **Vocabulary Strategy: Specialized Vocabulary**, page 940.*

10 Using Reference Sources

10.1 DICTIONARIES

A **general dictionary** will tell you a word's definitions, spelling, syllables, pronunciation, parts of speech, and history and origin.

❶ **tan·gi·ble** (tănʹjə-bəl) *adj.* **1a.** Discernible by the touch; palpable. **b.** Possible to touch. **c.** Possible to be treated as fact; real or concrete. **2.** Possible to understand or realize. **3.** Law that can be valued monetarily [Late Latin *tangibilis*, from Latin *tangere*, to touch] ❺

❶ Entry word, syllabication
❷ Pronunciation
❸ Part of speech
❹ Definitions
❺ Etymology

A **specialized dictionary** focuses on terms related to a particular field of study or work.

10.2 THESAURI

A **thesaurus** (plural, *thesauri*) is a dictionary of synonyms. A thesaurus can be especially helpful when you find yourself using the same modifiers over and over again.

10.3 SYNONYM FINDERS

A **synonym finder** is often included in word-processing software. It enables you to highlight a word and be shown a display of its synonyms.

10.4 GLOSSARIES

A **glossary** is a list of specialized terms, their definitions, and sometimes their pronunciations. Many textbooks contain glossaries, which are found at the back of the book. In fact, this textbook has four glossaries: the **Glossary of Literary and Nonfiction Terms,** the **Glossary of Reading and Informational Terms,** the **Glossary of Academic Vocabulary in English and Spanish,** and the **Glossary of Vocabulary in English & Spanish.** Use these glossaries to help you understand how terms are used in this textbook. You can find electronic versions of many reference sources on the Internet, or in software programs at your school or library.

*For more information, see **Vocabulary Strategy: Using Reference Aids**, page 274, **Vocabulary Strategy: Using a Thesaurus**, page 503, **Vocabulary Strategy: Using a Dictionary**, page 672, **Vocabulary Strategy: Using a Glossary**, page 704, **Vocabulary Strategy: Dictionary Entries**, page 741.*

11 Spelling Rules

11.1 WORDS ENDING IN A SILENT *E*

Before adding a suffix beginning with a vowel or *y* to a word ending in a silent *e*, drop the *e* (with some exceptions).

amaze + -ing = amazing
love + -able = lovable
create + -ed = created
nerve + -ous = nervous

Exceptions: *change + -able = changeable; courage + -ous = courageous*

When adding a suffix beginning with a consonant to a word ending in a silent *e,* keep the *e* (with some exceptions).

late + -ly = lately
spite + -ful = spiteful
noise + -less = noiseless
state + -ment = statement

Exceptions: *truly, argument, ninth, wholly, awful,* and others

When a suffix beginning with *a* or *o* is added to a word with a final silent *e,* the final *e* is usually retained if it is preceded by a soft *c* or a soft *g.*

bridge + -able = bridgeable
peace + -able = peaceable
outrage + -ous = outrageous
advantage + -ous = advantageous

When a suffix beginning with a vowel is added to words ending in *ee* or *oe,* the final silent *e* is retained.

agree + -ing = agreeing free + -ing = freeing
hoe + -ing = hoeing see + -ing = seeing

11.2 WORDS ENDING IN Y

Before adding most suffixes to a word that ends in *y* preceded by a consonant, change the *y* to *i.*

easy + -est = easiest
crazy + -est = craziest
silly + -ness = silliness
marry + -age = marriage

Exceptions: *dryness, shyness,* and *slyness*

However, when you add *-ing,* the *y* does not change.

empty + -ed = emptied but
empty + -ing = emptying

When adding a suffix to a word that ends in *y* preceded by a vowel, the *y* usually does not change.

play + -er = player
employ + -ed = employed
coy + -ness = coyness
pay + -able = payable

11.3 WORDS ENDING IN A CONSONANT

In **one-syllable** words that end in one consonant preceded by one short vowel, double the final consonant before adding a suffix beginning with a vowel, such as *-ed* or *-ing.* These are sometimes called 1+1+1 words.

dip + -ed = dipped set + -ing = setting
slim + -est = slimmest fit + -er = fitter

The rule does not apply to words of one syllable that end in a consonant preceded by two vowels.

feel + -ing = feeling peel + -ed = peeled
reap + -ed = reaped loot + -ed = looted

In words of more than one syllable, double the final consonant when (1) the word ends with one consonant preceded by one vowel and (2) when the word is accented on the last syllable.

be•gin´ per•mit´ re•fer´

In the following examples, note that in the new words formed with suffixes, the accent remains on the same syllable:

be•gin´ + -ing = be•gin´ning = beginning
per•mit´ + -ed = per•mit´ted = permitted

Exceptions: In some words with more than one syllable, though the accent remains on the same syllable when a suffix is added, the final consonant is nevertheless not doubled, as in the following examples:

tra´vel + er = tra´vel•er = traveler
mar´ket + er = mar´ket•er = marketer

In the following examples, the accent does not remain on the same syllable; thus, the final consonant is not doubled:

re•fer´ + -ence = ref´er•ence = reference
con•fer´ + -ence = con´fer•ence = conference

11.4 PREFIXES AND SUFFIXES

When adding a prefix to a word, do not change the spelling of the base word. When a prefix creates a double letter, keep both letters.

dis- + approve = disapprove
re- + build = rebuild
ir- + regular = irregular
mis- + spell = misspell
anti- + trust = antitrust
il- + logical = illogical

When adding *-ly* to a word ending in *l,* keep both *l*'s. When adding *-ness* to a word ending in *n,* keep both *n*'s.

careful + -ly = carefully
sudden + -ness = suddenness
final + -ly = finally
thin + -ness = thinness

11.5 FORMING PLURAL NOUNS

To form the plural of most nouns, just add *-s.*
   prizes   dreams   circles   stations

For most singular nouns ending in *o,* add *-s.*
   solos   halos   studios   photos   pianos

For a few nouns ending in *o,* add *-es.*
   heroes   tomatoes   potatoes   echoes

When the singular noun ends in *s, sh, ch, x,* or *z,* add *-es.*
   waitresses   brushes   ditches
   axes   buzzes

When a singular noun ends in *y* with a consonant before it, change the *y* to *i* and add *-es.*
   army—armies   candy—candies
   baby—babies   diary—diaries
   ferry—ferries   conspiracy—conspiracies

When a vowel (*a, e, i, o, u*) comes before the *y,* just add *-s.*
   boy—boys   way—ways
   array—arrays   alloy—alloys
   weekday—weekdays   jockey—jockeys

For most nouns ending in *f* or *fe,* change the *f* to *v* and add *-es* or *-s.*
   life—lives   calf—calves   knife—knives
   thief—thieves   shelf—shelves   loaf—loaves

For some nouns ending in *f,* add *-s* to make the plural.
   roofs   chiefs   reefs   beliefs

Some nouns have the same form for both singular and plural.
   deer   sheep   moose   salmon   trout

For some nouns, the plural is formed in a special way.
   man—men   goose—geese
   ox—oxen   woman—women
   mouse—mice   child—children

For a compound noun written as one word, form the plural by changing the last word in the compound to its plural form.
   stepchild—stepchildren   firefly—fireflies

If a compound noun is written as a hyphenated word or as two separate words, change the most important word to the plural form.
   brother-in-law—brothers-in-law
   life jacket—life jackets

11.6 FORMING POSSESSIVES

If a noun is singular, add *'s.*
   mother—my mother's car   Ross—Ross's desk

Exception: The *s* after the apostrophe is dropped after *Jesus', Moses',* and certain names in classical mythology (*Zeus'*). These possessive forms can thus be pronounced easily.

If a noun is plural and ends with *s,* just add an apostrophe.
   parents—my parents' car
   the Santinis—the Santinis' house

If a noun is plural but does not end in *s,* add *'s.*
   people—the people's choice
   women—the women's coats

11.7 SPECIAL SPELLING PROBLEMS

Only one English word ends in *-sede: supersede.* Three words end in *-ceed: exceed, proceed,* and *succeed.* All other verbs ending in the sound "seed" are spelled with *-cede.*
   concede   precede   recede   secede

In words with *ie* or *ei,* when the sound is long *e* (as in *she*), the word is spelled *ie* except after *c* (with some exceptions).

i before *e*	thief	relieve	field
	piece	grieve	pier
except after *c*	conceit	perceive	ceiling
	receive	receipt	
Exceptions:	either	neither	weird
	leisure	seize	

12 Commonly Confused Words

WORDS	DEFINITIONS	EXAMPLES
accept/except	The verb *accept* means "to receive or believe"; *except* is usually a preposition meaning "excluding."	Did the teacher **accept** your report? Everyone smiled for the photographer **except** Jody.
advice/advise	*Advise* is a verb; *advice* is a noun naming that which an *adviser* gives.	I **advise** you to take that job. Whom should I ask for **advice?**
affect/effect	As a verb, *affect* means "to influence." *Effect* as a verb means "to cause." If you want a noun, you will almost always want *effect*.	How deeply did the news **affect** him? The students tried to **effect** a change in school policy. What **effect** did the acidic soil produce in the plants?
all ready/already	*All ready* is an adjective meaning "fully ready." *Already* is an adverb meaning "before or by this time."	He was **all ready** to go at noon. I have **already** seen that movie.
desert/dessert	*Desert* (dĕz´ərt) means "a dry, sandy, barren region." *Desert* (dĭ-zûrt´) means "to abandon." *Dessert* (dĭ-zûrt´) is a sweet, such as cake.	The Sahara, in North Africa, is the world's largest **desert.** The night guard did not **desert** his post. Alison's favorite **dessert** is chocolate cake.
among/between	*Between* is used when you are speaking of only two things. *Among* is used for three or more.	**Between** ice cream and sherbet, I prefer the latter. Gary Soto is **among** my favorite authors.
bring/take	*Bring* is used to denote motion toward a speaker or place. *Take* is used to denote motion away from such a person or place.	**Bring** the books over here, and I will **take** them to the library.
fewer/less	*Fewer* refers to the number of separate, countable units. *Less* refers to bulk quantity.	We have **less** literature and **fewer** selections in this year's curriculum.
leave/let	*Leave* means "to allow something to remain behind." *Let* means "to permit."	The librarian will **leave** some books on display but will not **let** us borrow any.
lie/lay	To *lie* is "to rest or recline." It does not take an object. *Lay* always takes an object.	Rover loves to **lie** in the sun. We always **lay** some bones next to him.
loose/lose	*Loose* (lo͞os) means "free, not restrained"; *lose* (lo͞oz) means "to misplace or fail to find."	Who turned the horses **loose?** I hope we won't **lose** any of them.
passed/past	*Passed* is the past tense of *pass* and means "went by." *Past* is an adjective that means "of a former time." *Past* is also a noun that means "time gone by."	We **passed** through the Florida Keys during our vacation. My **past** experiences have taught me to set my alarm. Ebenezer Scrooge is a character who relives his **past.**
than/then	Use *than* in making comparisons; use *then* on all other occasions.	Ramon is stronger **than** Mark. Cut the grass and **then** trim the hedges.
two/too/to	*Two* is the number. *Too* is an adverb meaning "also" or "very." Use *to* before a verb or as a preposition.	Meg had **to** go **to** town, **too.** We had **too** much reading **to** do. **Two** chapters is **too** many.
their/there/they're	*Their* means "belonging to them." *There* means "in that place." *They're* is the contraction for "they are."	**There** is a movie playing at 9 P.M. **They're** going to see it with me. Sakara and Jessica drove away in **their** car after the movie.

Good speakers and listeners do more than just talk and hear. They use specific techniques to present their ideas effectively, and they are attentive and critical listeners.

COMMON CORE

Included in this handbook:
SL 1a–d, SL 2, SL 3, SL 4, SL 6

1 Speech

In school, in business, and in community life, a speech is one of the most effective means of communicating.

1.1 AUDIENCE, PURPOSE, AND OCCASION

Delivering a speech is an opportunity to share your ideas. Before you begin to prepare a speech, you will need to know *why* you are making the presentation and to *whom* you are presenting it. Understanding your purpose, the background and interests of your audience, and the occasion will help you select an appropriate focus and organizational structure for your speech.

- **Know Your Audience** What kind of group are you presenting to? Fellow classmates? A group of teachers? What are their interests and backgrounds? Understanding their different points of view can help you organize the information so that they understand and are interested in it.

- **Understand Your Purpose** Keep in mind your purpose for speaking. Are you trying to persuade the audience to do something? Perhaps you simply want to entertain them by sharing a story or experience. Your purpose directly affects your tone. Decide whether you'll best accomplish your purpose by being serious or humorous.

- **Know the Occasion** Are you speaking at a special event? Is it formal? Will others be giving speeches besides you? Knowing what the occasion is will help you choose the proper language and the right length for the event.

1.2 WRITING YOUR SPEECH

Once you understand your purpose and audience, you are ready to write your speech. Use the following guidelines to help you:

- **Create a Unified Speech** Do this first by organizing your speech into paragraphs, each of which develops a single main or central idea. Then make sure that just as all the sentences in a paragraph support the main idea of the paragraph, all the paragraphs in your speech support the main idea of the speech.

- **Clarify Your Ideas** Make sure that you show clear relationships between ideas. Transition words can help listeners follow your ideas.

For more information on transitions, see the **Writing Handbook,** *page R32.*

- **Use Appropriate Language** The subject of your speech—and the way you choose to present it—should match your audience, your purpose, and the occasion. You can use informal language, such as slang, to share a story with your classmates. For a persuasive speech in front of a school assembly, use formal, standard American English. If you are giving an informative presentation, be sure to explain any terms that the audience may not be familiar with.

- **Provide Evidence** Include relevant facts, statistics, and incidents; quote experts to support your ideas and opinions. Elaborate—provide specific details, perhaps with visual or media displays—to clarify what you are saying.

- **Arrange Details and Evidence Effectively** In a good presentation, your controlling idea, or thesis statement should be supported by clearly stated evidence. The evidence can be presented as details, reasons, descriptions, or examples. Use the following chart to help you arrange your ideas.

Introduction	• Focus on one strong example or statistic.
	• Make sure your evidence is intense or even surprising, so that it grabs the audience's attention.
Main Body	• Try to provide at least one piece of evidence for every new idea you introduce.
	• Define unfamiliar terms clearly.
	• When possible, include well-labeled diagrams or illustrations.
Conclusion	• Leave your audience with one strong piece of evidence or a powerful detail.

- **Use Figurative Language** Draw attention to important points with similes, metaphors, and sensory images.

- **Use Precise Language** Use precise language to convey your ideas. You can keep the audience's attention with a word that brings out strong emotion. You can use a question or interjection to make a personal connection with the audience.

- **Organize Effectively** Order your information in a way that helps you achieve your purpose. If you want to persuade, try starting with a "hook" (an interesting question or statement that captures your audience's attention) and finishing with your most compelling evidence. Which evidence is most important or interesting depends on your audience's background knowledge, experiences, and interests. You may need to reorganize your speech for different audiences.

- **Revise Your Speech** Revise, edit, and proofread it as you would for a written report. Check for correct subject-verb agreement and consistent verb tense. Correct run-on sentences and sentence fragments. Use parallel structure to emphasize ideas. Use complete sentences and correct punctuation and capitalization, even if no one else will see it. Your written speech should be clear and error free. If you notice an error in your notes during the speech, you may not remember what you actually wanted to say.

1.3 DELIVERING YOUR SPEECH

Use these techniques to help you prepare and present your speech:

Prepare

- **Review Your Information** Reread your notes and review any background research. You'll feel more confident during your speech.

- **Prepare Your Notes** Some people prefer to write down only key points. Others prefer the entire script. Write each main point, or each paragraph, of your speech on a separate numbered index card. Be sure to include your most important evidence and examples.

- **Plan Your Visual Aids** If you are planning on using visual aids, such as slides, posters, charts, graphs, video clips, overhead transparencies, or computer projections, now is the time to design them and decide how to work them into your speech.

Practice

- **Rehearse** Rehearse your speech several times, possibly in front of a practice audience. Maintain good **posture** by standing with your shoulders back and your head up. Glance at your notes to refresh your memory, but don't read them word for word. Instead, make **eye contact** with audience members. If you are using visual aids, arrange them in the order in which you will use them.

- **Use Speaking Techniques** Each time you rehearse, focus on a different speaking technique. **Voice modulation** means that your voice is clear and slightly varied—not too loud, not soft or mumbling, and not a monotone. Similarly, **inflection** refers to the tone of your voice. You may change your inflection to show how you feel about a particular point—happy, sad, and so on. **Tempo** means your rate of speed, and **enunciation** refers to how clearly you pronounce words.

- **Use Audience Feedback** If you had a practice audience, ask them specific questions about your delivery: Did I use enough eye contact? Was my voice at the right volume? Did I stand straight, or did I slouch? Use the audience's comments to evaluate the effectiveness of your delivery and to set goals for future rehearsals.

- **Evaluate Your Performance** When you have finished each rehearsal, evaluate your performance. Did you pause to let an important point sink in or use gestures for emphasis? Make a list of the aspects of your presentation that you will try to improve for your next rehearsal.

Present

- **Begin Your Speech** Try to look relaxed and smile.

- **Make Eye Contact** Try to make eye contact with as many audience members as possible. This will establish personal contact and help you determine if the audience understands your speech.

- **Remember to Pause** A slight pause after important points will provide emphasis and give your audience time to think about what you're saying.

- **Speak Clearly** Speak loud enough to be heard clearly, but not so loud that your voice is overwhelming. Use a conversational tone.

- **Maintain Good Posture** Stand up straight and avoid nervous movements that may distract the audience's attention from what you are saying.

- **Use Expressive Body Language** Use facial expressions to show your feelings toward your topic. Lean forward when you make an important point; move your hands and arms for emphasis. Use your body language to show your own style and reflect your personality.

- **Watch the Audience for Responses** If they start fidgeting or yawning, speak a little louder or get to your conclusion a little sooner. Use what you learn to evaluate the effectiveness of your speech and to decide what areas need improvement for future presentations.

Respond to Questions

Depending on the content of your speech, your audience may have questions. Follow these steps to make sure that you answer questions in an appropriate manner:

- Think about what your audience may ask and prepare answers before your speech.

- Tell your audience at the beginning of your speech that you will take questions at the end. This helps avoid audience interruptions.

- Call on audience members in the order in which they raise their hands.

- Repeat each question before you answer it to ensure that everyone has heard it. This step also gives you time to prepare your answer.

2 Different Types of Oral Presentations

2.1 INFORMATIVE SPEECH

When you deliver an informative speech, you give the audience new information or provide a better understanding of information. One example of an informative speech is a critique of a literary work, film, or dramatic production.

Use the following questions to evaluate the presentation of a peer or a public figure, or your own presentation.

Evaluate an Informative Speech

- Did the speaker maintain eye contact and speak clearly?

- Did the speaker explain the purpose of the presentation?

- Did the speaker take the audience's previous knowledge into consideration?

- Did the speaker cite a variety of sources for the information?

- Did the speaker communicate the information objectively?

- Did the speaker explain technical terms?

- Did the speaker use body language and visual aids effectively?

2.2 PERSUASIVE SPEECH

When you deliver a persuasive speech, you offer a thesis or clear statement on a subject, you provide relevant evidence to support your position, and you attempt to convince the audience to accept your point of view.

*For more information, see **Speaking and Listening Workshop: Presenting a Persuasive Speech,** pages 998–999.*

Use the following questions to evaluate the presentation of a peer or a public figure, or your own presentation.

Evaluate a Persuasive Speech

- Did the speaker state a clear position or perspective in support of an argument or proposal?
- Did the speaker describe supporting points coherently and use logical, clearly explained evidence?
- Did the speaker arrange supporting details, reasons, descriptions, and examples in a way that made sense to the audience?
- Did the speaker effectively use speaking techniques such as voice modulation, inflection, tempo, enunciation, and eye contact?
- What is your opinion of the speaker's content and delivery? What was the speech's overall impact on you?

2.3 DEBATE

A debate is a balanced argument covering both sides of an issue. In a debate, two teams compete to win the support of the audience. In a formal debate, two teams, each with two members, present their arguments on a given proposition or policy statement. One team argues for the proposition or statement and the other argues against it. Each debater must consider the proposition closely and must research both sides of it. To argue persuasively either for or against a proposition, a debater must be familiar with both sides of the issue.

Use the following guidelines to evaluate a debate.

Evaluate a Team in a Debate

- Did the team prove that a significant problem does or does not exist?
- How did the team convince you that the proposition is or is not the best solution to the problem?
- How effectively did the team present reasons and evidence supporting the case?
- How effectively did the team respond to arguments made by the opposing team?
- Did the speakers maintain eye contact and speak at an appropriate rate and volume?
- Did the speakers observe proper debate etiquette?

PRACTICE AND APPLY

View a political debate for a school, local, state, or national election. Use the preceding criteria to evaluate it.

2.4 NARRATIVE SPEECH

When you deliver a narrative speech, you tell a story or present a subject using a story-type format. A good narrative keeps an audience informed and entertained. It also allows you to deliver a message in a creative way.

Use the following guidelines to evaluate a speaker or your own presentation.

Evaluate a Narrative Speech

- Did the speaker establish a definite setting and a context, so audience members knew where and when events took place?
- Did the narrative include all the elements of a standard plot line—beginning, conflict, rising action, climax, and denouement?
- Did the plot line flow well?
- Did the speaker describe complex major and minor characters?
- Did the narrative have a consistent point of view, or did the speaker switch confusingly from *I* to *he* or *she*?
- Did the speaker maintain audience interest by using appropriate techniques, such as dialogue, suspense, movement, gestures, and expressions?

2.5 DESCRIPTIVE SPEECH

Description is part of most presentations. In a descriptive speech, you describe a subject that you are personally involved with.

Use the following questions to evaluate a speaker or your own presentation.

Evaluate a Descriptive Speech
- Did the speaker make clear his or her attitude (point of view) toward the subject? Think about words, tone of voice, gestures, and expressions.
- Did the speaker organize information to make the message clear and to appeal to audience members' interests and background?
- Did the speaker arrange supporting details, reasons, descriptions, and examples effectively?

2.6 ORAL INTERPRETATION

When you read a poem, play, or story aloud, your voice can bring the literature to life.

Oral Reading

An oral reading can be a monologue, during which you assume the voice of a character, the narrator, or the speaker in a poem. Or it may be a dialogue, during which you take the roles of two or more characters. Use the following techniques when giving an oral reading:

- **Speak Clearly** As you speak, pronounce your words carefully and clearly.

- **Control Your Volume** Make sure that you are loud enough to be heard but do not shout.

- **Pace Yourself** Read at a moderate rate, but vary your pace if it seems appropriate to the emotions of the character or to the action.

- **Vary Your Voice** Use a different voice for each character. Stress important words and phrases. Use your voice to express different emotions.

Dramatic Reading

In a dramatic reading, several speakers participate in the reading of a play or other work. Use the following techniques in your dramatic reading:

- **Prepare** Rehearse your material several times. Become familiar with the humorous and serious parts of the script. Develop a special voice that fits the personality of the character you portray.

- **Project** As you read your lines, aim your voice toward the back of the room to allow everyone to hear you.

- **Perform** React to the other characters as if you were hearing their lines for the first time. Deliver your own lines with the appropriate emotion. Use not only hand gestures and facial expressions but also other body movements to express your emotions.

Use the following questions to evaluate an artistic performance by a peer or public presenter, a media presentation, or your own performance.

Evaluate an Oral Interpretation
- Did the speaker speak clearly?
- Did the speaker maintain eye contact with the audience?
- Did the speaker project his or her voice without shouting?
- Did the speaker vary the rate of speech appropriately to express emotion, mood, and action?
- Did the speaker use a different voice for the character(s)?
- Did the speaker stress important words or phrases?
- Did the speaker use voice, tone, and gestures to enhance meaning?

PRACTICE AND APPLY

Listen to an oral reading by a classmate or view a dramatic performance in a theater or on television. Use the preceding criteria to evaluate it.

2.7 ORAL INSTRUCTIONS

You give oral instructions any time you are called upon to explain how to do something or how to fix a problem. When you give oral instructions, your goal is to teach the audience how to perform the task you are explaining. Make sure you present steps in order, speak clearly, and explain any terms your audience may not know.

If you are asked to follow a set of oral directions, remember to take notes, ask questions to clarify any confusing details, and restate the instructions in your own words.

Use the following questions to evaluate a speaker or your own presentation of directions.

Evaluate Oral Instructions

- Did the speaker make it clear what he or she was trying to explain?
- Did the speaker use a rate and volume of speech that made it easy for you to understand him or her?
- Did the speaker relate steps in a logical order?
- Did the speaker stay focused on the topic?
- Did the speaker monitor the audience's understanding by asking for and answering questions?

PRACTICE AND APPLY

Work with a classmate. As he or she gives a set of directions to follow, evaluate his or her delivery. Once you complete the task, determine how well you followed the directions. Then give the same set of directions while he or she evaluates your delivery.

3 Other Types of Communication

3.1 CONVERSATION

Conversations are informal, but they are important means of communicating. When two or more people exchange messages, it is equally important that each person contribute and actively listen.

3.2 GROUP DISCUSSION

Successful groups use guidelines for discussion and also assign a role to each member.

Role	Responsibilites
Chairperson	• Introduces topic • Explains goal or purpose • Participates in discussion and keeps it on track • Helps resolve conflicts • Helps group reach goal
Recorder	• Takes notes on discussion • Reports on suggestions and decisions • Organizes and writes up notes • Participates in discussion
Participants	• Contribute relevant facts or ideas to discussion • Respond constructively to one another's ideas • Reach agreement or vote on final decision

Guidelines for Discussion

- Agree on the role and responsibilities that each member of the discussion group will have.
- Plan an agenda with clear goals and deadlines.
- Set time limits for speakers.
- Don't talk while someone else is talking.
- Support statements and opinions with facts and examples.
- Avoid getting sidetracked by unrelated topics.
- Vote on any key issues.

For more information, see **Speaking and Listening Workshop: Participating in a Panel Discussion,** *pages 304–305.*

3.3 INTERVIEW

An **interview** is a formal type of conversation with a definite purpose and goal. To conduct a successful interview, use the following guidelines:

Prepare for the Interview

- Select your interviewee carefully. Identify who has the kind of knowledge and experience you are looking for.
- Set a time, a date, and a place. Ask permission to tape-record the interview.
- Learn all you can about the person you will interview or the topic you want information on.

- Prepare a list of questions. Create questions that encourage detailed responses instead of yes-or-no answers. Arrange your questions in order from most important to least important.
- Arrive on time with everything you need.

Conduct the Interview

- Ask your questions clearly and listen to the responses carefully. Give the person whom you are interviewing plenty of time to answer.
- Be flexible; follow up on any responses you find interesting.
- Avoid arguments; be tactful and polite.
- Even if you tape an interview, take notes on important points.
- Thank the person for the interview, and ask if you can call with any follow-up questions.

Follow Up on the Interview

- Summarize your notes or make a written copy of the tape recording as soon as possible.
- If any points are unclear or if information is missing, call and ask more questions while the person is still available.
- Select the most appropriate quotations to support your ideas.
- If possible, have the person you interviewed review your work to make sure you haven't misrepresented what he or she said.
- Send a thank-you note to the person in appreciation of his or her time and effort.

For more information, see **Speaking and Listening Workshop: Conducting an Interview,** *pages 890–891.*

Evaluate an Interview

You can determine how effective your interview was by asking yourself these questions:

- Did you get the type of information you were looking for?
- Were your most important questions answered to your satisfaction?
- Were you able to keep the interviewee focused on the subject?

4 Active Listening

Active listening is the process of receiving, interpreting, evaluating, and responding to a message.

Before Listening

- Learn what the topic is beforehand. You may need to read background information or learn new terms to understand the speaker's message.
- Think about what you know or want to know about the topic.
- Have a pen and paper to take notes.
- Establish a purpose for listening. You might listen to a funny story for enjoyment. Alternatively, you might listen to a formal speech to be informed about ideas that interest you.

While Listening

- Focus your attention on the speaker. Your facial expressions and body language should demonstrate your interest in hearing the topic.
- Listen for the speaker's purpose (usually stated at the beginning), which alerts you to main ideas.
- Listen for words or phrases that signal important points, such as *to begin with, in addition, most important, finally,* and *in conclusion.*
- Pay attention to explanations of unfamiliar terms. Use these terms to help you understand the speaker's message.
- Notice ideas that are repeated for emphasis.
- Jot down the most important points.
- Note comparisons and contrasts, causes and effects, or problems and solutions.
- As you take notes, use phrases, abbreviations, and symbols to keep up with the speaker.
- Note how the speaker uses word choice, voice pitch, posture, and gestures to convey meaning.

After Listening

- Ask questions to clarify anything that was unclear or confusing.
- Review your notes right away to make sure you understand what was said.

- Summarize and paraphrase the speaker's ideas.
- Compare your interpretation of the speech with others' reactions.

4.1 CRITICAL LISTENING

Critical listening involves evaluating a spoken message to judge its accuracy and reliability. You can use the following strategies as you listen to messages from public speakers:

- **Determine the Speaker's Purpose** Think about the background, viewpoint, and possible motives of the speaker. Separate facts from opinions. Listen carefully to details and evidence.

- **Determine the Speaker's Attitude** What point of view does the speaker have about the information he or she is presenting? Is the speaker enthusiastic and confident or bored and uncertain?

- **Listen for the Main Idea** Figure out the speaker's main message before allowing yourself to be distracted by seemingly convincing facts and details.

- **Recognize the Use of Persuasive Techniques** Speakers may present information in a particular way to persuade you to buy a product or accept an idea. Persuasive devices such as glittering generalities, either/or reasoning, and bandwagon or snob appeal may represent faulty reasoning and provide misleading information.

  *For more information, see **Recognizing Persuasive Techniques**, page R21.*

- **Observe Nonverbal Messages** A speaker's gestures, facial expressions, and tone of voice should reinforce the message. If they don't, you should doubt the speaker's sincerity and his or her message's reliability.

- **Give Appropriate Feedback** An effective speaker looks for verbal and nonverbal cues from you, the listener, to see how the message is being received. For example, if you understand or agree with the message, you might nod your head.

4.2 VERBAL FEEDBACK

At times you will be asked to give direct feedback to a speaker. You may be asked to evaluate the way the speaker delivers the presentation as well as the content of the presentation.

- **Ask Probing Questions** Examine the subject thoroughly and seek more information about it. Politely ask questions such as, "What evidence do you have to support the first point you made?" and "Could you give us details about X?"

- **Respond to Persuasive Messages** You may make a **challenge,** in which you respectfully disagree with the speaker and supply evidence that supports your viewpoint. Or you may respond with an **affirmation**—a positive comment about the main idea or about a significant detail.

Evaluate Delivery

- Did the speaker articulate words clearly and distinctly?
- Did the speaker pronounce words correctly?
- Did the speaker vary his or her rate?
- Did the speaker's voice sound natural and not strained?
- Was the speaker's voice loud enough?

Evaluate Content

Here's how to give constructive suggestions for improvement:

Be Specific Don't make statements like "Your charts need work." Offer concrete suggestions, such as "Please make the type bigger so we can read the poster from the back of the room."

Discuss Only the Most Important Points Don't overload the speaker with too much feedback. Focus on important points, such as

- Is the topic too advanced for the audience?
- Are the supporting details well organized?
- Is the conclusion weak?

Give Balanced Feedback Tell the speaker not only what didn't work but also what did work: "Consider dropping the last two slides, since you covered those points earlier. The first two slides got my attention."

What do you need to know to be a smart media consumer? Being media literate *means that you know what media products are, who created them, and what they mean. It means that you are able to analyze and evaluate media messages and how they influence you and your world. To become media literate, you'll need the tools to study media messages.*

COMMON CORE SL 2

1 Five Core Concepts in Media Literacy

from The Center for Media Literacy

The five core concepts of media literacy provide you with the basic ideas you can consider when examining media messages.

All media messages are "constructed." All media messages are made by someone. In fact, they are carefully thought out and researched and have attitudes and values built into them. Much of the information that you use to make sense of the world comes from the media. Therefore, it is important to know how a medium is put together so you can better understand the message it conveys.

Media messages are constructed using a creative language with its own rules. Each means of communication—whether it is film, television, newspapers, magazines, radio, or the Internet— has its own language and design. Therefore, the message must use the language and design of the medium that delivers the message. Thus, the medium actually shapes the message. For example, a horror film may use music to heighten suspense, or a newspaper may use a big headline to signal the importance of a story. Understanding the language of each medium can increase your enjoyment of it as well as help you recognize any subtle attempt to persuade you.

Different people experience the same media messages differently. Personal factors such as age, education, and experience will affect the way a person responds to a media message. How many times has your interpretation of a film or book differed from that of a friend? Everyone interprets media messages differently.

Media have embedded values and points of view. Media messages carry underlying values, which are purposely built into them by the creators of the message. For example, a commercial's main purpose may be to persuade you to buy something, but the commercial may also aim to convince you that the product is important to a particular way of life. Understanding not only the main message but also any other points of view will help you decide whether to accept or reject the message.

Most media messages are constructed to gain profit and/or power. The creators of media messages often provide a commodity, such as information or entertainment, in order to make money. The bigger the audience, the more the media outlet can charge for advertising. Consequently, media outlets want to build large audiences in order to bring in more revenue from advertising. For example, a television network will create programming to appeal to the largest audience possible, in the hope that the viewer ratings will attract more advertising dollars.

2 Media Basics

2.1 MESSAGE

When a film or TV show is created, it becomes a media product. Each media product is created to send a **message,** or an expression of a belief or opinion, that serves a specific purpose. In order to understand the message, you will need to deconstruct it.

Deconstruction is the process of analyzing a media presentation. To analyze a media presentation you will need to ask why and how it was created, who created it, and whom it is trying to influence.

2.2 AUDIENCE

A **target audience** is the specific group of people that a product or presentation is aimed at. The members of a target audience usually share certain characteristics, such as age, gender, ethnic background, values, or lifestyle. For example, a target audience may be kids ages 11 to 14 who like to eat hamburgers.

Demographics are the characteristics of a population, including age, gender, profession, income, education, ethnicity, and geographical location. Media decision makers use demographics to shape their content to suit the needs and tastes of a target audience.

2.3 PURPOSE

The **purpose,** or intent, of a media presentation is the reason it was made. All media products—from news programs to video games—are created for a specific purpose. Identifying why a media product was invented is the first step in understanding how it can influence you. The following chart shows purposes of different media products.

Purposes of Media Products	
Purpose	**Example**
Inform	news reports and articles, public service announcements, some Web sites
Persuade	advertisements, editorials, reviews, political cartoons
Entertain	most TV shows, films, recorded music; video games; most talk shows

Most media products have more than one purpose. For example, TV commercials are often entertaining, but their main purpose is to persuade you to buy something. If you aren't aware of all of a media products' purposes, you may become influenced without knowing it. This chart shows some examples.

Main and Other Purposes in Media		
Media Product	**Main Purpose**	**Other Purposes**
Sports coverage	To entertain	To inform you about sports or athletes
Advertisement	To persuade	To entertain you; to inform you about a product
News broadcast	To inform	To persuade you that an issue or idea is important

2.4 TYPES AND GENRES OF MEDIA

The term *media* refers to television, newspapers, magazines, radio, movies, and the Internet. Each is a **medium** or means for carrying information, entertainment, and advertisements to a large audience.

Media Tools — THINK central

Go to **thinkcentral.com**.
KEYWORD: HML7-R85

Each type of media has different characteristics, strengths, and weaknesses. The following chart shows how several types of media deliver their messages.

Type of Media	Characteristics
Newspaper Article	• Provides detailed information and dramatic photographs • Use **headlines** and **subheads** to give main ideas • Can't be updated until next edition or next day
Television News Report	• Uses an **announcer,** or "anchor," to guide viewers through the news report • Uses **video footage** to bring news to life or clarify what happened • Uses **graphics** to give information at a glance • Can be updated quickly
Documentary	• Tells about historic people and places, major events, and important social, political, or environmental issues • Uses **footage,** or shots of photographs, interviews, news reports, and film clips, to help viewers understand the subject • Features **interviews** of experts or people directly involved with the subject • Uses a **voice-over narrator,** the voice of an unseen speaker, who tells viewers why the subject is important and how the information about the subject is organized
Web Site	• Gives in-depth information on specialized subjects • Allows users to interact socially and to share files • Uses **text, still images,** and **video** • Allows users to select the information they want to receive by clicking on links • Allows users to see when the site was last updated • Can be updated quickly

*For more information, see **Types of Media**, page 10.*

2.5 PRODUCERS AND CREATORS

People who control the media are known as **gatekeepers.** Gatekeepers decide what information to share with the public and the ways it will be presented. The following diagram gives some examples.

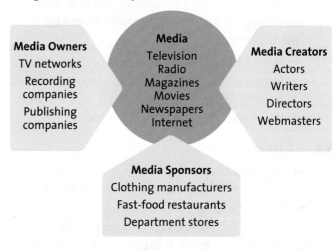

Media Owners
TV networks
Recording companies
Publishing companies

Media
Television
Radio
Magazines
Movies
Newspapers
Internet

Media Creators
Actors
Writers
Directors
Webmasters

Media Sponsors
Clothing manufacturers
Fast-food restaurants
Department stores

Media sponsors are companies that pay for their products to be advertised. It's important to be aware of sponsors and other gatekeepers, because they control much of what you see and hear. For example, if a soft-drink company sponsors a TV show, you probably won't see or hear about competing brands of soft drinks on that show.

2.6 INFLUENCE OF MEDIA

Everywhere you go, you're bombarded by the media—advertisements, newspapers, magazines, radio, and television. Different kinds of media are all competing for your attention, telling you, "Buy this product. Listen to this music. Read this story. Look at this image. Think about this opinion." The creators of these media products are selling messages. But they may also be sending subtle messages about values that they want you to believe in. For example, a car ad is meant to sell a car, but if you look closer, you will see that it is using a set of values, such as a luxurious lifestyle, to make the car attractive to the target audience. One message of the ad is that if you buy the car, you'll have the luxurious lifestyle. The other message is that the luxurious lifestyle is good and desirable. TV shows, movies, and news programs also convey values and beliefs.

Media can also shape your opinions about the world. For example, news about crime shapes our understanding about how much and what type of crime is prevalent in the world around us. TV news items, talk show interviews, and commercials may shape what we think of a political candidate, a celebrity, an ethnic group, a country, or a regional area. As a result, our knowledge of someone or someplace could be completely based on the information we receive from the television.

3 Film and TV

Films and television programs come in a variety of types. Films include comedies, dramas, documentaries, and animated features. Televison programs cover dramas, sitcoms, talk shows, reality shows, newscasts, and so on. Producers of films and producers of television programs rely on many of the same elements to make the action and settings seem real and to also affect the emotions of their audiences. Among these elements are scripts, visual and sound elements, special effects, and editing.

3.1 SCRIPT AND WRITTEN ELEMENTS

The writer and editor develop a story for television or film using a script and storyboard. A **script** is the text or words of a film or television show. A **storyboard** is a device used to plan the shooting of a movie or TV show. A storyboard is made up of drawings and brief descriptions of what is happening in each shot of a scene. The drawings of a storyboard help a director visualize how a finished scene might look before the scene is filmed. The following storyboard shows some scenes that a student created.

Shot 1
Marty is speeding down the street.

Shot 2
The hand moves on the clock

*For more information, see **Media Study: Produce Your Own Media,** page 157.*

3.2 VISUAL ELEMENTS

Visual elements in film and television include camera shots and angles. A **camera shot** is a single, continuous view taken by a camera. A **camera angle** is the angle at which the camera is positioned during the recording of a shot or image. Each azis carefully planned to create an effect. The chart shows what different shots are used for.

Camera Shot/Angle	Effect
Establishing shot introduces viewers to the location of a scene, usually by presenting a wide view of an area	establishes the setting of a film
Close-up shot shows a close view of a person or object	helps to create emotion and make viewers feel as if they know the character
Medium shot shows a view wider than a close-up but narrower than an establishing or long shot	shows part of an object, or a character from the knees or waist up
Long shot gives a wide view of a scene, showing the full figure(s) of a person or group and the surroundings	allows the viewer to see the "big picture" and shows the relationship between characters and the environment
Reaction shot shows in some way what he or she sees	allows the viewer to see how the subject feels in order to create empathy in the viewer
Low-angle shot looks up at an object or person	makes a character, object, or scene appear more important or threatening
High-angle shot looks down on an object or person	makes a character, object, or scene seem weak or unimportant
Point-of-view (POV) shot shows a part of the story through a character's eyes	helps viewers identify with that character

3.3 SOUND ELEMENTS

Sound elements in film and television include music, voice-over, and sound effects.

Music may be used to set the mood and atmosphere in a scene. Music can have a powerful effect on the way viewers feel about a story. For example, fast-paced music helps viewers feel excited during an action scene.

Voice-over is the voice of the unseen commentator or narrator of a film, TV program, or commercial.

Sound effects are the sounds added to films, TV programs, and commercials during the editing process. Sound effects, such as laugh tracks or the sounds of punches in a fight scene, can create humor, emphasize a point, or contribute to the mood.

3.4 SPECIAL EFFECTS

Special effects include computer-generated animation, manipulated video images, and fast- or slow-motion sequences in films, TV programs, and commercials.

Animation on film involves the frame-by-frame photography of a series of drawings or objects. When these frames are projected—at a rate of 24 per second—the illusion of movement is achieved.

A **split screen** is a special-effects shot in which two or more separate images are shown in the same frame. One example is when two people, actually a distance apart, are shown talking to each other.

3.5 EDITING

Editing is the process of selecting and arranging shots in a sequence. Moviemakers put shots together in ways that help you follow the action of a story. The editor decides which scenes or shots to use, as well as the length of each shot, the number of shots, and their sequence.

Cut is the transition from one shot to another. To create excitement, editors often use quick cuts, which are a series of short shots strung together.

Dissolve is a device in which one scene fades into another.

Fade-in is a device in which a white or black shot fades in to reveal the beginning of a new scene.

Fade-out is a device in which a shot fades to darkness to end a scene.

Jump cut is an abrupt and jarring change from one shot to another. A jump cut shows a break in time.

Pace is the length of time each shot stays on the screen and the rhythm that is created by the transitions between shots. Short, quick cuts create a fast pace in a story. Long cuts slow down a story.

4 News

The **news** is information on events, people, and places in your community, the region, the nation, and the world. It can be found in local newspapers, newscasts, online wire services, magazines, and documentaries. Because it's impossible to publish all the news that happens in one day in any one source, journalists have to make decisions about which stories will appear in newspapers and on newscasts. They use several factors to help them choose stories.

4.1 CHOOSING THE NEWS

Newsworthiness is the importance of an event or action that makes it worthy of media reporting. Journalists and their editors often use the following criteria in determining which stories should make the news:

Timeliness is the quality of being very current. Timely events usually take priority over previously reported events. For example, a car accident with deaths will be timely on the day it occurs. Because of its timeliness it may be on the front page of a newspaper or may be the lead story on a newscast.

Widespread impact is a characteristic of an event that could affect a number of people. The more widespread the impact of an event, the more likely it is to be newsworthy.

Proximity measures the nearness of an event to a particular city, region, or country. People tend to be more interested in stories that take place close to where they live and that thus may affect them directly.

Human interest is a quality of stories that cause readers or listeners to feel emotions such as happiness, anger, or sadness. People are interested in reading stories about other people.

Uniqueness is the condition of being the only one of a kind. Unique or uncommon events or circumstances are likely to be interesting to an audience.

Compelling video and **photographs** grab people's attention and stay in their minds.

4.2 REPORTING THE NEWS

While developing a news story, a journalist makes a variety of decisions about how to construct the story, such as what information to include and how to organize it. The following elements are commonly used in news stories:

5 W's and H are the six questions reporters answer when writing news stories—*who, what, when, where, why,* and *how.* It is a journalist's job to answer these questions in any type of news report. These questions also provide a structure for writing and editing a story.

Inverted pyramid is the means of organizing information according to importance. In the inverted-pyramid diagram below, the most important information (the answers to the 5 W's and H) appears at the top of the pyramid. The less important details appear at the bottom. Not all stories are reported using the inverted-pyramid form. The form remains popular, however, because it helps a reader to get the important information without reading the entire story. Notice the following example.

> Soft-drink makers announced that they would work to limit the availability of soft drinks in schools around the country.
>
> The industry feels it needs to help fight childhood obesity.
>
> The president of the Soft Drink Association formally announced the new policy last week.

Angle or slant is the point of view from which a story is written. Even an objective report must have an angle.

Consider these two headlines that describe the same house fire.

The first headline focuses on a fact. The second headline focuses on an opinion and has a negative slant.

Standards for News Reporting

The ideal of journalism is to present news in a way that is objective, accurate, and thorough. The best news stories contain the following elements:

- **Objectivity** The story takes a balanced point of view on the issues. It is not biased, nor does it reflect a specific attitude or opinion.

- **Accuracy** The story presents factual information that can be verified.

- **Thoroughness** The story presents all sides of an issue. It includes background information, telling *who, what, when, where, why,* and *how.*

Balanced Versus Biased Reporting

Objectivity in news reporting can be measured by how balanced or biased the story is.

Balanced reporting represents all sides of an issue equally and fairly.

A balanced news story

- represents people and subjects in a neutral light

- treats all sides of an issue equally

- does not include inappropriate questions, such as "Will you seek counseling after this terrible tragedy?"

- does not show stereotypes or prejudice toward people of a particular race, gender, age, religion, or other group
- does not leave out important background information that is needed to establish a context or perspective

Biased reporting is reporting in which one side is favored over another or in which the subject is unfairly represented. Biased reporting may show an overly negative view of a subject, or it may encourage racial, gender, or other stereotypes and prejudices. Sometimes biased reporting is apparent in the journalist's choice of sources.

Sources are the people interviewed for the news report and also any written materials and documents the journalist used for background information. From each source, the journalist gets a different point of view. To decide whether news reporting is balanced or biased, you will need to pay attention to the sources. Consider a news story on a new snack food, for instance. If the journalist's only source is a representative from the company that made the snack, the report may be biased. But if the journalist also includes the perspective of someone neutral, such as a scientist who is studying the nutritional value of the snack, the report may be more balanced. The following chart shows which sources are reliable.

Sources for News Stories	
Reliable Sources	**Weak Sources**
• experts in a field • people directly affected by the reported event (eyewitnesses) • published reports that are specifically mentioned or shown	• unnamed or anonymous sources • people who are not involved in the reported event (for example, people who heard about a story from a friend) • research, data, or reports that are not specifically named or are referred to only in vague terms (for example, "Research shows that . . .")

5 Advertising

Advertising is a sponsor's paid use of various media to promote products, services, or ideas. Some common forms of advertising are shown in the chart.

Type of Ad	Description
Billboard	a large outdoor advertising sign
Print ad	typically appears in magazines and newspapers; uses eye-catching graphics and persuasive copy
Flyer	a print ad that is circulated by hand or mail
Infomercial	an extended ad on TV that usually includes detailed product information, demonstrations, and testimonials
Public service announcement	a message aired on radio or TV to promote ideas that are considered to be in the public interest
Political ad	broadcast on radio or TV to promote political candidates
Trailer	a short film promoting an upcoming movie, TV show, or video game

Marketing is the process of transferring products and services from producer to consumer. It involves determining the packaging and pricing of a product, how it will be promoted and advertised, and where it will be sold. One way companies market their products is by becoming media sponsors.

Sponsors pay for their products to be advertised. These companies hire advertising agencies to create and produce specific campaigns for their products. They then buy television or radio airtime or magazine, newspaper, or billboard space to feature ads where the target audience is sure to see them. Because selling time and space to advertisers produces much of the income the media need to function, the media need advertisers just as much as advertisers need the media.

Product placement is the intentional and identifiable featuring of brand-name products in movies, television shows, video games, and

"That will be fine, Dad," I said.

"Good show, old man," my father said. "Now about this room. I don't see how you can stand it. Maybe you'd like us to drag your mattress into our room, where it's nice and cool."

My parents' bedroom had a little dinky air conditioner that puffed air about three degrees cooler than what was outside. It was pathetic.

"I'll be fine here, Dad," I said.

40 "Good lad. Now do you want to help us scrape paint off the woodwork or just explore around?"

"I think I'll do some exploring," I said.

—from *Looking for Bobowicz*
Daniel Pinkwater

Directions: Answer these questions about the selection from *Looking for Bobowicz*.

① stem

1. What can you infer about the narrator from his description of the two houses in lines 8–19?

   A. He is unhappy about moving.

   B. He wants to run away.

   C. He is spoiled.

   D. He likes city life. **④**

2. Which statement best describes the *theme* of this passage? **②**

   A. Suburban life is better than city life.

   B. Parents don't listen to their children.

   C. Crime is a big part of urban life.

   D. Change is difficult to accept.

3. In this passage, the narrator and his parents have different feelings about

   ③

   choices

   A. household chores

   B. the benefits of city life

   C. the importance of honesty

   D. family finances

4. The summer heat wave in this passage symbolizes the **⑤**

   A. danger of the city

   B. narrator's intense feelings

   C. run-down house

   D. father's enthusiasm

Tips: Multiple Choice

A multiple-choice question consists of a stem and a set of choices. The stem is in the form of a question or an incomplete sentence. One of the choices correctly answers the question or completes the sentence. Many tests offer four answer choices, but no matter how many choices are given, you can use the same strategies to guide you to the best answer.

① Read the stem carefully and try to answer the question before you look at the choices.

② Pay attention to key words in the stem. They may direct you to the correct answer. Note that question 2 is looking for the *theme*, or main idea, of the passage.

③ Don't jump to conclusions about the correct answer until you've read all of the choices. In question 3, you might decide to stop at choice A, because the narrator does talk about the modern house he moved out of and the 120-year-old house he lives in now, but that is not the correct answer.

④ After reading all of the choices, eliminate any that you know are incorrect. In question 1, you can safely eliminate choice D, because the narrator expresses his strong dislike of city life throughout the passage.

⑤ Some questions ask you to interpret a symbol.

Answers: 1. A, **2.** D, **3.** B, **4.** B

3 Vocabulary

Most standardized tests include items that ask about the meanings of words. Some questions might refer to a passage you just read, while others might provide a sentence or paragraph of context followed by the answer choices.

1. Which one of the following words from the passage on pages R94–R95 has a negative connotation? ❶
   A. stuff (line 2)
   B. modern (line 8)
   C. egad (line 20)
   D. dinky (line 37)

2. Which word from the passage comes from the Latin root meaning "city"?
   A. house (line 3)
   B. street (line 10)
   C. sidewalk (line 12)
   D. urban (line 15) ❷

3. Which line from the passage contains a simile? ❸
   A. "She said life was real in cities." (lines 18–19)
   B. "It's hot as an oven in here, old pal" (lines 20–21)
   C. "Good show, old man" (line 34)
   D. "It was pathetic." (line 38)

4. Read this dictionary entry for the word *chap*. Which noun definition represents the meaning of *chap* as used in line 25 of the passage?

   DEFINITION

   n. **1.** The roughening of the skin caused especially by cold. **2.** (*Chiefly Brit.*) fellow. **3.** The face.

   A. *n.* meaning 1
   B. *n.* meaning 2
   C. *n.* meaning 3
   D. *v.* meaning 1 ❹

Tips: Word Meaning

❶ Connotation is the suggestion or feeling a word carries beyond its literal meaning. *Small* is a neutral word. *Compact* is a more positive word for small, but the word *dinky* has a negative connotation.

❷ If you don't know the exact meaning of a word, look for clues in nearby sentences. For the word *urban* in line 15, read the description in the preceding paragraph and ask yourself where you will find houses with small yards and busy streets with buses. *Urban*, choice C, is the best answer to that question. *Urban* means "relating to the city."

❸ A simile is a figure of speech. The words *like* and *as* are clues that a comparison is a simile.

❹ Eliminate any answers that are not the same part of speech as the meaning of the word in the passage. *Chap* is used as a noun in the passsage, so you can rule out answer choice D.

Answers: 1. D, **2.** D, **3.** B, **4.** B

4 Writing and Language

You will be asked to write essays and even research papers in middle school. When it comes to writing, good ideas aren't enough. You need to know how to express them. That requires knowledge of English grammar, sentence structure, and usage. To measure that skill, many standardized tests ask you to identify errors or to improve sentences and paragraphs.

Directions: Read this passage and then answer the questions.

PASSAGE

(1) On May 1 and October 1 you might see two or three moving trucks on a single city block. (2) These are the busiest moving days of the year. (3) The longest trucks are usually from companies that supply movers and sturdy packing boxes. (4) You have to reserve these trucks weeks in advance. (5) They won't be available. (6) Professional movers use thick pads <u>for furniture protection from scratches</u>. (7) Sometimes people try to save money by renting a truck and moving himself. (8) Their things often get broken because they aren't packed properly.

1. The correct coordinating conjunction to join sentences 4 and 5 is
- **A.** but
- **B.** for
- **C.** or
- **D.** while

2. What is the best way to rewrite the underlined part of sentence 6?
- **A.** to protect furniture from scratches
- **B.** for scratch protection on furniture
- **C.** for the protection of furniture from scratches
- **D.** in order to protect from scratches on furniture

3. What change, if any, should be made to sentence 7?
- **A.** Change *try* to *trying*
- **B.** Change *renting* to *getting*
- **C.** Change *himself* to *themselves*
- **D.** Make no change

4. What change, if any, should be made to sentence 8?
- **A.** Change *their* to *there*
- **B.** Change *broken* to *broke*
- **C.** Change *aren't* to *are'nt*
- **D.** Make no change

Tips: Grammar

❶ Read the entire passage to grasp its overall meaning. Pay particular attention to any underlined parts.

❷ Before choosing a revision, read through all of the choices to decide which one is best. Your selection should produce a sentence that is grammatically correct.

❸ If you are asked to combine sentences, think about how the ideas relate to each other. When you understand the connection between the thoughts, you will know how to join them. The word *but* (choice A) can be used to show how two different ideas are related, but it is not the right word to use to join sentences 4 and 5.

❹ Some items will test your knowledge of language conventions. Make sure that pronouns agree with antecedents and that verbs agree with subjects.

❺ Some items will also test your knowledge of commonly confused words. In test item 4, choice A is a possible revision. Read sentences carefully to determine how each word is used before deciding which choice is best.

❻ In test items 3 and 4, choice D says, "Make no change." Choose this answer only if the sentence is correct as it is originally written.

Answers: 1. C, **2.** A, **3.** C, **4.** D

5 Responding to Writing Prompts

Not all tests are multiple choice. Sometimes you have to develop your ideas into a paragraph or a short essay. You might be asked to interpret, summarize, or react to a reading selection.

> **Directions:** Reread the selection from *Looking for Bobowicz* on pages R94–R95 and follow the directions for the short and extended constructed responses.

SHORT CONSTRUCTED RESPONSE

Write a well-organized paragraph comparing and contrasting the narrator's old and new homes.

> **SAMPLE SHORT CONSTRUCTED RESPONSE**
>
> The narrator's two homes are very different. ❶ In Happy Valley he lived on a tree-lined street in a quiet suburb. In Hoboken he lives in a noisy urban neighborhood where bicycles get stolen. The house in Happy Valley was modern and was surrounded by greenery. The house in Hoboken is an old, run-down building surrounded by busy streets. ❷ The name Happy Valley suggests a cool, rural locale that is free from the stifling heat and close quarters of Hoboken.

EXTENDED CONSTRUCTED RESPONSE

Discuss in two or three paragraphs what the narrator's mother means when she says life is "real" in cities.

> **SAMPLE EXTENDED CONSTRUCTED RESPONSE**
>
> When the narrator's mother says life is real in cities, she probably means that the city is a reflection of life itself. ❸
>
> Variety is what makes a city real. As you travel through a big city you can hear many languages being spoken, and you can sample foods from different parts of the world. ❹ You can rub shoulders with executives on one street and panhandlers on the next. You find people living in penthouses, modest homes, and public housing. You see mosques, churches, and synagogues.
>
> The challenges of urban life are also very real. ❸ People in cities, including children, learn to cope with overcrowding, noise, air pollution, traffic, and crime. ❺

Tips: Responding to Writing Prompts

❶ Short-constructed-response prompts are often fact based rather than interpretive. Get right to the point in your answer, and stick to the facts.

❷ Make sure that you write about the assigned topic. Support your answer with details from the passage, such as a quotation, a paraphrase, or an example.

❸ When you are writing an extended constructed response, build your paragraphs around clear topic sentences that will pull your ideas together.

❹ If you are asked to interpret a passage, don't just copy the author's words. Try to express the ideas in your own words. Express your ideas clearly so that the reader understands your viewpoint.

❺ Proofread your response for errors in capitalization, punctuation, spelling, or grammar.

6 Writing an Essay

Many tests will ask you to read a prompt and write an essay in response to it. You might be asked to write a narrative, persuasive, or expository essay. You might be asked to write a story, summarize an article, or respond to a piece of writing. It is important to read the prompt carefully and look for direction words that tell you what to write about. Because of the time constraints, an impromptu essay will not be polished. It will represent a first draft. Even so, it should be complete. Essays are scored on the following criteria:

- **Focus** Establish a point of view in the opening paragraph. Stay with that topic throughout the essay.

- **Organization** Maintain a logical progression of ideas.

- **Support for ideas** Use details and examples to develop an argument or line of thinking.

- **Style/word choice** Use words accurately and vary sentences.

- **Grammar** Use standard English and proofread for errors.

Writing Prompt

In 2004, a bill was introduced to the California legislature that proposed lowering the voting age to 14. Under the "Training Wheels for Citizenship" concept, votes cast by 14- and 15-year-olds would be counted as one-fourth of a full vote, and those cast by 16- and 17-year-olds would be counted as one-half. Write a persuasive essay of four or five paragraphs supporting or rejecting this idea.

SAMPLE PERSUASIVE ESSAY

Lowering the voting age is not a good idea, especially if our votes wouldn't count as full votes. A lot of high school students aren't interested in politics. It seems that many adults aren't either, because less than half of them vote in most elections. Teenagers are focused on getting into college. Events on Capitol Hill seem a long way off. Most of us probably wouldn't vote even if we could. **①** **②**

Voter independence is another issue. I generally listen to my parents, but sometimes they have their ideas and I have mine. If I were allowed to vote, I'm afraid they would try to influence my decision. Voting is supposed to be private, but my mom can always get the truth out of me.

As for counting our votes as fractions of a vote, that is an insult. For teenagers to have an impact on an election, four times as many of us would have to vote. It's almost un-American, because our nation was founded on the idea that everyone's vote has the same weight, whether we are rich or poor.

A lot of political issues affect young people. Most of the people living in poverty, for example, are kids. And of course the government pays more attention to the needs of people who vote. But money also influences government policies, and money is one thing young people don't have. **③**

In conclusion, young people lack the interest, the independence, and the economic power to make a difference in the voting booth. **④**

Tips: Writing an Essay

Before you begin writing, take a minute or two to gather your thoughts. You don't need to prepare a complete outline, but write the main points you want to make. In the essay here on lowering the voting age, the lack of interest, independence, and equality of voters are key issues.

① When writing a persuasive essay, state your point of view in the introduction.

② Facts and examples make your writing come to life, no matter what the topic is. Use them in the body of your essay to clarify your points and to strengthen your arguments. The writer of this essay uses statistics to demonstrate voter apathy among adults.

③ Try to consider the opposing point of view and respond to it. In the sample essay, the student notes that "the government pays more attention to the needs of people who vote."

④ Make sure your essay has a conclusion, even if it's just a single sentence. A conclusion pulls your ideas together and lets the reader know you have finished.

⑤ Allow time to reread what you have written. If you have to make a correction, do so neatly and legibly.

Act An act is a major division within a play, similar to a chapter in a book. Each act may be further divided into smaller sections, called scenes. Plays can have as many as five acts. *The Monsters Are Due on Maple Street* by Rod Serling has two acts.

Adventure Story An adventure story is a literary work in which action is the main element. An **adventure novel** usually focuses on a main character who is on a mission and is facing many challenges and choices.

Alliteration Alliteration is the repetition of consonant sounds at the beginning of words. Note the repetition of the *b* sound in these lines.

> Crusts of <u>b</u>lack <u>b</u>urned <u>b</u>uttered toast,
> Gristly <u>b</u>its of <u>b</u>eefy roasts . . .
> —Shel Silverstein, "Sarah Cynthia Sylvia Stout Would
>   Not Take the Garbage Out"

See pages 556, 608.

Allusion An allusion is a reference to a a famous person, place, event, or work of literature. In "Names/Nombres," Julia Alvarez makes an allusion to a line from the play *Romeo and Juliet* by William Shakespeare. She also makes an allusion to *Hey Jude,* a hit song by the Beatles.

See page 808.

Analogy An analogy is a point-by-point comparison between two things that are alike in some respect. Often, writers use analogies in nonfiction to explain unfamiliar subjects or ideas in terms of familiar ones.

See also **Extended Metaphor; Metaphor; Simile.**

Anecdote An anecdote is a short account of an event that is usually intended to entertain or make a point. In "Names/Nombres," Julia Alvarez uses an anecdote about arriving at the immigration office to show how her name began changing once she entered the United States.

See page 805.

Antagonist The antagonist is a force working against the protagonist, or main character, in a story, play, or novel. The antagonist is usually another character but can be a force of nature, society itself, or an internal force within the main character. In Michael Morpurgo's retelling of "Sir Gawain and the Green Knight," the Green Knight is the antagonist.

See page 692.
See also **Protagonist.**

Assonance Assonance is the repetition of vowel sounds within nonrhyming words. An example of assonance is the repetition of the *i* sound in the following line.

> is a d<u>i</u>amond bl<u>i</u>nd in the black belly of coal
>   —Lucille Clifton, "the earth is a living thing"

Author's Perspective An author's perspective is the unique combination of ideas, values, feelings, and beliefs that influences the way the writer looks at a topic. **Tone,** or attitude, often reveals an author's perspective. Peter Benchley writes "Great White Sharks" from a perspective that reflects his fascination with the sea and his regret that his novel *Jaws* caused misconceptions about sharks.

See page 920.
See also **Author's Purpose; Tone.**

Author's Purpose A writer usually writes for one or more of these purposes: to express thoughts or feelings, to inform or explain, to persuade, and to entertain. For example, in his "Remarks at the Dedication of the Aerospace Medical Health Center," President John F. Kennedy's purpose was to persuade Americans that the United States should lead the world in space research.

See also **Author's Perspective; Writer's Point of View.**

Autobiography An autobiography is a writer's account of his or her own life. In almost every case, it is told from the first-person point of view. Generally, an autobiography focuses on the most significant events and people in the writer's life over a period of time. Lance Armstrong's *It's Not About the Bike* is an autobiography.

See pages 8, 778, 816.
See also **Memoir.**

Ballad A ballad is a type of narrative poem that tells a story and was originally meant to be sung or recited. Because it tells a story, a ballad has a setting, a plot, and characters. **Folk ballads** were composed orally and handed down by word of mouth from generation to generation. "The Highwayman" by Alfred Noyes is an example of a **literary ballad,** which takes its form from the folk ballad but is not composed orally.

Biography A biography is the true account of a person's life, written by another person. As such, biographies are usually told from a third-person point of view. The writer of a biography usually researches his or her subject in order to present accurate information. The best biographers strive for honesty and balance in their accounts of their subjects' lives. William Jay Jacobs's "Eleanor Roosevelt" is an example of a biography.

Cast of Characters In the script of a play, a cast of characters is a list of all the characters in the play, usually in order of appearance. It may include a brief description of each character.

Character Characters are the people, animals, or imaginary creatures who take part in the action of a work of literature. Like real people, characters display certain qualities, or **character traits,** that develop and change over time, and they usually have **motivations,** or reasons, for their behaviors.

> **Central character:** Central or main characters are the most important characters in literary works. Generally, the plot of a short story focuses on one main character, but a novel may have several main characters.
>
> **Minor characters:** The less important characters in a literary work are known as minor characters. The story is not centered on them, but they help carry out the action of the story and help the reader learn more about the main character.
>
> **Dynamic character:** A dynamic character is one who undergoes important changes as a plot unfolds. The changes occur because of the character's actions and experiences in the story. The changes are usually internal and may be good or bad. Main characters are usually, though not always, dynamic.
>
> **Static character:** A static character is one who remains the same throughout a story. The character may experience events and have interactions with other characters, but he or she is not changed because of them.

See pages 5, 28, 184, 191, 249.
See also **Characterization; Character Traits.**

Characterization The way a writer creates and develops characters is known as characterization. There are four basic methods of characterization:

- The writer may make direct comments about a character through the voice of the narrator.
- The writer may describe the character's physical appearance.
- The writer may present the character's own thoughts, speech, and actions.

- The writer may present thoughts, speech, and actions of other characters.

See pages 186, 267.
See also **Character; Character Traits.**

Character Traits Character traits are the qualities shown by a character. Traits may be physical (brown eyes) or expressions of personality (shyness). Writers reveal the traits of their characters through methods of characterization. Sometimes writers directly state a character's traits, but more often readers need to infer traits from a character's words, actions, thoughts, appearance, and relationships. Examples of words that describe traits include *courageous, humble, generous,* and *wild.*

Climax The climax stage is the point of greatest interest in a story or play. The climax usually occurs toward the end of a story, after the reader has understood the **conflict** and become emotionally involved with the characters. At the climax, the conflict is resolved and the outcome of the plot usually becomes clear.

See pages 30, 35.
See also **Plot.**

Comedy A comedy is a dramatic work that is light and often humorous in tone, usually ending happily with a peaceful resolution of the main conflict.

Conflict A conflict is a struggle between opposing forces. Almost every story has a main conflict—a conflict that is the story's focus. An **external conflict** involves a character who struggles against a force outside him- or herself, such as nature, a physical obstacle, or another character. An **internal conflict** is one that occurs within a character.

Examples: In Rudyard Kipling's "Rikki-tikki-tavi," the mongoose Rikki is in conflict with the cobras Nag and Nagaina. In Robert D. San Souci's retelling of *Young Arthur,* Arthur is torn between wanting to escape punishment when he thinks he has stolen the king's sword and wanting to accept responsibility as a true knight should.

See pages 5, 28, 67, 78, 682.
See also **Plot.**

Connotation A word's connotations are the ideas and feelings associated with the word, as opposed to its dictionary definition. For example, the word *mother,* in addition to its basic meaning ("a female parent"), has connotations of love, warmth, and security.

Couplet A couplet is a rhymed pair of lines. A couplet may be written in any rhythmic pattern.

> Masons, when they start upon a building,
> Are careful to test out the scaffolding;
> —Seamus Heaney, "Scaffolding"

See also **Stanza**.

Critical Essay See **Essay**.

Denotation A word's denotation is its dictionary definition.
See also **Connotation**.

Description Description is writing that helps a reader to picture events, objects, and characters. To create descriptions, writers often use **imagery**—words and phrases that appeal to the reader's senses.

Dialect A dialect is a form of a language that is spoken in a particular place or by a particular group of people. Dialects may feature unique pronunciations, vocabulary, and grammar. For example, when Antonio and Felix speak to each other in Piri Thomas's story "Amigo Brothers," they use dialect that reflects their Puerto Rican community in New York. Their dialect includes informal grammar and slang words drawn from both American Spanish and English.

> "Same here. It ain't natural not to think about the fight. I mean, we both are *cheverote* fighters, and we both want to win."

Dialogue Dialogue is written conversation between two or more characters. Writers use dialogue to bring characters to life and to give readers insights into the characters' qualities, traits, and reactions to other characters. In fiction, dialogue is usually set off with quotation marks. In drama, stories are told primarily through dialogue.

Diary A diary is a daily record of a writer's thoughts, experiences, and feelings. As such, it is a type of autobiographical writing. The terms *diary* and *journal* are often used synonymously.

Drama A drama, or play, is a form of literature meant to be performed by actors in front of an audience. In a drama, the characters' dialogue and actions tell the story. The written form of a play is known as a script. A script usually includes dialogue, a cast of characters, and stage directions that give instructions about performing the drama. The person who writes the drama is known as the playwright or dramatist.

Dynamic Character See **Character**.

Epic Poem An epic poem is a long narrative poem about the adventures of a hero whose actions reflect the ideals and values of a nation or a group of people.

Essay An essay is a short work of nonfiction that deals with a single subject. There are many types of essays. An **expository essay** presents or explains information and ideas. A **personal essay** usually reflects the writer's experiences, feelings, and personality. A **persuasive essay** attempts to convince the reader to adopt a certain viewpoint. A **critical essay** evaluates a situation or a work of art.
See pages 8, 512.

Exaggeration An extreme overstatement of an idea is called an exaggeration. It is often used for purposes of emphasis or humor. In "Sally Ann Thunder Ann Whirlwind," Mary Pope Osborne exaggerates Sally's size, strength, and cleverness to create a humorous, memorable impression of the character.

Exposition Exposition is the first stage of a typical story plot. The exposition provides important background information and introduces the setting and the important characters. The conflict the characters face may also be introduced in the exposition, or it may be introduced later, in the rising action.
See pages 30, 35.
See also **Plot**.

Expository Essay See **Essay**.

Extended Metaphor An extended metaphor is a figure of speech that compares two essentially unlike things at some length and in several ways. It does not contain the word *like* or *as*.
See also **Metaphor**.

External Conflict See **Conflict**.

Fable A fable is a brief tale told to illustrate a moral or teach a lesson. Often the moral of a fable appears in a distinct and memorable statement near the tale's beginning or end. "The Race Between Toad and Donkey" by Roger D. Abrahams is an example of a fable from Jamaica.
See also **Moral**.

Falling Action The falling action is the stage of the plot in which the story begins to draw to a close. The falling action comes after the climax and before the resolution. Events in the falling action show the results of the important decision or action that happened at the climax. Tension eases as the falling action begins; however, the final outcome of the story is not yet fully worked out at this stage.

See page 30.
See also **Climax; Plot.**

Fantasy Fantasy is a type of fiction that is highly imaginative and portrays events, settings, or characters that are unrealistic. The setting might be a nonexistent world, the plot might involve magic or the supernatural, and the characters might have superhuman powers.

Farce Farce is a type of exaggerated comedy that features an absurd plot, ridiculous situations, and humorous dialogue. The main purpose of a farce is to keep an audience laughing. Comic devices typically used in farces include mistaken identity, wordplay (such as puns and double meanings), and exaggeration.

Fiction Fiction is prose writing that tells an imaginary story. The writer of a fictional work might invent all the events and characters or might base parts of the story on real people and events. The basic elements of fiction are plot, character, setting, and theme. Fiction includes short stories, novellas, and novels.

See also **Novel; Novella; Short Story.**

Figurative Language In figurative language, words are used in an imaginative way to express ideas that are not literally true. "Tasha's money is burning a hole in her pocket" is an example of figurative language. The sentence does not really mean that Tasha's pocket is on fire. Instead, it means that Tasha is anxious to spend her money. Figurative language is used for comparison, emphasis, and emotional effect.

See pages 558, 567, 613.
See also **Metaphor; Onomatopoeia; Personification; Simile.**

First-Person Point of View *See* **Point of View.**

Flashback In a literary work, a flashback is an interruption of the action to present events that took place at an earlier time. A flashback provides information that can help a reader better understand a character's current situation.

Example: In "The Last Dog," Katherine Paterson uses flashback to explain how Brock became interested in the "ancient fictions" and the world outside the dome.

Foil A foil is a character who provides a striking contrast to another character. By using a foil, a writer can call attention to certain traits possessed by a main character or simply enhance a character by contrast. In Avi's "What Do Fish Have to Do with Anything?" the mother acts as a foil to the main character, Willie.

Folklore The traditions, customs, and stories that are passed down within a culture are known as its folklore. Folklore includes various types of literature, such as legends, folk tales, myths, trickster tales, and fables.

See **Fable; Folk Tale; Myth.**

Folk Tale A folk tale is a story that has been passed from generation to generation by word of mouth. Folk tales may be set in the distant past and involve supernatural events. The characters in them may be animals, people, or superhuman beings. "Waters of Gold" is an example of a folk tale.

Foreshadowing Foreshadowing occurs when a writer provides hints that suggest future events in a story. Foreshadowing creates suspense and makes readers eager to find out what will happen. For example, in the myth "Icarus and Daedalus," Daedalus' warnings about flying close to the sun hint at Icarus' fate.

See pages 30, 77.

Form The structure or organization of a work of writing is often called its form. The form of a poem includes the arrangement of its words and lines on the page.

Free Verse Poetry without regular patterns of rhyme and rhythm is called free verse. Some poets use free verse to capture the sounds and rhythms of ordinary speech. The

> Yesterday, I lay awake in the palm of the night.
> A soft rain stole in, unhelped by any breeze,
> And when I saw the silver glaze on the windows,
> I started with A, with Ackerman, as it happened,
> Then Baxter and Calabro, . . .
> —Billy Collins, "The Names"

poem "The Names" by Billy Collins is written in free verse.

See pages 554, 561.
See also **Rhyme.**

Genre The term *genre* refers to a category in which a work of literature is classified. The major genres in literature are fiction, nonfiction, poetry, and drama.

Haiku Haiku is a form of Japanese poetry in which 17 syllables are arranged in three lines of 5, 7, and 5 syllables. The rules of haiku are strict. In addition to following the syllabic count, the poet must create a clear picture that will evoke a strong emotional response in the reader. Nature is a particularly important source of inspiration for Japanese haiku poets, and details from nature are often the subjects of their poems.

> On sweet plum blossoms
> The sun rises suddenly.
> Look, a mountain path!
>
> —Bashō

Hero A hero is a main character or protagonist in a story. In older literary works, heroes tend to be better than ordinary humans. They are typically courageous, strong, honorable, and intelligent. They are protectors of society who hold back the forces of evil and fight to make the world a better place. In modern literature, a hero may simply be the most important character in a story. Such a hero is often an ordinary person with ordinary problems.

Historical Dramas Historical dramas are plays that take place in the past and are based on real events. In many of these plays, the characters are also based on real historical figures. The dialogue and the action, however, are mostly created by the playwright.

Historical Fiction A short story or a novel can be called historical fiction when it is set in the past and includes real places and real events of historical importance. The novel *Crispin: The Cross of Lead* by Avi is an example of historical fiction.

See page 706.

Humor Humor is a quality that provokes laughter or amusement. Writers create humor through exaggeration, amusing descriptions, irony, and witty and insightful dialogue. In his essay "Breaking the Ice," Dave Barry uses humor to tell the story of his first date.

See pages 512, 605.

Hyperbole Hyperbole is a figure of speech in which the truth is exaggerated for emphasis or humorous effect.

Idiom An idiom is an expression that has a meaning different from the meaning of its individual words. For example, "to go to the dogs" is an idiom meaning "to go to ruin."

Imagery Imagery consists of words and phrases that appeal to a reader's five senses. Writers use sensory details to help the reader imagine how things look, feel, smell, sound, and taste.

> When the sun paints the desert
> with its gold,
> I climb the hills.
> Wind runs round boulders, ruffles
> my hair. . . .
>
> —Pat Mora, "Gold"

See pages 558, 561, 571.

Internal Conflict *See* **Conflict.**

Interview An interview is a conversation conducted by a writer or reporter, in which facts or statements are elicited from another person, recorded, and then broadcast or published. This book includes an interview with Ray Bradbury.

See page 478.

Journal *See* **Diary.**

Legend A legend is a story handed down from the past about a specific person, usually someone of heroic accomplishments. Legends usually have some basis in historical fact. *Young Arthur* by Robert D. San Souci is an example of a legend.

Limerick A limerick is a short, humorous poem composed of five lines. It usually has the rhyme scheme *aabba*, created by two rhyming couplets followed by a fifth line that rhymes with the first couplet. A limerick typically has a sing-song rhythm.

> There was an old man with a light,   *a*
> Who was dressed in a garment of white;   *a*
> He held a small candle,   *b*
> With never a handle,   *b*
> And danced all the merry long night.   *a*
>
> —Edward Lear

Lyric Poetry Lyric poetry is poetry that presents the personal thoughts and feelings of a single speaker. Most poems, other than narrative poems, are lyric poems. Lyric poetry can be in a variety of forms and cover many subjects, from love and death to everyday experiences. Mary Oliver's "Sleeping in the Forest" is an example of a lyric poem.

Memoir A memoir is a form of autobiographical writing in which a writer shares his or her personal experiences and observations of significant events or people. Often informal or even intimate in tone, memoirs usually give readers insight into the impact of historical events on people's lives. *An American Childhood* by Annie Dillard is a memoir.
See page 124.
See also **Autobiography.**

Metaphor A metaphor is a comparison of two things that are basically unlike but have some qualities in common. Unlike a simile, a metaphor does not contain the word *like* or *as.* In "The Delight Song of Tsoai-Talee," the speaker of the poem compares himself to different things in nature, including "a feather on the bright sky" and "the hunger of a young wolf."
See pages 558, 613.
See also **Extended Metaphor; Figurative Language; Simile.**

Meter In poetry, meter is the regular pattern of stressed (ˊ) and unstressed (˘) syllables. Although poems have rhythm, not all poems have regular meter. Each unit of meter is known as a **foot** and is made up of one stressed syllable and one or two unstressed syllables. Notice the meter marked in the following lines.

> The wind was a torrent of darkness among the gusty trees.
> The moon was a ghostly galleon tossed upon cloudy seas.
>
> —Alfred Noyes, "The Highwayman"

See pages 556, 583.
See also **Rhythm.**

Minor Character *See* **Character.**

Mood Mood is the feeling or atmosphere that a writer creates for the reader. Descriptive words, imagery, and figurative language all influence the mood of a work. In "Dark They Were, and Golden-Eyed," Ray Bradbury creates a mood of fearfulness and dread.
See pages 454, 461, 613.
See also **Tone.**

Moral A moral is a lesson that a story teaches. A moral is often stated at the end of a fable. For example, the stated moral of the Liberian fable "Two Ways to Count to Ten" is "It is not always the biggest nor the strongest, but sometimes the cleverest who wins the prize."
See also **Fable.**

Motivation *See* **Character.**

Myth A myth is a traditional story that attempts to answer basic questions about human nature, origins of the world, mysteries of nature, and social customs. For example, "Prometheus" is a Greek myth that explains how humans received the gift of fire.

Narrative Nonfiction Narrative nonfiction is writing that reads much like fiction, except that the characters, setting, and plot are real rather than imaginary. Narrative nonfiction includes autobiographies, biographies, and memoirs. *Exploring the Titanic* by Robert D. Ballard is an example of narrative nonfiction.

Narrative Poetry Poetry that tells a story is called narrative poetry. Like fiction, a narrative poem contains characters, a setting, and a plot. It might also contain such elements of poetry as rhyme, rhythm, imagery, and figurative language. Ernest Lawrence Thayer's "Casey at the Bat" is a narrative poem.

Narrator The narrator is the voice that tells a story. Sometimes the narrator is a character in the story. At other times, the narrator is an outside voice created by the writer. The narrator is not the same as the writer.
   An **unreliable narrator** is one who tells a story or interprets events in a way that makes readers doubt what he or she is saying. An unreliable narrator is usually a character in the story. The narrator may be unreliable for a number of different reasons. For example, the narrator may not have all the facts or may be too young to understand the situation.
See also **Point of View.**

Nonfiction Nonfiction is writing that tells about real people, places, and events. Unlike fiction, nonfiction is mainly written to convey factual information. Nonfiction includes a wide range of writing—newspaper articles, textbooks, instructional manuals, letters, essays, biographies, movie reviews, speeches, true-life adventure stories, advertising, and more.

Novel A novel is a long work of fiction. Like a short story, a novel is the product of a writer's imagination. Because a novel is considerably longer than a short story, a novelist can develop the characters and story line more thoroughly.
See also **Fiction.**

Novella A novella is a short prose tale, or short novel. It is longer than a short story and often teaches a moral, or satirizes a subject.
See also **Short Story; Novel.**

Ode An ode is a type of lyric poem that deals with serious themes, such as justice, truth, or beauty.

Onomatopoeia Onomatopoeia is the use of words whose sounds echo their meanings, such as *buzz, whisper, gargle,* and *murmur.* In "Amigo Brothers," the word *bong* is used to indicate the bell sounding at the beginning and end of each round of the boxing match.

> *Bong! Bong! Bong!* **The bell sounded over and over again.**
> —Piri Thomas, "Amigo Brothers"

Oral Literature Oral literature consists of stories that have been passed down by word of mouth from generation to generation. Oral literature includes folk tales, legends, and myths. In more recent times, some examples of oral literature have been written down or recorded so that the stories can be preserved.

Personal Essay *See* **Essay.**

Personification The giving of human qualities to an animal, object, or idea is known as personification. In "Rikki-tikki-tavi," for example, the animals are personified. They have conversations with each other as if they were human.

> "Don't kill me," said Chuchundra, almost weeping. "Rikki-tikki, don't kill me!"
> "Do you think a snake killer kills muskrats?" said Rikki-tikki scornfully.
> —Rudyard Kipling, "Rikki-tikki-tavi"

See pages 78, 558.
See also **Figurative Language.**

Persuasive Essay *See* **Essay.**

Play *See* **Drama.**

Playwright *See* **Drama.**

Plot The series of events in a story is called the plot. The plot usually centers on a **conflict,** or struggle, faced by the main character. The action that the characters take to solve the problem builds toward a climax in the story. At this point, or shortly afterward, the problem is solved and the story ends. Most story plots have five stages: exposition, rising action, climax, falling action, and resolution.
See pages 5, 28, 30, 35.
See also **Climax; Exposition; Falling Action; Rising Action.**

Poetry Poetry is a type of literature in which words are carefully chosen and arranged to create certain effects. Poets use a variety of sound devices, imagery, and figurative language to express emotions and ideas.
See also **Alliteration; Assonance; Ballad; Free Verse; Imagery; Meter; Narrative Poetry; Rhyme; Rhythm; Stanza.**

Point of View Point of view refers to how a writer chooses to narrate a story. When a story is told from the **first-person** point of view, the narrator is a character in the story and uses first-person pronouns, such as *I, me,* and *we.* In a story told from the **third-person** point of view, the narrator is not a character. Third-person narration makes use of pronouns such as *he, she, it,* and *they.* A writer's choice of narrator affects the information readers receive.

It is also important to consider whether a writer is writing from a **subjective** or an **objective** point of view. When writing from a subjective point of view, the writer includes personal opinions, feelings, and beliefs. When writing from an objective point of view, the writer leaves out personal opinions and instead presents information in a straightforward, unbiased way.
See pages 184, 225, 235, 780.
See also **Narrator.**

Prop The word *prop,* originally an abbreviation of the word *property,* refers to any physical object that is used in a drama. In the play based on Charles Dickens's *A Christmas Carol,* the props include a turkey and a dove.

Prose The word *prose* refers to all forms of writing that are not in verse form. The term may be used to describe very different forms of writing—short stories as well as essays, for example.

Protagonist A protagonist is the main character in a story, play, or novel. The protagonist is involved in the main conflict of the story. Usually, the protagonist undergoes changes as the plot runs its course. In "A Retrieved Reformation" by O. Henry, Jimmy Valentine is the protagonist.

Radio Play A radio play is a drama that is written specifically to be broadcast over the radio. Because the audience is not meant to see a radio play, sound effects are often used to help listeners imagine the setting and the action. The stage directions in the play's script indicate the sound effects.

Recurring Theme *See* **Theme.**

Refrain A refrain is one or more lines repeated in each stanza of a poem.
See also **Stanza.**

Repetition Repetition is a technique in which a sound, word, phrase, or line is repeated for emphasis or unity. Repetition often helps to reinforce meaning and create an appealing rhythm. Note how the use of repetition in the following lines emphasizes the rhythm of battle.

> Cannon to right of them,
> Cannon to left of them,
> Cannon in front of them
> —Alfred, Lord Tennyson, "The Charge of
> the Light Brigade"

See page 133.
See also **Alliteration; Sound Devices.**

Resolution *See* **Falling Action.**

Rhyme Rhyme is the repetition of sounds at the end of words. Words rhyme when their accented vowels and the letters that follow have identical sounds. *Cat* and *hat* rhyme, as do *feather* and *leather*. The most common type of rhyme in poetry is called **end rhyme,** in which rhyming words come at the ends of lines. Rhyme that occurs within a line of poetry is called **internal rhyme.** The following lines include examples of end rhyme.

> 'Twas brillig, and the slithy toves
> Did gyre and gimble in the wabe:
> All mimsy were the borogroves,
> And the mome raths outgrabe.
> —Lewis Carroll, "Jabberwocky"

See pages 133, 556, 605.

Rhyme Scheme A rhyme scheme is a pattern of end rhymes in a poem. A rhyme scheme is noted by assigning a letter of the alphabet, beginning with *a,* to each line. Lines that rhyme are given the same letter.

> It was many and many a year ago,   *a*
>   In a kingdom by the sea,   *b*
> That a maiden there lived whom you may know   *a*
>   By the name of Annabel Lee;   *b*
>   —Edgar Allan Poe, "Annabel Lee"

See page 575.

Rhythm Rhythm is a pattern of stressed and unstressed syllables in a line of poetry. Poets use rhythm to bring out the musical quality of language, to emphasize ideas, and to create moods. Devices such as alliteration, rhyme, assonance, and consonance often contribute to creating rhythm.
See pages 133, 583.
See also **Meter.**

Rising Action The rising action is the stage of the plot that develops the **conflict,** or struggle. During this stage, events occur that make the conflict more complicated. The events in the rising action build toward a **climax,** or turning point.
See page 30.
See also **Plot.**

Scene In drama, the action is often divided into acts and scenes. Each scene presents an episode of the play's plot and typically occurs at a single place and time.
See also **Act.**

Scenery Scenery is a painted backdrop or other structures used to create the setting for a play.

Science Fiction Science fiction is fiction in which a writer explores unexpected possibilities of the past or the future, using known scientific data and theories as well as his or her creative imagination. Most science fiction writers create believable worlds, although some create fantasy worlds that have familiar elements. Ray Bradbury, the author of "Dark They Were, and Golden-Eyed," is a famous writer of science fiction.
See also **Fantasy.**

Screenplay A screenplay is a play written for film.

Script The text of a play, film, or broadcast is called a script.

Sensory Details Sensory details are words and phrases that appeal to the reader's senses of sight, hearing, touch, smell, and taste. Note the sensory details in the following line. These details appeal to the senses of touch and smell.

> There was a cool breeze blowing and a sweet smell of
> mesquite fruit in the air, but I didn't appreciate it.
> —Marta Salinas, "The Scholarship Jacket"

See also **Imagery.**

Setting The setting of a story, poem, or play is the time and place of the action. Sometimes the setting is clear and well-defined. At other times, it is left to the reader's imagination.

Elements of setting include geographic location, historical period (past, present, or future), season, time of day, and culture.
See pages 5, 30, 47.

Short Story   A short story is a work of fiction that centers on a single idea and can be read in one sitting.   Generally, a short story has one main conflict that involves the characters and keeps the story moving.
See also **Fiction.**

Simile   A simile is a figure of speech that makes a comparison between two unlike things using the word *like* or *as.*

> The fingers were all there, but <u>like dead leaves that never fell</u>, the ring and little fingers were rigid and curled, the others barely moved.
> —Chaim Potok, "Zebra"

See pages 192, 558.
See also **Figurative Language; Metaphor.**

Sonnet   A sonnet is a poem that has a formal structure, containing 14 lines and a specific rhyme scheme and meter. The sonnet, which means "little song," can be used for a variety of topics.
See also **Rhyme Scheme.**

Sound Devices   Sound devices are ways of using words for the sound qualities they create.   Sound devices can help convey meaning and mood in a writer's work.   Some common sound devices include **alliteration, assonance, meter, onomatopoeia, repetition, rhyme,** and **rhythm.**
See pages 556, 575, 605.
See also **Alliteration; Assonance; Meter; Onomatopoeia; Repetition; Rhyme; Rhythm.**

Speaker   In poetry the speaker is the voice that "talks" to the reader, similar to the narrator in fiction.   The speaker is not necessarily the poet.   For example, in Carl Sandburg's "Washington Monument by Night," the experiences described may or may not have happened to the poet.
See pages 517, 554, 575, 878.

Speech   A speech is a talk or public address.   The purpose of a speech may be to entertain, to explain, to persuade, to inspire, or any combination of these purposes.   President John F. Kennedy's speech "Remarks at the Dedication of the Aerospace Medical Health Center" was written and delivered in order to persuade his audience.
See pages 8, 977.

Stage Directions   In the script of a play, the instructions to the actors, director, and stage crew are called the stage directions.   Stage directions might suggest scenery, lighting, sound effects, and ways for actors to move and speak.   Stage directions often appear in parentheses and in italic type.

> (*As soon as* Scrooge *shouts, the* girl *and the* carolers *vanish and* Cratchit *begins to close up the shop.*)
> —Frederick Gaines, *A Christmas Carol*

See pages 7, 399.

Stanza   A stanza is a group of two or more lines that form a unit in a poem.   Each stanza may have the same number of lines, or the number of lines may vary.
See also **Couplet; Form; Poetry.**

Static Character   *See* **Character.**

Stereotype   In literature, characters who are defined by a single trait are known as stereotypes.   Such characters do not usually demonstrate the complexities of real people. Familiar stereotypes in popular literature include the absent-minded professor and the busybody.

Structure   The structure of a work of literature is the way in which it is put together.   In poetry, structure involves the arrangement of words and lines to produce a desired effect.   One structural unit in poetry is the stanza.   In prose, structure involves the arrangement of such elements as sentences, paragraphs, and events.   "Dark They Were, and Golden-Eyed," for example, has a circular structure, in which the end mirrors the beginning.

Style   A style is a manner of writing.   It involves how something is said rather than what is said.   For example, "A Day's Wait" by Ernest Hemingway is written in a style that makes use of vivid verbs, precise nouns, long descriptive sentences, and realistic dialogue.

Surprise Ending   A surprise ending is an unexpected plot twist at the end of a story.   The surprise may be a sudden turn in the action or a piece of information that gives a different perspective to the entire story.   The short story writer O. Henry is famous for using this device.
See page 236.

Suspense   Suspense is a feeling of growing tension and excitement felt by a reader.   Suspense makes a reader curious about the outcome of a story or an event within a story.   A writer creates suspense by raising questions in the reader's mind. The use of **foreshadowing** is one way that writers create suspense.

See pages 77, 93, 103.

See also **Foreshadowing.**

Symbol A symbol is a person, a place, an object, or an activity that stands for something beyond itself. For example, a flag is a colored piece of cloth that stands for a country. A white dove is a bird that represents peace.

Example: In "What Do Fish Have to Do with Anything?" by Avi, money represents happiness, opportunity, and freedom to Willie's mother.

See pages 351, 595.

Tall Tale A tall tale is a humorously exaggerated story about impossible events, often involving the supernatural abilities of the main character. Stories about folk heroes such as Pecos Bill and Paul Bunyan are typical tall tales.

Teleplay A teleplay is a play written for television. In a teleplay, scenes can change quickly and dramatically. The camera can focus the viewer's attention on specific actions. The camera directions in teleplays are much like the stage directions in stage plays.

See page 139.

Theme A theme is a message about life or human nature that the writer shares with the reader. In many cases, readers must infer what the writer's message is. One way of figuring out a theme is to apply the lessons learned by the main characters to people in real life. For example, a theme of "A Crush" by Cynthia Rylant is that simple acts of kindness can make a positive difference in people's lives.

   Recurring themes are themes found in a variety of works. For example, authors from different backgrounds might express similar themes having to do with the importance of family values. **Universal themes** are themes that are found throughout the literature of all time periods. For example, *The Lord of the Rings* contains a universal theme relating to the hero's search for truth, goodness, and honor.

See pages 5, 316, 339, 375, 393, 743.

See also **Moral.**

Third-Person Point of View *See* **Point of View.**

Title The title of a piece of writing is the name that is attached to it. A title often refers to an important aspect of the work. For example, the title "The War of the Wall" refers to Lou and the narrator's conflict with the "painter lady."

Tone The tone of a literary work expresses the writer's attitude toward his or her subject. Words such as *angry, sad,* and *humorous* can be used to describe different tones.

See pages 456, 512.

See also **Author's Perspective; Mood.**

Tragedy A tragedy is a dramatic work that presents the downfall of a dignified character or characters who are involved in historically or socially significant events. The events in a tragic plot are set in motion by a decision that is often an error in judgment on the part of the hero. Succeeding events are linked in a cause-and-effect relationship and lead inevitably to a disastrous conclusion, usually death. William Shakespeare's *Romeo and Juliet* is a famous tragedy.

Traits *See* **Character.**

Turning Point *See* **Climax.**

Understatement Understatement is a technique of creating emphasis by saying less than is actually or literally true. It is the opposite of **hyperbole,** or exaggeration. Understatement is often used to create a humorous effect.

Universal Theme *See* **Theme.**

Unreliable Narrator *See* **Narrator.**

Voice The term *voice* refers to a writer's unique use of language that allows a reader to "hear" a human personality in the writer's work. Elements of style that contribute to a writer's voice can reveal much about the author's personality, beliefs, and attitudes.

See page 22.

Word Choice The success of any writing depends on the writer's choice of words. Words not only communicate ideas but also help describe events, characters, settings, and so on. Word choice can make a writer's work sound formal or informal, serious or humorous. A writer must choose words carefully depending on the goal of the piece of writing. For example, a writer working on a science article would probably use technical, formal words; a writer trying to establish the setting in a short story would probably use more descriptive words.

See also **Style.**

Writer's Point of View A writer's point of view is the writer's opinion about a topic.

Analogy An analogy is a comparison between two things that are alike in some way. Often, writers use analogies in nonfiction to explain an unfamiliar subject or idea by showing how it is like a familiar one.

Argument An argument is speaking or writing that expresses a position on a problem and supports it with reasons and evidence. An argument often takes into account other points of view, anticipating and answering objections that opponents might raise.
See also **Claim; Counterargument; Evidence.**

Assumption An assumption is an opinion or belief that is taken for granted. It can be about a specific situation, a person, or the world in general. Assumptions are often unstated.

Author's Message An author's message is the main idea or theme of a particular work.
See also **Main Idea; Theme,** *Glossary of Literary and Nonfiction Terms, page R109.*

Author's Perspective *See Glossary of Literary and Nonfiction Terms, page R100.*

Author's Position An author's position is his or her opinion on an issue or topic.
See also **Claim; Writer's Point of View,** *Glossary of Literary and Nonfiction Terms, page R109.*

Author's Purpose *See Glossary of Literary and Nonfiction Terms, page R100.*

Autobiography *See Glossary of Literary and Nonfiction Terms, page R100.*

Bias In a piece of writing, the author's bias is the side of an issue that he or she favors. Words with extremely positive or negative connotations are often a signal of an author's bias.

Bibliography A bibliography is a list of related books and other materials used to write a text. Bibliographies can be good sources for further study on a subject.
See also **Works Consulted.**

Biography *See Glossary of Literary and Nonfiction Terms, page R100.*

Business Correspondence Business correspondence is written business communications such as business letters, e-mails, and memos. In general, business correspondence is brief, to the point, clear, courteous, and professional.

Cause and Effect Two events are related by cause and effect when one event brings about, or causes, the other.

The event that happens first is the **cause**; the one that follows is the **effect.** Cause and effect is also a way of organizing an entire piece of writing. It helps writers show the relationships between events or ideas.
See also **False Cause,** *Reading Handbook, page R24.*

Chronological Order Chronological order is the arrangement of events by their order of occurrence. This type of organization is used in fictional narratives and in historical writing, biography, and autobiography.

Claim In an argument, a claim is the writer's position on an issue or problem. Although an argument focuses on supporting one claim, a writer may make more than one claim in a text.

Clarify Clarifying is a reading strategy that helps readers understand or make clear what they are reading. Readers usually clarify by rereading, reading aloud, or discussing.

Classification Classification is a pattern of organization in which objects, ideas, and/or information are presented in groups, or classes, based on common characteristics.

Cliché A cliché is an overused expression. "Better late than never" and "hard as nails" are common examples. Good writers generally avoid clichés unless they are using them in dialogue to indicate something about a character's personality.

Compare and Contrast To compare and contrast is to identify the similarities and differences of two or more subjects. Compare and contrast is also a pattern of organizing an entire piece of writing.

Conclusion A conclusion is a statement of belief based on evidence, experience, and reasoning. A valid conclusion is one that logically follows from the facts or statements upon which it is based.

Connect Connecting is a reader's process of relating the content of a text to his or her own knowledge and experience.

Consumer Documents Consumer documents are printed materials that accompany products and services. They usually provide information about the use, care, operation, or assembly of the product or service they accompany. Some common consumer documents are applications, contracts, warranties, manuals, instructions, labels, brochures, and schedules.

Context Clues When you encounter an unfamiliar word, you can often use context clues to understand it. Context clues are the words or phrases surrounding the word that provide hints about the word's meaning.

Counterargument A counterargument is an argument made to oppose another argument. A good argument anticipates opposing viewpoints and provides counterarguments to disprove them.

Credibility Credibility is the believability or trustworthiness of a source and the information it provides.

Critical Review A critical review is an evaluation or critique by a reviewer, or critic. Types of reviews include film reviews, book reviews, music reviews, and art show reviews.

Database A database is a collection of information that can be quickly and easily accessed and searched and from which information can be easily retrieved. It is frequently presented in an electronic format.

Debate A debate is basically an argument—but a very structured one that requires a good deal of preparation. In school settings, debate usually is a formal contest in which two opposing teams defend and attack a proposition.
See also **Argument.**

Deductive Reasoning Deductive reasoning is a way of thinking that begins with a generalization, presents a specific situation, and then moves forward with facts and evidence toward a logical conclusion. The following passage has a deductive argument embedded in it: "All students in the math class must take the quiz on Friday. Since Lana is in the class, she had better show up." This deductive argument can be broken down as follows: generalization: All students in the math class must take the quiz on Friday; specific situation: Lana is a student who is in the math class; conclusion: Therefore, Lana must take the math quiz.
See also **Analyzing Logic and Reasoning,** *Reading Handbook, pages R22–R25.*

Dictionary *See* **Reference Works.**

Draw Conclusions To draw a conclusion is to make a judgment or arrive at a belief based on evidence, experience, and reasoning.

Editorial An editorial is an opinion piece that usually appears on the editorial page of a newspaper or as part of a news broadcast. The editorial section of the newspaper presents opinions rather than objective news reports.
See also **Op/Ed Piece.**

Either/Or Fallacy An either/or fallacy is a statement that suggests that there are only two choices available in a situation when in fact there are more than two.
See also **Identifying Faulty Reasoning,** *Reading Handbook, page R24.*

Emotional Appeals Emotional appeals are messages that create strong feelings to make a point. An appeal to fear is a message that taps into people's fear of losing their safety or security. An appeal to pity is a message that taps into people's sympathy and compassion for others to build support for an idea, a cause, or a proposed action. An appeal to vanity is a message that attempts to persuade by tapping into people's desire to feel good about themselves.
See also **Recognizing Persuasive Techniques,** *Reading Handbook, pages R21–R22.*

Encyclopedia *See* **Reference Works.**

Essay *See Glossary of Literary and Nonfiction Terms, page R102.*

Evaluate To evaluate is to examine something carefully and to judge its value or worth. Evaluating is an important skill. A reader can evaluate the actions of a particular character, for example. A reader can also form opinions about the value of an entire work.

Evidence Evidence is a specific piece of information that supports a claim. Evidence can take the form of a fact, a quotation, an example, a statistic, or a personal experience, among other things.

Expository Essay *See* **Essay,** *Glossary of Literary and Nonfiction Terms, page R102.*

Fact Versus Opinion A **fact** is a statement that can be proved, or verified. An opinion, on the other hand, is a statement that cannot be proved because it expresses a person's beliefs, feelings, or thoughts.
See also **Generalization; Inference.**

Fallacy A fallacy is an error—usually in reasoning. Typically, a fallacy is based on an incorrect inference or a misuse of evidence.
See also **Either/Or Fallacy; Logical Appeal; Overgeneralization.**
See also **Identifying Faulty Reasoning,** *Reading Handbook, page R24.*

Faulty Reasoning *See* **Fallacy.**

Feature Article A feature article is a main article in a newspaper or a cover story in a magazine.

Generalization A generalization is a broad statement about a class or category of people, ideas, or things based on a study of, or a belief about, some of its members.
See also **Overgeneralization; Stereotyping.**

Government Publications Government publications are documents produced by government organizations. Pamphlets, brochures, and reports are just some of the many forms these publications take. Government publications can be good resources for a wide variety of topics.

Graphic Aid A graphic aid is a visual tool that is printed, handwritten, or drawn. Charts, diagrams, graphs, photographs, and maps are examples of graphic aids.
See also **Graphic Aids**, *Reading Handbook, pages R4–R7.*

Graphic Organizer A graphic organizer is a "word picture"—a visual illustration of a verbal statement—that helps a reader understand a text. Charts, tables, webs, and diagrams can all be graphic organizers. Graphic organizers and graphic aids can look the same. However, graphic organizers and graphic aids do differ in how they are used. Graphic aids help deliver important information to students using a text. Graphic organizers are actually created by students themselves. They help students understand the text or organize information.

Historical Documents Historical documents are writings that have played a significant role in human events. The Declaration of Independence, for example, is a historical document.

How-To Book A how-to book explains how to do something—usually an activity, a sport, or a household project.

Implied Main Idea *See* **Main Idea.**

Index The index of a book is an alphabetized list of important topics covered in the book and the page numbers on which they can be found. An index can be used to quickly find specific information about a topic.

Inductive Reasoning Inductive reasoning is the process of logical reasoning that starts with observations, examples, and facts and moves on to a general conclusion or principle.
See also **Analyzing Logic and Reasoning,** *Reading Handbook, pages R22–R25.*

Inference An inference is a logical guess that is made based on facts and one's own knowledge and experience.

Informational Text Informational text is writing that provides factual information. Examples include news reports, a science textbook, manuals, lab reports, and signs. Informational text also includes literary nonfiction, such as personal essays, opinion pieces, speeches, biographies, and historical accounts.

Internet The Internet is a global, interconnected system of computer networks that allows for communication through e-mail, listservs, and the World Wide Web. The Internet connects computers and computer users throughout the world.

Journal A journal is a periodical publication issued by a legal, medical, or other professional organization. The term may also be used to refer to a diary or daily record.

Loaded Language Loaded language consists of words with strongly positive or negative connotations, intended to influence a reader's or listener's attitude.

Logical Appeal A logical appeal is a way of writing or speaking that relies on logic and facts. It appeals to people's reasoning or intellect rather than to their values or emotions. Flawed logical appeals—that is, errors in reasoning—are called logical fallacies.
See also **Fallacy.**

Logical Argument A logical argument is an argument in which the logical relationship between the support and claim is sound.

Main Idea The main idea, or central idea, is the most important idea about a topic that a writer or speaker conveys. It can be the central idea of an entire work or of just a paragraph. Often, the main idea of a paragraph is expressed in a topic sentence. However, a main idea may just be implied, or suggested, by details. A main idea is typically supported by details.

Make Inferences *See* **Inference.**

Monitor Monitoring is the strategy of checking your comprehension as you read and modifying the strategies you are using to suit your needs. Monitoring often includes the following strategies: questioning, clarifying, visualizing, predicting, connecting, and rereading.

Narrative Nonfiction *See Glossary of Literary and Nonfiction Terms, page R105.*

News Article A news article is writing that reports on a recent event. In newspapers, news articles are usually brief and to the point, presenting the most important facts first, followed by more detailed information.

Nonfiction *See Glossary of Literary and Nonfiction Terms, page R105.*

Op/Ed Piece An op/ed piece is an opinion piece that typically appears opposite ("op") the editorial page of a newspaper. Unlike editorials, op/ed pieces are written and submitted by readers.

Organization *See* **Pattern of Organization.**

Overgeneralization An overgeneralization is a generalization that is too broad. You can often recognize overgeneralizations by the appearance of words and phrases such as *all, everyone, every time, any, anything, no one,* or *none.* An example is "None of the city's workers really cares about keeping the environment clean." In all probability, there are many exceptions. The writer can't possibly know the feelings of every city worker.
See also **Identifying Faulty Reasoning,** *Reading Handbook, page R24.*

Overview An overview is a short summary of a story, a speech, or an essay.

Paraphrase Paraphrasing is the restating of information in one's own words.
See also **Summarize.**

Pattern of Organization The term *pattern of organization* refers to the way ideas and information are arranged and organized. Patterns of organization include cause-and-effect, chronological, compare-and-contrast, classification, and problem-solution, among others.
See also **Cause and Effect; Chronological Order; Classification; Compare and Contrast; Problem-Solution Order; Sequential Order.**
See also **Reading Informational Texts: Patterns of Organization,** *Reading Handbook, pages R8–R13.*

Periodical A periodical is a magazine or other publication that is issued on a regular basis.

Personal Essay *See* **Essay,** *Glossary of Literary and Nonfiction Terms, page R102.*

Persuasion Persuasion is the art of swaying others' feelings, beliefs, or actions. Persuasion normally appeals to both the mind and the emotions of readers.
See also **Emotional Appeals; Loaded Language; Logical Appeal.**

See also **Recognizing Persuasive Techniques,** *Reading Handbook, pages R21–R22.*

Predict Predicting is a reading strategy that involves using text clues to make a reasonable guess about what will happen next in a story.

Primary Source *See* **Sources.**

Prior Knowledge Prior knowledge is the knowledge a reader already possesses about a topic. This information might come from personal experiences, expert accounts, books, films, and other sources.

Problem-Solution Order Problem-solution order is a pattern of organization in which a problem is stated and analyzed and then one or more solutions are proposed and examined.

Propaganda Propaganda is a form of communication that may use false or misleading information.

Public Documents Public documents are documents that were written for the public to provide information that is of public interest or concern. They include government documents, speeches, signs, and rules and regulations.
See also **Government Publications.**

Reference Works Reference works are sources that contain facts and background information on a wide range of subjects. Most reference works are good sources of reliable information because they have been reviewed by experts. The following are some common reference works: encyclopedias, dictionaries, thesauri, almanacs, atlases, and directories.

Review *See* **Critical Review.**

Rhetorical Questions Rhetorical questions are those that have such obvious answers that they do not require a reply. Writers often use them to suggest that their claim is so obvious that everyone should agree with it.

Scanning Scanning is the process used to search through a text for a particular fact or piece of information. When you scan, you sweep your eyes across a page, looking for key words that may lead you to the information you want.

Secondary Source *See* **Sources.**

Sequential Order Sequential order is a pattern of organization that shows the order of steps or stages in a process.

Setting a Purpose The process of establishing specific reasons for reading a text is called setting a purpose. Readers can look at a text's title, headings, and illustrations to guess what it might be about. They can then use these guesses to figure out what they want to learn from reading the text.

Sidebar A sidebar is additional information set in a box alongside or within an article. Popular magazines often make use of sidebars.

Signal Words In a text, signal words are words and phrases that help show how events or ideas are related. Some common examples of signal words are *and, but, however, nevertheless, therefore,* and *in addition.*

Sources A source is anything that supplies information. **Primary sources** are materials written by people who witnessed or took part in an event. Letters, diaries, autobiographies, and speeches are primary sources. Unlike primary sources, **secondary sources** are made by people who were not directly involved in an event or present when it occurred. Encyclopedias, textbooks, biographies, and most newspaper and magazine articles are examples of secondary sources.

Speech *See Glossary of Literary and Nonfiction Terms, page R108.*

Stereotyping Stereotyping is a dangerous type of overgeneralization. It can lead to unfair judgments of people based on their ethnic background, beliefs, practices, or physical appearance.

Summarize To summarize is to briefly retell the main ideas of a piece of writing in one's own words. *See also* **Paraphrase.**

Support Support is any information that helps to prove a claim.

Supporting Detail *See* **Main Idea.**

Synthesize To synthesize information means to take individual pieces of information and combine them in order to gain a better understanding of a subject.

Text Features Text features are elements of a text, such as boldface type, headings, and subheadings, that help organize and call attention to important information. Italic type, bulleted or numbered lists, sidebars, and graphic aids such as charts, tables, timelines, illustrations, and photographs are also considered text features.

Thesaurus *See* **Reference Works.**

Thesis Statement A thesis statement, or controlling idea, is the main proposition that a writer attempts to support in a piece of writing.

Topic Sentence The topic sentence of a paragraph states the paragraph's main idea; all other sentences in the paragraph provide supporting details.

Visualize Visualizing is the process of forming a mental picture based on written or spoken information.

Web Site A Web site is a collection of "pages" on the World Wide Web, usually devoted to one specific subject. Pages are linked together and accessed by clicking hyperlinks or menus, which send the user from page to page within a Web site. Web sites are created by companies, organizations, educational institutions, branches of the government, the military, and individuals.

Workplace Documents Workplace documents are materials that are produced or used within a work setting, usually to aid in the functioning of the workplace. They include job applications, office memos, training manuals, job descriptions, and sales reports.

Works Cited The term *works cited* refers to a list of all the works a writer has referred to in his or her text. This list often includes not only books and articles but also Internet sources.

Works Consulted The term *works consulted* refers to a list of all the works a writer consulted in order to create his or her text. It is not limited just to those cited in the text. *See also* **Bibliography.**

The Glossary of Academic Vocabulary in this section is an alphabetical list of the Academic Vocabulary words found in this textbook. Use this glossary just as you would use a dictionary—to find out the meanings of words used in your literature class, to talk about and write about literary and informational texts, and to talk about and write about concepts and topics in your other academic classes.

For each word, the glossary includes the pronunciation, syllabication, part of speech, and meaning. A Spanish version of each word and definition follows the English version. For more information about the words in this glossary, please consult a dictionary.

analyze (ăn′ə-līz) *v.* to separate, or break into parts and examine
 analizar *v.* separar o dividir en partes y examinar

area (âr′ē-ə) *n.* a division of experience, activity, or knowledge; a field
 área *sust.* división de experiencia, actividad o conocimiento; campo

attribute (ə-trĭb′yo͞ot) *n.* a quality thought of as a natural part of someone or something
 atributo *sust.* cualidad considerada como parte natural de alguien o algo

aware (ə-wâr′) *adj.* having knowledge of; informed about
 consciente *adj.* con conocimiento; informado

clause (klôz) *n.* a group of words containing a subject and predicate and forming a compound or complete sentence
 cláusula *sust.* grupo de palabras que contiene un sujeto y un predicado y forma una oración compuesta o completa

conduct (kən-dŭkt′) *v.* to direct the course of something; to manage or control
 conducir *v.* dirigir el curso de algo; guiar o controlar

contemporary (kən-tĕm′pə-rĕr′ē) *adj.* current; modern
 contemporáneo *adj.* actual; moderno

context (kŏn′tĕkst′) *n.* the words that surround a particular word or passage that make the meaning of that word or passage clear; the circumstances in which an event occurs; a setting
 contexto *sust.* palabras que rodean una palabra o un pasaje en particular y aclaran el significado de esa palabra o pasaje; circunstancias en las que ocurre un evento; entorno

cultural (kŭl′chər-əl) *adj.* the attitudes and behavior that characterize a group
 cultural *adj.* actitudes y conductas que caracterizan a un grupo

communicate (kə-myo͞o′nĭ-kāt) *v.* to pass along information about; to make known
 comunicar *v.* transmitir información; dar a conocer algo

demonstrate (dĕm′ən-strāt) *v.* to show clearly and purposefully
 demostrar *v.* mostrar en forma clara y con determinación

describe (dĭ-skr īb′) *v.* to tell or write about in detail
 describir *v.* decir o escribir algo en detalle

develop (dĭ-vĕl′əp) *v.* to grow or expand; to improve the quality of
 desarrollar *v.* crecer o expandir; mejorar la calidad de algo

domain (dō-mān′) *n.* a geographical area over which rule or control is exercised
 dominio *sust.* área geográfica sobre la que se ejerce poder o control

element (el′ə mənt) *n.* one necessary or basic part of a whole
 elemento *sust.* parte necesaria o básica de un todo

encounter (ĕn-koun′tər) *n.* an unexpected meeting
 encuentro *sust.* reunión inesperada

evaluate (ĭ-văl′yo͞o-āt) *v.* to find out the value or worth of something; to judge or examine
 evaluar *v.* hallar el valor o el precio de algo; juzgar o examinar

focus (fō′kəs) *n.* any center of interest or activity
 foco *sust.* centro de interés o actividad

goal (gōl) *n.* an aim, purpose, or specific result one tries to achieve
 meta *sust.* fin, propósito o resultado específico que se busca alcanzar

hypothesis (hī-pŏth′ĭ-sĭs) *n.* a suggested explanation for an observation or scientific problem that needs further testing or investigation

    hipótesis *sust.* explicación sugerida para una observación o problema científico que necesita más pruebas o investigación

identify (ī-dĕn′tə-fī) *v.* to find or name the characteristics, nature, or qualities of someone or something

    identificar *v.* hallar o nombrar las características, la naturaleza o las cualidades de alguien o algo

interpret (ĭn-tûr′prĭt) *v.* to explain the meaning of

    interpretar *v.* explicar el significado de algo

illustrate (ĭl′ə-strāt′) *v.* to make clear by use of examples or comparisons

    ilustrar *v.* aclarar por medio de ejemplos o comparaciones

impact (ĭm′păkt) *n.* the effect or impression of one thing on another

    impacto *sust.* efecto o impresión de una cosa con respecto a otra

influence (ĭn′flōō-əns) *n.* power or sway that affects people or things

    influencia *sust.* poder o dominio que afecta a las personas o las cosas

integrity (ĭn-tĕg′rĭ-tē) *n.* the quality in a person of having a strict moral code; complete, whole, undivided

    integridad *sust.* cualidad de una persona que posee un código moral estricto; cualidad de algo completo, entero, total

link (lĭngk) *v.* to connect, or join

    unir *v.* conectar o enlazar

locate (lō′kāt) *v.* to find something by searching

    ubicar *v.* hallar algo mediante una búsqueda

objective (əb-jĕk′tĭv) *n.* something worked toward or striven for

    objetivo *sust.* finalidad del trabajo o el esfuerzo

physical (fĭz′ĭ-kəl) *adj.* of or relating to the body, or material things

    físico *adj.* perteneciente al cuerpo o las cosas materiales o que se relaciona con éstos

primary (prī′mĕr-ē) *adj.* highest in rank, or first in importance

    primario *adj.* de categoría superior, primero en importancia

process (prŏs′ĕs) *n.* a series of steps performed in making or doing something

    proceso *sust.* serie de pasos que se siguen para hacer algo

react (rē-ăkt′) *v.* to act in response to something

    reaccionar *v.* actuar en respuesta a algo

resolve (rĭ-zŏlv′) *v.* to make a decision about, or to solve a problem

    resolver *v.* tomar una decisión con respecto a algo o solucionar un problema

respond (rĭ-spŏnd′) *v.* to answer, or make a reply

    responder *v.* contestar o dar una respuesta

specific (spĭ-sĭf′k) *adj.* definite; of a special sort

    específico *adj.* definitivo; de un tipo especial

status (stăt′əs) *n.* standing, position, or rank in comparison with others

    estado *sust.* grado, posición o categoría en comparación con otros

structure (strŭk′chər) *n.* something constructed or built, such as a building

    estructura *sust.* algo que se construye, como un edificio

style (stīl) *n.* the unique way in which something is said, done, expressed, or performed

    estilo *sust.* manera especial en que se dice, hace, expresa o representa algo

symbol (sĭm′bəl) *n.* something that represents something else; an object, mark, or sign

    símbolo *sust.* algo que representa otra cosa; objeto, marca o signo

task (tăsk) *n.* a function to be performed

    tarea *sust.* función a realizar

theme (thēm) *n.* a topic or subject of a discussion or piece of writing

    tema *sust.* materia o asunto de un debate o un escrito

tradition (trə-dĭsh′ən) *n.* a practice passed down from generation to generation

    tradición *sust.* práctica que se transmite de generación en generación

undertake (ŭn′dər-tāk′) *v.* to take upon oneself; enter into

    asumir *v.* tomar para sí; comprometerse

vary (vâr′ē) *v.* to modify or alter; to change the characteristics of something

    variar *v.* modificar o alterar; cambiar las características de algo

This glossary is an alphabetical list of vocabulary words found in the selections in this book. Use this glossary just as you would use a dictionary—to determine the meanings, syllabication, pronunciations, and parts of speech of words.

Many words in the English language have more than one meaning. The meanings provided here are those that apply to the words as they are used in the selections in this book. When closely related words are listed together in one entry (for instance, *automated* and *automate*), the definition given applies to the first form of the word, which is also the entry word.

Each entry word's English pronunciation is given in parentheses. These pronunciations also indicate the syllabication of the words. For help interpreting pronunciation symbols and stress marks, see the Pronunciation Key at the end of this glossary.

The parts of speech are noted with the following abbreviations:

adj. adjective
adv. adverb
n. noun
v. verb

For more information about the words in this glossary, consult a dictionary.

accommodations (ə-kŏm′ə-dā′shənz) *n.* rooms and food, especially in a hotel or on a ship or train
alojamiento *s.* habitaciones para que duerman y coman viajeros en hoteles, barcos o trenes

accost (ə-kôst′) *v.* to approach a person and speak unpleasantly or aggressively
importunar *v.* acercarse a una persona y hablarle de modo desagradable o agresivo

adjoining (ə-joi′nĭng) *adj.* next to or in contact with **adjoin** *v.*
colindante *adj.* al lado; contiguo **colindar** *v.*

agile (ăj′əl) *adj.* quick and light in movement
ágil *adj.* que puede moverse con facilidad

amenable (ə-mē′nə-bəl) *adj.* open; agreeable
dispuesto *adj.* que está de acuerdo

anecdotal (ăn′ĭk-dōt′l) *adj.* based on observations rather than scientific analysis
anecdótico *adj.* basado en observaciones más que en análisis científico

anonymous (ə-nŏn′ə-məs) *adj.* having an unknown or withheld name
anónimo *adj.* de nombre desconocido u oculto

antagonism (ăn-tăg′ə-nĭz′əm) *n.* hostility; unfriendliness
antagonismo *s.* hostilidad; oposición

appalling (ə-pô′lĭng) *adj.* outrageous; terrible **appall** *v.*
terrible *adj.* espantoso; atroz

aptitude (ăp′tĭ-tōōd′) *n.* natural ability
aptitud *s.* habilidad natural

aquatic (ə-kwăt′ĭk) *adj.* growing or living in the water
acuático *adj.* que crece o vive en el agua

aroma (ə-rō′mə) *n.* a smell; odor
aroma *s.* olor, generalmente agradable

artisan (är′tĭ-zən) *n.* a person who is skilled in a trade
artesano *s.* persona que hace objetos a mano siguiendo un método tradicional

ascend (ə-sĕnd′) *v.* to go or move upward; rise
ascender *v.* subir

assent (ə-sĕnt′) *n.* agreement
asentimiento *s.* acuerdo

automated (ô′tə-mā′tĭd) *adj.* able to function with little or no assistance from people **automate** *v.*
automatizado *adj.* que funciona por su cuenta con poca ayuda humana **automatizar** *v.*

bacterium (băk-tîr′ē-əm) *n.* the singular form of *bacteria*, microscopically small living things that may cause disease
bacteria *s.* organismo microscópico que puede causar enfermedades

balk (bôk) *v.* to refuse to move or act
resistirse *v.* rehusarse

barrage (bə-räzh′) *n.* a rapid, heavy attack
descarga *s.* sucesión rápida de golpes o balas

barren (băr′ən) *adj.* empty; lacking interest or charm
estéril *adj.* vacío; sin interés o encanto

beckon (běk′ən) *v.* to summon or call, usually by a gesture or nod
   llamar *v.* atraer con un gesto

bedlam (běd′ləm) *n.* a noisy confusion
   pandemonio *s.* confusión y ruido

brevity (brěv′ĭ-tē) *n.* shortness
   brevedad *s.* concisión

brooding (brōō′dĭng) *adj.* full of worry; troubled **brood** *v.*
   inquietante *adj.* pertubador; preocupante **inquietar** *v.*

brusque (brŭsk) *adj.* abrupt or blunt in speaking
   brusco *adj.* abrupto o contundente al hablar

buoyancy (boi′ən-sē) *n.* the ability to remain afloat in liquid
   flotabilidad *s.* capacidad de flotar en un líquido

camouflage (kăm′ə-fläzh′) *v.* to disguise or portray falsely in order to conceal
   camuflar *v.* disfrazar o disimular

capitalize (kăp′ĭ-tl-īz′) *v.* to take advantage of
   capitalizar *v.* sacar provecho

carcass (kär′kəs) *n.* the dead body of an animal
   cadáver *s.* esqueleto de animal muerto

cascade (kă-skād′) *n.* a waterfall or something that resembles a waterfall
   cascada *s.* caída de agua

chafe (chāf) *v.* to irritate by rubbing
   rozar *v.* frotar e irritar

chaotic (kā-ŏt′ĭk) *adj.* confused; disordered
   caótico *adj.* confuso; desordenado

cherish (chĕr′ĭsh) *v.* to care for deeply
   apreciar *v.* querer; valorar

chronicle (krŏn′ĭ-kəl) *n.* a record of historical events in the order in which they took place
   crónica *s.* registro de sucesos históricos en el orden en que se dan

claret (klăr′ĭt) *adj.* dark red
   granate *adj.* color vino tinto

clarity (klăr′ĭ-tē) *n.* clearness of mind
   claridad *s.* lucidez

cohort (kō′hôrt′) *n.* a companion or associate
   compinche *s.* compañero o socio

commence (kə-mĕns′) *v.* to start or begin
   comenzar *v.* empezar

compassionate (kəm-păsh′ə-nĭt) *adj.* wanting to help those who suffer
   compasivo *adj.* que siente pena por los que sufren y desea ayudar

compensation (kŏm′pən-sā′shən) *n.* payment
   remuneración *s.* pago

compulsory (kəm-pŭl′sə-rē) *adj.* forced; required
   obligatorio *adj.* forzoso

consensus (kən-sĕn′səs) *n.* general agreement
   consenso *s.* acuerdo general

consolation (kŏn′sə-lā′shən) *n.* a comfort
   consuelo *s.* alivio

contemplate (kŏn′təm-plāt′) *v.* to consider carefully and at length
   contemplar *v.* considerar con atención

contorted (kən-tôr′tĭd) *adj.* twisted or strained out of shape **contort** *v.*
   contorsionado *adj.* torcido **contorsionar** *v.*

contour (kŏn′tōŏr′) *n.* the outline of a figure or body
   contorno *s.* conjunto de líneas que limitan una figura

conventional (kən-vĕn′shə-nəl) *adj.* usual; traditional
   convencional *adj.* usual; tradicional

converge (kən-vûrj′) *v.* to come together
   convergir *v.* unirse

convivial (kən-vĭv′ē-əl) *adj.* enjoying the company of others; sociable
   cordial *adj.* sociable; simpático

convoluted (kŏn′və-lōō′tĭd) *adj.* difficult to understand; complicated
   enrollado *adj.* difícil de entender; complicado

cope (kōp) *v.* to struggle with and overcome
   superar *v.* hacer frente y vencer

copious (kō′pē-əs) *adj.* more than enough; plentiful
   copioso *adj.* abundante

covey (kŭv′ē) *n.* a small group or flock of birds, especially partridges or quail
nidada *s.* grupo de aves, especialmente de perdices o codornices

cower (kou′ər) *v.* to crouch or shrink down in fear
encogerse *v.* doblarse con miedo

croon (krōōn) *v.* to sing softly
canturrear *v.* cantar suavemente

culminate (kŭl′mə-nāt′) *v.* to reach the highest point or degree
culminar *v.* llegar a su momento o grado más alto

cumbersome (kŭm′bər-səm) *adj.* awkward; hard to manage
incómodo *adj.* pesado y díficil de manejar

cunning (kŭn′ĭng) *adj.* skillful, clever
astuto *adj.* ingenioso, listo

cunningly (kŭn′ĭng-lē) *adv.* in a clever way that is meant to trick or deceive
astutamente *adv.* de modo ingenioso con el fin de engañar

currency (kûr′ən-sē) *n.* money
moneda *s.* dinero

cynically (sĭn′ĭ-kəl-lē) *adv.* in a way that shows mistrust in the motives of others
cínicamente *adv.* con desconfianza de los motivos ajenos

daunting (dôn′tĭng) *adj.* frightening; intimidating **daunt** *v.*
sobrecogedor *adj.* desalentador; asustador **sobrecoger** *v.*

decimate (dĕs′ə-māt′) *v.* to kill or destroy a large part of
diezmar *v.* matar o destruir una gran parte

decoy (dē′koi′) *n.* a person or thing used to distract others or lead them in a different direction
señuelo *s.* persona o cosa que se usa para distraer o desviar

deference (dĕf′ər-əns) *n.* respect and honor
deferencia *s.* respeto y honor

demeaning (dĭ-mē′nĭng) *adj.* lowering one's dignity or standing **demean** *v.*
degradante *adj.* que reduce la dignidad o posición de una persona **degradar** *v.*

demonize (dē′mə-nīz′) *v.* to give evil, demonic qualities to
demonizar *v.* atribuir características muy negativas

despair (dĭ-spâr′) *v.* to lose hope
desesperar *v.* perder la esperanza

detached (dĭ-tăcht′) *adj.* separated; disconnected **detach** *v.*
separado *adj.* alejado; distanciado **separar** *v.*

devastating (dĕv′ə-stā′tĭng) *adj.* very effective in causing pain or destruction **devastate** *v.*
devastador *adj.* que causa gran dolor o destrucción **devastar** *v.*

diffuse (dĭ-fyōōz′) *v.* to spread out or through
difundir *v.* difuminar; diseminar

disarray (dĭs′ə-rā′) *n.* a state of disorder; confusion
desorganización *s.* desorden; confusión

disciplinarian (dĭs′ə-plə-nâr′ē-ən) *n.* someone who enforces strict discipline, or rules
ordenancista *s.* persona que impone reglas estrictas de orden y disciplina

discreetly (dĭ-skrēt′lē) *adv.* in a manner that shows caution and good judgment
discretamente *adv.* de modo moderado y sensato

disembodied (dĭs′ĕm-bŏ′dēd) *adj.* separated from or lacking a body **disembody** *v.*
incorpóreo *adj.* que no tiene cuerpo

disillusionment (dĭs′ĭ-lōō′zhən-mənt) *n.* disappointment; loss of hope
desilusión *s.* decepción; pérdida de la esperanza

dismay (dĭs-mā′) *n.* distress caused by trouble or something unexpected
consternación *s.* angustia por problemas o por sucesos inesperados

dismount (dĭs-mount′) *v.* to get down or off
desmontarse *v.* bajarse

disorientation (dĭs-ôr′ē-ĕn-tā′shən) *n.* mental confusion or impaired awareness
desorientación *s.* confusión mental

dispel (dĭ-spĕl′) *v.* to get rid of
disipar *v.* hacer desaparecer

dissenter (dĭ-sĕn′tər) *n.* one who disagrees or holds a different opinion
   disidente *s.* el que no está de acuerdo o tiene una opinión distinta

dissuade (dĭ-swād′) *v.* to persuade not to do something
   disuadir *v.* convencer de no hacer algo

dominate (dŏm′ə-nāt′) *v.* to have control over
   dominar *v.* mandar

dwindle (dwĭn′dl) *v.* to become less, until little remains
   disminuir *v.* reducir hasta que no queda casi nada

eavesdrop (ēvz′drŏp′) *v.* to listen secretly to a private conversation of others
   fisgonear *v.* escuchar en secreto conversaciones privadas

ecosystem (ē′kō-sĭs′təm) *n.* a physical environment, such as an ocean, and the community of things that live in it
   ecosistema *s.* ambiente físico, como un océano, y las comunidades que viven en él

eloquence (ĕl′ə-kwəns) *n.* forceful, convincing speech or writing
   elocuencia *s.* facultad de hablar o escribir de modo convincente

elusive (ĭ-lōō′sĭv) *adj.* tending to elude capture
   evasivo *adj.* escurridizo; difícil de capturar

eminent (ĕm′ə-nənt) *adj.* famous; well-respected
   eminente *adj.* muy famoso

endeavor (ĕn-dĕv′ər) *n.* purposeful or serious activity; enterprise
   empeño *s.* esfuerzo serio y resuelto

entitlement (ĕn-tīt′l-mənt) *n.* the state of having a right or claim to something
   derecho *s.* prerrogativa o atribución

epidemic (ĕp′ĭ-dĕm′ĭk) *n.* an outbreak of a disease that spreads quickly among many people
   epidemia *s.* enfermedad que ataca a mucha gente al mismo tiempo

evasive (ĭ-vā′sĭv) *adj.* tending or trying to avoid
   evasivo *adj.* que tiende a evitar

evidently (ĕv′ĭ-dənt-lē) *adv.* obviously; clearly
   evidentemente *adv.* obviamente; claramente

excess (ĭk-sĕs′) *adj.* too much or too many
   excesivo *adj.* que tiene demasiado

exhilarating (ĭg-zĭl′ə-rā′tĭng) *adj.* stimulating; making one feel thrilled or inspired **exhilarate** *v.*
   estimulante *adj.* tonificante; que hace sentir entusiasmo **estimular** *v.*

exuberantly (ĭg-zōō′bər-ənt-lē) *adv.* in a manner showing enthusiasm or joy
   exuberantemente *adv.* con mucho entusiasmo o alegría

falsify (fôl′sə-fī′) *v.* to make false by adding to or changing
   falsificar *v.* falsear

ferocity (fə-rŏs′ĭ-tē) *n.* fierceness; extreme intensity
   ferocidad *s.* fiereza; extrema intensidad

fester (fĕs′tər) *v.* to become an increasing source of irritation or poisoning
   enconarse *v.* volverse más irritante o venenoso

feverishly (fē′vər-ĭsh-lē) *adv.* in a way marked by intense emotion or activity
   febrilmente *adv.* con intensa emoción o actividad

flail (flāl) *v.* to wave wildly
   agitar *v.* ondear fuertemente

fledgling (flĕj′lĭng) *n.* a young bird that has recently grown its flight feathers
   polluelo *s.* pichón que acaba de echar plumas

flimsy (flĭm′zē) *adj.* not solid or strong
   ligero *adj.* insubstancial; débil

flinching (flĭn′chĭng) *n.* drawing back from difficulty or danger **flinch** *v.*
   reculada *s.* titubeo; vacilación **recular** *v.*

forage (fôr′ĭj) *v.* to search around for food or other supplies
   hurgar *v.* buscar lo que se necesita, especialmente alimento

foray (fôr′ā′) *n.* a trip into an unknown area
   incursión *s.* viaje a un territorio desconocido

forerunner (fôr′rŭn′ər) *n.* person or thing that came before
   precursor *s.* persona o cosa que precede algo que se desarrollará más tarde

foresighted (fôr′sī′tĭd) *adj.* having the ability to anticipate the future and prepare for it
   visionario *adj.* que anticipa el futuro y se prepara

forlorn (fər-lôrn′) *adj.* appearing lonely or sad
  desdichado *adj.* de aspecto triste y solo

frail (frāl) *adj.* delicate; weak and fragile
  frágil *adj.* delicado; débil

fray (frā) *n.* a fight; a heated dispute
  refriega *s.* lucha

gait (gāt) *n.* a manner of walking or moving on foot
  paso *s.* modo de andar

gaunt (gônt) *adj.* thin and bony
  enjuto *adj.* delgado y huesudo

genially (jēn′yəl-lē) *adv.* in a pleasant, friendly manner
  cordialmente *adv.* de modo amistoso

ghastly (găst′lē) *adj.* terrifyingly horrible
  espantoso *adj.* horrendo

gigantic (jī-găn′tĭk) *adj.* extremely large
  gigantesco *adj.* enorme

glinty (glĭn′tē) *adj.* sparkling
  destellante *adj.* brillante

grave (grāv) *adj.* solemn and dignified
  grave *adj.* solemne y digno

grievous (grē′vəs) *adj.* painful; serious
  penoso *adj.* doloroso; serio

grimace (grĭm′ĭs) *v.* to twist one's face to show pain or disgust
  hacer una mueca *v.* retorcer la cara de dolor o desagrado

hierarchy (hī′ə-rär′kē) *n.* an organization of people according to rank
  jerarquía *s.* organización por rango

homage (hŏm′ĭj) *n.* a display of loyalty and respect
  homenaje *s.* demostración de lealtad y respeto

humor (hyōō′mər) *v.* to give in to the wishes of
  llevar la corriente *v.* acceder; satisfacer

hustle (hŭs′əl) *v.* to gain by energetic effort
  conseguir *v.* obtener con mucho esfuerzo

impairment (ĭm-pâr′mənt) *n.* the condition of being damaged, injured, or harmed
  deterioro *s.* daño o herida

impasse (ĭm′păs′) *n.* a situation in which no progress can be made; a deadlock
  impasse *s.* situación en que no se avanza; punto muerto

impetus (ĭm′pĭ-təs) *n.* a driving force; a motivation
  ímpetu *s.* fuerza motriz; motivación

impoverished (ĭm-pŏv′ər-ĭsht) *adj.* very poor **impoverish** *v.*
  empobrecido *adj.* muy pobre **empobrecer** *v.*

improbable (ĭm-prŏb′ə-bəl) *adj.* not likely
  improbable *adj.* poco probable

improvise (ĭm′prə-vīz′) *v.* to make up on the spur of the moment, without preparation
  improvisar *v.* inventar en el momento

inadvertence (ĭn′əd-vûr′tns) *n.* a lack of attention; carelessness
  inadvertencia *s.* descuido; omisión

incoherent (ĭn′kō-hîr′ənt) *adj.* confused; lacking logical connections
  incoherente *adj.* confuso; carente de conexiones lógicas

inconsolable (ĭn′kən-sō′lə-bəl) *adj.* impossible or difficult to comfort
  inconsolable *adj.* que no se puede consolar

incredulously (ĭn-krĕj′ə-ləs-lē) *adv.* in a way that shows doubt or disbelief
  incrédulamente *adj.* con incredulidad

incriminate (ĭn-krĭm′ə-nāt′) *v.* to cause to appear guilty
  incriminar *v.* hacer parecer culpable

inevitably (ĭn-ĕv′ĭ-tə-blē) *adv.* unavoidably; without fail
  inevitablemente *adv.* que no se puede evitar; sin falta

infinitely (ĭn′fə-nĭt-lē) *adv.* extremely; greatly
  infinitamente *adv.* sumamente; enormemente

infuriated (ĭn-fyŏŏr′ē-ā′tĭd) *adj.* very angry **infuriate** *v.*
  enfurecido *adj.* furioso **enfurecer** *v.*

inscription (ĭn-skrĭp′shən) *n.* something written, carved, or engraved on a surface
  inscripción *s.* cosa escrita, tallada o gravada en una superficie

insinuation (ĭn-sĭn′yōō-ā′shən) *n.* a suggestion or hint intended to insult
  insinuación *s.* manera sutil de insultar

insolently (ĭn′sə-lənt-lē) *adv.* boldly and insultingly
  insolentemente *adv.* de modo grosero

integrated (ĭn′tĭ-grā′tĭd) *adj.* open to people of all races and groups **integrate** *v.*
  integrado *adj.* abierto a personas de todas las razas o grupos étnicos **integrar** *v.*

integrity (ĭn-tĕg′rĭ-tē) *n.* honesty or sincerity
  integridad *s.* honestidad o sinceridad

intricate (ĭn′trĭ-kĭt) *adj.* arranged in a complex way; elaborate
  intrincado *adj.* presentado de una manera compleja; elaborado

ironically (ī-rŏn′ĭk-lē) *adv.* in a way that is contrary to what is expected or intended
  irónicamente *adv.* de manera contraria a lo esperado

jauntily (jôn′tə-lē) *adv.* in a light and carefree way
  gallardamente *adv.* de manera ligera y despreocupada

jostling (jŏs′ə-lĭng) *n.* roughly bumping, pushing, or shoving **jostle** *v.*
  empujón *s.* empellón **empujar** *v.*

languish (lăng′gwĭsh) *v.* to remain unattended or be neglected
  languidecer *v.* debilitarse o perder fuerza por abandono

lanky (lăng′kē) *adj.* tall and thin
  largirucho *adj.* alto y flaco

linger (lĭng′gər) *v.* to continue to stay; delay leaving
  vacilar *v.* quedarse; tardar en partir

masterpiece (măs′tər-pēs′) *n.* a great work of art
  obra maestra *s.* obra de arte magistral

melancholy (mĕl′ən-kŏl′ē) *n.* sadness; depression
  melancolía *s.* tristeza; depresión

merge (mûrj) *v.* to blend together
  combinarse *v.* unirse

metabolism (mĭ-tăb′ə-lĭz′əm) *n.* all the processes a living thing uses to continue to grow and live
  metabolismo *s.* conjunto de procesos que se producen en las células de los seres vivos

migrant (mī′grənt) *adj.* moving from place to place
  migratorio *adj.* que se muda de un sitio a otro

mistrust (mĭs-trŭst′) *v.* to think of without confidence or trust
  desconfiar *v.* no tener confianza

moderate (mŏd′ər-ĭt) *adj.* not excessive or extreme; average
  moderado *adj.* mediano; módico

muse (myo͞oz) *v.* to say thoughtfully
  contemplar *v.* decir de modo pensativo

novelty (nŏv′əl-tē) *n.* something new, original, or unusual
  novedad *s.* algo nuevo, original o inusual

oblige (ə-blīj′) *v.* to force; require
  obligar *v.* forzar; requerir

optimistic (ŏp′tə-mĭs′tĭk) *adj.* hopeful about the future
  optimista *adj.* con esperanzas del futuro

partisan (pär′tĭ-zən) *adj.* relating to or in support of one political party
  partidario *adj.* que apoya un partido político

pendulum (pĕn′jə-ləm) *n.* a weight hung so that it can swing freely, sometimes used in timing the workings of certain clocks
  péndulo *s.* cuerpo que oscila libremente usado para regular el movimiento de las manecillas de los relojes

pensively (pĕn′sĭv-lē) *adv.* thoughtfully
  pensativamente *adv.* reflexivamente

perception (pər-sĕp′shən) *n.* insight; ability to understand people and situations
  percepción *s.* comprensión; capacidad de entender personas y situaciones

perfunctorily (pər-fŭngk′tə-rĭ-lē) *adv.* in a mechanical or unconcerned way
  mecánicamente *adv.* superficialmente; como por obligación

perilously (pĕr′ə-ləs-lē) *adv.* dangerously
  arriesgadamente *adv.* peligrosamente

perpetual (pər-pĕch′o͞o-əl) *adj.* continual; unending
  perpetuo *adj.* eterno; sin fin

portly (pôrt′lē) *adj.* stout or overweight
  corpulento *adj.* grueso o con exceso de peso

posterity (pŏ-stĕr′ĭ-tē) *n.* future generations
  posteridad *s.* generaciones futuras

precipitous (prĭ-sĭp′ĭ-təs) *adj.* very steep
　escarpado *adj.* muy pendiente

predatory (prĕd′ə-tôr′ē) *adj.* given to stealing from or hurting others for one's own gain
　rapaz *adj.* propenso a robar o hacer daño por beneficio propio

preoccupied (prē-ŏk′yə-pīd′) *adj.* lost in thought; distracted
　absorto *adj.* ensimismado; distraído

presentable (prĭ-zĕn′tə-bəl) *adj.* fit to be seen by people
　presentable *adj.* en condiciones de ser visto

prestigious (prĕ-stē′jəs) *adj.* having a high reputation
　prestigioso *adj.* que tiene renombre o importancia

prime (prīm) *adj.* first in quality or value
　óptimo *adj.* de primera calidad o valor

prominent (prŏm′ə-nənt) *adj.* well-known; widely recognized
　prominente *adj.* bien conocido; reconocido en muchas partes

prophecy (prŏf′ĭ-sē) *n.* a prediction of the future
　profecía *s.* predicción del futuro

proponent (prə-pō′nənt) *n.* a person who supports something
　defensor *s.* el que apoya una posición

prospective (prə-spĕk′tĭv) *adj.* likely to be or become
　potencial *adj.* posible

punctual (pŭngk′chōō-əl) *adj.* on time; prompt
　puntual *adj.* a tiempo

puny (pyōō′nē) *adj.* weak and small
　enclenque *adj.* débil y raquítico

quiver (kwĭv′ər) *v.* to shake with a slight, rapid movement
　temblar *v.* vibrar con un movimiento rápido y sutil

radar (rā′där) *n.* a method of detecting distant objects through the use of radio waves
　radar *s.* método de detectar objetos distantes por medio de ondas de radio

rampage (răm′pāj′) *n.* a wild or violent outbreak
　alboroto *s.* tumulto violento

rash (răsh) *adj.* reckless and careless
　precipitado *adj.* impetuoso e imprudente

rationality (răsh′ə-năl′ĭ-tē) *n.* reasonableness
　racionalidad *s.* lógica; conformidad con la razón

raucous (rô′kəs) *adj.* loud and harsh-sounding
　escandaloso *adj.* fuerte y estridente

recede (rĭ-sēd′) *v.* to become fainter or more distant
　desvanecerse *v.* alejarse

recessed (rē′sĕst′) *adj.* set-in or set back **recess** *v.*
　empotrado *adj.* metido en la pared **empotrar** *v.*

reclaim (rĭ-klām′) *v.* to get back; recover
　recuperar *v.* recobrar

recurrence (rĭ-kûr′əns) *n.* the act of happening again; return
　reaparición *s.* repetición; regreso

redeem (rĭ-dēm′) *v.* to set free
　redimir *v.* liberar

redundant (rĭ-dŭn′dənt) *adj.* not needed; more than necessary
　redundante *adj.* más de lo necesario

reel (rēl) *v.* to feel unsteady or dizzy
　tambalearse *v.* sentirse mareado

rehabilitate (rē′hə-bĭl′ĭ-tāt′) *v.* to restore to useful life, as through therapy and education
　rehabilitar *v.* restaurar a través de terapia y educación

renounce (rĭ-nouns′) *v.* to give up
　renunciar *v.* dejar o abandonar

reproof (rĭ-prōōf′) *n.* criticism for a fault
　reprobación *s.* crítica por una falta

retaliate (rĭ-tăl′ē-āt′) *v.* to get revenge; get even
　vengarse *v.* tomar represalias

retort (rĭ-tôrt′) *v.* to reply sharply
　replicar *v.* contestar con brusquedad

retribution (rĕt′rə-byōō′shən) *n.* punishment for bad behavior
　castigo *s.* pena al que ha cometido una falta

revelation (rĕv′ə-lā′shən) *n.* something made known
　revelación *s.* algo que se da a conocer

revere (rĭ-vîr′) *v.* to honor or worship
　venerar *v.* honrar o adorar

revert (rĭ-vûrt′) *v.* to return to a former condition
  revertir *v.* regresar a una condición anterior

revive (rĭ-vīv′) *v.* to return to life or consciousness
  revivir *v.* recobrar la conciencia; despertarse

righteous (rī′chəs) *adj.* based on one's sense of what is right
  recto *adj.* correcto; honrado

saunter (sôn′tər) *v.* to stroll in a casual manner
  pasear *v.* caminar lentamente

scrutiny (skrōōt′n-ē) *n.* close examination or study
  examen *s.* estudio detallado

sever (sĕv′ər) *v.* to cut off or apart
  cortar *v.* separar

shanty (shăn′tē) *n.* a rundown house; a shack
  choza *s.* casucha

sheepishly (shē′pĭsh-lē) *adv.* with a bashful or embarrassed look
  tímidamente *adv.* con una expresión tímida o avergonzada

shrewdly (shrōōd′lē) *adv.* wisely; in a clever way
  astutamente *adv.* inteligentemente; con astucia

shuffle (shŭf′əl) *v.* to slide the feet along the ground while walking
  arrastrar los pies *v.* rozar el suelo con los pies al caminar

simultaneously (sī′məl-tā′nē-əs-lē) *adv.* at the same time
  simultáneamente *adv.* al mismo tiempo

singe (sĭnj) *v.* to burn lightly
  chamuscar *v.* quemar en la superficie

slack (slăk) *adj.* not firm or tight; loose
  flojo *adj.* fláccido

smugly (smŭg′lē) *adv.* in a self-satisfied way
  presumidamente *adv.* con satisfacción vanidosa

snag (snăg) *v.* to catch and tear
  enganchar *v.* agarrarse y romperse

somber (sŏm′bər) *adj.* serious; gloomy
  sombrío *adj.* serio; triste

specify (spĕs′ə-fī′) *v.* to make known or identify
  especificar *v.* detallar o identificar

speculate (spĕk′yə-lāt′) *v.* to view or consider different possibilities; to guess what might happen
  especular *v.* pensar en distintas posibilidades; imaginar lo que puede pasar

spherical (sfîr′ĭ-kəl) *adj.* having the shape of a sphere or round ball
  esférico *adj.* con forma de esfera o de pelota

stance (stăns) *n.* posture; position
  postura *s.* posición

subtly (sŭt′lē) *adv.* not obviously; in a manner hard to notice or perceive
  sutilmente *adv.* veladamente; con discreción

sustain (sə-stān′) *v.* to keep up; to support
  sustentar *v.* preservar; mantener

tantalizing (tăn′tə-lī′zĭng) *adj.* tempting but out of reach **tantalize** *v.*
  tentador *adj.* que inspira interés sin satisfacer **tentar** *v.*

taskmaster (tăsk′măs′tər) *n.* a person who sets tasks for others to do
  supervisor *s.* persona que reparte tareas

taunt (tônt) *v.* to make fun of
  burlar *v.* provocar con burlas; ridiculizar

taut (tôt) *adj.* not loose or flabby
  tirante *adj.* tenso; terso

tawny (tô′nē) *adj.* a warm, sandy shade of brownish orange
  leonado *adj.* color pardo rojizo

tedious (tē′dē-əs) *adj.* tiresome; boring
  tedioso *adj.* aburrido

terse (tûrs) *adj.* speaking little; communicating in few words
  seco *adj.* lacónico; que se comunica con pocas palabras

threshold (thrĕsh′ōld′) *n.* a doorway or entrance
  umbral *s.* entrada

torrent (tôr′ənt) *n.* a violent, rushing stream
  torrente *s.* corriente rápida y veloz

trance (trăns) *n.* a condition of daydreaming or being unconscious of one's surroundings
   trance *s.* ensoñación; ensimismamiento

translucent (trăns-lōō'sənt) *adj.* allowing light to pass through
   translúcido *adj.* que deja pasar la luz

travesty (trăv'ĭ-stē) *n.* a degraded or grotesque likeness
   parodia *s.* imitación burlesca de una cosa seria; distorsión

unbridled (ŭn-brīd'ld) *adj.* lacking restraint or control
   desenfrenado *adj.* sin restricciones

unison (yōō'nĭ-sən) *n.* harmony or agreement; as with one voice
   unísono *s.* armonía o acuerdo; dicho con una voz

unperceived (ŭn-pər-sēvd') *adj.* not seen or noticed
   desapercibido *adj.* no visto

unperturbed (ŭn'pər-tûrbd') *adj.* not troubled or distressed
   impasible *adj.* que no se molesta

upstart (ŭp'stärt') *adj.* suddenly risen to wealth or power
   advenedizo *adj.* arribista

urgency (ûr'jən-sē) *n.* a condition of pressing importance; necessity
   urgencia *s.* gran necesidad

usher (ŭsh'ər) *v.* to guide in a certain direction
   conducir *v.* llevar en cierta dirección

valiant (văl'yənt) *adj.* brave; courageous
   valiente *adj.* valeroso

varmint (vär'mĭnt) *n.* a troublesome person or wild animal
   alimaña *s.* persona o animal que causa problemas

veer (vîr) *v.* to change direction; to shift
   virar *s.* cambiar de dirección; dar un viraje

venerable (vĕn'ər-ə-bəl) *adj.* deserving respect because of age, character, or importance
   venerable *adj.* que merece respeto por edad, carácter o importancia

vengeance (vĕn'jəns) *n.* the infliction of punishment in return for an offense
   venganza *s.* imposición de castigo por una ofensa

vile (vīl) *adj.* disgusting; unpleasant
   repugnante *adj.* desagrable; asqueroso

virtuous (vûr'chōō-əs) *adj.* morally good; honorable
   virtuoso *adj.* de buen carácter moral; honorable

visceral (vĭs'ər-əl) *adj.* instinctive
   visceral *adj.* instintivo

voracious (vô-rā'shəs) *adj.* possessing an insatiable desire; greedy
   voraz *adj.* que tiene un deseo insaciable; glotón

wavering (wā'vər-ĭng) *adj.* hesitating between two choices **waver** *v.*
   vacilante *adj.* que duda entre dos alternativas **vacilar** *v.*

wince (wĭns) *v.* to draw back, as in pain or distress
   estremecerse *v.* encogerse o contraerse por dolor

writhe (rīth) *v.* to twist or move painfully
   retorcerse *v.* contorsionarse de dolor

Pronunciation Key

Symbol	Examples	Symbol	Examples	Symbol	Examples
ă	at, gas	m	man, seem	v	van, save
ā	ape, day	n	night, mitten	w	web, twice
ä	father, barn	ng	sing, hanger	y	yard, lawyer
âr	fair, dare	ŏ	odd, not	z	zoo, reason
b	bell, table	ō	open, road, grow	zh	treasure, garage
ch	chin, lunch	ô	awful, bought, horse	ə	awake, even, pencil,
d	dig, bored	oi	coin, boy		pilot, focus
ĕ	egg, ten	ŏŏ	look, full	ər	perform, letter
ē	evil, see, meal	ōō	root, glue, through		
f	fall, laugh, phrase	ou	out, cow		**Sounds in Foreign Words**
g	gold, big	p	pig, cap	KH	*German* ich, auch;
h	hit, inhale	r	rose, star		*Scottish* loch
hw	white, everywhere	s	sit, face	N	*French* entre, bon, fin
ĭ	inch, fit	sh	she, mash	œ	*French* feu, cœur;
ī	idle, my, tried	t	tap, hopped		*German* schön
îr	dear, here	th	thing, with	ü	*French* utile, rue;
j	jar, gem, badge	*th*	then, other		*German* grün
k	keep, cat, luck	ŭ	up, nut		
l	load, rattle	ûr	fur, earn, bird, worm		

Stress Marks

′   This mark indicates that the preceding syllable receives the primary stress. For example, in the word *language,* the first syllable is stressed: lăng′gwĭj.

′   This mark is used only in words in which more than one syllable is stressed. It indicates that the preceding syllable is stressed, but somewhat more weakly than the syllable receiving the primary stress. In the word *literature,* for example, the first syllable receives the primary stress, and the last syllable receives a weaker stress: lĭt′ər-ə-chŏŏr′.

Adapted from *The American Heritage Dictionary of the English Language,* fourth edition. Copyright ©2006 by Houghton Mifflin Harcourt Publishing Company. Used with the permission of Houghton Mifflin Harcourt Publishing Company.

Index of Skills

A

Abbreviations, 850, R49, R82
Abstract nouns, R46, R52
Academic vocabulary, 16–19, 27, 183, 315, 453, 553, 639, 777, 901, 1009
   in speaking, 63, 131, 348, 366, 672, 704, 731, 927, 966, 975, 982
   in writing, 44, 74, 94, 120, 214, 233, 246, 264, 274, 286, 336, 385, 480, 490, 503, 592, 659, 688, 741, 799, 812, 825, 845, 916, 940
Act, in a play, R100
Acting performance, 429, 430
Action verbs, R47, R55
Active listening, R82–R83
Active voice, 590, 593, R57
Ad hominem attacks, 954
Adjective clauses, 169, 282, 287, R62
Adjectives, 883, R47, R57
   adjective clauses, 169, 282, 287, R62
   capitalization, R51
   coordinate, 626
   comparative forms of, 535
   superlative forms of, 535
Adventure novels, 96–101, R100
Adverb clauses, R62–R63
Adverbs, R47, R58
   adverb clauses, R62
   comparative forms of, 535
   conjunctive adverbs, 873
   superlative forms of, 535
Advertising, 4, 10, 984–987, R90–R91
   billboard, R90
   celebrities in, R91
   explicit and implicit messages, 985–986
   flyer, R90
   infomercial, R90
   marketing, R90
   persuasive techniques in, 10, R91
   political ad, R90
   print ad, 987, R90
   product placement, R90–R91
   public service announcement, R90
   sponsors, R90
   target audience, 10, 985, R85
   television commercials, 984–987, R90
   trailer, R90
   types of, R90
Affixes. *See* Prefixes; Suffixes.
Agreement
   antecedent-pronoun agreement, 91, 95, 301, R52–R53

subject-verb agreement, 481, R65–R67
Alliteration, 556, 557, 605, R100
Allusions, FM56, 808, R100
Almanacs, 1020, R110
Ambiguous pronoun references, R55
Analogies, 120, 335, 688, 982, R24, R71, R100, R110
Analysis, writing, R39
Analytical essays, 855, 873
Analyzing Point of View, FM40
Anecdotes, 805, 993, R100
Anglo-Saxon affixes, 825
Anglo-Saxon roots, 799
Animation, R87, R88
Antagonists, R100
Antecedent-pronoun agreement, 91, 95, 301, R52–R53
Antonyms, 63, 655, 752, R70, R71
Apostrophes, 75, R50
Appeals, 954, 985, R21, R91
   by association, R21
   bandwagon, 954, 985, R21, R83, R91
   emotional, R21, R91, R111
   ethical, R21
   to fear, R21, R91, R111
   logical, R21, R22–R25, R91, R112
   to loyalty, R21
   to pity, R21, R91, R111
   to vanity, R21, R111
Appendixes, 1022
Appositives and appositive phrases, 243, 247, 908, 917, R61
Approaches to literature. *See* Text criticism.
Archives, 1026
Argument: Supporting an Opinion, 162–171
Arguments, 8, 952–957, R20–R23, R110.
     See also Appeals; Persuasive techniques; Persuasive writing.
   analysis of, 952–957, R22–R26
   claims, R20, R26
   counterarguments, 959, 965, 969–974, 977, 981, 990, R20, R26, R27, R79
   deductive, R23, R111
   editorials and, 959–965, R20–R21
   evaluating, FM51, R26
   evidence, 919–926, 952–957, 988–997, R20, R22, R25, R26
   faulty, 954, 971, R24, R25, R26, R83
   general principle, R23
   inductive, R22, R112
   logical, R21, R22–R25, R26, R112
   opposing. *See* counterarguments *above.*

reasons, 990, R20, R26
speaking strategies for determining strong, R22–R26
in speeches, 977–981
strategies for reading, R20–R21
support, 952–957, 959, 963, 965, R20
writing, R40–R41, R99
Art. *See* Visuals, analyzing.
Articles. *See* Magazine articles; News articles.
Art projects, 581, 879, 915
Assessment Practice, 174–179, 306–311, 444–449, 544–549, 630–635, 768–773, 892–897, 1000–1005
   reading comprehension, 174–177, 306–309, 444–447, 544–547, 630–633, 768–771, 892–895, 1000–1003
   revising and editing, 179, 311, 449, 549, 635, 773, 897, 1005
   short constructed response, 177, 309, 447, 547, 633, 771, 895, 1003
   vocabulary, 178, 310, 448, 548, 634, 772, 896, 1004
   writing for assessment, 265, 397, 619, 755, 941
Assonance, R100, R107, R108
Assumptions, R110
Atlases, 1018, 1020
Audience
   comparison-contrast essay, 294, 295
   feature article, 620, 621
   how-to explanation, 756, 757
   literary analysis, 532, 533
   media and, 985, R85, R88–R89
   oral presentation, 542, 766
   personal narrative, 880, 881
   persuasive essay, 988, 989
   persuasive podcast, 172
   research paper, 1028, 1029
   short story, 432, 433
   speeches and, 981, R80
   supporting an opinion, 162, 163
   writing process, 20, 441
Audio and video resources, 1018
Author's background, 35, 47, 67, 77, 96, 103, 123, 133, 139, 191, 225, 235, 249, 267, 277, 289, 323, 339, 351, 375, 386, 393, 399, 461, 483, 497, 504, 511, 517, 523, 561, 567, 575, 583, 594, 605, 613, 647, 661, 675, 681, 691, 706, 717, 733, 743, 785, 805, 815, 826, 833, 857, 875, 907, 919, 929, 959, 969, 977

Classification, R110

Clauses
 adjective, 169, 282, 287, 883, R46, R54,
  R62, R67
 adverb, R62–R63
 dependent (subordinate), FM57, 287, 355,
  367, 427, 439, 698, 705, R49, R62, R64
 essential, R62
 independent (main), FM57, 287, 427,
  439, 673, R32, R62, R63, R64
 nonessential, R49, R62
 noun, R63
 punctuation of, 64, 522, R32, R49, R62,
  R63

Clichés, 168, R110

Climax, 30, 33, 35, 42, 435, R2, R101. See
  also Plot.

Close-up shots, films and, 155

Cluster diagrams, 1029

Coherence, FM48, 121, 162, 432, R29,
  R31–R32

Collective nouns, R46, R52, R67

Colons, 979, 983, R50

Combining sentences. See Coordinating
  conjunctions.

Comedy, R101. See also Humor; Tragedy.

Commas, 233, 873
 in addresses, R49
 adjectives and, R49
 appositives and, 247, 917, R61
 to avoid confusion, R49
 with clauses, 64, R32, R49, R62, R63
 in compound sentences, 673, R32, R49,
  R65
 with coordinating conjunctions, 64
 in dates, R49
 with definitions, 233
 in dialogue, 337
 in direct address, R49
 after introductory words or phrases, 962,
  967
 in letters, R49
 with phrases, 292, R49
 quick reference chart, R49
 with quotation marks, 337,
 in series, R49

Commercials. See Advertising.

Common Core Traits
 blogs, 442
 argumentative essay, 162, 170, 988, 996
 comparison-contrast essay, 294, 302
 conducting interviews, 890
 creating a wiki, 1044
 how-to explanation, 756, 764
 informative article, 620
 literary analysis, 532, 540
 oral instructions, 766
 panel discussion, 304

personal narrative, 880, 888
persuasive speech, 998
podcast, 172–173
presenting a critique, 542–543
research paper, 1028, 1043
short story, 432, 440
writing rubrics, 22

Common nouns, 808, 813, R46, R52

Commonplace assertions, 492, 919

Comparatives, using, 535, R58

Compare and contrast, R110
 biography and autobiography, 824
 characters, 43, 247, 248–265, 335, 361,
  365, 591, 730, 879
 films and drama, 430
 historical drama and diary, 857, 871, 872
 legends, 703
 literary works, 73, 93, 213, 658, 857–872
 magazine articles, 935, 939
 memoirs and, 285
 mood, 612–619
 opinions, 715, 981
 poetry, 293, 572
 points of view, 232, 245
 problem-solution essays, 373
 reading skills and strategies, 323–335
 theme, 396, 742, 743–754
 transitions and, 121

Compare-and-contrast writing, 75, 161,
  294–302, 373, R37–R38

Comparing Texts on the Same Topic, FM42

Comparison-and-contrast organization,
  294–300, R8, R11–R13, R32. See also
  Analogy; Arguments.
 point-by-point, 296, R11–R13, R37, R41
 signal words for, R11, R32
 subject-by-subject, 296, R11–R13, R38
 of texts, R11–R13

Complements, R60

Complex sentences, 427, 698, 705, 1042,
  R64

Composition, photographs, 529, 530

Compound-complex sentences, R64

Compound nouns, R46, R52

Compound sentences, 673, R60, R63–R64,
  R65–R66

Comprehension, monitoring, R112
 poetry, 523–527
 reading skills and strategies, 12, 605–611
 short stories, 13, 191–213, 339–347

Computers. See Online resources; Web sites.

Conclusions, drawing, R33, R110
 autobiographies, 844
 biographies and, 824
 about characters, 62, 232, 273, 426, 489,
  740
 Greek myths and, 658
 history-related writings, 872

magazine articles, 915
memoirs and, 285
multiple themes, 661–671
reading for information and, 803
about speakers, 396, 581
teleplays, 153

Conclusions, writing, 300, 538, 542, R33,
  R110

Concrete nouns, R46, R52

Conflict, 5, 28, 29, 47–63, R2, R37, R101.
  See also Falling action; Plot; Rising
  action.
 analyzing, 67, 68, 70, 73, 88, 116, 117,
 central, R37
 characterization and, 28, 84, 88, 117, 153
 at climax, R101
 in drama, 139–153
 external, 28, 29, 67, 73, R101
 identifying, 29, 31, 33, 67, 68, 70, 73,
  84, 114, 136, 153, 328, 339, 340, 497,
  500, R2
 in informative writing, 30, 35, R102
 internal, 28, 31, 67, 70, 73, 328, 335,
  R101
 in narrative nonfiction, 103, 114, 116,
  117
 in narrative writing, 432–441, R37
 in plot, 28, 30, 35, 67–73, 84, 88, R101,
  R106, R107
 resolution of, 30, 92, 339, 501
 setting and, 318
 theme and, 318, 328, 339, 340, 342

Conjunctions, 741, R64
 coordinating, 54, 64, 673, R32, R47,
  R49, R60, R62, R65
 correlative, R47, R66
 subordinating, 705, R47, R62, R63

Conjunctive adverbs, 873

Connecting, 11, 12, 35–43, 72, 212, 267–
  273, 368, 492, 522, 527, 600, 657,
  712, 800, 946, R2, R21, R28, R77,
  R110, R112. See also Cross-curricular
  connections.

Connotations, 348, 812, R71, R101

Consumer documents, 8, R16, R110

Content-specific vocabulary, 916

Context clues, 19, 44, 63, 103, 178, 214,
  233, 235, 246, 286, 310, 366, 385,
  448, 455, 490, 503, 548, 605, 634,
  731, 758, 785, 805, 845, 896, 959,
  1004, R15, R68, R72, R110. See also
  Vocabulary, in context.
 antonyms as, 63
 cause-and-effect, R68
 comparison, R68
 contrast, R68
 definition or restatement, 233, R68
 examples as, R68

N

Name-calling, faulty reasoning and, R24
Narrative and expressive writing, R36–R37
    anecdotes, R30, R41, R77, R100
    characterization, 433, 436, R36
    conflict, organization for, 433–436, R37
    descriptive, R102
    dialogue, 7, 435, 437, R36
    options for organization, R36–R37
    personal narrative, 880–889
    short stories, 432–441, R36–R37
Narrative elements and devices. *See*
    Characters; Conflict; Plot; Point of
    View; Setting; Theme.
Narrative nonfiction, 102, 103–119, 814,
    R105. *See also* Literary nonfiction.
Narrative poetry, 4, 133, 583, 675, R105
    analysis of, 133–137, 583–591
    characters in, 133, 137
    conflict in, 133, 136
    strategies for reading, 583–591
Narrative speeches, R79
Narrators 184, 185, 186, 188, 347, R105
    drawing conclusions about, 185, 342, 347
    first-person, 184, 185, 225–232, 347,
        880–889, R106
    point of view of, 184, 185, 225–232,
        235–245, 384, R106
    third-person, 184, 185, 235–245, 384,
        R106
    third-person limited, 184, 185
    third-person omniscient, 184, 185,
        235–245, 384
News, 4, 8. *See also* Media genres and types.
    accuracy, R89
    angle, R89
    balance in reporting, R89
    bias in reporting, 10, 919, R25, R89, R90
    choosing the news, 942–943, R88
    editorials, R13, R20, R40, R85, R111,
        R113
    features, 4, 8, 9, R112
    five *W*'s and *H,* R89
    inverted pyramid, R89
    newscast, 942–943, R86, R87–R88
    newsworthiness, 942–943, R88
    objectivity, R89
    op/ed, R113. *See also* Editorials.
    reporting, R89–R90
    slant, R89
    sources for, R90
    standards for reporting, R89
    thoroughness, R89
News articles, 8, 847–851, R14, R112
    evaluating sources and, 1023
    reading for information, 65, 478, 565,
        846–851

    writing, 384
News media, 10, 942–945, R88–R90
Newspapers and periodicals, 8, 10, 1018,
    1023–1024, R84, R85, R86,
    R88–R90, R113. *See also* News articles.
    articles in, 4, 8, 10, 478, R14, R86,
        R105, R112, R114
    editorials in, 960–961, 962–964, R111
    evaluating, 1024, R25–R26, R92
    op/ed pieces in, R113
Newsworthiness, 943, 944, R88
Nonsense poetry, 604, 605–611
Nonverbal techniques
    descriptive speeches, 173
    oral presentations, 543
    panel discussions, 305
    persuasive speeches, 999
Note taking, 600, 767, 833, 904, 1012, 1033
Noun clauses, R63
Nouns, 741, R52
    as antecedent, 95
    capitalization of, 808, 813
    common, 813, R52
    plural, R52
    possessive, 70, 75, R46, R50, R52, R53,
        R54, R74
    precise, 483, R29
    predicate, R60, R67
    proper, 808, 813, 887, R51, R52
    singular, R52
Novellas, 5
Novels, 5, 386–391, R105
    adventure novels, 96–101
    dramatizations of, 398, 399–424, 426
    historical novels, 706–711
    verse novels, 504–509

O

Objections, anticipating. *See*
    Counterarguments.
Objectivity, 780, 915
Objects
    direct, R48, R53, R60, R61, R63
    indirect, R48, R53, R60, R62, R63
    of prepositions, R53, R62, R63
    use of *whom* as, in sentence, R54
Odes, R106
Online articles, 65, 425
    writing, 620–627
Online resources
    research and, 1013–1015, 1018, 1026
    source lists, 1032
Onomatopoeia, 557, 605, 626, R106
Op/ed pieces, R113. *See also* Editorials.
Open-ended response. *See* Extended
    constructed response, Short
    constructed response.

Open form, in poetry, 554
Opinions, R84, R85, R89–R90
    claims and, 919
    compare-and-contrast, 981
    facts and, 492–495, R111
    identifying, 712–715, 935
    synthesizing information and, 800
    writing, 162–171
Oral fluency, 41, 108, 358, 381, 685, 746
Oral literature, R106
Oral presentations, R78–R81
    debates, R79
    interviews and, 891
    oral instructions, 766–767
    panel discussions, 304–305
    podcasts, 172–173
    presenting a critique, 542–543
Order of importance, R32, R35
Order of impression, R35
Organization, patterns of. *See* Patterns of
    organization.
Organizing. *See* Graphic organizers; Patterns
    of organization.
Origin, of words. *See* Etymologies; Word
    roots.
Outlines, 1035
    creating, 907–915, 1035
    drafting from, R28
    for taking notes, R4
Overgeneralization, R24, R113
Oversimplification, R24
Overview, R4, R93, R113

P

Pace. *See* Reading rate.
Panel discussions, 304–305, 965
Papers. *See* Research papers.
Paragraphs, R31–R32
    coherence of, R31–R32
    organizing, R31–R32
    topic sentence in, 495, 904, R31, R98,
        R114
    transitions in, 121, R31, R35
    unity of, R31
Parallelism, 623, R64, R77
    creating parallel structure in writing,
        623, 626, R64
    as a rhetorical device, R77
Paraphrasing, 675–679, 969–974, R113. *See*
    also Plagiarism.
    figurative language and, 875
    research papers, 1033, 1034
Parentheses, 139, R50
Participles and participial phrases, 491, R55,
    R56, R61
    dangling, 491, R59, R61
    misplaced, 491, R59, R61

past, 491, R55, R56, R57
present, 491, R55, R56
Parts of a book, 1021
Parts of speech, 741, R47, R52–R59. *See also*
    Grammar in context; *specific parts of
    speech.*
    reference chart of, R46
Passive voice, 593, R57
Past tense verbs, 209
Patterns of organization, 164, 165, 296, 907,
    R2, R8–R13, R42, R113
    cause-effect, R10–R11, R32–R33
    chronological, 103–119, 681–687,
        785–798, R8, R9–R10, R32, R35,
        R36, R40, R110, R113
    classification, R113
    comparison-contrast, R11–R13, R32
    deductive, R23, R111
    inductive, R22, R112
    main idea and supporting details,
        R8–R9, R31
    order of importance, R32, R35
    order of impression, R35
    point-by-point, 296, R11–R13, R37, R41
    problem-solution, R13, R39, R113
    sequential, R9, R32
    spatial order, 759, R32, R35
    subject-by-subject, 290, 296, R11–R13,
        R38
Peer review, 23, 990, 992, R30
    argumentative essay, 164, 166
    comparison-contrast essay, 296, 298
    how-to explanation, 758, 760
    informative article, 622, 624
    literary analysis, 534, 536
    personal narrative, 882, 884
    research paper, 1030, 1038
    short story, 434, 436
Periodicals, 8, 10, 1023–1024, R112, R113.
    See also Newspapers and periodicals.
Periods, 573, R29, R49
    in abbreviations, R49
    to fix run-ons, R64–R65
    with quotation marks, 337
Personal essay, 804, 805–811, 809
Personal narrative, writing, 880–889
Personification, 85, 195, 558, 567, 613,
    R106
Perspective, author's, R100. *See also* Point of
    view; Writer's point of view.
Persuasive speeches, 998–999, R79
Persuasive techniques, 954, 977–981,
    984–987, R20–R26
    in advertising, 10, 955, 984–987, R91
    anecdotes, 990
    appeals by association, R21
    appeals to fear, pity, or vanity, 954, R21,
        R91, R111

appeals to loyalty, R21
bandwagon appeals, 954, 985, R21, R91
celebrity ads, 906, R91
emotional appeals, R21, R91, R111
ethical appeals, R21
evaluating, R25–R26
glittering generality, R21, R83
loaded language, 954, R25, R112
logical appeals, 952, R21, R22–R25,
    R91, R112
media messages and, R92
slogans, R91
snob appeal, R21, R83
testimonials, 954, R21, R90
TV commercials, 985, 986
word choice in, R21
Persuasive essay, writing essay, 162–171,
    988–997, R40–R41, R94, R99, R102.
    See also Arguments.
    key traits, 988, R40–R41
    opinion statement, 989, R33
    options for organizing, 991, R20, R26
    rubric for, 996
Photographs, analyzing, 528–531
Phrases
    adjective, 883, R60
    adverb, R60
    appositive, 243, 247, 908, 917, R61, R62
    gerund, R61–R62
    infinitive, R59, R61
    introductory, 962, 967
    participial, 491, R55, R61
    prepositional, 471, 481, 967, R48, R59,
        R60
    verbal, R61–R62
Picture diagram, R6
Pie graphs, R5. *See also* Graphic aids.
Plagiarism, 1034
Planning, research and, 1011–1012
Planning/prewriting, 21, 23
    argumentative essays, 163–164, 989–990
    comparison-contrast essay, 295–296
    how-to explanation, 757–758
    informative article, 621–622
    literary analysis, 533–534
    personal narrative, 881–882
    research paper, 1029–1030
    short story, 433–434
    writing for assessment, 619
Plays. *See* Drama.
Plot, 5, 28–33. *See also* Climax; Exposition;
    Falling action; Flashbacks;
    Foreshadowing; Resolution; Rising
    action; Sequence.
    analysis of, 35–43
    characters and, 30–31, 191–213
    climax of, 30, 33, 35, 42, 43, 586, R2,
        R101

conflict in, 28, 29, 30, 35, 67–73, 84, 88,
    92, R37, R101, R106, R107
development of, 30
in drama, 399–426
exposition of, 30, 31, 32, 35, 36, 38, 43,
    R2, R102, R106
falling action in, 30, 33, 35, 42, 43, R2,
    R103, R106
in films, 154–156
in narrative nonfiction, 103–119
in narrative poetry, 133–137, 583–591
resolution in, 30, 33, 35, 42, 43, 92, 139,
    318, 497, 501, R2, R37, R101, R103,
    R106
rising action in, 30, 31, 32, 35, 40, R2,
    R102, R106, R107
sequence in, 399, 426
stages of, 30–31
Plot chart. *See* Plot diagram.
Plot diagram, 30, 43, R2, R36
Podcasts, 172–173
Poetic elements and devices. *See also* Literary
    elements and devices; Poetic forms.
    alliteration, 556, 557, 605, R100
    assonance, R100
    characterization, 289–293
    figurative language, 558, 559, 567–572,
        875–879, R68
    form, R2
    form in, 517–521, 523, 554–555, 559, R2
    graphical components, 554–555, 581
    humor, 605–611
    imagery, 558, 559, 561–564
    internal rhyme, R107
    lines, 289, 293, 517, 554, 575–581
    meter, 583–591, R105
    onomatopoeia, 557, 605, R106
    personification, 85, 195, 558, 567, 613,
        R106
    repetition, 133, 137, 556, 557, 599, 605,
        614, R107
    rhyme, 133, 517, 556, 557, 605, R107
    rhyme schemes, 575–581, R107
    rhythm, 133, 289, 556, 557, 583–591,
        R107
    sound devices, 556–557, 559, 575, 599
    sound elements, 556–557
    speakers, 396, 517–521, 575–581, 875–
        879, R108
    stanzas, 137, 517, 518, 521, 554, 575–
        581, R108
    style, 523–527
    symbols, 594–599
Poetic forms
    ballads, 591, R100
    couplets, R102
    epic poems, 674, R102

INDEX OF TITLES & AUTHORS

Page numbers that appear in italics refer to biographical information.

ACKNOWLEDGMENTS

INTRODUCTORY UNIT

Marian Reiner: "Thumbprint," from *A Sky Full of Poems* by Eve Merriam. Copyright © 1964, 1970, 1973 by Eve Merriam. All rights renewed and reserved. Used by permission of Marian Reiner.

The Barbara Hogenson Agency: Excerpt from *A Young Lady of Property* by Horton Foote. Copyright © 1955, 1983 by Horton Foote. Reprinted by arrangement with Horton Foote and The Barbara Hogenson Agency.

KidsHealth: Excerpt from "Stress" by the Memours Foundation, from KidsHealth.com. Copyright © KidsHealth.com. Reprinted with permission.

Atheneum Books for Young Readers: Excerpt from "Shells," from *Every Living Thing* by Cynthia Rylant. Copyright © 1985 by Cynthia Rylant. Reprinted with permission of Atheneum Books for Young Readers, an imprint of Simon & Schuster Children's Publishing Division.

UNIT 1

Hill and Wang: "The Last Cover," from *The Pride of Lions and Other Stories* by Paul Annixter. Copyright © 1960 by Hill and Wang, renewed copyright © 1988 by Hill and Wang. Reprinted by permission of Hill and Wang, a division of Farrar, Straus and Giroux, LLC.

Brandt & Hochman Literary Agents: Excerpt from "The Third Wish," from *More Than You Bargained For* by Joan Aiken. Copyright © 1957, renewed © 1985 by Joan Aiken. Reprinted by permission of Brandt & Hochman Literary Agents, Inc.

Houghton Mifflin Harcourt: "Seventh Grade," from *Baseball in April and Other Stories* by Gary Soto. Copyright © 1990 by Gary Soto. All rights reserved. Reprinted by permission of Houghton Mifflin Harcourt Publishing Company.

Scholastic: "The Last Dog" by Katherine Paterson. Copyright © 1999 by Minna Murra, Inc. Published in *Tomorrowland: 10 Stories about the Future* compiled by Michael Cart. Copyright © 1999 by Michael Cart. Reprinted by permission of Scholastic, Inc.

ABCNews: Excerpts from "'Spot' Goes High-Tech" by Jackie Judd, from ABCNEWS.com. Copyright © 2002 by ABCNews Internet Ventures. Courtesy of ABCNEWS.com.

Hill and Wang: "Thank You, M'am," from *Short Stories* by Langston Hughes. Copyright © 1996 by Ramona Bass and Arnold Rampersad. Reprinted by permission of Hill and Wang, a division of Farrar, Straus and Giroux, LLC.

Harvard University Press: "If I can stop one heart from breaking," from *The Poems of Emily Dickinson*, edited by Thomas H. Johnson. Copyright © 1951, 1955, 1979, 1983 by the President and Fellows of Harvard College. Reprinted by permission of the publishers and the Trustees of Amherst College.

Farrar, Straus and Giroux and Bloomsbury Publishing: Excerpt from *Holes* by Louis Sachar. Copyright © 1998 by Louis Sachar. Jacket design by Vladimir Radunsky from *Holes* by Louis Sachar. Jacket art and design copyright © 1998 by Vladimir Radunsky. Reprinted by permission of Farrar, Straus and Giroux, LLC and Bloomsbury Publishing Plc.

Madison Press Books: Excerpts from *Exploring the Titanic* by Robert D. Ballard. Copyright © 1988 by Ballard & Family. Reprinted by permission of Madison Press Books.

HarperCollins Publishers: Excerpt from *An American Childhood* by Annie Dillard. Copyright © 1987 by Annie Dillard. Reprinted by permission of HarperCollins Publishers.

The Estate of Rod Serling: "The Monsters Are Due on Maple Street" by Rod Serling. Copyright © 1960 by Rod Serling. Copyright © 1988 by Carolyn Serling, Jody Serling, and Anne Serling Sutton. Reprinted by permission of Code Entertainment and Carol Serling, on behalf of the Estate of Rod Serling.

Daniel Briney: Excerpts from "The Unnatural Course of Time" by Daniel Briney, from CultureDose.net. Copyright © 2002 by Daniel Briney. Reprinted with permission.

Simon & Schuster Books for Young Readers: "Papa's Parrot," from *Every Living Thing* by Cynthia Rylant. Copyright © 1985 by Cynthia Rylant. Reprinted with the permission of Simon & Schuster Books for Young Readers, an imprint of Simon & Schuster Children's Publishing Division.

UNIT 2

Scholastic: Excerpt from "An Hour with Abuelo," from *An Island Like You: Stories of the Barrio* by Judith Ortiz Cofer. Copyright © 1995 by Judith Ortiz Cofer. Reprinted by permission of Scholastic, Inc.

Melanie Jackson Agency: Excerpt from "The White Umbrella" by Gish Jen. Copyright © 1984 by Gish Jen. First published in *The Yale Review*. Reprinted with permission by Melanie Jackson Agency, LLC.

Random House Children's Books: Excerpt from "Kitty and Mack: A Love Story," from *145th Street: Short Stories* by Walter Dean Myers. Copyright © 2000 by Walter Dean Myers. Used by permission of Random House Children's Books, a division of Random House, Inc.

Curtis Brown: "Birthday Box" by Jane Yolen, from *Birthday Surprises: Ten Great Stories to Unwrap*, published by Morrow Junior Books. Copyright © 1995 by Jane Yolen. Reprinted by permission of Curtis Brown, Ltd.

William Morris Endeavor Entertainment: "Zebra," from *Zebra and Other Stories* by Chaim Potok. Copyright © 1998 by Chaim Potok. Reprinted by permission of William Morris Endeavor Entertainment, LLC. on behalf of the author.

Naomi Shihab Nye: "The Rider" by Naomi Shihab Nye, first published in *Invisible*. Reprinted by permission of the author.

Brent Ashabranner: "A Wall of Remembrance" by Brent Ashabranner. Reprinted by permission of the author.

National Park Service: Mrs. Eleanor Wimbish Letter to Her Son, William "Billy" Stocks. Reprinted by permission of the National Park Service, Vietnam Veterans Memorial Collection.

Bilingual Press/Editorial Bilingüe: "The Scholarship Jacket" by Marta Salinas, from *Nosotras: Latina Literature Today* (1986), edited by María del Carmen Boza, Beverly Silva, and Carmen Valle. By permission of Bilingual Press/Editorial Bilingüe, Arizona State University, Tempe, AZ.

Sheldon Fogelman Agency: "The Three-Century Woman" by Richard Peck. Copyright © 1996 by Richard Peck. First published in *Second Sight: Stories For a New Millennium* by Philomel Books. All rights reserved. Used with permission of Sheldon Fogelman Agency, Inc.

Farrar, Straus and Giroux: "Charles," from *The Lottery* by Shirley Jackson. Copyright © 1948, 1949 by Shirley Jackson, renewed © 1976, 1977 by Laurence Hyman, Barry Hyman, Mrs. Sarah Webster, and Mrs. Joanne Schnurer. Reprinted by permission of Farrar, Straus and Giroux, LLC.

Random House and Little, Brown Group: Excerpt from *The Heart of a Woman* by Maya Angelou. Copyright © 1981 by Maya Angelou. Used by permission of Random House, Inc. and Little, Brown Group Ltd.

Estate of Martin Luther King Jr.: Excerpt from Crusade for Citizenship Mass Meeting, February 12, 1958. Copyright © 1958 by Martin Luther King Jr. Copyright renewed © 1991 by Coretta Scott King. Reprinted by arrangement with the Estate of Martin Luther King Jr., c/o Writers House as agent for the proprietor New York, NY.

Jennifer Flannery Literary Agency: Excerpt from *My Life in Dog Years* by Gary Paulsen. Copyright © 1998 by Gary Paulsen. Used by permission of Jennifer Flannery Literary Agency.

Wylie Agency: "It Was a Long Time Before," from *Storyteller* by Leslie Marmon Silko. Copyright © 1981 by Leslie Marmon Silko. Reprinted with permission of the Wylie Agency, Inc.

Susan Bergholz Literary Services: "Abuelito Who," from *My Wicked Wicked Ways* by Sandra Cisneros. Copyright © 1987 by Sandra Cisneros. Published by Third Woman Press and in hardcover by Alfred A. Knopf. Reprinted by permission of Third Woman Press and Susan Bergholz Literary Services of New York and New Mexico. All rights reserved.

Puffin Books: Excerpt from "The Man Who Was a Horse," from *Long Journey Home* by Julius Lester. Copyright © 1972 by Julius Lester. Reprinted by permission of Puffin Books, a division of Penguin Group (USA) Inc. and the author.

Simon & Schuster: Excerpt from "A Mother in Mannville," from *When the Whippoorwill* by Marjorie Kinnan Rawlings. Copyright © 1936, 1940 by Marjorie Kinnan Rawlings, copyright renewed © 1964, 1968 by Norton S. Baskin. Reprinted with the permission of Simon & Schuster.

UNIT 3

Rowan Barnes-Murphy, Ltd.: "The Lion and the Mouse," from *Fables of Aesop* retold by Frances Barnes-Murphy. Copyright © 1994 by Frances Barnes-Murphy. Used by permission of Rowan Barnes-Murphy.

Curtis Brown: "Little Sister" by Nikki Grimes. First appeared in *Something On My Mind* published by Peter Smith Publisher. Copyright © 1978 by Nikki Grimes. Reprinted by permission of Curtis Brown, Ltd.

Piri Thomas: Excerpt from *Stories from El Barrio* by Piri Thomas. Copyright © 1978 by Piri Thomas. Reprinted by permission of the author.

Pantheon Books: "The War of the Wall," from *Deep Sightings and Rescue Missions* by Toni Cade Bambara. Copyright © 1996 by the Estate of Toni Cade Bambara. Used by permission of Pantheon Books, a division of Random House, Inc.

Time: "Back to the Wall," from *People Weekly,* May 27, 2004. Copyright © 2004 by People Weekly. Used by permission of Time, Inc. All rights reserved.

Candlewick Press: "What Do Fish Have to Do With Anything?" from *What Do Fish Have to Do With Anything? and Other Stories* by Avi. Copyright © 1994 by Avi. Used by permission of Candlewick Press.

Random House and International Creative Management: "Homeless," from *Living Out Loud* by Anna Quindlen. Copyright © 1987 by Anna Quindlen. Used by permission of Random House, Inc. and International Creative Management.

Scholastic: "A Crush," from *A Couple of Kooks and Other Stories About Love* by Cynthia Rylant. Copyright © 1990 by Cynthia Rylant. Published by Orchard Books/Scholastic, Inc. Used by permission.

Houghton Mifflin Harcourt: Excerpt from *The Giver* by Lois Lowry. Copyright © 1993 by Lois Lowry. Reprinted by permission of Houghton Mifflin Harcourt Publishing Company. All rights reserved.

Harvard University Press: "Spring Harvest of the Snow Peas," from *To Be the Poet* by Maxine Hong Kingston, pp. 86–87, Cambridge, Mass., Harvard University Press. Copyright © 2002 by Maxine Hong Kingston. Reprinted by permission of the publisher.

BOA Editions: "Eating Alone," from *Rose* by Li-Young Lee. Copyright © 1986 by Li-Young Lee. Reprinted with the permission of the author and BOA Editions, Ltd., www.BOAEditions.org.

University of Minnesota Press: *A Christmas Carol* by Charles Dickens, adapted by Frederick Gaines, from *Five Plays from the Children's Theatre Company of Minneapolis,* published by the University of Minnesota Press. Copyright © 1975 by Frederick Gaines. All rights reserved.

David A. Perdue: *A Christmas Carol Review* by David A. Perdue, from the Charles Dickens Page. Used by permission of the author.

Stanford University Libraries: Excerpt from "The Hummingbird that Lived Through Winter," from *My Kind of Crazy, Wonderful People: Seventeen Stories and a Play* by William Saroyan. Copyright © 1944 and renewed 1972 by William Saroyan. Reprinted by permission of Stanford University Libraries.

UNIT 4

Bantam Books: Excerpt from "One Ordinary Day, with Peanuts," from *Just An Ordinary Day: The Uncollected Stories* by Shirley Jackson. Copyright © 1979 by the Estate of Shirley Jackson. Used by permission of Bantam Books, a division of Random House, Inc.

Don Congdon Associates: "Dark They Were, and Golden-Eyed" as "The Naming of Names," from *Thrilling Wonder Stories* by Ray Bradbury. Copyright © 1949 by Standard Magazines, renewed 1976 by Ray Bradbury. Reprinted by permission of Don Congdon Associates, Inc.

The Charlotte Observer: Excerpt from "Ray Bradbury, Science Fiction Supernova, Has Little Use for the Internet" by Sandy Hill, the *Charlotte Observer,* October 12, 1997. Copyright © 1997 by the Charlotte Observer. Reprinted with permission of the Charlotte Observer.

Scribner: "A Day's Wait," from *The Short Stories of Ernest Hemingway.* Copyright 1933 by Charles Scribner's Sons. Copyright © 1961 by Mary Hemingway. Reprinted with permission of Scribner, an imprint of Simon & Schuster Adult Publishing Group.

Bruce Rettman: "How Hemingway Wrote" by Bruce Rettman. Reprinted by permission of the author.

Alfred A. Knopf Children's Books: Excerpt from *The People Could Fly: American Black Folktales* by Virginia Hamilton. Text copyright © 1985 by Virginia Hamilton. Reprinted by permission of Alfred A. Knopf Children's Books, a division of Random House, Inc.

Scholastic: "Fields of Flashing Light" and "Wild Boy of the Road," from *Out of the Dust* by Karen Hesse. Copyright © 1997 by Karen Hesse. Published by Scholastic Press/Scholastic, Inc. Reprinted by permission.

Crown Publishers: "Breaking the Ice," from *Dave Barry Is Not Making This Up* by Dave Barry. Copyright © 1994 by Dave Barry. Used by permission of Crown Publishers, a division of Random House, Inc.

Viking Penguin: "One Perfect Rose" by Dorothy Parker, from *The Portable Dorothy Parker,* edited by Brendan Gill. Copyright © 1926, copyright renewed © 1954 by Dorothy Parker. Used by permission of Viking Penguin, a division of Penguin Group (USA), Inc.

National Association for the Advancement of Colored People: "Song for an April Dusk" by Dorothy Parker, from *Dorothy Parker: Complete Poems.* Copyright © 1999 by The NAACP. The publisher wishes to thank the National Association for the Advancement of Colored People for this use of Dorothy Parker's work.

Liveright Publishing Corporation: "maggie and milly and molly and may," from *Complete Poems: 1904–1962* by E. E. Cummings, edited by George J. Firmage. Copyright © 1956, 1984, 1991 by the Trustees for the E. E. Cummings Trust. "who are you, little i?" from *Complete Poems: 1904–1962* by E. E. Cummings, edited by George J. Firmage. Copyright © 1963, 1991 by the Trustees for the E. E. Cummings Trust. "old age sticks," from *Complete Poems: 1904–1962* by E. E. Cummings, edited by George J. Firmage. Used by permission of Liveright Publishing Corporation.

UNIT 5

Henry Holt and Company: Excerpt from "A Minor Bird," from *The Poetry of Robert Frost,* edited by Edward Connery Lathem. Copyright © 1956 by Robert Frost. Copyright © 1928, 1969 by Henry Holt and Company. Reprinted by permission of Henry Holt and Company, LLC.

Arnold Adoff: "Under the Back Porch" by Virginia Hamilton. Copyright © 1992, 1999 by Virginia Hamilton Adoff. Copyright © 2009 by The Arnold Adoff Revocable Living Trust. Used by permission.

Scribner: "Faults" by Sara Teasdale, from *The Collected Poems of Sara Teasdale.* Copyright © 1937 by the Macmillan Company. Reprinted with the permission of Scribner, an imprint of Simon & Schuster Adult Publishing Group.

Alfred A. Knopf and Harold Ober Associates: Excerpt from "Winter Moon," from *The Collected Poems of Langston Hughes* by Langston Hughes. Copyright © 1994 by The Estate of Langston Hughes. Used by permission of Alfred A. Knopf, a division of Random House, Inc. and Harold Ober Associates, Inc.

Harvard University Press: "A word is dead" and "Fame is a bee," from *The Poems of Emily Dickinson,* edited by Thomas H. Johnson. Copyright © 1951, 1955, 1979, 1983 by the President and Fellows of Harvard College. Reprinted by permission of the publishers and the Trustees of Amherst College.

HarperCollins Publishers: "Cynthia in the Snow," from *Bronzeville Boys and Girls* by Gwendolyn Brooks. Copyright © 1956 by Gwendolyn Brooks Blakely. Used by permission of HarperCollins Publishers.

Houghton Mifflin Harcourt: Excerpt from "Ode to Mi Gato," from *Neighborhood Odes* by Gary Soto. Copyright © 1992 by Gary Soto. Reprinted by permission of Houghton Mifflin Harcourt Publishing Company. This material may not be reproduced in any form or by any means without the prior written permission of the publisher.

Houghton Mifflin Harcourt: "Primer Lesson," from *Slabs of the Sunburnt West* by Carl Sandburg. Copyright © 1922 by Houghton Mifflin Harcourt Publishing Company, and renewed 1950 by Carl Sandburg. Reprinted by permission of the publisher. This material may not be reproduced in any form or by any means without the prior written permission of the publisher.

The Millay Society: "The Courage That My Mother Had," from *Collected Poems* by Edna St. Vincent Millay. Copyright © 1954, 1982 by Norma Millay Ellis. Reprinted by permission of Elizabeth Barnett, Literary Executor, The Millay Society. All rights reserved.

Sterling Lord Literistic: "The Names" by Billy Collins. Copyright © 2002 by Billy Collins. Reprinted by permission of Sll/Sterling Lord Literistic, Inc.

Copper Canyon Press: "the earth is a living thing," from *The Book of Light* by Lucille Clifton. Copyright © 1993 by Lucille Clifton. Reprinted with the permission of Copper Canyon Press, P.O. Box 271, Port Townsend, WA 98368-0271.

Curtis Brown: "Gold" by Pat Mora. Copyright © 1998 by Pat Mora. First appeared in *Home: A Journey Through America,* published by Silver Whistle Books. Reprinted by permission of Curtis Brown, Ltd.

Little, Brown and Company: "Sleeping in the Forest," from *Twelve Moons* by Mary Oliver. Copyright © 1972, 1973, 1974, 1976, 1977, 1978, 1979 by Mary Oliver. By permission of Little, Brown and Company, Inc.

Faber and Faber: "Scaffolding," from *Death of a Naturalist* by Seamus Heaney. Copyright © 1966 by Seamus Heaney. Reprinted by permission of Faber and Faber, Ltd.

HarperCollins Publishers: "The World Is Not a Pleasant Place to Be," from *My House* by Nikki Giovanni. Copyright © 1972 by Nikki Giovanni. Reprinted by permission of HarperCollins Publishers.

Hugh Noyes: "The Highwayman," by Alfred Noyes. Reprinted by permission of Hugh Noyes for the Society of Authors as the Literary Representative of the Estate of Alfred Noyes.

HarperCollins Publishers: One haiku by Basho, from *The Essential Haiku: Versions of Basho, Buson & Issa,* edited and with an introduction by Robert Hass. Copyright © 1994 by Robert Hass. Reprinted by permission of HarperCollins Publishers.

Japan Publications Trading Co.: "One sweet plum blossoms" by Basho, from *One Hundred Famous Haiku* selected and translated by Daniel C. Buchanan. Used by permission of Japan Publications Trading Company, Ltd.

HarperCollins Publishers: "Fireflies," from *Joyful Noise* by Paul Fleischman. Text copyright © 1988 by Paul Fleischman. Used by permission of HarperCollins Publishers.

Henry Holt and Company: "Fireflies in the Garden," from *The Poetry of Robert Frost* edited by Edward Connery Lathem. Copyright 1956 by Robert Frost. Copyright 1928, 1969 by Henry Holt and Company. Reprinted by permission of Henry Holt and Company, LLC.

Organic Gardening: "Stars and Wings," by Therese Ciesinski from *Organic Gardening,* July/August 2000. Copyright © 2000 by Rodale, Inc. USA. Reprinted by permission of Organic Gardening magazine. All rights reserved. www.organicgardening.com

HarperCollins Children's Books: "Sarah Cynthia Sylvia Stout Would Not Take the Garbage Out," from *Where the Sidewalk Ends* by Shel Silverstein. Copyright © 1974, renewed 2002 by Evil Eye LLC. Reprinted with permission from the Estate of Shel Silverstein and HarperCollins Children's Books.

N. Scott Momaday: "The Delight Song of Tsoai-talee," from *The Gourd Dancer* by N. Scott Momaday. Copyright © 1976 by N. Scott Momaday. Reprinted by permission of the author.

Susan Bergholz Literary Services: "Four Skinny Trees," from *The House on Mango Street* by Sandra Cisneros. Copyright © 1984 by Sandra Cisneros. Published by Vintage Books, a division of Random House, Inc., and in hardcover by Alfred A. Knopf in 1994. Reprinted by permission of Susan Bergholz Literary Services, New York. All rights reserved.

Little, Brown and Company: "Ode to enchanted light," from *Odes to Opposites* by Pablo Neruda. Copyright © 1995 by Pablo Neruda and Fundación Pablo Neruda (Odes in Spanish). Copyright © 1995 by Ken Krabbenhoft (Odes in English). Copyright © 1995 by Ferris Cook (Illustrations and Compilation). Used by permission of Little, Brown and Company.

UNIT 6

Philomel Books: "Bess Call," from *Cut From the Same Cloth* by Robert D. San Souci. Copyright © 1993 by Robert D. San Souci. Used by permission of Philomel Books, a division of Penguin Young Readers Group, a member of Penguin Group (USA) Inc., 345 Hudson Street, New York, NY 10014. All rights reserved.

Scholastic: "Racing the Great Bear," from *Flying with the Eagle, Racing the Great Bear* by Joseph Bruchac. Copyright © 1993 by Joseph Bruchac. Reprinted by permission of Scholastic Inc.

Simon & Schuster Books for Young Readers: "Echo," from *The Macmillan Book of Greek Gods and Heroes* by Alice Low. Copyright © 1985 by Macmillan Publishing Company. Reprinted with the permission of Simon & Schuster Books for Young Readers, an imprint of Simon & Schuster Children's Publishing Division.

Scholastic: Excerpt from *The Greek Gods* by Bernard Evslin. Copyright © 1966 by Scholastic, Inc. Reprinted by permission of Scholastic, Inc.

Houghton Mifflin Harcourt: "Orpheus and Eurydice" from *Greek Myths* by Olivia E. Coolidge. Copyright © 1949 by Olivia E. Coolidge. Copyright renewed © 1977 by Olivia E. Coolidge. Adapted by permission of Houghton Mifflin Harcourt Publishing Company. All rights reserved.

"Phaëthon, Son of Apollo," from *Greek Myths* by Olivia E. Coolidge. Copyright © 1949 by Olivia E. Coolidge. Copyright renewed © 1977 by Olivia E. Coolidge. Reprinted by permission of Houghton Mifflin Harcourt Publishing Company. All rights reserved.

Dutton Signet: Excerpt from *Beowulf,* translated by Burton Raffel. Translation copyright 1963 by Burton Raffel. Used by permission of Dutton Signet, a division of Penguin Group (USA) Inc.

Barbara S. Kouts Literary Agent: *Young Arthur* by Robert D. San Souci. Copyright © 1977 by Robert D. San Souci. Reprinted by permission of Barbara S. Kouts Literary Agent.

National Geographic Society: Excerpts from "Looking for King Arthur" by Jerry Dunn, from *National Geographic World,* March 1997. Copyright © 1997 by National Geographic. Reprinted with permission from the National Geographic Society.

David Higham Associates: *Sir Gawain and the Green Knight* by Michael Morpurgo. Text copyright © 2004 by Michael Morpurgo. Reproduced by permission of the publisher David Higham Associates, Limited, on behalf of Walker Books Ltd., London.

Disney-Hyperion: Excerpt from *Crispin: The Cross of Lead* by Avi. Copyright © 2002 by Avi. Reprinted by permission of Disney-Hyperion, an imprint of Disney Book Group, LLC.

Voya Magazine: "Crispin: The Cross of Lead" book review by Rebecca Barnhouse, from *Voya,* Vol. 25, No. 2, June 2002. Copyright © 2002 by Rowman & Littlefield Publishing Group. Reprinted with permission of Voya Magazine.

School Library Journal: "Crispin: The Cross of Lead" book review by Cheri Estes, from *School Library Journal,* Vol. 48, No. 6, June 2002. Copyright © 2002 by School Library Journal. Reprinted with permission.

Estate of Jackie Torrence: "Brer Possum's Dilemma" by Jackie Torrence. Copyright © by Jackie Torrence. Used by permission of Rowan Blues and Jazz Society on behalf of the Estate of Jackie Torrence.

Curtis Brown: *Waters of Gold* by Laurence Yep. Text copyright © 1991 by Laurence Yep. First appeared in *Tongues of Jade,* published by HarperCollins. Reprinted by permission of Curtis Brown, Ltd.

Alfred A. Knopf: "Sally Ann Thunder Ann Whirlwind," from *American Tall Tales* by Mary Pope Osborne. Copyright © 1991 by Mary Pope Osborne. Used by permission of Alfred A. Knopf, an imprint of Random House Children's Books, a division of Random House, Inc.

Doubleday: "Two Ways to Count to Ten," from *African Wonder Tales* by Frances Carpenter Huntington. Copyright © 1963 by Frances Carpenter Huntington. Used by permission of Doubleday, a division of Random House, Inc.

Pantheon Books: "The Race Between Toad and Donkey," from *Afro-American Folktales,* edited by Roger D. Abrahams. Copyright © 1985 by Roger D. Abrahams. Used by permission of Pantheon Books, a division of Random House, Inc.

HarperCollins Publishers: Excerpt from "The King Who Wished for Gold, " from *The Robber Babies: Stories from the Greek Myths* retold by Anne Rockwell. Copyright © 1994 by Ann Rockwell. Reprinted by permission of HarperCollins Publishers.

Ricardo E. Alegría: Excerpt from "The Three Wishes," from *The Three Wishes: A Collection of Puerto Rican Folk Tales* by Ricardo E. Alegría. Copyright © 1969 by Ricardo E. Alegría. Reprinted by permission of the author.

Justin Hjelm: "Do Professional Athletes Get Paid Too Much?" by Justin Hjelm. Copyright © 2004 by Justin Hjelm. Used by permission of the author.

Time: "Why We Shouldn't Go to Mars" by Gregg Easterbrook, from *Time,* January 26, 2004. Copyright © 2004 by Time, Inc. Reprinted by permission.

SmartGirl.org: "Teen Reading Survey" from SmartGirl.org. Used by permission of SmartGirl.org.

Brandt and Hochman Literary Agents: "Take a Book Wherever You Go" by Joan Aiken, *Bookbird,* April 1973. Copyright © 1973 by Joan Aiken. Reprinted by permission of Brandt & Hochman Literary Agents, Inc.

UNIT 9

The Boston Herald: "The Difference a City Year Makes," by Lauren Beckham, from *The Boston Herald,* June 10, 1996. Used by permission of The Boston Herald.

CONSULTANTS

Janet Allen © Duane McCubrey; *Arthur Applebee* © Mark Schmidt; *Kylene Beers* © Sam Dudgeon/Houghton Mifflin Harcourt; *Jim Burke* © Bruce Forrester; *Douglas Carnine* © Houghton Mifflin Harcourt; *Carol Jago* Maggie's Photography, Pacific Palisades, CA *Yvette Jackson* © Howard Gollub; *Robert Jimenez* © Tamra Stallings; *Judith Langer* © Mark Schmidt; *Robert Marzano* © Robert J. Marzano; *Donna Ogle* © Houghton Mifflin Harcourt; *Carol Booth Olson* © Dawson & Associates Photography; *Carol Tomlinson* © Gitchell's Studio; *May Lou McClosky* © Michael Romeo; *Lydia Stack* © Monica Ani; *William McBride* © William McBride; *David Considine* © Bill Caldwell; *Larkin Pauluzzi* © Gabriel Pauluzzi; *Lisa Scheffler* © Steven Scheffler.

TABLE OF CONTENTS

FM9 © Getty Images; **FM12** *left* Illustration by Erika O'Rourke/Elm Studios; *right* © Artville; **FM13** *top* The Newbery Awards are administered by the American Library Service to Children, a division of the American Library Association. Seal image used by permission of American Library Association; *bottom* © PunchStock; **FM14** *right, Boy with Orange,* Murray Kimber. © Murray Kimber/Illustrationworks.com; *left* Library of Congress; **FM15** © PunchStock; **FM16** *left* © Adrian Arbib/Alamy Images; *right* Detail of *Birds XII* (2003), Barbara Weldon. Oil, gold leaf and wax on canvas; **FM17** *top* The Newbery Awards are administered by the American Library Service to Children, a division of the American Library Association. Seal image used by permission of American Library Association; *bottom* © PunchStock; **FM18** *left* © Ferdinando Scianna/Magnum Photos; *right* Detail of *Figures Crossing River on Gold Coins,* Andrew Judd. © Andrew Judd/Masterfile; *bottom* The Newbery Awards are administered by the American Library Service to Children, a division of the American Library Association. Seal image used by permission of American Library Association; **FM19** © Punchstock; **FM20** *left* © The Image Bank/Getty Images; *right, Dragon,* Greg Spalenka. © Greg Spalenka; **FM21** © PunchStock; **FM22** *left, Falling Figure (Icarus)* (1944), Henri Matisse. Color lithograph after a paper cut-out and gouache. Published on the back cover of the deluxe art review *Verve.* © 2008 Succession H. Matisse, Paris/Artists Rights Society (ARS), New York; *right* Illustration © Juan Wijngaard (1981) from *Sir Gawain and the Green Knight* by Selina Hastings. Reproduced by permission of Walker Books, Ltd., London; **FM23** *top* The Newbery Awards are administered by the American Library Service to Children, a division of the American Library Association. Seal image used by permission of American Library Association; *bottom* © PunchStock; **FM24** *top left* © Marvin Koner/Corbis; *top right* AP/Wide World Photos; *bottom* The Coretta Scott King Book Awards are administered by the Ethic and Multicultural Information Exchange Round Table of the American Library Association. Seal image used by permission of American Library Association; **FM25** © PunchStock; **FM26** *left* © Jeff Rotman/Alamy Images; *right* © Stephen Frink Collection/Alamy Images; **FM27** Punchstock; **FM28** *left* © Photo courtesy of Seattle Public Library; *right* Photo by Sharon Hoogstraten; *chambered nautilus* © Siede Preis/Getty Images; *spiny shell* © Jupiterimages Corporation; *conch shell* © Jupiterimages Corporation; *sea urchin* © Siede Preis/Getty Images; *polished nautilus* © Siede Preis/Getty Images; *pink conch shell* © Jupiterimages Corporation; *chambered shell* © Jupiterimages Corporation; *fighting conch shell* © Jupiterimages Corporation.

STUDENT GUIDE TO ACADEMIC SUCCESS

FM33 © Jupiterimages/Getty Images; **FM34** Maggie's Photography, Pacific Palisades; **FM36** © Punchstock.

POWER OF IDEAS

1 *left* From *The People Could Fly.* Illustrations © 1985 by Leo and Diane Dillon. Used by permission of Alfred A. Knopf, an imprint of Random House Children's Books, a division of Random House, Inc.; *top right* © MCA/Universal Pictures/

Courtesy Everett Collection; *bottom right* © 2008 VisionsofAmerica.com; **2** *left* © 1997 by Jerry Pinkney. Used by permission of HarperCollins Publishers; *right* © Alan Powdrill/Getty Images; **3** *left* © Images.com/Corbis; *right* AP/Wide World Photos; **8** *1* © Bettmann/Corbis; *2* © Bill Pierce/Time Life Pictures/Getty Images; *3* © Corbis; *4 top* Courtesy Westmont College (Santa Barbara) Student Newspaper, *The Horizon; 4 bottom* © Photographer's Choice/Getty Images; *5* © Judith Collins/Alamy Images; **10** *1* © MCA/Universal Pictures; *2* Courtesy of ABC NEWS; *3* © CBS Photo Archive; *4 Kibbles n' Bits Commercial* © Del Monte Corporation; *5* The Granger Collection, New York; **11** © Garry Hunter/Getty Images; **15** *top* © Brian Hagiwara/Getty Images; *bottom* © Thinkstock/Getty Images; **20** *left* © Jose Luis Pelaez, Inc./Corbis; *center* © Yellow Dog Productions/Getty Images; *right, magazine* © Time Life Pictures/Getty; *right, article* © 2005 The Summer Northwestern; **23** *left* © Image Source/Getty Images; *center* © Rob Brimson/Getty Images; *right* © Flying Colours, Ltd./Getty Images.

UNIT 1

25 *left* Detail of *Snowball Fight,* William Low. © William Low; *right* © Galen Rowell/Corbis; **26–27** *foreground* © Kelly Reno/Photofest; *background* © Paul Edmondson/Corbis; **26** *left* From *The Black Stallion* by Walter Farley. Cover art © 2002 John Rowe. Used by permission of Random House; **30** © Getty Images; **34** © Ed Bock/Corbis; **35** © Gary Soto; **37** © Lisa Pines/Getty Images; **40** *left* © Jose Luis Pelaez, Inc./Corbis; *center* © Jupiterimages Corporation; *background* © Doug Wilson/Corbis; **46** *foreground* © Getty Images; *background* © Doug Wilson/Corbis; **47** © Samantha Loomis Paterson; **49** Illustration by Erika O'Rourke/Elm Studios; **50** © Javier Larrea/Age Fotostock America, Inc.; **53, 56, 60–61** Illustration by Erika O'Rourke/Elm Studios; **66** © David M. Grossman/Jupiterimages Corporation; **67** © Corbis; **69** *Faith Ringgold* (1977), Alice Neel. Oil on canvas, 48″ × 36″. Private collection. © 2004 Estate of Alice Neel/Courtesy Robert Miller Gallery, New York/Philadelphia Museum of Art, Special Exhibition (Accession: *The Art of Alice Neel,* Page 150, Plate 70); **71** *Gamin* (about 1929), Augusta Savage. Painted plaster, 9″ × 5¾″ × 4⅜″. Gift of Benjamin and Olya Margolin © Smithsonian American Art Museum, Washington, D.C./Art Resource, New York; **76** *foreound* © Marc Romanelli/Getty Images; *background* © Artbeats; **77** © Getty Images; **79** © 1997 by Jerry Pinkney. Used by permission of HarperCollins Publishers; **80** © Jeremy Horner/Corbis; **81** *top* © GeoNova LLC; *bottom* © 1997 by Jerry Pinkney. Used by permission of HarperCollins Publishers; **86, 89, 90** © 1997 by Jerry Pinkney. Used by permission of HarperCollins Publishers; **96–97** © Jeff Hunter/Getty Images; **96** *top left* © Les Cunliffe/Age Fotostock America, Inc.; *center left* © Carla Sachar; **97** *top right* From *Holes* by Louis Sachar. Cover illustration by Vladimir Radunsky. Reprinted by permission of Yearling Books, a division of Random House, Inc.; *center right* The Newbery Awards are administered by the American Library Service to Children, a division of the American Library Association. Seal image used by permission of American Library Association; **98–99** © Corbis; **100–101** © Digital Vision/Getty Images; **102** *foreground* © Richard Cummins/Corbis; *background* © C. Lee/Photolink/Getty Images; **103** © Bettmann/Corbis; **105** *Titanic, Olympic, White Star Line* (1912), Montague B. Black. Christie's Images/Corbis; **107** *left* © Onslow Auctions Limited/Mary Evans Picture Library; *top right, Ruth* © Don Lynch Collection/*frame* © Kimball Art Museum/Corbis; *bottom right, Jack* © From the Collections of the University of Pennsylvania Archives/*frame* © Kimball Art Museum/Corbis; **108–109** Illustration by Steve Noon © Dorling Kindersley; **110** Museum of Science and Industry, Chicago; **111** *left, The Titanic,* Gordon Johnson. Oil on paper. © Margaret Johnson/SuperStock; *right* The Granger Collection, New York /*frame* © Kimball Art Museum/Corbis; **112, 115** *left* Illustration by Steve Noon © Dorling Kindersley; **115** *right* © The National Archives of the UK; **117** Illustration by Steve Noon © Dorling Kindersley; **119** 20th Century Fox/

Paramount © Photofest; **122** © S. Beaudet/zefa/Corbis; **123** © Jerry Bauer; **125** Detail of *Snowball Fight*, William Low. © William Low; **128** © Helen Norman/Corbis; **132** © Joe Robbins/Getty Images; **133** HUP Thayer, Ernest L. (1), Courtesy of the Harvard University Archives; **135** *Mighty Casey Advancing to the Bat* (1912), Dan Sayre Groesbeck. From illustration series for *Casey at the Bat* by Phineas Thayer. © Mary Evans Picture Library; **137** © Bettmann/Corbis; **138** © Enrique Algarra/Age Fotostock America, Inc.; **139** © Bettmann/Corbis; **141** *Empire of Lights* (1954), René Magritte. Oil on canvas, 146 cm × 114 cm. Musée d'Art Moderne, Brussels. Photo © Phototheque R. Magritte/ADAGP, Paris/Art Resource, New York. © 2008 C. Herscovici, Brussels/Artists Rights Society (ARS), New York; **143, 144, 147, 148, 151** © CBS Photo Archive; **154** © MCA/Universal Pictures/Courtesy Everett Collection; **155** *top* © 2008 by Universal Studios Licensing LLLP. Courtesy of Universal Studios Licensing LLLP. All rights reserved; *center* © MCA/Universal Pictures/Courtesy Everett Collection; *bottom* © 2008 by Universal Studios Licensing LLLP. Courtesy of Universal Studios Licensing LLLP. All rights reserved; **156** *top, center* © 2008 by Universal Studios Licensing LLLP. Courtesy of Universal Studios Licensing LLLP. All rights reserved; *background* © A & J Verkaik/Corbis; **159** © MCA/Universal Pictures/Courtesy The Everett Collection; **162** © Craig Aurness/Corbis; **173** © Bob Daemmrich/PhotoEdit; **180** © Siede Preis/Getty Images.

UNIT 2

181 *left* Detail of *Bernadita* (1922), Robert Henri. Oil on canvas, 24⅛″ × 20⅛″. Gift of the San Diego Wednesday Club. © San Diego Museum of Art (1926:138); *right* © Michael Goldman/Taxi/Getty Images; **182–183** © 20th Century Fox/ZUMA/Lucasfilm Ltd/Photofest; **190** *center* © Alexander Walter/Getty Images; *background* © Getty Images; **191** © Bettmann/Corbis; **193** *center* © Joshua Sheldon/Getty Images; *zebras* © James Gritz/www.jamesgritz.com; **197** © Alan Powdrill/Getty Images; **200** © Peter Finger/Corbis; **203** © GeoNova LLC; **205** *center* AP/Wide World Photos; *background* © Joe Raedle/Getty Images; **207** © Corbis; **211** © Alamy Images; **212** © Thinkstock/Getty Images; **217** AP/Wide World Photos; **218, 219** © Nathan Benn/Corbis; **222** *top* © David J. and Janice L. Frent Collection/Corbis; *bottom left* © Leif Skoogfors/Corbis; *bottom right* © Corbis Sygma; **224** © Alan Schein Photography/Corbis; **225** © David H. Wells; **227** *Bernadita* (1922), Robert Henri. Oil on canvas, 24⅛″ × 20⅛″. Gift of the San Diego Wednesday Club. © San Diego Museum of Art (1926:138); **230** *Portrait of Patience Escalier* (1888), Vincent van Gogh. Oil on canvas. Private collection. © Lefevre Fine Art Ltd., London/Bridgeman Art Library; **234** AP/Wide World Photos; **235** © Bettmann/Corbis; **237** Detail of *Tides of Memory* (1936), Norman Rockwell. Oil on board, 18¾″ × 15¼″. Collection of Mr. and Mrs. Norman Rockwell. Reproduced by permission of the Norman Rockwell Family Agency, Inc. Photo courtesy of the Norman Rockwell Museum at Stockbridge, Massachusetts; **240** *Eleanor* (1907), Frank Weston Benson. Oil on canvas, 64.13 cm × 76.83 cm. The Hayden Collection-Charles Henry Hayden Fund. © Museum of Fine Arts, Boston (08.326); **242** *Hill, Main Street, Gloucester* (1916), John Sloan. Oil on canvas, 25¾″ × 39⅞″. The Parrish Art Museum, Southampton, NY, Littlejohn Collection, 1961.3.208; **248** © Reuters/Corbis; **249** *top, bottom* AP/Wide World Photos; **251** *Red Hat* (2003), Deidre Scherer. Fabric and thread. © Deidre Scherer; **254** Library of Congress, Prints and Photographs Division; **256** © Getty Images; **258** © Images.com/Corbis; **266** Louis Lanzano/AP/Wide World Photos; **267** © Mitchell Gerber/Corbis; **269** *background* © Bettmann/Corbis; *bottom right* © Reg Lancaster/Express/Getty Images; **270, 271** *Martin Luther King, Jr.* Library of Congress; *signs* © Bettmann/Corbis; **276** Photo by Sharon Hoogstraten; **277** © C.E. Mitchell/stockphoto.com; **279** *Boy with Orange*, Murray Kimber. © Murray Kimber/Illustrationworks.com; **282** © Peter Weimann/Animals Animals-Earth Scenes. All rights reserved; **283** *Street Corner* (1991), Daniel Bennett Schwartz. Oil on canvas, 91.4 cm × 71.1 cm. Private collection. Photo © Bridgeman Art Library; **288** © Walter Hodges/Corbis; **289** *top* © Nancy Crampton; *bottom* © Gene Blevins/Corbis; **290** *Rosita Johnson*

(1958), Lee Marmon. Laguna, New Mexico. © Lee Marmon; **292** © Chris Dyball/Getty Images; **294** © Joseph Sohm; ChromoSohm Inc./Corbis; **305** © Inspirestock/Jupiterimages Corporation; **312** © Siede Preis/Getty Images.

UNIT 3

313 *left* Detail of *Birds XII* (2003), Barbara Weldon. Oil, gold leaf and wax on canvas; *right* © Adrian Arbib/Alamy Images; **314–315** MGM/The Kobal Collection; **314** The Granger Collection, New York; **316** *left, Faith Ringgold* (1977), Alice Neel. Oil on canvas, 48″ × 36″. Private collection. © 2004 Estate of Alice Neel/Courtesy Robert Miller Gallery, New York/Philadelphia Museum of Art, Special Exhibition (Accession: *The Art of Alice Neel*, Page 150, Plate 70); *right, Mighty Casey Advancing to the Bat* (1912), Dan Sayre Groesbeck. From illustration series for *Casey at the Bat* by Phineas Thayer. Mary Evans Picture Library; **322** *foreground* © Corbis; *background* © Getty Images; **323** © Nic Paget-Clarke; **325** *The Boxers*, Roger Coleman. Tempera. Private Collection. Photo © The Bridgeman Art Library; **326** © GeoNova LLC; **327** *left, Moose*, (1956), Alice Neel. © Estate of Alice Neel. Courtesy Robert Miller Gallery, New York; *right, Call Me Joe* (1955), Alice Neel. Oil on canvas, 34″ × 32″ © Estate of Alice Neel. Courtesy Robert Miller Gallery, New York; **329** *Still Open* (1994), Douglas Safranek. Egg tempera on panel, 4⅝″ × 4″. © Museum of the City of New York (95.6); **332** *Seated Fighter* (1985), Joseph Sheppard. Bronze, height 21″; **335** AP/Wide World Photos; **338** © Jim West/The Image Works, Inc.; **339** © The New York Public Library/Art Resource, New York; **341** Detail of *Harlem Street Scene* (1942), Jacob Lawrence. Gouache on paper, 21″ × 20¾″. Private collection. © Art Resource, New York. © 2008 The Jacob and Gwendolyn Lawrence Foundation, Seattle/Artists Rights Society (ARS), New York; **345** © Andre Jenny/Alamy Images; **346** © Bettmann/Corbis; **349** Judith F. Baca, *Triumph of the Hearts* from *World Wall: A Vision of the Future Without Fear* 1986–present © SPARC www.sparcmurals.org; **350** © Alex James Photographic/Getty Images; **351** Photo by Russ Wright/Courtesy Avi; **353** *Gregory. Los Angeles, March 31st 1982* (1982), David Hockney. Composite Polaroid. 14½″ × 13¾″. © David Hockney/The David Hockney No. 1 U.S. Trust; **357** *At the Aquarium* (2003), Jim Macbeth. Digital collage. Photo © Jim Macbeth/SuperStock; **359** © 2002 Gueorgui Pinkhassov/Magnum Photos; **362** *Celia. Los Angeles, April 10th 1982* (1982), David Hockney. Composite Polaroid. 18″ × 30″. © David Hockney/The David Hockney No. 1 U.S. Trust; **369** *top* The New York Times Company; *bottom* © Bill Pierce/Time Life Pictures/Getty Images; **370** *top* The New York Times Company; *bottom* © Jeff Dunn/Jupiterimages Corporation; **371** The New York Times Company; **372** *top* The New York Times Company; *bottom* © Gloria H. Chomica/Masterfile; **374** © Cassy Cohen/PhotoEdit; **375** Photo by Margaret Miller/Writers House LLC; **377** *Bladen's Hardware* (2002), Bill Firestone. © Bill Firestone; **380** *left* © Comstock Images/Alamy Images; *center* © John McAnulty/Corbis; *right* © Richard Cummins/Corbis; **383** Detail of *Zinnias* (2001), Bill Firestone. © Bill Firestone; **386–387** © Hulton-Deutsch Collection/Corbis; **386** *top* © Les Cunliffe/Age Fotostock America, Inc.; *center* © Lois Lowry; *left* Illustration by Ruben Ramos; *right* The Newbery Awards are administered by the American Library Service to Children, a division of the American Library Association. Seal image used by permission of American Library Association; **388–389** © Horace Bristol/Corbis; **390–391** © Laurence Mouton/PhotoAlto; **392** © Al Petteway /National Geographic Image Collection; **393** *top* © Christopher Felver/Corbis; *bottom* © 2002 Margaretta K. Mitchell; **394** Detail of *Birds XII* (2003), Barbara Weldon. Oil, gold leaf and wax on canvas; **395** Detail of *Birds III* (2002), Barbara Weldon. Oil, gold leaf and wax on canvas, 40″ × 40″; **398** © Thierry Dosogne/Iconica/Getty Images; **399** The Granger Collection, New York; **400–401, 403, 405, 407, 409, 411, 415, 416, 419, 420–421, 423** © Michael Rasbury; **425, 426** The Granger Collection, New York; **428** © Bettmann/Corbis; **429** *top* © Bettmann/Corbis; *center* © John Springer Collection/Corbis; *bottom* © MGM/The Kobal Collection; **430** *top* © The Everett Collection; *center* © United Artists/Photofest; **432** © Daryl Benson/Masterfile; **450** © Siede Preis/Getty Images.

UNIT 4

451 *left* Detail of *Mural Painting for the Terrace Plaza Hotel, Cincinnati* (1947), Joan Miró. Oil on canvas. Cincinnati Art Museum, Cincinnati, Ohio. Gift of Thomas Emery's Sons, Inc. Photo by Tony Walsh. © 2008 Successio Miró/Artists Rights Society (ARS), New York/ADAGP, Paris; *right* © Jeff Greenberg/Age Fotostock America, Inc.; **452–453** © Getty Images; **453** © Ben Edwards/Getty Images; **454** *left* © Joel Sartore/National Geographic Image Collection; *right* © Micheline Pelletier/Corbis; **456** © Gary Soto; **460** © Image Bank/Getty Images; **461** © Bassouls Sophie/Corbis Sygma; **463** *Sugar Sphinx* (1933), Salvador Dali. Oil on canvas. © 2008 Salvador Dali/Gala-Salvador Dali Foundation/Artists Rights Society (ARS), New York; **465** NASA/JPL/Caltech; **467** *Shellfish Flowers* (1929), Max Ernst. Oil on canvas, 129 cm × 129 cm. Inv.: R 19 P. Photo Jean-Francois Tomasian. Musée National d'Art Moderne, Centre Georges Pompidou, Paris. Photo © CNAC/MNAM/Dist. Réunion des Musées Nationaux/Art Resource, New York. © 2008 Artist Rights Society (ARS), New York/ADAGP, Paris; **470** *The Forest* (1950), Alberto Giacometti. Bronze, painted, 22″ × 24″ × 19¼″. Gift of Enid Haupt. National Gallery of Art, Washington, D.C. Photo © National Gallery of Art, Washington, D.C. © 2008 Artists Rights Society (ARS), New York/ADAGP, Paris; **473** © Araldo de Luca/Corbis; **474** Detail of *Figures Crossing River on Gold Coins,* Andrew Judd. ©Andrew Judd/Masterfile; **477** *The Whole City* (1935), Max Ernst. Oil on canvas, 60 cm × 81 cm. Kunsthaus, Zurich, Switzerland. © 2008 Artists Rights Society (ARS), New York/ADAGP, Paris; **478** *top* © *Charlotte Observer.* Reprinted by permission of the *Charlotte Observer; bottom* AP/Wide World Photos; **479** NASA; **482** © Thinkstock/Getty Images; **483** © Time Life Pictures/Getty Images; **485** *Contemplation* (1930), Alice Kent Stoddard. Oil on canvas. © SuperStock; **487** *Chair in the Sun* (2000), Pam Ingalls. © Pam Ingalls/Corbis; **488** © Dave King/Dorling Kindersley Images; **493** Photo by Robert Capa. © 2001 Cornell Capa/Magnum Photos; **496** © G. Rossenbach/zefa/Corbis; **497** © Ron Rovtar; **499** From *The People Could Fly.* Illustrations © 1985 by Leo and Diane Dillon. Used by permission of Alfred A. Knopf, an imprint of Random House Children's Books, a division of Random House, Inc.; **501** Photo by Gordon Lewis; **502** © 1975 David C. Conrad; **504–505** © Three Lions/Getty Images; **504** *top* © Les Cunliffe/Age Fotostock America, Inc.; *center* Courtesy Karen Hesse; **505** *right* The Newbery Awards are administered by the American Library Service to Children, a division of the American Library Association. Seal image used by permission of American Library Association; *left* From *Out of the Dust* by Karen Hesse. Published by Scholastic Press, a division of Scholastic Inc. Jacket illustration © 1997 by Scholastic Inc. Used by permission. Jacket photo courtesy of Library of Congress Prints and Photographs division, Farm Security Administration; **506–507** © Time Life Pictures/Getty Images; **508–509** © Getty Images; **510** © Yellow Dog Productions/Getty Images; **511** © Bob Daemmrich/Corbis; **512** © Diana Ong/SuperStock; **516** © Corbis; **517** The Granger Collection, New York; **519** © Matthias Kulka/Corbis; **520** © Robert Stahl/Getty Images; **521** © Bettmann/Corbis; **522** © Topham/The Image Works, Inc.; **523** © Bettmann/Corbis; **524–525** *Mural Painting for the Terrace Plaza Hotel, Cincinnati* (1947), Joan Miró. Oil on canvas. Cincinnati Art Museum, Cincinnati, Ohio. Gift of Thomas Emery's Sons, Inc. Photo by Tony Walsh. © 2008 Successio Miró/Artists Rights Society (ARS), New York/ADAGP, Paris; **526** *Painting* (1953), Joan Miró. Oil on canvas, 75⅞″ × 51″. Collection Mr. and Mrs. Richard K. Weil, St. Louis, Missouri. © 2008 Successio Miró/Artists Rights Society (ARS), New York/AGAGP, Paris; **528** © Laura Ciapponi/Getty Images; **529** *top, bottom* © Ferdinando Scianna/Magnum Photos; **530** *top left, Musician in the Rain,* Robert Doisneau. © Estate of Robert Doisneau/Rapho; *bottom left, The Cellist, 1957,* Robert Doisneau. © Estate of Robert Doisneau/Rapho; *background* © Peter Jon Hamann/Getty Images; **531** © Corinne Mudge; **532** © Richard Sisk/Jupiter Images; **543** © Mary Kate Denny/PhotoEdit; **550** © Siede Preis/Getty Images.

UNIT 5

551 *left* Detail of *Hacienda* (2002), Vanessa Julian. Acrylic on matteboard, 23″ × 19″. © Vanessa Julian; *right* © The Image Bank/Getty Images; **552–553** © Alex Webb/Magnum Photos; **560** © Photorush/Corbis; **561** © Christopher Felver/Corbis; **562** © 2008 VisionsofAmerica.com; **564** © Ruth Fremson/Pool/Reuters/Corbis; **565** © Joe Raedel/Getty Images; **566** © Paula Borchardt/Age Fotostock America, Inc.; **567** *top* © Michael S. Glaser, St. Mary's College of Maryland; *center* © Barbara Savage Cheresh; *bottom* Courtesy Pat Mora/Photo by Cheron Bayna; **569** *Bear with Houses,* Michael Wertz. Pastel. © Michael Wertz; **570** *The Orchard* (1997), Peter Davidson. Oil on paper, 37.5 cm × 44 cm. Private collection. Photo © Bridgeman Art Library; **571** *Hacienda* (2002), Vanessa Julian. Acrylic on matteboard, 23″ × 19″. © Vanessa Julian; **574** © Peter Byron/PhotoEdit; **575** *top* © David Levenson/Getty Images; *center* © Mike Simons/Getty Images; *bottom* © Bettmann/Corbis; **577** *Stages II,* Paul Davis. Oil, 10″ × 8″. Courtesy Coda Gallery. © Paul Davis; **578** Detail of *Family in the Park* (1999), Colin Bootman. Oil on canvas. Private collection. Photo © Bridgeman Art Library; **579** *The Seashore* (1900), William Henry Margetson. Oil on canvas. Private collection. Photo © The Maas Gallery, London/ Bridgeman Art Library; **581** © Todd Davidson/Images.com/Corbis; **582** AP/Wide World Photos; **583** *top* © Bettmann/Corbis; *bottom* The Granger Collection, New York; **585** © Time Life Pictures/Getty Images; **587** Detail of *Equestrian Portrait of a Man with a Page* (1600s), Thomas de Keyser. Oil on canvas, 94.6 cm × 77.2 cm. Private collection. Photo © Bridgeman Art Library; **588** Public Domain; **594** © Steve Satushek/Getty Images; **595** *top* © Roger-Viollet/The Image Works, Inc.; *center* © Dana Fleischman; *bottom* National Archives; **596** *Plum Garden, Kameido* from *One Hundred Views of Famous Places in Edo* (1857), Utagawa Hiroshige. Photo © Christie's Images/Corbis; **598** Stephen Alvarez/National Geographic Image Collection; **601** Illustration by Ken Oliver/The Art Agency; **604** © Shannon Burns/www.CartoonStock.com; **605** *top* © Bettmann/Corbis; *center* © Jeff Albertson/Corbis; *bottom, Edward Lear* (1857), William Holman Hunt. Pencil on paper, 63.3 cm × 50 cm. Photo © Walker Art Gallery, National Museums, Liverpool/Bridgeman Art Library; **607** *Dragon,* Greg Spalenka. © Greg Spalenka; **608** © Richard Downs; **610** Illustration by Alberto Ruggieri; **612** © Owen Franken/Corbis; **613** *top* © N. Scott Momaday/Courtesy of Royce Carlton, Inc.; *bottom* © Gene Blevins/Corbis; **615** Detail of *Four Directions* (1995), Jaune Quick-to-See Smith. Lithograph with linocut collage, 44.5″ × 30″. Photo provided by The Lawrence Lithography Workshop. Artwork courtesy Jaune Quick-to-See Smith (An enrolled Flathead Salish, member of the Salish and Kootenal Nation Montana); **617** Detail of *Houses, Trees, Bike,* Anne Lavine Dimeur. © Anne Lavina Dimeur/Images.com; **620** © Daryl Benson/Masterfile; **629** © Monica Stevenson Photography/Getty Images **638** © Siede Preis/Getty Images.

UNIT 6

637 *left* Study of *Almanach Der Blaue Reiter (*1911), Wassily Kandinsky. Watercolor, gouache, and black ink. Inv. AM 1994–70. Photo by Philippe Migeat. Musée National d'Art Moderne, Centre Georges Pompidou, Paris. Photo © CNAC/MNAM/Dist. Réunion des Musées Nationaux/Art Resource, New York. © 2008 Artists Rights Society (ARS), New York/ADAGP, Paris; *right* © Jim Zuckerman/Corbis; **638–639** © Tom Smart/Liaison/Getty Images; **646** © Paul A. Souders/Corbis; **647** *top* © Dorothy Evslin; *bottom* Courtesy of Julian Coolidge; **648** Detail from *Prometheus Carrying Fire,* Jan Cossiers. Prado, Madrid. © Art Resource, New York; **650** © GeoNova LLC; **653** *Orpheus in the Underworld* (1863), Louis Jacquesson de la Chevreuse. Oil on canvas, 115 cm × 145 cm. Musée des Augustins. Toulouse, France. © akg-images; **654** Museo della Civilta Romana, Rome. © Dagli Orti/The Art Archive; **655** *Orpheus Leading Eurydice from the Underworld* (1861), Jean Baptiste Camille Corot. Oil on canvas, 112.3 cm × 137.1 cm. © Museum of Fine Arts, Houston.

© Bridgeman Art Library; **657** *Orpheus* (1618), Marcello Provenzale. © Massimo Listri/Corbis; **660** © Creatas/JupiterImages Corporation; **661** *top* © The Schlesinger Library, Radcliffe Institute, Harvard University. http://www. radcliffe.edu/schles; *bottom* Courtesy of Julian Coolidge; **663** *The Fall of Icarus* (1944), Henri Matisse. Stencil print after a gouache and paper collage. © 2008 Succession H. Matisse, Paris/Artists Rights Society (ARS), New York; **665** *Falling Figure (Icarus)* (1944), Henri Matisse. Color lithograph after a paper cut-out and gouache. Published on the back cover of the deluxe art review *Verve*. © 2008 Succession H. Matisse, Paris/Artists Rights Society (ARS), New York; **667** Study of *Almanach Der Blaue Reiter* (1911), Wassily Kandinsky. Watercolor, gouache, and black ink. Inv. AM 1994–70. Photo by Philippe Migeat. Musée National d'Art Moderne, Centre Georges Pompidou, Paris. Photo © CNAC/MNAM/ Dist. Réunion des Musées Nationaux/Art Resource, New York. © 2008 Artists Rights Society (ARS), New York/ADAGP, Paris; **670** *The Cavalier,* Wassily Kandinsky. Staedtische Galerie im Lenbachhaus, Munich, Germany. © 2008 Artists Rights Society (ARS), New York/ADAGP, Paris. Photo © Giraudon/ Art Resource, New York; **674** © Jim West/PhotoEdit; **675** Text from *Beowulf* (about 1000). Page of manuscript in old English from the heroic poem *Beowulf.* British Library, London.© HIP/Art Resource, New York; **677** BEOWULF, Ray Winstone, 2007. © Paramount/Courtesy Everett Collection; **680** © Mason Morfit/Workbookstock/Jupiterimages Corporation; **681** © Robert D. San Souci; **683** Illustration by Walter Crane in *King Arthur's Knights* by Henry Gilbert, 1911. © Edwin Wallace/Mary Evans Picture Library; **686** © Arte & Immagini srl/Corbis; **689** © Francis G. Mayer/Corbis; **690** © Kelvin Murray/Getty Images; **691** © Getty Images; **692** Detail from illustration © Juan Wijngaard (1981) from *Sir Gawain and the Green Knight* by Selina Hastings. Reproduced by permission of Walker Books, Ltd., London; **694** © Heritage-Images/The Image Works, Inc.; **696–697, 701** Illustrations © Juan Wijngaard (1981) from *Sir Gawain and the Green Knight* by Selina Hastings. Reproduced by permission of Walker Books, Ltd., London; **706–707** © Robert Estall/Corbis; **706** *top left* © Les Cunliffe/Age Fotostock America, Inc.; *center* Photo by Russ Wright/Courtesy Avi; **707** *top right* The Newbery Awards are administered by the American Library Service to Children, a division of the American Library Association. Seal image used by permission of American Library Association; *top left* Cover image from *Crispin, The Cross of Lead* by Avi. © 2002. Reprinted with permission of Hyperion Books for Children, New York, New York; **708–709** © Bruno Morandi/Age Fotostock America, Inc.; **710–711** © Santiago Yaniz/ Age Fotostock America, Inc.; **713** Dover Publications; **714** Cover image from *Crispin, The Cross of Lead* by Avi. © 2002. Reprinted with permission of Hyperion Books for Children, New York, New York; **716** © Digital Vision/Getty Images; **717** *top* Courtesy Jackie Torrence; *bottom* Courtesy Laurence Yep; **719** Illustration by Ingrid Hess; **723** *Orchard* (2000), Chen Jia Qi. Watercolor. Red Lantern Folk Art, Mukashi Collection. © The Mukashi Collection/SuperStock; **725** Detail from *Spring in the Old Village* (2001), Chen Jia Qi. Watercolor. Red Lantern Folk Art, Mukashi Collection. © The Mukashi Collection/SuperStock; **729** Detail from *Sunny Spring* (1999), Zhang Min. Watercolor. Red Lantern Folk Art, Mukashi Collection. © The Mukashi Collection/SuperStock; **732** *foreground* © Eric and David Hosking/Corbis; *background* © Getty Images; **733** © 2003 Paul Coughlin; **735** *Man Leaning on Tree* © 1991 Michael McCurdy. From *American Tall Tales* by Mary Pope Osborne. Used by permission of Alfred A. Knopf, an imprint of Random House Children's Books, a division of Random House, Inc.; **737** *Woman and Bear* © 1991 Michael McCurdy. From *American Tall Tales* by Mary Pope Osborne. Used by permission of Alfred A. Knopf, an imprint of Random House Children's Books, a division of Random House, Inc.; **738** *Woman Beating Up Man* © 1991 Michael McCurdy. From *American Tall Tales* by Mary Pope Osborne. Used by permission of Alfred A. Knopf, an imprint of Random House Children's Books, a division of Random House, Inc.; **742** © Warner Bros. Entertainment, Inc. All Rights Reserved; **743** *top* Detail of photograph of Frances Carpenter with statue of Buddha, n.d., by Smithsonian Institution, Museum of Natural History (Neg #: 12520). Used in *The Elephant's Bathtub*. Record 2121/Sophia Smith Collection, Smith College; *bottom* Courtesy

Roger D. Abrahams; **745** *background* © Gallo Images/Corbis; *center* © Paul A. Souders/Corbis; **746** © GeoNova LLC; **751** *left* © Tracy Kahn Photography, Inc./Workbookstock.com/Jupiterimages Corporation; *right* © Image Source/ Workbookstock.com/Jupiterimages Corporation; *background* © David Reddick/ Workbookstock.com/Jupiterimages Corporation; **753** © GeoNova LLC; **756** © J. David Andrews/Masterfile; **767** © Zigy Kaluzny/Getty Images; **774** © Siede Preis/Photodisc/Getty Images.

UNIT 7

775 *left* Detail of *Alma Sewing* (about 1935), Francis Criss. Oil on canvas, 33″ × 45″. High Museum of Art, Atlanta, Georgia. Purchase with funds from the Fine Art Collectors, Mr. and Mrs. Henry Schwob, the Director's Circle, Mr. and Mrs. John L. Huber, High Museum of Art Enhancement Fund, Stephen and Linda Sessler, General Acquisitions Fund, the J.J. Haverty Fund, and through prior acquisitions. 2002.70; *right* © Jim Cornfield/Corbis; **776–777** *teen girls* Photos by Amy Carneghi; *teen guy* Photos by Erik Koelle; *scissors, scrapbook pages* Photos by Sharon Hoogstraten; *gerbera daisies* © Bezkorovayny Dmitry/ ShutterStock; *grass* © Donna Middlemiss/ShutterStock; *baseball, baseball glove, bat* © Getty Images; *peanuts* © Neil Webster/ShutterStock; *popcorn* © Scott Rothstein/ShutterStock; **780** *left* © Marvin Koner/Corbis; *right* © Bettmann/ Corbis; **783** © Reuters/Corbis; **784** © Viviane Moos/Corbis; **785** © Darien High School, Darien, Connecticut; **787** © Marvin Koner/Corbis; **789** © Corbis; **790** © Corbis; **793, 794** © Bettmann/Corbis; **795** © Hulton Archive/ Getty Images; **797** The Granger Collection, New York; **801, 802** © Bettmann/ Corbis; **804** *left, center* © SuperStock, Inc./SuperStock; *right* © Michael Rougier/ Getty Images; **805** AP/Wide World Photos; **807** *West 17th Street, New York City* (20th century), Patti Mollica. © Patti Mollica/SuperStock; **809** © GeoNova LLC; **814** South Bend Tribune/AP/Wide World Photos; **815** © Duomo/Corbis; **817** © James Startt; **819** Courtesy LaTrice (Haney) Vaughn; **821** AP/Wide World Photos; **822–823** AP/Wide World Photos; **824** © AFP/Getty Images; **826–827** AP/Wide World Photos; **826** *top left* © Les Cunliffe/Age Fotostock America, Inc.; *center* © Jerry Bauer; **827** *top left* From *By Any Means Necessary* by Malcolm X. Cover photograph © John Launois/Black Star/stockphoto.com. Used with permission of the publisher Scholastic Inc., New York; *top right* The Coretta Scott King Book Awards are administered by the Ethic and Multicultural Information Exchange Round Table of the American Library Association. Seal image used by permission of American Library Association; **828–829** © Bruce Davidson/Magnum Photos; **830–831** © James P. Blair/National Geographic Image Collection; **832** AP/Wide World Photos; **833** © Bettmann/Corbis; **834** Library of Congress Serial and Government Publications Division, [LC-USZC4-6144 DLC] ; **837** *left* Library of Congress Prints and Photographs Division, [LC-USZ62-119886 DLC]; *right* © Barros & Barros/Getty Images; **839** *left* National Archives; *right* © Lake County Museum/Corbis; **841** *left* © Bettmann/Corbis; *right* © Getty Images; **843** *left* © Bettmann/Corbis; *right* © Blank Archives/Getty Images; **847, 848** AP/Wide World Photos; **849** *top* The New York Times Company; *bottom* © Bettmann/Corbis; **852** © Getty Images; **853** *top* © Bettmann/Corbis; *center, bottom* Footage from *Biography: Jackie Robinson,* A & E Television Networks; **854** *top left, bottom left* Footage from *Biography: Jackie Robinson,* A & E Television Networks; *background* © Jerry Driendl/Getty Images; **856** AP/Wide World Photos; **857** *top* Courtesy The Lilly Library, Indiana University, Bloomington, Indiana; *bottom* Library of Congress, Prints and Photographs Division, [LC-USZ62-19319]; **859, 860, 863, 865, 867, 868** Illustrations by Dove (David) McHargue; **870** Brady-Hand Photographic Collection/Library of Congress, Prints and Photographs Division, [LC-DIG-cwpbh-02075]; *frame* Library of Congress, Prints and Photographs Division, [LC-USZC4-111323]; **871** Library of Congress, Prints and Photographs Division, [LC-USZC4-6307/LOT 8494]; *frame* Library of Congress, Prints and Photographs Division, [LC-USZC4-111323]; **874** © Bettmann/Corbis; **875** *top* © Fred Viebahn; *bottom* © Bettmann/Corbis; **877** *Alma Sewing* (about 1935), Francis Criss. Oil on canvas, 33″ × 45″. High